HANDBOOK OF AUTISM AND
PERVASIVE DEVELOPMENTAL DISORDERS

Handbook of Autism and Pervasive Developmental Disorders

Third Edition

Volume 1: Diagnosis, Development, Neurobiology, and Behavior

Edited by

Fred R. Volkmar

Rhea Paul

Ami Klin

Donald Cohen

JOHN WILEY & SONS, INC.

Library of Congress Cataloging-in-Publication Data:

Handbook of autism and pervasive developmental disorders / edited by Fred R. Volkmar . . .
    [et al.].—3rd ed.
        p.   cm.
    Includes bibliographical references and index.
    Contents: V. 1. Diagnosis, development, neurobiology, and behavior—v. 2. Assessment, interventions, and policy.
        ISBN 0-471-71696-0 (cloth : v. 1)—ISBN 0-471-71697-9 (cloth : v. 2)—ISBN 0-471-71698-7 (set)
    1. Autism in children. 2. Developmental disabilities. 3. Autistic children—Services for. 4. Developmentally disabled children—Services for. I. Volkmar, Fred R.
    RJ506.A9H26   2005
    618.92′85882—dc22

                                                                            2004059091

Printed in the United States of America.

10 9 8 7 6 5 4 3 2

To the Memory of Donald Cohen

At the time of his death, Donald Cohen was actively involved in the planning of this edition of the *Handbook*. His untimely passing made it impossible for him to see the final product. We are deeply grateful to him for his thoughtful counsel and mentorship as well as the truly impressive example he presented as a clinician-researcher. We hope that this *Handbook* is a testament to his vision and a fitting tribute to his memory.

Photo: Michael Marsland, Yale University

Contributors

M. Cherro Aguerre, MD
University of the Republic
School of Medicine
Cavia
Montevideo, Uruguay

George M. Anderson, PhD
Child Study Center
Yale University School of Medicine
New Haven, Connecticut

Joel R. Arick, PhD
Special Education
Portland State University
Portland, Oregon

Chris Ashwin, PhD
Autism Research Centre
University of Cambridge
Departments of Experimental Psychology
and Psychiatry
Cambridge, England

Grace T. Baranek, PhD, OTR/L
Division of Occupational Science
Department of Allied Health Sciences
University of North Carolina at Chapel Hill
Chapel Hill, North Carolina

Simon Baron-Cohen, PhD
Autism Research Centre
University of Cambridge
Departments of Experimental Psychology
and Psychiatry
Cambridge, England

Margaret L. Bauman, MD
Harvard Medical School
Massachusetts Hospital
Boston, Massachusetts

Jac Billington, BSc
Autism Research Centre
University of Cambridge
Cambridge, England

James W. Bodfish, PhD
Department of Psychiatry
University of North Carolina at Chapel Hill
Chapel Hill, North Carolina

Joel D. Bregman, MD
Center for Autism
North Shore Long Island Jewish Health
   System
Bethpage, New York

Courtney Burnette, MS
Department of Psychology
University of Miami
Coral Gables, Florida

Alice S. Carter, PhD
Department of Psychology
University of Massachusetts Boston
Boston, Massachusetts

Bhismadev Chakrabarti, BA, BSc
Autism Research Centre
University of Cambridge
Cambridge, England

KATARZYNA CHAWARSKA, PhD
Child Study Center
Yale University School of Medicine
New Haven, Connecticut

SOO CHURL CHO, MD
Division of Child and Adolescent Psychiatry
Seoul National University Hospital
Seoul, Korea

IAN COOK, MD
Department of Psychiatry and Behavioral
    Sciences
David Geffen School of Medicine at UCLA
Los Angeles, California

ELAINE E. COONROD, MS
Department of Psychology and Human
    Development
Vanderbilt University
Nashville, Tennessee

CHRISTINA CORSELLO, PhD
Autism and Communication Disorders Center
University of Michigan
Ann Arbor, Michigan

NAOMI ORNSTEIN DAVIS, MA
Boston University School of Medicine
Boston, Massachusetts

RUTH FALCO, PhD
Special Education
Portland State University
Portland, Oregon

PIERRE FERRARI, MD
Centre Hospitalier Public De Psychiatrie
    De L'Enfant Et De L'Adolescent
Foundation Vallee
Gentilly Cedex, France

PAULINE A. FILIPEK, MD
Department of Pediatrics and Neurology
University of California
Irvine College of Medicine
Orange, California

ERIC FOMBONNE, MD
McGill University
Department of Psychiatry at the Montreal
    Children's Hospital
Montreal, Quebec, Canada

JOAQUIN FUENTES, MD
GUATENA
San Sebastian, Spain

ANN FULLERTON, PhD
Special Education
Portland State University
Portland, Oregon

JOHN GERDTZ, PhD
Saint Mary's College of California
Moraga, California

PETER F. GERHARDT, EdD
Gerhardt Autism/Aspergers Consultation
    Group, LLC
Baltimore, Maryland

TEMPLE GRANDIN, PhD
Department of Animal Science
Colorado State University
Fort Collins, Colorado

RICHARD GRIFFIN, BA
Autism Research Centre
University of Cambridge
Cambridge, England

JAN S. HANDLEMAN, EdD
Douglas Developmental Disabilities Center
Rutgers, The State University of New Jersey
New Brunswick, New Jersey

FRANCESCA HAPPÉ, PhD (ALSO BA HONS
    OXFORD)
Social, Genetic and Developmental
    Psychiatry Centre
Institute of Psychiatry
King's College, London

SANDRA L. HARRIS, PhD
Douglas Developmental Disabilities Center
Rutgers, The State University of New Jersey
New Brunswick, New Jersey

PETER HOBSON, MD
The Tavistock Clinic
Adult Department
London, United Kingdom

DAVID L. HOLMES, EdD
Lifespan Services, LLC
Princeton, New Jersey

YOSHIHIKO HOSHINO, MD
Department of Neuropsychiatry
Hikarigaoka
Fukushima-shi, Japan

PATRICIA HOWLIN, MD
St. George's Hospital Medical School
Cranmer Terrace
London, United Kingdom

BROOKE INGERSOLL, PhD
Oregon Institute on Disability and
    Development Child Development and
    Rehabilitation
Center Oregon Health and Science University
Portland, Oregon

HEATHER K. JENNETT, MS
Douglas Developmental Disabilities Center
Rutgers, The State University of New Jersey
New Brunswick, New Jersey

WARREN JONES, BA
Child Study Center
Yale University School of Medicine
New Haven, Connecticut

AMI KLIN, PhD
Child Study Center
Yale University School of Medicine
New Haven, Connecticut

KATHY KOENIG , MSN
Child Study Center
Yale University School of Medicine
New Haven, Connecticut

JASON B. KONIDARIS
Norwalk, Connecticut

DAVID A. KRUG, PhD
Special Education
Portland State University
Portland, Oregon

LINDA J. KUNCE, PhD
Department of Psychology
Illinois Wesleyan University
Bloomington, Illinois

AMY LAURENT, OTR/L
Communication Crossroads
North Kingstown, Rhode Island

JOHN LAWSON, PhD
Autism Research Centre
University of Cambridge
Cambridge, England

GABRIEL LEVI, MD
Departimento di Scienze Neurologische e
Psichiatriche dell'eta Evolutina
Rome, Italy

JENNIFER A. LONCOLA, PhD
DePaul University
School of Education
Chicago, Illinois

LAUREN LOOS, MS
Autism Specialist
Oregon Department of Education
Salem, Oregon

CATHERINE LORD, PhD
UMACC
University of Michigan
Ann Arbor, Michigan

KATHERINE A. LOVELAND, PhD
University of Texas Health Sciences Center
    at Houston
Department of Psychiatry and Behavioral
    Sciences
Houston, Texas

MYRNA R. MANDLAWITZ, BA, MEd, JD
MRM Associates
Washington, DC

WENDY D. MARANS, MS, CCC/SLP
Child Study Center
Yale University School of Medicine
Private Practice
New Haven, Connecticut

LEE M. MARCUS, PhD
Division TEACCH
Department of Psychiatry
University of North Carolina School
    of Medicine
Chapel Hill, North Carolina

ANDRÉS MARTIN, MD
Child Study Center
Yale University School of Medicine
New Haven, Connecticut

MEGAN P. MARTINS, BA
Douglas Developmental Disabilities Center
Rutgers, The State University of New Jersey
New Brunswick, New Jersey

GAIL G. MCGEE, PhD
Emory University School of Medicine
Department of Psychiatry and Behavioral
    Sciences
Atlanta, Georgia

JAMES MCPARTLAND, MS
Child Study Center
Yale University School of Medicine
New Haven, Connecticut

ADRIENNE MERYL, BA
M.I.N.D. Institute
U.C. Davis Medical Center
Sacramento, California

GARY B. MESIBOV, PhD
Division TEACCH
University of North Carolina at Chapel Hill
Chapel Hill, North Carolina

RICHARD MILLS, CQSW, RMPA, MA, FRSA
NAS Southern Region Office
Church House, Church Road
Filton, United Kingdom

NANCY J. MINSHEW, MD
Western Psychiatric Institute and Clinic
Pittsburgh, Pennsylvania

MICHAEL J. MORRIER, MA
Emory University School of Medicine
Department of Psychiatry and Behavioral
    Sciences
Atlanta, Georgia

PETER MUNDY, PhD
Department of Psychology
University of Miami
Coral Gables, Florida

J. GREGORY OLLEY, PhD
Clinical Center for the Study of Development
    and Learning
University of North Carolina at Chapel Hill
Chapel Hill, North Carolina

SALLY OZONOFF, PhD
M.I.N.D. Institute
U.C. Davis Medical Center
Sacramento, California

VAYA PAPAGEORGIOU, MD
Medical Psychopedagogical Center of
    North Greece
Greece

L. DIANE PARHAM, PhD, OTR, FAOTA
Department of Occupational Science and
    Occupational Therapy
University of Southern California
Los Angeles, California

RHEA PAUL, PhD, CCC-SLP
Department of Communication Disorders
Southern Connecticut State University
New Haven, Connecticut

MICHAEL D. POWERS, MD
Center for Children with Special Needs
Glastonbury, Connecticut
and
Child Study Center
Yale University School of Medicine
New Haven, Connecticut

BARRY M. PRIZANT, PhD
Childhood Communication Services
Cranston, Rhode Island
and
Center for the Study of Human Development
Brown University
Providence, Rhode Island

SHERRI PROVENCAL, PhD
Department of Psychology
University of Utah
Salt Lake City, Utah

ISABELLE RAPIN
Albert Einstein College of Medicine
Bronx, New York

DIANA L. ROBINS, PhD
Department of Psychology
Georgia State University
Atlanta, Georgia

SALLY J. ROGERS, PhD
M.I.N.D. Institute
U.C. Davis Medical Center
Sacramento, California

EMILY RUBIN, MS, CCC/SLP
Communication Crossroads
Carmel, California

MICHAEL RUTTER, CBE, MD, FRCP,
    FRCPSYCH, FRS
Social, Genetic and Developmental
    Psychiatry Centre
Institute of Psychiatry
DeCrespigny Park
Denmark Hill
King's College, London

ANDERS RYDELIUS, MD, PhD
Karolinska Institute
Department of Woman and Child Health
Child and Adolescent Psychiatry Unit
St. Goran's Children's Hospital
Stockholm, Sweden

CELINE SAULNIER, PhD
Child Study Center
Yale University School of Medicine
New Haven, Connecticut

LAWRENCE SCAHILL, MSN, PhD
Child Study Center
Yale University School of Medicine
New Haven, Connecticut

MARTIN SCHMIDT, MD
Kinder Jundenpsychiatrische Klinik
Zentralinstitut fur Seelische Genundheit
Mannheim, Germany

ERIC SCHOPLER, PhD
Division TEACCH
Department of Psychiatry
University of North Carolina School
    of Medicine
Chapel Hill, North Carolina

LAURA SCHREIBMAN, PhD
Department of Psychology
University of California, San Diego
La Jolla, California

ROBERT T. SCHULTZ, PhD
Child Study Center
Yale University School of Medicine
New Haven, Connecticut

VICTORIA SHEA, PhD
Division TEACCH
The University of North Carolina at
    Chapel Hill
Chapel Hill, North Carolina

MIKLE SOUTH, MS
Department of Psychology
University of Utah
Salt Lake City, Utah

VIRGINIA WALKER SPERRY, MA
Child Study Center
Yale University School of Medicine
New Haven, Connecticut

MATTHEW STATE, MD, PhD
Child Study Center
Yale University School of Medicine
New Haven, Connecticut

WENDY L. STONE, PhD
Vanderbilt Children's Hospital
Nashville, Tennessee

RUTH CHRIST SULLIVAN, PhD
Autism Services Center
Huntington, West Virginia

DEAN SUTHERLAND, MS
Department of Speech Therapy
Canterbury University
Christchurch, New Zealand

JOHN A. SWEENEY, PhD
University of Pittsburgh
Western Psychiatric Institute and Clinic
Pittsburgh, Pennsylvania

PETER SZATMARI, MD
McMaster University
Department of Psychiatry
Faculty Health Sciences
Hamilton, Ontario, Canada

HELEN TAGER-FLUSBERG, PhD
Department of Anatomy and Neurobiology
Boston University School of Medicine
Boston, Massachusetts

KUO-TAI TAO, MD
Division of Nanging
Child Mental Health Research Center
Nanging, China

BRUCE TONGE, MD
Centre for Developmental Psychiatry
Monash Medical Center
Australia

KENNETH E. TOWBIN, MD
Mood and Anxiety Disorders Program
National Institute of Mental Health
Bethesda, Maryland

KATHERINE D. TSATSANIS, PhD
Child Study Center
Yale University School of Medicine
New Haven, Connecticut

BELGIN TUNALI-KOTOSKI, PhD
Center for Human Development Research
University of Texas Health Sciences Center
    at Houston
Houston, Texas

SAM TYANO
The Geha Psychiatric Hospital
The Beilinson Medical Center
Tel Aviv University Medical School
Tel Aviv, Israel

ERYN Y. VAN ACKER
College of Education
University of Illinois at Chicago
Chicago, Illinois

RICHARD VAN ACKER, PhD
College of Education
University of Illinois at Chicago
Chicago, Illinois

FRED R. VOLKMAR, MD
Child Study Center
Yale University
New Haven, Connecticut

HERMAN VAN ENGELAND, MD
Divisie Psychiatrie Kinder en
    Jeugdpsychiatrie
Utrecht, The Netherlands

SARA JANE WEBB, PhD
Center for Human Development and Disability
Autism Center Psychophysiology Laboratories
University of Washington
Seattle, Washington

AMY M. WETHERBY, PhD
Department of Communication Disorders
Executive Director, Center for Autism and
    Related Disorders
Florida State University
Tallahassee, Florida

SALLY WHEELWRIGHT, MA
Autism Research Centre
University of Cambridge
Cambridge, England

LORNA WING, MD
National Autistic Society Centre for Social
    and Communication Disorders
Bromley, Kent, United Kingdom

DIANNE ZAGER, PhD
Pace University
New York, New York

Editorial Board

Preface

A comprehensive *Handbook* devoted to *autism and pervasive developmental disorders* testifies to the volume of research, services, theory, and advocacy related to children and adults with the most severe disorders of development. Indeed, the third edition of this work is now literally two books. The expansion in size and sophistication reflects substantial advances in knowledge during the one decade that separates it from its predecessor published in 1997.

Autism has attracted remarkable interest and concern of clinicians and researchers from the time of its first scientific description over 60 years ago by Leo Kanner (1943). As a disorder that afflicts the core of socialization, it has posed scientific challenges to theories of developmental psychology and neurobiology as well as therapy and education. Virtually every type of theory relating to child development—cognitive, social, behavioral, affective, neurobiological—has been applied to understanding the enigmatic impairments and competencies of autistic individuals. And the results of empirical studies inspired by these diverse theoretical perspectives have enriched not only the field of autism but also the broad field of developmental psychopathology. Indeed, autism has served as a paradigmatic disorder for theory testing and research on the essential preconditions for normal social-cognitive maturation—expression and recognition of emotions, intersubjectivity, sharing a focus of interest with other people, the meaning and uses of language, forming first attachments and falling in love, empathy, the nuanced understanding of the minds of others—indeed, the whole set of competencies and motivations that allow a child to become a family member and social being.

This *Handbook* is guided by a developmental psychopathological orientation (Cicchetti & Cohen, 1995). Within this framework, principles and findings about normal development are used to illuminate how development may become derailed and lead to pathological conditions, and, conversely, studies of disorders such as autism are used to cast light on normal developmental processes. Autism and similar developmental disorders may serve as "experiments of nature." Their underlying biology and psychology, as well as the types of adaptations that individuals can use to compensate for their difficulties, may reveal mechanisms and processes that are otherwise concealed from awareness or scientific scrutiny.

As a serious, generally lifelong condition, autism has generated important challenges to the systems that relate to individuals with disabilities, including educational, vocational, medical, and psychiatric systems, as well as to social policy, legislation, and the legal systems. Because of its multifaceted impact on development, autism also has focused the attention of all the professions concerned with children and adults with difficulties, including psychology, education, psychiatry, physical rehabilitation, recreational therapy, speech and language, nursing, pediatrics, neurology, occupational therapy, genetics, social work, law, neuroradiology, pharmacology—indeed, virtually every caring profession. By drawing these disciplines together in the clinic and laboratory, autism has helped forge the multidisciplinary approach to developmental disabilities. One goal of this *Handbook* is to provide an orientation of shared concepts and knowledge to facilitate the future collaboration among the disciplines and professionals who work with autistic individuals and their families.

Nothing strikes more at the core of a family's functioning than the birth of a child with a serious disability. Kanner recognized the central involvement of families in his first reports when he described the peculiarities of social relations in families who came for his consultation and care. In his first accounts, he misread the data presented to him and postulated an etiologic role of parental behavior in the pathogenesis of autism. This mistake haunted the field and pained families for many years; it still may arise in certain places, as ghosts tend to do. However, Kanner soon righted his theory and emphasized the central message of his initial report that autism is essentially a reflection of an inborn dysfunction underlying affective engagement. Because social interaction is a two-way street, parents and others who spend time with an autistic child will no doubt relate differently than with his or her socially engaged, ebullient, linguistically gifted siblings. Of interest, more recent genetic information about autism and Asperger syndrome, discussed in the *Handbook,* returns us to Kanner's observations about social variations and impairments running within families. New findings of aggregation of autism, cognitive problems, and social difficulties within families suggest that an underlying vulnerability may be transmitted from one generation to the next. If so, explicating the interaction between genetic and environmental factors in the course of these disorders will bring us back to questions not too far from where Kanner started his speculations.

The impact of autistic individuals on family life has changed with the creation of more adequate services. Burdens on families have been eased by early identification, initiation of educational and other treatments during the first years of life, suitable family guidance and support, high-quality educational and other programs, respite care, supportive living and other arrangements for adults with autism, effective pharmacological treatments, and knowledge that can guide lifetime planning. Yet, with perhaps rare exception, an autistic child in the

family is experienced by parents, siblings, and extended family as profoundly painful. There can, of course, be consolations in dealing well with adversity; yet, however well a family and individual cope, a lifetime with autism brings with it more than a fair share of disappointment, sadness, and emotional scarring for all involved. Only with scientific advances that will prevent, greatly ameliorate, or even cure these conditions will this pain be fully eased. Clinicians and researchers have been drawn to autism in the hope of achieving this result, and their remarkable commitments are also reflected in this *Handbook* and in services throughout the world.

At times, however, therapeutic zeal has exceeded the knowledge available. The *Handbook* aims at providing authentic knowledge, broadly accepted by experts. Yet, we recognize that there are sometimes sharp differences of opinion and theoretical perspective and that today's wisdom may be tomorrow's delusion. Thus, it is important to foster diversity while encouraging everyone to pursue rigorous, empirical research that will improve future treatments. Scientific progress oddly leads to many divergent ideas and findings for a long time before a deeper level of clarity is achieved.

While we encourage tolerance of differing scientific views, we do not think that "anything goes." Virtually every month or two, parents and others who care for autistic children and adults are likely to hear announcements of new, miraculous treatments. They may be confused by the options and feel guilty for not making the sacrifices necessary to try still another approach. Today, within a stone's throw of our own university, parents are engaged in a medley of divergent treatments. As the recent review by the National Research Council (2001) has shown, a variety of treatments have now been shown to be effective for individuals with autism. The efficacy of a host of other treatments, commonly referred to as complementary or alternative treatments, remains to be scientifically well established. Often, such treatments compete with more traditional ones. Parents, and sometimes professionals, may feel at a loss in terms of evaluating such treatments and making sound, empirically based decisions about which treatment(s) should be pursued with respect to an individual child. Occasionally, differences between advocates and skeptics in relation to treatment ethics and efficacy arouse passions, including legal proceedings and splits between professionals or within the family. How are parents and professionals best able to make informed decisions?

Like other areas of science, the field of autism will advance when we adopt, whenever possible, the rigorous standards of scientific research. Indeed, our own work as clinician-researchers has led us to the conclusion that we should offer no less. Thus, in the *Handbook* we have attempted to provide a comprehensive account of current, scientific thinking and findings and to mark out speculation and theory for what these are. We also have eschewed accounts of ideas and treatments, however fascinating they might be, that are too far from the mainstream of scientific research and empirically guided practice. Such decisions are our responsibility and may leave some advocates feeling shortchanged or even angry; they retain their right to free speech and, who knows, may yet be vindicated.

In underlining the importance of data in guiding decisions about treatment, we also recognize that clinical care always occurs within a social context and is shaped by beliefs, values, and other historical and cultural values. Prevailing views about the rights of individuals with disabilities and their role in society have changed dramatically over the past decades. Embodied in legislation and judicial decision, the emergent viewpoints about rights to education, services, access, job opportunities—to basic human respect—have shaped services and improved the quality of the lives of individuals who would only decades ago have been subject to abuses of various types that limited freedom, stigmatized, or dehumanized. We have been delighted to see this view gaining increasingly wide acceptance around the world.

Parents and individuals with disabilities have been effective advocates. Communities and professionals have been sensitized to the subtle ways in which individuals with disabilities may be deprived of autonomy and are made to be more handicapped by lack of provision for their special needs. This trend has had

a major impact on the care and treatment of individuals with autism, as well. Far more than most experts believed possible 20 or even 10 years ago, many individuals with autism have not only the right but also the capacities to participate within their communities—to study, work, live, recreate, and share in family life. The *Handbook* reflects this important educational and cultural evolution in which a philosophy of despair has given way to one of hope.

We also appreciate that there are enormous differences among individuals with autism and related conditions in their abilities and needs, among families in their strengths and resources, and among communities and nations in their own viewpoints and histories. These differences should be respected, and policy and discussion should recognize that "autistic people" do not form a homogeneous class. Clinicians and practitioners generally are able to keep the individual at the focus of concern, as we do when we think together with families about their unique child or with an adult with autism about his or her special life situation. At such times, broader issues of social policy recede into the background as the fullness of the individual's needs and interests are paramount. In shaping social policy and planning regional and national systems, however, there is a clear consensus for the approach to treatment and lifetime planning captured by the ideology of autonomy and community-based living and working. We hope that this orientation is conveyed by this *Handbook*. At the same time, there is no single, right formula for every child or adult with autism: A community and nation should strive to have available a spectrum of services to satisfy the varied and changing needs and values of individuals with autism and their families.

Clearly defined concepts are essential for communication among scientists, especially for interdisciplinary and international collaboration. In the field of autism and other behavioral disorders, there has been substantial progress in nosology and diagnosis. This progress has enhanced discussion, research, and cross-disciplinary exchange. It had the merit of underlining the concept of developmental disorder and the breadth of dysfunctions in social, cognitive, language, and other domains. Similarly, the introduction of multiaxial diagnosis underscored the need for patients to be seen from varied points of view and the need to supplement "categorical disorders" (e.g., autism) with knowledge about other aspects of functioning, including medical status and adaptive abilities. As we discuss in the first section of this *Handbook,* advances in classification have led new knowledge and increasingly focused and refined research. The consensus exemplified in *Diagnostic and Statistical Manual of Mental Disorders,* fourth edition (*DSM-IV;* American Psychiatric Association, 1994), and *International Classification of Diseases,* 10th edition, (*ICD-10;* World Health Organization, 1992), has stimulated a tremendous increase in research over the past decade. Today the two internationally recognized systems provide a consistent approach to the diagnosis of the most severe disorders of early onset. While there are still some regional or national diagnostic alternatives, the trend is, fortunately, toward consensus. At the same time, the universal acceptance of a standard meter and of Greenwich time does not ensure great science or lack of debate and much work remains to be done, but the current approach has helped provide a solid framework on which future refinements can sensibly be made.

The thousands of publications—scientific papers, monographs, chapters, books—about autism and pervasive developmental disorder are evidence of its intrinsic interest to researchers and clinicians and to the human importance of these disorders for those who suffer from them and their families. The growing body of books and resources specifically designed for parents and family members has been a noteworthy achievement of the past several years. At the same time, you could reasonably ask why a revision of the *Handbook* is needed now.

This third edition of the *Handbook of Autism and Pervasive Developmental Disorders* is the second revision of a book that first appeared in 1987. This edition quickly became established as an important scholarly resource. Within a decade much had changed, and the second edition of this volume appeared. The rapid pace of scientific progress was reflected in the second edition, which was expanded to increase coverage of new research and treatment methods. Preparations for this version of the *Handbook* began in 2000 with an expansion of the number of editors in light of the increasingly diverse and sophisticated body of research that was becoming available.

In this edition, we have retained the best features of the second edition with expanded coverage in selected areas. In many instances, authors have kindly revised earlier contributions in light of current research; in other cases, we have solicited new contributors and chapters. As a result of the expanded coverage, the book has expanded into two volumes with a total of nine sections. This more extensive coverage reflects the increasing depth and breadth of work within the field.

In creating this *Handbook,* we invited chapters from recognized scholars. The responses to the invitations were gratifying. Each completed chapter was reviewed by the editors and by two members of a distinguished editorial committee. The use of peer review is not typical for volumes such as this, and we are grateful that all authors of chapters welcomed this process. The reviewers wrote careful critiques, sometimes many pages in length; these reviews were provided to the authors for their consideration during revision. The interactive process of revising chapters has helped ensure that the contributions are as good as the field allows.

The past several years have seen a major increase in the funding of research on autism. While we are gratified by this increased support, we hope for even more because only through research will we be able to change incidence and alter the natural history of autistic and other pervasive disorders. The cost of caring for one autistic individual over a lifetime may be more than any single investigator will ever have to spend during a career of research. Many hundreds of millions of dollars are spent internationally on direct services; only a tiny percentage of this expenditure is devoted to any type of formal research. It is as if the United States committed all of its funding to building iron lungs and considered virology to be a secondary concern in relation to polio. To fully exploit the many new methods for studying brain development and brain-behavior relations and to attempt to translate biological and behavioral research findings into treatments will require substantial investment of research funds. The recent network of federal centers through the Collaborative Program of Excellence in Autism (CPEA) and the Studies to Advance Autism Research and Treatment (STAART) as well as through the Research Units on Psychopharmacology (RUPP) and the Centers for Disease Control (CDC) have already had major benefits. These benefits will eventually include not only a reduction in suffering and in costs for those with autism, but also important knowledge that will benefit a far larger group of children and adults with other serious neuropsychiatric and developmental disorders. We hope that one contribution of the *Handbook* will be to underscore the gains from systematic research and the importance of sustained support for multidisciplinary clinical research groups.

We wish to recognize the support that has been provided over the decades to our own clinical and research program by the National Institute of Child Health and Human Development, National Institute of Deafness and Communication Disorders, and the National Institute of Mental Health, as well as by the Korczak Foundation, the W. T. Grant Foundation, the Doris Duke Foundation, the Simon's Foundation, Cure Autism Now, the National Alliance for Autism Research, and private donors.

We thank the members of our editorial board for their excellent contributions to this process and Lori Klein, who helped us coordinate this effort, as well as the wonderful editorial staff at Wiley, who have consistently sought to help us deliver the best possible work. We have been very fortunate in being able to work within the scholarly environment provided by the Yale School of Medicine and the Child Study Center. The unique qualities of the Child Study Center reflect the contributions of generations of faculty who have committed themselves to clinical scholarship, teaching, and service. We particularly wish to acknowledge the guidance and support of senior mentors—Albert J. Solnit, Sally Provence, Sam Ritvo, Sara Sparrow, and Edward Zigler—as well as many colleagues and collaborators in this work, including Robert Schultz, Cheryl Klaiman, Larry Scahill, Matt State, Elenga Grigorenko, George Anderson, James Leckman, Kasia Chawarska, Katherine Tsatsanis, Wendy Marans, and Emily Rubin.

A *Handbook* portrays what is known and reveals what is poorly understood. Although many studies have been conducted and areas explored, there is no hard biological or behavioral finding that can serve as a reliable compass point to guide research; in spite of great efforts and decades of commitment by researchers and clinicians, the fate of many autistic individuals remains cloudy; and even with new knowledge, there are still too many areas of controversy. That investigators and clinicians, working alongside families and advocates, have learned so much, often with very tight resources, speaks to their commitment to understanding and caring for autistic children and adults. The goal of this *Handbook* is to document their achievements and inspire their future efforts.

FRED R. VOLKMAR, MD
AMI KLIN, PHD
RHEA PAUL, PHD

Yale Child Study Center
New Haven, Connecticut
November, 2004

REFERENCES

American Psychiatric Association. (1980). *Diagnostic and statistical manual of mental disorders* (3rd ed.). Washington, DC: Author.

American Psychiatric Association. (1994). *Diagnostic and statistical manual of mental disorders* (4th ed.). Washington, DC: Author.

Cohen, D. J., & Donnellan, A. M. (1987). *Handbook of Autism and Pervasive Developmental Disorders*. New York: Wiley.

Cicchetti D., & Cohen D. J. (1995). *Developmental Psychopathology.* (Vols. 1–2). New York: Wiley.

Kanner, L. (1943). Autistic disturbances of affective contact. *Nervous Child 2*, 217–250.

Volkmar, F., Klin, A., Siegel, B., et al. (1994). Field trial for autistic disorder in *DSM-IV. American Journal of Psychiatry, 151*, 1361–1367.

World Health Organization. (1977). *Manual of the international statistical classification of diseases, injuries and causes of death* (9th ed., Vol. 1). Geneva, Switzerland: Author.

World Health Organization. (1992). *The ICD-10 classification of mental and behavioral disorders. Clinical descriptions and diagnostic guidelines.* Geneva, Switzerland: Author.

World Health Organization. (1993). *The ICD-10 classification of mental and behavioral disorders. Diagnostic criteria for research.* Geneva, Switzerland: Author.

Contents

VOLUME 1: DIAGNOSIS, DEVELOPMENT, NEUROBIOLOGY, AND BEHAVIOR

SECTION I
DIAGNOSIS AND CLASSIFICATION

Chapter 1.   Issues in the Classification of Autism and Related Conditions   5
              Fred R. Volkmar and Ami Klin

Chapter 2.   Epidemiological Studies of Pervasive Developmental Disorders   42
              Eric Fombonne

Chapter 3.   Childhood Disintegrative Disorder   70
              Fred R. Volkmar, Kathy Koenig, and Matthew State

Chapter 4.   Asperger Syndrome   88
              Ami Klin, James McPartland, and Fred R. Volkmar

Chapter 5.   Rett Syndrome: A Pervasive Developmental Disorder   126
              Richard Van Acker, Jennifer A. Loncola, and Eryn Y. Van Acker

Chapter 6.   Pervasive Developmental Disorder Not Otherwise Specified   165
              Kenneth E. Towbin

Chapter 7.   Outcomes in Autism Spectrum Disorders   201
              Patricia Howlin

SECTION II
DEVELOPMENT AND BEHAVIOR

Chapter 8.   Autism in Infancy and Early Childhood   223
              Katarzyna Chawarska and Fred R. Volkmar

Chapter 9.   The School-Age Child with an Autistic Spectrum Disorder   247
              Katherine A. Loveland and Belgin Tunali-Kotoski

Chapter 10. Adolescents and Adults with Autism   288
            Victoria Shea and Gary B. Mesibov

Chapter 11. Social Development in Autism   312
            Alice S. Carter, Naomi Ornstein Davis, Ami Klin, and Fred R. Volkmar

Chapter 12. Language and Communication in Autism   335
            Helen Tager-Flusberg, Rhea Paul, and Catherine Lord

Chapter 13. Neuropsychological Characteristics in Autism and Related Conditions   365
            Katherine D. Tsatsanis

Chapter 14. Imitation and Play in Autism   382
            Sally J. Rogers, Ian Cook, and Adrienne Meryl

Chapter 15. Autism and Emotion   406
            Peter Hobson

SECTION III
NEUROLOGICAL AND MEDICAL ISSUES

Chapter 16. Genetic Influences and Autism   425
            Michael Rutter

Chapter 17. Neurochemical Studies of Autism   453
            George M. Anderson and Yoshihiko Hoshino

Chapter 18. Neurologic Aspects of Autism   473
            *Nancy J. Minshew, John A. Sweeney, Margaret L. Bauman,
            and Sara Jane Webb*

Chapter 19. Functional Neuroimaging Studies of Autism Spectrum Disorders   515
            Robert T. Schultz and Diana L. Robins

Chapter 20. Medical Aspects of Autism   534
            Pauline A. Filipek

SECTION IV
THEORETICAL PERSPECTIVES

Chapter 21. Problems of Categorical Classification Systems   583
            Lorna Wing

Chapter 22. Executive Functions   606
            Sally Ozonoff, Mikle South, and Sherri Provencal

Chapter 23. Empathizing and Systemizing in Autism Spectrum Conditions   628
            *Simon Baron-Cohen, Sally Wheelwright, John Lawson, Richard Griffin,
            Chris Ashwin, Jac Billington, and Bhismadev Chakrabarti*

Chapter 24.   The Weak Central Coherence Account of Autism   640
              Francesca Happé

Chapter 25.   Joint Attention and Neurodevelopmental Models of Autism   650
              Peter Mundy and Courtney Burnette

Chapter 26.   The Enactive Mind—From Actions to Cognition: Lessons from Autism   682
              Ami Klin, Warren Jones, Robert T. Schultz, and Fred R. Volkmar

Author Index   I•1

Subject Index   I•39

VOLUME 2: ASSESSMENT, INTERVENTIONS, AND POLICY

SECTION V
ASSESSMENT

Chapter 27.   Screening for Autism in Young Children   707
              Elaine E. Coonrod and Wendy L. Stone

Chapter 28.   Diagnostic Instruments in Autistic Spectrum Disorders   730
              Catherine Lord and Christina Corsello

Chapter 29.   Clinical Evaluation in Autism Spectrum Disorders: Psychological
              Assessment within a Transdisciplinary Framework   772
              Ami Klin, Celine Saulnier, Katherine Tsatsanis, and Fred R. Volkmar

Chapter 30.   Assessing Communication in Autism Spectrum Disorders   799
              Rhea Paul

Chapter 31.   Behavioral Assessment of Individuals with Autism: A Functional
              Ecological Approach   817
              Michael D. Powers

Chapter 32.   Sensory and Motor Features in Autism: Assessment and Intervention   831
              Grace T. Baranek, L. Diane Parham, and James W. Bodfish

SECTION VI
INTERVENTIONS

Chapter 33.   Curriculum and Classroom Structure   863
              J. Gregory Olley

Chapter 34.   Behavioral Interventions to Promote Learning in Individuals with Autism   882
              Laura Schreibman and Brooke Ingersoll

Chapter 35.   Behavioral Interventions   897
              Joel D. Bregman, Dianne Zager, and John Gerdtz

Chapter 36. Critical Issues in Enhancing Communication Abilities for Persons with
            Autism Spectrum Disorders   925
            Barry M. Prizant and Amy M. Wetherby

Chapter 37. Enhancing Early Language in Children with Autism Spectrum Disorders   946
            Rhea Paul and Dean Sutherland

Chapter 38. Addressing Social Communication Skills in Individuals with
            High-Functioning Autism and Asperger Syndrome: Critical Priorities
            in Educational Programming   977
            Wendy D. Marans, Emily Rubin, and Amy Laurent

Chapter 39. School-Based Programs   1003
            Joel R. Arick, David A. Krug, Ann Fullerton, Lauren Loos, and Ruth Falco

Chapter 40. Helping Children with Autism Enter the Mainstream   1029
            Jan S. Handleman, Sandra L. Harris, and Megan P. Martins

Chapter 41. Models of Educational Intervention for Students with Autism: Home, Center,
            and School-Based Programming   1043
            Sandra L. Harris, Jan S. Handleman, and Heather K. Jennett

Chapter 42. Working with Families   1055
            Lee M. Marcus, Linda J. Kunce, and Eric Schopler

Chapter 43. Employment: Options and Issues for Adolescents and Adults with
            Autism Spectrum Disorders   1087
            Peter F. Gerhardt and David L. Holmes

Chapter 44. Psychopharmacology   1102
            Lawrence Scahill and Andrés Martin

SECTION VII
PUBLIC POLICY PERSPECTIVES

Chapter 45. Preparation of Autism Specialists   1123
            Gail G. McGee and Michael J. Morrier

Chapter 46. Educating Children with Autism: Current Legal Issues   1161
            Myrna R. Mandlawitz

Chapter 47. Cross-Cultural Program Priorities and Reclassification of Outcome
            Research Methods   1174
            Eric Schopler

SECTION VIII
INTERNATIONAL PERSPECTIVES

Chapter 48. International Perspectives   1193
            Fred R. Volkmar

SECTION IX
PERSONAL PERSPECTIVES

Chapter 49.   Community-Integrated Residential Services for Adults with Autism:
A Working Model (Based on a Mother's Odyssey)   1255
Ruth Christ Sullivan

Chapter 50.   A Sibling's Perspective on Autism   1265
Jason B. Konidaris

Chapter 51.   A Personal Perspective of Autism   1276
Temple Grandin

Chapter 52.   A Teacher's Perspective: Adult Outcomes   1287
Virginia Walker Sperry

Chapter 53.   Autism: Where We Have Been, Where We Are Going   1304
Isabelle Rapin

Author Index   I•1

Subject Index   I•39

SECTION I

DIAGNOSIS AND CLASSIFICATION

The paired processes of diagnosis and classification are fundamental to research and intervention. The diagnostic *process* includes all of the activities in which a clinician engages in trying to understand the nature of an individual's difficulty. The result of this process is often a narrative account—a portrait of the individual's past, the current problems, and the ways in which these problems can be related to each other and to possible, underlying causes. A useful diagnostic process also suggests methods for being helpful, including specific treatments. In the course of the diagnostic process, a clinician will learn about the patient's history, talk to others about the patient, observe the patient, engage in specialized examinations, and use laboratory and other methods for helping define patients' problems and their causes. The clinician will integrate the findings from these activities, based on specialized, scientific knowledge. Often, a patient will have several types of problems; the diagnostic process may lead to a narrative that links these to an underlying, common cause or may separate the problems on the basis of their differing causes or treatments. Often, more than one clinician may be involved in the diagnostic process; then, the final clinical, diagnostic formulation will integrate the pooled information into a coherent and consensual narrative that reflects the varied information.

One component of the diagnostic process is the assignment of the patient's difficulties—his or her signs, symptoms, pains, troubles, worries, dysfunctions, abnormal tests—to a specific class or category of illness or disorder. Through classification, the patient's individualized, unique signs and symptoms are provided a context. They are given a more general meaning. For example, the clinician will assign the patient's coughing and fever to the category *pneumonia*. This categorical diagnosis is placed within the narrative of the patient's life and current problems. It may be related to the patient's family or genetic background, experiences, exposures, vulnerabilities, and the like, and it will be used to explain why the patient has come for help and what type of treatment may be useful.

The diagnostic process is based on current knowledge, technologies, and skills; it can sometimes be quite brief (as in the diagnostic processes for an earache) or remarkably extensive (as in the diagnostic process for autism). Diagnostic classifications, also, are based on available knowledge and laboratory methods; they also embody conventions, the consensus among clinicians and experts about a *useful* way for sorting illnesses and troubles.

New knowledge and methodologies change the diagnostic process as well as the classification system. The advent of methods such as molecular genetic testing, magnetic resonance imaging of the brain, and structured, formal assessment of cognitive processes have changed the diagnostic process and classification and will continue to do so in the future.

The skillful diagnostic process, and the resultant account about the patient and his illness, often is broad-based, nuanced, and individualized. The clinical formulation, the full statement of findings, may capture the many dimensions of a person's life, including his or her competencies as well as specific

1

impairments and difficulties. However, a diagnostic categorization—a label or classification of specific troubles and their designation as a *syndrome, disorder* or *disease*—is delimited. Providing the label of a specific disease delimits individuality for the sake of being able to utilize general knowledge gained from scientific study and experience with others with similar problems. In this important respect, it is useful to think that *individuals are engaged in the process of diagnosis* and *symptoms and signs are classified* and labeled. A diagnostic label is not able or meant to capture the fullness of an individual. Diagnostic classification systems and specific assignment to a disease or disorder category are tools, which when combined with other tools should lead to helpful understanding and treatment.

The newer methods of classification of developmental, psychiatric, behavioral, or mental disorders respect the distinction between diagnosing an individual and classifying his or her problems. They are also multidimensional and elicit information about other domains of the patient's life, in addition to areas of leading impairment. This approach shapes and has been shaped by the two international systems of classification in which autism and pervasive developmental disorders are included: the *Diagnostic and Statistical Manual of Mental Disorders* of the American Psychiatric Association and the *International Statistical Classification of Diseases and Related Health Problems* of the World Health Organization (WHO). The introductions to the recent editions of these two systems (*DSM-IV,* American Psychiatric Association, 1994; and *ICD-10,* WHO, 1992) provide helpful overviews of the goals of classification and the roles of diagnostic categories in clinical understanding.

A new diagnostic term was introduced in the *DSM-III* in 1980: the concept of pervasive developmental disorder (PDD). The umbrella term PDD gained broad popularity among professionals from various disciplines as well as with parents and advocates. Without a previous history in psychiatry, psychology, or neurology, the novel term PDD had the advantage of not carrying excessive theoretical baggage or controversy. It also had a broad inter-disciplinary appeal and a nice emphasis on *development* and *disorders of development.* No specific diagnostic

criteria were provided for PDD, but the clinical description conveyed a sense of the contour of its clinical territory. To be a citizen of this territory, a child had to exhibit difficulties from the first several years of life involving several domains (social, language, emotional, cognitive) and with significant impairment of functioning. In 1980, and again when *DSM-III* was revised in 1987 (*DSM-III-R*), the only example of a specifically defined example of PDD was autism. Indeed, autism remains the paradigm or model form of PDD. From 1980 to 1994, other children whose difficulties were captured by the sense of PDD, but who were not diagnosed as having autism, were described as having "pervasive developmental disorder that is not otherwise specified" (PDD-NOS). Although not an official diagnostic term, the phrase autism spectrum disorder (ASD) is now in widespread use and is synonymous with the term PDD.

The 1994 edition of the *Manual of Mental Disorders* (*DSM-IV*), based on new evidence and international field testing, refined the diagnostic criteria for autism and formalized three new classes or types of pervasive developmental disorders: childhood disintegrative disorder, Asperger's disorder, and Rett's disorder. Also, a consensus was reached between the two major systems, *DSM* and *ICD,* for the system of classification and specific diagnostic criteria. Thus, for the first time, there is happily an internationally accepted, field-tested, diagnostic system for the most severe disorders of development. The *DSM-IV* and *ICD-10* systems form the epistemological backbone of this *Handbook.*

The chapters in this section of the *Handbook* describe current frameworks for classification, the four forms of pervasive developmental disorders for which specific criteria are provided in *DSM-IV,* and the kinds of disturbances that remain within the territory of pervasive developmental disorders that are not further classified. This section also provides a review of studies of natural history and outcome.

It is our expectation that advances in understanding the pathogenesis of pervasive developmental disorders will continue to have a major impact on the diagnostic and classification processes. Thus, in any discussion about diagnosis and nosology, it is important to recognize their provisional nature. Advances in knowledge may lead to changes in diagnostic approaches. It is also critical to remember the importance of balancing categorical approaches to diagnosis with a fuller understanding of the many dimensions of individual children and adults, that is, as whole people.

REFERENCES

American Psychiatric Association. (1980). *Diagnostic and statistical manual of mental disorders* (3rd ed.). Washington, DC: Author.

American Psychiatric Association. (1987). *Diagnostic and statistical manual of mental disorders* (3rd ed., rev.). Washington, DC: Author.

American Psychiatric Association. (1994). *Diagnostic and statistical manual of mental disorders* (4th ed.). Washington, DC: Author.

World Health Organization. (1992). *International classification of diseases* (10th ed.). Geneva, Switzerland: Author.

CHAPTER 1

Issues in the Classification of Autism and Related Conditions

FRED R. VOLKMAR AND AMI KLIN

Clinicians and researchers have achieved consensus on the validity of autism as a diagnostic category and the many features central to its definition (Rutter, 1996). This has made possible the convergence of the two major diagnostic systems: the fourth edition of the American Psychiatric Association's *Diagnostic and Statistical Manual of Mental Disorders* (*DSM-IV*, 1994) and the 10th edition of the International Classification of Diseases (*ICD-10;* World Health Organization [WHO], 1992). Although some differences remain, these major diagnostic systems have become much more alike than different; this has facilitated the development of diagnostic assessments "keyed" to broadly accepted, internationally recognized guidelines (Rutter, Le Couteur, & Lord, 2003; see Chapter 28, this *Handbook,* Volume 2). It is somewhat surprising that, as greater consensus has been achieved on the definition of strictly defined autism, an interesting and helpful discussion on issues of "broader phenotype" or potential variants of autism has begun (Bailey, Palferman, Heavey, & Le Couteur, 1998; Dawson et al., 2002; Pickles, Starr, Kazak, Bolton, Papanikolaou,

et al., 2000; Piven, Palmer, Jacobi, Childress, & Arndt, 1997; Volkmar, Lord, Bailey, Schultz, & Klin, 2004).

Today, autism is probably the complex psychiatric or developmental disorder with the best empirically based, cross-national diagnostic criteria. Data from a number of research groups from around the world have confirmed the usefulness of current diagnostic approaches, and, even more importantly, the availability of a shared clinical concept and language for differential diagnosis is a great asset for clear communication among clinicians, researchers, and advocates alike (Buitelaar, Van der Gaag, Klin, & Volkmar, 1999; Magnusson & Saemundsen, 2001; Sponheim, 1996; Sponheim & Skjeldal, 1998). In the future, the discovery of biological correlates, causes, and pathogenic pathways will, no doubt, change the ways in which autism is diagnosed and may well lead to new nosological approaches that, in turn, will facilitate further scientific progress (Rutter, 2000). Simultaneously, considerable progress has been made on understanding the broader range of difficulties included within the autism

The authors acknowledge the support of the National Institute of Child Health and Human Development (CPEA program project grant 1PO1HD3548201, grant 5-P01-HD03008, and grant R01-HD042127-02), the National Institute of Mental Health (STAART grant U54-MH066494), the Yale Children's Clinical Research Center, and of the National Alliance of Autism Research, Cure Autism Now, and the Doris Duke Foundation as well as the Simons Foundation. We also gratefully acknowledge the helpful comments of Professor Michael Rutter on an earlier version of this manuscript.

spectrum; that is, as our knowledge of autism has advanced, so has our understanding of a broader range of conditions with some similarities to it. Table 1.1 lists categories of pervasive developmental disorders (PDDs) as classified by *ICD-10* and *DSM-IV*.

In addition to the international and cross-disciplinary agreement about diagnostic criteria for autism, a consensus has emerged about other issues that were once debated. Today, there is broad agreement that autism is a developmental disorder, that autism and associated disorders represent the behavioral manifestations of underlying dysfunctions in the functioning of the central nervous system, and that sustained educational and behavioral interventions are useful and constitute the core of treatment (National Research Council, 2001).

In this chapter, we summarize the development of current diagnostic concepts with a particular focus on autism and on the empirical basis for its current official definition. We address the rationale for inclusion of other nonautistic PDDs/autism spectrum disorders (ASDs), which are discussed in detail in other chapters in this section. We also note areas in which knowledge is lacking, such as the relationships of autism to other comorbid conditions and the ongoing efforts to provide alternative approaches to subtyping these conditions.

DEVELOPMENT OF AUTISM AS A DIAGNOSTIC CONCEPT

Although children with what we now would describe as autism had probably been described much earlier as so called wild or feral children (Candland, 1993; Simon, 1978) it was Leo Kanner who first elaborated what today would be termed the syndrome of childhood autism.

Kanner's Description—Early Controversies

Kanner's (1943) seminal clinical description of 11 children with "autistic disturbances of affective contact" has endured in many ways. His description of the children was grounded in data and theory of child development, particularly the work of Gesell, who demonstrated that normal infants exhibit marked interest in social interaction from early in life. Kanner suggested that early infantile autism was an inborn, constitutional disorder in which children were born lacking the typical motivation for social interaction and affective comments. Using the model of inborn errors of metabolism, Kanner felt that individuals with autism were born without the biological preconditions for psychologically metabolizing the social world. He used the word *autism* to convey this self-contained quality. The term

TABLE 1.1   Conditions Currently Classified as Pervasive Developmental Disorders Correspondence of *ICD-10* and *DSM-IV* Categories

ICD-10	DSM-IV
Childhood autism	Autistic disorder
Atypical autism	Pevasive developmental disorder not otherwise specified (PDD-NOS)
Rett syndrome	Rett's disorder
Other childhood disintegrative disorder	Childhood disintegrative disorder
Overactive disorder with mental retardation	No corresponding category with stereotyped movements
Asperger syndrome	Asperger's disorder
Other pervasive developmental disorder	PDD-NOS
Pervasive developmental disorder, unspecified	PDD-NOS

Sources: Diagnostic and Statistical Manual of Mental Disorders, fourth edition, by American Psychiatric Association, 1994, Washington, DC: Author; and *International Classification of Diseases: Diagnostic Criteria for Research,* tenth edition, by the World Health Organization, 1992, Geneva, Switzerland: Author.

was borrowed from Bleuler (1911/1950), who used *autism* to describe idiosyncratic, self-centered thinking. Autism for Kanner was intended to suggest that autistic children, too, live in their own world. Yet, the autism of individuals with autism is distinct from that of schizophrenia: It represents a failure of development, not a regression, and fantasy is impoverished if present at all. The sharing of the term increased early confusion about the relationship of the conditions.

In addition to the remarkable social failure of autistic individuals, Kanner observed other unusual features in the clinical histories of the children. Kanner described the profound disturbances in communication. In the original cohort, three of the children were mute. The language of the others was marked by echolalia and literalness, as well as a fascinating difficulty with acquiring the use of the first person, personal pronoun ("I"), and referral to self in the third person ("he" or by first name). Another intriguing feature was the children's unusual responses to the inanimate environment; for example, a child might be unresponsive to parents, yet overly sensitive to sounds or to small changes in daily routine.

While Kanner's brilliant clinical accounts of the unusual social isolation, resistance to change, and dysfunction in communication have stood the test of time, other aspects of the original report have been refined or refuted by further research.

A contentious issue early in the history of autism research concerned the role of parents in pathogenesis. Kanner observed that parents of the initial cases were often remarkably successful educationally or professionally; he also appreciated that there were major problems in the relations between these parents and their child. In his initial paper, he indicated that he believed autism to be congenital, but the issue of potential psychological factors in causing autism was taken up by a number of individuals; this issue plagued the history of the field for many years. From the 1960s, however, it has been recognized that parental behavior as such played no role in pathogenesis. Yet, the pain of parents having been blamed for a child's devastating disorder tended to linger in the memories of families, even those whose

children were born long after the theory was dead; unfortunately, this notion still prevails in some countries.

Two types of information went against the psychogenic theories. It is now known that children with autism are found in families from all social classes if studies control for possible factors that might bias case ascertainment (e.g., Wing, 1980); while additional data on this topic are needed, more recent and rigorous research has failed to demonstrate associations with social class (see Chapter 2, this *Handbook,* this volume, for a review). A more central issue relevant to psychogenic etiology concerns the unusual patterns of interaction that children with autism and related conditions have with their parents (and other people as well). The interactional problems of autistic individuals clearly can be seen to arise from the side of the child and not the parents (Mundy, Sigman, Ungerer, & Sherman, 1986) although parents may be at risk for various problems (see Chapter 15, this *Handbook,* this volume). Probably most important, data support the role of dysfunction in basic brain systems in the pathogenesis of the disorder (see Volkmar et al., 2004). Today, the data appear to support the concept that biological factors, particularly genetic ones, convey a vulnerability to autism; as Rutter (1999) has noted, the issue of interaction between genetic and environmental vulnerabilities of all types remains an important one relevant to a host of disorders in addition to autism.

Kanner speculated that autism was not related to other medical conditions. Subsequent research has shown that various medical conditions can be associated with autism (see Chapter 2, this *Handbook,* this volume) and, most importantly, that approximately 25% of persons with autism develop a seizure disorder (Rutter, 1970; Volkmar & Nelson, 1990; see also Chapters 18 & 20, this *Handbook,* this volume). With the recognition of the prevalence of medical problems, some investigators proposed a distinction between "primary" and "secondary" autism depending on whether associated medical conditions, for example, congenital rubella (Chess, Fernandez, & Korn, 1978), could be demonstrated. As time went on, it became apparent that, in some basic sense, all cases were "organic," and designations such as primary and secondary autism are no longer generally made.

Kanner also misconstrued the relation between autism and intellectual disability. His first cases were attractive youngsters without unusual physical features, who performed well on some *parts* of IQ tests (particularly those that test rote memory and copying, such as block design, rather than comprehension of abstract, verbal concepts). Kanner felt that autistic children were not mentally retarded, and he, and many psychologists after him, invoked motivational factors to explain poor performance. Autistic individuals were called "functionally retarded." Decades of research have now shown that when developmentally appropriate tests are given in their entirety, full-scale intelligence and developmental scores (IQ and DQ scores) are in the mentally retarded range for the majority of individuals with autism (Rutter, Bailey, Bolton, & Le Couter, 1994) and maintain stability over time (Lockyer & Rutter, 1969, 1970). Kanner's impression of potentially normal intelligence, even in the face of apparent retardation, was based on what has proven to be a consistent finding on psychological testing. Children with autism often have unusually scattered abilities, with nonverbal skills often significantly advanced over more verbally mediated ones (see Chapter 29, this *Handbook,* Volume 2); at the same time, children with autism differ in their pattern of behavior and cognitive development from children with severe language disorders (Bartak, Rutter, & Cox, 1977). On the other hand, when the focus shifts from autism, strictly defined, to the broader autistic spectrum, a much broader range of IQ scores is observed (Bailey et al., 1998).

The severity of the autistic syndrome led some clinicians in the 1950s to speculate that autism was the earliest form of schizophrenia (Bender, 1946). Clinicians during the first decades of the study of autism tended to attribute complex mental phenomena such as hallucinations and delusions to children who were, and remained, entirely mute (Volkmar & Cohen, 1991a). In the 1970s, research findings began to show that these two conditions are quite disparate in terms of onset patterns, course, and family genetics (Kolvin, 1971; Rutter, 1972).

Other Diagnostic Concepts

In contrast to autism, the definition of *autistic-like* conditions remains in need of more clarification (Rutter, 1996; Szatmari, 2000; Szatmari, Volkmar, & Walther, 1995). Although the available research is less extensive than that on autism, several of these autistic-like conditions were well enough studied, broadly recognized, and clinically important enough to be included in *DSM-IV* and *ICD-10.* We anticipate that further studies will improve the definition of these conditions and that new disorders may well be delineated within the broad and heterogeneous class of PDD.

Diagnostic concepts with similarities to autism were proposed before and after Kanner's clinical research. Shortly after the turn of the century, Heller, a special educator in Vienna, described an unusual condition in which children appeared normal for a few years and then suffered a profound regression in their functioning and a derailment of future development (Heller, 1908). This condition was originally known as *dementia infantilis* or *disintegrative psychosis;* it now has official status in *DSM-IV* as childhood disintegrative disorder (see Chapter 3, this *Handbook,* this volume). Similarly, the year after Kanner's original paper, Hans Asperger, a young physician in Vienna, proposed the concept of autistic psychopathy or, as it is now known, Asperger's disorder (Asperger, 1944; see Chapter 4, this *Handbook,* this volume). Although Asperger apparently was not aware of Kanner's paper or his use of the word autism, Asperger used this same term in his description of the marked social problems in a group of boys he had worked with. Asperger's concept was not widely recognized for many years, but it has recently received much greater attention and is now included in both *DSM-IV* and *ICD-10.* Another clinician, Andreas Rett, observed an unusual developmental disorder in girls (Rett, 1966) characterized by a short period of normal development and then a multifaceted form of intellectual and motor deterioration. Rett's disorder is also now officially included in the PDD class (see Chapter 5, this *Handbook,* this volume).

The descriptions proposed by some other clinicians have not fared as well. For example,

Mahler, a child psychoanalyst, proposed the concept of symbiotic psychosis (Mahler, 1952) for children who seemed to fail in the task of separating their psychological selves from the hypothesized early fusion with their mothers. This concept now has only historical interest, as does her view of a "normal autistic phase" of development. In contrast, Rank (1949), also working from the framework of psychoanalysis, suggested that there is a spectrum of dysfunctions in early development that affects children's social relations and their modulation of anxiety. Her detailed descriptions of atypical personality development are of continuing interest in relation to the large number of children with serious, early-onset disturbances in development who are not autistic. These ideas were developed by Provence in her studies of young children with atypical development (Provence & Dahl, 1987; see also Chapter 6, this *Handbook,* this volume).

In the first (1952) and second (1968) editions of the American Psychiatric Association's Diagnostic and Statistical Manuals only the term *childhood schizophrenia* was officially available to describe autistic children. Much of the early work on autism and related conditions is, therefore, difficult to interpret because it is unclear exactly what was being studied. As information on life course and family history became available (Kolvin, 1971; Rutter, 1970), it became clear that autism could not simply be considered an early form of schizophrenia, that most autistic individuals were retarded, that the final behavioral expression of the autistic syndrome was potentially the result of several factors, and that the disorder was not the result of deviant parent-child interaction (Cantwell, Baker, & Rutter, 1979; DeMyer, Hingtgen, & Jackson, 1981). These findings greatly influenced the inclusion of autism in the third edition of *DSM* (American Psychiatric Association, 1980), to which we return later.

ISSUES IN CLASSIFICATION

Systems for classification exist for many different reasons, but a fundamental purpose is to enhance communication (Rutter, 2002). For researchers, this is essential to achieve reliability and validity of findings from research

studies, to share knowledge among investigators, and to encourage the development of a body of knowledge. For clinicians and educators, classification helps guide selection of treatments for an individual and the evaluation of the benefits of an intervention for groups of individuals with shared problems (Cantwell, 1996). For the legal system, government regulation, insurance programs, and advocates, classification systems define individuals with special entitlements. If a diagnostic classification system is to be effective in these varied domains, the system must be clear, broadly accepted, and relatively easy to use. Diagnostic stability is an important goal; difficulties arise if diagnostic systems are changed too rapidly, for example, interpretation of previous research becomes a problem. A classification system should provide descriptions that allow disorders to be differentiated from one another in significant ways, for example, in course or associated features (Rutter, 1996). Official classification systems must be applicable to conditions that afflict individuals of both sexes and of different ages; at different developmental levels; and from different ethnic, social, and geographical backgrounds. Finally, a system must be logically consistent and comprehensive (Rutter & Gould, 1985). Achieving these divergent goals is not always easy (Volkmar & Schwab-Stone, 1996).

The clinical provision of a diagnosis or multiple diagnoses is only one part of the *diagnostic process* (Cohen, 1976). The diagnostic process provides a richer description of a child or adult as a full person; it includes a historical account of the origins of the difficulties and changes over time, along with other relevant information about the individual's development, life course, and social situation. The diagnostic process highlights areas of competence, as well as difficulties and symptoms; it notes the ways the individual has adapted; it describes previous treatments, available resources, and other information that will allow a fuller understanding of the individual and his or her problems. Also, the diagnostic process may suggest or delineate biological, psychological, and social factors that may have placed the individual at risk, led to the disorder, changed its severity, or modified the symptoms and course. The result of the diagnostic process should be a rich formulation—an account that will be elaborated with new knowledge, including the response of the individual to intervention. It cannot be overemphasized that while the diagnostic label or labels provide important and helpful information, they do not substitute for a full and rich understanding of the individual's strengths and weaknesses and life circumstances. Thus, programs should be designed *around individuals* rather than labels.

A diagnostic formulation, based on an extended diagnostic process, is provisional and subject to change with new information and experience. In this sense, it is a continuing activity involving the individual, family, clinicians, and educators. The diagnostic process, as a clinical activity, depends on a body of scientific knowledge and is enriched when there is a common diagnostic language used for clinical and research purposes. Information provided by this process is useful at the level of the individual case but also has important public health and social policy implications, for example, in formulating intervention strategies and allocating resources.

Diagnostic systems lose value if they are either overly broad or overly narrow. The classification system must provide sufficient detail to be used consistently and reliably by clinicians and researchers across settings. When they achieve "official" status, as is the case for *ICD* and *DSM,* classification schemes have important regulatory and policy implications. Sometimes, there may be conflicts between scientific and clinical needs, on one hand, and the impact of definitions on policy, on the other. For example, there may be good scientific reasons for a narrowly defined categorical diagnosis that includes only individuals who *definitely and clearly* have a specifically defined condition and excludes individuals where there is less certainty. From the point of view of service provision, however, broader diagnostic concepts may be most appropriate. Unfortunately, there has often been a failure to recognize the validity of these two tensions around aspects of diagnosis.

Classification schemes of an "official" nature may have unintended, but important, implications, for example, in terms of legal mandates for services; this is particularly true in the United States where federal regulations

may be tied to specific diagnostic categories (Rutter & Schopler, 1992). Such an approach tends, unfortunately, to emphasize the diagnostic *label,* rather than the diagnostic *process.* On the other hand, if a governmental body adopts a broad diagnostic concept, the available resources may be diluted and individuals most in need of intensive treatment may be deprived while those with less clearly definable service requirements are included in programs (Rutter & Schopler, 1992).

There are many misconceptions about diagnosis and classification (see Rutter, 1996; Volkmar & Schwab-Stone, 1996; Volkmar, Schwab-Stone, & First, 2002). For example, *DSM-IV* and similar systems of classification are organized around dichotomous categories; in these systems, an individual either has or does not have a disorder. Yet, classification can also be dimensional, in which an individual has a problem, group of problems, or dysfunction to a certain degree. Dimensional approaches offer many advantages, as exemplified by the use of standard tests of intelligence, adaptive behavior, or communication; in many ways, such approaches have dominated in other branches of medicine and frequently coexist with categorical ones (see Rutter, 2002, for a review). Not only can the disease process (e.g., hypertension) be dimensional but also various risk factors may be dimensional, and a dimensional focus has important advantages for advancing knowledge in this regard. On the other hand, at some point qualitative and dimensional changes (as in blood pressure) may lead either to functional impairment or specific symptoms (e.g., a high blood pressure can lead to angina), and the categorical approach is needed to address this important implication of what is basically a dimensional phenomenon. Depression is a relevant example from psychiatry; for example, all of us have the experience of mood fluctuations during the course of our daily lives, but when depression becomes so significant that it begins to interfere with functioning or causes impairment in other ways, we can consider use of specific treatments for depression.

Dimensional and categorical classification systems are not incompatible. It is possible to set a boundary point along a dimension that can be used to define when a disorder is diagnosed. This boundary can be determined by empirical studies that indicate that an important threshold has been crossed that will influence functional status or impairment; or the boundary can be defined by convention reached by clinicians, researchers, those who establish policy, or some combination of factors. For example, disorders such as depression are readily amenable to dimensional definitions. To some extent, all of us have experience of the symptoms of depression, yet, for the clinical syndrome of depression, a threshold must be surpassed. There must be a sufficient number and range of symptoms that cause suffering, interfere with daily functioning, and persist (see Rutter, 2002; Chapter 28, this *Handbook,* Volume 2).

For studies of autism and associated conditions, various dimensional approaches have been employed. Some instruments used for purposes of screening or diagnostic assessment focus on behaviors or historical features (or both) that may be highly suggestive of a diagnosis of autism. Such approaches have not (with some notable exceptions—see Chapter 28, this *Handbook,* Volume 2) typically tried to relate in a straightforward way with categorical approaches. Given the issues of focusing on highly unusual behaviors, other problems are posed in the development and standardization of such instruments. At the same time, such instruments have had a very significant role in research as well as clinical work, for example, in screening for persons likely to have autism (see Chapter 27, this *Handbook,* Volume 2).

Another example of the dimensional approach is embodied in the use of traditional tests of intelligence or communicative ability (see Chapters 29 & 30, this *Handbook,* Volume 2). For such instruments, the provision of good normative data is an important benefit. A growing body of work has focused on the dimensional metrification of social competence using the Vineland Adaptive Behavior Scales (see Chapter 29, this *Handbook,* Volume 2).

The role of theory in guiding development of classification systems is a source of confusion. Many assume that a classification system must be based on a theoretical model. To some degree, all accounts of an event, process, clinical set of findings, or disorder relate to a "theory" (or what more probably might be called a hypothesis or theory in the making). Such prototheories focus on what to the viewer is the most important thing to convey about a phenomenon or set of observations. Such notions provide us with a sense of orderliness or narrative coherence. However, there is no truly naive form of description or a naive description of what clinicians and researchers mean by symptoms of a disorder. Even the decision about what to consider a disorder of an individual presupposes a theory of what should be considered a disorder or dysfunction.

The boundaries of the nosology for *DSM IV* and *ICD* reflect a history of the professions of neurology, psychiatry, and general medicine as well as preconceptions of where the current lines should be drawn. For example, the inclusion of Rett's disorder in *DSM-IV* raised the question of why a disorder with such clear neurological aspects should be classified within the PDDs (Gillberg, 1994). However, neurological factors play a strong role in many disorders (including autism), but that does not mean that they are *only* neurological. Much of the issue of where disorders such as autism or Rett's are placed has to do with a practical issue of usage (see Rutter, 1994, for a discussion). A similar argument could be had about Alzheimer's disease, which clearly falls within the professional purview of both psychiatrists and neurologists. One important effect of the decision to include Rett's disorder has been the ability to focus specifically on this group in terms of genetic mechanisms (see Chapter 5, this *Handbook,* this volume).

No nosology, including *DSM-IV* or *ICD-10,* can be totally free of theory, although there are good reasons for current psychiatric systems to aspire to be as atheoretical and descriptive as possible. This is illustrated in the earlier versions of *DSM* (American Psychiatric Association, 1952, 1968) where theory was so much part of definition that research work was impeded. Theoretically oriented classification systems often are difficult to use since there may be differences even among those who share a theoretical perspective. Since 1980, the trend in psychiatry has been toward descriptive, operational definitions that emphasize observable behaviors and discrete clinical findings (Frances, Widiger, & Pincus, 1989); indeed, such an approach is represented, in many respects, by Kanner's original description of autism. Such an approach to diagnosis is often called *phenomenological* although this term is confusing, since phenomenology is a branch of philosophy that concerns the underlying structures of experience and the modes of learning about mental and psychological phenomena (including the use of introspection and dense description). Phenomenology represents a theoretical approach to diagnosis that has an important history in psychology and psychiatry. When contemporary researchers and clinicians speak of *phenomenological* systems, they usually mean something quite different: descriptions of the surface (signs and symptoms) or accounts of observable phenomena. In any event, *DSM-IV* and *ICD-10* attempt to avoid all encompassing, grand theories of pathogenesis and concepts that require adherence to a particular viewpoint about the functioning of the mind or the origins of psychopathology. In this sense, they attempt to provide a relatively common language and framework that can be used by adherents of different theoretical points of view.

Another misunderstanding is that classification systems require etiologies and causes. Here, too, the trend within psychiatry has been toward systems that recognize that the causes of most psychiatric, developmental, and emotional disorders remain uncertain and complex (Rutter, 1996). Also, there is a realization that many different causes may lead to the apparently very similar clinical condition while one specific cause may be associated with various conditions. Scientific studies will reveal new causes for old diseases, and there often are surprises as different underlying factors are revealed for what has appeared to be a simple, homogeneous clinical condition. The increasing knowledge and the disparity between *genotype* (underlying cause) and *phenotype* (clinical presentation) indicate the importance of not basing a classification system only on purported causes. However, as etiologies are elucidated, it makes sense to consider including them within a diagnostic framework. In *DSM-IV,* a causal framework is most clear in the definition of posttraumatic stress disorder (PTSD), a condition in which a clear precipitant (a traumatic experience) is related to a range of persistent symptoms. For autism, a causal nosology is not yet available, although genetic, neuroimaging, behavioral, or other

findings during the next years may make this more feasible in diagnosing and subtyping autism.

Like other human constructions, classification systems can be misused (Hobbs, 1975). One misuse is to confuse the person with the diagnostic label. A person with a disorder is a person first: An individual with autism is not an "autistic." A label does not capture the fullness of the person, nor his or her humanity. There is a risk that categorical terms may minimize the tremendous differences among persons who have a particular condition. The very broad range of syndrome expression in autism requires the provision of multiple kinds of information in addition to the categorical diagnosis, for example, level of communicative speech, intellectual abilities, interests, and capacity for independent living.

Another misuse of a categorical diagnosis occurs when it is elevated to the status of being an *explanation* or when its use obscures lack of knowledge. In Moliere's plays, the physician would mystify and impress the patients with long Latin terms that were offered as explanations but were merely redescriptions of the patient's symptoms. For many diagnoses, this is still the case. For example, it is helpful to parents to know that their 2-year-old child is not talking because he or she has a disorder. However, it is different when this disorder is deafness—which may explain the muteness, at some interesting level of understanding—than when the disorder is autism. The diagnosis of autism clarifies some aspects of the nature of an individual child's muteness by placing this child within a class of individuals about whom a great deal of valuable information about treatment and course has been learned. But the classification does not really explain the language disorder any more than the diagnosis of attention deficit/hyperactivity disorder explains a child's overactivity and frustration intolerance. When a label is mistaken for an explanation, areas of ignorance may be covered over and the search for underlying causes may end prematurely.

The final misuse of classification is the potential for stigmatization. Parents and advocates are anxious about the ways in which classification may negatively skew how the child or adult is seen by others or the limitations and adversities that may follow upon being labeled. Unfortunately, this danger is real. When a child has been classified as mentally retarded or intellectually disabled, this has sometimes meant removal from the mainstream of education and a lifelong reduction of opportunity. The diagnosis of schizophrenia has had negative connotations associated with madness and danger. Autism, too, has had its social disadvantages; for example, at one time it may have implied a particular view of etiology in which parents were placed at fault. A diagnostic label may exclude individuals from programs or reduce chances in purchasing insurance. For these reasons, parents and advocates have sometimes felt that inclusion of autism as a mental disorder may imply that autism is the result of some type of emotional upset within the child or family—when it clearly is not—or that it stigmatizes the child. Dealing with these issues is a continuing process, and there have been major advances in destigmatization over the past years. Public education, professional awareness of the potential abuse of diagnostic labels, and legal imperatives are all important in reducing prejudice against individuals with handicaps and disabilities. These issues also have had important implications for studies of epidemiology and service planning, particularly when the available data related to labels are used for educational or intervention purposes; in such contexts, parents might, for example, chose to utilize the term *autism* to entitle their child to additional services even if full criteria for autism are not met or when the child might just as readily receive another label for service provision (a problem referred to as diagnostic substitution—see Chapter 2, this *Handbook,* this volume). Conversely, the well-intentioned attempt to destigmatize a child by describing his or her disability simply as a different style of learning or being has the potential to reduce entitlements and services and opportunities for the gains associated with treatment (National Research Council, 2001).

In summary, categorical diagnoses organize professional experience and data, promote communication, and facilitate the provision of suitable treatments and interventions. They are always open to improvement. They derive their full meaning within the context of a continuing diagnostic process. They may also be misused. However, they can be helpful in clarifying the nature of an individual's difficulties and thus suggest care and indicate course.

THE ROLE OF RESEARCH

Initial descriptions of disorders such as autism and related conditions were invariably made by a clinician-investigator who noticed some seeming element(s) of commonality among children with very complex developmental difficulties. Although modifications in early descriptions of these conditions have, not surprisingly, often been made over time, there usually has been a fundamental continuity of basic aspects of definitions with the historical definition. Over the past several decades, empirical research has assumed a progressively greater role in refining diagnostic criteria and categories. In this regard, even when empirical research suggests that some feature or features are central to the definition, these need not, necessarily, have a central etiological role. Conversely, features less critical for purposes of definition may have major importance for intervention. In autism, the unusual pattern of social deficit originally described by Kanner (1943) remains the central defining core of the condition (Klin, Jones, Schultz, & Volkmar, 2003); stereotyped motor mannerisms, on the other hand, do not as clearly separate autism from other conditions with severe and profound mental handicap (Volkmar, Klin, Siegel, Szatmari, Lord, et al., 1994). Similarly, unusual sensory experiences are commonly observed in individuals with autism; they, too, may be a focus of intervention, but they are not a robust, defining feature of the condition (see Chapter 32, this *Handbook,* Volume 2, and Rogers & Ozonoff, in press, for reviews). Other symptoms may be highly predictive of the presence of autism, but they are of such low frequency that they are not included in usual definitions. For example, a child's unusual attachment to a physical object—such as a string or a frying pan—is highly suggestive of the diagnosis of autism, but this preoccupation is not included in official diagnostic criteria because the behavior is not invariably present and even when present tends to be observed only in younger individuals.

Developmental aspects of syndrome expression are particularly important in autism and related conditions. A developmental approach to classification views specific behaviors within the context of normative development. For example, the echolalia of autistic individuals is similar in some respects to the repetitions observed in the speech of typically developing 2- and 3-year-olds (see Chapter 30, this *Handbook,* Volume 2). From this perspective, echolalia is not simply a symptom but also is seen among typical children at a particular phase of development; when an older, mute, autistic child begins to use echolalia, it may be a sign of progress in language development. On the other hand, as originally noted by Kanner, some aspects of the functioning of individuals with autism are fundamentally not developmentally appropriate at any age (see Chapters 28, 30, & 32, this *Handbook,* Volume 2). This is specifically true of the social dysfunction and lack of engagement. Even infants are engaged socially. The typical aloofness of autism and lack of reciprocity are distinctly abnormal at any age and appear especially so when these social disabilities are far out of proportion to the individual's functioning in other domains of daily living (see Chapter 11, this *Handbook,* this volume).

Behavioral deviance, such as lack of social reciprocity or abnormal preoccupations, is often the focus of the criteria used in defining a categorical diagnosis. Such deviance is also a focus of rating scales and other assessment instruments used in relation to autism. This diagnostic approach may be combined with an assessment of how the individual compares to typical children and adults, for example, in relation to language use. The multiaxial system of *DSM-IV* is an attempt to systematically convey the value of considering an individual from multiple perspectives. This includes assessment of the individual's personality, educational and social resources, ongoing stresses, medical problems and diseases, and adaptive functioning as well as impairment (Rutter & Schopler, 1992). Multiaxial diagnostic approaches are especially helpful in understanding individuals who have disorders that start during childhood and are persistent, like autism, and have major impact on all spheres of development and increase the

child's vulnerability to other difficulties (Rutter, Shaffer, & Shepherd, 1975). Multiaxial systems help to ensure that in the search for a single, encompassing, categorical diagnosis, the rich and multifaceted diagnostic process is not undervalued.

APPROACHES TO CATEGORICAL DEFINITIONS OF AUTISM

In contrast to many conditions in child psychiatry, strictly defined autism does not "shade off" into normalcy in the usual sense (Rutter & Garmezy, 1983) and thus represents one of the more robust disorders for purposes of categorical diagnosis; at the same time, the body of genetic research has raised the important issue of a "broader" phenotype, that is, of a continuum of social and related vulnerabilities (Volkmar et al., 2004).

Even for strictly defined autism, there are problems in the development of explicit definitions. These include the tremendous range in syndrome expression and change in symptoms over the course of development. Since the person with autism may not always be able to provide a direct, verbal report, the reports of parents or caregivers must be relied on, as with very young children, raising other potential problems including reliability and validity of historical information. Methods have been proposed for diagnosis that focus on very early development. These methods, which sometimes use dimensional ratings scales (see Chapter 28, this *Handbook,* Volume 2), may be problematic in relation to providing a categorical diagnosis for an adolescent or adult with autism. In the absence of an accepted measure of diagnostic pathophysiology, one would wish to consider both the historical information as well as course and current functioning in conferring a diagnosis of a severe developmental or psychiatric disorder. Yet, the use of development and history raises practical problems for categorical diagnostic systems. In general, history has been overlooked in the current official nosologies (with the exception of noting the age of onset)—a topic to which we return later.

There are interesting and relevant questions, too, about what should be included in a categorical diagnostic set of criteria. Should such a set emphasize only those symptoms and signs that most clearly differentiate one condition from another, or should the set of criteria also include important symptoms (e.g., rushes of panic and anxiety or overactivity and impulsiveness) that are also found among other conditions? Should the criteria capture the largest number of children who may have the condition or be more selective? What about symptoms that may be infrequent but of great clinical importance when they occur, such as self injurious behavior? To what degree should diagnostic criteria also be fuller descriptions of the condition?

Investigators began to propose more explicit categorical definitions of autism in the 1970s as a consensus on the validity of autism emerged. This was parallel to attempts in adult psychiatry to provide better definitions of psychiatric disorders for research purposes (Spitzer, Endicott, & Robins, 1978). The importance of a multiaxial or multidimensional approach to diagnosis became increasingly appreciated (Rutter et al., 1975). Rutter (1978) synthesized Kanner's original report and subsequent research in a highly influential definition of autism as having four essential features: (1) early onset by age 22 years, (2) impaired social development, (3) impaired communication, and (4) unusual behaviors consistent in many ways with Kanner's concept of "insistence on sameness" (resistance to change, idiosyncratic responses to the environment, motor mannerisms and stereotypes, etc.). Rutter specified that the social and communication impairments were distinctive and not just a function of associated mental retardation. In contrast, the National Society for Autistic Children (NSAC; Ritvo, 1978) in the United States proposed a definition that included disturbances in (1) rates and sequences of development, (2) responses to sensory stimuli, (3) speech, language-cognition, and nonverbal communication, and (4) the capacity to relate appropriately to people, events, and objects. This definition also emphasized the neurobiological basis of autism. While clinically providing more detail, the Ritvo-NSAC definition proved rather less influential than the Rutter synthesis, probably because the latter seemed conceptually clearer and closer to Kanner's original description.

DSM-III

DSM-III (1980) was a landmark in the development of psychiatric taxonomy based on research findings and emphasizing valid, reliable descriptions of complex clinical phenomena. Autism was included along with several other disorders in a newly designated class of childhood onset disorders, Pervasive Developmental Disorders (PDD). Other disorders included residual infantile autism, childhood onset pervasive developmental disorder (COPDD), and residual COPDD. A subthreshold condition was included as well, atypical PDD. The class name *pervasive developmental disorder* was newly coined and was meant to convey that individuals with these conditions suffered from impairment in the development and unfolding of multiple areas of functioning. The term also was meant to avoid a theoretical presupposition about etiology, and it quickly achieved broad acceptance. Subsequently, the choice of the term PDD has been debated (see Gillberg, 1991; Volkmar & Cohen, 1991b), and other terms, for example, autism spectrum disorder (ASD), have also come into common usage; the two terms are used synonymously here.

The *DSM-III* system was a major advance. It extended official recognition to autism, discarded the earlier presumption of a relation between autism and childhood schizophrenia, and provided a useful definition largely reflecting Rutter's (1978) approach. The use of a multiaxial system also facilitated research. However, some shortcomings with this system were relatively quickly apparent. The rationale for the inclusion of COPDD was apparently to account for those relatively rare children who developed an autistic-like disorder after age 30 months (Kolvin, 1971); this disorder was not, however, meant to be analogous with the concept of Heller's syndrome (disintegrative psychosis) since it was assumed (incorrectly) that the latter was invariably a function of some related general medical condition (Volkmar, 1992). The definition of autism itself was rather sparse and tended, perhaps not surprisingly given the official name of the disorder (infantile autism), to focus very much on autism as it is exhibited in younger children. The use of the term *residual autism* was included to account for cases where the child once met the criteria for infantile autism but no longer did so; this seemed, at some level, to imply that the individual no longer had autism. The term *atypical PDD* was used for subthreshold conditions, that is, for a constellation of difficulties that appeared to most appropriately be placed within the PDD class but which did not meet criteria for infantile autism or another explicitly defined condition, unintentionally suggesting Rank's earlier (1949) concept. Individuals with hallucinations and delusions were specifically excluded from the PDD diagnoses. While it is unlikely that many persons with autism will develop schizophrenia, it might be anticipated that individuals with autism would develop schizophrenia at least as often as other individuals in the general population, a hypothesis that seems to be sustained by available evidence (Volkmar & Cohen, 1991a).

The multiaxial placement of disorders in *DSM-III* also was a source of controversy; that is, autism and other PDDs were placed on Axis I as was mental retardation although other specific developmental disorders were listed on Axis II of the multiaxial system. The problems with *DSM-III* were widely recognized, and a major revision was undertaken for *DSM-III-R* (American Psychiatric Association, 1987).

DSM-III-R

Preparations for the revision of *DSM-III* began soon after it appeared. What started as revision soon became a major renovation. Radical changes were introduced into the concept of autism in *DSM-III-R* (American Psychiatric Association, 1987; see Waterhouse, Wing, Spitzer, & Siegel, 1993, for discussion of these changes). The rapid revision of the official nosology posed problems for researchers who were required to rediagnose their patients if they wished to remain *au courant.*

The definition of autistic disorder in *DSM-III-R* was more consistent with that of Wing (Wing & Gould, 1979) and others who advocated a somewhat broader view of the diagnostic concept (see Chapter 21, this *Handbook,* this volume). Three major domains of dysfunction were still included, with specific criteria provided for each domain: qualitative impairment in reciprocal social interaction, qualita-

tive impairment in verbal and nonverbal communication and in imagination, and restricted repertoire of activities and interests.

A small national field trial was conducted to finalize scoring rules for the *DSM-III-R* definition of autism (Spitzer & Siegel, 1990). Sixteen proposed criteria for autistic disorder were grouped into the three broad categories. Based on this field trial, the diagnosis of autism required that an individual child or adult had to exhibit at least 8 of these 16 criteria, in total, with a specified distribution over the three areas of disturbance. This requirement for an early onset of the condition was dropped in *DSM-III-R* because of the wish to provide a generally applicable criterion set, regardless of age, and partly for the philosophical reason that the age of onset should not be considered a diagnostic feature, that is, that clinicians should rely on present examination rather than history in making the diagnosis. This change would make it possible to diagnose autism in children who, for example, appeared to develop autism or something suggestive of it much later in development (Weir & Salisbury, 1980); such cases have never, however, been very common and it seemed problematic that their uniqueness was not flagged in some way (e.g., through diagnostic coding).

DSM III-R was attentive to changes in the expression of autism with age and developmental level. This represented a clear improvement over *DSM-III* (Volkmar, Cicchetti, Cohen, & Bregman, 1992) where the concept of residual autism had been an unsatisfactory attempt to deal with this issue. Criteria in *DSM-III-R* were offered for autistic disorder and were applicable to the entire range of the expression of the syndrome. Thus, an individual could retain the diagnosis of autism even if he or she was functioning at a higher developmental level or had experienced an amelioration of symptoms with age, perhaps as a result of educational intervention or maturation. The name of the condition was changed from infantile autism to reflect these changes. Finally, in *DSM-III-R,* the problematic COPDD category was dropped, leaving those children who had carried this diagnosis suspended in limbo or, in practice, placed within the PDD-not otherwise specified (NOS) category. The term for all subthreshold categories was changed to "Not otherwise specified" (NOS) throughout

DSM. Individuals with autism were no longer, by definition, excluded from also exhibiting schizophrenia.

The ambitious goal of a heuristic definition in *DSM-III-R* was a conceptual advance over *DSM-III,* but carried unforeseen consequences. *DSM-III-R* criteria expanded the diagnostic concept (Factor, Freeman, & Kardash, 1989; Hertzig, Snow, New, & Shapiro, 1990; Szatmari, 1992a; Volkmar et al., 1992). The rate of false-positive cases (if clinician judgment is taken as the standard) diagnosed according to *DSM-III-R* was nearly 40% (Rutter & Schopler, 1992; Spitzer & Siegel, 1990). This tendency to overdiagnose autism in more intellectual handicapped individuals likely also had the inadvertent effect of diverting clinical attention from autism as it appeared in intellectually more able individuals.

Other problems with *DSM-III-R* also were noted. First, the criteria set was more complex and detailed, and the inclusion of specific examples within the actual criteria seemed to limit clinician judgment. The elimination of age of onset as a central diagnostic feature was not consistent with Kanner's original report (1943) nor subsequent research that firmly established that autism was an early-onset disorder (e.g., Harper & Williams, 1975; Kolvin, 1971; Short & Schopler, 1988; Volkmar, Cohen, Hoshino, Rende, & Paul, 1988; Volkmar, Stier, & Cohen, 1985). Probably the main issue with *DSM-III-R,* however, was the major changes introduced in the diagnostic concept. These changes severely complicated the interpretation of studies that used different diagnostic criteria. This issue was particularly acute relative to the pending changes in the classification of autism and similar conditions in the 10th edition of the *ICD-10* (WHO, 1992), since it appeared that *DSM-III-R* markedly overdiagnosed autism relative to the draft *ICD-10* definition (Volkmar, Cicchetti, Bregman, & Cohen, 1992).

FROM *ICD-9* TO *ICD-10*

Since it was first introduced toward the end of the nineteenth century, the *ICD* has undergone many revisions (Kramer, 1968). The limitations of the psychiatric section were increasingly recognized, and extensive revision was undertaken in the eighth edition of *ICD,* which appeared in 1968 (see Rutter et al., 1975; Spitzer & Williams, 1980). At the same time, there was general agreement that future refinement would be needed and, over the next decade, a series of steps were undertaken to improve the *ICD* system (Sartorius, 1988). One important aspect was the development of a multiaxial system for the psychiatric disorders of childhood (Rutter et al., 1975). By 1978, the ninth edition of *ICD* appeared and plans for a revision were put into place. The *ICD-9* accorded official recognition to infantile autism as well as disintegrative psychosis (or what would now be termed *childhood disintegrative disorders*); both conditions were included in a category of childhood psychotic conditions—a category that also included other specific psychotic conditions of childhood and unspecified psychotic conditions. This approach reflected the historical view (then beginning to change) that autism represented one of the first manifestations of childhood psychosis.

The plan for revision of *ICD-10* was well underway at the time that *DSM-IV* was being developed. An important aspect of *ICD-10* has been its conceptualization as a group of documents written specifically for different users; for example, in contrast to the *DSM-IV* approach, research criteria for disorders are provided separately from clinical guidelines for primary health care providers. *ICD-10* offers comprehensive descriptions of clinical concepts underlying the disorder, followed by points of differential diagnosis, and then presents the main symptoms that should be present for a diagnosis. As a result, the *ICD-10* system offers, in some important respects, more flexibility to the clinician; this is particularly valuable given the intended international and cross-cultural use of the system.

DSM-IV AND *ICD-10*

The process of revision in the *ICD-10* was closely related to the development of the *DSM-IV* (American Psychiatric Association, 1994). The International (*ICD*) and American (*DSM*) systems are fundamentally related, and by formal agreements must share, to some degree, a common approach to diagnostic coding. There are, however, important general and specific differences between the two major diagnostic systems (Volkmar & Schwab-Stone,

1996). For example, the *ICD-10* system highlighted the importance of an individual's history in making a diagnosis while *DSM-III-R* relied on contemporaneous examination. Also in contrast to *DSM-IV, ICD-10* was specifically designed to have one set of research diagnostic criteria and a separate set of clinical guidelines. The American and International approaches would probably have resulted in very different patterns of diagnosis.

Preparations for the creation of the new, fourth edition of *DSM* began very shortly after *DSM-III-R* appeared, partly due to the pending changes in the *ICD-10*. As part of the revision process, work groups reviewed the current classification systems in light of existing research and identified areas both of consensus and controversy. They considered various issues, including clinical utility, reliability, and descriptive validity of categories and criteria as well as coordination with the *ICD-10* revision (Frances et al., 1991). As part of the process of creating *DSM-IV*, clinical investigators conducted literature reviews for each of the potential diagnostic categories. These reviews were particularly helpful for some of the new diagnostic categories. For example, although childhood disintegrative disorder (Heller's syndrome) is apparently much less common than autism, the data supported the view that it differed from autism in a number of important ways (Volkmar, 1992; Volkmar & Cohen, 1989). Asperger's disorder was included in *ICD-10*, but the text indicated that the validity of the syndrome as a disorder, distinct from autism, was not yet fully established (Rutter & Schopler, 1992; Szatmari, 1992a, 1992b). The absence of official or other generally agreed upon definitions for Asperger's disorder had contributed to markedly different uses of the term in clinical and research work (see Chapter 4, this *Handbook,* this volume). With Rett's disorder, the issues revealed by the review process had less to do with the validity of the diagnostic concept and more with the question of whether Rett's should be included in the PDD class rather than as a neurological disorder (Gillberg, 1994; Rutter, 1994; Tsai, 1992). Although the literature identified major gaps in knowledge and persistent issues, the consensus of workers in the field favored the inclusion of additional diagnostic categories within the PDD class; there was also agreement about the desirability of compatibility of *DSM-IV* and *ICD-10* (Rutter & Schopler, 1992).

In addition to these literature reviews, a series of data reanalyses were undertaken with regard to autism. These reanalyses used previously collected data and indicated that the *DSM-III-R* definition of autistic disorder was overly broad (Volkmar, Cicchetti, & Bregman, 1992). Several issues were identified during this process of analysis of the literature and of available data that needed clarification for *DSM-IV*, including issues of overdiagnosis in the more intellectually challenged and underdiagnosis in more able individuals. Consistent with the empirical principles guiding the creation of *DSM-IV*, the working group decided that the clarification of these and other issues would be based on the findings from a large, multinational field trial (Volkmar, Klin, Siegel, Szatmari, Lord, et al., 1994).

DSM-IV Field Trial

As part of the *DSM-IV* field trial for autism, 21 sites and 125 raters participated from the United States and around the world. By design, the raters had a range of experience in the diagnosis of autism and a range of professional backgrounds. The field trial included information on nearly 1,000 cases seen by one or more raters. In cases where the same case was rated by multiple raters to assess reliability, the rating by one clinician was chosen at random to be included in the main database. The preference for the entire field trial was for cases rated on the basis of contemporaneous examination and not just on review of records. By design, five contributing sites provided ratings on approximately 100 consecutive cases of individuals either with autism or other disorders in which the diagnosis of autism would reasonably be included in the differential diagnosis while the other 16 sites provided ratings of a minimum of about 20 cases. Cases were included only if it appeared that the case exhibited difficulties that would reasonably include autism in the differential diagnosis. The availability of clinical ratings of cases seen at clinical centers around the world was of interest in terms

TABLE 1.2   *DSM-IV* Autistic Disorder Field Trial
Group Characteristics

	Clinically Autistic ($N = 454$)	Other PDDs ($N = 240$)	Non-PDD ($N = 283$)
Sex Ratio (M:F)	4.49:1	3.71:1	2.29:1
Mute	54%	35%	33%
Age	8.99	9.68	9.72
IQ	58.1	77.2	66.9

Notes: Cases grouped by clinical diagnosis. Diagnoses of the "other PDD" cases included: Rett syndrome (13 cases), childhood disintegrative disorder (16 cases), Asperger syndrome (48 cases), PPD-NOS (116 cases), and atypical autism (47 cases). Diagnoses of the non-PDD cases included mental retardation (132 cases), language disorder (88 cases), childhood schizophrenia (9 cases), other disorders (54 cases).

of issues of compatibility between *DSM-IV* and *ICD-10*. Characteristics of the field trial sample are presented in Table 1.2.

Typically, multiple sources of information were available to the rater, and the quality of the information available to the rater was judged to be excellent or good in about 75% of cases. Individuals from a variety of ethnic backgrounds and in various educational settings were included. This approach differed in important respects from that employed in *DSM-III-R* where, for example, children with conduct disorders (without development disorder) were included in the comparison group.

A standard system of coding was used to elicit information on basic characteristics of the case (age, IQ, communicative ability, educational placement), the rater, and various diagnostic criteria. The coding form also provided possible criteria for Asperger's disorder, Rett's disorder, and childhood disintegrative disorder, based on the draft *ICD-10* definitions.

The field trial provided data for studying the patterns of agreement among the various diagnostic systems. These results are presented in Table 1.3. As shown, the *DSM-III* diagnoses of infantile autism and residual autism had a reasonable balance of sensitivity and specificity; the use of the residual autism category in *DSM-III* was associated with other problems. In contrast, *DSM-III-R* criteria had a higher sensitivity but lower specificity and a relatively high rate of false-positive cases, especially among individuals with retardation where the rate reached 60%. The *ICD-10* draft definition,

designed to be a research diagnostic system, had, as expected, higher specificity.

As mentioned earlier, one of the major differences between *DSM-III-R* and both *DSM-III* and *ICD-10* was the failure to include history in the diagnostic process, for example, early age of onset as an explicit diagnostic feature. Reported age of onset of autism was examined. The mean reported age at onset for autism was early. The data on reported age of onset are presented in Figure 1.1.

Age at onset had a modest, positive relationship with measured intelligence. Individuals with slightly later onset were more likely to have higher IQ scores. If onset by 36 months was added as an essential feature to *DSM-III-R,* the sensitivity of that system was increased. Thus, inclusion of age of onset as

TABLE 1.3   Table IV-2: Sensitivity (Se)/Specificity (Sp) by IQ Level

By IQ Level	N	*DSM-III*[a] Se	Sp	*DSM-III-R* Se	Sp	*ICD-10*[b] Se	Sp
<25	64	.90	.76	.84	.39	.74	.88
25–39	148	.88	.76	.90	.60	.88	.92
40–54	191	.79	.76	.93	.74	.84	.83
55–69	167	.86	.78	.84	.77	.78	.89
70–85	152	.79	.81	.88	.81	.74	.96
>85	218	.78	.83	.78	.78	.78	.91
Overall		.82	.80	.86	.83	.79	.89

[a] "Lifetime" diagnosis (current IA or "residual" IA).

[b] Original *ICD-10* criteria and scoring.

Adapted from "Field Trial for Autistic Disorder in *DSM-IV*," by F. R. Volkmar et al., 1994, *American Journal of Psychiatry, 151,* 1361–1367. Used with permission.

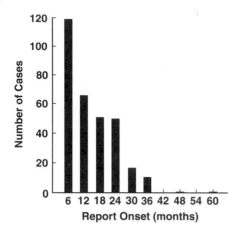

Figure 1.1 Age of onset: Cases with clinical diagnosis of autism.

an essential diagnostic feature for autism was supported and was consistent with the *ICD-10* draft criteria.

Aspects of the reliability of criteria and of diagnoses made by the various diagnostic systems were examined using chance corrected statistics. Since raters with a range of experience had participated in the field trial, it was possible to address rater experience in relation to reliability. In general, the interrater reliability of individual diagnostic criteria was in the good to excellent range. Only one criterion had poor interrater reliability. Typically, the more detailed *ICD-10* criteria had, as expected, greater reliability. Also as expected, experienced evaluators usually had excellent agreement among themselves and were more likely to agree with one another than with less experienced raters. The experience of the raters rather than their professional discipline had the greatest impact on reliability (Klin, Lang, Cicchetti, & Volkmar, 2000).

The temporal stability of ratings was assessed in two ways. A small number of cases for test-retest reliability were collected as part of the field trial; in addition, follow-up information was available on the cohort of 114 cases originally reported earlier (Volkmar, Bregman, Cohen, & Cicchetti, 1988). Criteria and diagnostic assignments were highly stable over relatively short periods of time in the range of less than one year. Findings with the cases followed up by Volkmar et al. (1988) suggested more diagnostic instability for those

individuals who were assigned a diagnosis of autism only by *DSM-III-R*. This instability of diagnostic classification was most apparent for younger children and for individuals with lower IQ.

The field trial data were also analyzed using signal detection methods and principal components analyses. The various approaches to the data suggested that certain items could be eliminated from the *ICD-10* definition, particularly items with low base rates or strong developmental associations (see later discussion). Before final decisions could be made on the *DSM-IV* definition, it was necessary to address the broader issue of whether other explicitly defined disorders would be included in the PDD class in *DSM-IV*. While the *DSM-IV* autism field trial was not primarily focused on the definition (much less the validity) of these conditions, the issues of the definition and validity were relevant to the *DSM-IV* and *ICD-10* definitions of autism. The boundaries for autism and the nonautistic PDD were mutually related: A narrow definition of autism would force some cases into the nonautistic PDD group. The broad definition of autism in *DSM-III-R* had certain advantages, for example, in ensuring access to services; but a narrower definition might be important for research studies that require greater homogeneity.

Definition of Autism in DSM-IV and ICD-10

The field trial data provided an important empirical basis for constructing the definition of autism for *DSM-IV*. The data showed that the *DSM-III-R* definition could be substantially improved by addition of a criterion relating to age of onset and by raising the diagnostic threshold. Similarly, various combinations of *DSM-III, DSM-III-R,* and new criteria all could have been used to provide a reasonably balanced diagnostic system. Given the concern about the importance of compatibility with *ICD-10* and the implications for research of a universally accepted definition, the working group of *DSM-IV* considered the benefits of the *ICD-10* system. Possible modifications in the *ICD-10* system were examined. The goal was to establish a definition for *DSM-IV* that balanced clinical and research needs, was reasonably concise and easy to use, provided reasonable coverage over the range of syndrome expression in autism, and was applicable over the full life span, from early childhood through adulthood.

Of the original 20 *ICD-10* criteria, four were identified for possible elimination. Alternatives to specific criteria were examined, and a modified definition was developed. This modified definition worked well both overall and over different levels of age and associated mental retardation; it also could be readily used by less experienced examiners.

Diagnostic criteria for autism in *DSM-IV* and *ICD-10* are presented in Table 1.4.

For the diagnosis of autism, at least six criteria must be exhibited, including at least two criteria relating to social abnormalities (group one) and one each relating to impaired communication (group 2) and range of interests and activities (group 3). In addition, the onset of the condition must have been prior to age 3 years as evidenced by delay or abnormal functioning in social interaction, language as used in social interaction, and symbolic/imaginative play. In addition, *DSM-IV* accepted the diagnostic convention that the disorder could not better be accounted for by the diagnosis of Rett's disorder or childhood disintegrative disorder (the definitions of these concepts are discussed subsequently).

Qualitative impairment in social interaction can take the form of markedly impaired nonverbal behaviors, failure in developmentally expectable peer relationships, lack of shared enjoyment or pleasure, or lack of social-emotional reciprocity. The stronger weighting of the impairments in socialization was noted during the field trial to be important in avoiding overdiagnosis of autism in more intellectually handicapped persons. This is also consistent with extensive previous clinical work, from the time of Kanner onward (e.g., Rutter, 1978; D. Cohen, 1980; Siegel, Vukicevic, Elliott, & Kraemer, 1989) that highlighted social dysfunction as the critical domain of impairment in autism.

Impairments in communication can take the form of delay or lack of spoken language, impairment in conversational ability, stereotyped language use, and deficits in imaginative play. For persons with autism, the delay or lack of spoken language must not be accompanied by compensations through other communicative means, for example, the use of

gesture. The domain of restricted patterns of behavior, interests, and activities includes encompassing preoccupations that are abnormal either in focus or intensity, adherence to nonfunctional routines or rituals, stereotyped motor movements, and persistent preoccupation with parts of objects.

The Definition of the Nonautistic PDDs

In contrast to *DSM-III-R*, a number of conditions other than autism and subthreshold autism (i.e., PDD-NOS) are now officially recognized in both *DSM-IV* and *ICD-10*. Given that these are newer disorders (at least in terms of their official recognition), it is not surprising that the substantive body of work on their definitions is less extensive than that for autism.

Rett's Disorder

There were few concerns about the validity of the entity explicated by Rett. It was clear that the transient, autistic-like phase of social withdrawal occurred early in the child's development and presented the primary problem for differentiation from autism (and one of the main arguments for its placement in the PDD class). However, there were some objections to including it in the PDD class (Gillberg, 1994) although it was also clear that it should be included somewhere (Rutter, 1994). The importance of its inclusion has been underscored by the subsequent discovery of a gene involved in the pathogenesis of the disorder (Amir, Van den Veyver, Wan, Tran, Francke, et al., 1999; also see Chapter 5, this *Handbook,* this volume).

Childhood Disintegrative Disorder

Although this condition had been included in *ICD-9* the presumption in *DSM-III-R* was that individuals with childhood disintegrative disorder (also known as Heller's syndrome or disintegrative psychosis) usually suffered from a neurological or other progressive process that accounted for their marked behavioral and developmental deterioration. The literature, however, did not support this association (Volkmar, 1992). While rare, childhood disintegrative disorder appeared to be a disorder that could be distinguished from autism and that was, like autism, of generally unknown etiology. The rationale for including

TABLE 1.4 *ICD-10* **Criteria for Autism**

Childhood Autism (F84.0)

A. Abnormal or impaired development is evident before the age of 3 years in at least one of the following areas:
  (1) receptive or expressive language as used in social communication;
  (2) the development of selective social attachments or of reciprocal social interaction;
  (3) functional or symbolic play.

B. A total of at least six symptoms from (1), (2) and (3) must be present, with at least two from (1) and at least one from each of (2) and (3)
  (1) Qualitative impairment in social interaction are manifest in at least two of the following areas:
    (a) failure adequately to use eye-to-eye gaze, facial expression, body postures, and gestures to regulate social interaction;
    (b) failure to develop (in a manner appropriate to mental age, and despite ample opportunities) peer relationships that involve a mutual sharing of interests, activities and emotions;
    (c) lack of socio-emotional reciprocity as shown by an impaired or deviant response to other people's emotions; or lack of modulation of behaviour according to social context; or a weak integration of social, emotional, and communicative behaviors;
    (d) lack of spontaneous seeking to share enjoyment, interests, or achievements with other people (e.g., a lack of showing, bringing, or point out to other people objects of interest to the individual).
  (2) Qualitative abnormalities communication as manifest in at least one of the following areas:
    (a) delay in or total lack of, development of spoken language that is *not* accompanied by an attempt to compensate through the use of gestures or mime as an alternative mode of communication (often preceded by a lack of communicative babbling);
    (b) relative failure to initiate or sustain conversational interchange (at whatever level of language skill is present), in which there is reciprocal responsiveness to the communications of the other person;
    (c) stereotyped and repetitive use of language or idiosyncratic use of words or phrases;
    (d) lack of varied spontaneous make-believe play or (when young) social imitative play.
  (3) Restricted, repetitive, and stereotyped patterns of behaviour, interests, and activities are manifested in at least one of the following:
    (a) an encompassing preoccupation with one or more stereotyped and restricted patterns of interest that are abnormal in content or focus; or one or more interests that are abnormal in their intensity and circumscribed nature though not in their content or focus;
    (b) apparently compulsive adherence to specific, nonfunctional routines or rituals;
    (c) stereotyped and repetitive motor mannerisms that involve either hand or finger flapping or twisting or complex whole body movements;
    (d) preoccupations with part-objects or non-functional elements of play materials (such as their odour, the feel of their surface, or the noise or vibration they generate).

C. The clinical picture is not attributable to the other varieties of pervasive developmental disorders; specific development disorder of receptive language (F80.2) with secondary socio-emotional problems' reactive attachment disorder (F94.1) or disinhibited attachment disorder (F94.2); mental retardation (F70-F72) with some associated emotional or behavioral disorders; schizophrenia (F20.-) of unusually early Onset; and Rett's syndrome (F84.12).

F84.1 Atypical autism

A. Abnormal or impaired development is evident at or after the age of 3 years (criteria as for autism except for age of manifestation).

B. There are qualitative abnormalities in reciprocal social interaction or in communication, or restricted, repetitive, and stereotyped patterns of behavior, interests, and activities. (Criteria as for autism except that it is unnecessary to meet the criteria for number of areas of abnormality.)

C. The disorder does not meet the diagnostic criteria for autism (F84.0).

Autism may be atypical in either age of onset (F84.10) or symptomatology (F84.11); the two types are differentiated with a fifth character for research purposes. Syndromes that are typical in both respects should be coded F84.12.

F84.10 Atypicality in age of onset

A. The disorder does not meet criterion A for autism (F84.0); that is, abnormal or impaired development is evident only at or after age 3 years.

B. The disorder meets criteria B and C for autism (F84.0).

TABLE 1.4   *(Continued)*

F84.11 Atypicality in symptomatology
A. The disorder meets criterion A for autism (F84.0); that is abnormal or impaired development is evident before age 3 years.
B. There are qualitative abnormalities in reciprocal social interactions or in communication, or restricted, repetitive, and stereotyped patterns of behavior, interests, and activities. (Criteria as for autism except that it is unnecessary to meet the criteria for number of areas of abnormality.)
C. The disorder meets criterion C for autism (F84.0).
D. The disorder does not fully meet criterion B for autism (F84.0).   '

F84.12 Atypicality in both age of onset and symptomatology
A. The disorder does not meet criterion A for autism (F84.0); that is, abnormal or impaired development is evident only at or after age 3 years.
B. There are qualitative abnormalities in reciprocal social interactions or in communication, or restricted, repetitive, and stereotyped patterns of behavior, interests, and activities. (Criteria as for autism except that it is unnecessary to meet the criteria for number of areas of abnormality.)
C. The disorder meets criterion C for autism (F84.0).
D. The disorder does not fully meet criterion B for autism (F84.0).

DSM-IV Criteria for Autistic Disorder (299.0)
A. A total of at least six items from (1), (2), and (3), with at least two from (1), and one each from (2) and (3):
   (1) Qualitative impairment in social interaction, as manifested by at least two of the following:
      (a) marked impairment in the use of multiple nonverbal behaviors such as eye-to-eye gaze, facial expression, body postures, and gestures to regulate social interaction,
      (b) failure to develop peer relationships appropriate to developmental level,
      (c) markedly impaired expression of pleasure in other people's happiness,
      (d) lack of social or emotional reciprocity,
   (2) Qualitative impairments in communication as manifested by at least one of the following:
      (a) delay in or total lack of, the development of spoken language (not accompanied by an attempt to compensate through alternative modes of communication such as gestures or mime)
      (b) in individuals with adequate speech, marked impairment in the ability to initiate or sustain a conversation with others
      (c) stereotyped and repetitive use of language or idiosyncratic language
      (d) lack of varied spontaneous make-believe play or social imitative play appropriate to developmental level
   (3) Restricted repetitive and *stereotyped patterns of behavior, interests, and activities,* as manifested by at least one of the following:
      (a) encompassing preoccupation with one or more stereotyped and restricted patterns of interest that is abnormal either in intensity or focus
      (b) apparently compulsive adherence to specific, nonfunctional routines or rituals
      (c) stereotyped and repetitive motor mannerisms (e.g., hand or finger flapping or twisting, or complex whole body movements)
      (d) persistent preoccupation with parts of objects
B. Delays or abnormal functioning in at least one of the following areas, with onset prior to age three: (1) social interaction, (2) language as used in social communication, or (3) symbolic or imaginative play.
C. Not better accounted for by Rett's Disorder or Childhood Disintegrative Disorder.

Sources: From *Diagnostic and Statistical Manual of Mental Disorders,* fourth edition, by American Psychiatric Association, 1994, Washington, DC: Author; and *International Classification of Diseases: Diagnostic Criteria for Research,* tenth edition, by the World Health Organization, 1992, Geneva, Switzerland: Author. Reprinted with permission.

this condition had less to do with its potential importance for research, for example, relative to the search for a gene or genes that might be involved, than its frequency. The limited data available also suggested some important potential differences from autism in terms of course and prognosis (Volkmar & Rutter, 1995) although others (e.g., Hendry, 2000) have questioned the recognition of the category; these issues are discussed in greater detail in Chapter 3, this *Handbook,* of this volume.

Asperger's Disorder

In many ways, the inclusion and definition of this condition have been the source of the greatest continuing confusion and controversy (e.g., Klin, Sparrow, & Volkmar, 1997; see also Chapter 4, this *Handbook,* this volume). Although Asperger's original paper (Asperger, 1944) and his subsequent clinical work (Hippler & Klicpera, 2003) emphasized the presence of circumscribed interests and motor delays, they were technically not required in either the *ICD-10* or *DSM-IV* definition that was eventually adopted. Indeed, in *DSM-IV,* it was emphasized that autism should take diagnostic precedence; difficulties in the use of these criteria were quickly noted (Miller & Ozonoff, 1997, 2000). As a result, final closure on the best definition of this disorder has not yet been achieved.

Given the general dissatisfaction with the definition of Asperger's disorder (see Chapter 4, this *Handbook,* this volume), the unfortunate problem of markedly different approaches to the definition of the disorder has continued complicating comparisons of results across studies.

There are now a least five rather different conceptualizations of Asperger's disorder in addition to those provided by *ICD-10* and *DSM-IV* (Ghaziuddin, Tsai, & Ghaziuddin, 1992; Klin & Volkmar, 1997; Leekam, Libby, Wing, Gould, & Gillberg, 2000; Szatmari, Bryson, Boyle, Streiner, & Duku, 2003; Tsai, 1992; Wing, 1981). Unfortunately, these definitions are not always easy to operationalize. Several major sources of disagreement are apparent. The first issue has to do with the precedence rule, which (in *DSM-IV* and *ICD-10*) excludes an individual from Asperger's if the person ever met the criteria for autism. (As a practical matter, this ends up, largely, revolving around the age at which parents were first concerned about the child's development.) The second issue concerns the approach to language delay (usually operationalized by whether the child spontaneously used meaningful words by 24 months and phrases by 36 months; Howlin, 2003; Klin, Schultz, Pauls, & Volkmar, in press). A third major issue has to do with whether the unusual circumscribed interests originally described by Asperger (1944) must be present for diagnosis; in *DSM-IV* and *ICD-10,* these *may* be present but are

not required. In the *DSM-IV* field trial, the presence of such interest was one of the features that discriminated individuals with clinical diagnoses of autism from Asperger's disorder. The limited available data (see Chapter 4, this *Handbook,* this volume, and Klin et al., in press) suggest, not surprisingly, rather poor overall agreement of these different diagnostic approaches.

To some extent, these disparities in diagnostic approach parallel broader differences in the way the disorder is conceptualized. For example, is Asperger best thought of as a milder form of autism (Leekam et al., 2000), is it characterized by a rather different neuropsychological profile than autism (Klin, Volkmar, Sparrow, Cicchetti, & Rourke, 1995), or are the social difficulties different from autism (Tsai, 1992)? Yet another issue is how and whether motor skills problems are taken into account (Ghaziuddin & Butler, 1998) or whether some other feature, for example, prosody, might differentiate autism and Asperger's disorder (Ghaziuddin & Gerstein, 1996). Perhaps the one thing that can be said with certainty about current diagnostic approaches is that there is general agreement that the current official approach (as in *DSM-IV* and *ICD-10*) has not been easy to operationalize and has not proven useful for research. Miller and Ozonoff (1997) have raised the cogent point that Asperger's own cases likely would not meet current official criteria for the disorder; a recent report (Hipller & Klicpera, 2003) of cases seen by Asperger may help inform the current debate (see also Eisenmajer et al., 1996; Howlin, 2003; Szatmari et al., 2003).

It must, however, also be noted that even given the lack of general agreement on a general diagnostic approach, emerging data are beginning to suggest some important potential differences between Asperger's and higher functioning autism, for example, in terms of neuropsychological profiles (Klin et al., 1995; Lincoln, Courchesne, Kilman, Elmasian, & Allen, 1998), comorbidity with other psychiatric disorders (Klin et al., in press), neuropsychological profiles and family genetics (Volkmar & Klin, 1998) and outcome (Szatmari et al., 2003). The critical issue is whether Asperger's can be shown to differ in important respects from either autism or PDD-NOS on measures other than those used in selecting cases in the first place; that is, information on the validity of the disorder is needed in areas such as differences in patterns of comorbidity, outcome, response to treatment, family history, or neuropsychological profiles. The relationship of Asperger's disorder to various other diagnostic concepts—for example, schizoid disorder, right hemisphere learning disability, and semantic pragmatic processing disorder— remains an important topic for research (see Klin, Volkmar, & Sparrow, 2000 for a review). Replication of findings based on the same diagnostic criteria used across sites is critical for progress to be made in this area. Until the time when a consensus on the definition of the condition emerges, it will be critical for researchers to employ very clear, operational depictions to allow for replication of findings.

Atypical Autism/PDD-NOS

Somewhat paradoxically, studies of what is undoubtedly the more frequent of the PDDs are uncommon (see Chapter 6, this *Handbook,* this volume). This subthreshold category receives considerable clinical use, and its importance

has been increasingly recognized in research studies (Bailey et al., 1998). *DSM-IV* and *ICD-10* take slightly different approaches to this category with *ICD-10* providing the possibility for more fine-grained distinctions based on the way in which full criteria for autism or another of the explicitly defined PDDs are not met. An unfortunate editorial change in *DSM-IV* produced some difficulties, which have now been rectified in *DSM-IV-TR.* Specifically, prior to *DSM-IV,* an individual had to have problems in social interaction *and* in communication *or* restricted interests. In *DSM-IV,* this criterion was changed leading to an unintended further broadening of the concept.

Table 1.5 provides a concise summary and comparison of the various disorders presently included within the overarching PDD category.

CURRENT CONTROVERSIES IN DIAGNOSIS

Although considerable progress has been made further work is needed in several areas.

TABLE 1.5   Differential Diagnostic Features of Autism and Nonautistic Pervasive Developmental Disorders

	Disorder				
Feature	Autistic Disorder	Asperger's	Rett's	Childhood Disintegrative Disorder	Pervasive Developmental Disorder-NOS
Age at recognition (months)	0–36	Usually >36	5–30	>24	Variable
Sex ratio	M > F	M > F	F (?M)	M > F	M > F
Loss of skills	Variable	Usually not	Marked	Marked	Usually not
Social skills	Very poor	Poor	Varies with age	Very poor	Variable
Communication skills	Usually poor	Fair	Very poor	Very poor	Fair to good
Circumscribed interests	Variable (mechanical)	Marked (facts)	NA	NA	Variable
Family history— similar problems	Sometimes	Frequent	Not usually	No	Unknown
Seizure disorder	Common	Uncommon	Frequent	Common	Uncommon
Head growth decelerates	No	No	Yes	No	No
IQ range	Severe MR to normal	Mild MR to normal	Severe MR	Severe MR	Severe MR to normal
Outcome	Poor to good	Fair to good	Very poor	Very poor	Fair to good

Adapted from "Nonautistic Pervasive Developmental Disorders," chap. 27.2, p. 4, by F. R. Volkmar & D. Cohen, in *Psychiatry,* R. Michaels et al., eds. Used with permission from Lippincott-Raven Publishers. NA = Not Applicable.

Comorbid Conditions and Autism

The issue of comorbidity with autism has assumed increasing importance in recent years; it is intimately related to the search for subgroups of autism. It appears likely that having any serious disability—such as autism or intellectual disability—increases the risk for other problems, and it is likely that, in the past, autism has tended to overshadow the presence of other difficulties (see Dykens, 2000). Autism has now been reported to co-occur with various other developmental, psychiatric, and medical conditions (Gillberg & Coleman, 2000). However, much of this literature rests on case reports, and this literature fails to address the more central question of whether associations are observed at greater than chance levels and, when this is done, results are generally much less striking (Rutter et al., 1994). An additional problem is that only positive associations are typically reported; for example, it is somewhat surprising that failure to thrive in infancy is so *uncommonly* reported in infants who go on to have autism.

Evolving diagnostic concepts and research findings have sometimes clarified such associations. For example, Kanner's original impression (1943) that persons with autism had normal intellectual potential has been shown to be incorrect; although the pattern of cognitive and adaptive abilities in autism is unusual, for the majority of children with autism, overall scores on cognitive testing are stable within the mentally retarded range (see Chapter 29, this *Handbook,* Volume 2). On the other hand, a substantial minority of persons with autism has cognitive abilities in the average or above-average range. Similarly, it is now well recognized that seizure disorders of various types are associated with autism in about 25% of cases (see Chapter 18, this *Handbook,* this volume). A much smaller proportion of autistic individuals exhibit fragile X syndrome or tuberous sclerosis (see Chapter 18, this *Handbook,* this volume). Apart from these well-recognized associations, the association of autism with other medical and behavioral conditions is much less convincing (Rutter, Bailey, et al., 1994).

Issues relating to comorbidity arise from a major difference between approaches to diagnosis in *DSM-IV* and *ICD-10.* Both systems are meant to be comprehensive in coverage. However, any system that attempts to move past the level of symptom description must deal with complicated problems of ensuring clinical utility, reliability, and validity. As a practical matter, this leads to decisions, sometimes fairly obvious and sometimes much less so, about relationships between categories, including whether one condition takes precedence over another in a diagnostic hierarchy. The *ICD-10* system reflects a nosological tradition of searching for a single, parsimonious diagnostic label to explain a patient's problems. This top-down approach tends to be concerned with broader, heuristic diagnoses and is less focused on symptoms as such. On the other hand, *DSM-IV* and its immediate predecessors have tended to be more bottom up in orientation. They start with symptoms and move toward broader categories. No single diagnosis is expected to convey the entire range of a patient's major problems, and there is more comfort with multiple categorical diagnoses, each covering a smaller domain of difficulties. In other words, *ICD* may miss some trees, and *DSM* may not capture the forest: Each approach has inherent advantages and limitations (see Volkmar & Schwab-Stone, 1996). The *DSM-IV* approach has some advantages for clinical utility; that is, important symptoms are less likely to be overlooked. It also does not prejudge the issue of comorbid relationships. The *ICD-10* approach has the advantage of providing a more robust big picture less focused on single symptoms and minimizing what are often spurious or meaningless associations.

The issue of comorbidity in relation to autism is further complicated by the nature of the syndrome. While autism is a lifelong disorder and probably one of the best examples of a disorder in psychiatry, symptoms change with age and developmental level. If the approach to diagnosis focuses on symptoms, an individual with autism will receive a large number of additional diagnoses over the course of the life span, including diagnoses that focus on anxiety, language, social problems, and the like. Such a list of additional diagnoses might serve a useful function by cataloging behaviors in need of clinical attention. But the list does not basically change the fundamental conception that the person has autism.

Given the wide range and severity of the disabilities experienced by individuals with autism, it is not surprising that they are vulnerable to many types of behavioral difficulties, including hyperactivity, obsessive-compulsive phenomena, self-injury and stereotypy, tics, and affective symptoms (Brasic, Barnett, Kaplan, Sheitman, Aisemberg et al., 1994; Ghaziuddin et al., 1992; Ghaziuddin, Alessi, & Greden, 1995; Jaselskis, Cook, & Fletcher, 1992; Nelson & Pribor, 1993; Poustka & Lisch, 1993; Quintana et al., 1995; Realmuto & Main, 1982). Interpretation of the available data is more complex when you move past the level of behavioral observation and try to consider these associations within a causal framework. For example, the diagnosis of Tourette's syndrome requires only the history of motor and vocal tics for a year or more. Do the compulsive behaviors and vocalizations emitted by many individuals with autism and intellectual disability warrant a second diagnosis of Tourette's syndrome? When should obsessive-compulsive disorder be diagnosed in a retarded, autistic individual with many perseverative behaviors?

Diagnostic systems like *DSM-IV* and *ICD-10* strive for logical consistency in their approach to the problem of diagnosis; this usually means that some degree of hierarchical decision must be employed when, for example, features that are part of the definition of autism are observed in other disorders. Thus, since stereotyped behaviors are common in autism and are included as a diagnostic feature in both *DSM-IV* and *ICD-10,* persons with autism cannot also receive a diagnosis of stereotyped movement disorder. Similarly, diagnostic problems arise with difficulties that are commonly observed to be "associated features" of autism, for example, unusual affective responses. On the other hand, mental retardation is not an essential diagnostic feature of autism, and it is thus possible (and important) for this diagnosis and one of autism to be made when both sets of criteria are satisfied.

The task of moving from the level of behavioral problems and symptoms to formal psychiatric/developmental diagnosis is complicated by the nature of autism itself. Half of autistic persons are largely or entirely mute, and for some disorders, this presents a profound diagnostic problem (Tsai, 1996). For example, early investigators incorrectly assumed continuity between autism and schizophrenia. While persons with autism may also develop schizophrenia (Petty, Ornitz, Michelman, & Zimmerman, 1985), this does not appear to be above the level expected in the general population (Volkmar & Cohen, 1991a). Similarly, the issue of comorbid obsessive-compulsive disorder and autism has been of interest given the use of new pharmacological treatments such as the selective serotonin reuptake inhibitors (SSRIs; see Chapter 44, this *Handbook,* Volume 2; Gordon, Rapoport, Hamburger, State, & Mannheim, 1992; Gordon, State, Nelson, Hamburger, & Rapoport, 1993; McDougle, Price, Volkmar, & Goodman, 1992). While phenomena suggestive of obsessions or compulsions are often observed in adults with autism (Rumsey, Rapoport, & Sceery, 1985), levels of such phenomena vary considerably across samples (Brasic et al., 1994; Fombonne, 1992; McDougle et al., 1995), and response to medication may not be specific to diagnosis. In general, it appears that the ritualistic phenomena of autism and typical obsessions and compulsions cannot simply be equated (Baron-Cohen, 1989).

Stereotyped motor movements and other mannerisms are very common in autism but do not qualify a case for the additional diagnosis of stereotyped movement disorder. However, a number of case reports and some case series have suggested a potentially more interesting association between autism and Tourette's disorder. In the latter condition, the child exhibits persistent motor *and* vocal tics (Burd, Fisher, Kerbeshian, & Arnold, 1987; Leckman, Peterson, Pauls, & Cohen, 1997; Nelson & Pribor, 1993; Realmuto & Main, 1982). It remains to be seen whether such an association is more frequent than would be expected by chance alone, particularly since differentiation of tics and stereotyped motor mannerisms can be confusing for less experienced clinicians.

Affective symptoms are frequently observed in persons with autism. These symptoms include affective lability, inappropriate affective responses, anxiety, and depression.

For higher functioning autistic persons, an awareness of their difficulties may result in overt clinical depression. There is some suggestion that adolescents with Asperger's are at particularly high risk for depression (Klin, Volkmar, & Sparrow, 2000). Bipolar disorders have also been reported and may respond to drug treatment (Gillberg, 1985; Kerbeshian, Burd, & Fisher, 1987; Komoto, Usui, & Hirata, 1984; Lainhart & Folstein, 1994; Steingard & Biederman, 1987).

Given the characteristic difficulties in social interaction and communication, as well as the frequent association of autism with mental retardation, it is not surprising that deployment and sustaining of attention would be problematic for individuals with autism (see Chapter 13, this *Handbook,* this volume). In *DSM-III-R,* the convention was established that autism and attention deficit disorder were made mutually exclusive diagnoses. This was based on the clinical belief that attentional problems in autism were better viewed as an aspect of the autistic condition and developmental level; there was a clinical impression that stimulant medications used in the treatment of attention deficit disorder often led to deterioration in the behavior of individuals with autism. The latter notion has now been called into question (see Towbin, 2003, for a review), and there is little doubt that attentional difficulties are observed in children with autism (Charman, 1998), but the question of whether such difficulties are sufficient to justify an additional diagnosis of attention deficit disorder remains unclear. Attentional difficulties may be intrinsically associated with developmental problems and may reflect broader difficulties in cognitive organization (Iacoboni, 2000) without necessarily implying attention deficit disorder. While some have suggested that attention deficit/hyperactivity disorder should be considered an additional diagnosis and target of treatment in persons with autism (Tsai, 1999), firm empirical data on this issue are lacking.

Barkley (1990) has noted that the issue of attentional problem is of much greater interest in children with PDD-NOS. Such children do not exhibit classical autism but have persistent problems in social interaction and the regulation of affective responses and behavior, which may suggest disorders of attention. Hellgren, Gillberg, and Gillberg (1994) have described a putative condition characterized by problems in attention, motor control and perception (DAMP) with features of both PDD and attention deficit disorder.

Autistic individuals are not immune to any other known medical conditions (Chapters 16 & 18, this *Handbook,* this volume). Yet, specific associations between autism and general medical conditions generally have not been sustained by formal research. Although some investigators (e.g., Gillberg, 1990) suggest that many different associations are common, studies that employ stringent diagnostic criteria have not supported this view (e.g., Rutter, Bailey, Bolton, & Le Couter, 1994). In one sense, this issue is simply definitional. If you take a very broad view of autism, a large number of persons with profound intellectual disability will be included in samples of autistic individuals; this population has a marked increase in the number of medical conditions that may be significantly involved in the person's developmental difficulties. The difficulties inherent in including such cases among those with more strictly defined autism are exemplified in the early reports about the association of autism with congenital rubella. Children with congenital rubella initially were reported to have many autistic-like features and to be very low functioning; over time, however, the diagnoses of these cases have proven questionable.

Subtypes of Autism

Investigators have used various approaches to subtype autism and the broader PDD class of conditions. Essentially, these attempts have fallen into two broad categories. The more common approach rests on clinical experience and the ability of clinician-investigators to notice features that are then used to delineate a specific diagnostic concept. Kanner's description of autism and the work of Asperger, Rett, and Heller are all examples of this approach. More recent examples include the proposed typology based on social characteristics proposed by Wing and colleagues (Wing & Gould, 1979). The major alternative is to utilize more complex statistical procedures to derive subgroups or subtypes empirically. It might seem more likely that the latter approach would be more productive, but, somewhat surprisingly, this really has not been the case.

Statistical Approaches to Subtyping

Complex statistical approaches have been helpful in developing and validating screening and assessment instruments, as well as in developing criteria to operationalize diagnostic concepts. Their value in developing *new* diagnostic categories has been limited by several factors. Approaches such as cluster and factor analysis, in the first place, are very dependent on the characteristic of the sample being studied and on the information originally provided; you cannot identify relevant variables or combinations of variables if they are not measured in the sample in the first place. Since our knowledge regarding the underlying neuropathological basis of autism and its relationship to development and behavior remains limited, it is not clear exactly what measures would best be included in such analyses. Another set of issues surrounds a set of interrelated problems: the marked range in syndrome expression associated with age and developmental level and issues related to sample selection and sample size. Nosological research using complex statistical models generally requires large and representative samples of patients. Unfortunately, the samples used in most studies are small and not representative. Results may be highly dependent on the original sample and may not generalize to other samples. This problem is compounded by the fact that the meaning of behaviors may change with age and with developmental level. The diagnosis of autism may be particularly difficult to make in very young children below the age of 3 years. You might assume that the purest form of autism is exhibited at this young age. However, as Lord (1995) has shown, the characteristic symptoms of autism such as repetitive behaviors often do not clearly develop before age 3 years while significant social deficits, suggestive of autism, may markedly improve after the first two years of life (see also Rogers, 2001).

The strong developmental nature of changes in syndrome expression means that variables such as age, developmental level, or IQ themselves become important variables in statistical analyses. It is a testament to the creativity of engaged clinicians and to the human capacity to notice regularities that at least so far the diagnostic concepts we are presently familiar with have emerged from clinical work and not from complex statistical analyses. On the other hand, such analyses may be helpful in examining current diagnostic concepts and alternative ways to conceptualize syndrome boundaries. It is possible, in the future, that better diagnostic concepts will be derived, for example, within the broad category of PDD-NOS.

Despite these problems, cluster and factor analytic approaches have been used with some frequency. For example, in an early study, Prior and colleagues (Prior, Boulton, Gajzago, & Perry, 1975) observed two clusters of cases. One cluster was more similar to Kanner's original syndrome in terms of early onset and clinical features and the other with later onset and more complex features. Similarly, Siegel, Anders, Ciaranello, Bienenstock, and Kramer (1986) identified four possible subgroups in a larger group of children with PDDs. Two groups appeared to correspond roughly to low and higher functioning autism while the other two groups were characterized either by schizotypal features or affective symptoms and behavior problems. Dahl, Cohen, and Provence (1986) identified two clusters of children in the PDD spectrum who had similar behavior problems but somewhat different patterns of language functioning and onset. Depending on sample and range of variables included in the analyses, various numbers of clusters have been derived. The less robust clusters—those with fewer cases and very complex clinical features—are less likely to be observed in subsequent studies. Eaves, Eaves, and Ho (1994) used data from over 150 children with autism spectrum disorders. In their sample, four meaningful subtypes emerged with different behavioral and cognitive profiles. Over half the sample fell into the subtype described as typically autistic; approximately 20% were also autistic but were lower functioning cognitively. The remaining cases formed two subtypes: One was a higher functioning group with similarities to Asperger's and another with less severe difficulties. Fein, Waterhouse, Lucci, and Snyder (1985) identified eight cognitive profiles that could be related to handedness (Soper et al., 1986) but not to more usual autistic features. More recently, Waterhouse and colleagues (1996) studied a relatively large group of children with some form of PDD not associated with an overt medical condition; they suggested that at least two overlapping continua were present, corresponding roughly to lower and higher functioning autism.

Methods other than cluster and factor analysis have been employed as well in the search for subgroups. For example, I. Cohen, Sudhalter, Landon-Jimenez, and Keogh (1993) utilized a novel system of pattern recognition (neural networks) as well as discriminant analyses; they argued that the neural network procedure was superior in correctly identifying whether autism was or was not present. In a well-controlled study by Cicchetti, Volkmar, Klin, and Showalter (1995), however, the neural networks procedure was not as effective as the simple diagnostic algorithm proposed in *ICD-10* and *DSM-IV*.

Multivariate methods have also been utilized to validate existing diagnostic groupings and new possible subgroups, for example, within the broad PDD-NOS category (see also Chapter 6, this *Handbook,* this volume). Van der Gaag et al. (1995) utilized a multivariate cluster analysis and demonstrated differences between cases with autistic disorder and a specific subtype of PDD-NOS (multiplex or multiple complex developmental disorder) on the basis of clinical and developmental features.

Clinical Approaches to Subtyping

The issue of subtypes has also been approached from a clinical standpoint. Wing and Gould (1979) proposed a classification scheme based on the nature of observed patterns of social interaction (aloof, passive, active-but-odd; see also Chapter 7, this *Handbook,* this volume). Other classifications have focused on cognitive profiles (Fein et al., 1985), language problems (Rapin, 1991; Rapin & Allen, 1983), presence of signs of overt central nervous system dysfunction (Tsai, Tsai, & August, 1985), and so forth. A decade ago, it appeared that possible associations of autism with various medical conditions would have major implications for understanding subtypes and etiology. At present, however, it appears that distinctions based on the presence of a strictly defined etiology or

associated medical condition do not simply correspond to obvious behavioral subtypes (Rutter, 1996). As Rutter has noted (2000), conditions such as autism are defined on the basis of their clinical features, and it is likely that complex, multifactorial models will be needed to understand underlying pathophysiology. That is, systems such as *DSM* and *ICD* are strongly influenced by pathophysiology when this is known but should not simply be thought of as classifying by cause.

As with the more statistically based approaches, clinically inspired approaches also must deal with the major confounding problem of intellectual level. For example, the three-group subtyping (aloof, passive, active-but-odd) proposed by Wing and Gould (1979) appears to sort children into relatively reliable groups; the typology has some measure of validity as well as potential benefits for planning interventions (Borden & Ollendick, 1994; Castelloe & Dawson, 1993; Volkmar & Cohen, 1989). However, differences among the subgroups appear to be largely a function of associated IQ. When IQ is controlled for, differences among the groups largely vanish (Volkmar & Cohen, 1989).

Individuals with profound mental retardation exhibit a number of autistic-like features (Wing & Gould, 1979) without, however, meeting full criteria for autism. Such cases have many of the same service needs as those with more strictly defined autism. Various investigators have, accordingly, proposed a distinction among primary, higher, and lower functioning autism given the very different patterns of educational need, associated medical problems, outcome, family history, and so forth associated with lower and higher IQ (Cohen, Paul, & Volkmar, 1986; Rutter, 1996; Tsai, 1992; Waterhouse et al., 1996). This important issue remains unresolved. Similarly, it is clear that, over time, children with severe developmental language disorders go on to exhibit marked social difficulties (Howlin, Mawhood, & Rutter, 2000) so that the issue of the connection between language disorders and autism remains an important area of study.

Developmental Regression

Various studies have suggested that perhaps 20% to 25% of children with autism have some degree of developmental regression (see Chapter 3, this *Handbook,* this volume). Unfortunately, this phenomenon remains poorly understood and, in part as a result, controversial. Most studies have utilized parent report with all the attendant problems of definition, reliability, and validity. In some cases, parents report a pattern less of regression and more one of developmental stagnation; in other cases, the report is of a regression but the history may also be remarkable for prior developmental delays. Finally, in some cases a dramatic regression is observed (Siperstein & Volkmar, 2004). The most common pattern is one in which a few words are apparently acquired and then lost. The more dramatic cases (e.g., where hundreds of words are acquired and then lost) are often more consistent with a diagnosis of childhood disintegrative disorder; however, the latter condition, by definition, has its onset after age 2. It is possible that some of the earlier and more dramatic cases of regression are expressions of the earliest forms of childhood disintegrative disorder. In any event, the study of this phenomenon (ideally at the time it happens) using various methodologies (genetics, neuroimaging, EEG, etc.) is critically needed.

Developmental Change

Important issues of developmental change in syndrome expression (over both age and IQ level) have been recognized for many years (Rutter, 1970). Diagnostic systems such as *DSM-IV* and *ICD-10* have generally adopted the stance of providing criteria that are specifically meant to cover this range of syndrome expression. An alternative, if rather unwieldy, approach is to provide different diagnostic criteria either for different age groups or for different levels of impairment (e.g., depending on level of communicative ability).

Examination of the data from the *DSM-IV* field trial illustrates some of these issues. For example, if we utilize the phi statistic to evaluate the ability of criteria to predict autism, the criteria included in *DSM-IV* and *ICD-10* are generally comparably powerful predictors across age and developmental level with some expectable but not overly dramatic exceptions; for example, stereotyped language use and problems in conversation would be expected to become more common as children become

older (and make communicative gains). Stereotyped mannerisms also become somewhat more common when children become older while other features (e.g., persistent preoccupation with parts of objects) are consistently observed.

Examination of some of the items *not* included in *DSM-IV/ICD-10* also illustrates this issue. Abnormal pitch/tone is largely a phenomenon observed in older individuals while attachments to unusual objects are less commonly observed in older individuals. Similarly, the phenomenon of hyper- or hyposensitivity to the inanimate environment has a complicated developmental course with features exhibited at some ages and not others (see Chapter 32, this *Handbook,* Volume 2).

Autism in Infants and Young Children

Increased awareness (on the part of both the general public and health care providers) and advances in early diagnosis have led to a change in the age at which autism is first diagnosed. A decade ago, diagnosis at age 4 was relatively typical (Siegel, Pliner, Eschler, & Elliott, 1988)—even when parents had been concerned much earlier. It is now more common for specialized diagnostic centers to see children at age 2 years (Lord, 1995; Moore & Goodson, 2003) or even younger (Klin, Cahawarska, Paul, Rubin, Morgan, et al., 2004). The increased interest in early diagnosis and the increasing numbers of younger children presenting for assessment present special problems for diagnosis. In contrast to older individuals, the diagnosis of infants and very young children is more complex (Charman & Baird, 2002; Cox et al., 1999; Stone et al., 1999) with diagnostic stability increasing after about age 2 years (Courchesne, 2002; Dawson et al., 2002). However, developmental changes in this age group can be marked (Szatmari, Merette, Bryson, Thivierge, Roy, et al., 2002). For example, the repetitive behaviors typical of older children are much less common in very young children (Charman & Baird, 2002; Cox et al., 1999; Lord, 1995; Moore & Goodson, 2003; Stone et al., 1999). Social abnormalities may become more striking as the child matures (Lord, Storoschuk, Rutter, & Pickles, 1993).

A few studies have addressed the applicability of *DSM-IV* and *ICD-10* criteria in infants and young children. It appears that some young children will meet criteria for autism, but some may not necessarily fulfill the required repetitive behavior criteria until around their third birthday (Lord, 1996). Less commonly, a child appears to meet criteria for autism but then, over time, makes substantial gain. Some alternatives to *DSM-IV* and *ICD-10* have been proposed (e.g., National Center for Clinical Infant Programs [NCCIP], 1994) but have not met with wide acceptance due to both practical and theoretical concerns.

Considerable efforts have gone into the development of methods to facilitate screening and early diagnosis (see Chapter 27, this *Handbook,* Volume 2). Given the apparent association of early identification and intervention with improved outcome (NRC, 2001) the issues of early diagnosis have assumed increasing importance. In addition to the various approaches for screening based on history and direct observation, new approaches are needed in which screening becomes more behavioral and less subjective (and thus more readily available in nonspecialist settings; see Chawarska, Klin, & Volkmar, 2003).

Cultural Issues and Diagnosis

The issue of cultural factors in the diagnosis of autism has been the subject of remarkably little discussion. As Brown and Rogers (2003) point out, this is somewhat paradoxical given the various governmental and other mandates for the study of cultural factors. While by no means excusing the dearth of studies, several factors likely have operated to reduce interest in this area. First, the general impression of clinicians seeing children from a range of cultures and subcultures around the world is one of how much more alike than different children are. While variations in treatment and, to some extent, theoretical conceptualizations differ (see Chapter 48, this *Handbook,* Volume 2), it is a testament to the robustness of autism as a diagnostic concept that cultural influences are not more striking. One potential exception (although one tending to prove the rule) relates to the high levels of autistic-like behavior in individuals who suffer severe early institutional deprivation (Rutter, 1999). More rigorous and well-controlled studies on the issue of social-cultural factors in autism are clearly

critically needed. Given the very limited literature on the topic of cultural factors, this area is one ripe for future research. Chapter 48 (this *Handbook,* Volume 2) provides an international perspective on this problem.

Defining the Broader Phenotype

Somewhat paradoxically as the definition of autism has become more elaborated, interest has also increased in the broader spectrum of difficulties apparently inherited in families (see Chapter 16, this *Handbook,* this volume). Most investigators would now agree what is transmitted genetically includes not only classical autism (Kanner, 1943) but a broader range of difficulties variously impacting on social development, communication, and/or behavior. Attempts are now being made to stratify families based on various measures initially designed for use in more stringently diagnostic autistic samples (Bishop, 1998; Constantino & Todd, 2003; Lord, 1990; Lord et al., 2000; Shao et al., 2002; Tadevosyan-Leyfer et al., 2003; Tanguay, Robertson, & Derrick, 1998). Such approaches hold promise for identifying broader dimensions of function/dysfunction in families. The development of new methods for assessing the broader phenotype (e.g., Bishop, 1998; Constantino & Todd, 2003) is of great interest in this regard.

In addition to both the more strictly defined cases of autism, the broader range of autism spectrum disorders includes difficulties that do not fit neatly into our current classification scheme. Such cases of atypical autism test the boundaries of our classification system but also serve to underscore the important point that individuals with these conditions have not always read the textbooks and may exhibit unusual patterns of difficulty suggestive of autism in some ways but also with important differences. Children reared in profoundly impoverished environments may exhibit marked social difficulties and other problems suggestive of autism (Rutter, 1999). Similar issues arise with respect to children who are congenitally blind (Hobson & Bishop, 2003). Yet another set of issues arises with regard to children who, at least initially, seem to exhibit problems more suggestive of a language disorder but, over time, exhibit a course and outcome in some ways more suggestive of autism (Mawhood, Howlin, & Rutter, 2000). Issues with regard to differentiation of autism and Asperger's and language disorders have been noted (Bishop, 2000; Bishop & Norbury, 2002). Cases with unusual features or presentations are of great interest in that they may help to clarify syndrome boundaries, underscore areas where knowledge is lacking, and may clarify alternative mechanisms or developmental pathways. For example, while there is little disagreement that higher functioning autism and Asperger's disorder both are characterized by significant problems in social interaction in the face of average overall cognitive ability, the social difficulties appear to arise in the context of rather different developmental pathways and trajectories, for example, with preservation of language skills early on, and possibly later, in Asperger's but not in higher functioning autism (see Chapter 5, this *Handbook,* this volume).

CONCLUSION

Leo Kanner's description (1943) of the syndrome of early infantile autism has proven to be robust and enduring. To a remarkable degree, his observations and intuitions remain fresh and inspiring. False leads in the original work have been clarified by research. We are also aware of how much work remains 60 years later.

Studies have clarified that the disintegrative PDDs (Rett's disorder and childhood disintegrative disorder) differ from strictly defined autism in various ways (Tsai, 1992; Volkmar & Rutter, 1995); the study of these unusual conditions may be helpful in clarifying mechanisms of pathogenesis relevant to autism (see Chapters 3 & 5, this *Handbook,* this volume). The validity of the newest PDD—Asperger's disorder—apart from higher functioning autism is less clearly established and results contradictory (although often based on markedly differing definitions of the disorder; Gilchrist et al., 2001; Klin et al., 1995; Manjiviona & Prior, 1999; Miller & Ozonoff, 2000; Ozonoff, Pennington, & Rogers, 1991). The boundaries of Asperger's disorder with autism and other disorders, such as schizoid disorder of childhood (Wolff, 1998, 2000) and semantic-pragmatic

disorder (Bishop, 1989, 2002), also remain to be clearly established.

While *DSM-IV* and *ICD-10* are the most recent and most extensively evaluated diagnostic approaches for autism, they are undoubtedly not the last word on diagnosis. The present *DSM-IV* and *ICD-10* systems have the considerable advantage of being based on a relatively extensive set of data; they have clearly facilitated research and service. The dual-use constraints on *DSM,* that is, the use of the same criteria for both research and service, meant that brevity and ease of use were important considerations. The *ICD-10* system does not, at least for the research definitions, have this constraint. It remains to be seen whether the more detailed *ICD-10* research definition will, in the end, predominate. From the point of view of research, the attempt to link diagnostic instruments specially to diagnostic criteria is a considerable advantage and may mean that for research purposes, in effect, the more detailed research definition will come to dominate.

Probably the greatest nosological need at present is the classification of conditions that appear to fall within the broad class of the PDDs but do not meet criteria for presently recognized disorders. This group of conditions, referred to either as "atypical autism" or "pervasive developmental disorder not otherwise specified," includes a larger number of children than those who are stringently defined as autistic. Their nosological status is much less well defined (see Chapter 6, this *Handbook,* this volume). Concepts such as multiplex developmental disorder have been proposed for some of these individuals. A large subgroup of such cases is associated with severe mental handicap. These conditions require special services similar to those required for autism (Wing & Gould, 1979); their relationship to strictly defined autism remains an area of considerable interest and may have particular importance for family-genetic studies (Rutter, 1996). Biological and behavioral research depends on well-defined groups of patients and rigorous application of diagnostic methodologies. For example, genetic studies require clear definition of affected individuals and exclusion of false-positive cases. In turn, we can hope that future nosologies will be enriched by the inclusion of other types of data, including genetic, neuroimaging, neurochemical, and other behavioral and biological markers. Thus, there is a critical dialectic between research in nosology and research of other types. Advances in both fields are mutually dependent and have the same goal: enhancing the understanding and care of individuals and advancing our understanding of autism and related conditions (Rutter, 1999).

Cross-References

Other syndromes presently included as PDDs are discussed in Chapters 3 through 6; Chapter 21 provides an alternative view of issues of diagnosis and classification; changes in syndrome expression are discussed in Chapters 8 through 10.

REFERENCES

American Psychiatric Association. (1952). *Diagnostic and statistical manual of mental disorders*. Washington, DC: Author.

American Psychiatric Association. (1968). *Diagnostic and statistical manual of mental disorders* (2nd ed.). Washington, DC: Author.

American Psychiatric Association. (1980). *Diagnostic and statistical manual of mental disorders* (3rd ed.). Washington, DC: Author.

American Psychiatric Association. (1987). *Diagnostic and statistical manual of mental disorders* (3rd ed., rev.). Washington, DC: Author.

American Psychiatric Association. (1994). *Diagnostic and statistical manual of mental disorders* (4th ed.). Washington, DC: Author.

Amir, R. E., Van den Veyver, I. B., Wan, M., Tran, C. Q., Francke, U., & Zoghbi, H. Y. (1999). Rett syndrome is caused by mutations in X-linked MECP2, encoding methyl-CpG-binding protein 2 [See comment]. *Nature Genetics, 23*(2), 185–188.

Asperger, H. (1944). Die "autistichen Psychopathen" im Kindersalter. *Archive fur psychiatrie und Nervenkrankheiten, 117,* 76–136.

Bailey, A., Palferman, S., Heavey, L., & Le Couteur, A. (1998). Autism: The phenotype in relatives. *Journal of Autism and Developmental Disorders, 28*(5), 369–392.

Barkely, R. A. (1990). *Attention deficit hyperactivity disorder: A handbook for diagnosis and treatment.* New York: Guilford Press.

Baron-Cohen, S. (1989). Do autistic children have obsessions and compulsions? *British Journal of Clinical Psychology, 28*(3), 193–200.

Bartak, L., Rutter, M., & Cox, A. (1977). A comparative study of infantile autism and specific developmental receptive language disorders—III. Discriminant function analysis. *Journal of Autism and Childhood Schizophrenia, 7,* 383–396.

Bender, L. (1946). Childhood schizophrenia. *American Journal of Orthopsychiatry, 17,* 40–56.

Bishop, D. V. (1989). Autism, Asperger's syndrome and semantic-pragmatic disorder: Where are the boundaries? [Special issue: Autism]. *British Journal of Disorders of Communication, 24*(2), 107–121.

Bishop, D. V. (1998). Development of the Children's Communication Checklist (CCC): A method for assessing qualitative aspects of communicative impairment in children. *Journal of Child Psychology and Psychiatry and Allied Disciplines, 39*(6), 879–891.

Bishop, D. V. (2000). What's so special about Asperger syndrome? The need for further exploration of the borderlands of autism. In A. Klin & F. R. Volkmar (Eds.), *Asperger syndrome* (pp. 254–277). New York: Guilford Press.

Bishop, D. V., & Norbury, C. F. (2002). Exploring the borderlands of autistic disorder and specific language impairment: A study using standardised diagnostic instruments. *Journal of Child Psychology and Psychiatry and Allied Disciplines, 43*(7), 917–929.

Bleuler, E. (1951). Dementia Praecox, or the Group of Schizophrenia. Translated by J. Zinkin. New York: International Universities Press. (Original work published 1911)

Borden, M. C., & Ollendick, T. H. (1994). An examination of the validity of social subtypes in autism. *Journal of Autism and Developmental Disorders, 24*(1), 23–37.

Brasic, J. R., Barnett, J. Y., Kaplan, D., Sheitman, B. B., Aisemberg, P., Lafargue, R. T., et al. (1994). Clomipramine ameliorates adventitious movements and compulsions in prepubertal boys with autistic disorder and severe mental retardation. *Neurology, 44*(7), 1309–1312.

Brown, J. R., & Rogers, S. J. (2003). Cultural issues in autism. In R. L. Hendren, S. Ozonoff, & S. Rogers (Eds.), *Autism spectrum disorders* (pp. 209–226). Washington, DC: American Psychiatric Press.

Buitelaar, J. K., Van der Gaag, R., Klin, A., & Volkmar, F. (1999). Exploring the boundaries of Pervasive Developmental Disorder Not Otherwise Specified: Analyses of data from the *DSM-IV* autistic field trial. *Journal of Autism and Developmental Disorders, 29*(1), 33–43.

Burd, L., Fisher, W. W., Kerbeshian, J., & Arnold, M. E. (1987). Is development of Tourette disorder a marker for improvement in patients with autism and other pervasive developmental disorders? *Journal of the American Academy of Child and Adolescent Psychiatry, 26*(2), 162–165.

Candland, D. K. (1993). Feral children and clever animals: Reflections on human nature. *Oxford University Press,* 411.

Cantwell, D. P. (1996). Classification of Child and Adolescent Psychopathology. *Journal of Child Psychiatry and Psychology, 37,* 3–12.

Cantwell, D. P., Baker, L., & Rutter, M. (1979). Families of autistic children and dysphasic children: Family life and interaction patterns. *Archives of General Psychiatry, 36,* 682–687.

Castelloe, P., & Dawson, G. (1993). Subclassification of children with autism and pervasive developmental disorder: A questionnaire based on Wing's subgrouping scheme. *Journal of Autism and Developmental Disorders, 23*(2), 229–241.

Charman, T. (1998). Specifying the nature and course of the joint attention impairment in autism in the preschool years: Implications for diagnosis and intervention. *Autism: International Journal of Research and Practice, 2*(1), 61–79.

Charman, T., & Baird, G. (2002). Practitioner review: Diagnosis of autism spectrum disorder in 2- and 3-year-old children. *Journal of Child Psychology and Psychiatry and Allied Disciplines, 43*(3), 289–305.

Chawarska, K., Klin, A., & Volkmar, F. (2003). Automatic attention cueing through eye movement in 2-year-old children with autism. *Child Development, 74*(4), 1108–1122.

Chess, S., Fernandez, P., & Korn, S. (1978). Behavioral consequences of congenital rubella. *Journal of Pediatrics, 93*(4), 699–703.

Cicchetti, D. V., Volkmar, F. R., Klin, A., & Showalter, D. (1995). Diagnosing autism using *ICD-10* criteria: A comparison of neural networks and standard multi variate procedures. *Journal of Child Neuropsychology, 1*(1), 26–37.

Cohen, D. J. (1976). The diagnostic process in child psychiatry. *Psychiatric Annals, 6*(9), 29–56.

Cohen, D. J. (1980). The pathology of the self in primary childhood autism and Gilles de la Tourette syndrome. In B. Blinder (Ed.), *Psychiatric clinics of North America* (pp. 383–402). Philadelphia: Saunders.

Cohen, D. J., Paul, R., & Volkmar, F. R. (1986). Issues in the classification of pervasive and other developmental disorders: Toward *DSM-IV. Journal of the American Academy of Child Psychiatry, 25*(2), 213–220.

Cohen, I. L., Sudhalter, V., Landon-Jimenez, D., & Keogh, M. (1993). A neural network approach to the classification of autism. *Journal of Autism and Developmental Disorders, 23*(3), 443–466.

Constantino, J. N., & Todd, R. D. (2003). Autistic traits in the general population: A twin study. *Archives of General Psychiatry, 60*(5), 524–530.

Courchesne, E. (2002). Abnormal early brain development in autism. *Molecular Psychiatry, 7*(Suppl. 2), S21–S23.

Cox, A., Klein, K., Charman, T., Baird, G., Baron-Cohen, S., Swettenham, J., et al. (1999). Autism spectrum disorders at 20 and 42 months of age: Stability of clinical and ADI-R diagnosis. *Journal of Child Psychology and Psychiatry and Allied Disciplines, 40*(5), 719–732.

Dahl, E. K., Cohen, D. J., & Provence, S. (1986). Clinical and multivariate approaches to the nosology of pervasive developmental disorders. *Journal of the American Academy of Child Psychiatry, 25*(2), 170–180.

Dawson, G., Munson, J., Estes, A., Osterling, J., McPartland, J., Toth, K., et al. (2002). Neurocognitive function and joint attention ability in young children with autism spectrum disorder versus developmental delay. *Child Development, 73*(2), 345–358.

DeMyer, M. K., Hingtgen, J. N., & Jackson, R. K. (1981). Infantile autism reviewed: A decade of research. *Schizophrenia Bulletin, 7*(3), 388–451.

Dykens, E. M. (2000). Psychopathology in children with intellectual disability. *Journal of Child Psychology and Psychiatry and Allied Disciplines, 41*(4), 407–417.

Eaves, L. C., Eaves, D. M., & Ho, H. H. (1994). Subtypes of autism by cluster analysis. *Journal of Autism and Developmental Disorders, 24*(1), 3–22.

Eisenmajer, R., Prior, M., Leekam, S., Wing, L., Ong, B., Gould, J., et al. (1996). Comparison of clinical symptoms in autism and Asperger's disorder. *Journal of the American Academy of Child and Adolescent Psychiatry, 35*(11), 1523–1531.

Factor, D. C., Freeman, N. L., & Kardash, A. (1989, December). A comparison of *DSM-III* and *DSM-III-R* criteria for autism. *Journal of Autism and Developmental Disorders, 19*(4), 637–640.

Fein, D., Waterhouse, L., Lucci, D., & Snyder, D. (1985). Cognitive subtypes in developmentally disabled children: A pilot study. *Journal of Autism and Developmental Disorders, 15*(1), 77–95.

Fombonne, E. (1992). Diagnostic assessment in a sample of autistic and developmentally impaired adolescents [Special issue: Classification and diagnosis]. *Journal of Autism and Developmental Disorders, 22*(4), 563–581.

Frances, A. J., Widiger, T. A., & Pincus, H. A. (1989). The development of *DSM-IV. Archives of General Psychiatry, 46,* 373–375.

Ghaziuddin, M., Alessi, N., & Greden, J. F. (1995). Life events and depression in children with pervasive disorders. *Journal of Autism and Developmental Disorders, 25*(5), 495–502.

Ghaziuddin, M., & Butler, E. (1998). Clumsiness in autism and Asperger syndrome: A further report. *Journal of Intellectual Disability Research, 42*(Pt. 1), 43–48.

Ghaziuddin, M., & Gerstein, L. (1996). Pedantic speaking style differentiates Asperger syndrome from high-functioning autism. *Journal of Autism and Developmental Disorders, 26*(6), 585–595.

Ghaziuddin, M., Tsai, L., & Ghaziuddin, N. (1992). Comorbidity of autistic disorder in children and adolescents. *European Child and Adolescent Psychiatry, 1*(4), 209–213.

Gilchrist, A., Green, J., Cox, A., Burton, D., Rutter, M., & Le Couteur, A. (2001). Development and current functioning in adolescents with Asperger syndrome: A comparative study. *Journal of Child Psychology and Psychiatry and Allied Disciplines, 42*(2), 227–240.

Gillberg, C. (1985). Asperger's syndrome and recurrent psychosis: A case study. *Journal of Autism and Developmental Disorders, 15*(4), 389–397.

Gillberg, C. (1990). Medical work-up in children with autism and Asperger syndrome. *Brain Dysfunction, 3*(5/6), 249–260.

Gillberg, C. (1991). Debate and argument: Is autism a pervasive developmental disorder? *Journal of Child Psychology and Psychiatry and Allied Disciplines, 32*(7), 1169–1170.

Gillberg, C. (1994). Debate and argument: Having Rett syndrome in the *ICD-10* PDD category does not make sense. *Journal of Child Psychology and Psychiatry and Allied Disciplines, 35*(2), 377–378.

Gillberg, C., & M. Coleman. (2000). The biology of the autistic syndromes (3rd ed.). London: Mac Keith Press.

Gordon, C. T., Rapoport, J. L., Hamburger, S. D., State, R. C., & Mannheim, G. B. (1992). Differential response of seven subjects with autistic disorder to clomipramine and desipramine. *American Journal of Psychiatry, 149*(3), 363–366.

Gordon, C. T., State, R. C., Nelson, J. E., Hamburger, S. D., & Rapoport, J. L. (1993). A double-blind comparison of clomipramine, desipramine, and placebo in the treatment of autistic disorder. *Archives of General Psychiatry, 50*(6), 441–447.

Harper, J., & Williams, S. (1975). Age and type of onset as critical variables in early infantile autism. *Journal of Autism and Childhood Schizophrenia, 5,* 25–35.

Heller, T. (1908). Dementia Infantilis. Zeitschrift fur die Erforschung und Behandlung des Jugenlichen. *Schwachsinns, 2,* 141–165.

Hellgren, L., Gillberg, C., & Gillberg, I. C. (1994). Children with deficits in attention, motor control and perception (DAMP) almost grown up: The contribution of various background to outcome at age 16 years. *European Child and Adolescent Psychiatry, 3*(1), 1–15.

Hendry, C. N. (2000). Childhood disintegrative disorder: Should it be considered a distinct diagnosis. *Clinical Psychology Review, 20,* 77–90.

Hertzig, M. E., Snow, M. E., New, E., & Shapiro, T. (1990). *DSM-III* and *DSM-III-R* diagnosis of autism and pervasive. *Journal of the American Academy of Child and Adolescent Psychiatry, 29*(1), 123–126.

Hippler, K., & Klicpera, C. (2003). A retrospective analysis of the clinical case records of "autistic psychopaths" diagnosed by Hans Asperger and his team at the University Children's Hospital, Vienna. In U. Frith & E. Hill (Eds.), *Autism: Mind and Brain* (pp. 21–42). Oxford, England: Oxford University Press.

Hobbs, N. (1975). *Issues in the classification of children.* San Francisco: Jossey-Bass.

Hobson, R. P., & Bishop, M. (2003). The pathogenesis of autism: Insights from congenital blindness. *Philosophical Transactions of the Royal Society of London—Series B: Biological Sciences, 358*(1430), 335–344.

Howlin, P. (2003). Outcome in high-functioning adults with autism with and without early language delays: Implications for the differentiation between autism and Asperger syndrome. *Journal of Autism and Developmental Disorders, 33*(1), 3–13.

Howlin, P., Mawhood, L., & Rutter, M. (2000). Autism and developmental receptive language disorders—a follow-up comparison in early adult life: II. Social, behavioural, and psychiatric outcomes. *Journal of Child Psychology and Psychiatry, 41,* 561–578.

Iacoboni, M. (2000). Attention and sensorimotor integration: Mapping the embodied mind. In A. W. Toga & J. C. Mazziotta (Eds.), *Brain mapping: The systems* (pp. 463–490). San Diego, CA: Academic Press.

Jaselskis, C. A., Cook, E. H., & Fletcher, K. E. (1992). Clonidine treatment of hyperactive and impulsive children with autistic disorder. *Journal of Clinical Psychopharmacology, 12*(5), 322–327.

Kanner, L. (1943). Autistic disturbances of affective contact. *Nervous Child, 2,* 217–250.

Kerbeshian, J., Burd, L., & Fisher, W. (1987). Lithium carbonate in the treatment of two patients with infantile autism and atypical bipolar symptomatology. *Journal of Clinical Psychopharmacology, 7*(6), 401–405.

Klin, A., Chawarska, K., Paul, R., Rubin, E., Morgan, T., Wiesner, L., & Volkmar, F. R. (2004). Autism in a 15 month old child. *American Journal of Psychiatry, 161,* 1981–1988.

Klin, A., Jones, W., Schultz, R., & Volkmar, F. (2003). The enactive mind, or from actions to cognition: Lessons from autism. *Philosophical Transactions of the Royal Society of London—Series B: Biological Sciences, 358*(1430), 345–360.

Klin, A., Lang, J., Cicchetti, D. V., & Volkmar, F. R. (2000). Brief report: Interrater reliability of clinical diagnosis and *DSM-IV* criteria for autistic disorder: Results of the *DSM-IV* autism field trial. *Journal of Autism and Developmental Disorders, 30*(2), 163–167.

Klin, A., Schultz, R., Pauls, D., & Volkmar, F. R. (in press). Three diagnostic approaches to Asperger's Disorder. *Journal of Autism and Developmental Disorders.*

Klin, A., Sparrow, S., & Volkmar, F. R. (1997). *Asperger's syndrome.* New York: Guilford Press.

Klin, A., & Volkmar, F. R. (1997). Asperger's Syndrome. In D. J. Cohen & F. R. Volkmar (Eds.), *Handbook of Autism and Pervasive Developmental Disorders* (2nd ed., pp. 94–122). New York: Wiley.

Klin, A., Volkmar, F. R., & Sparrow, S. S. (Eds.). (2000). *Asperger syndrome.* New York: Guilford Press.

Klin, A., Volkmar, F. R., Sparrow, S. S., Cicchetti, D. V., & Rourke, B. P. (1995). Validity and neuropsychological characterization of Asperger syndrome: Convergence with nonverbal learning disabilities syndrome. *Journal of Child Psychology and Psychiatry, 36*(7), 1127–1140.

Kolvin, I. (1971). Studies in childhood psychoses: Diagnostic criteria and classification. *British Journal of Psychiatry, 118,* 381–384.

Komoto, J., Usui, S., & Hirata, J. (1984). Infantile autism and affective disorder. *Journal of Autism and Developmental Disorders, 14*(1), 81–84.

Kramer, M. (1968). The history of the efforts to agree on an international classification of mental disorders. In *Diagnostic and statistical manual of mental disorders* (2nd ed.,

pp. xi–xx). Washington, DC: American Psychiatric Association.

Lainhart, J. E., & Folstein, S. E. (1994). Affective disorders in people with autism: A review of published cases. *Journal of Autism and Developmental Disorders, 24*(5), 587–601.

Leckman, J. F., Peterson, B. S., Pauls, D. L., & Cohen, D. J. (1997). Tic disorders. *Psychiatric Clinics of North America, 20*(4), 839–861.

Leekam, S., Libby, S., Wing, L., Gould, J., & Gillberg, C. (2000). Comparison of *ICD-10* and Gillberg's criteria for Asperger syndrome [Special issue: Asperger syndrome]. *Autism: Journal of Research and Practice, 4*(1), 11–28.

Lincoln, A. E., Courchesne, E., Kilman, B. A., Elmasian, R., & Allen, M. (1998). Neurobiology of Asperger syndrome: Seven case studies and quantitative magnetic resonance imaging findings. In E. Schopler, G. B. Mesibov, & L. J. Kunc (Eds.), *Asperger syndrome or high functioning autism?* (pp. 145–166). New York: Plenum Press.

Lockyer, L., & Rutter, M. (1969). A five to fifteen year follow-up study of infantile psychosis: III. Psychological Aspects. *British Journal of Psychiatry, 115,* 865–882.

Lockyer, L., & Rutter, M. (1970). A five to fifteen year follow-up study of infantile psychosis. *British Journal of Social and Clinical Psychology, 9,* 152–163.

Lord, C. (1995). Follow-up of two year olds referred for possible autism. *Journal of Child Psychology and Psychiatry, 36,* 1365–1382.

Lord, C., Storoschuk, S., Rutter, M., & Pickles, A. (1993). Using the ADI-R to diagnose autism in preschool children. *Infant Mental Health Journal, 14*(3), 234–252.

Magnusson, P., & Saemundsen, E. (2001). Prevalence of autism in Iceland. *Journal of Autism and Developmental Disorders, 31*(2), 153–163.

Mahler, M. (1952). On child psychoses and schizophrenia: Autistic and symbiotic infantiles psychoses. *Psychoanalytic Study of the Child, 7,* 286–305.

Manjiviona, J., & Prior, M. (1999). Neuropsychological profiles of children with Asperger syndrome and autism. *Autism: International Journal of Research and Practice, 3*(4), 327–356.

Mawhood, L., Howlin, P., & Rutter, M. (2000). Autism and developmental receptive language disorder—a comparative follow-up in early adult life. I: Cognitive and language outcomes. *Journal of Child Psychology and Psychiatry and Allied Disciplines, 41*(5), 547–559.

McDougle, C. J., Kresch, L. E., Goodman, W. K., Naylor, S. T., Volkmar, F. R., Cohen, D. J., et al. (1995). A case-controlled study of repetitive thoughts and behavior in adults with autistic disorder and obsessive-compulsive disorder. *American Journal of Psychiatry, 152*(5), 772–777.

McDougle, C. J., Price, L. H., Volkmar, F. R., & Goodman, W. K. E. (1992). Clomipramine in autism: Preliminary evidence of efficacy. *Journal of the American Academy of Child and Adolescent Psychiatry, 31*(4), 746–750.

Miller, J. N., & Ozonoff, S. (1997). Did Asperger's cases have Asperger disorder? A research note. *Journal of Child Psychology and Psychiatry, 38*(2), 247–251.

Miller, J. N., & Ozonoff, S. (2000). The external validity of Asperger disorder: Lack of evidence from the domain of neuropsychology. *Journal of Abnormal Psychology, 109*(2), 227–238.

Moore, V., & Goodson, S. (2003). How well does early diagnosis of autism stand the test of time? Follow-up study of children assessed for autism at age 2 and development of an early diagnostic service. *Autism: International Journal of Research and Practice, 7*(1), 47–63.

Mundy, P., Sigman, M. D., Ungerer, J., & Sherman, T. (1986). Defining the social deficits of autism: The contribution of non-verbal. *Journal of Child Psychology and Psychiatry and Allied Disciplines, 27*(5), 657–669.

National Center for Clinical Infant Programs. (1994). Diagnostic classification: 0–3. *National Center for Clinical Infant Programs.* Washington, DC: Author.

National Research Council. (2001). *Educating young children with Autism.* Washington, DC: National Academy Press.

Nelson, E. C., & Pribor, E. F. (1993). A calendar savant with autism and Tourette syndrome: Response to treatment and thoughts on the interrelationships of these conditions. *Annals of Clinical Psychiatry, 5*(2), 135–140.

Ozonoff, S., Pennington, B. F., & Rogers, S. J. (1991). Executive function deficits in high-functioning autistic individuals: Relationship to theory of mind. *Journal of Child Psychology and Psychiatry, 32*(7), 1081–1105.

Petty, L. K., Ornitz, E. M., Michelman, J. D., & Zimmerman, E. G. (1985). Autistic children who become schizophrenic. *Annual Progress in Child Psychiatry and Child Development.*

Pickles, A., Starr, E., Kazak, S., Bolton, P., Papanikolaou, K., Bailey, A., et al. (2000). Variable expression of the autism broader phenotype: Findings from extended pedigrees. *Journal of Child Psychology and Psychiatry and Allied Disciplines, 41*(4), 491–502.

Piven, J., Palmer, P., Jacobi, D., Childress, D., & Arndt, S. (1997). Broader autism phenotype: Evidence from a family history study of multiple-incidence autism families. *American Journal of Psychiatry, 154*(2), 185–190.

Poustka, F., & Lisch, S. (1993). Autistic behaviour domains and their relation to self-injurious behaviour. *Acta Paedopsychiatrica: International Journal of Child and Adolescent Psychiatry, 56*(2), 69–73.

Prior, M., Boulton, D., Gajzago, C., & Perry, D. (1975). The classification of childhood psychoses by numerical taxonomy. *Journal of Child Psychology and Psychiatry, 16*(4), 321–330.

Provence, S., & Dahl, K. (1987). Disorders of atypical development: Diagnostic issues raised by a spectrum disorder. In D. Cohen & A. Donnellan (Eds.), *Handbook of autism and pervasive developmental disorders* (pp. 677–689). New York: Wiley.

Quintana, H., Birmaher, B., Stedge, D., Lennon, S., Freed, J., Bridge, J., et al. (1995). Use of methylphenidate in the treatment of children with autistic disorder. *Journal of Autism and Developmental Disorders, 25*(3), 283–294.

Rank, B. (1949). Adaptation of the psychoanalytic technique for the treatment of young children with atypical development. *American Journal of Orthopsychiatry, 19,* 130–139.

Rapin, I. (1991). Autistic children: Diagnosis and clinical features. *Pediatrics, 87*(5, Pt. 2), 751–760.

Rapin, I., & Allen, D. A. (1983). Developmental language disorders: Nosologic considerations. In U. Kirk (Ed.), *Neuropsychology of language, reading and spelling* (pp. 155–184). New York: Academic Press.

Realmuto, G. M., & Main, B. (1982). Coincidence of Tourette's disorder and infantile autism. *Journal of Autism and Developmental Disorders, 12*(4), 367–372.

Rett, A. (1966). Uber ein eigenartiges hirntophisces Syndroem bei hyperammonie im Kindersalter. *Wein Medizinische Wochenschrift, 118,* 723–726.

Ritvo, E. R., & Freeman, B. J. (1977). National Society for Autistic Children definition of the syndrome of. *Journal of Pediatric Psychology, 2*(4), 142–145.

Rogers, S. (2001). Diagnosis of autism before the age of 3. *International review of research in mental retardation: Autism* (23), 1–31.

Rogers, S., & Ozonoff, S. (in press). What do we know about sensory dysfunction in autism? A critical review of the empirical evidence. *Journal of Child Psychology and Psychiatry.*

Rumsey, J. M., Rapoport, J. L., & Sceery, W. R. (1985). Autistic children as adults: Psychiatric, social, and behavioral. *Journal of the American Academy of Child Psychiatry, 24*(4), 465–473.

Rutter, M. (1970). Autistic children: Infancy to adulthood. *Seminars in Psychiatry, 2,* 435–450.

Rutter, M. (1978). Diagnostic validity in child psychiatry. *Advances in Biological Psychiatry, 2,* 2–22.

Rutter, M. (1994). Debate and argument: There are connections between brain and mind and it is important that Rett syndrome be classified somewhere. *Journal of Child Psychology and Psychiatry and Allied Disciplines, 35*(2), 379–381.

Rutter, M. (1996). Autism research: Prospects and priorities. *Journal of Autism and Developmental Disorders, 26,* 257–276.

Rutter, M. (1999). The Emmanual Miller Memorial Lectur 1998: Autism: Two-way interplay between research and clinical world. *Journal of Child Psychology and Psychiatry, 40,* 169–188.

Rutter, M. (2000). Genetic studies of autism: From the 1970s into the millennium. *Journal of Abnormal Child Psychology, 28*(1), 3–14.

Rutter, M. (2002). Classification: Conceptual issues and substantive findings. In E. Taylor & M. Rutter (Eds.), *Child and adolescent psychiatry* (4th ed., pp. 3–17). Oxford, England: Blackwell.

Rutter, M., Bailey, A., Bolton, P., & Le Couter, A. (1994). Autism and known medical conditions: Myth and substance. *Journal of Child Psychology and Psychiatry and Allied Disciplines, 35*(2), 311–322.

Rutter, M., & Garmezy, N. (1983). Developmental psychopathology. In E. M. Hetherington (Ed.), *Mussen's handbook of child psychology: Vol. 4. Socialization, personality and child development* (pp. 755–911). New York: Wiley.

Rutter M., & Gould, M. (1985). Classification. In M. Rutter & L. Hersov (Eds.), *Child and Adolescent Psychiatry: Modern Approaches* (2nd ed., pp. 304–321). Cambridge, MA: Blackwell.

Rutter, M., Le Couteur, A., & Lord, C. (2003). *Autism diagnostic interview-Revised.* Los Angeles: Western Psychological Services.

Rutter, M., & Schopler, E. (1992). Classification of pervasive developmental disorders: Some concepts and practical considerations [Special issue: Classification and diagnosis]. *Journal of Autism and Developmental Disorders, 22*(4), 459–482.

Rutter, M., Shaffer, D., & Shepherd, M. (1975). *A multiaxial classification of child psychiatric disorders.* Geneva, Switzerland: World Health Organization.

Sartorius, N. (1988). International perspectives of psychiatric classification. *British Journal of Psychiatry, 152*(Suppl.), 9–14.

Shao, Y., Raiford, K. L., Wolpert, C. M., Cope, H. A., Ravan, S. A., Ashley-Koch, A. A., et al. (2002). Phenotypic homogeneity provides increased support for linkage on chromosome 2 in autistic disorder. *American Journal of Human Genetics, 70*(4), 1058–1061.

Short, A., & Schopler, E. (1988). Factors relating to age of onset in autism. *Journal of Autism and Developmental Disorders, 18,* 207–216.

Siegel, B., Anders, T. F., Ciaranello, R. D., Bienenstock, B., & Kraemer, H. C. (1986). Empirically derived subclassification of the autistic syndrome. *Journal of Autism and Developmental Disorders, 16*(3), 275–293.

Siegel, B., Pliner, C., Eschler, J., & Elliott, G. R. (1988). How children with autism are diagnosed: Difficulties in identification of children with multiple developmental delays. *Journal of Developmental Behavioral Pediatrics, 9*(4), 199–204.

Siegel, B., Vukicevic, J., Elliott, G. R., & Kraemer, H. C. (1989). The use of signal detection theory to assess *DSM-III-R* criteria for autistic disorder. *Journal of the American Academy of Child and Adolescent Psychiatry, 28*(4), 542–548.

Simon, N. (1978). Kaspar Hauser's recovery and autopsy: A perspective on neurological and sociological requirements for language development. *Journal of Autism and Childhood Schizophrenia, 8*(2), 209–217.

Siperstein, R., & Volkmar, F. R. (2004). Parental reporting of regression in children with pervasive developmental disorders. *Journal of Autism and Developmental Disorders.*

Soper, H. V., Satz, P., Orsini, D. L., Henry, R. R., Zvi, J. C., & Schulman, M. (1986). Handedness patterns in autism suggest subtypes. *Journal of Autism and Developmental Disorders, 16*(2), 155–167.

Spitzer, R. L., Endicott, J. E., & Robins, E. (1978). Research diagnostic criteria. *Archives of General Psychiatry, 35,* 773–782.

Spitzer, R. L., & Siegel, B. (1990). The *DSM-III-R* field trial of pervasive developmental disorders. *Journal of the American Academy of Child and Adolescent Psychiatry, 29*(6), 855–862.

Spitzer, R. L., & Williams, J. B. W. (1980). Classification in psychiatry. In H. Kaplan, A. Freedman, & B. Sadock (Eds.), *The comprehensive textbook of psychiatry* (3rd ed.). Baltimore: Williams & Wilkins.

Sponheim, E. (1996). Changing criteria of autistic disorders: A comparison of the *ICD-10* research criteria and *DSM-IV* with *DSM-III-R,* CARS, and ABC. *Journal of Autism and Developmental Disorders, 26*(5), 513–525.

Sponheim, E., & Skjeldal, O. (1998). Autism and related disorders: Epidemiological findings in a Norwegian study using *ICD-10* diagnostic criteria. *Journal of Autism and Developmental Disorders, 28*(3), 217–227.

Steingard, R., & Biederman, J. (1987). Lithium responsive manic-like symptoms in two individuals with autism. *Journal of the American Academy of Child and Adolescent Psychiatry, 26*(6), 932–935.

Stone, W. L., Lee, E. B., Ashford, L., Brissie, J., Hepburn, S. L., Coonrod, E. E., et al. (1999). Can autism be diagnosed accurately in children under 3 years? *Journal of Child Psychology and Psychiatry and Allied Disciplines, 40*(2), 219–226.

Szatmari, P. (1992a). A review of the *DSM-III-R* criteria for autistic disorder [Special issue: Classification and diagnosis]. *Journal of Autism and Developmental Disorders, 22*(4), 507–523.

Szatmari, P. (1992b). The validity of autistic spectrum disorders: A literature review [Special issue: Classification and diagnosis]. *Journal of Autism and Developmental Disorders, 22*(4), 583–600.

Szatmari, P. (2000). Perspectives on the classification of Asperger syndrome. In A. Klin & F. R. Volkmar (Eds.), *Asperger syndrome* (pp. 403–417). New York: Guilford Press.

Szatmari, P., Bryson, S. E., Boyle, M. H., Streiner, D. L., & Duku, E. (2003). Predictors of outcome among high functioning children with autism and Asperger syndrome. *Journal of Child Psychology and Psychiatry and Allied Disciplines, 44*(4), 520–528.

Szatmari, P., Merette, C., Bryson, S. E., Thivierge, J., Roy, M. A., Cayer, M., et al. (2002). Quantifying dimensions in autism: a factor-analytic study [Comment]. *Journal of the American Academy of Child and Adolescent Psychiatry, 41*(4), 467–474.

Szatmari, P., Volkmar, F., & Walter, S. (1995). Evaluation of diagnostic criteria for autism using latent class models. *Journal of the American Academy of Child and Adolescent Psychiatry, 34*(2), 216–222.

Tadevosyan-Leyfer, O., Dowd, M., Mankoski, R., Winklosky, B., Putnam, S., McGrath, L., et al. (2003). A principal components analysis of the Autism Diagnostic Interview-Revised. *Journal*

of the American Academy of Child and Adolescent Psychiatry, 42(7), 864–872.

Tanguay, P. E., Robertson, J., & Derrick, A. (1998). A dimensional classification of autism spectrum disorder by social communication domains. *Journal of the American Academy of Child and Adolescent Psychiatry, 37*(3), 271–277.

Towbin, K. E. (2003). Strategies for pharmacologic treatment of high functioning autism and Asperger syndrome. *Child and Adolescent Psychiatric Clinics of North America, 12*(1) 23–45.

Tsai, L. (1992). Is Rett syndrome a subtype of pervasive developmental disorder? *Journal of Autism and Developmental Disorders, 22,* 551–561.

Tsai, L. (1996). Brief report: Comorbid psychiatric disorders of autistic disorders. *Journal of Autism and Developmental Disorders, 26,* 159–164.

Tsai, L. Y. (1999). Psychopharmacology in autism. *Psychosomatic Medicine, 61*(5), 651–665.

Tsai, L. Y., Tsai, M. C., & August, G. J. (1985). Brief report: Implication of EEG diagnoses in the subclassification of infantile autism. *Journal of Autism and Developmental Disorders, 15*(3), 339–344.

Van der Gaag, R. J., Buitelaar, J., Van den Ban, E., Bezemer, M., Njio, L., & Van Engeland, H. (1995). A controlled multivariate chart review of multiple complex developmental disorder. *Journal of the American Academy of Child and Adolescent Psychiatry, 34*(8), 1096–1106.

Volkmar, F. R. (1992). Childhood disintegrative disorder: Issues for *DSM-IV. Journal of Autism and Developmental Disorders, 22*(4), 625–642.

Volkmar, F. R., Cicchetti, D. V., Bregman, J., & Cohen, D. J. (1992). Three diagnostic systems for autism: *DSM-III, DSM-III-R,* and *ICD-10* [Special issue: Classification and diagnosis]. *Journal of Autism and Developmental Disorders, 22*(4), 483–492.

Volkmar, F. R., Cicchetti, D. V., Cohen, D. J., & Bregman, J. (1992). Brief report: Developmental aspects of *DSM-III-R* criteria for autism [Special issue: Classification and diagnosis]. *Journal of Autism and Developmental Disorders, 22*(4), 657–662.

Volkmar, F. R., & Cohen, D. J. (1989). Disintegrative disorder or "late onset" autism. *Journal of Child Psychology and Psychiatry and Allied Disciplines, 30*(5), 717–724.

Volkmar, F. R., & Cohen, D. J. (1991a). Comorbid association of autism and schizophrenia. *American Journal of Psychiatry, 148*(12), 1705–1707.

Volkmar, F. R., & Cohen, D. J. (1991b). Debate and argument: The utility of the term pervasive developmental disorder. *Journal of Child Psychology and Psychiatry and Allied Disciplines, 32*(7), 1171–1172.

Volkmar, F., Cohen, D., Hoshino, K., Rende, R., & Paul, R. (1988). Phenomenology and classification of the childhood psychoses. *Psychological Medicine, 18*(1), 191–201.

Volkmar, F. R., & Klin, A. (1998). Asperger syndrome and nonverbal learning disabilities. In E. Schopler & G. B. Mesibov (Eds.), *Asperger syndrome or high-functioning autism? Current issues in autism* (pp. 107–121). New York: Plenum Press.

Volkmar, F. R., Klin, A., & Pauls, D. (1998). Nosological and genetic aspects of Asperger Syndrome. *Journal of Autism and Developmental Disorders, 28*(5), 457–463.

Volkmar, F. R., Klin, A., Siegel, B., Szatmari, P., Lord, C., Campbell, M., et al. (1994). Field trial for autistic disorder in *DSM-IV*. *American Journal of Psychiatry, 151*(9), 1361–1367.

Volkmar, F. R., Lord, C., Bailey, A., Schultz, R. T., & Klin, A. J. (2004). Autism and Pervasive Developmental Disorders. *Journal of Child Psychology and Psychiatry, 45*(1), 135–170.

Volkmar, F. R., & Nelson, D. S. (1990). Seizure disorders in autism. *Journal of the American Academy of Child and Adolescent Psychiatry, 29*(1), 127–129.

Volkmar, F. R., & Rutter, M. (1995). Childhood disintegrative disorder: Results of the *DSM-IV* Autism Field Trial. *Journal of the American Academy of Child and Adolescent Psychiatry, 34*(8), 1092–1095.

Volkmar, F. R., & Schwab-Stone, M. (1996). Annotation: Childhood disorders in *DSM-IV*. *Journal of Child Psychology and Psychiatry and Allied Disciplines, 37*(7), 779–784.

Volkmar F. R., Schwab-Stone, M., & First, M. (2002). Classification in child and adolescent Psychiatry: Principles and issues. In M. Lewis (Ed.), *Child and adolescent psychiatry: A comprehensive textbook* (3rd ed., pp. 499–505). Baltimore: Williams & Wilkins.

Volkmar, F. R., Stier, D. M., & Cohen, D. J. (1985). Age of recognition of pervasive developmental disorder. *American Journal of Psychiatry, 142*(12), 1450–1452.

Waterhouse, L., Morris, R., Allen, D., Dunn, M., Fein, D., Feinstein, C., et al. (1996). Diagnosis and classification in autism. *Journal of Autism and Developmental Disorders, 26*(1), 59–86.

Waterhouse, L., Wing, L., Spitzer, R., & Siegel, B. (1993). Pervasive developmental disorders: From *DSM-III* to *DSM-III-R* [Special issue: Classification and diagnosis]. *Journal of Autism and Developmental Disorders, 22*(4), 525–549.

Weir, K., & Salisbury, D. M. (1980). Acute onset of autistic features following brain damage in a ten-year-old. *Journal of Autism and Developmental Disorders, 10,* 185–191.

Wing, L. (1980). Childhood autism and social class: A question of selection? *British Journal of Psychiatry, 137,* 410–417.

Wing, L. (1981). Asperger's syndrome: A clinical account. *Psychological Medicine, 11*(1), 115–129.

Wing, L., & Gould, J. (1979). Severe impairments of social interaction and associated abnormalities in children: Epidemiology and classification. *Journal of Autism and Developmental Disorders, 9*(1), 11–29.

Wolff, S. (1998). Schizoid personality in childhood: The links with Asperger syndrome, schizophrenia spectrum disorders, and elective mutism. In E. Schopler & G. B. Mesibov (Eds.), *Asperger syndrome or high-functioning autism? Current issues in autism* (pp. 123–142). New York: Plenum Press.

World Health Organization. (1992). *International classification of diseases: Diagnostic criteria for research* (10th ed.). Geneva, Switzerland: Author.

CHAPTER 2

Epidemiological Studies of Pervasive Developmental Disorders

ERIC FOMBONNE

Epidemiological surveys of autism started in the mid-1960s in England (Lotter, 1966, 1967) and have since been conducted in many countries. Most of these surveys have focused on a categorical-diagnostic approach to autism that has relied over time on different sets of criteria. All surveys, however, used a definition of autism that comprised severe impairments in communication and language, social interactions, and play and behavior. This chapter focuses on autism defined as a severe developmental disorder. It does not deal with subtle autistic features or symptoms that occur as part of other, more specific, developmental disorders, as unusual personality traits, or as components of the lesser variant of autism thought to index genetic liability to autism in relatives. With the exception of recent studies, other pervasive developmental disorders (PDD) falling short of diagnostic criteria for autistic disorder (PDDNOS, Asperger syndrome) were generally not included in the case definition used in earlier surveys although several epidemiological investigations yielded useful information on the rates of these particular PDDs. These data are summarized separately. This chapter provides an up-to-date review of the methodological features and substantive results of published epidemiological surveys. It also updates our previous review (Fombonne, 2003a) with the inclusion of eight new studies made available since then. A key feature of the review was to rely on summary statistics throughout to derive quantitative estimates for rates and correlates

of autism-spectrum disorders. This chapter addresses the following five questions:

1. What is the range of prevalence estimates for autism and related disorders?
2. What proportion of autism cases is attributable to specific associated medical disorders?
3. Is the incidence of autism increasing?
4. What are the other correlates of autistic-spectrum disorders, particularly with respect to race and ethnicity?
5. What is the role, if any, of cluster reports in causal investigations of autism?

DESIGN OF EPIDEMIOLOGICAL STUDIES

Epidemiology is concerned with the study of the repartition of diseases in human populations and of the factors that influence it. Epidemiologists use several measures of disease occurrence. Incidence rate refers to the number of new cases (numerator) of a disease occurring over a specified period in those at risk of developing the disease in the population (denominator, in person $\times$ years). Cumulative incidence is the proportion of those who were free of the disease at the beginning of the observation period and developed the disease during that period. Measures of incidence are required to properly estimate morbidity due to a disease, its possible changes over time, and the risk factors underlying disease status. Prevalence is a measure used in cross-sectional surveys (there is no passage of time) and reflects the proportion of subjects in a given population who, at that point in time, suffer from the disease. Most epidemiological studies of autism have been cross-sectional and are not informative on incidence (with a few recent exceptions). As a result, prevalence rates have been used to describe autism in populations.

It is useful to summarize how data are collected in a prevalence study (refer to Table 2.1; and also Fombonne, 2002a). The investigators first select a population of a given size (N), often in a circumscribed geographic area. Then, one or more screening stages are organized to identify possible cases designated as screen positives (a + b). In a second, diagnostic stage, the screen positives (a + b) undergo a thorough evaluation and are finally classified as cases (a, or true positives) or noncases (b, false positives). The probability that a screen positive is a case (a/a + b) is called the positive predictive value. The prevalence is then calculated by dividing the number of cases identified in the diagnostic stage by the size of the population (a/N). However, the imperfection of the screening process means that this calculation does not take into account the false negatives (c), true cases who were missed in the screening stage. In published autism surveys, there is often no way to estimate (c), although techniques exist that could allow for this. As a result, the prevalence estimate can be seriously underestimated. When comparing surveys over time, two factors may jeopardize the comparison. Better awareness of the disorder, improved screening techniques, and detection all contribute to reduce the false negatives (c) (and as a consequence to increase a). Changes in case definition, especially a broadening of

the concept of autism, a shift from autism to PDD, the recognition of autism in subjects of normal intelligence, and other similar factors will all contribute to increase (a) (subjects who are now regarded as cases, a, whereas, previously, they were included in b, or even d). Thus, even in the absence of a change in the incidence of the disorder, prevalence estimates (a/N) can go up merely for methodological reasons.

Selection of Studies

The studies were identified through systematic searches from the major scientific literature databases (MEDLINE, PSYCINFO) and from prior reviews (Fombonne, 1999, 2003a; Wing, 1993). Only studies published in the English language were included. Surveys that relied on a questionnaire-based approach to define whether a subject was a case or not a case were also excluded because the validity of the diagnosis is unsatisfactory in these studies. Overall, 42 studies published between 1966 and 2003 were selected that surveyed PDDs in clearly demarcated, nonoverlapping samples. Of these, 36 studies provided information on rates of autistic disorder, 3 studies provided estimates only on all PDDs combined, and 3 studies provided data only on high-functioning PDDs. For several studies, the publication listed in the tables is the most detailed account or the earliest one. When appropriate, however, other published articles were used to extract relevant information from the same study.

Survey Descriptions

Surveys were conducted in 14 countries, and half of the results have been published since 1997. Details on the precise sociodemographic composition and economical activities of the area surveyed in each study were generally lacking. Most studies were conducted in predominantly urban or mixed areas, however, with only two surveys (6 and 11) carried out in predominantly rural areas. The proportion of children from immigrant families was generally not available and very low in five surveyed populations (Studies 11, 12, 19, 23, and 26). Only in Studies 4, 34, and 38 was there a substantial minority of children with either an immigrant or different ethnic background living in the

Table 2.1   Hypothetical Prevalence Study of Autism

	Cases (D)	Noncases ($\bar{D}$)	
Screen positive	a	b	a + b
Screen negative	c	d	c + d
	a + c	b + d	a + b + c + d = N

False negatives (FN) = d; False positives (FP) = b; Positive predictive value (PPV); Prevalence (P) = a + c/N = p(D); Sensitivity (Se, rate of true positives) = a/a + c; Specificity (Sp, rate of true negatives) = d/b + d.

area. The age range of the population included in the surveys is spread from birth to early adult life, with an overall median age of 8.0. Similarly, in 39 studies, there is huge variation in the size of the population surveyed (range: 826–4,590,000), with a median population size of 63,860 subjects (mean = 255,000). About half of the studies relied on targeted populations ranging in size from 15,870 to 166,860.

Study Designs

A few studies have relied on existing administrative databases (i.e., Croen, Grether, Hoogstrate, & Selvin, 2002; Gurney et al., 2003) or on national registers (Madsen et al., 2002) for case identification. Most investigations have relied on a two-stage or multistage approach to identify cases in underlying populations. The first screening stage of these studies often consisted of sending letters or brief screening scales requesting school and health professionals to identify possible cases of autism. Each investigation varied in several key aspects of this screening stage. First, the coverage of the population varied enormously from one study to another. In some studies (3, 17, 20, 24, 33), only cases already known from educational or medical authorities could be identified. In other surveys, investigators achieved extensive coverage of the entire population, including children attending normal schools (Studies 1, 25, 40) or children undergoing systematic developmental checks (Studies 13, 19, 22, 32, 36). In addition, the surveyed areas varied in terms of service development as a function of the specific educational or health care systems of each country and of the year of investigation. Second, the type of information sent out to professionals invited to identify children varied from simple letters including a few clinical descriptors of autism-related symptoms or diagnostic checklists rephrased in nontechnical terms, to more systematic screening based on questionnaires or rating scales of known reliability and validity. Third, participation rates in the first screening stages provide another source of variation in the screening efficiency of surveys. Refusal rates were available for 13 studies (1, 5, 6, 9, 12, 14, 19, 20, 23, 25, 30, 37, and 40); the rate of refusal ranged from 0%

(Study 25) to 35% (Study 40), with a median value of 14%. Fewer studies could examine the extent to which uncooperative participation or outright refusal to participate in surveys is associated with the likelihood that the corresponding children have autism. Bryson, Clark, and Smith (1988; Study 12) provided some evidence that those families who refused to cooperate in the intensive assessment phase had children with ABC scores similar to other false positives in their study, suggesting that these children were unlikely to have autism. Webb, Morey, et al. (2003; Study 40) similarly produced data showing increasing refusal rate in those with fewer *ICD-10* PDD symptoms. By contrast, in a Japanese study (Sugiyama & Abe, 1989; Study 13) where 17.3% of parents refused further investigations for their 18-month-old children who had failed a developmental check, follow-up data at age 3 suggested that half of these children still displayed developmental problems. Whether these problems were connected to autism is unknown, but this study points to the possibility that higher rates of developmental disorders exist among nonparticipants to surveys. Similarly, in Lotter's study (1966; Study 1), 58 questionnaires covering schools for handicapped children were returned out of the 76 forms sent out, and an independent review of the records showed that 4 of the 18 missing forms corresponded to autistic children. It is difficult to draw firm conclusions from these different accounts. Although there is no consistent evidence that parental refusal to cooperate is associated with autism in their offspring, a small proportion of cases may be missed in some surveys as a consequence of noncooperation at the screening stage. One study (40) included a weighting procedure to compensate for nonresponse.

Only two studies (1 and 30) provided an estimate of the reliability of the screening procedure. The sensitivity of the screening methodology (a/(a + c) in Table 2.1) is also difficult to gauge in autism surveys. The usual epidemiological approach of sampling screened negative subjects at random to estimate the proportion of false negatives (c/(a + c) in Table 2.1) has not been used in these surveys because the low frequency of the disorder would make undertaking such estimations both imprecise and costly. The cases that were missed as a result of noncooperation or imperfect sensitivity of the screening procedure make it necessary to view the prevalence estimates as underestimates of the true rates. The magnitude of this underestimation is unknown in each survey.

Similar considerations about the methodological variability across studies apply to the intensive assessment phases. Participation rates in these second-stage assessments were not always available, either because they had simply not been calculated, or because the do sign and/or method of data collection did not lead easily to their estimation. When available (Studies 1, 5, 8, 12, 13, 15, 22, 23, 25, 29, 30, 32, 36), they were generally high, ranging from 76.1% (Study 12) to 98.6% (Study 25). The information used to determine final diagnostic status usually involved a combination of informants and data sources, with a direct assessment of the person with autism in 21 studies.

The assessments were conducted with various diagnostic instruments, ranging from a classical clinical examination to the use of batteries of standardized measures. The Autism Diagnostic Interview (Le Couteur et al., 1989) and/or the Autism Diagnostic Observational Schedule (Lord, Risi, et al., 2000) were used in the most recent surveys. The precise diagnostic criteria retained to define caseness vary according to the study and, to a large extent, reflect historical changes in classification systems. Thus, Kanner's criteria and Lotter's and Rutter's definitions were used in Studies 1 to 8 (all conducted before 1982), whereas *DSM*-based definitions took over thereafter as well as *ICD-10* since 1990. Some studies have relaxed partially some diagnostic criteria such as an age of onset before 30 months (Study 6) or the absence of schizophrenic-like symptoms (Studies 13 and 14). However, most surveys have relied on the clinical judgment of experts to arrive at the final case groupings. It is worth underlining that field trials for recent classifications such as *DSM-III-R* (Spitzer & Siegel, 1990) or *DSM-IV/ICD-10* (Volkmar, Klin, et al., 1994) have also relied on the judgment of clinical experts, taken as a gold standard to diagnose autism and calibrate diagnostic algorithms. Therefore, the heterogeneity of diagnostic criteria used across surveys is somewhat mitigated by reliance on expert clinical judgment for final

case determination. It is, furthermore, difficult to assess the impact of a specific diagnostic scheme or of a particular diagnostic criterion on the estimate of prevalence since other powerful method factors confound between-studies comparisons of rates. Surprisingly, few studies have built in a reliability assessment of the diagnostic procedure; reliability during the intensive assessment phase was high in seven surveys (4, 13, 16, 23, 24, 32, 36) and moderate in another one (14).

CHARACTERISTICS OF AUTISTIC SAMPLES

Data on children with autistic disorders were available in 36 surveys (1 to 36; see Table 2.2). In total, 7,514 subjects were considered to suffer from autism; this number ranged from 6 (Studies 18 and 25) to 5,038 (Study 34) across studies (median: 48; mean: 209). An assessment of intellectual function was obtained in 21 studies. These assessments were conducted with various tests and instruments; furthermore, results were pooled in broad bands of intellectual level that did not share the same boundaries across studies. As a consequence, differences in rates of cognitive impairment between studies should be interpreted with caution. Despite these caveats, some general conclusions can be reached (Table 2.2). The median proportion of subjects without intellectual impairment is 29.6% (range: 0% to 60%).[1] The corresponding figures are 29.3% (range: 6.6% to 100%) for mild-to-moderate intellectual impairments, and 38.5% (range: 0% to 81.3%) for severe-to-profound mental retardation. Gender repartition among subjects with autism was reported in 32 studies totaling 6,963 subjects with autism, and the male/female sex ratio varied from 1.33 (Study 7) to 16.0 (Study 4), with a mean male:female ratio of 4.3:1. Thus, no epidemiological study ever identified more girls than boys with autism, a finding that parallels the gender differences found in clinically referred samples (Lord, Schopler, & Revecki, 1982). Gender differences were more pronounced when autism was not associated with

---

[1] Study 23, which relied on different IQ groupings, has been excluded.

TABLE 2.2 Prevalence Surveys of Autistic Disorder

No.	Study	Country	Area	Size of Target Population	Age	Number of Subjects with Autism	Diagnostic Criteria	Percentage with Normal IQ	Gender Ratio (M:F)	Prevalence Rate/10,000	95% CI
1	Lotter, 1966	United Kingdom	Middlesex	78,000	8–10	32	Rating scale	15.6	2.6 (23/9)	4.1	2.7 ; 5.5
2	Brask, 1970	Denmark	Aarhus County	46,500	2–14	20	Clinical	—	1.4 (12/7)	4.3	2.4 ; 6.2
3	Treffert, 1970	United States	Wisconsin	899,750	3–12	69	Kanner	—	3.06 (52/17)	0.7	0.6 ; 0.9
4	Wing, Yeates, Brierly, & Gould, 1976	United Kingdom	Camberwell	25,000	5–14	17[a]	24 items rating scale of Lotter	30	16 (16/1)	4.8[b]	2.1 ; 7.5
5	Hoshino et al., 1982	Japan	Fukushima-Ken	609,848	0–18	142	Kanner's criteria	—	9.9 (129/13)	2.33	1.9 ; 2.7
6	Bohman, Bohman, Björck, & Sjöholm, 1983	Sweden	County of Västerbotten	69,000	0–20	39	Rutter criteria	20.5	1.6 (24/15)	5.6	3.9 ; 7.4
7	McCarthy, Fitzgerald, & Smith, 1984	Ireland	East	65,000	8–10	28	Kanner	—	1.33 (16/12)	4.3	2.7 ; 5.9
8	Steinhausen, Göbel, Breinlinger, & Wohlloben, 1986	Germany	West Berlin	279,616	0–14	52	Rutter	55.8	2.25 (36/16)	1.9	1.4 ; 2.4
9	Burd, Fisher, & Kerbeshan, 1987	United States	North Dakota	180,986	2–18	59	*DSM-III*	—	2.7 (43/16)	3.26	2.4 ; 4.1
10	Matsuishi et al., 1987	Japan	Kurume City	32,834	4–12	51	*DSM-III*	—	4.7 (42/9)	15.5	11.3 ; 19.8

11	Tanoue, Oda, Asano, & Kawashima, 1988	Japan	Southern Ibaraki	95,394	7	DSM-III	132	—	4.07 (106/26)	13.8	11.5 ; 16.2
12	Bryson, Clark, & Smith, 1988	Canada	Part of Nova-Scotia	20,800	6–14	New RDC	21	23.8	2.5 (15/6)	10.1	5.8 ; 14.4
13	Sugiyama & Abe, 1989	Japan	Nagoya	12,263	3	DSM-III	16	—	—	13.0	6.7 ; 19.4
14	Cialdella & Mamelle, 1989	France	1 district (Rhône)	135,180	3–9	DSM-III-like	61	—	2.3	4.5	3.4 ; 5.6
15	Ritvo et al., 1989	United States	Utah	769,620	3–27	DSM-III	241	34	3.73 (190/51)	2.47	2.1 ; 2.8
16	Gillberg, Steffenburg, & Schaumann, 1991[d]	Sweden	South-West Gothenburg + Bohuslän County	78,106	4–13	DSM-III-R	74	18	2.7 (54/20)	9.5	7.3 ; 11.6
17	Fombonne & du Mazaubrun, 1992	France	4 regions, 14 districts	274,816	9 and 13	Clinical-ICD-10-like	154	13.3	2.1 (105/49)	4.9	4.1 ; 5.7
18	Wignyosumarto, Mukhlas, & Skirataki, 1992	Indonesia	Yogyakarita (SE of Jakarta)	5,120	4–7	CARS	6	0	2.0 (4/2)	11.7	2.3 ; 21.1
19	Honda, Shimizu, Misumi, Niimi, & Ohashi, 1996	Japan	Yokohama	8,537	5	ICD-10	18	50.0	2.6 (13.5)	21.08	11.4 ; 30.8
20	Fombonne, du Mazaubrun, Cans, & Grandjean, 1997	France	3 districts	325,347	8–16	Clinical ICD-10-like	174	12.1	.81 112/62	5.35	4.6 ; 6.1

(continued)

47

TABLE 2.2 (*Continued*)

No.	Study	Country	Area	Size of Target Population	Age	Number of Subjects with Autism	Diagnostic Criteria	Percentage with Normal IQ	Gender Ratio (M:F)	Prevalence Rate/10,000	95% CI
21	Webb, Lobo, Hervas, Scourfield, & Fraser, 1997	United Kingdom	South Glamorgan, Wales	73,301	3–15	53	*DSM-III-R*	—	6.57 (46/7)	7.2	5.3 ; 9.3
22	Arvidsson, Danielsson, Forsberg, Gillberg, & Johansson, 1997	Sweden (West coast)	Mölnlycke	1,941	3–6	9	*ICD-10*	22.2	3.5 (7/2)	46.4	16.1 ; 76.6
23	Sponheim & Skjeldal, 1998	Norway	Akershus County	65,688	3–14	34	*ICD-10*	47.1[c]	2.09 (23/11)	5.2	3.4 ; 6.9
24	Taylor et al., 1999	United Kingdom	North Thames	490,000	0–16	427	*ICD-10*	—	—	8.7	7.9 ; 9.5
25	Kadesjö, Gillberg, & Hagberg, 1999	Sweden (Central)	Karlstad	826	6.7–7.7	6	*DSM-III-R/ ICD-10* Gillberg's criteria (Asperger syndrome)	50.0	5.0 (5/1)	72.6	14.7 ; 130.6
26	Baird, Charman, & Baron-Cohen, 2000	United Kingdom	South-East Thames	16,235	—	50	*ICD-10*	60	15.7 (47/3)	30.8	22.9 ; 40.6
27	Powell et al., 2000	United Kingdom	West Midlands	25,377	—	62	Clinical/ *ICD-10/DSM-IV*	—	—	7.8	5.8 ; 10.5
28	Kielinen, Linna, & Moilanen, 2000	Finland	North (Oulu et Lapland)	152,732	—	187	*ICD-8/ICD-9/ ICD-10*	49.8	4.12 (156/50)	12.2	10.5 ; 14.0

48

29	Bertrand et al., 2001	United States	Brick Township, New Jersey	8,896	—	36	DSM-IV	36.7	2.2 (25/11)	40.5	28.0 ; 56.0
30	Fombonne, Simmons, Ford, Meltzer, & Goodman, 2001	United Kingdom	Angleterre et Pays de Galles	10,438	5–15	27	DSM-IV/ICD-10	55.5	8.0 (24/3)	26.1	16.2 ; 36.0
31	Magnússon & Saemundsen, 2001	Iceland	Whole Island	43,153	5–14	57	Mostly ICD-10	15.8	4.2 (46/11)	13.2	9.8 ; 16.6
32	Chakrabarti & Fombonne, 2001	United Kingdom (Midlands)	Staffordshire	15,500	2.5–6.5	26	ICD-10/DSM-IV	29.2	3.3 (20/6)	16.8	10.3 ; 23.2
33	Davidovitch, Holtzman, & Tirosh, 2001	Israel	Haiffa	26,160	7–11	26	DSM-III-R/DSM-IV	—	4.2 (21/5)	10.0	6.6 ; 14.4
34	Croen, Grether, Hoogstrate, & Selvin, 2002a	United States	California DDS	4,950,333	5–12	5,038	CDER (Full syndrome)	62.8[e]	4.47 (4,116/921)	11.0	10.7 ; 11.3
35	Madsen et al., 2002	Denmark	National register	63,859	8	46	ICD-10	—	—	7.2	5.0–10.0
36	Chakrabarti & Fombonne, 2004	United Kingdom (Midlands)	Staffordshire	10,903	4–7	24	ICD-10/DSM-IV	33.3	3.8 (19/5)	22.0	14.4 ; 32.2

[a] This number corresponds to the sample described in Wing and Gould (1979).

[b] This rate corresponds to the first published paper on this survey and is based on 12 subjects among children age 5 to 14 years.

[c] In this study, mild mental retardation was combined with normal IQ, whereas moderate and severe mental retardation were grouped together.

[d] For the Goteborg surveys by Gillberg et al. (Gillberg, 1984; Gillberg et al., 1991; Steffenburg & Gillberg, 1986), a detailed examination showed that there was overlap among the samples included in the three surveys; consequently only the last survey has been included in this table.

[e] This proportion is likely to be overestimated and to reflect an underreporting of mental retardation in the CDER evaluations.

mental retardation. In 13 studies (865 subjects) where the sex ratio was available within the normal band of intellectual functioning, the median sex ratio was 5.5:1. Conversely, in 12 studies (813 subjects), the median sex ratio was 1.95:1 in the group with autism and moderate-to-severe mental retardation.

Prevalence Estimations for Autistic Disorder

Prevalence estimates ranged from 0.7/10,000 to 72.6/10,000 (Table 2.2). Confidence intervals were computed for each estimate; their width (difference between the upper and lower limit of the 95% confidence interval) indicates the variation in sample sizes and in the precision achieved in each study (range: 0.3 –115.9; mean = 11.3). Prevalence rates were negatively correlated with sample size (Spearman $r = -.73$; $p < .01$); small-scale studies tended to report higher prevalence rates.

When surveys were combined in two groups according to the median year of publication (1994), the median prevalence rate for 18 surveys published in the period 1966 to 1993 was 4.7/10,000, and the median rate for the 18 surveys published in the period 1994 to 2004 was 12.7/10,000. Indeed, the correlation between prevalence rate and year of publication reached statistical significance (Spearman $r = .65$; $p < .01$); and the results of the 22 surveys with prevalence rates over 7/10,000 were all published since 1987. These findings point toward an increase in prevalence estimates in the past 15 to 20 years. To derive a best estimate of the current prevalence of autism, it was therefore deemed appropriate to restrict the analysis to 28 surveys published since 1987. The prevalence estimates ranged from 2.5 to 72.6/10,000 (average 95% CI width: 14.1), with an average rate of 16.2/10,000 and a median rate of 11.3/10,000. Similar values were obtained when slightly different rules and time cutpoints were used, with median and mean rates fluctuating between 10 and 13 and 13 and 18/10,000 respectively. From these results, a conservative estimate for the current prevalence of autistic disorder is most consistent with values lying somewhere between 10/10,000 and 16/10,000. For further

calculations, we arbitrarily adopted the midpoint of this interval as the working rate for autism prevalence, that is, the value of 13/10,000.

Associated Medical Conditions

Rates of medical conditions associated with autism were reported in 15 surveys and the findings are summarized in Table 2.3. These medical conditions were investigated by very different means ranging from questionnaires to full medical workups.

Conditions such as congenital rubella and PKU account for almost no cases of autism. Prior studies suggesting an association of congenital rubella (Chess, 1971) and PKU (Knobloch & Pasamanick, 1975; Lowe, Tanaka, Seashore, Young, & Cohen, 1980) with autism were conducted before implementation of systematic prevention measures. Likewise, our nil estimate of 0% for autism and neurofibromatosis is consistent with the 0.3% rate found in a large series of 341 referred cases (Mouridsen, Bachmann-Andersen, Sörensen, Rich, & Isager, 1992). Similarly, the rates found for cerebral palsy and Down syndrome equally suggest no particular association. Recent reports (Bregman & Volkmar, 1988; Ghaziuddin, Tsai, & Ghaziuddin, 1992; Howlin, Wing, & Gould, 1995) have focused on the co-occurrence of Down syndrome and autism in some individuals. The epidemiological findings give further support

TABLE 2.3   Medical Disorders Associated with Autism in Recent Epidemiological Surveys

	Number of Studies	Median Rate	Range
Cerebral palsy	7	1.4	0–4.8
Fragile X	9	0.0	0–8.1
Tuberous sclerosis	11	1.1	0–3.8
Phenylketonuria	8	0	0–0
Neurofibromatosis	7	0	0–1.4
Congenital rubella	11	0.0	0–5.9
Down syndrome	12	0.7	0–16.7
At least one disorder	**16**	**5.5**	**0–16.7**
Epilepsy	12	16.7	0–26.4
Hearing deficits	8	1.3	0–5.9
Visual deficits	6	0.7	0–11.1

to the validity of these clinical descriptions (that the two conditions co-occur in some children), although they do not suggest that the rate of comorbidity is higher than that expected by chance once the effects of mental retardation are taken into account. For fragile X, the low rate available in epidemiological studies is almost certainly an underestimate because fragile X was not recognized until relatively recently, and the most recent surveys did not always include systematic screening for fragile X. In line with prior reports (Smalley, Tanguay, Smith, & Guitierrez, 1992), tuberous sclerosis (TS) has a consistently high frequency among autistic samples. Assuming a population prevalence of 1/10,000 for TS (Ahlsen, Gillberg, Lindblom, & Gillberg, 1994; Hunt & Lindenbaum, 1984; Shepherd, Beard, Gomez, Kurland, & Whisnant, 1991), it appears that the rate of TS is about 100 times higher than that expected under the hypothesis of no association. Whether epilepsy, localized brain lesions, or direct genetic effects mediate the association between TS and autism is a matter for ongoing research (Smalley, 1998).

The overall proportion of cases of autism that could be causally attributed to known medical disorders therefore remains low. From the 16 surveys where rates of one of seven clear-cut medical disorders potentially causally associated with autism (cerebral palsy, fragile X, TS, PKU, neurofibromatosis, congenital rubella, and Down syndrome) were available, we computed the proportion of subjects with at least one of these recognizable disorders. Because the overlap between these conditions is expected to be low and because the information about multiply-handicapped subjects was not available, this overall rate was obtained by summing directly the rates for each individual condition within each study. The resulting rate might, therefore, be slightly overestimated. The fraction of cases of autism with a known medical condition that was potentially etiologically significant ranged from 0% to 16.7%, with a median and mean values of 5.5% and 5.9% respectively. Even if some adjustment were made to account for the underestimation of the rate of fragile X in epidemiological surveys of autism, the attributable proportion of cases of autism would not exceed the 10%

figure for any medical disorder (excluding epilepsy and sensory impairments). Although this figure does not incorporate other medical events of potential etiological significance, such as encephalitis, congenital anomalies, and other rare medical syndromes, it is similar to that reported in a recent review of the question (Rutter, Bailey, Bolton, & Le Couteur, 1994). It is worth noting that epidemiological surveys of autism in very large samples (Studies 15, 17, and 20) provided estimates in line with our conservative summary statistics. By contrast, claims of average rates of medical conditions as high as 24% appear to apply to studies of smaller size and to rely on a broadened definition of autism (Gillberg & Coleman, 1996).

Rates of epilepsy are high among autism samples. The proportion suffering from epilepsy tends also to be higher in studies that have higher rates of severe mental retardation (as in Studies 16, 17, and 20). Age-specific rates for the prevalence of epilepsy were not available. The samples where high rates of epilepsy were reported tended to have a higher median age, although these rates seemed mostly to apply to school-age children. Thus, in light of the increased incidence of seizures during adolescence among subjects with autism (Deykin & MacMahon, 1979; Rutter, 1970), the epidemiological rates should be regarded as underestimates of the lifetime risk of epilepsy in autism. These rates are nonetheless high and support the findings of a bimodal peak of incidence of epilepsy in autistic samples, with a first peak of incidence in the first years of life (Volkmar & Nelson, 1990).

RATES OF OTHER PERVASIVE DEVELOPMENTAL DISORDERS

Several studies have provided useful information on rates of syndromes that are similar to autism, but fall short of strict diagnostic criteria for autistic disorder (Table 2.4). Because the screening procedures and subsequent diagnostic assessments differed from one study to another, these groups of disorders are not strictly comparable across studies. In addition, as they were not the group on which the attention was focused, details are often lacking on their phenomenological features in the available reports.

TABLE 2.4 Relative Rates of Autism and Other Pervasive Developmental Disorders

No.	Study	Rates of Autism	Prevalence Rate of Other PDDs	Combined Rate of Autism and Other PDDs	Prevalence Rate Ratio[a]	Case Definition for Other PDDs
1	Lotter, 1966	4.1	3.3	7.8	0.90	Children with some behavior similar to that of autistic children
2	Brask, 1970	4.3	1.9	6.2	0.44	Children with "other psychoses" or "borderline psychotic"
4	Wing, Yates, Brierly, & Gould, 1976	4.9	16.3	21.2	3.33	Socially impaired (triad of impairments)
5	Hoshino et al., 1982	2.33	2.92	5.25	1.25	Autistic mental retardation
9	Burd, Fisher, & Kerbeshan, 1987	3.26	>7.79[b]	>11.05[b]	2.39	Children referred by professionals with "autistic-like" symptoms, not meeting *DSM-III* criteria for IA, COPDD, or atypical PDD
14	Cialdella & Mamelle, 1989	4.5	4.7	9.2	1.04	Children meeting criteria for other forms of "infantile psychosis" than autism, or a broadened definition of *DSM-III*
17	Fombonne & du Mazaubrun, 1992[c]	4.6	6.6	11.2	1.43	Children with mixed developmental disorders
20	Fombonne, du Mazaubrun, Cans, & Grandjean, 1997	5.3	10.94	16.3	2.05	Children with mixed developmental disorders
26	Baird, Charman, & Baron-Cohen, 2000	30.8	27.1	57.9	0.9	Children with other PDDs
27	Powell et al., 2000	7.8	13.0	20.8	1.7	Children with other PDDs
29	Bertrand et al., 2001	40.5	27.0	67.4	0.7	Children with PDDNOS and Asperger disorder
32	Chakrabarti & Fombonne, 2001	16.8	36.1	52.9	2.15	Children with PDDNOS
35	Madsen et al., 2002	7.2	22.2	29.4	3.08	Children with PDDNOS
36	Chakrabarti & Fombonne, 2004	22.0	24.8	46.8	1.13	Children with PDDNOS

[a]Other PDD rate divided by autism rate.
[b]Computed by the author.
[c]These rates are derived from the complete results of the survey of three birth cohorts of French children (Rumeau-Rouquette et al., 1994).

Unspecified Pervasive Developmental Disorders

Different labels (see Table 2.4) have been used to characterize these conditions, such as the triad of impairments involving impairments in reciprocal social interaction, communication, and imagination (Wing & Gould, 1979). These groups would be overlapping with current diagnostic labels such as atypical autism and pervasive developmental disorders not otherwise specified (PDDNOS). Fourteen of the 36 surveys yielded separate estimates of the prevalence of these developmental disorders, with 10 studies showing higher rates for the nonautism disorders than the rates for autism. The ratio of the rate of nonautistic PDD to the rate of autism varied between from 0.44 to 3.33 (Table 2.4) with a mean value of 1.6, which translates into an average prevalence estimate of 20.8/10,000 if one takes 13/10,000 as the rate for autism. In other words, for two children with autism assessed in epidemiological surveys, three children were found with severe impairments that had a similar nature but that fell short of strict diagnostic criteria for autism. This group has been much less studied in previous epidemiological studies, but progressive recognition of its importance and relevance to autism has led to changes in the design of more recent epidemiological surveys (see later in this chapter). They now include these less typical children in the case definition adopted in surveys. It should be clear from these figures that they represent a substantial group of children whose treatment needs are likely to be as important as those of children with autism.

Asperger Syndrome and Childhood Disintegrative Disorder

The reader is referred to recent epidemiological reviews for these two conditions (Fombonne, 2002b; Fombonne & Tidmarsh, 2003). Epidemiological studies of Asperger syndrome (AS) are sparse, probably because it was acknowledged as a separate diagnostic category only recently in both *ICD-10* and *DSM-IV.* Only two epidemiological surveys have *specifically* investigated its prevalence (Ehlers & Gillberg, 1993; Kadesjö, Gillberg, & Hagberg, 1999).

Only a handful ($N < 5$) of cases were identified in these surveys, with the resulting estimates of 28 and 48/10,000 being extremely imprecise. By contrast, other recent autism surveys have consistently identified smaller numbers of children with AS than those with autism *within* the same survey. In Studies 23 to 27 and 32 (reviewed in Fombonne & Tidmarsh, 2003) and Study 36, the ratio of autism to AS rates in each survey was above unity, suggesting that the rate of AS was consistently *lower* than that for autism (Table 2.5). How much lower is difficult to establish from existing data, but a ratio of 5:1 would appear to be an acceptable, albeit conservative, conclusion based on this limited available evidence. Taking 13/10,000 as the rate for autism, this translates into a rate for AS that would be 2.6/10,000, a figure used for subsequent calculations. A recent survey of high-functioning PDDs in Welsh mainstream primary schools has yielded a relatively high (uncorrected) prevalence estimate of 14.5/10,000. Of the 17 children contributing to this figure, 10 had either Asperger's disorder or high-functioning autism as a primary diagnosis. Assuming than half of these would have Asperger's disorder, we could extrapolate a 4.3/10,000 prevalence, a figure that is in line with other studies. However, much caution should be applied to this calculation as it is based on several assumptions that are impossible to verify.

Childhood Disintegrative Disorder

Few surveys have provided data on childhood disintegrative disorder (CDD), also known as Heller syndrome, disintegrative psychosis (*ICD-9*), or late-onset autism (see Volkmar, 1992). In addition to the four studies (9, 23, 31, 32) of our previous review (Fombonne, 2002b), another survey has provided new data on CDD (36). Taking the five studies into account (Table 2.6), prevalence estimates ranged from 1.1 to 9.2/100,000. The pooled estimate based on seven identified cases and a surveyed population of 358,633 children, was 1.9/100,000. The upper-bound limit of the associated confidence interval (4.15/100,000) indicates that CDD is a rare condition, with 1 case occurring for every 65 cases of autistic disorder. As cases of CDD were both rare and already included in

TABLE 2.5 Asperger Syndrome (AS) in Recent Autism Surveys

Study	Size of Population	Age Group	Informants	Assessment — Instruments	Assessment — Diagnostic Criteria	Autism N	Autism Rate/10,000	Asperger Syndrome N	Asperger Syndrome Rate/10,000	Autism/AS Ratio
Sponheim & Skjeldal, 1998	65,688	3–14	Parent Child	Parental interview + direct observation, CARS, ABC	ICD-10	32	4.9	2	0.3	16.0
Taylor et al., 1999	490,000	0–16	Record	Rating of all data available in child record	ICD-10	427	8.7	71	1.4	6.0
Kadesjö, Gillberg, & Hagberg, 1999	826	6.7–7.7	Child Parent Professional	ADI-R, Griffiths Scale or WISC, Asperger Syndrome Screening Questionnaire	DSM-III-R/ICD-10 Gillberg's criteria (Asperger syndrome)	6	72.6	4	48.4	1.5
Powell et al., 2000	25,377	1– 4.9	Records	ADI-R Available data	DSM-III-R DSM-IV ICD-10	54	—	16	—	3.4
Baird, Charman, & Baron-Cohen, 2000	16,235	7	Parents Child Other data	ADI-R Psychometry	ICD-10 DSM-IV	45	27.7	5	3.1	9.0
Chakrabarti & Fombonne, 2001	15,500	2.5–6.5	Child Parent Professional	ADI-R, 2 weeks multidisciplinary assessment, Merrill-Palmer, WPPSI	ICD-10 DSM-IV	26	16.8	13	8.4	2.0
Chakrabarti & Fombonne, 2004	10,903	2.5–6.5	Child Parent Professional	ADI-R, 2 weeks multidisciplinary assessment, Merrill-Palmer, WPPSI	ICD-10 DSM-IV	24	22.0	12	11.0	2.0
Overall						**614**		**123**		**5.0**

TABLE 2.6 Surveys of Childhood Disintegrative Disorder (CDD)

Study	Country (Region/State)	Size of Target Population	Age Group	Assessment	N	M/F	Prevalence Estimate (/100,000)	95% CI1 (/100,000)
Burd, Fisher, & Kerbeshan, 1987	United States (North Dakota)	180,986	2–18	Structured parental interview and review of all data available–DSM-III criteria	2	2/—	1.11	0.13 ; 3.4
Sponheim & Skjeldal, 1998	Norway (Akershus County)	65,688	3–14	Parental interview and direct observation (CARS, ABC)	1	?	1.52	0.04 ; 8.5
Magnusson & Saemundsen, 2001	Iceland (whole island)	85,556	5–14	ADI-R, CARS, and psychological tests—mostly *ICD-10*	2	2/—	2.34	0.3 ; 8.4
Chakrabarti & Fombonne, 2001	United Kingdom (Staffordshire, Midlands)	15,500	2.5–6.5	ADI-R, 2 weeks' multidisciplinary assessment, Merrill-Palmer, WPPSI—*ICD-10/DSM-IV*	1	1/—	6.4	0.16 ; 35.9
Chakrabarti & Fombonne, 2004	United Kingdom (Staffordshire, Midlands)	10,903	2.5–6.5	ADI-R, 2 weeks' multidisciplinary assessment, Merrill-Palmer, WPPSI—*ICD-10/DSM-IV*		1/—	9.2	0–58.6
Pooled estimates		358,633				6/—	**1.9**	**0.87–4.15**

the numerator alongside autism cases in most surveys, we do not provide separate estimates of the numbers of subjects suffering from CDD in subsequent calculations.

Prevalence for Combined PDDs

Taking the aforementioned *conservative* estimates, the prevalence for all PDDs is at least 36.4/10,000 (the sum of estimates for autism [13/10,000], PDDNOS [20.8/10,000], and AS [2.6/10,000]). This global estimate is derived from a conservative analysis of existing data.

However, six out of eight recent epidemiological surveys yielded even higher rates (Table 2.7). The two surveys that did not show higher rates might have underestimated them. In the Danish investigation (Study 35), case finding depended on notification to a National Registry, a method that is usually associated with lower sensitivity for case finding. The Atlanta survey by the Centers for Disease Control and Prevention (CDC; Study 38) was based on a very large population (which typically yields lower prevalence, as described earlier) and age-specific rates were, in fact, in the 40-to-45/10,000 range in some birth cohorts (Fombonne, 2003b). The common design features of the four other epidemiological inquiries (Studies 26, 29, 32, 36) that yielded higher rates are worthy of mention. First, the case definition chosen for these investigations was that of a pervasive developmental disorder as opposed to the narrower approach focusing on autistic disorder typical of previous surveys. Investigators were concerned with any combination of severe developmental abnormalities occurring in one or more of the three symptomatic domains defining PDD and autism. Second, case-finding techniques employed in these surveys were proactive, relying on multiple and repeated screening phases, involving both different informants at each phase and surveying the same cohorts at different ages, which certainly maximized the sensitivity of case identification. Third, assessments were performed with standardized diagnostic measures (Autism Diagnostic Interview-Revised [ADI-R] and Autism Diagnostic Observation Schedule [ADOS]), which match well the dimensional approach retained for case definition. Finally, these samples comprised young children around their fifth birthday, thereby optimizing sensitivity of case-finding procedures. Furthermore, the size of targeted populations was reasonably small (between 9,000 and 16,000), probably allowing for the most efficient use of research resources. Conducted in different regions and countries by different teams, the convergence of estimates is striking. Two further results are worth noting. First, in sharp contrast with the prevalence for combined PDDs, the separate estimates for autistic disorder and PDD-NOS vary widely in studies where separate figures were available. It appears that the reliability of the differentiation between autistic disorder and PDD-NOS was mediocre at that young age, despite the use of up-to-date standardized measures. Second, the rate of mental retardation was, overall, much lower than in previous surveys of autism. Although this should not be a surprise for children in the PDD-NOS/AS groups, this trend was also noticeable within samples diagnosed with autistic disorder. To what extent this trend reflects the previously mentioned differential classification issues between autism and PDD-NOS or a genuine trend over time toward decreased rate of mental retardation within children with autistic disorder (possibly as a result as earlier diagnosis and intervention) remains to be established.

In conclusion, the convergence of recent surveys around an estimate of 60/10,000 for all PDD combined is striking, especially when coming from studies with improved methods. This estimate appears now to be the best estimate for the prevalence of PDDs currently available.

TIME TRENDS

The debate on the hypothesis of a secular increase in rates of autism has been obscured by a lack of clarity in the measures of disease occurrence used by investigators, or rather in their interpretation. In particular, it is crucial to differentiate prevalence (the proportion of individuals in a population who suffer from a defined disorder) from incidence (the number of new cases occurring in a population over time). Prevalence is useful for estimating needs and planning services; only incidence rates can be used for causal research. Both prevalence and incidence estimates will be inflated when

TABLE 2.7 Newer Epidemiological Surveys of PDDs

No.	Study	Age	AUTISM Rate/10,000	Gender Ratio (M:F)	IQ Normal (%)	PDDNOS and AS Rate/10,000	Gender Ratio (M:F)	IQ Normal (%)	All PDDs Rate/10,000
26	Baird, Charman, & Baron-Cohen, 2000	7	30.8	15.7	60	27.1	4.5	—	57.9
29	Bertrand et al., 2001	3–10	40.5	2.2	37	27.0	3.7	51	67.5
32	Chakrabarti & Fombonne, 2001	4–7	16.8	3.3	29	44.5	4.3	94	61.3
35	Madsen et al., 2002	8	7.7	—	—	22.2	—	—	30.0
36	Chakrabarti & Fombonne, 2004	4–7	22.0	4.0	33.3	35.8	8.7	91.6	58.7
37	Scott, Baron-Cohen, Bolton, & Brayne, 2002	5–11	—	—	—	—	—	—	58.3[a]
38	Yeargin-Allsopp et al., 2003	3–10	—	—	—	—	—	—	34.0
39	Gurney et al., 2003	6–11	—	—	—	—	—	—	52.0

[a]Computed by the author.

57

case definition is broadened and case ascertainment is improved. Time trends in rates can therefore only be gauged in investigations that hold these parameters under strict control over time. These methodological requirements must be borne in mind while reviewing the evidence for a secular increase in rates of PDDs.

Five approaches to assess this question have been used in the literature: (1) referral statistics, (2) comparison of cross-sectional epidemiological surveys, (3) repeat surveys in defined geographic areas, (4) successive birth cohorts, and (5) incidence studies.

Referral Statistics

Increasing numbers of children referred to specialist services or known to special education registers have been taken as evidence for an increased incidence of autism-spectrum disorders. However, trends over time in referred samples are confounded by many factors such as referral patterns, availability of services, heightened public awareness, decreasing age at diagnosis, and changes over time in diagnostic concepts and practices, to name only a few. Failure to control for these confounding factors was obvious in some recent reports (Fombonne, 2001), such as the widely quoted reports from California educational services (Department of Developmental Services, 1999, 2003).

First, these reports applied to numbers, not to rates, and failure to relate these numbers to meaningful denominators left the interpretation of an upward trend vulnerable to changes in the composition of the underlying population. For example, the population of California was 19,971,000 in 1970 and rose to 35,116,000 as of July 1, 2002, a change of 75.8%. Thus, part of the increase in numbers of subjects identified with autism merely reflects the change in population size, but the DDS reports have ignored or not adequately accounted for this change.

Second, the focus on the year-to-year changes in absolute numbers of subjects known to California state-funded services detracts from more meaningful comparisons. As of December 2002, the total number of subjects with a PDD diagnosis was 17,748 in the 0-to-19 age group (including 16,108 autism codes 1 and 2 and 1,640 other PDDs; Department of Developmental Services,

2003). The population of 0- to 19-year-olds of California was 10,462,273 in July 2002. If one applies a somewhat conservative PDD rate of 30/10,000, one would expect to have 31,386 PDD subjects within this age group living in California. These calculations do not support the "epidemic" interpretation, but instead suggest that children identified in the DDS database were only a subset of the population prevalence pool. The increasing numbers reflect merely an increasing proportion of children accessing services.

Third, no attempt was ever made to adjust the trends for changes in diagnostic concepts and definitions. However, major nosographic modifications were introduced during the corresponding years, with a general tendency in most classifications to broaden the concept of autism (as embodied in the terms *autism spectrum* or *pervasive developmental disorder*).

Fourth, age characteristics of the subjects recorded in official statistics were portrayed in a confusing manner where the preponderance of young subjects was presented as evidence of increasing rates in successive birth cohorts (see Fombonne, 2001). The problems associated with disentangling age from period and cohort effects in such observational data are well known in the epidemiological literature and deserve better statistical handling.

Fifth, the decreasing age at diagnosis leads to increasing numbers of young children being identified in official statistics or referred to already busy specialist services. Earlier identification of children from the prevalence pool may result in increased service activity; however, it does not mean increased *incidence*.

Another study of this dataset was subsequently launched to demonstrate the validity of the epidemic hypothesis (MIND Institute, 2002). The investigation was, however, flawed in its design. The authors relied on DDS data and aimed at ruling out changes in diagnostic practices and immigration into California as factors explaining the increased numbers. While immigration was reasonably ruled out, the study comparing diagnoses of autism and mental retardation over time was impossible to interpret in light of the extremely low (<20%) response rates. Furthermore, a study only based on cases registered for services cannot rule out that the proportion of cases within the general population who registered with services has changed over time. Assuming a constant incidence and prevalence at two different time points (meaning there is no epidemic), the number of cases known to a public agency delivering services could well increase by 200% if the proportion of cases from the community referred to services rises from 25% to 75% in the interval. To rule out this (likely, as mentioned) explanation, data over time are needed *both* on referred subjects *and* on nonreferred (or referred to other services) subjects. Failure to do that precludes drawing any inference to the California population from a study of the DDS database (Fombonne, 2003b). The conclusions of this report were therefore simply unwarranted.

A recent reanalysis of the California data has in fact strongly suggested that switches in diagnostic practices from mental retardation to autism could also account for increased numbers of subjects with an autism diagnosis in the California DDS datasets (Croen, Grether, Hoogstrate, & Selvin, 2002). Jick and Kaye (2003) obtained similar data in the United Kingdom. They showed that the incidence of specific developmental disorders (including language disorders) decreased by about the same amount that the incidence of diagnoses of autism increased in boys born from 1990 to 1997.

On the whole, evidence from these referral statistics is very weak and certainly does not deserve the media attention that it has received. Accordingly, proper epidemiological studies are needed to assess secular changes in the incidence of a disorder.

Comparison of Cross-Sectional Epidemiological Surveys

Due to their cross-sectional methodology, most epidemiological investigations of autism have been concerned with prevalence. As shown earlier, each epidemiological survey of autism possesses unique design features that could account almost entirely for between-studies variations in rates; time trends in rates of autism are therefore difficult to gauge from published prevalence rates. The significant correlation mentioned between prevalence rate and year of publication could merely reflect

increased efficiency over time in case identification methods used in surveys as well as changes in diagnostic concepts and practices. Thus, changes in diagnostic practices were reported in Magnusson and Saemundsen's study (2001) where *ICD-9* rates for the oldest cohorts born in the years 1964 to 1983 were lower than the *ICD-10* rates of the most recent 1984 to 1992 birth cohorts. Similarly, lower rates in the oldest birth cohorts were thought to reflect changes in diagnostic practices and boundaries in Webb, Lobo, Hervas, Scourfield, and Fraser's study (1997). One large survey recently conducted in the United Kingdom (Study 24) also documented a steep rise in the number of cases diagnosed with autism or atypical autism, and a similar trend for AS. The interpretation of these trends is, however, unclear because there was no control of drift over time in diagnostic practices nor of changes in service development.

The most convincing evidence that method factors could account for most of the variability in published prevalence estimates comes from a direct comparison of eight recent surveys conducted in the United Kingdom and the United States (Table 2.8). In each country, four surveys were conducted around the same year and with similar age groups. As there is no reason to expect huge between-area differences in rates, prevalence estimates should therefore be comparable within each country. However, an inspection of estimates obtained in each set of studies (Table 2.8: right-hand column) shows a 6-fold variation in rates for U.K. surveys, and a 14-fold variation in U.S. rates. In each set of studies, high rates derive from surveys that used intensive population-based screening techniques, whereas lower rates were obtained from studies relying on administrative methods for case finding. Since no passage of time was involved, the magnitude of these gradients in rates can only be attributed to differences in case identification methods across surveys, and the replication of the pattern in two countries provides even more confidence in this interpretation. This analysis of recent and contemporaneous studies shows that no inference on trends in the incidence of PDDs can be derived from a simple comparison of prevalence rates over time, since studies conducted at different periods

TABLE 2.8   Study Design Impact on Prevalence

	Location	Size	Age Group	Method	PDD Rate/ 10,000
U.K. Studies					
Chakrabarti & Fombonne, 2001	Staffordshire	15,500	$2\frac{1}{2}$–$6\frac{1}{2}$	Intense screening and assessment	62.6
Baird, Charman, & Baron-Cohen, 2000	South East Thames	16,235	7	Early screening and follow-up identification	57.9
Fombonne, Simmons, Ford, Meltzer, & Goodman, 2001	England and Wales	10,438	5–15	National household survey of psychiatric disorders	26.1
Taylor et al., 1999	North Thames	490,000	0–16	Administrative records	10.1
U.S. Studies					
Bertrand et al., 2001	Brick Township, New Jersey	8,896	3–10	Multiple sources of ascertainment	67
Sturmey & James, 2001	Texas	3,564,577	6–18	Educational services	16
DDS, 1999	California	3,215,000	4–9	Educational services	15
Hillman, Kanafani, Takahashi, & Miles, 2000	Missouri	—.	5–9	Educational services	4.8

are likely to differ even more with respect to their methodology.

The next two approaches are in essence equivalent to a comparison of cross-sectional surveys although specific attempts are made to maintain constant some design features in the surveys.

Repeat Surveys in Defined Geographic Areas

Repeated surveys, using the same methodology and conducted in the same geographic area at different points in time, can potentially yield useful information on time trends if the methods are kept relatively constant. The Göteborg studies (Gillberg, 1984; Gillberg, Steffenburg, & Schaumann, 1991; Steffenburg & Gillberg, 1986) provided three prevalence estimates that increased over a short period from 4.0 (1980) to 6.6 (1984) and 9.5/10,000 (1988). The gradient is even steeper if rates for the urban area alone are considered (4.0, 7.5, and 11.6/10,000; Gillberg, Steffenburg, & Schaumann, 1991). However, comparisons of these rates are not straightforward as different

age groups were included in each survey. The rate in the first survey for the youngest age group (which resembles more closely the children included in the other two surveys) was 5.1/10,000. Second, the increased prevalence in the second survey was explained by improved detection among the mentally retarded, and that of the third survey by cases born to immigrant parents. That the majority of the latter group was born abroad suggests that migration into the area could be a key explanation. Taken in conjunction with a change in local services and a progressive broadening of the definition of autism over time acknowledged by the authors (Gillberg, Steffenburg, & Schaumann, 1991), these findings do not provide evidence for an increased incidence of autism.

Two separate surveys conducted on children born 1992 to 1995 and 1996 to 1998 in Staffordshire in the United Kingdom (Table 2.2: Studies 32 and 36) were performed with rigorously identical methods for case definition and case identification. The prevalence for combined PDD was comparable and not statistically different in the two surveys (Chakrabarti

& Fombonne, in press), suggesting no upward trend in overall rates of PDD during the time interval of the studies.

Successive Birth Cohorts

In large surveys encompassing a wide age range, increasing prevalence rates among the most recent birth cohorts could be interpreted as indicating a secular increase in the incidence of the disorder, provided that alternative explanations can confidently be ruled out. This analysis was used in two French surveys (17 and 20), which derived from large sample sizes. In the first study (17), prevalence estimates were available for the two birth cohorts of children born in 1972 and 1976 and surveyed in 1985 and 1986. The rates were similar (5.1 and 4.9/10,000) and not statistically different (Fombonne & du Mazaubrun, 1992). Furthermore, in a subsequent investigation conducted in 1989 and 1990 in exactly the same areas, the age-specific rate of autism for the 1981 birth cohort was slightly lower (3.1/10,000; Rumeau-Rouquette et al., 1994). In any event, the findings were not suggestive of increasing rates in the most recent cohorts. Another survey conducted with the same methodology but in different French regions a few years later (Study 20) led to a similar overall prevalence estimate as the first survey (Table 2.2). The latter survey included consecutive birth cohorts from 1976 to 1985, and pooling the data of both surveys showed no upward trend in age-specific rates (Fombonne, du Mazaubrun, Cans, & Grandjean, 1997). Some weight should be given to these results as they derive from a total target population of 735,000 children, 389 of whom had autism. However, the most retarded children with autism were reflected in these studies and, as a consequence, any upward trend that would apply specifically to high-functioning subjects might have gone undetected.

An analysis of special educational disability from Minnesota showed a 16-fold increase in the number of children identified with a PDD from 2001 to 2002, as compared with 1991 to 1992 (Gurney et al., 2003; Study 39). The increase was not specific to autism since during the same period an increase of 50% was observed for all disability categories (except severe mental handicap), especially for the

category including ADHD. The large sample size allowed the authors to assess age, period, and cohort effects. Prevalence increased regularly in successive birth cohorts; for example, among 7-year-olds, the prevalence rose from 18/10,000 in those born in 1989, to 29/10,000 in those born in 1991 and to 55/10,000 in those born in 1993, suggestive of birth cohort effects. Within the *same* birth cohorts, age effects were also apparent since for children born in 1989 the prevalence rose with age from 13/10,000 at age 6, to 21/10,000 at age 9, and 33/10,000 at age 11. As argued by the authors, this pattern is not consistent with what one would expect from a chronic nonfatal condition diagnosed in the first years of life. Their analysis also showed a marked period effect that identified the early 1990s as the period when rates started to go up in all ages and birth cohorts. Gurney et al. (2003) further argued that this phenomenon coincided closely with the inclusion of PDDs in the federal Individual with Disabilities Educational Act (IDEA) funding and reporting mechanism in the United States. A similar interpretation of upward trends had been put forward by Croen, Grether, Hoogstrate, and Selvin (2002) in their analysis of the California DDS data.

Incidence Studies

Only three studies provided recent incidence estimates (Kaye, Melero-Montes, & Jick, 2001; Powell et al., 2000; Smeeth et al., 2004). All studies showed an upward trend in incidence over short periods. In the largest study of 1,410 subjects, there was a 10-fold increase in the rate of first recorded diagnoses of PDDs in United Kingdom general practice medical records from 1988 to 1992 and from 2000 to 2001 (Smeeth et al., 2004). The increase was more marked for PDDs other than autism but the increase in autism also was obvious. However, none of these investigations could determine the effect on the upward trend of changes over time in diagnostic criteria, improved awareness, and service availability.

Conclusion on Time Trends

The available epidemiological evidence does not strongly support the hypothesis that the incidence of autism has increased. As it stands now, the recent upward trend in rates of *prevalence* cannot be directly attributed to an increase in the *incidence* of the disorder. There is some evidence that diagnostic substitution and changes in the policies for special education as well as the increasing availability of services are responsible for the higher prevalence figures. Most of the existing epidemiological data are inadequate to properly test hypotheses on changes in the incidence of autism in human populations. Moreover, the low frequency of autism and PDDs seriously limits power in most investigations and variations of small magnitude in the incidence of the disorder are very likely to go undetected. Future investigations should aim at setting up surveillance programs that will allow estimates of the incidence of PDDs (as opposed to autism only) and the monitoring of its changes over time. It will be crucial to set up parallel investigations in different geographic areas to replicate findings across areas as a validating tool. Such programs should focus on age groups where the identification and diagnosis of the range of PDDs is less likely to fluctuate over time. Rapid changes in the age at first diagnosis and concerns about the validity and stability of diagnostic assessments among preschool samples require investigators to focus on older age groups. On the other hand, changes in the autistic symptomatology in adolescence and difficulties in service delivery to teenagers (and therefore in case identification) suggest a focus on younger children. The school-age years (7 to 12 years) should therefore be selected for efficient monitoring. Mandatory education at that age would facilitate identification and would minimize potential difficulties in diagnosing highfunctioning subjects at the upper end of this age range. Diagnostic assessments should rely on standardized measures of known reliability and validity. Furthermore, developmental and phenomenological data should be collected at a symptomatic level, and uniformly across the whole spectrum of PDDs, remaining free of particular nosological contingencies. Secondary application of diagnostic algorithms (current and/or future) on datasets containing detailed developmental and symptomatic data will then allow for performing meaningful comparisons over time, while holding diagnostic groupings

constant. Finally, good psychometric data on cognitive functioning will also be needed to assess trends in various subgroups in light of the preliminary evidence that patterns of mental retardation in autism may be changing. Obviously, surveillance programs should also incorporate measures of risk factors hypothesized to exert causal influences for this group of disorders.

IMMIGRANT STATUS, ETHNICITY, SOCIAL CLASS, AND OTHER CORRELATES

Some investigators have mentioned the possibility that rates of autism might be higher among immigrants (Gillberg, 1987; Gillberg, Schaumann, & Gillberg, 1995; Gillberg, Steffenburg, & Schaumann, 1991; Wing, 1980). Five of the 17 children with autism identified in the Camberwell study were of Caribbean origin (Study 4; Wing, 1980), and the estimated rate of autism was 6.3/10,000 for this group compared with 4.4/10,000 for the rest of the population (Wing, 1993). However, the wide confidence intervals associated with rates from this study (Table 2.2) indicate no statistically significant difference. This area of London had received a large proportion of immigrants from the Caribbean region in the 1960s; and when there is migration flux in and out of an area, estimation of population rates should be viewed with much caution. Yet, Afro-Caribbean children referred from the same area were recently found to have higher rates of autism than referred controls (Goodman & Richards, 1995). The sample again was very small ($N = 18$) and differential referral patterns to a tertiary center also providing services for the local area could not be ruled out. Only one child was born from British-born Afro-Caribbean parents in a recent U.K. survey (Study 21; Webb, Lobo, et al., 1997), providing little support to this particular hypothesis. Similarly, the findings from the Göteborg studies paralleled an increased migration flux in the early 1980s in this area (Gillberg, 1987); they, too, were based on relatively small numbers (19 children from immigrant parents). In the same geographic area, Arvidsson et al. (1997; Study 22) had five children out of nine in their sample with either both parents ($N = 2$) or one parent ($N = 3$) having immigrated to Sweden. However, there were no systematic comparisons with rates of immigrants in the population. A positive family history for developmental disorders was reported in three such cases and a chromosomal abnormality in one further case. In the Icelandic survey (Study 31), 2.5% of the autism parents were from non-European origin compared to a 0.5% corresponding rate in the whole population, but it was unclear if this represented a significant difference. In Study 23, the proportion of children with autism and a non-European origin was marginally but not significantly raised compared with the population rate of immigrants (8% vs. 2.3%), but this was based on a very small sample (two children of non-European origin). A U.K. survey found comparable rates in areas with contrasting ethnic composition (Powell et al., 2000). In the Utah survey, where a clear breakdown by race was achieved (Ritvo et al., 1989; Study 15, Table 2.2), the autism parents showed no deviation from the racial distribution of this state. The proportion of non-Whites in this study and state was, however, noticeably low, providing little power to detect departures from the null hypothesis. Other studies have not systematically reported the proportion of immigrant or ethnic groups in the areas surveyed. In four studies where the proportions of immigrant groups were low (11, 12, 19, 21), rates of autism were in the upper range of rates. Conversely, in studies of other populations (14, 17, and 20) where immigrants contributed substantially to the denominators, rates were in the rather low band. The analysis of a large sample ($N = 4,356$) of Californian PDD children showed a lower risk of autism in children of Mexico-born mothers and a similar risk for children of mothers born outside the United States compared with California-born mothers (Croen, Grether, & Selvin, 2002). In this study, the risk of PDD was raised in African American mothers with an adjusted rate ratio of 1.6 (95% CI: 1.5 to 1.8); by contrast, the prevalence was similar in White, Black, and other races in the population-based survey of Atlanta (Yeargin-Allsopp et al., 2003), where case ascertainment is likely to be more complete than in the previous study.

Taken altogether, the combined results of these reports should be interpreted in the specific methodological context of these investigations. Most studies had low numbers of identified cases, and especially small numbers of autistic children born from immigrant parents, and many authors in these studies relied on broadened definitions of autism. Statistical testing was not rigorously conducted and doubts could be raised in several studies about the appropriateness of the comparison data that were used. Thus, the overall proportion of immigrants in the population may be an inappropriate figure with which to compare observed rates of children from immigrant parents among autistic series. Fertility rates of immigrant families are likely to be different from those in the host populations and call for strict age-adjusted comparisons of individuals at risk for the disorder. The proportion of immigrants in the entire population might seriously underestimate that for younger age groups, and, in turn, this could have given rise to false positive results. In addition, studies sampling children through services or clinical sources may be biased because ethnicity, race and social class are likely to differentially affect access to these settings. Finally, studies were generally poor in their definition of immigrant status, with unclear amalgamation of information on country of origin, citizenship, immigrant status, race, and ethnicity. Finally, it is unclear what common mechanism could explain the putative association between immigrant status and autism, since the origins of the immigrant parents (especially in Study 16; see also Gillberg & Gillberg, 1996) were diverse and represented in fact all continents. With this heterogeneity in mind, what common biological features might these immigrant families share and what would be a plausible mechanism explaining the putative association between autism and immigrant status? The possibility of an increased vulnerability to intrauterine infections in nonimmunized immigrant mothers was raised, but not supported, in a detailed analysis of 15 autistic children from immigrant parents (Gillberg & Gillberg, 1996). These authors instead posited that parents, and in particular fathers, affected with autistic traits would be inclined to travel abroad to find female partners more naïve to their social difficulties. This speculation was based, however, on three observations only, and assessment of the autistic traits in two parents was not independently obtained.

The hypothesis of an association between immigrant status or race and autism, therefore, remains largely unsupported by the empirical results. Most of the claims about these possible correlates of autism were derived from post hoc observations of very small samples and were not subjected to rigorous statistical testing. Large studies have generally failed to detect such associations.

Autism and Social Class

Twelve studies provided information on the social class of the families of autistic children. Of these, four studies (1, 2, 3, and 5) suggested an association between autism and social class or parental education. The year of data collection for these four investigations was before 1980 (Table 2.2), and all studies conducted thereafter provided no evidence for the association. Thus, the epidemiological results suggest that the earlier findings were probably due to artifacts in the availability of services and in the case-finding methods, as already shown in other samples (Schopler, Andrews, & Strupp, 1979; Wing, 1980).

Cluster Reports

Occasional reports of space or time clustering of cases of autism have raised concerns in the general public. In fact, only one such report has been published in the professional literature (Baron-Cohen, Saunders, & Chakrabarti, 1999) that described seven children with either autism or PDD-NOS living within a few streets from each other in a small town of the Midlands (United Kingdom). The cluster was first identified by a parent, and the subsequent analysis was uninformed with proper statistical procedures and inconclusive as to whether this cluster could have occurred by chance only. The comparison of the incidence or prevalence rate within the cluster to that of the general population (as performed by Baron-Cohen & Wheelwright, 1999) is an inappropriate technique to assess cluster alarms. The reason is that, by definition, a preselection bias occurs in the delineation of the cluster boundaries (Kulldorff, 1999). Thus, finding an increased incidence or prevalence rate ratio in a cluster does *not* prove anything; this erroneous approach has been referred to in the literature as the "Texan sharpshooter" effect, referring to the gunman who shot first and then painted a target around the bullet hole. On the other hand, a negative finding would certainly suggest a random phenomenon.

When cluster alarms are associated to a possible causal mechanism, it is recommended to perform focused tests of clustering at other suspected sources of risk exposure. The cluster alarms for childhood leukemia occurring near a nuclear plant in England were followed by investigations of disease incidence at other nuclear plants, which proved to be negative (Hoffmann & Schlattmann, 1999). However, the potential source of the cluster alarm is not always identified and, in these instances, it is suggested to monitor the incidence of future cases in the area of first alarm. Chen, Connelly, and Mantel (1993) have outlined postalarm monitoring techniques that allow investigators to confirm or reject alarms, based on the observation of the time intervals preceding each of the first five cases diagnosed subsequent to the alarm. The approach is a confirmatory technique that ignores the cluster alarm data and thus avoids the aforementioned preselection bias. Other techniques, such as space-time scan statistics (Kulldorff, 1999), can confirm or reject a cluster alarm by extending the investigation to a larger area while avoiding selection biases, adjusting for population density, confounding variables and multiple testing, and allowing for the precise location of clusters. They require, however, the availability of regional or national geocoded data that are usually not available for autism. Other general statistical techniques to assess time and space clustering are reviewed in specialist journals.

Cluster alarms are likely to represent random occurrence in most instances, as illustrated by several recent investigations of cluster alarms for other rare disorders of childhood. Cluster alarms in autism have not been investigated with scientific rigor, whereas research strategies and ad hoc statistical procedures exist for that purpose. The approach to such cluster alarms should be to confirm the alarm in the first place, using the available techniques to assess the significance of clusters and to exclude random noise in spatial and time distribution of the disorder. Only when an alarm has been confirmed should researchers set up more complex epidemiological investigations to investigate risk factors and causal mechanisms.

CONCLUSION

Epidemiological surveys of autism and PDDs have now been carried out in several countries. Methodological differences in case definition and case-finding procedures make between-survey comparisons difficult to perform. Despite these differences, some common characteristics of autism and PDDs in population surveys have consistently emerged. Autism is associated with mental retardation in about 70% of the cases and is overrepresented among males (with a male/female ratio of 4.3:1). Autism is found in association with some rare and genetically determined medical conditions, such as tuberous sclerosis. Overall, the median value of about 5.5% for the combined rate of medical disorders in autism derived from this review is consistent with the 5% (Tuchman, Rapin, & Shinnar, 1991) to 10% (Rutter, Bailey, Bolton, & Le Couteur, 1994) figures available from other investigations. A majority of surveys has ruled out social class as a risk factor for autism, a result once supported by studies of clinical, that is, less representative, samples. The putative association of autism with immigrant status or race is, so far, not borne out by epidemiological studies. The conclusion of a lack of variation in the incidence of autism according to race or ethnicity is reached, however, from a weak empirical base, and future studies might address this issue more efficiently. In fact, epidemiological studies of autism and PDDs have generally been lacking sophistication in their investigation of most other risk factors.

The same considerations apply to the issue of secular changes in the incidence of autism. The little evidence that exists does not support this hypothesis, but power to detect time trends is seriously limited in existing datasets. The debate has been largely confounded by confusion between prevalence and incidence. Although prevalence estimates appear to have gone up over time, this increase most likely represents changes in the concepts, definitions, service availability, and awareness of autistic-spectrum disorders in both the lay and professional public. To assess whether the incidence has increased, method factors that account for an important proportion of the variability in rates must be tightly controlled.

Taking 35/10,000 and 60/10,000 as two working rates for the combination of all PDDs, and using U.S. population figures as of July 1, 2002, it can be estimated that about 284,000 and up to 486,000 subjects under the age of 20 suffer from a PDD in the United States. These figures carry straightforward implications for current and future needs in services and early educational intervention programs.

Cross-References

Issues of diagnosis of autism spectrum disorders are addressed in Chapter 1 and Chapters 3 through 6; medical aspects of autism are discussed in Chapter 20.

REFERENCES

Ahlsen, G., Gillberg, C., Lindblom, R., & Gillberg, C. (1994). Tuberous sclerosis in Western Sweden: A population study of cases with early childhood onset. *Archives of Neurology, 51,* 76–81.

Arvidsson, T., Danielsson, B., Forsberg, P., Gillberg, C., Johansson, M., & Kjellgren, G. (1997). Autism in 3–6-year-old children in a suburb of Goteborg, Sweden. *Autism, 2,* 163–173.

Baird, G., Charman, T., Baron-Cohen, S., Cox, A., Swettenham, J., Wheelwright, S., et al. (2000). A screening instrument for autism at 18 months of age: A 6 year follow-up study. *Journal of the American Academy of Child and Adolescent Psychiatry, 39,* 694–702.

Baron-Cohen, S., Saunders, K., & Chakrabarti, S. (1999). Does autism cluster geographically? A research note. *Autism, 3,* 39–43.

Bertrand, J., Mars, A., Boyle, C., Bove, F., Yeargin-Allsopp, M., & Decoufle, P. (2001). Prevalence of autism in a United States population: The Brick Township, New Jersey, investigation. *Pediatrics, 108,* 1155–1161.

Bohman, M., Bohman, I. L., Björck, P. O., & Sjöholm, E. (1983). Childhood psychosis in a northern Swedish county: Some preliminary findings from an epidemiological survey. In

M. H. Schmidt & H. Remschmidt (Eds.), *Epidemiological approaches in child psychiatry* (pp. 164–173). New York: George Thieme Verlag Stuttgart.

Brask, B. H. (1972). A prevalence investigation of childhood psychoses. In *Nordic Symposium on the Care of Psychotic Children.* Oslo: Barnepsychiatrist Forening.

Bregman, J. D., & Volkmar, F. R. (1988). Autistic social dysfunction and Down's syndrome. *Journal of the American Academy of Child and Adolescent Psychiatry, 27,* 440–441.

Bryson, S. E., Clark, B. S., & Smith, I. M. (1988). First report of a Canadian epidemiological study of autistic syndromes. *Journal of Child Psychology and Psychiatry, 4,* 433–445.

Burd, L., Fisher, W., & Kerbeshan, J. (1987). A prevalence study of pervasive developmental disorders in North Dakota. *Journal of the American Academy of Child and Adolescent Psychiatry, 26*(5), 700–703.

Chakrabarti, S., & Fombonne, E. (2001). Pervasive developmental disorders in preschool children. *Journal of the American Medical Association, 285*(24), 3093–3099.

Chakrabarti, S., & Fombonne, E. (in press). *Pervasive developmental disorders in preschool children: High prevalence confirmed.* American Journal of Psychiatry.

Chen, R., Connelly, R., & Mantel, N. (1993). Analysing post-alarm data in a monitoring system in order to accept or reject the alarm. *Statistics in Medicine, 12,* 1807–1812.

Chess, S. (1971). Autism in children with congenital rubella. *Journal of Autism and Childhood Schizophrenia, 1,* 33–47.

Cialdella, P., & Mamelle, N. (1989). An epidemiological study of infantile autism in a French department. *Journal of Child Psychology and Psychiatry, 30*(1), 165–175.

Croen, L. A., Grether, J. K., Hoogstrate, J., & Selvin, S. (2002). The changing prevalence of autism in California. *Journal of Autism and Developmental Disorders, 32*(3), 207–215.

Croen, L. A., Grether, J. K., & Selvin, S. (2002). Descriptive epidemiology of autism in a California population: Who is at risk? *Journal of Autism and Developmental Disorders, 32*(3), 217–224.

Davidovitch, M., Holtzman, G., & Tirosh, E. (2001, March). Autism in the Haifa area—an epidemiological perspective. *Israeli Medical Association Journal, 3,* 188–189.

Department of Developmental Services. (1999). *Changes in the population of persons with autism and pervasive developmental disorders in California's Developmental Services System: 1987 through 1998.* Retrieved July 16, 2004, from http://www.dds.ca.gov.

Department of Developmental Services. (2003). *Autism spectrum disorders: Changes in the California caseload—an update 1999 through 2002.* Retrieved July 16, 2004, from http://www.dds.ca.gov/Autism/pdf/AutismReport2003.pdf.

Deykin, E. Y., & MacMahon, B. (1979). The incidence of seizures among children with autistic symptoms. *American Journal of Psychiatry, 136*(10), 1310–1312.

Ehlers, S., & Gillberg, C. (1993). The epidemiology of Asperger syndrome: A total population study. *Journal of Child Psychology and Psychiatry, 34,* 1327–1350.

Fombonne, E. (1999). The epidemiology of autism: A review. *Psychological Medicine, 29,* 769–786.

Fombonne, E. (2001). Is there an epidemic of autism? *Pediatrics, 107,* 411–413.

Fombonne, E. (2002a). Case identification in an epidemiological context. In M. Rutter & E. Taylor (Eds.), *Child and adolescent psychiatry* (pp. 52–69). Oxford, England: Blackwell.

Fombonne, E. (2002b). Prevalence of childhood disintegrative disorder (CDD). *Autism, 6*(2), 147–155.

Fombonne, E. (2003a). Epidemiological surveys of autism and other pervasive developmental disorders: An update. *Journal of Autism and Developmental Disorders, 33*(4), 365–382.

Fombonne, E. (2003b). The prevalence of autism. *Journal of the American Medical Association, 289*(1), 1–3.

Fombonne, E., & du Mazaubrun, C. (1992). Prevalence of infantile autism in 4 French regions. *Social Psychiatry and Psychiatric Epidemiology, 27,* 203–210.

Fombonne, E., du Mazaubrun, C., Cans, C., & Grandjean, H. (1997). Autism and associated medical disorders in a large French epidemiological sample. *Journal of the American Academy of Child and Adolescent Psychiatry, 36*(11), 1561–1566.

Fombonne, E., Simmons, H., Ford, T., Meltzer, H., & Goodman, R. (2001). Prevalence of pervasive developmental disorders in the British nationwide survey of child mental health. *Journal of the American Academy of Child and Adolescent Psychiatry, 40*(7), 820–827.

Fombonne, E., & Tidmarsh, L. (2003). Epidemiological data on Asperger disorder. *Child and Adolescent Psychiatric Clinics of North America, 12,* 15–21.

Ghaziuddin, M., Tsai, L., & Ghaziuddin, N. (1992). Autism in Downs' syndrome: Presentation and diagnosis. *Journal of Intellectual Disability Research, 35,* 449–456.

Gillberg, C. (1984). Infantile autism and other childhood psychoses in a Swedish region: Epidemiological aspects. *Journal of Child Psychology and Psychiatry, 25,* 35–43.

Gillberg, C. (1987). Infantile autism in children of immigrant parents. A population-based study from Göteborg, Sweden. *British Journal of Psychiatry, 150,* 856–858.

Gillberg, C., & Coleman, M. (1996). Autism and medical disorders: A review of the literature. *Developmental Medicine and Child Neurology, 38,* 191–202.

Gillberg, C., & Gillberg, C. (1996). Autism in immigrants: A population-based study from Swedish rural and urban areas. *Journal of Intellectual Disability Research, 40,* 24–31.

Gillberg, C., Schaumann, H., & Gillberg, I. C. (1995). Autism in immigrants: Children born in Sweden to mothers born in Uganda. *Journal of Intellectual Disability Research, 39,* 141–144.

Gillberg, C., Steffenburg, S., & Schaumann, H. (1991). Is autism more common now than ten years ago? *British Journal of Psychiatry, 158,* 403–409.

Goodman, R., & Richards, H. (1995). Child and adolescent psychiatric presentations of second-generation Afro-Caribbeans in Britain. *British Journal of Psychiatry, 167,* 362–369.

Gurney, J. G., Fritz, M. S., Ness, K. K., Sievers, P., Newschaffer, C. J., & Shapiro, E. G. (2003). Analysis of prevalence trends of autism spectrum disorder in Minnesota [Comment]. *Archives of Pediatrics and Adolescent Medicine, 157*(7), 622–627.

Hillman, R., Kanafani, N., Takahashi, T., & Miles, J. (2000). Prevalence of autism in Missouri: Changing trends and the effect of a comprehensive state autism project. *Missouri Medicine, 97,* 159–163.

Hoffmann, W., & Schlattmann, P. (1999). An analysis of the geographical distribution of leukemia incidence in the vicinity of a suspected point source: A case study. In A. B. Lawson et al. (Eds.), *Disease mapping and risk assessment for public health* (pp. 396–409). Chichester, West Sussex, England: Wiley.

Honda, H., Shimizu, Y., Misumi, K., Niimi, M., & Ohashi, Y. (1996). Cumulative incidence and prevalence of childhood autism in children in Japan. *British Journal of Psychiatry, 169,* 228–235.

Hoshino, Y., Yashima, Y., Ishige, K., Tachibana, R., Watanabe, M., Kancki, M., et al. (1982). The epidemiological study of autism in Fukushi-maken. *Folia Psychiatrica et Neurologica Japonica, 36,* 115–124.

Howlin, P., Wing, L., & Gould, J. (1995). The recognition of autism in children with Down syndrome: Implications for intervention and some speculations about pathology. *Developmental Medicine and Child Neurology, 37,* 406–414.

Hunt, A., & Lindenbaum, R. H. (1984). Tuberous sclerosis: A new estimate of prevalence within the Oxford region. *Journal of Medical Genetics, 21,* 272–277.

Jick, H., & Kaye, J. A. (2003). Epidemiology and possible causes of autism. *Pharmacotherapy, 23*(12), 1324–1330.

Kadesjö, B., Gillberg, C., & Hagberg, B. (1999). Autism and Asperger syndrome in seven-year-old children: A total population study. *Journal of Autism and Developmental Disorders, 29*(4), 327–331.

Kaye, J., Melero-Montes, M., & Jick, H. (2001). Mumps, measles, and rubella vaccine and the incidence of autism recorded by general practitioners: A time trend analysis. *British Medical Journal, 322,* 0–2.

Kielinen, M., Linna, S. L., & Moilanen, I. (2000). Autism in Northern Finland. *European Child and Adolescent Psychiatry, 9,* 162–167.

Knobloch, H., & Pasamanick, B. (1975). Some etiologic and prognostic factors in early infantile autism and psychosis. *Pediatrics, 55,* 182–191.

Kulldorff, M. (1999). Statistical evaluation of disease cluster alarms. In A. B. Lawson et al. (Eds.), *Disease mapping and risk assessment for public health* (pp. 143–149). Chichester, West Sussex, England: Wiley.

Le Couteur, A., Rutter, M., Lord, C., Rios, P., Robertson, S., Holdgrafer, M., et al. (1989). Autism diagnostic interview: A standardized investigator-based instrument. *Journal of Autism and Developmental Disorders, 19,* 363–387.

Lord, C., Risi, S., Lembrecht, L., Cook, E., Leventhal, B., DiLavore, P., et al. (2000). The Autism Diagnostic Observation Schedule-Generic: A standard measure of social and communication deficits associated with the spectrum of autism. *Journal of Autism and Developmental Disorders, 30,* 205–223.

Lord, C., Schopler, E., & Revecki, D. (1982). Sex differences in autism. *Journal of Autism and Developmental Disorders, 12,* 317–330.

Lotter, V. (1966). Epidemiology of autistic conditions in young children: I. Prevalence. *Social Psychiatry, 1,* 124–137.

Lotter, V. (1967). Epidemiology of autistic conditions in young children: II. Some characteristics of the parents and children. *Social Psychiatry, 1*(4), 163–173.

Lowe, T. L., Tanaka, K., Seashore, M. R., Young, J. G., & Cohen, D. J. (1980). Detection of phenylketonuria in autistic and psychiatric children. *Journal of the American Medical Association, 243,* 126–128.

Madsen, K. M., Hviid, A., Vestergaard, M., Schendel, D., Wohlfahrt, J., Thorsen, P., et al. (2002). A population-based study of measles, mumps, and rubella vaccination and autism. *New England Journal of Medicine, 347*(19), 1477–1482.

Magnusson, P., & Saemundsen, E. (2001). Prevalence of autism in Iceland. *Journal of Autism and Developmental Disorders, 31,* 153–163.

Matsuishi, T., Shiotsuki, M., Yoshimura, K., Shoji, H., Imuta, F., & Yamashita, F. (1987). High prevalence of infantile autism in Kurume City, Japan. *Journal of Child Neurology, 2,* 268–271.

McCarthy, P., Fitzgerald, M., & Smith, M. A. (1984). Prevalence of childhood autism in Ireland. *Irish Medical Journal, 77*(5), 129–130.

MIND Institute. (2002, October 17). *Report to the Legislature on the Principal Findings from the epidemiology of autism in California: A comprehensive pilot study.* Davis: University of California.

Mouridsen, S. E., Bachmann-Andersen, L., Sörensen, S. A., Rich, B., & Isager, T. (1992). Neurofibromatosis in infantile autism and other types of childhood psychoses. *Acta Paedopsychiatrica, 55,* 15–18.

Powell, J., Edwards, A., Edwards, M., Pandit, B. S., Sungum-Paliwal, S. R., & Whitehouse, W. (2000). Changes in the incidence of childhood autism and other autistic spectrum disorders in preschool children from two areas of the West Midlands, UK. *Developmental Medicine and Child Neurology, 42,* 624–628.

Ritvo, E. R., Freeman, B. J., Pingree, C., Mason-Brothers, A., Jorde, L., Jensen, W. R., et al. (1989). The UCLA-University of Utah epidemiologic survey of autism: Prevalence. *American Journal of Psychiatry, 146*(2), 194–199.

Rumeau-Rouquette, C., du Mazaubrun, C., Verrier, A., Mlika, A., Bréart, G., Goujard, J., et al. (1994). *Prévalence des handicaps: Évolution dans trois générations d'enfants 1972, 1976, 1981.* Paris: Editions INSERM.

Rutter, M. (1970). Autistic children: Infancy to adulthood. *Seminars in Psychiatry, 2,* 435–450.

Rutter, M., Bailey, A., Bolton, P., & Le Couteur, A. (1994). Autism and known medical conditions: Myth and substance. *Journal of Child Psychology and Psychiatry, 35,* 311–322.

Schopler, E., Andrews, C. E., & Strupp, K. (1979). Do autistic children come from upper-middle-class parents? *Journal of Autism and Developmental Disorders, 9*(2), 139–151.

Scott, F. J., Baron-Cohen, S., Bolton, P., & Brayne, C. (2002). Brief report: Prevalence of autism spectrum conditions in children aged 5–11 years in Cambridgeshire, UK. *Autism, 6*(3), 231–237.

Shepherd, C. W., Beard, C. M., Gomez, M. R., Kurland, L. T., & Whisnant, J. P. (1991). Tuberous sclerosis complex in Olmsted County, Minnesota, 1950–1989. *Archives of Neurology, 48,* 400–401.

Smalley, S. (1998). Autism and tuberous sclerosis. *Journal of Autism and Developmental Disorders, 28,* 407–414.

Smalley, S. L., Tanguay, P. E., Smith, M., & Gutierrez, G. (1992). Autism and tuberous sclerosis. *Journal of Autism and Developmental Disorders, 22,* 339–355.

Smeeth, L., Cook, C., Fombonne, E., Heavey, L., Rodrigues, L., Smith, P., et al. (2004). *Rate of first recorded diagnosis of autism and other pervasive developmental disorders in United Kingdom general practice, 1988 to 2001.* Manuscript submitted for publication.

Spitzer, R. L., & Siegel, B. (1990). The *DSM-III-R* field trial of pervasive developmental disorders. *Journal of the American Academy of Child and Adolescent Psychiatry, 6,* 855–886.

Sponheim, E., & Skjeldal, O. (1998). Autism and related disorders: Epidemiological findings in a Norwegian study using *ICD-10* diagnostic criteria. *Journal of Autism and Developmental Disorders, 28,* 217–222.

Steffenburg, S., & Gillberg, C. (1986). Autism and autistic-like conditions in Swedish rural and urban areas: A population study. *British Journal of Psychiatry, 149,* 81–87.

Steinhausen H.-C., Göbel, D., Breinlinger, M., & Wohlloben, B. (1986). A community survey of infantile autism. *Journal of the American Academy of Child Psychiatry, 25*(2), 186–189.

Sturmey, P., & James, V. (2001). Administrative prevalence of autism in the Texas school system. *Journal of the American Academy of Child Psychiatry, 40*(6), 621.

Sugiyama, T., & Abe, T. (1989). The prevalence of autism in Nagoya, Japan: A total population study. *Journal of Autism and Developmental Disorders, 19*(1), 87–96.

Tanoue, Y., Oda, S., Asano, F., & Kawashima, K. (1988). Epidemiology of infantile autism in Southern Ibaraki, Japan: Differences in prevalence in birth cohorts. *Journal of Autism and Developmental Disorders, 18,* 155–166.

Taylor, B., Miller, E., Farrington, C. P., Petropoulos, M. C., Favot-Mayaud, I., Li, J., et al. (1999, June 12). Autism and measles, mumps, and rubella vaccine: No epidemiological evidence for a causal association. *Lancet, 353,* 2026–2029.

Treffert, D. A. (1970). Epidemiology of infantile autism. *Archives of General Psychiatry, 22,* 431–438.

Tuchman, R. F., Rapin, I., & Shinnar, S. (1991). Autistic and dysphasic children: II. Epilepsy. *Pediatrics, 88,* 1219–1225.

Volkmar, F. R. (1992). Childhood disintegrative disorder: Issues for *DSM-IV. Journal of Autism and Developmental Disorders, 22,* 625–642.

Volkmar, F. R., Klin, A., Siegel, B., Szatmark, I., Lord, Ou Campbell, M., et al. (1994). Field trial for autistic disorder in *DSM-IV. American Journal of Psychiatry, 151*(9), 1361–1367.

Volkmar, F. R., & Nelson, D. S. (1990). Seizure disorders in autism. *Journal of the American Academy of Child and Adolescent Psychiatry, 1,* 127–129.

Webb, E., Lobo, S., Hervas, A., Scourfield, J., & Fraser, W. I. (1997). The changing prevalence of autistic disorder in a Welsh health district. *Developmental Medicine and Child Neurology, 39,* 150–152.

Webb, E., Morey, J., Thompsen, W., Butler, C., Barber, M., & Fraser, W. I. (2003). Prevalence of autistic spectrum disorder in children attending mainstream schools in a Welsh education authority. *Developmental Medicine and Child Neurology, 45*(6), 377–384.

Wignyosumarto, S., Mukhlas, M., & Shirataki, S. (1992). Epidemiological and clinical study of autistic children in Yogyakarta, Indonesia. *Kobe Journal of Medical Sciences, 38*(1), 1–19.

Wing, L. (1980). Childhood autism and social class: A question of selection? *British Journal of Psychiatry, 137,* 410–417.

Wing, L. (1993). The definition and prevalence of autism: A review. *European Child and Adolescent Psychiatry, 2,* 61–74.

Wing, L., & Gould, J. (1979). Severe impairments of social interactions and associated abnormalities in children: Epidemiology and classification. *Journal of Autism and Developmental Disorders, 9*(1), 11–29.

Wing, L., Yeates, S. R., Brierly, L. M., & Gould, J. (1976). The prevalence of early childhood autism: Comparison of administrative and epidemiological studies. *Psychological Medicine, 6,* 89–100.

Yeargin-Allsopp, M., Rice, C., Karapurkar, T., Doernberg, N., Boyle, C., & Murphy, C. (2003). Prevalence of autism in a U.S. metropolitan area. *Journal of the American Medical Association, 289*(1), 49–55.

CHAPTER 3

Childhood Disintegrative Disorder

FRED R. VOLKMAR, KATHY KOENIG, AND MATTHEW STATE

Nearly 100 years ago, Theodore Heller, a Viennese educator, reported on six children who had exhibited severe developmental regression at ages 3 to 4 years following a period of apparently normal development. After the regression, recovery was quite limited. Initially, Heller (1908) termed this condition *dementia infantilis;* subsequently, other terms have been used for the concept, for example, Heller's syndrome, disintegrative psychosis, and, more recently, childhood disintegrative disorder (CDD). Over the past century, more than 100 cases have been reported in the world literature; not surprisingly, information on the condition is much more limited than that available on autism. In this chapter, we review the development of the diagnostic concept, current definitions, information on clinical features, epidemiology, course, and validity of the condition. We also note areas of controversy, and issues that remain to be clarified are reviewed.

DEVELOPMENT OF THE DIAGNOSTIC CONCEPT

Although only recently accorded official recognition in *DSM-IV* as a diagnostic concept, CDD has a long history.

Heller's work occurred shortly after the turn of this century, but many decades were to pass before his diagnostic concept was widely recognized. Debate initially centered on issues of continuity with schizophrenia and, more recently, with autism. The early confusion with schizophrenia reflected the general presumption that, more or less, all severe psychiatric disturbances reflected psychosis that was equated with schizophrenia (see Chapter 1, this *Handbook*, this volume, for a discussion). Only as various lines of evidence began to suggest the importance of making distinctions was it clear, for example, that autism differed from schizophrenia of childhood in a host of ways. The pioneering studies of Kolvin (1971) and Rutter (1972) were particularly important in this regard since they demonstrated that within a large group of "psychotic" children, there was a bimodal pattern of onset. The early-onset group had begun to have troubles at birth or within a year or so after birth while the late-onset group developed apparently normally for many years. Clinical features of the early-onset group included marked impairments in social, cognitive, and language development similar to those described by Kanner for autism, whereas the late-onset group exhibited delusions, hallucinations, and other features more similar to schizophrenia. There was no higher than expected frequency of schizophrenia among family members of the early-onset group, but there was such an increase among first-degree relatives in the late-onset group. This observation has been

The authors acknowledge the support of NICHD grant 5P01-HD-03008-28. The case report is reprinted with permission from *Psychoses and Pervasive Developmental Disorders in Childhood and Adolescence,* Fred R. Volkmar, MD, editor, American Psychiatric Association Press, 1996. The authors are grateful to Drs. Kurita, Malhotra, Gillberg, and Deonna for their kind provision of additional information.

well replicated (e.g., Makita, 1966; Volkmar, Cohen, Hoshino, Rende, & Paul, 1988). It is also of interest that in these studies a handful of cases did not seem to fall so simply either into the early- or late-onset group, for example, 3 of the 83 cases in Kolvin's series exhibited an intermediate age of onset between the autistic and schizophrenic groups.

These and other data on the validity of autism led to its official recognition in *DSM-III* (American Psychiatric Association, 1980), where it was placed in a new class of disorder, pervasive developmental disorder (PDD; see Chapter 1, this *Handbook*, this volume). Infantile autism was defined on the basis of marked social, language, and other problems arising by 30 months of age. Partly in recognition of the fact that a few children seemed to develop an autistic-like condition after that time, *DSM-III* also included a category, childhood onset pervasive developmental disorder (COPDD). This category was not meant to be analogous to Heller's diagnostic concept; the implicit presumption in *DSM-III* was that such cases invariably reflected some progressive neuropathological process. However, the ninth revision of the *International Classification of Diseases* (*ICD-9;* World Health Organization [WHO], 1978) had included a category for disintegrative psychosis or Heller's syndrome defined on the basis of "normal or near normal development in the first years of life, followed by a loss of social skills and of speech together with a severe disorder of emotion, behavior, and relationships." *ICD-9* did not, however, prove as influential as *DSM-III,* primarily because the latter system included explicit guidelines for diagnosis.

Although a very detailed definition of COPDD was included in *DSM-III,* it quickly became clear that this diagnostic concept was problematic in many respects (Volkmar, 1987), and only a handful of reports appeared in the literature (Burd, Fisher, & Kerbeshian, 1988). When *DSM-III* was revised (*DSM-III-R,* American Psychiatric Association, 1987), the COPDD concept was dropped. Diagnostic criteria for autism were expanded in number and conceptually, and early onset of autism was not an essential diagnostic feature; autistic disorder was the only operationally defined disorder within the PDD class. These changes meant that historical information, for example, on the pattern and time of onset, was not particularly relevant to the diagnosis of autism. Thus, children who would have been recognized as having disintegrative psychosis in *ICD-9* would usually have been said to have autistic disorder in *DSM-III-R*. This state of affairs became even more complex as the drafts of the *ICD-10* revision began to appear.

Childhood Disintegrative Disorder in *ICD-10* and *DSM-IV*

In contrast to *DSM-III-R, ICD-10* included a draft definition of CDD. This definition was largely consistent with earlier work (e.g., Heller, 1930; Zappert, 1921), which had generally suggested the following diagnostic features:

1. A distinctive pattern of syndrome onset (a period of several years of normal development before a marked deterioration)
2. Progressive deterioration (either gradual or abrupt) once the syndrome had its onset with loss of skills in multiple areas
3. Behavioral and affective symptoms
4. An absence of features of gross neurological dysfunction

Draft *ICD-10* criteria for the condition included apparently normal development for at least 2 years with age-appropriate social, communicative, and other skills; a definite loss of skills in more than one area; development of problems in social interaction, communication, and restricted patterns of interest or behavior of the type observed in autism; and a loss of interest in the environment. By definition, the disorder could not coexist with autism or any other explicitly defined PDD, schizophrenia, elective mutism, or the syndrome of acquired aphasia with epilepsy.

Using the draft *ICD-10* criteria, Volkmar and Cohen (1989) identified a series of 10 cases of apparent CDD from within a larger sample of individuals with the clinical features of autism. Characteristics of the CDD were then contrasted to cases of autism that had been identified before or after 24 months. This comparison was particularly appropriate to the issue of whether CDD simply represented late-onset autism since differences between the groups on some external measure(s) would tend to support the validity of CDD apart from late-onset autism. This was indeed the case. Cases with late-onset autism tended to be higher functioning while the CDD cases were more likely to be mute, more likely to be in residential placement, and so forth. Thus, it appeared that CDD was not simply late-onset autism; rather, it appeared to have distinctive features, clinical course, and even worse outcome.

The inclusion of CDD in *ICD-10* represented a marked divergence from *DSM-III-R* and clearly had implications for the definition of autism in *DSM-IV* (American Psychiatric Association, 1994). As part of the *DSM-IV* revision process, a review (Volkmar, 1992) of CDD identified 77 cases in the world literatures and suggested that while the condition was apparently relatively rare, it seemed to merit inclusion in *DSM-IV* because it appeared to differ from autism in important respects and because it was not (as had previously been assumed) always, or even usually, associated with an identifiable neurological condition that might account for the deterioration.

Inclusion of CDD in *DSM-IV* was also suggested by the results of the *DSM-IV* field trial for autism and related conditions (Volkmar et al., 1994; Volkmar & Rutter, 1995). Although the field trial was primarily concerned with the development and validation of the *DSM-IV* diagnosis of autism, 16 cases of CDD that had been previously evaluated at participating centers were included. Of even more interest, an additional 15 cases that met *ICD-10* criteria for CDD were identified in the field trial. In these cases, the clinician had not given CDD as the clinical diagnosis but had noted the presence of various diagnostic features of the condition. This is not surprising since, particularly in the United States, clinicians have been much less familiar with the diagnostic concept. Relative to cases with autism, in the field trial, cases with CDD were more likely to be mute and had greater degrees of associated mental handicap.

As noted by Volkmar and Rutter (1995), the *DSM-IV* and *ICD-10* criteria for the condition are conceptually very similar. However, for the sake of brevity, the *DSM-IV* system is somewhat less detailed and less truly operationalized. In addition, *ICD-10* includes loss of interest in the environment as a diagnostic criterion and is more explicit in indicating that the actual behavioral criteria for autism must be met. As a practical matter, it would appear that the diagnosis should probably *not* be made if the actual behavioral criteria for autism are not met. In both *DSM-IV* and *ICD-10,* the age and pattern of onset are particularly important for the definition of the condition; that is, there must be a marked regression after a period of prolonged normal development—arbitrarily set at 2 years of age. This regression is associated with the acquisition of behaviors commonly seen in autism. It is hoped that increased awareness of the condition will stimulate greater identification of cases and more research and that increasingly better guidelines for diagnosis will be developed (Kurita, 1989).

CLINICAL FEATURES

The following section provides a discussion of the essential clinical features of CDD.

Onset of Childhood Disintegrative Disorder

As noted previously, the onset of CDD is highly distinctive and an essential diagnostic feature.

Age of Onset

Development prior to the regression is relatively prolonged (several years) and should be reasonably normal; for example, the child has the capacity to speak in sentences by age 2 (WHO, 1990). Heller's (1930) impression was that onset was often between ages 3 and 5 years, and this range continues to be the case. Volkmar (1992) reported a mean age at onset of 3.4 years in his review of 77 reported cases. The issue of the time of onset is particularly relevant to distinctions of CDD from autism because it is clear that, in some cases, autism is recognized after 24 months of age (although almost invariably before age 3; Volkmar, Stier, & Cohen, 1985). For example, in the case series collected at Division TEACCH in North Carolina, over three-fourths of children with autism had been identified by their parents as having difficulties by 2 years of age (Short & Schopler, 1988). Diagnosis of autism is also sometimes delayed by the primary clinicians' lack of familiarity with the condition (Siegel, Pliner, Eschler, & Elliott, 1989).

Cases with late-onset autism (i.e., whose difficulties are apparent after age 2 but before age 3) tend to be higher functioning, and it seems likely that case detection may be delayed by the relative preservation of cognitive abilities (Volkmar & Cohen, 1989). Wohlgemuth, Kiln, Cohen, and Volkmar (1994) compared aspects of deterioration in autism and CDD. In their report, when deterioration in autism was reported, it typically involved the loss of ability to speak in single words or the failure of this ability to progress. In contrast, in CDD the previously acquired level of language was much higher, and deterioration was always observed in multiple areas, that is, not simply limited to speech.

Occasional ambiguities are sometimes observed, for example, a child with recurrent ear infections and delayed speech who then goes on to develop a more typical CDD presentation at age 3. Kurita (1988) has suggested that early development, that is, prior to age 2, may not always be perfectly normal, and there might be a history of mild delay (see also Kurita, Kita, & Miyake, 1992). Despite current diagnostic criteria, some cases of CDD might develop before age 2 although the diagnosis of such cases is problematic and may be the source of some confusion, that is, both with autism and with Rett disorder although the regression in Rett's is usually relatively early in life. Similarly, in Landau-Kleffner syndrome (of acquired aphasia with epilepsy), there may be occasional confusion with CDD or autism, but it appears that the clinical features of this condition and its course are relatively distinctive (Bishop, 1985, 1994). Further complicating the issue is the problem of potential early regression in autism, which is variably reported in 20% to 40% of cases (see Lainhart et al., 2002; Rogers & DiLalla, 1990; Siperstein & Volkmar, 2004; Volkmar et al., 1985, for a discussion). We return to the issue of differential diagnosis and current controversies later in this chapter. Data related to age of onset of autism and CDD as abstracted from the *DSM-IV* field trial data are summarized in Figure 3.1. There is a clear and significant difference in the two distributions of onset of the two conditions.

Characteristics of Onset

Several different patterns of onset of CDD have been observed. Occasionally, the condition has a relatively abrupt onset (days to weeks) but sometimes develops more gradually (weeks to months). There may be a premonitory phase prior to the marked deterioration; during this time, the child may be nonspecifically agitated, anxious, or dysphoric.

In several case series, the onset of CDD has been noted to be associated with some psychosocial stress or medical event (Evans-Jones & Rosenbloom, 1978; Kobayashi & Murata, 1998; Kurita, 1988; Volkmar, 1992). However, the significance of stressful events in syndrome pathogenesis is unclear. The group of stressors reported has been diverse, but all share the feature of being relatively common to preschool children, for example, birth of a sibling or death of a grandparent, hospitalization for elective surgery, or immunizations. It seems unlikely that such associations have etiological significance (Rutter, 1985). Davidovitch, Glick, Holtzman, Tirosh, and Safir (2000) noted that this phenomenon, that is, of attributing some etiological significance to an associated medical or psychosocial event, is common in parents of children with autism who regress as compared to those

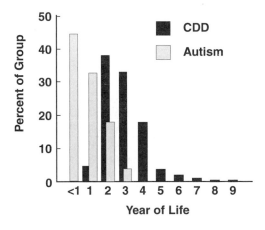

Figure 3.1 Age of onset in 160 cases with clinical diagnoses of CDD and 316 cases with clinical diagnoses of autism.

who do not. Kobayashi and Murata (1998) reported similar results in their study of children with *setback* autism.

BEHAVIORAL AND CLINICAL FEATURES

Table 3.1 provides a summary of clinical features in a number of reported cases as well as several cases seen by the authors and not previously reported.

Once CDD is established, it resembles autism in its phenomenological manifestations. Typically, social skills are markedly impaired. There is, however, some suggestion that the degree of impairment may be slightly less than that observed in autism (Kanner, 1973; Kurita, 1988; Kurita et al., 1992). Parents usually report that the loss of social interaction skill is dramatic and of great concern to them.

Given that the child typically has been speaking in full sentences, often quite well, the development of either total mutism or marked deterioration in verbal language is also very striking and frequent in CDD. Even for those individuals who subsequently regain speech, it does not typically return to previous levels of communicative ability. Rather, communicative abilities are more similar to those observed in autism with a sparsity of communicative acts, limited expressive vocabulary, and markedly impaired pragmatic skills.

Unusual behaviors including stereotyped behaviors, problems with transitions and change, and nonspecific overactivity are typically observed (Malhotra & Singh, 1993). As noted previously, various affective responses that appear inexplicable are often observed at the time of syndrome onset. As mentioned previously, *ICD-10* suggests that a general loss of interest in the environment is also usual. Dete-

TABLE 3.1   Characteristics of Disintegrative Disorder Cases

	Cases		
	1908–1975	1977–1995	1996–2004
Variable	N = 48	N = 58	N = 67
		Male/Female	
Sex ratio	35/12	49/9	53/14
		$\overline{X}$ SD	
Age at onset (years)	3.42 1.12	3.32 1.42	3.21 0.97
		$\overline{X}$ SD	
Age at follow-up	8.67 4.14	10.88 5.98	10.25 4.81
Symptoms		% of N Cases	
Speech deterioration/loss	100 47	100 58	100 54
Social disturbance	100 43	98 57	100 54
Stereotypy/resistance to change	100 38	85 54	68 54
Overactivity	100 42	77 37	59 54
Affective symptoms/anxiety	100 17	78 38	55 54
Deterioration self-help skills	94 33	82 49	66 54

Source: Adapted with permission from "Childhood Disintegrative Disorders: Issues for *DSM-IV*," by F. R. Volkmar, 1992, *Journal of Autistic Developmental Disorders 22*, 625–642; and "Childhood Disintegrative Disorder," by F. R. Volkmar, A. Klin, W. D. Marans, & D. J. Cohen, in *Autism and Pervasive Developmental Disorders,* second edition, 1997, New York: Wiley. Additional cases based on case series reported by Kurita et al., 1994; "Childhood Disintegrative Disorder: Re-Examination of the Current Concept," by S. Malhotra and N. Gupta, 2002, *European Child and Adolescent Psychiatry, 11*(3), pp. 108–114; Mourdisen et al., 2000, with additional cases supplied by C. Gillberg and F. R. Volkmar. *Note:* Results based on available data.

rioration in self-help skills, notably in toileting skills, is striking (Kurita, 1988; Volkmar, 1992) and in contrast to autism where such skills are often acquired somewhat late but are not typically dramatically lost.

EPIDEMIOLOGY

Epidemiological data on this condition are limited. This reflects both (1) the true relative and frequency of the condition apart from autism and (2) the likelihood that cases have been markedly underdiagnosed. In his review (see Chapter 2, this volume, 2002), Fombonne notes that estimates range from about 1 to 9 cases per 100,000 children. Data from case series (e.g., the series of consecutive cases reported by Volkmar & Cohen, 1989) indicate that the disorder was one-tenth as common as autism; however, these data were not based on a truly epidemiological sample. It is interesting that a rather similar rate was observed of children with autism who had regressed after age 3 (Rogers & DiLalla, 1990). A different study using a somewhat more epidemiologically based sample suggested a prevalence rate of 1 in 100,000 (Burd, Fisher, & Kerbeshian, 1989). It must be emphasized that the relative lack of familiarity of clinicians with this concept makes interpretation of the available data somewhat suspect.

Initially, it appeared that the condition was equally affecting males and females. However, more recent studies have noted a preponderance of males similar to that seen in autism (Lord, Schopler, & Revicki, 1982). It also is possible that some cases of Rett syndrome were originally misdiagnosed as having Heller's syndrome; that is, Rett's condition was described only in 1966, and the degree of the deterioration in Rett's cases may be suggestive of CDD (Burd et al., 1989; Hill & Rosenbloom, 1986; Millichap, 1987; Rett, 1966; Volkmar, 1992). In cases of CDD observed in the past 20 years, there is a high male predominance.

COURSE AND PROGNOSIS

Information on course and outcome is an important factor for evaluating the validity of psychiatric conditions. In approximately 75%

of CDD cases, the child's behavior and development deteriorate to the much lower level of functioning and remain there. On the one hand, no further deterioration occurs, but subsequent developmental gains appear to be minimal (Volkmar & Cohen, 1989). On the other hand, the marked developmental regression seems to be followed by a limited recovery; for example, a child regains the capacity to speak although usually only in a limited way (Volkmar & Cohen, 1989). Burd, Ivey, Barth, and Kerbeshian (1998) provided follow-up data on two children with CDD after 14 years; at the time of follow-up, both were severely impaired, exhibited seizure disorder, were nonverbal, and were in residential treatment. With greater awareness of the condition, more cases are being seen at younger ages and eventual longer term follow-up of these cases will be needed.

In a small number of cases, the developmental deterioration is progressive and does not plateau. This appears to be likely if some identifiable, neuropathological process can be identified. If the process is progressive, death may be the eventual result (Corbett, 1987), and there may be increased mortality if other medical conditions are present. For example, two cases reported by Mouridsen, Rich, and Isager (1998) died in association with subacute sclerosing panencephalitis (death at age 9 years) and with tuberous sclerosis (death at age 31 years). One case with whom the authors are familiar died in adolescence apparently following a seizure. In a handful of cases, the child has been observed to make a noteworthy recovery.

NEUROBIOLOGICAL FINDINGS AND ETIOLOGY

Although CDD was originally termed *dementia infantilis,* Heller's impression, and that of others, was that CDD was not associated with apparent organic disease; this was also originally Kanner's impression (1943) about autism. In both cases, this initial impression has had to be modified. It is now clear that about 25% of individuals with autism have seizures, often with an onset later than is typical in children, and another 25% have various other EEG abnormalities. In the Volkmar

(1992) review, EEGs had been obtained in 45 cases of apparent CDD. These data are supplemented by additional, more recent reports of CDD cases (Malhotra & Singh, 1993; Mouridsen, Rich, & Isager, 2000; Volkmar & Rutter, 1995). Seizures have been noted in various case reports, for example, Hill and Rosenbloom (1986; 2 of 9 cases), Volkmar and Cohen (1989; 2 of 10 cases), Malhotra and Singh (1993; 1 case), and Kurita, Osada, & Miyake (2004; 3 of 10 cases). In the Malhotra and Singh report (1993), the onset of developmental deterioration was associated with seizures. Tuchman and Rapin (1997) reported that regression in children with autism spectrum disorder occurred equally in individuals with and without seizures. Similarly, Shinnar and colleagues (2001) reported relatively high rates of seizures and autism spectrum disorder in a large cohort of children with language regression. Although these data are limited, the rates of seizure disorder and EEG abnormality appear to be similar to those observed in autism (e.g., Deykin & MacMahon, 1979; Rutter, 1985; Volkmar & Nelson, 1990) and suggest that an EEG is routinely indicated as part of clinical assessment.

CDD has been associated with various conditions such as tuberous sclerosis, neurolipidoses, metachromatic leukodystrophy, Addison-Schilder's disease, and subacute sclerosing panencephalitis along with literally hundreds of other possible causes including metabolic, infectious, genetic, immunopathic, environmental, and epileptogenic causes (see Dyken & Krawiecki, 1983; Mouridsen et al., 1998). As noted previously, the impression, for example, in *DSM-III* and *DSM-III-R* was that such associated conditions are generally found, but this view has not been supported by the data. Selected disorders associated with loss of developmental skills are listed in Table 3.2.

In Volkmar's (1992) review of published cases, specific neuropathological conditions were only occasionally identified. Late onset, for example, after age 6, of CDD appears more likely to be associated with some specific neuropathological process. Given the child's marked regression, it is now typical for parents to consult with many different specialists and for various tests, laboratory studies, and diagnostic procedures to be obtained. Other than EEG abnormalities and occasional seizure disorder, such tests usually are not particularly productive although they should be undertaken. However, usually even when very extensive medical investigations are undertaken, it is not possible to identify a specific general medical condition that accounts for the child's deterioration (Volkmar, 1992). Even if such an etiology can be identified, the diagnosis of CDD is made and the presence of the associated medical condition noted. This is similar to the approach in autism that may be associated with various general medical conditions (Rutter, Bayley, Boulton, & Le Couter, 1994).

Except for the EEG information and one study by Gillberg, Terenius, Hagberg, Witt-Engerstrom, and Eriksson (1990) on cerebrospinal fluid (CSF) beta-endorphins, there is a general absence of information regarding the neurochemistry, neuropsychology, neurophysiology, or neuroanatomy of CDD. Although the small sample sizes and differences in method complicate the interpretation of the limited available data, in general, striking differences in brain morphology and structure have not been observed (Mouridsen et al., 2000). Similarly, information on potential genetic factors is extremely limited. Mouridsen et al. (2000) reported one case of a boy with an inversion of chromosome 10 (46xy, inv(10) (p11, 21q21.2), but the child's mother also had the same anom-

TABLE 3.2   Selected Disorders Associated with Loss of Developmental Skills

Infections (HIV, measles, CMV)	Mitochondrial defects (e.g., Leigh disease)
Hypothyroidism	Subacute sclerosing panencephalitis
Neurolipidosis	Metachromatic Leukodystrophy
Addison-Schilder disease	Seizures
Angleman syndrome	Gangliosidoses
Lipofuscinosis	Aminoacidopathies (e.g., PKU)

Source: For an exhaustive list, see "Neurodegenerative Diseases of Infancy and Childhood," by P. Dyken and N. Krawiecki, 1983, "Neurodegenerative Diseases of Infancy and Childhood, *Annals of Neurology, 13,* 351–364.

aly and was a successful professional. In other reports, no unusual genetic findings have been noted (e.g., Burd et al., 1998; Russo, Perry, Kolodny, & Gillberg, 1996). This is particularly unfortunate because there is some reason to think that possibly the etiology (or etiologies) in CDD may be somewhat more homogeneous than those more typically seen in autism, that is, given the pattern of onset and the relative infrequency of such cases.

GENETICS OF CHILDHOOD DISINTEGRATIVE DISORDER

Given the relevance of genes for other PDDs, it is tempting to speculate about their role in this syndrome as well. Despite the paucity of direct evidence from population genetic or molecular studies, even the limited epidemiological and case report data do provide some basis for developing and testing hypotheses about disease etiology. In addition, the recent identification of Methyl CpG Binding Protein 2 (MECP2) as the cause of a majority of cases of classic Rett's disorder (Amir et al., 1999) may turn out to provide important clues about promising approaches to future genetic studies of CDD.

The literature reviewed in this chapter suggests that the prevalence of CDD is approximately 1 per 100,000 live births. In addition, case examples of subjects who have any family members with a PDD of any kind are unusual (Zwaigenbaum et al., 2000). Indeed, CDD appears in the majority of reported instances to be "sporadic"; that is, it seems to arise "out of nowhere" within a particular family (Malhotra & Gupta, 2002). These observations that CDD is rare and does not often cluster in families must be taken into account in formulating hypotheses about the role genes could conceivably play in the syndrome. Furthermore, Lainhart and colleagues (2002) reported that rates of the "broader autism phenotype" did not differ in parents of children with autism with and without regression, suggesting no increase in the genetic liability—at least in the autism phenotype characterized by regression.

Though the terms *familial* and *genetic* are often used interchangeably, they are not synonymous. There are multiple mechanisms that can result in the *de novo* appearance of genetic syndromes. In the realm of neuropsychiatric disorders, Down syndrome, Prader-Willi syndrome, and velocardiofacial syndrome are familiar examples of chromosomal disorders that are demonstrably genetic in etiology, but rarely pass through generations within a family. It is conceivable that CDD, as well, could be the result of rare sporadic chromosomal rearrangements. The fact that gross chromosomal abnormalities have so far not been found in cases of CDD does not rule out such a mechanism. The resolution of routine clinical cytogenetic exams in instances where a specific gene or locus is not known is on the order of 4 million base pairs of DNA. Any abnormality that involved substantially less genetic material than this could be missed, even in the face of the extensive clinical work-ups that usually accompany the diagnosis of developmental regression.

In addition, chromosomal abnormalities are certainly not the only form of sporadic mutation. The most pertinent recent example can be found in Rett's disorder. Mutations of single molecules in the DNA chain encoding the MECP2 gene account for about 80% of cases presenting with the classic phenotype (see Amir & Zoghbi, 2000, for review). These sporadic cases are most often the result of germline mutations in males (Girard et al., 2001). It is certainly possible that an analogous, rarely occurring mutation in ova or sperm could account for CDD.

The absence of reports of multigeneration CDD families suggests that it is unlikely that the syndrome is inherited in dominant fashion. Such disorders are transferred from one generation to the next, with only one copy of a defective gene necessary to cause the condition. While not everyone who inherits such a dominant gene develops the full-blown disorder, nonetheless, we would expect to see successive generations in a family having some evidence of the syndrome. To date, no such families have been reported. Alternative forms of Mendelian inheritance might better fit the available data but are not entirely satisfactory explanations either. Recessive disorders, in which one defective gene must be inherited from each of two parents, can often appear to be sporadic, particularly if the offending versions of a gene are found rarely in a population. In this circumstance, multiple generations in a family would be unaffected until the chance mating of two mutation carriers. If this were the case, however, the risk of having the disorder in a sibling of a child with CDD would be on the order of 25%. The fact that cases of CDD are not commonly reported among first-degree relatives would argue against this hypothesis but would not rule it out. A paucity of familial cases could also result if parents who have one child with CDD tend to stop having additional children. A similar explanation would have to be invoked if it was hypothesized that CDD was a rare X-linked disorder. The observed male preponderance of 4:1 (Malhotra & Gupta, 2002; Volkmar, 1992; Volkmar & Rutter, 1995) could be accounted for if girls were provided a measure of protection by a second X chromosome. Again, however, the recurrence risk for male offspring in an affected family would be on the order of 50%, far higher than what is observed in the available literature.

Data that are directly relevant to this issue are limited. In their study of the broader autistic phenotype, Lainhart and colleagues (2002) reported that parents of probands with regression and nonregressive autism exhibited similar rates of the broader autism phenotype. Zwaigenbaum and colleagues (2000) reported on two half brothers, one with autism and the other with CDD.

Finally, in the absence of any other compelling explanation, it could be hypothesized that CDD is a complex disorder resulting from either the chance accumulation of a number of rare genetic events, from some unknown environmental precipitant that alone or in concert with a genetic liability results in the apparently sporadic emergence of the syndrome, or from a novel genetic mechanism.

Lessons from Rett Syndrome

Dramatic advances in the understanding of the genetic basis of Rett's disorder may turn out to have considerable relevance for the study of CDD. While preliminary screenings of the MECP2 gene in CDD cases have not identified causative mutations (M. State and J. Greally, personal communication, 2004), more general lessons may be derived from the study of Rett's disorder. For instance, the strongly held notion that Rett's disorder was a rela-

tively homogeneous clinical entity confined to girls appears to have been mistaken. In reality, the phenotype can vary dramatically in females from the classic syndrome described in *DSM-IV* to mild learning disabilities. Moreover, a wide variety of phenotypes have now also been identified in males (Amir & Zoghbi, 2000; Couvert et al., 2001; Hammer, Dorrani, Dragich, Kudo, & Schanen, 2002; Kleefstra et al., 2002; Meloni et al., 2000). The current understanding of CDD could similarly turn out to be incomplete when and if a genetic contribution is identified, either because the manifestations of a CDD mutation could be quite variable or because there could be gender-related difference in how such an abnormality is expressed.

Recent studies of Rett's disorder have also called into question the notion of homogeneity from a genetic as well as clinical perspective. At present, only about 80% of patients with the classic Rett's disorder phenotype have been confirmed to have a MECP2 mutation. Familial or atypical cases have proven even more difficult to characterize. These findings could be the result of an incomplete understanding of the genomic structure and regulation of MECP2. However, it may be that there are other Rett's disorder loci apart from MECP2. The same could well apply to CDD. More than one genetic abnormality might result in similar clinical presentations, so any single mechanism might prove an unsatisfactory solution to the problem of understanding the transmission of CDD.

Finally, the identification of MECP2 as a major cause of developmental regression in girls came about in large part because of the identification of unusual families among the much more common sporadic cases of Rett's disorder (Amir et al., 1999). The search for "outlier" examples of an already unusual disorder could prove to be a similarly profitable strategy for studying the genetics of CDD.

Future Genetic Studies of Childhood Disintegrative Disorder

The combination of being a rare disorder and the absence of clear familial aggregation of CDD cases certainly presents obstacles to the study of the genetics of the disorder. Nonetheless, rapid advances in genetic technologies hold promise for the study of CDD. The advent of high-resolution chromosomal screening techniques, the development of extremely sensitive proteomic technologies, and the exponential growth in the ability to screen the genome for mutations will allow investigators to test hypotheses about the transmission of this disorder. As importantly, more concerted clinical and epidemiological research can help further refine our understanding of the nature of this disorder and provide a more solid foundation for future investigations of the potential role that genes play in the etiology of CDD.

Other Neurobiological Factors

Despite extensive medical evaluations, the *yield* in terms of discovering clearly potentially causative conditions for the developmental regression is surprisingly low. Russo and colleagues (1996) have speculated that a combination of genetic factors and environmental stress might be involved and, further, that a specific immune response might be involved. Shinnar and colleagues (2001) similarly speculate that the widespread parental report of associated stressful events with the onset of the condition might have some etiological significance. Supporting data for such hypotheses are limited. In general, the recent presumption has been that the stresses reported (e.g., birth of a sibling) are not highly unusual for children in this age group.

While the cause or causes of CDD remain unknown, the course of the disorder, the association with EEG abnormalities and seizure disorder, and the occasional association with known medical conditions suggest that neurobiological factors are likely central in pathogenesis. As with autism, it is possible that multiple pathogenic pathways may act to produce the condition, and the absence of clearly identified neuropathological mechanisms likely reflects more on current research techniques than the absence of such factors (Rivinus, Jamison, & Graham, 1975; Wilson, 1974). Despite the progress in our understanding of the central nervous system, much remains to be discovered. The absence of specific neurobiological mechanisms is probably more a reflection on the present state of science than the absence itself.

VALIDITY OF CHILDHOOD DISINTEGRATIVE DISORDER AS A DIAGNOSTIC CATEGORY

Diagnostic categories exist for different reasons and purposes (see Rutter, 2003; Rutter & Taylor, 2002, for discussion). There are understandable and legitimate tensions between those who wish to have broader diagnostic categories—for example, to ensure service provision—and those who advocate for more narrowly defined categories—for example, for research purposes (see Chapter 1, this volume). With regard to CDD, these issues and tensions also exist. The *validity* of the category has been the object of debate. In this section, we summarize some of the information on validity of the condition with respect to autism and other disorders.

Childhood Disintegrative Disorder and Autism

Although Kanner's original (1943) impression was that autism was congenital, subsequent work has consistently shown that in a minority of cases parents report some period of months, or even a year or more, of normal development before symptoms of autism are recognized (Kolvin, 1971; Kurita, 1985; Short & Schopler, 1988; Siperstein & Volkmar, 2004; Volkmar et al., 1985, 1988). The cases, sometimes referred to as *late-onset* autism or, particularly in the Japanese literature, as *setback* autism, have not, unfortunately, been commonly studied, and there is some potential for confusion (or even for overlap) with CDD. That is, although, by definition, CDD has its onset after age 2, with normal previous development, it is possible that this is an artificial distinction, and some cases of onset earlier than age 2 have indeed been reported in the literature (see Figure 3.1). Several other issues further complicate this problem. What is reported as "regression" often seems to be more adequately characterized as developmental stagnation; for example, the child says one or two words and then speech and subsequent development fail to progress normally. This state of affairs is rather different from that reported in prototypical development of CDD where a marked loss of functioning in multiple areas occurs. In a recent study, Siperstein and Volkmar (2004) noted that language loss and social skills loss are often prominent in autism when parents report loss of skills. Their report also notes that, when regression is strictly defined (e.g., based not only on parental report of regression but also of developmental milestones), demonstrable regression was relatively uncommon. In their follow-up study of nearly 200 cases of autism who had lost skills, Kobayashi and Murata (1998) reported that there were higher rates of seizure disorder and lower language levels associated with reported language setback. Davidovitch and colleagues (2000) examined differences between children with autism who were reported to have regressed and those who did not regress; they found little difference between the groups. Language regression is not as commonly reported among children with overall developmental delay (Shinnar et al., 2001).

In a recent study, Kurita et al. (2004) evaluated the clinical validity of CDD as defined by *DSM-IV* in 10 children with the condition who were compared to a larger group of age- and gender-matched children with *DSM-IV* autistic disorder with speech loss. Compared to the children with autism who had exhibited speech loss, those with CDD exhibited higher levels of anxiety/dysphoria as well as higher levels of stereotyped behavior. The CDD group also had a higher rate of seizure disorder, and there was a suggestion of differences in the profiles on psychological testing. Although differences in levels of retardation were not observed, the authors pointed out that the relative youth of the group (mean age of 8.2 years for the CDD cases) limited the value of such a comparison.

Childhood Disintegrative Disorder and Other Disorders

As noted previously, another area of controversy has centered on the view of CDD as reflecting a neuropathological process. There is little disagreement that some brain-based mechanism is responsible for the condition; most of the debate has centered either on the idea that CDD is commonly associated with one or more specific and identifiable other medical conditions. As noted earlier, a thorough search for any associated neurological or other general medical condition is clearly indicated in CDD although, somewhat surprisingly, even extensive evaluations often fail to reveal an associated medical condition. In their study of dementia using a large cohort of cases in Australia, Nunn, Williams, and Ouvrier (2002) estimated the prevalence of dementia in childhood to be 5.6 per 100,000 cases. Of the children identified, in 21% of cases a specific etiology could not be determined; they suggest the general utility of a broad conceptualization of childhood dementia.

In addition to the various metabolic and genetic disorders that can cause deterioration, the development of an autistic-like clinical picture can follow central nervous system infection or other insult (Weir & Salisbury, 1980). Occasionally, epileptic conditions may also mimic autism or CDD (Deonna, Ziegler, Malin-Ingvar, Ansermet, & Roulet, 1995). This issue has been most controversial with respect to the syndrome of acquired aphasia with epilepsy (Landau-Kleffner syndrome) in which aphasia develops in association with multifocal spike and spike/wave discharges on EEG (Beaumanoir, 1992). This syndrome is relatively well described but remains poorly understood, and, in general, the impression is of an aphasia rather than a PDD (this condition is included in *ICD-10* as a developmental language disorder but is not recognized in *DSM-IV*). Nonverbal abilities tend to be spared, and there can be considerable recovery (Bishop, 1985). In contrast to CDD where later onset of the disorder is usually associated with a worse prognosis, later onset in Landau-Kleffner is associated with better outcome (Bishop, 1985). Other epileptic conditions may also mimic autism or CDD (Deonna et al., 1995).

There seems little disagreement that, once established, CDD resembles autism in terms of clinical features and course (Militerni, Bravaccio, & D'Anuono, 1997; Volkmar & Cohen, 1989). Hendry (2000), however, has questioned the utility of CDD as a diagnostic concept, noting the strong overlap in symptoms with autism. Hendry rightly notes the limitations of the available data, which are very small as compared, for example, to that on autism. She also raises several relevant questions about the difficulties in reliance on parental report and so forth. In contrast, Volk-mar and Rutter (1995), in their review of the results of CDD in the *DSM-IV* field trial, came to a different conclusion, observing major differences both in the dramatic clinical presentation and course. As they noted, the major rationale for including CDD as a recognized diagnostic entity primarily related to its potential for clarifying basic mechanisms of pathogenesis.

DIFFERENTIAL DIAGNOSIS

The differential diagnosis of CDD includes the other PDDs and other conditions. Because of the very distinctive pattern of onset, historical information is critical in making the diagnosis.

Autism

Once established, CDD shares the same essential features on current clinical examination. Thus, historical information is particularly important in distinguishing the two conditions. In about 75% of cases of autism, parents do not report an unequivocally normal period of development; usually social development is markedly delayed and deviant, and language fails to develop in expected ways. In a smaller group of cases, the parents report either that the child seemed to develop normally, usually up to about 18 to 24 months of age, or that single words developed but the child did not go on to develop more complex speech; such cases should not be diagnosed with CDD. It is not uncommon for the presenting complaint in autism to center on language loss and then for a careful history to establish earlier preexisting abnormalities, for example, in terms of unusual environmental sensitivities or responses (e.g., Stein, Dixon, & Cowan, 2000). Complexities may arise if historical information is absent, the report of a truly prolonged period of normal development is questionable, the clinician fails to obtain an adequate history, or the autistic child is somewhat higher functioning. In the last case, it is possible that early language seems to develop in a near normal fashion, but the parent becomes concerned as more complex social-communicative difficulties become apparent. Careful history will usually reveal that no actual period of regression of the type seen in CDD occurred. The use of materials such as baby books, home videotapes, or movies may be helpful.

In CDD, it is essential that the early development be unequivocally normal with the child able to speak in sentences prior to the onset of the condition. If such a history cannot be documented, a diagnosis of CDD should not be made; in such cases, a diagnosis of atypical autism may be most appropriate. There are also the exceptions that tend to prove the rule, for example, children who were being reared in a bilingual context and whose language was slightly delayed but who otherwise appeared to be developing appropriately prior to the onset of the regression.

Rett's Disorder

Rett's disorder (see Chapter 5, this volume) is occasionally confused with CDD; this reflects the fact that some degree of regression is observed in both conditions and that the more autistic-like phase of Rett's disorder may be most prominent in the preschool years, that is, when diagnostic evaluations are first conducted. For individuals familiar with both conditions, misdiagnosis is relatively unlikely given the very different histories and clinical features of the conditions.

Asperger Syndrome

In this condition, early language and cognitive development may seem to have been normal or near normal. Sometimes parents become aware of the social and other difficulties as the child enters a preschool program. This may, incorrectly, lead some care providers to suspect that there was a marked regression in functioning. However, in Asperger, cognitive functions are relatively preserved, and the truly marked and severe regression of the kind seen in CDD is absent.

Childhood Schizophrenia

In rare instances, there may be confusion of CDD with other psychiatric disorders such as schizophrenia. Although very early onset schizophrenia (VERS) is very rare, the degree of regression and deterioration may suggest

CDD (see Werry, 1992). However, usually the characteristic findings of schizophrenia on clinical examination will clarify the diagnosis.

Landau-Kleffner Syndrome

The syndrome of acquired aphasia with epilepsy (Landau-Kleffner syndrome) has its onset in children and is characterized by acquired aphasia in association with multifocal spike and spike/wave discharges on EEG (Beaumanoir, 1992). This syndrome is relatively well described but remains poorly understood (S. Wilson, Djukic, Shinnar, Dharmani, & Rapin, 2003). Children with the Landau-Kleffner syndrome usually exhibit marked interest in communication using nonverbal modalities, and typically the regression is largely confined to the area of language. Nonverbal abilities tend to be spared, and there is often considerable recovery (Bishop, 1985). In contrast to CDD where later onset of the disorder is usually associated with a worse prognosis, later onset in Landau-Kleffner is associated with better outcome (Bishop, 1985). Other epileptic conditions may also mimic autism or CDD (Deonna et al., 1995), and, as noted previously, a history of language regression should prompt a careful assessment for possible seizure disorder (Shinnar et al., 2001).

Other Associated Medical Conditions

As noted earlier, a thorough search for any associated neurological or other general medical condition is indicated in CDD. Specific findings on examination or in the history may help guide the process of evaluation. If any such condition is identified, it is then specified on Axis III. Disorders with onset after some period of normal development include gangliosidosis, metachromatic leukodystrophy, Niemman-Pick disease, and so forth. Developmental deterioration and the development of an autistic-like clinical picture can follow central nervous system infection or other insult (Weir & Salisbury, 1980). Rarely clinically significant regression occur in the context of overt seizures (Tuchman & Rapin, 1997; S. Wilson et al., 2003).

EVALUATION AND MANAGEMENT

Assessment of the child with CDD may be most effectively accomplished by a group of professionals who work together as a team or in close collaboration with one another. Referrals usually come from primary care providers although occasionally mental health workers, educators, and others may question a diagnosis, for example, of autism, because of some features of the case that they know to be unusual. Given the potential for multiple assessments, it is important that the professionals involved in the child's care work effectively to avoid fragmentation and duplication of effort. Various professionals may be involved, for example, child psychiatrists, psychologists, speech pathologists, pediatric neurologists, occupational and physical therapists, and others. It is appropriate and desirable to engage parents actively in the assessment process.

Given the unusual history of the onset of CDD, a careful history is particularly critical. This history should include information related to the pregnancy and neonatal period, early developmental history, as well as medical and family history. As noted previously, the examination of videotapes may clearly document the child's early normal development. Information on the pattern and age of onset of the condition is central.

Although extensive medical investigations usually fail to reveal the presence of another specific medical condition or specific neurodegenerative disorder, a careful search for such conditions is indicated. This is particularly true if aspects of the case are unusual; for example, if the onset is rather later (after age 6), or if the deterioration is progressive and does not plateau. Initial consultation with a pediatric neurologist is always indicated. Given the severity of these conditions, an EEG and CT or MRI scan are also usually obtained.

Tests of communication and cognitive ability should be chosen with consideration of the child's current levels of functioning to obtain estimates of functioning useful in documenting subsequent developmental change as well as for educational and rehabilitative programming. The use of developmental and other tests typically given to younger children may be appropriate, for example (Bayley, 1969; Dunst, 1980; Uzgiris & Hunt, 1975). For somewhat higher functioning but nonverbal children, the Leiter International Performance Scale (Leiter, 1948) may be useful. As with children with autism, modifications in usual assessment procedures may have to be made. Communication scales that may be appropriate include the Receptive-Expressive Emergent Language Scale (REEL; Bzoch & League, 1971); the Sequenced Inventory of Communicative Development (SICD; Hedrick, Prather & Tobin, 1975), and the Reynell Developmental Language Scales (Reynell & Gruber, 1990).

The Vineland Adaptive Behavior Scales (expanded form; Sparrow, Balla, & Cicchetti, 1984) should be administered to document levels of adaptive behaviors. This instrument provides useful information both for diagnostic and programming purposes.

As part of the psychiatric or psychological assessment, the child should be observed in more and less structured activities, for example, during developmental assessment or while interacting with parents. As part of the history, the examiner should specifically inquire about the child's current and past social skills (e.g., deferential attachments, interest in parents and peers, use of gaze), communication (receptive and expressive, articulation problems, typical utterances, level of language organization prior to the regression, unusual features such as echolalia, and nature of language loss), and responses to the environment and motor behaviors (e.g., self-stimulatory behaviors, difficulties with change or transitions). The acquisition and any loss of adaptive skills, for example, toileting, self-care, or related skills, should also be reviewed. Observation of the child's play is helpful, for example, in documenting levels of language, cognitive, and social organization and in observing gross and fine motor skills. Problematic or unusual behaviors relevant to the diagnosis or likely to present obstacles for intervention should be noted.

Treatment of CDD is essentially the same as for autism. Methods such as behavior modification and special education should be used to help encourage the acquisition, or reacquisition, of basic adaptive skills. There are no

specific pharmacological treatments for CDD although it is likely that many of the same agents used with some benefit in autism will sometimes also be helpful. The use of any pharmacological agent should include a careful assessment of potential risks and benefits.

The families (parents, sibs, and extended family members) of patients should be supported. This includes provision of appropriate information about the condition, helping families make use of available local and other resources, and helping family members receive mutual support, for example, through support groups. Given that the prognosis of CDD appears, in general, to be somewhat worse than that of autism, the stresses experienced by parents and siblings may also be greater.

CASE REPORT

Donald was the youngest of three children born to college-educated parents. The pregnancy, labor and delivery, and early development were unremarkable. He appeared to be a normally active and sociable baby. He was smiling at 6 weeks, sitting at 7 months, crawling at 9 months, and walking without support at 15 months. He had several ear infections in the first year of life but said his first words by 12 months and was speaking in full sentences shortly after his second birthday. Videotapes provided by his parents confirmed his apparently normal developmental status.

Shortly after his third birthday, Donald's parents became concerned about his development as, over the course of several weeks, he lost both receptive and expressive language and became progressively less interested in interaction and the inanimate environment. He developed various self-stimulatory behaviors and lost the ability to use the toilet independently.

No apparent reason for the regression was identified. Extensive medical investigations were undertaken. Although he was noted to have a borderline abnormal EEG, no specific medical condition that might account for his developmental deterioration was identified. Subsequent evaluations at other centers and by other specialists (including pediatric neurologists and geneticists) similarly failed to identify such a condition. There was no family history of similar problems or developmental difficulties in members of the immediate or extended family.

Although he had previously been in a regular nursery school setting, his behavior and developmental deterioration warranted his placement in a special educational setting. At 4 years old, comprehensive evaluation revealed that his cognitive skills were at about the 18-month level with language and social skills at an even lower level. Over the course of many months, some, although highly limited, expressive language skills returned as he was able to say an occasional single word. His social unrelatedness, lack of interest in the environment, and unusual behaviors continued. At the time of follow-up, at age 16, he continues to be severely impaired.

CONCLUSION

Although described nearly 100 years ago, CDD remains infrequently reported and very uncommonly studied. As noted by Rapin (in press), the classification of children who develop an autistic-like condition after several years of normal development remains very poorly understood. It is clear that, once the condition is established, it behaviorally is very similar to autism. The condition differs from autism in the nature and pattern of its onset and in course and certain clinical features. While it appears very likely that some underlying neurobiological basis, or bases, of the condition exists, precise etiological mechanisms have not been identified. Past its obvious importance for affected children and their families, studies of such mechanisms may be important in providing a better understanding of mechanisms of syndrome pathogenesis that may have relevance to autism (Darby & Clark, 1992).

Cross-References

Issues of diagnosis and classification are discussed in Chapters 1 through 7; medical and neurological conditions potentially relevant to CDD are reviewed in Chapters 16, 18, 19, and 20.

REFERENCES

American Psychiatric Association. (1980). *Diagnostic and statistical manual of mental disorders* (3rd ed.). Washington, DC: Author.

American Psychiatric Association. (1987). *Diagnostic and statistical manual of mental disorders* (3rd ed., rev.). Washington, DC: Author.

American Psychiatric Association. (1994). *Diagnostic and statistical manual of mental disorders* (4th ed.). Washington, DC: Author.

Amir, R. E., Van den Veyver, I. B., Wan, M., Tran, C. Q., Francke, U., & Zoghbi, H. Y. (1999). Rett syndrome is caused by mutations in X-linked MECP2, encoding methyl-CpG-binding protein 2 [see comment]. *Nature Genetics, 23*(2), 185–188.

Amir, R. E., & Zoghbi, H. Y. (2000). Rett syndrome: Methyl-CpG-binding protein 2 mutations and phenotype-genotype correlations. *American Journal of Medical Genetics, 97*(2), 147–152.

Bayley, N. (1969). *Bayley scales of infant development.* New York: Psychological Corporation.

Beaumanoir, A. (1992). The Landau-Kleffner syndrome. In J. Roger, M. Bureau, C. Dravet, F. E. Dreifuss, A. Perret, & P. Wolf (Eds.), *Epileptic seizures in infancy, childhood, and adolescence* (2nd ed., pp. 231–243). London: John Libbey.

Bishop, D. V. M. (1985). Age on onset and outcome in "acquired aphasia with convulsive disorder" (Landau-Kleffner syndrome). *Developmental Medicine and Child Neurology, 27,* 705–712.

Bishop, D. V. M. (1994). Developmental disorders of speech and language. In M. Rutter, E. Taylor, & L. Hersov (Eds.), *Child and adolescent psychiatry: Modern approaches* (3rd ed., pp. 546–568). London: Blackwell.

Burd, L., Fisher, W., & Kerbeshian, J. (1988). Childhood onset pervasive developmental disorder. *Journal of Child Psychology and Psychiatry and Allied Disciplines, 29*(2), 155–163.

Burd, L., Fisher, W., & Kerbeshian, J. (1989). Pervasive disintegrative disorder: Are Rett syndrome and Heller dementia infantilis subtypes? *Developmental Medicine and Child Neurology, 31*(5), 609–616.

Burd, L., Ivey, M., Barth, A., & Kerbeshian, J. (1998). Two males with childhood disintegrative disorder: A prospective 14-year outcome study. *Developmental Medicine and Child Neurology, 40*(10), 702–707.

Bzoch, K., & League, R. (1971). *Receptive Expressive Emergent Language Scale.* Gainesville, FL: Language Educational Division, Computer Management Corporation.

Corbett, J. (1987). Development, disintegration and dementia. *Journal of Mental Deficiency Research, 31*(4), 349–356.

Couvert, P., Bienvenu, T., Aquaviva, C., Poirier, K., Moraine, C., Gendrot, C., et al. (2001). MECP2 is highly mutated in X-linked mental retardation. *Human Molecular Genetics, 10,* 941–946.

Darby, J. K., & Clark, L. (1992). Autism syndrome as a final common pathway of behavioral expression for many organic disorders. *American Journal of Psychiatry, 149*(1), 146.

Davidovitch, M., Glick, L., Holtzman, G., Tirosh, E., & Safir, M. P. (2000). Developmental regression in autism: Maternal perception. *Journal of Autism and Developmental Disorders, 30*(2), 113–119.

Deonna, T., Ziegler, A., Malin-Ingvar, M., Ansermet, F., & Roulet, E. (1995). Reversible behavioral autistic-like regression: A manifestation of a special (new?) epileptic syndrome in a 28 month old child: A 2 year longitudinal study. *Neurocase, 1,* 1–9.

Deykin, E. Y., & MacMahon, B. (1979). The incidence of seizures among children with autistic symptoms. *American Journal of Psychiatry, 136*(10), 1310–1312.

Dunst, C. (1980). *A clinical and educational manual for use with the Uzgiris and Hunt Scales* Baltimore: University Park Press.

Dyken, P., & Krawiecki, N. (1983). Neurodegenerative diseases of infancy and childhood. *Annals of Neurology, 13,* 351–364.

Evans-Jones, L. G., & Rosenbloom, L. (1978, August). Disintegrative psychosis in childhood. *Developmental Medicine and Child Neurology, 20*(4), 462–470.

Fombonne, E. (2002). Prevalence of childhood disintegrative disorder. *Autism: Journal of Research and Practice, 6*(2), 149–157.

Gillberg, C., Terenius, L., Hagberg, B., Witt-Engerstrom, I., & Eriksson, I. (1990). CSF beta-endorphins in childhood neuropsychiatric disorders. *Brain Development, 12*(1), 88–92.

Girard, M., Couvert, P., Carrie, A., Tardieu, M., Chelly, J., Beldjord, C., et al. (2001). Parental origin of de novo MECP2 mutations in Rett syndrome. *European Journal of Human Genetics, 9*(3), 231–236.

Hammer, S., Dorrani, N., Dragich, J., Kudo, S., & Schanen, C. (2002). The phenotypic consequences of MECP2 mutations extend beyond Rett syndrome. *Mental Retardation and Developmental Disabilities Research Reviews, 8,* 94–98.

Hedrick, D., Prather, F., & Tobin A. (1975). *Sequenced inventory of communicative development.* Seattle: University of Washington Press.

Heller, T. (1908). Dementia infantilis. *Zeitschrift fur die Erforschung und Behandlung des Jugenlichen Schwachsinns, 2,* 141–165.

Heller, T. (1930). Uber Dementia infantilis. *Zeitschrift fur Kinderforschung, 37,* 661–667.

Hendry, S. N. (2000). Childhood disintegrative disorder. *Clinical Psychology Review, 20,* 77–90.

Hill, A. E., & Rosenbloom, L. (1986). Disintegrative psychosis of childhood: Teenage follow-up. *Developmental Medicine and Child Neurology, 28*(1), 34–40.

Kanner, L. (1943). Autistic disturbances of affective contact. *Nervous Child, 2,* 217–250.

Kleefstra, T., Yntema, H. G., Oudakker, A. R., de Vries, B. B., van Bokhoven, H., Hamel, B. C., et al. (2002). Localization of a gene for nonspecific X-linked mental retardation (MRX 76) to Xp22.3-Xp21.3. *American Journal of Medical Genetics, 110,* 410–411.

Kobayashi, R., & Murata, T. (1998). Setback phenomenon in autism and long term prognosis. *Archives Psychiatrica Scandinavia, 98,* 296–303.

Kolvin, I. (1971). Studies in childhood psychoses: I. Diagnostic criteria and classification. *British Journal of Psychiatry, 118,* 381–384.

Kurita, H. (1985). Infantile autism with speech loss before the age of thirty months. *Journal of the American Academy of Child Psychiatry, 24*(2), 191–196.

Kurita, H. (1988). The concept and nosology of Heller's syndrome: Review of articles and report of two cases. *Japanese Journal of Psychiatry and Neurology, 42,* 785–793.

Kurita, H. (1989). Heller's syndrome as a type of pervasive developmental disorder. *Journal of Mental Health, 35,* 71–81.

Kurita, H., Kita, M., & Miyake, Y. (1992). A comparative study of development and symptoms among disintegrative psychosis and infantile autism with and without speech loss. *Journal of Autism and Developmental Disorders, 22*(2), 175–188.

Kurita, H., Osada, H., & Miyake, Y. (2004). External validity of childhood disintegrative disorder in comparison with autistic disorder. *Journal of Autism and Developmental Disorders, 34,* 355–362.

Lainhart, J. E., Ozonoff, S., Coon, H., Krasny, L., Dinh, E., Nie, J., et al. (2002). Autism, regression, and the broader autism phenotype. *American Journal of Medical Genetics, 113,* 231–237.

Leiter, R. G. (1948). *Leiter International Performance Scale.* Chicago: Stoelting.

Lord, C., Schopler, E., & Revicki, D. (1982). Sex differences in autism. *Journal of Autism and Developmental Disorders, 12,* 317–330.

Makita, K. (1966). The age of onset of childhood schizophrenia. *Folia Psychiatric Neurologica Japonica, 20,* 111–112.

Malhotra, S., & Gupta, N. (1999). Childhood disintegrative disorder. *Journal of Autism and Developmental Disorders, 29,* 491–498.

Malhotra, S., & Gupta, N. (2002). Childhood disintegrative disorder: Re-examination of the current concept. *European Child and Adolescent Psychiatry, 11*(3), 108–114.

Malhotra, S., & Singh, S. (1993). Disintegrative psychosis of childhood: An appraisal and case study. *Acta Paedopsychiatrica, 56,* 37–40.

Meloni, I., Bruttini, M., Longo, I., Mari, F., Rizzolio, F., D'Adamo, P., et al. (2000). A mutation in the Rett syndrome gene, MECP2, causes X-linked mental retardation and progressive spasticity in males. *American Journal of Human Genetics, 67,* 982–985.

Militerni, R., Bravaccio, C., & D'Anuono, P. (1997). Childhood disintegrative disorder: Review of cases and pathological consideration. *Developmental Brain Dysfunction, 10,* 67–74.

Millichap, J. G. (1987). Rett's syndrome: A variant of Heller's dementia? [Letter]. *Lancet, 1,* 440.

Mouridsen, S. E., Rich, B., & Isager, T. (1998). Validity of childhood disintegrative psychosis. General findings of a long-term follow-up study. *British Journal of Psychiatry, 172,* 263–267.

Mouridsen, S. E., Rich, B., & Isager, T. (2000). A comparative study of genetic and neurobiological findings in disintegrative psychosis and infantile autism. *Psychiatry and Clinical Neurosciences, 54*(4), 441–446.

Nunn, K., Williams, K., & Ouvrier, R. (2002). The Australian Childhood Dementia Study. *European Child and Adolescent Psychiatry, 11,* 63–70.

Rett, A. (1966). Uber ein eigenartiges hirntophisces Syndroem bei hyperammonie im Kindersalter. *Wein Medizinische Wochenschrift, 118,* 723–726.

Reynell, J., & Gruber, C. (1990). *Reynell Developmental Language Scales—US Edition.* Los Angeles, CA: Western Psychological Services.

Rivinus, T. M., Jamison, D. L., & Graham, P. J. (1975). Childhood organic neurological disease presenting as a psychiatric disorder. *Archives of Disease in Childhood, 50,* 115–119.

Rogers, S. J., & DiLalla, D. L. (1990). Age of symptom onset in young children with Pervasive Developmental Disorder. *Journal of the American Academy of Child and Adolescent Psychiatry, 29,* 863–872.

Russo, M., Perry, R., Kolodny, E., & Gillberg, C. (1996). Heller syndrome in a pre-school boy. Proposed medical evaluation and hypothesized pathogenesis. *European Child and Adolescent Psychiatry, 5*(3), 172–177.

Rutter, M. (1972, October). Childhood schizophrenia reconsidered. *Journal of Autism and Childhood Schizophrenia, 2*(4), 315–337.

Rutter, M. (1985). Infantile autism and other pervasive developmental disorders. In M. Rutter & L. Hersov (Eds.), *Child and adolescent psychiatry—Modern approaches* (pp. 545–566). London: Blackwell.

Rutter, M. (2003). Categories, Dimensions, and the Mental Health of Children and Adolescents. *Annals of the New York Academy of Science, 1008,* 1–12.

Rutter, M., Bailey, A., Bolton, P., & Le Couter, A. (1994). Autism and known medical conditions: Myth and substance. *Journal of Child Psychology and Psychiatry and Allied Disciplines, 35*(2), 311–322.

Rutter, M., & Taylor, E. (2002). Classification: Conceptual issues and substantive findings. In E. Taylor & M. Rutter (Eds.), *Child and adolescent psychiatry* (4th ed., pp. 3–17). Oxford, UK: Blackwell Publishing.

Shinnar, S., Rapin, I., Arnold, S., Tuchman, R., Shulman, L., Ballabasn-Gil, K., et al. (2001). Language regression in childhood. *Pediatric Neurology, 24,* 183–194.

Short, A., & Schopler, E. (1988). Factors relating to age of onset in autism. *Journal of Autism and Developmental Disorders, 18,* 207–216.

Siegel, B., Pliner, C., Eschler, J., & Elliott, G. R. (1989). How children with autism are diagnosed: Difficulties in identification of children with multiple developmental delays. *Developmental and Behavioral Pediatrics, 9,* 199–204.

Sparrow, S. S., Balla, D., & Cicchetti, D. V. (1984). *Vineland adaptive behavior scales (Survey Form).* Circle Pines, MN: American Guidance Service.

Stein, M. T., Dixon, S. D., & Cowan, C. (2000). A two-year-old boy with language regression and unusual social interactions. *Journal of Developmental and Behavioral Pediatrics, 21*(4), 285–290.

Tuchman, R. F., & Rapin, I. (1997). Regression in pervasive developmental disorders: Seizures and epileptiform electroencephalogram corre-lates. *Pediatrics, 99*(4), 560–566.

Uzgiris, I. C., & Hunt, J. M. (1975). *Assessment in infancy: Ordinal scales of psychological development.* Urbana: University of Illinois Press.

Volkmar, F. R. (1987). Diagnostic issues in the pervasive developmental disorders. *Journal of Child Psychology and Psychiatry and Allied Disciplines, 28*(3), 365–369.

Volkmar, F. R. (1992). Childhood disintegrative disorder: Issues for *DSM-IV*. *Journal of Autism Developmental Disorders, 22,* 625–642.

Volkmar, F. R. (1996). The "disintegrative" disorders. In F. Volkmar (Ed.), *Childhood psychoses and pervasive developmental disorders* (pp. 223–248). Washington, DC: American Psychiatric Association Press.

Volkmar, F. R., & Cohen, D. J. (1989). Disintegrative disorder or "late onset" autism. *Journal of Child Psychology and Psychiatry and Allied Disciplines, 30*(5), 717–724.

Volkmar, F. R., Cohen, D. J., Hoshino, Y., Rende, R. D., & Paul, R. (1988). Phenomenology and classification of the childhood psychoses. *Psychological Medicine, 18*(1), 191–201.

Volkmar, F. R., Klin, A., Marans, W. D., & Cohen, D. J. (1997). Childhood disintegrative disorder. In D. J. Cohen & F. R. Volkmar (Eds.), *Autism and pervasive developmental disorders* (2nd ed., pp. 47–59). New York: Wiley.

Volkmar, F. R., Klin, A., Siegel, B., Szatmari, P., Lord, C., Campbell, M., et al. (1994). Field trial for autistic disorder in *DSM-IV*. *American Journal of Psychiatry, 151*(9), 1361–1367.

Volkmar, F. R., & Rutter M. (1995). Childhood disintegrative disorder: Results of the *DSM-IV* autism field trial. *Journal of the American Academy of Child and Adolescent Psychiatry, 34,* 1092–1095.

Volkmar, F. R., Stier, D. M., & Cohen, D. J. (1985). Age of recognition of pervasive developmental

disorder. *American Journal of Psychiatry, 142*(12), 1450–1452.

Weir, K., & Salisbury, D. M. (1980). Acute onset of autistic features following brain damage in a ten-year-old. *Journal of Autism and Developmental Disorders, 10*(2), 185–191.

Werry, J. S. (1992). Child and adolescent (early onset) schizophrenia: A review in light of *DSM-III-R*. *Journal of Autism and Developmental Disorders, 22*(4), 601–624.

Wilson, J. (1974). Investigation of degenerative disease of the central nervous system. *Archives of Disease in Childhood, 47,* 163–170.

Wilson, S., Djukic, A., Shinnar, S., Dharmani, C., & Rapin, I. (2003). Clinical characteristics of language regression in children. *Developmental Medicine and Child Neurology, 45*(8), 508–514.

Wohlgemuth, D., Kiln, A., Cohen, D. J., & Volkmar, F. R. (1994, October). Childhood disintegrative disorder: Diagnosis and phenomenology. Paper presented at the annual meeting of the American Academy of Child and Adolescent Psychiatry, New York.

World Health Organization. (1978). Mental disorders: Glossary and guide to their classification in accordance with the ninth revision of the international classification of diseases. Geneva, Switzerland: Author.

World Health Organization. (1990). *International Classification of Diseases* (Draft version, 10th ed.). Geneva, Switzerland: Author.

Zappert, J. (1921). Dementia infatilies Heller. *Monatsschrift fur Kinderheilkunde, 22,* 389–391.

Zwaigenbaum, L., Szatmari, P., Mahoney, W., Bryson, S., Bartolucci, G., & MacLean, J. (2000). High functioning autism and childhood disintegrative disorder in half brothers. *Journal of Autism and Developmental Disorders, 30*(2), 121–126.

CHAPTER 4

Asperger Syndrome

AMI KLIN, JAMES MCPARTLAND, AND FRED R. VOLKMAR

Asperger syndrome (AS) is a severe and chronic developmental disorder closely related to autistic disorder and pervasive developmental disorder-not otherwise specified (PDD-NOS), and, together, these disorders comprise a continuum referred to as the *autism spectrum disorders* (ASDs). Having autism as the paradigmatic and anchoring disorder in this diagnostic category, the ASDs more generally are characterized by marked and enduring impairments within the domains of social interaction, communication, play and imagination, and a restricted range of behaviors or interests. Although the diagnostic criteria for AS are still evolving, the "official" definitions provided in the *International Classification of Diseases,* 10th edition (*ICD-10;* World Health Organization [WHO], 1993) and the *Diagnostic and Statistical Manual of Mental Disorders,* fourth edition (*DSM-IV;* American Psychiatric Association, 2000) distinguish it from autism primarily on the basis of a relative preservation of linguistic and cognitive capacities in the first 3 years of life. Both in practice and in research studies, however, the term AS has been used to refer to individuals with variedly defined manifestations of the ASDs, including autism without mental retardation (or higher functioning autism [HFA]), "milder" forms of autism marked by higher cognitive and linguistic abilities, and more socially motivated but socially vulnerable adolescents and adults with unusual and socially interfering circumscribed interests. AS has also been used as a conceptual bridge between autism and the general population in an attempt to define a continuum of social function ranging from severe autism to "normalcy."

The confusions and controversies surrounding the definition and validity of AS mean that the nosological status of AS as a discrete condition separate from autism is still uncertain (Frith, 2004; Volkmar & Klin, 2000). The usage of the term, however, has been justified in pragmatic terms to bring more attention to individuals with autism with higher verbal abilities (Wing, 2000) or to less disabled individuals but with social vulnerabilities accompanied by a learning style conducive of technical knowledge or skills (Baron-Cohen, Wheelwright, Stone, & Rutherford, 1999) and as a model illustrating the need for research on factors mediating specific manifestations and outcome in the ASDs (Szatmari, 2000). It is important to keep these various uses of the term AS as the backdrop to any discussion of its nosologic and validity status to avoid less productive lines of inquiry meant to reconcile clinical research data yielded by studies using different definitions, criteria, and approaches to this condition. The prevailing attitude among researchers, clinicians, and advocates alike, however, is that regardless of these various uncertainties, individuals with AS have an early-onset social disability that impairs their capacity for meeting the demands of everyday life and that this is an uncontroversial clinical fact necessitating, therefore, systematic research involving all tools available to clinical science.

In this chapter, we describe the historical background of AS, its clinical features, and special considerations for assessment and intervention. We review current diagnostic issues including validity studies and suggest potentially fruitful guidelines for future research.

ASPERGER'S ORIGINAL CLINICAL CONCEPT

Hans Asperger (1906–1980) was an Austrian pediatrician with interest in special education who in 1944 described four children ages 6 to 11 years who had difficulty integrating socially into groups despite seemingly adequate cognitive and verbal skills (1944; Frith provided an English translation of the original article in 1991, adding an account of Asperger's professional background). He originally termed the condition he described *Autistischen Psychopathen im Kindesalter,* or autistic personality disorders in childhood, echoing Bleuler's (1916) use of the term *autism in schizophrenia* to signify extreme egocentrism, or the shutting off of relations between the person affected and other people. He contrasted this condition from schizophrenia, however, by emphasizing the stable and enduring nature of the social impairments in autistic psychopathy and by voicing the optimistic view that unlike in schizophrenia, his patients were able to eventually develop some relationships. The term *psychopathy* is best translated as personality disorder (i.e., a group of stable personality traits). In Asperger's time and cultural ethos, this term did not have the negative connotation of its present usage. The choice of the label *autistic psychopathy* also reflected Asperger's belief that difficulties in socialization represented the defining feature of the condition. However, he also detailed various clusters of behavioral symptoms and clinical features that appeared in conjunction with the social disability. His observations continue to be incorporated into current definitions of the disorder and include:

- *Impairment in nonverbal communication:* There is a reduction in the quantity and diversity of facial expressions and limitations in the use of gesture, as well as difficulties in understanding nonverbal cues conveyed by others.

- *Idiosyncrasies in verbal communication:* Spontaneous communication is characterized by highly circumstantial utterances (e.g., failing to distinguish abstractions from autobiographical narration), long-winded and incoherent verbal accounts failing to convey a clear message or thought (e.g., tangential speech prompted by a series of associations), and one-sidedness (e.g. failing to communicate changes of topic or to introduce new material). Both the style of language and tone of delivery are pedantic, like a "little professor."

- *Social adaptation and special interests:* There are egocentric preoccupations with unusual and circumscribed interests that absorb most of the person's attention and energy, thus precluding the acquisition of practical skills necessary for self-help and social integration. Some of these interests, for example, in letters and numbers, are often quite precocious. Later in life, special interests tend to evolve into specific, topic-related collections of information abundant with encyclopedic knowledge, such as astronomy or geography.

- *Intellectualization of affect:* Emotional presentation is marked by poor empathy, the tendency to intellectualize feelings, and an accompanying absence of intuitive understanding of other people's affective experiences and communication.

- *Clumsiness and poor body awareness:* Motoric presentation is characterized by odd posture and gait, poor body awareness, and clumsiness. Asperger emphasized his patients' inability to participate in group sports or other self-help activities involving motor coordination and integration and described in detail their poor graphomotor skills.

- *Conduct problems:* The most common reason for clinical referral of Asperger's patients involved failure at school and associated behavioral problems including aggressiveness, noncompliance, and negativism, which were accounted for in terms of their deficits in social understanding and extreme pursuit of highly circumscribed interests. Asperger was particularly concerned about his patients' poor social adjustment and how they were mercilessly bullied and teased by peers.

- *Onset:* Asperger thought that the condition could not be recognized in early childhood. Speech and language skills as well as curiosity about the environment in general, including people, were thought not to be conspicuously deviant.
- *Familial and gender patterns:* Some 30 years prior to the first publication revealing genetic contributions to the etiology of the ASDs, Asperger highlighted the familial nature of the condition affecting his patients, suggesting that similar traits in parents or relatives were found in almost every single case. His patients were almost exclusively boys.

The year before Asperger's article on autistic psychopathy appeared in the German child psychiatry literature, Leo Kanner (1943) had published his classic description of 11 children with "autistic disturbances of affective contact." Though both authors were unaware of the other's work, there were many commonalities between their patients, including problems with social interaction, affect, and communication, as well as unusual and idiosyncratic patterns of interest. The main differences related to Asperger's observations that his patients' speech and language acquisition were less commonly delayed, motor deficits were more likely, onset was later in childhood, and all the initial cases occurred in boys. More importantly, however, there were significant differences in terms of aspects and severity of symptomatology in the areas of social-emotional functioning, speech, language and cognitive skills, motor mannerisms, and circumscribed interests, which to a great extent may have been a function of the specific patients seen by Kanner (who were primarily preschoolers, less verbal, and more cognitively disabled) and by Asperger (who were primarily school-age children, highly verbal, and cognitively able). Consequently, Kanner's description became associated with the "classically" cognitively impaired or "lower functioning" child with autism, whereas Asperger's description lends itself more readily to an association with the more cognitively able and highly verbal older child with autism.

EVOLVING CONCEPTUALIZATION OF ASPERGER SYNDROME

Discussions of Asperger's work were not available in English until the 1970s. Prior to that, however, a handful of related publications in English with some relevance to his work had appeared. For example, Robinson and Vitale (1954) described three cases of children ages 8 to 11 who showed a pattern of circumscribed interests reminiscent of Asperger's patients. The children were interested in developmentally precocious topics such as chemistry, nuclear fission, transportation systems, astronomy, electricity, and mortgages, about which they talked incessantly in one-sided conversations with adults and peers. These children were generally socially isolated, play with other children had to revolve around their interests, and they had overly blunt manners and no concern about their grooming and other social niceties. Kanner (1954) was the invited discussant of this paper. The descriptions reminded him of infantile autism, but he felt that these children were less socially withdrawn and more affectively engaged with others, although they lacked friends and did not participate in group activities. The circumscribed interests dominated the lives of these children, monopolizing their learning and interfering with their ability to engage others in reciprocal relationships. Yet, the interests were often unusual, consisting of collections of facts rather than conceptual inquiries, making them even more difficult to share with others as a hobby or to build on as a possible vocational possibility. It is of interest, therefore, that Kanner's incisive clinical observations greatly resembled those of Asperger's when he was called to describe children similar to those encountered by Asperger in his original case studies.

The concept of autistic psychopathy was introduced to a wider English-speaking readership by Van Krevelen (1963), who made a deliberate attempt to distinguish it from Kanner's autism. In Van Krevelen's view (1971), the conditions are sharply different. Kanner's autism is manifested from the first months of life, the child walks before he or she talks, speech is delayed or absent, language never attains the function of communication, there is a lack of interest in others, and prognosis is poor. In contrast, Asperger's condition is manifested from the third year of life or later, the child talks before he or she walks, language aims at communication but remains one-sided, the child seeks interaction but in an awkward fashion, and prognosis is rather good. In many ways, van Krevelen's distinctions remain the core argument for those supporting a separation between the two conditions. Neither Kanner (1954) nor Asperger (in at least most of his early writings) ever appeared to make a strong argument for a more categorical separation of the two conditions (though Kanner never published an explicit account of his views of Asperger's work, and Asperger both limited the use of *autistic psychopathy* to cognitively able and highly verbal individuals and appeared to support a distinction later in life; see Asperger, 1979; and Hippler & Klicpera, 2003).

An influential review and series of case reports by Lorna Wing (1981) finally popularized Asperger's work among English readers. She reported 34 cases, ages 5 to 35, of whom 19 had a clinical presentation similar to Asperger's account, whereas 19 had a consistent current presentation but did not have the characteristic onset patterns and early history. Concerned that the term *psychopathy* might connote sociopathic behavior rather than the intended personality disorder and hoping to ground the condition in developmental terms, she renamed the disorder *Asperger's syndrome.* Wing summarized Asperger's description and proposed some modifications for the syndrome based on her case studies. Though Asperger thought the condition was unrecognizable prior to 3 years of age, Wing suggested the following difficulties were present in the *first 2 years of life:* (1) a lack of normal interest and pleasure in other people, (2) babbling that is limited in quantity and quality, (3) reduced sharing of interests and activities, (4) absence of an intense drive to communicate, both verbally and nonverbally, with others, (5) speech that is abnormal in terms of delayed acquisition or impoverished content consisting mainly of stereotyped utterances, and (6) failure to develop a full repertoire of imaginative pretend play. Wing also suggested that AS can be found in individuals with mild mental retardation and that, although in her sample males outnumbered females, around 20% were girls. These modifications blurred the distinctions originally suggested by Van Krevelen (1971) and reiterated by Asperger (1979), bringing the syndrome into an autism spectrum of disabilities defined by Wing in terms of the triad of impairments involving social, communication, and imaginative activities (Wing, 2000).

Wing's (1981) publication sparked a great deal of interest, and the quantity of research publications and clinical studies addressing AS has continued to grow steadily (Klin, Volkmar, & Sparrow, 2000). Much of this literature concerns an attempt to define the distinction (or lack thereof) between AS and HFA. Historically, researchers have used the label idiosyncratically, taking liberties to modify or to emphasize elements of the syndrome depending on their clinical experiences or theoretical stance. This variability renders it virtually impossible to compare findings of studies adopting different definitions known to yield, not surprisingly, different groups for comparison (e.g., Ghaziuddin, Tsai, & Ghaziuddin, 1992; Klin, Pauls, Schultz, & Volkmar, in press). Some progress has been made toward this end through the establishment of "official," though tentative, diagnostic criteria now incorporated in *ICD-10* (WHO, 1993) and *DSM-IV* (American Psychiatric Association, 1994), although this definition has itself been very controversial.

Issues in Definition of Asperger Syndrome

Although Wing (1981) did not provide a specific set of categorical diagnostic criteria, many case reports and research studies derived such criteria from her publication and used these to characterize their respective patient or subject population. However, accounts often included different sets of criteria, reflecting the author's decision as to which behaviors were necessary, only suggestive, or altogether irrelevant. As noted, such variability in diagnostic assignment suggested that comparisons among studies would be difficult and pointed to the need for a uniform nosology of AS (Rutter & Gould, 1985). Despite Wing's (2000) repeated attempts to slow the process that she unwittingly started and echoing Van Krevelen's (1971) initial approach, the stage was set for the field to test the validity status of AS relative to HFA. In this context, there was a need for consensual criteria for the definition of AS to be universally adopted by clinical researchers. Following the framework of current diagnostic systems such as *ICD-10* (WHO, 1993) and *DSM-IV* (1994), this definition had to be categorical (i.e., AS and autism should be defined in terms of mutually exclusive criteria) rather than dimensional (i.e., AS and autism should not differ simply in terms of degree of symptomatology). This task was complicated by the fact that Wing's (1981) account, from which most subsequent definitions were derived (Gillberg & Gillberg, 1989; Szatmari, Bartolucci, & Bremner, 1989; Tantam, 1988a), implied that the two conditions could not be separated and that AS was a subtype of autism with only minor differences in clinical manifestation. Many case reports and research studies avoided this issue altogether, particularly by failing to state whether subjects also fulfilled criteria for autism. While the designation of Asperger syndrome as a "variant" or "subtype" of autism (e.g., as highly verbal individuals with autism with normative or superior IQs) is justifiable from several practical perspectives (e.g., to bring attention to a subgroup of people with autism thus facilitating advocacy, to provide a concept around which clients and their families can more easily coalesce and share experiences; Wing, 2000; Szatmari, 2000), this is not so in formal diagnostic systems, which are meant, among other things, to provide mutually exclusive categories to facilitate research. Thus, the central issue in recent years has been whether AS and HFA (and, by necessity, PDD-NOS) are distinctive in ways that *are independent of the definition used to assign group membership.* In other words, research has focused on whether these concepts are associated with a different developmental course; different neurocognitive, neurobiological, or genetic underpinnings; or a different outcome (Klin et al., in press; Volkmar, Lord, Bailey, Schultz, & Klin, 2004). The end result of this process was the tentative inclusion of AS in *ICD-10* (WHO, 1993). And because *ICD-10* and *DSM-IV* were intended to be equivalent, AS was also included in the *DSM-IV* autism/PDD field trials (Volkmar, Klin, Seigel, et al., 1994).

The *ICD-10* (WHO, 1993) and *DSM-IV* definitions attempted to bridge over the differences among previous definitions and to contrast AS with autism, without which validation work would be impossible. To do so, it focused primarily on the number of overall symptoms (greater in autism and lower in AS, which was intended to capture variable degrees of severity), excluded the language cluster included in the diagnosis of autism (indicating the absence of severe language impairment in AS while sidestepping an attempt to define the peculiarities typical of verbal communication in AS), and specified onset criteria that contrasted with those for autism (the absence of clinically significant delays in speech, language, and cognitive development in AS). In many respects, this definition was both stricter than some (particularly relative to the onset criteria) and less specific than others (as it subsumed the more unique symptoms of AS under the autism clusters of social impairment and restricted areas of interest). In essence, AS was defined in terms of the criteria for autism (either presence or absence). The *ICD-10* criteria for AS are given in Table 4.1.

In practice, the *ICD-10* and *DSM-IV* definitions make a distinction between autism and AS solely on the basis of the onset criteria. In autism, any concerns prior to the age of 3 years involving social interaction, social communication, or symbolic/imaginative play are sufficient for the criteria to be met. In contrast, any concern involving cognitive development (in essence, typical exploration of and curiosity about the environment given that the majority of children are not developmentally assessed prior to age 3), self-help skills, or more broadly defined adaptive behavior (other than social interaction but including social communication) would rule out the diagnosis of AS. The possibly overinclusive nature of onset criteria for autism and overexclusive nature of onset criteria for AS (and any ambiguities left in the definition, e.g., how to distinguish social interaction from social communication) are resolved in terms of the *precedence rule*— if an individual meets criteria for autism, he or she cannot be assigned the diagnosis of AS (Volkmar & Klin, 2000).

Although the advent of the *DSM-IV* definition was intended to create a consensual

TABLE 4.1   ICD-10 Research Diagnostic Guidelines for Asperger Syndrome

1. There is no clinically significant general delay in spoken or receptive language or cognitive development. Diagnosis requires that single words should have developed by 2 years of age or earlier and that communicative phrases be used by 3 years of age or earlier. Self-help skills, adaptive behavior, and curiosity about the environment during the first 3 years should be at a level consistent with normal intellectual development. However, motor milestones may be somewhat delayed and motor clumsiness is usual (although not a necessary diagnostic feature). Isolated special skills, often related to abnormal preoccupations, are common, but are not required for the diagnosis.
2. There are qualitative abnormalities in reciprocal social interaction (criteria for autism).
3. The individual exhibits an unusually intense, circumscribed interest or restricted, repetitive, and stereotyped patterns of behavior interests and activities (criteria for autism; however, it would be less usual for these to include either motor mannerisms or preoccupations with part-objects or nonfunctional elements of play materials).
4. The disorder is not attributable to other varieties of pervasive developmental disorder; simple schizophrenia schizotypal disorder, obsessive-compulsive disorder, anakastic personality disorder; reactive and disinhibited attachment disorders of childhood.

Source: Reprinted with permission from World Health Organization (1993). *Disorders of psychological development* (Criteria for Research) (Geneva: WHO), pp. 154–155.

diagnostic starting point for research, it has been consistently criticized as overly narrow (Eisenmajer et al., 1996; Szatmari, Archer, Fisman, Streiner, & Wilson, 1995), rendering the diagnostic assignment of AS improbable or even "virtually impossible" according to some authors (Leekam, Libby, Wing, Gould, & Gillberg, 2000; Mayes, Calhoun, & Crites, 2001; Miller & Ozonoff, 2000). While this critique has reinforced the approach of some researchers to cluster all ASDs together in search of common underlying factors, other researchers are pursuing subgrouping efforts because of their recognition that autism is a clinically heterogeneous disorder and that the characterization of subtypes of PDD might help behavioral and biological research by allowing the identification of clinically more homogeneous groups (Bailey, Palferman,

Heavey, & Le Couteur, 1998; Rutter, 1999; Volkmar, Klin, & Cohen, 1997). For the purpose of this chapter, however, this process has highlighted the differences among some influential definitions of AS. Table 4.2 presents a comparison of key diagnostic features among the most widely used definitions, which include Asperger's (1944) original account and later emphases and changes (Asperger, 1979; Van Krevelen, 1971), as well as those of Wing (1981), Gillberg and Gillberg (1989), Tantam (1988a), and Szatmari, Bremner, and Nagy (1989a, 1989b). These definitions are compared with the one formalized in *DSM-IV* (American Psychiatric Association, 1994), which, as noted, is conceptually equivalent to the one included in *ICD-10* (WHO, 1993; Volkmar et al., 1994). Items in bold are those features deemed *necessary* for the diagnosis of AS according to the given diagnostic system.

It is evident from Table 4.2 that a direct comparison among the various diagnostic systems is not straightforward. Ghaziuddin and colleagues (1992) attempted to compare some of these systems. Having simplified the criteria for comparison, the study compared Asperger's (1944) definition with Wing's (1981)—which was made to be equivalent to Gillberg and Gillberg's (1989) and Tantam's (1988)—and the definitions of Szatmari and colleagues' (1989a, 1989b) and *ICD-10* (WHO, 1993). Of 15 patients identified as having AS according to Wing's criteria, only 10 patients met Szatmari et al.'s criteria, and only 8 patients met the description by Asperger as well as *ICD-10* criteria. The primary reason that seven patients did not fulfill *ICD-10* (and Asperger's) criteria was their failure to meet the onset criteria, specifically the lack of clinically significant delay in speech and language acquisition. Therefore, despite the lack of required specific social, language and communication, and absorbing interests criteria (which differ form Asperger's account), the *ICD-10* definition is, in practice, more restrictive than other systems because of its emphasis on specific onset patterns (which is consistent with Asperger's account).

This state of affairs raises several issues for nosology research:

1. By simultaneously emphasizing the lack of communication and cognitive delays in the

TABLE 4.2   Comparison of Six Sets of Clinical Criteria Defining Asperger Syndrome

Clinical Feature*	Asperger (1944, 1979)	Wing (1981)	Gillberg & Gillberg (1989)	Tantam (1988)	Szatmari et al. (1989)	DSM-IV (APA, 1994)
Social Impairment						
Poor nonverbal communication	**Yes**	**Yes**	**Yes**	**Yes**	**Yes**	Yes
Poor empathy	**Yes**	**Yes**	**Yes**	**Yes**	**Yes**	Yes
Failure to develop friendship	**Yes**	**Yes**	**Yes**	**Yes** (implied)	**Yes**	Yes
Language/Communication						
Poor prosody and pragmatics	**Yes**	**Yes**	**Yes**	**Yes**	**Yes**	Not stated
Idiosyncratic language	**Yes**	**Yes**	Not stated	Not stated	**Yes**	Not stated
Impoverished imaginative play	Yes	**Yes**	Not stated	Not stated	Not stated	Not stated
All Absorbing Interest	**Yes**	**Yes**	**Yes**	**Yes**	Not stated	Often
Motor Clumsiness	**Yes**	**Yes**	**Yes**	**Yes**	Not stated	Often
Onset (0–3 years)						
Speech delays/deviance	**No**	May be present	May be present	Not stated	Not stated	**No**
Cognitive delays	**No**	May be present	Not stated	Not stated	Not stated	**No**
Motor delays	Yes	Sometimes	Not stated	Not stated	Not stated	May be present
Exclusion of Autism	**Yes** (1979)	No	No	No	**Yes**	**Yes**
Mental Retardation	**No**	May be present	Not stated	Not stated	Not stated	Not stated

* Symptoms that are defined as necessary for the presence of the condition are given in bold.

first years of life while failing to specify required social, communication, motor, and absorbing interest features that are thought to be typical in AS, the *ICD-10* definition differentiates autism from AS solely based on the onset criteria, in fact, irrespective of the nature of the patient's social impairment later in life. Whether individuals diagnosed in this manner will have a later presentation consistent with Asperger's description remains to be documented. Various authors (Gillberg & Gillberg, 1989; Leekam, Libby, Wing, Gould, & Gillberg, 2000; Wing, 1981) have reported cases that would not meet the *ICD-10* onset criteria and yet presented with what they thought was AS. However, even higher functioning individuals with autism appear to have the onset of their condition before age 3 years (Volkmar & Cohen, 1989). In summary, while it is interesting to study eventual clinical presentations on the basis of early profiles of development, there is no assurance that later onset will lead to individuals conforming

with Asperger's description. Also, if pursuing this strategy, it is unlikely that such poorly detailed, "all or nothing" description of onset characteristics will capture meaningful variability of developmental concepts of interest (e.g., social motivation, joint attention, nonverbal communication), which are likely to mediate outcome.

2. By failing to include social, communicative, or restricted interest patterns more specific to AS (by subsuming those under general clusters defining autism), the *ICD-10* definition of AS disregards features that could serve as discriminative factors and may be unique among AS patients. For example, Tantam (1988a) suggests that in contrast to the prevailing view of individuals with autism, individuals with AS may wish to be sociable and yet fail to establish relationships. Although this may also be true for older adolescents and adults with autism, it would be unusual for a younger child with autism. This was an important point raised by Van Krevelen (1971), who

thought children with autism disregarded others while children with AS approached others in an eccentric fashion. Both were socially impaired, but qualitatively different.

3. Just as autistic social dysfunction can be defined only in the context of the child's overall developmental level (Rutter, 1978), there may be a host of developmental factors that should be considered in attempts to differentiate the social, affective, and communication presentation of individuals with HFA from those with AS. These include chronological age (e.g., less pronounced contrast in older adolescents and adults), IQ and language level (e.g., less pronounced contrast in individuals with higher IQ and language abilities), and the presence of any medical condition disrupting speech and language acquisition early in life independently from psychiatric diagnosis (e.g., cleft palate, intermittent hearing loss resulting from chronic ear infection)

In summary, the different diagnostic systems have provided different sets of criteria but have not resolved the key issue dominating research on AS since the early 1970s, namely, its validity status relative to autism. That some influential authors had not meant to suggest that AS was a distinguishable diagnostic entity is unlikely to quell this debate. There is a need to go beyond the current sterile impasse fueling so much of the current classification debate, which is still based on rather arbitrary decisions and vague semantics rather than empirical validation of operationalized definitions that reflect more sophisticated developmental constructs.

Three approaches appear to be emerging from this discussion. The first, here called the *spectrum approach,* disregards the nosologic discussion entirely by equating AS with higher functioning ASDs or with some social vulnerability of the kind seen in ASDs (some individuals with this characterization may not meet clinical criteria for a PDD). Proponents of this approach make the assumptions that all early-onset and chronic social vulnerabilities share some factors in common and that research is best invested in better examining and possibly quantifying these factors seen as the

dimensions creating the autism spectrum (e.g., Baron-Cohen, 2002; Constantino & Todd, 2003). The second approach—here called the *early language approach,* makes a distinction between AS and HFA by dividing children with ASD and apparently normal cognitive development into two groups in terms of language development in the first 3 years of life. A diagnosis of AS is given if the child achieved single words by age 2 years and phrase speech (typically defined as nonecholalic three-word combinations used meaningfully for communication) by the age of 3 years. A diagnosis of autism is given if the child does not meet these criteria (Gilchrist et al., 2001; Szatmari et al., 1995, 2000). The third approach criticizes the first two and offers an alternative (Klin et al., in press). As to the spectrum approach, it is unlikely, though not entirely impossible, that single underlying factors or dimensions could generate the highly complex and heterogeneous spectrum of autism-related disorders in a predictable, quantified manner. As to the early language approach, there is concern that it greatly narrows the potential lines of distinction between autism and AS in that other aspects of onset (e.g., social engagement and social cognitive patterns), as well as any unique features in current presentation (e.g., social motivation, verbosity), are disregarded (Volkmar & Klin, 2000). More practically, there is concern that because individuals with HFA may not present with speech delays as defined in this diagnostic scheme, there is a potential for the resultant samples (of individuals with HFA and AS) to overlap considerably in terms of other symptomatology, thus increasing the potential for type II errors (i.e., not finding differences).

To address these potential limitations, the third approach—here called the *unique features approach* (possibly better described as "bell-ringers" approach)—emphasizes the features more specifically associated with AS highlighted by Asperger (1944) and several other authors (e.g., Klin & Volkmar, 1997; Tantam, 1988a). These features are included in the narratives accompanying the definition of AS in *ICD-10* (WHO, 1993) and in *DSM-IV-TR* (American Psychiatric Association, 2000) but are not included in the respective sets of diagnostic criteria. In this approach, onset criteria are given in more detail. For example, distinctions are made between children who isolate themselves (more typical of autism) and those who seek others, sometimes incessantly, but in a socially insensitive manner (more typical of AS); and between children whose language is delayed, echolalic, or otherwise stereotyped (more typical of autism) and those whose language is adequate or even precocious and whose difficulties in this area are limited to the communicative use of language (i.e., pragmatics; more typical of AS). The added details are meant to facilitate research into developmental paths of social disabilities with a greater degree of specificity. Additional modifications proposed involve the inclusion of one-sided verbosity as a necessary communication criterion in AS and the presence of factual, circumscribed interests that interfere with both general learning and reciprocal social conversation. These communication symptoms were introduced with a view to capture the observed greater social motivation seen in individuals with AS (relative to HFA).

Research systematically assessing the utility of these approaches is still limited. One recent study (Klin et al., in press), however, has shown that three diagnostic schemes for AS used simultaneously—*DSM-IV*, the early language approach, and the unique features approach—have low agreement in case assignment and lead to different results in comparisons of IQ profiles, patterns of comorbidity, and familial aggregation of psychiatric symptoms across the approach-specific resultant groups of HFA, AS, and PDD-NOS.

ASPERGER'S WORK REVISITED

Hippler and Klicpera (2003) recently conducted a retrospective analysis of the clinical case records of individuals with *autistic psychopathy* (AP) diagnosed by Hans Asperger and his team in the various clinics that they practiced. Although there are obvious limitations in using current concepts to reanalyze data generated through the lens of a different era (with its unique system of diagnostic concepts and debates), this paper helps us better understand Asperger's work and development of his diagnostic concept. For example, he saw approximately 9,800 children between 1951

and 1980. Only an estimated 1.15% was diagnosed with AP. Thus, the condition that he described was likely to be quite specific. The estimate of cases falling within the autism spectrum, but without an explicit diagnosis of AP, was double that number. Of the AP cases, 95% were boys, a manifold increase in the typical autism gender ratio (4 boys for every girl), larger but closer to the ratio reported for higher functioning ASDs, and closer still to the gender ratio reported for individuals with AS (Volkmar et al., 2004). The clinical concepts used to describe patients suggested the notion that these children had social motivation but were very awkward in approaching others, leading to failure to establish relationships. For example, "contact disorder" or "instinct disorder" were used to refer to a lack of common sense, impaired "practical intelligence" in everyday situations, and a need to learn these skills through their intellect (Hippler & Klicpera, 2003, p. 294). Fifty-four percent of cases showed excellent verbal abilities (e.g., fund of information) but impaired nonverbal abilities (e.g., visual-spatial skills), echoing a learning profile thought to be more typical of individuals with AS than of those with HFA (Klin, Volkmar, Sparrow, Cicchetti, & Rourke, 1995). On IQ tests, higher verbal IQ (VIQ) than performance IQ (PIQ) was more than twice as common as the reverse (44% versus 18%), and almost the totality of cases had full-scale IQs within or above the normative range. Some resemblance between the child with AP and one or more family members was observed in 53% of the sample, with 52% of fathers being reported as being similar to their child in aspects of social dysfunction, a much higher estimate of familiality than observed in autism but similar to some recent family genetic data using the more specific feature of AS to define the proband (Klin et al., in press). Eighty-two percent of AP cases were reported to have circumscribed interests of the kinds subsequently described as particularly specific to AS (e.g., topic-based obsessions). An attempt to apply the *ICD-10* criteria for AS resulted in a diagnosis of AS in 68% of cases; 25% did not meet the requirement of absence of clinical symptoms before the age of 3; of these, half had some language delays.

Hippler and Klicpera's article (2003) is very helpful in showing the very specific profile of children singled out by Asperger over his lifetime, which contrasts markedly with some of the current definitions of AS. Still, there is little to gain from an exegetic analysis of this nature, if the validity and utility of the construct cannot be assessed relative to predictions independent of definitions for case assignment. The development of our understanding of autism offers an interesting contrast. Despite the remarkably enduring quality of Kanner's (1943) original description, many key issues have been modified as a result of subsequent research. The fact that Rutter's (1978) codification of Kanner's prose proved to be an effective and reliable diagnostic tool is partially thanks to Kanner's brilliance, but it is also a function of the severity of the condition he described. Given that the syndrome described by Asperger is more equivocal than Kanner's autism—overlapping with autism to some extent but also maybe shading into eccentric normalcy, it is appropriate that additional work is needed to create an effective and reliable definition.

ALTERNATIVE DIAGNOSTIC CONCEPTS

Professionals from diverse disciplines such as adult psychiatry, neuropsychology, and neurology have dealt with individuals with significant problems in social interaction who did not seem to precisely fit Kanner's (1943) concept of infantile autism (Klin & Volkmar, 1997). Wolff and colleagues (Wolff & Barlow, 1979; Wolff & Chick, 1980) proposed the term *schizoid personality in childhood* in their description of children with social isolation and emotional detachment, unusual communicative style, and rigidity of thought and behavior. Although the initial emphasis on the condition as a personality disorder resulted in more sketchy accounts of developmental course, attempts to reconstruct the developmental history of these children were made (e.g., Wolff, 1991, 1995). Several attempts have been made to compare this concept with AS (e.g., Nagy & Szatmari, 1986; Tantam, 1988b), showing some areas of similarity (e.g., abnormalities in empathy and nonverbal communication) but also some areas

of difference (e.g., level and pervasiveness of social disability, more severe in AS), outcome (less positive in AS), and relatedness to the schizophrenia spectrum of disorders (the association is stronger in schizoid personality in childhood).

The concept of nonverbal learning disabilities (NLD) was originally proposed by Johnson and Myklebust (1971; Myklebust, 1975) and was subsequently elaborated and thoroughly researched by Rourke (1989). NLD refers to a profile of neuropsychological assets and deficits that have a significant negative impact on a person's social and communication skills (see Chapter 13, this *Handbook,* this volume). Deficits in neuropsychological skills such as tactile perception, psychomotor coordination, visual-spatial organization, and nonverbal problem solving occur in the presence of preserved rote verbal abilities. The particular profile of strengths and deficits results in a characteristic learning style such as the tendency to overly rely on overlearned behaviors when dealing with novel or complex situations. Poor pragmatics and prosody in speech are seen in the presence of relatively preserved formal language skills such as vocabulary and syntax and single-word reading abilities. Difficulties in appreciating the subtle, and sometimes obvious, nonverbal aspects of social interaction lead to major deficits in social perception and judgment, which often result in social isolation and rejection and increased risk for social withdrawal and serious mood disorders (Rourke, Young, & Leenaars, 1989). Although potentially associated with a number of different conditions (Rourke, 1995), it is often seen in individuals with AS but less so in individuals with autism (Gunter, Ghaziuddin, & Ellis, 2002; Klin, Sparrow, Volkmar, Cicchetti, & Rourke, 1995; Lincoln, Courchesne, Allen, Hanson, & Ene, 1998; Siegel, Minshew, & Goldstein, 1996).

Another influential concept was proposed by Rapin and Allen (1983), who used the term *semantic-pragmatic disorder* to describe cases in which speech and language skills were adequate in form (syntax and phonology) but impoverished in content and use (semantics and pragmatics). Bishop (1989, 1998) refined the descriptions and assessment instrumentation used in the characterization of communicative difficulties exhibited by these children. More recent research (Bishop, 2000) has shown that the association between semantic and pragmatic deficits is not a necessary one and that a term such as *pragmatic language impairment* might be preferable to refer to these children.

Other concepts, such as developmental learning disability of the right hemisphere (Denckla, 1983; Weintraub & Mesulam, 1983), have been proposed. Although the number of labels available and the diversity of disciplines from which they arose are a testament to the robustness of the underlying clinical phenomena, these various labels have the potential for introducing confusion in nosologic discussion of AS. Their discipline-specific nature may also inhibit the kinds of interdisciplinary research that could provide an integrated and comprehensive understanding of individuals with AS. Confusion is particularly an issue for parents whose child might receive any of several different diagnostic labels depending on the training and discipline of the clinician with whom they consult. Given that the various conditions described reflect primarily differences in discipline-specific emphasis (language and communication versus neuropsychological profiles versus neurological profiles), thus mapping on different levels of discourse, it is clear that these are not mutually exclusive concepts. In other words, they describe an overlapping group of children with social vulnerabilities. Therefore, it is likely more helpful if they are not used as competing diagnostic concepts but as methodological approaches to better understand aspects of the social, communicative, neuropsychological, and neurologically based disabilities evidenced in individuals with AS.

CLINICAL FEATURES OF ASPERGER SYNDROME

Onset Patterns

Children with AS do not present with clinically significant delays in language acquisition, cognitive development, or self-help skills in the first years of life. In fact, language acquisition, in terms of vocabulary and sentence construction, may be precocious in some cases and parents may report that the child began to talk before learning to walk. Vocabulary acquisition, however, may be unusual as children may learn complex or adult-like words, typically associated with a special interest prior to learning more typical, child-like vocabulary associated with social play and experiences. Parents may report that once the child began to talk, there was a pedantic quality to their speech, both in terms of their choice of words and sentence construction (more formal than seen in typical peers) and in terms of the tone of voice and phrasing (sometimes assuming a "teaching" quality). Attachment patterns to family members are often seen as unremarkable, and in contrast to autism, there are few visible signs of social disability in the highly familiar environment of the child's home. In many ways, these children appear to orient to others although they may use them more instrumentally than reciprocally, for example, to speak to them rather than to truly engage them in a shared pursuit. The social disability becomes more apparent when the child is outside the home environment, particularly in group situations involving same-age children. In such situations, they may approach other children in inappropriate or awkward ways, for example, speaking loudly when in close proximity, or otherwise becoming very upset when other children are not willing to play with them following their agenda, which typically involves the pursuit of play or games restricted to a narrow and often developmentally atypical interest. The contrast in presentation in the home and family setting relative to social group settings is likely explained by the nature of the social partners. At home, interactions with parents are highly scaffolded by the adults, who mold their behavior to adjust to the child's approaches, guiding the interaction and preventing communication breakdown. In social group settings involving peers, there is a need for more conventional and socially appropriate behavior because peers show little tolerance for deviation from usual expectations. It is typical, therefore, for parents to first become concerned about their children's behavior at the time of transitions to school-like settings (e.g., informal play groups, nursery, or preschool).

During preschool years, some children may develop intense interests about which they begin to learn a great deal. Some of these may be unusual for their age (e.g., geography, arrows, storm drains). They may acquire a wealth of facts and information related to a given interest, choosing to talk a great deal to other children, who fail to show the same interest and, consequently, distance themselves from such approaches. Typical experiences anchoring a child's understanding of his or her day (e.g., routines at preschool, transition times, social rituals) may not convey a sense of familiarity, prompting the child to rely (often precociously) on more formal definitions of experiences such as time (e.g., a 3-year-old may repeatedly ask, "What time is it?"), rigid rules (an explicitly and verbally defined schedule), or repeated questions of adults. To some children, these behaviors appear to be related to incapacity to make intuitive sense of their own experiences, of nonexplicit nonverbal cues conveyed by others, and of the changeable behavior of people who make sense only within the overall context of a social situation, yet another construct adding to the experience of confusion in these children. The pursuit of unchangeable phenomena (that remain the same and do not depend on context) may have earlier led the child to exhibit a fascination with letters and numbers, which subsequently may evolve into precocious reading abilities and fascination with facts, all of which may serve to ground the child in what otherwise would be an overwhelmingly perplexing, constantly shifting, and primarily implicit social environment.

Social Functioning

In some contrast to the social presentation in autism, individuals with AS find themselves socially isolated but are not usually withdrawn in the presence of other people, typically approaching others but in an inappropriate or eccentric fashion. For example, they may engage the interlocutor, usually an adult, in one-sided conversation characterized by long-winded, pedantic speech about a favorite and often unusual and narrow topic. They may express interest in friendships and in meeting people, but their wishes are often thwarted by their awkward approaches and insensitivity to the other person's feelings, intentions, and nonliteral

and implied communications (e.g., signs of boredom, haste to leave, and need for privacy). Chronically frustrated by their repeated experiences of failure to engage others and form friendships, some individuals with AS develop symptoms of a mood disorder that may require treatment, including medication. They also may react inappropriately to, or fail to interpret the valence of, the context of the affective interaction, often conveying a sense of insensitivity, formality, or disregard for the other person's emotional expressions. They may be able to describe correctly, in a cognitive and often formalistic fashion, other people's emotions, expected intentions, and social conventions; yet, they are unable to act on this knowledge in an intuitive and spontaneous fashion, thus losing the tempo of the interaction. Their poor intuition and lack of spontaneous adaptation are accompanied by marked reliance on formalistic rules of behavior and rigid social conventions. This presentation is largely responsible for the impression of social naiveté and behavioral rigidity that is so forcefully conveyed by these individuals (Klin & Volkmar, 1997).

Communication Patterns

Although significant abnormalities of speech and language are not typical of individuals with AS, there are at least three aspects of these individuals' communication patterns that are of clinical interest (Klin, 1994). First, speech may be marked by poor prosody, although inflection and intonation may not be as rigid and monotonic as in autism (Ghaziuddin & Gerstein, 1996). They often exhibit a constricted range of intonation patterns that is used with little regard to the communicative functioning of the utterance (e.g., assertions of fact, humorous remarks). Rate of speech may be unusual (e.g., too fast) or may lack in fluency (e.g., jerky speech), and there is often poor volume modulation (e.g., voice is too loud despite physical proximity to the conversational partner). The latter feature may be particularly noticeable in the context of a lack of adjustment to the given social setting (e.g., in a library or a noisy crowd). Second, speech may often be tangential and circumstantial, conveying a sense of looseness of associations and incoherence. Even though in a very small number of cases this symptom may be an indicator of a possible thought disorder, the lack of contingency in speech is a result of the one-sided, egocentric conversational style (e.g., unrelenting monologues about the names, codes, and attributes of innumerable TV stations in the country), failure to provide the background for comments and to clearly demarcate changes in topic, and failure to suppress the vocal output accompanying internal thoughts. Third, the communication style of individuals with AS is often characterized by marked verbosity. The child may talk incessantly, usually about a favorite subject, often in complete disregard to whether the listener might be interested, engaged, or attempting to interject a comment, or change the subject of conversation. Despite such long-winded monologues, the individual may never come to a point or conclusion. Attempts by the interlocutor to elaborate on issues of content or logic or to shift the interchange to related topics are often unsuccessful.

Circumscribed Interests

Individuals with AS typically amass a large amount of factual information about a topic in a very intense fashion. The actual topic may change from time to time but often dominates the content of social exchange. Frequently, the entire family may be immersed in the subject for long periods of time. This behavior is peculiar in the sense that oftentimes extraordinary amounts of factual information are learned about very circumscribed topics (e.g., snakes, names of stars, TV guides, deep fat fryers, weather information, personal information on members of Congress) without a genuine understanding of the broader phenomena involved. This symptom may not always be easily recognized in childhood because strong interests in certain topics, such as dinosaurs or fashionable fictional characters, are so ubiquitous. However, in both younger and older children the special interests typically interfere with learning in general because they absorb so much of the child's attention and motivation, and they have a very negative impact on their ability to engage others in reciprocal social interaction because the interest intrudes and often dominates conversation with others.

Motoric Difficulties

Individuals with AS often present with a history of motor difficulties and delayed acquisition of skills requiring sophisticated motor coordination, such as pedaling a bike, catching a ball, opening jars, and climbing outdoor play equipment. They are often visibly awkward and poorly coordinated and may exhibit unusual gait patterns, odd posture, poor manipulative and handwriting skills, and significant deficits in visual-motor skills (Gillberg, 1990; Tantam, 1988a). When tested, children with AS have been shown to experience difficulties on measures of apraxia, balance, tandem gait, and finger-thumb apposition, suggesting difficulties in proprioception (Weimer, Schatz, Lincoln, Ballantyne, & Trauner, 2001). It is not clear, however, whether "clumsiness" or poor motor coordination skills differentiate individuals with AS from those with HFA (Green, Gilchrist, Burton, & Cox, 2002; Smith, 2000), who may show similar difficulties.

Comorbid Features

From a clinical standpoint, the most common comorbid conditions impacting on individuals with AS are anxiety and depression (Klin & Volkmar, 1997). In many cases, anxiety seems to be secondary to a sense of being overwhelmed by the fast pace and competitive social demands of typical peer interactions coupled with a sense of lack of control over the outcome of such social events. Similarly, depression appears to emerge as a result of increased awareness of repeated experiences of failure despite an intent, which can be quite intense, to establish relationships, make friends, or have a romantic experience. Research estimates of comorbid anxiety and/or depression in individuals with AS are as high as 65% (Ellis, Ellis, Fraser, & Deb, 1994; Fujikawa, Kobayashi, Koga, & Murata, 1987; Ghaziuddin, 2002; Ghaziuddin, Ghaziuddin, & Greden, 2002; Ghaziuddin, Weidmer-Mikhail, & Ghaziuddin, 1998; Green et al., 2000; Howlin & Goode, 1998). Some data suggest, however, that individuals with AS and HFA are equally at increased risk for problems with anxiety and depression, with no differences between the groups (Kim, Szatmari, Bryson, Streiner,

& Wilson, 2000). In some respects, these results are difficult to reconcile with our experience, according to which individuals with autism are likely to suffer less anxiety and depression because of their lack of involvement with others, which in turn, makes them (1) less vulnerable to the challenges inherent in trying to navigate a complex social world and (2) less vulnerable to experiences of inadequacy resulting from failure to establish relationships despite repeated (and painful) attempts.

Several other conditions have been described in association with AS, although these descriptions are more typical of early published reports that tended to be case studies rather than case-control series. These early reports emphasized possible associations with Tourette's syndrome (e.g., Gillberg & Rastam, 1992; Kerbeshian & Burd, 1986; Littlejohns, Clarke, & Corbett, 1990; Marriage, Miles, Stokes, & Davey, 1993) and obsessive-compulsive disorder (Thomsen, 1994). Reports of associations with psychotic conditions have included reports of psychotic depression and bipolar disorder (manic depressive psychosis; Gillberg, 1985).

Some reports, though primarily case studies, have focused on conduct problems, more specifically on violent and criminal behavior (e.g., Baron-Cohen, 1988; Everall & Le Couteur, 1990; Mawson, Grounds, & Tantam, 1985; Scragg & Shah, 1994; Tantam, 1988c; Wing, 1986). However, the hypothesis that the combination of high intelligence and verbal skills with poor empathy and social cognition fosters violent or criminal behavior has not been empirically borne out. Ghaziuddin and colleagues (1991) reviewed the literature and found a lack of support for this speculation. Our own experience suggests that individuals with AS do not present with antisocial or sociopathic characteristics; the absence of empathy connotes poor insight into the social and emotional nature of other people, not an absence of compassion for their welfare. Individuals with AS often transgress rules at school, with people, and in the community at large, and their behavior may indeed lead to formal encounters with school authorities or law enforcement officers. However, they typically do not engage in these acts willfully or maliciously. Their social ineptitude and unawareness of social rules and expectations may lead them, for example, to make blunt requests of a sexual nature; or their intense and all-absorbing circumscribed interests may lead them to commit eccentric acts associated with those interests (e.g., accumulate clutter in the backyard of a multifamily home). More typically, however, these individuals are too naïve to become "competent criminals." In fact, individuals with AS are much more likely to be victims than victimizers due to their inability to read the intents of others, which in a typical school environment may involve repeated mocking and cruel singling out of the child because of his or her eccentricities, poor grooming, or social clumsiness. Adults may eventually grow despondent in social situations, eventually gravitating toward the periphery of society.

Another association suggested by early reports was the presence of schizophrenia in some individuals with AS. In fact, there was some suggestion that AS might, in some sense, be a "bridging" condition between autism and schizophrenia (Wolff, 1995). Though several research studies have suggested an association between the disorders (e.g., Nagy & Szatmari, 1986; Tantam, 1991), the preponderance of empirical evidence fails to support this speculation. Ghaziuddin, Leininger, and Tsai (1995) found that patients with AS had greater levels of disorganized thinking than an HFA comparison group, but they were not more likely to exhibit a thought disorder. Reviews of large case series reveal that schizophrenia is no more common among individuals with AS than in the general population (Volkmar & Cohen, 1991). And in family genetic studies, there is no evidence of larger aggregation of schizophrenia-related symptoms in families of probands with ASD or of ASD-related symptoms in families of probands with schizophrenia (see Chapter 16, *Handbook,* this volume). Though research has not supported a relationship between AS and schizophrenia, several factors have contributed to this enduring misperception. The combination of excessive verbalization and poor social judgment and social monitoring in AS or the tendency of persons with AS to speak excessively about special interests may result in highly inappropriate and bizarre behavior that mimics psychotic behavior (e.g., incoherent or accelerated speech). Additionally, there has been an overreliance on single-case studies as well as some ascertainment biases (Bejerot & Duvner, 1995; Ryan, 1992; Taiminen, 1994).

PREVALENCE

Studies of prevalence in general, and of psychiatric disorders in particular, are greatly affected by the quality and nature of the definition used to single out cases from the general population (e.g., precise versus vague, discrete versus overlapping with other conditions). As discussed earlier, varying criteria continue to be employed in the diagnosis of AS, constituting a major confound in any attempt to interpret epidemiological studies of AS (Ehlers & Gillberg, 1993). Nevertheless, consistent with the trend observed in ASDs in general (Fombonne & Tidmarsh, 2003) rates of AS appear to be on the rise. Twenty years ago, an epidemiological study in an area of London (Wing, 1981; Wing & Gould, 1979) reported a prevalence rate of 0.6 to 1.1 per 10,000. However, this study assessed only children under the age of 15 *with mild mental retardation,* clearly a minority among individuals assigned the label AS, thereby very likely underestimating the true prevalence. Gillberg and Gillberg (1989) reported rates of 10 to 26 children per 10,000 among children with normal intelligence, with an additional 0.4 per 10,000 showing the combination of AS and mental retardation. A subsequent study (Ehlers & Gillberg, 1993) calculated a minimum prevalence rate of 3.6 per 1,000 children (7 to 16 years of age) for a diagnosis of AS and 7.1 per 1,000 children when including suspected cases. Fombonne and Tidmarsh (2003) reviewed a number of epidemiological studies that included the diagnostic category of AS and reported a wide range of prevalence rates, from 0.3 to 48.4 per 10,000, which clearly reflected methodologic differences across studies. Illustrating a common problem in epidemiological research, the highest estimate derived from the study with the smallest sample size. Making allowances for the methodological shortcomings of the available studies and for the great ambiguity associated with the definition of the phenomenon itself, Fombonne and Tidmarsh suggested a working prevalence rate of 2 per 10,000 pending further research. Prevalence estimates will always depend on the definition of AS and the adoption of operationalized concepts that can be applied by epidemiologists with a degree of reliability. Hence there is a need for progress in defining consensual approaches to this condition because, from a purely practical standpoint, prevalence estimates have profound implications for allocation of resources and service provision.

VALIDITY OF ASPERGER SYNDROME

As amply documented in the previous sections, the validity of AS as distinct from other conditions, notably HFA, but also PDD-NOS, remains controversial (Ozonoff & Griffith, 2000; Volkmar & Klin, 2000). A lack of uniformity in usage of the term also characterizes definitions adopted for the purpose of research, as different sets of diagnostic criteria have been used by different researchers with resulting complications for interpretation of research (Ghaziuddin et al., 1992; Klin et al., in press). There is little disagreement about the fact that AS is on a phenomenological continuum with autism, particularly in relation to the problems in the areas of social and communication functioning (Wing, 1991). For example, within the *DSM-III-R* (American Psychiatric Association, 1987) diagnostic system, persons with AS would either meet criteria for autistic disorder or would be said to exhibit PDD-NOS (Tsai, 1992). What is less clear is whether the condition is qualitatively different from, rather than just a milder form of, autism.

Several studies investigating different aspects of the disorder have attempted to identify discriminating criteria between the two conditions with only mixed results to date. These studies have involved the neuropsychological, social-cognitive, neurobiological, genetic, and prognostic aspects of the disorders.

Neuropsychological Studies

A number of studies have attempted to distinguish AS from other ASDs, and HFA in particular, by demonstrating a pattern of neuropsychological performance that uniquely characterizes the disorders (e.g., Wing, 1998). Though findings are not wholly consistent, these studies suggest that individuals with HFA tend to have greater impairment within the domains of language and verbal comprehension (Lincoln, Allen, & Kilman, 1995; Siegel et al., 1996) while exhibiting relative strength in nonverbal areas (Klin, Carter, & Sparrow, 1997). Several studies have empirically demonstrated significant distinctions between groups. In one study (Klin, Volkmar, Sparrow, Cicchetti, & Rourke, 1995), a group of individuals with AS and HFA of comparable chronological age and full-scale IQ were compared in multiple domains of neuropsychological function. On average, individuals with AS exhibited a significant VIQ-PIQ differential with stronger verbal abilities, while individuals in the HFA group tended to have comparable verbal and performance abilities. With respect to other domains of neuropsychological function, 11 areas were shown to discriminate between the two groups. Some neuropsychological skills represented areas of strength in AS and weakness in HFA, whereas the converse was true for other domains of ability. Six areas of psychological deficit were associated with a diagnosis of AS: fine and gross motor skills, visual motor integration, visual-spatial perception, nonverbal concept formation, and visual memory. Five areas of psychological deficits were negatively correlated with a diagnosis of AS: articulation, verbal output, auditory perception, vocabulary, and verbal memory. Finally, all but three subjects with AS presented with a neuropsychological profile consistent with an NLD (Rourke, 1989). In contrast, only one subject in the HFA group did so. These results indicated an overlap between AS, but not HFA, and NLD, suggesting an empirical distinction between AS and HFA based on neurocognitive profiles.

Since this study was published, a number of publications have replicated, or partially replicated, its findings. Ehlers et al. (1997) compared results on an intelligence test across groups with AS and autism. The authors found that individuals with AS exhibited stronger verbal ability with a weakness in subtests measuring visual-spatial organization and graphomotor skills (WISC-R Object Assembly,

Coding Subtests). In contrast, individuals with autism displayed an isolated skill on a measure of visual parts-to-whole reasoning (Block Design subtest). Lincoln and colleagues (1998) carried out a meta-analysis of several studies addressing neuropsychological profiles differentiating AS from HFA. Results indicated that individuals with AS showed a pattern of stronger VIQ relative to PIQ. In contrast, individuals with HFA exhibited the reverse pattern, with stronger nonverbal abilities and weaker verbal skills. The authors concluded that autism is characterized by impaired verbal skills, which are intact in AS. Miller and Ozonoff (2000) also compared groups with HFA and AS with similar results but with an important caveat. The AS group had higher VIQ and full-scale IQ and exhibited a greater difference between verbal and nonverbal abilities (with verbal abilities being stronger). However, this study also observed better visual-perceptual skills in individuals with AS, suggesting a more general effect of higher performance or IQ in the group with AS rather than reverse profiles, suggesting that "AS is simply high-IQ autism." Evidence was suggestive but inconclusive regarding a trend toward poorer motor performance in the group with AS. Considering the fact that many studies demonstrating this pattern of verbal strengths specific to AS had used varying diagnostic criteria, Ghaziuddin and Mountain-Kimchi (2004) compared AS with HFA using unmodified, official diagnostic criteria. The study found that, overall, individuals with AS had higher VIQ with greater strengths in fund of knowledge and vocabulary relative to individuals with HFA. A recent review of the literature (Reitzel & Szatmari, 2003) confirmed this pattern of differential neuropsychological profiles, with individuals with HFA consistently demonstrating lower scores on measures of verbal functioning. Importantly, however, it was noted that studies have not consistently demonstrated that individuals with AS possess nonverbal weaknesses or increased spatial or motor problems relative to individuals with HFA, echoing Miller and Ozonoff's conclusions (2000). In other words, differences in neuropsychological profiles were explained in terms of an overriding effect of higher IQ in individuals with AS relative to those with HFA, rather than a double dissociation of strengths and deficits suggested by the NLD model.

Several studies have failed to detect significant differences in neuropsychological profiles between individuals with AS and HFA. One of the earliest investigations in this area was conducted by Szatmari, Tuff, Finlayson, and Bartolucci (1990), who administered a comprehensive test battery including intelligence, achievement, and neuropsychological measures to groups with AS and HFA matched on full-scale IQ. Few differences were detected; the AS group tended to perform better on a test of verbal concept formation (WISC-R Similarities subtest), while the HFA group showed higher performance on a test of motor speed and coordination (Grooved Pegboard, nondominant hand). The authors concluded that the lack of differentiation on the neurocognitive battery suggested that the AS and HFA groups could be combined in a more general PDD category. A second study was conducted by Ozonoff, Rogers, and Pennington (1991). A neuropsychological battery was administered to groups with HFA and AS, matched on full-scale IQ and PIQ, as well as chronological age. Although both groups differed on some measures from typical control subjects, they differed from each other only in regard to verbal memory, likely an artifact of the significantly higher verbal skills in individuals with AS (Ozonoff, Rogers, & Pennington, 1991). The authors concluded that the two groups could not be reliably differentiated in terms of their neuropsychological profiles.

Though much of the research into neuropsychological distinctions has focused on verbal versus nonverbal abilities, concurrent work has addressed a particular aspect of neuropsychological skills, namely executive functions. One marginally significant finding in Szatmari and colleagues' (1990) study was that individuals with autism performed less well than those with AS on a single measure of executive functions (Wisconsin Card Sort Test, perseverative errors). Rinehart, Bradshaw, Tonge, Brereton, and Bellgrove (2002) assessed executive functions using visual-spatial tasks subserved by fronto-striatal brain regions. On this measure, individuals with AS were found to have intact performance, while those with HFA exhibited inhibitory deficits that became evident with increased cognitive demands. Ozonoff and colleagues (1991a) found that executive function did not differ between individuals with AS and HFA; however, it was the most reliable distinction between both groups and typical controls, suggesting the primacy of deficits in this area underlying a more broadly defined PDD group.

The differences in results and conclusions reported in these studies of neurocognitive functioning in AS and HFA most likely reflect different diagnostic approaches and ascertainment procedures adopted by the various groups of investigators. In general, studies adopting the most stringent diagnostic procedures, that is, selecting the most phenomenologically prototypical cases, found maximal distinctions between groups (e.g., Klin et al., 1995; Lincoln et al., 1998). Studies that failed to find distinctions between groups (e.g., Ozonoff, Rogers, & Pennington, 1991; Szatmari et al., 1990) tended to adopt broadened or otherwise modified definitions, thereby possibly reducing power to detect results (however, see Miller & Ozonoff, 2000, for an exception). This assumption, however, cannot be systematically tested until investigators from different research groups begin to adopt consensual definitions and standardized procedures for case assignment. For example, one study (Klin et al., in press) applying three diagnostic schemes *simultaneously* to the same pool of subjects with AS and HFA found significant differences in IQ differential (VIQ relative to PIQ) when case assignment followed two of the three diagnostic systems (the *DSM-IV* approach and the *unique features* approach, as discussed previously), but not when case assignment followed the third system (the *early language* approach).

Social-Cognitive Studies

A number of research studies have explored autistic children's ability to impute mental states such as beliefs, desires, and intentions to others and to themselves or to have a theory of other people's (and their own) subjectivity—a *theory of mind* (ToM; Baron-Cohen, Tager-Flusberg, & Cohen, 1999). The major hypothesis emerging from this work is that individuals with autism lack this capacity and that this fundamental deficit may explain Wing's

(Wing & Gould, 1979) triad of symptoms defining autism, namely, impairment of social and communicative functioning and imaginative activities (see Chapter 47, this *Handbook*, Volume 2, for a review). Problems in these abilities, as measured by joint attention and pretend play, are evident in children with autism as early as 18 months (Baron-Cohen, Cox, Baird, Sweettenham, & Nightingale, 1996; Charman et al., 1997).

Several studies have found evidence suggesting that differential abilities in ToM may help to distinguish AS from autism. Ozonoff, Pennington, and Rogers (1991) and Ozonoff, Rogers, and Pennington (1991) investigated "first- and second-order theory of mind." *First-order attributions* refer to a situation in which a subject must attribute a mental state—for example, a false belief—to another person, whereas *second-order attributions* require recursive thinking about mental states, in which a subject is required to predict one person's thought about another person's thoughts. First-order tasks begin to be mastered by age 4 in normally developing children, whereas the ability to make second-order attributions develops later, at around the age of 7 (Perner & Wimmer, 1985). In this study, the autistic group exhibited significant impairment in relation to both the AS and an age- and IQ-matched control group, and the AS group showed intact ToM abilities. Bowler (1992) also found that, on similar tasks, individuals with AS showed no impairment in ToM abilities relative to both IQ-matched typical individuals and a group of schizophrenic patients. Ziatas, Durkin, and Pratt (2003) reported that children with AS showed lesser impairments in mentalizing abilities than children with autism. Several publications indicate that these patterns may be evident early in development; assessments at 18 months failed to detect impairments in joint attention and pretend play in children subsequently diagnosed with AS (Baird et al., 2000; Cox et al., 1999). Studies of adults have also indicated that patients with AS exhibit more subtle impairments in ToM abilities, as demonstrated by inconsistent or delayed responses on more sophisticated and naturalistic assessments (Royers, Buysse, Ponnet, & Pichal, 2001; Kaland et al., 2002). One study (Happé et al., 1996) used positron emission tomography to examine brain activity in individuals with AS during performance of a ToM task. Patients with AS, like typical controls, showed selective activation in the medial prefrontal cortex; however, in subjects with AS the activity was localized in a slightly different region of the PFC (lower and more anterior). This finding is consistent with behavioral data suggesting existing, but abnormal, ToM abilities in AS.

Though much research suggests differential ToM abilities in individuals with AS and autism, several studies have obtained results inconsistent with this conclusion. Dahlgren and Trillingsgaard (1996) found that individuals with AS demonstrated intact ToM skills relative to typical individuals, but so did the HFA group; ToM performance was not useful in differentiating between the two diagnoses. A third pattern of results was obtained by Baron-Cohen, Wheelwright, and Jolliffee (1997), who found that individuals with AS and HFA were comparably impaired on advanced tasks of ToM.

Although at least some individuals with AS demonstrate intact abilities in many of these laboratory studies, their ability to take the perspective of another person—to adequately evaluate other people's interests, beliefs, intentions and feelings—is typically impaired in real-life contexts. This observation was originally made by Asperger himself (1944) and was reiterated by Van Krevelen (1971), who captured this phenomenon in terms of a lack of an intuitive understanding of other people's social behavior or to avail themselves from empathic feelings and from negotiating social interaction by means of quick-paced, nonverbal means. In this context, individuals with AS were said to mediate their social and emotional exchange through explicit verbal and logical means, cognitively, rigidly, and in a rule-governed fashion, rather than affectively, intuitively, and in a self-adjusting fashion (see also Klin, Jones, Schultz, & Volkmar, 2003).

Studies to date offer provocative intimations of ToM as a useful differentiator between AS and autism, but results are not fully consistent with clinical observations of social experiences of people with AS. Furthermore, these findings are vulnerable to several methodological criticisms. Frith (2004) suggested that findings pointing to a milder impairment in ToM among individuals with AS may simply reflect high verbal ability and intelligence; these cognitive characteristics provide individuals with AS with an advantage in that they may be able to succeed on ToM tasks by means of well-reasoned responses based on logical inference, rather than true social intuition. Indeed, several studies of ToM abilities have highlighted the important role played by verbal skills on subjects' performance (e.g., Happé, 1995; Sparrevohn & Howie, 1995). To avoid the formulation of an explicit task and possible verbal mediation, several studies have examined the *tendency* to attribute social meaning (including ToM) to ambiguous visual displays (geometric shapes moving and interacting in a "social manner"; e.g., Klin, 2000), showing significant deficits in ToM skills in individuals with AS, which were similar to those with HFA. One study (Grossman, Klin, Carter, & Volkmar, 2000) used a paradigm deliberately created to test the impact of verbal mediation in processing social stimuli. In this case, the task involved the processing of facial expressions, rather than ToM, although its results are relevant to the present discussion. Individuals with AS were found to be particularly susceptible to language interference in their performance when facial expressions were presented simultaneously with mismatching written verbal labels. While typical controls' accuracy and reaction time when identifying facial expressions were by and large unaffected by this "strooplike" phenomenon, this was not so for the individuals with AS, for whom the faces appeared less salient than the verbal labels.

In this context, Klin, Jones, Schultz, and Volkmar (2002) proposed that the success evidenced by individuals with AS in laboratory measures may be a function of the poor ecological validity of the paradigms used. In other words, these individuals may be able to "solve" social problems if they are explicitly formulated to them, whereas in real life there is a need to naturally seek salient social cues and generate the problem to be solved, and many such "problems" are not necessarily amenable to logical translation or verbal mediation because this process would imply very slow, sequential, piecemeal, and laborious processing, whereas real-life social situations demand fast, simultaneous, holistic, and intuitive reactions (e.g., highly synchronized and constantly changing facial expressions, posture, and prosodic cues among a host of other dynamic elements). Thus, traditional ToM tasks may oversimplify social problem solving, creating an illusion of competence not commensurate with demonstrated abilities in real-life social contexts. Aware of this problem, Tager-Flusberg (2001) contrasted two aspects of ToM competence: first, the ability to successfully acquire social information from the environment (social perception) and, second, the ability to reason about it (social cognition). She hypothesized that autism entails impairment in both aspects, but AS involves only problems with social perception. This conceptualization offers a potential explanation for the problems experienced by individuals with AS in real life that are not replicated in lab studies; real-life situations entail fluid, ambiguous, contextually defined information, while laboratory studies tend to provide more explicit information.

These criticisms indicate that to truly assess ToM ability as a differentiating factor between AS and HFA, there is a need for more naturalistic and ecologically valid studies. Investigators interested in ToM capacities must devise experimental situations less amenable to logical and verbal solutions. Optimally, these should involve processing of more visual rather than verbal stimuli and more naturalistic and socially contextualized rather than abstract and logical situations, and processing time (i.e., latency of response) should be an important parameter to be considered given that, clinically, individuals with AS typically cannot avail themselves of their formal social knowledge in quick-paced, simultaneously shifting, social situations.

Medical and Neurobiological Studies

A number of studies have attempted to differentiate AS from HFA based on neurobiological measures. Several reports of neurobiological abnormalities associated with AS have appeared, although no consensus has been reached because many of these reports have been case studies or involved very small samples and because of the ubiquitous nosologic issues discussed earlier. Wing (1981) noted a higher than expected frequency of perinatal problems (nearly half of her original sample) among this population. However, Gillberg and Gillberg (1989) concluded that reduced obstetric optimality was more common in autism than in AS. Other reports have associated certain medical conditions with individual cases of AS—for example, aminoaciduria (Miles & Capelle, 1987) and ligamentous laxity (Tantam, Evered, & Hersov, 1990). Casanova, Buxhoeveden, Switala, and Roy (2002) found abnormalities in the organization of minicolumns in both AS and autism, suggesting common underlying neural pathology. A case series by Gillberg (1989) reported high frequencies of medical anomalies, also common to both diagnostic groups; however, these results have been challenged (Rutter, Bailey, Bolton, & Le Couteur, 1994).

Neuroimaging studies of AS and autism have become one of the most prolific areas of research in the field. Nevertheless, there is scant data to differentiate neuroanatomical structures and functions between AS and autism. Most studies have sampled one group or the other or collapsed them into an ASD group. Some studies have, however, focused on individuals with AS as compared to typical controls and found discrepancies in brain structure. Berthier, Starkstein, and Leiguarda (1990) reported MRI results indicating left frontal macrogyria and bilateral opercular polymicrogyria in patients with AS. These findings were linked to cortical migration abnormalities in a first-degree relative with bipolar disorder. Other studies have reported gray tissue anomalies in subjects with AS as compared to typical controls (McAlonan et al., 2002). Several case studies have revealed left temporal lobe damage (Jones & Kerwin, 1990; CT scan) and left occipital hypoperfusion (Ozbayrak, Kapucu, Erdem, & Aras, 1991; SPECT) in patients with AS. In a case study by Volkmar and colleagues (1996), a father and son with AS showed virtually identical abnormalities on their MRIs. The father's images showed a large, bilateral, V-shaped wedge of missing tissue just superior to the ascending ramus of the Sylvian fissure, at about the level where the middle frontal gyrus normally intersects with the precentral sulcus. The son's images showed similar dysmorphology in the

same area, although it was larger on the right side; his images also showed decreased tissue in the anterior-inferior right temporal lobe, suggesting an atrophic process or a regional neurodevelopmental growth failure. Both father and son exhibited a similar neuropsychological profile, and the similarity of brain anomalies and symptoms is suggestive of potential familial transmission.

A more limited set of studies has employed functional imaging and spectroscopy to demonstrate differences in brain function and neurotransmitter concentrations between individuals with AS and typical controls. Murphy and colleagues (2002) used proton magnetic resonance spectroscopy to examine the relationship between abnormalities in frontal and parietal lobes and clinical symptomatology. Compared to typical controls, patients with AS had higher levels of N-acetylaspartate (NAA), creatine and phosphocreatine, and choline, neurotransmitters that serve as indicators of neuronal density, mitochondrial metabolism, phosphate metabolism, and membrane turnover. Furthermore, there were positive correlations between neurotransmitter levels and clinical presentation: Higher levels of prefrontal NAA were associated with obsessional behavior, and increased prefrontal choline was associated with social function. The authors concluded that individuals with AS exhibit abnormalities in neuronal integrity of the prefrontal cortex, which relates to their unique pattern of symptoms. McKelvey, Lambert, Mottron, and Shevell (1995) reported on three patients with abnormal right hemisphere functioning on SPECT imaging, a finding consistent with the NLD neurocognitive model of AS.

A handful of studies have attempted to study differential brain structure in individuals with AS and autism. Studies have suggested that, across diagnosis, higher functioning individuals on the autism spectrum tend not to exhibit hypoplasia of the neocerebellar vermis, a finding more common in lower functioning people on the spectrum that may be associated more with mental retardation than with autism (e.g., Piven et al., 1992; Piven, Palmer, Jacobi, Childress, & Arndt, 1997). In some contrast, Lincoln and colleagues (1998) reported that individuals with autism (relative to AS) exhibited more consistent pathology of the cerebellar vermis, thinner posterior corpus callosum, and smaller anterior corpus callosum. One recent study has provided exciting information about potential neuroanatomical distinctions between subgroups of ASDs. Lotspeich et al. (2004) compared individuals with HFA and low-functioning autism (LFA) and AS. The study indicated enlarged cerebral gray matter volumes in HFA and LFA relative to controls. The AS group showed enlargement that was intermediate with respect to patients with autism and typical controls but was not significantly different from either. The authors inferred that cerebral gray matter may correlate with symptom severity, suggesting that AS represents the mild end of the continuum. This study also detected differential relationships between brain structure and neurocognitive function; cerebral white matter volume was positively correlated with PIQ only in subjects with AS, and gray matter correlated with PIQ in both HFA and AS, but in different directions (positive correlation in AS, negative correlation in HFA). Another study added a comorbid component, namely Tourette's syndrome (TS) to this discussion. Berthier, Bayes, and Tolosa (1993) used MRI to study brain structure in patients with comorbid AS and TS and with patients with TS alone. Results revealed cortical and subcortical abnormalities in 5 of the 7 patients with AS and TS, but only in 1 of the 9 patients with TS only.

Findings to date do not present a clear picture of the neurobiological underpinnings of AS or replicated distinctions among the ASDs. In many ways, issues of definition of the ASD subgroups make it impossible to derive firm conclusions from the available data. Additionally, there are methodological issues related to intersite differences in imaging techniques (e.g., Lotspeich et al., 2004). Nevertheless, this growing volume of literature holds great promise, particularly in those studies in which a more specific brain-behavior relationship is found. In this context, neuroimaging studies, and particularly functional MRI research, should be guided by neuropsychological and social-cognitive models that hold the potential to explain core aspects of the presentation of individuals with ASDs. And although analyses have often been performed on the basis of

categorical subgrouping, dimensional analyses (e.g., association between quantified brain activation and measurable aspects of the phenotype) may prove more powerful in the long run. Equally important are the initial efforts to move to measures of interconnectivity of key brain systems subserving cognitive and social processing (see Chapter 19, this *Handbook,* this volume).

Genetics

From its original description by Asperger (1944), there has been evidence for familial vulnerabilities in AS. As noted, Asperger observed similar characteristics in family members, particularly in fathers. This genetic predisposition is in keeping with more recent findings demonstrating that the ASDs are among the most heritable of psychiatric conditions (Rutter, Bailey, Simonoff, & Pickles, 1997), although knowledge about patterns of inheritability and genetic etiologies is still limited (see Chapter 16, this *Handbook,* this volume). Given the heterogeneity of the ASDs, it is of little surprise, but of great importance, to consider the fact that the ASDs are the more severe manifestations of a broader and possibly more prevalent phenotype of social-communicative difficulties and behavioral rigidities (e.g., Bailey et al., 1995; Le Couteur et al., 1996).

Consistent with Asperger's original observation, a number of case reports have reported similar traits in family members, especially among fathers (Bowman, 1988; DeLong & Dwyer, 1988; Gillberg, Gillberg, & Steffenburg, 1992; Volkmar et al., 1996). Others have reported data on social vulnerabilities in other relatives. Multiple births concordant for AS have been observed (Burgoine & Wing, 1983). Volkmar and colleagues (1997) examined family history data and found that nearly half of the families surveyed reported information positive to AS, ASDs, and the broader autism phenotype in first-degree relatives, most commonly among males. The probands with AS were more likely (relative to general population rates) to have a sibling diagnosed with autism or an ASD; this was twice as likely in male siblings as in female siblings. Rates of autism and ASD were also increased in first cousins. Klin et al. (in press) reported similar results. When using the unique features diagnostic scheme (as described earlier), it was of interest that the rates of ASDs or the broader autism phenotype in parents and grandparents (males and females) of probands with AS was over triple the rate found for the same relatives of probands with HFA (17% versus 5%). This finding suggests even stronger genetic contributions in families of probands of AS relative to those of probands with autism (Volkmar & Klin, 2000).

Though still limited, there are some reports of autism and AS co-occurring in different members of the same family (e.g., Wing, 1981). In our clinical experience and in a preliminary report (Klin et al., in press), we have observed some sibships in which one brother has autism and the other has AS. The fact that the triplets reported by Burgoine and Wing (1983) had some aspects of their history more similar to patterns observed in autism also suggests a common familial link between autism and AS. Collectively, these findings point to genetic mechanisms in common not only between autism and AS but also among all ASDs (Frith, 2004).

In addition to evidence of familial patterns in AS, direct evidence of a genetic component has been published. Specific genetic abnormalities have been reported in case studies of patients with AS—for example, one case with a balanced de novo translocation (Anneren, Dahl, Uddenfeldt, & Janols, 1995), one case with an autosomal fragile site (Saliba & Griffiths, 1990), and a possible association with fragile X syndrome (Bartolucci & Szatmari, 1987). Tentler and colleagues (2003) found two patients with AS with balanced translocations on chromosome 17, perhaps suggesting a candidate sequence. Although these findings are only preliminary, they provide guidelines for future research studies and concrete sources for explicating the shared genetic components of AS and other ASDs.

Fast-accruing genetic data have the promise of moving research on ASD subtypes from the rather imprecise phenotypic comparisons to date to potential endophenotypes mediating syndrome expression. For this to happen, however, there is a need for much more refined phenotypic characterization of both core symptoms and hypothesized neuropsychological, social-cognitive, or neurobiological patterns.

Outcome

Asperger's (1944) initial description predicted a positive outcome for many of his patients, largely based on his hope that they would be able to use their special talents for the purpose of obtaining employment and leading self-supporting lives. His observation of similar traits in family members encouraged the notion that patients could marry and raise families. Although his account was tempered somewhat by experience (Asperger, 1979), Asperger continued to believe that a more positive outcome was a central criterion differentiating individuals with his syndrome from those with Kanner's autism. In considering autism inclusive of low-functioning cases, this would certainly be the case (Gillberg, 1991). When compared with individuals with HFA, outcome of individuals with AS is more likely to be more positive on the basis of case reports, anecdotal evidence, and some preliminary studies, but data supporting this hypothesis are still scant. More positive outcomes for individuals with AS could simply reflect the overall effects of the preserved language and cognitive skills required for the diagnosis (for at least the first years of life). Nevertheless, some studies support the notion of differential outcomes in individuals with AS and HFA. Several studies examined outcome in young adults with AS (Newson, Dawson, & Everaard, 1984/1985; Tantam, 1991) and reported that although most remained at home despite high cognitive potential, a minority of them had married and/or held regular employment. Though a comparable sample with autism was not assessed, this outcome appears better than typically expected for individuals with HFA. Gillberg (1998) suggested that patients with AS experience more positive outcomes, especially in the domains of academics and self-help skills. In contrast, Szatmari, Bartolucci, et al. (1989b) compared outcomes in children with AS and HFA and noted minimal differences. Others have reported that older individuals and adults with AS and HFA are so similar that they are difficult or impossible to distinguish on the basis of outcome (Gilchrist et al., 2001; Howlin, 2003; Szatmari et al., 2000). All of these three studies, however, used the early language approach as a diagnostic scheme for case assignment, which, at least in our experience, yields the least contrast between the two groups (Klin et al., in press). A recent study (Szatmari, Bryson, Boyle, et al., 2003) looked into predictors of outcome by ASD subtype by following children with autism and AS between the ages of 4 and 6 years through 10 to 13 years using adaptive behavior (i.e., levels of ability, which are norm-based) and measures of autistic symptoms (i.e., levels of disability) and found that the power of prediction was stable over time but different for the two groups. The authors found that the association between language skills and outcome was stronger in the autism group than in the AS group, suggesting that for the individuals with AS, higher language skills did not confer any advantage. Of great practical importance, however, was that the explanatory power of the predictor variables was greater for communication and social skills than for autistic symptoms, suggesting the possibility that adaptive competence (levels of self-sufficiency) and autistic symptomatology (levels of disability) may constitute rather independent facets of these children's development. This finding was corroborated in a recent study (Klin, Saulnier, Sparrow, Cicchetti, Lord, & Volkmar, in press). From a practical perspective, this point suggests that intervention programs should emphasize *both* reduction of symptoms and improvement of self-sufficiency skills given that the focus on the former does not necessarily imply advancement of the latter.

Despite these interesting preliminary data, it is important to recognize that the status of research into differential outcomes is still quite limited (Howlin, 1997). This is particularly regrettable given that of all the possible reasons to separate these two conditions, differential outcome would probably be the one with the greatest practical relevance. There is a need to ensure, however, that well-known mediators of outcome, and particularly IQ and language levels past the first years of life, are not components of the diagnostic definitions, which would create circularity in the study design and would likely result in spurious differences between the two groups.

Summary of Validation Studies

A common thread throughout the reviewed validation studies is the sore need for consensual and reliable diagnostic criteria for AS and demonstration of the fidelity of the concept across sites. Future research should attempt to:

1. *Ensure that differences between AS and other conditions are independent of the criteria defining disorders.* Historically, studies have employed circular reasoning, with results reflecting the diagnostic criteria rather than providing additional information. Dependent variables should be independent of (i.e., not a function of, not highly correlated with, not associated with, and not a result of) diagnostic criteria.

2. *Adopt an agreed-on definition, and* operationalize *it in much greater detail (including the process used to obtain data used in diagnostic decision making).* One possibility is to modify well-proven diagnostic instrumentation such as the Autism Diagnostic Interview-Revised (Rutter, Le Couteur, & Lord, 2003) and the Autism Diagnostic Observation Schedule (Lord, Rutter, DiLavore, & Risi, 1999; see Chapter 28, this *Handbook,* Volume 2) to include an "AS module" covering the more unique features of AS in every domain of characterization (i.e., onset, social, communication, and narrow interests and behaviors), as well as differential diagnostic algorithms keyed to the consensually adopted defining criteria. It is indeed very unlikely that any of the issues related to the nosologic status of AS discussed in this chapter will be resolved in the absence of an effort of this kind.

3. *Include larger samples and multisite comparisons.* Much of our understanding of the putative differences between AS and HFA stems from reports involving case studies or small case series. Larger studies will not only improve power to detect differences but also increase the likelihood that results are meaningful and replicable. And there have been striking differences in findings across research groups, which may reflect not only different methodologies but also different biases in subject recruitment. To overcome this critical difficulty, there is a need for cross-site studies using tools of the

kinds described earlier within a common effort to carry out a well-controlled, multi-center field trial.

4. *Avoid oversimplifications of key clinical phenomena.* Historically, research on AS has failed to acknowledge, describe, operationalize, or quantify the complex set of clinical phenomena involved in key concepts defining AS such as circumscribed interests, social awkwardness in the presence of social motivation, pedantic style, and verbosity as a strategy for social adaptation among others. Many studies gloss over these phenomena, providing limited or no description of the sample beyond rather vague statements.

5. *Ensure the achievement of, and report data on, interrater reliability of procedures used in diagnostic process (e.g., semistructured interviews, best-estimate diagnoses) and, if possible, document the entire process to make possible the replication of the various procedures by members of a different research team.*

Additionally, it may be useful for investigators to depart from the prevalent model of validation research in which data are collected and compared on the basis of clinical groups formed by a priori diagnostic assignments. Because the validity of ASD subtypes is still uncertain (see Chapter 1, this *Handbook,* this volume), much could be learned by reversing the process. Researchers could assess meaningful and interesting patterns (e.g., detailed onset and early development patterns, specific neuropsychological, social-cognitive, or neurobiological profiles) and then carefully chart the range of phenotypic expressions associated with them. This approach would redefine phenotype as a dependent variable and open the door for the use of statistical techniques to empirically define the existence of true categories.

CLINICAL ASSESSMENT OF INDIVIDUALS WITH ASPERGER SYNDROME

The topic of clinical assessment of children with ASD is reviewed in much greater detail in Chapters 28 through 32, Volume 2, of this *Handbook.* In this section, we briefly discuss assessment procedures uniquely relevant to

individuals with AS. For a more comprehensive discussion of the issues outlined here, the reader is referred to a more complete text (Klin, Sparrow, Marans, Carter, & Volkmar, 2000) and Chapter 29, Volume 2, of this *Handbook.*

AS, like the other PDDs, involves delays and deviant patterns of behavior in multiple areas of functioning. Thorough evaluation of all relevant domains requires different areas of expertise, including overall developmental functioning, neuropsychological features, language and communication skills, adaptive functioning, and behavioral status. Therefore, the clinical assessment of individuals with this disorder is most effectively conducted by an experienced, interdisciplinary team.

In the majority of cases, a comprehensive interdisciplinary assessment will involve the following components: a thorough developmental and health history, psychological and communication assessments, and a diagnostic work-up including differential diagnosis. Further consultation regarding behavioral management, motor disabilities, possible neurological concerns, comorbidities and associated psychopharmacology, and assessment related to advanced studies or vocational training may also be needed. Given the prevailing difficulties in the definition of AS and the great heterogeneity of the condition, it is crucial that the aim of the clinical assessment be a comprehensive and detailed profile of the individual's assets, deficits, and challenges, rather than simply a diagnostic label. Effective educational and treatment programs can be devised only on the basis of such a profile, given the need to address specific deficits while capitalizing on the person's various resources and strengths.

The psychological assessment aims at establishing the overall level of intellectual functioning, profiles of psychomotor functioning, verbal and nonverbal cognitive strengths and weaknesses, style of learning, and adaptive behaviors (or independent living skills). At a minimum, the psychological assessment should include assessments of intelligence and adaptive functioning, although the assessment of more detailed neuropsychological skills can be of great help to further delineate the child's profiles of strengths and deficits (e.g., in regard to organizational skills). A description of results should include not only quantified information but also a judgment as to how representative the child's performance was during the assessment procedure and a description of the conditions that are likely to foster optimal and diminished performance. For example, the child's responses to the amount of structure imposed by the adult, the optimal pace for presentation of tasks, successful strategies to facilitate learning from modeling and demonstrations, and effective ways of containing off-task and maladaptive behaviors such as cognitive and behavioral rigidity (e.g., verbal perseverations, perfectionism), distractibility (e.g., difficulty inhibiting irrelevant responses, tangentiality), and anxiety are all important observations that can be extremely useful for designing and optimizing intervention programs. Within the psychological assessment, particular emphasis should be placed on the assessment of adaptive functioning, which refers to capacities for personal and social self-sufficiency in real-life situations. The importance of this component of the clinical assessment cannot be overemphasized. Its aim is to obtain a measure of the child's typical patterns of functioning in familiar and representative environments such as the home and the school, which may contrast markedly with the demonstrated level of performance and presentation in the clinic. It provides the clinician with an essential indicator of the extent to which the child is able to use his or her potential (as measured in the assessment) in the process of adaptation to environmental demands. A large discrepancy between intellectual level and adaptive level signifies that a priority should be made of instruction within the context of naturally occurring situations to foster and facilitate the use of skills to enhance quality of life.

The communication assessment should examine nonverbal forms of communication (e.g., gaze, gestures), nonliteral language (e.g., metaphor, irony, absurdities, and humor), suprasegmental aspects of speech (e.g., patterns of inflection, stress, and volume modulation), pragmatics (e.g., turn taking, sensitivity to cues provided by the interlocutor), and content, coherence, and contingency of conversation. Particular attention should be given to perseveration on circumscribed topics, metalinguistic skills (e.g., understanding of the language of mental states including intentions, emotions, and beliefs), reciprocity, and rules of conversation.

The diagnostic assessment should integrate information obtained in all components of the comprehensive evaluation, with a special emphasis on developmental history and current symptomatology. It should include observations of the child during more and less structured periods. This effort should take advantage of observations in all settings, including the clinic's reception area (e.g., contacts with other children or with family members), the halls (e.g., how the child interacts initially with the examiners), as well as in the testing room during breaks, periods of silence, or otherwise unstructured situations. Often, the child's disability is much more apparent during such periods in which the child is not given any instruction and has no adult-imposed expectation as to how to behave. Specific areas for observation and inquiry include the patient's patterns of special interest and leisure time, social and affective presentation, quality of attachment to family members, development of peer relationships and friendships, capacities for self-awareness, perspective-taking and level of insight into social and behavioral problems, typical reactions in novel situations, and ability to intuit another person's feelings and infer another person's intentions and beliefs. Problem behaviors that are likely to interfere with remedial programming should be noted (e.g., anxiety, temper tantrums). The child's ability to understand ambiguous, nonliteral communications (particularly teasing and sarcasm) should be further examined, particularly in regard to the child's patterns of response (e.g., misunderstandings of such communications may elicit aggressive behaviors). Other areas of observation involve the presence of obsessions or compulsions, ritualized behaviors, depression and panic attacks, integrity of thought, and reality testing.

One important aspect of the diagnostic characterization of individuals with AS relates to the need to differentiate diagnostic instruments from diagnostic screeners. The former typically involve comprehensive, semistructured procedures including both information provided by parents or caregivers and direct examination and aim at producing a detailed profile of developmental patterns and current behavioral presentation needed for diagnostic assignment. The latter typically involve the completion of a brief checklist by parents, caregivers, teachers, or other professionals, or by self-report, and aim at identifying those with a higher probability of having the condition from the general population. It is critical to emphasize that screeners are not meant to replace the diagnostic process. Rather, they are meant to provide the basis for further referral. Currently, the only diagnostic instrument available that considers the distinction of autism from AS is the Asperger Syndrome (and high-functioning autism) Diagnostic Interview (ASDI; Gillberg, Gillberg, Rastam, & Wentz, 2001), although there are no data supporting this instrument's validity insofar as the distinction between AS and HFA is concerned. There are no other diagnostic instruments developed for the specific purpose of subtyping the ASDs into autism, AS, and PDD-NOS. As mentioned earlier, there seems to be a great need for modification of current instruments to make possible this differentiation, although this recommendation is closely tied to other developments in validity studies of AS. In contrast, there are a large number of diagnostic screeners purported to identify individuals with AS, some of which appear to be of help in identifying vulnerabilities within the autism spectrum, but none has been shown to differentiate (nor has that been a stated objective) individuals with AS from those with autism or PDD-NOS.

TREATMENT AND INTERVENTIONS

The topic of treatment and interventions is briefly summarized here, with an emphasis on issues that are uniquely relevant to individuals with AS. More comprehensive guidelines are reviewed in Chapters 33 through 44, Volume 2, of this *Handbook*.

As in autism, treatment of AS is essentially supportive and symptomatic, and to a great extent, overlaps with the treatment guidelines applicable to individuals with HFA (Mesibov, 1992). Though a similar set of recommendations applies to individuals with both conditions, interventionists are often

more optimistic about individuals with AS given the common finding of relatively preserved social motivation. Unfortunately, there is currently a paucity of systematic data demonstrating the effectiveness of particular interventions, although some progress has been made in this area (see Klin & Volkmar, 2003, for a summary of treatment studies and of treatment approaches). Medications may be effective in treating associated features of the disorder, such as inattention, anxiety, or depression, although psychopharmacology cannot yet target core impairments in AS or, for that matter, other ASDs. In recent years, clinicians and educators experienced with this population have published a number of volumes proffering useful education and intervention strategies (e.g., Attwood, 1998; Bashe & Kirby, 2001; Howlin, 1999; Myles & Simpson, 1997; Ozonoff, Dawson, & McPartland, 2002; Powers & Poland, 2002; Wing, 2001). In general, recommended interventions focus on: (1) devising strategies to take advantage of the unique constellation of strengths characteristic of AS to compensate for areas of difficulty and (2) modifying contexts (i.e., environments) to maximally support the learning and behavioral styles of this population. The recommended content or treatments should be tailored, based on a thorough assessment, to the individual needs of the patient. However, nearly universally applicable foci include acquisition of basic social and communication skills, adaptive functioning, organizational skills, and, depending on what is developmentally appropriate, academic or vocational skills. It is also crucial that any intervention program incorporate techniques to encourage generalization of acquired skills to ensure the use of learned abilities in novel contexts.

Securing Services

Despite the great progress in dissemination of awareness and understanding of AS, the authorities deciding on eligibility for services may fail to appreciate the severity of the various disabilities exhibited by individuals with AS. Proficient verbal skills, overall IQ usually within the normal range, and a solitary lifestyle often mask outstanding deficiencies observed primarily in novel or otherwise socially demanding situations, thus decreasing the perception of the very salient needs for supportive intervention. Hence there is a need for active participation on the part of the clinician, together with parents and possibly an advocate, to forcefully pursue the student's access to appropriately supportive programs. The formalization of the diagnosis in *ICD-10* and *DSM-IV,* together with the directives from the National Research Council report (2001) that individuals with all forms of ASDs (including AS) should be provided with intensive and comprehensive educational programs of the kinds prescribed for individuals with autism, has facilitated this process somewhat. In the past, many individuals with AS were diagnosed as having learning disabilities with some eccentric features, a nonpsychiatric diagnostic label that is much less effective in securing services. Others, who were given the diagnosis of autism or PDD-NOS, had often to contend with educational programs designed for much lower functioning children, thus failing to have their relative strengths and unique disabilities properly addressed. Yet another group of individuals with AS is sometimes characterized as exhibiting *social-emotional maladjustment* (SEM), an educational label that is often associated with conduct problems and volitional maladaptive behaviors. These individuals are often placed in educational settings for individuals with conduct disorders, thus allowing for the worse mismatch possible, namely, of individuals with a very naïve understanding of social situations with those who can and do manipulate social situations to their advantage without the benefit of self-restraint.

Learning

In educating students with AS, it is crucial to take advantage of their typically strong language skills and concrete style of thinking. Skills, concepts, appropriate procedures, cognitive strategies, and behavioral norms may be most effectively taught in an explicit and rote fashion using a parts-to-whole verbal instruction approach, where the verbal steps are in the correct sequence for the behavior to be effective. The educational program should be tailored to the child, not to the diagnosis, and derived from the individual's neuropsycholog-

ical profile of assets and deficits; specific intervention techniques should be similar to those usually employed for many subtypes of learning disabilities, with an effort to circumvent the identified difficulties by means of compensatory strategies relying on areas of strength, in this case, usually verbal abilities. If significant motor and visual-motor deficits exist, the individual should receive physical and occupational therapies and, where available, assistive technologies (e.g., using a laptop to type assignments rather than writing). Occupational therapy should not only focus on traditional techniques designed to remediate motor deficits but also reflect an effort to integrate these activities with learning of visual-spatial concepts, visual-spatial orientation, and body awareness.

Adaptive Functioning

The acquisition of self-sufficiency skills in all areas of functioning should also be a priority. Because individuals with AS tend to rely on rigid rules and routines, these can be used to foster positive habits and enhance the person's quality of life and that of family members. The teaching approach should follow closely the guidelines set earlier (see preceding Learning subsection) and should be practiced routinely in naturally occurring situations and across different settings to maximize generalization of acquired skills.

Behavioral Management

Challenging behaviors are common among individuals with AS. As noted, their motivations are rarely malicious and are more likely to stem from difficulties with arousal regulation and poor emotional insight into self and others. Specific problem-solving strategies, usually following a verbal algorithm, may be taught for handling the requirements of frequently occurring, troublesome situations (e.g., involving novelty, intense social demands, or frustration). Training is usually necessary for recognizing situations as troublesome and for selecting the best available learned strategy to use in such situations. Cognitive and behavioral strategies for anxiety management (e.g., breathing exercises) are often helpful in teaching students to control negative emotions. In designing any intervention to control problematic behaviors, it is important to collect data to both understand the function that they are serving to the child (i.e., using functional behavior analysis) and to ascertain a true estimate of the efficacy of treatment.

Communication and Social Skills Training

Because individuals with AS experience communication deficits predominantly within the domain of pragmatics, these skills are best taught by or with the support of a communication specialist with expertise in this area. Conversation skills should be taught directly including self-monitoring level of diction and volume, taking turns in conversation, topic introduction, and maintenance.

The interrelationship between language and social ability makes it helpful to interweave communicative training with interventions to specifically address social skills. A general principle for teaching social skills is to explicitly define rules for social behavior; individuals with AS lack the intuition and social wherewithal to detect and respond to social information effectively, and this strategy helps them to compensate for these deficits. On an individual basis, teaching explicit scripts that can be used in social situations (e.g., approaching a peer) capitalizes on strong rote memory abilities; these scripts can then be rehearsed in role play. For children requiring more basic social interventions, practicing expression and recognition of facial expressions is useful; in students with higher levels of ability, this may involve teaching them to read more subtle social cues. Many aids, including software programs, have been developed to facilitate such goals; in this domain and, more generally, it is helpful to move from static to dynamic. For example, children may practice recognizing affect in pictures or cartoons, subsequently moving on to videotapes, then finally during in vivo role modeling. A number of excellent guidelines have been published to guide parents and interventionists in teaching social skills.

Social skills training groups are an effective and increasingly common intervention for working on pragmatics and social abilities. Such groups involve a small number of children with social impairments (they may include typical peer models, but it is important that typical peers receive prior training) working in concert with one or more educators. They are uniquely beneficial in allowing for didactic training and practice with peers in a single setting. Furthermore, they may foster development of supportive relationships (for both children and their parents) that endure after group has concluded. Teaching may include the following:

1. Appropriate nonverbal behavior (e.g., the use of gaze for social interaction, monitoring and patterning inflection of voice). This may involve imitative drills, working with a mirror, and so forth.
2. Verbal decoding of nonverbal behaviors of others (e.g., the meaning of social and affective cues, posture, voice patterns).
3. Processing of visual information simultaneously with auditory information (to foster integration of competing stimuli and facilitate the creation of the appropriate social context of the interaction).
4. Social and self-awareness.
5. Social norms and expectations.
6. Perspective-taking skills.
7. Correct interpretation of ambiguous communications (e.g., nonliteral language).

All of these should be taught, practiced, and fostered in multiple environments.

Assistive Technology

Recent advances in computer technology and the expansion of the Internet offer everexpanding opportunities for individuals with ASDs. The intellectual capabilities of people with AS render them viable computer users, and, for many individuals, computer-based work is intrinsically very rewarding. Computers are now considered useful in numerous aspects of intervention. Given the frequency of graphomotor problems, typing academic assignments or employment-related tasks alleviates much of the difficulty associated with manual penmanship. Organizational software and personal data assistants can be immensely useful in helping individuals with schedules, to-do lists, and a variety of other organizational tasks that are very challenging for those with executive dysfunction (Ozonoff, 1998).

The Internet is an excellent medium for parents and educators to communicate regarding academic goals and behavior management, thereby increasing consistency across people and settings, which is so vital to maximize the effectiveness of interventions for individuals with AS. Finally, the computer skills acquired through these activities may, and often do, become a valuable asset in the context of vocational opportunities later in life.

Vocational Training

Adults with AS often fail to meet entry requirements for jobs in their area of training or fail to maintain a job because of their poor interview skills, social disabilities, eccentricities, anxiety attacks, and, at times, poor grooming. All of these areas may require appropriate interventions and preparation prior to challenging events. To ensure success, it is also important that they are trained for and are placed in jobs for which they are not neuropsychologically impaired and in which they will enjoy a certain degree of support and shelter. It is also preferable that the job does not involve intensive social demands, time pressures, or the need to quickly improvise or generate solutions to novel situations.

Self-Support

Because individuals with AS are usually self-described loners despite an often intense wish to make friends and have a more active social life, there is a need to facilitate social contact within the context of an activity-oriented group (e.g., church communities, hobby clubs, and self-support groups). The little experience available with the latter suggests that individuals with AS enjoy the opportunity to meet others with similar problems and may develop relationships around an activity or subject of shared interest. Internet support groups and chat rooms have proved to be excellent forums for individuals with AS and their families to make contact with others who may share an interest in AS or may simply partake in a common enjoyed activity. For many individuals with AS, a strategy that may help in the management of an individual's everyday needs is to maintain long-term supportive contact with a counselor. Therapy can focus on problems of

empathy, social difficulties, and depressive symptoms, and a more direct, problem-solving focus can at times be more beneficial than an insight-oriented approach.

Pharmacotherapy

No medications have been shown to decrease the core social and communicative symptomatology of individuals with ASDs. However, pharmacological approaches, typically combined with behavioral interventions and appropriate adaptations in the child's environment, can be very helpful in allaying comorbid symptoms involving anxiety, depression, inattention, and others, thus making the child more available to educational and therapeutic activities. Physicians prescribing medications should be knowledgeable not only of the comorbid conditions that they are treating but also, and especially, of the nature of the ASDs. Multifaceted symptoms should be treated with a minimal number of agents, and planning of pharmacological intervention should include clear definitions of targeted symptoms and evaluative procedures to ensure that the medication is having a positive impact on the child's functioning and well-being (Towbin, 2003). Continued follow-up is required to adjust treatment (e.g., to slowly reach therapeutic levels), evaluate effects, and possibly discontinue or change the intervention if there are prohibitive side effects or if there is no demonstrated benefit.

CONCLUSION

Since the previous edition of the *Handbook* in 1997, the major positive changes involving the diagnostic construct of AS occurred in areas other than progress in clinical research. First, there has been an ever-increasing awareness by the general public and authorities deciding on supportive services of the needs and strengths of individuals with this condition. Lorna Wing's influential introduction of the term in 1981 has, 2 decades later, accomplished its stated goal of bringing individuals with severe social disabilities accompanied by preserved cognitive and language skills to the attention of the clinical community and educational systems. And although misperceptions remain, there is a general consensus that these individuals require special services without which they cannot fulfill their potential and live more independent and fulfilling lives. Second, with the formalization of the disorder and the entitlements associated with it, there has been a great need for practical resources addressing these individuals' needs for social and communication skills training and other areas of intervention throughout their life span. In response to this need, there has been an exponential growth in the past few years of publications meant to set guidelines and strategies for teaching skills necessary for social adaptation, learning, self-regulation, and vocational success. Most of these strategies have not been systematically examined, and indeed, this is a great priority for the next decade.

In contrast to these developments, clinical research has been hindered by lack of progress as to the validity status of AS. Much of this research has been flawed due in great degree to a lack of a consensual, validated, and well-operationalized definition of the condition. While the question of whether AS can be differentiated from autism without intellectual disabilities may have originated from the chance referrals to Leo Kanner and Hans Asperger, it has endured for more substantial reasons. The ASDs refer to a highly heterogeneous phenotype, which nevertheless is primarily defined by the pronounced and early emerging social disability. Given the complexity of social behavior, it is not unreasonable to expect that there may be more than one developmental pathway generating the variable manifestations of these conditions. Therefore, the successful identification of more homogeneous subtypes can potentially be of great benefit to behavioral and neurobiological research seeking to yield more effective treatment strategies and to elucidate the causative processes underlying the etiologies of these conditions. In the face of this challenge, however, research studies have failed to produce the level of substantive detail in phenotypic characterization and of documentation of longitudinal outcomes required for true progress in the understanding of developmental mechanisms mediating syndrome expression. It is premature to close the door on this debate because the data are still limited as to whether the ASDs, and autism and AS in particular, should be considered the same or different.

Two general lines of research may be adopted to elucidate this issue.

First, if we consider the possibility that the two conditions are the same or simply variable manifestations of the same underlying construct—the ASDs—then there is a need to clarify the dimensions creating this spectrum. With the exception of IQ and language skills, there has not been much progress in elucidating the potential factors mediating expression of the syndrome and determining eventual outcomes. To this goal, there is a need for research relating, in a quantified manner, specific neuropsychological, social-cognitive, or neurobiological models to phenotypic expression including measures of outcome such as levels of symptomatology and of ability or adaptation. All ASDs have their onset in the early years of a child's life. Longitudinal research is needed in which key developmental processes hypothesized to mediate phenotypic expression are evaluated relative to the range of phenotypic variability later in life. The rather vague onset criteria established for the ASDs could hardly be expected to elucidate the thorny diagnostic issues presented by these conditions later in life. And there are still very few studies that have attempted to examine prospectively the early years of individuals later diagnosed as having AS. As these individuals typically come to the attention of specialized clinics later in childhood (given the absence of the more common reasons for referral such as language delays and social isolation), most of what we know about the onset of this condition is based on retrospective information. Yet, the formal definitions of AS depend entirely on onset patterns as a way of differentiating it from autism. In summary, there is a need for much greater knowledge about the eventual impact on phenopic expression of variables ranging from social motivation to joint attention skills, from sensory and psychomotor adaptation and self-regulation to executive abilities, and from different learning styles to different language profiles to gain more knowledge of different pathways to social disabilities.

Second, if we consider the possibility that AS and autism are different conditions, then there is a need to clarify what is meant by the word *different*. There are various practical reasons that a person may justifiably choose to see two conditions as different (Szatmari, 2000), but the most important ones concern the fact that they may have different etiologies or pathogenetic pathways (e.g., genetic mechanisms), they may respond differently to different kinds of treatment (e.g., because of different neurocognitive, social-cognitive, or neurobiological profiles), or they may imply differential outcomes (which would signify more detailed guidelines for intervention to better address the eventual challenges and maximize factors promoting eventual success). None of these important areas of research can, however, be dramatically advanced without a much more detailed, standardized, and quantified description of the two conditions. There is a great deal of knowledge about autism in general, but much less about the group of higher functioning individuals, most of whom are seen in clinics at a later age for the same reasons that individuals with AS are also not seen in early childhood. As suggested earlier, given the current status of the diagnostic process feeding into research studies of AS, it is unlikely that progress will be made without a concerted multisite effort adopting rigorous diagnostic procedures. These should include new and especially developed diagnostic instrumentation operationalized around a consensual set of defining criteria.

Finally, interest in AS has opened the door to debates that had been until recently very limited. Broader attention to individuals with AS who are rather eccentric and socially awkward but who may also have special talents in domains of factual knowledge or technological skills raises questions about the borderlands of this condition. For example, to what extent should we stretch the spectrum to encompass a much larger group of more successful and not necessarily disabled people whose social ineptness has had, nevertheless, great impact over their internal, social, and affective lives (Asperger, 1954, as cited in Bosch, 1970; Baron-Cohen, 2002)? Whether an approach taking this larger view of the phenotype, larger in fact than the commonly accepted *broader autism phenotype,* might contribute to a better understanding of genetic mechanisms needs to be answered. But to do so, there will be a need for increasingly more refined phenotypic measures of sociability.

Cross-References

Other diagnostic concepts are discussed in Chapters 1, 3, 5, and 6; outcome studies in Chapter 7; and assessment issues in Chapters 27 through 32.

REFERENCES

American Psychiatric Association. (1987). *Diagnostic and statistical manual of mental disorders* (3rd ed., rev.). Washington, DC: Author.

American Psychiatric Association. (1994). *Diagnostic and statistical manual of mental disorders* (4th ed.). Washington, DC: Author.

American Psychiatric Association. (2000). *Diagnostic and statistical manual of mental disorders* (4th ed., text rev.). Washington, DC: Author.

Anneren, G., Dahl, N., Uddenfeldt, U., & Janols, L. O. (1995). Asperger syndrome in a boy with a balanced de novo translocation: T(17;19)(p13.3;p11) [letter]. *American Journal of Medical Genetics, 56*(3), 330–331.

Asperger, H. (1944). Die "Autistischen Psychopathen" im Kindesalter. *Archiv für Psychiatrie und Nervenkrankheiten, 117,* 76–136.

Asperger, H. (1979). Problems of infantile autism. *Communication, 13,* 45–52.

Attwood, T. (1998). *Asperger's syndrome: A guide for parents and professionals.* Philadelphia: Jessica Kingsley.

Bailey, A., Le Couteur, A., Gottesman, I., Bolton, P., Simonoff, E., Yuzda, E., et al. (1995). Autism as a strongly genetic disorder: Evidence from a British twin study. *Psychological Medicine, 25,* 63–77.

Bailey, A., Palferman, S., Heavey, L., & Le Couteur, A. (1998). Autism: The phenotype in relatives. *Journal of Autism and Developmental Disorders, 28,* 369–392.

Baird, G., Charman, T., Baron-Cohen, S., Cox, A., Swettenham, J., Wheelwright, S., et al. (2000). A screening instrument for autism at 18 months of age: A 6 year follow-up study. *Journal of the American Academy of Child and Adolescent Psychiatry, 39*(6), 694–702.

Baron-Cohen, S. (1988). An assessment of violence in a young man with Asperger's syndrome. *Journal of Child Psychology and Psychiatry, 29,* 351–360.

Baron-Cohen, S. (2002). The extreme male brain theory of autism. *Trends in Cognitive Sciences, 6,* 248–254.

Baron-Cohen, S., Cox, A., Baird, G., Swettenham, J., & Nightingale, N. (1996). Psychological markers in the detection of autism in infancy in a large population. *British Journal of Psychiatry, 168*(2), 158–163.

Baron-Cohen, S., Tager-Flusberg, H., & Cohen, D. J. (Eds.). (1999). *Understanding other minds: Perspectives from autism* (2nd ed.). Oxford, England: Oxford University Press.

Baron-Cohen, S., Wheelwright, S., & Jolliffee, T. (1997). Is there a "language of the eyes"? Evidence from normal adults and adults with autism or Asperger syndrome. *Visual Cognition, 4,* 311–331.

Baron-Cohen, S., Wheelwright, S., Stone, V., & Rutherford, M. (1999). A mathematician, a physicist and a computer scientist with Asperger syndrome: Performance on folk psychology and folk physics tests. *Neurocase, 5*(6), 475–483.

Bartolucci, G., & Szatmari, P. (1987). Possible similarities between the fragile, X., and Asperger's syndrome [letter]. *American Journal of Disorders of Childhood, 141*(6), 601–602.

Bashe, P. R., & Kirby, B. L. (2001). *The OASIS guide to Asperger syndrome.* New York: Crown.

Bejerot, S., & Duvner, T. (1995). Asperger's syndrome or schizophrenia? *Nordic Journal of Psychiatry, 49*(2), 145.

Berthier, M. L., Bayes, A., & Tolosa, E. S. (1993). Magnetic resonance imaging in patients with concurrent Tourette's disorder and Asperger's syndrome. *Journal of the American Academy of Child and Adolescent Psychiatry, 32*(3), 633–639.

Berthier, M. L., Starkstein, S. E., & Leiguarda, R. (1990). Developmental cortical anomalies in Asperger's syndrome: Neuroradiological findings in two patients. *Journal of Neuropsychiatry and Clinical Neurosciences, 2*(2), 197–201.

Bishop, D. V. M. (1989). Autism, Asperger's syndrome and semantic-pragmatic disorder: Where are the boundaries? *British Journal of Disorders of Communications, 24,* 107–121.

Bishop, D. V. M. (1998). Development of the Children's Communication Checklist (CCC): A method for assessing qualitative aspects of communicative impairment in children. *Journal of Child Psychology and Psychiatry, 39*(6), 879–891.

Bishop, D. V. M. (2000). What's so special about Asperger syndrome? The need for further exploration of the borderlands of autism. In A. Klin, F. R. Volkmar, & S. S. Sparrow (Eds.), *Asperger syndrome* (pp. 278–308). New York: Guilford Press.

Bleuler, E. (1951). Lehrbuch der psychiatrie. In A. A. Brill (Ed. & Trans.), *Textbook of psychiatry.* New York: Dover. (Original work published 1916)

Bosch, G. (1970). *Infantile autism.* New York: Springer-Verlag.

Bowler, D. M. (1992). "Theory of Mind" in Asperger's syndrome. *Journal of Child Psychology and Psychiatry, 33*(5), 877–893.

Bowman, E. P. (1988). Asperger's syndrome and autism: The case for a connection. *British Journal of Psychiatry, 152,* 377–382.

Burgoine, E., & Wing, L. (1983). Identical triplets with Asperger's syndrome. *British Journal of Psychiatry, 143,* 261–265.

Casanova, M., Buxhoeveden, D. P., Switala, A. E., & Roy, E. (2002, February). Minocolumnar pathology in autism. *Neurology, 58*(3), 428–432.

Charman, T., Swettenham, J., Baron-Cohen, S., Cox, A., Baird, G., & Drew, A. (1997). Infants with autism: An investigation of empathy, pretend play, joint attention, and imitation. *Developmental Psychology, 33*(5), 781–789.

Constantino, J., & Todd, R. D. (2003). Autistic traits in the general population: A twin study. *Archives of General Psychiatry, 60*(5), 524–530.

Cox, A., Klein, K., Charman, T., Baird, G., Baron-Cohen, S., Swettenham, J., et al. (1999). Autism spectrum disorders at 20 and 42 months of age: Stability of clinical and ADI-R diagnosis. *Journal of Child Psychology and Psychiatry, 40*(5), 719–732.

Dahlgren, S. O., & Trillingsgaard, A. (1996). Theory of mind in non-retarded children with autism and Asperger's syndrome. A research note. *Journal of Child Psychology and Psychiatry, 37,* 759–763.

DeLong, G. R., & Dwyer, J. T. (1988). Correlation of family history with specific autistic subgroups: Asperger's syndrome and bipolar affective disease. *Journal of Autism and Developmental Disorders, 18*(4), 593–600.

Denckla, M. B. (1983). The neuropsychology of social-emotional learning disabilities. *Archives of Neurology, 40,* 461–462.

Ehlers, S., & Gillberg, C. (1993). The epidemiology of Asperger syndrome: A total population study. *Journal of Child Psychology and Psychiatry, 34*(8), 1327–1350.

Ehlers, S., Nyden, A., Gillberg, C., & Dahlgren Sandberg, A. (1997). Asperger syndrome, autism and attention disorders: A comparative study of the cognitive profiles of 120 children. *Journal of Child Psychology and Psychiatry, 2,* 207–217.

Eisenmajer, R., Prior, M., Leekam, S., Wing, L., Gould, J., Welham, M., et al. (1996). Comparison of clinical symptoms in autism and

Asperger's disorder. *Journal of the American Academy of Child and Adolescent Psychiatry, 35,* 1523–1531.

Ellis, H. D., Ellis, D. M., Fraser, W., & Deb, S. (1994). A preliminary study of right hemisphere cognitive deficits and impaired social judgments among young people with Asperger syndrome. *European Child and Adolescent Psychiatry, 3*(4), 255–266.

Everall, I. P., & Le Couteur, A. (1990). Firesetting in an adolescent with Asperger's Syndrome. *British Journal of Psychiatry, 157,* 284–287.

Fombonne, E., & Tidmarsh, L. (2003). Epidemiologic data on Asperger disorder. *Child and Adolescent Psychiatric Clinics of North America, 12,* 15–22.

Frith, U. (Ed.). (1991). *Autism and Asperger syndrome.* Cambridge, England: Cambridge University Press.

Frith, U. (2004). Emanuel Miller lecture: Confusions and controversies about Asperger syndrome. *Journal of Child Psychology and Psychiatry, 45*(4), 672–686.

Fujikawa, H., Kobayashi, R., Koga, Y., & Murata, T. (1987). A case of Asperger's syndrome in a nineteen-year-old who showed psychotic breakdown with depressive state and attempted suicide after entering university. *Japanese Journal of Child and Adolescent Psychiatry, 28*(4), 217–225.

Ghaziuddin, M. (2002). Asperger syndrome: Associated psychiatric and medical conditions. *Focus on Autism and Other Developmental Disabilities, 17*(3), 138–144.

Ghaziuddin, M., Butler, E., Tsai, L., & Ghaziuddin, N. (1994). Is clumsiness a marker for Asperger Syndrome? *Journal of Intellectual Disabilities Research, 38*(5), 519–527.

Ghaziuddin, M., & Gerstein, L. (1996). Pedantic speaking style differentiates Asperger syndrome from high-functioning autism. *Journal of Autism and Developmental Disorders, 26*(6), 585–595.

Ghaziuddin, M., Ghaziuddin, N., & Greden, J. (2002). Depression in persons with autism: Implications for research and clinical care. *Journal of Autism and Developmental Disorders, 32*(4), 299–306.

Ghaziuddin, M., Leininger, L., & Tsai, L. (1995). Brief report: Thought disorder in Asperger syndrome [Comparison with high-functioning autism]. *Journal of Autism and Developmental Disorders, 25*(3), 311–317.

Ghaziuddin, M., & Mountain-Kimchi, K. (2004). Defining the intellectual profile of Asperger syndrome: Comparison with high-functioning autism. *Journal of Autism and Developmental Disorders, 34*(3), 279–284.

Ghaziuddin, M., Tsai, L. Y., & Ghaziuddin, N. (1991). Brief report: Violence in Asperger Syndrome, a critique. *Journal of Autism and Developmental Disorders, 21*(3), 349–354.

Ghaziuddin, M., Tsai, L. Y., & Ghaziuddin, N. (1992). Brief report: A comparison of the diagnostic criteria for Asperger Syndrome. *Journal of Autism and Developmental Disorders, 22*(4), 643–649.

Ghaziuddin, M., Weidmer-Mikhail, E., & Ghaziuddin, N. (1998). Comorbidity of Asperger syndrome: A preliminary report. *Journal of Intellectual Disability Research 42*(4), 279–283.

Gilchrist, A., Green, J., Cox, A., Burton, D., Rutter, M., & Le Couteur, A. (2001). Development and current functioning in adolescents with Asperger syndrome: A comparative study. *Journal of Child Psychology and Psychiatry, 42,* 227–240.

Gillberg, C. (1985). Asperger's syndrome and recurrent psychosis: A case study. *Journal of Autism and Developmental Disorders, 15*(4), 389–397.

Gillberg, C. (1989). Asperger syndrome in 23 Swedish children. *Developmental Medicine and Child Neurology, 31,* 520–531.

Gillberg, C. (1990). Autism and the pervasive developmental disorders. *Journal of Child Psychology and Psychiatry, 31*(1), 99–119.

Gillberg, C. (1991). Outcome in autism and autistic-like conditions. *Journal of the American Academy of Child and Adolescent Psychiatry, 30*(3), 375–382.

Gillberg, C. (1998). Asperger syndrome and high-functioning autism. *British Journal of Psychiatry, 172,* 200–209.

Gillberg, C., Gillberg, I. C., Rastam, M., & Wentz, E. (2001). The Asperger Syndrome (and high-functioning autism) Diagnostic Interview (ASDI): A preliminary study of a new structured clinical interview. *Autism: Journal of Research and Practice, 5*(1), 57–66.

Gillberg, C., Gillberg, I. C., & Steffenburg, S. (1992). Siblings and parents of children with autism: A controlled population-based study. *Developmental Medicine and Child Neurology, 34*(5), 389–398.

Gillberg, C., & Rastam, M. (1992). Do some cases of anorexia nervosa reflect underlying autistic-like. *Behavioural Neurology, 5*(1), 27–32.

Gillberg, I. C., & Gillberg, C. (1989). Asperger syndrome: Some epidemiological considerations. *Journal of Child Psychology and Psychiatry, 30,* 631–638.

Green, J., Gilchrist, A., Burton, D., & Cox, A. (2000). Social and psychiatric functioning in adolescents with Asperger syndrome compared with conduct disorder. *Journal of Autism and Developmental Disorders, 30,* 279–293.

Grossman, J. B., Klin, A., Carter, A. S., & Volkmar, F. R. (2000). Verbal bias in recognition of facial emotions in children with Asperger syndrome. *Journal of Child Psychology and Psychiatry, 41*(3), 369–379.

Gunter, H. L., Ghaziuddin, M., & Ellis, H. D. (2002). Asperger syndrome: Tests of right hemisphere functioning and interhemispheric communication. *Journal of autism and Developmental Disorders, 32*(4), 263–281.

Happé, F. G. (1995). The role of age and verbal ability in the theory of mind task performance of subjects with autism. *Child Development, 66*(3), 843–855.

Happé, F., Ehlers, S., Fletcher, P., Frith, U., Johansson, M., Gillberg, C., et al. (1996). "Theory of mind" in the brain: Evidence from a PET scan study of Asperger syndrome. *NeuroReport, 8*(1), 197–201.

Hippler, K., & Klicpera, C. (2003). A retrospective analysis of the clinical case records of "autistic psychopaths" diagnosed by Hans Asperger and his team at the University Children's Hospital, Vienna. [Philosophical Transactions of the Royal Society]. *Biological Sciences, 358,* 291–301.

Howlin, P. (1997). Prognosis in autism: Do specialist treatments affect long-term outcome. *European Child and Adolescent Psychiatry, 6*(2), 55–72.

Howlin, P. (1999). *Children with autism and Asperger syndrome: A guide for practitioners and carers.* New York: Wiley.

Howlin, P. (2003). Outcome in high-functioning adults with autism with and without early language delays: Implications for the differentiation between autism and Asperger syndrome. *Journal of Autism and Developmental Disorders, 33,* 3–13.

Howlin, P., & Goode, S. (1998). Outcome in adult life for people with autism and Asperger's syndrome. In F. R. Volkmar (Ed.), *Autism and pervasive developmental disorders* (pp. 209–241). Cambridge, England: Cambridge University Press.

Johnson, D. J., & Myklebust, H. R. (1971). *Learning disabilities.* New York: Grune & Stratton.

Jones, P. B., & Kerwin, R. W. (1990). Left temporal lobe damage in Asperger's syndrome. *British Journal of Psychiatry, 156,* 570–572.

Kaland, N., Moller-Nielsen, A., Callesen, K., Mortensen, E. L., Gottlieb, D., & Smith, L. (2002, May). A new "advanced" test of theory of mind: Evidence from children and adolescents with Asperger syndrome. *Journal of Child Psychology and Psychiatry, 43*(4), 517–528.

Kanner, L. (1943). Autistic disturbances of affective contact. *Nervous Child, 2,* 217–253.

Kanner, L. (1954). Discussion of Robinson & Vitale's paper on "Children with circumscribed interests." *American Journal of Orthopsychiatry, 24,* 764–766.

Kerbeshian, J., & Burd, L. (1986). Asperger's syndrome and Tourette syndrome: The case of the pinball wizard. *British Journal of Psychiatry, 148,* 731–736.

Kim, J., Szatmari, P., Bryson, S., Streiner, D. L., & Wilson, F. J. (2000). The prevalence of anxiety and mood problems among children with autism and Asperger syndrome. *Autism: Journal of Research and Practice, 4,* 117–132.

Klin, A. (1994). Asperger syndrome. *Child and Adolescent Psychiatry Clinic of North America, 3,* 131–148.

Klin, A. (2000). Attributing social meaning to ambiguous visual stimuli in higher-functioning autism and Asperger syndrome: The Social Attribution Task. *Journal of Child Psychology and Psychiatry, 41*(7), 831–846.

Klin, A., Carter, A., & Sparrow, S. S. (1997). Psychological assessment of children with autism. In D. J. Cohen & F. R. Volkmar (Eds.), *Handbook of autism and pervasive developmental disorders* (2nd ed., pp. 418–427). New York: Wiley.

Klin, A., Jones, W., Schultz, R. T., & Volkmar, F. R. (2003). The enactive mind: From actions to cognition—lessons from autism. [Philosophical Transactions of the Royal Society]. *Biological Sciences, 358,* 345–360.

Klin, A., Jones, W., Schultz, R., Volkmar, F., & Cohen, D. (2002). Defining and quantifying the social phenotype in autism. *American Journal of Psychiatry, 159*(6), 895–908.

Klin, A., Pauls, D., Schultz, R., & Volkmar, F. (in press). Three diagnostic approaches to Asperger syndrome: Implications for research. *Journal of Autism and Developmental Disorders.*

Klin, A., Sparrow, S. S., Marans, W. D., Carter, A., & Volkmar, F. R. (2000). Assessment issues in children and adolescents with Asperger syndrome. In A. Klin, F. R. Volkmar, & S. S. Sparrow (Eds.), *Asperger syndrome* (pp. 309–339). New York: Guilford Press.

Klin, A., Sparrow, S. S., Volkmar, F. R., Cicchetti, D. V., & Rourke, B. P. (1995). Asperger syndrome. In B. P. Rourke (Ed.), *Syndrome of nonverbal learning disabilities: Neurodevelopmental manifestations* (pp. 93–118). New York: Guilford Press.

Klin, A., & Volkmar, F. R. (1996). The pervasive developmental disorders: Nosology and profiles of development. In S. Luthar, J. Burack, D. Cicchetti, & J. Wiesz (Eds.), *Developmental perspectives on risk and psychopathology.* New York: Cambridge University Press.

Klin, A., & Volkmar, F. R. (1997). Asperger syndrome. In D. J. Cohen & F. R. Volkmar (Eds.), *Handbook of autism and pervasive developmental disorders* (pp. 94–122). New York: Wiley.

Klin, A., & Volkmar, F. R. (Eds.). (2003). Asperger syndrome. *Child and adolescent psychiatric clinics of North America.* Philadelphia: Saunders.

Klin, A., Volkmar F. R., & Sparrow, S. S. (Eds.). (2000). *Asperger syndrome.* New York: Guilford Press.

Klin, A., Volkmar, F. R., Sparrow, S. S., Cicchetti, D. V., & Rourke, B. P. (1995). Validity and neuropsychological characterization of Asperger syndrome. *Journal of Child Psychology and Psychiatry, 36*(7), 1127–1140.

Le Couteur, A., Bailey, A., Goode, S., Pickles, A., Robertson, S., Gottesman, I., et al. (1996). A broader phenotype of autism: The Clinical spectrum in twins. *Journal of Child Psychology and Psychiatry, 37*(7), 785–801.

Leekam, S., Libby, S., Wing, L., Gould, J., & Gillberg, C. (2000). Comparison of *ICD-10* and Gillberg's criteria for Asperger syndrome. *Autism: Journal of Research and Practice, 4,* 11–28.

Lincoln, A., Courchesne, E., Allen, M., Hanson, E., & Ene, M. (1998). Neurobiology of Asperger syndrome: Seven case studies and quantitative magnetic resonance imaging findings. In E. Schopler, G. Mesibov, & L. J. Kunce (Eds.), *Asperger syndrome or high-functioning autism?* (pp. 145–166). New York: Plenum Press.

Lincoln, A. J., Allen, M., & Kilman, A. (1995). The assessment and interpretation of intellectual abilities in people with autism. In E. Schopler & G. Mesibov (Eds.), *Learning and cognition in autism* (pp. 89–117). New York: Plenum Press.

Littlejohns, C. S., Clarke, D. J., & Corbett, J. A. (1990). Tourette-like disorder in Asperger's syndrome. *British Journal of Psychiatry, 156,* 430–433.

Lord, C., Rutter, M. J., DiLavore, P., & Risi, S. (1999). *Autism diagnostic observation schedule.* Los Angeles: Western Psychological Services.

Lotspeich, L., Kwon, H., Schumann, C. M., Fryer, S. L., Goodlin-Jones, B. L., Buonocore, M. H., et al. (2004). Investigation of Neuroanatomical Differences Between Autism and Asperger Syndrome. *Archives of General Psychiatry, 61*(3), 291–298.

Marriage, K., Miles, T., Stokes, D., & Davey, M. (1993). Clinical and research implications of the co-occurrence of Asperger's and Tourette syndrome. *Australian and New Zealander Journal of Psychiatry, 27*(4), 666–672.

Mawson, D., Grounds, A., & Tantam, D. (1985). Violence and Asperger's syndrome: A case study. *British Journal of Psychiatry, 147,* 566–569.

Mayes, S. D., Calhoun, S. L., & Crites, D. L. (2001). Does *DSM-IV* Asperger's disorder exist? *Journal of Abnormal Child Psychology, 29,* 263–271.

McAlonan, G., Daly, E., Kumari, V., Critchley, H. D., van Amelsvoort, T., Suckling, J., et al. (2002). Brain anatomy and sensorimotor gating in Asperger's syndrome. *Brain, 125*(7), 1594–1606.

McKelvey, J. R., Lambert, R., Mottron, L., & Shevell, M. I. (1995). Right-hemisphere dysfunction in Asperger's syndrome. *Journal of Child Neurology, 10*(4), 310–314.

Mesibov, G. B. (1992). Treatment issues with high-functioning adolescents and adults with autism. In E. Schopler & G. B. Mesibov (Eds.), *High-functioning individuals with autism* (pp. 143–156). New York: Plenum Press.

Miles, S. W., & Capelle, P. (1987). Asperger's syndrome and aminoaciduria: A case example. *British Journal of Psychiatry, 150,* 397–400.

Miller, J., & Ozonoff, S. (2000). The external validity of Asperger disorder: Lack of evidence from the domain of neuropsychology. *Journal of Abnormal Psychology, 109,* 227–238.

Murphy, D. G. M., Critchley, H. D., Schmitz, N., McAlonan, G., van Amelsvoort, T., Robertson, D., et al. (2002). Asperger syndrome: A proton magnetic resonance spectroscopy study of brain. *Archives of General Psychiatry, 59*(10), 885–892.

Myklebust, H. R. (1975). Nonverbal learning disabilities: Assessment and intervention. In H. R. Myklebust (Ed.), *Progress in learning disabilities* (Vol. 3, pp. 85–121). New York: Grune & Stratton.

Myles, B. S., & Simpson, R. (1997). *Asperger syndrome: A guide for educators and parents.* Austin, TX: ProEd.

Nagy, J., & Szatmari, P. (1986). A chart review of schizotypal personality disorders in children. *Journal of Autism and Developmental Disorders, 16*(3).

National Research Council. (2001). *Educating children with autism.* Washington, DC: National Academies Press.

Newson, E., Dawson, M., & Everaard, T. (1984–1985). The natural history of able autistic people: Their management and functioning in a social context. *Communication,* 19–21.

Ozbayrak, K. R., Kapucu, O., Erdem, E., & Aras, T. (1991). Left occipital hypoperfusion in a case with Asperger Syndrome. *Brain Development, 13*(6), 454–456.

Ozonoff, S. (1998). Assessment and remediation of executive dysfunction in autism and Asperger syndrome. In E. Schopler, G. Mesibov, & L. J. Kunce (Eds.), *Asperger syndrome or high functioning autism?* (pp. 263–289). New York: Plenum Press.

Ozonoff, S., Dawson, G., & McPartland, J. (2002). *A parent's guide to Asperger syndrome and high-functioning autism.* New York: Guilford Press.

Ozonoff, S., & Griffith, E. M. (2000). Neuropsychological function and the external validity of Asperger syndrome. In A. Klin, F. R. Volkmar, & S. S. Sparrow (Eds.), *Asperger syndrome* (pp. 72–96). New York: Guilford Press.

Ozonoff, S., Pennington, B. F., & Rogers, S. J. (1991). Executive function deficits in high-functioning autistic individuals: Relationship to Theory of Mind. *Journal of Child Psychology and Psychiatry, 32*(7), 1081–1105.

Ozonoff, S., Rogers, S. J., & Pennington, B. F. (1991). Asperger's syndrome: Evidence of an empirical distinction from high-functioning autism. *Journal of Child Psychology and Psychiatry, 32*(7), 1107–1122.

Perner, J., & Wimmer, H. (1985). "John thinks that Mary thinks that . . .": Attribution of second-order beliefs by 5–10 year old children. *Journal of Experimental Child Psychology, 39,* 437–471.

Piven, J., Nehme, E., Simon, J., Barta, P., Pearlson, G., & Folstein, S. E. (1992). Magnetic resonance imaging in autism: Measurement of the cerebellum, pons, and fourth ventricle. *Biological Psychiatry, 31,* 491–504.

Piven, J., Palmer, P., Jacobi, D., Childress, D., & Arndt, S. (1997). The broader autism phenotype: Evidence from a family study of multiple-incidence autism families. *American Journal of Psychiatry, 154,* 185–190.

Piven, J., Saliba, K., Bailey, J., & Arndt S. (1997). An MRI study of autism: The cerebellum revisited. *Neurology, 49*(2), 546–551.

Powers, M., & Poland, J. (2002). *Asperger syndrome and your child: A parent's guide.* New York: HarperCollins.

Rapin, I., & Allen, D. (1983). Developmental language disorders. In U. Kirk (Ed.), *Neuropsychology of language, reading and spelling.* New York: Academic Press.

Reitzel, J.-A., & Szatmari, P. (2003). Cognitive and academic problems. In M. Prior (Ed.), *Learning and behavior problems in Asperger syndrome* (pp. 35–54). New York: Guilford Press.

Rinehart, N. J., Bradshaw, J. L., Tonge, B. J., Brereton, A. V., & Bellgrove, M. A. (2002). A neurobehavioral examination of individuals with high-functioning and Asperger disorder using a fronto-striatal model of dysfunction. *Behavioral and Cognitive Neuroscience Reviews, 1*(2), 164–177.

Robinson, J. F., & Vitale, L. J. (1954). Children with circumscribed interests. *American Journal of Orthopsychiatry, 24,* 755–764.

Rourke, B. (1989). *Nonverbal learning disabilities: The syndrome and the model.* New York, Guilford Press.

Rourke, B. (Ed.). (1995). *Syndrome of nonverbal learning disabilities: Manifestations in neurological disease disorder and dysfunction.* New York: Guilford Press.

Rourke, B., Young, G. C., & Leenaars, A. A. (1989). A childhood learning disability that predisposes those afflicted to adolescent and adult depression and suicide risk. *Journal of Learning Disabilities, 22,* 169–185.

Royers, H., Buysse, A., Ponnet, K., & Pichal, B. (2001). Advancing advanced mind-reading tests: Empathic accuracy in adults with a pervasive developmental disorder. *Journal of Child Psychology and Psychiatry, 42*(2), 271–278.

Rutter, M. (1978). Diagnosis and definition of childhood autism. *Journal of Autism and Childhood Schizophrenia, 8*(2), 139–161.

Rutter, M. (1999). The Emmanual Miller Memorial Lecture 1998: Autism: Two-way interplay between research and clinical world. *Journal of Child Psychology and Psychiatry, 40,* 169–188.

Rutter, M., Bailey, A., Bolton, P., & Le Couteur, A. (1994). Autism and known medical conditions: Myth and substance. *Journal of Child Psychology and Psychiatry, 35*(2), 311–322.

Rutter, M., Bailey, A., Simonoff, E., & Pickles, A. (1997). Genetic influences in autism. In D. J. Cohen & F. R. Volkmar (Eds.), *Handbook of autism and pervasive developmental disorders* (2nd ed., pp. 370–387). New York: Wiley.

Rutter, M., & Gould, M. (1985). Classification. In M. Rutter & L. Herson (Eds.), *Child and adolescent psychiatry: Modern approaches* (2nd ed., pp. 304–321). Oxford, England: Blackwell.

Rutter, M., Le Couteur, A., & Lord, C. (2003). *ADI-R autism diagnostic interview* (Revised). Los Angeles: Western Psychological Services.

Ryan, R. M. (1992). Treatment-resistant chronic mental illness: Is it Asperger's syndrome? *Hospital and Community Psychiatry, 43*(8), 807–811.

Saliba, J. R., & Griffiths, M. (1990). Brief report: Autism of the Asperger type associated with an autosomal fragile site. *Journal of Autism and Developmental Disorders, 20*(4), 569–575.

Scragg, P., & Shah, A. (1994). Prevalence of Asperger's syndrome in a secure hospital. *British Journal of Psychiatry, 165*(5), 679–682.

Siegel, D. J., Minshew, N. J., & Goldstein, G. (1996). Wechsler IQ profiles in diagnosis of high-functioning autism. *Journal of Autism and Developmental Disorders, 26*(4), 389–406.

Smith, I. M. (2000). Motor functioning in Asperger syndrome. In A. Klin, F. R. Volkmar, & S. S. Sparrow (Eds.), *Asperger syndrome* (pp. 97–124). New York: Guilford Press.

Sparrevohn, R., & Howie, P. M. (1995). Theory of mind in children with autistic disorder: Evidence of developmental progression and the role of verbal ability. *Journal of Child Psychology and Psychiatry, 36*(2), 249–263.

Szatmari, P. (2000). Perspectives on the classification of Asperger syndrome. In A. Klin, F. R. Volkmar, & S. S. Sparrow (Eds.), *Asperger syndrome* (pp. 403–417). New York: Guilford Press.

Szatmari, P., Archer, L., Fisman, S., Streiner, D. L., & Wilson, F. (1995). Asperger's syndrome and autism: Differences in behavior, cognition, and adaptive functioning. *Journal of the American Academy of Child and Adolescent Psychiatry, 34,* 1662–1671.

Szatmari, P., Bartolucci, G., & Bremner, R. (1989a). Asperger's syndrome and autism: Comparison of early history and outcome. *Developmental Medicine and Child Neurology, 31*(6), 709–720.

Szatmari, P., Bremner, R., & Nagy, J. N. (1989b). Asperger's syndrome: A review of clinical features. *Canadian Journal of Psychiatry, 34*(6), 554–560.

Szatmari, P., Bryson, S. E., Boyle, M. H., Streiner, D. L., & Duku, E. (2003). Predictors of outcome among high functioning children with autism and Asperger syndrome. *Journal of Child Psychology and Psychiatry, 44*(4), 520–528.

Szatmari, P., Bryson, S. E., Streiner, D. L., Wilson, F., Archer, L., & Ryerse, C. (2000). Two-year outcome of preschool children with autism or Asperger's syndrome. *American Journal of Psychiatry, 157,* 1980–1987.

Szatmari, P., Tuff, L., Finlayson, M. A. J., & Bartolucci, G. (1990). Asperger's syndrome and autism: Neurocognitive aspects. *Journal of the American Academy of Child and Adolescent Psychiatry, 29,* 130–136.

Tager-Flusberg, H. (2001). A reexamination of the theory of mind hypothesis of autism. In J. A. Burack & T. Charman (Eds.), *The development of autism: Perspectives from theory and research* (pp. 173–193). Mahwah, NJ: Erlbaum.

Taiminen, T. (1994). Asperger's syndrome or schizophrenia: Is differential diagnosis necessary for adult patients? *Nordic Journal of Psychiatry, 48*(5), 325–328.

Tantam, D. (1988a). Annotation: Asperger's syndrome. *Journal of Child Psychology and Psychiatry, 29*(3), 245–255.

Tantam, D. (1988b). Lifelong eccentricity and social isolation: II. Asperger's syndrome or schizoid personality disorder? *British Journal of Psychiatry, 153,* 783–791.

Tantam, D. (1988c). Lifelong eccentricity and social isolation: I. Psychiatric, social, and forensic aspects. *British Journal of Psychiatry, 153,* 777–782.

Tantam, D. (1991). Asperger's syndrome in adulthood. In U. Frith (Ed.), *Autism and Asperger syndrome* (pp. 147–183). Cambridge, England: Cambridge University Press.

Tantam, D., Evered, C., & Hersov, L. (1990). Asperger's syndrome and ligamentous laxity. *Journal of the American Academy of Child and Adolescent Psychiatry, 29*(6), 892–896.

Tantam, D., Evered, C., & Hersov, L. (1990). Asperger's syndrome and ligamentous laxity. *Journal of the American Academy of Child and Adolescent Psychiatry, 29*(6), 892–896.

Tentler, D., Johannesson, T. M., Johansson, M., Rastamm, M., Gillberg, C., Orsmark, C., et al. (2003). A candidate region for Asperger syndrome defined by two 17p breakpoints. *European Journal of Human Genetics, 11*(2), 189–195.

Thomsen, P. H. (1994). Obsessive-compulsive disorder in children and adolescents: A 6–22-year follow-up study: Clinical descriptions of the course and continuity of obsessive-compulsive symptomatology. *European Child and Adolescent Psychiatry, 3*(2), 82–96.

Towbin, K. E. (2003). Strategies for pharmacologic treatment of high-functioning autism and Asperger syndrome. *Child and Adolescent Psychiatric Clinics of North America, 12*(1), 23–45.

Tsai, L. Y. (2002). Diagnostic issues in high-functioning autism. In E. Schopler & G. B. Mesibov (Ed.), *High-functioning individuals with autism* (pp. 11–40). New York: Plenum Press.

Van Bourgondien, M. E., & Woods, A. V. (1992). Vocational possibilities for high-functioning adults with autism. In E. Schopler & G. B. Mesibov (Eds.), *High-functioning individuals with autism* (pp. 227–239). New York: Plenum Press.

Van Krevelen, D. A. (1963). On the relationship between early infantile autism and autistic psychopathy. *Acta Paedopsychiatrica, 30,* 303–323.

Van Krevelen, D. A. (1971). Early infantile autism and autistic psychopathy. *Journal of Autism and Child Schizophrenia, 1*(1), 82–86.

Volkmar, F. R., & Cohen, D. J. (1989). Disintegrative disorder or "late onset" autism. *Journal of Child Psychology and Psychiatry, 30*(5), 717–724.

Volkmar, F. R., & Cohen, D. J. (1991). Comorbid association of autism and schizophrenia. *American Journal of Psychiatry, 148*(12), 1705–1707.

Volkmar, F. R., & Klin, A. (2000). Diagnostic issues in Asperger syndrome. In A. Klin, F. R. Volkmar, & S. S. Sparrow (Eds.), *Asperger syndrome* (pp. 25–71). New York: Guilford Press.

Volkmar, F. R., Klin, A., & Cohen, D. J. (1997). Diagnosis and classification of autism and related conditions: Consensus and issues. In D. J. Cohen & F. R. Volkmar (Eds.), *Handbook of autism and pervasive developmental disorders* (pp. 5–40). New York: Wiley.

Volkmar, F. R., Klin, A., & Pauls, D. (1998). Nosological and genetic aspects of Asperger Syndrome. *Journal of Autism and Developmental Disorders, 28*(5), 457–463.

Volkmar, F. R., Klin, A., Schultz, R. B., Bronen, R., Marans, W. D., Sparrow, S. S., et al. (1996). Grand rounds in child psychiatry: Asperger syndrome. *Journal of the American Academy of Child and Adolescent Psychiatry, 35,* 118–123.

Volkmar, F. R., Klin, A., Siegel, B., Szatmari, P., Lord, C., Campbell, M., et al. (1994). *DSM-IV Autism/Pervasive Developmental Disorder Field Trial. American Journal of Psychiatry, 151,* 1361–1367.

Volkmar, F. R., Lord, C., Bailey, A., Schultz, R. T., & Klin, A. (2004). Autism and pervasive developmental disorders. *Journal of Child Psychology and Psychiatry, 45*(1), 1–36.

Weimer, A. K., Schatz, A. M., Lincoln, A., Ballantyne, A. O., & Trauner, D. A. (2001). "Motor" impairment in Asperger syndrome: Evidence for a deficit in proprioception. *Journal of Developmental and Behavioral Pediatrics, 22*(2), 92–101.

Weintraub, S., & Mesulam, M. M. (1983). Developmental learning disabilities of the right hemisphere: Emotional, interpersonal, and cognitive components. *Archives of Neurology, 40,* 463–468.

Wing, L. (1981). Asperger's syndrome: A clinical account. *Psychological Medicine, 11,* 115–129.

Wing, L. (1986). Clarification on Asperger's Syndrome (Letters to the Editor). *Journal of Autism and Developmental Disorders, 16*(4), 513–515.

Wing, L. (1998). The history of Asperger syndrome. In E. Schopler & G. Mesibov (Eds.), *Asperger syndrome or high-functioning autism?* (pp. 11–28). New York: Plenum Press.

Wing, L. (2000). Past and future of research on Asperger syndrome. In A. Klin, F. R. Volkmar, & S. S. Sparrow (Eds.), *Asperger syndrome* (pp. 418–432). New York: Guilford Press.

Wing, L., & Gould, J. (1979). Severe impairments of social interaction and associated abnormalities in children: Epidemiology and classification. *Journal of Autism and Childhood Schizophrenia, 9,* 11–29.

Wolff, S. (1991). "Schizoid" personality in childhood and adult life: III. The childhood picture. *British Journal of Psychiatry, 159,* 629–635.

Wolff, S. (1995). *Loner's: The life path of unusual children.* London: Routledge.

Wolff, S., & Barlow, A. (1979). Schizoid personality in childhood: A comparative study of schizoid, autistic and normal children. *Journal of Child Psychology and Psychiatry, 20,* 19–46.

Wolff, S., & Chick, J. (1980). Schizoid personality in childhood: A controlled follow-up study. *Psychological Medicine, 10,* 85–100.

World Health Organization. (1993). *International classification of diseases* [Chapter V. Mental and behavioral disorders (including disorders of psychological development): Diagnostic criteria for research] (10th ed.). Geneva, Switzerland: Author.

Ziatas, K., Durkin, K., & Pratt, C. (2003). Differences in assertive speech acts produced by children with autism, Asperger syndrome, specific language impairment, and normal development. *Development and Psychopathology, 15*(1), 73–94.

CHAPTER 5

Rett Syndrome: A Pervasive Developmental Disorder

RICHARD VAN ACKER, JENNIFER A. LONCOLA, AND ERYN Y. VAN ACKER

At least in its classical form, Rett syndrome is a phenotypically distinct progressive X-linked dominant neurodevelopmental disorder that almost exclusively affects females. The characteristic pattern of cognitive and functional stagnation with subsequent deterioration profoundly impairs postnatal brain growth and development. Rett syndrome represents one of the most common causes of mental retardation in females, second only to Down syndrome (Ellaway & Christodoulou, 1999). Stereotypic hand movements, typically at midline, are one of the most prominent symptoms. The disorder is the first human disease that has been found to result from defects in a protein involved in the regulation of gene expression through its interaction with methylated DNA. As such, Rett syndrome could hold the key to our understanding of human disorders ranging from some forms of learning disability to autism.

Andreas Rett, an Austrian physician, first described the disorder following his serendipitous discovery of two girls seated in his waiting room who displayed strikingly similar hand-wringing mannerisms. When he discussed this with his receptionist, they were able to review patient records and identify six additional patients with similar behavioral characteristics and developmental histories. Unable to find a known classification for the disorder, Rett (1966) published a report (in German) describing 22 girls with a syndrome consisting of stereotypic hand movements, dementia, autistic behavior, ataxia, cortical atrophy, and hyperammonemia (blood ammonia). The reported increased levels of hyperammonemia were subsequently found to be only rarely associated

with this disorder. This false lead, coupled with very limited exposure (Rett, 1969, 1977) of this information in the English language medical literature, resulted in a general failure to recognize Rett syndrome, previously termed cerebroatrophic hyperammonemia as a nosological entity.

Unaware of Rett's work, Bengt Hagberg was working with patients displaying similar symptoms in Sweden. In 1980, he presented a paper at the European Federation of Child Neurology Societies describing 16 girls he had observed (Hagberg, 1980). Later, he and several colleagues (Hagberg, Aicardi, Dias, & Ramos, 1983) published in the *Annals of Neurology* their report of 35 girls from France, Portugal, and Sweden with Rett syndrome. This landmark account awakened the recognition and interest of clinicians and researchers and provided credit to Dr. Rett for his pioneering efforts on the disorder that bears his name. Researchers have learned much about this disorder over the past 2 decades; however, much remains to be discovered.

CLINICAL PRESENTATION AND NATURAL HISTORY

Individuals with Rett syndrome exhibit a unique and characteristic course of development (Naidu, Murphy, Moser, & Rett, 1986). Prenatal and perinatal histories of these persons are generally unremarkable. Although minor pre- and perinatal problems (e.g., mild hypotonia, tremulous neck movements, a low intensity of interpersonal contact, and abnormal hand use and language development) can be identified retrospectively in as many as 80% of the girls (Burford, Keer, & Macleod, 2003; Charman et al., 2002; Hanefeld, 1985; Leonard & Bower, 1998; Nomura & Segawa, 1990; Opitz & Lewin, 1987; Sekul & Percy, 1992), it is unlikely that these mild symptoms would be detected as relevant even with detailed neurological or developmental assessment. Excess levels of hand patting, waving, and involuntary movements including alternate opening and closing of the fingers, twisting of the wrists and arms, or nonspecific circulating hand-mouth movements appear to be the most characteristic early warning signals for the syndrome (Holm, 1985; Kerr, Montague, & Stephenson, 1987; Witt-Engerstrom, 1987). Given the wide range of functioning at this age, such soft signs would generally be dismissed. Thus, parents generally report normal physical and mental development for the first 6 to 8 months of life as evidenced by physical growth and psychomotor and verbal behavior (Gillberg, 1987; Sekul & Percy, 1992). This apparently normal period of development is followed by a slowing or cessation of the acquisition of developmental milestones with significant deviations in the acquisition of skills requiring balance (e.g., walking) in many cases. By 15 months, approximately half of the girls demonstrate serious developmental delays and abnormal neurological signs or symptoms. By 3 years of age, the children have experienced a rapid deterioration of behavior as evidenced by

loss of acquired speech, voluntary grasping, and the purposeful use of the hands (Charman et al., 2002). The girls begin to lack sustained interest in persons or objects and demonstrate limited interpersonal contact; however, they maintain eye contact (Holm, 1985; Trevathan & Naidu, 1988; Witt-Engerstrom, 1987). This deterioration occurs very quickly, typically within 1 year or less, resulting in severe-to-profound disabilities and stereotyped behaviors. Deceleration of head growth (acquired microcephaly), coarse, jerky movements of the trunk and limbs, a stiff-legged, broad-based gait with somewhat short steps and swaying movements of the shoulders when walking accompany the developmental deterioration (Coleman & Gillberg, 1985; Hanefeld, 1985; Kerr & Stephenson, 1986; Naidu et al., 1986; Percy, Zoghbi, & Riccardi, 1985). With the loss of purposeful hand movements, the most prominent symptom of the syndrome appears, in the form of stereotypic hand-to-mouth movements, hand clasping, and "hand washing" (see Figure 5.1; Ishikawa et al., 1978; Leiber, 1985).

The developmental regression seems to plateau during the early school years. In some cases, parents report their daughters attempt to increase their functional use of retained skills. The girls become more responsive to their environment. As children with Rett syndrome approach adolescence, they are frequently subject to increased spasticity and

 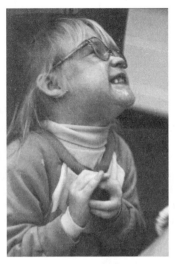 

Figure 5.1   Stereotypic hand movements in Rett syndrome.

vasomotor disturbances of the lower limbs, possible loss of existing ambulation, scoliosis, and a diminished rate of growth. Facial grimacing, bruxism (teeth grinding), hyperventilation, apnea (breath holding), aerophagia (air swallowing), constipation, and seizure activity also may accompany the syndrome (Trevathan & Naidu, 1988).

Hagberg and Witt-Engerstrom (1986) proposed a staging system to facilitate the characterization of the disorder patterns and profiles from infancy through adolescence. Their system suggests four clinical stages and was derived from a synthesis of clinical observations over the years in 50 Swedish cases of Rett syndrome. The stage patterns provide average guidelines for use when confronted with the diagnostic problems resulting from the complex symptomatology and longitudinal profile of the condition. The four stages are Early Onset Stagnation Stage, Rapid Destructive Stage, Pseudostationary Stage, and Late Motor Degeneration Stage. This staging system has gained general acceptance; however, the names assigned to each stage have been criticized (Opitz, 1986; Trevathan & Naidu, 1988), and the stages are commonly referred to simply by number. The symptoms and features of each of the four stages are as follows:

Stage 1 (onset 6 to 18 months): The clinical profile at this stage suggests a deterioration, or at least a general slowing down (stagnation) of motor development. Hypotonia is typically noted. Deviation from normal development is often compensated for or hidden, in part, by the rapid developmental speed of infancy. For example, most of the children can sit independently prior to the initiation of this stage but many fail to develop the subsequent postural skills needed for balance when crawling, standing, and walking. Yet, Sekul and Percy (1992) report that as many as 60% of the girls appear to compensate for this delay with alternative means of locomotion (e.g., rolling, creeping, or shuffling). Approximately 80% of persons with Rett syndrome will attain independent ambulation. Thus, additional gross motor abilities often are learned during this stage, but are delayed in their appearance, even as others are lost. The symptoms of

Stage 1 are nonspecific and are not predictive of subsequent deterioration.

Stage 2 (onset 1 to 4 years): During this stage, the syndrome becomes significantly more pronounced as the children lose previously acquired abilities. A relatively well-demarcated period of rapidly declining social interaction, stagnation or loss of acquired cognitive abilities, and loss of purposeful hand use and speech is evident in most cases. Stereotypic movements, often virtually continuous during waking hours, become a prominent symptom. The intellectual functioning of the girl with Rett syndrome during this stage is generally reported to fall within the severe-to-profound range of mental retardation. Ataxic/apraxic gait abnormalities are observed in ambulatory girls. Also when the child is awake, she may display aberrant breathing patterns. Hyperventilation and respiratory pauses (generally lasting 30 to 40 seconds) are most common.

This deterioration frequently has been sufficiently dramatic to simulate a toxic or encephalitic state (Hagberg & Witt-Engerstrom, 1986). Parents frequently report that their children seem irritable. Unprovoked episodes of screaming and spontaneous tantrums are common (Coleman et al., 1988). Seizure activity is present in approximately one-fourth of the girls during this stage. Sleep abnormalities including delayed sleep onset and increased night awakenings are manifested by more than three-fourths of the girls (Piazza, Fisher, Kiesewetter, Bowman, & Moser, 1990).

Stage 3 (onset 2 to 10 years): Persons with Rett syndrome generally demonstrate diminishing autistic symptomatology and improved social interaction during this period. They appear to be more aware of their surroundings and seem to make attempts at using residual functional skills. Communication skills are reported to improve with better interaction. Some girls employ eye pointing, babbling, or even word pieces to signal communicative intent (Sekul & Percy, 1992). Seizures occur in up to 80% of the girls with Rett syndrome (Coleman et al., 1988). Spasticity or rigidity and scoliosis tend to progress, and jerky, truncal ataxia and apraxia become prominent.

Stage 4 (onset 10+ years): Progressive muscle wasting, scoliosis, spasticity, and rigidity frequently are displayed during this late stage. Decreasing mobility and late-stage second neuron abnormalities (e.g., drop-foot abnormalities, remarkably plantar-flexed feet) may require the use of a wheelchair. Spinal cord dysfunction appears to act in conjunction with extrapyramidal features to lessen mobility (Witt-Engerstrom & Hagberg, 1990). Interestingly, this stage is marked by increased motor deterioration only. The person's cognitive functioning remains stable, while social interaction (eye contact) and attentiveness improve. Seizure activity often becomes less problematic, allowing for a decrease in the anticonvulsant regimen for some girls.

Although persons over the age of 25 have been identified, the oldest being 76 years of age (International Rett Syndrome Association, personal communication, 2002), little systematic research has been conducted with this group to provide information on the course of the disorder past adolescence. There is some evidence to suggest that the life expectancy of persons with Rett syndrome may be diminished; however, precise information is not available at this time. A recent case study of a 60-year-old woman with Rett syndrome was reported by Jacobsen, Viken, and von Tetzchner (2001). With proper attention and care, this person was able to regain numerous lost skills including ambulation. The report stresses the importance of environmental adaptations necessary for rehabilitation. Failure to keep accurate developmental histories, infrequent diagnostic evaluations of adults, and the probability of secondary contractures masking the more classic signs of the disorder impede the identification of older persons with Rett syndrome. Malnutrition, uncontrolled seizures, swallowing difficulties, and health problems secondary to immobility increase the risk for a shortened life span in persons with Rett syndrome. Premature deaths in ambulatory girls thought to be healthy, except for demonstrating Rett syndrome, and whose seizures were under control have been reported (Hagberg, 1989;

Hagberg, Berg, & Steffenburg, 2001; Iyama, 1993). These deaths are reported throughout the first 3 decades of the life span with their peak occurrence falling in the second decade of life. Cardiac disturbances (Percy, 1992; Sekul et al., 1991), breathing dysfunctions, and seizures (Hagberg, 1989) have been suggested as possible causes for these premature deaths.

The four-stage clinical pattern and profile for Rett syndrome has been reported to be "a sometimes crude and a somewhat simplistic frame" for specifically characterizing and covering the whole profile in all cases (Hagberg & Witt-Engerstrom, 1986, p. 58). Transitions between stages are often indistinct and may be difficult to discern precisely for research purposes (Philippart, 1986). Even so, the staging system has been found to be a useful instrument for a more systematic registration, thought, and approach to the complex clinical manifestations of individuals with the Rett syndrome as they progress through the disorder.

DIAGNOSTIC CRITERIA

The diagnostic criteria for Rett syndrome, initially developed in the mid-1980s (Hagberg, Goutieres, Hanefeld, Rett, & Wilson, 1985; The Rett Syndrome Diagnostic Criteria Work Group, 1988), have recently been revised (Hagberg, Hanefeld, Percy, & Skjeldal, 2002). The fourth edition (revised) of the *Diagnostic and Statistical Manual of Mental Disorders* (*DSM-IV-TR*) has included Rett syndrome (termed Rett's Disorder) as a subcategory of Pervasive Developmental Disorder (American Psychiatric Association, 1994). The *DSM-IV-TR* diagnostic criteria for 299.80 Rett's Disorder generally coincide with those initially proposed by the Rett Syndrome Diagnostic Criteria Work Group (1988). The *DSM-IV-TR* criteria, however, differ in some significant ways from the most recent revision of the diagnostic criteria developed by members of an international panel of experts convened by the International Rett Syndrome Association (IRSA: Hagberg et al., 2002). For example, the *DSM-IV-TR* indicates "apparently normal psychomotor development through the first 5 months after birth" whereas Hagberg and his associates (2002) indicate that psychomotor development is "largely normal through the first six months or may be delayed from birth" (p. 295). Deceleration of head growth between 5 and 48 months of age is a necessary criterion within the *DSM-IV-TR*. The revised IRSA diagnostic criteria, on the other hand, indicate that postnatal deceleration of head growth will be evident in the majority of cases, but not all. A slight variation between the *DSM-IV-TR* and the IRSA diagnostic criteria involves the established age limits for various symptoms. The *DSM-IV-TR* has adopted a 5-month upper age level for normal psychomotor development and the lower age limit for loss of purposeful hand skills. Thus, these criteria coincide with the 5-month lower limit for the appearance of decelerated head growth. The adoption of the 5-month upper age limit for normal development may prove too restrictive. The Rett Syndrome Diagnostic Criteria Work Group (1988) provided a footnote to their criteria to indicate that "apparently normal development may appear for up to 18 months" (p. 426). No such notation is provided within the current *DSM-IV* criteria.

The Hagberg et al. (2002) criteria specify supportive criteria such as disturbances in breathing when awake, bruxism, impaired sleep patterns, impaired muscle tone, muscle wasting, and dystonia, to mention a few. The *DSM-IV-TR* includes EEG abnormalities, seizures, nonspecific brain-imaging abnormalities, and severe or profound mental retardation (Axis II) as associated features and disorders. Thus, the two sources differ in the associated and supportive features of the disorder. Moreover, the current *DSM-IV-TR* criteria fail to indicate exclusionary criteria that are critical for differential diagnosis. Table 5.1 provides the revised diagnostic criteria for Rett syndrome specified by Hagberg and his associates (2002) and Rett's Disorder as provided in the *DSM-IV-TR*.

Classical Rett syndrome, to date, is almost exclusively described in female patients. Some researchers (Clayton-Smith, Watson, Ramsden, & Black, 2000; Coleman, 1990; Eeg-Olofsson, Al-Zuhair, Teebi, Zaki, & Daoud, 1990; Jan, Dooley, & Gordon, 1999; Philippart, 1990; Topcu et al., 2002; Topcu, Topaloglu, Renda, Berker, & Turanli, 1991), however, have presented case studies of males displaying behavioral symptoms and developmental histories similar to those reported for Rett syndrome. In fact, six males have been registered with the International Rett Syndrome Association (personal communication, 2002). All but one of these male cases, however, fail to meet the strict criteria necessary to be included as confirmed classical cases of Rett syndrome. One report (Topcu et al., 2002) describes a male who does, in fact, display classical Rett syndrome and is mosaic (somatic mosaicism) for the truncating MECP2 mutation. Nevertheless, Rett syndrome is almost exclusively seen in girls due to the predominant occurrence of mutations on the paternal X chromosome, and also the presumed early postnatal lethal effect of the disease-causing mutations in hemizygous boys (Topcu et al., 2002).

VARIANTS OF RETT SYNDROME

The mutation of MECP2, a regulating gene on the X chromosome, has been linked to the Rett syndrome (Amir et al., 1999; Hoffbuhr, Moses, Jerdonek, & Naidu, 2002). A number of researchers have completed surveys of the mutations found in various populations of individuals with Rett syndrome (e.g., Bieber Nielsen et al., 2001; Bienvenu et al., 2000; Cheadle, Gill, & Fleming, 2000; Wan, Lee, & Zhang, 1999; Xiang et al., 2000) and have reported the identification of mutations in MECP2 in 35% to 87% of those tested.

Although mutations of the MECP2 gene appear to play a critical role in the development of Rett syndrome, they cannot yet serve as distinctive diagnostic markers because other disorders have been linked to mutations of the MECP2 gene. These mutations have been documented in persons affected with severe encephalopathy (Hoffbuhr, Devaney, et al., 2001; Wan et al., 1999), X-linked mental retardation (Meloni, Bruttini, & Longo, 2000), infantile autism (Beyer et al., 2002), mild learning disability (Hoffbuhr, Devaney, et al., 2001), and an Angelman syndrome-like phenotype (P. Watson, Black, & Ramsden, 2001). Therefore, as no specific diagnostic marker variable has yet been identified for Rett syndrome, clinical homogeneity is essential for epidemiological and research purposes. The strict diagnostic criteria previously discussed, however, may result in a failure to recognize the spectrum of pheno-

TABLE 5.1 Diagnostic Criteria for Rett Syndrome and Rett's Disorder

Diagnostic Criteria	*DSM-IV-TR* Rett's Disorder

Necessary Criteria
1. Apparently normal prenatal and perinatal history
2. Psychomotor development largely normal through the first 6 months or may be delayed from birth[a]
3. Normal head circumference at birth
4. Postnatal deceleration of head growth in the majority
5. Loss of achieved purposeful hand skills between ages 6 months and 2½ years
6. Stereotypic hand movements such as hand wringing/squeezing, clapping/tapping, mouthing and washing/rubbing automatisms
7. Emerging social withdrawal, communication dysfunction, loss of learned words, and cognitive impairment
8. Impaired (dyspraxic) or failing locomotion
 	
Supportive Criteria
1. Disturbances of breathing while awake (hyperventilation, breath holding, forced expulsion of air or saliva, air swallowing)
2. Bruxism (teeth grinding)
3. Impaired sleep pattern from early infancy
4. Abnormal muscle tone successively associated with muscle wasting and dystonia
5. Peripheral vascomotor disturbances
6. Scoliosis/kyphosis progressing through childhood
7. Growth retardation
8. Hypotrophic small and cold feet: small, thin hands
 	
Exclusionary Criteria
1. Organomegaly or other signs of storage disease
2. Retinopathy, optic atrophy, or cataract
3. Evidence of perinatal or postnatal brain damage
4. Existence of identifiable metabolic or other progressive neurological disorder
5. Acquired neurological disorder resulting from severe infections or head trauma
	Necessary criteria
	A. All of the following:
	  1. Apparently normal prenatal and perinatal development
	  2. Apparently normal psychomotor development through the first 5 months after birth
	B. Onset of all of the following after the period of normal development:
	  1. Deceleration of head growth between ages 5 and 48 months
	  2. Loss of previously acquired purposeful hand skills between ages 5 and 30 months with subsequent development of stereotyped hand movements (e.g., hand-wringing and hand-washing)
	  3. Loss of social engagement early in the course (although often social interaction develops later)
	  4. Appearance of poorly coordinated gait or trunk movements
	  5. Severely impaired expressive and receptive language development with severe psychomotor retardation
	
	Associated Features and Disorders
	1. Severe or profound mental retardation (Axis II)
	2. Increased frequency of EEG abnormalities and seizure disorders
	3. Nonspecific brain imaging abnormalities

[a] Development may appear to be normal for up to 18 months.

Source: From "An Update on Clinically Applicable Diagnostic Criteria in Rett Syndrome," by B. Hagberg, F. Hanefeld, A. Percy, and O. Skjeldal, 2002, *European Journal of Paediatric Neurology, 6,* pp. 292–297; the diagnostic criteria and information on Rett's Disorder is from *Diagnostic and Statistical Manual of Mental Disorders,* fourth edition, text revision, American Psychiatric Association, 1994, Washington, DC: Author. Reprinted with permission.

typic manifestations that might be included under the Rett syndrome classification.

Clinical variants of children with similar clinical courses who do not fulfill all the current diagnostic criteria have been recognized in the literature (Hagberg, 1995; Hagberg & Skjeldal, 1994; Huppke, Held, Laccone, & Hanefeld, 2003; Zappella, 1992). Hagberg and

his associates (2002) have developed revised criteria for the delineation of variant phenotypes. These criteria are provided in Table 5.2. Atypical forms include individuals with developmental delays prior to regression or who lack the initial period of normal development (congenital variant) or who display an early psychomotor delay but without regression until

TABLE 5.2   Diagnostic Criteria for the Delineation of Variant Phenotypes

A. Must meet at least three of the following Main Criteria:
 1. Absence or reduction of hand skills
 2. Reduction or loss of babble speech
 3. Monotonous pattern of hand stereotypies
 4. Reduction or loss of communication skills
 5. Deceleration of head growth from first years of life
 6. Rett syndrome disease profile: a regression stage followed by a recovery interaction contrasting with slow neuromotor regression

B. Must meet at least 6 of the following Supportive Criteria
 1. Breathing irregularities
 2. Bloating/air swallowing
 3. Bruxism (harsh sounding teeth grinding)
 4. Abnormal locomotion
 5. Scoliosis/kyphosis
 6. Lower limb amyotrophy (weakening and wasting of the muscle)
 7. Cold, purplish feet, usually growth impaired
 8. Sleep disturbances including night screaming outbursts
 9. Laughing/screaming spells
 10. Diminished response to pain
 11. Intense eye contact/eye pointing

Note: From "An Update on Clinically Applicable Diagnostic Criteria in Rett Syndrome," by B. Hagberg, F. Hanefeld, A. Percy, and O. Skjeldal, 2002, *European Journal of Paediatric Neurology, 6,* pp. 292–297.

school age (delayed onset variant); a group whose supportive characteristics do not appear until late childhood (atypical or "form fruste"); those with a family recurrence (familial variant); and those who have retained some speech ("preserved speech variant"). In the latter group, words or even short sentences may be retained, although they are typically not employed in a functional manner. The head circumference of individuals with the form fruste variant often fall within normal limits, yet significantly below the norm (Hagberg, Stenbom, & Witt-Engerstrom, 2000). Individuals with the congenital variant often display a more severe phenotype than that found in classical Rett syndrome (Hagberg et al., 2000). Mutations in the MECP2 gene have been identified in as many as 50% of the individuals tested with variant forms of Rett syndrome (Bieber Nielsen et al., 2001; Cheadle et al., 2000). The lower percentage of identified MECP2 mutations in the variant forms of Rett syndrome may indicate the presence of genocopying mutations or (yet unidentified) mutations in regulatory elements of MECP2 (Shahbazian & Zoghbi, 2002).

DIFFERENTIAL DIAGNOSIS

The presentation of Rett syndrome differs considerably depending on the stage and age of observation. For example, a child 4 or 5 years of age with classical Rett syndrome can be correctly diagnosed with relative ease. Due to vague symptomology, diagnosis during infancy is frequently misinterpreted. Likewise, the late stage in adolescence displays a common, complex picture of severe multiple disabilities with secondary contractures resembling any number of disorders and, therefore, often is misdiagnosed. To fully understand this condition, the diagnostician must recognize and consider the entire disease process (Trevathan & Naidu, 1988).

Only 18% to 23% of the estimated 8,000 to 10,000 individuals in the United States afflicted with Rett syndrome have been identified thus far (International Rett Syndrome Association, personal communication, 2002; Moser, 1986). Lack of awareness of this disorder on the part of physicians and clinicians is undoubtedly a major contributing factor to this state of affairs. Even when physicians are aware of the Rett syndrome, an accurate diagnosis is not always forthcoming. Table 5.3 presents some of the clinical characteristics by stage and differential diagnoses often assigned to persons with Rett syndrome.

The most common nonspecific diagnosis for children with Rett syndrome above age 1 year is reported to be early infantile autism (*DSM-IV-TR*—299.00 Autistic Disorder; Olsson, 1987). In fact, many children with Rett syndrome seem to fulfill the necessary criteria to establish the diagnosis of infantile autism (Gillberg, 1987; Olsson, 1987; Olsson & Rett, 1985). Thus, some researchers (Allen, 1988; Gillberg, 1989) argued that perhaps Rett syndrome might best be thought of as a subtype of autism or overlapping diagnostic entities. The *DSM-IV-TR* includes Autistic Disorder and Rett's Disorder as subcategories of Pervasive Developmental Disorder. The behavioral patterns, progression, and prognosis of these two

TABLE 5.3   Rett Syndrome: Clinical Characteristics and Differential Diagnosis by Stage

Stage	Clinical Characteristics	Differential Diagnosis
Early onset stagnation stage Onset: 6 to 18 months Duration: months	Developmental stagnation Deceleration of head/brain growth Disinterest in play activity Hypotonia	Benign congenital hypotonia Prader-Willi syndrome Cerebral palsy
Rapid destructive stage Onset: 1 to 4 years Duration: weeks to months	Rapid developmental regression with irritability Loss of hand use Seizures Hand stereotypies: wringing, clapping, tapping, mouthing Autistic manifestations Loss of expressive language Insomnia Self-abusive behavior (e.g., chewing fingers, slapping face)	Autism Psychosis Hearing or visual disturbance Encephalitis Infantile spasms (West syndrome) Tuberous sclerosis Ornithine carbamoyl transferase deficiency Phenylketonuria Infantile neuronal ceroid lipofuscinosis (INCL)
Plateau stage Onset: 2 to 10 years Duration: months to years	Severe mental retardation/apparent dementia Amelioration of autistic features Seizures Typical hand stereotypies: wringing, tapping, mouthing Prominent ataxia and apraxia Spasticity Hyperventilation, breath-holding, aerophagia Apnea during wakefulness Weight loss with excellent appetite Early scoliosis Bruxism	Spastic ataxic cerebral palsy Spinocerebral degeneration Leukodystrphies or other storage disorders Neuroaxonal dystrophy Lennox-Gastaut syndrome Angelman syndrome
Late motor deterioration Onset: 10+ years Duration: years	Combined upper and lower motor neuron signs Progressive scoliosis, muscle wasting, and rigidity Decreasing mobility: wheelchair-bond Growth retardation Improved eye contact Staring, unfathomable gaze Virtual absence of expressive and receptive language Trophic disturbance of feet Reduced seizure frequency	Unknown degenerative disorder

Source: "Diagnostic Criteria for Rett Syndrome," by The Rett Syndrome Diagnostic Criteria Work Group, 1988, *Annals of Neurology, 23,* pp. 425–428. Reprinted with permission.

conditions, nevertheless, differ significantly. Clinically important differences have been identified between the Rett syndrome (especially during the latter two stages) and other conditions with autism or autistic traits (Naidu et al., 1990; Olsson, 1987; Olsson & Rett, 1985, 1990; Percy, Zoghbi, Lewis, & Jankovic, 1988). A basic distinction between the two disorders can be made on the basis of motor behavioral analysis (Olsson & Rett, 1985, 1987; Percy, Zoghbi, et al., 1988). "Whereas autism represents a regression of verbal but not motor skills; Rett syndrome involves the simultaneous regression of both skills" (Percy, Zoghbi, et al., 1988, p. S67). Stereotypic behavior associated with infantile autism is generally more complex and, unlike that in Rett syndrome, often involves the manipulation of an object with preservation of the pincer grasp. Children with Rett syndrome reportedly differ from children with infantile autism with respect to their respiratory pattern (displaying breath-holding, hyperventilation, and air-saliva expulsion); the presence of ataxia and apraxia, bruxism, hypoactivity, and a general slowness of movements; and an absence of purposeful hand movement (Gillberg, 1986; Olsson, 1987; Percy, Zoghbi, et al., 1988; Sekul & Percy, 1992). Persons with Rett syndrome demonstrate a very restricted repertoire of movements that appear monotonous in both form and speed (Olsson & Rett, 1985). Van Acker (1987) reported that the stereotypic behaviors of persons with Rett syndrome were displayed in patterned sequences with significant conditional probabilities, whereas those of persons with infantile autism were displayed in a random fashion. Budden (1986) has presented another critical feature that may help in the differential diagnosis of Rett syndrome and infantile autism: Persons with Rett syndrome frequently develop appropriate speech before the onset of symptoms. On the other hand, children with autism differ from those with Rett syndrome in that they display overactivity and inappropriate vocalizations, and tend to replicate simple motor activities or complex movements within a rich repertoire of motor behavior (Percy, Zoghbi, et al., 1988). Table 5.4 presents a comparison of the clinical manifestations differentiating Rett syndrome from infantile autism.

TABLE 5.4   Comparison of Rett Syndrome and Infantile Autism

Rett Syndrome
1. Normal development to 6 to 18 months
2. Progressive loss of speech and hand function
3. Profound mental retardation in all functional areas
4. Acquired microcephaly, growth retardation, decreased weight gain
5. Stereotypic hand movements always present
6. Progressive gait difficulties, with gait and truncal apraxia and ataxia; some may become nonambulatory
7. Language always absent
8. Eye contact present, and sometimes very intense
9. Little interest in manipulating objects
10. Seizures in at least 70% in early childhood (various seizure types)
11. Bruxism, hyperventilation with air-swallowing and breath-holding common
12. Choreoathetoid movements and dystonia may be present

Infantile Autism
1. Onset from early infancy
2. Loss of previously acquired skills does not occur
3. More scatter of intellectual function. Visual-spatial and manipulative skills often better than apparent verbal skills
4. Physical development normal in the majority
5. Stereotypic behavior is more varied in manifestation and is always more complex; midline manifestations rare
6. Gait and other gross motor functions normal in first decade of life
7. Language sometimes absent; if present, peculiar speech patterns always present; markedly impaired nonverbal communication
8. Eye contact with others typically avoided or inappropriate
9. Stereotypic ritualistic behavior usually involves skillful but odd manipulation of objects or sensory self-stimulation
10. Seizures (usually temporal-limbic complex partial) in 25% in late adolescence and adulthood
11. Bruxism, hyperventilation, and breath-holding not typical
12. Dystonia and chorea not present*

*Extrapyramidal signs may appear in some patients with autism after puberty.

Source: "The Clinical Recognition and Differential Diagnosis of Rett Syndrome," by E. Trevathan and S. Naidu, 1988, *Journal of Child Neurology, 3*(Suppl.), pp. S6–S16. Reprinted with permission.

Considering the present concept of infantile autism as a behavioral syndrome, the initial differential diagnosis of Rett syndrome for some children may prove somewhat problematic. Infantile autism, however, is very rare in a female, which means that the mere presence of severe autistic symptomology in a girl under 2 years should prompt the consideration of Rett syndrome in the differential diagnosis. One must also be aware, however, that "a large percentage of children with Rett syndrome age 0 to 6 months or older than 3 to 5 years are not autistic" (Olsson & Rett, 1987). Thus, physicians and clinicians alike must realize that the presence of an autistic behavioral syndrome is not an obligatory condition for a diagnosis of Rett syndrome (Olsson & Rett, 1987).

Millichap (1987) has suggested that Rett syndrome might represent a variant of Childhood Disintegrative Disorder (Heller's syndrome). Children with Childhood Disintegrative Disorder develop their symptoms later (e.g., at least age 2 and typically age 3 or 4 years) than individuals with Rett syndrome and normal neurological findings are reported in persons with the former disease. In a comparison of two boys with Childhood Disintegrative Disorder and six girls with Rett syndrome, Burd, Fisher, and Kerbeshian (1989) reported persons afflicted with these disorders differed from children with classic autism. Children with Childhood Disintegrative Disorder (Heller's syndrome) and Rett syndrome displayed normal prenatal and perinatal periods, followed by marked developmental regression after which they acquired few or no new skills. The authors have suggested that these children should be distinguished from those with classic autism, and should be classified as "pervasive disintegrative disorder, Heller type" and "pervasive disintegrative disorder, Rett type." The *DSM-IV-TR* has included both Rett's Disorder (Rett syndrome) and Childhood Disintegrative Disorder (Heller's syndrome) as subcategories of Pervasive Developmental Disorders.

Stage 2 developmental regressions often suggest neurodegenerative diseases. The earliest stages of Rett syndrome are difficult to distinguish from infantile neuronal ceroid lipofuscinsis (INCL), an autosomal recessive disease especially frequent in the Finnish population.

Both disorders cause a rapid regression of psychomotor development and the manifestation of hand and finger stereotypies at approximately the same age. As INCL progresses, however, myoclonus and retinal degeneration becomes apparent and differentiates the two disorders (Sekul & Percy, 1992). Failure to designate retinopathy or optic atrophy as exclusionary criteria for Rett's Disorder within the *DSM-IV-TR* may complicate the differential diagnosis of this disorder.

A report by Philippart (1993) links Rett syndrome with tuberous sclerosis, a nerocutaneous disorder. Although this disorder may show initial similarities to Rett syndrome, close examination of the skin with a Wood's lamp and the presence of serial computed tomography abnormalities will distinguish this disorder (Sekul & Percy, 1992). Chromosomal disorders, such as Angelman syndrome ("happy puppet syndrome") can display similar features to Rett syndrome. Children with Angelman syndrome, however, fail to display a period of normal development and subsequent rapid regression. Acute and chronic encephalitis may be distinguished by examination of the cerebrospinal fluid (CSF) and by a characteristic electroencphalography. The loss of language and the development of seizures in preschool-age children are similar in both Rett syndrome and the Landau-Kleffner syndrome. Head circumference growth and motor skills are preserved in the Landau-Kleffner syndrome.

In summary, the clinical identification of Rett syndrome rests on the careful exploration of clinical manifestations and the specific pattern of symptom progression. The differential diagnosis based on clinical observation, although frequently difficult at presentation (especially during the earliest stages), becomes much easier after follow-up over several months to a few years. A diagnosis of Rett syndrome should involve a molecular genetic analysis to identify mutations in the MECP2 gene.

EPIDEMIOLOGY

Rett syndrome has been reported to exist on all the populated continents and in most countries of the world (e.g., Budden, 1986; Gouticrcs & Aicardi, 1985; Hanaoka, Ishikawa, &

Kamoshita, 1985; Kerr & Stephenson, 1986; Moodley, 1992). Thus, the literature supports the view that Rett syndrome does not seem to be a rare disorder and that it is more or less universal; additionally less than 2 per 100 cases of Rett syndrome display familial relationships (Zoghbi, 1988). Thus, the pattern of occurrence of Rett syndrome is dissimilar to that of traditional inborn errors of metabolism (e.g., glactosemia, Hartnup's disease, ketoaciduria, phenylketonuria), which often display strong geographic, ethnic, and familial accumulation.

Approximately 2,329 cases of the Rett syndrome worldwide are registered with the International Rett Syndrome Association, with the following distribution: United States, 1,887; Canada, 101; Mexico, 9; and other foreign, 312 (International Rett Syndrome Association, personal communication, 2002). The prevalence of the Rett syndrome has been studied, based on the Swedish registry for mental retardation and surveys of neuropediatricians, in a part of southwestern Sweden comprising five counties and the city of Gothenburg (Hagberg, 1985). In a population of 315,469 children and adolescents, 6 to 17 years of age, 13 cases were detected, all girls. The corresponding prevalence was about 1 per 15,000 live female births. In their study of 5,400 consecutive referrals to the pediatric neurology center in western Scotland, Kerr and Stephenson (1985) identified 19 cases of Rett syndrome. The resulting prevalence rate was very similar to that reported by Hagberg (1985); 1 per 12,000 to 13,000 females (Kerr & Stephenson, 1986).

A prevalence study was conducted within several geographic areas of the state of Texas in the United States by researchers at the Baylor College of Medicine (Kozinetz et al., 1993). The study employed the Texas Rett Syndrome Registry and explored females ages 2 through 18 years. This study was the first with a large ethnic mix that would allow an exploration of racial/ethnic group-specific prevalence of Rett syndrome. A prevalence estimate of approximately 1 per 22,800 live female births was reported with no significant differences in prevalence estimates by race/ethnicity (African American, Caucasian, and Hispanic). This estimate is lower than that reported in earlier studies suggesting the prevalence of Rett syndrome has perhaps been overestimated.

No matter which estimate is employed, Rett syndrome seems to be significantly more prevalent among girls than phenylketonuria (PKU), a condition for which all neonates are screened in the majority of developed countries (Hagberg, 1985). As progressive brain disorders and metabolic diseases together constitute only 5% to 6% (1.5 to 2.0 per 10,000 children) of the etiologies in persons with severe or profound mental retardation, the Rett syndrome should be considered as an important etiologic factor in females, second only to Down syndrome. In fact, this syndrome might well be responsible for one-fourth to one-third of progressive developmental disabilities among females (Hagberg, 1985).

ETIOLOGY

Since Rett syndrome, at least in its classical form, had only been reported in females coupled with a number of familial cases (represented in Table 5.5), researchers suspected the existence of an X-linked dominant genetic inheritance as the basis for this disorder. It was hypothesized that the genetic mutation would be lethal in males, resulting in a spontaneous abortion of the fetus (Comings, 1986; Riccardi, 1986). Genetic mapping in the familial cases identified a mutation at the Xq28 locus (Sirianni, Naidu, Pereira, Pillotto, & Hoffman, 1998). In 1999, researchers (Amir et al., 1999) identified mutations in the MECP2 gene as the cause of Rett syndrome.

During normal human development, many genes are expressed in a tissue-specific manner. That is, the gene must only function in the creation of specific cells. In fact, more than one-third of our genes are expressed only within the brain. Many of these genes are needed during critical periods of central nervous system (CNS) development, and then their expression must be turned off. Other genes are required only after birth and turning these genes on and off at appropriate times is critical for normal and proper development (Lombroso, 2000). The MECP2 gene encodes the development of the transcriptional silencing methyl-CpG binding protein-2. This protein plays an important role

TABLE 5.5   Familial Cases in Rett Syndrome

	Number of Pairs
Monozygotic twins	
Both females afflicted	8
Only one female afflicted	1
Dizygotic twins (female/female)	
Both females afflicted	2
Only one female afflicted	5
Dizygotic twins (female/male)	
Female afflicted	8
Full sisters	6
Half-sisters	2
Full cousins	1
Second cousins	2
Second half-cousins	1
Aunt—niece	1
Great-grand aunt—niece	1
Sister and half-brother, both have children with Rett syndrome	1
Mother—daughter	1

Source: "Genetic Aspects of Rett Syndrome," by H. Y. Zoghbi, 1988, Journal of Child Neurology, 3(Suppl.), pp. S76–S78. Adapted with permission.

in the "silencing" of various genes during CNS development. This protein binds to prescribed methylated cytosine nucleotides (CpG dinucleotides) on the DNA. The bound DNA-MECP2 complex then interacts with a histone deacetylase complex and the transcriptional co-repressor Sin3A. Together, these repressors alter the chromatin making the genes inaccessible to transcriptional activators—in essence, silencing the further transcription of that gene. The mutations in the MECP2 gene in Rett syndrome result in a failure to produce the MECP2 protein. Thus, the genes that MECP2 would normally silence continue to engage in ongoing transcription. The number and nature of the genes for which MECP2 is meant to suppress throughout the genome is as yet unknown (Singer & Naidu, 2001); although there is reason to believe these genes regulate the development and mature function of the brain and central nervous system (Shahbazian & Zoghbi, 2002; Webb & Latif, 2001). Genetic analyses have reported as many as 87% of the females displaying the classical Rett syndrome and 50% of those displaying a variant form test positive for mutations of the MECP2 gene (Bieber Nielsen et al., 2001). These numbers suggest strong support for the current criteria used for clinical diagnosis of Rett syndrome. Kerr,

Belichenko, Woodcock, and Woodcock (2001) suggest the need to explore further those cases in which no mutations of the MECP2 gene have been identified for individuals who have been clinically diagnosed with Rett syndrome. They suggest that additional novel MECP2 mutations, other genetic mutations, or external factors may yet be identified to play a role in the occurrence of Rett syndrome.

Numerous different mutations of the MECP2 gene have been identified in individuals with Rett syndrome. Van den Veyver and Zoghbi (2001) found 30 missense mutations (single-base changes that result in the substitution of one amino acid for another in the protein product), 22 of which are in the methyl-CpG binding domain (MBD) of MECP2. Additionally they found 35 nonsense mutations (single-base changes that create a termination condon resulting in a shortened, dysfunctional protein product), 12 frameshift mutations (changes in the DNA chain that occur when the number of nucleotides inserted or deleted is not a multiple of three, so that every condon beyond that point is read incorrectly during translation), and 1 splice-site mutation (failure to remove intron, or noncoding DNA, sequences prior to protein translation altering the sequence of the protein product).

Most mutations occur de novo (as new spontaneous mutations in the generation of the sperm or ovum; Dragich, Houwink-Manville, & Schanen, 2000). Kondo et al. (2000) propose that Rett syndrome is more frequent in females since 88% of the sporadic or de novo cases in their study appeared to have paternally derived mutations in MECP2. In contrast, the familial cases and mutations in a number of males suspected of displaying a variant of Rett syndrome were determined to be maternally derived. Girard et al. (2001) report that de novo MECP2 mutations with paternal origin were identified in 71% of the families studied. Two cases of maternal origin MECP2 mutation were reported. The high frequency of male germ-line transmission of the mutation is consistent with a predominant occurrence of the disease in females (as males do not inherit their X chromosome from their father).

If separate mutations affect a single gene, the condition is termed allelic heterogeneity, and this is found in the majority of disease-causing mutations studied to date. Interestingly, even when different regions of the same gene are mutated, they often result in the same clinical phenotype among affected individuals. Occasionally, however, different mutations within the same gene will result in different clinical presentations. This may explain some of the Rett syndrome variants. One study (Huppke, Laccone, Kramer, Engel, & Hanefeld, 2000), however, failed to correlate the type of mutation and the phenotype. Thus, factors other than type or position of the mutation may influence the severity of the symptoms.

Another factor hypothesized to play an important role in the symptoms associated with Rett syndrome involves the pattern of X chromosome inactivation (XCI; Amir et al., 2000; Hoffbuhr et al., 2001; Takagi, 2001; Zoghbi, Percy, Schultz, & Fill, 1990). At conception, females have two X chromosomes, with similar genes on each (a gene pair). Having the genes on both X chromosomes remain active results in severe effects; thus, one of the genes in each pair must be inactivated. Typically, the pattern of inactivation is random between the genes on the X chromosome provided by the mother and those on the X chromosome provided by the father. In some cases, however, the pattern of inactivation is skewed. That is, a greater number of the genes on either the paternal or maternal X chromosome remain active. Approximately 10% of females in the general population displayed skewed inactivation of their X chromosomes (Lyon, 1972). As the cell reproduces, the same gene on each X chromosome remains active (or inactive) in each copy. The severity of the symptoms in Rett syndrome may be related to both the number and the location of the genes with the mutated MECP2 gene. If the active gene in most cells holds the mutation (skewed XCI); symptoms will likely be more severe. Likewise, if the cells with the active gene displaying the mutation are more often involved in the encoding for the development of critical tissues (e.g., brain cells) symptoms would be more dramatic. Bieber Nielsen et al. (2001), however, failed to identify any correlation between the X chromosome inactivation pattern in peripheral blood samples with the clinical presentation or severity of symptoms in a group of Danish women with Rett syndrome.

To date, mutations in the MECP2 gene have been identified in many, but not all individuals diagnosed with the Rett syndrome (e.g., Bienvenu et al., 2000; Hoffbuhr et al., 2001; Xiang et al., 2000). MECP2 mutations have been identified in 70% to 90% of sporadic or de novo cases and approximately 50% of familial cases of Rett syndrome (Shahbazian & Zoghbi, 2001). Failure to identify the mutation may result from many factors including the accuracy of the original diagnosis and the methodology used to screen for the mutations (e.g., secondary structural content prediction [SSCP], gene sequencing, denaturing high performance liquid chromatography [DHPLC]). Failure to identify mutations in the MECP2 gene in individuals displaying Rett syndrome also might indicate that mutations will be found in other genes within the same enzymatic pathway as the MECP2 gene. Thus, genes encoding for other proteins required in the proper methylation of the specific DNA sequences, or the deacetylation of histones might be involved (Lombroso, 2000). Only the coding region of the MECP2 gene has been carefully analyzed, so mutations in regulatory elements (similar to other known $C \rightarrow T$ transition mutation disorders) could account for those cases in which no mutation has been identified (Shahbazian & Zoghbi, 2002).

As mentioned, mutations of the MECP2 gene have also resulted in disorders that are phenotypically distinct from Rett syndrome (e.g., nonspecific X-linked mental retardation, congenital encephalopathy with respiratory arrest; e.g., Clayton-Smith et al., 2000; Hoffbuhr et al., 2001). Thus, the mutation in the MECP2 gene cannot serve as a diagnostic marker variable for Rett syndrome. Genetic research will need to further explore the correlation of genotype and phenotype. More importantly, work to identify the "downstream" genes that are affected by the mutation of the MECP2 gene and any other gene along the enzymatic pathway will help improve our understanding of the pathomechanisms of the disorder.

NEUROPATHOLOGY

Neuropathological studies have been conducted in Rett syndrome that may assist in a better understanding of how ineffective MECP2 activity produces Rett syndrome. Although individuals with Rett syndrome are typically small for their age, only the brain weighs less than expected for the height and weight of the individual (Armstrong, Dunn, Schultz, et al., 1999). This supports the view that the MECP2 gene appears to have its greatest impact on downstream genes that code for the development and mature function of brain tissue. Accumulated autopsy studies (e.g., Brucke, Sofic, Killian, Rett, & Riederer, 1988; Harding, Tudmay, & Wilson, 1985; Jellinger & Seiteberger, 1986; Missliwetz & Depastas, 1985) suggest that the brain of the individual with Rett syndrome weighs significantly less than that of controls matched for both age and height. The weight of the average brain from an individual with classical Rett syndrome weighed 950g, which is the brain weight of a normal 1-year-old child (Armstrong, 2001). This researcher goes on to note that many individuals with form fruste and preserved speech variants of Rett syndrome display head circumferences (and presumably brain weights) within normal limits. The decrease in brain size and weight appears to begin after birth (in most cases), starting at 3 to 4 months of age. Brain size and weight appear to stabilize in later childhood, and the absence of markers for significant degenerative disorder support the idea that the decreased brain size is

the result of arrested brain development (Armstrong, 2001).

Brucke et al. (1988) report the most conspicuous finding from their autopsy studies was the underpigmentation of the substantia nigra (especially the zona compacta). It contained many fewer well-pigmented neurons for the age of the person (53% to 73%), and fewer pigmented granules per neuron, whereas the total number of nigral neurons and the triphasic substructure of neuromelanin were within the normal range. The basal ganglia of some patients showed mild gliosis. These findings were supported in a study of 38 patients with Rett syndrome conducted in Sweden by Lekman et al. (1989). Brucke et al. (1988) also reported low melanin content in the locus coeruleus. As the melanin pigmentation in the substantia nigra normally increases with age, this lack of pigmentation serves as "evidence of a retardation in maturation of these neurons (in the substantia nigra and locus coeruleus) which possibly leads to a decreased synthesis rate of dopamine and a compensatory enhancement in its turnover rate" (Brucke et al., 1988, p. 323). Increased levels of dopamine and serotonin metabolites in their subject support their hypothesis. The abnormalities of the substantia nigra and the related changes in dopamine synthesis could account for the prominent movement disorder associated with Rett syndrome.

Receptors for serotonin are hugely increased in the brain stem at all ages in persons with Rett syndrome (Kerr & Witt-Engerstrom, 2001). Serotonin plays an early role in the determination of later cortical function (Lagercrantz & Srinivasan, 1991) and is also an important neuromodulator and neurotransmitter in the mature brain.

Jellinger, Armstrong, Zoghbi, and Percy (1988) presented evidence from electron microscopic studies of abnormal neurites in the frontal cortex and caudate nucleus with greatly reduced axonal or dendritic connections. In a study of two females with Rett syndrome (Armstrong, 1992), the cortical neurons appeared to be less mature and demonstrated significantly decreased dendritic arborization that did not appear to be age related. This could be the result of the general growth arrest manifested in Rett syndrome and may, in part, explain the acquired microcephaly witnessed in Stage 1 of the disorder.

Golgi studies of cerebral cortical dendrites (Armstrong, Dunn, Antalffy, & Trivedi, 1995) have identified a reduced dendritic arborization in the pyramidal neurons of Layers III, IV, and V in frontal motor and inferior temporal regions in the brains of individuals with Rett syndrome. In the affected regions, apical and basal dendrites are selectively reduced; basal dendrites of Layers III and V in the frontal and motor cortex; basal dendrites of Layer IV of the subiculum, and apical dendrites of Layer V of the motor cortex. The dendrites of the hippocampal and occipital regions are not significantly reduced. The decreased dendritic branching in Rett syndrome suggests that the synaptic input is reduced.

A study by Cornford, Philippart, Jacobs, Scheibel, and Vinters (1994) reports on the neuronal changes in the brain of a girl with Rett syndrome observed in a frontal lobe biopsy performed at age 3 years and in the postmortem brain at age 15 years. Widespread neuronal mitochondrial inclusions and the appearance of dendritic retraction in Golgi-stained cortical pyramidal and Purkinji neurons were the most significant neuropathological features. The Golgi preparations of the frontal cortex and cerebellar folia (autopsy brain) manifested truncation and thickening of the dendrites and a degenerate appearance of cortical pyramidal neurons similar to that of an aged brain. Thus, neuronal and mitochondrial deterioration appeared to continue after stabilization of the neurological deterioration (at 3 years) in Rett syndrome. This has led these authors to speculate, "Rett syndrome could result from inadequate maintenance of a full array of neuronal contacts, similar to the aging process, in which such dendritic regression apparently occurs over the span of many years" (p. 430).

The pathogenic mechanisms of the morphological brain lesions and their relations to clinical and neurochemical findings in Rett syndrome remain unknown. Neuropathological studies at autopsy serve a critical role in attempts to better understand Rett syndrome. The International Rett Syndrome Association urges parents of persons with this disorder to consider the gift of autopsy should their children die prematurely. To this end, a uniform procedure has been developed for the postmortem examination (Percy, Hass, Kolodnyu, Moser, & Naidu, 1988), and is available from IRSA. Advance arrangements must be made with a pathologist so that tissues can be frozen, optimally within 4 to 6 hours following death.

NEUROANATOMY

The development of sophisticated methods for visualization of the human central nervous system in vivo has provided a means to quantify brain structure and function in persons with brain dysfunction. Routine neuroimaging studies in persons with Rett syndrome, however, have only revealed occasional nonspecific changes. Serial computed tomography (CT) and magnetic resonance imaging (MRI) studies have shown evidence of progressive brain atrophy, particularly in the frontal and temporal regions, in some girls after age 2 years (Krageloh-Mann, Schroth, Niemann, & Michaelis, 1989; Nihei & Naitoh, 1990; Nomura, Segawa, & Hasegawa, 1984; Yano et al., 1991). These findings are consistent with the pathological findings of Jellinger and Seiteberger (1986) reported earlier.

Decreased cerebral blood flow (to 88% of that noted in age-matched controls) was reported in seven persons with Rett syndrome (Nielsen, Friberg, Lou, Lassen, & Sam, 1990). Single photon emission computed tomography demonstrated significantly decreased cerebral blood flow to the prefrontal and temporal regions, whereas that to the primary sensorimotor cortex remained unaffected. A similar pattern of cerebral blood flow is observed in infants (Chugani, Phelps, & Mazziotta, 1987) suggesting that this finding may reflect the growth arrest noted in Rett syndrome. Further evidence of abnormal cerebral blood flow in Rett syndrome was reported by Yoshikawa et al. (1991). The developmental increase of the frontal-to-temporal cerebral blood flow ratio demonstrated in age-matched controls was not observed in six females with Rett syndrome.

Employing quantitative methods of analysis in neuroimaging, Cassanova and associates (1991) reported smaller cerebral hemispheres in 8 persons with Rett syndrome when compared with controls. A decreased area of caudate nucleus, even when the overall smaller brain area was taken into account, also was noted in the girls with Rett syndrome. Smaller cerebral hemispheres, basal ganglia, corpus callosum, cerebellar hemispheres, inferior olive, and anterior vermis were reported in 13 females with Rett syndrome compared with 10 female control subjects (Murakami et al., 1992). Reiss et al. (1993) completed a quantitative neuroimaging study that provided in vivo neuroanatomical correlates of the neurological and developmental features of Rett syndrome. This group reports reduced cerebral volume, a disproportionate reduction in brain tissue volumes, with a greater decrease of gray matter to white, regional variation in the percentage of cortical gray matter (with frontal regions showing the greatest decrease), reduced volume of subcortical gray matter (with the caudate nucleus showing significant volume reduction), and increased cerebrospinal fluid volume when controlling for brain volume differences in the females with Rett syndrome. These findings, especially those related to the caudate nucleus, are of interest from a clinical standpoint as they may help explain the significant motor and cognitive-developmental symptoms present in Rett syndrome.

Magnetic resonance imaging (MRI) studies have compared volumetric brain analyses of individuals with Rett syndrome to age-matched controls (Gotoh et al., 2001; Subramaniam, Naidu, & Reiss, 1997). Global reductions in grey matter volumes are reported; with exaggerated loss within the prefrontal, posterior frontal, and anterior temporal regions. Subramaniam et al. (1997) reported a preferential reduction in the volume of the caudate nucleus. Gotoh et al. (2001) identified thinning of the corpus callosum, widening of the prepontin cistern, a narrowing of the brain stem, and cerebellar atrophy in some individuals with Rett syndrome. No evidence of active degenerative disease, however, had been seen, and the whole brain seemed to be affected by the atrophy.

The consistency of data obtained through the neuroimaging research with results from neuropathological investigations supports the need for continued neuroimaging studies in Rett syndrome. Longitudinal studies of subjects from the time the children manifest the earliest signs of the syndrome would be especially enlightening. Information gained from neuroimaging studies could make a significant contribution to our understanding of the etiology, homogeneity, and pathogenesis of this disorder. Segawa (2001) has presented a rather interesting discussion of the pathophysiology of Rett syndrome by attempting to relate many of the neuropathological findings to clinical characteristics of the disorder.

NEUROCHEMICAL ALTERATIONS

The progressive nature of Rett syndrome after an apparently normal pre- and neonatal period is highly suggestive of a metabolic disorder similar to PKU. The pathogenesis of the disorder, however, remains a mystery. Extensive research exploring biogenic amines and endorphins through the analyses of serum amino acids, urine amino and organic acids, lysosomal enzymes, and routine chemistries has been undertaken. One hypothesis is that symptoms result from an abnormality in the dopamine system, a neurotransmitter system that regulates the control of voluntary movements in the extrapyramidal system. This hypothesis, based on the decreased pigmentation of the substantia nigra and the prominent movement disorders suggestive of extrapyramidal dysfunction (Zoghbi, Percy, Glaze, Butler, & Riccardi, 1985), led Nomura and her associates (Nomura et al., 1984; Nomura, Segawa, & Higurashi, 1985) to speculate that as the disease progresses the dopamine system becomes hyperactive due to postsynaptic supersensitivity caused by hypoactive dopamine neurons. Abnormality in the dopamine system is supported by the finding of a decrease of biogenic amine metabolites in cerebrospinal fluid in six children with Rett syndrome, the most significant reductions being in homovanillic acid (HVA), the major dopamine metabolite (Zoghbi et al., 1985). These findings were extended to 32 girls found to have significant reductions in HVA and 4-hydroxy-3-methoxyphenylethylene glycol (HMPG), the metabolites of dopamine and norepinephrine (Zoghbi et al., 1989; Zoghbi et al., 1985). An abnormality in this system is further supported by demonstration in an autopsy study of decreasing binding of 3H spiperone, a ligand with high affinity for dopamine D2 receptors, in the putamen (Riederer et al., 1985). Hand-mouth stereotypies, hypotonia, and ataxia similar to that seen in Rett syndrome are demonstrated in boys with the Lesch Nyhan syndrome. In that disorder, all biochemical aspects of the function of dopamine neuron terminals in the corpus striatum have been found to be decreased up to 10% to 30% of control values in autopsy studies of three affected cases (Lloyd et al., 1981).

Studies, however, have failed to replicate the findings that abnormal neurotransmitter levels characterize the Rett syndrome. Unlike the six cases reported by Zoghbi et al. (1985) where norepinephrine and dopamine metabolites were reduced in comparison to control individuals, subjects in a more recent investigation (Harris et al., 1986) did not demonstrate a reduction in metabolites of either of these neurotransmitter substances. Reduction of dopamine D2 receptor binding in the putamen, as found in the autopsy study by Riederer et al. (1985) with 3H spiperone, was not demonstrated in living subjects by in vivo positron-emission tomography (PET) scanning. Additionally, low normal receptor binding instead of dopamine receptor supersensitivity was reported (in direct opposition to the results reported by Nomura et al., 1985). Similar findings are reported in a second study (Riederer et al., 1986), where preliminary biochemical analyses on plasma, urine, cerebrospinal fluid, and postmortem brain areas indicated no disturbance of neurotransmitter function. These researchers suggest various drug therapies administered to the girls prior to sample testing and undernutrition (a problem common to girls with the Rett syndrome) might influence the synthesis and turnover of these biogenic amines. An alternative hypothesis suggests that such a deficit might also be triggered as a primary consequence of the disease process. Efforts to understand the often contradictory results are complicated further by the differing laboratory procedures employed by investigators throughout the world.

Rett syndrome appears to share neurochemical features (without the associated neuropathological features) with some age-related neurodegenerative diseases such as Alzheimer's and Parkinson's diseases. Wenk and his associates (Wenk, Naidu, Casanova, Kitt, & Moser, 1991; Wenk, O'Leary, Nemeroff, Bissette, Moser, & Naidu, 1993) have reported decreased cortical and subcortical levels of choline acetyl-transferase (ChAT) activity in a series of postmortem brain studies. The decreased ChAT activity may be related to loss of cholinergic cells, qualitatively similar to the loss in Alzheimer's disease. These studies (Wenk et al., 1991, 1993) also report decreased ChAT activity in the hippocampus and thalamus consistent with a loss of cholinergic cells in the medial septum and vertical limb of the Broca and the pedunculopontine tegmental nucleus. This loss of cholinergic cells throughout the basal forebrain might well be responsible for the cognitive stagnation and memory loss characteristic of Rett syndrome, as has been suggested for the dementia associated with Alzheimer's and Parkinson's diseases (Collerton, 1986; Whitehouse, Price, Clark, Coyle, & DeLong, 1981).

Persons with Rett syndrome have been reported to display a remarkable tolerance for pain and a high rate of stereotyped behavior, seizure activity, and respiratory disturbances. These symptoms have been induced in laboratory animals exposed to elevated endorphin levels. Several research groups have therefore studied the ß-endorphin system in females with Rett syndrome. Budden, Myer, and Butler (1990) found elevated ß-endorphin immunoreactivity in the cerebrospinal fluid of 11 out of the 12 girls studied. These findings were extended as elevated cerebrospinal fluid ß-endorphins were reported in 90% of more than 150 persons with Rett syndrome (Myer, Tripathi, Brase, & Dewey, 1992). The degree of elevation of the ß-endorphins, however, did not correlate with the severity of the symptoms (e.g., stereotypy, breathing disturbance) or stage of the disorder. Contradictory results, however, have been reported (Genazzani, Zappella, Nalin, Hayek, & Facchinetti, 1989; Gillberg, Terenius, Hagberg, Witt-Engerstrom, & Eriksson, 1990). These researchers report significantly lower levels of ß-endorphins in girls with Rett syndrome compared with age-matched controls. As in the biogenic amine studies reported earlier, the basis for these contradictory findings remains unknown.

Perhaps the most promising lead for a neurochemical marker for Rett syndrome has developed from a study of five autopsied cases exploring brain and cerebrospinal fluid glycolipids (Lekman, Hagberg, & Svennerholm, 1991). The concentrations of two major brain gangliosides, GD1a in frontal gray matter and GD1b in temporal gray matter, appear to be lowered selectively in the cerebral cortex and cerebellum in girls with Rett syndrome. The ganglioside GD1a is thought to play an important role in synaptogenesis since it is prominent in synaptic membranes and high concentrations are reported during the time when nerve ending growth and synapse formation are most intense (25th fetal week until age 2 years). Ganglioside GD1b is rich in axons and accrues more slowly, reaching maximum concentration at age 20 years. The reduction in GD1a would help explain the pathogenic findings of decreased dendritic arborization reported by Armstrong (1992). These findings appear to be specific for Rett syndrome; however, replication of a larger series is required to validate the results.

Synapses within the cerebral cortex, basal ganglia, and brain stem responsible for movement and breathing employ the excitatory amino acid neurotransmitter glutamate. Glutamate-mediated neurotransmission appears to be disrupted in persons with Rett syndrome. Two studies (Hamberger, Gillberg, Palm, & Hagberg, 1992; Lappalainien & Riikonen, 1996) of the cerebrospinal fluid in girls with Rett syndrome report elevated levels of glutamate in young children and significantly reduced levels in older individuals. A study using MR spectroscopy (Pan, Lane, Hetherington, & Percy, 1999) also replicated these findings. This would suggest that the synaptic levels of glutamate may be elevated and could account for the cortical hyperexcitability, seizures, and possibly dendritic pathology and abnormalities in Rett syndrome.

DRUG THERAPY

To date, there is no cure for the Rett syndrome, and therapeutic interventions directed at the fundamental mechanisms underlying Rett syndrome, while limited in number and scope, have failed to demonstrate any lasting or substantive improvements.

Treatment of Underlying Causes

Based on the biochemical findings in the research, the effect of bromocriptine, a dopamine agonist, has been explored in 12 girls with Rett syndrome (Zappella, 1990; Zappella & Genazzani, 1986; Zappella, Genazzani, Facchinetti, & Hayek, 1990). Improvements in communication and a decreased frequency of agitation episodes were initially reported; however, these improvements failed to recur following the "washout" phase of the study. Uncontrolled studies exploring the effect of other anti-Parkinsonian drugs aimed at the monoamine system (e.g., L-dopa, pergolide, deprenyl) have been undertaken but have failed to provide evidence of improvement on a consistent basis. L-dopa and Sinemet (DuPont) have been reported to show benefit for a limited number of patients in the later stages of the disorder when increasing rigidity appeared (Percy & Hagberg, 1992). Tetrabenazine, a monoamine depleter and blocker, resulted in an exacerbation of symptoms in one patient (Sekul & Percy, 1992). Egger, Hofacker, Schiel, and Holthausen (1992), reported that magnesium orotate or citrate (4 to 10 mg/kg/day) initially given as an anticonvulsant (after more traditional anticonvulsants had failed) resulted in a decrease in hyperventilation in a girl with Rett syndrome. They extended their findings to six additional patients with Rett syndrome. A decrease in hyperventilation was reported in all girls and parents reported a decrease in their daughters' hand stereotypies and episodes of agitation. Convulsions were reduced in four of the girls. Serum magnesium levels were normal for all patients prior to the start of the treatment, suggesting that the magnesium was acting pharmacologically rather than correcting a deficit. The researchers suggest that the magnesium is counteracting intracellular lactic acidosis and serving as a N-methyl-D-asparate channel blocker, thus reducing excitotoxic neuronal damage.

A randomized double-blind controlled crossover trial of L-carnitine (a natural amino acid that breaks down long-chain fatty acids in the blood transporting the particles to the mitochondrial membrane for increased energy production) was performed with 35 girls with Rett syndrome (Ellaway et al., 1999). The study reported improvements in eye contact, concentration and attention span, reduced daytime somnolence, increased vocalization, and increased mobility; assessments by both medical personnel and caregivers indicated that the girls appeared happier.

Neurotransmitter precursor therapy has been attempted with the amino acids tyrosine (the precursor for dopamine and norepinephrine) and tryptophan (precursor for serotonin) in nine girls (Nielsen, Lou, & Andresen, 1990). No clinical performance or EEG pattern changes were observed as a result of treatment.

A double-blind controlled crossover trial of melatonin (a natural hormone secreted by the pineal gland to help promote drowsiness) was conducted by McArthur and Budden (1998) to explore its efficacy on sleep disturbances associated with Rett syndrome. They report the melatonin decreased sleep onset latency, improved total sleep, and improved sleep efficiency—especially in those subjects with the most disturbed sleep patterns during baseline.

Naltrexone, an opiate antagonist, was employed in a double-blind crossover trial (Percy et al., 1991). The use of an opiate antagonist was attempted due to the reports of elevated levels of ß-endorphins in girls with Rett syndrome. The motor behavior and other symptoms of the disorder displayed no improvement during the naltrexone treatment phase. In fact, the girls' performance on the Bayley Scales of Infant Development worsened during the phase of naltroxone treatment (Percy & Hagberg, 1992). Given the lack of a biochemical marker and a limited understanding of the biological basis of Rett syndrome, it may not be surprising that drug therapy has not proven particularly effective.

EEG Profile and Seizure Control

At this time, we must be satisfied to provide suitable medication aimed at symptomatic relief (e.g., seizure activity). The electroencephalogram (EEG) has been demonstrated to be significantly abnormal for persons with Rett syndrome throughout all but the earliest stage of the disorder. A study based on the EEG records of 44 persons with Rett syndrome found abnormal EEG tracings to be almost universal (Niedermeyer, Rett, Renner, Murphy, & Naidu, 1986). Abnormal sleep patterns have also been noted. Haas, Rice, Trauner, and Merritt (1986) report the "presence of intermittent episodes of high amplitude bursts of spike wave or slow wave discharges followed by a brief period of relative suppression of background activity"

(p. 238) during sleep. Robb, Harden, and Boyd (1989) report, that in their study of 52 girls with Rett syndrome, discharges, consisting of short waves or spikes, were a common feature. These discharges could be infrequent or almost continuous and characteristically were most prominent around the middle third of the head.

Pronounced EEG abnormalities were most often found from 3 to 10 years of age and tended to become less severe during the second decade of life (Niedermeyer et al., 1986; Rett, 1986). Glaze and associates (1987), described the progressive changes in the EGG and correlated it with the clinical staging system. Their work is summarized in Table 5.6. The EEG changes generally appear at the beginning of Stage 2 and then follow a stepwise progression, with slowing, loss of normal sleep characteristics, multifocal abnormalities, and, finally, generalized slow spike and wave activity (Verma, Chheda, & Nigro, 1986).

Although all girls with Rett syndrome demonstrate abnormal EEG tracings, seizure activity is not universal. Naidu et al. (1986) reported that approximately 84% of the girls in their study demonstrated seizures. The most common types of clinical seizures include generalized tonic-clonic and partial complex seizures. Infantile spasms with hypsaarrythmia, however, may be an early symptom (Iyama, 1993). Selection of a specific medication should be based on clinical seizure type and EEG pattern. Several clinicians (Adkins, 1986; Budden, 1986; Naidu et al., 1986; Philippart, 1986) agree that standard dosages of Tegretol (carbamazepine) constitute the best seizure management program. Adrenocorticotrphic hormone or prednisone has been helpful in treating infantile spasms (Sekul & Percy, 1992). Hagberg (1985) warns, however, that many girls with Rett syndrome overreact and must therefore be taken off the medication. Haas and his associates (1986) have employed the ketogenic diet to reduce seizures in girls with seizures failing to respond to medications. As the girls enter late adolescence, seizure activity may decrease allowing modification of their medication regimen. Staring spells, eye rolling, and other episodic behavior may be observed in individuals with Rett syndrome and do not always indicate seizure activity (Garofalo, Drury, & Goldstein, 1988). Therefore,

TABLE 5.6   Correlation of EEG Characteristics with Clinical Stages

| State | EEG Characteristics | | | |
	Stage 1	Stage 2	Stage 3	Stage 4
Awake	Normal or minimal slowing of occipital-dominant rhythm and background activity	Marked slowing of occipital-dominant rhythm and back-ground activity; rare focal spike or sharp-wave discharges	Further, gradual slowing of occipital-dominant rhythm, with its subsequent disap-pearance; moderate-to-marked slowing of background activity; appearance of multifocal spike and sharp-wave discharges; during latter part of this stage, appearance of generalized slow spike-wave pattern	Absence of occipital-dominant rhythm; marked slowing of background activity (delta frequencies); multifocal spike and/or sharp-wave discharges or generalized slow spike-wave pattern
Asleep	Normal, with well-defined vertex trans-ients and sleep spindles	Less well-defined vertex transients and spindles and subsequent loss of these sleep characteristics; ap-pearance of focal or multifocal spike and/or sharp-wave dis-charges	Absent vertex transients and spindles during NREM sleep; multifocal spike and/or sharp-wave discharges, with later development of generalized slow spike-wave pattern during NREM sleep	Almost continuous generalized slow spike-wave activity

Source: "Rett Syndrome in the Electroencephalographic Characteristics with Clinical Staging," by D. G. Glaze, J. D. Frost, H. Y. Zoghbi, & A. K. Percy, 1987, *Archives of Neurology, 44,* pp. 1053–1056. Copyright 1987, American Medical Association.

these behaviors should not be treated as seizures without EEG documentation.

GROWTH PATTERNS AND NUTRITION

A pattern of deceleration across all growth measurements, following the first 6 months of life, is witnessed in most persons with Rett syndrome (Schultz et al., 1993). The exact cause of this remains unknown. A systemic deficiency in mitochondrial energy production as reported from muscle biopsy tissue has been suggested (Coker & Melnyk, 1991; Schultz et al., 1993). The best evidence to date, however, suggests nutritional, rather than chromosomal, neurological, or hormonal factors underlie this failure to grow. Some evidence suggests defects in carbohydrate (Clark et al., 1990; Haas & Rice, 1985; Haas et al., 1986), ascorbic acid, and glutathione (Sofic, Riederer, Killian, & Rett, 1987) metabolism. Malabsorption of critical nutrients and failure to

benefit from adequate caloric intake must be considered when examining the malnutrition displayed in some persons with Rett syndrome (Missliwetz & Depastas, 1985). Motil, Schultz, Brown, Glaze, and Percy (1994) report that energy expenditure associated with involuntary motor movement places these girls in a situation of lower energy balance (energy intake versus expenditure) than controls. The lowered energy balance in girls with Rett syndrome paralleled their degree of height and weight deficits, despite similar dietary energy intakes between groups. Haas and his associates (Haas & Rice, 1985; Haas et al., 1986) have reported improved weight gain in conjunction with diminished stereotyped behavior and better seizure control with the implementation of a high-calorie, high-fat ketogenic diet.

Reilly and Cass (2001) explored the issue of growth failure in Rett syndrome. They paid special attention to the impact of the feeding problems experienced by many of these individuals.

Through their own clinical experience and the results of a questionnaire, these researchers identified several common feeding problems (see Table 5.7). They have developed a series of management protocols involving dietary supplementation, food texture modifications, and posture modifications. A nutritionist should be available to consult with parents and program staff relative to diet if weight gain is a problem.

Constipation is a common problem experienced by persons with Rett syndrome. Many of the girls fail to consume adequate fluids and fiber which may result in an impacted bowel (Hunter, 1987). Dietary measures (ingestion of fiber, mineral oil, fruit with high liquid content, etc.) may prove adequate, although artificial laxatives, enemas, or suppositories are often required (Naidu et al., 1990).

COGNITIVE AND ADAPTIVE FUNCTIONING

Rett syndrome is characterized by an especially debilitating combination of an extrapyramidal movement disorder, delayed response latencies, and the loss of acquired speech. Such a combination of disabilities significantly limits our ability to estimate the cognitive functioning of persons with this disorder. Traditional methods of cognitive assessment require either unimpaired motor or verbal responses from the individual to generate valid estimates. If the person is required to employ a means of responding that in itself is impaired, we can never be certain whether the assessed functioning is a

TABLE 5.7   Feeding Problems Common in Persons with Rett Syndrome

Inability to consume adequate calories orally to meet energy requirements.

Evidence of ongoing aspiration during oral feeding.

Oral feeding is stressful for the caregiver, the individual with Rett syndrome, or both.

Mealtimes are protracted, leaving limited time for other daily activities.

Oral intake is erratic.

Oral supplementation has failed.

Chronic food/liquid refusal or aversive behavior during mealtime has developed.

A safe route for providing regular medication is required (e.g., with food or liquid intake).

measure of cognitive ability or of the motor and verbal disability. Thus, the assessment of cognitive functioning in persons with Rett syndrome is particularly problematic.

Given the effect of Rett syndrome on verbal and motor behavior, assessment employing traditional standardized measures of cognitive ability is counterindicated. These measures would be invalid because they would generate scores that would be indicative of the verbal and motor disability instead of cognitive ability. For this reason, the cognitive abilities of girls with Rett syndrome traditionally have been assessed with instruments designed for evaluating infants. These measures can be administered to persons with very little verbal and motor ability. Generally, however, they require caregivers and others familiar with the child to make judgments about the child's ability and developmental functioning level to support data collected through direct observation. Many of these measures allow flexibility in the materials employed in testing to maximize child interest. Thus, these assessments are thought to provide a more accurate picture of developmental functioning than traditional IQ tests. Although using infant assessments for older children with severe impairments is a common practice, these tests were normed and standardized on infants. Thus, the score attained might best be interpreted as an estimate.

Along those lines, Demeter (2000) cautions that when assessing individuals with severe or profound disabilities such as those found in Rett syndrome, a standardized instrument is unlikely to measure the full range of a child's ability. Noting that discrepancies exist between parental reports of ability and the ability levels indicated by test results, Demeter suggests that persons with Rett syndrome often show situation-specific skills that traditional measures miss. Some children can and do learn to interact within their environment to get their needs met, yet this capacity may be missed by assessment or assumed to be nonexistent. Demeter suggests that when attempting to assess a child with Rett syndrome, researchers should use criterion-referenced tests to measure a child's ability to learn new skills as well as multiple observations in natural environments. Further, because children with Rett syndrome are highly social, assessment should use social interests or people versus objects to elicit responses.

Physical and neurological impairments inherent in Rett syndrome (e.g., apraxia) may impede a person's ability to act on or respond to stimuli in the consistent manner often necessitated in standardized testing situations. As a result, scoring should be completed in a way that does not penalize these individuals for instances when there is no response. Test administrators should take into account the child's successful attempts divided by the total number of actual attempts, omitting the times the child was nonresponsive. For example, if a child was asked to point to a particular picture and was only able to do so 6 of the 10 times requested, and got 4 of the 6 attempts correct, then the percentage would be calculated using $\frac{4}{6}$ as the raw score instead of $\frac{4}{10}$. The end result is an exploration of the ratio of correct to incorrect responses free of trials in which the movement disorders associated with Rett syndrome precluded item selection.

One assessment tool suggested by the International Rett Syndrome Association (IRSA, 2002) for assessing cognitive ability in persons with Rett syndrome is the Peabody Picture Vocabulary Test-Revised (PPVT-R). The PPVT-R requires that students point to the one picture that the test administrator verbally labels, out of four displayed. The IRSA suggests a modified test protocol (enlarging pictures and spreading them farther apart to ease the interpretation of eye-gaze responses, testing over multiple days to guard against "down days" and possible misinterpretation) to assist in providing an accurate picture of the child's skill level. One must note, however, that the PPVT-R ". . . is not a comprehensive test of general intelligence, instead it measures only one important facet of intelligence: vocabulary" (Dunn & Dunn, 1981, p. 2). Like other measures employed to assess the cognitive ability of persons with Rett syndrome, the validity of the scores attained must be explored further.

Assessment measures that employ eye gaze or switch activation may be useful for persons with Rett syndrome. The question remains whether the score attained could be replicated if the same measure were administered again: Does the test measure cognitive ability or simply provide an opportunity for responding (e.g., the student is aware that she should activate a switch but does so randomly)? Further, the small amount of stimuli provided as distracters in measures such as the PPVT-R allow for a 25% chance that the student will select the correct answer. Administration of assessment instruments to persons with severe disabilities typically requires that the individual be familiar with the response capabilities of the person being tested. Problems can arise when the administrator scores an item as correct based on a vague implied response or assumed capabilities based on previous knowledge of the child.

Another consideration when assessing the cognitive abilities with Rett syndrome is visual acuity. In a 1996 study, von Tetzchner et al., used the Fagen Test of Infant Intelligence to assess visual function and visual information processing in a group of girls with Rett syndrome and then compared them with a control group of age-matched typically developing children. Results indicated that all the girls in the study ($n = 41$) displayed a visual acuity below what would be expected in fully developed vision. The authors suggest this may be due to syndrome-related arrested cortical and retinal development or attentional deficits that cause misleading results. Either way, the authors suggest that persons with Rett syndrome need additional time to process information be it novel or familiar. Additional response time must be incorporated into any assessment involving children with Rett syndrome.

Much of the research on Rett syndrome suggests that the individuals function within the severe-to-profound range of mental retardation. Perry, Sarlo-McGarvey, and Haddad (1991) employed the Cattell Infant Intelligence Scale (Cattell, 1940) to assess the cognitive functioning of 15 girls with Rett syndrome. Each of the girls tested below the 8-month cognitive functioning level, with an average of 3 months, suggesting profound cognitive deficits. There is, however, considerable debate about whether children with Rett syndrome experience a true dementia involving cognitive degeneration that results in severe or profound mental retardation (e.g., Budden, Meek, & Henighan, 1990; Charnov, Stach, & Didonato, 1989; Rolando, 1985) or a cognitive arrest or stagnation at the point of the initial motor and language regression (e.g., Fontanesi & Haas, 1988; Kerr et al.,

1987; Naidu et al., 1986). Charnov and her associates (Charnov et al., 1989) evaluated the developmental histories of 16 girls with Rett syndrome through parent interview (of preregression development) and current functioning assessment employing the Birth to Three Developmental Scale (Bangs & Dodson, 1979). In all developmental areas, they report that the current functioning of each subject was substantially below that which the children were attributed to have achieved prior to the onset of the disorder. Interestingly, the developmental skills profile at the time of testing mirrored that of the preregression skills, although at a lower level of functioning.

There is some support for a hypothesis that Rett syndrome results in cognitive arrest or stagnation at the developmental level achieved at the age of onset of the condition in combination with a severe extrapyramidal movement and expressive language disorder as opposed to cognitive dementia (Hagberg & Witt-Engerstrom, 1986; Kerr & Stephenson, 1986; Stephenson & Kerr, 1987). The extent and timing of the cognitive stagnation may be the result of the differential timing of the genetic mutation and the number and location of the cells impacted with the defective MECP2 gene (Hoffbuhr et al., 2001). Fontanesi and Haas (1988) evaluated the cognitive functioning of 18 girls with Rett syndrome. They administered the Vineland Adaptive Behavior Scales and the Bayley Scales of Adaptive Abilities in addition to examining medical and developmental histories and interviewing parents regarding the age at which their daughters attained developmental milestones. Their results indicated that "skills not dependent on either language or fine motor function are retained at a developmental level equivalent to the age of onset" (p. S23). Gross motor functioning, daily living skills, and object permanence were found to be relatively preserved, whereas fine motor control and language functioning displayed substantial degeneration from preregression developmental levels.

In a longitudinal study of the cognitive skills in six girls with Rett syndrome, Woody-att and Ozanne (1993) reported patterns of similarity across the group as well as individual variations across subjects and within subjects over a period of 3 years. Using the Uzgiris and Hunt Scales of Infant Psychological Development (1975), they found the girls resembled one another and remained relatively stable over the 3 years in the sensorimotor domains of Object Permanence (Piagetian Stages I and II), Vocal Imitation (Piagetian Stages 0 and I), Gestural Imitation (Piagetian Stages 0 and I), and Scheme Actions (Piagetian Stages II and III). There was considerable individual variation among the girls in relation to the sensorimotor domain of Means Ends Abilities, ranging from Piagetian Stages I to IV. The girls also demonstrated the greatest level of individual improvement over the 3-year study (from Piagetian Stage I to Stages II and IV for three of the girls).

Current best estimates suggest that persons with Rett syndrome function within the severe-to-profound range of mental retardation following the regression in Stage 2 of the disorder. The areas of gross motor activity and daily living skills appear to be more advanced than other adaptive functions and the girls are capable of some cognitive improvement over time. Further research is needed to gain a fuller understanding of the cognitive abilities of girls with Rett syndrome. Multidisciplinary assessments of children with Rett syndrome are required to gather information on factors that may influence cognitive development and performance. Inconsistency of response in the test situation is a common report across the studies. This makes standardized testing difficult, and care should be taken not only to provide standardized administrations of cognitive tests, but also to look across the daily functioning of the individuals to identify actions that indicate target abilities. For example, in one of our studies (Van Acker & Grant, 1995), one of the girls failed to demonstrate awareness of a covered object during testing, suggesting a lack of object permanence. Later in the testing situation, however, she dropped a toy and it rolled under the table. She repeatedly looked under the table for the missing item.

COMMUNICATION

Communication abilities and subsequent programming for persons with Rett syndrome have been the topic of very limited empirical research. Prior to regression, most of the girls with this disorder are reported to have developed single spoken words and/or word combinations. Comprehension skills appropriate to the child's age also are typically noted (Budden, Meek, et al., 1990; Woodyatt & Ozanne, 1992). The loss of language skills during regression is sufficiently rapid to be mistaken for hearing loss. Following the regression phase of the disorder, speech and language skills are observed to be severely impaired. Verbalizations are typically nonexistent or limited to "nonfunctional" consonant-vowel combinations, except in the estimated 2% to 4% of girls who fall within the preserved speech variant of Rett syndrome (Budden, Meek, et al., 1990; Skjeldal, von Tetzchner, Jacobsen, Smith, & Heilberg, 1995; Zappella, 1992). Girls with the preserved speech variant may retain full sentence use and may even slowly show an increase in vocabulary (von Tetzchner, 1997). However, for the most part, these girls employ their language in a nonfunctional manner. They continue to display significant communication impairment with pronounced pragmatic difficulties (Gillberg, 1997). As the girls approach adolescence, improved eye contact, social interaction, and communicative intentionality are reported (Woodyatt & Ozanne, 1993).

Individuals with Rett syndrome become a part of the estimated one million children and adults in the United States who are unable to communicate orally (Diggs, 1981). Most successful communication programs for these girls take advantage of their limited communicative behaviors (e.g., Donnellan, Mirenda, Mesaros, & Fassbender, 1984). Vocalizations, facial expressions, gestures, walking toward a desired item or activity, and eye gaze are common communicative behaviors displayed by persons with Rett syndrome. Parents and educators must attune themselves to their child's communicative behavior and respond contingently to these signals. As with any child, the critical element in the development of a meaningful communication system depends on the contingent interaction of the person and her environment (Lewis, Alessandri, & Sullivan, 1990). When others learn to detect the communicative behaviors and to respond to them in a systematic fashion, a formal and effective system of communication can be developed. Parents have taken photographs of their daughter's

facial and gestural communicative behaviors and developed a "dictionary" for those who interact frequently with their child (International Rett Syndrome Association, 1990).

Until recently, persons with multiple disabilities, such as those displayed in Rett syndrome, would have been deemed unlikely candidates to benefit from formal communication intervention. In the past, the literature has asserted a powerful relationship between cognition and language development. Intentional communication was thought to require performance at Piaget's (1929) sensorimotor development Stage V (Bates, Benigni, Bretherton, Camaioni, & Volterra, 1979; Bates, Camaioni, & Volterra, 1975; Kahn, 1977, 1981, 1984). Formal testing suggests that girls with Rett syndrome function at a presymbolic language level (Woodyatt & Ozanne, 1992, 1993). Again, one cannot determine whether these results relate primarily to cognitive deficits or to an expressive language and/or motor disorder. Numerous anecdotal reports however, suggest that these girls may well understand more than they can express (Weisz, 1987). Moreover, the assumption that intentional communication requires Stage V functioning has been called into question (Reichle & Keogh, 1986; Rice, 1983).

Persons with Rett syndrome, in fact, have been taught to employ augmentative communication systems that involve eye pointing, communication boards (pictures), facial expressions, gestures, and the activation of switches or computers to indicate some limited volitional gestures. Van Acker and Grant (1995) employed a dynamic computer-graphic presentation contingent on touch-screen activation with three girls to select desired food items. Results indicated that two of the three girls demonstrated a reduction in stereotypic hand use and significantly increased item requesting when provided computer-based requesting instruction. Interestingly, cognitive assessment of all three girls indicated a functioning level below the Piagetian Sensorimotor Stage V, yet benefit from instruction was obvious.

Similarly, Hetzroni, Rubin, and Konkol (2002) were able to teach three girls with Rett syndrome to match picture symbols (PCS or orthography) or picture symbols plus text to the spoken request to "touch _____ ." Their results suggested the girls were able to demonstrate a steady learning curve over the symbols employed and to display a partial retention of these symbols over time.

Speech and language services appear to be warranted for persons with Rett syndrome. Programming should emphasize functional receptive and expressive language skills, as well as cognitive, social pragmatic, and affective communication skills. Early intervention could target eye contact and attending to the environment. Cause-and-effect relationships that allow the children to gain an understanding of their ability to affect their environment are essential for communication training. Though Rett syndrome affects a person's ability to attend to objects and stimuli, seemingly reducing the capability to discriminate between items and therefore making communication intervention difficult, there is evidence that children with Rett syndrome can sustain attention in preferred activities for longer than average periods of time (J. Watson, Umansky, Marcy, & Repacholi, 1996). Implications of this research support the idea that interventions should strive to identify and use activities, people, and items preferred by the child to enhance motivation to learn. Simple switches to activate toys or computer monitors may enhance an awareness of cause-and-effect relationships. Musical instruments also have been shown to promote the child's desire to interact with her environment (Wesecky, 1986; Zappella, 1986). Given the importance of communication skills, researchers need to identify the range of communication functioning in, and effective methods to teach improved communication skills to, persons with Rett syndrome.

ORTHOPEDIC ASPECTS AND INTERVENTION

Persons with Rett syndrome exhibit multiple orthopedic and motor movement disorders. These disorders can vary significantly across the different phases of the syndrome. Physical and occupational therapists, therefore, must play an important role in the care of individuals with Rett syndrome (Braddock, Braddock, & Graham, 1993; Hanks, 1986, 1990). Intensive therapy, while failing to alter the actual course of the disease, has been successful in addressing symptoms by maintaining or improving functional movement, mobility, preventing deformities, and keeping the girls in contingent contact with their environments. During the periods of regression associated with the disorder, therapeutic intervention is especially important and should be more frequent, because transition skills are at risk (Hanks, 1990). Although persons with Rett syndrome display numerous similarities, their specific therapeutic problems and responses to treatment vary dramatically (Hanks, 1986, 1990; Lieb-Lundell, 1988; Sponseller, 1989). The therapeutic intervention program, therefore, must be highly individualized.

Apraxia and *ataxia* are frequently the earliest manifestations of motor problems in Rett syndrome. Hypotonia interferes with postural stability. Fitzgerald, Jankovic, Glaze, Schultz, and Percy (1990) suggest that the typical "jerky truncal tremors" may reflect a derangement of postural reflexes rather than cerebellar pathology. The girls develop compensatory increased tone to achieve stability, resulting in abnormal movement patterns. A marked fixing or locking of their joints into positions of stability to counter disruption in balance is typical, inhibiting their ability to shift positions. Thus, the legs are often kept in wide abduction while sitting and standing (see Figure 5.2) and weight shift is absent (Hanks, 1986).

The girls often demonstrate expressions of agitation and fear in response to any movements

Figure 5.2 Stereotypic hand movements in Rett syndrome.

that are not self-initiated. Similar voluntary movements, however, are not related to these stress reactions. Lieb-Lundell (1988) reports, "No amount of practice or exposure alters this response of fear to extrinsically initiated movement" (p. 533).

Several therapeutic interventions have been found to be successful in the treatment of apraxia-ataxia. Tone reduction techniques similar to those used with patients afflicted with cerebral palsy or impaired through a stroke are appropriate. Interventions might include (1) use of the therapy ball, (2) balance-stimulating floor activities, (3) segmental rolling, and (4) rotation and weight shift activities (Hanks, 1986, 1990). Vestibular movement activities (e.g., merry-go-rounds, swings) have also been reported as helpful if the child will tolerate this intervention (Havlak & Covington, 1989).

Efforts to facilitate normal movement while maintaining reduced tone are usually not successful, however (Hanks, 1990). As the girls often resist being moved, close physical contact and a slow, firm approach aimed to reduce the child's anxiety during physical assistance is suggested. Individuals with Rett syndrome often have very long response latency. Therapists must provide verbal directions and encouragement and provide the time needed for a response.

Stereotyped hand movements represent one of the most distinguishing characteristics of the Rett syndrome. Hand wringing, hand washing, hand tapping, and hand-to-mouth movements are common stereotypies resulting in the loss of purposeful hand function. These movements appear to evolve with age, proceeding from simple, rapid movements to a slower, more complex form and ultimately to slow, less complicated repetitive movements (Clare, 1986). Most researchers consider the stereotypic hand movements to represent primary circular reactions resulting from an underlying extrapyramidal disorder. Thus, they represent nonvolitional movements. Persons with Rett syndrome appear to require great concentration and effort to break out of the stereotypic movements for even brief attempts at purposeful hand use.

Stereotypic behaviors are more remarkable under stressful situations and diminish or disappear momentarily when changing posture or eating. In some individuals, periods of respiratory dysrhythmia (hyperventilation and apnea; Kerr et al., 1990) exacerbated stereotypic movements. Increased stereotypic hand movements in Rett syndrome have been reported to coincide with improved EEG tracings. Niedermeyer and Naidu (1990) have suggested that this passive finger movement may block focal and multifocal spike activity. This phenomenon has been reported previously in Rolandic epilepsy (Sekul & Percy, 1992).

Despite their neurological origin, the stereotypic behaviors of persons with Rett syndrome appear to be influenced, at least minimally, by environmental stimuli. An analogue study of the stereotypic behavior of two young women with Rett syndrome demonstrated that their moment-to-moment expression appeared to be influenced by environmental contingencies (Wehmeyer, Bourland, & Ingram, 1993). They found that both participants increased or decreased their level of stereotypic responding as the result of various consequences within their social setting. For example, one of the girls would demonstrate a significant increase in stereotypy when placed in a task demand situation. The authors speculated that escape and/or avoidance of task engagement was negatively reinforcing her stereotypy. Van Acker (1987) reported a 40% reduction in the stereotypic hand movements displayed by one girl when involved in computer-assisted instruction. These findings were extended in a later study where the stereotypic behavior of two additional girls displayed a significant decrease during computer-assisted requesting.

Though stereotypic hand movements are an intrinsic part of Rett syndrome, there is some evidence that girls with the preserved speech variant of Rett syndrome retain more functional hand use than girls with classical Rett syndrome. The preserved speech variant is usually associated with a higher ability level in the cognitive, speech, and motor domains. Umansky et al. (2001) suggest that differing levels of MECP2 protein function may account for differences in object-oriented hand use in girls with the preserved speech variant. Furthermore, as a result of an intervention study conducted with one 6-year-old girl with the preserved speech variant of Rett syndrome, Umansky et al. believe that social facilitation of object-oriented hand use is an important factor in preservation of this function. Outside encouragement of hand use contributes to a child's ability to retain hand movements and skill.

The suspected neurophysiological etiology of stereotypy in Rett syndrome has led researchers to caution practitioners attempting to modify these behaviors. As these behaviors appear to represent basically involuntary movements, efforts to change this behavior, especially through the use of aversive consequences, seem ill advised (Hanks, 1990). Moreover, previous attempts to use operant conditioning procedures to alter symptomatic behaviors of persons with Rett syndrome have not proven particularly promising. For example, differential reinforcement, response interruption, and contingent hand restraint have been used to decrease self-injurious behavior (Iwata, Pace, Willis, Gamache, & Hyman, 1986). They reported that the hand biting of these girls, though moderately reduced through intervention, appeared to "be related to organic predisposition rather than being shaped inadvertently by the environment" (p. 164). Facial screening has been attempted, without success, to decrease breathing irregularities (Lugaresi, Cirignotta, & Montagna, 1985). Recently, however, operant approaches employing prompting, backward chaining, shaping, and positive reinforcement have shown success (Bat-Haee, 1994; Piazza, Anderson, & Fisher, 1993; Van Acker & Grant, 1995). Piazza and her associates (1993) were able to reestablish functional self-feeding in three girls with Rett syndrome through the use of graduated prompting and positive reinforcement. These researchers suggest that feeding may represent a good first step in developing improved hand use as the girls generally enjoy eating and the food serves as a natural positive reinforcer. They caution parents and practitioners to be aware that the period needed for skill acquisition may be longer than that displayed in other children with severe or profound disabilities. Moreover, because these girls display variable progress from day to day, data collection to plot change over the course of the training can help parents avoid becoming discouraged. Thus, operant procedures, especially nonaversive approaches, may prove effective in the treatment of some behavioral characteristics of the Rett syndrome; however,

maintenance of treatment effects has not been documented. Treatments with various medications such as L-dopa, haloperidol, 5-HTP, and various anticonvulsants have proved unrewarding thus far (Percy et al., 1985).

Splinting has been found to be successful in interrupting hand-to-mouth (Hanks, 1986) and hand wringing (Aron, 1990; Naganuma, 1988) movements, thus allowing the girls to direct their attention to tasks and persons in their environment and to reduce the risk of skin breakdown related to these high-rate behaviors. In fact, some persons with Rett syndrome have demonstrated improved functional hand use while splints were in use (Naganuma, 1988). Tuten and Miedaner (1989), however, were unable to replicate the effectiveness of hand splints. The two subjects involved in this study displayed no decrease in stereotyped hand wringing, nor any subsequent increase in functional hand use as a result of hand splint application. Sharpe (1992) employed an alternating treatments design to compare the effectiveness of bilateral hand splints and an elbow orthosis for two girls with Rett syndrome. Both girls demonstrated a decrease in stereotypic hand movements and a corresponding increase in toy play with the use of the elbow orthosis. The bilateral hand splints had no obvious treatment effect. No studies have demonstrated any maintenance effects of hand splints over time once the splints have been removed. Additionally, many persons with Rett syndrome are unable to tolerate the application of hand or arm splints for even short periods.

Instructional strategies that reinforce behaviors incompatible with stereotypic movements are recommended. Many of the girls accept having the stereotypic behavior interrupted. In fact, they often seem to relax when their stereotypic behavior is stopped for short periods. This can be accomplished by having the girls placed into the prone position or by simply holding one hand while assisting functional hand use (see Figure 5.3). Hanks (1986) reports, "Toys that combine bright colors and sound and require input from the child are helpful in keeping the child involved with the environment and making attempts to use her hands" (p. 250). Encouraging the child to use her hands for reaching or switch activation can potentially reduce stereotypic hand movements

Figure 5.3 Interruption of stereotypic behavior to promote functional hand use.

as reaching for an object and hand-wringing behaviors are incompatible (J. Watson, Umansky, Marcy, Johnston, & Repacholi, 1996). Music therapy has also proved useful in the promotion of functional hand use. The music appears to increase the level of awareness and the instruments motivate efforts to reach out and interact (Wesecky, 1986). Battery-operated toys and computers modified to respond to an easily activated switch provide an almost limitless array of possibilities not only to decrease stereotyped behavior (Van Acker, 1987; Van Acker & Grant, 1995) but also to increase functional hand use, communication, and cognitive development (Hanks, 1986; Sponseller, 1989; Zappella, 1986).

Bumin, Uyanik, Yilmaz, Kayihan, and Topcu (2003) report that following 8 weeks of exposure to the Halliwick method of hydrotherapy, an 11-year-old girl with Rett syndrome displayed increased balance while walking, decreased stereotypic movements, and improved purposeful hand use (e.g., improved self-feeding).

Spasticity has been reported as a typical problem during Stage II of the disorder. This spasticity may "vary from a mild increase in tone in the gastroc-soleus complex, resulting in toe walking, to severe involvement throughout the body affecting even respiration and swallowing" (Hanks, 1986, p. 248). The resulting muscle imbalance may lead to severe contractures, especially distally (e.g., a downward pointing of the foot). This spasticity may also be responsible, at least in part, for the high incidence of scoliosis in girls with Rett syndrome (Hanks, 1986; Sponseller, 1989).

Hydrotherapy emphasizing movement in the water, range of motion, and basic water skills has been helpful in the improvement of range of motion and the reduction of discomfort (Hanks, 1986; Lieb-Lundell, 1988; Schleichkorn, 1987). Tone reduction activities such as rotation, weight shift, and vibration have been reported to result in a temporary reduction of spasticity (Hanks, 1986, 1990).

Ambulation remains one of the critical skills to develop and maintain in persons with Rett syndrome. Many of the girls fail to develop this skill prior to Stage II, while others lose this ability as part of the rapid motor degeneration. As spasticity and apraxia increase, the girls often lose many functional gross motor skills that they had previously achieved. Additionally, these girls often manifest spatial disorientation. Their perception of an upright posture results in a forward, backward, or lateral leaning. Ambulation may be lost, especially for girls with an orientation toward backward leaning, as they are unable to initiate their forward weight shift. They fear falling when attempting weight shift in a forward direction. The abnormal gait pattern typically displayed in this syndrome results from a combination of spasticity, ataxia, apraxia, compensatory spinal rigidity, and spatial disorientation. Asymmetries may develop as one leg becomes stiffer or weaker. Weight shift is accomplished through lateral rocking and trunk rotation is lost. More simply, because the center of balance is off, girls often think they are falling forward when they are standing normally. They try to compensate by leaning back, fall over, and over time may lose the ability to stand (Kerr et al., 1990).

Independent standing and ambulation represent a realistic therapy goal, especially in the early years. Many girls while unable to walk independently can do so with assistance. Such aided ambulation should be encouraged. Weight-bearing exercises, walking, and gait training have been successful (Hanks, 1986, 1989, 1990). If appropriate, activities designed to elicit righting and equilibrium responses might include use of the large therapy ball (prone positioning and then standing, leaning forward), weight shifting (seating the child on a bench and then tipping the bench slightly backward), and ultimately active shift forward to come from sitting to standing (Hanks, 1990).

Frequently, foot deformities (e.g., ankle pronation, plantar flexion inversion and toe curling) must be corrected with polypropylene ankle-foot orthosis, hinged to allow dorsiflexion. Attempts to correct pronation foot deformities with below-ankle orthosis has not proven effective as they destabilize the child's gait. Gentle manual stretching, night splints, and weight shifting in controlled standing with the heels down have all proven useful if started prior to signs of actual contractures (Hanks, 1990).

Individuals with the ability to ambulate must engage in activities that will maintain this skill and promote stimulation of the joints and muscles (Kjoerholt & Salthammer, 1989). Walking and stair climbing should be a regular part of the daily routine to maximize these skills. Kjoerholt and Salthammer (1989) caution that therapists must be patient as the girls walk "very slowly and will often stop without any noticeable reason, probably due to apraxia" (p. 84). Many of the common devices for assisting ambulation (e.g., push-type walker) are of limited usefulness due to loss of purposeful hand function.

Scoliosis (a side-to-side curvature of the spine) in individuals with Rett syndrome is well documented (Hagberg et al., 1983; Hanks, 1986, 1989; Harrison & Webb, 1990; Loder, Lee, & Richards, 1989; Sponseller, 1989), and kyphosis ("hunchback") is common (Rett, 1977; Sponseller, 1989). Together, these deformities represent the primary musculoskeletal concern in Rett syndrome. There are no rigid guidelines to predict deformity or to recommend treatment. Standard criteria (e.g., sex of patient, curve pattern, onset of menarche, Risser sign) typically useful in determining an appropriate intervention strategy do not appear to be helpful with this syndrome (Hennessy & Haas, 1988). Scoliosis results in a muscle imbalance in the area around the curve. The muscles on one side of the spinal column will be spastic and hypertonic, whereas one may notice atrophic or hypotonic musculature on the other side. The person often will tend to lean toward the hypotonic side. Initially, tone reduction activities, such as gentle lengthening of the concave side and activation of the convex side through elicitation of equilibrium reactions are recommended (Hanks, 1990).

Placing the child on her side with the apex of the curve down may prove helpful. Exercises designed to maximize use of the muscles the girl avoids using are in order (e.g., feed and lead the child by the hand on her hypotonic side). Good positioning is vital; and strollers, wheelchairs, and high chairs should be fitted properly to produce a symmetrical sitting posture and an erect spine (Hanks, 1986; Kjoerholt & Salthammer, 1989).

EDUCATIONAL IMPLICATIONS

Children, even those with severe disabilities, must be provided an appropriate education within the least restrictive environment. As a result, school personnel are called on to make judgments about the appropriateness of curriculum and associated instructional strategies for children with exceptional needs. To plan effectively, educators must be cognizant of a child's current level of functioning, capacity for learning, and potential for meeting reasonable instructional objectives.

Given the cognitive, communicative, and physical limitations of Rett syndrome, the educational prognosis is guarded at best. Though children may not attain developmental milestones at appropriate times, and indeed may never attain many skills typical for other children their age, children with Rett syndrome can and do benefit from educational intervention.

Koppenhaver, Erickson, and Skotko (2001) promote the merits of early literacy learning through mother and child storybook reading. They compared the ability of four girls with Rett syndrome to label common items in picture books using picture symbols and augmentative communication systems before and after parent training. They report that "access to communication symbols, assistive technologies, and parent training" consistently enhanced children's frequency of attending to and "responding" through the use of various augmentative communication devices. Koppenhaver et al., used four intervention strategies with the parents in his study, all of which would be useful for educators. First, they suggest attributing meaning to a child's attempts to communicate, even if the meaning is uncertain. Second, prompt the use of communication symbols or devices through natural questions and comments, instead of commands. Third, they believe in providing a sufficient wait time after asking questions and then providing a hierarchy of prompts, rather than a complete physical guidance after the child is nonresponsive. Finally, Koppenhaver and his associates believe that interventionists (be they parents or educators) should consistently ask questions of children that maximize their ability to use the adaptive equipment they have in front of them. Ask questions that have answers on the communication board the child is using (Koppenhaver et al., 2001). The key to any successful intervention is to get the child involved in the process, and even though it may take more effort to engage a child with Rett syndrome, the endeavor is worthwhile. Though these children may not be able to read a story on their own, they can participate in and enjoy the activity of reading.

Individualized Education Plan goals related to developing a viable communication system are worthwhile. Study of seemingly meaningless routines and actions of girls with Rett syndrome can help develop communication systems based on intent and caregivers can make inferences to help establish meaning and develop goal-directed behaviors. Through structured overinterpretation, where adults consistently respond to a certain gaze or gesture as an indication of some need or want, we can help children with Rett syndrome gain control over their environment and make it a safe, predictable setting (von Tetzchner, 1997).

Writing Individual Education Plan (IEP) goals related to functional skills such as drinking, eating, and oral motor skills, hand use, dressing, cognition, communication, and social skills have all been suggested by the International Rett Syndrome Association (www .rettsyndrome.org). These goals provide an excellent starting point for educators and parents seeking to build an educational program for a child with Rett syndrome, but it is important to remember that goals must be individualized and appropriate for the targeted student. Not all goals are appropriate for all children.

Though intervention styles and methodology vary from disability to disability, Rett syndrome falls under the same pervasive developmental disorder umbrella as autism.

Some intervention techniques often used for children with autism have been adopted for use with Rett syndrome. Although there is very little empirical evidence that children with Rett syndrome benefit from these intervention techniques, anecdotal reports from parents are often encouraging. These methods include applied behavior analysis, which uses a discrete trial format to teach new skills, floor time, a relationship-based approach focusing on opening and closing communication circles, and PECS, a picture exchange communication system (Hunter, 1999). On the other hand, published empirical studies of some of these intervention approaches (e.g., discrete trial format instruction, applied behavior analysis techniques to increase functional hand use) have failed to document their effectiveness with students displaying Rett syndrome (Iwata et al., 1986; Smith, Klevstrand, & Lovaas, 1995).

CONCLUSION

Only a small percentage of the estimated 10,000 individuals in the United States afflicted with the Rett syndrome have been identified thus far. Lack of awareness of this disorder on the part of physicians and clinicians is undoubtedly a major contributing factor to this state of affairs. Even when physicians are aware of the Rett syndrome, an accurate diagnosis is not always forthcoming. There is often a hesitation to accept, as a specific entity, a disorder for which there is no definitive diagnostic marker. Today, a diagnosis of Rett syndrome continues to require a careful analysis of the clinical signs and symptoms (often supported by the identification of a MECP2 mutation).

Rett syndrome does not, as first suspected, appear to be a degenerative disease but rather a disorder characterized by arrested neurodevelopment caused by a mutation of the MECP2 gene and the resulting failure to silence various yet unknown genes during development. The discovery of MECP2 as a gene involved in Rett syndrome will potentially lead to the development of a diagnostic test for early diagnosis and prenatal testing. Further research into the cause, pathogenesis, effective treatment, and ultimately prevention of this disorder is ongoing. Future research could refine our understanding of the pathogenesis of this disorder.

When this happens, there will be increased hope for the development of an effective treatment (e.g., medication), and, perhaps, a cure (e.g., gene therapy). The development of mouse models for Rett syndrome will facilitate the molecular dissection of the pathogenesis of this disorder. Increased research related to treatment of symptoms, communication development, and educational "best practices" with individuals displaying Rett syndrome are sorely needed. As one of the slogans of the International Rett Syndrome Association states, "If we care today, we can cure tomorrow."

Cross-References

Issues in diagnosis of other pervasive developmental disorders are discussed in Chapters 1, 3, 4, and 6; assessment issues are discussed in Chapters 27 through 33; issues in health care are reviewed in Chapter 20.

REFERENCES

Adkins, W. N. (1986). Rett syndrome at an institution for the developmentally disabled. *American Journal of Medical Genetics, 24*(Suppl. 1), 85–97.

Allen, D. A. (1988). Autistic spectrum disorders: Clinical presentation in preschool children. *Journal of Child Neurology, 3*(Suppl.), S48–S56.

American Psychiatric Association. (1994). *Diagnostic and statistical manual of mental disorders* (4th ed.). Washington, DC: Author.

Amir, R. E., Van den Veyver, I. B., Schultz, R., Malicki, D. M., Tran, C. Q., Dahle, E. J., et al. (2000). Influence of mutation type and X chromosome inactivation on Rett syndrome phenotypes. *Annals of Neurology, 47*, 670–679.

Amir, R. E., Van den Veyver, I. B., Wan, M., Tran, C. Q., Francke, U., & Zoghbi, H. Y. (1999). Rett syndrome is caused by mutations in X-linked MECP2, encoding methyl-CpG-binding protein 2. *Nature Genetics, 23*, 185–188.

Armstrong, D. (1992). The neuropathology of the Rett syndrome. *Brain and Development, 14*(Suppl.), S89–S100.

Armstrong, D. (2001). Rett syndrome neuropathology review 2000. *Brain and Development, 23*, S72–S76.

Armstrong, D., Dunn, J. K., Antalffy, B., & Trivedi, R. (1995). Selective dendritic alterations in the cortex of Rett syndrome. *Journal of Neuropathology and Experimental Neurology, 54*, 195–201.

Armstrong, D., Dunn, J. K., Schultz, R. J., Herbert, D. A., Glaze, D. G., & Motile, K. J. (1999). Organ growth in Rett syndrome: A postmortem examination analysis. *Pediatric Neurology, 20*(2), 125–129.

Aron, M. (1990). The use and effectiveness of elbow splints in the Rett syndrome. *Brain and Development, 12*, 162–163.

Bangs, T., & Dodson, S. (1979). *Birth to Three Developmental Scale.* Hingham, MA: Teaching Resources.

Bates, E., Benigni, L., Bretherton, I., Camaioni, L., & Volterra, V. (1979). *The emergence of symbols: Cognitive communication in infancy.* New York: Academic Press.

Bates, E., Camaioni, L., & Volterra, V. (1975). The acquisition of performatives prior to speech. *Merrill-Palmer Quarterly, 26*, 407–423.

Bat-Haee, M. A. (1994). Behavioral training of a young woman with Rett syndrome. *Perceptual and Motor Skills, 78*, 314.

Beyer, K. S., Blasi, F., Bacchelli, E., Klauck, S. M., Maestrini, E., & Poustka, A. (2002). Mutation analysis of the coding sequence of the MECP2 gene in infantile autism. *Human Genetics, 111*, 305–309.

Bieber Nielsen, J., Henriksen, K. F., Hansen, C., Silahtaroglu, A., Schwartz, M., & Tommerup, N. (2001). MECP2 mutations in Danish patients with Rett syndrome: High frequency of mutations but no consistent correlations with clinical severity or with X chromosome inactivation pattern. *European Journal of Human Genetics, 9*, 178–184.

Bienvenu, T., Carrie, A., de Roux, N., Vinet, M. C., Jonveaux, P., Couvert, P., et al. (2000). MECP2 mutations account for most cases of typical Rett syndrome. *Human Molecular Genetics, 9*(9), 1377–1384.

Braddock, S. R., Braddock, B. A., & Graham, J. M. (1993, October). Rett syndrome: An update and review for the primary pediatrician. *Clinical Pediatrics, 43*, 613–625.

Brucke, T., Sofic, E., Killian, W., Rett, A., & Riederer, P. (1988). Reduced concentrations and increased metabolism of biogenic amines in a single case of Rett syndrome: A postmortem brain study. *Journal of Neural Transmission, 68*, 315–324.

Budden, S. S. (1986). Rett syndrome: Studies of 13 affected girls. *American Journal of Medical Genetics, 24*(Suppl. 1), 99–109.

Budden, S. S., Meek, M., & Henighan, C. (1990). Communication and oral-motor function in Rett syndrome. *Developmental Medicine and Child Neurology, 32*, 51–55.

Budden, S. S., Myer, E., & Butler, I. (1990). Cerebrospinal fluid studies in the Rett syndrome:

Biogenic amines and ß-endorphins. *Brain and Development, 12,* 81–84.

Bumin, G., Uyanik, M., Yilmaz, I., Kayihan, H., & Topcu, M. (2003). Hydrotherapy for Rett syndrome. *Rehabilitation Medicine, 35*(1), 44–45.

Burd, L., Fisher, W., & Kerbeshian, J. (1989). Pervasive disintegrative disorder: Are Rett syndrome and Heller dementia infantilis subtypes? *Developmental Medical Child Neurology, 31*(5), 609–616.

Burford, B., Keer, A. M., & Macleod, H. A. (2003). Nurse recognition of early deviation in development in home videos of infants with Rett disorder. *Journal of Intellectual Disability Research, 47,* 588–589.

Cassanova, M. F., Naidu, S., Goldberg, T. E., Moser, H. W., Khoromi, S., Kumar, A., et al. (1991). Quantitative magnetic resonance imaging in Rett syndrome. *Journal of Neuropsychiatry, 3,* 66–72.

Cattell, P. (1940). *Infant intelligence scale.* New York: Psychological Corporation.

Charman, T., Cass, H., Owen, L., Wigram, T., Slonims, V., Weeks, L., et al. (2002). Regression in individuals with Rett syndrome. *Brain and Development, 24,* 281–283.

Charnov, E. K., Stach, B. A., & Didonato, R. M. (1989, November). *Pre and post onset developmental levels in Rett syndrome.* Paper presented at the American Speech-Language-Hearing Association Convention. St. Louis, MO.

Cheadle, J. P., Gill, H., & Fleming, N. (2000). Long-read sequence analysis of the MECP2 gene in Rett syndrome patients: Correlation of disease severity with mutation type and location. *Human Molecular Genetics, 9,* 1119–1129.

Chugani, H. T., Phelps, M. E., & Mazziotta, J. C. (1987). Positron emission tomography study of human brain functional development. *Annals of Neurology, 22,* 487–497.

Clare, A. J. (1986). *Rett syndrome: Behind their eyes is more than they can show us.* Dissertation, Thames Polytechnic Incorporating Avery Hill College, Kent, United Kingdom.

Clark, A., Gardner, Medwin, D., Richardson, J., McGann, A., Bonham, J. R., et al. (1990). Abnormalities of carbohydrate metabolism and of OCT gene function in the Rett syndrome. *Brain and Development, 12,* 119–124.

Clayton-Smith, J., Watson, P., Ramsden, S., & Black, G. C. (2000). Somatic mutation in MECP2 as a non-fatal neurodevelopmental disorder in males. *Lancet, 356,* 830–832.

Coker, S. B., & Melnyk, A. R. (1991). Rett syndrome and mitochondrial enzyme deficiencies. *Journal of Child Neurology, 6,* 164–166.

Coleman, M. (1990). Is classical Rett syndrome ever present in males? *Brain and Development, 12,* 31–32.

Coleman, M., Brubaker, J., & Hunter, K. (1988). Rett syndrome: A survey of North American patients. *Journal of Mental Deficiency Research, 32,* 117–124.

Coleman, M., & Gillberg, C. (1985). *The biology of autistic syndromes* (pp. 45–50). New York: Praeger.

Collerton, D. (1986). Cholinergic function and intellectual decline in Alzheimer's disease. *Neuroscience, 19,* 1–28.

Comings, D. E. (1986). The genetics of Rett syndrome: The consequences of a disorder where every case is a new mutation. *American Journal of Medical Genetics, 24*(Suppl. 1), 383–388.

Cornford, M. E., Philippart, M., Jacobs, B., Scheibel, A. B., & Vinters, H. V. (1994). Neuropathology of Rett syndrome: Case report with neuronal and mitochondrial abnormalities in the brain. *Journal of Child Neurology, 9*(4), 424–431.

Demeter, K. (2000). Assessing the developmental level in Rett syndrome: An alternative approach. *European Child and Adolescent Psychiatry, 9*(3), 227–233.

Diggs, C. C. (1981). School services. *Language, Speech, and Hearing Services in Schools, 4,* 269–271.

Donnellan, A. M., Mirenda, P. L., Mesaros, R. A., & Fassbender, L. L. (1984). Analyzing the communicative functions of aberrant behavior. *Journal of the Association for Persons with Severe Handicaps, 9*(3), 201–212.

Dragich, J., Houwink-Manville, I., & Schanen, C. (2000). Rett syndrome: A surprising result of a mutation in MECP2. *Human Molecular Genetics, 9,* 2365–2375.

Dunn, L. M., & Dunn, L. M. (1981). *Peabody Picture Vocabulary Test-Revised.* Circle Pines: MN: American Guidance Service.

Eeg-Olofsson, O., Al-Zuhair, A. G. H., Teebi, A. S., Zaki, M., & Daoud, A. S. (1990). A boy with Rett syndrome. *Brain Development, 12*(5), 529–532.

Egger, J., Hofacker, N., Schiel, W., & Holthausen, H. (1992). Magnesium for hyperventilation in Rett's syndrome. *Lancet, 340,* 621–622.

Ellaway, C., & Christodoulou, J. (1999). Rett syndrome: Clinical update and review of recent genetic advances. *Journal of Paediatric and Child Health, 35,* 419–426.

Ellaway, C. J., Williams, K., Leonard, H., Higgins, G., Wilcken, B., & Chritodoulou, J. (1999). Rett syndrome: Randomized controlled trial of L-carnitine. *Journal of Child Neurology, 14,* 162–167.

Fitzgerald, P. M., Jankovic, J., Glaze, D. G., Schultz, R., & Percy, A. K. (1990). Extrapyramidal involvement in Rett's syndrome. *Neurology, 40,* 293–295.

Fontanesi, J., & Haas, R. H. (1988). Cognitive profile of Rett syndrome. *Journal of Child Neurology, 3*(Suppl.), S20–S24.

Garofalo, E., Drury, I., & Goldstein, G. (1988). EEG abnormalities aid diagnosis of Rett syndrome. *Pediatric Neurology, 4,* 350–353.

Genazzani, A., Zappella, M., Nalin, A., Hayek, Y., & Facchinetti, F. (1989). Reduced cerebrospinal fluid ß-endorphin levels in Rett syndrome. *Child Nervous System, 5,* 111–113.

Gillberg, C. (1986). Autism and Rett syndrome: Some notes on differential diagnosis. *American Journal of Medical Genetics, 24*(Suppl. 1), 127–131.

Gillberg, C. (1987). Autistic symptoms in Rett syndrome: The first two years according to mother reports. *Brain and Development, 9*(5), 499–501.

Gillberg, C. (1989). The borderland of autism and Rett syndrome: Five case histories to highlight diagnostic difficulties. *Journal of Autism and Developmental Disorders, 19*(4), 545–559.

Gillberg, C. (1997). Communication in Rett syndrome complex. *European Child and Adolescent Psychology, 6*(Suppl. 1), 21–22.

Gillberg, C., Terenius, L., Hagberg, B. Witt-Engerstrom, I., & Eriksson, I. (1990). CSF ß-endorphins in childhood neuropsychiatric disorders. *Brain and Development, 12,* 88–92.

Girard, M., Couvert, P., Carrie, A., Tardieu, M., Chelly, J., Beldjord, C., et al. (2001). Paternal origin of *de novo* MECP2 mutations in Rett syndrome. *European Journal of Human Genetics, 9,* 231–236.

Glaze, D. G., Frost, J. D., Zoghbi, H. Y., & Percy, A. K. (1987). Rett syndrome in the electroencephalographic characteristics with clinical staging. *Archives of Neurology, 44,* 1053–1056.

Gotoh, H., Susuki, I., Maruki, K., Mitomo, M., Hirasawa, K., & Sasaki, N. (2001). Magnetic resonance imaging and clinical findings examined in adulthood studies on three adults with Rett syndrome. *Brain and Development, 23,* S118–S121.

Goutieres, F., & Aicardi, J. (1985). Rett syndrome: Clinical presentation and laboratory investigations in 12 further French patients. *Brain and Development, 7*(3), 305–306.

Haas, R., & Rice, M. L. A. (1985). Is Rett's syndrome a disorder of carbohydrate metabolism? Hyperpyruvic acidemia and treatment by ketogenic diet. *Annals of Neurology, 18,* 418.

Haas, R. H., Rice, M. A., Trauner, D. A., & Merritt, A. (1986). Therapeutic effects of a ketogenic diet in Rett syndrome. *American Journal of Medical Genetics, 24*(Suppl. 1), 225–246.

Hagberg, B. (1980, June). *Infantile autistic dementia and loss of hand use: A report of 16 Swedish girl patients.* Paper presented at the Research Session of the European Federation of Child Neurology Societies, Manchester, England.

Hagberg, B. (1985). Rett syndrome: Swedish approach to analysis of prevalence and cause. *Brain and Development, 7*(3), 277–280.

Hagberg, B. (1989). Rett syndrome: Clinical peculiarities, diagnostic approach, and possible cause. *Pediatric Neurology, 5,* 75–83.

Hagberg, B. (1995). Clinical delineation of Rett syndrome variants. *Neuropaediatrics, 26,* 62.

Hagberg, B., Aicardi, J., Dias, K., & Ramos, O. (1983). A progressive syndrome of autism, dementia, ataxia, and loss of purposeful hand use in girls: Rett syndrome: Report of 35 cases. *Annals of Neurology, 14*(4), 471–479.

Hagberg, B., Berg, M., & Steffenburg, U. (2001). Three decades of sociomedical experiences from West Swedish Rett females 4–60 years of age. *Brain and Development, 23,* S28–S31.

Hagberg, B., Goutieres, F., Hanefeld, F., Rett, A., & Wilson, J. (1985). Rett syndrome: Criteria for inclusion and exclusion. *Brain and Development, 7*(3), 372–373.

Hagberg, B., Hanefeld, F., Percy, A., & Skjeldal, O. (2002). An update on clinically applicable diagnostic criteria in Rett syndrome. *European Journal of Paediatric Neurology, 6,* 292–297.

Hagberg, B., & Skjeldal, O. H. (1994). Rett variant: A suggested model for inclusion criteria. *Pediatric Neurology, 11,* 5–11.

Hagberg, B., Stenbom, Y., & Witt-Engerstrom, I. (2000). Head growth in Rett syndrome. *Acta Paediatr, 89,* 198–202.

Hagberg, B., & Witt-Engerstrom, I. (1986). Rett syndrome: A suggested staging system for describing impairment profile with increasing age towards adolescence. *American Journal of Medical Genetics, 24*(Suppl. 1), 47–59.

Hamberger, A., Gillberg, C., Palm, A., & Hagberg, B. (1992). C.S.F. elevated glutamate in Rett syndrome. *Neuropediatrics, 23,* 212–213.

Hanaoka, S., Ishikawa, N., & Kamoshita, S. (1985). Three cases of Rett syndrome. In S. Kamoshita (Ed.), *Abstracts for the workshop on Aicardi syndrome and Rett syndrome.* Tokyo.

Hanefeld, F. (1985). The clinical pattern of the Rett syndrome. *Brain and Development, 7*(3), 320–325.

Hanks, S. B. (1986). The role of therapy in Rett syndrome. *American Journal of Medical Genetics, 24*(Suppl. 1), 247–252.

Hanks, S. B. (1989, May). *Motor disabilities and physical therapy strategies in Rett syndrome.* Paper presented at the 5th annual conference of the International Rett Syndrome Association, Washington, DC.

Hanks, S. B. (1990). Motor disabilities in the Rett syndrome and physical therapy strategies. *Brain and Development, 12,* 157–161.

Harding, B. N., Tudmay, A. J., & Wilson, J. (1985). Neuropathological studies in a child showing some features of the Rett syndrome. *Brain and Development, 7*(3), 342–344.

Harris, J. C., Wong, D. F., Wagner, H. N., Rett, A., Naidu, S., Dannals, R. F., et al. (1986). Positron emission tomographic study of D2 dopamine receptor binding and CSF biogenic amine metabolites in Rett syndrome. *American Journal of Medical Genetics, 24*(Suppl. 1), 201–210.

Harrison, D. J., & Webb, P. J. (1990). Scoliosis in the Rett syndrome: Natural history and treatment. *Brain and Development, 12,* 154–156.

Havlak, C., & Covington, C. (1989). *Motor function: Physical and occupational therapy strategies. Education and therapeutic intervention in Rett syndrome.* Ft. Washington, MD: International Rett Syndrome Association.

Hennessy, M. J., & Haas, R. H. (1988). The orthopedic management of Rett syndrome. *Journal of Child Neurology, 3*(Suppl.), S43–S47.

Hetzroni, O., Rubin, C., & Konkol, O. (2002). The use of assistive technology for symbol identification by children with Rett syndrome. *Journal of Intellectual and Developmental Disability, 27,* 57–71.

Hoffbuhr, K., Devaney, J. M., LaFluer, B., Sirianni, N., Scacheri, C., Giron, J., et al. (2001). MECP2 mutations in children with and without the phenotype of Rett syndrome. *Neurology, 56,* 1496–1495.

Hoffbuhr, K. C., Moses, L. M., Jerdonek, M. A., & Naidu, S. (2002). Associations between MECP2 mutations, X-chromosome inactivation and phenotype. *Mental Retardation and Developmental Disabilities, 8,* 99–105.

Holm, V. A. (1985). Rett syndrome: A case report from an audiovisual program. *Brain and Development, 7*(3), 297–299.

Hunter, K. (1987). Rett syndrome: Parents' views about specific symptoms. *Brain and Development, 9*(5), 535–538.

Hunter, K. (1999). *The Rett syndrome handbook.* Clinton, MD: International Rett Syndrome Association.

Huppke, P., Held, M., Laccone, F., & Hanefeld, F. (2003). The spectrum of phenotypes in females with Rett syndrome. *Brain and Development, 25,* 346–351.

Huppke, P., Laccone, F., Kramer, N., Engel, W., & Hanefeld, F. (2000). Rett syndrome: Analysis of MECP2 and clinical characterization of 31 patients. *Human Molecular Genetics, 9,* 1369–1375.

International Rett Syndrome Association. (1990). *Parent idea book: Managing Rett syndrome.* Ft. Washington, MD: Author.

International Rett Syndrome Association. (2002). *Testing methods.* Retrieved October 1, 2002, from http://rettsyndrome.org/main/testing.htm.

Ishikawa, A., Goto, T., Narasaki, M., Yokochi, K., Kitahara, H., & Fukuyama, Y. (1978). A new syndrome (?) of progressive psychomotor deterioration with peculiar stereotyped movement and autistic tendency: A report of three cases. *Brain and Development, 3,* 258.

Iwata, B. A., Pace, G. M., Willis, K. D., Gamache, T. B., & Hyman, S. L. (1986). Operant studies of self-injurious hand biting in the Rett syndrome. *American Journal of Medical Genetics, 24,* 157–166.

Iyama, C. M. (1993). Rett syndrome. *Advances in Pediatrics, 40,* 217–245.

Jacobsen, K., Viken, A., & von Tetzchner, S. (2001). Rett syndrome and ageing: A case study. *Disability and Rehabilitation, 23,* 160–166.

Jan, M. M. S., Dooley, J. M., & Gordon, K. E. (1999). Male Rett syndrome variant: Application of diagnostic criteria. *Pediatric Neurology, 20,* 238–240.

Jellinger, K., Armstrong, D., Zoghbi, H. Y., & Percy, A. K. (1988). Neuropathology of Rett syndrome. *Acta Neuropathologica, 76,* 142–158.

Jellinger, K., & Seiteberger, F. (1986). Neuropathology of Rett syndrome. *American Journal of Medical Genetics, 24*(Suppl. 1), 259–288.

Kahn, J. V. (1977). Comparison of manual and oral language training. *Mental Retardation, 12,* 3–5.

Kahn, J. V. (1981). A comparison of sign and verbal language training with nonverbal retarded children. *Journal of Speech and Hearing Sciences, 47,* 113–119.

Kahn, J. V. (1984). Cognitive training and initial use of referential speech. *Topics in Language Disorders, 5,* 14–28.

Kerr, A. M., Belicohenko, P., Woodcock, T., & Woodcock, M. (2001). Mind and brain in Rett disorder. *Brain and Development* (Suppl. 1), S44–S49.

Kerr, A. M., Montague, J., & Stephenson, J. B. P. (1987). The hands, and the mind, pre- and post-regression, in Rett syndrome. *Brain and Development, 9*(5), 487–490.

Kerr, A., Southall, D., Amos, P., Cooper, R., Samuels, M., Mitchell, J., et al. (1990).

Correlation of electroencephalogram, respiration, and movement in the Rett syndrome. *Brain and Development, 12,* 61–68.

Kerr, A., & Stephenson, J. B. P. (1985). Rett's syndrome in the west of Scotland. *British Medical Journal, 291,* 579–582.

Kerr, A., & Stephenson, J. B. P. (1986). A study of the natural history of Rett syndrome in 23 girls. *American Journal of Medical Genetics, 24,* 77–83.

Kerr, A. M., & Witt-Engerstrom, I. (2001). *Rett disorder and the developing brain.* Oxford, England: Oxford University Press.

Kjoerholt, K., & Salthammer, E. (1989). *Kjoerholt Salthammer Fysioterapi: Educational and therapeutic intervention in Rett syndrome.* Ft. Washington, MD: International Rett Syndrome Association.

Kondo, I., Morishita, R., & Fukuda, T. (2000). The spectrum and paternal origin of de novo mutants of methyl-CpG-binding protein 2 gene (MECP2) in Rett syndrome. *American Journal of Human Genetics, 67*(Suppl. 2), 386.

Koppenhaver, D. A., Erickson, K. A., & Skotko, B. G. (2001). Supporting the communication of girls with Rett syndrome and their mothers in storybook reading. *International Journal of Disability, Development and Education, 48*(4), 395–410.

Kozinetz, C. A., Skender, M. L., MacNaughton, N., Almes, M. J., Schultz, R. J., Percy, A. K., et al. (1993). Epidemiology of Rett syndrome: A population-based registry. *Pediatrics, 91,* 445–450.

Krageloh-Mann, I., Schroth, G., Niemann, G., & Michaelis, R. (1989). The Rett syndrome: Magnetic resonance imaging and clinical findings in four girls. *Brain and Development, 11,* 175–178.

Lagercrantz, H., & Srinivasan, M. (1991). Development and function of neurotransmitters/modulator systems in the brain stem. In M. A. Birke (Ed.), *The fetal and neonatal brain stem* (pp. 1–20). Cambridge, England: Cambridge University Press.

Lappalainien, R., & Riikonen, R. S. (1996). High levels of cerebrospinal fluid glutamate in Rett syndrome. *Pediatric Neurology, 15,* 213–216.

Leiber, B. (1985). Rett syndrome: A nosological entity. *Brain and Development, 7*(3), 275–276.

Lekman, A., Hagberg, B., & Svennerholm, B. A. (1991). Membrane cerebral lipids in Rett syndrome. *Pediatric Neurologist, 7,* 186–190.

Lekman, A., Witt-Engerstrom, I., Gottfries, J., Hagberg, B. A., Percy, A. K., & Svennerholm, L. (1989). Rett syndrome: Biogenic amines and metabolites in postmortem brain. *Pediatric Neurology, 5*(6), 357–362.

Leonard, H., & Bower, C. (1998). Is the girl with Rett syndrome normal at birth? *Developmental Medicine and Child Neurology, 49,* 115–121.

Lewis, M., Alessandri, S. M., & Sullivan, M. W. (1990). *Expectancy, loss of control, and anger expression in young infants.* Report of the Institute for the Study of Child Development, Robert Wood Johnson Medical School Department of Pediatrics, New Brunswick, NJ.

Lieb-Lundell, C. (1988). The therapist's role in the management of girls with Rett syndrome. *Journal of Child Neurology, 3*(Suppl.), S31–S34.

Lloyd, K. G., Hornykiewicz, O., Davidson, L., Shannak, K., Farley, I., Goldstein, M., et al. (1981). Biochemical evidence of dysfunction of brain neurotransmitters in the Lesch-Nyhan syndrome. *New England Journal of Medicine, 305,* 1106–1111.

Loder, R. T., Lee, C. L., & Richards, B. S. (1989). Orthopedic aspects of Rett syndrome: A multicenter review. *Journal of Pediatric Orthopedics, 9*(5), 557–562.

Lombroso, P. J. (2000). Genetics of childhood disorders: A gene for Rett syndrome. *Journal of the American Academy of Child and Adolescent Psychiatry, 39,* 671–674.

Lugaresi, E., Cirignotta, F., & Montagna, P. (1985). Abnormal breathing in the Rett syndrome. *Brain and Development, 7,* 328–333.

Lyon, M. F. (1972). X chromosome inactivation and developmental patterns in mammals. *Biological Review, 47,* 1–35.

McArthur, A. J., & Budden, S. (1998). Sleep dysfunction in Rett syndrome: A trial of exogenous melatonin. *Developmental Medicine and Child Neurology, 40,* 186–192.

Meloni, L., Bruttini, M., & Longo, I. (2000). A mutation in the Rett syndrome gene, MECP2, causes X-linked mental retardation and progressive spasticity in males. *American Journal of Human Genetics, 67,* 982–983.

Millichap, J. G. (1987). Rett's syndrome: A variant of Heller's dementia? *Lancet, 1,* 440.

Missliwetz, J., & Depastas, G. (1985). Forensic problems in Rett syndrome. *Brain and Development, 7*(3), 326–328.

Moodley, M. (1992). Rett syndrome in South Africa. *Annals of Tropical Paediatrics, 12,* 409–415.

Moser, H. W. (1986). Preamble to the workshop on Rett syndrome. *American Journal of Medical Genetics, 24*(Suppl. 1), 1–20.

Motil, K. J., Schultz, R., Brown, B., Glaze, D. G., & Percy, A. K. (1994). Altered energy balance may account for growth failure in Rett syndrome. *Journal of Child Neurology, 9*(3), 315–319.

Murakami, J. W., Courchesne, E., Haas, R. H., Press, G. A., & Yeung-Courchesne, R. (1992). Cerebellar and cerebral abnormalities in Rett syndrome: A quantitative MR analysis. *American Journal of Roentgenology, 159,* 177–183.

Myer, E. C., Tripathi, H. L., Brase, D. A., & Dewey, W. L. (1992). Elevated CSF beta-endorphin immunoreactivity in Rett's syndrome: Report of 158 cases and comparison with leukemic children. *Neurology, 42,* 357–360.

Naganuma, G. (1988). Motor functions. Physical therapy strategies. *Educational and therapeutic intervention in Rett syndrome.* Ft. Maryland, MD: International Rett Syndrome Association.

Naidu, S., Hyman, S., Piazza, K., Savedra, J., Perman, J., Wenk, G., et al. (1990). The Rett syndrome: Progress report on studies at the Kennedy Institute. *Brain and Development, 12,* 5–7.

Naidu, S., Murphy, M., Moser, H. W., & Rett, A. (1986). Rett syndrome: Natural history in 70 cases. *American Journal of Medical Genetics, 24*(Suppl. 1), 61–72.

Niedermeyer, E., & Naidu, S. (1990). Further EEG observations in children with Rett syndrome. *Brain and Development, 12,* 53–54.

Niedermeyer, E., Rett, A., Renner, H., Murphy, M., & Naidu, S. (1986). Rett syndrome and the electroencephalogram. *American Journal of Medical Genetics, 24*(Suppl. 1), 195–200.

Nielsen, J. B., Friberg, L., Lou, H., Lassen, N. A., & Sam, I. L. (1990). Immature pattern of brain activity in Rett syndrome. *Archives of Neurology, 47,* 982–986.

Nielsen, J. B., Lou, H. C., & Andresen, J. (1990). Biochemical and clinical effects of tyrosine and tryptophan in the Rett syndrome. *Brain and Development, 12,* 143–148.

Nihei, K., & Naitoh, H. (1990). Cranial computed tomographic and magnetic resonance imaging studies on the Rett syndrome. *Brain and Development, 12,* 101–105.

Nomura, Y., & Segawa, M. (1990). Clinical features of the early stage of the Rett syndrome. *Brain and Development, 12,* 16–19.

Nomura, Y., Segawa, M., & Hasegawa, M. (1984). Rett syndrome—Clinical studies and pathophysiological consideration. *Brain and Development, 6,* 475–486.

Nomura, Y., Segawa, M., & Higurashi, M. (1985). Rett syndrome—An early catecholamine and indolamine deficient disorder? *Brain and Development, 7*(3), 334–341.

Olsson, B. (1987). Autistic traits in the Rett syndrome. *Brain and Development, 9*(5), 491–498.

Olsson, B., & Rett, A. (1985). Behavioral observations concerning differential diagnosis between the Rett syndrome and autism. *Brain and Development, 7*(3), 281–289.

Olsson, B., & Rett, A. (1987). Autism and Rett syndrome: Behavioral investigations and differential diagnosis. *Developmental Medicine and Child Neurology, 29,* 429–441.

Olsson, B., & Rett, A. (1990). A review of the Rett syndrome with a theory of autism. *Brain and Development, 12,* 11–15.

Opitz, J. M. (1986). Rett syndrome: Some comments on terminology and diagnosis. *American Journal of Medical Genetics, 24,* 27–37.

Opitz, J. M., & Lewin, S. (1987). Rett syndrome—A review and discussion of syndrome delineation. *Brain and Development, 9*(5), 445–450.

Pan, J. W., Lane, J. B., Hetherington, H., & Percy, A. K. (1999). Rett syndrome: H spectroscopic imaging at 4:1 Tesla. *Journal of Child Neurology, 14,* 524–528.

Percy, A. K. (1992, May). *Medical updates and overviews.* Paper presented at the International Rett Syndrome Association meeting, San Diego, CA.

Percy, A. K., & Hagberg, B. (1992). *Therapy in Rett syndrome: Drug trials and failures* (pp. 108–110).

Percy, A. K., Hass, R., Kolodny, E., Moser, H., & Naidu, S. (1988). Recommendations regarding handling of the necropsy in Rett syndrome. *Journal of Child Neurology, 3* (Suppl.), 91–93.

Percy, A. K., Schultz, R., Glaze, D. G., Skender, M., del Junco, D., Waring, S. C., et al. (1991). Trail of the opiate antagonist, naltrexone, in children with Rett syndrome. *Annals of Neurology, 30,* 486.

Percy, A. K., Zoghbi, H. Y., Lewis, K. R., & Jankovic, J. (1988). Rett syndrome: Qualitative and quantitative differentiation from autism. *Journal of Child Neurology, 3*(Suppl.), S65–S67.

Percy, A. K., Zoghbi, H., & Riccardi, V. M. (1985). Rett syndrome: Initial experience with an emerging clinical entity. *Brain and Development, 7*(3), 300–304.

Perry, A., Sarlo-McGarvey, N., & Haddad, C. (1991). Brief report: Cognitive and adaptive functioning in 28 girls with Rett syndrome. *Journal of Autism and Developmental Disorders, 21*(4), 551–556.

Philippart, M. (1986). Clinical recognition of Rett syndrome. *American Journal of Medical Genetics, 24*(Suppl. 1), 111–118.

Philippart, M. (1990). The Rett syndrome in males. *Brain and Development, 12,* 33–36.

Philippart, M. (1993). Rett syndrome associated with tuberous sclerosis in a male and in a female: Evidence for arrested motor and mental development. *American Journal of Medical Genetics, 48,* 229–230.

Piaget, J. (1929). *The child's conception of the world.* New York: Harcourt, Brace and Jovanovich.

Piazza, C. C., Anderson, C., & Fisher, W. (1993). Teaching self-feeding skills to patients with Rett syndrome. *Developmental Medicine and Child Neurology, 35,* 991–996.

Piazza, C. C., Fisher, W., Kiesewetter, K., Bowman, L., & Moser, H. (1990). Aberrant sleep patterns in children with Rett syndrome. *Brain and Development, 12,* 488–493.

Reichle, J., & Keogh, W. (1986). Communication instruction for learners with severe handicaps: Some unresolved issues. In R. Horner, L. Meyer, & B. Fredricks (Eds.), *Education of learners with severe handicaps: Exemplary services* (pp. 189–220). Baltimore: Paul H. Brookes.

Reilly, S., & Cass, H. (2001). Growth and nutrition in Rett syndrome. *Disability and Rehabilitation, 23,* 118–128.

Reiss, A. L., Faruque, F., Naidu, S., Abrams, M., Beaty, T., Bryan, R. N., et al. (1993). Neuroanatomy of Rett syndrome: A volumetric imaging study. *Annals of Neurology, 34*(2), 227–234.

Rett, A. (1966). Uber ein eigenartiges hirnatrophisches syndrom bei hyperammonamie im kindesalter (On an unusual brain atrophy syndrome in hyperammonaemia in childhood). *Wien Med Wochenschr, 116,* 723–738.

Rett, A. (1969). Ein zerebral-atrophisches Syndrom bei Hyperammonamie im Kindesalter (Hyperammonaemia and cerebral atrophy in childhood). *Forschr Med, 87,* 507–509.

Rett, A. (1977). A cerebral atrophy associated with hyperammonaemie. In P. J. Vinken & G. W. Bruyn (Eds.), *Handbook of clinical neurology.* Amsterdam, North Holland: Elsevier Science Publishing Company.

Rett, A. (1986). History and general overview. *American Journal of Medical Genetics, 24*(Suppl. 1), 21–26.

Riccardi, V. M. (1986). The Rett syndrome: Genetics and the future. *American Journal of Medical Genetics, 24*(Suppl. 1), 389–402.

Rice, M. (1983). Contemporary accounts of the cognitive/language relationship: Implications for speech-language clinicians. *Journal of Speech and Hearing Disorders, 48,* 347–359.

Riederer, P., Brucke, T., Sofic, E., Kienzl, E., Schnecker, K., Eng, D., et al. (1985). Neurochemical aspects of the Rett syndrome. *Brain and Development, 7*(3), 351–360.

Riederer, P., Wieser, M., Wichart, I., Schmidt, B., Killian, W., & Rett, A. (1986). Preliminary brain autopsy findings in progredient Rett syndrome. *American Journal of Medical Genetics, 24*(Suppl. 1), 305–315.

Robb, S. A., Harden, A., & Boyd, S. G. (1989). Rett syndrome: An EEG study in 52 girls. *Neuropediatrics, 20*(4), 192–195.

Rolando, S. (1985). Rett syndrome: Report of eight cases. *Brain and Development, 7*(3), 290–296.

Schleichkorn, J. (1987). Rett syndrome: A neurological disease largely undiagnosed here. *Physical Therapy Bulletin, 2,* 16–18.

Schultz, R. J., Glaze, D. G., Motil, K. J., Armstrong, D. D., del Junco, D. L., Hubbard, C. R., et al. (1993). The pattern of growth failure in Rett syndrome. *American Journal of Disabilities in Children, 147*(6), 633–637.

Segawa, M. (2001). Pathophysiology of Rett syndrome from the standpoint of clinical characteristics. *Brain and Development, 23,* S94–S98.

Sekul, E. A., Moak, J. P., Schultz, R., Glaze, D. G., Dunn, J. K., & Percy, A. K. (1991). Electrocardiographic changes in Rett syndrome. *Annals of Neurology, 30,* 496.

Sekul, E. A., & Percy, A. K. (1992). Rett syndrome: Clinical features, genetic considerations, and the search for a biological marker. *Current Neurology, 12,* 173–198.

Shahbazian, M. D., & Zoghbi, H. Y. (2001). Molecular genetics of Rett syndrome and clinical spectrum of MECP2 mutations. *Current Opinions in Neurology, 14,* 171–176.

Shahbazian, M. D., & Zoghbi, H. Y. (2002). Rett syndrome and MECP2: Linking epigenetics and neuronal function. *American Journal of Human Genetics, 71,* 1259–1272.

Sharpe, P. A. (1992). Comparative effects of bilateral hand splints and an elbow orthosis on stereotypic hand movements and toy play in two children with Rett syndrome. *American Journal of Occupational Therapy, 46,* 134–140.

Singer, H. S., & Naidu, S. (2001). Rett syndrome: "We'll keep the genes on for you." *Neurology, 56*(5), 611–617.

Sirianni, N., Naidu, S., Pereira, J., Pillotto, R. F., & Hoffman, E. P. (1998). Rett syndrome: Confirmation of X-linked dominant inheritance, and localization of the gene to Xq28. *American Journal of Human Genetics, 63,* 1552–1558.

Skjeldal, O. H., von Tetzchner, S., Jacobsen, K., Smith, L., & Heiberg, A. (1995). Rett syndrome: Distribution of phenotypes with special attention to the preserved speech variant. *Neuropediatrics, 26,* 87.

Smith, T., Klevstrand, M., & Lovaas, O. I. (1995). Behavioral treatment of Rett's disorder: Ineffectiveness in three cases. *American Journal of Mental Retardation, 100,* 317–322.

Sofic, E., Riederer, P., Killian, W., & Rett, A. (1987). Reduced concentrations of ascorbic acid and glutathione in a single case of Rett syndrome: A postmortem brain study. *Brain and Development, 9*(5), 529–531.

Sponseller, P. D. (1989). *Orthopaedic problems in Rett syndrome.* Ft. Washington, MD: International Rett Syndrome Association.

Stephenson, J. B., & Kerr, A. M. (1987). Rett syndrome: Disintegration not dementia. *Lancet, 1,* 741.

Subramaniam, B., Naidu, S., & Reiss, A. L. (1997). Neuroanatomy in Rett syndrome. *Neurology, 48,* 399–407.

Takagi, N. (2001). The role of X-chromosome inactivation in the manifestation of Rett syndrome. *Brain and Development* (Suppl. 1), S182–S185.

The Rett Syndrome Diagnostic Criteria Work Group. (1988). Diagnostic criteria for Rett syndrome. *Annals of Neurology, 23,* 125–128.

Tpocu, M., Akyerli, C., Sayi, A., Toruner, G. A., Kocoglu, S. R., Cimbis, M., et al. (2002). Somatic mosaicism for a MECP2 mutation associated with classic Rett syndrome in a boy. *European Journal of Human Genetics, 10,* 77–81.

Topcu, M., Topaloglu, H., Renda, Y., Berker, M., & Turanli, G. (1991). The Rett syndrome in males. *Brain and Development, 13*(1), 62.

Trevathan, E., & Naidu, S. (1988). The clinical recognition and differential diagnosis of Rett syndrome. *Journal of Child Neurology, 3*(Suppl.), S6–S16.

Tuten, H., & Miedaner, J. (1989). Effect of hand splints on stereotypic hand behavior of girls with Rett syndrome: A replication study. *Physical Therapy, 69*(12), 1099–1103.

Umansky, R., Watson, R., Hoffbuhr, K., Painter, K. M., Devaney, J., & Hoffman, E. (2001). Social facilitation of object-oriented hand use in a Rett syndrome variant girl: Implications for partial preservation of a hypothesized specialized cerebral network. *Developmental and Behavioral Pediatrics, 22*(2), 119–122.

Uzgiris, I. C., & Hunt, J. M. (1975). *Assessment in infancy: Ordinal scales of psychological development.* Urbana: University of Illinois Press.

Van Acker, R. (1987). *Stereotypic responding associated with Rett Syndrome: A comparison of girls with this disorder and matched subject controls without the Rett Syndrome* (Doctoral dissertation). DeKalb: Northern Illinois University.

Van Acker, R., & Grant, S. B. (1995). An effective computer-based requesting system for persons with Rett syndrome. *Journal of Childhood Communication Disorders, 16,* 31–38.

Van den Veyver, I. B., & Zoghbi, H. Y. (2001). Mutations in the gene encoding methyl-CpG-binding protein 2 cause Rett syndrome. *Brain and Development, 23,* S147–S151.

Verma, N. P., Chheda, R. L., & Nigro, M. A. (1986). Electroencephalographic findings in Rett syndrome. *Electroencephalograhy and Clinical Neurophysiology, 64,* 394–401.

von Tetzchner, S. (1997). Communication skills among females with Rett syndrome. *European Child and Adolescent Psychology, 6,* 33–37.

von Tetzchner, S., Jacobsen, K. H., Smith, L., Skjeldal, O. H., Heiberg, A., & Fagen, J. A. (1996). Vision, cognition and developmental characteristics of girls and women with Rett syndrome. *Developmental Medicine and Child Neurology, 38,* 212–225.

Wan, M., Lee, S. S. J., & Zhang, X. (1999). Rett syndrome and beyond: Recurrent spontaneous and familial MECP2 mutations at CpG hotspots. *American Journal of Human Genetics, 65,* 1520–1529.

Watson, J. S., Umansky, R., Marcy, S., Johnston, C., & Repacholi, B. (1996). Behavioral competition in a case of Rett syndrome. *Journal of Applied Developmental Psychology, 17,* 553–575.

Watson, J. S., Umansky, R., Marcy, S., & Repacholi, B. (1996). Intention and preference in a 3-year-old girl with Rett syndrome. *Journal of Applied Developmental Psychology, 17,* 69–84.

Watson, P., Black, G., & Ramsden, S. (2001). Angelman syndrome phenotype associated with mutations in MECP2, a gene encoding a methyl CpG binding protein. *Journal of Medical Genetics, 38,* 224–228.

Webb, T., & Latif, R. (2001). Rett syndrome and the MECP2 gene. *Journal of Medical Genetics, 38,* 217–223.

Wehmeyer, M., Bourland, G., & Ingram, D. (1993). An analogue assessment of hand stereotypies in two cases of Rett syndrome. *Journal of Intellectual Disability Research, 37,* 95–102.

Weisz, C. L. (1987). Range of emotion. *Brain and Development, 9*(5), 543–545.

Wenk, G. L., Naidu, S., Casanova, M. F., Kitt, C. A., & Moser, H. (1991). Altered neurochemical markers in Rett syndrome. *Neurology, 41,* 1753–1756.

Wenk, G. L., O'Leary, M., Nemeroff, C. B., Bissette, G., Moser, H., & Naidu, S. (1993). Neurochemical alterations in Rett syndrome. *Developmental Brain Research, 74,* 67–72.

Wesecky, A. (1986). Music therapy for children with Rett syndrome. *American Journal of Medical Genetics, 24*(Suppl. 1), 253–257.

Whitehouse, P. J., Price, D. L., Clark, A. W., Coyle, J. T., & DeLong, M. R. (1981). Alzheimer disease: Evidence for selective loss of cholinergic neurons in the nucleus basalis. *Annals of Neurology, 10,* 122–126.

Witt-Engerstrom, I. (1987). Rett syndrome: A retrospective pilot study on potential early predictive symptomatology. *Brain and Development, 9*(5), 481–486.

Witt-Engerstrom, I., & Hagberg, B. (1990). The Rett syndrome: Gross motor disability and neural impairment in adults. *Brain and Development, 12,* 23–26.

Woodyatt, G. C., & Ozanne, A. E. (1992). Communication abilities and Rett syndrome. *Journal of Autism and Developmental Disorders, 22,* 155–173.

Woodyatt, G. C., & Ozanne, A. E. (1993). A longitudinal study of cognitive skills and communication behaviors in children with Rett syndrome. *Journal of Intellectual Disability Research, 37,* 419–435.

Xiang, F., Buervenich, S., Nicolao, P., Bailey, M. E., Zhang, Z., & Anvret, M. (2000). Mutation screening in Rett syndrome patients. *Journal of Medical Genetics, 37,* 250–255.

Yano, S., Yamashita, Y., Matsuishi, T., Abe, T., Yamada, S., & Shinohara, M. (1991). Four adult Rett patients at an institution for the handicapped. *Pediatric Neurology, 7,* 289–292.

Yoshikawa, H., Fueki, N., Suzuki, H., Sakuragawa, N., & Masaaki, I. (1991). Cerebral blood flow and oxygen metabolism in Rett syndrome. *Journal of Child Neurology, 6,* 237–242.

Zappella, M. (1986). Motivational conflicts in Rett syndrome. *American Journal of Medical Genetics, 24*(Suppl. 1), 143–151.

Zappella, M. (1990). A double-blind trial of bromocriptine in the Rett syndrome. *Brain and Development, 12,* 148–150.

Zappella, M. (1992). The Rett girls with preserved speech. *Brain Development, 14,* 98–101.

Zappella, M., & Genazzani, A. (1986). Girls with Rett syndrome tested with bromocriptine. *Wiener Klinische Wochenschrift, 98,* 780.

Zappella, M., Genazzani, A., Facchinetti, F., & Hayek, G. (1990). Bromocriptine in the Rett syndrome. *Brain and Development, 12,* 221–225.

Zoghbi, H. Y. (1988). Genetic aspects of Rett syndrome. *Journal of Child Neurology, 3*(Suppl.), S76–S78.

Zoghbi, H. Y., Milstien, S., Butler, I. J., Smith, E. O., Kaufman, S., Glaze, D. G., et al. (1989). Cerebrospinal fluid biogenic amines and biopterin in Rett syndrome. *Annals of Neurology, 25,* 56–60.

Zoghbi, H. Y., Percy, A. K., Glaze, D. G., Butler, I. J., & Riccardi, V. M. (1985). Reduction of biogenic amine levels in the Rett syndrome. *New England Journal of Medicine, 313,* 921–924.

Zoghbi, H. Y., Percy, A. K., Schultz, R. J., & Fill, C. (1990). Patterns of X chromosome inactivation in the Rett syndrome. *Brain and Development, 12,* 131–135.

CHAPTER 6

Pervasive Developmental Disorder Not Otherwise Specified

KENNETH E. TOWBIN

The diagnostic term for conditions that share the central feature of a severe deficit in social learning and reciprocity is Pervasive Developmental Disorder Not Otherwise Specified (PDD-NOS). Individuals with PDD-NOS have social deficits similar to autism and may have, in addition, fundamental disturbances in communication, social behavior, emotion regulation, cognition, and interests. The symptoms of these deficits arise during the first years of life, yet their severity or scope do not meet the more restrictive criteria for the other PDDs—Autistic, Asperger's, Rett's, or Childhood Disintegrative Disorder. Like all these diagnostic terms, PDD-NOS is based on clinical presentation and developmental history. It is likely that PDD-NOS is not just one condition. Until recently, the paucity of biological evidence in support of PDD-NOS created the impression that the diagnosis was more of a concept—a theoretical mild form of autism—than a valid condition. Some argued that the presentation of individuals with PDD-NOS was so diverse that the term was not meaningful and did not convey practical information about impairment and prognosis. Robust findings from recent genetic and family history studies of autism, as well as mounting psychophysiological and imaging evidence, have provided a substantial counterargument to these propositions. In the past several years, genetic studies of Autism Spectrum Disorders (ASDs; Autistic disorder, Asperger's disorder, and PDD-NOS) have revealed similarities among them all, and underscored the connection between PDD-NOS and autism. Clinically, although individuals with PDD-NOS may display milder symptoms than individuals with autism, the biological features and genetic risks suggest remarkable similarities. Contemporary questions now focus on the relationships between ASDs and a widening Broader Autism Phenotype (BAP; Dawson, Webb, et al., 2002).

PDD-NOS is similar, not identical, to autism. There is reliable evidence that individuals diagnosed with PDD-NOS have milder deficits and a better prognosis than those diagnosed with autism (Gillberg, 1991). It is less clear whether these differences hold up when one compares those with PDD-NOS to individuals with autism who are matched on nonverbal IQ and basic grammatical and syntactical language. It is also unknown whether the definitions and demarcations of subtypes of PDD in the *Diagnostic and Statistical Manual of Mental Disorders* (*DSM-IV-TR*) and *World Health Organization International Classification of Diseases* (*ICD-10*) are valid or meaningful. Logically, a comprehensive classification system (Rutter & Gould, 1985) must provide for conditions that fall short of the severity or range of symptoms of the other PDDs but nevertheless exhibit impairment as a consequence of problems in social reciprocity. It is unclear whether the current divisions are biologically valid. The ASDs are often viewed as stratifying along a hypothetical spectrum or continuum covering the broad clinical range from those with profound aloofness and mental retardation to those who appear neurotypical but nevertheless display a distinctive lifelong social or empathic blindness (Wing, 1992). On this hypothetical spectrum, PDD-NOS is a paradoxical clinical entity. Despite its amorphous clinical boundaries and the subtlety of the clinical presentation, PDD-NOS is one of the most important PDDs. Its importance stems from its relationship to autism, its prevalence, and most of all, the impairment that it imparts to those who have it.

In this chapter, PDD will be the term for the spectrum that includes all the Pervasive Developmental Disorders including Autistic disorder, PDD-NOS, Asperger's disorder, and so on. The chapter offers an overview of PDD-NOS as a conceptual and clinical entity. It begins with a conceptual view and review of how *DSM-IV-TR* and *ICD-10* represent PDD-NOS. Since PDD-NOS is synonymous with "not anything else in PDD," it cannot be understood without competent knowledge of the alternative diagnoses and conditions defined under PDD. For this reason, a detailed account of the differential diagnosis is offered. Explication of descriptive elements such as epidemiology, etiology, and natural history follow; and the review ends with a condensed discussion of treatments and future research directions.

NOSOLOGY

The term PDD first surfaced in *DSM-III.* Within the group of PDDs, there were three conditions: infantile autism, childhood onset PDD, and atypical PDD. In *DSM-III-R,* this was modified once again and PDD was redefined with only two subtypes: Autistic Disorder and PDD-NOS. *DSM-IV* and *ICD-10* created new subgroup diagnoses that previously were under the umbrella term PDD-NOS in *DSM-III-R* or *ICD-9.* The new subgroups with separate designations include Asperger's disorder (*ICD-10* and *DSM-IV-TR*), atypical autism (*ICD-10*), Childhood Disintegrative Disorder (*ICD-10* and *DSM-IV-TR*), and Rett's Disorder (*ICD-10* and *DSM-IV-TR*).

DSM-IV and *ICD-10* use diagnostic terms and guidelines for PDD-NOS in different ways.

ICD-10 has a category of PDD-unspecified (F84.9), but this description is not as broad as *DSM-IV* PDD-NOS. Closer scrutiny of the clinical guidelines and descriptions in *ICD* reveal that a more complete analogue to *DSM-IV*'s PDD-NOS is the combination of PDD-unspecified and atypical autism (F84.1; World Health Organization [WHO], 1992). *DSM-IV-TR* declares that "atypical autism" is included under their term of PDD-NOS (p. 84). *DSM-IV* states that individuals in this category fail to meet age criteria, do not display all the key elements of autism or the other subtypes of PDD, or that when these other elements are present, they may not be of sufficient severity to meet the full criteria for autism or the other subtypes of PDD. In *DSM-IV-TR,* PDD-NOS was one major exception to the policy of making no more than minimal changes from *DSM-IV. DSM-IV-TR* rectifies the *DSM-IV* error that would allow the diagnosis of PDD-NOS in the absence of social impairments. *DSM-IV-TR* makes clear that PDD-NOS is, foremost, a disorder of "reciprocal social interaction that is associated with" impairments in "either verbal or non-verbal communication," or with repetitive behaviors, and/or restricted interests.

Despite this clarification, the guidelines for PDD-NOS in *DSM-IV-TR* continue to be problematic because they are vaguely worded and difficult to translate into clear definitions or explicit operational criteria. By definition, individuals with PDD-NOS present with fewer or less severe symptoms than those who have Autistic or Asperger's disorder, and do not meet criteria for Rett's Disorder or Childhood Disintegrative Disorder. Buitelaar and coworkers (1998) offered an operationalized definition of PDD-NOS although this has not been generally embraced in clinical or research activities. Like individuals with Autistic or Asperger's disorder, persons with PDD-NOS can have restricted interests, dedication to nonfunctional routines, limited imaginary play, and stereotyped behavior. Unlike those with Autistic or Asperger's disorder, these features may all be mild or absent. Compared to those with Autistic disorder, individuals with PDD-NOS may or may not exhibit deficits in expressive or receptive language.

CONCEPTUAL BACKGROUND

Although terminology has changed, the existence of an intermediate or mild PDD condition is not a new discovery. Individuals with autism-like developmental disorders have been recognized for over 100 years (Itard, 1962). After Leo Kanner identified the features of autism (1943), a series of reports appeared describing individuals who were nearly but not quite like those characterized by Kanner (Bender, 1946; Despert, 1958). The individuals in these reports all exhibited early-onset, profound deficits in relating, but they displayed other features that were different from those seen in autism, particularly in language and stereotyped movement.

The unquestionable existence of these conditions calls for a comprehensive system of classification to provide a corresponding diagnosis that is clear, logical, practical, and relevant. Those who wish for such a meaningful definition of PDD-NOS have had to revise the definition as the concepts of the PDD change. Consequently, the clinical application of PDD-NOS has been open to criticism on at least two fronts. On the one side, some claim that PDD-NOS should be removed because the inherent vagueness of criteria (particularly under the current criteria) conveys so little information about the person's deficits, prognosis, and course that it renders the diagnosis unhelpful or meaningless. On another side, there is criticism that PDD-NOS should be folded into Autistic disorder because it is so completely continuous with autism that it does not make sense to give it a separate diagnostic standing. If PDD-NOS is simply a segment of the continuum of "Autism Spectrum Disorders," it is a redundancy.

Wing and coworkers proposed the concept of a continuum of autistic conditions that are differentiated by the degree of impairment in social reciprocity (Wing & Gould, 1979). In that view, individuals who are aloof and resist interactions with others represent the most severe end of the spectrum. Next, in order of decreasing severity, are individuals who are passive but accept interactions when others initiate and continue to press on with them. The least severe group is termed "active but odd," insofar as they approach others and desire interaction, but exhibit idiosyncratic and egocentric social exchanges. Early in childhood these active-but-odd individuals might shrink from social interactions or be shunned by their young age-mates because of intrusive behaviors, excessively restrictive demands, or overreaction to rebuffs and refusals. In later childhood, they display a failure to comprehend and apply ordinary social rules; as adults their deficits become relatively milder and subtler. Wing and Gould suggested that it takes more time and interaction to recognize the deficits in the active-but-odd group than in the other groups (Wing & Gould, 1979).

Wing's vision may be accurate on several counts, but it is not without flaws. First, Wings' concept of the spectrum is broader than that of current diagnostic systems (Wing, 1997), and she has not offered cut points that would enable one to differentiate subgroups and boundaries. Second, to relate the spectrum to diagnostic categories, one must make untested suppositions. The social skills dimension may not be sufficient to enable division in the PDD diagnostic system. The prevailing view is that autism is the most severe end of the continuum, followed by Asperger's disorder, and then PDD-NOS at the mildest end (Prior et al., 1998). There are others who suggest that the order should be Autistic disorder, PDD-NOS, and Asperger's disorder (Kurita, 1997). However, empirical studies fail to support either generalization. Robertson and coworkers (Robertson, Tanguay, L'Ecuyer, Sims, & Waltrip, 1999) found only a weak correlation between social communication and clinical diagnosis. Similarly, Gilchrist and coworkers (2001) found prognosis and adaptive function failed to differentiate high-functioning autism (HFA) from Asperger's disorder.

A further problem with the continuum model is that it is exceedingly difficult to reconcile with a categorical diagnostic system. Systems of nosology require compiling conditions into relatively homogeneous phenotypic subgroups. Imposing categorical diagnostic boundaries on dimensional characteristics requires the sacrifice of important details and data—the entire procedure becomes a procrustean bed. The effort to define boundaries that capture the comparative distinctions between points on a spectrum cannot help but generate blurry, confusing definitions with qualifiers like "relatively," "significantly," and "limited amount." Conversely, the imposition of specific boundaries (and terms) where none exist creates illusory, false dichotomies that give official sanction to fictional differences. As Cantwell and Rutter suggested (1994), psychology divides IQ ranges into subdivisions such as *mild, moderate,* and *severe* mental retardation. Consider the absence of real difference between someone with an IQ of 68 who is diagnosed with "mild mental retardation" and another person with an IQ of 72 whose condition is called "borderline IQ." Even so, as Cantwell and Rutter (1994) have discussed, categorical systems offer the benefits of efficient communication and conceptual clarity, which may facilitate treatment. In addition, historically, science has condoned imposing categorical distinctions on known dimensional variables. Another example is the way we divide the electromagnetic wave spectrum into colors. There are legitimate reasons to harbor uncertainty about the validity and significance of the distinctions among the current subtypes of PDD.

It follows logically from these conceptual considerations, that the diagnosis of PDD-NOS generates ambiguity and confusion in clinical work. The label fails to position a patient's current functioning on this extensive continuum. *DSM-IV-TR* reflects this nebulous quality by, on the one hand, designating PDD-NOS as a diagnosis, but on the other, offering only a description without specific operationalized criteria. The text describing PDD-NOS is a tautology. The *DSM-IV-TR* description restates a logically fundamental criterion of any valid diagnosis—a collection of disorders that are not other disorders (Rutter & Gould, 1985). Any diagnostic category that fails this criterion is redundant. Were it not for its clinical legitimacy, the distress of families, and the impairment of those with this condition, the *definition of* PDD-NOS would be a mere logical absurdity.

Despite its inherent diagnostic circularity and imprecision, the category (and concept) of PDD-NOS is indispensable. (Ambiguity may

be relevant and instructive, nevertheless.) PDD-NOS encompasses a unique region in the spectrum of PDD and conveys important clinical information about persons who are so diagnosed. PDD-NOS is the diagnosis for a collection of conditions that share important features resembling the primary PDDs but to a milder degree. Other PDD diagnoses do not accommodate the phenomena exhibited by this group of individuals. Furthermore, PDD-NOS denotes a link between this important group of disorders and the other more narrowly defined PDD subtypes. Whether the relationship is valid is being resolved by longitudinal, pathophysiological, cognitive, etiologic, and genetic studies. Some headway is being made on these fronts and may lead to a different system of grouping these conditions. It might be said that PDD-NOS is a work in progress that needs further investigation. Yet without a place in the diagnostic system, the relationships among these disorders cannot be explored.

In clinical use, it appears that PDD-NOS takes on multiple meanings, each of which is supported by official diagnostic guidelines. PDD-NOS has at least four different definitions that diagnosticians can employ under different circumstances:

1. PDD-NOS is not actually a clinical entity but a label to use under unfavorable diagnostic conditions. For some authorities, PDD-NOS is to be used as a default diagnosis when information is inadequate or as a last resort when the developmental history is unreliable. In this view, PDD-NOS may be a temporary designation or delaying strategy when the absence of reliable information prevents asserting a more specific PDD diagnosis or until the clinician can acquire a trustworthy history.

2. On the continuum of PDD, PDD-NOS is a collection of entities that are relatively higher functioning, but not qualitatively distinct. PDD-NOS includes conditions in which impairment in language or restricted interests/repetitive behaviors are mild or perhaps absent. In this view, PDD-NOS is a group of disorders in which, by stringent criteria, the impairment in one of these domains is too mild to permit one to assign another diagnosis; yet the impairments in

social relating are far too severe to be considered a variant of normal (Allen et al., 2001). This is congruent with *ICD-10* Atypical Autism and advances the idea that PDD-NOS is "mild" autism, that is, "differences in severity rather than type"(Szatmari, 1997). The boundaries separating "high-functioning autism" and this kind of PDD-NOS are exceedingly uncertain. This definition of PDD-NOS has evolved from an acceptance of an autism spectrum disorder and relies on such factors as prognosis and range of disturbance to define its points.

3. PDD-NOS is the diagnosis for individuals who present with a late age of onset of autistic symptoms. Rutter and Schopler (1988) suggest that the positive criteria for autism include the three core features plus early age of onset. Seen this way, PDD-NOS is the diagnosis when this fourth feature is absent, just as in Definition 2. Volkmar and coworkers (Volkmar, Steir, & Cohen, 1985) reported that there may be a wide gap in age of onset and age of clinical diagnosis and depend on the reliability of parents' memories. There are, however, rare reports of individuals in whom the age of onset occurs after age 30 months and who do not meet criteria for Childhood Disintegrative Disorder (Volkmar & Cohen, 1989).

4. The heterogeneous clinical entities that comprise PDD-NOS share two critical features—early onset of symptoms and impairment in social reciprocity. Such a definition implies that the theoretical span of the autistic spectrum from severe autism (and aloofness) to much milder, but nevertheless impairing, deficits in social reciprocity, may not be continuous. It focuses on conditions other than autism that display prominent impairment in relatedness. However, these other conditions also present with additional symptoms that are not part of the spectrum of autism per se, such as impairments in understanding affect, affective modulation, and patterns of attachment. From this perspective, PDD-NOS, in the current official nosology, includes conditions with core features of impairment in both reciprocal social interactions and the capacity to develop empathy; these are re-

lated to PDD, but with further study may be determined to be clinically distinct from autism (Volkmar & Cohen, 1988).

This last view proposes that there are other disorders of social relating that are not well characterized currently and might temporarily be placed under PDD-NOS. The evolution of Asperger's disorder (ASP) as a clinical diagnosis illustrates this idea. The relationship between ASP and autism remains uncertain; some believe it is a variant of autism (Frith, 2004), or the same as high-functioning autism (Szatmari, Bartolucci, Bremner, Bond, & Rich, 1989; HFA), whereas others, including Asperger himself (1979), assert that the condition is quite separate from autism. PDD-NOS may be the best temporary location for disorders like this that have yet to be fully characterized yet display features along the spectrum of moderate to severe impairment in social reciprocity. Some candidates for inclusion in this perspective would include schizoid disorders in children (Wolff & Chick, 1980), Multiple Complex Developmental Disorder (Buitelaar et al., 1998; Cohen, Paul, & Volkmar, 1986; Towbin, Dykens, Pearson, & Cohen, 1993), Multiple Developmental Impairment (MDI; McKenna et al., 1994), Pragmatic Language Impairment (Bishop, 1989), some Infant Regulatory Disorders, and some Reactive Attachment Disorders (Richters & Volkmar, 1994).

BIOLOGICAL STUDIES OF PDD-NOS

There are no biological markers that measure the "dose" of autism risk or social reciprocity impairment. Attempts to refine the spectrum using phenomenological features have tended to reinforce evidence favoring a spectrum or continuum among the *DSM-IV* diagnoses of autism to PDD-NOS, rather than any meaningful separation between them (Robertson et al., 1999; Tanguay, Robertson, & Derrick, 1998). Moving away from the *DSM-IV* view of PDDs, Lord and coworkers (Lord, Leventhal, & Cook, 2001) have suggested that the phenomenology better reflects a multidimensional view of the autism spectrum in which there are three independent dimensions—nonverbal intellectual ability, expressive language ability, and social reciprocity with repetitive behaviors/restricted interests. They propose that genetic studies would benefit from applying such a model instead of relying on *DSM-IV* subtypes. Further significant promise in redefining the spectrum of PDD has come from using information from genetics (Spiker, Lotspeich, Dimiceli, Myers, & Risch, 2002), neuropsychological results (Klin et al., 1999), and functional behavior (Gillham, Carter, Volkmar, & Sparrow, 2000). Although exciting neuropsychological and neuroimaging findings are being produced (Piggott et al, 2004; Schultz et al., 2000; Sparks et al., 2002; Wang et al., 2004), the effectiveness of these measures to create meaningful distinctions within PDD (diagnostic specificity) has yet to be demonstrated. The emerging view is that in the future, PDD may be divided in a different way, perhaps along dimensions of higher versus lower grammatical/syntactic language acquisition and cognitive ability. This approach would replace the systems that are based on the amount of stereotypy/restricted interests, social use of language, and severity of social impairment (Howlin, 2003; Lord et al., 2001; Szatmari et al., 2002). Another possibility is that receptive and expressive language impairment may be used to differentiate higher and lower functioning ASDs (Walker et al., 2004).

There is growing biological evidence to support a close relationship between PDD-NOS and autism. Robust support comes from family and genetic studies of PDDs. Twin studies that ascertain the presence of autistic *and* nonautistic PDD have reliably demonstrated increased rates of ASP and PDD-NOS among monozygotic co-twins of probands with autism (Bailey et al., 1995; Le Couteur et al., 1996; MacLean et al., 1999). In Folstein and Rutter's twin study (1977), the reported concordance for narrowly defined autism in monozygotic (MZ) twins was 36% (versus 0% in dyzygotic [DZ] twins). When the data were reanalyzed, examining concordance that included higher functioning, socially impaired relatives, the rate increased to 82% (Folstein & Rutter, 1987). Bailey and coworkers (1995) evaluated concordance in 45 twin pairs in which one twin had autism (25 MZ and 20 DZ). The concordance rate of autism among MZ twins was 60% and among DZ twins was 0%. Concordance for the broader autism spectrum phenotype was 92% versus 0% for MZ and DZ twins, respectively. Le Couteur and coworkers expanded the original cohort ascertained by Folstein and Rutter (1977) to include 20 additional MZ males and 14 additional DZ male twin pairs. They reported that among MZ co-twins of probands with autism, there was a concordance rate of 60% for autistic disorder and 72% for all PDDs. Among dizygotic twins, rates concordance for autism was 0% and for the broader phenotype (all PDDs), 10%.

Family studies offer another method of discovering genetic relationships. Most studies indicate that a PDD-NOS diagnosis is as likely as autism in sibs of probands with autism. Using rigorous family study methodology, Piven and coworkers (1990) noted higher rates of "severe social dysfunction and isolation" among adult siblings of children with autism. This was replicated in a subsequent controlled sample of parents (Piven, Palmer, et al., 1997). Bolton and coworkers' (1994) study of 99 probands with autism found an overall rate of 5.8% of siblings had a PDD—2.9% Autistic disorder and 2.9% nonautistic PDD. MacLean and coworkers (1999) suggest that a stronger case can be made for inheritance of the severity of impairment or level of function than for the subtype of PDD. They examined 94 children in 46 "multiplex" (more than one sibling diagnosed with a PDD) families using rigorous diagnostic methods and comparing IQ and adaptive functioning. For 31 of 50 sibling pairs, both children received the same diagnoses and thus did not reflect significant aggregation of PDD subtypes within families. Their analyses revealed that the only moderate or greater correlations were for nonverbal IQ, adaptive behaviors of socialization, and communication. Thus, they propose that it is more important to stratify according to level of function than PDD subtype in genetic studies.

These studies are vulnerable to the criticism that environmental contributions have made significant contributions to the results (Szatmari et al., 2000). One remedy is to use extended pedigree studies that control for the bias introduced by environmental contributions. Using this method, Szatmari and coworkers found that rates of lesser variant features of autism (i.e., communication impairments, social impairments, and repetitive activities) were significantly more likely in biological versus nonbiological relatives of PDD probands. Moreover, rates of these lesser variant features were as common in relatives of the higher IQ, higher functioning probands as among those of lower functioning probands. It is particularly valuable that the investigators examined genetic risk for lesser variant features in relatives of *nonautistic* as well as autistic PDD. Similar to findings reported by Bolton and coworkers (1994), rates of lesser variant features were unrelated to the subtype of PDD diagnosis. The genetic risk to relatives was independent of PDD subtype, and lesser variant features were as common among relatives of nonautistic PDD ("atypical autism" or ASP) as among relatives of individuals with autism. A noteworthy design limitation of this study is its reliance on reports of relatives about other relatives, rather than direct interviews of all relatives. This may be partially offset by use of a control population and good evidence that family report designs tend to underreport, not inflate, the presence of symptoms and disorders. In addition, a similar study of an epidemiological cohort (Micali et al., 2004) revealed similar results. In that study there was a sixfold increase in the prevalence of PDDs among family members of probands with a PDD. These rates were across all PDD subtypes (Micali et al., 2004).

Neuropsychological Studies

Several lines of evidence suggest that individuals who have PDD-NOS share neuropsychological features with those who are diagnosed with Autistic disorder (Dawson, Webb, et al., 2002). Dawson and coworkers (Dawson, Munson, et al., 2002) found that the performance of preschool-age children with PDD-NOS was not different from that of children with autism in measures of joint attention, ventromedial prefrontal cortex function, or dorsolateral frontal cortex tasks. The performance on joint attention tasks was clearly different in the group of children with PDD compared to mental age-matched control groups. However, the primary aim of the study was to investigate the relationship between joint attention skills and executive functions in the frontal lobes. It is

notable that there were no differences between PDD and control groups in performance on dorsolateral or ventromedial frontal lobe function tasks at this age. In another series of studies, Dawson, Carver, and coworkers (2002) measured event-related potentials (P400 and Nc) when processing familiar and unfamiliar faces, in the same cohort of 3- to 4-year-olds and two comparison groups (children with developmental disorders and healthy children). The autism spectrum group did not demonstrate the typical pattern of P400 and Nc response to familiar versus unfamiliar faces although they did display typical differences to familiar versus unfamiliar objects. There were no differences in responses between those with autism and those with PDD-NOS. Similarly, van der Geest and coworkers (van der Geest, Kemner, Verbaten, & van Engeland, 2002) found no differences in gaze fixation to upside-down faces between children with autism and PDD-NOS children. Both were abnormal compared to age-matched healthy volunteers. Neither group was abnormal in gaze fixation for upright faces.

Investigations using theory of mind (ToM) tasks may distinguish high-functioning from low-functioning PDD, but do not differentiate diagnostic subtypes. Poor performance on ToM tasks is not unique to autism or PDD (Pickup & Frith, 2001; Pilowsky, Yirmiya, Arbelle, & Mozes, 2000). Differences in performance between individuals with autism and those with PDD-NOS appear to be related more to overall IQ and adaptive function than to anything that is specific in these diagnoses (Buitelaar et al., 1999; Serra, Loth, van Geert, Hurkens, & Minderaa, 2002).

Neuroimaging

There is one SPECT study that compares individuals who have "high-functioning autism" (perhaps ASP and PDD-NOS) with normals (C. Gillberg, 1992). The results suggested that the affected individuals displayed temporal lobe hypoperfusion. Comparing epileptic and nonepileptic ASD individuals revealed equivalent temporal lobe perfusion patterns, implying that seizures were not likely to cause hypoperfusion. Similarly, a large cohort ($N = 112$) of children, adolescents, and adults with autism and age-matched controls were examined with magnetic resonance imaging (MRI; Hashimoto et al., 1995). Fifteen percent of the ASD cohort was considered "high-functioning" (e.g., IQ > 80). Results suggested that individuals with ASD had diminished volumes in the cerebellar vermian lobes VI and VII as well as hypoplasia of the brain stem. These findings are in agreement with other studies of individuals with ASDs, which have previously reported vermian hypoplasia, though none heretofore have used controls or a cohort size as convincing as that of the Hashimoto study (Courchesne, 1995).

Sparks and coworkers (2002) compared structural MRI among 3- to 4-year-old children with autism (both high and low functioning), developmental delays, and healthy volunteers. Children with PDDs demonstrated significantly increased total cerebral volume, and increased (bilateral) hippocampi and amygdala volumes compared to total cerebral volume. There were no differences in higher versus lower functioning children with PDDs, but those with autism appeared to have even larger amygdala volumes bilaterally, compared to those with PDD-NOS (Sparks et al., 2002).

Summary of Biological Studies

Considered altogether, studies of patterns of inheritance or neuroimaging offer no support for differences among Autistic disorder, Asperger's disorder, and PDD-NOS. Future nosological systems may base the divisions of the PDD along dimensions related to cognitive and language abilities or higher versus lower functioning (Prior et al., 1998; Szatmari et al., 2002).

DIFFERENTIAL DIAGNOSIS

Table 6.1 offers diagnoses that may overlap or be confused with PDD-NOS. Ordinarily, confusion arises because a patient's presentation shares one or more features of impairment in socialization, language, and restricted patterns of behavior. PDD-NOS may be overlooked when excessive or premature emphasis is placed on a prominent feature that is associated with another diagnosis. A more comprehensive assessment should consider current

TABLE 6.1   Conditions to Be Considered in the Differential Diagnosis of PDD-NOS

A. Conditions within PDD
　　Asperger syndrome
　　Autism
　　Childhood disintegrative disorders
B. Other Developmental Disorders
　　Developmental language disorder
　　Mental retardation
　　Semantic pragmatic disorder
C. Disorders That May Onset in Early Childhood
　　Attention deficit hyperactivity disorder
　　Avoidant disorder
　　Generalized anxiety disorder (childhood type)
　　Obsessive compulsive disorder
　　Overanxious disorder
　　Reactive attachment disorder
　　Schizophrenia (childhood onset type)
　　Schizotypal disorder
　　Social phobia

functioning, the broad range of symptoms, and history related to each domain of social reciprocity, language, and patterns of stereotyped behavior or restricted interests (Filipek et al., 2000).

PDD-NOS and Other PDD Entities

Although experienced clinicians can reliably recognize a PDD from a disorder that is not a PDD (kappa of 0.67, 91% agreement), their ability to differentiate PDD-NOS, ASP, and Autistic disorder is much weaker (kappa = 0.51, 73% agreement; Mahoney et al., 1998). In Mahoney and coworkers' study, the largest disagreements came in discerning PDD-NOS from the two other PDD diagnoses. This is particularly pertinent because PDD-NOS is defined in relationship to these other PDD diagnoses: Whether one observes PDD-NOS depends on the definitions and boundaries of the other PDDs. As definitions (and boundaries) change, one may legitimately perceive an individual as having one diagnosis or another. This stretches one's conviction in the meaning of diagnostic terms. Ordinarily, PDD-NOS implies that the clinical presentation is nearly like some other PDD subtype. Therefore, diagnosing PDD-NOS demands that the clinician have a good understanding of the boundaries and subtleties of each PDD. After a discussion of the relationship between

PDD-NOS and the other specific diagnoses within PDD, this section takes up other developmental disorders outside PDD, and then other psychiatric disorders that may arise in infancy and early childhood.

As Mahoney and coworkers (1998) and Tanguay and coworkers (1998) discovered, the vagueness of PDD-NOS is most evident when clinicians must divine the boundaries between it, other PDDs, and other syndromes. A source of uncertainty is that the three major developmental domains that define impairment in autistic conditions—impairment in social relatedness, communication disorder and/or restriction in imaginative play, and repetitive patterns of behavior or restricted interests—are highly qualitative and largely independent of one another; each might be understood as a separate continuous variable (Tanguay et al., 1998). These complex domains have thwarted attempts to find meaningful demarcations within the spectrum of PDD conditions. Diagnostic guidelines for any of the PDD diagnoses do not offer threshold measures and do not declare how much impairment (or competence) is necessary in each domain to justify being included in the diagnosis. Each domain lacks precise definitions and introduces a measure of uncertainty into the deliberation. Thus, the experience, training, and procedures used by a diagnostician influence whether an individual with an atypical presentation is diagnosed with PDD-NOS, autism, or another PDD.

In addition, even when the domains can be clearly defined, there is uncertainty over how much (or little) impairment is consistent with the diagnosis of PDD-NOS. For research purposes, most investigators now turn to the ADI-R and ADOS-G and define their own algorithms to clarify the boundaries with PDD-NOS and other PDDs (Tanguay et al., 1998). At the present time, there is no agreed-on cut point for obtaining scores on the ADI-R and ADOS-G for PDD-NOS or ASP. Furthermore, the extensive training necessary to attain reliability on these instruments has made them impractical for day-to-day clinical use, despite their recent ready availability. Autism research has not yet produced practical, reliable, quick instruments to make these distinctions. Without these instruments and reliable measures of "how much autism" an individual

may possess, this differential diagnostic decision will be unreliable. There continues to be disagreement over how much impairment in each of these three domains is needed to make a reliable conclusion. The implications of how much these differences in functioning contribute to the prognosis or treatment also have yet to be spelled out. As long as this uncertainty persists, cautious consideration of the differential diagnosis will be critical to every evaluation.

Asperger's Disorder

Prior to 1980 and the creation of *DSM-IV* and *ICD-10,* there was no distinction between PDD-NOS and ASP and thus no need for practitioners (or researchers) to differentiate between them. Current criteria offer little direction or guidance for separating PDD-NOS from ASP. It is not yet clear whether phenomenological features represent valid differences between these entities. As yet, there is no evidence pointing to difference in etiology or to specific features that influence prognosis, treatment, or genetic recurrence risk. As reviewed previously, evidence suggests that mild degrees of social dysfunction may be more common in first-degree relatives of individuals with autism, ASP, or PDD-NOS than in control populations (Piven et al., 1990, 1997; Szatmari et al., 2000; Walker et al., 2004). Kurita (1997) suggests that differences in imitation and auditory responsiveness may be lower in those with ASP than in individuals with atypical autism akin to PDD-NOS. The current diagnostic guidelines state that language development and motor coordination in ASP may be distinctive (Klin & Shepard, 1994). Individuals with PDD-NOS may or may not show delays in language development (Walker et al., 2004) and may or may not be clumsy. The diagnostic guidelines proposed by Klin and coworkers (1995) are that individuals with ASP show normal grammatical and syntactic language development, normal adaptive functioning aside from socialization, all-absorbing special interests/skills, and awkwardness in motor tasks. However, there is reason to question whether motor clumsiness or all-absorbing interests/skills reliably discriminate between PDD-NOS and Asperger syndrome (Manjiviona &

Prior, 1995). Furthermore, it may be that motor clumsiness is closely linked to early language delay (Bishop, 2002). Further studies will be needed to clarify the relevance of motor clumsiness. *ICD-10* declares that the validity of the ASP construct (as an entity different from high-functioning autism) remains in doubt (*ICD-10*), and this is supported by some investigation (Frith, 2004; Howlin, 2003; Macintosh & Dissanayake, 2004; Miller & Ozonoff, 2000). There are disagreements about whether "language development" can be termed "normal" in ASP when pragmatic functions, prosody, or intonation are so disturbed (Frith, 2004; Howlin, 2003; Szatmari, 1997; Szatmari, Bryson, Boyle, Streiner, & Duku, 2003; Szatmari, Tuff, Finlayson, & Bartolucci, 1990). A great deal must be learned about ASP before its unique features can be specified. The Task Force on Nomenclature in *DSM-IV-TR* reflected the ambivalence over whether ASP and PDD-NOS are separate. On the one hand, they created a new unique category for ASP; but they supplied the same numerical code (299.80) for it and for PDD-NOS. As a result, numerical coding searches relying on *DSM-IV-TR* will fail to distinguish individuals with PDD-NOS and ASP.

Autistic Disorder

Determining whether an individual has autism or PDD-NOS can baffle even experienced clinicians. This is only partially a result of attempting to subdivide a continuum into discrete parts. The absence of measurable standards and specific cut points defining levels of impairment within domains is particularly problematic when deciding between autism and PDD-NOS. It is not as difficult to make the diagnosis in mentally retarded individuals who are relatively skilled nonverbally and strikingly aloof, but the confusion over which diagnosis is most appropriate can be enormous when evaluating high-functioning individuals. This was borne out in the *DSM-IV* field trials (Volkmar et al., 1994). In that study, 125 raters who had a range of experience reviewed histories of 977 patients who were thought to have autism or for whom autism was a reasonable question in the differential diagnosis. Half the raters had considerable experience in the diagnosis of autism. The

field trial results suggested that clinicians reliably could make distinctions between autism, ASP, and PDD-NOS. However, for PDD-NOS more than the other PDD subtypes, there was greater disagreement about how individuals would be diagnosed under the different diagnostic systems. Within the group of individuals with PDD-NOS diagnoses, 71 of 153 cases (46%) met criteria for autism in one of the three diagnostic systems (*DSM-III, DSM-III-R, ICD-10*) but were beneath criteria for autism in one or more of the other systems. There was agreement in only 55 of 153 (36%) cases that individuals did not meet criteria for autism according to any of the diagnostic schemes. Mahoney and coworkers' investigations (1998) noted a similar pattern of difficulties. In those studies, 143 children with autism, Asperger syndrome, atypical autism, or developmental disorders that were not part of PDD were evaluated using ADI-R, ADOS, Vineland Adaptive Behavior Scales, and age-appropriate Weschler IQ measures. Comparing consensus best estimate diagnoses, clinician diagnoses, and independent blind expert rater diagnoses, the investigators reported good agreement for autism and Asperger syndrome, but not for PDD-NOS. For autism, the false positive rate was acceptable at 0.20, 0.03 for Asperger syndrome, and 0.06 for PDD-NOS. However, the false negative rates told another story with autism at 0.05, Asperger syndrome at 0.13, and PDD-NOS at 0.49, revealing "49% of the 'true' cases of atypical autism were misdiagnosed as autism by the [expert] raters."

Uncertainty over the definition and quantification of relatedness compound this difficulty. Thus, clinicians frequently must face the question of how much relatedness is compatible with autism or PDD-NOS. Experienced clinicians know that children with autism may enjoy cuddling, seek comfort when injured, or make eye contact, but may also exhibit other features of aberrant and delayed social interaction. However, less knowledgeable clinicians may hold to the idea that certain behaviors such as proximity seeking of caretakers under stress, ability to follow simple commands, or eye contact precludes the diagnosis of autism. Just how much relatedness and reciprocity are necessary to place one into PDD-NOS or out of autism remain ambiguous.

A common conundrum for clinicians arises when reassessing persons previously diagnosed with autism, who now show some, though much less, impairment in one or two domains. When a child or adolescent displays mild, significant impairment in social skills but previously exhibited all the profound delays and deviance of an autistic disorder, is it more appropriate to diagnose Autistic disorder (high-functioning) or PDD-NOS? There are no conventions for how one reconciles disparities in the presentation when comparing the past and present. An outmoded view is that improvement itself argues against the diagnosis of autism. There is now good evidence that autistic individuals usually increase their skills over time, including social reciprocity (Lord, 1995). Moreover, if the developmental history is unobtainable or unreliable, then it is likely that an individual would be diagnosed PDD-NOS. However, diagnostic guidelines are inconsistent. Generally, the *DSM* convention for other diagnoses (e.g., depression, anxiety disorders) is that individuals who display persistent impairment, albeit less severe than at the time of the *original* diagnosis, are considered to have partial improvement rather than a new, less specific, diagnosis (e.g., Anxiety Disorder NOS).

Childhood Disintegrative Disorder

Childhood Disintegrative Disorder (CDD) is a rare condition (Malhotra & Gupta, 2002; Volkmar et al., 1994; Volkmar & Rutter, 1995). Typically, as in Heller's original descriptions (Heller, 1908), patients with CDD have a 3-to-4-year history of early unequivocally normal development followed by intellectual (particularly language skill) decline leading to profound impairment, including social impairment and unrelatedness. Such a history is distinctive in comparison with PDD-NOS and is not likely to lead to confusion. However, a clear-cut history such as this is rare; a decline in function between 18 and 24 months is offered for many autistic and PDD-NOS patients who also display a plateau or mild decline in social development (Volkmar et al., 1985). Consequently, a history of onset after 30 months, language delay, and milder declines in function lead most clinicians to use PDD-NOS rather than CDD

(Volkmar et al., 1994). However, such history should raise the possibility of CDD, and among these, Landau-Kleffner syndrome, inborn errors of metabolism, glycogen storage disorders, and mitochondrial disorders should be considered. With the characteristic motor impairments, head circumference deceleration, and loss of language skills, one must also consider Rett syndrome, particularly in females. Landau-Kleffner syndrome (acquired aphasia; Beaumanior, 1992) periodically receives particularly wide attention. Concomitant medical conditions should not preclude the diagnosis of autism or PDD-NOS; when both are displayed, then both the medical and PDD-NOS diagnoses should be used. No phenomenological guidelines specifically distinguish between PDD-NOS and CDD or spell out the conditions under which a decline in function warrants diagnosing one over the other. In practice, patients with later onset routinely receive diagnosis of PDD-NOS in preference to CDD, although in the *DSM-IV* field trials, a period of normal development up to age 2 years, current mutism, and placement in residential facilities were salient features that led clinicians to diagnose CDD (Volkmar & Rutter, 1995; Volkmar et al., 1994). Recently, this group of conditions has received attention fueled by unsupported theories postulating vaccine-related increases in PDD (Fombonne & Chakrabarti, 2001).

PDD-NOS and Other Developmental Disorders

The descriptions of Developmental Language Disorders, particularly Semantic-Pragmatic Disorder (Adams & Bishop, 1989; Bishop & Adams, 1989) or Pragmatic Language Impairment (PLI; Bishop & Norbury, 2002) accurately portray language impairments seen in some individuals with PDD, particularly PDD-NOS. As defined by Rapin and Allen (1983), Semantic-Pragmatic Disorder is a condition in which complex language is intact, but use, content, and understanding of language are impaired. There is active debate over whether Semantic-Pragmatic Disorder should remain as a description, separate from PDDs (Bishop, 1989, 2000), or is synonymous with PDD-NOS (Brook & Bowler, 1992). It is likely that there are other conditions described by neuropsychology or speech and language pathology, such as auditory processing disorders, that also overlap with PDD.

Taking a methodical and judicious approach, Bishop has argued that it is premature to consider all PLI to be equivalent to PDD-NOS although she is unequivocal that individuals with PDD-NOS commonly exhibit this type of language disorder. One problem is that PLI is not unique to PDDs and may be seen in the context of specific language impairment (SLI). To explore this, Bishop and Norbury (2002) studied children with high-functioning autism, PLI, typical SLI (i.e., not mixed SLI & PLI), and healthy volunteers, using measures of basic language, pragmatic language, the Autism Diagnostic Interview (ADI-R), and Autism Diagnostic Observation Schedule (ADOS-G). Acknowledging that the metric for PDD-NOS is not codified for the ADI-R, Bishop found that only 3 of 18 children with PLI met criteria for autism on these instruments. Only 1 child among 18 in the PLI group met criteria for PDD-NOS with a modified ADI-R (checklist) and the ADOS-G. An important question that emerges is whether the diagnosis based on only current functioning (as opposed to history) is accurate; if the ADI checklist alone had been used, then 4 of 18 would have met criteria for PDD-NOS and 5 of 18 met criteria for autism (a total of 9/18 [50%] having been diagnosed with a PDD). Based on the modified ADI checklist, 6 of 18 (33%) of the PLI and 2 of 11 (18%) SLI-T children had PDD features at 4 to 5 years of age that no longer were apparent at the time of the study. Nevertheless, it is also apparent that 50% of PLI children did not exceed criteria for PDD currently or in the past based on parent report. Bishop and Norbury underscore that the PDD features PLI children exhibited were almost exclusively related to language criteria (such as failing to ask for information, using stereotyped or idiosyncratic words). They did not display impairment in use of imagination, and less than 25% had excessive interests or ritualized behaviors by history (Bishop & Norbury, 2002). Thus, all PLI may not be a part of the autism spectrum, and until this has been clarified through further study, continued use of this descriptive, though not diagnostic, term is warranted.

One source of confusion stems from the separate, parallel, autonomous diagnostic systems that are used in communication pathology and pediatric psychiatry. Communication pathologists do not use psychiatric diagnoses; they provide accurate descriptions of language skills. As a result, they may not consider the broader context of impairments related to social skills and stereotyped movements that might shed light on an autistic spectrum condition. Thus, the accurate description by communication pathologists may not correspond to medical nosology. Conversely, psychiatric nosology has collapsed the wide, and richly varied range of expressive, receptive, and pragmatic language into three mutually exclusive categories that may not have empirical validity. If communication pathologists held themselves to the current system of medical nosology, they would be forced to dilute their observations and conclusions at the expense of considerable breadth and precision. The characterization of communication disorders in current psychiatric nosology does not reflect the precision of modern speech pathology and, understandably, most speech and language experts shun it.

In addition, the diagnostic objectives of the two fields are dissimilar. The conclusions offered by communication pathology focus predominantly on elements of language and seek to provide a clear description of their "piece" of the disorder; whereas the aim for the psychiatrist is to furnish a comprehensive, parsimonious diagnostic formulation for the entire panoply of symptoms. A communication pathologist may recognize syntactic, prosodic, and linguistic impairments but view information regarding circumscribed interests or restricted patterns of behavior to be outside his or her scope. Should this occur, the PDD-NOS patient will be viewed as suffering from a language disorder—a description that is accurate as far as it goes though it may be insufficient as a complete diagnostic formulation.

Mental Retardation

Young children who exhibit mental retardation, language delay or impairment, and delays in social reciprocity occupy a position at another boundary with PDD-NOS. There is general agreement that language delays, deficient social skills, and stereotyped mannerisms are very common among retarded persons (Bregman, 1991; Fraser & Rao, 1991) and abilities decline as IQ level descends. When social delays are severe, then autism becomes a serious consideration; but milder impairments in social reciprocity, language impairments, or the absence of imaginative play create a dilemma. When are these delays or deficits consonant with mental retardation and when is an additional diagnosis of PDD-NOS appropriate? The impairments must be considered in the context of the child's general level of retardation. Even when standardized screening devices such as the Vineland Adaptive Behavior Scales are employed (Volkmar et al., 1993), they provide little help in determining whether delays are commensurate with the level of retardation or represent manifestations and a developmental disorder. Standardized measures alone cannot answer questions of how much lower social performance must be, compared with communication or daily living skills, for PDD-NOS to be a legitimate consideration. There is considerable uncertainty over how great a discrepancy must exist in specific domains of socialization, language, and stereotyped interests compared with the general level of retardation among retarded individuals with PDD-NOS. This uncertainty surfaces in studies of prevalence rates of PDD among retarded persons. Some researchers have reported that as many as 30% of mentally retarded individuals have a PDD (Gillberg et al., 1986). This is to be contrasted with the figure of 5 to 10 per 10,000 reported among the general population. It is evident that considerable work is necessary to understand the distribution of these features among the general population of retarded persons. We still do not know how much impairment a retarded or nonretarded patient must exhibit to be appropriately considered as having PDD-NOS.

PDD-NOS and Conditions with Onset in Childhood

It may not be intuitive that Attention Deficit Hyperactivity Disorder (ADHD) could be confused with PDD-NOS. Unlike the child with PDD-NOS, the typical child with ADHD does not display extensive problems with relating to others although problems with milder deficits

in misreading affects and impulsive behavior can discourage social relationships (Greene et al., 2001; Jensen, Larrieu, & Mack, 1997; Matthys, Cuperus, & van Engeland, 1999; Pfiffner, Calzada, & McBurnett, 2000). In an investigation designed to study this question, Luteijn and coworkers (2000) reported that checklist scores for attentional problems in ADHD children were not different from those for children with PDD-NOS and there were large overlaps in scores on social problems. Jensen and coworkers also saw this in a study of 44 children. Although PDD-NOS children exhibited more withdrawal behavior, those who were diagnosed with "PDD-NOS *plus* ADHD" did not show withdrawal. Moreover, a highly distractible child can seem as if he is "in his own world" and unrelated (Roeyers, Keymeulen, & Buysse, 1998). Consequently, it is not unusual for children with higher functioning PDD to be diagnosed with only ADHD (Perry, 1998; Roeyers et al., 1998). This is particularly the case when a careful developmental history has not been obtained (Perry, 1998; Roeyers et al., 1998). Sometimes these children are seen as "the worst case ever" of ADHD or "treatment refractory ADHD." Although there may be similar impairments in disruptive behaviors, the children with PDD-NOS appear to have significantly more difficulties in social understanding and in emotional and behavioral problems related to excessive affective reactions (Jensen et al., 1997).

Distinguishing between PDDs and ADHD can be difficult in individuals who have concurrent moderate-to-severe mental retardation (MR), developmental language disorder, or severe hyperactivity (as in *ICD-10* hyperkinesis). Impairment and delays in social relationships are common in individuals with ADHD plus MR or ADHD plus developmental language disorders (Bagwell et al., 2001; Noterdaeme, Amorosa, Mildenberger, Sitter, & Minow, 2001). Moreover, there is a relatively high frequency of symptoms of impulsiveness or inattention in higher functioning individuals with PDD (Luteijn et al., 2000) and those with PDD-NOS (Roeyers et al., 1998). Under *DSM-III-R* and *DSM-IV,* hierarchical rules prohibit the diagnosis of both conditions, since autism or PDD-NOS is understood to be primary and symptoms of inattention or distractibility are viewed in the context of this larger syndrome.

In the absence of a detailed developmental history or when children are very young, ADHD can be a common preliminary diagnosis or presenting complaint.

Obsessive-Compulsive Disorder

There has always been some ambiguity about how one separates obsessions and compulsions from stereotyped movements and restricted interests. There are suggestions that some constellations of symptoms are more likely in those with PDDs compared with OCD patients, but there are no pathognomonic symptoms in either group (McDougle et al., 1995). When developmentally delayed or retarded persons display habits and repetitive behaviors, the dividing line can become very vague. This becomes complicated when trying to understand these behaviors in individuals who possess some language but whose developmental ages are so low that one would not expect a capacity for self-reflection or an ability to formulate concepts of anxiety, senselessness, or resistance to performing the acts. Thus, some clinicians will diagnose comorbid OCD and mental retardation without eliciting information about early developmental features of social relating, language, other unusual interests, and patterns of behavior. It can compound the uncertainty when reverse logic is used, such as citing a favorable response to serotonin reuptake inhibitors (SRIs) as justification of the diagnosis of OCD. Certainly, it is possible for persons with developmental disabilities to develop habit disorders or OCD. However, a wider scope of inquiry that includes a detailed behavioral and developmental history (including language development) is indicated.

Generalized Anxiety Disorder

Excessive concern about past events, needs for constant reassurance, feelings of tension or inability to relax, and self-consciousness may be viewed as Generalized Anxiety Disorder (GAD) in children with PDD-NOS. Generalized anxiety can also produce constant worry, sleep disturbance, and excessive fatigue. Higher functioning individuals with PDD-NOS may exhibit these symptoms, but individuals with GAD do not exhibit impairments in social

functioning, or restricted interests that are disabling for individuals with PDDs. Hierarchical rules in *DSM-IV* underscore the primacy of PDD symptoms in persons with anxiety by prohibiting the diagnosis of GAD in persons with PDD conditions. Nevertheless, GAD occasionally surfaces as the presenting diagnosis in higher functioning children with lifelong social delays, restricted patterns of behavior, and narrow interests. Important features that can distinguish GAD are well-developed abilities to understand the wishes, desires, and interests of others and to read nonverbal social interactions. Often, major problems in persons with GAD stem from an excessive focus on these elements. Children with GAD have social interactions that may be excessively personalized or unveil self-disparaging worries over past or future interactions. However, as a rule, they are able to engage in reciprocal conversation, share interests and emotions, and to accurately recognize another's pleasure. They tend to see annoyance in others, even when it is not present, in contrast to those with PDDs, who are likely to fail to recognize it.

Personality Disorders

Several personality disorder diagnoses may be ascribed to persons with developmental histories and childhood onset features of PDD-NOS. Older children, adolescents, or young adults with PDD-NOS who exhibit avoidance of social contact but possess more developed language skills may be viewed as having either Schizoid or Avoidant Personality Disorder. Although some argue that the desire for social relationships precludes PDD, many higher functioning ASP and PDD-NOS individuals wish for social contact and are aware that they are different from others (Wing, 1992). The awareness of this difference can be a source of distress to individuals with PDD-NOS (Wing, 1992). Their inability to enter social situations successfully can make them appear shy and in need of considerable reassurance before venturing into novel social situations, thereby suggesting Avoidant Personality Disorder. Somewhat lower functioning individuals with PDD-NOS may harbor more wariness and prefer to avoid social interaction altogether. This more aloof group resembles the schizoid children described by Wolff and

Chick (1980). When a child displays language disorder, poor pragmatic behaviors (such as unrelated or circumstantial utterances) he may be erroneously considered to have Schizotypal Personality Disorder, or Schizophrenia. This is particularly likely when circumscribed interests and preoccupations are prominent (Rumsey, Andreasen, & Rapoport, 1986). Some consider that ASP should be a subtype of Schzoid Personality Disorder (Tantam, 1988b). When a reliable developmental history cannot be obtained, clinicians might presume that an adolescent or young adult has a personality disorder.

Experience in diagnosing autistic spectrum disorders is important in learning to differentiate between developmental disorders and personality disorders (Volkmar et al., 1994). Features of very early onset with enduring impairment in imaginary play, socialization, and restricted patterns of behavior throughout childhood would point toward diagnosis of a developmental disorder. There are too few investigations of the developmental history of adults with unequivocal Avoidant, Schizoid, or Schizotypal Personality Disorder to compare developmental histories with persons with PDD-NOS. Consequently, it is unknown whether characteristic features of PDD are displayed through childhood and adolescence in persons with Avoidant, Schizoid, or Schizotypal Personality Disorder. Tantam (1988b) suggests that differences do exist, insofar as elevated scores on measures of abnormal nonverbal expression were correlated with early developmental disturbances, whereas schizoid features were not. Tantam (1988b) report that features of developmental delays and abnormal nonverbal expression clustered together, but schizotypal features did not correlate with developmental abnormalities. It is also unclear whether there are other typical features in the childhood course or natural history of Schizoid, Schizotypal, or Avoidant Personality Disorder that would permit differentiation of these conditions from PDD-NOS. *DSM-IV* itself points to the complexity of differentiating high-functioning autism and ASP from Schizoid Personality Disorder (*DSM-IV*).

Consider a hypothetical individual who presents with mild-to-moderate impairment in socialization and a history of significant progress in social reciprocity following profound delays in early childhood. This person's developmental achievements introduce a diagnostic problem resembling the one for autistic persons described earlier. This is a predicament for the clinician who must decide whether this person suffers from one or more of these personality disorders or PDD-NOS. Many clinicians will favor a personality diagnosis in the face of such a history. If a history of language development, restricted patterns of behavior, and narrow interests is not pursued, the assessment may yield a personality disorder diagnosis. However, when there is still impairment resulting from limited social reciprocity, it is inappropriate to reject the diagnosis of PDD-NOS or autism based on gains in language, or social interest.

Discarding the diagnosis of PDD-NOS because of improvements and replacing it with a personality diagnosis promotes two illogical concepts. The first proposes that the patient recovered from PDD-NOS and went on to develop a new, separate disorder affecting personality. This is illogical insofar as the same symptoms, present continuously, are viewed as resulting from one disorder in childhood and a different disorder later on. The natural history of PDD-NOS shows that individuals improve. It is contradictory to suggest, therefore, that when a person with PDD-NOS improves, a different diagnosis should be applied.

An alternative formulation is that the individual has displayed a personality disorder throughout his or her lifetime with features of language delay, social impairment, and restricted interests or patterns of behavior. If this were true, this hypothetical personality disorder would be hierarchically related to PDD, continuous with PDD, or a muted form of PDD. Empirical, longitudinal studies of such "personality disorders" do not confirm this formulation (Kolvin, 1971). Conceptually, this view takes a regressive step by reverting to the pre-Kolvin era in which the disorders in the autism spectrum, the schizophrenia spectrum, and conditions exhibiting social isolation, were all presumed to be related and nosologically warranted being lumped into a single entity. Wolff and Chick (1980) have favored a view that autism and schizophrenia are on a continuum, although this dismisses findings suggesting the two are distinct (Kolvin, 1971; Volkmar & Cohen, 1991; Werry, 1992).

Reactive Attachment Disorder

According to *DSM-IV,* a child who has a verified history of psychosocial adversity, termed "pathogenic care" during the first years of life and displays disinhibited or inhibited responses in social situations, may have Reactive Attachment Disorder (RAD). Closer scrutiny reveals that many children who undergo profound neglect or abuse subsequently show substantial physical and emotional improvement when they receive compassionate, nurturing care (O'Connor, Rutter, Beckett, Keaveney, & Kreppner, 2000). Others show a protracted or intractable course, "quasi-autistic features," and present a clinical conundrum (Rutter, Kreppner, & O'Connor, 2001). Reliable data suggest that overactivity, inattention, stereotyped behaviors, and eating problems may persist in a small minority of children and are highly correlated with the duration of privation (Beckett et al., 2002; Roy, Rutter, & Pickles, 2000). Quasi-autistic features, such as social aloofness or social impairment symptoms of PDD that arise in a small minority of children, are not likely to persist (Rutter et al., 1999). Thus, at times, the social dysfunction of RAD may resemble PDD-NOS and it may be difficult to decide which is the more suitable diagnosis. As suggested by Richters and Volkmar (1994), there are several reasons to reflect carefully on the relationship between PDD-NOS and RAD. The first reason is clinical. Children who receive profoundly detrimental parenting in early life are often just the ones for whom it is most difficult to obtain a reliable developmental history or to determine whether there has been pathogenic care. In the absence of an accurate, reliable developmental history, clinicians may prematurely or hastily decide that the symptom picture is exclusively the result of adversity during the child's early years. The consequence of a hasty decision is that the educational plan for such a child and the expectations of care providers are very different when RAD, as opposed to PDD-NOS, is the working diagnoses. Second, although most abused and neglected children are not developmentally delayed, a developmentally delayed

child may be more likely to receive abuse. Children with impairments in language and relatedness who display inflexible patterns and routines may be more likely to experience mistreatment or neglect by angry parents who do not understand why their child is so exhausting and unrewarding. An aloof child who does not sleep or eat well, refuses to comply with rules and limits, and does not become calm when held or reciprocate a smile or greeting may further inflame abusive or neglectful handling. An uninformed parent may believe the child is oppositional or willfully disobedient. Thus, a child's developmental delays could aggravate and incite as readily as emanate from profound mistreatment. Third, RAD may require reconsideration in light of a broader concept of PDD. The biological determinants of protracted RAD are poorly understood; the acute and chronic course of RAD could be explained on the basis of constitutional vulnerability to impairment in social relatedness. It seems possible that the children who display a protracted course have a larger dose of deprivation and this may further stress biological susceptibilities. In this model, abuse and neglect become impediments leading to suboptimal adjustment but are not the exclusive cause of it.

Schizophrenia

The hierarchical rules for handling co-occurring PDD and schizophrenia are contradictory in *DSM-IV* and do not stem from empirical data. When premorbid autism or another PDD exists, the *DSM* requires the presence of prominent hallucinations and delusions for at least a month. If these criteria are met in the context of autism, then both diagnoses are warranted. However, if another PDD is present (ASP or PDD-NOS), then the diagnosis of schizophrenia *supplants* the prior PDD diagnosis and the only diagnosis is schizophrenia. The *DSM* offers no rationale for this decision. Generally, the guidelines for making diagnoses suggest that a more specific diagnosis is preferred to one that is "not otherwise specified." The problem in schizophrenia is the implication that once hallucinations and delusions set in, individuals with early-onset deficits in social reciprocity are no different from those without such a history. There is no empirical evidence to support eliminating this distinction and some evidence to suggest that individuals with insidious onset and early premorbid social and language deficits exhibit a poorer prognosis and different neuropathological features (Cannon et al., 2002; Silverstein, Mavrolefteros, & Close, 2002). It seems more congruous to follow the practice of applying both diagnoses (e.g., schizophrenia *plus* PDD-NOS) instead of discarding nonautistic PDD (Volkmar & Cohen, 1991).

This is not a trivial consideration. Watkins and coworkers (Watkins, Asarnow, & Tanguay, 1988) reviewed histories of 18 children diagnosed with schizophrenia. They reported that 7 subjects (39%) had symptoms that would have been sufficient to meet criteria for autism before 30 months. This is somewhat greater than the 17% rate (13% autism plus 4% with impairment in two domains) reported by Alaghband-Rad and coworkers (1995) at the National Institute of Mental Health (NIMH) in their cohort of schizophrenic children. The NIMH group did not report which domains within the Autism Diagnostic Interview (ADI) were impaired. If all subjects with impairment in social reciprocity showed this before 36 months and exhibited this premorbid-to-prominent hallucinations/delusions, the rate for premorbid PDD could be as high as 63% (McKenna et al., 1994). A third of the entire schizophrenic cohort also exhibited developmental language delays (Alaghband-Rad et al., 1995). In an early paper, the NIMH group (Gordon et al., 1994) emphasized the complexity of differentiating a PDD from childhood-onset schizophrenia and the need for rigorous methodology in discovering features of a PDD in individuals with schizophrenia, although they did not report on ADI domains. This was even more relevant to their later descriptive data on children with "multiple developmental impairment," a type of Psychosis Not Otherwise Specified (McKenna et al., 1994). In that subgroup, the rate of PDD symptoms at the time of presentation was 39%. This is particularly important when the diagnosis of schizophrenia relies on negative symptoms, and hallucinations and delusions are only weakly evident (Minshew, 2001).

Bipolar disorder is often diagnosed in persons with PDDs who have irritability, aggression, and reactivity to disruption in routines. It is particularly more likely to be diagnosed in those with chronic agitation, distractibility, and/or sleep difficulties. It should be underscored that decreased need for sleep is not the same as the difficulties initiating sleep that are often seen in persons with PDDs. As with other disorders, there is a growing awareness that the concept of bipolar disorder may be applied more narrowly by some investigators than others. Leibenluft and coworkers (Leibenluft, Charney, Towbin, Bhangoo, & Pine, 2003) have suggested ways of understanding these different views. If bipolar disorders are to be narrowly defined, then episodicity must be a cardinal feature (Geller et al., 2002; Leibenluft et al., 2003). In applying the narrow phenotype diagnoses to those with PDDs, one must then consider whether chronic symptoms such as agitation, irritability, and distractibility are all significantly increased during a period of elevated mood and decreased need for sleep. Otherwise, there is a high risk that overlapping, chronic symptoms will be used redundantly to make multiple diagnoses (e.g., ADHD, PDD, bipolar disorder; Geller et al., 2002). This leaves open the question of how the broader phenotype condition may be related to narrow phenotype bipolar disorder.

Social Phobias

Social phobias are the least common anxiety disorders of childhood onset and a very uncommon early childhood-onset disorder (Beidel, 1991). Patients typically begin having symptoms in their teens, although childhood-onset cases certainly occur. Of the group with generalized social phobias, at least 50% will experience onset prior to age 12 years (Mannuzza et al., 1995; Velting & Albano, 2001; Wittchen & Fehm, 2001). As with several of the other conditions previously discussed, a clinician who narrows the range of possibilities too quickly risks making a diagnostic error. It is critical to recognize the difference between the social aloofness of higher functioning autistic individuals and the extreme shyness or avoidance accompanied by anxiety that is characteristic of social phobias or avoidant disorders. The obstruction of PDD-NOS or social phobia may lead a child to display anxiety and to attempt refraining from social interactions. However, the concept of social phobia has traditionally been reserved for individuals who have preservation of development in other domains of their lives and have socially appropriate relationships within a small circle of family and friends (Beidel, 1991). The typical individual with social phobia enjoys the company of others and will experience loneliness. It is less clear whether the loneliness of high-functioning autistic PDD-NOS persons has these same qualities although they certainly may wish to participate and fit in with their peer group. Individuals with social phobias ought to display a strong capacity for understanding complex emotional situations and to exhibit spontaneous empathy in social situations. A history of normal language, imaginative play, flexibility in facing novel situations, and ordinary social development are crucial. Comorbid depressive, anxiety, or substance abuse disorders were common in adult subjects with social phobia (Mannuzza et al., 1995; Velting & Albano, 2001; Wittchen & Fehm, 2001), but they did not have the pervasive impairment in relationships and restricted interests characteristic of high-functioning autistic or Aspergerian individuals. Complicating this picture is the elevated rate of social phobia among relatives of probands with autism (Piven & Palmer, 1997, 1999; Smalley, McCracken, & Tanguay, 1995) suggesting that social phobia could reside within the broader phenotype of the autism spectrum.

Two Potential Subgroups within PDD-NOS: Multiplex Developmental Disorder and Disorders of Attention, Motor Control, and Perception

Neither Multiple Complex (or Multiplex) Developmental Disorder (MCDD) nor Disorders of Attention, Motor Control, and Perception (DAMP) is a term in the *DSM-IV* or *ICD-10*. However, they may be closely related to or be viewed as part of a PDD spectrum.

MCDD is an early-onset syndrome in which there are basic deficits in affective modulation, capacity for relating, and thinking. The characteristics of onset in infancy or very early childhood, sustained limitations in the

capacity to form reciprocal relationships, and impoverished affective regulation suggest that MCDD might be appropriately placed in the category of PDD. These children display extreme impairments in the capacity to interact successfully with peers and adults, capacity for empathy, and in their ability to tolerate negative affects such as frustration or anxiety. When distressed, they become highly disorganized in their behavior and thinking (Dahl, Cohen, & Provence, 1986). MCDD has specific criteria and can be reliably diagnosed and differentiated from other childhood-onset disorders of behavior or affect (Buitelaar et al., 1998; Towbin et al., 1993). Impairments in social relating are reflected in the diminished amounts and a primitive quality of peer relationships as well as fundamental impairments in the child's manner of relating to primary caretakers. Children with MCDD syndrome exhibit consistent features of avoidance, detachment, high degrees of ambivalence, clinging, or intense irritability. Deficits in affective regulation result in peculiar fears, chronic anxiety, frequent incidents of intense anger, and extreme behavioral reactions. These demonstrate limitations in modulation of internal affective states and affective expression. In addition, recurrent episodes of disorganization in thinking or perceptual distortions are characteristic (Cohen et al., 1986; Towbin et al., 1993). This is ordinarily episodic, but thought disorganization may be more consistent. Problems in thinking reach neither the proportions nor sustained intensity that are sufficient for chronic delusional or psychotic conditions. Changes in routine or structure often precipitate disorganization. This vulnerability is reminiscent of the patterned behavior and inflexibility typical of PDDs. As the condition is characterized and its boundaries are explored, it is appropriate to place it under the wider umbrella of PDD-NOS (Cohen et al., 1986).

MCDD emerged from observations of a large number of preschool-age children who presented for developmental evaluations (Dahl et al., 1986). Rescorla (1986) conducted standardized evaluations that suggested these children were an "intermediate group" between children with autism and so-called reactive children who appeared anxious and depressed. The MCDD group showed high scores on a factor of "bizarre" features (confusion, having strange ideas, exhibiting strange behaviors, and being lost in thoughts). This bizarre factor was more common among children in an MCDD group and a group of children with high-functioning autism (HFA) or Asperger syndrome than a comparison reactive group (Rescorla, 1986). Unlike those with HFA, the MCDD individuals scored highly on a factor measuring anxiety and depression that included items like worrying, being tense and anxious, and demanding attention (Rescorla, 1986; van der Gaag et al., 1995) similar to comparison "highly reactive" children.

The impairments of children with MCDD have suggested to some investigators that MCDD is an early appearing form of bipolar illness, Borderline Personality Disorder, Schizotypal Personality Disorder, or Schizophrenia. Although the affective dysregulation and impairment in thinking and interpersonal relationships are reminiscent of these conditions, it is not evident that MCDD is continuous with these Axis I or II conditions or that linking MCDD to them is appropriate. Until we have stronger biological markers or endophenotypes (Crosbie & Schachar, 2001; Milberger et al., 1996), it is premature to make these associations. Reading descriptions of these conditions, one is struck by how much their clinical presentations resemble one another (Caplan, 1994; Tantam, 1988a; Watkins et al., 1988). Investigators have commented on the persistent confusion between so-called childhood-onset schizophrenia and high-functioning autism or schizophrenia (Szatmari et al., 1990; Tantam, 1988b; Watkins et al., 1988).

There is some support from biological studies for differentiating MCDD from other PDDs. Lincoln and coworkers evaluated 30 children with MCDD, ADHD, and healthy volunteers on measures of behavior, psychophysiological tasks, and event-related potentials (Lincoln, Bloom, Katz, & Boksenbaum, 1998). Results suggested that the 11 MCDD children displayed a distinct profile of auditory processing impairment. In a similar vein, Kemner and coworkers (Kemner, van der Gaag, Verbaten, & van Engeland, 1999) reported that visual event-related potentials to P3 at multiple leads, and Nc in frontal regions differentiated MCDD children from those with autism and healthy volunteers on a visual oddball task. Following in this same effort to discover biological endophenotypes, Jansen and coworkers (2000; Jansen, Gispen-de Wied, van der Gaag, & van Engeland, 2003) examined cortisol responses to psychological and physical stress in 10 children with MCDD, HFA, and healthy volunteers. Results suggested that individuals with HFA had an increased cortisol response to psychological stress, whereas MCDD children had a decreased response compared to healthy volunteers. There were no differences between groups in response to physical stress. It is particularly interesting that the pattern of reduced cortisol response is frequently observed in adults with schizophrenia (Jansen et al., 1998, 2000).

The neurodevelopmental perspective of schizophrenia has promoted greater interest in MCDD (Bloom, 1993; Fish, Marcus, Hans, Auerbach, & Perdue, 1992). This concept proposes that early-onset neural defects associated with stable cognitive impairments set the stage for an increased risk of schizophrenia. What is not clear is whether these developmental adversities routinely generate schizophrenia, or whether they are nonspecific risk factors that profoundly and adversely affect adjustment in adulthood. Sparrow and coworkers (1986) reported that measures of social immaturity and dysfunction had stability and persistence, but that deterioration in function overall was not seen at 7-year follow-up. Similarly, Kestenbaum (1983) reported a variety of outcomes, with psychosis only rarely ensuing in a similar albeit small cohort. Lofgren and coworkers (Lofgren, Bemporad, King, Lindem, & O'Driscoll, 1991) also found no specific outcome in children identified as having a borderline syndrome. In support of this view, Nicholson and coworkers (2001) reported that children ascertained for schizophrenia but showing a variation of MCDD called Multiple Developmental Impairment (MDI), went on to develop affective disorders or had a continuation of their presenting symptoms (Nicholson et al., 2001). Despite being ascertained for schizophrenia, none of the cohort went on to develop schizophrenia. Diagnostically, at 2- to 8-year follow-up, 12% had developed Schizoaffective Disorder; 15%, Bipolar Disorder; 24%, major depression; and 50% were clinically unchanged. Children with MCDD may resemble those described with schizoid conditions (Wolff & Chick, 1980) or Asperger syndrome (Tantam, 1988b). A syndrome of poor interpersonal relatedness, odd language, and idiosyncratic thinking may be a stable, persistent trait.

DAMP, a disorder first described by Gillberg, is a comorbid condition of ADHD and Developmental Coordination Disorder (Gillberg, 2003). Gillberg has suggested a close link between DAMP and PDD spectrum disorders, based on overlapping symptoms. Two-thirds of patients with severe DAMP will resemble those with ASP or PDD-NOS (Gillberg, 2003). In a population study of Swedish 7-year-olds, those with coordination deficits were more likely to display symptoms of social impairment; and those with DAMP were even more likely to have these symptoms (Kadesjo & Gillberg, 1999). Children with DAMP were also more likely to display problems in speech production, phonological processing, and reading than children with only ADHD symptoms (Kadesjo & Gillberg, 1999).

EPIDEMIOLOGY

The prevalence rates reported for PDD-NOS have been heavily influenced by changes in diagnostic criteria, in the same fashion as the rates for all the PDDs. Definitions of Autistic disorder are particularly relevant; a broader or narrower definition will influence the size of the population that is ascertained, and may inversely influence the size of the nonautistic PDD. A methodologically weak study suggested that definitions may also influence population classified as mentally retarded (Croen et al., 2002). Consequently, the interpretation of epidemiological studies must consider the diagnostic system and methods employed.

In *DSM-III,* the alternatives to AD were Childhood-Onset PDD and Atypical PDD. Under *DSM-III-R,* these latter two categories were collapsed into PDD-NOS. It can be seen that a simple comparison of prevalence rates of Atypical PDD (*DSM-III*) and PDD-NOS (*DSM-III-R*) will not draw from congruent populations. *DSM-III-R* criteria were broader than those in *DSM-III* (Spitzer & Siegel, 1990; Volkmar et al., 1994). Compared to *DSM-III,* *DSM-III-R* increased the portion of children

with a PDD who received the diagnosis of AD (Hertzig, Snow, New, & Shapiro, 1990; Spitzer & Siegel, 1990). Also, changes in *DSM-III-R* criteria classified individuals as having a PDD who would not have met *DSM-III* criteria (Spitzer & Siegel, 1990).

Aside from definitions, prevalence rates are heavily influenced by the investigation's methodology. Different methods have produced widely disparate prevalence rates of autism. The discrepancies in results can be explained on the basis of methods of ascertainment, diagnostic criteria, and diagnostic procedures. Investigators who combine infantile autism and other, more broadly defined PDD subtypes in their cohort reported estimates of AD 1.9 to 4.9 per 10,000 (Bryson, Clark, & Smith, 1988; Ritvo, Freeman, & Pingree, 1989; Steinhausen, Gobel, Berinlinger, & Wohlleben, 1986; Wing & Gould, 1979). The studies that limited their ascertainment to narrow or strict definitions of infantile (or Kanner's) autism ("nuclear autism") gave a fairly consistent estimates of 2.0 to 2.2 per 10,000 (C. Gillberg & Coleman, 1992; Steffenberg & Gillberg, 1986; Steinhausen et al., 1986). Gillberg went on to suggest that rising prevalence rates of AD over the past 10 years were a consequence of changes in the diagnosis and broadening of definitions. Ritvo and coworkers suggested that widely disseminating information led to better recognition of autism. The Canadian study (Bryson et al., 1988), the first to employ a broad definition and research criteria, reported a prevalence rate of 10 per 10,000 and heralded the current period of higher rates.

Initial studies, like those undertaken by Wing and Gould (1979), reported prevalence rates for nonautistic PDD of 21 per 10,000. They went on to suggest that approximately 16 per 10,000 children had disorders of "reciprocal social interaction" other than "typical autism."

As a result of concerns about rising rates of autism and claims that PDDs are reaching epidemic proportions, several rigorous studies, using operationalized definitions and careful methods, were conducted. The stated objective of these studies was to determine rates for autism, but the growing importance of autism spectrum disorders (ASD) led investigators to seek rates for nonautistic PDD as well. Chakrabarti and Fombonne (2001) scrupulously examined rates of PDDs in preschoolers among a population of 320,000 (15,500 children 3 to 5 years old) in the United Kingdom. Results showed 97 children with a PDD: 26 (17/10,000) were noted to have AD; 13 (8.4/10,000) had ASP; 1 had Rett syndrome; 1 had CDD; and 56 (36/10,000) were noted to have PDD-NOS. The United States Centers for Disease Control were commissioned to examine rates in Brick Township, New Jersey (Bertrand et al., 2001). The New Jersey study relied primarily on school records, and then also on clinicians' reports, self-referral of parents, and lists of children provided by parent groups. Children were then directly evaluated using modern techniques and definitions. Results showed 53 children were evaluated directly—22 were diagnosed through records. The overall rate was 67/10,000 for all ASDs among children 3 to 10 years old. The rate for combined Asperger syndrome and PDD-NOS was 27/10,000. The authors suggested that the rates for nonautistic PDD were an underestimate resulting from the methods and may have overestimated AD at the expense of nonautistic PDD (Bertrand et al., 2001). Fiona and coworkers (Fiona, Baron-Cohen, Bolton, & Brayne, 2002) examined rates in Cambridge, United Kingdom, among 5- to 11-year-olds. Rates for ASD were 57/10,000.

Taken together, these studies suggest that the combined total for all other forms of nonautistic PDD are more common than autism. Fombonne's (2003) meta-analysis suggested that a conservative estimate for the prevalence rate of PDD-NOS was 15/10,000—150% of the rate for autism and 600% of the rate for Asperger's disorder. However, until positive, specific criteria are applied to large community-based populations the prevalence of PDD-NOS must remain tentative. In addition, problems demarcating the boundary between severe developmental language disorder and PDD continue to plague efforts to obtain accurate prevalence rates.

ETIOLOGY

The same genetic, neurochemical, and cognitive abnormalities that have been proposed for AD are likely to produce PDD-NOS. The current models suggest that no single contribution is sufficient and that PDDs result from combinations of genetic and life events (Jones & Szatmari, 2002). No neurochemical findings have been shown to correlate with PDD subtypes.

The search for biological mechanisms has cataloged many genetic and medical conditions and anomalies that arise in autistic individuals. Specific genetic disorders have been observed with more than chance frequency in cohorts of children with autism (C. Gillberg & Coleman, 1992). The most common is fragile X syndrome, but a long list of other disorders of probable genetic etiology including Cornelia de Lang syndrome, tuberous sclerosis (I. C. Gillberg, Gillberg, & Ahlsen, 1994; Smalley, 1998), Cohen syndrome (Howlin, 2001), and PKU have also been identified in association with autism (Gillberg & Coleman, 1992). However, no condition has been identified that might be considered a principal or specific cause of a PDD. Every genetic condition that has been reported in conjunction with AD has also been reported in individuals who do not have autism. It appears that some genetic or metabolic conditions may increase the risk for autism, but none have been shown to invariably result in a PDD (Lauritsen, Mors, Mortensen, & Ewald, 2002). It is likely that the outcome runs a gamut. For example, fragile X syndrome appears to produce a range of social impairments from severe autism to PDD-NOS to developmentally near-appropriate social reciprocity (Reiss et al., 1986). Most cohorts typically have pooled individuals diagnosed as PDD-NOS or Autistic disorder into a single group (e.g., "autistic syndromes"; C. Gillberg, 1992).

There has been a sustained effort to better characterize the cognitive features of children with autism (Prior, 1979; Sigman, Ungerer, Mundy, & Sherman, 1987). During the past decade, investigation has resulted in a more precise characterization of the complex cognitive deficits that arise in autistic individuals (Baron-Cohen, Tager-Flusberg, & Cohen, 1993, Minshew et al., 2002). Individuals with autism display limitations in attention to emotional expression (Piggott et al., 2004), and in the capacity for affective imitation (Rogers & Pennington, 1991). They also display relative strengths on visual-spatial tasks (Caron et al.,

2004). Until recently, the connection between these impairments and the profound social impediments of autism was obscure. However, more detailed study has suggested that autistic persons display consistent, profound limitations in the capacity to understand that other persons have a mental apparatus with thoughts, desires, and intentions that influence their actions (Baron-Cohen et al., 1985). This capacity for recognition of others' thoughts and mental apparatus has been termed "theory of mind" [ToM]). It is the cognitive function that permits a child to perceive and relate to the mental state of another.

Klin and coworkers (Klin, Volkmar, & Sparrow, 1992) have suggested that the study of autistic subjects may be unsuitable for investigating ToM problems because most autistic individuals have the onset of extreme social impairment prior to the period when ToM skills emerge. Thus it is only logical to expect that primary abilities to recognize subtle social signals would be severely impaired as well. They propose that it would be more appropriate to study individuals with better language and communication skills such as those with high-functioning autism, MCDD, or ASP. Such an approach would permit more detailed examinations of processes underlying social decisions. Klin and coworkers have suggested that impairment in theory of mind is more likely to be a consequence than the cause of ASDs.

Persons with PDD-NOS or high-functioning autism could be particularly suitable subjects for researchers who want to learn more about ToM hypotheses. Bowler (1992) suggests that high-functioning autistic individuals were able to correctly identify the mental state of another in an experimental paradigm, but could not explain their success by applying an understanding of mental state. Moreover, successful performance under experimental conditions did not correlate with adaptive social function. Possessing a theory of mind did not engender social competence among these subjects (Miller & Ozonoff, 2000; Ozonoff & Miller, 1995). Serra and coworkers (2002) found in a 3-year longitudinal study that children with PDD-NOS displayed delays in development of theory of mind compared to healthy volunteers. They noted that children with

PDD-NOS were able to predict others' behavior as well as control children, but they had greater difficulty than control children in understanding wishes and desires in others (Serra et al., 2002). They also suggest that children with PDD-NOS may perceive emotional or psychological characteristics, but do not apply them (Serra, Minderaa, van Geert, & Jackson, 1999).

NATURAL HISTORY

There have been few longitudinal studies of disorders comprising PDD-NOS, particularly when compared to numerous studies of individuals with autism. Narrowly defined autism exhibits a wide range of outcomes (Gillberg & Steffenberg, 1987). A very small number of autistic persons are able to attend college and live independently. Although many more make obvious strides in achieving greater social awareness, they remain socially odd, require lifelong supervision, and need educational support. The largest portion, perhaps 60%, make modest gains or remain severely impaired (Gillberg, 1991). The outcome of autism has been directly correlated with overall IQ, language development, and appearance of seizures. Seizures occur in as many as 30% of cases and are more frequent among individuals with lower IQ scores.

Most studies of nonautistic PDD assemble cohorts of persons with ASP. Relative to lower functioning children with autism, the prognosis for those with ASP can be fairly good, although findings of most studies favor restrained optimism. Szatmari and coworkers (1989) reported a high overall adaptive level on follow-up, but methodological flaws in selection and diagnoses may have compromised the generalizability of these findings. Most others give disappointing results though still reporting better outcomes among those with higher IQ and verbal skills (Venter, Lord, & Schopler, 1991). Asperger believed that the disorder bearing his name remained stable throughout adolescence and adulthood (1944). Although a majority of the individuals in his cohort made good academic adjustments, throughout life they sustained the social deficits first displayed in childhood. It appears that deficits in social impairment improve but do not keep pace with gains in IQ among these higher functioning individuals (Schatz & Hamdan-Allen, 1995).

There are many opinions on whether ASP increases the risk of developing other disorders. Schizophrenia occurred in only one of 200 cases in Asperger's original cohort (1944). One individual in Wing's cohort (1981) was thought to have schizophrenia. Wolff and Chick (1980) conducted a controlled follow-up study of individuals with schizoid personality who were ascertained using operational criteria. This generally has been regarded as a longitudinal study of ASP. In this sample, 2 of 22 persons developed schizophrenia and nearly half had suicidal ideation. However, "mystical or psychotic symptoms" were evident in nearly half the cohort (Wolff & Chick, 1980). Szatmari and coworkers (1989) suggested that anxiety, obsessive-compulsive symptoms, conduct symptoms, and schizotypal symptoms were more common in persons with ASP than in those with autism. In their studies, bizarre ideation was less common in ASP than in autism. Wing (1981), too, found anxiety symptoms to be prominent in her ASP sample. C. Gillberg (1992) cautioned that clinicians unfamiliar with the disorder may misinterpret the bizarre, concrete, and idiosyncratic thoughts and behaviors of adolescents or adults with ASP as signs of schizophrenia. This has also been borne out in work that directly ascertains elements of thought disorder in higher functioning autistic individuals with language (Dykens, Volkmar, & Glick, 1991; Ghaziuddin, Leininger, & Tsai, 1995).

These studies suggest that individuals with PDD-NOS appear to have a better prognosis than persons with autism, but they do not fare as well as persons with ASP. This appears to be directly correlated with the cognitive and language abilities. Differences appear less related to diagnoses than functional abilities (Serra et al., 2002; Szatmari, 1997; Szatmari et al., 2000). Obviously, lower functioning autistic persons have the most limited prognosis. Estimating the prognosis of persons with high-functioning autism, compared to those with PDD-NOS, cannot be reliably accomplished at this point. The most reliable factors to consider are overall IQ; social skills, measured by standardized measures; and language abilities.

Only one investigation has been published on the outcome of individuals diagnosed with multiplex developmental disorder (van der Gaag, 1993). Van der Gaag reported a variety of outcome results ascertained with a standardized diagnostic assessment of 43 adolescents and 12 adults previously identified as MCDD. Seven adolescents (16%) were free of any Axis I or II diagnoses. The most common adolescent Axis I diagnoses were anxiety disorders (17%) and mood disorders (10%). Axis II diagnoses in the adolescents identified PDD-NOS (37%), schizoid (12%), and schizotypal (2%) personality disorders most commonly. Of the 12 adults, 2 (17%) developed schizophrenia, 30% had schizoid personality, and 17% had Schizotypal Personality Disorder. Apparently, MCDD may produce varied outcomes; however, it is equally evident that it is associated with a great risk of chronic mental disorder.

TREATMENT

No one treatment, method, or approach has been shown to be effective for individuals with PDD-NOS. The decision to implement a treatment is based on the individual's strengths, symptoms, the setting, and the limitations that exist at the time (Towbin, 2003). This approach reflects the polymorphic symptoms, diverse deficits, and the wide range of impairments exhibited by children with PDD-NOS.

For every patient, treatment begins with a thoughtful and comprehensive evaluation (Filipek et al., 2000). It cannot be completed in a single session. The objectives of evaluation are to detect the predominant symptoms that are impeding the patient's development; the capacities, talents, and resources that can be recruited in support of the patient's care; and the principal limitations under which he or she operates (Towbin, 1994). Such an evaluation must include direct interviews with primary caretakers and others who are knowledgeable about the patient's early development. In addition, information from others familiar with the patient, including pediatricians, teachers, and extended family can be extremely helpful. Standardized measures can provide useful information

(Filipek et al., 2000) and are discussed elsewhere in this *Handbook*. In addition, laboratory studies including electroencephalogram, karyotype, fragile-X testing, blood studies for quantitative amino acids, and urine for organic acids may be important, although these studies yield negative results in more than 90% of children with autism (Lauritsen et al., 2002; Wassink, Piven, & Patil, 2001). In children with any focal neurological findings, documented decline in skills, or onset of seizures, magnetic resonance imaging (MRI) scans allow clinicians to visualize brain structure without radiation risk. For children with PDD-NOS who do not exhibit these features, the value of these studies for therapeutic care is highly questionable (Filipek et al., 2000).

Compiling the history must include participation of family members. Once the history has been collected and a formulation prepared, the interpretation must permit parent and family members to raise concerns about the findings and discuss their implications. This, too, is a process that unfolds over time and requires supplemental meetings to reiterate the formulation, correct misunderstandings, and refine the prognosis and plans for the patient. Misconceptions and distortions beset the cause and treatment of PDD-NOS. Parents and family members have the best opportunity to discuss their fears and doubts in an atmosphere of candor and compassion. The opportunity to explore their fears and hopes permits the family to approach treatments that are consistent with the child's optimal requirements and the family's basic values, beliefs, and capacities. It also facilitates the family's collaboration with the wider environment that includes the extended family, community, and school system.

Appropriate treatment rests on a foundation of educational instruction that relates to the patient's capacities and limitations. The educational curriculum should assure that there is adequate emphasis on objectives related to language and social skills development. However, each child is different; each one possesses particular skills and requires interventions aimed toward specific maladaptive behaviors. This individuality demands a tailored program conducted by teachers who are experienced in the education of students with developmental delays. Ordinarily, it is appropriate to integrate language and social skills training into a unitary program of instruction that includes achievement of academic skills. Such an integrated approach facilitates the child's ability to generalize language and social skills across settings, persons, and situations. In contrast to the traditional resource room or "pull-out" methods used to assist children with specific learning or speech/language disorders, the integrated classroom model provides children with PDD opportunities to practice skills across a variety of domains in the same setting with the same people. This reduces the number of novel persons, experiences, and settings to which the child must become accustomed.

There are no generalizable guidelines on classroom assignments and classmate mixtures. Some children benefit most from being placed in classrooms with ordinary children. Others cannot manage without the consistent specialized instruction that comes from full-time assignment to special programs in contained classrooms with small classes. Still others learn best from a mix of mainstream and specialized classroom placements. The tendency to assign children based on their highest or lowest functional domain tends to obscure their specific needs. Therefore a child with good academic progress may still require the support and skills of a specialized classroom setting, while a lower functioning child might do well in a mainstream remedial class for some topics, or mainstream in nonacademic areas.

Cognitive and behavioral methods are the most investigated and commonly used interventions in the treatment of autistic individuals and likely are applicable across the spectrum of PDD conditions. They have been directed toward decreasing self-injury, perseverative behaviors, and other behaviors that impede social interaction. They have also been implemented to promote social competence and relating (Mesibov, 1984). An example of the application of these methods is the Treatment and Education of Autistic and Related Communication Handicapped CHildren (TEACCH) program in North Carolina (Schopler, 1994). As defined by Schopler, a primary aim of the program is to improve skill levels in socialization and communication. This is achieved through manipulation of the environment in an effort to accommodate the child's deficit. These can be integrated successfully into a school curriculum and reinforced at home and in other social settings. Alternative approaches attempt to increase social interaction indirectly by increasing language learning (Lovaas, 1987). This is achieved by modifying the child's behavior using parents or hired assistants as therapists in intensive one-on-one teaching sessions (Lovaas, 1987). Use of cognitive techniques has been applied to teaching imaginative play and toward efforts to have children understand "other minds" in false belief paradigms. The development of prosocial behaviors may have enduring effects that will influence adaptation in adulthood (Mesibov, 1983). However, it remains to be demonstrated that these interventions improve social functioning in spontaneous interaction or increase motivation for social interaction (Bowler, 1992; Rutter & Bailey, 1993).

Pharmacotherapy can play a useful role in the treatment of PDD-NOS and has been reviewed recently elsewhere (Towbin, 2003) and in this *Handbook* (see Chapter 44). There is no specific agent or class of agents that can affect the core deficit of PDD-NOS nor one that is useful generically for every symptom that may arise. Nevertheless, specific symptoms may be responsive to particular agents (Towbin, 2003). Assessment of the symptoms rather than the diagnoses presented by a patient becomes much more critical in making decisions about pharmacological intervention (Towbin, 2003). Frequent symptoms that lead patients or their families to consider pharmacological interventions include aggressive or self-injurious behaviors; repetitive stereotypic behaviors; hyperkinesis, inattention, and distractibility; emotional lability; withdrawal; or extreme tantruming.

Self-injury is one of the most troubling symptoms that patients display. These injuries may be related to compulsive or repetitive stereotypical patterns of behavior (Zubieta & Alessi, 1993). Atypical neuroleptic agents have been employed for the treatment of self-injurious behaviors (Barnard, Young, Pearson, Geddes, & O'Brien, 2002; McCracken et al., 2002). Case reports and small studies suggested that naltrexone might be useful in some patients (Leboyer, Bouvard, & Dugas, 1988; Sandman, Barron, & Colman, 1990), but attempts to replicate efficacy in controlled trials have been unsuccessful. Some even suggest naltrexone may be harmful (Campbell et al., 1993; Willemsen-Swinkels, Buitelaar, Nijhof, & van Engeland, 1995). There is no simple formula for the management of these symptoms. There is some evidence that selective serotonergic reuptake inhibitor (SSRI) agents, such as clorimipramine, fluvoxamine, and sertraline, may be helpful (McDougle, Price, & Volkmar, 1994). The SSRIs may also be useful for treating extreme inflexibility in those with PDDs. Tantruming in response to changes in routine or the presence of novel stimuli would be another indication for these agents.

Symptoms of hyperactivity, inattention, and distractibility may respond to stimulant agents (Birmaher, Quintana, & Greenhill, 1988; Handen, Johnson, & Lubetsky, 2000; Quintana et al., 1995). However, there may be a greater risk of adverse reactions to stimulants in PDD patients (Handen et al., 2000) than in children with ADHD. Some studies suggest this may not be the case (Quintana et al., 1995), and further study is warranted.

Children with PDD-NOS who are aggressive may receive benefit from atypical neuroleptic agents (Barnard et al., 2002) such as risperidone (McCracken et al., 2002), ziprasidone (McDougle, Kem, & Posey, 2002), lithium (Steingard & Biederman, 1987), valproate, carbamazepine, SSRIs (Zubieta & Alessi, 1993), or propranolol (Ratey et al., 1987). There is some suggestion that trazodone may be useful as well (Zubieta & Alessi, 1992). Disorganization, agitation, and aggression may respond to neuroleptics although one wants to minimize the dosage and total duration of treatment with agents like haloperidol and pimozide (Perry et al., 1989).

Approaching pharmacological treatment for PDD-NOS requires exceptional care and thoroughness (Towbin, 2003). Individuals with PDD-NOS are a particularly vulnerable patient population; they often have difficulty reporting side effects and identifying their fears and worries about medication. As a group, they are more susceptible to misapplication of medications for extended periods. Safeguarding their care requires thoughtful consideration and painstaking technique, and it is necessary to move through pharmacological treatment patiently and steadily. This requires attention to symptom targets, vigilant tracking of responses, administration of sufficient doses over an adequate duration for each agent, and the limiting of polypharmacy to a minimum as much as possible (Towbin, 2003).

Reassessment and attending to areas of strength are keystones of responsible care. Although the deficits of PDD-NOS appear to be stable over time, persons who have PDD-NOS do grow and develop. As they do, the nature and severity of their symptoms and limitations change. Educational regulations require periodic reevaluation of the child's academic progress. These should also serve as reminders for reevaluation of the patient's overall development and symptom profile. Reassessment of developmental and adaptive functioning are important for correcting unwanted side effects of therapeutic interventions or symptomatic misinterpretations that have become clearer since initial diagnosis and planning. This is particularly important if plans were laid when the child was young or had very limited verbal capacities. Repeated psychological and developmental assessments should be conducted routinely, perhaps at 2- to 3-year intervals.

SUMMARY

A review of PDD-NOS reveals that some gains have been made in the past decade in the nature of PDD-NOS and its biological implications. At this point, there are several avenues for moving the field ahead. Foremost is that the diagnostic entity of PDD-NOS must be sustained. Only by maintaining PDD-NOS will the field allow for further characterization and research that can move us toward a better understanding of the basic neuroscience, course, and treatments that pertain to individuals with these disorders.

The field is also in a better position to make more specific recommendations about the diagnosis of PDD-NOS. For research purposes, it would be helpful to have a consensus about how a benchmark instrument like the ADI-R and ADOS-G could be used to make reliable diagnosis of PDD-NOS.

More work is needed to reach a consensus about operational definitions for clinical use,

like those worked out for Autistic disorder, but it is possible to make specific statements about when the diagnosis is appropriate and when it is not. PDD-NOS should continue to be used when social deficits are a prominent, impairing feature of the clinical picture. The correction to the text in *DSM-IV-TR* has served to emphasize that social deficits are necessary for PDD-NOS. There is general agreement that this means using *DSM-IV* Group A-1 Criteria or their equivalent from *ICD-10*. Thus, individuals without social deficits but with other features of PDD, such as those with only specific language impairment or with SLI and stereotyped movements should not be diagnosed with PDD-NOS. Also, the impairment criterion is crucial, particularly for establishing a boundary between relative weaknesses that properly fall within the broader autism phenotype (BAP) rather than PDDs.

There is an emerging consensus that an adaptation of the Autistic disorder DSM criteria could serve as a rough guide to making the diagnosis of PDD-NOS. Implications from the proposals from Buitelaar and coworkers (1998), or Walker and coworkers (2004) are that (after excluding all other PDD disorders) a total of at least three *DSM-IV* Autistic disorder symptoms, at least one of which must be in the social impairment (Group A-I) cluster, might form a template for future PDD-NOS research. In addition, this guideline would omit the criterion for age of onset.

Careful research still must answer myriad questions, many of them absolutely basic. Among the most important are explorations of the continuity and demarcations within the wider spectrum of PDD. Longitudinal studies of the course and prognosis of a well-characterized cohort of children with PDD-NOS would be an extremely valuable contribution. Similarly, studies that compare high- and low-functioning PDD spectrum children should employ prospective longitudinal designs. In addition, we need to understand more about the relationship between symptoms and physiology. Further work is needed to identify markers that relate to genetic endowment ("endophenotypes"). These might stem from neurophysiological, functional magnetic resonance imaging, or neuropsychological studies, such as those relying on facial recognition (Baron-Cohen, Wheelwright, Hill,

Raste, & Plumb, 2001; Schultz et al., 2000), eye gaze (Klin, Jones, Schultz, Volkmar, & Cohen 2002), auditory social recognition (Rutherford, Baron-Cohen, & Wheelwright, 2002), or neuropsychological performance (Dawson, Webb, et al., 2002). In each case, validation of these tasks demands that they be applied across the continuum of PDDs.

Genetic studies hold out the hope of learning how core autism might be related to high-functioning autism, Asperger syndrome, and milder PDD conditions. In particular, genetic studies that ascertain PDD-NOS probands and employ state-of-the-art family study methods are needed. The relationships between multiple complex developmental disorder, other PDD conditions, and schizophrenia are an additional fruitful research area (McCellan & Werry, 1994). Carefully crafted epidemiological investigations will bring us closer to understanding the prevalence of these conditions and highlight the breadth of treatment and educational needs. Effective treatments such as cognitive approaches, social skills training, pharmacological agents, and educational modifications continue to be indispensable for higher functioning individuals in this group.

Overall, clinicians continue to be better informed and able to diagnose and treat higher functioning PDD disorders than ever before. New treatments and clearer definitions have provided opportunities for patients previously viewed as merely idiosyncratic to be understood in a more constructive and positive way. Kanner's articulation promoted sensitivity to those with autism. Now those with higher functioning PDDs may benefit from thoughtful interdisciplinary approaches. Modern educational models, cognitive strategies, pharmacotherapies, and social skills training that have been offered to those with autism can be extended to others who may have even better prognoses. Instead of being seen as treatment refractory, psychotic, conduct disordered, or oppositional, there are now opportunities to place the symptoms of those with higher functioning PDDs into a developmental and social-emotional context and to consider each individual's potential. This process highlights treatments that are most likely to be helpful and focuses the efforts of those who teach or treat these individuals. It

promotes understanding and compassion for the complex social, emotional, and cognitive symptoms experienced by those with PDD-NOS. For those closest to individuals with PDD-NOS, such knowledge also provides a coherent framework and creates an opportunity for collaboration in their pursuit to find help for their loved ones.

Cross-References

Specific diagnostic concepts are discussed in Chapters 1 to 5, longitudinal and follow-up studies in Chapter 7, assessment issues are reviewed in Chapters 27 to 32, behavioral interventions are discussed in Chapters 32 and 35, and pharmacological issues reviewed in Chapter 44.

REFERENCES

Adams, C., & Bishop, D. V. (1989). Conversational characteristics of children with semantic-pragmatic disorder: Part I. Exchange structure, turntaking, repairs and cohesion. *British Journal of Disorders of Communication, 24*(3), 211–239.

Alaghband-Rad, J., McKenna, K., Gordon, C. T., Albus, K. E., Hamburger, S. D., Rumsey, J. M., et al. (1995). Childhood-onset schizophrenia: The severity of premorbid course. *Journal of the American Academy of Child and Adolescent Psychiatry, 34*(10), 1273–1283.

Allen, D. A., Steinberg, M., Dunn, M., Fein, D., Feinstein, C., Waterhouse, L., et al. (2001). Autistic disorder versus other pervasive developmental disorders in young children: Same or different? *European Child and Adolescent Psychiatry, 10*(1), 67–78.

Asperger, H. (1944). Autistic psychopathy in childhood (U. Frith, Trans.). In U. Frith (Ed.), *Autism and Asperger syndrome* (pp. 37–92). Cambridge, England: Cambridge University Press.

Asperger, H. (1979). Problems of infantile autism. *Communication, 13,* 45–52.

Bagwell, C. L., Molina, B. S., Pelham, W. E., Jr., & Hoza, B. (2001). Attention-deficit hyperactivity disorder and problems in peer relations: Predictions from childhood to adolescence. *Journal of the American Academy of Child and Adolescent Psychiatry, 40*(11), 1285–1292.

Bailey, A., Le Couteur, A., Gottesman, I., Bolton, P., Simonoff, E., Yuzda, E., et al. (1995). Autism as a strongly genetic disorder: Evidence from a

British twin study. *Psychological Medicine, 25*(1), 63–77.

Barnard, L., Young, A. H., Pearson, J., Geddes, J., & O'Brien, G. (2002). A systematic review of the use of atypical antipsychotics in autism. *Journal Psychopharmacology, 16*(1), 93–101.

Baron-Cohen, S., Leslie, A. M., & Frith, U. (1985). Does the autistic child have a "theory of mind"? *Cognition, 21*(1), 37–46.

Baron-Cohen, S., Tager-Flusberg, H., & Cohen, D. J. (1993). *Understanding other minds: Perspectives from autism.* Oxford, England: Oxford Medical Publications.

Baron-Cohen, S., Wheelwright, S., Hill, J., Raste, Y., & Plumb, I. (2001). The "Reading the Mind in the Eyes" Test revised version: A study with normal adults, and adults with Asperger syndrome or high-functioning autism. *Journal of Child Psychology and Psychiatry, 42*(2), 241–251.

Beaumanoir, A. (1992). The Landau-Kleffner syndrome. In J. Roger, M. Bureau, F. E. Dravet, A. Dreyfus, A. Perret, & P. Wolf (Eds.), *Epileptic syndromes in infancy, childhood, and adolescence* (2nd ed., pp. 231–243). London: Libbey.

Beckett, C., Bredenkamp, D., Castle, J., Groothues, C., O'Connor, T. G., & Rutter, M. (2002). Behavior patterns associated with institutional deprivation: A study of children adopted from Romania. *Journal of Developmental and Behavioral Pediatrics, 23*(5), 297–303.

Beidel, D. C. (1991). Social phobia and overanxious disorder in school age children. *Journal of the American Academy of Child and Adolescent Psychiatry, 30,* 545–552.

Bender, L. (1946). Childhood schizophrenia. *American Journal of Orthopsychiatry, 17,* 40–56.

Bertrand, J., Mars, A., Boyle, C., Bove, F., Yeargin-Allsopp, M., & Decoufle, P. (2001). Prevalence of autism in a United States population: The Brick Township, New Jersey, investigation. *Pediatrics, 108*(5), 1155–1161.

Birmaher, B., Quintana, H., & Greenhill, L. (1988). Methylphenidate treatment of hyperactive autistic children. *Journal of the American Academy of Child Psychiatry, 27,* 248–251.

Bishop, D. V. (1989). Autism, Asperger's syndrome, and pragmatic semantic disorder: Where are the boundaries? *British Journal of Disorders of Communication, 24,* 107–121.

Bishop, D. V. (2000). Pragmatic language impairment: A correlate of SLIA, distinct subgroup or part of the autistic continuum? In D. V. Bishop & L. B. Leonard (Eds.), *Speech and language impairments in children: Causes characteristics, intervention and outcome* (pp. 99–114). Philadelphia: Taylor & Francis.

Bishop, D. V. (2002). Motor immaturity and specific speech and language impairment: Evidence for a common genetic basis. *American Journal of Medical Genetics, 114*(1), 56–63.

Bishop, D. V., & Adams, C. (1989). Conversational characteristics of children with semantic-pragmatic disorder: Part II. What features lead to a judgement of inappropriacy? *British Journal of Disorders of Communication, 24*(3), 241–263.

Bishop, D. V., & Norbury, C. F. (2002). Exploring the borderlands of autistic disorder and specific language impairment: A study using standardised diagnostic instruments. *Journal of Child Psychology and Psychiatry, 43*(7), 917–929.

Bloom, F. E. (1993). Advancing a neurodevelopmental etiology for schizophrenia. *Archives of General Psychiatry, 50,* 224–227.

Bolton, P., Macdonald, H., Pickles, A., Rios, P., Goode, S., Crowson, M., et al. (1994). A case-control family history study of autism. *Journal of Child Psychology and Psychiatry, 35*(5), 877–900.

Bowler, D. M. (1992). "Theory of mind" in Asperger's syndrome. *Journal of Child Psychology and Psychiatry, 33*(5), 877–893.

Bregman, J. D. (1991). Current developments in the understanding of mental retardation. Part II: Psychopathology. *Journal of the American Academy of Child and Adolescent Psychiatry, 30*(6), 861–872.

Brook, S. L., & Bowler, D. M. (1992). Autism by another name? Semantic and pragmatic impairments in children. *Journal of Autism and Developmental Disorders, 22*(1), 61–81.

Bryson, S. E., Clark, B. S., & Smith, I. M. (1988). First report of a Canadian epidemiological study of autistic syndromes. *Journal of Child Psychology and Psychiatry, 29,* 433–445.

Buitelaar, J. K., & van der Gaag, R. J. (1998). Diagnostic rules for children with PDD-NOS and multiple complex developmental disorder. *Journal of Child Psychology and Psychiatry, 39*(6), 911–919.

Buitelaar, J. K., van der Wees., M., Swaab-Barneveld, H., & van der Gaag, R. J. (1999). Verbal memory and performance IQ predict theory of mind and emotion recognition ability in children with autistic spectrum disorders and in psychiatric control children. *Journal of Child Psychology and Psychiatry, 40*(6), 869–881.

Campbell, M., Anderson, L. T., Small, A. M., Adams, P., Gonzalez, N. M., & Ernst, M. (1993). Naltrexone in autistic children: Behavioral symptoms and attentional learning.

Journal of the American Academy of Child and Adolescent Psychiatry, 32, 1283–1291.

Cannon, M., Caspi, A., Moffitt, T. E., Harrington, H., Taylor, A., Murray, R. M., et al. (2002). Evidence for early-childhood, pan-developmental impairment specific to schizophreniform disorder: Results from a longitudinal birth cohort. *Archives of General Psychiatry, 59*(5), 449–456.

Cantwell, D. P., & Rutter, M. (1994). Classification: Conceptual issues and substantive findings. In M. Rutter, E. Taylor, & L. Hersov (Eds.), *Child and adolescent psychiatry: A modern approach* (3rd ed., pp. 3–21). London: Blackwell.

Caplan, R. (1994). Childhood schizophrenia assessment and treatment: A developmental approach. *Child and Adolescent Psychiatry Clinics of North America, 3*(1), 15–30.

Caron, M. J., Mottron, L., Rainville, C., & Chouinard, S. (2004). Do high-functioning persons with autism present superior spatial abilities? *Neuropsychologia, 42*(4), 467–481.

Chakrabarti, S., & Fombonne, E. (2001). Pervasive developmental disorders in preschool children. *Journal of the American Medical Association, 285*(24), 3093–3099.

Cohen, P. R., & Volkmar, F. R. (1986). Issues in the classification of pervasive developmental disorders: Toward *DSM-IV. Journal of the American Academy of Child Psychiatry, 25,* 213–229.

Courchesne, E. (1995). New evidence of cerebellar and brainstem hyppoplasia in autistic infants, children and adolescents: The MR imaging study by Hashimoto and colleagues. *Journal of Autism and Developmental Disorders, 25*(1), 19–22.

Croen, L. A., Grether, J. K., Hoogstrate, J., & Selvin, S. (2002). The changing prevalence of autism in California. *Journal of Autism and Developmental Disorders, 32*(3), 207–215.

Crosbie, J., & Schachar, R. (2001). Deficient inhibition as a marker for familial ADHD. *American Journal of Psychiatry, 158*(11), 1884–1890.

Dahl, E. K., Cohen, D. J., & Provence, S. (1986). Clinical and multivariate approaches to the nosology of pervasive developmental disorders. *Journal of the American Academy of Child Psychiatry, 25*(2), 170–180.

Dawson, G., Carver, L., Meltzoff, A. N., Panagiotides, H., McPartland, J., & Webb, S. J. (2002). Neural correlates of face and object recognition in young children with autism spectrum disorder, developmental delay, and typical development. *Child Development, 73,* 700–717.

Dawson, G., Munson, J., Estes, A., Osterling, J., McPartland, J., Toth, K., et al. (2002). Neurocognitive function and joint attention ability in young children with autism spectrum disorder versus developmental delay. *Child Development, 73*(2), 345–358.

Dawson, G., Webb, S., Schellenberg, G. D., Dager, S., Friedman, S., Aylward, E., et al. (2002). Defining the broader phenotype of autism: Genetic, brain, and behavioral perspectives. *Development and Psychopathology, 14*(3), 581–611.

Despert, J. L., & Sherwin, A. C. (1958). Further examination of diagnostic criteria in schizophrenic illness and psychoses of infancy and early childhood. *American Journal of Psychiatry, 114,* 784–790.

Dykens, E., Volkmar, F., & Glick, M. (1991). Thought disorder in high-functioning autistic adults. *Journal of Autism and Developmental Disorders, 21*(3), 291–301.

Filipek, P. A., Accardo, P. J., Ashwal, S., Baranek, G. T., Cook, E. H., Jr., Dawson, G., et al. (2000). Practice parameter: Screening and diagnosis of autism: Report of the Quality Standards Subcommittee of the American Academy of Neurology and the Child Neurology Society. *Neurology, 55*(4), 468–479.

Fiona, J. S., Baron-Cohen, S., Bolton, P., & Brayne, C. (2002). Brief report: Prevalence of autism spectrum conditions in children aged 5–11 years in Cambridgeshire, U.K. *Autism, 6*(3), 231–237.

Fish, B., Marcus, J., Hans, S. L., Auerbach, J. G., & Perdue, S. (1992). Infants at risk for schizophrenia: Sequelae of a genetic neurointegrative defect. *Archives of General Psychiatry, 49,* 221–235.

Folstein, S., & Rutter, M. (1977). Infantile autism: A genetic study of 21 twin pairs. *Journal of Child Psychology and Psychiatry, 18,* 297–321.

Folstein, S., & Rutter, M. (1987). Autism: Familial aggregation and genetic implications. *Journal of Autism and Developmental Disorders, 18,* 3–29.

Fombonne, E. (2003). Epidemiological surveys of autism and other pervasive developmental disorders: An update. *Journal of Autism and Developmental Disorders, 33*(4), 365–382.

Fombonne, E., & Chakrabarti, S. (2001). No evidence for a new variant of measles-mumps-rubella-induced autism. *Pediatrics, 108*(4), E58.

Fraser, W. I., & Rao, J. M. (1991). Recent studies of mentally handicapped young people's behavior. *Journal of Child Psychology and Psychiatry, 32,* 79–108.

Frith, U. (2004). Emanuel Miller lecture: Confusions and controversies about Asperger syndrome. *Journal of Child Psychology and Psychiatry, 45*(4), 672–686.

Geller, B., Zimerman, B., Williams, M., Delbello, M. P., Bolhofner, K., Craney, J. L., et al. (2002). *DSM-IV* mania symptoms in a prepubertal and early adolescent bipolar disorder phenotype compared to attention-deficit hyperactive and normal controls. *Journal of Child and Adolescent Psychopharmacology, 12*(1), 11–25.

Ghaziuddin, M., Leininger, L., & Tsai, L. (1995). Brief report: Thought disorder in Asperger's syndrome: Comparison with high-functioning autism. *Journal of Autism and Developmental Disorders, 25*(3), 311–318.

Gilchrist, A., Green, J., Cox, A., Burton, D., Rutter, M., & Le Couteur, A. (2001). Development and current functioning in adolescents with Asperger syndrome: A comparative study. *Journal of Child Psychology and Psychiatry, 42*(2), 227–240.

Gillberg, C. (1991). Outcome in autism and autistic-like conditions. *Journal of the American Academy of Child and Adolescent Psychiatry, 30*(3), 375–382.

Gillberg, C. (1992). The Emanuel Miller Memorial Lecture 1991: Autism and autistic-like conditions: Subclasses among disorders of empathy. *Journal of Child Psychology and Psychiatry, 33,* 813–842.

Gillberg, C. (2003). Deficits in attention, motor control, and perception: A brief review. *Archives of Disease in Childhood, 88*(10), 904–910.

Gillberg, C., & Coleman, M. (1992). *The biology of autistic syndromes: Clinics in developmental medicine, Number 126* (2nd ed.). Oxford, England: Blackwell.

Gillberg, C., Persson, E., Grufman, M., & Themner, U. (1986). Psychiatric disorders in mildly and severely mentally retarded urban children and adolescents: Epidemiological aspects. *British Journal of Psychiatry, 149,* 68–74.

Gillberg, C., & Steffenburg, S. (1987). Outcome and prognostic factors in infantile autism and similar conditions: A population-based study of 46 cases followed through puberty. *Journal of Autism and Developmental Disorders, 17*(2), 273–287.

Gillberg, I. C., Gillberg, C., & Ahlsen, G. (1994). Autistic behavior and attention deficits in tuberous sclerosis: A population based survey. *Developmental Medicine and Child Neurology, 36,* 50–56.

Gillham, J. E., Carter, A. S., Volkmar, F. R., & Sparrow, S. S. (2000). Toward a developmental operational definition of autism. *Journal of Autism and Developmental Disorders, 30*(4), 269–278.

Gordon, C. T., Frazier, J. A., McKenna, K., Giedd, J., Zametkin, A., Zahn, T., et al. (1994). Childhood-onset schizophrenia: An NIMH study in progress. *Schizophrenia Bulletin, 20*(4), 697–712.

Greene, R. W., Biederman, J., Faraone, S. V., Monuteaux, M. C., Mick, E., DuPre, E. P., et al. (2001). Social impairment in girls with ADHD: Patterns, gender comparisons, and correlates. *Journal of the American Academy of Child and Adolescent Psychiatry, 40*(6), 704–710.

Handen, B. L., Johnson, C. R., & Lubetsky, M. (2000). Efficacy of methylphenidate among children with autism and symptoms of attention-deficit hyperactivity disorder. *Journal of Autism and Developmental Disorders, 30*(3), 245–255.

Hashimoto, T., Tayama, M., Murakawa, K., Yoshimoto, T., Miyazaki, M., Harada, M., et al. (1995). Development of the brainstem and cerebellum in autistic patients. *Journal of Autism and Developmental Disorders, 25*(1), 1–18.

Heller, T. (1908). Dementia infantilis. *Zeitschrift fur die Erforschung und Behandlung des Jugenlichen Schwachsinns (Journal of Research and Treatment of Children with Mental Retardation), 2* 141–165.

Hertzig, M., Snow, M. E., New, E., & Shapiro, T. (1990). *DSM-III* and *DSM-III-R* diagnosis of autism and pervasive developmental disorder in nursery school children. *Journal of the American Academy of Child and Adolescent Psychiatry, 29,* 123–126.

Howlin, P. (2001). Autistic features in Cohen syndrome: A preliminary report. *Developmental Medicine and Child Neurology, 43*(10), 692–696.

Howlin, P. (2003). Outcome in high-functioning adults with autism with and without early language delays: Implications for the differentiation between autism and Asperger syndrome. *Journal of Autism and Developmental Disorders, 33*(1), 3–13.

Itard, J. (1962). *The wild boy of Aveyron.* New York: Appleton-Century-Crofts.

Jansen, L. M., Gispen-de Wied, C. C., van der Gaag, R. J., ten Hove, F., Willemsen-Swinkels, S. W., Harteveld, E., et al. (2000). Unresponsiveness to psychosocial stress in a subgroup of autistic-like children, multiple complex developmental disorder. *Psychoneuroendocrinology, 25*(8), 753–764.

Jansen, L. M., Gispen-de Wied, C. C., Gademan, P. J., De Jonge, R. C., van der Linden, J. A., & Kahn, R. S. (1998). Blunted cortisol response to a psychosocial stressor in schizophrenia. *Schizophrenia Research, 33*(1/2), 87–94.

Jansen, L. M., Gispen-de Wied, C. C., van der Gaag, R. J., & van Engeland, H. (2003). Differentiation between autism and multiple complex developmental disorder in response to psychosocial stress. *Neuropsychopharmacology, 28*(3), 582–590.

Jensen, V. K., Larrieu, J. A., & Mack, K. K. (1997). Differential diagnosis between attention-deficit/hyperactivity disorder and pervasive developmental disorder: Not otherwise specified. *Clinical Pediatrics, 36*(10), 555–561.

Jones, M. B., & Szatmari, P. (2002). A risk-factor model of epistatic interaction, focusing on autism. *American Journal of Medical Genetics, 114*(5), 558–565.

Kadesjo, B., & Gillberg, C. (1999). Developmental coordination disorder in Swedish 7-year-old children. *Journal of the American Academy of Child and Adolescent Psychiatry, 38*(7), 820–828.

Kanner, L. (1943). Autistic disturbances of affective contact. *Nervous Child, 2,* 217–250.

Kemner, C., van der Gaag, R. J., Verbaten, M. N., & van Engeland, H. (1999). ERP differences among subtypes of pervasive developmental disorders. *Biological Psychiatry, 46*(6), 781–789.

Kestenbaum, C. (1983). The borderline child at risk for major psychiatric disorder in adult life: Seven case reports with follow-up. In K. Robson (Ed.), *The borderline child: Approaches to etiology, diagnosis, and treatment* (pp. 49–81). New York: McGraw-Hill.

Klin, A., Jones, W., Schultz, R., Volkmar, F., & Cohen, D. (2002). Visual fixation patterns during viewing of naturalistic social situations as predictors of social competence in individuals with autism. *Archives of General Psychiatry, 59*(9), 809–816.

Klin, A., & Shepard, B. A. (1994). Psychological assessment of autistic children. *Child and Adolescent Psychiatry Clinics of North America, 3*(1), 53–70.

Klin, A., Sparrow, S. S., de Bildt, A., Cicchetti, D. V., Cohen, D. J., & Volkmar, F. R. (1999). A normed study of face recognition in autism and related disorders. *Journal of Autism and Developmental Disorders, 29*(6), 499–508.

Klin, A., Volkmar, F. V., & Sparrow, S. S. (1992). Autistic social dysfunction: Some limitations of the theory of mind hypothesis. *Journal of Child Psychology and Psychiatry, 33,* 861–876.

Klin, A., Volkmar, F. V., Sparrow, S. S., Ciccehetti, D. V., & Rourke, B. P. (1995). Validity and neuropsycholgical characterization of Asperger Syndrome: Convergence with Nonverbal Learning Disabilities Syndrome. *Journal of Child Psychology and Psychiatry, 36,* 1127–1140.

Kolvin, I. (1971). Studies in the childhood psychoses: Part I. Diagnostic criteria and classification. *British Journal of Psychiatry, 118,* 381–384.

Kurita, H. (1997). A comparative study of Asperger syndrome with high-functioning atypical autism. *Psychiatry and Clinical Neurosciences 51*(2), 67–70.

Landa, R., Piven, J., Wzorek, M. M., Gayle, J. O., Chase, G. A., & Folstein, S. E. (1992). Social language use in parents of autistic individuals. *Psychological Medicine, 22*(1), 245–254.

Lauritsen, M. B., Mors, O., Mortensen, P. B., & Ewald, H. (2002). Medical disorders among inpatients with autism in Denmark according to *ICD-8:* A nationwide register-based study. *Journal of Autism and Developmental Disorders, 32*(2), 115–119.

Leboyer, M., Bouvard, M. P., & Dugas, M. (1988). Effects of naltrexone on infantile autism. *Lancet, 26,* 715.

Le Couteur, A., Bailey, A., Goode, S., Pickles, A., Robertson, S., Gottesman, I., et al. (1996). A broader phenotype of autism: The clinical spectrum in twins. *Journal of Child Psychology and Psychiatry, 37*(7), 785–801.

Leibenluft, E., Charney, D. S., Towbin, K. E., Bhangoo, R. K., & Pine, D. S. (2003). Defining clinical phenotypes of juvenile mania. *American Journal of Psychiatry, 160*(3), 430–437.

Lincoln, A. J., Bloom, D., Katz, M., & Boksenbaum, N. (1998). Neuropsychological and neurophysiological indices of auditory processing impairment in children with multiple complex developmental disorder. *Journal of the American Academy of Child and Adolescent Psychiatry, 37*(1), 100–112.

Lofgren, D. P., Bemporad, J., King, J., Lindem, K., & O'Driscoll, G. (1991). A prospective follow-up study of so-called borderline children. *American Journal of Psychiatry, 148*(11), 1541–1547.

Lord, C. (1995). Follow-up of two-year-olds referred for possible autism. *Journal of Child Psychology and Psychiatry, 36*(8), 1365–1382.

Lord, C., Leventhal, B. L., & Cook, E. H., Jr. (2001). Quantifying the phenotype in autism spectrum disorders. *American Journal of Medical Genetics, 105*(1), 36–38.

Lord, C., Risi, S., Lambrecht, L., Cook, E. H., Jr., Leventhal, B. L., DiLavore, P. C., et al. (2000). The autism diagnostic observation schedule-generic: A standard measure of social and communication deficits associated with the spectrum of autism. *Journal of Autism and Developmental Disorders, 30*(3), 205–223.

Lovaas, O. I. (1987). Behavioral treatment and normal intellectual and educational functioning in young autistic children. *Journal of Consulting and Clinical Psychology, 55,* 3–9.

Luteijn, E. F., Serra, M., Jackson, S., Steenhuis, M. P., Althaus, M., Volkmar, F., et al. (2000). How unspecified are disorders of children with a pervasive developmental disorder not otherwise specified? A study of social problems in children with PDD-NOS and ADHD. *European Child and Adolescent Psychiatry, 9*(3), 168–179.

Macintosh, K. E., & Dissanayake, C. (2004). Annotation: The similarities and differences between autistic disorder and Asperger's disorder: A review of the empirical evidence. *Journal of Child Psychology and Psychiatry, 45*(3), 421–434.

MacLean, J. E., Szatmari, P., Jones, M. B., Bryson, S. E., Mahoney, W. J., Bartolucci, G., et al. (1999). Familial factors influence level of functioning in pervasive developmental disorder. *Journal of the American Academy of Child and Adolescent Psychiatry, 38*(6), 746–753.

Mahoney, W. J., Szatmari, P., Maclean, J. E., Bryson, S. E., Bartolucci, G., Walter, S. D., et al. (1998). Reliability and accuracy of differentiating pervasive developmental disorder subtypes. *Journal of the American Academy of Child and Adolescent Psychiatry, 37,* 278–285.

Malhotra, S., & Gupta, N. (2002). Childhood disintegrative disorder: Re-examination of the current concept. *European Child and Adolescent Psychiatry, 11*(3), 108–114.

Manjiviona, J., & Prior, M. R. (1995). Comparison of Asperger's syndrome and high-functioning autistic children on a test of motor impairment. *Journal of Autism and Developmental Disorders, 25*(1), 23–40.

Mannuzza, S., Schneier, F. R., Chapman, T. F., Liebowitz, M. R., Klein, D. F., & Fyer, A. J. (1995). Generalized social phobia. *Archives of General Psychiatry, 52,* 230–237.

Matthys, W., Cuperus, J. M., & van Engeland, H. (1999). Deficient social problem solving in boys with ODD/CD, with ADHD, and with both disorders. *Journal of the American Academy of Child and Adolescent Psychiatry, 38*(3), 311–321.

McCellan, J., & Werry, J. (1994). Practice parameters for the assessment and treatment of children and adolescents with schizophrenia. *Journal of the American Academy of Child and Adolescent Psychiatry, 33*(5), 616–635.

McCracken, J. T., McGough, J., Shah, B., Cronin, P., Hong, D., Aman, M. G., et al. (2002). Risperidone in children with autism and serious behavioral problems. *New England Journal of Medicine, 347*(5), 314–321.

McDougle, C. J., Kem, D. L., & Posey, D. J. (2002). Use of ziprasidone for maladaptive symptoms in youths with autism. *Journal of the American Academy of Child and Adolescent Psychiatry, 41,* 921–927.

McDougle, C. J., Kresch, L. E., Goodman, W. K., Naylor, S. T., Volkmar, F. R., Cohen, D. J., et al. (1995). A case-controlled study of repetitive thoughts and behavior in adults with autistic disorder and obsessive-compulsive disorder. *American Journal of Psychiatry, 152*(5), 772–777.

McDougle, C. J., Price, L. H., & Volkmar, F. R. (1994). Recent advances in the pharmacotherapy of autism and related conditions. *Child and Adolescent Psychiatry Clinics of North America, 3*(1), 71–89.

McKenna, K., Gordon, C. T., Lenane, M., Kaysen, D., Fahey, K., & Rapoport, J. L. (1994). Looking for childhood onset schizophrenia: The first 71 cases screened. *Journal of the American Academy of Child and Adolescent Psychiatry, 33,* 636–644.

Mesibov, G. B. (1983). Current perspectives and issues in autism and adolescence. In E. Schopler & G. B. Mesibov (Eds.), *Autism in adolescents and adults* (pp. 37–53). New York: Plenum Press.

Mesibov, G. B. (1984). Social skills training with verbal autistic adolescents and adults: A program model. *Journal of Autism and Developmental Disorders, 14,* 395–404.

Micali, N., Chakrabarti, S., & Fombonne, E. (2004). The broad autism phenotype: Findings from an epidemiological survey. *Autism, 8*(1), 21–37.

Milberger, S., Faraone, S. V., Biederman, J., Testa, M., & Tsuang, M. T. (1996). New phenotype definition of attention deficit hyperactivity disorder in relatives for genetic analyses. *American Journal of Medical Genetics, 67*(4), 369–377.

Miller, J. N., & Ozonoff, S. (2000). The external validity of Asperger disorder: Lack of evidence from the domain of neuropsychology. *Journal of Abnormal Psychology, 109*(2), 227–238.

Minshew, N. J. (2001). Editorial preface. *Journal of Autism and Developmental Disorders, 31*(1), 1–3.

Minshew, N. J., Sweeney, J., & Luna, B. (2002). Autism as a selective disorder of complex information processing and underdevelopment of neocortical systems. *Molecular Psychiatry, 7*(Suppl 2), S14–S15.

Nicholson, R., Lenane, M., Brookner, F., Gochman, P., Kumra, S., Spechler, L., et al. (2001). Children and adolescents with psychotic disorder not otherwise specified: A 2-to 8-year follow-up study. *Comprehensive Psychiatry, 42*(4), 319–325.

Noterdaeme, M., Amorosa, H., Mildenberger, K., Sitter, S., & Minow, F. (2001). Evaluation of attention problems in children with autism and children with a specific language disorder. *European Child and Adolescent Psychiatry, 10*(1), 58–66.

O'Connor, T. G., Rutter, M., Beckett, C., Keaveney, L., & Kreppner, J. M. (2000). The effects of global severe privation on cognitive competence: Extension and longitudinal follow-up: English and Romanian adoptees study team. *Child Development, 71*(2), 376–390.

Ozonoff, S., & Miller, J. N. (1995). Teaching theory of mind: A new approach to social skills training for individuals with autism. *Journal of Autism and Developmental Disorders, 25,* 415–434.

Perry, R. (1998). Misdiagnosed ADD/ADHD: Rediagnosed PDD. *Journal of the American Academy of Child and Adolescent Psychiatry, 37*(1), 113–114.

Perry, R., Campbell, M., Adams, P. I., Lynch, N., Spencer, E. K., Curen, E. L., et al. (1989). Long-term efficacy of haloperidol in autistic children: Continuous versus discontinuous drug administration. *Journal of the American Academy of Child and Adolescent Psychiatry, 28,* 87–92.

Pfiffner, L. J., Calzada, E., & McBurnett, K. (2000). Interventions to enhance social competence. *Child and Adolescent Psychiatric Clinics of North America, 9*(3), 689–709.

Pickup, G. J., & Frith, C. D. (2001). Theory of mind impairments in schizophrenia: Symptomatology, severity and specificity. *Psychological Medicine, 31*(2), 207–220.

Piggot, J., Kwon, H., Mobbs, D., Blasey, C., Lotspeich, L., Menon, V., et al. (2004). Emotional attribution in high-functioning individuals with Autistic Spectrum Disorder: A functional imaging study. *Journal of the American Academy of Child and Adolescent Psychiatry, 43*(4), 473–480.

Pilowsky, T., Yirmiya, N., Arbelle, S., & Mozes, T. (2000). Theory of mind abilities of children with schizophrenia, children with autism, and normally developing children. *Schizophrenia Research, 42*(2), 145–155.

Piven, J., Chase, G., Landa, R., Wzorek, M., Gayle, J., Cloud, D., et al. (1991). Psychiatric disorders in parents of autistic individuals. *Journal of the American Academy of Child and Adolescent Psychiatry, 30*(3), 471–478.

Piven, J., Gayle, J., Chase, G. A., Fink, B., Landa, R., Wzorek, M. M., et al. (1990). A family study of neuropsychiatric disorders in the adult siblings of autistic individuals. *Journal of the American Academy of Child and Adolescent Psychiatry, 29,* 177–189.

Piven, J., & Palmer, P. (1997). Cognitive deficits in parents from multiple-incidence autism families. *Journal of Child Psychology and Psychiatry, 38*(8), 1011–1021.

Piven, J., & Palmer, P. (1999). Psychiatric disorder and the broad autism phenotype: Evidence from a family study of multiple-incidence autism families. *American Journal of Psychiatry, 156*(4), 557–563.

Piven, J., Palmer, P., Landa, R., Santangelo, S., Jacobi, D., & Childress, D. (1997). Personality and language characteristics in parents from multiple-incidence autism families. *American Journal of Medical Genetics, 25*(4), 398–411.

Prior, M. R. (1979). Cognitive abilities and disabilities in infantile autism: A review. *Journal of Abnormal Child Psychology, 7,* 357–380.

Prior, M. R., Eisenmajer, R., Leekam, S., Wing, L., Gould, J., Ong, B., et al. (1998). Are there subgroups within the autistic spectrum? A cluster analysis of a group of children with autistic spectrum disorders. *Journal of Child Psychology and Psychiatry, 39*(6), 893–902.

Quintana, H., Birmaher, B., Stedge, D., Lennon, S., Freed, J., Bridge, J., et al. (1995). Use of methylphenidate in treatment of children with autistic disorder. *Journal of Autism and Developmental Disorders, 25*(3), 283–295.

Rapin, I., & Allen, D. A. (1983). Developmental language disorders: Nosologic considerations. In U. Kirk (Ed.), *Neuropsychology of language, reading and spelling* (pp. 155–184). New York: Academic Press.

Ratey, J. J., Bemporad, J., Sorgi, P., Bick, P., Polatkoff, S., O'Driscoll, G., et al. (1987). Brief report: Open trial effects of beta-blockers on speech and social behaviors in 8 autistic adults. *Journal of Autism and Developmental Disorders, 17,* 439–446.

Reiss, A. L., Feinstein, C., Toomey, K. E., Goldsmith, B., Rosenbaum, K., & Caruso, M. A.

(1986). Psychiatric disability associated with the fragile X chromosome. *American Journal of Medical Genetics, 23,* 393–402.

Rescorla, L. A. (1986). Preschool psychiatric disorders: Diagnostic classification and symptom patterns. *Journal of the American Academy of Child Psychiatry, 25*(2), 162–169.

Richters, M. M., & Volkmar, F. R. (1994). Case study: Reactive attachment disorder of infancy or early childhood. *Journal of the American Academy of Child and Adolescent Psychiatry, 33*(3), 328–332.

Ritvo, E. R., Freeman, B. J., & Pingree, C. (1989). University of Utah epidemiological survey of autism: Prevalence. *American Journal of Psychiatry, 146,* 194–199.

Robertson, J. M., Tanguay, P. E., L'Ecuyer, S., Sims, A., & Waltrip, C. (1999). Domains of Social Communication Handicap in Autism Spectrum Disorder. *Journal of the American Academy of Child and Adolescent Psychiatry, 38,* 738–745.

Roeyers, H., Keymeulen, H., & Buysse, A. (1998, November/December). Differentiating attention-deficit/hyperactivity disorder from pervasive developmental disorder not otherwise specified. *Journal of Learning Disabilities, 31*(6), 565–571.

Rogers, S. J., & Pennington, B. F. (1991). A theoretical approach to the deficits in infantile autism. *Development and Psychopathology, 3,* 137–162.

Roy, P., Rutter, M., & Pickles, A. (2000). Institutional care: Risk from family background or pattern of rearing? *Journal of Child Psychology and Psychiatry, 41*(2), 139–149.

Rumsey, J. M., Andreasen, N., & Rapoport, J. L. (1986). Thought, language, communication, and affective flattening in autistic adults. *Archives of General Psychiatry, 43,* 771–777.

Rutherford, M. D., Baron-Cohen, S., & Wheelwright, S. (2002). Reading the mind in the voice: A study with normal adults and adults with Asperger syndrome and high-functioning autism. *Journal of Autism and Developmental Disorders, 32*(3), 189–194.

Rutter, M. L., Andersen-Wood, L., Beckett, C., Bredenkamp, D., Castle, J., Groothues, C., et al. (1999). Quasi-autistic patterns following severe early global privation: English and Romanian Adoptees (ERA) study team. *Journal of Child Psychology and Psychiatry, 40*(4), 537–549.

Rutter, M. L., & Bailey, A. (1993). Thinking and relationships: Mind and brain (some reflections on theory of mind and autism). In S. Baron-Cohen, H. Tager-Flusberg, & D. J. Cohen (Eds.), *Understanding other minds:*

Perspectives from autism (pp. 481–504). Oxford, England: Oxford Medical Publications.

Rutter, M., & Gould, M. (1985). Classification. In M. Rutter, & L. Hersov (Eds.), *Child and adolescent psychiatry: Modern approaches* (pp. 304–321). Oxford, England: Blackwell Scientific Publications.

Rutter, M. L., Kreppner, J. M., & O'Connor, T. G. (2001). Specificity and heterogeneity in children's responses to profound institutional privation. *British Journal of Psychiatry, 179,* 97–103.

Rutter, M., & Schopler, E. (1988). Autism and pervasive developmental disorders. In M. Rutter, A. H. Tuma, & I. S. Lann (Eds.), *Assessment and diagnosis in child psychopathology* (pp. 408–434). New York: Guilford Press.

Sandman, C. A., Barron, J. L., & Colman, H. (1990). An orally administered opiate blocker, naltrexone, attenuates self-injurious behavior. *American Journal of Mental Retardation, 95,* 93–102.

Schatz, J., & Hamdan-Allen, G. (1995). Effects of age and IQ on adaptive behavior domains for children with autism. *Journal of Autism and Developmental Disorders, 25,* 51–60.

Schopler, E. (1994). A statewide program for treatment and education of autistic and related communication handicapped children (TEACCH). *Child and Adolescent Psychiatry Clinics of North America, 3*(1), 91–103.

Schultz, R. T., Gauthier, I., Klin, A., Fulbright, R. K., Anderson, A. W., Volkmar, F., et al. (2000). Abnormal ventral temporal cortical activity during face discrimination among individuals with autism and Asperger syndrome. *Archives of General Psychiatry, 57*(4), 331–340.

Serra, M., Loth, F. L., van Geert, P. L., Hurkens, E., & Minderaa, R. B. (2002). Theory of mind in children with "lesser variants" of autism: A longitudinal study. *Journal of Child Psychology and Psychiatry, 43*(7), 885–900.

Serra, M., Minderaa, R. B., van Geert, P. L., & Jackson, A. E. (1999). Social-cognitive abilities in children with lesser variants of autism: Skill deficits or failure to apply skills? *European Child and Adolescent Psychiatry, 8*(4), 301–311.

Sigman, M., Ungerer, J. A., Mundy, P., & Sherman, T. (1987). Cognition in autistic children. In D. J. Cohen & A. M. Donnellan (Eds.), *Handbook of autism and pervasive developmental disorders* (pp. 103–120). New York: Wiley.

Silverstein, M. L., Mavrolefteros, G., & Close, D. (2002). Premorbid adjustment and neuropsychological performance in schizophrenia. *Schizophrenia Bulletin 28*(1), 157–165.

Smalley, S. L. (1998). Autism and tuberous sclerosis. *Journal of Autism and Developmental Disorders, 28*(5), 407–414.

Smalley, S. L., McCracken, J. T., & Tanguay, P. E. (1995). Autism, affective disorders, and social phobia. *American Journal of Medical Genetics, 60*(1), 19–26.

Sparks, B. F., Friedman, S. D., Shaw, D. W., Aylward, E. H., Echelard, D., Artru, A. A., et al. (2002). Brain structural abnormalities in young children with autism spectrum disorder. *Neurology, 59*(2), 184–192.

Sparrow, S. S., Rescorla, L. A., Provence, S., Condon, S. O., Goudreau, D., & Cicchetti, D. V. (1986). Follow-up of "atypical" children—A brief report. *Journal of the American Academy of Child Psychiatry, 25*(2), 181–185.

Spiker, D., Lotspeich, L. J., Dimiceli, S., Myers, R. M., & Risch, N. (2002). Behavioral phenotypic variation in autism multiplex families: Evidence for a continuous severity gradient. *American Journal of Medical Genetics, 114*(2), 129–136.

Spitzer, R., & Siegel, B. (1990). The *DSM-III-R* field trials of pervasive developmental disorders. *Journal of the American Academy of Child and Adolescent Psychiatry, 29,* 855–862.

Steffenburg, S., & Gillberg, C. (1986). Autism and autistic-like conditions in Swedish rural and urban areas: A population study. *British Journal of Psychiatry, 149,* 81–87.

Steingard, R., & Biederman, J. (1987). Lithium responsive manic like symptoms in two individuals with autism and mental retardation: Case report. *Journal of the American Academy of Child and Adolescent Psychiatry, 26,* 932–935.

Steinhausen, H., Gobel, D., Berinlinger, M., & Wohlleben, B. (1986). A community survey of infantile autism. *Journal of the American Academy of Child Psychiatry, 25*(2), 186–189.

Szatmari, P. (1997). Pervasive developmental disorder not otherwise specified. In T. A. Widiger, A. J. Frances, H. A. Pincus, R. Ross, M. B. First, & W. Davis (Eds.), *DSM-IV sourcebook* (Vol. 3, pp. 43–54). Washington, DC: American Psychiatric Press.

Szatmari, P., Bartolucci, G., Bremner, R. S., Bond, S., & Rich, S. (1989). A follow-up study of high-functioning autistic children. *Journal of Autism and Developmental Disorders, 19,* 213–225.

Szatmari, P., Bryson, S. E., Boyle, M. H., Streiner, D. L., & Duku, E. (2003). Predictors of outcome among high-functioning children with autism and Asperger syndrome. *Journal of Child Psychology and Psychiatry, 44*(4), 520–528.

Szatmari, P., MacLean, J. E., Jones, M. B., Bryson, S. E., Zwaigenbaum, L., Bartolucci, G., et al. (2000). The familial aggregation of the lesser variant in biological and nonbiological relatives of PDD probands: A family history study. *Journal of Child Psychology and Psychiatry, 41*(5), 579–586.

Szatmari, P., Merette, C., Bryson, S. E., Thivierge, J., Roy, M. A., Cayer, M., et al. (2002). Quantifying dimensions in autism: A factor-analytic study. *Journal of the American Academy of Child and Adolescent Psychiatry, 41*(4), 467–474.

Szatmari, P., Tuff, L., Finlayson, A. J., & Bartolucci, G. (1990). Asperger's syndrome and autism: Neurocognitive aspects. *Journal of the American Academy of Child and Adolescent Psychiatry, 29*(1), 130–136.

Tanguay, P. E., Robertson, J., & Derrick, A. (1998). A dimensional classification of autism spectrum disorder by social communication domains. *Journal of the American Academy of Child and Adolescent Psychiatry, 37*(3), 271–277.

Tantam, D. (1988a). Asperger's syndrome: Annotation. *Journal of Child Psychology and Psychiatry, 29,* 245–255.

Tantam, D. (1988b). Lifelong eccentricity and social isolation: II Asperger's syndrome or schizoid personality disorder? *British Journal of Psychiatry, 153,* 783–791.

Towbin, K. E. (1994). Pervasive developmental disorder not otherwise specified: A review and guidelines for clinical care. *Child and Adolescent Psychiatry Clinics of North America, 3*(1), 149–161.

Towbin, K. E. (2003). Strategies for pharmacologic treatment of high-functioning autism and Asperger syndrome. *Child and Adolescent Psychiatric Clinics of North America, 12*(1), 23–45.

Towbin, K. E., Dykens, E. D., Pearson, G. S., & Cohen, D. J. (1993). Conceptualizing "Borderline Syndrome of Childhood" and "Childhood Schizophrenia" as a developmental disorder. *Journal of the American Academy of Child and Adolescent Psychiatry, 32*(4), 775–782.

van der Gaag, R. J. (1993). *Multiplex development disorder: An exploration of the borderlines on the autistic spectrum.* Unpublished master's thesis, University of Utrecht, The Netherlands.

van der Gaag, R. J., Buitelaar, J. K., Van den Ban, E., Bezemer, M., Njio, L., & van Engeland, H. (1995). A controlled multivariate chart review of multiple complex developmental disorder. *Journal of the American Academy of Child and Adolescent Psychiatry, 34*(8), 1096–1106.

van der Geest, J. N., Kemner, C., Verbaten, M. N., & van Engeland, H. (2002). Gaze behavior of children with pervasive developmental disorder toward human faces: A fixation time study. *Journal of Child Psychology and Psychiatry, 43*(5), 669–678.

Velting, O. N., & Albano, A. M. (2001). Current trends in the understanding and treatment of social phobia in youth. *Journal of Child Psychology and Psychiatry, 42*(1), 127–140.

Venter, A., Lord, C., & Schopler, E. (1991). A follow-up study of high-functioning autistic children. *Journal of Child Psychology and Psychiatry, 33*(3), 489–507.

Volkmar, F. R., Carter, A., Sparrow, S. S., & Cicchetti, D. V. (1993). Quantifying social development in autism. *Journal of the American Academy of Child and Adolescent Psychiatry, 32,* 627–632.

Volkmar, F. R., & Cohen, D. J. (1988). Classification and diagnosis of childhood autism. In E. Schopler & G. B. Mesibov (Eds.), *Diagnosis and assessment in autism* (pp. 71–76). New York: Plenum Press.

Volkmar, F. R., & Cohen, D. J. (1989). Disintegrative disorder or "late onset" autism. *Journal of Child Psychology and Psychiatry, 30,* 717–724.

Volkmar, F. R., & Cohen, D. J. (1991). Comorbid association of autism and schizophrenia. *American Journal of Psychiatry, 148,* 1705–1707.

Volkmar, F. R., Klin, A., Siegel, B., Szatmari, P., Lord, C., Campbell, M., et al. (1994). Field trial for autistic disorder in *DSM-IV. American Journal of Psychiatry, 151,* 1361–1367.

Volkmar, F. R., & Rutter, M. (1995). Childhood disintegrative disorder: Results from the field trials for *DSM-IV. Journal of the American Academy of Child and Adolescent Psychiatry, 34,* 1092–1097.

Volkmar, F. R., Shaffer, D., & First, M. (2000). PDDNOS in *DSM-IV. Journal of Autism and Developmental Disorders, 30*(1), 74–75.

Volkmar, F. R., Steir, D., & Cohen, D. J. (1985). Age of onset of pervasive developmental disorder. *American Journal of Psychiatry, 142,* 1450–1452.

Walker, D. R., Thompson, A., Zwaigenbaum, L., Goldberg, J., Bryson, S. E., Mahoney, W. J., et al. (2004). Specifying PDD-NOS: A comparison of PDD-NOS, Asperger syndrome, and autism. *Journal of the American Academy of Child and Adolescent Psychiatry, 43*(2), 72–80.

Wang, A. T., Dapretto, M., Hariri, A., Sigman, M., & Bookheimer, S. (2004). Neural correlates of facial affect processing in children and adolescents with autism spectrum disorder. *Journal of the American Academy of Child and Adolescent Psychiatry, 43*(4), 481–490.

Wassink, T. H., Piven, J., & Patil, S. R. (2001). Chromosomal abnormalities in a clinic sample of individuals with autistic disorder. *Psychiatric Genetics, 11*(2), 57–63.

Watkins, J. M., Asarnow, R. F., & Tanguay, P. E. (1988). Symptom development in childhood-onset schizophrenia. *Journal of Child Psychology and Psychiatry, 29,* 865–878.

Werry, J. (1992). Child and adolescent (early onset) schizophrenia: A review in light of *DSM-III-R. Journal of Autism and Developmental Disorders, 22*(4), 601–624.

Willemsen-Swinkels, S. H. N., Buitelaar, J. K., Nijhof, G. J., & van Engeland, H. (1995). Failure of naltrexone hydrochloride to reduce self-injurious and autistic behavior in mentally retarded adults. *Archives of General Psychiatry, 52,* 766–773.

Wing, L. (1981). Asperger's syndrome: A clinical account. *Psychological Medicine, 11*(1), 115–129.

Wing, L. (1997). The autistic spectrum. *Lancet, 350*(9093), 1761–1766.

Wing, L. (1992). Manifestations of social problems in high-functioning autistic people. In E. Schopler & G. B. Mesibov (Eds.), *high-functioning individuals with autism* (pp. 129–142). New York: Plenum Press.

Wing, L., & Gould, J. (1979). Severe impairments in social interaction and associated abnormalities in children: Epidemiology and classification. *Journal of Autism and Developmental Disorders, 9,* 11–29.

Wittchen, H. U., & Fehm, L. (2001). Epidemiology, patterns of comorbidity, and associated disabilities of social phobia. *Psychiatric Clinics of North America, 24*(4), 617–641.

Wolff, S., & Chick, J. (1980). Schizoid personality in childhood: A controlled follow-up study. *Psychological Medicine, 10,* 85–100.

World Health Organization. (1992). *International classification of diseases* (10th ed.). Geneva, Switzerland: Author.

Zubieta, J. K., & Alessi, N. E. (1992). Acute and chronic administration of trazodone in the treatment of disruptive behavior disorders in children. *Journal of Clinical Psychopharmacology, 12,* 346–351.

Zubieta, J. K., & Alessi, N. E. (1993). Is there a role of serotonin in the disruptive behavior disorders? A literature review. *Journal of Child and Adolescent Psychopharmacology, 3,* 11–35.

CHAPTER 7

Outcomes in Autism Spectrum Disorders

PATRICIA HOWLIN

In the decades following Kanner's first accounts of children with autism, there have been many hundreds of publications dealing with this disorder. However, only a relatively small proportion has focused on adults, and fewer still have systematically studied the progress of individuals with autism as they move through adolescence and into adulthood. In the following chapter, the prognosis for individuals with autism in terms of their social outcomes, cognitive functioning, employment status, and mental health is explored. The overall pattern of change is also considered, and evidence of deterioration in function during the adolescent or early adult years is assessed. Finally, factors that appear to influence outcome in adulthood are reviewed.

SOCIAL OUTCOMES

Information on life for adults with autism comes from a variety of sources. First, there are the fascinating autobiographical accounts by higher functioning individuals (e.g., Gerland, 1996; Grandin, 1995; Holliday-Willey, 1999; Jolliffe, Landsdown, & Robinson, 1992; Lawson, 2002; O'Neill, 1999; Williams, 1992), but these apply to only a minority of people within the autistic spectrum. Second, there is a substantial number of clinically based descriptions of young adults. Although often very interesting, these tend to be somewhat unsystematic (e.g., Creak, 1963; Eisenberg, 1956; Mittler, Gillies, & Jukes, 1966; Newson, Dawson, & Everard, 1982), and because they do not provide data on functioning in childhood, there

is no information on the trajectory that individuals follow over the years.

By far the most informative studies are those that have traced development from childhood to adulthood. One of the earliest of these, a follow-up of 96 children reassessed in their 20s and 30s, was by Kanner himself (1973). The majority of his patients had remained highly dependent, living with parents, in sheltered communities, in state institutions for people with learning disabilities, or in psychiatric hospitals. Outcome was more positive for those with better developed communication skills, and among this group just over half were functioning relatively well. Eleven such individuals had jobs and one was at college. Seven had their own homes and one man (a successful music composer) was married with a child.

The first systematic outcome studies were conducted by Rutter and his colleagues (Lockyer & Rutter, 1969, 1970; Rutter, Greenfeld, & Lockyer, 1967; Rutter & Lockyer, 1967). Thirty-eight individuals, first diagnosed with autism as children in the 1950s or 1960s, were reassessed at age 16 years or older. At follow-up, more than half were in long-term hospital care, and 3 were living in residential communities. Of the 11 who still lived with their parents, 7 had no outside occupation and only 3 had paid jobs. Overall, 14% were said to have made a "good" social adjustment; 25% were rated as "fair" and 61% as "poor."

Lotter (1974a, 1974b) followed up 29 individuals, ages 16 to 18 years, who had been diagnosed as autistic in childhood. Among the 22 who had left school, only one had a job, and almost half were in long-term hospital care. Two individuals were living at home, and five were attending day training centers. Outcome ratings were very similar to those reported in the study of Rutter.

More than a decade later, Gillberg and Steffenburg (1987) reported on a group of 23 individuals age 16 or over living in Sweden. Only one person was found to be fully self-supporting; of the remainder, around half were rated as having a "fair" outcome and half as "poor" or "very poor."

Kobayashi, Murata, and Yashinaga (1992) used a postal survey to follow up 201 people, ages 18 to 33 years, in Japan. The average follow-up period was 15 years. Five percent were still attending school or college; 20% were employed, mostly in food and service industries. All but three of those with jobs still lived with their parents; one was in a group home, and two had their own apartments; none were married. Around a quarter of the group were rated as having a "good" or "very good" outcome; the same proportion were rated as "fair," and just under half were rated as "poor" or "very poor."

A telephone survey by Ballaban-Gil, Rapin, Tuchman, and Shinnar (1996) found that among 45 adults initially diagnosed as children, more than half (53%) were in residential placements and only one was living independently. Eleven percent were in regular employment (all in menial jobs), and a further 16% were in sheltered placements. Rates of behavioral difficulties were high, and only three adults were rated as having no social deficits.

Even among individuals of higher IQ, outcome is often very limited. Rumsey, Rapoport, and Sceery (1985) followed up 14 men between 18 and 39 years of age, seven of whom had originally been diagnosed by Kanner, and all of whom fulfilled *DSM-III* criteria for autism. Despite their mean IQ being around 99, all continued to have marked social difficulties. Only one individual had friends, and only four were in independent employment. Most of the group (71%) remained very dependent on their parents or others for support, and one person was in a state hospital.

Venter, Lord, and Schopler (1992) described outcomes for 22 individuals age 18 years or over who had a preschool IQ of 60+ and a mean IQ of around 90 at follow-up. Around a third were

competitively employed, but, again, jobs were generally at a very low level and the majority were in sheltered employment or special training programs; three had no occupation. Only four individuals lived more or less independently. However, Szatmari and his colleagues (Szatmari, Bartolucci, Bremner, Bond, & Rich, 1989) reported more positive findings for a group of 12 men and 4 women, all diagnosed as high functioning (IQ above 65). At follow-up, they were between 17 and 31 years of age with a mean WAIS IQ of 92. Half had attended college or university, and over a third were in regular, full-time employment. Half were described as being completely independent, although some of these still lived at home. Over half had never formed close relationships, but a quarter had dated regularly or had long-term relationships, and one was married.

Rutter and his colleagues (Howlin, Goode, Hutton, & Rutter, 2004; Howlin, Mawhood, & Rutter, 2000; Mawhood, Howlin, & Rutter, 2000) also conducted two long-term follow-up studies of individuals first seen in childhood. The first (Howlin et al., 2000; Mawhood et al., 2000) focused on a group of 19 young men who had initially been involved in a comparison study of children with receptive language disorder when between 4 and 9 years of age. At initial assessment, all had a nonverbal IQ of 70 or above, and as adults their mean performance IQ was in the mid 80s. Although the majority had improved over time, all showed continuing problems in communication; almost half remained socially isolated, only three lived independently, and more than two-thirds had significant difficulties associated with obsessional or ritualistic tendencies. Only five individuals were considered to have a good or moderately good outcome; the remainder showed substantial impairments.

A subsequent study (Howlin et al., 2004) described outcome in 61 men and 7 women (average age 29 years) who had initially been diagnosed at a mean age of 7 years. Only individuals with a childhood IQ of at least 50 were included in the study, and as adults their average performance IQ was 75. By follow-up, almost one-third of the group were in paid employment, although jobs were mostly poorly paid and low level. Around a quarter had developed some form of friendship with another person in their own age group, but close sexual relationships were rare and only three individuals were (or had been) married. Eight individuals had achieved relatively high levels of independence as adults, but most remained very dependent on their families or other support services and few were able to live entirely alone. Overall, around a fifth of the group was rated as having a "very good" or "good" outcome, and a similar proportion was rated as "fair"; almost half was rated as having a "poor" outcome, and 10% were in hospital care.

These and other studies of adult functioning summarized in Table 7.1 show that many adults continue to remain highly dependent on their families or other support services well into their late 20s and beyond. Only a minority achieved totally independent living, and even among the most able groups (e.g., Mawhood et al., 2000; Newson et al., 1982; Rumsey et al., 1985; Szatmari et al., 1989; Tantam, 1991; Venter et al., 1992), most still lived with their parents or were in sheltered residential placements. Outings and other social activities tended to be organized by parents or care workers, with very little initiative or choice on the part of the people with autism themselves. As a consequence, close friendships were rare; and Kanner himself noted that although several of his patients had achieved relatively highly in work-related areas, their attempts to form personal friendships "were much less successful." In most studies, fewer than 5% of participants had married or had long-term sexual relationships, although the proportions were higher in the groups described by Szatmari et al. and Larsen and Mouridsen (1997). In the latter study, two individuals were also noted as having children of their own. Generally, however, few follow-up studies have extended beyond the late 20s to early 30s; hence, information about marriage and parenting is very limited. A few personal accounts by individuals such as Lawson (2002) or Holliday-Willey (1999) describe the problems experienced by individuals with autism in coping with marriage and the demands of bringing up a family, especially when the children, too, share this condition. Nevertheless, the fact that autism is largely inherited (International Molecular Genetic Study of Autism Consortium, 2001; Rutter, 2000) means that many parents of children with autism will

themselves have an autistic spectrum disorder. Thus, marriage rates must be far higher than follow-up studies have previously suggested, and much more needs to be known about patterns of functioning within "autistic" families and what variables are related to success or difficulties.

CHANGES IN OUTCOME OVER RECENT YEARS

Many follow-up reports have attempted to summarize outcome among their participants, using ratings such as "good," "fair," "poor," or "very poor." However, comparisons between studies need to be treated with caution because of differences in sample selection and in the measures used. Most investigations have involved relatively small groups of subjects, diagnostic criteria are sometimes imprecise, and/or the quality of data on early intellectual functioning is poor. Overall judgments of whether outcome is "good," "fair," or "poor" also tend to be based on variable criteria, and these are often poorly defined and rarely backed up by assessments of reliability or validity. Generally, however, a "good" rating indicates moderate to high levels of independence in living and work, with some friends/acquaintances. "Fair" indicates need of support in work and/or daily living but with some limited autonomy. "Poor" usually means living in residential care, hospital provision, or the parental home with close supervision.

As shown in Table 7.1, these ratings vary widely between studies. "Good" ratings, for example, range from 0% to 38%, and "poor" ratings from 16% to over 80%. There is some suggestion, however, that the overall outcome may have improved somewhat over the past 2 decades, compared with that found in the 1960s and 1970s. Thus, whereas the mean percentage of those rated as having a "good" outcome in follow-up studies conducted before 1980 was around 10%, over the following 2 decades the proportion had risen to 20%. "Poor" outcome ratings declined from an average of 65% to 46% over the same period. "Fair" ratings remained around 25% to 30%. One particularly noticeable change has been in the frequency of admissions to long-term hospital care. Around 40% to 50% of individuals

TABLE 7.1 Independence and Social Outcomes in Follow-Up Studies of Adults*

Study (N)	Semi/Independent Living (%)	With Parents (%)	Residential Provision (%)	Hospital Care (%)	Married (%)	Some Friends (%)	Outcome Summary (%)		
							"Good"	"Fair"	"Poor"
Eisenberg, 1956 (63)	0	46		54			5	21	74
Creak, 1963 (100)							17	40	43
Mitler, Gillies, & Jukes, 1966 (26)	0			74			0	26	74
Lockyer & Rutter, 1970 (38)	0	18	19	53			14	25	61
Kanner, 1973 (96)	8				1 (1 child)	2	11		
DeMeyer, Barton, DeMeyer, Norton, Allan, & Steele, 1973 (120)	0			42			10	16	74
Lotter, 1974 (29)	0	28		48			14	24	62
Newson, Dawson, & Everard, 1982 (93)	7	71	16	7	1	15	7	77	16
Rumsey, Rapoport, & Sceery, 1985 (14)	21	64	7	7			35	35	28
Gillberg & Steffenberg, 1987 (23)	4	61	35				4	48	35
Szatmari, Bartolucci, Bremner, Bond, & Rich, 1989 (16)	33	63	12	0	29	21	38	31	31
Tantam, 1991 (46)	3	41	53	2	2	1			
Kobayashi, Murata, & Yashinaga, 1992 (201)	1	97		2	0		27	27	46
Venter, Lord, & Schopler, 1992 (22)	21			0	0				
von Knorring & Häglöf, 1994 (34)							3	9	88
Ballaban-Gil, Rapin, Tuchman, & Shinnar, 1995 (45)	2	45	53				6	?	?
Larsen & Mouridsen, 1997 (18)	44	17	12	17	22 (2 with children)		28	28	44
Mawhood, Howlin, & Rutter, 2000 (19)	16	32	47	5	5	21	26		74
Howlin, 2003 (68)	10	38	38	12	4	19	22	19	57

* Summary ratings based on authors' own classification where provided. Otherwise "Good" = Moderate to high levels of independence in living and/or job; some friends/acquaintances. "Fair" = Needing support in work and/or daily living but some limited autonomy. Poor = Living in residential care or hospital provision (or parental home but with close supervision in most activities).

in the earlier studies moved into such placements as adults, but there was a marked decline from the 1980s onward, with the mean being around 6% and, in many cases, far less. However, despite the general trend toward the closure of large residential institutions, for some individuals it has proved extremely difficult to find an alternative to hospital care because their behavioral problems, and especially their lack of social understanding, greatly limit their ability to settle into community-based provision (Howlin et al., 2004).

CHANGES IN COGNITIVE ABILITY

Young children with autism are not a particularly easy group to assess using formal psychometric measures. Their problems in verbal expression and comprehension, together with impaired social understanding and motivation, are all potential sources of difficulty. Moreover, few cognitive tests are designed for children whose development is markedly delayed or uneven, as occurs in autism. Indeed, the use of standardized tests with children with autism has been criticized by some practitioners as being inappropriate and misleading. Nevertheless, it has been demonstrated that if appropriate tests are used, the results can be both valid and reliable (Clark & Rutter, 1979, 1981) and prove remarkably stable over the long term. Howlin et al. (2004), for example, found little overall change in IQ scores from childhood to adulthood over an average period of 22 years. Overall correlations between child and adult verbal IQ were also high ($r = .68$). This relative stability in IQ was also noted by Ballaban-Gil et al. (1996) with only 18% of their sample showing a marked change in IQ from childhood to adolescence or adulthood. When change did occur, this usually represented an improvement rather than a decline in intellectual ability. Moreover, a study by Hutton (1998) of apparent deterioration in cognitive ability from childhood to adulthood found that the variable most predictive of decline was the type of test that had been used to assess IQ in childhood. Individuals who as children were assessed only on verbal tests or on small numbers of subtests from nonverbal scales were far more likely to have shown a significant "deterioration" in IQ than those

tested on nonverbal scales and a wider range of subtests. Other factors, such as gender, initial IQ, or presence of epilepsy were not significantly associated with a decline in scores.

A significant relationship between childhood IQ and adult outcome has been reported in several follow-up studies (e.g., Gillberg, 1991; Howlin et al., 2002; Lockyer & Rutter, 1969, 1970; Lotter, 1978; Rutter, Greenfield, & Lockyer, 1967; Rutter & Lockyer, 1967). Indeed, Nordin and Gillberg (1998) in their review of outcome research suggest that measured IQ at the time of diagnosis is one of the best single predictors of outcome. However, although in many cases, IQ scores appear to show little change over the years, there are exceptions. For example, in the study by Howlin et al. (2004), *mean* scores tended to remain very stable over time, but these could conceal individual changes. Thus, around one-third of the group showed a drop in performance IQ, and 16% showed an improvement. On verbal tests, the pattern was in the opposite direction, with over 40% showing an increase and 7% a decline. The association between childhood IQ and prognosis in adult life is also a complex one (see later Predictors of Outcome section).

EDUCATION AND EMPLOYMENT

One major factor affecting outcome in adulthood is the adequacy, or otherwise, of educational provision, and the importance of access to appropriate education for later employment and social and economic independence is widely recognized. However, research in the field of disability indicates that although inclusive education can succeed in the infant years, successful integration becomes progressively more difficult to achieve as children grow older. Acceptance, both by mainstream peers and teachers, tends to decrease with age and the risk of rejection is particularly high for children with more pervasive problems, such as those with autism (Deno, Maruyama, Espin, & Cohen, 1990; Farrell, 1997). Spontaneous social interactions with typically developing peers do not tend to occur unless the environment, teaching materials, and children's activities are appropriately structured (Lord, 1995), and, even then, close, reciprocal friendships are unlikely to develop (Burack, Root, & Zigler, 1997).

There can be no doubt that schooling for children with autism has improved substantially over recent decades. In early studies (DeMeyer et al., 1973; Lockyer & Rutter, 1969, 1970; Rutter & Lockyer, 1967), the majority of children, even those who were of higher IQ, had received less than 5 years' schooling in all. One-third of children in the Rutter and Lockyer studies, for example, had never attended school. In more recent outcome studies, almost all the children, whatever their intellectual level, had remained in school of some sort for at least 10 years. Nevertheless, full inclusion in schools still appears to be the exception rather than the rule (Howlin et al., 2004; Mawhood et al., 2000; Venter et al., 1992), and many students with autism leave school without any formal academic or vocational qualifications. Rates of entry to college are even lower, and in the majority of the outcome studies reviewed in Table 7.2, none of the individuals concerned had attended college or

TABLE 7.2   Educational and Employment Outcomes in Follow-Up Studies of Adults with Autism*

Study (n)	Age (Years)	IQ	College/ University (%)	Jobs (%)	Highest Level Jobs	Lowest Level Jobs
Lockyer & Rutter, 1969, 1970 (38)	16+	X = 62		8	Factory work	Unpaid shop work
Kanner, 1973 (96)	22–29		7	9	Military, banking, chemist, accountant	Store/kitchen work
Lotter, 1974 (29)	16–18	55–90		4	No information	
Newson, Dawson, & Everard, 1982 (93)	X = 23	High functioning	11	22	Few details	
Rumsey, Rapoport, & Sceery, 1985 (14)	18–39	55–129	14	29	Librarian, cab driver, computing	Janitor, most in sheltered workshops
Szatmari, Bartolucci, Bremner, Bond, & Rick, 1989 (16)	17–34	68–110	50	47	Librarian, teacher, salesman	Factory workshop
Tantam, 1991 (46)	X = 24	High functioning	4	9	No information	
Kobayashi, Murata, & Yashinaga, 1992 (201)	18–33	23% > 70	2	22	Bus conductor, cook, mechanic	Industrial work
Venter, Lord, & Schopler, 1992 (22)	18+	X = 90	7	27	Bartender	Rest "low level"
Ballaban-Gil, Rapin, Tuchman, & Shinnar, 1996 (45)	18+	31% > 70	11			All "menial"
Larsen & Mouridsen, 1997 (18)	32–43	78% > 50	0	22	Driver, office boy, gardener	Sheltered factory
Mawhood, Howlin, & Rutter, 2000 (19)	21–26	70–117	22	16	Lab technician	Voluntary sheltered work
Howlin, Goode, Hutton, & Rutter, 2004 (68)	21+	51–137	7	34	Scientific officer; computing, accounts, electronics	Washing up, supermarket, grave digger

* Includes follow-up studies in which majority of participants are 16+ and in which specific data on further education/employment are presented.

university or obtained a degree or similar qualification. Overall, the average proportion attending college was around 12% (range 0% to 50%). The numbers obtaining university degrees ranged from zero to 43%, with the proportions being greater in groups of higher ability (e.g., Mawhood et al., 2000; Rumsey et al., 1985; Szatmari et al., 1989).

Lack of higher education results in individuals falling progressively further behind their peers, but even for those who do successfully complete mainstream education and go on to obtain college or university qualifications, follow-up studies indicate that employment levels in adulthood are disappointing. Indeed, for people with any form of disability, the chances of finding or keeping employment in the open work market are limited. It is estimated, for example, that even individuals with mild intellectual disabilities have unemployment rates as high as 60% to 70%. If employment is found, job status and stability are typically low (Zetlin & Murtaugh, 1990), and work experience is frequently very negative (Szivos, 1990). The situation is much the same for individuals with autism, including those who are intellectually very able. Even if they are successful in getting through the interview process (a major stumbling block for many), jobs tend to be poorly paid and/or to end prematurely—often because of difficulties related to social competence.

Table 7.2 summarizes data on rates of employment in adult follow-up studies. Although, over the years, there appears to have been some increase in the proportion of individuals with autism who do find work, the numbers are still relatively low, with the average percent in studies post-1980 around only 24%. Even in the studies with a focus on high-functioning individuals, the highest proportion reported in work is 47% (Szatmari et al., 1989), and in other studies (e.g., Mawhood et al., 2000) the figure is well below 20%. Moreover, although some individuals were reported to have obtained high-level, well-paid, and responsible jobs, the majority had rather menial positions, such as kitchen hands, unskilled factory workers, or backroom supermarket staff. In addition, jobs had often been procured through the personal contacts of families rather than through the normal channels (Howlin & Goode, 1998). Employment stability, too, was poor, with many individuals experiencing lengthy periods without paid work.

Although the effectiveness of the supported employment model for individuals with intellectual disabilities is well established (Kilsby & Beyer, 1996; McCaughrin, Ellis, Rusch, & Heal, 1993; Pozner & Hammond, 1993), it is only relatively recently that such schemes have been extended to meet the specific needs of clients with autism. Smith, Belcher, and Juhrs (1995) describe a wide variety of successful job placements in their Maryland support scheme. These included manufacturing jobs, such as simple assembly-type work (25 clients); backroom retail work (44 clients); printing and mailing jobs (31); food services (23); warehouse work (20); recycling and delivery (12); and jobs with government organizations, mainly janitors and office clerks (15). The program is remarkable, not only for the large number of clients finding work but also because of its success in placing individuals with very limited language, low intellectual ability, and challenging behavior, as well as those who were more able. In another U.S.-based program, Keel, Mesibov, and Woods (1997), evaluating job outcomes for 100 clients enrolled in the TEACCH program (Treatment and Education of Autistic and Related Communication-handicapped Children) found that almost all were in work of some kind. Sixty-nine were in individual placements, 20 worked in "enclaves" (i.e., small groups with a job coach in one setting), and 7 of the least able clients worked in "mobile crews" providing housecleaning services. Jobs were mostly in the food service field, but around a quarter involved clerical or technical posts.

However, although often highly successful, the focus of such schemes has tended to be on relatively low-level jobs, and few programs have been specifically designed to meet the needs of more intellectually able adults with autism, despite their considerable potential. Nevertheless, specialist support for this particular group can prove highly effective. Mawhood and Howlin (1999) evaluated a supported employment program for 30 high-functioning individuals with autistic spectrum disorders living in London. All had a formal diagnosis of autism or Asperger syndrome, a WAIS IQ score of 70 or above, and had been actively seeking work for some time. Twenty percent had a university degree, and two-thirds had other academic or vocational qualifications. Their work outcomes were compared to those of a nonsupported, matched comparison group. During the course of a 2-year pilot program, more than two-thirds of the supported group obtained paid employment, compared with only one-quarter of the control group. Moreover, in the supported group, the majority of jobs were clerical or administrative in nature while only one individual in the comparison group obtained a job at this level. Earnings were significantly higher in the supported group, and there was a high level of satisfaction with the scheme, both among employers and the people with autism themselves.

In the course of the following 5 to 6 years, more than 90 positions have been found, with more than 80% being in computing, accounting, or administration. Other jobs have included secretarial, nursery, film processing, and consultancy work; jobs in science and government departments; and positions in housekeeping, sales, warehouses, and telephone and postal services. Moreover, at a time when temporary work contracts are becoming the norm, more than 50% of these placements were permanent; none have yet been dismissed from their job, and several employers have offered work to more than one autistic client.

Schemes such as this demonstrate conclusively how far the employment situation for people with autism can be improved by means of specialist help. However, in the absence of such support, it is all too easy for individuals to drift into a life of isolation and loneliness. Without work, opportunities to meet with peers or make friends will be severely restricted, and without money most individuals are obliged to remain living with their parents (or in some form of state-provided residential care). Leisure activities are limited, and failure to find suitable work, sometimes despite many years of trying, also results in frustration, loss of self-esteem, and, for some, entry into a cycle of anxiety and depression or other psychiatric disturbance (Howlin, 2004).

PSYCHIATRIC DISORDERS

On the whole, data on mental health problems in autism are based on clinical case reports or small group studies, and there are no systematic studies of incidence. However, although estimates vary (ranging from 4% to 58%; Lainhart, 1999), by far the most prevalent psychiatric disturbances reported are those related to anxiety and depression. As early as 1970, Rutter noted the risk of depressive episodes occurring in adolescents or older individuals with autism, and subsequent reviews have reported a high frequency of affective disorders both among individuals with autism (Lainhart & Folstein, 1994) and within their families (Bolton, Pickles, Murphy, & Rutter, 1998; Smalley, McCracken, & Tanguay, 1995). Abramson and colleagues (1992) suggest that around one-third of people with autism suffer from affective disorders, and high rates of depression are found among high-functioning individuals, as well as those of lower ability. Thus, Tantam (1991), in his study of 85 adults with Asperger syndrome, noted that 2% had a depressive psychosis and 5% had a bipolar disorder. A further 13% suffered from nonpsychotic depression and/or anxiety. In the study of Rumsey et al. (1985) of 14 relatively high-functioning individuals, generalized anxiety problems were found in half the sample. Similar figures were reported by Wing (1981), who found that around a quarter of her group of 18 individuals with Asperger syndrome showed signs of an affective disorder. Bipolar affective disorders or mania without depression tends to be reported less frequently than depression alone, although Wozniak et al. (1997) found that up to 21% of their autism/pervasive developmental disorder (PDD) sample had been diagnosed as having mania.

In reviewing case reports of psychiatric disorder in individuals with autism and related disorders (Howlin, 2004), 35 different studies involving 200 patients age 14 years and older were identified. Eighty-six cases were diagnosed with autism or PDD; 114 were described as having Asperger syndrome or were within the high-functioning range of the autistic spectrum. As shown in Figure 7.1, by far, the most frequent psychiatric diagnoses given (in 56% of cases) related to depression or anxiety disorders (including major and minor depression, mood disorders or bipolar affective disorder, depression plus anxiety, severe social withdrawal, and attempted suicide). Mania alone

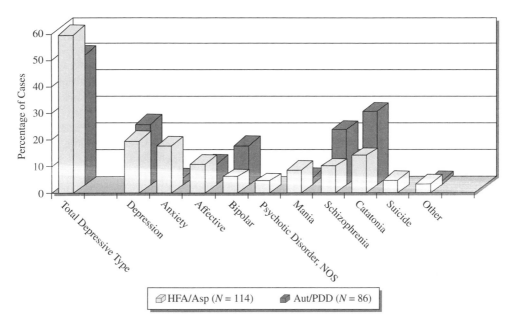

Figure 7.1 Psychiatric diagnoses reported in individuals with autism and those with Asperger syndrome or high-functioning autism.

occurred much less frequently, in under 3% of the total. The relatively high number of cases of catatonia reported largely reflects the special interest in this disorder of Lorna Wing and her colleagues (Wing and Shah, 2000). This also illustrates how case reports cannot be used to determine the prevalence of psychiatric illness since the researchers' particular area of expertise or interest will lead to systematic bias in the types of cases seen. However, the figure does provide a *rough* guide to the relative frequency of different disorders, and data from this and other reviews consistently suggest that while depressive types of disorder are relatively common, schizophrenic illness is much less prevalent.

Schizophrenia in ASD

Understanding of the links between autism and schizophrenia has come a long way since Szurek and Berlin (1956) suggested that clinically there was no reason to make any sharp distinctions between psychosis, autism, atypical development, or schizophrenia. Rutter (1972) was among the first of many to highlight a number of crucial variables relating to onset, course, prognosis, treatment, and family history that

differentiated between autism and schizophrenia. That is not to say that autism and schizophrenia never coexist; and, as the present review indicates, there is a number of case reports on the comorbidity of the two conditions (Clarke, Baxter, Perry, & Prasher, 1999; Petty, Ornitz, Michelman, & Zimmerman, 1984; Sverd, Montero, & Gurevich, 1993). However, larger scale studies of individuals with autism have failed to find any evidence of increased rates of schizophrenia (Chung, Luk, & Lee, 1990; Ghaziuddin, Weidmer-Mikhail, & Ghaziuddin, 1998). None of the cases followed up by Kanner, over a period of 40 years, was reported as showing positive psychiatric symptoms (delusions or hallucinations), and Volkmar and Cohen (1991) found only one individual with an unequivocal diagnosis of schizophrenia in a sample of 163 cases.

Schizophrenia also appears to be uncommon among more able individuals or those with Asperger syndrome. Asperger (1944) noted that only one of his 200 cases developed schizophrenia, and Wing (1981), in a study of 18 individuals with Asperger syndrome, describes one with an unconfirmed diagnosis of schizophrenia. Rumsey et al. (1985), in their detailed psychiatric study, found no evidence of schizophrenia. None of the relatively able subjects in the studies of Mawhood and colleagues (2000) or Howlin et al. (2004) had developed a schizophrenic illness, and only one individual in a similar group studied by Szatmari et al. (1989) had been treated for chronic schizophrenia. Tantam (1991) diagnosed three cases of schizophrenia among 83 individuals with Asperger syndrome, but these were all psychiatric referrals.

Volkmar and Cohen (1991) have concluded that the frequency of schizophrenia in individuals with autism is around 0.6% (roughly comparable to that in the general population) and, thus, the rate of comorbidity of the two conditions is no greater than would be expected by chance. Similar findings are reached in the more recent overview by Lainhart (1999). Thus, although some studies have suggested that there may be an excess of schizophrenia among individuals with Asperger syndrome (Wolff & McGuire, 1995), there is little evidence for such claims (Wing, 1986).

Other Psychotic Conditions

Although the occurrence of first-rank schizophrenic symptoms is relatively unusual, there are reports of individuals who show isolated psychotic symptoms, including delusional thoughts. Tantam (1991) suggests that the delusional content is often linked with autistic-type preoccupations. For example, one young man described by Wing (1981) could not be deterred from his conviction that some day Batman was going to come and take him away as his assistant. Ghaziuddin, Tsai, and Ghaziuddin (1992) describe another who was unduly concerned about the ozone layer and believed the air in Michigan was not pure enough to breathe. One of my patients was threatening to take revenge on the U.S. president and the U.K. prime minister because he believed the American and British Air Control authorities had conspired to prevent him from qualifying as an airline pilot. Another young man since childhood had "voices" to whom he could talk when he was particularly angry or upset. He believed firmly that the voices were real, but they did not provoke any distress or make him do things that he did not wish to do. Instead, they appeared to offer him a means of working through difficult situations, and if he became particularly agitated, his parents would send him off to "talk to his voices."

A number of other authors have described cases of delusional disorder, various unspecified psychoses (occasionally associated with epilepsy), paranoid ideation, catatonia, and hallucinations (Clarke, Littlejohns, Corbett, & Joseph, 1989; Ghaziuddin et al., 1992; Rumsey et al., 1985; Szatmari et al., 1989; Tantam, 1991, 2000; Wing & Shah, 2000). Obsessive-compulsive disorders have also been reported although it can often prove very difficult to distinguish between these and the ritualistic and stereotyped behaviors that are characteristic of autism (Szatmari et al., 1989).

As noted in the earliest descriptions of autism (Kanner, 1971; Lockyer & Rutter, 1970; Lotter, 1966) epilepsy is another complicating psychiatric factor, and it occurs in around 25% to 30% of cases (Lord & Bailey, 2002). The risk of developing fits appears to be higher among those who are profoundly retarded, but there does not seem to be a marked difference between groups of normal IQ and those with mild-moderate retardation. Eleven (16%) of the adults with an IQ of 50 or above assessed by Howlin et al. (2004) had at least one fit. In four cases, IQ was between 50 and 69; in seven, IQ was in the normal range. Occasionally, the onset of epilepsy is associated with marked behavioral changes and regression in adolescence (see later discussion), although this is by no means always the case.

ARE HIGHER FUNCTIONING INDIVIDUALS AT GREATER RISK OF PSYCHIATRIC DISTURBANCE?

It is often suggested that the risk of psychiatric disturbance, especially related to depression and anxiety, is particularly great among higher functioning individuals with autism or those with Asperger syndrome. There are several reasons for this view. First, because of these individuals' relatively good cognitive ability and *apparently* competent use of language, they frequently fail to receive the level of support they need. Second, despite their superficially good expressive skills, many have extensive linguistic and comprehension difficulties (especially involving abstract or complex concepts), and their understanding of the more subtle aspects of social interaction is often profoundly limited. Such deficits frequently prove an almost insurmountable barrier to social integration. Third, others' expectations of their social and academic potential are often unrealistically high, and there may be constant pressure for them to "fit into normal society." Finally, their own awareness of their difficulties and the extent to which they are isolated from others can result in great sadness and very low self-esteem. All these factors can place enormous pressures on the individuals concerned and sometimes result in intolerable levels of anxiety and stress. Nevertheless, there is little evidence of differential rates of mental health problems among subgroups within the autistic spectrum. On the whole, the findings from the case studies summarized in Figure 7.1, did not indicate a higher incidence of such problems in higher functioning compared to less able individuals. And, although the former group were somewhat more likely to be diagnosed as having mania or anxiety disorders, this may be because it is much more difficult to diagnose these conditions in individuals who have little ability to describe their moods and feelings effectively (Sturmey, 1998). In their case, the problems may simply be labeled as unspecified "mood disorders" (see Figure 7.1).

However, many of the clinical case studies reviewed did not distinguish clearly between high-functioning and low-functioning individuals or between those with autism and Asperger syndrome. Even if separate categories were used, diagnostic criteria were rarely specified, and very few reports provided information on the IQ levels of the individuals concerned. Szatmari et al. (1989), in one of the few well-controlled studies in this area, failed to find any marked differences in rates of psychiatric disturbance between adults with a diagnosis of Asperger syndrome and those with high-functioning autism although the autism group tended to show more bizarre preoccupations.

In summary, crucial data on the prevalence and nature of mental health problems across the autistic spectrum are still lacking, and there is a particular need for epidemiological studies in this area. Better research is needed,

too, into ways of improving the identification and treatment of psychiatric disorders because many clinicians working in adult psychiatric services often know relatively little about people with autism. Thus, the obsessionality, flattened affect, poor eye contact, unusual body movements, and echoed speech that are typical of autism may be misinterpreted as symptoms of psychosis (Volkmar & Cohen, 1991). Impoverished language (Howlin, 2004), literal interpretation of questions (Wing, 1986), and concrete thinking (Dykens, Volkmar, & Glick, 1991) are all additional sources of confusion. For example, if asked, "Do you ever hear voices when there is no one in the room?" individuals with autism are almost certain to reply in the affirmative, since they can obviously hear voices coming from many other sources. It is also important that isolated "symptoms," such as the unusual ideas or fixations noted earlier, be kept in perspective. For example, when a psychiatric nurse heard of the voices experienced by the young man described earlier, his parents were warned that he was seriously mentally ill. Their attempts to persuade medical staff that this was not a crisis, but typical behavior, were dismissed as collusion and denial, and it was with great difficulty that they prevented his being compulsorily detained in a psychiatric hospital. This failure to understand the characteristic communication and social difficulties associated with autism can give rise to potentially serious misunderstandings and misdiagnosis, even in the case of relatively able individuals. For those with little or no speech, the risks of an incorrect diagnosis (or failure to diagnose when problems do exist) are even higher.

Finding the appropriate treatment for people with autism who develop additional psychiatric disorders can also prove difficult. Clinical experience suggests that delays in diagnosis and treatment are particularly undesirable within this group because behavior patterns that are established during the course of the illness (e.g., disturbed waking and sleeping patterns) can then be very difficult to alter, even when the patient's condition generally has improved (Howlin, 2004). Medication can be helpful (McDougle, 1997) but rarely works in isolation. There is little evidence for the effectiveness of psychoanalytically based interventions (Campbell, Schopler, Cueva, & Hallin, 1996). Individual psychotherapy or counseling may be beneficial for higher functioning people, but clinical experience suggests that these approaches *must* be combined with direct practical advice on how to deal with problems. If appropriately adapted, cognitive behavioral strategies seem to be of potential benefit (Hare, Jones, & Paine, 1999; Stoddart, 1999) although there is very little systematic research in this area, and even single case studies are rare.

MORTALITY AND CAUSES OF DEATH

Long-term follow-up studies of children and adolescents with psychiatric disorders have demonstrated above-average mortality rates compared to age- and sex-matched controls, especially concerning death from "unnatural causes" (suicide, accidents, etc.; Kuperman, Black, & Burns, 1988; Larsen, Dahl, & Hallum, 1990; Östman, 1991; Strauss, 1996). Research also suggests that death rates are higher in individuals with autistic spectrum disorders (Gillberg & Coleman, 2000; Shavelle, Strauss, & Picket, 2001). Isager, Mouridsen, and Rich (1999) followed 207 cases with autism or autism-like conditions over a 24-year period and found that seven individuals had died, giving a crude mortality rate of 3.4%—approximately double the expected rate. Mortality was highest in those with severe-profound learning disabilities or those of higher intelligence. In the former group ($n = 4$), all of whom were in residential institutions, two deaths were attributed to choking while unsupervised, one to pneumonia, and one to meningitis. In the more able group ($n = 3$), who lived either independently or with parents, one death followed an epileptic attack, and two were due to drug overdoses (one deliberate; the other *probably* accidental). Occasional deaths have been reported, too, in general follow-up studies of individuals with autism (Lotter, 1978). Causes of death include car accidents (Kanner, 1973; Larsen & Mouridsen, 1997); encephalopathy, self-injury, nephritic syndrome, and asthma (Kobayashi et al., 1992); unrecognized volvulus (in a woman in a long-term psychiatric institution, Larsen & Mouridsen, 1997); status epilepticus (Howlin et al., 2004); and cases of drowning,

pneumonia, and complications arising from long-term psychotropic medication (Ballaban-Gil et al., 1996).

The largest single study of mortality rates (Shavelle et al., 2001), based on more than 13,000 individuals with autism registered on the California Department of Developmental Services database, concluded that average mortality rates were more than double those of the general population. In individuals with mild mental retardation or those of normal IQ, deaths from seizures, nervous system dysfunction, drowning, and suffocation were three times more common than in nondisabled controls. Among individuals with more severe mental retardation, there was a threefold increase in deaths from all causes (other than cancer).

Suicide as a cause of death has been noted in a number of studies. Among the "schizoid" individuals (several of whom appeared to meet criteria for Asperger syndrome) studied by Wolff and McGuire (1995), 10 of 17 women and 17 of 32 men had attempted suicide. Tantam (1991) described the case of one man who threw himself into the river Thames because the government refused to abolish British Summer Time, and he believed that watches were damaged by the necessity of being altered twice a year. In Wing's group of 18 individuals with Asperger syndrome, three had attempted suicide although, fortunately, their attempts had not been successful. One young man, who had become very distressed by minor changes in his work routine, tried to drown himself but failed because he was a good swimmer. When he tried to strangle himself, the attempt also failed because, as he said, "I am not a very practical person."

Nordin and Gillberg (1998) have suggested that higher death rates of individuals with autistic spectrum disorders may be due to the association of autism with severe mental retardation and epilepsy. However, the preceding examples indicate that many other causes are also operating. The number of deaths related to the inadequate medical and physical care of individuals living in institutions is a particular cause of concern, and awareness of the importance of basic health care could well help to reduce deaths within this group. Better understanding of the difficulties that lead some young people to attempt suicide could also avoid unnecessary loss of life.

ARE THERE DIFFERENCES IN OUTCOME BETWEEN INDIVIDUALS WITH AUTISM AND ASPERGER SYNDROME?

The issue of whether autism and Asperger syndrome are different conditions (albeit part of the same spectrum of disorders) has been a source of continuing debate over recent years (cf. Klin, Volkmar, & Sparrow, 2000; Schopler, Mesibov, & Kunce, 1998). However, when IQ is adequately controlled for, comparisons between the two groups have failed to find any *consistent* evidence of major group differences in rates of social, emotional, and psychiatric problems; current symptomatology; motor clumsiness; or neuropsychological profiles (see Howlin, 2003; Macintosh & Dissanayake, 2004, for reviews). Moreover, any differences that may be found in early childhood tend to diminish with age (Gilchrist, Green, Cox, Rutter, & Le Couteur, 2001; Howlin, 2003; Ozonoff, South, & Miller, 2000; Szatmari, Archer, Fisman, Streiner, & Wilson, 1995). On the basis of current research evidence, there is little to support the view that Asperger syndrome and high-functioning autism are essentially different conditions. Certainly, there is no justification for differentiating between the groups in terms of access to support services. Instead, it should be recognized that for *all* high-functioning individuals with an autistic disorder, there is a need for much improved services throughout childhood and adulthood if the long-term outcome is to be significantly enhanced.

HOW COMMON IS DETERIORATION IN ADULTHOOD?

The transition to adulthood can be a time of upheaval and difficulties for many young people and their families. It is not surprising, therefore, that parents of children with autism approach this life stage with considerable trepidation and anxiety. In a number of long-term studies, there have been accounts of an increase in disruptive behaviors in adolescence, and these can undoubtedly prove very difficult

for families to deal with. Lockyer and Rutter (1970), for example, noted that five individuals (out of 64) in his follow-up studies showed a marked deterioration in their communication, together with progressive inertia, and general cognitive decline. Three of these cases had also developed epilepsy. Gillberg and Steffenburg (1987) reported that around a third of their sample of 23 autistic individuals presented with a temporary (1 to 2 years) aggravation of symptoms, such as hyperactivity, aggressiveness, destructiveness, and ritualistic behaviors. In another five cases, the symptoms had persisted, resulting in continuing deterioration, increased inertia, loss of language skills, and slow intellectual decline. This pattern was more likely to occur in females than males. Von Knorring and Häglöf (1993) also noted that of the four individuals in their sample of 34 who showed a "mildly deteriorating course," three were women. Ballaban-Gil et al. (1996) noted that ratings of problem behaviors had increased in almost 50% of their adult sample, although the nature of these is not defined. In the Japanese follow-up of 201 young adults, Kobayashi and his colleagues (1992) found that 31% showed a worsening of symptoms, mainly after the age of 10 years, but there was no difference in the proportions of males and females who experienced a loss of skills. Larsen and Mouridsen (1997), in a comparative study of autism and Asperger syndrome, reported that three of the nine cases with Asperger syndrome and two of the nine with autism had shown deterioration, mostly occurring in late puberty. In both of these latter studies, the pattern of deterioration described was very similar to that outlined by Rutter and Gillberg and Steffenburg.

In one of the very few systematic investigations of deterioration over time, Hutton (1998) examined data on the emergence of problems in adulthood for 125 individuals. Over a third were reported to have developed new behavioral or psychiatric difficulties including psychosis, obsessive-compulsive disorder, anxiety, depression, tics, social withdrawal, phobias, and aggression. The average age when these symptoms developed was 26 years, with most people developing symptoms prior to the age of 30. "Periodicity," that is, episodes of disturbance occurring at fairly regular and frequent intervals, was noted in eight individuals. The increase in problems of this nature was not associated with epilepsy, cognitive decline, or residential placement. However, women were more likely to show an increase in problems than men, and individuals with a lower verbal IQ in childhood were also at greater risk of developing new problems in adulthood. Marked deterioration in cognitive abilities occurred mostly among individuals in long-term hospital placements.

Although it is clear that some individuals with autism do show an increase in problems as they grow older, in many studies tracing progress from childhood to adulthood, the overriding picture is one of *improvement* over time. This was reported in the early follow-up studies of Rutter and his group and by Kanner himself, who noted that for some individuals, particularly those who become more aware of their difficulties, mid-adolescence was often a period of "remarkable improvement and change" (Kanner, 1973). Although a third of the individuals in the Kobayashi et al. (1992) study had shown some increase in problems during adolescence, over 40% were rated as showing marked improvement, generally between 10 and 15 years. Even in the Ballaban-Gil study (1996), where increases in ratings of behavioral disturbance were higher than in other groups, 16% had improved, and 35% had shown no deterioration in behavior from childhood to adulthood. Many other studies, both retrospective and prospective, indicate that change over time is more likely to be positive, rather than negative. Studies using standardized assessment instruments such as the Autism Diagnostic Interview-Revised (ADI-R; Lord, Rutter, & Le Couteur, 1994) or the Autism Diagnostic Observation Schedule-Generic (ADOS-G; Lord et al., 2000) have found the severity and frequency of many symptoms decrease significantly with time (Gilchrist et al., 2001; Howlin, 2002; Piven, Harper, Palmer, & Arndt, 1996). In a study of more than 400 individuals with autism from 10 to 53 years of age, Seltzer et al. (2002) found clear evidence of improvement on ADI-R scores from childhood to adolescence and adulthood. Verbal and nonverbal communication had improved, as had scores on the Reciprocal Social Interaction domain. Scores on *all* the items in the Restricted, Repetitive Behaviors and Interests Domain had also decreased from childhood

to adulthood. Similar improvements have been reported in individuals with severe learning disabilities. Thus, Beadle-Brown, Murphy, Wing, Shah, and Holmes (2000) reported changes in scores on the Handicaps, Behaviours and Skills schedule (HBS; Wing & Gould, 1978) for 146 young adults with severe learning disabilities and/or autism over a period of 12 years (age at initial assessment 2 to 18 years; age at follow-up, 13 to 30 years). Although there was no marked change in IQ, self-care skills (toileting, feeding, grooming, washing, dressing, etc.) had improved significantly, and there had also been progress in certain areas related to educational achievement (e.g., reading, writing, numbers, money, and time). There were fewer significant changes in communication skills as measured by the HBS although both expressive and receptive scores on the Reynell Developmental Language scale had increased significantly. Improvements were related to initial IQ level, with those individuals with an IQ below 55 (or who were untestable) as children showing less improvement than those with an IQ of 55 or above.

Follow-up studies with a focus on more able individuals have also documented steady improvements over time. For example, in the studies of Mawhood and her colleagues (Howlin et al., 2000; Mawhood et al., 2000), of 19 young men followed up from 7 to 23 years of age, verbal ability on formal IQ tests had increased significantly, and in terms of general social competence, almost one-third of the group had moved from a rating of "poor" functioning in childhood to a "good" rating as adults. There was relatively little change, however, in ratings of friendship quality.

In summary, while it is evident that skills may be lost or problem behaviors increase in adolescence or early adulthood, it is also essential to get the picture into perspective. Conclusions about "improvement" or "deterioration" may depend on the particular measures used, and whereas individuals may fail to make progress in certain areas (e.g., in the ability to form close friendships), other skills, notably those related to communication, may show positive and significant change. The numbers of adults who show marked deterioration in all aspects of their functioning are, fortunately, very small and overall regression appears to be the exception, not the rule.

PREDICTORS OF OUTCOME

The variability in outcome among individuals with autism has been noted since the very earliest follow-up studies of Eisenberg and Kanner (Eisenberg, 1956; Kanner & Eisenberg, 1956), and there have been many attempts to try to isolate the variables that best predict later functioning. As noted earlier, educational placement can have a major influence on outcome; and Kanner, in his follow-up (1973), noted that lack of appropriate education was highly damaging. Subsequent studies (e.g., Lockyer & Rutter, 1969, 1970; Lotter, 1974a, 1974b; Rutter, Greenfeld, & Lockyer, 1967; Rutter & Lockyer, 1967) also noted the association between years of schooling and later outcome. The most positive outcomes are generally reported for individuals who have attended mainstream schools, but since outcomes are directly affected by pupils' linguistic and cognitive levels, the influence of schooling, per se, on long-term functioning remains obscure.

The relationship between the severity of autistic symptomatology in early childhood and later outcome is also unclear. Rutter and colleagues (Lockyer & Rutter, 1969, 1970; Rutter & Lockyer, 1967) found no significant correlation between individual symptoms in childhood (other than lack of speech) and adult outcome, although there was a significant relationship with the total number of major symptoms rated. DeMeyer et al. (1973) also reported a relationship between overall severity of autistic symptoms and later progress. In contrast, Lord and Venter (1992) found no association between prognosis and total number of early symptoms as rated on the ADI. Of greater predictive value were the degree of language *abnormality* and the level of disruption caused by stereotyped and repetitive behaviors.

The possible impact of many other variables remains uncertain. In almost every follow-up study in which women have been involved (many studies are exclusively male), outcome has been poorer for females than males. However, the number of women participants has generally been very small and the differences found rarely reach significance; the tendency for females to be of lower IQ also complicates the issue (Lord & Schopler, 1985). In some studies, the presence of epilepsy has been associated with a poorer outcome but, again, epilepsy is more likely to occur in individuals with more severe cognitive impairments. Socioeconomic factors and ratings of family adequacy have also been correlated with prognosis in some studies (DeMeyer et al., 1973; Lotter, 1974a, 1974b), but there is little evidence of a direct causal relationship between an impoverished or disruptive family background and later outcome, although, as with any other condition, disruption at home may well result in an increase in problems generally.

The two factors that have been consistently associated with later prognosis are early language development and IQ. Very few children who have not developed some useful speech by the age of 5 to 6 years are reported to have a positive outcome, although occasionally older children may develop relatively good communication skills. The relationship between long-term outcome and cognitive ability in childhood has also been noted in many follow-up studies (Gillberg & Steffenburg, 1987; Lockyer & Rutter, 1969, 1970; Lotter, 1974a, 1974b; Rutter, Greenfeld, & Lockyer, 1967; Rutter & Lockyer, 1967). Thus, individuals who were either untestable as children or who had nonverbal IQ scores below 50 were almost invariably reported as remaining highly dependent. However, more recent studies suggest that a minimum childhood IQ of 70 is necessary for a positive outcome in adulthood. Howlin et al. (2004) found that on virtually every adult measure (academic attainments, communication skills, reading and spelling, employment status, social independence), individuals with a childhood IQ below 70 were significantly more impaired than those with an initial IQ of 70+. Only one individual with an IQ between 50 and 69 obtained a "good" outcome rating in adulthood. Nevertheless, even among the 45 individuals in this study with an initial IQ above 70, outcome was very mixed. Thus, although almost one-third of this subgroup were rated as having a "good" or "very good" outcome, 22% were rated as only "fair" and 44% obtained ratings of "poor" or "very poor." Moreover, those individuals with an IQ above 100 did no better as a group than those with an IQ in the 70 to 99 range. Indeed, several individuals in this lower range achieved considerably more highly as adults than many with a childhood IQ of above 100.

Childhood performance on nonverbal tests of intelligence, while being a *relatively* good predictor of outcome, is by no means a perfect one, and Lord and Bailey (2002) have proposed that childhood *verbal* IQ is a far more reliable indicator of later functioning. However, in the Howlin et al. study, although correlations between child and adult verbal IQ were highly significant, there was a sizable subgroup of individuals who, despite being unable to score at all on verbal tests when younger, subsequently made considerable improvement in this area. Over a third of individuals who were "untestable" on verbal measures initially obtained a verbal IQ equivalent of at least 70 at follow-up, and several of these children were subsequently rated as having a "good" or "very good" outcome as adults. In the case of other children, who *were* able to obtain a verbal IQ score when first assessed, the relationship with adult outcome was very variable. While a third of those who scored above 50 on verbal IQ tests as children obtained outcome ratings of "good" or "very good" in adulthood; one-third were rated as "fair" and a further third as having a "poor" or "very poor" outcome. Even among the few children who scored above 70 on a verbal IQ test initially, less than half were rated as having a "good"/"very good" outcome as adults. Thus, again, although statistically there is a positive correlation between early verbal IQ and later prognosis, from an individual, clinical perspective, this variable has only limited predictive value.

Lord and Bailey (2002) have also suggested that the presence of useful speech by age 5 is highly predictive of later outcome. Certainly, for many young children it is much easier to obtain information of this kind than to obtain a verbal IQ score, although there may be some problems of recall if interviewing parents of older individuals. However, in the Howlin et al. (2004) study, even this variable was only weakly associated with adult outcome. Over 40% of children who had little or no language when first diagnosed had subsequently developed useful language, and, the higher their linguistic levels as adults, the more likely were they to do well on a range of other outcome measures. Other research has pointed to the impact that improvements in language may have on the developmental trajectory of children with autism (Szatmari, 2000), but we

have little information on what is associated with such improvement.

To some extent, it may prove easier to identify correlates of "poor" outcome than the variables predictive of good prognosis. In the Howlin et al. study, as already noted, most individuals with an initial performance IQ below 70 remained highly dependent as adults. Moreover, *no one* with a childhood performance IQ below 70 and a verbal IQ below 30 achieved even a "fair" rating in adulthood, and only one individual with a performance IQ below 70 coupled with a verbal IQ below 50 did so.

Identifying the reasons that some individuals make significant improvements in their general levels of functioning over time while others show little or no change has major implications for our understanding of autism and of the factors influencing the trajectory from childhood to adulthood. It may be, as Kanner postulated, that the presence of *additional* skills or interests (e.g., specialized knowledge in particular areas or competence in mathematics, music, or computing), which allow individuals to find their own "niche" in life and thus enable them to be more easily integrated into society, is of crucial importance. Alternatively, the ability to function adequately in adult life may depend as much on the degree of support offered (by families, educational, employment, and social services) as much as basic intelligence (Lord & Venter, 1992; Mawhood & Howlin, 1999).

CONCLUSION

Although admissions to hospital care have fallen and expectations about the future for people with disabilities generally have risen over the years, dedicated services for adults with autism would not seem to have kept pace with the growth in specialist provision for children with this disorder. Overall, it is evident that the majority of individuals with autism, regardless of their intellectual level, continue to experience many problems in adult life. However, it is also clear that outcome can depend crucially on the degree and appropriateness of support that is provided beyond the school years and into adulthood. Thus, although the focus of much recent research has been on the importance of early intervention programs (National Research Council, 2001), true social inclusion will only be possible if the long-term needs of adults, as well as children with autism, are fully recognized and adequately supported.

REFERENCES

Abramson, R. K., Wright, H. H., Cuccara, M. L., Lawrence, L. G., Babb, S., Pencarinha, D., et al. (1992). Biological liability in families with autism. *Journal of the American Academy of Child and Adolescent Psychiatry, 31,* 370–371.

Asperger, H. (1944). Autistic psychopathy in childhood (U. Frith, Trans.). In U. Frith (Ed.), *Autism and Asperger syndrome* (pp. 37–92). Cambridge, England: Cambridge University Press.

Ballaban-Gil, K., Rapin, I., Tuchman, R., & Shinnar, S. (1996). Longitudinal examination of the behavioral, language, and social changes in a population of adolescents and young adults with autistic disorder. *Pediatric Neurology, 15,* 217–223.

Beadle-Brown, J., Murphy, G., Wing, L., Shah, A., & Holmes, N. (2000). Changes in skills for people with intellectual disability: A follow-up of the Camberwell Cohort. *Journal of Intellectual Disability Research, 44,* 12–24.

Bolton, P., Pickles, A., Murphy, M., & Rutter, M. (1998). Autism, affective and other psychiatric disorders: Patterns of familial aggregation. *Psychological Medicine, 28,* 385–395.

Burack, J. A., Root, R., & Zigler, E. (1997). Inclusive education for children with autism: Reviewing ideological, empirical and community considerations. In D. Cohen & F. Volkmar (Eds.), *Handbook of autism and pervasive developmental disorders* (2nd ed., pp. 796–807). New York: Wiley.

Campbell, M., Schopler, E., Cueva, J. E., & Hallin, A. (1996). Treatment of autistic disorder. *Journal of the American Academy of Child and Adolescent Psychiatry, 35,* 134–143.

Chung, S. Y., Luk, F. L., & Lee, E. W. H. (1990). A follow-up study of infantile autism in Hong Kong. *Journal of Autism and Developmental Disorders, 20,* 221–232.

Clark, P., & Rutter, M. (1979). Task difficulty and task performance in autistic children. *Journal of Child Psychology and Psychiatry, 20,* 271–285.

Clark, P., & Rutter, M. (1981). Autistic children's responses to structure and to interpersonal demands. *Journal of Autism and Developmental Disorders, 11,* 201–217.

Clarke, D. J., Baxter, M., Perry, D., & Prasher, V. (1999). The diagnosis of affective and psychotic disorders in adults with autism. *Autism: International Journal of Research and Practice, 3,* 149–164.

Clarke, D. J., Littlejohns, C. S., Corbett, J. A., & Joseph, S. (1989). Pervasive developmental disorders and psychoses in adult life. *British Journal of Psychiatry, 155,* 692–699.

Creak, M. (1963). Childhood psychosis: A review of a 100 cases. *British Journal of Psychiatry, 109,* 84–89.

DeMyer, M. K., Barton, S., DeMeyer, W. E., Norton, J. A., Allan, J., & Steele, R. (1973). Prognosis in autism: A follow-up study. *Journal of Autism and Childhood Schizophrenia, 3,* 199–246.

Deno, S., Maruyama, G., Espin, G., & Cohen, C. (1990). Educating students with mild disabilities in general education classrooms: Minnesota alternatives. *Exceptional Children, 572,* 150–161.

Dykens, E., Volkmar, F. R., & Glick, M. (1991). Thought disorder in high functioning autistic adults. *Journal of Autism and Developmental Disorders, 21,* 303–314.

Eisenberg, L. (1956). The autistic child in adolescence. *American Journal of Psychiatry, 112,* 607–612.

Farrell, P. (1997). The integration of children with severe learning difficulties: A review of the recent literature. *Journal of Applied Research in Intellectual Disabilities, 10,* 1–14.

Gerland, G. (1996). *A real person: Life on the outside.* London: Souvenir Press.

Ghaziuddin, M., Tsai, L. Y., & Ghaziuddin, N. (1992). Co-morbidity of autistic disorder in children and adolescents. *European Journal of Child and Adolescent Psychiatry, 1,* 209–213.

Ghaziuddin, M., Weidmer-Mikhail, E., & Ghaziuddin, N. (1998). Comorbidity in Asperger syndrome: A preliminary report. *Journal of Intellectual Disability Research, 42,* 279–283.

Gilchrist, A., Green, J., Cox, A., Rutter, M., & Le Couteur, A. (2001). Development and current functioning in adolescents with Asperger syndrome: A comparative study. *Journal of Child Psychology and Psychiatry, 42,* 227–240.

Gillberg, C. (1991). Outcome in autism and autistic-like conditions. *Journal of the American Academy of Child and Adolescent Psychiatry, 30,* 375–382.

Gillberg, C., & Coleman, M. (2000). *The biology of the autistic syndromes* (3rd ed.). Oxford, England: MacKeith Press.

Gillberg, C., & Steffenburg, S. (1987). Outcome and prognostic factors in infantile autism and similar conditions: A population-based study of 46 cases followed through puberty. *Journal of Autism and Developmental Disorders, 17,* 272–288.

Grandin, T. (1995). The learning style of people with autism; An autobiography. In K. A. Quill (Ed.), *Teaching children with autism: Strategies to enhance communication and socialization* (pp. 33–52). New York: Delmar.

Hare, D., Jones, J. P. R., & Paine, C. (1999). Approaching reality: The use of personal construct assessment in working with people with Asperger syndrome. *Autism; International Journal of Research and Practice, 3,* 165–176.

Holliday-Willey, L. (1999). *Pretending to be normal.* London: Jessica Kingsley.

Howlin, P. (2003). Outcome in high functioning adults with autism with and without early language delays: Implications for the differentiation between autism and Asperger syndrome. *Journal of Autism and Developmental Disorders, 33,* 3–13.

Howlin, P. (2004). *Autism and Asperger syndrome: Preparing for adulthood* (2nd ed.). London: Routledge.

Howlin, P., & Goode, S. (1998). Outcome in adult life for individuals with autism. In F. Volkmar (Ed.), *Autism and developmental disorders* (pp. 209–241). New York: Cambridge University Press.

Howlin, P., Goode, S., Hutton, J., & Rutter, M. (2004). Adult outcomes for children with autism. *Journal of Child Psychology and Psychiatry 45,* 212–229.

Howlin, P., Mawhood, L. M., & Rutter, M. (2000). Autism and developmental receptive language disorder: A follow-up comparison in early adult life: II. Social, behavioural and psychiatric outcomes. *Journal of Child Psychology and Psychiatry, 41,* 561–578.

Hutton, J. (1998). *Cognitive decline and new problems arising in association with autism.* Unpublished doctoral dissertation, University of London.

International Molecular Genetic Study of Autism Consortium. (2001). A genomewide screen for autism: Strong evidence for linkage to chromosome 2q, 7q, and 16p. *American Journal of Human Genetics, 69,* 570–581.

Isager, T., Mouridsen, S. E., & Rich, B. (1999). Mortality and causes of death in pervasive developmental disorders. *Autism: International Journal of Research and Practice, 3,* 7–16.

Jolliffe, T., Landsdown, R., & Robinson, T. (1992). *Autism: A personal account.* London: National Autistic Society.

Kanner, L. (1971). Follow-up study of eleven autistic children originally reported in 1943.

Journal of Autism and Childhood Schizophrenia, 1, 119–145.

Kanner, L. (1973). *Childhood psychosis: Initial studies and new insights.* New York: Winston/Wiley.

Kanner, L., & Eisenberg, L. (1956). Early infantile autism 1943–1955. *American Journal of Orthopsychiatry Psychiatry, 26,* 55–65.

Keel, J. H., Mesibov, G., & Woods, A. V. (1997). TEACCH-Supported employment programme. *Journal of Autism and Developmental Disorders, 27,* 3–10.

Kilsby, M., & Beyer, S. (1996). Engagement and interactions: A comparison between supported employment and day service provision. *Journal of Intellectual Disability Research, 40,* 348–358.

Klin, A., Volkmar, F. R., & Sparrow, S. S. (Eds.). (2000). *Asperger syndrome.* New York: Guilford Press.

Kobayashi, R., Murata, T., & Yashinaga, K. (1992). A follow-up study of 201 children with autism in Kyushu and Yamaguchi, Japan. *Journal of Autism and Developmental Disorders, 22,* 395–411.

Kuperman, S., Black, D. W., & Burns, T. L. (1988). Excess mortality among formerly hospitalized child psychiatric patients. *Archives of General Psychiatry, 45,* 277–282.

Lainhart, J. E. (1999). Psychiatric problems in individuals with autism, their parents and siblings. *International Review of Psychiatry, 11,* 278–298.

Lainhart, J. E., & Folstein, S. E. (1994). Affective disorders in people with autism: A review of published cases. *Journal of Autism and Developmental Disorders, 24,* 587–601.

Larsen, F. W., Dahl, V., & Hallum, E. (1990). A 30-year follow-up study of a child psychiatric clientele: I. Demographic description. *Acta Paediatrica Scandinavica, 81,* 39–45.

Larsen, F. W., & Mouridsen, S. E. (1997). The outcome in children with childhood autism and Asperger syndrome originally diagnosed as psychotic: A 30-year follow-up study of subjects hospitalized as children. *European Child and Adolescent Psychiatry, 6,* 181–190.

Lawson, W. (2002). *Understanding and working with the spectrum of autism: An insider's view.* London: Jessica Kingsley.

Lockyer, L., & Rutter, M. (1969). A five to fifteen year follow-up study of infantile psychosis: III. Psychological aspects. *British Journal of Psychiatry, 115,* 865–882.

Lockyer, L., & Rutter, M. (1970). A five to fifteen year follow-up study of infantile psychosis: IV. Patterns of cognitive abilities. *British Journal of Social and Clinical Psychology, 9,* 152–163.

Lord, C. (1995). Facilitating social inclusion: Examples from peer intervention programs. In E. Schopler & G. Mesibov (Eds.), *Learning and cognition in autism* (pp. 221–239). New York: Plenum Press.

Lord, C., & Bailey, A. (2002). Autism spectrum disorders. In M. Rutter & E. Taylor (Eds.), *Child and adolescent psychiatry* (4th ed., pp. 636–663). Oxford, England: Blackwell.

Lord, C., Rutter, M., & Le Couteur, A. (1994). Autism Diagnostic Interview-Revised: A revised version of a diagnostic interview for carers of individuals with possible pervasive developmental disorders. *Journal of Autism and Developmental Disorders, 24,* 659–685.

Lord, C., Rutter, M., Di Lavore, P. C., & Risi, S. (2000). Autism Diagnostic Observation Schedule (ADOS). Los Angeles: Western Psychological Services.

Lord, C., & Schopler, E. (1985). Differences in sex ratios in autism as a function of measured intelligence. *Journal of Autism and Development Disorders, 15,* 185–193.

Lord, C., & Venter, A. (1992). Outcome and follow-up studies of high functioning autistic individuals. In E. Schopler & G. B. Mesibov (Eds.), *High functioning individuals with autism* (pp. 187–200). New York: Plenum Press.

Lotter, V. (1966). Epidemiology of autistic conditions in young children. I: Prevalence. *Social Psychiatry, 1,* 163–173.

Lotter, V. (1974a). Factors related to outcome in autistic children. *Journal of Autism and Childhood Schizophrenia, 4,* 263–277.

Lotter, V. (1974b). Social adjustment and placement of autistic children in Middlesex: A follow-up study. *Journal of Autism and Childhood Schizophrenia, 4,* 11–32.

Lotter, V. (1978). Follow-up studies. In M. Rutter & E. Schopler (Eds.), *Autism: A reappraisal of concepts and treatment* (pp. 475–496). New York: Plenum Press.

Macintosh, K. E., & Dissanayake, C. (2004). Annotation: The similarities and differences between autistic disorder and Asperger's disorder. *Journal of Child Psychology and Psychiatry, 45,* 419–420.

Mawhood, L. M., & Howlin, P. (1999). The outcome of a supported employment scheme for high functioning adults with autism or Asperger syndrome. *Autism; International Journal of Research and Practice, 3,* 229–253.

Mawhood, L. M., Howlin, P., & Rutter, M. (2000). Autism and developmental receptive language disorder—a follow-up comparison in early adult life: I. Cognitive and language outcomes.

Journal of Child Psychology and Psychiatry, 41, 547–559.

McCaughrin, W., Ellis, W., Rusch, F., & Heal, L. (1993). Cost-effectiveness of supported employment. *Mental Retardation, 31,* 41–48.

McDougle, C. J. (1997). Psychopharmacology. In D. J. Cohen & F. R. Volkmar (Eds.), *Handbook of autism and pervasive developmental disorders* (2nd ed., pp. 707–729). New York: Wiley.

Mittler, P., Gillies, S., & Jukes, E. (1966). Prognosis in psychotic children: Report of a follow-up study. *Journal of Mental Deficiency Research, 10,* 73–83.

National Research Council. (2001). *Educating children with autism* (Committee on Educational Interventions for Children with Autism). Washington, DC: National Academy Press.

Newson, E., Dawson, M., & Everard, T. (1982). *The natural history of able autistic people: Their management and functioning in a social context.* Unpublished report to the Department of Health and Social Security, London.

Nordin, V., & Gillberg, C. (1998). The long-term course of autistic disorders: Update on follow-up studies. *Acta Psychiatrica Scandinavica, 97,* 99–108.

O'Neill, J. L. (1999). *Through the eyes of aliens: A book about autistic people.* London: Jessica Kingsley.

Östman, O. (1991). Child and adolescent psychiatric patients in adulthood. *Acta Paediatrica Scandinavica, 84,* 40–45.

Ozonoff, S., South, M., & Miller, J. N. (2000). *DSM-IV* defined Asperger syndrome: Cognitive, behavioural and early history differentiation from high-functioning autism. *Autism: International Journal of Research and Practice, 4,* 29–46.

Petty, L. K., Ornitz, E. M., Michelman, J. D., & Zimmerman, E. G. (1984). Autistic children who become schizophrenic. *Archives of General Psychiatry, 41,* 129–135.

Piven, J., Harper, J., Palmer, P., & Arndt, S. (1996). Course of behavioural change in autism: A retrospective study of high-IQ adolescents and adults. *Journal of the American Academy of Child and Adolescent Psychiatry, 35,* 523–529.

Pozner, A., & Hammond, J. (1993). *An evaluation of supported employment initiatives for disabled people.* Research Series No. 17. London: Department of Employment.

Rumsey, J. M., Rapoport, J. L., & Sceery, W. R. (1985). Autistic children as adults: Psychiatric social and behavioural outcomes. *Journal of the American Academy of Child Psychiatry, 24,* 465–473.

Rutter, M. (1972). Childhood schizophrenia reconsidered. *Journal of Autism and Childhood Schizophrenia, 2,* 315–337.

Rutter, M. (2000). Genetic studies of autism: From the 1970s into the Millennium. *Journal of Abnormal Child Psychology, 28,* 3–14.

Rutter, M., Greenfeld, D., & Lockyer, L. (1967). A five to fifteen year follow-up of infantile psychosis: II. Social and behavioural outcome. *British Journal of Psychiatry, 113,* 1183–1189.

Rutter, M., & Lockyer, L. (1967). A five to fifteen year follow-up study of infantile psychosis: I. Description of the sample. *British Journal of Psychiatry, 113,* 1169–1182.

Schopler, E., Mesibov, G. B., & Kunce, L. J. (1998). *Asperger syndrome or high functioning autism?* New York: Plenum Press.

Seltzer, M. M., Krauss, M. W., Shattuck, P. T., Orsmond, G., Swe, A., & Lord, C. (2002). *The symptoms of autism spectrum disorders in adolescence and adulthood.* Manuscript submitted for publication.

Shavelle, R. M., Strauss, D. J., & Pickett, J. (2001). Causes of death in autism *Journal of Autism and Developmental Disorders, 6,* 569–576.

Smalley, S., McCracken, J., & Tanguay, P. (1995). Autism, affective disorders, and social phobia. *American Journal of Medical Genetics (Neuropsychiatric Genetics), 60,* 19–26.

Smith, M., Belcher, R., & Juhrs, P. (1995). *A guide to successful employment for individuals with autism.* Baltimore: Paul H. Brookes.

Stoddart, K. (1999). Adolescents with Asperger syndrome: 3 case studies of individual and family therapy. *Autism: International Journal of Research and Practice, 3,* 255–272.

Sturmey, P. (1998). Classification and diagnosis of psychiatric disorders in persons with developmental disabilities. *Journal of Developmental and Physical Disabilities, 10,* 317–330.

Sverd, J., Montero, G., & Gurevich, N. (1993). Brief report: Case for an association between Tourette's syndrome, autistic disorder and schizophrenia-like disorder. *Journal of Autism and Developmental Disorders, 23,* 407–414.

Szatmari, P. (2000). Perspectives on the classification of Asperger syndrome. In A. Klin, F. R. Volkmar, & S. S. Sparrow (Eds.), *Asperger syndrome* (pp. 403–417). New York: Guilford Press.

Szatmari, P., Archer, L., Fisman, S., Streiner, D., & Wilson, F. (1995). Asperger's syndrome and autism: Differences in behaviour, cognition and adaptive functioning. *Journal of the American Academy of Child and Adolescent Psychiatry, 34,* 1662–1670.

Szatmari, P., Bartolucci, G., Bremner, R. S., Bond, S., & Rich, S. (1989). A follow-up study of high functioning autistic children. *Journal of Autism and Developmental Disorders, 19,* 213–226.

Szivos, S. E. (1990). Attitudes to work and their relationship to self-esteem and aspirations among young adults with a mild mental handicap. *British Journal of Mental Subnormality, 36,* 108–117.

Szurek, S., & Berlin, I. (1956). Elements of psychotherapeutics with the schizophrenic child and his parents. *Psychiatry, 19,* 1–19.

Tantam, D. (1991). Asperger's syndrome in adulthood. In U. Frith (Ed.), *Autism and Asperger syndrome* (pp. 147–183). Cambridge, England: Cambridge University Press.

Tantam, D. (2000). Psychological disorder in adolescents and adults with Asperger's syndrome. *Autism: International Journal of Research and Practice, 4,* 47–62.

Venter, A., Lord, C., & Schopler, E. (1992). A follow-up study of high functioning autistic children. *Journal of Child Psychology and Psychiatry, 33,* 489–507.

Volkmar, F. R., & Cohen, D. J. (1991). Comorbid association of autism and schizophrenia. *American Journal of Psychiatry, 148,* 1705–1707.

von Knorring, A.-L., & Häglöf, B. (1993). Autism in northern Sweden. A population based follow-up study: Psychopathology. *European Child and Adolescent Psychiatry, 2,* 91–97.

Williams, D. (1992). *Nobody nowhere.* London: Corgi Books.

Wing, L. (1981). Asperger's syndrome: A clinical account. *Psychological Medicine, 11,* 115–129.

Wing, L. (1986). Clarification on Asperger's syndrome [Letter to the Editor]. *Journal of Autism and Developmental Disorders, 16,* 513–515.

Wing, L., & Gould, J. (1978). Systematic recording of behaviors and skills of retarded and psychotic children. *Journal of Autism and Childhood Schizophrenia, 8,* 79–97.

Wing, L., & Shah, A. (2000). Catatonia in autistic spectrum disorders. *British Journal of Psychiatry, 176,* 357–362.

Wolff, S., & McGuire, R. J. (1995). Schizoid personality in girls: A follow-up study. What are the links with Asperger's syndrome? *Journal of Child Psychology and Psychiatry, 36,* 793–818.

Wozniak, J., Biederman, J., Faraone, S. V., Frazier, J., Kim, J., Millstein, R., et al. (1997). Mania in children with pervasive developmental disorder revisited. *Journal of the American Academy of Child and Adolescent Psychiatry, 36,* 1552–1559.

Zetlin, A., & Murtaugh, M. (1990). Whatever happened to those with borderline IQs? *American Journal on Mental Retardation, 94,* 463–469.

SECTION II

DEVELOPMENT AND BEHAVIOR

The concept of pervasive developmental disorders (PDDs) implies that individuals with autism and related conditions display difficulties across a range of developmental domains, rather than simply in one or another aspect of development. The unfolding and maturation of basic competencies are affected to a greater or lesser degree, and there are varied downstream behavioral consequences of earlier difficulties. The patterns of dysfunction, the extent of impairment, and the areas of relatively better or even normal functioning differ among individuals within one category of disorder and also among the types of disorders. While the pathways of development—socialization, communication, perception and attention, and cognition—are separated in theoretical discussion and research, the minds of children are not so neatly divisible by chapter headings or disciplinary designations. Thus, the complex interactions between the domains and changing relations among them at different phases of development also need to be considered.

The scientific study of development and behavior of individuals with autism and other disorders aims at defining the nature of the underlying dysfunctions. What are the specific types of social dysfunctions exhibited by individuals with autism and how do these differ from those seen in Asperger syndrome, Rett's, or other forms of mental retardation? In autism, what accounts for the relatively better performance on some cognitive tasks (e.g., those that call upon rote memory) in contrast with others (e.g., those that require particular types of social judgment)? What is the mean-

ing of the disparity between verbal and performance skills in Asperger's syndrome, and how does this pattern relate to social difficulties?

To understand the behavioral and developmental findings among individuals with pervasive developmental disorders, it is necessary to study individuals with different levels of cognitive ability (from profoundly retarded through normal intelligence); at different chronological ages (from early childhood through adulthood); and with various observational, laboratory, interview, and other approaches that have demonstrated reliability and validity. The interpretation of findings requires thoughtful consideration of possible methodological problems, including how representative the sample is of the full population of individuals with the disorder, the adequacy of control and contrast groups, how well the behavioral measure captures the function that is to be studied, and the validity or the measures as well as other issues concerning design of instruments and studies. Research in developmental psychopathology must be as rigorous and replicable as in any other area of psychological study.

The developmental psychopathological perspective on autism and similar conditions explains the empirical findings concerning atypical behavior and development within the context of normal principles of development. From this perspective, the concepts of normal development highlight the specific types of deviations, abnormalities, rates, and patterns of development of individuals and groups with pervasive disorders. In turn, the study of individuals with autism and other conditions is used to test and expand hypotheses about preconditions of normal development and the unfolding of basic competencies, for example, the relations among cognitive, social, and affective development.

Autism and the other pervasive disorders almost always are chronic conditions; however, the functioning of individuals is not static. While intellectual abilities tend to remain relatively stable, individuals with autism and other pervasive disorders mature and change during their lives, just as other children and adolescents do. For example, individuals with strictly defined autism usually tend to become increasingly social during their later childhood and adolescent years; occasionally, children with pervasive disorders show dramatic improvements in social and adaptive functioning and may seem only odd or eccentric in adulthood. For some individuals, progress is slow or, sadly, in some cases minimal. Furthermore, new difficulties can also emerge over time.

Adolescence may be quite difficult for these children as they experience an upsurge of sexual and aggressive behavior; for higher functioning individuals, young adulthood may be a time of heightened loneliness and depression as they recognize the profound nature of their difficulties, their differences from others, and their limited opportunities. This can be a particular problem for more able individuals with higher functioning autism, Asperger's, or PDD-NOS. The study of development during the lifespan is important for practical as well as theoretical reasons. The chapters in this Section describe the major domains in which individuals with pervasive disorders manifest their cardinal problems. A fuller understanding of behavioral changes throughout development is critical for understanding not only the natural history of these disorders, but also for designing interventions appropriate for each developmental level.

CHAPTER 8

Autism in Infancy and Early Childhood

KATARZYNA CHAWARSKA AND FRED R. VOLKMAR

Autism is a neurodevelopmental disorder characterized by symptom onset prior to the third birthday. Until relatively recently, its early symptoms have usually been ascertained retrospectively through parent reports because the majority of children did not receive the diagnosis until preschool or early school age. In the past decade, however, advances in early diagnosis research and the reports stressing the efficacy of early intervention made the transition to studying autism in the first 3 years of life both possible and imperative (National Research Council, 2001). In addition to the importance of early identification of autism for treatment, particularly in families where there is a known genetic risk, early identification provides the opportunity for studying the disorder before confounding effects of treatment, development of compensatory strategies, and comorbid disorders have begun to impact its manifestation. This chapter contains a review of research regarding the symptoms of autism in infancy and early childhood, specific developmental profiles observed in this population, stability of the diagnosis, and a brief discussion of the challenges and opportunities that earlier diagnosis of the condition will present.

SYMPTOMS OF AUTISM IN EARLY CHILDHOOD

Studies on parental recognition of developmental abnormalities in autism suggest that approximately 30% (De Giacomo & Fombonne, 1998) to 54% (Volkmar, Stier, & Cohen, 1985) of parents of children diagnosed with autism register their first concerns before their child's first birthday and at least 80% to 90% recognize their child's abnormalities by 24 months (De Giacomo & Fombonne, 1998). These estimates are based primarily on parents' retrospective reports and, thus, may be confounded by passage of time, limited expertise regarding typical development, and possible underestimation of the significance of perceived difficulties in early development. For that reason, they are likely to represent the upper-bound limit of the actual age of symptom onset in autism (De Giacomo & Fombonne, 1998; Volkmar et al., 1985).

First Year of Life

Defining a set of developmentally sensitive diagnostic criteria for autism in infants and toddlers is an inherently difficult task (Lord &

The authors gratefully acknowledge the support of the National Institute of Child Health and Human Development (grants 1-PO1-HD35482-01, 5 P01-HD042127-02), the National Institute of Mental Health (STAART grant U54-MH066594), and the National Alliance of Autism Research grants. The authors thank Amy Sanchez for her help in the preparation of this chapter.

Risi, 2000). Infancy is a period of the most dynamic growth and change; thus, the same behavior (or absence thereof) in one narrowly defined period of time gains clinical significance and becomes indicative of abnormal development only a few months later. For instance, predominance of exploratory play is typical and adaptive for children under the age of 12 months but may signify developmental difficulties when it extends into the second year of life and is not followed by symbolic and generative forms of play (Losche, 1990; Piaget, 1954). The preintentional use of physical gestures such as reach and grasp to pursue desirable objects is typical of children under the age of 9 months. It is expected, however, that this gesture becomes synchronized with eye contact soon thereafter as an index of emerging intentional communication (Bates, 1979). A persistent lack of such synchronization becomes symptomatic of disruption in social communication in the second year of life. Moreover, some early symptoms of autism become less pronounced over time as children acquire language and begin to benefit from intervention programs targeting, among others, play or specific joint attention skills. Situational factors such as variability of clinical presentation depending on the extent of attentional, cognitive, and behavioral difficulties, amount of structure and support provided during testing, nature of the task (e.g., verbal versus nonverbal), and novelty and complexity of the environment may also have impact on early diagnosis (National Research Council, 2001).

Among other factors that might hinder the early detection of autism is the regression or, as it is sometimes termed, the *setback* phenomenon. While the initial observations of cases of autism suggested the presence of social development abnormalities from birth (Kanner, 1943/1968), further clinical observations revealed a subgroup of children who reportedly developed normally though the first 18 to 20 months of life, but then experienced loss of language skills and decreased interest in usual activities along with withdrawal from social interactions (Eisenberg & Kanner, 1956; Volkmar & Cohen, 1989). Recent estimates suggest that between 20% and 40% of children with autism experience regression prior to the second birthday (Fombonne & Chakrabarti, 2001;

Kurita, 1985; Lord, Shulman, & DiLavore, 2004; Rogers & DiLalla, 1990; Tuchman & Rapin, 1997). It is not clear whether regressive autism constitutes a neurobiological subtype of autism, represents variable expression of the same genetic factors, or is an even earlier manifestation of essentially the same phenomenon seen in childhood disintegrative disorder (see Volkmar, Koenig, & State, Chapter 3, this *Handbook,* this volume).

Despite the fact that a significant proportion of parents report concerning behaviors prior to the first birthday, the direct evidence regarding clinical presentation of infants with autism in this age range is still very limited. Apart from a series of clinical case studies and parent retrospective report, the most direct evidence comes from studies analyzing videotapes of children who were subsequently diagnosed with autism.

Case Studies

In his description of 11 cases of autism, Kanner (1943/1968) noted that while abnormalities of speech and cognitive functions, as well as repetitive behaviors and insistence on sameness, emerge over time as the child acquires motor and cognitive skills necessary for the abnormalities to manifest themselves, the autistic aloneness, or the "inability to relate themselves in the ordinary way to people and situations" (p. 243), is present since birth. This social isolation is evident from very early on in their self-sufficiency and ability to occupy themselves for long periods of time. Moreover, Kanner suggested that these children have difficulties in adjusting body posture while being held by another person and in assuming an anticipatory posture in preparation of being picked up. Others reported limited eye contact and decreased social responsivity (Dawson, Osterling, Meltzoff, & Kuhl, 2000; Klin et al., 2004; Sparling, 1991), as well as lack of motor imitation and imitative babbling (Dawson et al., 2000). Among other symptoms described in case studies are those relating to arousal regulation and motor development. More specifically, infants that are later diagnosed with autism may demonstrate excessive tremulousness and excessive startle response in the perinatal period (Sparling, 1991), arousal regulation difficulties, sleep difficulties, unusual sensitivity to stimuli (particularly hypersensitivity to touch), oral-motor problems, as well as motor difficulty related to both hypo- and hypertonia present by 6 months of age (Dawson et al., 2000). Although intriguing, case studies have a number of profound limitations, including lack of data regarding universality of the described symptoms, as well as their specificity to autism (see also Stone, 1997, for review).

Parent Report

Retrospective parent report studies suggest that the early symptoms cluster around deficits in early emerging social interaction skills and may include arousal regulation difficulties. In a retrospective interview study by Klin, Volkmar, and Sparrow (1992), parents of preschoolers with autism were interviewed with the Vineland Adaptive Behaviors Scale (Sparrow, Balla, & Cicchetti, 1984) to determine whether children with autism exhibit impairments in social behaviors that typically emerge prior to the first birthday. Five behaviors were the most frequently endorsed as never performed by children with autism as compared with a developmentally delayed control group matched for mental age (MA), chronological age (CA), and intelligence quotient (IQ): showing anticipation of being picked up, showing affection toward familiar people, showing interest in children or peers other than siblings, reaching for a familiar person, and playing simple interaction games with others. Rogers and DiLalla (1990) addressed the question of the earliest manifestations of autism in a group of 39 children (mean age 45 months) referred to a specialized clinic and diagnosed with infantile autism or pervasive developmental disorder (PDD). Parents of children with symptom onset before 12 months expressed concerns primarily about their abnormal temperamental characteristics, as the children were described as either extremely difficult or very passive. Reported symptoms included irritability, inability to be soothed, and erratic physiological patterns, or being too good, undemanding, and happy to play alone in a crib. Other symptoms included lack of stranger anxiety that typically emerges around 8 months. It is not clear, however, to what extent these symptoms related to self-regulation are specific to autism in the first year of life.

Videotape Analysis Studies

Several studies of home videos suggest that infants with autism are distinguishable both from their typical and developmentally delayed peers in the first year of life.

Autism versus Typical Development Maestro and colleagues (2002) studied videotapes of infants 6 months and younger who were later diagnosed with autism and compared the results with video recordings of typical controls matched for CA. Among the characteristics considered were visual attention and affective responsiveness to social and nonsocial stimuli. Infants with autism showed diminished visual attention to people, sought others less frequently, and were less likely to smile at others and vocalize as compared to typically developing infants. They were also less likely to anticipate others' aim and to explore objects orally or manually. At the same time, there were no differences between the groups in terms of visual attention and affective responses to objects. Moreover, behaviors related to communication or repetitive behaviors occurred in the same frequency in both groups.

In slightly older infants (8 to 10 months), the only behavior that distinguished children with early-onset autism from typical peers was diminished response to their name, while other social behaviors (looking at others, looking at the face while smiling, and orienting to name), communication behaviors (vocalizations consisting of vowel and vowel-consonant combinations), and functional and nonfunctional repetitive behaviors did not (Werner et al., 2000). The diminished response to name persisted and retained its power to differentiate between the two groups at the age of 12 months (Osterling & Dawson, 1994). Thus, it appears that already in the first months of life, there is a lower sensitivity to and salience of social stimuli as compared with typical children. However, approximately 70% of children with autism also experience delays in various areas of development; thus, to identify what is uniquely due to autism, the behavior of infants with autism must be compared to that of infants without autism who have developmental delays.

Autism versus Mental Retardation   Baranek (1999) rated the videotaped material of 39 children ages 9 to 12 months on early-emerging social-cognitive behaviors (looking, gaze aversion, response to name, social touch responses, and affective expressions), as well as various repetitive and sensory-seeking and avoiding behaviors. The only behavior that reliably distinguished infants with autism from the two other groups was poor response to name. However, when a profile of predictor variables was considered, infants with autism tended to exhibit excessive mouthing, aversion to social touch, lower frequency of orienting to visual stimuli, and poor response to name as compared to MR and typical controls. The study suggested that in the last quarter of the first year of life, autism might manifest not only in social communication difficulties (response to name) but also in diminished interest in nonsocial visual stimuli and unusual sensory behaviors.

Behavior of 12-month-old infants with autism as well as infants later diagnosed with MR and 20 typically developing infants was analyzed for a wide range of social-communicative as well as motor and sensory behaviors (Osterling, Dawson, & Munson, 2002). The behaviors of interest included gaze (looking at faces, attention to people, attention to objects not held by others), joint attention (looking at an object held by another, alternating gaze between a person and an object, and pointing), communication and language (seeking contact with an adult, participation in reciprocal social games, immediate imitation, orienting to name), as well as motor behaviors (repetitive motor actions, sitting unassisted, crawling, pulling to a stand, standing unassisted, and walking). Infants with autism and MR differed from those with only MR in terms of the frequency and duration of two behaviors: orienting to name and looking at people. Infants with autism (both with and without MR) differed from typical controls on the same items and use of gestures, looking at objects held by others, and repetitive actions, but not on rate of vocalizations or looking at objects not held by others. A discriminant function analysis iden-

tified three behaviors that were particularly useful for identifying infants with autism: orienting to name, looking at people, and looking at objects held by people.

Summary

Based on the analysis of samples of videotaped diaries, it appears that in the first year of life infants with early-onset autism can be distinguished from typical and developmentally delayed children matched for CA. During the first 6 to 8 months, the affected infants show diminished visual attention to people, which may signify limited salience of and interest in the social environment. They tend to seek others less frequently and are less likely to engage in early social communicative exchanges involving smiling at others and vocalizing. At the same time, they are no different from typical children where interest in and exploration of objects are concerned. This pattern is consistent with the hypothesis of the earliest disruption of social development in autism, but the present evidence is not sufficient to determine whether diminished social orientation in the first months of life is unique to autism or whether it is shared with other developmental disorders. In the second half of the first year when typically developing infants begin to respond differentially to verbal stimuli in general and to the sound of their own name in particular, infants with autism begin to show a startling lack of such sensitivity. This particular deficit sets them apart consistently from both typical and developmentally delayed peers and persists throughout the early preschool years (Lord, 1995). In the visual domain, affected infants continue to be less responsive and pay less attention to people in their environment. At about the same time, typically developing infants become capable of integrating their interactions with people with the exploration of objects and begin to engage in visual joint attention behaviors (Bruner, 1981). Although deficits in visual joint attention are one of the most reliable symptoms of autism in the second year of life and beyond, at 12 months they are only beginning to emerge and might manifest in a lower frequency of looking at objects held by others. Despite reports of difficulties in sensory sensitivities, arousal regulation, motor difficulties, and impaired vocal and motor imitation based on parent report and single-case studies, none of these factors have been reported as a result of analysis of the videotaped materials. This discrepancy may be due to selective taping, but it may also suggest that these symptoms are not unique to infants with autism.

Second and Third Years

A majority of parents of children with autism begin to recognize and seek medical or psychological advice about their children's developmental disturbances in the second and third years of life (De Giacomo & Fombonne, 1998; Rogers & DiLalla, 1990; Short & Schopler, 1988). Concerns are usually triggered by a lack of skill progress (e.g., speech does not develop as expected), loss of skills (e.g., loss of words, eye contact, or interest in others), and emergence of abnormal behaviors (e.g., proclivity for spinning things or motor mannerisms).

Parent Retrospective Report

Studies comparing clinical presentation of children with autism with typical children (Hoshino et al., 1982; Ornitz, Guthrie, & Farley, 1977) and children with other developmental disabilities (Wimpory, Hobson, Williams, & Nash, 2000) suggest that the differences between groups begin to cluster around the core areas of autistic psychopathology. While the abnormalities in the area of social interaction and communication continue to unfold, unusual sensory interests and repetitive behaviors begin to emerge (e.g., Ornitz et al., 1977). A study on parents of preschool children with autism and developmental delays employing the Detection of Autism by Infant Sociability Interview (DAISI) suggests that behaviors that differentiated the two diagnostic groups fell into two categories: dyadic or social interaction (i.e., raising arms up to be picked up, frequency and intensity of eye contact, preverbal turn taking, and using noises communicatively), as well as triadic or person-object-person interactions (joint attention, i.e., referential use of eye contact, offering and giving objects, pointing to objects, and following others' pointing) (Wimpory et al., 2000). Others reported symptom clusters

present in children under the age of 24 months including social behaviors (limited imitation, preference for being alone, not looking at others, lack of interest in interactive games), affective behaviors (no social smile, limited facial expressions, and empty smile), and sensory behaviors (no response to name, behaving as if deaf, insensitivity to pain, hypersensitivity to the taste of food; Hoshino et al., 1982).

Parent Prospective Report

Parental reports regarding current developmental concerns are less likely to be affected by selective recollection and can be compared with direct clinical observations (Cox et al., 1999; Dahlgren & Gillberg, 1989; Gillberg et al., 1990; Klin et al., 1992; Lord, 1995; Stone, Lee, et al., 1999).

Autism versus Language Disorder   A longitudinal study by Cox and his colleagues (Cox et al., 1999) followed a group of forty-six 20-month-old infants identified through a screening with the Checklist for Autism in Toddlers (CHAT; Baird et al., 2000; Baron-Cohen, Allen, & Gillberg, 1992; Baron-Cohen, Cox, Baird, Sweettenham, & Nighingale, 1996) as being at risk for autism. The *ICD-10* diagnosis at 42 months indicated that the sample contained 8 children with autism, 13 with nonautistic PDD, 9 with language disorder, and 15 typical children. Parents were interviewed with the Autism Diagnostic Interview-Revised (ADI-R; Lord, Rutter, & Le Couteur, 1994), a structured investigator-based interview used in differential diagnosis of autism. Two items of the ADI-R consistently differentiated the autism group at 20 and 42 months: point for interest and use of conventional gestures. At 20 months, the range of facial expressions item was also consistently endorsed. At 42 months, several new items—seeking to share enjoyment, offering comfort, nodding, and imaginative play—were endorsed as more pathological by parents of children with autism. No items from the repetitive behaviors and stereotypical patterns of behaviors scale differentiated between the groups at any time point.

Autism versus Developmental Delay   Lord (1995) reported a follow-up study of thirty

2-year-old children who were referred for a clinical evaluation to a multidisciplinary developmental disabilities clinic for a differential diagnosis of autism. Parents were interviewed with the Autism Diagnostic Interview-Revised ADI-R (Le Couteur et al., 1989) supplemented with the items appropriate for children under age 2. All children were reevaluated a year later. The item-by-item analysis of 30 of the ADI questions (29 items from the original Le Couteur et al. diagnostic algorithm and one additional item, attention to voice) identified a set of items that discriminated 2-year-old children with autism from other children with developmental delays. These items in the social domains were: seeking to share own enjoyment, directing attention, use of other's body as a tool, interest in other children, greeting, and social reciprocity. In the area of communication, attention to voice, pointing, and understanding of gestures discriminated between the groups. Among the items comprising the repetitive and restricted behaviors domain, hand and finger mannerisms as well as unusual sensory behaviors discriminated between the groups. Two of these behaviors, directing attention (showing) and attention to voice, were found particularly useful in differentiating between the diagnostic groups, as they identified correctly 82.8% of children.

At age 3, four items correctly classified all the subjects: use of other's body, attention to voice, pointing, and finger mannerisms. At this age, more children with autism showed abnormalities in gaze, limited range of facial expressions, and limited comfort-seeking behaviors. In addition, the number of children with nonautistic disorders showing abnormal behaviors decreased from the age of 2 to 3, allowing for clearer differentiation between the two groups. Behaviors related to directing attention, abnormal gaze, and facial expressions have been found equally disturbed across the range of language skills and nonverbal functioning (Lord & Pickles, 1996).

Observational Studies

Direct observational and experimental studies provide the most reliable source of information regarding syndrome expression in young children.

Autism Only   Stone, Hoffman, Lewis, and Ousley (1994) examined behavioral characteristics of a group of 26 children between the ages of 24 and 44 months diagnosed with autism. The majority of children in this age range exhibited lack of awareness of others, impaired imitation, abnormal social play, abnormal nonverbal communication, and absence of imaginative play. Deficits in social interaction and nonverbal communication were more prominent than presence of repetitive behaviors and restricted interests and activities. Parents and clinicians rarely endorsed abnormal speech production, abnormal speech content, and impaired conversational skills, as most of the children in this age group were nonverbal. At the same time, children with autism showed no abnormality in comfort seeking, suggesting they were able to use their parents as a source of reassurance, and they enjoyed cuddling and affection. In addition, no increase in distress over change and insistence on routines was noted, suggesting that the need for sameness may emerge and become more apparent later in development.

Autism versus Developmental Delay   One of the most well-known and widely used instruments for diagnostic observation is the Autism Diagnostic Observation Scale-Generic (ADOS-G). The ADOS-G is composed of four modules designed for children with different levels of language skills, with Module 1 designed for preverbal and nonverbal children (Lord et al., 2000). The ADOS-G provides a DSM-IV-based algorithm for the diagnosis of autism, nonautistic PDD, and non-PDD. Module 1 of the ADOS-G was modeled directly on its prelinguistic (PL) precursor, the PL-ADOS (DiLavore, Lord, & Rutter, 1995). Using the PL-ADOS, DiLavore and colleagues examined social and communicative behaviors as well as the presence of unusual sensory interests and stereotypical behaviors in a group of 38- to 61-month-old preschool children diagnosed clinically with autism or developmental delay. Children with autism consistently showed impaired use of nonverbal behaviors to regulate social interactions, including eye contact, facial expressions directed to others, and social smile, combined with impaired ability to share pleasure with others. Lack of social reciprocity and spontaneous joint attention was notable, along with increased use of other's body to communicate, and decreased ability to differentiate between parent and examiner. They were also less likely to direct their vocalizations at others, use gestures, and respond to name. Increased frequency of restricted, repetitive, and stereotyped patterns of behaviors was noted as well. Adrien and colleagues (Adrien et al., 1992) studied the validity and reliability of the Infant Behavioral Summarized Scale (IBSS) for assessment of 6- to 48-month-old children with autism, children with developmental delays, and typical controls. They identified 19 out of 33 items that reliably differentiated children with autism from their developmentally delayed peers. The items were related to socialization (e.g., ignores people, prefers aloneness), communication (lack of vocal communication, lack of appropriate facial expressions, poor imitation of gestures or voices), attention and perception (e.g., easily distracted, none or bizarre reaction to auditory stimuli, abnormal eye contact), stereotyped behaviors and unusual postures, as well as inappropriate use of objects. These findings suggest besides abnormalities in the key diagnostic areas, young children with autism show significant attentional deficits, and hyposensitivity to auditory stimuli.

Prospective Screeners

Reports regarding early manifestations of autism in infancy and early childhood have been put to the test in a series of prospective studies attempting to identify children at risk in general (Baird et al., 2000; Baron-Cohen et al., 1992, 1996; Charman, Baron-Cohen, Baird, et al., 2001; Robins, Fein, Barton, & Green, 2001) and referred populations (Robins et al., 2001; Scambler, Rogers, & Wehner, 2001; Stone, Coonrod, & Ousley, 2000). The early reports on the use of the Checklist for Autism in Toddlers (CHAT), a measure combining parent report and physician observation, suggested that at 18 months, symptoms of autism are likely to include abnormalities in the development of protodeclarative pointing, abnormalities in gaze monitoring, as well as pretend play (Baron-Cohen et al., 1992, 1996). However, a subsequent follow-up study indi-

cated that although these behaviors are highly specific to autism, 80% of parents of children who were later diagnosed with autism did not report these behaviors as being abnormal at 18 months (Baird et al., 2000). It is plausible that early on, parents have difficulties in detecting and reporting abnormalities in these specific behaviors, or the difficulties are not universal in children with autism at this age. Moreover, the population screened in the original Baron-Cohen et al. (1996) study did not include children with more severe developmental delays and disabilities further limiting generalizability of the finding to a broader population of infants with autism. A report based on the use of the CHAT with parents of 3-year-olds with autism and developmental delays suggests that further modification of the critical set of items may lead to increased sensitivity without significant loss in specificity (Scambler et al., 2001), but the utility of the new criteria for primary screening remains to be tested in the general population.

To address some of the shortcomings of the CHAT, Robins et al. developed a 23-item extension of the original screening instrument designed for screening 24-month-old children (Modified Checklist for Autism in Toddlers [M-CHAT]; Robins et al., 2001). It was tested on a large group of children screened at well-baby visits as well as children enrolled in early intervention programs. A discriminant function analysis identified a set of predictors that included joint attention items (protodeclarative pointing, following a point, and bringing objects to show), social relatedness items (interest in other children, imitation), and communication (responding to name) consistent with other reports regarding symptoms of autism at the age of 2 (Baron-Cohen et al., 1996; Lord, 1995). The actual rates of false negative and false positive cases remain to be determined on completion of a follow-up assessment of the cohort (see also Stone, Chapter 27, this *Handbook,* Volume 2).

Summary

Retrospective studies on early manifestations of autism relying on parent report and videotape analysis suggest that in the first year of life, a set of developmentally sensitive diagnostic signs of autism is likely to include decreased visual attention to people and diminished response to name (see Table 8.1). The abnormal sensory responses, including excessive mouthing and aversion to touch, have been reported less consistently in the first year of life. In the second and third years of life, symptoms of autism in most children intensify and spread to multiple areas of functioning. In the small minority of children experiencing a developmental regression, the onset of difficulties is often marked by loss of language skills and a decrease in social interest by 18 to 24 months. In the second year, typical infants undergo a tremendous growth spurt regarding social interactions, imaginative play, and nonverbal and verbal communication, while infants with autism begin to show syndrome-specific difficulties in these areas. In the social domain, the most frequently reported symptoms are diminished eye contact; limited interest in peers, social games and turn-taking exchanges; low frequency of looking referentially at parents; and preference for being alone. Vocal and motor imitation appear delayed compared to the children's overall developmental level. A limited range of facial expressions and infrequent instances of sharing affect have been reported as well. In the area of communication, the most striking differences relate to early emerging social communicative exchanges through nonverbal and vocal or verbal means. Affected children have difficulties using conventional gestures. They do not point spontaneously to show things and have difficulties in understanding or responding to such gestures by others. They continue to have difficulties in responding to speech in general and to their name in particular by, for instance, reorienting and looking at an adult. Moreover, the reports stress that children have

TABLE 8.1 Symptoms Differentiating Infants and Toddlers with Autism from Typical and Developmentally Delayed Peers

	Social Interaction	Communication	Stereotypical Behaviors and Repetitive Patters
First year	Limited ability to anticipate being picked up Low frequency of looking at people Little interest in interactive games Little affection toward familiar people Content to be alone	Poor response to name Infrequent looking at objects held by others	Excessive mouthing Aversion to social touch
Second and third year	Abnormal eye contact Limited social referencing Limited interest in other children Limited social smile Low frequency of looking at people Limited range of facial expressions Limited sharing of affect/enjoyment Little interest in interactive games Limited functional play No pretend play Limited motor imitation	Low frequency of verbal or nonverbal communication Failure to share interest (e.g., through pointing, giving, and showing) Poor response to name Failure to respond to communicative gestures (e.g., pointing, giving, and showing) Use of others' body as tool Unusual vocalizations	Hand and finger mannerisms Inappropriate use of objects Repetitive interests/play Unusual sensory behaviors (hyper or hyposensitivity to sounds, textures, taste, visual stimuli)

difficulties using words and vocalizations communicatively. In verbal children, unusual features such as echolalia may be present. Although still infrequent, some stereotypic and repetitive behaviors begin to emerge, especially as children reach 3 years of age. Among them are hand and finger mannerisms, as well as unusual sensory-seeking or avoidance behaviors. The symptoms in children with autism intensify with time and become more pronounced. At the same time, in children with developmental delays, some of the autistic-like behaviors observed early in development appear to diminish in frequency and intensity, allowing for clearer discrimination between the groups.

Methodological Limitations

The results of the studies targeting symptoms of autism in the first 3 years of life are very encouraging and, in many respects, convergent. Nonetheless, several methodological limitations inherent in both the type of available sources of information and selection of comparison groups are worth highlighting. The primary sources of information regarding the earliest syndrome expression continue to be parent retrospective reports and video diaries. Parent interview data, although invaluable, may be confounded by selective recall, limited knowledge about normal development, or denial. Moreover, studies comparing parental reports of concurrent symptoms and expert clinical observations suggest that while parents tend to be accurate in reporting negative symptoms, they do much worse as far as the positive symptoms are concerned (Stone et al., 1994). Specifically, parents often report reliably on a failure to participate in early social games, songs and routines, and preference for solitary activities. However, they have more difficulties judging typicality and reporting deficits in joint attention behaviors and pretend play, the most prototypical symptoms of autism in the second and third years of life (Charman, Baron-Cohen, Baird, et al., 2001). Further, changes in the syndrome expression over time based on parent report can be misleading because it is not clear to what extent the changes reflect true increase in frequency and intensity of the symptoms, grow-

ing parental expectations, or more accurate observation and reporting (Lord, 1995).

The videotaped material collected by parents provides the most direct window into the behavior of the youngest infants subsequently diagnosed with autism. However, these data can be biased by selective taping. For instance, case studies as well as parent reports suggest the presence of abnormalities in arousal regulation, extreme fussiness or placidity, and a lack of stranger anxiety in the first year of life. None of these qualities have been reported based on the analysis of videotaped materials, and it is not clear whether they are not specific to autism or whether such episodes are selectively excluded from the family video diaries.

Although the specific sets of behavioral criteria differentiating children with autism from other disabled populations in the first 3 years of life are slowly beginning to emerge, making direct comparisons and seeking commonalities across studies are still difficult for several reasons. First, there is a limited consistency among studies in terms of specific behaviors selected for observation and their operational definitions, which makes comparisons between the studies problematic at times. Second, the comparison groups vary, which, combined with a very limited number of studies, limits the generalizability of the results. While in some studies autism is compared to language disorders, others select groups with developmental delays of mixed origin, including known genetic syndromes. Still other studies focus on consecutive referrals to clinics specializing in PDD and subsequently compare those diagnosed with PDD to non-PDD disorders. Naturally, the sets of symptoms differentiating the diagnostic groups in these studies are likely to differ. Nonetheless, the progress in studies on early symptoms and diagnosis of autism in recent years has been impressive and marks the beginning of intensive and interdisciplinary research programs targeting infants and toddlers with PDD.

Longitudinal studies of very young children with autism (e.g., 12 to 24 months of age) as well as studies on high-risk populations of younger siblings of children with autism will help elucidate these diagnostic conundrums in the near future.

EARLY DIAGNOSIS

Lowering the age of autism diagnosis raises a question of both sensitivity and specificity of the state-of-the-art diagnostic instruments and procedures, which have been created for and used successfully in older children.

Early Diagnosis and *DSM-IV*

Although the diagnostic criteria for autism in the *DSM-IV* have very good sensitivity and specificity and cover a range of syndrome expression with regard to age and degree of MR, especially when applied to children 4 years and older (Volkmar et al., 1994), they may be of limited use in the diagnosis of the youngest population of children with autism (Lord, 1995; Stone, Lee, et al., 1999). Diagnostic criteria, such as failure to develop peer relationships, impaired conversational skills, and stereotyped language, are usually not applicable to children under 3 years of age (Stone, Lee, et al., 1999). Among the criteria most frequently and consistently endorsed by clinicians in this study were impaired use of nonverbal behaviors and lack of social reciprocity in the social domain and delayed development of spoken language in the communication domain. Children in this age range displayed fewer symptoms from the stereotyped and repetitive behaviors domain; the most commonly (but not necessarily consistently) endorsed symptom was preoccupation with stereotyped and repetitive patterns of interests. These results suggest that further research on the utility of the *DSM-IV* criteria in children under the age of 3 is needed; if only some of the diagnostic criteria are applicable, a different algorithm for the youngest group may be considered necessary (Stone, Lee, et al., 1999).

Early Diagnosis and Autism Diagnostic Interview-Revised

Despite the fact that the ADI-R (Lord et al., 1994) has been found highly effective in diagnosing autism in individuals over the age of 4 years, its utility for diagnosis of very young children (specifically, individuals with MA below 2 years) is rather problematic (Cox et al., 1999; Lord, 1995; Rutter, Le Couteur, & Lord, 2003). In 2-year-olds, ADI-R tends to overdiagnose children with severe developmental delays and underdiagnose higher functioning children with some emerging gestures and words (Lord, 1995). Both sensitivity (proportion of children with autism identified correctly by ADI) and specificity (proportion of children without autism classified correctly by ADI) in children under the age of 3 years were around 50% (Chawarska, Klin, Paul, & Volkmar, submitted; Cox et al., 1999; Lord, 1995).

At the age of 3 years, the ADI-R appears to yield results more consistent with the clinical diagnosis (Cox et al., 1999; Lord, 1995). The higher functioning children who at the age of 2 did not meet diagnostic criteria were reported to have more autistic features in their language, and they met all diagnostic criteria; however, the overdiagnosis of children with severe developmental delays in 3-year-olds remained an issue (Lord, 1995). It is not clear if the improvement in the sensitivity and specificity of the ADI-R was due to the emergence of more consistent patterns of symptoms (e.g., deficits in understanding of gestures, limited range of facial expressions, and shared enjoyment, as well as unusual features of language), higher parental expectations, or higher accuracy of parental reporting in older, previously diagnosed children (Lord & Magill-Evans, 1995).

Early Diagnosis and Clinical Experience

Diagnosis of autism in children under the age of 3 based on clinical observation appears to be the most stable and reliable method (Adrien et al., 1992; Chawarska et al., submitted; Cox et al., 1999; Gillberg et al., 1990; Klin et al., in press; Lord, 1995; Stone, Lee, et al., 1999). Results of the only two studies reporting on diagnosis of autism in children under 24 months suggests that in this age group, clinical diagnosis was relatively stable, with 75% to 90% children diagnosed with autism retaining the diagnosis at follow-up, and the remaining cases receiving another PDD diagnosis (Chawarska et al., in press-a; Cox et al., 1999). Thus, when a broader concept of "autistic spectrum disorder" (ASD) was applied to the diagnosis in the second year of life all children positively identified as on the spectrum continued to exhibit symptoms of ASD at 3 years. However, the rate of cases identified falsely as not on the spectrum at 20 months was very high in this study (Cox et al., 1999). It is not clear whether the high rates of false negative cases at 20 months is due to problems with diagnostic criteria used at this age or whether they might be attributed to a later onset or increase in severity of symptoms.

In 2- and 3-year-old children, the clinical diagnosis continues to be stable and the rate of false negatives diminishes (Lord, 1995; Stone, Lee, et al., 1999). Lord (1995) examined stability of autism diagnosis in a sample of 2-year-olds referred for a differential diagnosis and reassessed at the age of 4. At follow-up, 88% of 4-year-olds retained the diagnosis. The remaining 12% children were rediagnosed with a nonautism disorder (developmental delay and specific language disorder). Only 14% of children who were initially diagnosed with a nonautistic disorder at the age of 2 received a diagnosis of autism at age 3. Stone and her colleagues (1999) also examined the reliability and stability of the clinical diagnosis over a 1-year period in a group of children under the age of 3 years diagnosed with autism or PDD-NOS. A follow-up assessment indicated that the clinical diagnosis was the most reliable and stable for children exhibiting symptoms of autism, as 72% of children retained the diagnosis, 24% improved and received a PDD-NOS diagnosis, and only 4% were diagnosed with a disorder outside the autism spectrum. Children diagnosed at age 2 with PDD-NOS had a more variable outcome. Although 92% of them remained on the spectrum, in about half of the children, symptoms worsened and they were diagnosed with autism. The remaining half showed no or only slight improvement. Because only children with an ASD diagnosis were included in this study, the rate of false negative cases was not examined.

Summary

Clinical diagnosis continues to constitute the gold standard in diagnosis of ASDs not only in school-age children (Volkmar et al., 1994) but also in infants, toddlers, and preschoolers (Chawarska et al., submitted; Cox et al., 1999; Lord, 1995; Stone, Ousley, et al., 1999). Not surprisingly, the reliability of clinical diagnosis is highly correlated with the extent of clinicians' experience evaluating young children (Stone, Ousley, et al., 1999). Expert clinicians are likely to simultaneously consider a number of complementary factors, including the child's history, developmental level, adaptive functioning, verbal and nonverbal communication, and level of social engagement and imagination, leading to a more accurate estimate of the probability of the child's having autism (Lord & Risi, 2000). In general, the short-term stability of clinical diagnosis is very high. Consistent with the findings reported on older children (Volkmar et al., 1994), the PDD-NOS diagnosis is less stable (Stone, Lee, et al., 1999). Although most of these children remain on the spectrum at the age of 3, in some children the symptoms worsen and become consistent with the diagnosis of autism. The rate of false negative cases; that is, the proportion of children who were classified either as typical or as having various non-PDD disabilities, varies highly depending on the study and is likely to be negatively correlated with the age at first diagnosis and the child's cognitive level. Late onset of autism in children and limited sensitivity of the diagnostic procedures are among the factors responsible for cases that go undetected in the first 3 years of life.

SPECIFIC AREAS OF FUNCTIONING

Early observations (Kanner, 1943/1968) and more recent experimental studies (Charman et al., 1997; Chawarska, Klin, Paul, & Volkmar, in press-b; Cox et al., 1999; Dawson & Adams, 1984; Dawson, Meltzoff, Osterling, & Rinaldi, 1998; Dawson, Munson, et al., 2002; Mundy, Sigman, & Kasari, 1990; Mundy, Sigman, Ungerer, & Sherman, 1986; Sigman & Ungerer, 1981, 1984) suggest that in the first years of life, development of children with autism progresses at varying rates and, in some cases, is characterized by significant delays and abnormalities in certain areas of development but not others. This developmental decalage persists over time, and in school-age children manifests in syndrome-specific patterns of cognitive, communication, and adaptive skills (Ehlers et al., 1997; Freeman, Ritvo, Yokota, Childs, & Pollard, 1988; Joseph et al., 2002; Klin, Volkmar, Sparrow, Cicchetti, et al., 1995; Volkmar et al., 1994).

Although young children with autism present with many syndrome-specific deficits, delays in sensorimotor development and executive function in infants and preschool children with autism do not appear either specific or universal. The sensorimotor stage of cognitive development extends from birth through the age of language acquisition and symbolic thinking (Piaget, 1954) and in typical development concludes by the end of the second year of life. In the classic Piagetian sense, sensorimotor intelligence encompasses concepts of object permanence, as well as space and causality. A number of studies indicate that although young children with autism experience delays in these areas, these deficits are not syndrome specific (Chawarska et al., in press; Cox et al., 1999; Dawson, Munson, et al., 2002; Sigman & Ungerer, 1984), and eventually, most children with an MA above 24 months master the central sensorimotor concepts (Morgan, Cutrer, Coplin, & Rodrigue, 1989).

Executive function (EF) skills encompass a broad range of cognitive abilities including planning, flexibility of thought and action, inhibition of irrelevant responses and stimuli, as well as working memory (i.e., holding online mental representations). A number of studies on adults, school-age children, and adolescents with autism suggest impairments in EF (Bennetto, Pennington, & Rogers, 1996; Ozonoff, Pennington, & Rogers, 1991; Pennington & Ozonoff, 1996), but the relationship between autism and EFs is unclear (Bennetto et al., 1996; Russell, Jarrold, & Henry, 1996; Russell, Jarrold, & Hood, 1999). Several studies employing a wide range of tasks tapping EF skills—such as prepotent response inhibition, spatial or object working memory, set shifting and action monitoring—indicate that deficits in preschool children with autism are not syndrome specific and are comparable to those observed in developmentally delayed controls matched for MA (Dawson, Munson, et al., 2002; Griffith, Pennington, Wehner, & Rogers, 1999). Specific deficits in EF become more

apparent at the age of 5 years and are expressed in impaired performance on tasks concerning rule learning, visual recognition memory, working spatial memory, and prepotent response inhibition (Dawson, Meltzoff, Osterling, & Rinaldi, 1998; McEvoy, Rogers, & Pennington, 1993). Such developmental trends suggest that the elementary EF skills emerging early in development may not be affected differentially in autism (Dawson, Munson, et al., 2002).

Attentional Functioning

Although a number of attentional abnormalities in autism have been documented, their extent, as well as their centrality to autism, remains to be clarified (see Burack, Enns, Stauder, Mottron, & Randolph, 1997; Tsatsanis, Chapter 13, this *Handbook,* this volume, for a review). One of the important aspects of attention is the ability to select salient elements or features of the environment for further processing (James, 1890/1950). Studies on older individuals with autism suggest that their spontaneous visual attention to people in general and to faces in particular is diminished as compared with developmentally delayed groups (Klin, Jones, Schultz, Volkmar, & Cohen, 2002; Volkmar & Mayes, 1990). A similar trend has been observed in infants and toddlers with autism. In the first year of life, affected infants visually orient less frequently to people as compared with typical and developmentally delayed controls (Baranek, 1999; Maestro et al., 2002; Osterling et al., 2002). This selective bias persists in the second year and beyond (Dawson, Meltzoff, Osterling, & Rinaldi, 1998; Dawson, Meltzoff, Osterling, Rinaldi, & Brown, 1998; Swettenham et al., 1998). For instance, Swettenham and colleagues examined frequency and distribution of spontaneous visual attention directed at people and objects during a free play session in a group of 20-month-old children with autism, developmental delays, and typical peers. Infants with autism spent a greater proportion of their play focused on objects and a significantly smaller proportion of time fixating visually on people and monitoring their behavior as compared with the two control groups. Similarly, preschool children with autism have been found to monitor communicative behaviors of adults interacting with them much less frequently than matched children with developmental language disorder and typical children (McArthur & Adamson, 1996). At the age of 5, children with autism were less likely to orient to both social and nonsocial stimuli than the two comparison groups, but this impairment was more severe when social stimuli were concerned (Dawson, Meltzoff, Osterling, Rinaldi, & Brown, 1998). Several hypotheses have been proposed to account for such patterns of visual attention. One such hypothesis suggests that children with autism may avoid complex visual stimuli such as faces (Swettenham et al., 1998). Another suggests that children with autism may have a preference for perfect contingencies and, thus, avoid inherently unpredictable and variable social stimuli (Dawson & Lewy, 1989). Yet another hypothesis suggests that the deficit in social attention might be related to motivation and salience of social rewards (Dawson, Carver, et al., 2002).

Preverbal Communication

Delays in development of speech and communication are usually the first to be noticed by parents (53.7%) and the most frequently reported (74.4%; De Giacomo & Fombonne, 1998). Compared to typically developing children, most children with autism develop language later, and their language development is marked by the presence of unusual features (see Tager-Flusberg, Lord, & Paul, Chapter 12, this *Handbook,* this volume).

Vocalizations

The available data suggest that preverbal children with autism show abnormal patterns of sound production. Based on the analysis of vocalizations of three prelinguistic children with autism ages 2.5 to 4 years, Wetherby, Yonclas, and Bryan (1989) noted that although their rate of communication was within the normal range for their stage of language development, they had defects in well-formed syllable production and displayed overproduction of atypical vocalizations such as growling, tongue clicking, and trills. More recently, Sheinkopf, Mundy, Oller, and Steffens (2000) studied vowel-like and consonant-like sounds and into-

nation in a group of preschool children with MA of approximately 22 months and expressive language age of 14 to 15 months. Although children with autism had a similar rate of well-formed canonical vocalizations (babbling), their vocalizations had more abnormal vocal quality than the developmentally delayed comparison group and included squeals, growls, and yells.

Nonverbal Communication

Disturbances in the emergence of nonverbal communication are one of the most prototypical and most extensively studied features of autism in infants and preschool children. Nonverbal communication skills reflect motivation to communicate, understanding of how to communicate, and basic representational skills (Bates, 1979; Sigman & Ruskin, 1999). In the first 9 months of typical development, infants are able to effectively communicate their needs by a variety of means, including reaching for a desirable object or fussing and crying. These communicative attempts are usually directed at the goal itself and not at the person that might be instrumental in attaining the goal. At about 9 months, infants begin to direct their communicative attempts at adults by, for instance, making eye contact with an adult while reaching for a distant toy. Along with this change, infants begin to substitute the early emerging physical gestures (e.g., an open-hand reach) with conventional gestures such as pointing or showing. Their communicative behavior becomes protoimperative, as it involves using human agents to attain nonsocial goals, as well as protodeclarative, involving the use of nonsocial means for social purposes of, for instance, sharing attention (Bates, 1979). Emergence of these behaviors at the end of the first year of life marks, according to Bates, the beginnings of intentional communication, communication in which a child is aware a priori that his or her behavior will have an effect on a listener.

This developmental transition is of particular importance for the discussion of deficits in nonverbal communication in autism. As compared with children with MR or Down syndrome matched for MA, preverbal children with autism communicate less frequently (Stone, Ousley, Yoder, Hogan, & Hepburn,

1997; Wetherby, Cain, Yonclas, & Walker, 1988) and use less complex combinations of nonverbal behaviors to communicate (Stone et al., 1997). Specifically, 2-year-old children with autism are less likely to use eye contact, conventional gestures such as distal and proximal pointing and showing gestures; are more likely to manipulate the examiner's hand using hand-over-hand gestures; and are less likely to pair their communicative gestures with eye contact and vocalizations compared with their developmentally delayed peers (Stone et al., 1997). At the same time, the autism and MR groups do not differ in terms of the proportion of communicative acts that involve reaching, giving objects, touching objects, or vocalizing.

A disproportionately high number of the communicative behaviors that are observed in young children with autism serve a purpose of requesting objects or actions (i.e., protoimperative communication) with very few communicative behaviors aimed at directing another's attention to an object or event (i.e., protodeclarative communication) (Baron-Cohen, 1989; Curcio, 1978; Dawson, Meltzoff, Osterling, Rinaldi, & Brown, 1998; Loveland & Landry, 1986; Mundy & Crowson, 1997; Mundy, Sigman, & Kasari, 1994; Mundy et al., 1986, 1990; Roeyers, Van Oost, & Bothuyne, 1998; Sigman, Mundy, Sherman, & Ungerer, 1986; Sigman & Ruskin, 1999; Stone et al., 1997). This act of recruiting or following the attention of another person for the purpose of sharing interest or enjoyment is often referred to as joint attention (Bruner, 1975; Mundy & Sigman, 1989; Tomasello, 1995). Joint attention behaviors have strong predictive relationships with receptive and expressive language development and nonverbal communication, as well as social-cognitive development. (see Mundy & Burnette, Chapter 25, this *Handbook,* this volume, for a review).

Although the ability to respond to and initiate joint attention bids in autism increases over time, especially in highly structured contexts (Leekam, Hunnisett, & Moore, 1998; Leekam, Lopez, & Moore, 2000), individuals with autism continue to have difficulties using these skills adaptively and spontaneously in more naturalistic situations (Baron-Cohen, Baldwin, & Crowson, 1997; Baron-Cohen, Campbell, Karmiloff-Smith, Grant, & Walker, 1995; Klin et al., 2002; Leekam, Baron-Cohen, Perrett, Milders, & Brown, 1997; Volkmar & Mayes, 1990; Whalen & Schreibman, 2003). Moreover, the sequence of skill acquisition appears to differ from that observed in typical development, which may be suggestive of the development of alternative compensatory processing strategies (Carpenter, Pennington, & Rogers, 2002).

Exploration and Play

Piaget (1962) was the first to stress the progressive nature of mental representation in play and its role in developing and understanding symbols. In the first year of life, play consists of nonsymbolic, undifferentiated exploration of sensorimotor characteristics of objects, their texture, color, details, and the sounds they produce. In the second year of life, play evolves into functional-relational play closely tied to the conventional functions of objects, which then gives way to pretend play. This form of play becomes increasingly generative as children enact activities first in simple and then in multistep pretend scenarios using, first, objects, then placeholders (Tamis-LeMonda & Bornstein, 1991). The onset of symbolic play usually coincides with the beginning of language; in both cases, the child manifests the ability to represent an arbitrary stimulus (e.g., a block or a word) as something else (e.g., an airplane), ignoring, in a sense, the primary, or first-order representation of a block as a block and focusing on its secondary, symbolic aspect (Piaget, 1962).

The videotape analysis studies do not provide strong evidence regarding disrupted object exploration in the first year of life. Infants with autism appear to attend visually to objects with similar frequency as their typical and developmentally delayed peers (Baranek, 1999; Maestro et al., 2002; Osterling et al., 2002). However, 9- to 12-month-old infants with autism have been reported to mouth objects more frequently (Baranek, 1999), which might suggest emerging sensory-seeking behaviors or an extended phase of low-level sensory exploration. Although at 12 months the behaviors of children with autism tend to be more repetitive than those of typical peers, this attribute does not differentiate them from developmentally delayed peers (Baranek, 1999; Osterling et al., 2002).

The second year of life is dominated by increasingly complex functional play with some elements of pretense emerging toward the second birthday. While syndrome-specific impairments in play have been widely described in preschool and school-age children, it is not clear whether they are already present in the second year of life. A study of a small group of 20-month-old infants with autism (MA = 17 months) suggests that at this age, the impairments in play may not be fully differentiated, as infants with autism engage in functional play with a similar frequency as the CA- and MA-matched developmentally delayed controls (Charman et al., 1997). Likewise, their rate of pretend play does not differ from MA-matched developmentally delayed controls but is lower than CA-matched typical peers. These findings are congruent with a longitudinal analysis of videotapes focused on the development of presymbolic play in a small group of children with autism and typical controls followed between 4 and 42 months of age (Losche, 1990). The study suggested that up to 21 months of age, children with autism engaged in various explorations of objects with frequency and quality similar to their typical peers, but starting at 22 months, the frequency of goal-oriented exploration reached a plateau in infants with autism, while it continued to diversify and increase in frequency in typical controls.

Deficits in functional and symbolic play in relation to other cognitive skills have been well documented in preschool children with autism (McDonough, Stahmer, Schreibman, & Thompson, 1997; Mundy et al., 1986; Sigman & Ruskin, 1999; Sigman & Ungerer, 1984; Stone & Caro-Martinez, 1990). While during the preschool period, play skills continue to develop and can be enhanced through prompts, scaffolding, and modeling, children with autism continue to engage in little spontaneous functional and pretend play and their play lacks in generativity (Lewis & Boucher, 1988; McDonough et al., 1997; see Chapter 14, this *Handbook,* this volume).

Motor Imitation

Motor imitation and emulation play an important role in the emergence of both symbolic and social-cognitive skills (Tomasello, Kruger, & Ratner, 1993) and thus are central for studies of autistic psychopathology (Rogers & Pennington, 1991). Motor imitation, or copying a feature of the body movements of a model, requires detection and analysis of movements, that is, the ability to translate visual information regarding body movements of others into matching motor output as well as appreciation for an intentional aspect of such movement (Tomasello et al., 1993). In contrast, in emulation the action copied has to do with reproduction of the object movement rather than the model's body movement.

Studies on imitation in school-age children with autism consistently report deficits in this area as compared to other developmentally challenged populations (Bartak, Rutter, & Cox, 1975; Rogers, 1999; Rogers & Pennington, 1991). Specifically, difficulties with imitation but not emulation of actions of others (Hobson & Lee, 1999), including imitation of both meaningful and meaningless hand and face movements (Rogers, Bennetto, McEvoy, & Pennington, 1996; Smith & Bryson, 1998), have been reported.

While it is not clear whether, in children with autism, deficits in imitation and emulation are already present in the first year of life, the existing evidence suggests that such deficits are detectable at the end of the second year of life (Charman, Baron-Cohen, Swettenham, et al., 2001; Charman et al., 1997). Twenty-month-old infants with autism were able to emulate fewer actions with objects than their matched developmentally delayed controls. The frequency of emulation was associated with the level of nonverbal functioning, but impairments observed in the autism group appeared syndrome specific. Syndrome-specific impairments in gesture imitation in toddlers and preschoolers with autism (Dawson & Adams, 1984; Dawson, Meltzoff, Osterling, & Rinaldi, 1998; Roeyers et al., 1998; Rogers, Hepburn, Stackhouse, & Wehner, 2003; Sigman & Ungerer, 1984) and emulation of actions with objects (Dawson et al., 1998; Roeyers et al., 1998; Rogers et al., 2003) have been reported as well. Finally, imitation skills tend to be below the level expected based on other aspects of sensorimotor development, such as object permanence, and they are positively correlated with frequency of spontaneous social and communicative behaviors

(Dawson & Adams, 1984) and language skills (Sigman & Ungerer, 1984).

Adaptive Functioning

Studies of adaptive functioning, or the development and application of abilities in order to achieve personal independence and social sufficiency (Cicchetti & Sparrow, 1990) in school-age children with autism, suggest that compared with MA- or IQ-matched controls, these children have overall lower scores (Lord & Schopler, 1989) and present with greater variability in the profile of adaptive skills (Burack & Volkmar, 1992; Klin et al., 1992; Volkmar et al., 1987). In particular, they show specific deficits in the area of socialization relative to other areas of adaptive behaviors as well as cognitive skills (Volkmar, Carter, Sparrow, & Cicchetti, 1993). This pattern of relative social impairment as compared to other adaptive skills and cognitive levels appears highly characteristic of autism but not other nonautistic PDD disorders (Gillham, Carter, Volkmar, & Sparrow, 2000).

Parent retrospective interview data suggest that young children with autism show deficits in the development of social adaptive skills that include skills usually mastered in the first year of life (Klin et al., 1992). Klin and colleagues examined the adaptive behaviors of a group of 4-year-old children with autism, and children with developmental delays matched for MA, CA, and IQ, using the Vineland Adaptive Behaviors Scale (Vineland; Sparrow et al., 1984). They reported difficulties in skills usually mastered by 6 to 8 months including, the ability to anticipate being picked up, interest in other children, playing simple interactive games with others, and showing affection toward others. A specific pattern of delays in the development of adaptive behaviors has been reported in toddlers and preschoolers with autism (Stone, Ousley et al., 1999). Stone and her colleagues documented that compared to CA- and MA-matched controls, 2-year-old children with autism had significantly lower age equivalent scores in the Communication and Socialization domains. Their scores in these areas were also significantly lower as compared to their overall mental level, suggesting profound difficulties in translating their cognitive potential into real-life functioning.

Thus, similar to older children, young children with autism exhibit syndrome-specific patterns of developmental and adaptive skills.

Attachment

Attachment, or affective bond between a child and a mothering figure (Ainsworth, Blehar, Waters, & Wall, 1978), has been extensively studied in children with autism. The results of numerous studies using the Strange Situation paradigm provide limited evidence of syndrome-specific deficits in this area (Capps, Sigman, & Mundy, 1994; Rogers, Ozonoff, & Maslin-Cole, 1993; Waterhouse & Fein, 1998). These findings appear counterintuitive considering numerous reports regarding parental perception of their children's impoverished affective bond with their mother, as well as presence of attachments to unusual transitional objects (e.g., hard objects or objects of specific classes; Volkmar, Cohen, & Paul, 1986). It has been hypothesized that children with autism, although capable of developing a strategic form of attachment, may lack the affiliative form of social behaviors and, thus, may differentiate parents from strangers and seek their proximity for comfort but are less likely to display affiliative behaviors for purely social purposes (Waterhouse & Fein, 1998).

EARLY INTERVENTION

A growing body of work has highlighted the importance of early intervention in autism and related disorders. As summarized in the National Research Council (2001) review of early intervention, a number of programs have been able to provide reasonably strong evidence on intervention efficacy. Differences among the programs include aspects of theoretical orientation, the degree to which the child or teacher sets the learning agenda, and the degree to which the approach is based on developmental principles. Areas of similarity have included intensity of treatment (averaging about 27 hours a week), the importance of treatment structure, and intensive teaching approaches as well as a focus on helping the child become more able to learn independently.

The most widely studied intervention approach has been applied behavioral analysis

(ABA), although a growing body of work has focused on more eclectic intervention models (National Research Council, 2001). It is gratifying that controlled studies are beginning to appear (Eikeseth, Smith, Jahr, & Eldevik, 2002; Smith, Groen, & Wynn, 2000). Much of the available research is based on older (i.e., preschool) children, and it remains unclear how easily current approaches can be adapted to work with infants and very young children.

The problem of early intervention in infancy will likely increase substantially over the next decade as the age of first diagnosis continues to fall (Volkmar, Lord, Bailey, Schultz, & Klin, 2004). It is even possible that more physiologically or genetically based methods may be able to detect potential risk for autism in the first months of life. The observation that the age at which treatment is begun may be an important factor in predicting outcome (Harris & Handleman, 2000) highlights the urgency of this problem. It will be important for treatment studies in this population to focus on specific processes; for example, attempts have been made to focus on developmental skills, which are presumed to underlie other areas of difficulty (Kasari, 2002). Data on outcome from older children enrolled in intervention also make it clear that even with good interventions, some children do not improve as well as others; understanding this phenomenon remains an important focus of theory and research (Mundy, 2003). Although there has been a growing interest in teaching social skills to older children with autism, the applicability of such approaches to younger children remains to be explored. It is likely that more effective methods will focus on the social-communicative underpinnings of subsequent development. Such work will force both clinicians and researchers to attempt to disentangle the complex interrelationships of early developmental process and to address issues of mechanisms and treatment moderators as well an individual response differences.

CONCLUSION

In the past decade, interest in early diagnosis and developmental profiles of children with PDDs has increased substantially. Studies based on parent report, analysis of videotaped diaries, and direct observations have advanced the field toward identification of developmentally sensitive diagnostic criteria for infants and toddlers with autism. These symptoms cluster around deficits in early emerging social reciprocity and nonverbal communication skills. Although unusual responses to sensory stimuli and motor mannerisms are often present in the second and third years of life, their frequency and intensity are highly variable. Clinical diagnosis, particularly when determined by an experienced clinician, continues to constitute the gold standard as compared to traditional diagnostic instruments. Its short-term stability as well as specificity and sensitivity is high, particularly in children over the age of 24 months. Similar to older children, infants and preschoolers with autism present with highly variable profiles of strengths and weaknesses. Although young children with autism frequently experience developmental delays, some areas of development appear specifically affected in autism. These include abnormalities in selective visual attention to social stimuli, nonverbal communication, delays and abnormalities in play development, deficits in imitation and emulation skills, and delays in acquisition of social and communicative adaptive skills. In contrast, although delays in sensorimotor and EF skills have been reported, they do not appear to be syndrome specific.

Early detection of autism and other PDDs is likely to remain a focus of autism research. National Institutes of Health as well as numerous private foundations set early detection of autism and its underlying mechanisms as one of their priorities. The future directions of research are likely to include efforts toward refinement of the diagnostic criteria including other PDD disorders as well as identification of predictors of outcome. It will be critical to turn attention to high-risk populations of siblings of children with autism and address essential questions regarding their developmental trajectories and the mechanisms underlying the emergence of autism.

Cross-References

Issues of diagnosis and classification are discussed in Section I (Chapters 1 through 7);

development in school-age children and in adolescents and adults with autism spectrum disorders are addressed in Chapters 9 and 10, respectively; screening and diagnostic instruments are reviewed in Chapters 27 and 28. Also, see Chapter 14 for a review of play and imitation development and Chapter 25 for review of issues related to joint attention in autism.

REFERENCES

Adrien, J. L., Barthelemy, C., Perrot, A., Roux, S., Lenoir, P., Hameury, L. et al. (1992). Validity and reliability of the Infant Behavioral Summarized Evaluation (IBSE): A rating scale for the assessment of young children with autism and developmental disorders. *Journal of Autism and Developmental Disorders, 22*(3), 375–394.

Adrien, J. L., Lenoir, P., Martineau, J., Perrot, A., Hameury, L., Larmande, C., et al. (1993). Blind ratings of early symptoms of autism based upon family home movies. *Journal of the American Academy of Child and Adolescent Psychiatry, 32*(3), 617–626.

Ainsworth, M. S., Blehar, M. C., Waters, E., & Wall, S. (1978). *Patterns of attachment: A psychological study of the strange situation.* Hillsdale, NJ: Erlbaum.

Baird, G., Charman, T., Baron-Cohen, S., Cox, A., Swettenham, J., Wheelwright, S., et al. (2000). A screening instrument for autism at 18 months of age: A 6-year follow-up study. *Journal of the American Academy of Child and Adolescent Psychiatry, 39*(6), 694–702.

Baranek, G. T. (1999). Autism during infancy: A retrospective video analysis of sensory-motor and social behaviors at 9–12 months of age. *Journal of Autism and Developmental Disorders, 29*(3), 213–224.

Baron-Cohen, S. (1989). Joint-attention deficits in autism: Towards a cognitive analysis. *Development and Psychopathology, 1*(3), 185–189.

Baron-Cohen, S., Allen, J., & Gillberg, C. (1992). Can autism be detected at 18 months? The needle, the haystack, and the CHAT. *British Journal of Psychiatry, 161,* 839–843.

Baron-Cohen, S., Baldwin, D. A., & Crowson, M. (1997). Do children with autism use the speaker's direction of gaze strategy to crack the code of language? *Child Development, 68*(1), 48–57.

Baron-Cohen, S., Campbell, R., Karmiloff-Smith, A., Grant, J., & Walker, J. (1995). Are children with autism blind to the mentalistic significance of the eyes? *British Journal of Developmental Psychology, 13*(4), 379–398.

Baron-Cohen, S., Cox, A., Baird, G., Sweettenham, J., & Nighingale, N. (1996). Psychological markers in the detection of autism in infancy in a large population. *British Journal of Psychiatry, 168*(2), 158–163.

Bartak, L., Rutter, M., & Cox, A. (1975). A comparative study of infantile autism and specific developmental receptive language disorder: I. The children. *British Journal of Psychiatry, 126,* 127–145.

Bates, E. (1979). *The emergence of symbols: Cognition and communication in infancy.* New York: Academic Press.

Bennetto, L., Pennington, B. F., & Rogers, S. J. (1996). Intact and impaired memory functions in autism. *Child Development, 67*(4), 1816–1835.

Bruner, J. S. (1975). The ontogenesis of speech acts. *Journal of Child Language, 2*(1), 1–19.

Bruner, J. S. (1981). The social context of language acquisition. *Language and Communication, 1*(Suppl. 2/3), 155–178.

Burack, J. A., Enns, J., Stauder, J., Mottron, L., & Randolph, B. (1997). Attention in autism: Behavioral and electrophysiological evidence. In D. J. Cohen, & F. R. Volkmar (Eds.), *Handbook of autism and pervasive developmental disorders.* New York: Wiley.

Burack, J. A., & Volkmar, F. R. (1992). Development of low- and high-functioning autistic children. *Journal of Child Psychology and Psychiatry and Allied Disciplines, 33*(3), 607–616.

Capps, L., Sigman, M., & Mundy, P. (1994). Attachment security in children with autism. *Development and Psychopathology, 6*(2), 249–261.

Carpenter, M., Pennington, B. E., & Rogers, S. J. (2002). Interrelations among social-cognitive skills in young children with autism. *Journal of Autism and Developmental Disorders, 32*(2), 91–106.

Charman, T., Baron-Cohen, S., Baird, G., Cox, A., Wheelwright, S., Swettenham, J., et al. (2001). Commentary: The Modified Checklist for Autism in Toddlers. *Journal of Autism and Developmental Disorders, 31*(2), 145–148.

Charman, T., Baron-Cohen, S., Swettenham, J., Baird, G., Cox, A., & Drew, A. (2001). Testing joint attention, imitation, and play as infancy precursors to language and theory of mind. *Cognitive Development, 15*(4), 481–498.

Charman, T., Swettenham, J., Baron-Cohen, S., Cox, A., Baird, G., & Drew, A. (1997). Infants with autism: An investigation of empathy, pretend play, joint attention, and imitation. *Developmental Psychology, 33*(5), 781–789.

Chawarska, K., Klin, A., Paul, R., & Volkmar, F. R. (in press-a). Autism spectrum disorders under the age of 2 years: Stability and change over time in syndrome expression. *Journal of Child and Psychology and Psychiatry.*

Chawarska, K., Klin, A., Paul, R., & Volkmar, F. R. (in press-b). Diagnostic and developmental profiles of 2-year-olds with Autism Spectrum Disorders. *Journal of the American Academy of Child and Adolescent Psychiatry.*

Christopher, J. A., Sears, L. L., Williams, P. G., Oliver, J., & Hersh, T. (2004). Familial, medical and developmental patterns of children with autism and a history of language regression. *Journal of Developmental and Physical Disabilities, 16*(2), 163–170.

Cicchetti, D. V., & Sparrow, S. S. (1990). Assessment of adaptive behavior in young children. In J. H. Johnson & J. Goldman (Eds.), *Developmental assessment in clinical child psychology: A handbook. Pergamon general psychology series* (Vol. 163, pp. 173–196). New York: Pergamon Press.

Cox, A., Klein, K., Charman, T., Baird, G., Baron-Cohen, S., Swettenham, J., et al. (1999). Autism spectrum disorders at 20 and 42 months of age: Stability of clinical and ADI-R diagnosis. *Journal of Child Psychology and Psychiatry and Allied Disciplines, 40*(5), 719–732.

Curcio, F. (1978). Sensorimotor functioning and communication in mute autistic children. *Journal of Autism and Childhood Schizophrenia, 8*(3), 281–292.

Dahlgren, S. O., & Gillberg, C. (1989). Symptoms in the first two years of life: A preliminary population study of infantile autism. *European Archives of Psychiatry and Neurological Sciences, 238*(3), 169–174.

Dawson, G., & Adams, A. (1984). Imitation and social responsiveness in autistic children. *Journal of Abnormal Child Psychology, 12*(2), 209–225.

Dawson, G., Carver, L., Meltzoff, A. N., Panagiotides, H., McPartland, J., & Webb, S. J. (2002). Neural correlates of face and object recognition in young children with autism spectrum disorder, developmental delay and typical development. *Child Development, 73*(3), 700–717.

Dawson, G., & Lewy, A. (1989). Arousal, attention, and the socioemotional impairments of individuals with autism. In G. Dawson (Ed.), *Autism: Nature, diagnosis, and treatment* (pp. 49–74). New York: Guilford Press.

Dawson, G., Meltzoff, A. N., Osterling, J., & Rinaldi, J. (1998). Neuropsychological correlates of early symptoms of autism. *Child Development, 69*(5), 1276–1285.

Dawson, G., Meltzoff, A. N., Osterling, J., Rinaldi, J., & Brown, E. (1998). Children with autism fail to orient to naturally occurring social stimuli. *Journal of Autism and Developmental Disorders, 28*(6), 479–485.

Dawson, G., Munson, J., Estes, A., Osterling, J., McPartland, J., Toth, K., et al. (2002). Neurocognitive function and joint attention ability in young children with autism spectrum disorder versus developmental delay. *Child Development, 73*(2), 345–358.

Dawson, G., Osterling, J., Meltzoff, A. N., & Kuhl, P. (2000). Case study of the development of an infant with autism from birth to two years of age. *Journal of Applied Developmental Psychology, 21*(3), 299–313.

De Giacomo, A., & Fombonne, E. (1998). Parental recognition of developmental abnormalities in autism. *European Child and Adolescent Psychiatry, 7*(3), 131–136.

DiLavore, P. C., Lord, C., & Rutter, M. (1995). Prelinguistic autism diagnostic observation schedule. *Journal of Autism and Developmental Disorders, 25*(4), 355–379.

Ehlers, S., Nyden, A., Gillberg, C., Sandberg, A., Dahlgren, S., Hjelmquist, E., et al. (1997). Asperger syndrome, autism and attention disorders: A comparative study of the cognitive profiles of 120 children. *Journal of Child Psychology and Psychiatry and Allied Disciplines, 38*(2), 207–217.

Eikeseth, S., Smith, T., Jahr, E., & Eldevik, S. (2002). Intensive behavioral treatment at school for 4- to 7-year-old children with autism: A 1-year comparison controlled study. *Behavior Modification, 26*(1), 49–68.

Eisenberg, L., & Kanner, L. (1956). Early infantile autism, 1943–55. *American Journal of Orthopsychiatry, 26,* 556–566.

Fombonne, E., & Chakrabarti, S. (2001). No evidence for a new variant of measles-mumps-rubella-induced autism. *Pediatrics, 108*(4), 1–8.

Freeman, B., Ritvo, E. R., Yokota, A., Childs, J., & Pollard, J. (1988). WISC-R and Vineland Adaptive Behavior Scale scores in autistic children. *Journal of the American Academy of Child and Adolescent Psychiatry, 27*(4), 428–429.

Gillberg, C., Ehlers, S., Schaumann, H., Jakobsson, G., Dahlgren, S. O., Lindblom, R., et al. (1990). Autism under age 3 years: A clinical study of 28 cases referred for autistic symptoms in infancy. *Journal of Child Psychology and Psychiatry and Allied Disciplines, 31*(6), 921–934.

Gillham, J. E., Carter, A. S., Volkmar, F. R., & Sparrow, S. S. (2000). Toward a developmental operational definition of autism. *Journal of Autism and Developmental Disorders, 30*(4), 269–278.

Griffith, E. M., Pennington, B. F., Wehner, E. A., & Rogers, S. J. (1999). Executive functions in young children with autism. *Child Development, 70*(4), 817–832.

Harris, S. L., & Handleman, J. S. (2000). Age and IQ at intake as predictors of placement for young children with autism: A four- to six-year follow-up. *Journal of Autism and Developmental Disorders, 30*(2), 137–142.

Hobson, R., & Lee, A. (1999). Imitation and identification in autism. *Journal of Child Psychology and Psychiatry and Allied Disciplines, 40*(4), 649–659.

Hoshino, Y., Kumashiro, H., Yashima, Y., Tachibana, R., Watanabe, M., & Furukawa, H. (1982). Early symptoms of autistic children and its diagnostic significance. *Folia Psychiatrica et Neurologica, 36*, 367–374.

James, W. (1950). *The principles of psychology.* New York: Dover. (Original work published 1890)

Joseph, R. M., Tager-Flusberg, H., & Lord, C. (2002). Cognitive profiles and social-communicative functioning in children with autism spectrum disorder. *Journal of Child Psychology and Psychiatry and Allied Disciplines, 43*(6), 807–821.

Kanner, L. (1968). Autistic disturbances of affective contact. *Acta Paedopsychiatrica: International Journal of Child and Adolescent Psychiatry, 35*(4–8), 98–136. (Original work published 1943)

Kasari, C. (2002). Assessing change in early intervention programs for children with autism. *Journal of Autism and Developmental Disorders, 32*(5), 447–461.

Klin, A., Chawarska, K., Paul, R., Rubin, E., Morgan, T., Wiesner, L., et al. (2004). Clinical case conference: Autism at the age of 15 months. *American Journal of Psychiatry, 161*(11): 1981–1988.

Klin, A., Jones, W., Schultz, R., Volkmar, F., & Cohen, D. (2002). Visual fixation patterns during viewing of naturalistic social situations as predictors of social competence in individuals with autism. *Archives of General Psychiatry, 59*(9), 809–816.

Klin, A., Volkmar, F. R., & Sparrow, S. S. (1992). Autistic social dysfunction: Some limitations of the theory of mind hypothesis. *Journal of Child Psychology and Psychiatry and Allied Disciplines, 33*(5), 861–876.

Klin, A., Volkmar, F., Sparrow, S., Cicchetti, D., & Rourke, B. (1995). Validity and neuropsychological characterization of Asperger syndrome: Convergence with nonverbal learning disabilities syndrome. *Journal of Child Psychology and Psychiatry and Allied Disciplines, 36*(7), 1127–1140.

Kurita, H. (1985). Infantile autism with speech loss before the age of thirty months. *Journal of the American Academy of Child Psychiatry, 24*(2), 191–196.

Le Couteur, A., Rutter, M., Lord, C., Rios, P., Robertson, S., Holdgrafer, M., et al. (1989). Autism diagnostic interview: A standardized investigator-based instrument. *Journal of Autism and Developmental Disorders, 19*(3), 363–387.

Leekam, S., Baron-Cohen, S., Perrett, D., Milders, M., & Brown, S. (1997). Eye-direction detection: A dissociation between geometric and joint attention skills in autism. *British Journal of Developmental Psychology, 15*(Pt. 1), 77–95.

Leekam, S., Hunnisett, E., & Moore, C. (1998). Targets and cues: Gaze-following in children with autism. *Journal of Child Psychology and Psychiatry and Allied Disciplines, 39*(7), 951–962.

Leekam, S., Lopez, B., & Moore, C. (2000). Attention and joint attention in preschool children with autism. *Developmental Psychology, 36*(2), 261–273.

Lewis, V., & Boucher, J. (1988). Spontaneous, instructed and elicited play in relatively able autistic children. *British Journal of Developmental Psychology, 6*(4), 325–339.

Lord, C. (1995). Follow-up of two-year-olds referred for possible autism. *Journal of Child Psychology and Psychiatry and Allied Disciplines, 36*(8), 1365–1382.

Lord, C., & Magill-Evans, J. (1995). Peer interactions of autistic children and adolescents. *Development and Psychopathology, 7*(4), 611–626.

Lord, C., & Pickles, A. (1996). Language level and nonverbal social communicative behaviors in autistic and language-delayed children. *Journal of the American Academy of Child & Adolescent Psychiatry, 35*(11), 1542–1550.

Lord, C., & Risi, S. (2000). Diagnosis of autism spectrum disorders in young children. In A. M. Wetherby & B. M. Prizant (Eds.), *Autism spectrum disorders: A transactional de-*

velopmental perspective. *Communication and language intervention series* (Vol. 9, pp. 11–30). Baltimore: Paul H. Brookes.

Lord, C., Risi, S., Lambrecht, L., Cook, E. H., Leventhal, B. L., DiLavore, P. C., et al. (2000). The Autism Diagnostic Observation Schedule—Generic: A standard measure of social and communication deficits associated with the spectrum of autism. *Journal of Autism and Developmental Disorders, 30*(3), 205–223.

Lord, C., Rutter, M., & Le Couteur, A. (1994). Autism Diagnostic Interview Revised: A revised version of a diagnostic interview for caregivers of individuals with possible pervasive developmental disorders. *Journal of Autism and Developmental Disorders, 24*(5), 659–685.

Lord, C., & Schopler, E. (1989). The role of age at assessment, developmental level, and test in the stability of intelligence scores in young autistic children. *Journal of Autism and Developmental Disorders, 19*(4), 483–499.

Lord, C., Shulman, C., & DiLavore, P. (2004). Regression and word loss in autistic spectrum disorders. *Journal of Child Psychology and Psychiatry, 45*(5), 936–955.

Losche, G. (1990). Sensorimotor and action development in autistic children from infancy to early childhood. *Journal of Child Psychology and Psychiatry, 31,* 749–761.

Loveland, K. A., & Landry, S. H. (1986). Joint attention and language in autism and developmental language delay. *Journal of Autism and Developmental Disorders, 16*(3), 335–349.

Maestro, S., Muratori, F., Barbieri, F., Casella, C., Cattaneo, V., Cavallaro, M., et al. (2001). Early behavioral development in autistic children: The first 2 years of life through home movies. *Psychopathology, 34*(3), 147–152.

Maestro, S., Muratori, F., Cavallaro, M. C., Pei, F., Stern, D., Golse, B., et al. (2002). Attentional skills during the first 6 months of age in autism spectrum disorder. *Journal of the American Academy of Child and Adolescent Psychiatry, 41*(10), 1239–1245.

McArthur, D., & Adamson, L. B. (1996). Joint attention in preverbal children: Autism and developmental language disorder. *Journal of Autism and Developmental Disorders, 26*(5), 481–496.

McDonough, L., Stahmer, A., Schreibman, L., & Thompson, S. J. (1997). Deficits, delays, and distractions: An evaluation of symbolic play and memory in children with autism. *Development and Psychopathology, 9*(1), 17–41.

McEvoy, R. E., Rogers, S. J., & Pennington, B. F. (1993). Executive function and social communication deficits in young autistic children. *Journal of Child Psychology and Psychiatry and Allied Disciplines, 34*(4), 563–578.

Morgan, S. B., Cutrer, P. S., Coplin, J. W., & Rodrigue, J. R. (1989). Do autistic children differ from retarded and normal children in Piagetian sensorimotor functioning? *Journal of Child Psychology and Psychiatry and Allied Disciplines, 30*(6), 857–864.

Mundy, P. (2003). The neural basis of social impairments in autism: The role of the dorsal medial-frontal cortex and anterior cingulate system. *Journal of Child Psychology and Psychiatry and Allied Disciplines, 44*(6), 793–809.

Mundy, P., & Crowson, M. (1997). Joint attention and early social communication: Implications for research on intervention with autism. *Journal of Autism and Developmental Disorders, 27*(6), 653–676.

Mundy, P., & Sigman, M. (1989). The theoretical implications of joint-attention deficits in autism. *Development and Psychopathology, 1*(3), 173–183.

Mundy, P., Sigman, M., & Kasari, C. (1990). A longitudinal study of joint attention and language development in autistic children. *Journal of Autism and Developmental Disorders, 20*(1), 115–128.

Mundy, P., Sigman, M., & Kasari, C. (1994). Joint attention, developmental level, and symptom presentation in autism. *Development and Psychopathology, 6*(3), 389–401.

Mundy, P., Sigman, M., Ungerer, J., & Sherman, T. (1986). Defining the social deficits of autism: The contribution of non-verbal communication measures. *Journal of Child Psychology and Psychiatry and Allied Disciplines, 27*(5), 657–669.

National Research Council (Ed.). (2001). *Educating children with autism.* Washington, DC: National Academy Press.

Ornitz, E. M., Guthrie, D., & Farley, A. H. (1977). The early development of autistic children. *Journal of Autism and Childhood Schizophrenia, 7*(3), 207–229.

Osterling, J. A., & Dawson, G. (1994). Early recognition of children with autism: A study of first birthday home videotapes. *Journal of Autism and Developmental Disorders, 24*(3), 247–257.

Osterling, J. A., Dawson, G., & Munson, J. A. (2002). Early recognition of 1-year-old infants with autism spectrum disorder versus mental retardation. *Development and Psychopathology, 14*(2), 239–251.

Ozonoff, S., Pennington, B. F., & Rogers, S. J. (1991). Executive function deficits in high-functioning autistic individuals: Relationship to theory of mind. *Journal of Child Psychology and Psychiatry and Allied Disciplines, 32*(7), 1081–1105.

Pennington, B. F., & Ozonoff, S. (1996). Executive functions and developmental psychopathology. *Journal of Child Psychology and Psychiatry and Allied Disciplines, 37*(1), 51–87.

Piaget, J. (1954). *The construction of reality in the child.* New York: Basic Books.

Piaget, J. (1962). The stages of the intellectual development of the child. *Bulletin of the Menninger Clinic, 26*(3), 120–128.

Robins, D. L., Fein, D., Barton, M. L., & Green, J. A. (2001). The modified checklist for autism in toddlers: An initial study investigating the early detection of autism and pervasive developmental disorders. *Journal of Autism and Developmental Disorders, 31*(2), 131–144.

Roeyers, H., Van Oost, P., & Bothuyne, S. (1998). Immediate imitation and joint attention in young children with autism. *Development and Psychopathology, 10*(3), 441–450.

Rogers, S. J. (1999). An examination of the imitation deficit in autism. In J. Nadel & G. Butterworth (Eds.), *Imitation in infancy* (pp. 254–283). New York: Cambridge University Press.

Rogers, S. J., Bennetto, L., McEvoy, R., & Pennington, B. F. (1996). Imitation and pantomime in high-functioning adolescents with autism spectrum disorders. *Child Development, 67*(5), 2060–2073.

Rogers, S. J., & DiLalla, D. L. (1990). Age of symptom onset in young children with pervasive developmental disorders. *Journal of the American Academy of Child and Adolescent Psychiatry, 29*(6), 863–872.

Rogers, S. J., Hepburn, S. L., Stackhouse, T., & Wehner, B. (2003). Imitation performance in toddlers with autism and those with other developmental disorders. *Journal of Child Psychology and Psychiatry, 44*(5), 763–781.

Rogers, S. J., Ozonoff, S., & Maslin-Cole, C. (1993). Developmental aspects of attachment behavior in young children with pervasive developmental disorders. *Journal of the American Academy of Child and Adolescent Psychiatry, 32*(6), 1274–1282.

Rogers, S. J., & Pennington, B. F. (1991). A theoretical approach to the deficits in infantile

autism. *Development and Psychopathology, 3*(2), 137–162.

Russell, J., Jarrold, C., & Henry, L. (1996). Working memory in children with autism and with moderate learning difficulties. *Journal of Child Psychology and Psychiatry and Allied Disciplines, 37*(6), 673–686.

Russell, J., Jarrold, C., & Hood, B. (1999). Two intact executive capacities in children with autism: Implications for the core executive dysfunctions in the disorder. *Journal of Autism and Developmental Disorders, 29*(2), 103–112.

Rutter, M., Le Couteur, A., & Lord, C. (2003). Autism Diagnostic Interview-Revised: WPS Edition [Manual]. Los Angeles: Western Psychological Services.

Scambler, D., Rogers, S. J., & Wehner, E. A. (2001). Can the Checklist for Autism in Toddlers differentiate young children with autism from those with developmental delays? *Journal of the American Academy of Child and Adolescent Psychiatry, 40*(12), 1457–1463.

Sheinkopf, S. J., Mundy, P., Oller, D., & Steffens, M. (2000). Vocal atypicalities of preverbal autistic children. *Journal of Autism and Developmental Disorders, 30*(4), 345–354.

Short, A. B., & Schopler, E. (1988). Factors relating to age of onset in autism. *Journal of Autism and Developmental Disorders, 18*(2), 207–216.

Sigman, M., Mundy, P., Sherman, T., & Ungerer, J. (1986). Social interactions of autistic, mentally retarded and normal children and their caregivers. *Journal of Child Psychology and Psychiatry and Allied Disciplines, 27*(5), 647–656.

Sigman, M., & Ruskin, E. (1999). Continuity and change in the social competence of children with autism, Down syndrome, and developmental delays. *Monographs of the Society for Research in Child Development, 64*(1), 1–114.

Sigman, M., & Ungerer, J. (1981). Sensorimotor skills and language comprehension in autistic children. *Journal of Abnormal Child Psychology, 9*(2), 149–165.

Sigman, M., & Ungerer, J. A. (1984). Cognitive and language skills in autistic, mentally retarded, and normal children. *Developmental Psychology, 20*(2), 293–302.

Smith, I. M., & Bryson, S. E. (1998). Gesture imitation in autism I: Nonsymbolic postures and sequences. *Cognitive Neuropsychology, 15*(6–8), 747–770.

Smith, T., Groen, A. D., & Wynn, J. W. (2000). Randomized trial of intensive early intervention for children with pervasive developmental disorder. *American Journal on Mental Retardation, 105*(4), 269–285.

Sparling, J. W. (1991). A prospective case report of infantile autism from pregnancy to four years. *Journal of Autism and Developmental Disorders, 21*(2), 229–236.

Sparrow, S. S., Balla, D. A., & Cicchetti, D. V. (1984). *Vineland Adaptive Behavior Scales: Interview edition, survey form manual.* Circle Pines, MN: American Guidance Service.

Stone, W. L. (1997). Autism in infancy and early childhood. In D. J. Cohen, & F. R. Volkmar (Eds.), Handbook of autism and pervasive developmental disorders. New York: Wiley.

Stone, W. L., & Caro-Martinez, L. M. (1990). Naturalistic observations of spontaneous communication in autistic children. *Journal of Autism and Developmental Disorders, 20*(4), 437–453.

Stone, W. L., Coonrod, E. E., & Ousley, O. Y. (2000). Screening Tool for Autism Two-Year-Olds (STAT): Development and preliminary data. *Journal of Autism and Developmental Disorders, 30*(6), 607–612.

Stone, W. L., Hoffman, E. L., Lewis, S. E., & Ousley, O. Y. (1994). Early recognition of autism. *Archives of Pediatric and Adolescent Medicine, 148,* 174–179.

Stone, W. L., Lee, E. B., Ashford, L., Brissie, J., Hepburn, S. L., Coonrod, E. E., et al. (1999). Can autism be diagnosed accurately in children under 3 years? *Journal of Child Psychology and Psychiatry and Allied Disciplines, 40*(2), 219–226.

Stone, W. L., Ousley, O. Y., Hepburn, S. L., Hogan, K. L., & Brown, C. S. (1999). Patterns of adaptive behavior in very young children with autism. *American Journal on Mental Retardation, 104*(2), 187–199.

Stone, W. L., Ousley, O. Y., Yoder, P. J., Hogan, K. L., & Hepburn, S. L. (1997). Nonverbal communication in two- and three-year-old children with autism. *Journal of Autism and Developmental Disorders, 27*(6), 677–696.

Swettenham, J., Baron-Cohen, S., Charman, T., Cox, A., Baird, G., Drew, A., et al. (1998). The frequency and distribution of spontaneous attention shifts between social and nonsocial stimuli in autistic, typically developing, and nonautistic developmentally delayed infants. *Journal of Child Psychology and Psychiatry and Allied Disciplines, 39*(5), 747–753.

Tamis-LeMonda, C. S., & Bornstein, M. H. (1991). Individual variation, correspondence, stability, and change in mother and toddler play. *Infant Behavior and Development, 14*(2), 143–162.

Tomasello, M. (1995). Joint attention as social cognition. In C. Moore & P. J. Dunham (Eds.), *Joint attention: Its origins and role in development* (pp. 103–130). Hillsdale, NJ: Erlbaum.

Tomasello, M., Kruger, A. C., & Ratner, H. H. (1993). Cultural learning. *Behavioral and Brain Sciences, 16*(3), 495–552.

Tuchman, R. F., & Rapin, I. (1997). Regression in pervasive developmental disorders: Seizures and epileptiform electroencephalogram correlates. *Pediatrics, 99*(4), 560–566.

Volkmar, F. R., Carter, A., Sparrow, S. S., & Cicchetti, D. V. (1993). Quantifying social development in autism. *Journal of the American Academy of Child and Adolescent Psychiatry, 32*(3), 627–632.

Volkmar, F. R., & Cohen, D. J. (1989). Disintegrative disorder or "late onset" autism. *Journal of Child Psychology and Psychiatry and Allied Disciplines, 30*(5), 717–724.

Volkmar, F. R., Cohen, D. J., & Paul, R. (1986). An evaluation of *DSM-III* criteria for infantile autism. *Journal of the American Academy of Child Psychiatry, 25*(2), 190–197.

Volkmar, F. R., Klin, A., Siegel, B., Szatmari, P., Lord, C., Campbell, M., et al. (1994). Field trial for autistic disorder in *DSM-IV. American Journal of Psychiatry, 151*(9), 1361–1367.

Volkmar, F. R., Lord, C., Bailey, A., Schultz, R. T., & Klin, A. (2004). Autism and pervasive developmental disorders. *Journal of Child Psychology and Psychiatry and Allied Disciplines, 45*(1), 135–170.

Volkmar, F. R., & Mayes, L. C. (1990). Gaze behavior in autism. *Development and Psychopathology, 2*(1), 61–69.

Volkmar, F. R., Sparrow, S. S., Goudreau, D., Cicchetti, D. V., Paul, R., & Cohen, D. J. (1987). Social deficits in autism: An operational approach using the Vineland Adaptive Behavior Scales. *Journal of the American Academy of Child and Adolescent Psychiatry, 26*(2), 156–161.

Volkmar, F. R., Stier, D. M., & Cohen, D. J. (1985). Age of recognition of pervasive developmental disorder. *American Journal of Psychiatry, 142*(12), 1450–1452.

Waterhouse, L., & Fein, D. (1998). Autism and the evolution of human social skills. In F. R. Volkmar (Ed.), *Autism and pervasive developmental disorders Cambridge monographs in child and adolescent psychiatry* (pp. 242–267). Cambridge, UK: Cambridge University Press.

Werner, E., Dawson, G., Osterling, J., & Dinno, N. (2000). Brief report: Recognition of autism spectrum disorder before one year of age—A retrospective study based on home videotapes. *Journal of Autism and Developmental Disorders, 30*(2), 157–162.

Wetherby, A. M., Cain, D. H., Yonclas, D. G., & Walker, V. G. (1988). Analysis of intentional communication of normal children from the prelinguistic to the multiword stage. *Journal of Speech and Hearing Research, 31*(2), 240–252.

Wetherby, A. M., Yonclas, D. G., & Bryan, A. A. (1989). Communicative profiles of preschool children with handicaps: Implications for early identification. *Journal of Speech and Hearing Disorders, 54*(2), 148–158.

Whalen, C., & Schreibman, L. (2003). Joint attention training for children with autism using behavior modification procedures. *Journal of Child Psychology and Psychiatry and Allied Disciplines, 44*(3), 456–468.

Wimpory, D. C., Hobson, R., Williams, J., & Nash, S. (2000). Are infants with autism socially engaged? A study of recent retrospective parental reports. *Journal of Autism and Developmental Disorders, 30*(6), 525–536.

CHAPTER 9

The School-Age Child with an Autistic Spectrum Disorder

KATHERINE A. LOVELAND AND BELGIN TUNALI-KOTOSKI

For the child with an autistic spectrum disorder (ASD), the elementary school years bring challenges associated with the changing expectations that accompany increasing physical and behavioral maturity. During the period from ages 6 to 12, the child with ASD faces transitions to new learning environments, contact with new peers and adults, and departures from familiar places and routines. These changes affect many domains of functioning, as the child is required to adapt to more complex and demanding social environments, to learn more sophisticated skills, to communicate at a higher level, and to process more information. Such experiences, which are common to children of school age, are particularly challenging for those with ASD, who have not only developmental delays in multiple domains but also difficulty adjusting to changes in their environments.

At the same time, however, most children with ASD make progress during the school years, acquiring new skills and learning to cope with new people, places, and events. The developmental path followed by an individual child during this period will be difficult to predict: It is the complex product of a dynamic process linking neural maturation with environmental influences, learning, and the child's own self-regulatory activity (Cicchetti & Tucker, 1994). However, some trends in development can be outlined.

By the age of 6, children with ASD have already begun to diverge from one another according to characteristics such as degree of language delay and intellectual deficit. These divergent developmental paths have much to do with later outcome; perhaps the best-known example of this divergence is the better outcome observed for those children who have acquired some oral language by age 5 (Rutter, Greenfield, & Lockyer, 1967). Thus, we can expect that children with ASD but without mental retardation will respond differently to the challenges of the school years than those with both ASD and mental retardation.

Often the behavior of the child with ASD in the school years is more obviously discrepant from that of nondisabled age-mates than it was earlier in life. That is, domains of development such as social and communicative functioning may become more rather than less divergent from their expected trajectories during this period, particularly in the child with more severe autistic behavior. A lack of normal peer relationships, the absence or paucity of pretend play, the presence of repetitive behaviors or focused interests, and a marked impairment of social relatedness become clearly delineated in contrast to normative expectations for children in this age group. This apparently increasing discrepancy is due in part to changes in expectations for the child's behavior: For example, the inability to follow directions, to

The authors thank Emese Nagy, MD, PhD, for her invaluable help in the preparation of this chapter and Stacy Reddoch for her editorial assistance.

initiate interactions, or to inhibit motor stereotypies is more obvious in an 8-year-old than in
a 3-year-old. It is also partly due to the cumulative effect of environmental experiences on
the child with ASD, whose social and emotional experiences of the world and opportunities to learn have differed sharply from those
of typically developing children, because of
the child's own tendency to interact differently with the world (Loveland, 2001).

Although it is possible to identify such
broad trends as those discussed earlier, the picture of "typical" development in the school-age
child with ASD is complicated by the fact that
classification of some children on the autistic
spectrum of disorder remains controversial
(Tsai, 1992). Although there are now well-
accepted methods for reliable and valid diagnosis of autism (Lord, Rutter, DiLavore, & Risi,
1999; Lord, Rutter, & Le Couteur, 1994), there
is today a surprising amount of disagreement
about the possibility of subcategories of the
autistic spectrum and about the relationship of
autistic disorder to other diagnostic categories,
such as Asperger syndrome, or proposed categories such as nonverbal learning disability
or semantic-pragmatic language disorder. This
lack of agreement reflects in part a tension between categorical and dimensional approaches
to classification, with research tending to support a picture of ASD as multidimensional and
multiply determined, but with clinical and educational practice based on assignment to discrete diagnostic categories within the larger
category of pervasive developmental disorders
(*DSM-IV*). Despite the persistence of discrete
diagnostic categories of ASD in clinical practice, there is considerable heterogeneity among
persons diagnosed with ASD (Gillberg & Coleman, 1992; Klin, Jones, Schultz, Volkmar, &
Cohen, 2002a) even within the same category.
The autistic spectrum of disorder (Wing &
Gould, 1979) may include subtypes differing
in etiology, clinical presentation, or developmental course, as well as in the level of cognitive, social, or language disability (Volkmar
et al., 1994). (These issues are explored in
greater depth in the following section.) For example, although both *DSM-IV* and *ICD-10* distinguish between autistic disorder (AD) and
Asperger syndrome (AS; Asperger, 1944), in

practice it is difficult to distinguish these categories reliably and without overlap (Volkmar
& Klin, 2000). In addition, there remain individuals who, although manifesting some symptoms of ASD, do not clearly meet criteria for
the diagnosis of AD or AS, either because they
lack some required symptoms or because their
severity of autistic symptoms is not great
enough. Although advances are being made in
the study of the broader autism phenotype, at
present it is difficult to interpret the research
literature as to the development of children in
these possible subtypes, because of inconsistent methods of categorization across studies
and insufficient information about the taxo-
nomic validity of various categories. This state
of affairs contributes to difficulty in identifying developmental expectations for individual
children with ASD in the school years.

In this review, we provide a picture of development in school-age children with ASD
with and without mental retardation, keeping
in mind that the relevant literature includes
studies of children diagnosed not only with
AD (*DSM-IV*) but also with other pervasive
developmental disorders, such as pervasive developmental disorder-not otherwise specified
(PDD-NOS) or Asperger syndrome. We should
expect, in considering development during this
age period, that the organization and trajectory of development in any number of domains
may differ among children with ASD of varying intellectual ability. At the same time, however, it is possible to look for continuities as
well as discontinuities between development of
autistic spectrum behaviors in the school years
and earlier and later development (Michelotti,
Charman, Slonims, & Baird, 2002). Although
there is a wide-ranging literature on the behavioral development of children with ASD, we
focus in this chapter on several areas of particular interest to the development of the child
with ASD from ages 6 to 12.

DEVELOPMENTAL ISSUES FOR
THE SCHOOL-AGE CHILD WITH
AUTISTIC SPECTRUM DISORDER

In the following section several areas are
discussed that are of special importance for
the development of children with ASD. These

include social and adaptive behavior, play, language and communication, emotion, school adjustment, and academic achievement.

Social and Adaptive Behavior

Deficits in social behavior and social understanding are particularly characteristic of persons with ASD. Since autism was first described by Kanner (1943), these deficits have been recognized as an essential component of the syndrome. They first become obvious in the preschool years, when a failure to establish peer relationships, a lack of normal relatedness with familiar people, a preference for aloneness, poor eye contact and gesture, tactile defensiveness, and lack of initiative in communication become evident in most children with ASD (Rutter, 1978; Wing & Gould, 1979). In some respects, social deficits may gradually decrease in severity during the school years, as the child begins to benefit from intervention and from learning to cope in familiar situations and with familiar people (Gillberg, 1984; Gillberg & Coleman, 1992). However, in general, the social deficits seen in the preschool child with ASD tend to persist through the school years and beyond, changing the form in which they are manifested and showing the effects of maturation and development of the individual (Rutter & Garmezy, 1983). Even children who have made excellent progress in multiple domains as a result of early interventions are likely to retain some socioemotional differences (Bailey, 2001).

Although there is considerable heterogeneity among children with ASD in the presentation of their social behavior (Klin et al., 2002a), some generalizations can be made. For example, Wing and colleagues have described three subtypes of social behavior that capture many of the manifestations of ASD seen in the school-age child (Wing & Attwood, 1987; Wing & Gould, 1979).

The *aloof* children are those most likely to be described as "classically autistic." They do not seek, and may actively avoid, contact with others, and they may become very distressed if it is thrust on them. They do not initiate communication (even though some can speak), and much of their time may be occupied with stereotypies or other repetitive interests. These children with ASD are noted for unresponsiveness and failure to initiate interactions with both peers and adults (Freitag, 1970; Loveland & Landry, 1986; Trad, Bernstein, Shapiro, & Hertzig, 1993). They often do not play with other children or demonstrate interest in friendships (Rutter, 1974). Deficits in their ability to use gaze and gesture appropriately in social situations lead to frequent failures to communicate (Buitelaar, van Engeland, de Kogel, de Vries, & van Hooff, 1991). Aloof children with ASD may be sufficiently unresponsive that it is very difficult to direct and maintain their attention; thus, it may be easier to get their attention using proximal rather than distal stimulation (e.g., touching the child's hand rather than pointing to something). They may seem at times to be deaf, even though they are not. Lacking a complete participation in the usual set of social signals and routines that govern human interactions, aloof children with ASD are distinctly handicapped in social situations. Although they may exhibit emotion, their emotions are not necessarily tied to contexts easily interpreted by others and thus can be puzzling and frustrating to caregivers. Tantruming is common, particularly when the child is frustrated by disruption of a routine or by other circumstances the child cannot control. Individuals with these characteristics are most often seen in the preschool age group, but some continue in this manner into later childhood, adolescence, and adulthood; these are most likely to be persons with significant mental retardation. Quite often these children have a difficult and lengthy adjustment to a new school placement, and social problems are likely to arise in the classroom.

The *passive* group includes children who do not actively avoid social contact with others but who nevertheless lack the spontaneous and intuitive grasp of social interaction that is shared by normally developing children. They will accept the social approaches of others, but often do not have the skills to respond appropriately. Their communication and play behaviors are rigid and sometimes stereotyped. These individuals tend to function at a somewhat higher developmental level than those in the aloof group, with more language and fewer motor stereotypies, and they are in general "easier to manage." Although passive children with ASD can be easier to manage than those who are aloof, they require considerable help to relate to peers in the classroom or other situations. Some children who start out displaying the aloof pattern of behavior later have a better fit with the passive group. Thus, presentation as aloof versus passive may depend to some extent on the child's developmental level or IQ, and a transition from one category to the other may reflect maturation as well as accumulation of social experiences.

The *active-but-odd* children are those who are usually described as having high-functioning autism or Asperger syndrome. They actively seek out contact with others, but the form and quality of their social approaches are unusual and often inappropriate. These more able children with ASD experience difficulty in relating socially to peers and others, even though they may have considerable language skills and may be interested in communicating with others. Characteristic of this group are behaviors such as repetitive questioning, inappropriate touching, conversation focused exclusively on the child's own narrow interests, and odd postures, gestures, and facial expressions. Their social behavior and communication seem to reflect a view of the social world that is literal and concrete, and they show a limited awareness of the feelings, thought, and motives of others. However, these individuals are more intellectually able, and as a consequence, their autistic spectrum characteristics are sometimes identified later than those of other children with ASD. In contrast to less intellectually able children, active-but-odd children may be aware to some extent that they are different and not always accepted by others, which can be a source of distress. They also tend to prefer rigid and predictable routines in their daily life, such that unexpected events, new people, and unfamiliar surroundings can be very stressful. When they are highly stressed, they may regress to behaviors displayed at earlier ages (e.g., tantruming, self-stimulatory behaviors) or even exhibit signs of psychosis (Wing & Attwood, 1987). Moreover, because they are relatively able, they are often placed in classes or other situations in which they are expected

to exercise age-appropriate social judgment and social behavior. These situations can lead to difficulties for the school-age child who cannot meet the social expectations of peers. Such children are at high risk for peer victimization or shunning (Little, 2002), although there is a great deal of variation in how well accepted children with ASD are when placed with peers in regular classes (inclusion). Some research suggests that despite the fact that they are frequently less liked, able children with ASD are no more likely than other students to report feeling lonely and that their limited awareness of social factors may in some cases insulate them from feeling excluded (Chamberlain, 2002). A recent study found that persons with ASD do not make the same judgments about other people's trustworthiness as controls (Adolphs, Sears, & Piven, 2001). The authors concluded that the amygdala, a structure in the temporal lobe of the brain, is dysfunctional in autism and that its dysfunction impairs the ability to perceive socially relevant information and link it to social knowledge and self-regulation of social behavior. If so, it is possible to see how difficulty judging the meaning of peers' facial expressions and social behaviors could lead to incorrect judgments about social situations, as well as inappropriate behavior.

Some of the social difficulties experienced by children with ASD may be related to cognitive limitations, such as differences in patterns of attention. Pierce, Glad, and Schreibman (1997) found that the ability of verbal children with ASD to interpret social situations is reduced when they must attend to multiple aspects of the situation. Also, research on visual fixations has shown that individuals with autism do not necessarily attend to the same aspects of situations, as do other people. In viewing scenes of social behavior, adolescents with autism showed reduced time attending to eyes and more time attending to mouths than did controls (Klin, Jones, Schultz, Volkmar, & Cohen, 2002b).

Despite their many social deficits, there are a number of areas of social behavior in which children with ASD do appear to have strengths and to make progress during the school years. For example, children with ASD usually display signs of attachment to parents and other caregivers, including distress upon separation (Volkmar, Cohen, & Paul, 1986). Studies have suggested that a basic capacity for attachment exists in children with ASD and that their attachment behavior is not different in kind from that of other developmentally delayed children or that of younger typically developing children (Ozonoff & South, 2001; Shapiro, Sherman, Calamari, & Koch, 1987; Sigman & Mundy, 1989; Sigman & Ungerer, 1984). Most children with ASD do form attachments, although some aspects of attachment, particularly more cognitive aspects, may be impaired in these children (Dissanayake & Sigman, 2001). Moreover, children with ASD respond differently to different persons and in different situations (Landry & Loveland, 1988; Sigman & Ungerer, 1984). These findings suggest that children with ASD are not actually indifferent to other persons, but are aware to varying extents that different persons hold different significance for them. In addition, studies have found that children with ASD in the preschool and school years demonstrate mirror self-recognition, provided they have reached a mental age level comparable to that at which young nondisabled children achieve self-recognition (G. Dawson & McKissick, 1984; Ferrari & Matthews, 1983). These studies suggest that whatever the basis of the social deficits in persons with ASD, it is probably not a failure to distinguish self from other. Thus, at least some of the foundations for normal social behavior appear to be present in children with ASD.

Efforts to support and increase the use of appropriate social behavior in children with ASD have used a variety of methods. Verbal children with ASD can benefit from being taught strategies such as self-monitoring during social interactions (Morrison, Kamps, Garcia, & Parker, 2001) and may benefit from social training that involves peers without ASD (Kamps et al., 2002).

Although there is considerable clinical and research evidence that children with ASD are deficient in social skills, there is a need to document the consequences of these deficits as they affect the everyday life of children with ASD. One approach to studying the impact of social deficits on the lives of children with ASD is by use of standardized test instruments (Volkmar & Klin, 1993). Such studies have the potential to reveal patterns of development across age groups and with reference to normative data. Studies using adaptive behavior scales to study social behavior in ASD have clearly shown that social and interpersonal skills of persons with ASD are poorer than would be expected based on their IQ and overall developmental level and that persons with ASD are usually weaker in this area than are comparable persons with other developmental disabilities (Ando & Yoshimura, 1979; Ando, Yoshimura, & Wakabayashi, 1980; Klin, Volkmar, & Sparrow, 1992; Loveland & Kelley, 1988, 1991; Rodrigue, Morgan, & Geffken, 1991; Rumsey, Rapoport, & Sceery, 1985; Schatz & Hamden-Allen, 1995; Sparrow & Cicchetti, 1987; Volkmar et al., 1987). Such differences have even been found as early as ages 2 to 3 years (Stone, Ousley, Hepburn, Hogan, & Brown, 1999) and are thought to continue into adulthood (Njardvik, Matson, & Cherry, 1999). Deficits in adaptive and social skills may extend to those children and adults who have developmental disorders that are closely related to or may co-occur with ASD, such as fragile X syndrome (Cohen, 1995; Fisch, Simensen, & Schroer, 2002).

The adaptive deficits of ASD do not appear to be a result of developmental delay alone (Rodrigue et al., 1991), but rather a robust pattern associated with the syndrome of ASD and one that persists over development in both higher and lower functioning persons of both genders (Freeman et al., 1991; Kraijer, 2000; McLennan, Lord, & Schopler, 1993). Some differences have been found between children with ASD of lower and higher IQ, however, as to the relationships among domains of cognitive and adaptive behaviors. There is some evidence that social delays are more severe, relative to other domains of functioning, for those children with ASD who also have mental retardation (Burack & Volkmar, 1992) and that for them, adaptive levels are more closely related to IQ than for children with mental retardation who do not have ASD (Carpentieri & Morgan, 1996). Liss et al. (2001) compared higher and lower functioning children with autism to IQ and age-matched controls without autism and found that for lower functioning children with autism, adaptive levels were highly related to

IQ. However, for the more able children, adaptive skills were more closely related to verbal ability and were strongly related to autistic symptomatology. Other studies have found that individuals with a diagnosis of Asperger syndrome have better developed adaptive skills than those with a diagnosis of autism (McLaughlin-Cheng, 1998; Szatmari, Archer, Fisman, Streiner, & Wilson, 1995).

In general, the social/adaptive skills of children with ASD do not necessarily continue to increase with advancing age, as would ordinarily be expected. Some studies have found little or no relationship between level of social/adaptive skills and chronological age in children or adolescents with ASD (Jacobson & Ackerman, 1990; Loveland & Kelley, 1988, 1991). This pattern may reflect a tendency to regress or to reach plateaus in development, or it may reflect the wide variability in performance often seen among children with ASD. However, other studies have found that certain adaptive skills, such as communication and self-care, have a more predictable relationship with age, with older children having more skills than younger ones (Ando & Yoshimura, 1979; Ando et al., 1980; Loveland & Kelley, 1991). Thus, although the literature clearly shows that the development of social skills is delayed in persons with ASD, it is less clear what to expect for the development of these skills in individual children. For this reason, population-specific norms for adaptive skills have begun to be developed for persons with ASD so that progress of individual children with ASD can be compared with that of age peers with a similar diagnosis (A. S. Carter et al., 1998).

Conclusions: Social and Adaptive Skills

Although deficits in social skills relative to other areas of functioning are characteristic of children with ASD, their manifestations vary widely in the school-age child. These manifestations are linked to the severity of ASD and the child's level of cognitive functioning. Some children with ASD, particularly those with mental retardation, may exhibit regressions or plateaus in social development, where little progress is made over a period of time. In general, children with ASD can be expected to make progress in social skills during the school years, but they will do so at a slower pace than nondisabled age-mates.

Play

Play is an important complex motivated behavior through which children learn to practice a wide variety of new skills in their social environment. Sensory-motor play provides knowledge about the child's own body and helps in developing a frame of reference for the world. Manipulative games lead infants to learn about objects, to control their environments, and to develop fine-motor skills. From infancy onward, children learn about basic social behavioral patterns and social relationships from social play, as well as practicing and increasing language and gestural communication and other skills. Therefore, if children lack developmentally appropriate play skills, as is true of many children with ASD, they will be placed at a serious disadvantage in their development (Boucher, 1999).

Typically developing children ordinarily begin to engage in reciprocal social play (such as tickle games) in the first year of life and in functional play with objects shortly thereafter. Pretend or symbolic play, in which one thing or person is used to represent another in an imaginary action sequence, is usually present by 2 to 3 years. Though the youngest children play together in parallel, cooperative play gradually develops, so that by school age most typically developing children engage in elaborated pretend play and games with others. As children mature, these cooperative types of play require increasing levels of sophistication in social cognition and social interaction skills, as well as in language, memory, motor skills, and self-regulation.

By contrast, young children with ASD are often observed not to engage in reciprocal play, pretend play, or cooperative play well past the age and developmental levels at which such play would ordinarily be expected to emerge. Instead, they may play repetitively with objects (e.g., lining up, spinning, or mouthing them) or engage primarily in passive activities such as watching television or videos. Young children with ASD have been found to have different patterns of interest and attention to toys than do other children and to behave differently during toy-related communicative interactions (D. K. O'Neill & Happé, 2000). More developed children may pursue with great absorption a topic of special interest to them that is not shared with others (e.g., see the case of James, discussed later). Engagement in pretend and in cooperative activities with peers tends to be lacking unless specifically encouraged and supported. It has been hypothesized that early social, cognitive, and affective deficits in ASD such as in affective attunement (Hobson, 1990), metarepresentational ability (Craig & Baron-Cohen, 1999), and social orienting (Mundy, Sigman, Ungerer, & Sherman, 1987) adversely affect development of the social and cognitive skills necessary for the development of play. Early nonverbal communication skills have been found to be a predictor of the extent to which children with ASD initiate play interactions when they are school age (Sigman & Ruskin, 1999). It is difficult to imagine how cooperative play can occur in a child who lacks the ability to engage in joint attention interactions. Similarly, a child who lacks adequate empathy and social self-regulation skills will have difficulty taking part in both dyadic play and organized games with larger groups. In addition, children with ASD are not necessarily motivated to play with other children, to interact, and share experiences with others; hence, they often do not do so, even when they possess cognitive and motor skills sufficient to engage in shared play activities.

To varying extents, play does develop over time in most children with an ASD. Many children with ASD do acquire functional play and some symbolic play by the time they reach school age, but the level of their play is frequently behind that of age peers (McDonough, Stahmer, Schreibman, & Thompson, 1997; Riguet, Taylor, Benaroya, & Klein, 1981; E. Williams, Reddy, & Costall, 2001). A number of studies have examined methods to increase appropriate play behavior in preschool and school-age children with an ASD.

Behavioral reinforcement techniques have been found to be effective in increasing cooperative and interactive play behavior in children with ASD. When children with ASD were given a choice whether to play alone with toys or move to a play area common with other children and share toys with them, they increased their play with other children if the toys were more attractive in that play area or more play time was allotted in that play area (Hoch, McComas, Johnson, Faranda, & Guenther, 2002). Children in a study by Nuzzolo-Gomez, Leonard, Ortiz, Rivera, and Greer (2002) received reinforcement for playing with toys; the children's time spent in passive behavior decreased, and they spent significantly more time with toys.

Another approach to improving play has been to emphasize interventions designed to improve early social-communication skills, the development of which is thought to be important to development of play and other skills. Because socioemotional skills are interrelated in development, training some basic skills, such as joint attention, can indirectly affect others, such as play, empathy, imitation, and language skills in children with ASD (Whalen, 2001). Development of other social skills such as imitation may also enhance play behavior. In an intervention in which adults imitated them, children with ASD increased their engagement in reciprocal social play (Field, Field, Sanders, & Nadel, 2001). In a review of 16 empirical studies, Hwang and Hughes (2000) found that early training in social communication skills positively affected a wide range of socioemotional and cognitive skills, including imitative play, in children with ASD although there was limited generalization of skills to settings other than that in which training was received.

Modeling play and communication can be a highly effective intervention to teach children to make more conversation and social initiations during play interactions. Verbal children with ASD have been found to be able to learn appropriate play comments and to apply these in play activities with their siblings (Taylor, Levin, & Jasper, 1999). Typically developing peers are also important resources for children with ASD to learn about play and to practice socioemotional skills. Children with ASD can be motivated by various methods to choose to play with other children (Smith, Lovaas, & Lovaas, 2002). When playing with typically developing children, high-functioning children with ASD engaged in interactive play and produced more interactive speech with their peers. After a 16-week playgroup intervention, children with ASD displayed more symbolic play and improved language skills, and they maintained these behavioral changes well beyond the therapy (Zercher, Hunt, Schuler, & Webster, 2001).

Some studies suggest that children with ASD benefit more from interventions to increase play when they are given an active role. When children with ASD were allowed to make choices about the toys or games used during a language intervention session, they showed significantly greater engagement in social play than did those for whom clinicians chose the games and toys, even if the clinician's choices were based on the child's preferences (C. M. Carter, 2001). Jahr, Eldevik, and Eikeseth (2000) found that modeling of cooperative play interactions was not effective in increasing appropriate play behavior in verbal children with ASD unless the children were required to describe the modeled interaction verbally before attempting it themselves.

Numerous studies have found that the capacity to pretend is impaired in children with ASD (e.g., Scott, Baron-Cohen, & Leslie, 1999). However, some studies have found that children with ASD are able to engage in pretend play, if play is structured for them and if they are prompted to do so (Jarrold, Boucher, & Smith, 1996). There is some evidence that themes from the child's own focused interests can be used in interventions to enhance the child's motivation to play (e.g., a child who is preoccupied with airplanes may be more engaged in games about flying and planes; Baker, 2000).

Although socioemotional problems in autism do not originate from insensitive parenting, parental sensitivity can positively affect the development of communication, play, and imagination in children with ASD. Siller and Sigman (2002) measured synchronization of caregivers' behavior when they played with control children, with children with developmental delays, and with children with ASD. Caregivers of children with ASD demonstrated similar synchronization with the children's behavior as did caregivers of control children or children with developmental delays. However, children whose caregivers showed good behavioral synchronization during play had better developed socioemotional skills in later years.

Perhaps in response to the child's perceived social difficulties, parents of children with ASD often make more initiations in play with their children than do parents of control children (El-Ghoroury & Romanczyk, 1999). As a result, children with ASD are less likely to initiate when playing with their parents than when playing with their siblings. This finding suggests that to encourage cooperative play in children with ASD, it is more effective to allow the child time to initiate play activities than to attempt to direct the course of play. With intervention, play interaction can be synchronized to an optimal level that allows sufficient space for children's initiations. Mother-child play sessions can, therefore, be an excellent way to facilitate interaction and can lead to increased cooperative play (Sasagawa, Oda, & Fujita, 2000).

Conclusions: Play

Children with ASD are usually delayed in the development of play skills, particularly pretend and cooperative play, although in most children play continues to develop and improve during the school years. Delays in play development appear to be related in part to delays in social communication skills. Interventions to improve social communication and imitation skills may benefit development of play, and likewise play-based interventions have been shown to benefit development of social communication skills. The play of children with ASD may be enhanced by allowing them an active role in choosing games, toys, and play themes that interest them.

Language and Communication

Deficits in language and communication are characteristic of the school-age child with ASD. Many children with ASD still have little language by age 5 or 6, and in those children, deficits in nonverbal communication are usually also evident (Loveland & Landry, 1986). For example, lower IQ and younger school-age children with ASD may have continued difficulty in joint attention interactions, where gestures such as pointing, showing, and gaze-following are used to direct attention and establish a shared focus of interest (Landry & Loveland, 1988; Loveland & Landry, 1986; Mundy et al., 1986). These children may fail to use or respond to such gestural behaviors or may do so inconsistently, leading to marked difficulty in maintaining social-communicative interactions. These deficits in social communication are a significant barrier to learning, as much effort must be expended just to direct and maintain the child's attention. Some children without oral language do successfully acquire a vocabulary of signs or learn to use communicative aids such as pictures representing common requests (e.g., a picture of a toilet to represent a request to go to the bathroom).

By contrast, the presence of speech before age 5 is an indicator for a better prognosis in children with ASD (Rutter, 1983) and is characteristic of those who become higher functioning. In those school-age children with ASD who do develop language, speech is likely to be pragmatically inappropriate as well as developmentally delayed. Among the characteristic features of language in children with ASD are immediate and delayed echolalia; pronoun reversals; unusual intonation; bizarre, idiosyncratic, or "metaphorical" speech including neologisms; and stereotyped or repetitive speech. However, those children who are high functioning and develop considerable language skills may primarily exhibit more subtle manifestations of language disorder, such as oddities of conversational interaction. These latter children, despite their pragmatic difficulties, may exhibit unusual strengths in some aspects of language development, such as word decoding skills leading to unusually early reading or *hyperlexia* (Frith & Snowling, 1986; O'Connor & Hermelin, 1994). Some of the characteristics of language in children with ASD are discussed in more detail next.

Echolalia

Echolalia, the repetition of others' or one's own speech, is a feature of normal language acquisition in infants. Up to 75% of verbal persons with ASD exhibit echolalia at some point (Prizant, 1983). Although echolalic speech is considered characteristic of children with ASD (Rutter, 1968), it is by no means present in all of them, nor is it independent of developmental level (Fay & Butler, 1968; Howlin, 1982; McEvoy, Loveland, & Landry, 1988). Echolalia also is not present only in persons with ASD. It persists or reappears in some forms of pathological development and in various psychiatric conditions (schizophrenia, Tourette's syndrome). It can be a symptom of brain damage, dementia, Alzheimer's, or Pick's disease, and can appear after a circumscribed lesion in the left medial frontal lobe and the supplemental motor area (Hadano, Nakamura, & Hamanaka, 1998). Echolalia resulting from the isolated impairment of the speech area in the brain can occur despite the presence of an inability to produce spontaneous speech or to comprehend language (Mendez, 2002). Some echolalic speech may be a result of the disinhibition of an acoustic-verbal motor reflex following isolation of the language network from the surrounding networks, resulting in a "closed loop" for speech that is heard (Linetsky, Planer, & Ben-Hur, 2000). Unintentional, or nonfunctional, echolalia of this kind could be a phenomenon similar to unintentional imitation occurring after the disinhibition of frontal network, most likely involving the mirror neuron system (Gallese, Fadiga, Fogassi, & Rizzolatti, 1996; Lhermitte, 1983). However, some echolalic speech in children with ASD appears to have a functional role in communication and thus may be differently mediated in the brain.

A number of studies have suggested that echolalia serves a purpose in the development of language in children with ASD, possibly by allowing the child to take a conversational turn and thereby remain involved in a social-communicative exchange (Fay, 1973; Prizant & Duchan, 1981). Prizant and Duchan and McEvoy et al. (1988) found that immediate and delayed echolalia can serve a variety of functions in conversational exchanges, including turn taking, declarative statements, rehearsal, self-regulatory utterances, yes answers, and requests. However, one should be cautious in assigning specific meanings to the echolalic utterances of children with ASD; such meanings depend to a large extent on contextual cues and the responses of the listener; thus, they can be open to a variety of interpretations (Loveland, Landry, Hughes, Hall, & McEvoy, 1988; McEvoy et al., 1988; Rydell & Mirenda, 1994). The findings of these studies suggest that echolalia may be best viewed as a communicative strategy used by children with ASD who cannot consistently produce spontaneous speech. It is also possible that echolalia itself aids the process of language acquisition, perhaps by sustaining the social-interactional context in which conversation (and learning) takes place (Rydell & Mirenda, 1994). However, a study by Tager-Flusberg and Calkins (1990) in which the utterances of children with ASD were transcribed over the period of a year found that their imitative utterances are not necessarily of greater length or complexity than their spontaneous speech. Thus, although echolalia may facilitate conversational skills, it does not necessarily facilitate grammatical development. Nevertheless, echolalic speech may be related in predictable ways to the development of language in children with ASD. McEvoy et al. found that the proportion of echolalic language by children with ASD was greatest at lower language levels, suggesting that as children acquire more language, less and less of it is echolalic. We should, therefore, expect to see a gradual replacement of echolalic communication with spontaneous speech over time in school-age children with ASD who are continuing to acquire language.

Characteristics of Speech

The speech of children with ASD often sounds different from that of other children. Verbal children with autistic disorder or Asperger syndrome have been found to produce frequent articulation errors or unintelligible utterances or utterances that are inappropriate in phrasing (Shriberg, Paul, McSweeny, Klin, & Cohen, 2001). Ordinarily, prosody helps to clarify the meaning of utterances within a conversation and thus adds an important channel of communication. Compared with the speech of agemates without ASD, the speech of children with ASD may sound more erratic and lacking in the prosodic characteristics of normal speech; at times, prosodic patterns may seem to conflict with meaning as, for example, when a question intonation appears with a statement or a greeting. Persons with ASD also have difficulties using information from prosody to understand what others say (Baltaxe, 1984). Children with ASD are able to use stress for emphasis in an utterance—but it may appear in an atypical place in the sentence (Baltaxe & Simmons, 1985; Fine, Bartolucci, Ginsberg, & Szatmari, 1991). Verbal children with autism were found to use significantly more words

with atypical stress in two intonation patterns, whereas children with Asperger syndrome differed from control children in only a few intonation patterns. These findings suggest that in general, the speech and auditory comprehension of children with ASD are compromised by deficits in the ability to use and understand the prosody of language in a meaningful way.

Personal Pronouns

Errors in use of personal pronouns (particularly, I/you pronoun reversals) have long been described as characteristic of verbal children with ASD (Bartak & Rutter, 1974; Fay, 1979; Kanner, 1944). Many typically developing children do make some pronoun reversals at around age 2, but only for a limited time (Charney, 1980; Chiat, 1982; Loveland, 1984). Similarly, most persons with ASD do not make pronoun reversals consistently or frequently (Lee, Hobson, & Chiat, 1994; Loveland & Landry, 1986; Tager-Flusberg, 1989), and some may instead substitute proper names for I and you pronouns (Jordan, 1989). Some evidence suggests pronoun errors are more common in children with higher functioning autism than with Asperger syndrome (Szatmari, Bartolucci, & Bremner, 1989). These errors are particularly striking when they occur in school-age children with ASD, because they usually appear inconsistent with the child's overall level of language development. Although in the past, pronoun errors in autism were interpreted as indicating a confusion between the concepts of "I" and "you" (i.e., self and other; Bettleheim, 1967), more recently they have been interpreted to show that there is a confusion of social roles, cognitive perspectives, or linguistic means of representing them (Charney, 1981; Fay, 1979; Loveland & Landry, 1986). Loveland and Landry showed that appropriate use of I and you by preschool and school-age children with autism was positively related to their ability to initiate joint attention interactions by means of gesture, suggesting that use of these terms is in fact closely tied to the achievement of a basic social reciprocity. Lee et al. (1994) found that although school-age children and adolescents with autism made few pronoun reversal errors in tests of pronoun use, they were reported to make them sporadically in their everyday life. This suggested that they *know* how to use the pronouns but that they may have difficulty identifying their own or others' social roles in some situations, resulting in errors. Research suggests that although children with autism do often have difficulty learning to use first- and second-person pronouns correctly, they acquire personal pronouns in the same order as do children with language delays or no disability: first-person, third-person, and then second-person pronouns (Baltaxe & D'Angiola, 1996).

Conversational Skills

Many children with ASD do not reach a level of language development at which true conversational exchanges are possible. However, as described earlier, some forms of echolalic or stereotyped speech can function communicatively, and children with ASD who have little spontaneous language may nevertheless use these forms of speech to engage in reciprocal communicative interactions (Hurtig, Ensrud, & Tomblin, 1982; Prizant & Duchan, 1981). This skill is a highly important one for the school-age child with ASD, who, with its advent, has acquired one of the keys for accessing the social world. Thus, it is important that less verbal children with ASD be encouraged to engage in whatever level of conversational interaction is possible for them, using echolalia, stereotyped questions, delayed echoes, and other kinds of speech to scaffold their entry into this essential social experience.

Numerous strategies have been used to facilitate verbal and nonverbal communication in children with ASD who are learning language. In younger and less verbal children, behavioral approaches have been helpful in teaching children to use language in functional ways. For example, a time-delay strategy can be used in which a trainer presents a stimulus (e.g., food) and waits a few seconds before prompting the child to respond. This technique, along with reinforcement and social interactive training techniques, has been successful in increasing the verbal communication of children who already have some language, including the frequency of verbal requests, greetings, expression of affection, and naming pictures (Ingenmey & Van Houten, 1991; Taylor & Harris, 1995). Charlop and Trasowech (1991) successfully taught a time-delay technique to parents to help increase greeting and requesting skills of children. Other techniques, such as contingent imitation and modeling, have been successful in increasing positive affect and gaze behavior (Harris, Handleman, & Fong, 1987). Functional communication training can be helpful to less verbal children with ASD in reducing the expression of difficult, disruptive behaviors. For example, if disruptive behaviors are followed by a break session and children can ask for and receive a break, gradually they will produce fewer disruptive behaviors and will increase the number of requests for breaks (R. E. O'Neill & Sweetland-Baker, 2001). Attaining the ability to communicate needs in socially acceptable ways is an important developmental step for children with ASD, which greatly facilitates their adjustment to the classroom and other settings.

In more verbally able children with ASD, a delay in social skills related to language use (i.e., in language pragmatics) may be present together with relatively preserved grammar, a large vocabulary, and a high degree of fluency (Tager-Flusberg et al., 1990). This pattern of development in high-functioning persons with ASD may reflect an adequate development of basic language skills such as phonetics but a specific impairment of more complex and interpretive language skills, including comprehension (Minshew, Goldstein, & Siegel, 1995). As a result, the high-functioning school-age child with ASD is commonly described as "very verbal" but at the same time "a poor communicator."

Conversational speech of more verbally able children with ASD is usually described as deficient in a variety of ways. For example, the child's conversation may focus on limited topics of interest to no one but the child (e.g., reading maps), speech may be pedantic and formal in situations where this style is out of place, socially inappropriate statements or questions may be produced (e.g., "You've sure gotten fat!"), references may be difficult to follow because of a failure to consider the speaker's point of view, intonation and prosody may be odd or uninformative (Fine et al., 1991), and neologisms or other idiosyncratic speech may be used (Baltaxe, 1977; Fine et al., 1991; Loveland, Tunali, Kelley, & McEvoy, 1989). In addition, children with ASD may be somewhat unresponsive to the speech of conversational partners, or they may respond in unexpected ways that suggest they have difficulty identifying and maintaining a topic of discourse. Even when children with ASD are gaining structural language skills over development, they may not be gaining discourse skills at a comparable rate (Tager-Flusberg & Anderson, 1991).

The conversational deficiencies of children with ASD have been well described. Research by Fine, Bartolucci, Szatmari, and Ginsberg (1994) on cohesive links in the conversational discourse of children and adolescents with high-functioning autism or Asperger syndrome found that the high-functioning autism group did not tend to link their utterances to earlier statements in the conversation, suggesting they may not be as attuned to the conversational context as a speaker without ASD would be. The Asperger group, by contrast, made errors such as referring to things for which there was no prior referent. These individuals seemed to be insufficiently aware of the listener's need for information. During conversation, children with ASD were found to be less likely to offer new or relevant information, to produce fewer narratives, and sometimes not to respond to questions, although they were not different from control children in gesture use (Capps, Kehres, & Sigman, 1999). Similar findings have resulted from studies of referential communication in verbal persons with ASD. Loveland et al. (1989) asked children and adolescents with ASD or Down syndrome (DS) to learn a game and teach it (verbally) to another person, with the learner giving three levels of increasingly specific prompts as needed. Even though both groups had learned the game equally well, those with ASD required much more specific prompting to convey the necessary target information to another person, suggesting that they had difficulty selecting and organizing information to convey to a listener. This study also suggested that verbal persons with ASD are insufficiently aware of the listener's need for information. Further, a study on the ability to make conversational responses within an accepted social framework (social scripts) found that children and adolescents with ASD were less likely to give helpful or empathetic responses to a conversational partner's distress than

were comparison subjects with DS, but that some did so after seeing such responses modeled (Loveland & Tunali, 1991). This study suggested that at least some persons with ASD may be to some extent aware of a listener's point of view, but they may not know how to respond appropriately.

One of the most important skills related to social communication is the ability to make appropriate inferences about the other's communicative intentions (Sabbagh, 1999). In conversation, verbal children with ASD frequently misinterpret the intentions of others (Hough, 1990) and are often literal and concrete as well as socially inappropriate, even though they may speak fluently (Joanette, Goulet, & Hannequinn, 1990). Even high-functioning children and adolescents with ASD have considerable difficulty adjusting to the needs of conversational partners, for example, by providing appropriate amounts of information, judging when information is relevant or interesting, and avoiding ambiguity. Ordinarily, conversational partners can read and interpret each other's communicative intentions. Children with ASD have been found to have difficulty identifying conversational violations (Loveland, Pearson, Tunali-Kotoski, Ortegon, & Gibbs, 2001; Surian, Baron-Cohen, & Van der Lely, 1996) and to have special difficulty in recognizing another person's communicative intentions. Not surprisingly, children with ASD have been found to have difficulty on tasks measuring humor or indirect speech. For example, they have been found to make significantly more errors in understanding jokes, even if they understand the difference between jokes and simple stories (Ozonoff & Miller, 1996). St. James and Tager-Flusberg (1994) found that when interacting with their mothers, children with autism were unlikely to use humor. Happé (1993) found that only subjects with autism who passed a second-order theory of mind task were able to recognize sarcasm. Understanding irony and sarcasm requires some ability to reason about other persons' thoughts and feelings, since the intention of the speaker is at variance with the surface meaning of what is said. Thus, the well-documented deficiency of persons with ASD in understanding mental states may well contribute to deficiencies in conversational skills (Baron-Cohen, 1995).

However, the relationship between conversational skills and understanding mental states is not completely straightforward. Using various methods, children can be taught to improve their conversational abilities, to initiate conversation, to take turns, to listen more attentively, and to maintain or change a topic. However, these changes do not necessarily improve understanding of mental states or other complex sociocognitive skills. Even after successful communication training, children with ASD did not improve their performance on false belief tasks (Chin & Bernard-Opitz, 2000), and, similarly, following mental state teaching, children with autism showed little improvement on communication measures (Hadwin, Baron-Cohen, Howlin, & Hill, 1997).

Research indicates that school-age children with ASD are likely to have difficulty making the social judgments that ordinarily guide conversation. Although this difficulty is likely to have something to do with a failure to understand other persons, their mental states, and intentions, research also suggests conversational difficulties may be related to children's confusion about how to act on what they know about others. When children with ASD are given added structure or prompts, they can frequently speak more informatively (Loveland & Tunali, 1991; Loveland et al., 1989). It is thus somewhat encouraging to conclude that in many cases, children with ASD know more than they say, and with appropriate external structuring, they can communicate more effectively.

Narrative Storytelling

There is a small but growing literature documenting that verbal children with ASD can tell stories of various kinds. Story narratives are of special interest for the study of ASD because they are an example of discourse for which fairly well-defined cultural expectations exist (e.g., stories are expected to have a distinct beginning, middle, and end) and because they presuppose considerable interpersonal awareness between speakers, if the story is to be understood. Children with ASD, however, might be expected to have an imperfect grasp of cultural expectations as well as impaired interpersonal awareness. Thus, we should expect to see differences between the story narratives of children with and without ASD.

Several studies have focused on this issue. Tager-Flusberg and Quill (1987) and Bruner and Feldman (1993) found that persons with ASD told stories that were less complex, shorter, and contained more grammatical errors than those of nondisabled persons of similar developmental level. A later study by Tager-Flusberg (1995) also found that stories of children with autism and mental retardation were shorter and less complex and contained fewer causal statements and that they were less likely to include a resolution or introduce new characters. Other studies have examined the content of stories, concluding that children with ASD are likely to talk less about characters' mental states (Baron-Cohen, Leslie, & Frith, 1986) and that their narratives are pragmatically deficient, including neologisms and idiosyncratic expressions not usually found in the narratives of other children (Loveland, McEvoy, Tunali, & Kelley, 1990). Children with autism have been found to be less creative and to provide fewer imaginative elements during storytelling than control children do. Children with Asperger syndrome, however, have been found to be better able to produce imaginative characters (Craig & Baron-Cohen, 2000). Children with autism and children with developmental delays were found to be less able than typically developing children to identify the causes of their characters' internal states when narrating stories; instead, they tended simply to label emotions or actions (Capps, Losh, & Thurber, 2000). When children with autism and children with mental retardation but without autism were matched on language ability, Tager-Flusberg and Sullivan (1995) found no group differences in narrative length, lexical elements, and mental state terms in spontaneous narratives. However, compared with controls, children with autism and children with mental retardation or learning disability gave fewer emotion-related responses to questions about their stories, and children with autism had difficulty explaining emotional states. When retelling stories, children with autism were found to perform similarly to children with Williams syndrome, but worse than control children, when talking about informational elements of the story. However, when talking about emotional elements, children with autism performed worse than both children with Williams syndrome and control children (Pearlman-Avnion & Eviatar, 2002). Thus, children with ASD may have special difficulty with imaginative and emotional aspects of stories, including mental states, even though structural aspects of storytelling may be intact. It is not surprising that success on theory of mind tasks has been found to be closely related to narrative abilities of children with ASD but not in those with other developmental delay (Capps et al., 2000; Tager-Flusberg & Sullivan, 1995).

Some evidence suggests verbal children and adolescents with ASD, particularly those of lower IQ, may not have a grasp of the conventional, culturally determined story "schema." Loveland, McEvoy, et al. (1990) reported that some of their subjects with ASD, when asked to tell the story of a puppet show, responded by describing the shape, color, or movements of the puppets ("Puppets. They are red and green. They go up and down . . .") but without conveying any kind of story. This type of response may indicate that these individuals lack a grasp of what a story *is,* perhaps reflecting a failure of acculturation (Bruner & Feldman, 1993; Loveland & Tunali, 1993).

Studying narratives in children with autism can be a powerful tool to explore aspects of discourse and pragmatics that are not usually accessible with standard language tests. The study of story narratives in children with ASD, though now only beginning, may eventually provide a window into the child's growing social and cultural awareness.

Conclusions: Language and Communication

Like their social skills, the communication skills of school-age children with ASD vary widely according to degree of autistic impairment and level of development. Although many children with ASD make considerable progress in communication during the school years, impairments of social aspects of communication remain a significant problem for most. Recent research suggests that verbal children with ASD are capable of more sophisticated use of language (e.g., storytelling) than was previously thought; that they may communicate more effectively when given prompting or modeling of appropriate conversational language; and that even echolalic speech may contribute to the development of conversational skills.

Emotion

Emotional behavior is an essential part of the child's social development, providing a basis for communication and for an understanding of self and others. Children without ASD engage in affective interactions from early in infancy (e.g., Stern, 1985), and before they reach preschool, they can not only produce readily recognizable facial expressions but also identify simple emotions in others. However, some more advanced skills, such as matching auditory and facial expressions of emotion or elicited imitation of emotional expressions, may not be fully mastered until after the age of 6 (Brun, 2001; Brun, Nadel, & Mattlinger, 1998). During the school years, emotional skills continue to develop and may reach a ceiling in later childhood when they become similar to those of adults.

In individuals with ASD, however, the picture of emotional development may be quite different. Because it has been hypothesized that children with ASD are centrally deficient in relating emotionally to others (Hobson, 1993), much of the research on emotion in people with ASD has been devoted to determining whether they have a special deficit in understanding or expressing emotion. This point remains controversial, and the evidence suggests that emotional differences in development are not unique to those with an ASD (W. Jones, Bellugi, et al., 2001). For example, persons with developmental disabilities other than ASD (e.g., Down syndrome, learning disabilities) have also been found to have affective deficiencies in some studies (Hobson, Ouston, & Lee, 1989; Loveland, Fletcher, & Bailey, 1990).

Nevertheless, it is clear that children with ASD display emotional responses that seem unusual, inappropriate, excessive, or inadequate compared with the responses of other children in similar situations (Capps, Kasari, Yirmiya, & Sigman, 1993; Joseph & Tager-Flusberg, 1997; Yirmiya, Kasari, Sigman, & Mundy, 1989). Also, they often behave in ways that suggest they are not aware of or concerned with the feelings of others or that they do not understand the consequences of feelings in other people. Self-reports of high-functioning persons with autism indicate that their experiences of emotional life are often confusing and aversive, including fear, anxiety, sadness, and frustration (Grandin, 1995; R. S. Jones, Zahl, & Huws, 2001; Wahlberg & Rotatori, 2001). Some research suggests that autism can be categorized along the spectrum of empathy disorders (Gillberg & Coleman, 1992). Disorders such as autism, Asperger syndrome, attention deficit disorder, Tourette's syndrome, obsessive-compulsive disorder (OCD), and anorexia nervosa share a profile of impairment in understanding and interpreting other people's thoughts, feelings, and intentions. Although empathy requires well-developed theory of mind skills and well-functioning emotion perception and recognition, it is much more than these subskills separately.

Many studies have found persons with ASD to have difficulty recognizing the affective expressions of others and in sharing affect in communicative situations (Hobson et al., 1988; Loveland et al., 1995; Snow, Hertzig, & Shapiro, 1987; Weeks & Hobson, 1987). Persons with ASD have also been found to have differences in their production of spontaneous and elicited affective expressions, with fewer positive expressions and more unusual or anomalous expressions than comparison subjects (Loveland et al., 1994; Yirmiya et al., 1989). Although some studies have suggested there may be an underlying deficit in perception of affect in children with ASD (e.g., Loveland et al., 1995), other studies have not always found specific affective deficits in ASD or have found no differences between persons with ASD and comparison subjects matched for verbal mental age (MA; Ozonoff, Pennington, & Rogers, 1990; Prior, Dahlstrom, & Squires, 1990). Thus, the affective deficiencies of children and adults with ASD may reflect, in part, developmental delay, and their affective development may be closely related to their level of language development.

Another possible reason for inconsistent findings on emotion tasks in ASD is differences in strategies used to perform tasks. Some evidence from functional brain imaging suggests that individuals with ASD may process facial and affective information differently than typically developing peers (Pierce, Muller, Ambrose, Allen, & Courchesne, 2001). Moreover, when emotional perception skills are challenged with information coming through multiple sensory channels, as with vocal and facial expressions of emotion together, the socio-emotional impairment of children with ASD is more apparent. When asked to match emotional expressions from faces and voices, children with autism have been found to be less able to identify the pictures that match the voices (Hobson et al., 1988; Loveland et al., 1995) and to spend less time looking at pictures that match the voices (Haviland, Walker-Andrews, Huffman, & Toci, 1996). Although children with ASD seem to find emotional expression easier to perceive in moving faces than in static ones (Gepner, Deruelle, & Grynfeltt, 2001), increased complexity in a situation, such as information from more than modality or more rapid presentation, may make emotion perception (and social perception in general) more difficult for them (Loveland et al., 2001; Pierce et al., 1997).

Efforts to teach children with ASD to understand or recognize emotions have met with varying success. Verbally able children with ASD can be taught to improve their performance on tasks of emotional understanding, although this improvement was not followed by improvement in conversational skills, pretend play, or other domains (Hadwin, Baron-Cohen, Howlin, & Hill, 1996; Hadwin et al., 1997). Behavioral techniques (Gena, Krantz, McClannahan, & Poulson, 1996; Okuda, Inoue, & Yamamoto, 1999; Shaw, 2001; Stafford, 2000) and computer-based training programs (Silver & Oakes, 2001) have been used to train specific emotional recognition and responding skills. Such methods can result in increased appropriate responding, but they vary in their effectiveness among children and the results have not always generalized to performance in real-life settings.

Conclusions: Emotion

Although there is abundant clinical evidence that the emotional development of children with ASD differs from that of other children, laboratory research studies on this topic have not consistently found evidence of deficiencies in recognizing, understanding, or expressing emotion. In the school-age child with ASD, affective deficiencies likely contribute to difficulties forming peer relationships. For example, a child who fails to recognize when he or she has offended others will have difficulty making friends. More research is needed to explore the affective behavior and perceptions of children with ASD in natural settings to iden-tify the consequences of affective deficiencies for the child's social development.

School Adjustment and Academic Achievement

Beginning with the initial transition to school, children with ASD face numerous challenges in the complex school environment, both social-emotional and academic. The social-emotional and academic challenges faced by children with ASD appear to share many of the same roots.

As they develop, children must learn to negotiate the changing social expectations of both peers and adults. Because of their dif-ficulty in interpreting social subtleties and regulating their own social behavior, however, children with ASD have difficulty meeting social expectations at an age-appropriate level. This limitation can adversely affect peer relationships in school, participation in group activities, and even ability to learn in the classroom setting. As a consequence, many children with ASD feel puzzled, frustrated, anxious, and inadequate in the social context of the school.

A rigid work style and cognitive in-flexibilities can also contribute to difficulty adjusting to the school environment at an age-appropriate level, such that for some chil-dren, even small departures from expected routines (such as a change in classroom seat-ing) may result in major adjustment difficul-ties as well as feelings of insecurity and anxiety. The well-documented impairment in executive functioning common to more intel-lectually able children with ASD (Pennington & Ozonoff, 1996) can make it difficult for them to keep track of assignments, complete homework and test papers, and allocate their time. It can also adversely affect social and emotional functioning, as children experience limitations in coping and problem solving. Other common vulnerabilities such as atten-tion/concentration difficulties, impulsivity, and abnormalities in various sensory modali-ties (e.g., tendency to become overstimulated or specific auditory, tactile, or visual sensitivi-ties) only contribute to the self-management difficulties of children with ASD. For example,

many children with ASD have symptoms of hyperactivity (Eaves & Ho, 1997), which can adversely affect academic achievement. How-ever, teaching self-monitoring of attention and performance can help to improve the aca-demic performance of children with ASD. Sixth-grade students with autism significantly improved the accuracy and productivity of their classroom work as well as their achieve-ment test scores after an intervention in-voking self-monitoring of attention (Takeuchi & Yamamoto, 2001). Students with ASD can also improve their academic performance when they are given the opportunity to make choices in the process of learning, for exam-ple, deciding the order in which they will com-plete tasks (Moes, 1998).

Academically, while some students with ASD experience no special difficulties, others display learning problems, to varying degrees. Many children with ASD who have significant developmental delays are nonverbal and may not be developmentally ready for instruction in academic subjects. For these children, a pri-mary goal may be the establishment of basic communication skills, along with the ability to attend to instruction and participate in a learn-ing situation. Behavioral techniques and spe-cialized communication therapy have proven effective in promoting these goals. When lan-guage is attained, most still require structure and individualized assistance in many, if not all, academic areas.

Many verbal children with ASD have better-developed nonverbal than verbal skills, performing relatively well on visual-spatial tasks but having difficulty with those that depend more on language, particularly oral and written expression. Unfortunately, much of what happens in the classroom depends on reading, listening, and speaking, and even arithmetic involves reading numerals. As a re-sult, children whose nonverbal skills are much better developed than their verbal skills (par-ticularly oral language) may be viewed as less intellectually able than they really are and thus may be placed in classes that do not challenge them sufficiently in their areas of strength. Others, particularly those who meet criteria for Asperger syndrome, may excel at language-based tasks and be less strong in the nonverbal area. These children are also difficult to serve appropriately in the school, since their intellectual abilities and need for academic challenge may greatly exceed their social maturity and self-management abilities. As a result, they, too, may be placed in less than ideal classroom settings. For example, a very bright child may be ready for the intellectual demands of a gifted-track class but may find the social and attentional demands of the class too stressful and frustrating. In both instances, it is important that multiple aspects of the child's functioning—not only academic test scores or speech—be considered in arriving at an optimal placement. It is also important that the appropriate level of supports be available to the child in the classroom and at home and necessary modifications be considered. For example, some children are helped by the presence of an aide in the classroom who provides help and redirection as needed. Others benefit from longer time to complete work, assistive writing devices such as keyboards, lists and schedules, special seating arrangements, and the presentation of work in small units.

In general, children with ASD do not necessarily share a characteristic set of academic difficulties, but instead, exhibit deficits that appear related to their individual patterns of strengths and weaknesses over development. As a result, individual educational needs vary considerably. Even intellectually able students with ASD can have different academic profiles than typically developing individuals (Siegal, Goldstein, & Minshew, 1996). Minshew, Goldstein, Taylor, and Siegel (1994) compared the academic achievement levels of high-functioning males with autism and a comparison group without autism, matched on variables such as age, gender, IQ, race, and SES. As compared to the comparison group, those with autism had significantly more difficulty on reading comprehension tasks. However, there were no significant differences on spelling, computational tasks, and mechanical reading. Great care is needed in the evaluation of profiles of ability for children with ASD, whose individual educational needs may not fit readily with the prepared programs of their home school districts.

Some higher functioning school-age children with ASD do not have significant delays in basic reading, spelling, and arithmetic skills.

Instead, for such children, these skills are intact or even precocious (Rumsey, 1992). For instance, a number of investigators have studied hyperlexia, in which the child displays exceptionally well-developed reading skills relative to IQ or mental age (Goldberg, 1987; O'Connor & Hermelin, 1994; Whitehouse & Harris, 1984). Hyperlexia is commonly found in a subgroup of high-functioning children with ASD. O'Connor and Hermelin studied two children with high-functioning ASD and hyperlexia, ages 5 and 9. They were paired for comparison with two normally developing children of average reading level and tested at 6-month intervals over 2 years and later at ages 9 and 12. The reading ability of the children with ASD was very advanced for their chronological and mental ages, especially in phonological decoding skills. Their comprehension was also good but at a level more commensurate with mental age. Their reading was much faster than comparison subjects' reading, especially with difficult material. These findings suggest some degree of dissociation between phonological decoding skills and semantic comprehension in these children. In another study, Grigorenko et al. (2002) studied a sample of 80 children with developmental delays, ages 2 to 12, for incidence of hyperlexia. While the frequency of hyperlexia was not significantly different for boys and girls, the children with PDD had significantly more incidents of hyperlexia as compared to children with non-PDD diagnoses. Additional research is needed to clarify the role of hyperlexia in the cognitive and language development of higher functioning children with ASD and its implications for education.

Like hyperlexia, dyslexia has also been studied to better understand the specific academic differences seen in some school-age children with ASD. In their comparative study of children with ASD and children with dyslexia matched for reading age, Frith and Snowling (1983) found that the children with dyslexia had superior skills in comprehension and use of semantic context but had difficulties with phonological processing. The children with ASD, by contrast, had problems in comprehension and the use of semantic context. This finding is consistent with the findings from Rumsey and Hamburger's (1990) study in which high-functioning men with

ASD had better phonological and rote auditory memory skills than comparison subjects with severe dyslexia. These findings, taken together, suggest that many verbal children with ASD may have an advantage in some aspects of reading (i.e., phonological decoding) and a disadvantage in others (e.g., comprehension), relative to children without ASD of comparable mental age.

During the school years, children with ASD experience significant changes in cognitive, emotional, social, and adaptive development, and, consequently, it is important that their educational programs be adapted to their changing needs over time. To study the effects of age on academic functioning, Goldstein, Minshew, and Siegel (1994) examined a group of high-functioning individuals with autism and control subjects with no autism (mean ages, 16 and 15, respectively). Younger subjects with or without autism performed equally well on psychoeducational measures of procedural skills, even on complex tasks that required interpretation, while children with autism performed more poorly on tasks administered with complex linguistic instructions. Older children with autism, however, performed poorly on interpretive tasks. These developmental changes and their implications for academic performance underscore the need for individualized educational plans and the need to monitor children's educational plans closely over time.

During recent years, there has been a significant increase in the body of literature that focuses on specific academic needs and service delivery to individuals with ASD and their families. As we have come to understand more about ASD and the special needs of these children and their families, educational approaches to this group have changed significantly; however, it was not until the mid-1970s that educational systems began to respond to their specific needs. Before this period, many public school programs were not accessible to children with ASD (Schreibman, 1988). Families had to create their own resources through private organizations and were often left without guidance and support. Given this history, difficulties in dealing with the school systems, finding the appropriate programs, and gaining access to the available services have histori-

cally been a source of frustration and stress for parents of school-age children with ASD (Tunali & Power, 1993; Unger & Powell, 1980).

More recently, however, research on educating children with ASD has provided a number of new and important educational directions (Schreibman, 1988). Among the major developments in education is emphasis on comprehensive and functional curricula, teacher training, and education (Dunlap, Koegel, & Egel, 1979; Halle, 1982); home-based intervention programs that involve parent training (Ozonoff & Cathcart, 1998); focus on the optimal educational environment and classroom instructions (e.g., inclusion; McDonnell, Thorson, & McQuivey, 1998); mainstreaming and emphasis on learning in the natural setting (Kamps, Walker, Maher, & Rotholtz, 1992); transitioning to small group formats with a modified curriculum (Kamps et al., 1992), integrating choice-making opportunities (Moes, 1998); peer tutoring (Kamps, Locke, Delquadri, & Hall, 1989); transition of the child and the services to less restrictive and more productive community-based settings (Schopler & Mesibov, 1983); and a more comprehensive treatment/intervention that is longitudinal and age appropriate (Schreibman, 1988). Despite these exciting changes, appropriate programs, much-needed services, and the research to improve our knowledge in teaching the school-age child with ASD remain limited. As the number of children needing ASD-related services increases, schools are increasingly called on to stretch their already limited resources to provide these services. In many areas of the United States, children with ASD cannot easily obtain access to appropriate classroom placements, teachers, and aides trained to work with children with ASD, needed assistive devices and modifications, or supportive programs such as home-based interventions and social skills training.

Despite the limited availability of services, individuals with ASD are now more widely served in both public and private schools than in the past. As a result, more of them are completing academic high school programs and even college. The challenges for these individuals and their families continue as they move into greater independence and vocational choices.

Conclusions: School Adjustment and Academic Achievement

Although it presents opportunities for learning and development, school also presents many challenges for the child with ASD, both academic and social in nature. Children with ASD often benefit from school placements in which educators are sensitive to their social and emotional as well as their academic needs. Because children with ASD vary widely in skills and profiles of ability, it is often difficult to meet their educational needs in the classroom. Both lower functioning and higher functioning children with ASD are difficult to serve, in that they do not necessarily learn or develop in the same ways as other children (e.g., children with hyperlexia). There is a need for continued research, both on the neurodevelopmental basis of learning in children with ASD and on techniques to facilitate learning of academic skills. At the same time, children and adolescents with ASD have greater opportunities today than in the past, and many have attained educational success at an unprecedented level.

PSYCHIATRIC AND BEHAVIORAL PROBLEMS

Although children with ASD exhibit behavioral and developmental characteristics specific to the autistic spectrum, they may have additional behavioral and psychiatric disorders such as obsessive-compulsive or ritualistic behaviors, hyperactivity/inattention, psychosis, mood disorders, or anxiety. Such disorders can be of equal or even greater concern to families than are autistic behaviors, because they can lead to increased difficulty with behavior management, learning, and social relationships. By the later school years, many children with ASD are receiving treatment for comorbid disorders, whether through psychotropic medication, behavior modification techniques, or other modalities. However, given the complexity and varying degrees of severity of autistic symptoms, it can be a challenge to identify and separate these symptoms from those of a potentially coexisting psychiatric disorder. In the developing child with ASD, this task is particularly difficult because of the changing manifestations of the disorder over time as well as the child's

limited ability to give self-report. As the issue of comorbidity in ASD begins to receive more interest and attention, studies have begun to focus on the relationship between ASD and disorders such as attention deficit/ hyperactivity disorder (ADHD), anxiety and mood disorders, and OCD. For instance, it has been reported that the risk of psychosis is higher than expected in Asperger syndrome (Clarke, Littlejohns, Corbett, & Joseph, 1989; Gillberg, 1985). Anxiety disorders, sometimes associated with depression, are also common in ASD (Frith, 1991). These findings and others serve to emphasize that school-age children with ASD are at risk for psychiatric disorders and that it is important to identify and treat these disorders whenever possible. In this section, we review several of the most common disorders that affect children with ASD.

Stereotyped, Repetitive, and Ritualistic Behaviors

Stereotyped, repetitive, or ritualistic behaviors are an essential diagnostic feature in ASD (Gray & Tonge, 2001; Lord et al., 1994; Militerni, Bravaccio, Falco, Fico, & Palermo, 2002; Rutter, 1985; Turner, 1999; Wing & Gould, 1979). Although repetitive movements such as handclapping and rocking are often observed in younger or less able children with autism, stereotyped or ritualistic behaviors of various kinds are also present in older or more developed individuals. Bartak and Rutter (1976), in their study of 19 children with autism of average intelligence, found that almost half had stereotypical movements and resisted changes in the environment. Unusual but intense interests such as weather systems, maps, and geography, as well as unusual and repetitive play activity (e.g., reading the telephone book or train/bus schedules for fun, playing with the same toy[s] repetitively), were all common. Despite their diagnostic significance, abnormal repetitive behaviors have received much less interest from researchers than the social and communication deficits associated with this group of disorders, and the exploration of these behaviors in ASD has not been approached as systematically (Bodfish, Symons, Parker, & Lewis, 2000). A recurring question is the relationship of such behaviors in ASD to the symptoms of OCD, that is, whether they may be viewed as belonging on the same continuum of disorder, whether they share common origins, and whether they have a similar role in the psychological life of the individual.

There is some evidence that the presentation of repetitive, stereotyped, and ritualistic behaviors in persons with ASD changes with development (Militerni et al., 2002), progressing from repetitive sensory motor activities to more complex and elaborated activities that may take many forms and may resemble the symptoms of OCD. A number of studies indicate that even though some characteristically autistic behaviors, such as impaired social interaction and communication and motor stereotypies, are prominent in young children, complex stereotyped behaviors and routines resembling OCD behaviors are less frequent (Cox et al., 1999; Kroeker, 2001; Vostanis et al., 1998). In other words, these manifestations of repetitive behavior and thought may be evidenced only in children of a more advanced developmental level (Kroeker, 2001). This consistent finding suggests that a developmental process may be involved in the emergence of obsessional symptoms, and a greater level of maturity may be needed for the development of these obsessional features (Gray & Tonge, 2001). Although some studies have found that ritualistic and repetitive behaviors are more common and more intense during middle childhood and tend to diminish during adolescence and adulthood (Mesibov & Shea, 1980), other investigators report that these symptoms are often retained during adulthood. For instance, Rumsey et al. (1985) found that many adult autistic men, regardless of their level of intellectual functioning, exhibited a number of ritualistic behaviors and compulsions, such as putting objects in certain places, hand washing, and stereotyped touching. These behaviors can closely resemble those of persons with OCD, raising the question of a possible relationship between ASD and OCD, as well as the issue of differential diagnosis and treatment.

In studies that compared the ritualistic obsessive-compulsive behaviors observed in ASD to those observed in OCD, it has been argued that the stereotypies seen in ASD, while superficially resembling the stereotypies of OCD, are less organized and less complex (Swedo & Rapoport, 1989). Whereas OCD behaviors are usually described as egodystonic (i.e., recognized by the individual as undesirable), the similar behaviors present in individuals with ASD are thought to be egosyntonic (i.e., recognized by the individual as acceptable and desirable; Baron-Cohen, 1989; Swedo & Rapoport, 1989). However, research has challenged this view of OCD in persons without ASD. For instance, children with OCD do not always present with anxiety (Berg, Zahn, & Behar, 1986); also, many persons with OCD have egosyntonic obsessions and compulsions and may lack insight into the senselessness of their behaviors (Insel & Akiskal, 1986). Moreover, due to their social and communication difficulties, even high-functioning individuals with ASD may not appear to be resisting their compulsions or to be affected by associated emotional distress, making it difficult to identify a coexisting OCD (Tsai, 1992). Thus, the relationship between ASD and OCD is not clear at this time and is deserving of further study.

A number of investigators have focused on the neurobiology of stereotypic (and self-injurious) behaviors in ASD as well as other diagnostic categories such as mental retardation (Stein & Niehaus, 2001) and have attempted to identify their basis in the child's developing brain. For instance, Pierce and Courchesne (2001) found that in children with autism, but not in controls, the rate of stereotyped behavior was negatively related to the size of the cerebellar vermis lobules VI-VII and positively related to frontal lobe volume. J. H. Williams, Whiten, Suddendorf, and Perrett (2001) argued that early developmental failure in a recently discovered class of neurons in frontal cortex (mirror neurons) is likely to create a number of developmental impairments observed in ASD, including stereotyped mimicking, such as echolalia.

Stereotypical and repetitive behaviors, including motor stereotypies, are not unique to ASD. They are also commonly found in persons with a variety of other developmental disorders such as mental retardation (Rojahn & Sisson, 1990), psychiatric disorders (e.g., OCD, schizophrenia), and neurological conditions such as Parkinson's disease and Tourette's syndrome

(Bodfish et al., 2000). J. E. Dawson, Matson, and Cherry (1998) examined the most common maladaptive behaviors (i.e., aggression, self-injurious behaviors, and stereotypies) in three diagnostic groups: autism, PDD-NOS, and mental retardation. They found that these behaviors had similar functions in the life of the individual, regardless of diagnostic group. However, Bodfish et al. found that adults with autism had significantly more and severe compulsions, stereotypy, and self-injury than those without autism. They also found that the repetitive behavior severity and severity of autism were closely related. The authors concluded that although abnormal repetition is observed in disorders other than autism, there is a pattern of higher frequency of occurrence and greater severity associated with autism. Thus, these behaviors remain a source of significant concern for individuals with ASD through the school years and beyond.

Although repetitive and ritualistic behaviors are not unique to ASD, they are among the most troubling features of the syndrome, from the standpoint of parents, teachers, and peers. The need to reduce or manage these behaviors has generated a significant number of studies on intervention and treatment using both psychopharmacologic and behavioral interventions. Some investigators have conducted controlled trials of the efficacy of selective serotonin reuptake inhibitors (SSRIs) such as fluvoxamine (Kauffmann, Vance, Pumariega, & Miller, 2001), clomipramine (Gordon, Rapoport, Hamburger, State, & Mannheim, 1992), naltrexone (Anderson et al., 1997; P. G. Williams, Allard, Sears, Dalrymple, & Bloom, 2001), mirtazapine (Posey, Guenin, Kohn, Swiezy, & McDougle, 2001), and risperidone (McDougle et al., 1998), among others, with varying but promising results for the reduction of stereotypical, repetitive behaviors. A group of behavioral intervention studies that focused on changing children's environments (e.g., teaching orienting responses to environmental stimuli) also reported positive outcomes (Frea & Hughes, 1997; Hall, 1997; Shabani, Wilder, & Flood, 2001). In their studies on the function and treatment of stereotypical behaviors, Kennedy, Meyer, Knowles, and Shukla (2000) concluded that the causes of stereotypy in children and adolescents with ASD are complex,

and the function of a specific behavior may be less important than previously believed.

Conclusions: Stereotyped, Repetitive, and Ritualistic Behaviors

Ritualistic, stereotyped, and repetitive behaviors can vary widely in presentation in children with ASD, in part because of the developmental level of the individual child. There is a need to investigate whether developmental continuities exist between the stereotyped movements commonly seen in younger and lower functioning individuals with ASD and the OCD-like behaviors observed in more developed individuals with ASD. The resemblance of the ritualistic, stereotyped, and repetitive behaviors of ASD to those of persons with mental retardation and those with other psychiatric disorders such as OCD suggests possible similarities in underlying pathophysiology among these disorders that require further investigation. Both pharmacological and behavioral approaches have been used with some success to reduce the severity of ritualistic, stereotyped, and repetitive behaviors in children with ASD.

Attention Deficit/Hyperactivity Disorder

School-age children with ASD frequently display characteristics that are associated with ADHD (Goldstein, Johnson, & Minshew, 2001). Symptoms such as inattention, hyperactivity, or impulsivity as well as some associated features (e.g., low frustration tolerance, temper outbursts, mood lability, poor concentration, excessive insistence that requests be met) are observed in many settings, including school. For example, compared with boys with Down syndrome, boys with autism were found to move more rapidly between different activities when in their usual environments and to be more likely to engage in one activity at a time in a sequential manner (Ruble, 1998). This style of activity may reflect attentional limitations. These behaviors are among those most frequently reported by parents of children with ASD, and they can negatively affect the child's emotional well-being as well as social and academic performance. They can be observed early in life and tend to continue through the school years, adolescence, and adulthood.

As in children without ASD, attention deficits and hyperactivity in children with ASD may present differently at different ages or levels of development. Whereas preschoolers may display a great deal of motor activity, older children are likely to become gradually less active, but to remain inattentive or distractible. Symptoms of attention deficit and hyperactivity often result in the placement of children with ASD in self-contained or other highly structured classroom settings where distractions are minimized and tasks are presented in small steps.

Despite these clinical observations, there is limited literature on comorbidity of ASD and ADHD. One of the reasons for this is the way the *DSM* system defines these disorders. Like the *DSM-III-R, DSM-IV* specifies that if the symptoms of inattention and hyperactivity occur during the course of a PDD, an additional diagnosis of ADHD is not given. This discourages the clinician from thinking of the child with ASD as having an attention deficit disorder, even when symptoms are severe. Nevertheless, many children with ASD are identified and treated for such symptoms. One study found 30% of their sample of higher functioning children with ASD were being treated with psychotropic medication for symptoms of inattention, distractibility, or hyperactivity, and 20.2% were taking stimulants (Martin, Scahill, Klin, & Volkmar, 1999). In an attempt to explore the comorbidity issue, Clark, Feehan, Tinline, and Vostanis (1999) examined a group of children with ADHD, asking their parents to rate them on a measure of autism. In this study, 65% to 80% of the parents reported significant difficulties in socialization and peer interactions as well as nonverbal and pragmatic communication in their children with ADHD. Luteijn et al. (2000) reported that according to parent report, children with PDD-NOS and those with ADHD both have problems in behaving appropriately in social situations. However, the children with PDD-NOS have more significant difficulties than do children with ADHD alone in social interaction and communication. Children with ASD and children with ADHD have also been found to differ in their pattern of responding to sensory experiences (Ermer & Dunn, 1998). Thus, while children with ADHD

and those with ASD tend to share some characteristics, they can be clearly differentiated by the type and severity of other characteristics.

Studies of cognitive processes in children with ASD have suggested that information processing differences may be involved in the expression of ADHD symptoms in these children. There is also some evidence that impairments of attention and arousal may be involved in the underlying neurodevelopmental mechanisms of ASD (G. Dawson & Lewy, 1989; Hutt, Hutt, Lee, & Ounsted, 1964; Rimland, 1964; Wainwright-Sharp & Bryson, 1993). Some investigators have studied the autonomic correlates of attention and arousal, while others have investigated attention at the behavioral level in children with ASD. Although it is not yet clear whether abnormalities in arousal play a role in ASD (James & Barry, 1980), research suggests that persons with ASD are impaired in basic information processing and attentional operations (Wainwright-Sharp & Bryson, 1993), such that the response to sensory stimuli may be delayed or attenuated (Courchesne, 1987; Zahn, Rumsey, & Van Kannen, 1987). Given that a number of studies have found attenuated responding on tasks requiring selective attention (Ciesielski, Courchesne, & Elmasian, 1990), it has been suggested that although children with ASD may not have difficulty registering information, they may instead have difficulties in processing it (Courchesne, Lincoln, Yeung-Courchesne, Elmasian, & Grillon, 1989; Wainwright-Sharp & Bryson, 1993). Goldstein et al. (2001) found that higher functioning children and adults with autism had deficits on measures of psychomotor speed and cognitive flexibility, but not on measures representative of sustaining and encoding factors of attention. Another reported difficulty in this population is overselectivity and a resulting limited use of incoming information (Lovaas, Schreibman, Koegel, & Rehm, 1971; Rincover & Ducharme, 1987). Executive function deficits have been found in both ADHD and autism, but not in conduct disorder or Tourette's syndrome (Pennington & Ozonoff, 1996). Impairments in motor inhibition were found to be specific to ADHD, while impairment in verbal working memory was found to be specific to autism. These studies serve to emphasize that problems with attention and information processing more generally may be present in all persons with ASD to some degree and that they are likely to affect numerous areas of functioning.

Conclusions: Attention Deficit/Hyperactivity Disorder

Attention deficits and hyperactivity are among the most frequently reported and pervasive problems for children with ASD. These symptoms are also widely treated with medication, although there are few studies on ADHD in ASD and its treatment. In the school years, hyperactivity usually diminishes, but problems in attention are likely to remain. Although current diagnostic practice discourages dual diagnosis of ASD and ADHD, recent research on the brain and attention in ASD suggests impairment of attention may play an important role in the development of the syndrome. The relationship of ASD to attention deficits on a clinical level should receive further investigation.

Anxiety

Anxiety is an important but little-studied problem in children and adults with ASD (Lainhart, 1999). The effect of anxiety on children with ASD can be severe, and it may be manifested in tantruming, aggression, agitation, irritability, noncompliance, fearfulness, and other undesirable behaviors. Families and teachers commonly report that challenging behaviors increase when children with ASD experience situations that produce anxiety, such as unexpected changes in routine or new social situations. In fact, as Groden, Cautela, Prince, and Berryman (1994) argued, anxiety and stress may contribute to many of the typical behavioral manifestations of autism, including unusual fears, stereotypies, and symptoms resembling those of OCD.

Children with ASD, particularly those with higher functioning autism or Asperger syndrome, are reported to have higher rates of anxiety problems than children without an ASD (Gillott, Furniss, & Walter, 2001; Kim, Szatmari, Bryson, Streiner, & Wilson, 2000). Although the reasons for increased anxiety in children with ASD have not been established, difficulties in cognition and self-regulation may be involved. For example, cognitive limitations such as impairment in executive function-

ing may contribute to anxiety problems in ASD; anxiety can arise when a child has difficulty generating new solutions to problems or changing strategies or when a child becomes overwhelmed by too many alternatives or demands. Although some situations that produce anxiety in children with ASD could be expected to do so in other children as well (e.g., meeting peers at a new school, answering difficult questions), children with ASD typically have more difficulty than other children in regulating their emotions and behavior in response to such situations. As a result, they may be more likely to react to the escalating anxiety of such a situation by "acting out" in some way.

Biological vulnerabilities may also play a role in increased anxiety in children with ASD. Studies of the families of persons with ASD have suggested that they have a higher than expected level of psychiatric disorders, including anxiety disorders (Abramson et al., 1992; Piven & Palmer, 1999). Personality traits present in families of ASD, including anxiety, shyness, irritability, and oversensitivity, may be associated with a genetic liability for ASD (Murphy et al., 2000). Even among children with related disorders, autistic behavior can be associated with anxiety; in school-age girls with fragile X, social communication deficits similar to those seen in ASD have been found to be associated with the presence of anxiety (Mazzocco, Kates, Baumgardner, Freund, & Reiss, 1997). Although these and other studies suggest that symptoms of anxiety may be closely related to the neurobiological differences that lead to ASD, it remains for further research to determine the mechanisms of such a relationship.

The treatment of anxiety in children with ASD must be a high priority for research. In a study of psychotropic medications used by individuals with ASD, Martin et al. (1999) found that 65% of those taking medication did so for treatment of anxiety-related disorders. Among the commonly used medications for anxiety in ASD are antidepressants such as fluoxetine (Koshes, 1997) and buspirone (Buitelaar, van der Gaag, & van der Hoeven, 1998). Some children are also reported to respond well to cognitive or behavioral approaches to reducing anxiety and associated behavior problems (Cullain, 2002).

Conclusions: Anxiety

Anxiety is very common among children with ASD, and it may lead to various maladaptive behaviors, including acting out. Because anxiety is so pervasive among children with ASD, it is important that families, clinicians, and educators recognize its effects and its contribution to the expression of other behavioral problems. Although cognitive and self-regulatory deficits may contribute to anxiety, research suggests that a vulnerability to anxiety may be linked to the biological basis of ASD.

Affective Disorders

Depression is one of the most common psychiatric disorders in persons with ASD, particularly in those who are higher functioning. Despite their average to above-average abilities in intellectual, language, adaptive, and academic areas, higher functioning individuals with ASD experience chronic difficulties in social interactions and relatedness and are often painfully aware of their impairment. In the school years, when peer relationships and social skills become a crucial developmental task, developmental delays in this area generate a great deal of frustration, anxiety, and distress, which in turn increase the likelihood of psychiatric difficulties. However, when symptoms that are suggestive of an affective disorder develop, it is often difficult to make a formal diagnosis because of the individual's difficulty in communicating feelings and experiences (Lainhart & Folstein, 1994).

Comorbidity of affective disorders with Asperger syndrome has been reported (DeLong & Dwyer, 1988; Gillberg, 1985), as has the case of an individual with autism who also had depression and trichotillomania (Hamdan-Allen, 1991). Kurita and Nakayasu (1994) reported a rare case of a 20-year-old male with autism presenting with seasonal affective disorder and trichotillomania. Lainhart and Folstein (1994) reviewed previously published cases of individuals with ASD and an additional diagnosis of affective disorder. Half of these individuals were female, and almost all subjects had some degree of mental retardation. The onset of affective disorder was during childhood for 35% of the subjects, and 50% had a family history of affective disorder or suicide. After their review, the investigators noted that the three critical features of an affective disorder (i.e., a change in mood, a change in the individual's view of himself and the world, and the appearance of vegetative symptoms) were rarely reported by these individuals, making the diagnostic assessment particularly challenging. These rare but important cases help emphasize the fact that both high- and low-functioning individuals with ASD are vulnerable to affective disorders.

Conclusions: Affective Disorders

Though apparently common in persons with ASD, affective disorders are not easy to diagnose, particularly in children. There is a great need for research on methods of diagnosis and treatment of affective disorders in both higher and lower functioning individuals with ASD.

EXAMPLES OF DEVELOPMENT IN THE SCHOOL-AGE CHILD WITH AUTISTIC SPECTRUM DISORDER

The trends in development of the child with ASD during the school years are best observed through longitudinal follow-up. The following cases, each of whom was seen from preschool through adolescence, illustrate some of the issues that arise in development of children with ASD with and without mental retardation, respectively. (Names and some details of these individuals have been changed to protect confidentiality.)

Joan, a Girl with Autistic Spectrum Disorder and Moderate Mental Retardation

Joan was first seen at a medical center psychiatric clinic at the age of 4 years, 8 months (4;8). At the time of her first assessment, Joan lived with her mother and stepfather. Her parents were divorced the year before. As an infant, Joan was reported to have had recurrent ear infections and delayed motor milestones. Between the ages of 12 and 18 months, she was reported to have displayed a sudden change in behavior, with loss of previously acquired language and onset of screaming episodes, running, twirling, spinning, and social withdrawal.

Joan was enrolled in an early childhood intervention program through her school district at age 3;6 on the basis of her documented language delay. She was initially referred to the clinic for developmental evaluation and diagnosis, and she continued to receive follow-up evaluations at intervals over the succeeding 12 years. The records of this series of assessments depict the trends in her cognitive, social, and language development.

When first examined, Joan was restless, hyperactive, and uncooperative, with little eye contact and few signs of social relatedness. She explored her environment in an aimless manner, touching objects and spinning them. It was easier to get her attention using proximal rather than distal stimulation (e.g., touching her hand rather than pointing). She did not initiate social or communicative interaction by speech or gesture but sometimes responded to initiations by others. Developmental testing required frequent breaks and the presentation of items in small units. She frequently did not attend and had to be reminded to look at what her hands were doing. She often perseverated, and self-stimulatory and challenging behaviors tended to interfere with testing. Joan often responded impulsively but did not like to be asked to redo her work. However, with considerable structuring her score fell above the 30-month level on the nonverbal items of the Bayley Scales of Infant Development, Mental Scale; she demonstrated receptive and expressive language at approximately a 24- to 30-month level, including both spontaneous language and echolalic speech. It was recommended that she receive speech/language intervention and continue in a structured early childhood intervention program.

Joan was next seen at age 7;1, after having been enrolled in school-based intervention for several years. She was then in a self-contained special education first-grade classroom for children with severe disabilities, where she was reported to display hyperactivity, short attention span, and behavior problems. Motor, cognitive, and social delays prevented her participation in age-appropriate physical play, such as riding bicycles and taking part in team sports. Joan also was not yet independent in toileting, dressing, or eating. Upon assessment, her expressive language was characterized primarily by echolalia, but she was sometimes able to respond to direct questions or commands and could point to named colors and parts of the body. Responses to gestures such as pointing were inconsistent, and she displayed little expressive gesture. Her language was found to be at a 30- (expressive) to 36-month (receptive) level, although nonverbal intelligence was at a mental age of 4;9. At this point, Joan's behavior was characterized by repetitive behaviors such as spinning objects, hyperactivity and distractibility, some inappropriate affect, and poor social relatedness.

At Joan's next evaluation at the clinic, she was 10;7 years old. In the interval, she continued to be served in self-contained special education classrooms and to receive speech/language intervention. She was reported to have no friendships with peers at school at this time, although her behavior problems there had decreased. Her cooperativeness was distinctly improved since the previous evaluation, and she required much less external structuring to complete the assessment. She required more structure on tasks that were more difficult for her (verbal tasks) and less on those that were easier (nonverbal tasks). She exhibited little affect, but seemed to know when she was performing well; she said, "Good!" to herself whenever she responded correctly to an item. Despite continued problems in attention, Joan was able to attain a nonverbal mental age of 5;9 on the Leiter International Performance Scale (nonverbal, NV, IQ 55), demonstrating skills in matching by color, shape, and number, and in reproducing simple block designs. However, more abstract items, such as matching by use, were too difficult for her. Language skills had improved to a 3- to 4-year level, with greater vocabulary, increased ability to respond to more complex questions and requests, skilled repetition of word and number strings, and decreased echolalia. More of Joan's language was now spontaneous, in two- and three-word utterances, although delayed echoes also appeared. Joan still rarely initiated communication, but her responsiveness to others had increased. Receptive language was still better developed than expressive. Assessment of adaptive behavior (Vineland Adaptive Behavior Scales) indicated that Joan had few skills for self-care (although she was now toilet trained) and that her social skills were at a 2½-year level.

Joan was seen again a year later at age 11;6. Her cooperation at this evaluation was excellent, with considerably reduced distractibility and hyperactivity. Social relatedness with examiners was also improved, as shown by Joan's responsiveness to attempts to redirect her attention. Socially inappropriate behaviors were fewer, but still present (e.g., pulling her dress up over her head). Nonverbal intelligence showed developmental progress (NVMA 6;3, NVIQ 59), but language remained at a 3- to 4-year level, with echolalia and perseveration present in much of her speech. At the same time, Joan began to show signs of growing insight into her own behavior. For example, when frustrated by being unable to answer a question, she once said, "Joan is sad." Joan's adaptive skills also showed progress, with improvement in self-care and social skills, and notable strength in written communication skills, relative to oral.

At age 15;2, Joan was seen again. At this time, she was enrolled in a self-contained life skills class at her local high school, with individual speech therapy, occupational therapy, and adaptive physical education, but was mainstreamed for lunch, music, drama, and typing. During the school day, an educational aide accompanied Joan and assisted her individually in most of her activities. Joan was reported to have made significant advances in social behavior. For example, although she still rarely initiated conversation, she interacted with other students if placed in a group situation. Joan also seemed more interested in pleasing the examiners during her assessment, and she responded well to praise. Although Joan had greatly improved in her ability to attend and to remain on task, she still required structuring to complete more difficult tasks, both at school and during her assessment. In contrast to her earlier assessments, Joan's problems with attention and persistence now tended to take the form of distractibility and impulsive responding rather than hyperactivity. Her behavior also was improved, although some inappropriate affect and speech were still present. Joan's assessment revealed continued progress in nonverbal skills (NVMA 7;5; NVIQ 57) but little progress in oral language skills, although

vocabulary had increased to about a 6-year level. Immediate and delayed echolalia was still present. Her academic achievement was found to be in the range of kindergarten to second grade, with strengths in spelling, word attack, and letter-word identification (Woodcock-Johnson). Joan's adaptive skills had increased to a 4- to 7-year level, with particular weakness in interpersonal relationships.

Joan was evaluated again at age 16;4. She had made some progress in all areas, but her expressive language and social adaptive skills were still in the 4-year range. Joan continued to have significant difficulty with attention and concentration, expressive and receptive language, social skills, and adaptive behavior. Her overall IQ was in the moderate range of mental retardation. She was involved in extracurricular activities at her church and in Special Olympics, and she had begun to have friends in her class at school.

Interpretation

The case of Joan illustrates progression from a classical autism presentation in the preschool years to a significantly improved presentation in adolescence, though still on the autistic spectrum of disorder. Joan exhibits many features typical of the child with ASD who is moderately to severely impaired: She has a history of repetitive motor activities such as spinning objects; her language and communication are significantly more impaired than her nonverbal skills; it is difficult to direct and maintain her attention; she has been hyperactive, and her behavior has been difficult to control; she has had few social relationships with peers; her play and exploration are very immature; and she has inappropriate affect and poor social judgment. However, her development from the preschool years through the school years and into adolescence reveals developmental trends in a number of areas. First, Joan gained nonverbal cognitive skills at a fairly constant rate throughout the period of study, with a nonverbal IQ remaining stable between 55 and 60. Thus, she continued to gain skill in nonverbal reasoning, visual motor, and constructional skills from preschool through adolescence. By contrast, her language has apparently reached a plateau at about a 4-year developmental level that was attained by about age 12, with greater weakness in expressive than receptive language. As a result, on reaching adolescence, Joan is further behind age-mates in academic progress than might be expected based on her nonverbal IQ. In addition, her significant language delay and autistic social deficits have combined to make her seem somewhat less intellectually able than she may actually be; this has meant that over the years she has received fewer opportunities to mix socially with nondisabled age-mates and has had somewhat lower expectations set for her in school than would be desirable. During the years from ages 6 to 12, the primary priorities of Joan's educational program were to develop language and control behavior.

Joan's adaptive skills have also increased over the years she has been assessed, but like her language skills, they have progressed more slowly than her nonverbal skills and have reached an apparent plateau in adolescence. By age 12, she had mastered most basic self-care skills and had increased her social and communication skills; however, her recent slow progress in adaptive behavior may indicate that she is having difficulty making a transition to the greater independence, social judgment, and peer-oriented activities expected of adolescents.

Dramatic changes have taken place in Joan's attention and behavior. Starting from a state of hyperactivity, uncooperativeness, and frequent motor self-stimulation behaviors as a preschooler, she became in the school years significantly better controlled, better able to focus attention and persist on tasks, and less disruptive in class. By adolescence, she was no longer hyperactive, although she still needed external structuring to persist on difficult tasks. Thus, over time Joan developed improved *self*-control in a variety of situations, partly as a result of structured intervention and partly as a result of maturation.

Less dramatic but still significant changes have taken place in Joan's social behavior from preschool to adolescence. As a preschooler, Joan resembled the passive type of individual described by Wing, in that she rarely initiated but did respond to others. She has continued to be a relatively passive communicator, although her interest in others and her communication skills have both increased. Her assessments document steady increases in responsiveness, cooperativeness, social awareness, and relatedness, as well as the beginnings of social insight and peer friendships. Some of these changes may have been facilitated by Joan's gradual increase in attentional and behavioral self-control, which may have helped her to benefit both from instruction and from social experience.

James, a Boy with an Autistic Spectrum Disorder and Above-Average Intelligence

James, the only child of his parents, was first brought to a medical center psychiatric outpatient clinic for an evaluation at the age of 5. The presenting problems were severe and frequent temper tantrums, extreme inattention and hyperactivity, restlessness, sleep difficulties, sensory abnormalities (e.g., did not like to be touched, was overly sensitive to loud noises), extreme discomfort in response to changes in routines, and some self-stimulatory behaviors. Up to the age of 1 year, James reportedly had recurrent ear infections and was diagnosed with asthma at the age of 13 months. However, he reportedly never had a severe attack and did not have any asthma symptoms after age 2. Developmental milestones including language were met within the expected time frames, with some delays in socialization and toilet training. His parents reported that James was not very interested in interacting with his peers. They also reported that James taught himself how to read and write, could tell the day of the week that various dates fell on, and had an outstanding memory, recalling past events with every minor detail. At the age of 5, his level of nonverbal intelligence was measured by the Leiter International Performance Scale at an IQ of 145. Although exact scores were not available, both his receptive and expressive language scores had been previously assessed to be "above age level." His preacademic skills assessed by the Wide Range Achievement Test were also significantly above average. During this time, James was described as a "somewhat anxious" child who was concerned about nuclear war and had some other fears (e.g., fear of heights). These anxieties were not severe enough to create concern for his parents. Because he had some significant autistic-like behaviors but did not fit the picture of the typical child with autism, James was given a formal diagnosis of PDD-NOS at the end of this evaluation.

At age 9, James came for a follow-up evaluation with a set of more specific concerns. His parents reported that James had started to exhibit many unusual behaviors and did not respond to medication (i.e., Ritalin) that was prescribed for his attentional difficulties and hyperactivity. He was often extremely anxious and would suddenly dwell on a given thought and become restless and (through a chain of associations) would reach a catastrophic conclusion that would create a state described as "panicky." For example, while at school, he would look out the window on a sunny day and think of possible rain later. For James, rain meant destructive weather, which made him think of tornados. Consequently, he would become so anxious that he would not be able to remain in the classroom. James also displayed a significant amount of oppositional behavior and severe temper tantrums that lasted for hours. During the time since his previous evaluation, James also developed a number of ritualistic and obsessive-compulsive behaviors that kept him preoccupied for long periods of time (e.g., touching the trash can a certain number of times before leaving the house, watching the Weather Channel for hours to avoid unexpected tornados).

During this time, James also became more interested in his age-mates and developed an intense but unrequited attachment to a female classmate that triggered the development of paranoid beliefs and experiences. These difficulties, which interfered significantly with his and his family's daily lives, necessitated pharmacological and psychotherapeutic interventions. His second assessment at this time yielded a much more uneven profile, with intellectual skills in the high average range (Wechsler Intelligence Scale for Children-Revised, Full Scale IQ=111) but with social skills and social comprehension in the impaired range. His self-help and coping skills (Vineland Adaptive Behavior Scales) were also assessed to be much lower than expected levels. His academic scores, however, were significantly above average in all major areas. James was in regular classes (honors classes in some subjects) with no remedial academic assistance.

James was evaluated again at age 12. At this time, despite significant improvement in many difficult behaviors (e.g., tantrums), he had become more and more socially isolated, spending hours every day involved in a fantasy world of imaginary cities and countries. He began to draw complicated maps of these places, discussing in great detail their populations, climates, imports, exports, and so on. Although he showed an obvious desire to be with his peers, he simply did not know how to approach them. During this time, James also started to display appetite and sleep disturbances, decreased energy, and difficulty concentrating and was prescribed antidepressant medication with a good response. His assessment scores continued to indicate above-average intellectual and language skills and extremely well-developed academic skills. James was in honors classes in almost every subject. However, his adaptive behavior scores were in the impaired range in socialization and self-help skills. As a teenager, he worked closely with one of the authors (BT), receiving supportive therapy, medications, and social skills training. Difficulties in socialization continued to be the major issue. James graduated from high school and later enrolled in a community college, where he pursued studies in information technology.

Interpretation

James's case highlights the many puzzling but fascinating developmental and diagnostic challenges of ASDs. At the age of 5, James presented as an extremely bright youngster who did not display many obvious developmental delays. Moreover, some skills such as visuospatial memory and academic skills were precocious. However, he exhibited a number of unusual behaviors consistent with an ASD that were relatively easy to identify. Although there was a gap between James and his peers in social skills, it was not the major concern when compared with his other difficulties such as lack of control in behavior (e.g., severe temper tantrums, no delay of gratification, inattention, hyperactivity).

Over the years between preschool and adolescence, James continued to acquire skills in the cognitive and academic domains that kept him at or above the level of his nondisabled age-mates. Like Joan, he learned to control his behavior better in a variety of contexts. However, while his nondisabled age-mates made progress in the cognitive domain and overtook some of his early achievements, James's initial mild difficulties in the adaptive domain, especially socialization, became major handicaps over the years, making the gap between him and his age peers significantly wider.

Perhaps the most interesting aspect of this case is the different presentation of "autistic-like" behaviors/characteristics over development. As James faced challenging developmental tasks (e.g., peer interaction and socialization experiences), his well-developed intellectual capacity made him painfully aware of his deficiencies. This in turn made him more vulnerable to additional emotional discomfort with feelings of isolation, withdrawal, sadness, and overall emotional distress. After his third evaluation, James met the diagnostic criteria for major depression in addition to his ASD diagnosis. Similarly, the intensity and the complexity of his "obsessive" rituals raised the question of comorbidity of OCD and an ASD. A further consideration is the changing nature of diagnostic standards during James's lifetime. His early diagnosis of PDD-NOS reflected the fact that his presentation was not classically autistic and that at the time it was difficult to be certain whether he entirely met criteria for autism. It is possible, but not certain, that were he assessed as a young child today, he would be classified with Asperger syndrome. Taken altogether, James's case forces us to examine the relationships among different manifestations of his impaired functioning across the stages of development. While we can explain some of the changes in terms of James's developmental maturation, we are left with many puzzling questions about the development of his ASD and the eventual outcome for this intelligent young man.

CONCLUSION

ASD, like other developmental disorders, is not a static condition that once visited upon the child, remains the same with increasing age. Instead, ASD is manifested differently as the child develops, reflecting the maturation of neural and behavioral systems, the effects of learning and experience, the activity of the individual, and their reciprocal interactions.

This review of developmental issues for the school-age child with ASD suggests important directions for future research.

Despite the recent research emphasis on lack of social understanding in persons with ASD, we still do not know enough about how children with ASD actually view their world. Little is known about how they attend to and perceive social and emotion information, interpret situations, make social judgments, understand what is said to them, and interpret the impact of their behaviors on others, or about the person with ASD as a member of a society or culture. The complexities and subtleties involved in real-time social interactions may not be adequately captured in the laboratory with simple, easily controlled tasks (Klin et al., 2002a; Loveland, 2001). Moreover, the infrequent occurrence of certain behaviors (e.g., neologisms in speech, pronoun errors) may be highly important, even though these behaviors are not readily observed in the laboratory. Studies that are based on more natural situations, while still informed by current theoretical issues, will provide us with richer data, allowing a more realistic understanding of social functioning in ASD and can make it possible to gain a better understanding of the more subtle social and communicative deficits observed in high-functioning persons with ASD.

At present, much remains to be learned about brain development in children with ASD with respect to specific, known changes in the behavioral and clinical manifestations of ASD over time. Although approaches to studying brain and behavior in ASD have become increasingly more sophisticated over the years, we have not yet succeeded in integrating these approaches to form a more comprehensive neurodevelopmental model of ASD. In constructing such a model, it will be important also to consider not only the changing and reciprocal nature of the relationship between brain and behavior over development but also the self-organizing activities of the developing child (Cicchetti & Tucker, 1994). The advent of behavioral genetics approaches to ASD, as well as animal models, opens new avenues through which the neurodevelopmental basis of ASD can be addressed. A greater understanding of these factors in ASD may help to explain the comorbidity or overlap in symptoms with other conditions such as ADHD and anxiety disorders, as well as the reasons that mental retardation is present in most individuals with ASD.

Finally, as identification of children with ASD has taken place at earlier and earlier ages, both the need and the opportunity for early intervention have increased. Although treatments using methods such as applied behavior analysis, psychotropic medication, and social skills training have all benefited children with ASD, additional research to develop more effective programs and services is critically needed. The challenges faced by the school-age child with ASD are many and multidimensional, and they vary with the needs and developmental levels of the individual. To help the child with ASD deal successfully with school, peers, physical maturation, changing family relationships, and other challenges of the school years, programs must reflect an awareness not only of the deficits characteristic of ASD but also of the growing capabilities of the developing child.

Cross-References

Autism in infancy and in adolescence and adulthood is discussed in Chapters 8 and 10, respectively; model programs are discussed in Chapter 41, and health care issues are reviewed in Chapter 20.

REFERENCES

Abramson, R. K., Wright, H. H., Cuccaro, M. L., Lawrence, L. G., Babb, S. P., Pencrinha, D., et al. (1992). Biological liability in families with autism. *Journal of the American Academy of Child and Adolescent Psychiatry, 31,* 370–371.

Adolphs, R., Sears, L., & Piven, J. (2001). Abnormal processing of social information from faces in autism. *Journal of Cognitive Neuroscience, 13,* 232–240.

Anderson, S., Hanson, R., Malecha, M., Oftelie, A., Erickson, C., & Clark, J. M. (1997). The effectiveness of naltrexone in treating task attending, aggression, self-injury and stereotypic mannerisms of six young males with autism or pervasive developmental disorders. *Journal of Developmental and Physical Disabilities, 9*(3), 211–242.

Ando, H., & Yoshimura, I. (1979). Effects of age on communication skill levels and prevalence of maladaptive behaviors in autistic and mentally retarded children. *Journal of Autism and Developmental Disorders, 9,* 83–93.

Ando, H., Yoshimura, I., & Wakabayashi, S. (1980). Effects of age on adaptive behavior levels and academic skill levels in autistic and mentally retarded children. *Journal of Autism and Developmental Disorders, 10,* 173–184.

Asperger, H. (1944). Die "autistischen psychopathen" im Kindesalter. *Archiv fur Psychiatrie und Nervenkrakheiten [Autistic psychopathology in childhood], 117,* 76–136.

Bailey, K. J. (2001). Social competence of children with autism classified as best-outcome following behavior analytic treatment. *Dissertation Abstracts International, 61*(12-B), 6696.

Baker, M. J. (2000). Incorporating children with autism's thematic ritualistic behaviors into games to increase social play interactions with siblings. *Dissertation Abstracts International, 60*(12-B), 6353.

Baltaxe, C. (1977). Pragmatic deficits in the language of autistic adolescents. *Journal of Pediatric Psychology, 2,* 176–180.

Baltaxe, C. (1984). Use of contrastive stress in normal, aphasic and autistic children. *Journal of Speech and Hearing Research, 27,* 97–105.

Baltaxe, C., & D'Angiola, N. (1996). Referencing skills in children with autism and specific language impairment. *European Journal of Disorders of Communication, 31,* 245–258.

Baltaxe, C., & Simmons, J. Q. (1985). Prosodic development in normal and autistic children. In E. Schopler & G. Mesibov (Eds.), *Issues in autism: Communication problems in autism* (pp. 95–125). New York: Plenum Press.

Baron-Cohen, S. (1989). Do autistic children have obsessions and compulsions? *British Journal of Child Psychology, 28,* 193–200.

Baron-Cohen, S. (1995). *Mindblindness: An essay on autism and theory of mind.* Cambridge, MA: MIT Press.

Baron-Cohen, S., Leslie, A., & Frith, U. (1986). Mechanical, behavioral, and intentional understanding of picture stories in autistic children. *British Journal of Developmental Psychology, 4,* 113–125.

Bartak, L., & Rutter, M. L. (1974). The use of personal pronouns by autistic children. *Journal of Autism and Childhood Schizophrenia, 4,* 217–222.

Bartak, L., & Rutter, M. L. (1976). Differences between mentally retarded and normally intelligent autistic children. *Journal of Autism and Childhood Schizophrenia, 6,* 109–120.

Berg, C. J., Zahn, T. P., & Behar, D. (1986). Childhood obsessive-compulsive disorder: An anxiety disorder. In R. Gittelman (Ed.), *Anxiety* disorders of childhood (pp. 126–135). New York: Guilford Press.

Bettleheim, B. (1967). The empty fortress. New York: Free Press.

Bodfish, J. W., Symons, F. J., Parker, D. E., & Lewis, M. H. (2000). Varieties of repetitive behavior in autism: Comparisons to mental retardation. Journal of Autism and Developmental Disorders, 30, 237–243.

Boucher, J. (1999). Editorial: Interventions with children with autism—methods based on play. Child Language Teaching and Therapy, 15, 1–5.

Brun, P. (2001). The psychopathology of emotions in children: The importance of typical development [Psychopathologie de l'emotion chez l'enfant: L'importance des donnees developpementales typiques]. Enfance, 53, 281–291.

Brun, P., Nadel, J., & Mattlinger, M. J. (1998). The emotional hypothesis in autism [L'hypothese emotionnelle dans l'autisme.] Psychologie Francaise, 43, 147–156.

Bruner, J., & Feldman, C. (1993). Theories of mind and the problem of autism. In S. Baron-Cohen, H. Tager-Flusberg, & D. Cohen (Eds.), Understanding other minds: Perspectives from autism (pp. 267–291). Oxford, England: Oxford University Press.

Buitelaar, J. K., van der Gaag, J., & van der Hoeven, J. (1998). Buspirone in the management of anxiety and irritability in children with pervasive developmental disorders: Results of an open-label study. Journal of Clinical Psychiatry, 59, 56–59.

Buitelaar, J. K., van Engeland, H., de Kogel, K., de Vries, H., & van Hooff, J. A. (1991). Differences in the structure of social behaviour of autistic children and non-autistic retarded controls. Journal of Child Psychology and Psychiatry and Allied Disciplines, 32, 995–1015.

Burack, J., & Volkmar, F. (1992). Development of low- and high-functioning autistic children. Journal of Child Psychology and Psychiatry and Allied Disciplines, 33, 607–616.

Capps, L., Kasari, C., Yirmiya, N., & Sigman, M. (1993). Parental perception of emotional expressiveness in children with autism. Journal of Consulting and Clinical Psychology, 61, 475–484.

Capps, L., Kehres, J., & Sigman, M. (1998). Conversational abilities among children with autism and children with developmental delays. Autism: International Journal of Research and Practice, 2, 325–344.

Capps, L., Losh, M., & Thurber, C. (2000). The frog ate the bug and made his mouth sad: Narrative competence in children with autism. Journal of Abnormal Child Psychology, 28, 193–204.

Carpentieri, S., & Morgan, S. B. (1996). Adaptive and intellectual functioning in autistic and nonautistic retarded children. Journal of Autism and Developmental Disorders, 26, 611–620.

Carter, A. S., Volkmar, F. R., Sparrow, S. S., Wang, J. J., Lord, C., Dawson, G., et al. (1998). The Vineland Adaptive Behavior Scales: Supplementary norms for individuals with autism. Journal of Autism and Developmental Disorders, 28, 287–302.

Carter, C. M. (2001). Using choice with interactive play to increase language skills in children with autism. Dissertation Abstracts International, 61(12-A), 4730.

Chamberlain, B. O. (2002). Isolation or involvement? The social networks of children with autism included in regular classes. Dissertation Abstracts International, 62(8-A), 2680.

Charlop, M. H., & Trasowech, J. E. (1991). Increasing autistic children's daily spontaneous speech. Journal of Applied Behavior Analysis, 24, 747–761.

Charney, R. (1980). Speech roles and the development of personal pronouns. Journal of Child Language, 7, 509–528.

Charney, R. (1981). Pronoun errors in autistic children: Support for a social explanation. British Journal of Disorders of Communication, 15, 39–43.

Chiat, S. (1982). If I were you and you were me: The analysis of pronouns in a pronoun-reversing child. Journal of Child Language, 9, 359–379.

Chin, H. H., & Bernard-Opitz, V. (2000). Teaching conversational skills to children with autism: Effect on the development of a theory of mind. Journal of Autism and Developmental Disorders, 30, 569–583.

Cicchetti, D., & Tucker, D. (1994). Development and self-regulatory structures of the mind. Development and Psychopathology, 6, 533–549.

Ciesielski, K. T., Courchesne, E., & Elmasian, R. (1990). Effects of focused selective attention tasks on event-related potentials in autistic and normal individuals. Electroencephalography and Clinical Neurophysiology, 75, 207–220.

Clark, T., Feehan, C., Tinline, C., & Vostanis, P. (1999). Autistic symptoms in children with attention deficit-hyperactivity disorder. European Child and Adolescent Psychiatry, 8, 50–55.

Clarke, D. J., Littlejohns, C. S., Corbett, J. A., & Joseph, S. (1989). Pervasive developmental disorders and psychoses in adult life. British Journal of Psychiatry, 155, 692–699.

Cohen, I. L. (1995). Behavioral profiles of autistic and nonautistic fragile X males. *Developmental Brain Dysfunction, 8,* 252–269.

Courchesne, E. (1987). A neurophysiological view of autism. In E. Schopler & G. B. Mesibov (Eds.), *Neurobiological issues in autism* (pp. 285–324). New York: Plenum Press.

Courchesne, E., Lincoln, A. J., Yeung-Courchesne, R., Elmasian, R., & Grillon, C. (1989). Pathophysiologic findings in nonretarded autism and receptive developmental language disorder. *Journal of Autism and Developmental Disorders, 19,* 1–17.

Cox, A., Klein, K., Charman, T., Baird, G., Baron-Cohen, S., Swettenham, J., et al. (1999). Autism spectrum disorders at 20 and 42 months of age: Stability of clinical and ADI-R diagnosis. *Journal of Child Psychology and Psychiatry, 40,* 719–732.

Craig, J., & Baron-Cohen, S. (1999). Creativity and imagination in autism and Asperger syndrome. *Journal of Autism and Developmental Disorders, 29,* 319–326.

Craig, J., & Baron-Cohen, S. (2000). Story-telling ability in children with autism or Asperger syndrome: A window into the imagination. *Israeli Journal of Psychiatry and Related Sciences, 37,* 64–70.

Cullain, R. E. (2002). The effects of social stories on anxiety levels and excessive behavioral expressions of elementary school-aged children with autism. *Dissertation Abstracts International, 62*(7-A), 2383.

Dawson, G., & Lewy, A. (1989). Arousal, attention, and the socio-emotional impairments of individuals with autism. In G. Dawson (Ed.), *Autism: Nature, diagnosis and treatment* (pp. 49–79). New York: Guilford Press.

Dawson, G., & McKissick, F. C. (1984). Self-recognition in autistic children. *Journal of Autism and Developmental Disabilities, 14,* 383–395.

Dawson, J. E., Matson, J. L., & Cherry, K. E. (1998). An analysis of maladaptive behaviors in persons with autism, PDD-NOS, and mental retardation. *Research in Developmental Disabilities, 19*(5), 439–448.

DeLong, G. R., & Dwyer, J. J. (1988). Correlation of family history with specific autistic subgroups: Asperger's syndrome and bipolar affective disease. *Journal of Autism and Developmental Disabilities, 18,* 593–600.

Dissanayake, C., & Sigman, M. (2001). Attachment and emotional responsiveness in children with autism. In L. M. Glidden (Ed.), *International review of research in mental retardation: Autism* (Vol. 23, pp. 239–266). San Diego, CA: Academic Press.

Dunlap, G., Koegel, R., & Egel, A. (1979). Autistic children in school. *Exceptional Children, 45,* 552–558.

Eaves, L. C., & Ho, H. H. (1997). School placement and academic achievement in children with autistic spectrum disorders. *Journal of Developmental and Physical Disabilities, 9,* 277–291.

El-Ghoroury, N. H., & Romanczyk, R. G. (1999). Play interactions of family members towards children with autism. *Journal of Autism and Developmental Disorders, 29,* 249–258.

Ermer, J., & Dunn, W. (1998). The sensory profile: A discriminant analysis of children with and without disabilities. *American Journal of Occupational Therapy, 52,* 283–290.

Fay, W. (1973). On the echolalia of the blind and of the autistic child. *Journal of Speech and Hearing Disorders, 38,* 478–489.

Fay, W. (1979). Personal pronouns and the autistic child. *Journal of Autism and Developmental Disorders, 9,* 247–260.

Fay, W., & Butler, B. (1968). Echolalia, IQ, and the developmental dichotomy of speech and language systems. *Journal of Speech and Hearing Research, 11,* 365–371.

Ferrari, M., & Matthews, W. S. (1983). Self-recognition deficits in autism: Syndrome specific or general developmental delay. *Journal of Autism and Developmental Disabilities, 13,* 317–324.

Field, T., Field, T., Sanders, C., & Nadel, J. (2001). Children with autism display more social behaviors after repeated imitation sessions. *Autism: International Journal of Research and Practice, 5*(3), 317–323.

Fine, J., Bartolucci, G., Ginsberg, G., & Szatmari, P. (1991). The use of intonation to communicate in pervasive developmental disorders. *Journal of Child Psychology and Psychiatry, 32,* 771–782.

Fine, J., Bartolucci, G., Szatmari, P., & Ginsberg, G. (1994). Cohesive discourse in pervasive developmental disorders. *Journal of Autism and Developmental Disorders, 24,* 315–329.

Fisch, G. S., Simensen, R. J., & Schroer, R. J. (2002). Longitudinal changes in cognitive and adaptive behavior scores in children and adolescents with the Fragile X mutation or autism. *Journal of Autism and Developmental Disorders, 32*(2), 107–114.

Frea, W. D., & Hughes, C. (1997). Functional analysis and treatment of social-communicative behavior of adolescents with developmental disabilities. *Journal of Applied Behavioral Analysis, 30*(4), 701–704.

Freeman, B. J., Rahbar, B., Ritvo, E. R., Bice, T. L., Yokota, A., & Ritvo, R. (1991). The stability of cognitive and behavioral parameters in autism: A twelve-year prospective study. *Journal of the American Academy of Child and Adolescent Psychiatry, 30,* 479–482.

Freitag, G. (1970). An experimental study of the social responsiveness of children with autistic behaviors. *Journal of Experimental Child Psychology, 9,* 436–453.

Frith, U. (1991). *Autism and Asperger syndrome.* London: Cambridge University Press.

Frith, U., & Snowling, M. (1983). Reading for meaning and reading for sound in autistic and dyslexic children. *British Journal of Developmental Psychology, 1,* 329–342.

Frith, U., & Snowling, M. (1986). Comprehension in hyperlexic readers. *Journal of Experimental Child Psychology, 42,* 392–415.

Gallese, V., Fadiga, L., Fogassi, L., & Rizzolatti, G. (1996). Action recognition in the premotor cortex. *Brain, 119*(Pt 2):593–609.

Gena, A., Krantz, P. J., McClannahan, L. E., & Poulson, C. L. (1996). Training and generalization of affective behavior displayed by youth with autism. *Journal of Applied Behavior Analysis, 29*(3), 291–304.

Gepner, B., Deruelle, C., & Grynfeltt, S. (2001). Motion and emotion: A novel approach to the study of face processing by young autistic children. *Journal of Autism and Developmental Disorders, 31*(1), 37–45.

Gillberg, C. (1984). Autistic children growing up: Problems during puberty and adolescence. *Developmental Medicine and Child Neurology, 26,* 122–129.

Gillberg, C. (1985). Asperger's syndrome and recurrent psychosis—A neuropsychiatric case study. *Journal of Autism and Developmental Disorders, 15,* 389–397.

Gillberg, C., & Coleman, M. (1992). *The biology of the autistic syndromes* (2nd ed.). New York: Cambridge University Press.

Gillott, A., Furniss, F., & Walter, A. (2001). Anxiety in high-functioning children with autism. *Autism: International Journal of Research and Practice, 5,* 277–286.

Goldberg, T. E. (1987). On hermetic reading abilities. *Journal of Autism and Developmental Disorders, 17,* 29–44.

Goldstein, G., Johnson, C. R., & Minshew, N. J. (2001). Attentional processes in autism. *Journal of Autism and Developmental Disorders, 31*(4), 433–440.

Goldstein, G., Minshew, N. J., & Siegel, D. J. (1994). Age differences in academic achievement in high-functioning autistic individuals. *Journal of Clinical and Experimental Neuropsychology, 16*(5), 671–680.

Gordon, O. T., Rapoport, J. T., Hamburger, J. D., State, R. C., & Mannheim, G. B. (1992). Differential response of seven subjects with autistic disorder to clomipramine and desipramine. *American Journal of Psychiatry, 149,* 363–366.

Grandin, T. (1995). How people with autism think. In E. Schopler & G. B. Mesibov (Eds.), *Learning and cognition in autism: Current issues in autism* (pp. 137–156). New York: Plenum Press.

Gray, K. M., & Tonge, B. J. (2001). Are there early features of autism in infants and preschool children? *Journal of Pediatrics and Child Health, 37*(3), 221–226.

Grigorenko, E. L., Klin, A., Pauls, D. L., Senft, R., Hooper, C., & Volkmar, F. R. (2002). A Descriptive Study of Hyperlexia in a Clinically Referred Sample of Children with Developmental Delays. *Journal of Autism and Developmental Disorders, 32,* 3–12.

Groden, J., Cautela, J., Prince, S., & Berryman, J. (1994). The impact of stress and anxiety on individuals with autism and developmental disabilities. In E. Schopler & G. B. Mesibov (Eds.), *Behavioral issues in autism: Current issues in autism* (pp. 177–194). New York: Plenum Press.

Hadano, K., Nakamura, H., & Hamanaka, T. (1998). Effortful echolalia. *Cortex, 34,* 67–82.

Hadwin, J., Baron-Cohen, S., Howlin, P., & Hill, K. (1996). Can we teach children with autism to understand emotions, belief, or pretence? *Development and Psychopathology, 8,* 345–365.

Hadwin, J., Baron-Cohen, S., Howlin, P., & Hill, K. (1997). Does teaching theory of mind have an effect on the ability to develop conversation in children with autism? *Journal of Autism and Developmental Disorders, 27,* 519–537.

Hall, L. J. (1997). Effective behavioural strategies for the defining characteristics of autism. *Behaviour Change, 14*(3), 139–154.

Halle, J. W. (1982). Teaching functional language to the handicapped: An integrative model of the natural environment teaching techniques. *Journal of the Association for the Severely Handicapped, 7,* 29–36.

Hamden-Allen, G. (1991). Brief report: Trichotillomania in an autistic male. *Journal of Autism and Developmental Disorders, 21,* 79–82.

Happé, F. G. E. (1993). Communicative competence and theory of mind in autism: A test of relevance theory. *Cognition, 48,* 101–119.

Harris, S. L., Handleman, J. S., & Fong, P. L. (1987). Imitation of self-stimulation: Impact on the autistic child's behavior and affect. *Child and Family Behavior Therapy, 9,* 1–21.

Haviland, J. M., Walker-Andrews, A. S., Huffman, L. R., & Toci, L. (1996). Intermodal perception of emotional expressions by children with autism. *Journal of Developmental and Physical Disabilities, 8*(1), 77–88.

Hobson, R. P. (1990). On acquiring knowledge about people and the capacity to pretend: Response to Leslie. *Psychological Review, 97*(1), 114–121.

Hobson, R. P. (1993). *Autism and the development of mind.* Hove, England: Erlbaum.

Hobson, R. P., Ouston, J., & Lee, A. (1988). Emotion recognition in autism: Coordinating faces and voices. *Psychological Medicine, 18,* 911–923.

Hobson, R. P., Ouston, J., & Lee, A. (1989). Recognition of emotion by mentally retarded adolescents and young adults. *American Journal on Mental Retardation, 93,* 434–443.

Hoch, H., McComas, J. J., Johnson, L., Faranda, N., & Guenther, S. (2002). The effects of magnitude and quality of reinforcement on choice responding during play activities. *Journal of Applied Behavior Analysis, 35*(2), 171–181.

Hough, M. S. (1990). Narrative comprehension in adults with right and left hemisphere brain damage: Theme organization. *Brain and Language, 38,* 253–277.

Howlin, P. (1982). Echolalic and spontaneous phrase speech in autistic children. *Journal of Child Psychology and Psychiatry, 23,* 281–293.

Hurtig, R., Ensrud, S., & Tomblin, J. B. (1982). The communicative function of questions production in autistic children. *Journal of Autism and Developmental Disorders, 12,* 57–69.

Hutt, C., Hutt, S. J., Lee, D., & Ounsted, C. (1964). Arousal and childhood autism. *Nature, 204,* 908–909.

Hwang, B., & Hughes, C. (2000). The effects of social interactive training on early social communicative skills of children with autism. *Journal of Autism and Developmental Disorders, 30*(4), 331–343.

Ingenmey, R., & Van Houten, R. (1991). Using time delay to promote spontaneous speech in an autistic child. *Journal of Applied Behavioral Analysis, 24,* 591–596.

Insel, T. R., & Akiskal, H. S. (1986). Obsessive-compulsive disorder with psychotic features: A phenomenologic analyses. *American Journal of Psychiatry, 143,* 1527–1533.

Jacobson, J., & Ackerman, L. (1990). Differences in adaptive functioning among people with autism or mental retardation. *Journal of Autism and Developmental Disorders, 20,* 205–219.

Jahr, E., Eldevik, S., & Eikeseth, S. (2000). Teaching children with autism to initiate and sustain cooperative play. *Research in Developmental Disabilities, 21*(2), 151–169.

James, A. L., & Barry, R. J. (1980). A review of psychopathology in early onset psychosis. *Schizophrenia Bulletin, 6,* 506–525.

Jarrold, C., Boucher, J., & Smith, P. (1996). Generativity deficits in pretend play in autism. *British Journal of Developmental Psychology, 14,* 275–300.

Joanette, Y., Goulet, P., & Hannequinn, D. (1990). *Right hemisphere and verbal communication.* New York: Springer-Verlag.

Jones, R. S. P., Zahl, A., & Huws, J. C. (2001). First-hand accounts of emotional experiences in autism: A qualitative analysis. *Disability and Society, 16*(3), 393–401.

Jones, W., Bellugi, U., Lai, Z., Chiles, M., Reilly, J., Lincoln, A., et al. (2001). Hypersociability: The social and affective phenotype of Williams syndrome. In U. Bellugi & M. St. George (Eds.), *Journey from cognition to brain to gene: Perspectives from Williams' syndrome* (pp. 43–71). Cambridge, MA: MIT Press.

Jordan, R. R. (1989). An experimental comparison of the understanding and use of speaker-addressee personal pronouns in autistic children. *British Journal of Disorders of Communication, 24,* 169–179.

Joseph, R. M., & Tager-Flusberg, H. (1997). An investigation of attention and affect in children with autism and Down syndrome. *Journal of Autism and Developmental Disorders, 27*(4), 385–396.

Kamps, D., Locke, P., Delquadri, J., & Hall, R. V. (1989). Increasing academic skills of students with autism using fifth grade peers as tutors. *Education and Treatment of Children, 12,* 38–51.

Kamps, D., Royer, J., Dugan, E., Kravits, T., Gonzalez-Lopez, A., Garcia, J., et al. (2002). Peer training to facilitate social interaction for elementary students with autism and their peers. *Exceptional Children, 68,* 173–187.

Kamps, D., Walker, D., Maher, J., & Rotholtz, D. (1992). Academic and environmental effects of small group arrangements in classrooms for students with autism and other developmental disabilities. *Journal of Autism and Developmental Disorders, 22,* 277–293.

Kanner, L. (1943). Autistic disturbances of affective contact. *Nervous Child, 2,* 217–250.

Kanner, L. (1944). Early infantile autism. *Journal of Pediatrics, 25,* 211–217.

Kauffmann, C., Vance, H. B., Pumariega, A. J., & Miller, B. (2001). Fluvoxamine treatment of a child with severe PDD: A single case study. *Psychiatry: Interpersonal and Biological Processes, 64*(3), 268–277.

Kennedy, C. H., Meyer, K. A., Knowles, T., & Shukla, S. (2000). Analyzing the multiple functions of stereotypical behavior for students with autism: Implications for assessment and treatment. *Journal of Applied Behavioral Analysis, 33*(4), 559–771.

Kim, J. A., Szatmari, P., Bryson, S. E., Streiner, D. L., & Wilson, F. J. (2000). The prevalence of anxiety and mood problems among children with autism and Asperger syndrome. *Autism: International Journal of Research and Practice, 4,* 117–132.

Klin, A., Jones, W., Schultz, R., Volkmar, F. R., & Cohen, D. (2002a). Defining and quantifying the social phenotype in autism. *American Journal of Psychiatry, 159,* 909–916.

Klin, A., Jones, W., Schultz, R., Volkmar, F. R., & Cohen, D. (2002b). Visual fixation patterns during viewing of naturalistic social situations as predictors of social competence in individuals with autism. *Archives of General Psychiatry, 59,* 809–816.

Klin, A., Volkmar, F. R., & Sparrow, S. S. (1992). Autistic social dysfunction: Some limitations of the theory of mind hypothesis. *Journal of Child Psychology and Psychiatry, 33,* 861–876.

Koshes, R. J. (1997). Use of fluoxetine for obsessive-compulsive behavior in adults with autism. *American Journal of Psychiatry, 154,* 578.

Kraijer, D. (2000). Review of adaptive behavior studies in mentally retarded persons with autism/pervasive developmental disorder. *Journal of Autism and Developmental Disorders, 30*(1), 39–47.

Kroeker, R. (2001). Rhythmic behaviors in typically developing infants, and infants with later diagnosed autism or developmental delay. *Dissertation Abstracts International, 62*(5-B), 2517.

Kurita, H., & Nakayasu, N. (1994). Brief report: An autistic male presenting seasonal affective disorder (SAD) and trichotillomania. *Journal of Autism and Developmental Disorders, 24,* 687–692.

Lainhart, J. E. (1999). Psychiatric problems in individuals with autism, their parents and siblings. *International Review of Psychiatry, 11,* 278–298.

Lainhart, J. E., & Folstein, S. E. (1994). Affective disorders in people with autism: A review of published cases. *Journal of Autism and Developmental Disabilities, 24,* 587–601.

Landry, S. H., & Loveland, K. A. (1988). Communication behaviors in autism and developmental language delay. *Journal of Child Psychology and Psychiatry and Allied Disciplines, 29,* 621–634.

Lee, A., Hobson, R. P., & Chiat, S. (1994). I, you, me, and autism: An experimental study. *Journal of Autism and Developmental Disorders, 24,* 155–176.

Lhermitte, F. (1983). "Utilisation behaviour" and its relation to lesions of the frontal lobes. *Brain, 106,* 237–255.

Linetsky, E., Planer, D., & Ben-Hur, T. (2000). Echolalia-palilalia as the sole manifestation of nonconvulsive status epilepticus. *Neurology, 55,* 733–734.

Liss, M., Harel, B., Fein, D., Allen, D. S., Dunn, M., Feinstein, C., et al. (2001). Predictors and correlates of adaptive functioning in children with developmental disorders. *Journal of Autism and Developmental Disorders, 31*(2), 219–230.

Little, L. (2002). Middle-class mothers' perceptions of peer and sibling victimization among children with Asperger's syndrome and nonverbal learning disorders. *Issues in Comprehensive Pediatric Nursing, 25*(1), 43–57.

Lord, C., Rutter, M. L., DiLavore, P. C., & Risi, S. (1999). *Autism Diagnostic Observation Schedule—WPS* (WPS ed.). Los Angeles: Western Psychological Services.

Lord, C., Rutter, M. L., & Le Couteur, A. (1994). The Autism Diagnostic Interview—Revised: A revised version of a diagnostic interview for caregivers of individuals with possible pervasive developmental disorders. *Journal of Autism and Developmental Disorders, 24,* 659–685.

Lovaas, O. I., Schreibman, L., Koegel, R., & Rehm, R. (1971). Selective responding by autistic children to multiple sensory inputs. *Journal of Abnormal Psychology, 77,* 211–222.

Loveland, K. A. (1984). Learning about points of view: Spatial perspective and the acquisition of 'I/you.' *Journal of Child Language, 2,* 535–556.

Loveland, K. A. (2001). Toward an ecological theory of autism. In J. A. Burack, T. Charman, N. Yirmiya, & P. R. Zelazo (Eds.), *The development of autism: Perspectives from theory and research* (pp. 17–37). Hillsdale, NJ: Erlbaum.

Loveland, K. A., Fletcher, J., & Bailey, V. (1990). Verbal and nonverbal communication of events in learning-disability subtypes. *Journal of Clinical and Experimental Neuropsychology, 12,* 433–447.

Loveland, K. A., & Kelley, M. (1988). Development of adaptive behavior in adolescents and young adults with autism and Down syndrome. *American Journal of Mental Retardation, 93,* 84–92.

Loveland, K. A., & Kelley, M. (1991). Development of adaptive behavior in preschoolers with autism and Down syndrome. *American Journal of Mental Retardation, 96,* 13–20.

Loveland, K. A., & Landry, S. H. (1986). Joint attention and communication in autism and language delay. *Journal of Autism and Developmental Disorders, 16,* 335–349.

Loveland, K. A., Landry, S. H., Hughes, S. O., Hall, S. K., & McEvoy, R. E. (1988). Speech acts and the pragmatic deficits of autism. *Journal of Speech and Hearing Research, 31,* 593–604.

Loveland, K. A., McEvoy, R. E., Tunali, B., & Kelley, M. (1990). Narrative story-telling in autism and Down syndrome. *British Journal of Developmental Psychology, 8,* 9–23.

Loveland, K. A., Pearson, D. A., Tunali-Kotoski, B., Ortegon, J., & Gibbs, M. C. (2001). Judgments of social appropriateness by children and adolescents with autism. *Journal of Autism and Developmental Disorders, 31,* 367–376.

Loveland, K. A., & Tunali, B. (1991). Social scripts for conversational interactions in autism and Down syndrome. *Journal of Autism and Developmental Disorders, 21,* 177–186.

Loveland, K. A., & Tunali, B. (1993). Narrative language in autism and the theory of mind hypothesis: A wider perspective. In S. Baron-Cohen, H. Tager-Flusberg, & D. Cohen (Eds.), *Understanding other minds: Perspectives from autism* (pp. 247–266). Oxford, England: Oxford University Press.

Loveland, K. A., Tunali, B., Kelley, M., & McEvoy, R. E. (1989). Referential communication and response adequacy in autism and Down syndrome. *Applied Psycholinguistics, 10,* 401–413.

Loveland, K. A., Tunali-Kotoski, B., Chen, R., Brelsford, K., Ortegon, J., & Pearson, D. (1995). Intermodal perception of affect in persons with autism or Down syndrome. *Development and Psychopathology, 7,* 409–418.

Loveland, K. A., Tunali-Kotoski, B., Pearson, D., Brelsford, K., Ortegon, J., & Chen, R. (1994). Imitation and expression of facial affect in autism. *Development and Psychopathology, 6,* 433–444.

Luteijn, E. F., Serra, M., Jackson, S., Steenhuis, M. P., Althaus, M., Volkmar, F. R., et al. (2000). How unspecified are disorders of children with a pervasive developmental disorder not otherwise specified? A study of social problems in children with PDD-NOS and ADHD. *European Child and Adolescent Psychiatry, 9,* 168–179.

Martin, A., Scahill, L., Klin, A., & Volkmar, F. R. (1999). Higher-functioning pervasive developmental disorders: Rates and patterns of psychotropic drug use. *Journal of the American Academy of Child and Adolescent Psychiatry, 38,* 923–931.

Mazzocco, M. M., Kates, W. R., Baumgardner, T. L., Freund, L. S., & Reiss, A. L. (1997). Autistic behaviors among girls with fragile X syndrome. *Journal of Autism and Developmental Disorders, 27,* 415–435.

McDonnell, J., Thorson, N., & McQuivey, C. (1998). The instructional characteristics of inclusive classes for elementary students with severe disabilities: An exploratory study. *Journal of Behavioral Education, 8,* 415–437.

McDonough, L., Stahmer, A., Schreibman, L., & Thompson, S. J. (1997). Deficits, delays, and distractions: An evaluation of symbolic play and memory in children with autism. *Development and Psychopathology, 9*(1), 17–41.

McDougle, C. J., Holmes, J. P., Carlson, D. C., Pelton, G. H., Cohen, D. J., & Price, L. H. (1998). A double-blind, placebo-controlled study of risperidone in adults with autistic disorder and other pervasive developmental disorders. *Archives of General Psychiatry, 55*(7), 633–641.

McEvoy, R. E., Loveland, K. A., & Landry, S. H. (1988). Functions of immediate echolalia in autistic children. *Journal of Autism and Developmental Disorders, 18,* 657–688.

McLaughlin-Cheng, E. (1998). Asperger syndrome and autism: A literature review and meta-analysis. *Focus on Autism and Other Developmental Disabilities, 13*(4), 234–245.

McLennan, J. D., Lord, C., & Schopler, E. (1993). Sex differences in higher functioning people with autism. *Journal of Autism and Developmental Disorders, 23,* 217–227.

Mendez, M. F. (2002). Prominent echolalia from isolation of the speech area. *Journal of Neuropsychiatry and Clinical Neurosciences, 14*(3), 356.

Mesibov, G. B., & Shea, V. (1980. March). *Social and interpersonal problems of autistic adolescents and adults.* Meeting of the Southeastern Psychological Association, Washington, DC.

Michelotti, J., Charman, T., Slonims, V., & Baird, G. (2002). Follow-up of children with language delay and features of autism from preschool years to middle childhood. *Developmental Medicine and Child Neurology, 44,* 812–819.

Militerni, R., Bravaccio, C., Falco, C., Fico, C., & Palermo, M. T. (2002). Repetitive behaviors in autistic disorder. *European Journal of Child and Adolescent Psychiatry, 11*(5), 210–218.

Minshew, N. J., Goldstein, G., & Siegel, D. J. (1995). Speech and language in high-functioning autistic individuals. *Neuropsychology, 9,* 255–261.

Minshew, N. J., Goldstein, G., Taylor, G., & Siegel, D. J. (1994). Academic achievement in high functioning autistic individuals. *Journal of Clinical and Experimental Neuropsychology, 16,* 261–270.

Moes, D. (1998). Integrating choice-making opportunities within teacher-assigned academic tasks to facilitate the performance of children with autism. *Journal of the Association for Persons with Severe Handicaps, 23,* 319–328.

Morrison, L., Kamps, D., Garcia, J., & Parker, D. (2001). Peer mediation and monitoring strategies to improve initiations and social skills for students with autism. *Journal of Positive Behavior Interventions, 3,* 237–250.

Mundy, P., Sigman, M., Ungerer, J., & Sherman, T. (1986). Defining the social deficits of autism. *Journal of Child Psychology and Psychiatry, 27,* 657–669.

Mundy, P., Sigman, M., Ungerer, J., & Sherman, T. (1987). Nonverbal communication and play correlates of language development in autistic children. *Journal of Autism and Developmental Disorders, 17*(3), 349–364.

Murphy, M., Bolton, P. F., Pickles, A., Fombonne, E., Piven, J., & Rutter, M. L. (2000). Personality traits of the relatives of autistic probands. *Psychological Medicine, 30,* 1411–1424.

Njardvik, U., Matson, J. L., & Cherry, K. E. (1999). A comparison of social skills in adults with autistic disorder, pervasive developmental disorder not otherwise specified, and mental retardation. *Journal of Autism and Developmental Disorders, 29*(4), 287–295.

Nuzzolo-Gomez, R., Leonard, M. A., Ortiz, E., Rivera, C. M., & Greer, R. (2002). Teaching children with autism to prefer books or toys over stereotypy or passivity. *Journal of Positive Behavior Interventions, 4,* 80–87.

O'Connor, N., & Hermelin, B. (1994). Two autistic savant readers. *Journal of Autism and Developmental Disorders, 24,* 501–515.

Okuda, K., Inoue, M., & Yamamoto, J. (1999). Teaching reading comprehension for students with developmental disabilities: Acquisition of the inference of causal events and emotion in the sentence. *Japanese Journal of Behavior Therapy, 25*(1), 7–22.

O'Neill, D. K., & Happé, F. G. E. (2000). Noticing and commenting on what's new: Differences and similarities among 22-month-old typically developing children, children with Down syndrome and children with autism. *Developmental Science, 3*(4), 457–478.

O'Neill, R. E., & Sweetland-Baker, M. (2001). Brief report: An assessment of stimulus generalization and contingency effects in functional communication training with two students with autism. *Journal of Autism and Developmental Disorders, 31*(2), 235–240.

Ozonoff, S., & Cathcart, K. (1998). Effectiveness of a home program intervention for young children with autism. *Journal of Autism and Developmental Disorders, 28,* 25–32.

Ozonoff, S., & Miller, J. N. (1996). An exploration of right hemisphere contributions to the pragmatic impairments of autism. *Brain and Language, 52,* 411–434.

Ozonoff, S., Pennington, B. F., & Rogers, S. (1990). Are there specific emotion perception deficits in young autistic children? *Journal of Child Psychology and Psychiatry, 31,* 343–361.

Ozonoff, S., & South, M. (2001). Early social development in young children with autism: Theoretical and clinical implications. In G. Bremner & A. Fogel (Eds.), *Blackwell handbook of infant development: Handbooks of developmental psychology* (pp. 565–588). Malden, MA: Blackwell.

Pearlman-Avnion, S., & Eviatar, Z. (2002). Narrative analysis in developmental social and linguistic pathologies: Dissociation between emotional and informational language use. *Brain and Cognition, 48,* 494–499.

Pennington, B. F., & Ozonoff, S. (1996). Executive functions and developmental psychopathology. *Journal of Child Psychology and Psychiatry, 37*(1), 51–87.

Pierce, K., & Courchesne, E. (2001). Evidence for a cerebellar role in reduced exploration and stereotyped behavior in autism. *Biological Psychiatry, 49,* 655–664.

Pierce, K., Glad, K. S., & Schreibman, L. (1997). Social perception in children with autism: An attentional deficit? *Journal of Autism and Developmental Disorders, 27,* 265–282.

Pierce, K., Muller, R. A., Ambrose, J., Allen, G., & Courchesne, E. (2001). Face processing occurs outside the fusiform "face area" in autism: Evidence from functional MRI. *Brain, 124*(10), 2059–2073.

Piven, J., & Palmer, P. (1999). Psychiatric disorder and the broad autism phenotype: Evidence from a family study of multiple-incidence autism families. *American Journal of Psychiatry, 156,* 557–563.

Posey, D. J., Guenin, K. D., Kohn, A. E., Swiezy, N. B., & McDougle, C. J. (2001). A naturalistic open-label study of mirtazapine in autistic and other pervasive developmental disorders. *Journal of Child and Adolescent Psychopharmacology, 11*(3), 267–277.

Prior, M., Dahlstrom, B., & Squires, T. (1990). Autistic children's knowledge of thinking and feeling states in other people. *Journal of Child Psychology and Psychiatry and Allied Disciplines, 31,* 587–601.

Prizant, B. M. (1983). Language acquisition and communicative behavior in autism: Toward an understanding of the whole of it. *Journal of Speech and Hearing Disorders, 48,* 296–307.

Prizant, B. M., & Duchan, J. F. (1981). The functions of immediate echolalia in autistic children. *Journal of Speech and Hearing Disorders, 46,* 241–249.

Riguet, C. B., Taylor, N. D., Benaroya, S., & Klein, L. S. (1981). Symbolic play in autistic, Down's, and normal children of equivalent mental age. *Journal of Autism and Developmental Disorders, 11*(4), 439–448.

Rimland, B. (1964). *Infantile autism.* New York: Appleton-Century-Crofts.

Rincover, A., & Ducharme, J. M. (1987). Variables influencing stimulus overselectivity and "tunnel vision" in developmentally delayed children. *American Journal of Mental Deficiency, 91,* 422–430.

Rodrigue, J. R., Morgan, S. B., & Geffken, G. R. (1991). A comparative evaluation of adaptive behavior in children and adolescents with autism, Down Syndrome, and normal development. *Journal of Autism and Developmental Disabilities, 21,* 187–196.

Rojahn, J., & Sisson, L. A. (1990). Stereotyped behavior. In J. L. Matson (Ed.), *Handbook of behavior modification with the mentally retarded* (2nd ed., pp. 181–223). New York: Plenum Press.

Ruble, L. A. (1998). Comparative study of the natural habitat behaviors of children with autism and children with down syndrome: An ecological approach. *Dissertation Abstracts International, 59*(5-B), 2459.

Rumsey, J. M. (1992). Neuropsychological studies of high-level autism. In E. Schopler & G. Mesibov (Eds.), *High functioning individuals with autism* (pp. 41–64). New York: Plenum Press.

Rumsey, J. M., & Hamburger, S. D. (1990). Neuropsychological divergence of high-level autism and severe dyslexia. *Journal of Autism and Developmental Disorders, 20,* 155–168.

Rumsey, J. M., Rapoport, J. L., & Sceery, W. R. (1985). Autistic children as adults: Psychiatric, social, and behavioral outcomes. *Journal of the American Academy of Child Psychiatry, 24,* 465–473.

Rutter, M. L. (1968). Concepts of autism: A review of research. *Journal of Child Psychology and Psychiatry, 9,* 1–25.

Rutter, M. L. (1974). The development of infantile autism. *Psychological Medicine, 4,* 147–163.

Rutter, M. L. (1978). Diagnosis and definition. In M. Rutter & E. Schopler (Eds.), *Autism: A reappraisal of concepts and treatment* (pp. 1–25). New York: Plenum Press.

Rutter, M. L. (1983). Cognitive deficits in the pathogenesis of autism. *Journal of Child Psychology and Psychiatry, 24,* 513–531.

Rutter, M. L. (1985). Infantile autism and other pervasive developmental disorders. In M. Rutter & L. Hersov (Eds.), *Child and adolescent psychiatry: Modern approaches* (pp. 545–566). Oxford, England: Blackwell Scientific Publications.

Rutter, M. L., & Garmezy, N. (1983). Developmental psychopathology. In E. M. Hetherington (Ed.), *Handbook of child psychology* (Vol. 4, pp. 775–911). New York: Wiley.

Rutter, M. L., Greenfield, D., & Lockyer, L. (1967). A five to fifteen-year follow-up study of infantile psychosis: II. Social and behavioral outcome. *British Journal of Psychiatry, 113,* 1187–1199.

Rydell, P. J., & Mirenda, P. (1994). Effects of high and low constraint utterances on the production of immediate and delayed echolalia in young children with autism. *Journal of Autism and Developmental Disorders, 24,* 719–735.

Sabbagh, M. (1999). Communicative intentions and language: Evidence from right-hemisphere damage and autism. *Brain and Language, 70,* 29–69.

Sasagawa, E., Oda, H., & Fujita, T. (2000). Effectiveness of the Dohsa-Hou on mother-child interactions: Children with Down syndrome and autism. *Japanese Journal of Special Education, 38*(1), 13–22.

Schatz, J., & Hamdan-Allen, G. (1995). Effects of age and IQ on adaptive behavior domains for children with autism. *Journal of Autism and Developmental Disorders, 25*(1), 51–60.

Schopler, E., & Mesibov, G. B. (1983). *Autism in adolescents and adults.* New York: Plenum Press.

Schreibman, L. (1988). *Autism.* Newbury Park, CA: Sage.

Scott, F. J., Baron-Cohen, S., & Leslie, A. (1999). If pigs could fly: A test of counterfactual reasoning and pretence in children with autism. *British Journal of Developmental Psychology, 17*(3), 349–362.

Shabani, D. B., Wilder, D. A., & Flood, W. A. (2001). Reducing stereotypic behavior through discrimination training, differential reinforcement of other behavior, and self-monitoring. *Behavioral Interventions, 16,* 279–286.

Shapiro, T., Sherman, M., Calamari, G., & Koch, D. (1987). Attachment in autism and other developmental disorders. *Journal of the American Academy of Child Psychiatry, 26,* 480–484.

Shaw, S. (2001). Behavioral treatment for children with autism: A comparison between discrete trial training and pivotal response training in teaching emotional perspective-taking skills. *Dissertation Abstracts International, 61*(11-B), 6121.

Shriberg, L. D., Paul, R., McSweeny, J. L., Klin, A., & Cohen, D. J. (2001). Speech and prosody characteristics of adolescents and adults with high-functioning autism and Asperger syndrome. *Journal of Speech and Hearing Research, 44,* 1097–1115.

Siegal, D. J., Goldstein, G., & Minshew, N. (1996). Designing instruction for the high-functioning autistic individual. *Journal of Developmental and Physical Disabilities, 8,* 1–19.

Sigman, M., & Mundy, P. (1989). Social attachments in autistic children. *Journal of the American Academy of Child and Adolescent Psychiatry, 28,* 74–81.

Sigman, M., & Ruskin, E. (1999). Continuity and change in the social competence of children with autism, Down syndrome, and developmental delays. *Monographs of the Society for Research in Child Development, 64,* 1–114.

Sigman, M., & Ungerer, J. A. (1984). Attachment behaviors in autistic children. *Journal of Autism and Developmental Disorders, 14,* 231–244.

Siller, M., & Sigman, M. (2002). The behaviors of parents of children with autism predict the subsequent development of their children's communication. *Journal of Autism and Developmental Disorders, 32*(2), 77–89.

Silver, M., & Oakes, P. (2001). Author Evaluation of a new computer intervention to teach people with autism or Asperger syndrome to recognize and predict emotions in others. *Autism: International Journal of Research and Practice, 5*(3), 299–316.

Smith, T., Lovaas, N. W., & Lovaas, O. I. (2002). Behaviors of children with high-functioning autism when paired with typically developing versus delayed peers: A preliminary study. *Behavioral Interventions, 17*(3), 129–143.

Snow, M. E., Hertzig, M. E., & Shapiro, T. (1987). Expression of emotion in young autistic children. *Journal of the American Academy of Child and Adolescent Psychiatry, 26,* 836–838.

Sparrow, S. S., & Cicchetti, D. V. (1987). Adaptive behavior and the psychologically disturbed child. *Journal of Special Education, 21,* 89–100.

Stafford, N. (2000). Can emotions be taught to a low functioning autistic child? *Early Child Development and Care, 164,* 105–126.

Stein, D. J., & Niehaus, D. (2001). Stereotypic self-injurious behaviors: Neurobiology and psychopharmacology. In D. Simeon & E. Hollander (Eds.), *Self-injurious behaviors: Assessment and treatment* (pp. 29–48). Washington, DC: American Psychiatric Press.

Stern, D. (1985). *The interpersonal world of the infant.* New York: Basic Books.

St. James, P. J., & Tager-Flusberg, H. (1994). An observational study of humor in autism and Down syndrome. *Journal of Autism and Developmental Disorders, 24*(5), 603–617.

Stone, W. L., Ousley, O. Y., Hepburn, S. L., Hogan, K. L., & Brown, C. S. (1999). Patterns of adaptive behavior in very young children with autism. *American Journal on Mental Retardation, 104*(2), 187–199.

Surian, L., Baron-Cohen, S., & Van der Lely, H. (1996). Are children with autism deaf to gricean maxims? *Cognitive Neuropsychiatry, 1,* 55–72.

Swedo, S. E., & Rapoport, J. L. (1989). Phenomenology and differential diagnosis of obsessive-compulsive disorder in children and adolescents. In J. L. Rapoport (Ed.), *Obsessive-compulsive disorder in children and adolescents* (pp. 13–32). Washington, DC: American Psychiatric Press.

Szatmari, P., Archer, L., Fisman, S., Streiner, D. L., & Wilson, F. (1995). Asperger's syndrome and autism: Differences in behavior, cognition, and adaptive functioning. *Journal of the American Academy of Child and Adolescent Psychiatry, 34*(12), 1662–1671.

Szatmari, P., Bartolucci, G., & Bremner, R. (1989). Asperger's syndrome and autism: Comparison of early history and outcome. *Developmental Medicine and Child Neurology, 31,* 709–720.

Tager-Flusberg, H. (1989. April). *An analysis of discourse ability and internal state lexicons in a longitudinal study of autistic children.* Society for Research in Child Development, Kansas City, Missouri.

Tager-Flusberg, H. (1995). Once upon a ribbit: Stories narrated by autistic children. *British Journal of Developmental Psychology, 13,* 45–49.

Tager-Flusberg, H., & Anderson, M. (1991). The development of contingent discourse ability in autistic children. *Journal of Child Psychology and Psychiatry, 32,* 1123–1134.

Tager-Flusberg, H., & Calkins, S. (1990). Does imitation facilitate the acquisition of grammar? Evidence from a study of autistic, Down's syndrome, and normal children. *Journal of Child Language, 17,* 591–606.

Tager-Flusberg, H., Calkins, S., Nolin, T., Baumberger, T., Anderson, M., & Chadwick-Dias, A. (1990). A longitudinal study of language acquisition in autistic and Down's syndrome children. *Journal of Autism and Developmental Disorders, 20,* 1–21.

Tager-Flusberg, H., & Quill, K. (1987). *Storytelling and narrative skills in verbal autistic children.* Society for Research in Child Development, Baltimore, Maryland.

Tager-Flusberg, H., & Sullivan, K. (1995). Attributing mental states to story characters: A comparison of narratives produced by autistic and mentally retarded individuals. *Applied Psycholinguistics, 16*(3), 241–256.

Takeuchi, K., & Yamamoto, J. I. (2001). A case study of examining the effects of self-monitoring on improving academic performance by a student with autism. *Japanese Journal of Special Education, 38,* 105–116.

Taylor, B. A., & Harris, S. L. (1995). Teaching children with autism to seek information: Acquisition of novel information and generalization of responding. *Journal of Applied Behavior Analysis, 28,* 3–4.

Taylor, B. A., Levin, J., & Jasper, S. (1999). Increasing play-related statements in children with autism toward their siblings: Effects of video modeling. *Journal of Developmental and Physical Disabilities, 11,* 253–264.

Trad, P. V., Bernstein, D., Shapiro, T., & Hertzig, M. (1993). Assessing the relationship between affective responsivity and social interaction in children with pervasive developmental disorder. *Journal of Autism and Developmental Disorders, 23,* 361–377.

Tsai, L. Y. (1992). Diagnostic issues in high-functioning autism. In E. Schopler & G. Mesibov (Eds.), *High-functioning individuals with autism* (pp. 11–40). New York: Plenum Press.

Tunali, B., & Power, T. (1993). Creating satisfaction: A psychological perspective on stress and coping in families of handicapped children. *Journal of Child Psychology and Psychiatry, 34,* 945–957.

Turner, M. (1999). Annotation: Repetitive behavior in autism: a review of psychological research. *Journal of Child Psychology and Psychiatry, 40,* 839–849.

Unger, D. G., & Powell, D. R. (1980). Supporting families under stress: The role of social networks. *Family Relations, 29,* 566–574.

Volkmar, F. R., Cohen, D. J., & Paul, R. (1986). An evaluation of *DSM-III* criteria for infantile autism. *Journal of the American Academy of Child Psychiatry, 25,* 190–197.

Volkmar, F. R., & Klin, A. (1993). Social development in autism: Historical and clinical perspectives. In S. Baron-Cohen, H. Tager-Flusberg, & D. Cohen (Eds.), *Understanding other minds: Perspectives from autism* (pp. 40–55). Oxford, England: Oxford University Press.

Volkmar, F. R., & Klin, A. (2000). Diagnostic issues in Asperger syndrome. In *Asperger syndrome* (pp. 25–71). New York: Guilford Press.

Volkmar, F. R., Klin, A., Siegel, B., Szatmari, P., Lord, C., Campbell, M., et al. (1994). Field trial for autistic disorder in *DSM-IV. American Journal of Psychiatry, 151,* 1361–1367.

Volkmar, F. R., Sparrow, S. S., Goudreau, D., Cicchetti, D. V., Paul, R., & Cohen, D. J. (1987). Social deficits in autism: An operational approach using the Vineland Adaptive Behavior Scales. *Journal of the American Academy of Child and Adolescent Psychiatry, 26,* 156–161.

Vostanis, P., Smith, B., Corbett, J., Sungum-Paliwal, R., Edwards, A., Gingell, K., et al. (1998). Parental concerns of early development in children with autism and related disorders. *Autism: International Journal of Research and Practice, 2*(3), 229–242.

Wahlberg, T., & Rotatori, A. F. (2001). Interview with a high functioning adult with autism. In T. Wahlberg et al. (Eds.), *Autistic spectrum disorders: Educational and clinical interventions. Advances in special education* (Vol. 14, pp. 269–300). Oxford, England: Elsevier.

Wainwright-Sharp, J. A., & Bryson, S. E. (1993). Visual orienting deficits in high-functioning people with autism. *Journal of Autism and Developmental Disorders, 23,* 1–13.

Weeks, S., & Hobson, R. P. (1987). The salience of facial expression for autistic children. *Journal of Child Psychology and Psychiatry and Allied Disciplines, 28,* 137–151.

Whalen, C. M. (2001). Joint attention training for children with autism and the collateral effects on language, play, imitation, and social behaviors. *Dissertation Abstracts International, 61*(11-B), 6122.

Whitehouse, D., & Harris, J. C. (1984). Hyperlexia in infantile autism. *Journal of Autism and Developmental Disabilities, 14,* 281–289.

Williams, E., Reddy, V., & Costall, A. (2001). Taking a closer look at functional play in children with autism. *Journal of Autism and Developmental Disorders, 31*(1), 67–77.

Williams, J. H., Whiten, A., Suddendorf, T., & Perrett, D. I. (2001). Imitation, mirror neurons and autism. *Neuroscience and Biobehavioral Reviews, 25*(4), 287–295.

Williams, P. G., Allard, A., Sears, L., Dalrymple, N., & Bloom, A. S. (2001). Brief report: Case reports on naltrexone use in children with autism: controlled observations regarding benefits and practical issues of medication management. *Journal of Autism and Developmental Disorders, 31*(1), 103–108.

Wing, L., & Attwood, A. (1987). Syndromes of autism and atypical development. In D. Cohen, A. Donellan, & R. Paul (Eds.), *Handbook of autism and pervasive developmental disorders* (pp. 3–19). New York: Wiley.

Wing, L., & Gould, J. (1979). Severe impairments of social interaction and associated abnormalities in children: Epidemiology and classification. *Journal of Autism and Developmental Disorders, 9,* 11–29.

Yirmiya, N., Kasari, C., Sigman, M., & Mundy, P. (1989). Facial expressions of affect in autistic, mentally retarded, and normal children. *Journal of Child Psychology and Psychiatry, 30,* 725–736.

Zahn, T. P., Rumsey, J. M., & Van Kannen, D. P. (1987). Autonomic nervous system activity in autistic, schizophrenic, and normal men: Effects of stimulus significance. *Journal of Abnormal Psychology, 96,* 135–144.

Zercher, C., Hunt, P., Schuler, A., & Webster, J. (2001). Increasing joint attention, play and language through peer supported play. *Autism: International Journal of Research and Practice, 5*(4), 374–398.

CHAPTER 10

Adolescents and Adults with Autism

VICTORIA SHEA AND GARY B. MESIBOV

The clinical presentation and psychoeducational needs of adolescents and adults with autism have not yet been studied as extensively as those aspects of children with autism. However, there are some empirical follow-up studies of adolescents and adults who were initially diagnosed with autism as children, and there is also a growing professional literature of educational and other therapeutic interventions for adolescents and adults. This chapter reviews what is known about adolescents and adults with autism (the term *autism* is used in this chapter for the range of autism spectrum disorders or ASD) and then discusses significant clinical topics related to these age groups.

OUTCOME STUDIES

It is clear that almost all children with autism grow up to be adolescents and then adults with autism. From the Maudsley Hospital long-term study (Rutter, 1970) and Leo Kanner's (1973) collection of papers including follow-up reports of his patients, through Lotter's (1978) careful review of outcome studies, to current literature reviews (Howlin & Goode, 1998; Nordin & Gillberg, 1998), the consensus of the research and clinical literature is that autism is almost always a lifelong disabling condition. However, several authors have indicated that a small number of individuals diagnosed with autism as children would not meet diagnostic criteria for autism in later years (e.g., DeMyer et al., 1973; Lovaas, 2000; Nordin & Gillberg, 1998; Piven, Harper, Palmer, & Arndt, 1996; Rumsey, Rapoport, & Sceery, 1985; Rutter, 1970; Seltzer et al., 2003; Szatmari, Bartolucci, Bremner, Bond, & Rich,

1989; Von Knorring & Haeggloef, 1993), although in many cases there are some residual characteristics of social, communication, and/or behavioral idiosyncrasies.

Developmental Course

The research literature indicates that at adolescence some individuals with autism improve markedly, others experience deterioration in functioning (e.g., increased aggression, increasingly rigid or repetitive behavior, loss of skills), and many continue a stable, maturational course.

Improvement

A number of follow-up studies have reported general symptomatic improvement with increasing age. Kanner, Rodriguez, and Ashenden (1972) indicated that "a remarkable change took place" (p. 29) in early-mid teens for a subgroup of patients who, according to the authors, "became uneasily aware of their peculiarities and began to make a conscious effort to do something about them" (p. 29) and later went on, in most cases, to independent living and higher education or gainful employment.

Of the 201 Japanese families surveyed by Kobayashi, Murata, and Yoshinaga (1992), 43% reported "marked improvement" in their youngsters, generally between the ages of 10 to 15 years. Ballaban-Gil, Rapin, Tuchman, and Shinnar (1996) found that behavioral improvement was reported for 9% to 18% of their heterogeneous sample, depending on the behavior. Eaves and Ho (1996) reported cognitive or behavioral improvement in 37% of their sample of

76 children followed for 4 years into early adolescence. More optimistically, Piven et al. (1996) found that parents of their sample of 38 "high IQ" adolescents and adults reported that compared to their functioning at age 5 years, 82% had improved in communication, 82% had improved in social interactions, and 55% had improved in restricted and repetitive behaviors. Similarly, the MIND Institute (Byrd et al., 2002) study of 100 families with late adolescents with autism found that 88% of parents reported improvements in communication or language, 83% reported improvements in socialization, and 75% reported improvements in behavior, interests, or activities (although it should be noted that parents of school-age children were even more likely to indicate that their child's autism had improved). Piven et al. (1996) suggested that one developmental trajectory for early childhood autism involves significant improvement in all areas of symptomatology, to the point that "consideration should be given to diagnosing autism in adults who met criteria for autism as children and continue to have impairments in related domains of behavior" (p. 528) even if they don't currently meet diagnostic criteria.

In a study of 59 clients receiving treatment in North Carolina's Treatment and Education of Autistic and Related Communication-handicapped CHildren (TEACCH) program, scores on the Childhood Autism Rating Scale (Schopler, Reichler, DeVellis, & Daly, 1980) decreased (i.e., reflected improvement) by an average of three points (on a scale from 15 to 60) between mean age 8.7 years and mean age 15.9 years. Significant improvements were found for the group on ratings of imitation, body movement, use of objects, adapting to changes, responding to sounds, appropriate use of near sensors (touch, taste, and smell), verbal and nonverbal communication, and activity level (Mesibov, Schopler, Schaffer, & Michal, 1989).

Cross-sectional studies also suggest improvement with age. Ando and colleagues (Ando & Yoshimura, 1979; Ando, Yoshimura, & Wakabayashi, 1980), in a cross-sectional study of 24 younger (ages 6 to 9 years) and 14 older (ages 11 to 14 years) individuals with autism, reported higher skills levels in the older group in terms of toilet training, eating skills, language comprehension, conversational abilities, participation in group activities, and appropriate classroom behavior.

Most recently, Seltzer et al. (2003) reported comparisons of Autism Diagnostic Interview-Revised (ADI-R) "current" versus "lifetime" scores for a sample of 251 adolescents (mean age 15.71 years) and 154 adults (mean age 31.57 years) who had been diagnosed with autism in childhood. Significant symptom reduction was reported for both groups in all three domains of the ADI-R (Communication, Reciprocal Social Interaction, and Restricted, Repetitive Behaviors and Interests). Based on current scores, only 54.8% of the total sample met ADI-R cutoff scores in all three domains, whereas 96.5% met these cutoffs based on lifetime scores. In spite of the significant reduction in symptoms and increase in social and communication skills from childhood to adulthood, according to the authors:

> That the disorder changes in its manifestation over the life course does not . . . indicate that affected individuals have any less of a need for services and supports as they move through adolescence into adulthood and midlife than they did in childhood. Rather, developmentally appropriate services are needed for adolescents and adults with ASD diagnoses. (p. 579)

Deterioration

Nordin and Gillberg's (1998) review suggested that 12% to 22% of adolescents show cognitive or behavioral deterioration, although these figures were derived from retrospective reports, not prospective studies. In the follow-up study of Kobayashi et al. (1992), families indicated that 32% of their youngsters had shown behavioral deterioration during their teenage years, with a reported peak at ages 12 to 13 years. Venter, Lord, and Schopler (1992) reported that in a group of 58 high-functioning children, "Two adolescents (one male, one female) experienced gradual cognitive and behavioral deteriorations in their mid-teens that plateaued in late adolescence; neither had seizures or any evidence of hard neurological signs after extensive investigations" (p. 494). Ballaban-Gil et al. (1996) found that families reported that problem behaviors had worsened (or were being treated with medication) in 24 of 54 adolescents

(44%) and 22 of 45 adults (49%); further, increased rates of behavioral difficulties since childhood were reported at all cognitive levels except for "normal/near normal" adolescents (p. 218, Table 2). Eaves and Ho (1996), in a sample of 76 individuals first evaluated as children (ages 3 to 12 years), reported behavioral deterioration over a 4-year period in five individuals. Wing and Shah (2000) described, in a subgroup of adolescents, the development of catatonia, defined as "increased slowness affecting movement and verbal responses; difficulty in initiating and completing actions; increased reliance on physical or verbal prompting by others; and increased passivity and apparent lack of motivation" (p. 357) often associated with unusual gait, postures, or "freezing" at thresholds or in sitting positions, and in some cases preceded by periods of very agitated, at times aggressive, behavior. Gilchrist et al. (2001) reported that many of the individuals in their sample of 20 adolescents with Asperger syndrome were reported by their parents on the ADI to have more problems and symptoms in adolescence than in early childhood.

Seltzer et al. (2003) reported that 47 of 405 individuals developed symptoms in adolescence or adulthood that were not present in childhood, based on ADI-R interviews with parents.

Ongoing Behavioral Difficulties

Even if their skills have not deteriorated, many adolescents and adults with autism are reported by their parents to exhibit significant behavior problems, including resistance to change, compulsions, unacceptable sexual behavior, tantrums, aggression, and/or self-injurious behavior (DeMyer, 1979; Fong, Wilgosh, & Sobsey, 1993). Several authors have pointed out that even if the frequency of difficult behaviors decreases, the result of such behaviors on the part of individuals who are taller, heavier, and stronger can be more distressing or even dangerous than the same behaviors in childhood (Gillberg, 1991; Harris, Glasberg, & Delmolino, 1998; Mesibov, 1983; Nordin & Gillberg, 1998; Rutter, 1970). Marcus (1984) described the feelings of "burnout" experienced by many parents of older youngsters with autism. Seltzer, Krauss, Orsmond, and Vestal (2001) reported that mothers of 13 adults with autism and mental retardation were much more likely than mothers of adults with Down syndrome to report feeling that they were "walking on eggshells" (p. 285).

Various empirical studies have documented the prevalence of difficult behaviors in adolescents and adults. Rumsey et al. (1985) described a sample of 14 men with autism, 9 of whom had intelligence in the average range. Six individuals (five of them with average intelligence) had significant, although infrequent, temper outbursts. Ballaban-Gil et al. (1996) found that behavioral difficulties and/or behavioral medication were reported in 69% of their sample of 99 adolescents and adults. The number of individuals with problem behaviors or psychotropic medication was inversely related to estimated intelligence range, but even in the highest functioning group (adults with normal/near normal intelligence), 7 of 13 individuals were reported by their families to have behavioral difficulties.

Howlin, Mawhood, and Rutter (2000) reported assessment results for a group of 19 nonretarded adults with autism (mean age 23 years, 9 months; mean performance IQ 94). Family members of 18 of these 19 adults responded to the ADI and reported that 3 individuals (17%) showed "severe" levels of "autistic-type behavior," 10 individuals (56%) had "moderate" disturbances in this area, and 5 (28%) individuals had "no/minimal" problems.

Similarly, Howlin, Goode, Hutton, and Rutter (2004) assessed the adult functioning of a group of 68 individuals who had childhood nonverbal IQs of 50 or above and found that 23 (35%) were rated by their parents on the ADI as having moderate autism-related problem behaviors, and 7 (11%) were rated as having severe problems. The authors found that "autistic-type behaviors (routines, rituals, stereotypies, etc.)" were not strongly associated with IQ, and that:

Although the more able group was less likely to show very severe difficulties in these areas, the distribution of such symptoms was generally fairly evenly spread and within each IQ band, the majority of individuals continued to have at least mild to moderate problems associated with repetitive and stereotyped behaviors. (p. 226)

Intelligence

An important determinant of developmental course in autism is the individual's level of intelligence or mental retardation. The prevalence of mental retardation and the stability of IQ from childhood to adolescence or adulthood have been the focus of several investigations.

Autism and Mental Retardation

Historically, estimates of the prevalence of mental retardation in the population of individuals with autism have been in the range of 70% to 80% (Fombonne, 1999; National Research Council, 2001b; Tager-Flusberg, Joseph, & Folstein, 2001). However, because the broad autism spectrum includes so many individuals with intelligence in the average range or above (e.g., people with Asperger syndrome and some individuals with Pervasive Developmental Disorder-not otherwise specified [PDD-NOS]), the prevalence of mental retardation within the broad autism spectrum is now thought to be considerably lower than the figure of 70% to 80% (Bryson & Smith, 1998; Lord & Bailey, 2002). Chakrabarti and Fombonne (2001) reported that the rate of mental retardation in the preschool children diagnosed with PDD (i.e., the broad autism spectrum) in a region of England was 26%. Gillberg (1998) has suggested that the rate of mental retardation within the broad autism spectrum might be as low as 15%.

Further, there are indications that the current prevalence of mental retardation may be lower than the traditional figure of 70% to 80% for younger cohorts of individuals with autism because of the increased availability of early intervention and special education. Eaves and Ho (1996) described their sample of youngsters with ASD born between 1974 and 1984 as having "autism in the third generation" (p. 558), using the generational metaphor of Wakabayashi and Sugiyama (cited in Kobayashi et al., 1992) of the "first generation" (born before 1960 and without access to special education) and the "second generation" (born 1960 to 1972 when special education was only inconsistently available). In the Eaves and Ho sample of 76 "third-generation" youngsters, at adolescence only 52% had performance IQs less than 70, and 62% had verbal IQs below 70.

Similarly, Ballaban-Gil et al. (1996) published follow-up results of an unselected group of 54 adolescents and 45 adults with autism who had initially been diagnosed during childhood by one clinician (Isabelle

Rapin, MD). The distribution of estimated intelligence among *adults* was as follows: severe to profound mental retardation, 47%; mild to moderate mental retardation, 22%; normal to near normal intelligence, 29% (indeterminate, 2%). Among *adolescents,* the curve was shifted markedly higher: severe to profound mental retardation, 19%; mild to moderate mental retardation, 37%; normal to near normal intelligence, 42% (indeterminate, 2%).

The recent study for the California Legislature by the University of California's MIND Institute (Byrd, 2002) indicated that a record review revealed that mental retardation was diagnosed in 50% of a sample of individuals with autism born between 1983 and 1985, but in only 22% of a sample of individuals born between 1993 and 1995. In a different study of population trends in California, Croen, Grether, Hoogstrate, and Selvin (2002a, 2002b) found that only 37% of children with autism born between 1987 and 1994 and served by the California Department of Developmental Services also had diagnoses of mental retardation (although there were factors that suggested that this figure could be either an underestimate [because some etiologies of mental retardation were excluded] or an overestimate [because some findings of mental retardation were not included in the records]).

A different perspective on the relationship of autism and mental retardation is found in the work of Bryson and Smith (1998), who reported that approximately 25% of a population sample of adolescents and young adults with mental retardation also had autism. Similarly, Morgan et al. (2002) reported an autism prevalence rate of 30% in a large sample of adults with mental retardation. Steffenburg, Gillberg, and Steffenburg (1996) reported a rate of ASD of 38% in a sample of adolescents with both mental retardation and epilepsy.

Even without autism, having an IQ < 50 in childhood is almost always associated with significant limitations and dependence in adulthood (i.e., inability to earn a living, need for supervised residential situation and specialized vocational or day programming). Outcome is somewhat more variable for individuals with IQs between 50 and 70, although adult status of only marginal social and economic self-sufficiency is common (Baroff, 1999).

The combination of mental retardation and autism is particularly powerful in affecting the individual's developmental status as an adult. People with both autism and mental retardation have significantly poorer functioning in terms of education, work, living situation, and general independence than those with autism and average intelligence (Howlin & Goode, 1998; Howlin et al., 2004; Nordin & Gillberg, 1998; Rutter, 1970). Coexisting autism at all levels of intelligence adds difficulties in terms of comprehension and social use of language, understanding social cues and expectations, organizing behavior, and rigid attachment to routines (Mesibov, Shea, & Schopler, in press; Van Bourgondien, Mesibov, & Castelloe, 1989). Howlin et al. (2004) make the point that even for individuals without mental retardation, "Outcome tends to be very variable and it seems that the fundamental deficits associated with autism, in particular the degree of ritualistic and stereotyped behaviors may, at times, 'swamp' the effects of a relatively high IQ" (p. 226).

Stability of IQ

In general, IQ scores from childhood to adolescence and adulthood of *groups* of people with autism are stable (Lockyer & Rutter, 1969; Nordin & Gillberg, 1998). Most of the *individual* changes that do occur are in the direction of improvement (e.g., Freeman et al., 1991) with several exceptions: the incidents of significant deterioration in adolescence discussed previously and cases in which individuals with good nonverbal intelligence fail to develop verbal language (e.g., Howlin et al., 2004; Lord & Venter, 1992).

Ballaban-Gil et al. (1996) reported that in their heterogeneous sample of 99 children, two individuals went from the range of severe mental retardation in childhood to the normal/near normal range at follow-up as adolescents or adults (all ranges were estimates based on family report). Ten other individuals moved up to the next higher range (i.e., from severe to mild/moderate retardation or from mild/moderate to normal/near normal) while six individuals moved down one range.

Mawhood, Howlin, and Rutter (2000) reported the adult (ages 21 to 26 years) IQ scores of nine individuals with autism who were part of a larger group of children with normal nonverbal intelligence who had originally been studied at ages 4 to 9 years by Bartak, Rutter, and Cox (1975). These nine students had completed the Wechsler Intelligence Scale for Children (WISC) as children and the Wechsler Adult Intelligence Scale-Revised (WAIS-R) as adults. Their mean verbal IQ increased from 66 to 82 between early childhood and adulthood, while their performance IQ remained in the broadly normal range (mean performance IQ decreased from 94 to 83). There was marked individual variability in verbal IQ scores, and comparisons of test scores were somewhat difficult to interpret because of different test instruments used at different ages (i.e., WISC versus WAIS-R). Nevertheless, the results indicated that the verbal intelligence of the group of autistic youngsters with normal-near normal nonverbal intelligence generally improved substantially over the course of their adolescence.

Similarly, Howlin et al. (2004), in an adult outcome study of 68 children (ages 3 to 15 years) with autism and initial nonverbal IQ > 50, found that verbal IQ was quite stable for youngsters who initially had verbal IQs > 70 and that there were considerable increases among most (69%) of those with initial verbal IQs between 30 and 69. Further, even among the 31 individuals who were untestable or had verbal IQs < 30 at initial assessment, as adults four had verbal IQs of 50 to 69, and nine had verbal IQs above 70. Performance IQ in this study was more stable, with most individuals staying in the same band (i.e., > 100, 70 to 99, or 50 to 69) or changing by one band.

Overall, recent research indicates that while some individuals with autism make dramatic gains or experience significant losses in cognitive skills, typically, IQs are stable between childhood and adulthood.

Language

Various research reports have described the types of language impairments associated with ASD in adolescence and adulthood.

Patterns of Speech and Language Characteristics

Most adolescents and adults with autism continue to demonstrate abnormalities in speech and language (Baltaxe & Simmons, 1992; Howlin, 1997, 2003; Rumsey et al., 1985; Tager-Flusberg, 2001; Twachtman-Cullen, 1998), although the literature suggests overall improvements in language skills from childhood to adulthood.

Kobayashi et al. (1992) reported that in their sample of 197 young adults with autism, 16% communicated fluently with good vocabulary, 31% communicated with language that was unusual or inappropriate in some way, 32% understood some language but did not communicate verbally, 9% used echolalia, and 12% did not vocalize meaningfully.

Ballaban-Gil et al. (1996) reported improvement from childhood to adulthood in expressive and receptive language in most individuals with normal/near normal intelligence and similar improvement in some of those with mild/moderate mental retardation. In their sample of adolescents and adults, 23% of those with normal/near normal intelligence were described by their families as having essentially normal expressive language.

Seltzer et al. (2003) described the results of ADI-R interviews with 405 families of adolescents and adults as indicating: "There was a general pattern of abatement of symptoms, reflecting improved overall use of language, improved ability to communicate nonverbally, and reduced stereotyped, repetitive, or idiosyncratic speech" (p. 571). In particular, they reported that "nearly two-thirds (60.2%) of those who were not able to speak in three-word phrases on a daily basis at age 4–5 years [were] currently able to do so" (p. 575); in the overall sample, 70% currently demonstrated this level of language skill.

Similarly, according to Venter et al. (1992) in their study of 58 individuals who had nonverbal IQs of at least 60 as children, by the age of 5 years, only 39 of 58 had useful speech (defined as an age equivalent of 13 months on the Peabody Picture Vocabulary Test [PPVT] and expressive use of at least five words used daily for communication); but at follow-up an average age of 8 years later (mean age 14.69 years), all of the subjects had useful speech, 54 of 58 (93.1%) obtained a basal (approximately 2-year level) on the PPVT, and 52 of 58 (89.6%) could complete the verbal portion of a Wechsler test (Lord & Venter, 1992).

However, the Mawhood et al. (2000) study of 19 adults who had average nonverbal IQs as children found significant variability in adult language skills: Eight spoke in good sentences (although half had difficulty sustaining conversations), five had immature speech, and six were either mute, echolalic, or at the level of single-word utterances.

Shriberg et al. (2001) analyzed the speech patterns of a group of 30 adolescents and adults with either high-functioning autism or Asperger syndrome. Compared to a normal control group, these clinical groups had higher rates of misplaced stress, excessive loudness, nasality, articulation errors, and repetitions of sounds, syllables, or words, with additional indications of more high-pitched/falsetto voices and slower speech. The authors concluded:

Although the obtained differences did not suggest gross involvement, even infrequent voice and resonance differences can affect listeners' perceptions of a speaker's emotional status and attractiveness. These findings are consistent with the percept of a "pedantic" style of speech often attributed to individuals with HFA [high-functioning autism] and AS [Asperger syndrome]. (p. 1110)

Lord (1996) reported that a group of 20 high-functioning adolescents was developmentally delayed in their use of "mental" verbs (e.g., think, wonder) and that both higher and lower functioning adolescents used an increased number of unusual words or phrases compared to typical children.

Outcome Measures

The lack of meaningful, spontaneous speech by age 5 years has historically been associated with poor adult outcome (Eisenberg, 1956; Gillberg & Steffenberg, 1987; Lotter, 1974; Rutter, 1970). There are numerous reports of individuals who began speaking after this age (e.g., Ballaban-Gil et al., 1996; DeMyer et al., 1973; Howlin, 2003; Howlin et al., 2004; Nordin & Gillberg, 1998; Rumsey et al., 1985; Rutter, Greenfeld, & Lockyer, 1967; Venter et al., 1992; Windsor, Doyle, & Siegel, 1994). However, according to Lord and Bailey (2002):

A child who does not have fluent speech by age 5 years may still make significant gains, but the later these gains come, the less likely the child's language will be flexible and complex, and the more likely language delays of some sort may reduce his or her level of independence. (p. 639)

In the Mawhood et al. (2000) study, it is interesting that the best predictor of the adults' composite language score (which included expressive grammar, receptive understanding of complex instructions, and conversational abilities) was their childhood score on the PPVT (a test of receptive vocabulary only). Scores on this test were also a significant predictor of social relationships in adulthood in this sample (Howlin et al., 2000). Similarly, Venter et al. (1992) found that adding PPVT scores to a regression analysis significantly increased the power of early childhood measures to predict adolescent adaptive behavior scores. However, Gilchrist et al. (2001) found that early language milestones and abnormalities were not related to adolescent social functioning in a sample of high-functioning youngsters. Similarly, Mayes and Calhoun (2001), in a study of a slightly younger sample with average cognitive skills, reported that early delays in speech and language versus timely attainment of language milestones did not differentiate groups of children in terms of later clinical status in the areas of autistic symptoms, expressive language skills, or cognitive skills.

In summary, the research literature indicates that language skills generally improve markedly from childhood to adulthood in groups of people with autism (although not necessarily in all individuals), but impairments remain, even in individuals with average intelligence.

Adaptive Behavior

A robust finding in the research literature on individuals with autism is that adaptive behavior is usually markedly lower than intelligence, particularly among those with higher intelligence (Bölte & Poustka, 2002; Bryson & Smith, 1998; Carter et al., 1998; Freeman et al., 1991; Lockyer & Rutter, 1969; Rumsey et al., 1985). For example, Venter et al. (1992) reported that at follow-up (ages 10 to 37 years), their sample had a mean Full Scale IQ of 79.21, but mean Vineland standard scores of 47.57 (Communication), 49.05 (Daily Living Skills),

and 38.09 (Socialization). Similarly, Howlin et al. (2000) reported that their group of adults (ages 21 to 26 years) had a mean verbal IQ of 82 but mean Vineland standard scores of 51.11 (Communication), 65.1 (Daily Living Skills), and 46.4 (Socialization).

Similarly, the group of 20 adolescents (ages 11 to 19 years) studied by Green, Gilchrist, Burton, and Cox (2000) had a mean IQ of 92, but only 50% were independent in the most basic of self-care skills (i.e., bathing and brushing teeth). These authors further reported:

None of these normally intelligent young adults were considered by their parents capable of purchasing major items or engaging in leisure activities independently outside the home. Only a handful were able to travel at all independently, make any decisions about self-care, or even use the telephone. (p. 290)

This phenomenon of the discrepancy between cognitive skills and daily functioning was also described by Siegel:

Typically these young people *do* know how to make their bed, do laundry, microwave a pizza, and brush their teeth adequately. Left on their own, however, many never make their bed, wear only disheveled clothes, eat mainly lots of junk food, and have chronically bad breath. (Siegel, 1996, p. 296)

Several authors have stressed the clinical importance of assessing the adaptive behavior skills of individuals with autism and normal IQs, because these individuals may be denied various public services on the grounds that they are not mentally retarded. Assessment of adaptive functioning is important for all individuals with autism, but documenting significantly impaired adaptive functioning is particularly crucial for supporting more cognitively capable adolescents and adults with autism in obtaining needed services, such as special educational accommodations, residential supports, vocational training, and supplemental income (Bryson & Smith, 1998; Klin & Volkmar, 2000).

Academic Achievement and Higher Education

According to Venter et al. (1992), the academic achievement of groups of youngsters with autism has increased over the years, probably because of greater access to educational opportunities and services. However, their study and several others have also found that scores on academic achievement tests often reflect functional deficits relative to intelligence. For example, in their sample many of the adolescents and adults with IQs of 90 or above obtained academic achievement scores below age level on *all* of the achievement subtests except reading/decoding (i.e., they showed deficits in reading/comprehension, spelling, and basic computation skills).

Similarly, Mawhood et al. (2000) reported mean academic achievement age equivalents for their sample of adults with a mean IQ of 82 as follows: reading accuracy, 12.17 years; reading comprehension, 10.64 years; mean spelling, 10.82 years. Further, in the Howlin et al. (2004) sample of adults, the subgroup of individuals with average intelligence and "very good" outcome obtained the following age equivalents: reading accuracy, 12.2 years; reading comprehension, 10.5 years; spelling, 13.1 years.

Minshew, Goldstein, Taylor, and Siegel (1994) reported that a sample of 54 adult men with autism did not differ from a control group on tests of "mechanical" academic skills such as word attack, spelling, and computation, but did show significant deficits in reading comprehension. Similarly, Minshew, Goldstein, and Siegel (1997) found significant differences from carefully matched controls in a group of 33 adolescents and adults with autism (mean age 21 years) on several measures of reading comprehension.

Although historically many adults with autism have not developed functional reading and mathematics skills above the elementary school level, there are also numerous reports that a small percentage of individuals with autism have attended and graduated from college and graduate schools (Green et al., 2000; Howlin, 2003; Howlin et al., 2004; Kanner, 1973; Rumsey et al., 1985; Szatmari et al., 1989; Tantam, 1991; Venter et al., 1992). Individuals with autism spectrum disorders and advanced degrees include Temple Grandin, PhD (Grandin, 1995); Terese Jolliffe, PhD (Jolliffe, Lansdown, & Robinson, 1992); and Liane Holliday Willey, PhD (Willey, 1999).

Psychiatric and Emotional Problems

Bryson and Smith (1998) reported preliminary results from a population-based study of adolescents and young adults (ages 14 to 20 years) indicating that "at least 40% of individuals with ADI-R defined autism experienced psychiatric 'episodes' " (p. 100) with mood disorders being particularly common. Consistent with this finding, a number of researchers have reported that depression is the most common psychiatric condition in clinical samples of adults with autism spectrum disorders (Ghaziuddin, Ghaziuddin, & Greden, 2002; Ghaziuddin, Weidmer-Mikhail, & Ghaziuddin, 1998; Howlin, 2000). Although depression among people with autism is often thought to be a reaction to stresses and social isolation, there have also been several reports of increased incidence of depression among mothers of children with autism *prior to the births of these children,* suggesting a genetic loading for depressive illness in people with autism (Bolton, Pickles, Murphy, & Rutter, 1998; Piven & Palmer, 1999; Piven et al., 1991; Smalley, McCracken, & Tanguay, 1995). Anxiety disorders (including obsessive-compulsive disorder) are also frequently reported in samples of adolescents and adults with autism (Green et al., 2000; Rumsey et al., 1985; Seltzer et al., 2001; Szatmari et al., 1989).

In terms of more severe mental illness, most researchers have concluded that there is no strong evidence for *increased* risk for schizophrenia among adolescents and adults with autism (Ghaziuddin et al., 2002; Howlin & Goode, 1998), but there have been some reports of individuals with both conditions, as well as reports of isolated paranoid or delusional thinking or auditory hallucinations (Clarke, Baxter, Perry, & Prasher, 1999; Howlin, 2000, 2003; Rumsey et al., 1985; Szatmari et al., 1989; Wing, 1981). Bipolar disorder (manic-depression) has also been reported (Clarke et al., 1999; Howlin, 2000; Tantam, 2000).

Epilepsy

Reports of the prevalence of epilepsy vary (Shavelle, Strauss, & Pickett, 2001; Tuchman, 2000), but review articles generally indicate a rate of 20% to 33% (Bryson & Smith, 1998; Nordin & Gillberg, 1998; Rapin, 1997).

Epilepsy occurs at all levels of intelligence but is found most frequently in association with mental retardation (Rutter, 1970; Volkmar & Nelson, 1990; Wolf & Goldberg, 1986) or marked developmental regression (Gillberg & Steffenburg, 1987; Kobayashi & Murata, 1998; Rutter et al., 1967).

There seems to be a bimodal distribution of age of onset of seizures: before 5 years or during early adolescence (Howlin, 2000; Rutter, 1970; Tuchman, 2000; Volkmar & Nelson, 1990). Kobayashi et al. (1992) reported that 36 of 188 (19.1%) of their sample of 99 children with autism (of varying IQ levels) developed epilepsy, with onset for 17 of these 36 (47%) between 11 and 14 years. Giovanardi Rossi, Posar, and Parmeggiani (2000) reported that for a group of 27 adolescents and young adults with epilepsy or EEG paroxysmal abnormalities without seizures, onset for 66.7% was after age 12 years. The MIND Institute study (Byrd, 2002) indicated a prevalence rate of epilepsy of 9.8% among individuals with autism born between 1993 and 1995 (ages approximately 7 to 9 years at the time of the study) but 14.8% among individuals born between 1983 and 1985 (approximately 17 to 19 years of age); although this was a cross-sectional study, this finding could be interpreted to reflect additional diagnoses of epilepsy during the late childhood to adolescent period.

Mortality

Autism itself is not a degenerative disorder and, in fact, is typically characterized by developmental *progression,* but associated medical conditions (particularly epilepsy) and/or accidents related to significant mental retardation have been known to contribute to some early deaths. (Note that since autism was first described in the mid-1940s, most individuals diagnosed with autism as children are only now moving past middle age.)

Several studies have looked at the issues of rates and causes of death through middle age among people with autism. Isager, Mouridsen, and Rich (1999) reviewed the death records as of late 1993 of essentially all children with PDDs in Denmark who were born between 1945 and 1980. From a total group of 341 individuals, 324 were still living in Denmark, 4 had

emigrated, 1 had disappeared, and 12 had died. This number of deaths, although small, represented a significantly higher death rate within the group with PDDs than the expected mortality rate in the general population matched for age, gender, and length of follow-up. Of the 12 deaths, five were due to physical disease, one was suspected to be related to a seizure, four were accidents (three suspected of being related to a seizure), and two were suicides. Only one of the deaths was in the group with mild mental retardation; five of the individuals had moderate to severe mental retardation, and six had IQs at or above 84.

Shavelle et al. (2001) analyzed the causes of death over a 14-year period (1983 to 1997) of all ambulatory individuals with autism in the California state database (202 deaths among 13,111 individuals). Results indicated that the mortality rate for individuals with autism, particularly for females and for people with moderate, severe, or profound mental retardation, was elevated compared to that of the general population. Seizures, suffocation, and drowning were the causes of death that most accounted for this difference at all levels of intelligence. Similarly, Patja, Iivanainen, Vesala, Oksanen, and Ruoppila (2000) reported that in Finland epileptic seizures were a significant risk factor for decreased life expectancy, and Ballaban-Gil et al. (1996) commented on the high number of reported incidents of drowning among children with autism.

Causes of death reported in other follow-up studies of children with autism into adolescence or adulthood include 1 of a sample of 23 of a heart condition (Gillberg & Steffenberg, 1987); 1 of a sample of 32 from pneumonia subsequent to a diagnosis of "diffuse degenerative process" (Lotter, 1974); 1 of a sample of 79 from status epilepticus (Howlin et al., 2004); 2 of a sample of 64 during seizures (Rutter, 1970); 2 of a sample of 96, 1 unexpectedly (with a history of seizures) and 1 by being hit by a truck (Kanner, 1973); 3 of a sample of 106 from aspiration pneumonia, drowning, and "complications of chronic administration of psychotropic medications" (Ballaban-Gil et al., 1996, p. 219); and 4 of a sample of 201 from suspected encephalopathy, self-inflicted head injury, nephrotic syndrome, and asthma (Kobayashi et al., 1992).

The reports of Patja et al. (2000) and Shavelle et al. (2001) suggest that individuals with autism and mental retardation generally have fewer of the risk factors associated with typical adult lifestyles, such as smoking, drinking alcohol, traffic and occupational accidents, and suicide. Hardan and Sahl (1999) reported that suicidal ideation and behaviors were found in a handful of children and adolescents with mild-moderate mental retardation and autism or PDD-NOS, and suicidal thoughts or behavior in high-functioning adults has also been reported by Wing (1981) and Tantam (1991).

In spite of the statistically increased death rate in groups of individuals with autism spectrum disorders (with or without mental retardation), it is clear that *the vast majority of people with autism live at least through middle age and almost certainly beyond.* Therefore, many people with autism will outlive their parents, which has tremendous implications for living arrangements and other service needs for adults with autism.

Living Arrangements

In the general American culture, at the end of adolescence most individuals leave their family's home and either live independently or live with other young people, sometimes in personal relationships and sometimes as mutually chosen or temporarily assigned roommates. The living situations of adults with autism, however, are typically quite different: Independent living or living with peers is rare.

Seltzer et al. (2001) reported that direct inquiries of the state Mental Retardation/Developmental Disabilities agencies in New York and Massachusetts yielded the following information: In New York in 1998, 54% of agency clients with autism ages 20 to 29 still lived with their parents, and 34% of those ages 30 to 39 still did so. In Massachusetts in 1997, 42% of agency clients with autism ages 18 to 30 lived with their parents, and 23% of those older than 30 still did so. Although these figures reflected significant dependence on parents by adults with autism, the figures were low compared to adults of the same age with only mental retardation (Seltzer et al., 2001), many of whom remain at home even longer.

This suggested that many of these adults with autism were in residential placements because they were difficult for their parents to manage or live with.

For adults with both autism and mental retardation, the challenges of living completely independently are unlikely to be met (Nordin & Gillberg, 1998; Howlin et al., 2004). Household maintenance, money management, time management, and social self-protection are complex tasks that less capable adults with autism simply don't have the skills to manage successfully. If parents or other family members are not available to provide the needed support, guidance, and supervision, these must be provided from another, typically public, source. The specific forms these services take vary based on a number of factors, including finances, philosophical trends in public service delivery (Harris et al., 1998), and personal choice. The current trend toward "self-determination" (i.e., public financial support for services chosen or designed by individual consumers; www.self-determination.com) may sometimes result in situations of mutually chosen roommates, if all the variables of compatible individuals, finances, real estate, availability of other services, and transportation fall into place (and stay in place). However, for the most part, adults with both autism and mental retardation either remain at home with their families or live in group care settings arranged by others. Ideally, service providers in these settings have specialized knowledge of autism, in addition to knowledge of mental retardation (Persson, 2000; Van Bourgondien, Reichle, & Schopler, 2003).

Even adults with autism and average intelligence have difficulty with independent living. Howlin and Goode (1998) reviewed the living arrangements reported in several earlier studies (Mawhood, 1995, as cited in Howlin & Goode, 1998; Rumsey et al., 1985; Szatmari et al., 1989; Venter et al., 1992). According to this review, among 66 adults (ages 18 to 39 years) without mental retardation, only 11 individuals were described as living independently (one of these with daily contact and advice from his mother and one in a "sheltered accommodation" [p. 220]); 17 were in some kind of supervised or supported residential placement, and 38 individuals were still living with their parents, although some of these individuals were reportedly quite independent.

Similarly, Ballaban-Gil et al. (1996) reported that of 13 adults (ages 18 to 29 years) without mental retardation, 1 was living independently, 3 were in residential programs, and 9 were living with parents. In the Howlin et al. (2000) follow-up study of 19 nonretarded individuals with autism at ages 21 to 26 years, 3 were living independently, 9 were in residential programs, 1 was in a hospital, and 6 were living with their parents.

In the Howlin et al. (2004) study of 68 individuals (ages 21 to 48 years) who had childhood performance IQs above 50, approximately 10% were living independently or with minimal supervision as adults. However, the authors indicated that the sheltered residential arrangements for a number of individuals may have been a reflection of the limited availability of housing options or the limited wage-earning potential of these individuals rather than a reflection of their self-care and independent living skills.

Venter et al. (1992) summarized the issue of living arrangements in their sample:

Because of increasingly graded options for residential services, these placements are changing almost every day, but . . . placements have been the result of a great deal of work by parents and professionals to help the young adults with autism find the least restricted environment in which they can cope. (p. 540)

Employment

The ability to maintain full-time, independent employment is one of the defining criteria of "normal" adult functioning in our culture. Most reports of the adult employment status of individuals with autism spectrum disorders find that only a minority of these individuals meet this criterion (Howlin & Goode, 1998). Nevertheless, beginning with Kanner's own patients, some adults with ASD have independently held full-time jobs. This is rare enough that many studies list the specific jobs, which have included computer operator, clerk (Rutter, 1970); "bank teller, laboratory technician, duplicating machine operator, accountant, 'blue collar job' at an agricultural research station, general office worker, page in the foreign language section of a library, bus boy in a restaurant, truck loading supervisor, helper in a drug store" (Kanner et al., 1972, p. 28); music composer/former Navy meteorologist (Kanner, 1973); janitor, cab driver, library assistant, keypunch operator (Rumsey et al., 1985); library worker, physics tutor, salesman (semimanagerial), factory worker (Szatmari et al., 1989); astronomy professor, mathematician, chemist, technologist, civil servant, musician, expert in heraldry (Asperger, 1991); physiotherapist, bus conductor, automobile mechanic, cook, office worker (Kobayashi et al., 1992); laboratory technician (Howlin et al., 2000); and "scientific officer [for an] oil company; electrical work, cartographer, postal assistant, factory work, computing, accounts, fabric designer" (p. 216, Howlin et al., 2004).

Several researchers have noted that factors such as the local economy and the availability of specialized vocational training programs and supports significantly improve the vocational success of individuals with autism (Kobayashi et al., 1992; Lord & Venter, 1992; Mawhood & Howlin, 1999). Specific supported employment strategies and programs are described by Mawhood and Howlin (1999); McClannahan, MacDuff, and Krantz (2002); Keel, Mesibov, and Woods (1997); Smith, Belcher, and Juhrs (1995); and Van Bourgondien and Chapman (Mesibov, Shea, & Schopler, in press).

Smith et al. (1995) indicated that the stereotype that all people with autism require jobs with rigid routines, in quiet environments, is not true: "Workers with autism have managed to avoid jobs that emphasize their weaknesses in language and social skills and find employment under numerous job titles in a variety of industries" (p. 285). Similarly, Keel et al. (1997) indicated: "Most people with autism are able to handle a variety of tasks within their jobs as long as there is a predictable routine or [emphasis added] a schedule to follow and what is expected is clear to them at all times" (p. 6). Several authors stress that individualized support that facilitates communication and problem solving involving related aspects of life (e.g., transportation, social interests, stress management, money management) is important for successful employment of individuals with autism (Keel et al., 1997;

McClannahan et al., 2002; Mesibov, Shea, & Schopler, in press).

Marriage

A small number of individuals with autism are reported to have married. These reports have come from several sources: follow-up studies of children diagnosed with autism (Howlin, 2003; Howlin et al., 2004; Kanner, 1973; Szatmari et al., 1989; Tantam, 1991); reports of parents who have been diagnosed as a result of their children's diagnostic evaluation (Ritvo, Mason-Brothers, Freeman, & Pingree, 1988; Ritvo, Ritvo, Freeman, & Mason-Brothers, 1994); autobiographies (e.g., *An Asperger Marriage,* by Chris and Gisela Slater-Walker; *Pretending to be Normal: Living with Asperger's Syndrome,* by Liane Willey); and other professional literature (e.g., *Aspergers in Love: Couple Relationships and Family Affairs,* by Maxine Aston). The majority of adults with autism, however, are generally reported to have either limited social contacts, relatively superficial relationships, or social interactions mainly in the context of community groups and organizations (Ballaban-Gil et al., 1996; Howlin et al., 2000; Howlin et al., 2004; Rumsey et al., 1985).

Autism and the Criminal Justice System

Unfortunately, people with many types of developmental disabilities, including autism, are more likely than typically developing individuals to be victims of crime (Debbaudt, 2001; National Research Council, 2001a) and/or potentially criminal sexual or financial exploitation (e.g., Howlin et al., 2004; Murrie, Warren, Kristiansson, & Dietz, 2002). Further, people with autism may have more difficulty than others in interacting with the police, whether as victims, witnesses, or suspects, because of their limited communication skills, unusual behaviors, or social misperception of situations. Suggestions for increasing safety of both children and adults with autism are available from (1) materials from the South Carolina Autism Society (www.scautism.org/protect.html); (2) a special section of the 2003, second edition, *Advocate* publication of the Autism Society of America (scheduled to be available online in late 2004 for members at

www.autism-society.org); and (3) the book by Debbaudt (2001).

Higher functioning individuals are particularly vulnerable to being victims of crime or exploitation if they spend time in the community with inadequate support or supervision. Conversely, several reports have suggested an association between Asperger syndrome/high-functioning autism and criminal behavior (Baron-Cohen, 1988; Kohn, Fahum, Ratzoni, & Apter, 1998/2002; Mawson, Grounds, & Tantam, 1985; Murrie et al., 2002; O'Brien, 2002; Scragg & Shah, 1994; Siponmaa, Kristiansson, Jonson, Nydén, & Gillberg, 2001; Tantam, 1991), although this suggestion has also been disputed (Ghaziuddin, Tsai, & Ghaziuddin, 1991; Hall & Bernal, 1995; Howlin & Goode, 1998), and Murrie et al. (2002) have made the point that "the majority of persons with Asperger's syndrome are scrupulously law-abiding" (p. 66).

Nevertheless, Frith (1991) reported:

Autistic people, and particularly those of the Asperger type, have been involved in some difficult forensic cases. Sometimes their offenses are part of their single-minded pursuit of a special interest, sometimes the result of a defensive panic-induced action and sometimes the consequence of a complete lack of common sense. . . . Typically the Asperger individual, when apprehended, does not seem to feel guilt, does not try to conceal or excuse what he or she did, and may even describe details with shocking openness. (p. 25)

Similarly, in reviewing the literature, Howlin (1997, 2000) suggested that run-ins with the legal system were likely to be related to perseverative interests or unusual thinking patterns on the part of individuals with Asperger syndrome/high-functioning autism, *not* malicious or unscrupulous motives. For example, several "crimes" reportedly committed by individuals with high-functioning autism were related to a fascination with washing machines, trains, chemical reactions, fire, poisons, and other dangerous topics. Other crimes were apparently related to heightened sensory sensitivity (e.g., aggression toward a crying baby), extreme distress when routines were interrupted (leading to aggression toward the source of interruption), limited understanding of social norms (particularly related to sexual behavior), and social naiveté (such that the individuals with autism were "set up" to commit illegal acts that they didn't fully understand).

O'Brien (2002) reported on a comparison of offenders with mental retardation ("intellectual disability") either with or without autism. The offenses committed by people with both autism and mental retardation, compared to those of people with only mental retardation, were less likely to involve drugs or alcohol, were less likely to involve concrete gain, and were likely to be committed during daylight hours, consistent with the relative social naiveté associated with autism.

Overall, it appears that because of the social and communication difficulties of people with autism, they are unfortunately at increased risk for being victims of crime or being caught up in law enforcement or legal situations beyond their comprehension. Incidents of illegal behavior on the part of more cognitively advanced individuals with autism have also been reported.

CLINICAL ISSUES

The clinical issues that confront adolescents and adults with autism vary based on both age and developmental level, particularly intelligence level. Individuals with both autism and mental retardation have many issues and challenges in common irrespective of age, while age and legal independence play a greater role among those with autism and average intelligence.

Adolescents and Adults with Autism and Mental Retardation

Common challenges and clinical needs within the population of individuals with both autism and mental retardation include the continued development or refinement of self-help skills; issues related to sexuality; the need for ongoing supervision and legal protection; the skills and supports needed to engage in meaningful, productive work; and typical, but painful, life events such as grief and loss.

Self-Help Skills

For more impaired individuals with autism (and even some high-functioning individuals;

Green et al., 2000), independent self-help skills are often problematic. Sometimes these skills have not been mastered in childhood and continue to cause difficulties in adolescence and beyond.

In addition to the global delays associated with mental retardation, specific aspects of autism (e.g., sensory issues, difficulties with sequencing, and limited awareness of social expectations) can interfere with learning skills in the areas of dressing, eating, and bathing. Further, some individuals with autism and mental retardation, even if they do not have toileting accidents, have never completely mastered wiping themselves after using the toilet. This issue is particularly problematic to address in adolescence or adulthood, when privacy concerns and caregivers' modesty may interfere with direct instruction in the bathroom, even though this is likely to be necessary.

Further, there are increased needs in the area of personal hygiene beginning in adolescence. With females, issues related to menstruation can be difficult for families, teachers, and other caregivers to handle. For example, sensory sensitivities and dislike of changes in routine may lead to resistance or refusal to use sanitary napkins. Some girls and women with autism might not recognize that they have their periods or may not have the communication skills to inform their caregivers. Occasionally, some females with autism become fascinated with the sensory qualities of the menstrual blood. Further, learning to change sanitary napkins and dispose of the used ones requires individualized and private instruction for many adolescents. Finally, some girls and women may experience premenstrual distress that negatively affects their mood and behavior, yet they may not be able to communicate the nature of their discomfort. Another aspect of skill development that is important for adolescent females with autism is learning to put on and wear a bra.

Adolescent boys must generally learn to shave (or at least to tolerate being shaved), either with an electric razor (which has the advantage of being safe, but the disadvantage of being noisy and vibrating) or with a different kind of razor. Both boys and girls at this age need to learn to put on and wear deodorant.

Teaching hygiene and self-help skills to adolescents or adults with autism and mental retardation is typically best accomplished through the principles of:

- Individualizing goals and methods rather than relying on a standard curriculum
- Eliminating unpleasant sensory stimuli as much as possible
- Breaking skills down into small steps
- Using objects or pictures in sequence to communicate the sequence of steps
- Providing frequent practice
- Following the desired behavior with a clear finish and enjoyable activity or object

Sexuality

Van Bourgondien, Reichle, and Palmer (1997) reviewed the limited literature on sexuality and autism and indicated that while some professionals have questioned the sexual interests and sex education needs of individuals with autism, empirical research has revealed that sexuality is, in fact, an important issue for many of them.

The most typical sexual behavior among individuals with autism, both with and without mental retardation, is masturbation (DeMyer, 1979; Haracopos & Pedersen, 1992, as cited in Van Bourgondien et al., 1997; Ousley & Mesibov, 1991). Ruble and Dalrymple (1993) documented parents' concerns that many adolescents and adults with significant mental retardation and autism touched their genitals or masturbated in public without knowing that this behavior might disturb or offend others. Van Bourgondien et al. (1997) reported results of a survey of group home staff about the sexual behaviors of a group of 89 adults with mental retardation and autism who lived in the homes. Caregivers reported that overt sexual behavior was common, including masturbation (75% of men, 24% of women); masturbation with various objects (26% of the men who masturbated, but 0% of the women who masturbated); sexual arousal from visual stimulation, including other people (17% of men, 18% of women); and sexual behaviors involving or directed toward other people (35% of men, 29% of women). Additional sexually related interests (holding hands, hugging, kissing, petting, etc.) were reported in a study of 15 late adolescents and

adults with autism by Konstantareas and Lunsky (1997).

Many individuals can learn, after frequent redirection, to go to a specific private place to masturbate. Sometimes changing the individual's wardrobe (e.g., from sweatpants to jeans) is helpful. Also, keeping people engaged with other interesting, meaningful activities can reduce the frequency of masturbation in public. Sex education for individuals with adequate receptive language typically includes information about body parts, hygiene for genital areas, the concepts of privacy and degrees of relationships (i.e., stranger, staff or supervisor, family member, friend, casual date, boyfriend/girlfriend/going steady, fiancé/fiancée, husband/wife), acceptable public and private behaviors for various types of relationships, masturbation, sexual intercourse, and special topics based on the individual's interests, experiences, and questions (Koller, 2000; Melone & Lettick, 1983; Shea & Gordon, 1984).

Guardianship

In the United States, parents automatically cease to be a child's guardian when that child reaches the legal age of adulthood, which varies from state to state but is generally 18 years. At that point, children are legally independent unless guardianship has been arranged through the legal system. Parents of youngsters with significant mental retardation (with or without autism) may assume that continued guardianship is automatic, so the need for legal proceedings is an important issue for professionals to help families anticipate. Many states have various forms of guardianship, including full guardianship of the individual and his or her assets, as well as more limited guardianship involving only specified life decisions (e.g., medical decisions but not where the individual lives). It is important for families to obtain competent legal advice in their state *before* the child's legal age of adulthood in order to consider the most appropriate arrangements to safeguard both the individual's well-being and his or her rights.

Work

Typical Americans work at paying jobs for a variety of reasons: They need money to pay for shelter, food, clothes, and so on; they enjoy the work itself; they like the social aspects of their jobs; and they like to keep themselves occupied with productive activity. For many adults with both autism and mental retardation, some of these sources of motivation are not relevant. Because of their mental retardation, they may not understand the instrumental value of money or the costs of daily life, and, in addition, they may realistically not be able to earn enough money to pay for most of the things they need. Also, because of their cognitive disabilities, the work they can do may not be inherently interesting. Further, because of their autism, they may not enjoy the social aspects of jobs; in fact, social interactions at work might be experienced as stressful, albeit necessary, parts of their daytime life. However, with specialized supports, work can be made meaningful, productive, and satisfying for many adults with autism (Mawhood & Howlin, 1999; Smith, Belcher, & Juhrs, 1995).

The TEACCH supported employment program (Keel et al., 1997; Mesibov, Shea, & Schopler, in press) uses the principles of Structured Teaching (Schopler, Mesibov, & Hearsey, 1995) in work settings. Specifically, individualized visual strategies are used to answer four essential questions: (1) What work am I supposed to do? (2) How much work am I supposed to do? (3) How will I know that I am progressing toward being finished? (4) What happens next? For employees with autism and significant mental retardation, answering these questions generally includes some of the following strategies:

- Organizing work supplies into some kind of containers
- Organizing these materials in a way that encourages the employee to work from left to right or top to bottom
- Providing visual information about the work that is to be performed (e.g., a model of the finished product or a demonstration of how to manipulate the materials)
- Providing visual information that work is moving toward completion (e.g., the sight of the container of materials becoming emptier, a check-off picture list of the various steps of the task, or the sight of an hourglass emptying or a timer moving toward 0)
- A visual cue for what to do when the work is finished (e.g., a concrete reward, a symbol of a favored activity, or a cue to go to the break area)

These same principles are used in designing supported employment plans for more cognitively capable workers, for example:

- Teaching employees to organize their work materials (which can include file folders for office-type work)
- Teaching employees to use written lists both for organizing their work and for checking off items as they are completed
- Teaching employees to use a written daily or weekly schedule

Not all adults with autism and mental retardation find typical sheltered or supported work environments enjoyable, however. The TEACCH program has developed the Carolina Living Learning Center, set in a semirural location near the university town of Chapel Hill (Mesibov, Shea, & Schopler, in press; Van Bourgondien & Reichle, 1997). The setting provides a wide range of work activities (including various aspects of gardening, facility maintenance, and other outside work in addition to structured work activities indoors) and community recreation. The Autism Society of North Carolina has established the Creative Living program, which combines music and art activities, community recreation, prevocational activities, and volunteer jobs at local businesses and agencies (e.g., animal shelters and public libraries) with more traditional supported employment opportunities.

Difficult Life Events

Unfortunately, difficult life events such as illness and death of loved ones, undergoing medical procedures, being hurt or abused, and so on occur in the lives of individuals with autism. A series of picture books for adolescents and adults about such life events can be an important resource for families and counselors to help these individuals understand what is happening and perhaps ask questions or express feelings and concerns. This series, *Books Beyond Words,* by Sheila Hollins and colleagues, is available from www.rcpsych.ac.uk

/publications/bbw/index.htm (Royal College of Psychiatrists, 17 Belgrave Square, London SW1X 8PG).

Adolescents with Autism and Average Intelligence

Adolescents with autism and average intelligence face challenges similar to those of their typical peers, namely learning to deal with increased expectations at school and more complex social issues.

School

Adolescence presents more able adolescents with multiple challenges at school, since many capable adolescents spend at least part, or perhaps all, of their school day in regular education classes in typical middle schools and high schools. However, although high-functioning adolescents often perform academically at or above grade level in certain subjects, the organizational and social expectations in middle school and high school (e.g., keeping track of multiple assignments and long-term projects; moving quickly between classes; avoiding violation of subtle social taboos) can be overwhelming (Klin & Volkmar, 2000). Further, experiences of being teased, bullied, or ostracized, which are major sources of distress even for typical youngsters at this age, can be intense and excruciatingly painful for some adolescents with autism (Green et al., 2000).

Relationships with Peers

Many intellectually capable adolescents with autism are interested in having friends, but are not skilled at developing or maintaining friendships. The nuances of socially acceptable dress, speech, mannerisms, topics of conversation, and typical adolescent viewpoints on the world (e.g., "Rules are meant to be broken") are typically difficult for adolescents with autism to understand. Even those who want to have friends are often so unsuccessful at their daily social interactions that many eventually retreat to their rooms, their computers, their televisions, and their special interests. Sometimes, however, it appears that distress over limited social relationships is more of an issue for families than for the adolescents with autism themselves, who might be

genuinely satisfied with having only brief or focused contacts with other people.

Therapeutic interventions at this age include:

- Explicitly teaching adolescents about social and emotional topics and techniques for fitting in better, if not completely, with the customs of their social world
- Teaching organizational strategies (if these have not already been mastered), such as clarifying assignments, using checklists of needed books and materials, structuring homework time, following a checklist of chores, making a calendar of weekly plans, and so on
- Arranging, if needed, for modified assignments, additional time on tests and projects, reduced handwriting demands, alternative methods of testing, and so on
- Arranging time and encouragement for activities that are enjoyable and relaxing (even if they are solitary or somewhat atypical) to counteract the stresses of daily life at school
- Providing emotional support
- Providing supervision by adults to prevent bullying and reduce teasing

Sometimes medication for anxiety and/or depression is also indicated.

Adults with Autism and Average Intelligence

Clinical areas in which adults with autism and average intelligence may have special needs include going to college, keeping a job, and managing issues associated with adult relationships and sexuality.

College

As noted previously, it is clear from the research and clinical literature that some adults with autism can be successful at college and in some advanced graduate programs (typically in fields such as science and research, engineering, computer technology, library/information science, and accounting). Again, the organizational and social aspects of college and graduate school are almost always more problematic than the academic content. Williams and

Palmer ("Preparing for College: Tips for Students with HFA/Asperger's Syndrome," available at http://www.teacch.com/teacch_e.htm), described the following strategies:

- Preparing in advance for daily life on campus (e.g., living in a dorm, food service options, doing laundry, sharing a bathroom, using the library, time management)
- Having a single room
- Learning to use "to-do" lists and a small appointment book for time management
- Identifying helpful advisors about social and logistical issues
- Learning to ask for help (including support from the Disability Services office)
- Learning to identify stressors and coping mechanisms
- Choosing classes that provide a balanced and manageable workload
- Creating a social life around special interests
- Arranging time for exercise as a stress management tool

Work

Even adults with autism who have average intelligence have historically had limited vocational success without specialized supports (Howlin & Goode, 1998; Lord & Bailey, 2002; Nordin & Gillberg, 1998). Adults with autism who can master the intellectual aspects of jobs in competitive employment may have significant difficulties with the organizational aspects of their jobs (e.g., time management, accepting changes in routine, and keeping work materials organized) and with the social aspects (e.g., knowing how and when to chat or joke with coworkers, what to do during breaks, and how to ask for help as needed). In addition to the Structured Teaching strategies discussed earlier, some of the techniques used with higher functioning adults with autism in the TEACCH Supported Employment program include:

- Explaining social expectations in written form
- Providing supportive counseling sessions reinforced with written summaries of plans and suggestions

- Providing information about where to find help or guidance on a daily basis (and a fallback plan in case the regular supervisor is absent)
- Supplying employers with information about autism, the specific client, and a contact person from the supported employment program

Sexuality

Individuals with autism and average intelligence are likely to be involved in community-based social situations with the potential to lead to sexual opportunities and experiences. However, given the subtle and frequently unspoken communications and expectations in social/sexual situations, difficulties with understanding these situations and knowing how to behave are not surprising. According to Howlin (1997), problems related to sexuality in individuals with autism and average intelligence generally involve the social, rather than the physical, aspects of sexuality. Social/sexual problems outlined by Howlin can include an intense determination to date and marry in order to "be like everyone else" (p. 245), yet limited social understanding and skills necessary for establishing and maintaining intimate partnerships; "obsessions and infatuations" (p. 247) with desired partners which may not be reciprocated; simple, naïve understanding of sexual feelings; and vulnerability to sexual exploitation. Occasionally, there are also problems involving behaviors that are interpreted by others as sexual, even though they were not intended in this way (e.g., being inadequately dressed in public or touching other people with only friendly or helpful intentions, such as picking lint off their shirts). Further, the combination of social-communication differences and sensory sensitivities may make sexual expression within marriage less frequent and/or less "romantic" than spouses might wish (Aston, 2002). Very clear, explicit communication about socially desirable, effective behaviors and the perspectives of others may be needed to help more capable adults with autism find ways to meet their needs for social, physical, and sexual contact with others, while remaining safe from exploitation and abuse.

CONCLUSION

The developmental course and adult outcome of autism spectrum disorders can essentially be viewed in two ways. From the perspective of normal development and the independent adulthood that parents wish for their children, autism is a serious disability that usually does not permit those results. On the other hand, compared to their severely atypical early development, over time, many children with autism show improvements in skills and socially acceptable behavior, and most families adapt to the special needs of their offspring (Sanders & Morgan, 1997).

Adolescence can be a particularly challenging time for some individuals with autism spectrum disorders and their families, while for others it is a time of increased skill development and social awareness. Since the very first patients were identified by Kanner (1943) and Asperger (1991), a few individuals have developed extremely well in terms of living independently, working, supporting themselves, and even marrying. Many more who have average intelligence or mild mental retardation have been able to master academic skills in public schools, obtain and keep meaningful jobs (through specialized supports), and enjoy social and family activities and relationships, even if these are somewhat idiosyncratic. It is unfortunately true that some individuals with autism, particularly those with very significant mental retardation, limited functional language, and/or intense interests or rigid behaviors remain very disabled. Adults with co-existing autism and mental retardation need both specialized residential services and specialized supports for working or engaging in other meaningful and satisfying activities during the day. Both residential and vocational/day program services require money, trained staff, transportation, and a welcoming community.

Cross-References

Outcome in autism is discussed in Chapter 7; autism in young and school-age children is addressed in Chapters 8 and 9, respectively. Vocational supports are discussed in Chapter 43.

Clinical Web Sites

www.aspergersyndrome.org

www.TheGrayCenter.org

www.tonyattwood.com

www.teacch.com

Clinical Books

Attwood, T. (1998). *Asperger syndrome: A guide for parents and professionals.* Bristol, PA: Jessica Kingsley.

Bashe, P., & Kirby, B. (2001). *The OASIS guide to Asperger syndrome.* New York: Crown.

Bolick, T. (2001). *Asperger syndrome and adolescence: Helping preteens and teens get ready for the real world.* Gloucester, MA: Fair Winds Press.

Cumine, V., Leach, J., & Stevenson, G. (1998). *Asperger syndrome: A practical guide for teachers.* London: David Fulton.

Debbaudt, D. (2001). *Autism, advocates, and law enforcement professionals.* Bristol, PA: Jessica Kingsley.

Faherty, C. (2000). *What does it mean to me?* Arlington, TX: Future Horizons.

Fullerton, A., Stratton, J., Coyne, P., & Gray, C. (1996). *Higher functioning adolescents and young adults with autism.* Austin, TX: ProEd.

Hodgdon, L. (1999). *Solving behavior problems in autism.* Troy, MI: QuirkRoberts.

Howlin, P. (1997). *Autism: Preparing for adulthood.* New York: Rutledge.

Janzen, J. (2003). *Understanding the nature of autism: A guide to the autism spectrum disorders.* San Antonio, TX: Communication Skill Builders.

McAfee, J. (2001). *Navigating the social world.* Arlington, TX: Future Horizons.

Mesibov, G. B., Adams, L. W., & Klinger, L. G. (1998). *Autism: Understanding the disorder.* New York: Kluwer Academic/Plenum Press.

Mesibov, G. B., Shea, V., & Adams, L. W. (2001). *Understanding Asperger syndrome and high functioning autism.* New York: Kluwer Academic/Plenum Press.

Mesibov, G. B., Shea, V., & Schopler, E. (in press). *The TEACCH approach to autism spectrum disorders.* New York: Kluwer Academic/ Plenum Press.

Ozonoff, S., Dawson, G., & McPartland, J. (2002). *A parent's guide to Asperger syndrome and high-functioning autism: How to meet the challenges and help your child thrive.* New York: Guilford Press.

Powers, M., & Poland, J. (2002). *Asperger syndrome and your child*. New York: Harper Academic.

Smith, M. D., Belcher, R. G., & Juhrs, P. D. (1995). *A guide to successful employment for individuals with autism*. Baltimore: Paul H. Brookes.

REFERENCES

Ando, H., & Yoshimura, I. (1979). Effects of age on communication skill levels and prevalence of maladaptive behaviors in autistic and mentally retarded children. *Journal of Autism and Developmental Disorders, 9,* 83–93.

Ando, H., Yoshimura, I., & Wakabayashi, S. (1980). Effects of age on adaptive behavior levels and academic skill levels in autistic and mentally retarded children. *Journal of Autism and Developmental Disorders, 10,* 173–184.

Asperger, H. (1991). "Autistic psychopathy" in childhood. In U. Frith (Ed. & Trans.), *Autism and Asperger syndrome*. New York: Cambridge University Press. (Original work published 1944)

Aston, M. (2002). *The other half of Asperger syndrome: A guide to an intimate relationship with a partner who has Asperger syndrome*. Shawnee Mission, KS: Autism Asperger Publishing.

Ballaban-Gil, K., Rapin, I., Tuchman, R., & Shinnar, S. (1996). Longitudinal examination of the behavioral, language, and social changes in a population of adolescents and young adults with autistic disorder. *Pediatric Neurology, 15,* 217–223.

Baltaxe, C. A. M., & Simmons, J. Q., III. (1992). A comparison of language issues in high-functioning autism and related disorders with onset in childhood and adolescence. In E. Schopler & G. B. Mesibov (Eds.), *High functioning individuals with autism* (pp. 201–225). New York: Plenum Press.

Baroff, G. (1999). *Mental retardation: Nature, cause, and management* (3rd ed.). Philadelphia: Brunner/Mazel.

Baron-Cohen, S. (1988). An assessment of violence in a young man with Asperger's syndrome. *Journal of Child Psychology and Psychiatry, 29,* 351–360.

Bartak, L., Rutter, M., & Cox, A. (1975). A comparative study of infantile autism and specific developmental receptive language disorder: I. The children. *British Journal of Psychiatry, 126,* 127–145.

Bölte, S., & Poustka, F. (2002). The relation between general cognitive level and adaptive behavior domains in individuals with autism with and without co-morbid mental retardation. *Child Psychiatry and Human Development, 33,* 165–172.

Bolton, P. F., Pickles, A., Murphy, M., & Rutter, M. (1998). Autism, affective and other psychiatric disorders: Patterns of familial aggregation. *Psychological Medicine, 28,* 385–395.

Bryson, S. E., & Smith, I. M. (1998). Epidemiology of autism: Prevalence, associated characteristics, and implications for research and service delivery. *Mental Retardation and Developmental Disabilities Research Reviews, 4,* 97–103.

Byrd, R. (2002). *Report to the Legislature on the principle findings from the epidemiology of autism in California: A comprehensive pilot study*. University of California Davis, MIND Institute. Available from http://www.ucdmc.ucdavis.edu/mindinstitute/html/news/autismreport.htm.

Carter, A. S., Volkmar, F. R., Sparrow, S. S., Wang, J.-J., Lord, C., Dawson, G., et al. (1998). The Vineland Adaptive Behavior Scales: Supplementary norms for individuals with autism. *Journal of Autism and Developmental Disorders, 28,* 287–302.

Chakrabarti, S., & Fombonne, E. (2001). Pervasive developmental disorders in preschool children. *Journal of the American Medical Association, 285,* 3093–3099.

Clarke, D., Baxter, M., Perry, D., & Prasher, V. (1999). The diagnosis of affective and psychotic disorders in adults with autism: Seven case reports. *Autism, 3,* 149–164.

Croen, L. A., Grether, J. K., Hoogstrate, J., & Selvin, S. (2002a). The changing prevalence of autism in California. *Journal of Autism and Developmental Disorders, 32,* 207–215.

Croen, L. A., Grether, J. K., Hoogstrate, J., & Selvin, S. (2002b). Descriptive epidemiology of autism in a California population: Who is at risk? *Journal of Autism and Developmental Disorders, 32,* 217–224.

Debbaudt, D. (2001). *Autism, advocates, and the law enforcement professionals: Recognizing and reducing risk situations for people with autism spectrum disorders*. London: Jessica Kingsley.

DeMyer, M. K. (1979). *Parents and children in autism*. Washington, DC: Winston and Sons.

DeMyer, M. K., Barton, S., DeMyer, W. E., Norton, J. A., Allen, J., & Steele, R. (1973). Prognosis in autism: A follow-up study. *Journal of Autism and Childhood Schizophrenia, 3,* 199–246.

Eaves, L. C., & Ho, H. H. (1996). Brief report: Stability and change in cognitive and behavioral characteristics of autism through childhood.

Journal of Autism and Developmental Disorders, 26, 557–569.

Eisenberg, L. (1956). The autistic child in adolescence. *American Journal of Psychiatry, 1112,* 607–612.

Fombonne, E. (1999). The epidemiology of autism: A review. *Psychological Medicine, 29,* 769–786.

Fong, L., Wilgosh, L., & Sobsey, D. (1993). The experience of parenting an adolescent with autism. *International Journal of Disability, Development and Education, 40,* 105–113.

Freeman, B. J., Rahbar, B., Ritvo, E. R., Bice, T. L., Yokota, A., & Ritvo, R. (1991). The stability of cognitive and behavioral parameters in autism: A twelve-year prospective study. *Journal of the American Academy of Child and Adolescent Psychiatry, 30,* 479–482.

Frith, U. (1991). Asperger and his syndrome. In U. Frith (Ed.), *Autism and Asperger syndrome.* (pp. 1–36). New York: Cambridge Press.

Ghaziuddin, M., Ghaziuddin, N., & Greden, J. (2002). Depression in persons with autism: Implications for research and clinical care. *Journal of Autism and Developmental Disorders, 32,* 299–306.

Ghaziuddin, M., Tsai, L. Y., & Ghaziuddin, N. (1991). Brief report: Violence in Asperger syndrome: A critique. *Journal of Autism and Developmental Disorders, 21,* 349–354.

Ghaziuddin, M., Weidmer-Mikhail, E., & Ghaziuddin, N. (1998). Comorbidity of Asperger syndrome: A preliminary report. *Journal of Intellectual Disability Research, 42,* 279–283.

Gilchrist, A., Green, J., Cox, A., Burton, D., Rutter, M., & Le Couteur, A. (2001). Development and current functioning in adolescents with Asperger syndrome: A comparative study. *Journal of Child Psychology and Psychiatry and Allied Disciplines, 42,* 227–240.

Gillberg, C. (1991). Outcome in autism and autistic-like conditions. *Journal of the American Academy of Child and Adolescent Psychiatry, 30,* 375–382.

Gillberg, C. (1998). Asperger syndrome and high-functioning autism. *British Journal of Psychiatry, 172,* 200–209.

Gillberg, C., & Steffenberg, S. (1987). Outcome and prognostic factors in infantile autism and similar conditions: A population based study of 46 cases followed through puberty. *Journal of Autism and Developmental Disorders, 17,* 273–287.

Giovanardi Rossi, P., Posar, A., & Parmeggiani, A. (2000). Epilepsy in adolescents and young adults with autistic disorder. *Brain Development, 22,* 102–106.

Grandin, T. (1995). *Thinking in pictures: And other reports from my life with autism.* New York: Random House.

Green, J., Gilchrist, A., Burton, D., & Cox, A. (2000). Social and psychiatric functioning in adolescents with Asperger syndrome compared with conduct disorder. *Journal of Autism and Developmental Disorders, 30,* 279–293.

Hall, I., & Bernal, J. (1995). Asperger's syndrome and violence. *British Journal of Psychiatry, 166,* 262.

Hardan, A., & Sahl, R. (1999). Suicidal behavior in children and adolescents with developmental disorders. *Research in Developmental Disabilities, 20,* 287–296.

Harris, S. L., Glasberg, B., & Delmolino, L. (1998). Families and the developmentally delayed adolescent. In V. B. Van Hasselt & M. Hersen (Eds.), *Handbook of psychological treatment protocols for children and adolescents* (pp. 519–548). Mahwah, NJ: Erlbaum.

Howlin, P. (1997). *Autism: Preparing for adulthood.* London: Rutledge.

Howlin, P. (2000). Outcome in adult life for more able individuals with autism or Asperger syndrome. *Autism, 4,* 63–83.

Howlin, P. (2003). Outcome in high-functioning adults with autism with and without early language delays: Implications for the differentiation between autism and Asperger syndrome. *Journal of Autism and Developmental Disorders, 33,* 3–13.

Howlin, P., & Goode, S. (1998). Outcome in adult life for people with autism and Asperger's syndrome. In F. R. Volkmar (Ed.), *Autism and pervasive developmental disorders: Cambridge monographs in child and adolescent psychiatry* (pp. 209–241). New York: Cambridge University Press.

Howlin, P., Goode, S., Hutton, J., & Rutter, M. (2004). Adult outcome for children with autism. *Journal of Child Psychology and Psychiatry, 45,* 212–229.

Howlin, P., Mawhood, L., & Rutter, M. (2000). Autism and developmental receptive language disorder: A follow-up comparison in early adult life. II: Social, behavioural, and psychiatric outcomes. *Journal of Child Psychology and Psychiatry and Allied Disciplines, 41,* 561–578.

Isager, T., Mouridsen, S. E., & Rich, B. (1999). Mortality and causes of death in pervasive developmental disorders. *Autism, 3,* 7–16.

Jolliffe, T., Lansdown, R., & Robinson, T. (1992). Autism: A personal account. *Communication, 26,* 12–19. (Available from the National

Autistic Society, 393 City Road, London EC1V 1NG, United Kingdom)

Kanner, L. (1943). Autistic disturbances of affective contact. *Nervous Child, 2,* 217–250.

Kanner, L. (1973). *Childhood psychosis: Initial studies and new insights.* Washington, DC: Winston and Sons.

Kanner, L., Rodriguez, A., & Ashenden, B. (1972). How far can autistic children go in matters of social adaptation? *Journal of Autism and Childhood Schizophrenia, 2,* 9–33.

Keel, J. H., Mesibov, G. B., & Woods, A. (1997). TEACCH-supported employment program. *Journal of Autism and Developmental Disorders, 27,* 3–9.

Klin, A., & Volkmar, F. R. (2000). Treatment and intervention guidelines for individuals with Asperger syndrome. In A. Klin, F. R. Volkmar, & S. S. Sparrow (Eds.), *Asperger syndrome* (pp. 340–366). New York: Guilford Press.

Kobayashi, R., & Murata, T. (1998). Setback phenomenon in autism and long-term prognosis. *Acta Psychiatrica Scandinavica, 98,* 296–303.

Kobayashi, R., Murata, T., & Yoshinaga, K. (1992). A follow-up study of 201 children with autism in Kyushu and Yamaguchi areas, Japan. *Journal of Autism and Developmental Disorders, 22,* 395–411.

Kohn, Y., Fahum, T., Ratzoni, G., & Apter, A. (1998). Aggression and sexual offense in Asperger's syndrome. *Israel Journal of Psychiatry and Related Sciences, 35,* 293–299. Abstract obtained from *PsychINFO* database, 1999-10154-006, 2002.

Koller, R. (2000). Sexuality and adolescents with autism. *Sexuality and Disability, 18,* 125–135.

Konstantareas, M. M., & Lunsky, Y. J. (1997). Sociosexual knowledge, experience, attitudes, and interests of individuals with autistic disorder and developmental delay. *Journal of Autism and Developmental Disorders, 27,* 397–413.

Lockyer, L., & Rutter, M. (1969). A five- to fifteen-year follow-up study of infantile psychosis: III. Psychological aspects. *British Journal of Psychiatry, 115,* 865–882.

Lord, C. (1996). Language in high-functioning adolescents with autism: Questions about deviance and delay. In D. Cicchetti & S. L. Toth (Eds.), *Adolescence: Opportunities and challenges: Rochester symposium on developmental psychopathology* (Vol. 7, pp. 149–165). Rochester, NY: University of Rochester Press.

Lord, C., & Bailey, A. (2002). Autism spectrum disorders. In M. Rutter & E. Taylor (Eds.), *Child and adolescent psychiatry* (4th ed., pp. 636–663). Malden, MA: Blackwell Science.

Lord, C., & Venter, A. (1992). Outcome and follow-up studies of high-functioning autistic individuals. In E. Schopler & G. B. Mesibov (Eds.), *High-functioning individuals with autism* (pp. 187–199). New York: Plenum Press.

Lotter, V. (1974). Factors related to outcome in autistic children. *Journal of Autism and Childhood Schizophrenia, 4,* 263–277.

Lotter, V. (1978). Follow-up studies. In M. Rutter & E. Schopler (Eds.), *Autism: A reappraisal of concepts and treatment* (pp. 475–495). New York: Plenum Press.

Lovaas, O. I. (2000). Experimental design and cumulative research in early behavioral intervention. In P. J. Accardo, C. Magnusen, & A. J. Capute (Eds.), *Autism: Clinical and research issues* (pp. 133–161). Baltimore: York Press.

Marcus, L. M. (1984). Coping with burnout. In E. Schopler & G. B. Mesibov (Eds.), *The effects of autism on the family* (pp. 311–326). New York: Plenum Press.

Mawhood, L., & Howlin, P. (1999). The outcome of a supported employment scheme for high-functioning adults with autism or Asperger syndrome. *Autism, 3,* 229–254.

Mawhood, L., Howlin, P., & Rutter, M. (2000). Autism and developmental receptive language disorder: A comparative follow-up in early adult life. I: Cognitive and language outcomes. *Journal of Child Psychology and Psychiatry and Allied Disciplines, 41,* 547–559.

Mawson, D., Grounds, A., & Tantam, D. (1985). Violence and Asperger Syndrome: A case study. *British Journal of Psychiatry, 147,* 566–569.

Mayes, S. D., & Calhoun, S. L. (2001). Nonsignificance of early speech delay in children with autism and normal intelligence and implications for *DSM-IV* Asperger's disorder. *Autism, 5,* 81–94.

McClannahan, L. E., MacDuff, G. S., & Krantz, P. J. (2002). Behavior analysis and intervention for adults with autism. *Behavior Modification, 26,* 9–26.

Melone, M. B., & Lettick, A. L. (1983). Sex education at Benhaven. In E. Schopler & G. B. Mesibov (Eds.), *Autism in adolescents and adults* (pp. 169–186). New York: Plenum Press.

Mesibov, G. B. (1983). Current issues in autism and adolescence. In E. Schopler & G. B. Mesibov (Eds.), *Autism in adolescents and adults* (pp. 37–53). New York: Plenum Press.

Mesibov, G. B., Schopler, E., Schaffer, B., & Michal, N. (1989). Use of the Childhood Autism Rating Scale with autistic adolescents and adults. *Journal of the American Academy of Child and Adolescent Psychiatry, 28,* 538–541.

Mesibov, G. B., Shea, V., & Schopler, E. (in press). *The TEACCH approach to autism spectrum disorders*. New York: Kluwer Academic/ Plenum Press.

Minshew, N. J., Goldstein, G., & Siegel, D. J. (1997). Neuropsychologic functioning in autism: Profile of a complex information processing disorder. *Journal of the International Neuropsychological Society, 3,* 303–316.

Minshew, N. J., Goldstein, G., Taylor, H. G., & Siegel, D. J. (1994). Academic achievement in high functioning autistic individuals. *Journal of Clinical and Experimental Neurology, 16,* 261–270.

Morgan, C. N., Roy, M., Nasr, A., Chance, P., Hand, M., Mlele, T., et al. (2002). A community survey establishing the prevalence rate of autistic disorder in adults with learning disability. *Psychiatric Bulletin, 26,* 127–130.

Murrie, D. C., Warren, J. I., Kristiansson, M., & Dietz, P. E. (2002). Asperger's syndrome in forensic settings. *International Journal of Forensic Mental Health, 1,* 59–70.

National Research Council. (2001a). *Crime victims with developmental disabilities: Report of a workshop.* Committee on Law and Justice; Joan Persilia, Joseph Foote, and Nancy A. Crowell (Eds.), Commission on Behavioral and Social Sciences and Education. Washington, DC: National Academy Press.

National Research Council. (2001b). *Educating children with autism.* Committee on Educational interventions for children with autism, Division of Behavioral and Social Sciences and Education. Washington, DC: National Academy Press.

Nordin, V., & Gillberg, C. (1998). The long-term course of autistic disorders: Update on follow-up studies. *Acta Psychiatrica Scandinavica, 97,* 99–108.

O'Brien, G. (2002). Dual diagnosis in offenders with intellectual disability: Setting research priorities: A review of research findings concerning psychiatric disorder (excluding personality disorder) among offenders with intellectual disability. *Journal of Intellectual Disability Research, 46,* 21–30.

Ousley, O. Y., & Mesibov, G. B. (1991). Sexual attitudes and knowledge of high-functioning adolescents and adults with autism. *Journal of Autism and Developmental Disorders, 21,* 471–481.

Patja, K., Iivanainen, M., Vesala, H., Oksanen, H., & Ruoppila, I. (2000). Life expectancy of people with intellectual disability: A 35-year follow-up study. *Journal of Intellectual Disability Research, 44,* 591–599.

Persson, B. (2000). Brief report: A longitudinal study of quality of life and independence among adult men with autism. *Journal of Autism and Developmental Disorders, 30,* 61–66.

Piven, J., Chase, G. A., Landa, R., Wzorek, M., Gayle, J., Cloud, D., et al. (1991). Psychiatric disorders in the parents of autistic individuals. *Journal of the American Academy of Child and Adolescent Psychiatry, 30,* 471–478.

Piven, J., Harper, J., Palmer, P., & Arndt, S. (1996). Course of behavioral change in autism: A retrospective study of high-IQ adolescents and adults. *Journal of the American Academy of Child and Adolescent Psychiatry, 35,* 523–529.

Piven, J., & Palmer, P. (1999). Psychiatric disorder and the broad autism phenotype: Evidence from a family study of multiple-incidence autism families. *American Journal of Psychiatry, 156,* 557–563.

Rapin, I. (1997). Autism. *The New England Journal of Medicine, 337,* 97–104.

Ritvo, E. R., Mason-Brothers, A., Freeman, B. J., & Pingree, C. (1988). Eleven possibly autistic parents. *Journal of Autism and Developmental Disorders, 18,* 139–143.

Ritvo, E. R., Ritvo, R., Freeman, B. J., & Mason-Brothers, A. (1994). Clinical characteristics of mild autism in adults. *Comprehensive Psychiatry, 35,* 149–156.

Ruble, L. A., & Dalrymple, N. J. (1993). Social/sexual awareness of persons with autism: A parental perspective. *Archives of Sexual Behavior, 22,* 229–240.

Rumsey, J. M., Rapoport, J. L., & Sceery, W. R. (1985). Autistic children as adults: Psychiatric, social, and behavioral outcomes. *Journal of the American Academy of Child Psychiatry, 24,* 465–473.

Rutter, M. (1970). Autistic children: Infancy to adulthood. *Seminars in Psychiatry, 2,* 435–450.

Rutter, M., Greenfeld, D., & Lockyer, L. (1967). A five- to fifteen-year follow-up study of infantile psychosis: II. Social and behavioural outcome. *British Journal of Psychiatry, 113,* 1183–1199.

Sanders, J. L., & Morgan, S. B. (1997). Family stress and adjustment as perceived by parents of children with autism or Down syndrome: Implications for intervention. *Child and Family Behavior Therapy, 19,* 15–32.

Schopler, E., Mesibov, G. B., & Hearsey, K. (1995). Structured Teaching in the TEACCH system. In E. Schopler & G. B. Mesibov (Eds.), *Learning and cognition in autism* (pp. 243–268). New York: Plenum Press.

Schopler, E., Reichler, R. J., DeVellis, R. F., & Daly, K. (1980). Toward objective classification of childhood autism: Childhood Autism Rating Scale (CARS). *Journal of Autism and Developmental Disorders, 10,* 91–103.

Scragg, P., & Shah, A. (1994). Prevalence of Asperger's syndrome in a secure hospital. *British Journal of Psychiatry, 165,* 679–682.

Seltzer, M. M., Krauss, M. W., Orsmond, G. I., & Vestal, C. (2001). Families of adolescents and adults with autism: Uncharted territory. In L. M. Glidden (Ed.), *International review of research in mental retardation: Vol. 23. Autism* (pp. 267–294). San Diego, CA: Academic Press.

Seltzer, M. M., Krauss, M. W., Shattuck, P. T., Orsmond, G., Swe, A., & Lord, C. (2003). The symptoms of autism spectrum disorders in adolescence and adulthood. *Journal of Autism and Developmental Disorders, 33,* 565–581.

Shavelle, R. M., Strauss, D. J., & Pickett, J. (2001). Causes of death in autism. *Journal of Autism and Developmental Disorders, 31,* 569–576.

Shea, V., & Gordon, B. N. (1984). *Growing up: A social and sexual education picture book for young people with mental retardation.* Chapel Hill, NC: University of North Carolina–Chapel Hill. (Available from the Autism Society of North Carolina, 505 Oberlin Road, Suite 230, Raleigh, NC 27605 or www.autism-society.nc.org)

Shriberg, L. D., Paul, R., McSweeny, J. L., Klin, A., Cohen, D. J., & Volkmar, F. R. (2001). Speech and prosody characteristics of adolescents and adults with high-functioning autism and Asperger syndrome. *Journal of Speech, Language, and Hearing Research, 44,* 1097–1115.

Siegel, B. (1996). *The world of the autistic child.* New York: Oxford University Press.

Siponmaa, L., Kristiansson, M., Jonson, C., Nydén, A., & Gillberg, C. (2001). Juvenile and young adults mentally disordered offenders: The role of child neuropsychiatric disorders. *Journal of the American Academy of Psychiatry and the Law, 29,* 420–426. Abstract obtained from *PsychINFO* database, 2003, Abstract No. 2001-09782-008.

Smalley, S., McCracken, J., & Tanguay, P. (1995). Autism, affective disorders, and social phobia. *American Journal of Medical Genetics, 60,* 19–26.

Smith, M. D., Belcher, R. G., & Juhrs, P. D. (1995). *A guide to successful employment for individuals with autism.* Baltimore: Paul H. Brookes.

Steffenburg, S., Gillberg, C., & Steffenburg, U. (1996). Psychiatric disorders in children and adolescents with mental retardation and active epilepsy. *Archives of Neurology, 53,* 904–912.

Abstract obtained from PsychINFO database, 2003, Abstract No. 2000-00345-002.

Szatmari, P., Bartolucci, G., Bremner, R., Bond, S., & Rich, S. (1989). A follow-up study of high-functioning autistic children. *Journal of Autism and Developmental Disorders, 19,* 213–225.

Tager-Flusberg, H. (2001). Understanding the language and communicative impairments in autism. In L. M. Glidden (Ed.), *International review of research in mental retardation: Vol. 23. Autism* (pp. 185–205). San Diego, CA: Academic Press.

Tager-Flusberg, H., Joseph, R., & Folstein, S. (2001). Current directions in research on autism. *Mental Retardation and Developmental Disabilities Research Reviews, 7,* 21–29.

Tantam, D. (1991). Asperger syndrome in adulthood. In U. Frith (Ed.), *Autism and Asperger syndrome* (pp. 147–183). New York: Cambridge University Press.

Tantam, D. (2000). Psychological disorder in adolescents and adults with Asperger syndrome. *Autism, 4,* 47–62.

Tuchman, R. (2000). Treatment of seizure disorders and EEG abnormalities in children with autism spectrum disorders. *Journal of Autism and Developmental Disorders, 30,* 485–489.

Twachtman-Cullen, D. (1998). Language and communication in high functioning autism and Asperger syndrome. In E. Schopler, G. B. Mesibov, & L. J. Kunce (Eds.), *Asperger syndrome or high functioning autism?* (pp. 199–225). New York: Plenum Press.

Van Bourgondien, M. E., Mesibov, G. B., & Castelloe, P. (1989). *Adaptation of clients with autism to group home settings.* Paper presented at the National Conference of the Autism Society of America, Seattle, WA.

Van Bourgondien, M. E., & Reichle, N. C. (1997). Residential treatment for individuals with autism. In D. J. Cohen & F. R. Volkmar (Eds.), *Handbook of autism and pervasive developmental disorders* (2nd ed., pp. 691–706). New York: Wiley.

Van Bourgondien, M. E., Reichle, N. C., & Palmer, A. (1997). Sexual behavior in adults with autism. *Journal of Autism and Developmental Disorders, 27,* 113–125.

Van Bourgondien, M. E., Reichle, N. C., & Schopler, E. (2003). Effects of a model treatment approach on adult with autism. *Journal of Autism and Developmental Disorders, 33,* 131–140.

Venter, A., Lord, C., & Schopler, E. (1992). A follow-up study of high-functioning autistic children. *Journal of Child Psychology and Psychiatry and Allied Disciplines, 33,* 489–507.

Volkmar, F. R., & Nelson, D. S. (1990). Seizure disorders in autism. *Journal of the American Academy of Child and Adolescent Psychiatry, 29,* 127–129.

Von Knorring, A. L., & Haeggloef, B. (1993). Autism in northern Sweden: A population-based follow up study: Psychopathology. *European Journal of Child and Adolescent Psychiatry, 2,* 91–97. Abstract obtained from PsychINFO database, 2003, Abstract No. 1994-37828-001.

Willey, L. H. (1999). *Pretending to be normal.* Philadelphia: Jessica Kingsley.

Windsor, J., Doyle, S. S., & Siegel, G. M. (1994). Language acquisition after autism: A longitu-dinal case study of autism. *Journal of Speech and Hearing Research, 37,* 96–105. Abstract obtained from PsychINFO database, 2003, Abstract No. 1994-31255-001.

Wing, L. (1981). Asperger's syndrome: A clinical account. *Psychological Medicine, 11,* 115–129.

Wing, L., & Shah, A. (2000). Catatonia in autistic spectrum disorders. *British Journal of Psychiatry, 176,* 357–362.

Wolf, L., & Goldberg, B. (1986). Autistic children grow up: An eight to twenty-four year follow-up study. *Canadian Journal of Psychiatry, 31,* 550–556

CHAPTER 11

Social Development in Autism

ALICE S. CARTER, NAOMI ORNSTEIN DAVIS, AMI KLIN, AND FRED R. VOLKMAR

The syndrome of early infantile autism was first described in 1943 by Leo Kanner. In his remarkably enduring paper, he reported on 11 children who exhibited what Kanner thought to be a congenital lack of interest in other people, or *autism,* from the Greek *autos,* meaning "self." In contrast to the very limited interest these children had in the social environment, they often were highly interested in aspects of the inanimate environment. For example, a child might appear not to recognize his or her parents but would become panicked if the furniture were rearranged. Kanner regarded the social dysfunction and the unusual responses to the environment to be the two essential features of the syndrome. Throughout the broad range of syndrome expression, it is remarkable that now, 60 years later, the social disability of persons with autism remains probably the most striking, and poorly understood, aspect of the condition (Lord, 1993).

Social deficits have been repeatedly described in persons with autism (e.g., Rimland, 1964; Rutter, 1978; Wing, 1976). Although some social skills emerge over time, even adults with autism who are "higher functioning" have major problems in social relationships (Volkmar & Cohen, 1985). Subsequent work has modified Kanner's original description in important ways, but social deviance has continued to be recognized as a significant phenomenological aspect of the syndrome. Di-

agnostic and assessment instruments developed for autism typically emphasize social factors (Parks, 1984) as do current diagnostic criteria for the disorder (American Psychiatric Association, 1994).

Daily social encounters with persons with autism illustrate the severity of the social deficit seen in autism. In addition, social interaction with persons with autism who vary in chronological age and developmental level highlight the complex issues posed by developmental changes and syndrome heterogeneity. A young autistic child may prefer to spend most of his or her time engaged in solitary activities. He or she may fail to respond differentially to a strange person and, particularly in very young and the most impaired individuals, may have relatively little interest in social interaction—even with his or her parents. In contrast to normally developing infants, for whom the social environment is of greatest interest, the younger autistic child may be exquisitely sensitive to the nonsocial environment and may become profoundly distressed in response to a change in the manner in which food is organized on his or her plate. The older child with autism often exhibits evidence of specific attachments to parents and may passively accept bids for social interaction. However, rarely is social interaction initiated when there is no other nonsocial goal motivating the social initiation. The highest functioning indi-

The authors gratefully acknowledge the support of the National Institute of Child Health and Human Development (Grants 1-PO1-HD35482-01, 5 P01-HD042127-02) and the National Institute of Mental Health (STAART grant U54-MH066594). The support of the National Alliance of Autism Research is gratefully acknowledged.

viduals with autism may be very interested in social interaction, but their odd and eccentric social styles and limited capacities to understand or anticipate others' internal emotional states, intentions, and motivations make it very difficult to negotiate the nuances of social interaction (Klin, Jones, Schultz, & Volkmar, 2003).

Higher functioning persons with autism may evidence the following social deficits: (1) failure to establish a joint frame of reference for the transaction (e.g., may begin a discussion without providing the listener with adequate background information), (2) failure to take social norms or the listener's feelings into account (e.g., approaching an unfamiliar adult and remarking, "You're very fat"), and (3) exclusive reliance on limited, conventional conversational stratagems or stereotyped expressions as the child elaborates some idiosyncratic interest or echoes a previous statement (e.g., "Do you know about prime numbers?"). Failures in the use of nonverbal cues for modulating social interaction are common even in those individuals who never speak; mute persons with autism may fail to make appropriate use of eye contact, fail to respond to extralexical social signals, and seem to avoid interaction. As social relationships develop, they typically lack the richness and intimacy seen even in young normally developing children.

Significant progress has been made in the past 20 years in understanding developmental aspects of syndrome expression, understanding the nature of the social dysfunction as reflected in specific developmental processes, and formulating broader theoretical views of autistic social dysfunction. With the advent of improved instrumentation and shared diagnostic tools, the field has moved beyond disagreements over fundamental aspects of definition and diagnosis, resolving some of the core methodological problems that impeded research. Moreover, with enthusiasm for social neuroscience growing (Insel & Fernald, 2004), autism research is no longer characterized by what was previously a widely held, albeit implicit, "cognitive primacy hypothesis" (Cairns, 1979).

This chapter selectively reviews the topic of social development in autism. It is organized around several broad areas of interest: social dysfunction as a diagnostic feature of autism, specific aspects of social development in which individuals with autism evidence impairments, and theoretical models for understanding autistic social dysfunction. To the extent possible, research findings are presented within a developmental context. This approach helps to emphasize the distinctiveness and complexity of the course of social development in autism.

SOCIAL DYSFUNCTION AS A DIAGNOSTIC FEATURE OF AUTISM

While certain aspects of Kanner's original description proved to be false leads for research, his phenomenological report of autism has proven remarkably enduring. Several aspects of his initial report deserve particular mention. First, Kanner emphasized that social deviance and delay was a hallmark, if not the hallmark, of autism. He was careful to contrast the social interest of children with autism with that of normally developing infants and emphasized that it was the autistic social dysfunction that was distinctive. This emphasis has been continuously reflected in the various official and unofficial guidelines for the diagnosis of autism that have appeared since Kanner's original report. The need for diagnostic guidelines became more critical during the late 1970s as the validity of autism as a diagnostic category became more clearly established. Various attempts, both categorical and dimensional, have been made to specify the nature of the social deficit.

Rutter (1978) emphasized that the unusual social development observed in autism was one of the essential features for definition, was distinctive, and was not just a function of associated mental retardation. Early epidemiological studies, for example, Wing and Gould (1979), also highlighted some of the difficulties in assessing social development relative to overall cognitive ability, particularly among the more severely handicapped. By 1980, there was general agreement on the need to include autism in official diagnostic systems such as the American Psychiatric Association's *Diagnostic and Statistical Manual of Mental Disorders,* third edition (*DSM-III*; American Psychiatric Association, 1980). The

DSM-III definition of *infantile autism* labeled the social deficit as "pervasive"; the use of this term was really most appropriate for the youngest and most impaired children, that is, consistent with the name of the category. The term *residual autism* was available for persons who had once exhibited the pervasive social deficit but no longer did so. As a practical matter, it was clear that some social skills did emerge over time, and imprecision regarding the nature of the social deficit was clearly problematic (Volkmar, 1987a).

In the subsequent revision of the *DSM-III* (*DSM-III-R*, American Psychiatric Association, 1987), the nature of the social deficit in autism was defined with greater attention to developmental variation. Qualitative impairment in social interaction was retained as one of three essential diagnostic features for autistic disorder (in addition to impairments in communication and a restricted range of interests/activities). Within the social domain, an individual had to exhibit at least two items from a list of five criteria to demonstrate a social deficit (see Table 11.1). The *DSM-III-R* criteria also included many examples to clarify the nature of the social deficits that were described. The *DSM-III-R* approach to the definition of the social dysfunction in autism reflected an awareness of the developmental changes in syndrome expression and the recognition that the social skills that did emerge over time were unusual in quality and/or quantity. This change was also reflected in the official change of name of the disorder from infantile autism to autistic disorder.

Given the greater number and better specification of criteria for social dysfunction, the *DSM-III-R* system had the major advantage over previous *DSM* versions of suitability for statistical evaluation. For example, Siegel, Vukicevic, Elliott, and Kraemer (1989) reanalyzed clinician ratings of *DSM-III-R* criteria for autism by employing signal detection analysis, an approach designed to identify the most robust criterion or combination of criteria that can reliably be used for diagnosis. Consistent with Kanner's original impression and subsequent research, this analysis indicated that the social criteria were the most potent predictors of diagnosis. Unfortunately, however, the broader orientation of *DSM-III-R* also led to a change in the threshold of diagnosis, with many individuals who previously would not have met criteria for infantile autism classified with a diagnosis of autistic disorder. Major revisions were made in *DSM-IV* (American Psychiatric Association, 1994), which, in the end, paralleled the major changes in the International Classification of Diseases (*ICD-10;* World Health Organization [WHO], 1993, see Chapter 1). In both *DSM-IV* and *ICD-10* qualitative impairment in social interaction has been maintained as one of the essential diagnostic features (see Table 11.1). The *DSM-IV* revision included a reduction in the number of criteria and the detail of these criteria. Problems in at least two of the four

---

TABLE 11.1   Evolution of the Definition of Social Dysfunction in Autism

Rutter (1978)	Social delays/deviance but not just secondary to mental retardation
DSM-III (APA, 1980)	Pervasive social problems
DSM-III-R (APA, 1987)	Qualitative impairment in social interaction: at least two of the following: 1. Lack of awareness of others 2. Absent/abnormal comfort seeking 3. Absent/impaired imitation 4. Absent/abnormal social play 5. Gross deficits in ability to make peer friendships
DSM-IV (APA, 1994)	Qualitative impairment in social interaction:
ICD-10 (WHO, 1993)	at least two of the following: 1. Marked deficits in nonverbal behaviors used in social interaction 2. Absent peer relations relative to developmental level 3. Lack of shared enjoyment/pleasure 4. Problems in social-emotional reciprocity

areas listed in Table 11.1 are required for the autistic social dysfunction to be considered present. These same guidelines remain in place today and, with the exception of work to extend understanding of the social dysfunction and other aspects of the diagnosis to younger ages (Charman & Baird, 2002), have not been changed. The growing body of work on autism as it appears in infancy may have important implications for development of age-specific criteria in the future (see Chapter 8, this *Handbook,* this volume).

In addition to categorical approaches to the definition of social dysfunction, various rating scales, interviews, and checklists have been used to provide dimensional definitions (e.g., Constantino et al., 2003). Dimensional definitions are particularly important in the area of social dysfunction where, in contrast to cognitive or language ability, well-developed, norm-referenced tests of ability have not generally been available. Some instruments, such as the Autism Diagnostic Interview (ADI; Lord, Rutter, & Le Couteur, 1994), assess the individual's typical pattern of social engagement as well as highly unusual social features to determine whether a child meets criteria for disorder

via parent report. Although developed to address diagnostic caseness, attempts have been made to determine whether ADI scores might also be used as continuous phenotypes (e.g., Spiker, Lotspeich, Dimiceli, Myers, & Risch, 2002). Observational instruments to assess dimensional aspects of social-communication, such as the Early Social-Communication Scales (ESCS; Mundy, Hogan, & Doehring, 1994), have been extremely valuable in developing a more thorough understanding of the early emergence of social-communication deficits in autism (see Mundy & Burnette, Chapter 25, this *Handbook,* this volume). A widely available, norm-referenced test, the Vineland Adaptive Behavior Scales (Sparrow, Balla, & Cicchetti, 1984), has also been used to provide a metric for social dysfunction in autism. The Vineland is a semistructured parent interview that assesses day-to-day adaptive functioning in the areas of communication, daily living, and socialization. Volkmar and colleagues (1987) reported that, relative to overall cognitive abilities, children with autism exhibited much lower than expected social skills in comparison to a mental age-matched group (see Figure 11.1). Information collected from the

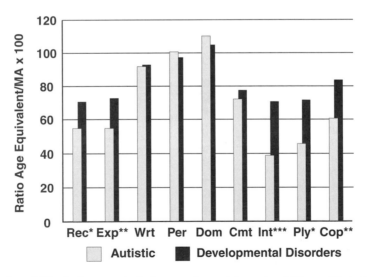

Figure 11.1 Ratios of Vineland age-equivalent scores to mental age in children with autism versus other developmental disorders. Cop = Coping; Cmt = Community; Dom = Domestic; Exp = Expressive communication; Int = Interpersonal relationships; Per = Personal skills; Ply = Play and leisure time; Rec = Receptive communication; Wrt = Written communication.
*$p < .05$, ** $p = < .01$. *** $p < .001$. Adapted from "Social Deficits in Autism: An Operational Approach Using the Vineland Adaptive Behavior Scales," by F. R. Volkmar et al., 1987, *Journal of the American Academy of Child and Adolescent Psychiatry, 26,* pp. 156–161.

Vineland and signal detection methodology has also been used to demonstrate that delays in social skills are robust predictors of the diagnosis of autism, even when compared to delays in communication (Gillham, Carter, Volkmar, & Sparrow, 2000; Volkmar, Carter, Sparrow, & Cicchetti, 1993). A series of studies using the Vineland generally supports the notion that individuals with autism demonstrate deficits in social skills that are greater than expected relative to overall developmental level (e.g., Freeman et al., 1991; Loveland & Kelley, 1991; Rodrigue, Morgan, & Geffken, 1991; Rumsey, Rapoport, & Sceery, 1985; Stone, Ousley, Hepburn, Hogan, & Brown, 1999). Table 11.2 presents Vineland items that distinguish between children with autism and both age and mental age-matched controls.

In contrast to many of the instruments focused specifically on autism, the Vineland is an important tool because it assesses more familiar and normative, developmentally appropriate skills. Supplementary norms for the Vineland have been developed for use with individuals with autism and may have potential utility in screening for autism (Carter, Volkmar, Sparrow, Wang, Lord, et al., 1998). The

Vineland is currently undergoing revision and has been expanded to include a larger number of items that are relevant to capture the social functioning of individuals with autism.

STUDYING SOCIAL BEHAVIOR IN AUTISM

Early studies of the social development of children with autism (e.g., Ornitz, Guthrie, & Farley, 1977; Volkmar, Cohen, & Paul, 1986) were often based on retrospective parent reports rather than direct observations. More recently, researchers have employed pediatric record review (e.g., Fombonne et al., 2004), used family videotaped records (e.g., Osterling, Dawson, & Munson, 2002), and studied infant siblings of children diagnosed with autism to examine early social functioning. Consistent with Kanner's impression that the social deviance associated with autism is present from birth, research suggests that, at least in retrospect, parents' reports often concern the child's development in the first year of life (cf. Rogers, 2004). In a minority of cases, the child's development is reported to be normal or near normal before the parents become concerned, usually between the ages of 18 months

TABLE 11.2   Vineland Socialization Items Differentiating Autistic Children from Age and MA-Matched Controls

Item	Expected Age (Years–Months)	p <
Shows interest in new objects/people	< 0-2	.05
Anticipates being picked up by caregiver	< 0-2	.01
Shows affection to familiar persons	0-4	.001
Shows interest in children/peers other than siblings	0-4	.001
Reaches for familiar person	0-5	.001
Plays simple interaction games	0-6	.001
Uses household objects for play	0-7	.05
Shows interest in activities of others	0-8	.01
Imitates simple adult movements	0-7	.01
Laughs/smiles in response to positive statements	0-11	.01
Calls at least two familiar people by name	0-11	.01
Participates in at least one activity/game with others	1-7	.05
Imitates adult phrases heard previously	1-11	.05

Sources: Items drawn from the Vineland Adaptive Behavior Scales, *Vineland Adaptive Behavior Scales,* by S. Sparrow, D. Balla, and D. Cicchetti, 1984, Circle Pines, Minnesota: American Guidance Service. Data abstracted from "Autistic Social Dysfunctions: Some Limitations of the Theory of Mind Hypothesis," by A. Klin, F. R. Volkmar, and S. S. Sparrow, 1992, *Journal of Child Psychology and Psychiatry, 33,* pp. 861–876. Expected age is the median age at which the behavior is present in the general population, cases matched on age and mental age and included in comparison only if mental age of the pair was equal to that typically associated with the behavior in the general population.

van Engeland, de Kogel, de Vries, & van Hooff, 1991).

Interest in Social Speech

Some of the earliest evidence of social drive is the typical newborn's preference for the human voice, especially its mother's voice, over other sounds (DeCasper & Fifer, 1980). Vocal communications between infants and caregivers constitute an important aspect of social interchange even before speech is acquired. For example, long before the infant can respond differentially to the verbal content of speech, he or she can respond with great accuracy to tone and pitch of voice (Lewis, 1963). While the precise mechanisms by which early reciprocal social interactions facilitate the emergence of lexical-communicative speech remain unclear, Bruner (1983) and other theorists have emphasized the role of such transactions for subsequent linguistic development.

However, in the case of autism, even very young children appear to lack a preference for speech sounds over other kinds of sounds (Klin, 1991, 1992; Osterling & Dawson, 1994). In addition to the typical delays in the onset of speech (Stone, Hoffman, Lewis, & Ousley, 1994), young children with autism exhibit atypical preverbal vocalizations (Sheinkopf, Mundy, Oller, & Steffens, 2000), depressed rates of preverbal communication (Wetherby, Prizant, & Hutchinson, 1998), as well as a restricted range of communicative behaviors—particularly those concerned with regulation (Mundy & Stella, 2000). Recent experimental work in toddlers (Paul, Chawarska, Klin, & Volkmar, 2004) suggests a general decrease in interest in listening to speech and a lack of development of preference for typical language patterns. If this lack of interest in social stimuli is in fact present from birth, it is likely that children with autism would fail to initiate and integrate the basic interpersonal patterns that are believed to be the foundation for all later communication.

Joint Attention

The absence or deviance of gaze behaviors and other forms of early nonverbal interchange in children with autism also interferes with the emergence of *intersubjectivity,* the coconstruction of shared emotional meaning between parent and caregiver (Stern, 1987; Trevarthen & Aitken, 2001). This failure to achieve intersubjectivity in persons with autism also results in a lack of a series of behaviors known as *joint attention,* which typically emerges in the 8- to 12-month age period (Bakeman & Adamson, 1984; Hannan, 1987). Joint attention is a preverbal social communicative skill that involves sharing with another person the experience of a third object or event (Bruner, 1983; Schaffer, 1984). Typically developing infants will, for instance, smile and point at a toy they find interesting, alternately looking at the toy and to their mother. Similarly, typically developing infants will follow the parent's eye gaze and/or point as they turn to show an object of interest in the distance. However, such triadic exchanges are consistently impoverished in children with autism of similar mental age (Mundy, Sigman, Kasari, 1990; see also Mundy, Chapter 25, this *Handbook,* this volume).

Given that this behavior typically emerges prior to 1 year of age, but diagnosis of autism is not typically made until sometime in the second year, a handful of studies have retrospectively reviewed home movies/videos of children with autism as infants. Osterling and Dawson (1994), for example, reviewed videotapes of first birthday parties of 22 children (11 with autism and 11 who were developing normally). Data were collected on social, affective, communicative, and joint attention behaviors as well as for symptoms suggestive of autism. The children with autism exhibited fewer social and joint attention behaviors and more autistic symptoms. Behaviors such as pointing, showing objects, looking at others, and orienting in response to name could be used to differentiate the groups. More recently, Osterling et al. (2002) studied the same phenomena among 20 children later diagnosed with autism spectrum disorder (ASD), 14 later diagnosed with mental retardation, and 20 typically developing children. This study replicated and extended the 1994 paper, demonstrating that the children with autism exhibited fewer social and joint attention behaviors and more atypical autism-specific behaviors than both the typically developing and developmentally delayed groups. Thus, the limited social and joint attention behaviors were not a function of developmental delays but appear to be central to the diagnosis of autism.

In autism, relative failures may be apparent in showing or pointing to objects. When children do show or point, they are much less likely to alternate gaze at the interactive partner and a desired or interesting object/activity than a typically developing child would. Indeed, deficits in joint attention are among the most striking and persistent problems in younger children with autism (Lewy & Dawson, 1992; Loveland & Landry, 1986; Mundy et al., 1994; Mundy, Sigman, Ungerer, & Sherman, 1986, Chapter 25, this *Handbook,* this volume). Even when joint attention is observed, its quality is unusual, with minimal coordination of gaze, vocalizations, and gestures. Further complicating the social interactions of children with autism is that they may also show less positive affect directed toward others in social exchanges and may even avoid positive praise (Kasari, Sigman, Mundy, & Yirmiya, 1990).

Rather than a complete deficit in joint attention skills, a specific pattern of joint attention skills and deficits is usually apparent in children and adults with autism. Individuals with autism may, for example, display *protoimperative* gesturing, while *protodeclarative* gesturing is usually completely absent (Baron-Cohen, 1989; Curcio, 1978; Gomez, Sarria, & Tamarit, 1993; Kasari et al., 1990). Protoimperatives involve the use of gaze and/or gestures to gain another person's aid in obtaining a particular object or outcome (e.g., pointing to a box of cookies on a high shelf). Protodeclaratives involve similar combinations of eye contact and gesturing, but solely with the aim of calling another person's attention to an object or experience, that is, without any instrumental purpose (e.g., showing a parent that he or she has found an interesting toy; Bates, 1976). Among children with autism who are preverbal, communication appears to be almost entirely *requestive.* Thus, even those children with autism who display coordination of eye contact with gestures and actions tend not to use it merely to share an awareness or an experience of an object or event, as do normal children and

developmentally matched children with mental retardation (see Tager-Flusberg, Paul, & Lord, Chapter 12, this *Handbook,* this volume).

As with other aspects of gaze behavior, developmental relationships and correlates of joint attention have been observed. Children with autism who are functioning at lower developmental levels across other domains also usually show lower levels of joint attention (Mundy et al., 1994). Joint attention has been related to language abilities (Mundy, Sigman, Ungerer, & Sherman, 1987), gains in language abilities over time (Charman et al., 2003; Siller & Sigman, 2002), and aspects of executive functioning (McEvoy, Rogers, & Pennington, 1993).

Finally, as with other social behaviors, deficits in joint attention skills have implications beginning very early in life, affecting the ability of children with autism to engage with others and to forge social relationships. In contrast, typically developing children are able to use joint attention to share their affective experiences with their caregivers vis-à-vis objects and events in the world long before they develop language.

Imitation

Deficits in the areas of imitation have important consequences for other aspects of development. The ability of an infant to share experiences with its caregiver with regard to an object of reference is an important context for symbolic development (Werner & Kaplan, 1963). The capacity to imitate also appears to be a prerequisite for the acquisition of subsequent symbolic activities. Children with autism display serious deficits across different types of imitation tasks (Prior, 1979). Various studies have documented deficits in this area (see Smith & Bryson, 1994, for a review).

Infants and children with autism produce less spontaneous imitation of the actions of their parents (Dawson & Adams, 1984; Meltzoff & Gopnik, 1993), and they are less adept at elicited imitation (Charman & Baron-Cohen, 1994; Stone & Caro-Martinez, 1990). Studies have consistently revealed that younger children with autism consistently have problems in the imitation of simple body movements and those that involve objects (e.g., DeMyer, Barton, & Norton, 1972; Stone,

Lemanek, Fishel, Fernandez, & Altemeier, 1990; Stone, Ousley, & Littleford, 1995). For example, in a recent study, Rogers, Hepburn, Stackhouse, and Wehner (2003) demonstrated that toddlers with autism evidenced delays relative to developmentally delayed and typically developing children in specific types of imitation skills including oral-facial imitation (e.g., extending and wiggling tongue) and imitation of actions on objects (e.g., patting a squeaky toy with elbow). Deficits in reciprocal social play, characterized by infant games such as peekaboo and patty-cake, which integrate imitation and social dialogue, are also noted by parents of children with autism (Klin, 1992). As with other social behaviors, important effects of developmental level and context are observed (Dawson & Adams, 1984; Sigman & Ungerer, 1984b). In Rogers' and colleagues recent study of toddlers (2003), oral-facial and object imitation skills were related to overall developmental level and to an estimate of autism severity, but results did not confirm Stone, Ousley, and Littleford's (1997) finding of relations between imitation and expressive language or play skills.

Play

Play skills normally develop within the first 2 years of life. At first, objects are simply manipulated, mouthed, or visually regarded. Later the child moves from simple manipulations and inspection to combining objects in play (e.g., stacking blocks) as spatial relationships are explored. Functional use of play objects, such as using a cup to feed a doll, typically develops toward the end of the first year of life. True symbolic play typically develops during the latter half of the second year of life as play objects become completely independent of action and play is no longer constrained by an object's physical properties (see Singer, 1996). The development of play skills parallels other aspects of cognitive development as the child acquires the capacity for symbolic thought (Piaget, 1951).

The autistic child's play stands in stark contrast to the richness of play in the typically developing child. Parents' reports of the play of children with autism suggest that it is characterized by lack of social engagement as well as repetitive and stereotyped object manipulation and nonfunctional use of objects (Black, Freeman, & Montgomery, 1975; Mundy et al., 1986; Sigman & Ungerer, 1984b; Stone et al., 1990). For example, a toy truck may interest the child only to the extent that parts of it may be spun or whirled. In comparison to children with mental retardation, comparatively less symbolic play is observed among children with autism (DeMyer, Mann, Tilton, & Loew, 1967; Stone & Lemanek, 1990; Wing, Gould, Yeates, & Brierley, 1977).

Consistent with a less developmentally mature capacity for play, materials may be of greater interest to children with autism because of the way they taste or feel, rather than their potential for symbolic or constructive play. In addition, play in younger children with autism is highly repetitive in nature (Sherman, Shapiro, & Glassman, 1983; Stone et al., 1990). Thus, deficits are observed in both functional and symbolic play (e.g., Sigman & Ungerer, 1984b; Stone et al., 1990). Consistent with the emergence of other social skills, symbolic play is sometimes present. However, when present, the qualitative nature of the play of children with autism differs from that observed among typically developing children and children with Down syndrome. Symbolic play acts of the majority of children with autism were characterized as object substitutions, and they evidenced fewer play acts involving attributions of false properties and no symbolic play acts involving a reference to an absent object.

The development of functional and symbolic play skills is intimately related to differentiation of objects and actions and the progressive independence of thought processes from concrete reality (Piaget, 1951) as children develop functional or symbolic play skills. Limited symbolic play in autism may emerge from social difficulties or as part of a more general problem of symbolic thought and language. Symbolic play skills may also be related to broader symbolic development, including the emergence of differential attachment (Sigman & Ungerer, 1984b) and the emergence of symbolic language (see Tager-Flusberg, Paul, & Lord, Chapter 12, this *Handbook,* this volume). In a recent paper, Rutherford and Rogers (2003) compared the role of two cognitive theories—theory of mind and executive function—in the development of pretend play skills. Although young children with autism did show expected deficits in pretend play, the authors were not able to establish a clear link with either of the two cognitive theories (see also Libby, Powell, Messer, & Jordan, 1998). Continued research in this area is needed to clarify the cognitive factors that affect play skills.

Many aspects of the play of children with autism remain to be studied, such as the developmental unfolding of patterns of social play, the extent to which children with autism can differentiate fantasy from reality, and developmental features of the relations of observed individual differences in play to cognitive and social factors. What is becoming clearer is that it is possible to teach discrete components of social play to children with autism (see Terpstra, Higgins, & Pierce, 2002, for a review). Studies that manipulate such skill acquisition have the potential to greatly inform understanding of associations among specific social play skills and other behaviors.

Attachment

By the end of the first year of life, typically developing infants have established a coherent pattern of social behaviors, referred to as *attachment,* that serve to maintain proximity to the caregiver and facilitate exploration (Bowlby, 1969). During their first year, typically developing infants learn to respond differentially to their caregivers and other individuals. The complex processes underlying attachment are one of the evolved characteristics on which infant survival is based (Freedman, 1974; see also Chapter 22, this *Handbook,* this volume). Attachment behaviors are characterized by the child's concern for maintaining proximity with its caregiver and extreme distress in the face of that caregiver's absence (Bowlby, 1969; Rutter, 1981). When the infant achieves a secure attachment organization, the caregiver acts as a "home base" from which the child may engage in exploration of the world. Early patterns of infant-caregiver interaction can be related to the quality of later attachment, which are, in turn, related to subsequent cognitive and social skills (see Seifer & Schiller, 1995). The strength of these

processes is suggested by the observation that even neglected or abused infants typically form attachments as do infants with mental handicap (Moser-Richters & Volkmar, 1996; Thompson, 1996), and such processes may be observed in various ways in infancy, for example, through specific attention to the mother's voice (Mills & Melhuish, 1974).

A recent meta-analytic analysis of studies employing the Strange Situation (Ainsworth, Blehar, Waters, & Wall, 1978) demonstrated that autism is compatible with a secure attachment organization (Rutgers, Bakermans-Kranenburg van Ijzendoorn, & van Berckelaer-Onnes, 2004). Moreover, Rutgers and colleagues revealed that, although children with autism were more likely to have insecure attachment organization than their typically developing peers, higher functioning individuals with autism were no more likely to be insecurely attached than their typically developing peers. Thus, the risk for insecurity appears limited to those individuals with autism and cognitive deficits.

It is important to emphasize that the behavior observed in the typical laboratory setting may not reflect behavior in more naturalistic settings; for example, children with autism may evidence diminished or odd attachment behaviors (Lord, 1993). Although younger children with autism often exhibit proximity seeking more frequently toward their mother relative to a stranger and increase their proximity to the mother following reunion with her (Sigman & Mundy, 1989; Sigman & Ungerer, 1984a), the quality of these behaviors may be unusual (Rogers, Ozonoff, & Maslin-Cole, 1993). Various developmental correlates of these behaviors have also been noted (Capps, Sigman, & Mundy, 1994; Rogers, Ozonoff, & Maslin-Cole, 1991, 1993; Sigman & Ungerer, 1984a). More recently, Dissanayake and Crossley (1997), examining separations and reunions in naturalistic settings, found that children with autism (and children with Down syndrome) showed fundamentally similar attachment behaviors but greater variability in behaviors across three observation sessions. The greater variability may impact parents' experience, such that they do not share in a working model of dyadic attachment security. Even though behavioral research has clearly documented the presence of attachment behaviors and a high rate of attachment security, it also is clear that the perception of parents with respect to attachment behaviors is very different (Volkmar et al., 1986).

In addition, although social attachments do not always develop when expected, idiosyncratic attachments to objects are sometimes seen (Volkmar, 1987b). Young children who are developing normally often form attachments to transitional objects, typically soft and cuddly materials that aid them with transitions of various sorts. When younger children with autism have attachments to objects, these attachments are almost always odd in quality. For example, younger children with autism may be attached to objects that are hard (e.g., cereal boxes, metal cars), or they may be attached to a class of objects rather than a specific object (e.g., a magazine of a certain type but not a specific magazine). In the *DSM-IV* field trial (Volkmar et al., 1994), attachments to unusual objects were noted to be of low frequency but, when present, very specific to the diagnosis of autism. The significance of such objects and their relation to the more typical transitional objects seen in normally developing children remains to be understood.

Peer Relations

Over the course of typical development, social skills become increasingly differentiated as children develop peer relations, prosocial skills, and an increasing capacity for self-regulation (Schaffer, 1984; Singer, 1996). Among individuals with autism, however, limited interest in social interaction and reduced initiation of social contact with peers remain apparent over time. Mutual or cooperative play of the type usually expected among school-age children is typically absent, and many children with autism prefer to be left alone to engage in self-stimulatory and other unusual activities. In older children, there is typically a failure to engage in social interchange with peers, and cooperative play is usually absent; they make far fewer approaches to peers than other children (Koning & Magill-Evans, 2001; Le Couteur et al., 1989). Some individuals may in fact become more passive or odd in their style of

interaction over time (Wing & Gould, 1979). In older children, the social failures in communication are most evident as children fail to initiate social interchange and have difficulties taking another person's point of view into account (Volkmar & Cohen, 1985).

Indeed, there is increasing evidence that children and adolescents with autism rarely develop typical peer relationships (Koning & Magill-Evans, 2001; Le Couteur et al., 1989; Orsmond, Krauss, & Seltzer, 2004). Observational studies highlight deficits in social initiations to peers relative to both typically developing and cognitively impaired peers (Jackson et al., 2003), and direct interviews of higher functioning children and adolescents reveal greater difficulty defining central elements of what determines friendship relationships as well as greater feelings of loneliness (Bauminger & Kasari, 2000).

Among individuals on the autism spectrum, those with less well-developed cognitive and verbal skills make fewer initiations to peers (Hauck, Fein, Waterhouse, & Feinstein, 1995; Sigman & Ruskin, 1999). In addition to making fewer initiations, some children with autism respond less often to the approaches of others and often appear more content when left alone (Attwood, Frith, & Hermelin, 1988; Volkmar, 1987b). In contrast to their interactions with peers, children with autism are more likely to approach adults than children (Hauck et al., 1995; Jackson et al., 2003). Perhaps due to this tendency to approach adults, when social relationships do develop, these tend to be with adults. It is also quite likely that adults will be more accepting of deviant social behaviors. It is notable that in a recent study of 235 adolescents and adults with autism living at home, only 8% of the sample were rated by mothers on the ADI (Lord et al., 1994) as having a friendship that involved varied, mutually responsive, and reciprocal activities, and almost half of the sample (46.4%) were reported to have no peer relationships (Orsmund et al., 2004). Using more relaxed criteria for defining friendships, an additional 20% of respondents had at least one "friend" with whom they engaged in a joint activity outside an organized setting. Approximately one-fourth of the sample had at least one peer relationship within an organized setting.

For some individuals with autism, social interest expands significantly during adolescence accompanied by continued gains in social skills (Rutter, 1970; Schopler & Mesibov, 1983). Unfortunately, however, even when social interest increases, marked problems usually remain as the individual has difficulty in dealing with social rules and conventions and with the reciprocal give-and-take inherent to social situations (Church, Alinsanski, & Amanullah, 2000; Rutter, 1983; Seltzer et al., 2003). There are often particular difficulties with learning, and then in generalizing, the rules of social interchange (Schopler & Mesibov, 1983). Even though gradual improvement is common, unfortunately, some individuals lose skills during adolescence.

Higher functioning adults may desire to make social contact. These individuals often have marked problems in developing friendships and relating to others because the practical ability to carry on the complex tasks related to intense social interaction is a source of much difficulty. Feelings of inadequacy and isolation are common (Bemporad, 1979; Kanner, Rodriquez, & Ashden, 1972; Volkmar & Cohen, 1985). Kanner et al. (1972) suggested that those individuals with good outcome on follow-up had learned, by adolescence, to perceive themselves as unusual and were able, in a rudimentary way, to develop strategies for coping with their disability.

A variety of intervention programs targeting peer and social skills have been developed. Despite some methodological flaws (e.g., small numbers of participants, lack of appropriate measures of outcome), a small body of research now documents the success of many of these programs (see McConnell, 2002, and Rogers, 2000, for reviews). However, many of the programs that have been studied empirically remain inaccessible to the general public, and many programs that are used more commonly (e.g., social stories and social skills groups in schools) need to be examined more rigorously for effectiveness (Rogers, 2000).

Affective Development

In the second or third year of life, typically developing children begin to recognize and label their own and others' emotional states (Bretherton & Beeghly, 1982). Children with autism appear to have difficulty recognizing emotions in others, although it is not clear whether there is truly a perceptual difficulty with recognizing facial affect or a more cognitive-affective inability to infer others' mental states (DeGelder, 1991; Hobson, 1986, 1990, 1993; Hobson, Chapter 15, this Handbook, this volume; Ozonoff, Pennington, & Rogers, 1990).

Children with autism have been observed to have difficulties in both the spontaneous expression and purposeful reproduction of affective responses. With respect to emotional expression, during early childhood the overall impression of young children with autism may be one of social aloofness or disengagement (Wing & Gould, 1979). Throughout the life span, their range of expression, frequency of different expressions, and integration of affective displays are unusual relative to typically developing and cognitively impaired individuals (Ricks & Wing, 1975; Snow, Hertzig, & Shapiro, 1987; Yirmiya, Kasari, Sigman, & Mundy, 1989). Moreover, the integration of appropriate affective displays into the ongoing social interaction is an area of particular difficulty (Dawson et al., 1990; Kasari, Sigman, Baumgartner, & Stipek, 1993; McGee, Feldman, & Chernin, 1991). Even when smiling is observed, it is much less likely to be coordinated with gaze toward others or to be elicited in social interactions (e.g., Dawson et al., 1990). Persons with autism have also been noted to have difficulties with the imitation of facial displays of emotion; relative to Down syndrome subjects, those with autism were more likely to produce unusual facial displays (Loveland et al., 1994).

Specific difficulties in facial recognition and processing information conveyed by human faces, and particularly human emotion, have been noted. In an early study, Langdell (1978) observed age-related changes in aspects of facial recognition in autism. Various studies have similarly suggested problems in the recognition of faces. These problems include the recognition of unfamiliar faces relative to nonsocial objects (Boucher & Lewis, 1992) and difficulties in utilizing contextual cues (Teunisse & de Gelder, 1994). At least some aspects of the face, at least as depicted in photographs, can be utilized as sources of information by children with autism (Volkmar, Sparrow, Rende, & Cohen, 1989). A more complete discussion of the controversies in this area is presented by Hobson (Chapter 15, this *Handbook,* this volume). Significant advances in understanding neural processes underlying facial recognition have also occurred (see Volkmar, Klin, Schultz, Chawarska, & Jones, 2003).

Differences in emotion expression, imitation, and recognition have implications for the development of empathy. Experiments designed to elicit empathic response on the part of autistic individuals have found an absence of expressed concern in response to a display of distress by an adult (Bacon, Fein, Morris, Waterhouse, & Allen, 1998; Sigman, Kasari, Kwon, & Yirmiya, 1992). This may be due in part to differences in attention to others' negative affective states. For example, children with autism may less frequently look at an adult who is demonstrating distress (Bacon et al., 1998; Sigman et al., 1992). Children with autism also usually fail to respond with prosocial behaviors such as giving, sharing, helping, or offering comfort or affection (Lord, 1993; Ohta, Nagai, Hara, & Sasaki, 1987), which suggests a diminished degree of awareness of a range of others' affective states.

Diminished affective social responsiveness, with respect to both disruption in emotion identification and expression, likely contributes to broader problems in social relations as parents, peers, and other interactive partners may have more difficulty reading the cues of the individual with autism as well as more difficulty anticipating the limits of the individual with autism with respect to empathy and ability to enter into intersubjective emotional states.

THEORETICAL MODELS OF AUTISTIC SOCIAL DYSFUNCTION

Over the past decade, several different theoretical approaches have been put forth to conceptualize the fundamental basis of social dysfunction in autism. A comprehensive, developmentally based theory that can address the changing presentation across the developmental course is critical for understanding the neurobiology of social deficits in autism. These theories vary with respect to viewing dysfunction in the social domain as either the catalyst for the wide range of deficits observed in multiple developmental domains in autism or as a result of, or part of, a cascade of developmental consequences caused by a primary deficit in another developmental domain. Challenges for theoretical models that attempt to explain social behavior in autism include: (1) the very broad range of syndrome expression in autism and related conditions, (2) the need to encompass observed developmental changes, and (3) the likelihood that different etiologies may underlie somewhat different phenotypes (Volkmar, Lord, Bailey, Schultz, & Klin, 2004). A brief review of several recent theoretical approaches serves to illustrate their advantages and disadvantages for understanding autistic social dysfunction.

Undoubtedly the most productive theoretical model has been the theory of mind (ToM) hypothesis (Baron-Cohen, 1995). This theory suggests that the characteristic deficits in social interaction arise due to a basic problem in intersubjectivity (Trevarthen & Aitken, 2001), that is, as a fundamental inability to conceptualize mental phenomena in self and other. Within this theory, individuals with ASDs are presumed to be unable to understand the beliefs, intentions, feelings, and desires of others and hence are unable to negotiate the social world successfully (Baron-Cohen, 1988). This theory view has a number of clear advantages; for example, it accounts for the marked social difficulties over the entire range of syndrome expression. Unfortunately, careful analysis of the hypothesis also reveals a number of difficulties. Theory of mind skills are strongly related to language so that many higher functioning individuals with autism or Asperger's can do the usual theory of mind tasks despite being very disabled socially (Bowler, 1992; Dahlgren & Trillingsgaard, 1996). Developmental issues pose another problem because the social difficulties of autism are ones that appear well before theory of mind skills, at least as the latter are usually conceptualized (Klin, Volkmar, & Sparrow, 1992; see also Frye, Zelazo, & Falfai, 1995).

An alternative theoretical approach has focused on executive functioning (EF) skills, which include a group of abilities that allow maintenance of the set for problem solving to solve an overarching goal. These abilities include the ability for forward planning and set shifting, which are presumed to be the skills most impacted in autism (Ozonoff, 1997). This theory encompasses a number of the difficulties that children with autism have in learning. These include the tendency to perseverate or engage in inappropriate, off-task responses and the tremendous trouble that individuals with autism often have in applying knowledge in real-world contexts (Volkmar et al., 2003). Furthermore, some aspects of the brain circuitry involved in EF skills have been identified, for example, the dorsolateral prefrontal cortex (Pennington & Ozonoff, 1996). There is also the suggestion that EF difficulties may aggregate within families (Hughes, Leboyer, & Bouvard, 1997; Hughes, Plumet, & Leboyer, 1999). However, difficulties with the EF hypothesis arise in several respects since EF deficits are not unique to autism but are observed in a number of disorders (Pennington & Ozonoff, 1996) and do not correlate straightforwardly with the degree of social impairment (Dawson & Meltzoff, 1998; see also Ozonoff, South, & Provencal, Chapter 22, this *Handbook,* this volume).

A third major theoretical approach has focused on difficulties in the ability of individuals with autism to integrate information into coherent or meaningful wholes, that is, in central coherence (Frith, 2003; Happe, 1996). Problems with attention, appreciation of context, and overall meaning are presumed to arise from weak central coherence. While attractive as a hypothesis, supportive empirical data have been sparse (Mottron, Peretz, & Menard, 2000). It could also easily be argued that difficulties in central coherence are the *result* of severe social disability rather than the reverse (Volkmar et al., 2003).

A new approach, the enactive mind (EM) model, takes a somewhat different theoretical view (Klin et al., 2003; Klin, Chapter 26, this *Handbook,* this volume), viewing the development of cognitive-symbolic capacities as resulting from action on the environment with social cognition emerging from within a social-interactive context. In this view, the disruption of these processes in autism produces a general orientation toward the world of things rather than specifically to people. As a result, individuals with autism and related disorders take a very different approach to learning the rules of social interaction. This model, embedded in emerging findings from cognitive neuroscience, has a number of potential advantages, particularly for understanding the apparent paradox of individuals with autism and Asperger's, who function at a high level cognitively, but remain profoundly impaired socially. Further empirical work is clearly needed on this hypothesis.

As evident from these descriptions, still needed is a comprehensive theoretical perspective that accounts for the multiple developmental trajectories and divergent patterns of social functioning observed among children, adolescents, and adults with ASDs. The dramatic increase in empirical research on social dysfunction among individuals with autism is increasing understanding of phenotypic aspects of social dysfunction in autism, which will inform advances in genetics and basic neurobiology. Reciprocally, the discovery of genetic and neurobiological markers will inform the identification of subtypes of phenotypes along the autism spectrum. It is quite likely that multiple neurobiological processes may result in similar phenotypic outcomes and that regulatory processes may cause differentiation in outcomes among individuals who share common neurobiological markers; in other words, multi- and equifinality (Cicchetti & Rogosch, 1996) likely characterize the social developmental processes that underlie ASDs (see also Brothers, 1989; Brothers & Ring, 1992, for a discussion of related issues).

CONCLUSION

Considerable research has been conducted that contributes to our understanding of social deficits in autism since the last publication of this *Handbook.* Major methodological advances have benefited from technological innovations that promote improved assessment of social behavior (e.g., see Insel, 1992; Insel & Fernald, 2004). For example, new technologies available to track eye gaze and to develop complex emotion stimuli have greatly enhanced knowledge about gaze and emotion recognition. In addition, the widespread use of integrated diagnostic tools (i.e., ADI and Autism Diagnostic Observation Schedule [ADOS]; Lord et al., 2000) enables more accurate comparisons across studies and samples. Further, earlier detection and improvements in diagnostic methods for very young children have encouraged studies of the early emergence of social dysfunction. Finally, dramatic advances in brain imaging techniques have led to the emergence of the new field of social neuroscience (Insel & Fernald, 2004).

Consistent with Kanner's (1943) earliest descriptions, social deficits remain a hallmark feature of the disorder. At the same time, in contrast to early depiction of the absence of social behaviors, it is now clear that there is great variability across individuals with autism with respect to both overall level of social functioning in day-to-day settings and performance on laboratory-based tasks, which may or may not be congruent with behavior in naturalistic settings. Because the social relatedness dysfunction remains a central, if not driving, component of autism, a current challenge facing researchers is to explain the relatedness that *is* present. Moreover, whereas more work is needed to further describe multiple aspects of social functioning in individuals with autism, it is critical to design studies that begin to focus on underlying mechanisms. Finally, longitudinal studies and intervention studies may begin to address the complex interplay observed among cognitive, communicative, and social deficits as well as within components of social behaviors.

Cross-References

Aspects of communication, attention, and cognition are discussed in Chapters 12 through 15; Chapters 8 through 10 provide a summary of aspects of natural history. Diagnostic features of autism are discussed in Chapters 1 through 7. Theoretical perspectives on social development are addressed in Chapters 21 through 26.

REFERENCES

Adamson, L. B. (1995). *Communication development in infancy.* Boulder, CO: Westview Press.

Ainsworth, M. S., Blehar, M., Waters, E., & Wall, S. (1978). *Patterns of attachment: A psychological study of the strange situation.* Oxford, England: Erlbaum.

American Psychiatric Association. (1980). *Diagnostic and statistical manual of mental disorders* (3rd ed.). Washington, DC: Author.

American Psychiatric Association. (1987). *Diagnostic and statistical manual of mental disorders* (3rd ed., rev.). Washington, DC: Author.

American Psychiatric Association. (1994). *Diagnostic and statistical manual of mental disorders* (4th ed.). Washington, DC: Author.

Ando, H., Yoshimura, I., & Wakabayashi, S. (1980). Effects of age on adaptive behavior levels and academic skill levels in autistic and mentally retarded children. *Journal of Autism and Developmental Disorders, 10,* 173–184.

Attwood, A., Frith, J., & Hermelin, B. (1988). The understanding and use of interpersonal gestures by autistic and down syndrome children. *Journal of Autism and Developmental Disorders, 18,* 241–258.

Bacon, A. L., Fein, D., Morris, R., Waterhouse, L., & Allen, D. (1998). The responses of children with autism to the distress of others. *Journal of Autism and Developmental Disorders, 28,* 129–142.

Bakeman, R., & Adamson, L. (1984). Coordinating attention to people and objects in mother-infant and peer-infant interaction. *Child Development, 55,* 1278–1289.

Baron-Cohen, S. (1988). Social and pragmatic deficits in autism: Cognitive or affective? *Journal of Autism and Developmental Disorders, 18*(3), 379–403.

Baron-Cohen, S. (1989). Perceptual role-taking and protodeclarative pointing in autism. *British Journal of Developmental Psychology, 7,* 113–127.

Baron-Cohen, S. (1995). *Mindblindness: An essay on autism and theory.* Cambridge, MA: MIT Press.

Bates, E. (1976). *Language and context: The acquisition of pragmatics.* New York: Academic Press.

Bauminger, N., & Kasari, C. (2000). Loneliness and friendship in high-functioning children with autism. *Child Development, 71,* 447–456.

Bemporad, J. R. (1979). Adult recollections of a formerly autistic child. *Journal of Autism and Developmental Disorders, 9,* 179–197.

Black, M., Freeman, B. J., & Montgomery, J. (1975). Systematic observation of play behavior in autistic children. *Journal of Autism and Childhood Schizophrenia, 5*(4), 363–371.

Bloom, K. (1974). Eye contact as a setting event for infant learning. *Journal of Experimental Child Psychology, 17,* 250–263.

Boucher, J., & Lewis, V. (1992). Unfamiliar face recognition in relatively able autistic children.

Journal of Child Psychology and Psychiatry and Allied Disciplines, 33(5), 843–859.

Bowlby, J. (1969). *Attachment and loss: Vol. 1. Attachment.* New York: Basic Books.

Bowler, D. M. (1992). "Theory of mind" in Asperger's syndrome. *Journal of Child Psychology and Psychiatry, 33*(5), 877–893.

Bretherton, I., & Beeghly, M. (1982). Talking about internal states: The acquisition of an explicit theory of mind. *Developmental Psychology, 19,* 906–921.

Brothers, L. (1989). A biological perspective on empathy. *American Journal of Psychiatry, 146,* 10–19.

Brothers, L., & Ring, B. (1992). A neuroethological framework for the representation of minds. *Journal of Cognitive Neuroscience, 4,* 107–118.

Bruner, J. (1983). *Child's talk: Learning to use language.* New York: Norton.

Buitelaar, J. K., van Engeland, H., de Kogel, K. H., de Vries, H., & van Hooff, J. (1991). Differences in the structure of social behaviour of autistic children and non-autistic retarded controls. *Journal of Child Psychology and Psychiatry and Allied Disciplines, 32*(6), 995–1015.

Burack, J. A., & Volkmar, F. R. (1992). Development of low- and high-functioning autistic children. *Journal of Child Psychology and Psychiatry and Allied Disciplines, 33*(3), 607–616.

Cairns, R. B. (1979). *Social development: The origins and plasticity of interchanges.* San Francisco: Freeman.

Capps, L., Sigman, M., & Mundy, P. (1994). Attachment security in children with autism. *Development and Psychopathology, 6,* 249–261.

Caron, R. F., Caron, A. J., Roberts, J., & Brooks, R. (1997). Infant sensitivity to deviation in dynamic facial-vocal displays: The role of eye regard. *Developmental Psychology, 33,* 802–813.

Carter, A. S., Volkmar, F. R., Sparrow, S. S., Wang, J. J., Lord, C., Dawson, G., et al. (1998). The Vineland Adaptive Behavior Scales: Supplementary norms for individuals with autism. *Journal of Autism and Developmental Disorders, 28*(4), 287–302.

Charman, T., & Baird, G. (2002). Practitioner review: Diagnosis of autism spectrum disorder in 2- and 3-year-old children. *Journal of Child Psychology and Psychiatry, 43*(3), 289–305.

Charman, T., & Baron-Cohen, S. (1994). Another look at imitation in autism. *Development and Psychopathology, 6,* 403–413.

Charman, T., Baron-Cohen, S., Swettenham, J., Baird, G., Drew, A., & Cox, A. (2003). Predicting language outcome in infants with autism and pervasive developmental disorder.

International Journal of Language and Communication Disorders, 38(3), 265–285.

Chawarska, K., Klin, A., & Volkmar, F. (2003). Automatic cueing through eye movement in 2-year-old children with autism. *Child Development, 74*(4), 1108–1122.

Church, C., Alinsanski, S., & Amanullah, S. (2000). The social, behavioral, and academic experiences of children with Asperger syndrome. *Focus on Autism and other Developmental Disabilities, 15,* 12–20.

Cicchetti, D., & Rogosch, F. A. (1996). Equifinality and multifinality in developmental psychopathology. *Development and Psychopathology, 8*(4), 597–600.

Constantino, J. N., Davis, S. A., Todd, R. D., Schindler, M. K., Gross, M. M., Brophy, S. L., et al. (2003). Validation of a brief quantitative measure of autistic traits: Comparison of the social responsiveness scale with the autism diagnostic interview-revised. *Journal of Autism and Developmental Disorders, 33*(4), 427–433.

Curcio, F. (1978). Sensorimotor functioning and communication in mute autistic children. *Journal of Autism and Childhood Schizophrenia, 8,* 282–292.

Dahlgren, S. O., & Trillingsgaard, A. (1996). Theory of mind in non-retarded children with autism and Asperger's syndrome. A research note. *Journal of Child Psychology and Psychiatry, 37,* 759–763.

Dawson, G., & Adams, A. (1984). Imitation and social responsiveness in autistic children. *Journal of Abnormal Child Psychology, 12,* 209–226.

Dawson, G., & Galpert, L. (1990). Mothers' use of imitative play for facilitating social responsiveness and toy play in young autistic children. *Development and Psychopathology, 2*(2), 151–162.

Dawson, G., Hill, D., Spencer, A., Galpert, L., & Watson, L. (1990). Affective exchanges between young autistic children and their mothers. *Journal of Abnormal Child Psychology, 18,* 335–345.

Dawson, G., & Meltzoff, A. N. (1998). Neuropsychological correlates of early symptoms of autism. *Child Development, 69*(5), 1276–1285.

DeCasper, A., & Fifer, W. (1980). Of human bonding: Newborns prefer their mothers' voices. *Science, 171,* 1174–1176.

DeGelder, B. (1991). Face recognition and lip-reading in autism. *European Journal of Cognitive Psychology, 3,* 69–86.

DeMyer, M. K., Barton, S., & Norton, J. A. (1972). A comparison of adaptive, verbal, and motor profiles of psychotic and non-psychotic sub-normal children. *Journal of Autism and Childhood Schizophrenia, 2*(4), 359–377.

DeMyer, M. K., Mann, N. A., Tilton, J. R., & Loew, L. H. (1967). Toy-play behavior and use of body by autistic and normal children as reported by mothers. *Psychological Reports, 21*(3), 973–981.

Dissanayake C., & Crossley, S. A. (1997). Autistic children's responses to separation and reunion with their mothers. *Journal of Autism and Developmental Disorders, 27*(3), 295–312.

Farroni, R., Csibra, G., Simion, F., & Johnson, M. (2002). Eye contact detection in humans from birth. *Proceedings of the National Academy of Sciences, 99,* 9602–9695.

Farroni, T., Johnson, M. H., Brockbank, M., & Simion, F. (2000). Infants use of gaze direction to cue attention: The importance of perceived motion. *Visual Cognition, 7,* 705–718.

Freedman, D. G. (1974). *Human infancy: An evolutionary perspective* New York: Erlbaum.

Freeman, B. J., Rahbar, B., Ritvo, E. R., Bice, T. L., Yokota, A., & Ritvo, R. (1991). The stability of cognitive and behavioral parameters in autism: A twelve-year prospective study. *Journal of the American Academy of Child and Adolescent Psychiatry, 30,* 479–482.

Fombonne, E., Heavey, L., Smeeth, L., Rodrigues, L. C., Cook, C., Smith, P. G., et al. (2004). Validation of the diagnosis of autism in general practitioner records. *BMC Public Health, 4,* 5.

Frith, U. (2003). *Autism: Explaining the enigma* (2nd ed.). Malden, MA: Blackwell.

Frye, D., Zelazo, P., & Falfai, T. (1995). Theory of mind and rule-based reasoning. *Cognitive Development, 10,* 483–527.

Gillberg, C., Ehlers, S., Schaumann, H., Jakobsson, G., Dahlgren, S. O., Lindbolm, R., et al. (1990). Autism under age 3 years: A clinical study of 28 cases referred for autistic symptoms in infancy. *Journal of Child Psychology and Psychiatry, 31,* 921–934.

Gillham, J. G., Carter, A. S., Volkmar, F. R., & Sparrow, S. S. (2000). Toward a developmental operational definition of autism. *Journal of Autism and Developmental Disabilities, 30*(4), 269–278.

Gomez, J., Sarria, E., & Tamarit, J. (1993). The comparative study of early communication and theories of mind: Ontogeny, phylogeny, and pathology. In S. Baron-Cohen, H. Tager-Flusberg, & D. Cohen (Eds.), *Understanding other minds: Perspectives from autism* (pp. 397–426). Oxford, England: Oxford University Press.

Hainline, L. (1978). Developmental changes in visual scanning of face and nonface patterns by infants. *Journal of Experimental Child Psychology, 25,* 90–115.

Hains, S. M. J., & Muir, D. W. (1996). Infant sensitivity to adult eye direction. *Child Development, 67,* 1940–1951.

Haith, M. M., Bergman, T., & Moore, M. (1977). Eye contact and face scanning in early infancy. *Science, 218,* 179–181.

Hannan, T. (1987). A cross-sequential assessment of the occurrences of pointing in 3- to 12-month-old human infants. *Infant Behavior and Development, 10,* 11–22.

Happe, F. G. (1996). Studying weak central coherence at low levels: Children with autism do not succumb to visual illusions. A research note. *Journal of Child Psychology and Psychiatry, 37*(7), 873–877.

Hauck, M., Fein, D., Waterhouse, L., & Feinstein, C. (1995). Social initiations by autistic children to adults and other children. *Journal of Autism and Developmental Disorders, 25*(6), 579–595.

Hobson, P. (1986). The autistic child's appraisal of expressions of emotion. *Journal of Child Psychology and Psychiatry, 27,* 321–342.

Hobson, P. (1990). On acquiring knowledge about people and the capacity to pretend: Response to Leslie (1987). *Psychological Review, 97,* 114–121.

Hobson, P. (1993). Understanding persons: The role of affect. In S. Baron-Cohen, H. Tager-Flusberg, & D. Cohen (Eds.), *Understanding other minds: Perspectives from autism* (pp. 204–227). Oxford, England: Oxford University Press.

Hood, B. M., Willen, J. D., & Driver, J. (1998). Adult's eyes trigger shifts of visual attention in human infants. *Psychological Science, 9,* 131–134.

Hughes, C., Leboyer, M., & Bouvard, M. (1997). Executive function in parents of children with autism. *Psychological Medicine, 27*(1), 209–220.

Hughes, C., Plumet, M. H., & Leboyer, M. (1999). Towards a cognitive phenotype for autism: Increased prevalence of executive dysfunction and superior spatial span amongst siblings of children with autism. *Journal of Child Psychology, Psychiatry and Allied Disciplines, 40*(5), 705–718.

Insel, T. (1992). Oxytocin: A neuropeptide for affiliation: Evidence from behavioral, receptor autoradiographic, and comparative studies. *Psychoneuroendocrinology, 17,* 3–35.

Insel, T. R., & Fernald, R. D. (2004). How the brain processes social information: Searching for the Social Brain. *Annual Review of Neuroscience, 27,* 697–722.

Jackson, C. T., Fein, D., Wolf, J., Jones, G., Hauck, M., Waterhouse, L., et al. (2003). Responses and sustained interactions in children with mental retardation and autism. *Journal of Autism and Developmental Disorders, 33*(2), 115–121.

Johnson, M. H., Dziurawiec, S., Ellis, H., & Morton, J. (1991). Newborn's preferential tracking of face-like stimuli and its subsequent decline. *Cognition, 40*(1/2), 1–19.

Kanner, L. (1943). Autistic disturbances of affective contact. *Nervous Child, 2,* 227–250.

Kanner, L., Rodriguez, A., & Ashden, B. (1972). How far can autistic children go in matters of social adaptation. *Journal of Autism and Childhood Schizophrenia, 2,* 9–33.

Kasari, C., Sigman, M., Baumgartner, P., & Stipek, D. J. (1993). Pride and mastery in children with autism. *Journal of Child Psychology and Psychiatry, 34*(3), 353–362.

Kasari, C., Sigman, M., Mundy, P., & Yirmiya, N. (1990). Affective sharing in the context of joint attention interactions of normal, autistic and mentally retarded children. *Journal of Autism and Developmental Disorders, 20,* 87–100.

Kasari, C., Sigman, M., & Yirmiya, N. (1993). Focused and social attention of autistic children in interactions with familiar and unfamiliar adults: A comparison of autistic, mentally retarded, and normal children. *Development and Psychopathology, 5*(3), 403–414.

Klin, A. (1991). Young autistic children's listening preferences in regard to speech: A possible characterization of the symptom of social withdrawal. *Journal of Autism and Developmental Disorders, 21,* 217–250.

Klin, A. (1992). Listening preferences in regard to speech in four children with developmental disabilities. *Journal of Child Psychology and Psychiatry, 33,* 763–769.

Klin, A., Jones, W., Schultz, R., & Volkmar, F. (2003). The enactive mind—from actions to cognition: Lessons from autism. In U. Frith & E. Hill (Eds.), *Autism: Mind and brain.* Oxford, England: Oxford University Press.

Klin, A., Volkmar, F. R., & Sparrow, S. S. (1992). Autistic social dysfunctions: Some limitations of the theory of mind hypothesis. *Journal of Child Psychology and Psychiatry, 33,* 861–876.

Koning, C., & Magill-Evans, J. (2001). Social and language skills in adolescent boys with Asperger syndrome. *Autism, 5,* 23–36.

Langdell, T. (1978). Recognition of faces: An approach to the study of autism. *Journal of Child Psychology and Psychiatry, 19,* 255–268.

Le Couteur, A., Rutter, M., Lord, C., Rios, P., Robertson, S., Holdgrafer, M., et al. (1989). Autism diagnostic interview: A standardized investigator-based instrument. *Journal of Autism and Developmental Disorders, 19,* 363–387.

Leekam, S. R., Lopez, B., & Moore, C. (2000). Attention and joint attention in preschool children with autism. *Developmental Psychology, 36,* 261–273.

Lewis, M. (1963). *Language, thought and personality in infancy and childhood.* London: G. Harapth.

Lewy, A. L., & Dawson, G. (1992). Social stimulation and joint attention in young autistic children. *Journal of Abnormal Child Psychology, 20*(6), 555–566.

Libby, S., Powell, S., Messer, D., & Jordan, R. (1998). Spontaneous play in children with autism: A reappraisal. *Journal of Autism and Developmental Disorders, 28,* 487–498.

Ling, D., & Ling, A. H. (1974). Communication development in the first three years of life. *Journal of Speech and Hearing Research, 17,* 146–159.

Lord, C. (1993). The complexity of social behavior in autism. In S. Baron-Cohen, H. Tager-Flusberg, & D. Cohen (Eds.), *Understanding other minds: Perspectives from autism* (pp. 292–316). Oxford, England: Oxford University Press.

Lord, C. (1996). Follow-up of two-year-olds referred for possible autism. *Journal of Child Psychology and Psychiatry, 36*(8), 1065–1076.

Lord, C., Risi, S., Lembrecht, L., Cook, E. H., Jr., Leventhal, B. L., DiLavore, P. C., et al. (2000). The Autism Diagnostic Observation Schedule—generic: A standard measure of social and communication deficits associated with the spectrum of autism. *Journal of Autism and Developmental Disorders, 30,* 205–223.

Lord, C., Rutter, M., & Le Couteur A. (1994). Autism diagnostic interview: A revised version of a diagnostic interview for caregivers of individuals with possible pervasive developmental disorders. *Journal of Autism and Developmental Disorders, 24,* 659–685.

Loveland, K. A., & Kelley, M. L. (1991). Development of adaptive behavior in preschoolers with autism or Down syndrome. *American Journal on Mental Retardation, 96*(1), 13–20.

Loveland, K., & Landry, S. (1986). Joint attention and communication in autism and language delay. *Journal of Autism and Developmental Disorders, 16,* 335–349.

Loveland, K. A., Tunali-Kotoski, B., Pearson, D. A., Brelsford, K. A., Ortegon, J., & Chen, R. (1994). Imitation and expression of facial affect in autism. *Development and Psychopathology, 6*(3), 433–444.

Mayes, L., Cohen, D., & Klin, A. (1993). Desire and fantasy: A psychoanalytic perspective on theory of mind and autism. In S. Baron-Cohen, H. Tager-Flusberg, & D. Cohen (Eds.), *Understanding other minds: Perspectives from autism* (pp. 450–464). Oxford, England: Oxford University Press.

McConnell, S. R. (2002). Interventions to facilitate social interaction for young children with autism: Review of available research and recommendations for educational intervention and future research. *Journal of Autism and Developmental Disorders, 32*, 351–372.

McEvoy, R. E., Rogers, S. J., & Pennington, B. F. (1993). Executive function and social communication deficits in young autistic children. *Journal of Child Psychology and Psychiatry, 34*, 563–578.

McGee, G. G., Feldman, R. S., & Chernin, L. (1991). A comparison of emotional facial display by children with autism and typical preschoolers. *Journal of Early Intervention, 15*(3), 237–245.

Meltzoff, A., & Gopnik, A. (1993). The role of imitation in understanding persons and developing a theory of mind. In S. Baron-Cohen, H. Tager-Flusberg, & D. Cohen (Eds.), *Understanding other minds: Perspectives from autism* (pp. 333–366). Oxford, England: Oxford University Press.

Mills, M., & Melhuish, E. (1974). Recognition of mother's voice in early infancy. *Nature, 252,* 123–124.

Moser-Richters, M., & Volkmar, F. R. (1996). Reactive attachment disorder. In M. Lewis (Ed.), *Child and adolescent psychiatry: A comprehensive textbook* (2nd ed., pp. 498–501). Baltimore: Williams & Wilkins.

Mottron, L., Peretz, I., & Menard, E. (2000). Local and global processing of music in high-functioning persons with autism: Beyond central coherence? *Journal of Child Psychology, Psychiatry and Allied Disciplines, 41*(8), 1057–1065.

Mundy, P., Hogan, A., & Doehring, P. (1994). *A preliminary manual for the abridged Early Social Communication Scales.* Miami, FL: Author.

Mundy, P., Sigman, M., & Kasari, C. (1990). A longitudinal study of joint attention and language disorders in autistic children. *Journal of Autism and Developmental Disorders, 20,* 115–123.

Mundy, P., Sigman, M., & Kasari, C. (1994). Joint attention, developmental level, and symptom presentation in autism. *Development and Psychopathology, 6,* 389–401.

Mundy, P., Sigman, M., Ungerer, J., & Sherman, T. (1986). Defining the social deficits of autism: The contribution of non-verbal communication measures. *Journal of Child Psychology and Psychiatry, 27*(5), 657–669.

Mundy, P., Sigman, M., Ungerer, J., & Sherman, T. (1987). Nonverbal communication and play correlates of language development in autistic children. *Journal of Autism and Developmental Disorders, 17,* 349–364.

Mundy, P., & Stella, J. (2000). Joint attention, social orienting, and nonverbal communication in autism. In A. M. Wetherby & B. M. Prizant (Eds.), *Autism spectrum disorders: A transactional developmental perspective* (pp. 55–77). Baltimore, MD: Paul H. Brookes.

Ohta, M., Nagai, Y., Hara, H., & Sasaki, M. (1987). Parental perception of behavioral symptoms in Japanese autistic children. *Journal of Autism and Developmental Disorders, 17,* 549–564.

Olson, G., & Sherman, T. (1983). Attention, learning, and memory in infants. In P. H. Mussen (Series Ed.), & M. M. Haith & J. J. Campos (Volume Eds.), *Handbook of child psychology: Infancy and developmental psychobiology* (Vol. 2, pp. 1001–1080). New York: Wiley.

Ornitz, E. M., Guthrie, D., & Farley, A. H. (1977). Early development of autistic children. *Journal of Autism and Childhood Schizophrenia, 7,* 207–229.

Orsmond, G. I., Krauss, M. W., & Seltzer, M. M. (2004). Peer relationships and social and recreational activities among adolescents and adults with autism. *Journal of Autism and Developmental Disorders, 34*(3), 245–256.

Osterling, J., & Dawson, G. (1994). Early recognition of children with autism: A study of 1st birthday home videotapes. *Journal of Autism and Developmental Disorders, 24,* 247–257.

Osterling, J. A., Dawson, G., & Munson, J. A. (2002). Early recognition of 1-year-old infants with autism spectrum disorder versus mental retardation. *Developmental Psychopathology, 14*(2), 239–251.

Ozonoff, S. (1997). Causal mechanisms of autism: Unifying perspectives from an information-processing framework. In D. J. Cohen & F. R. Volkmar (Eds.), *Handbook of Autism and Pervasive Developmental Disorders* (2nd ed., pp. 868–879). New York: Wiley.

Ozonoff, S., Pennington, B., & Rogers, S. (1990). Are there specific emotion perception deficits in young autistic children? *Journal of Child Psychology and Psychiatry, 31,* 343–361.

Parks, S. L. (1983). The assessment of autistic children: A selective review of available instruments. *Journal of Autism and Developmental Disorders, 13,* 255–267.

Paul, R., Chawarska, K., Klin, A., & Volkmar, F. (2004). *The development of preverbal communication in toddlers with autism spectrum disorders.* Paper presented at the annual meeting of the American Psychological Association, Honolulu, Hawaii, August, 2004.

Pennington, B. F., & Ozonoff, S. (1996). Executive functions and developmental psychopathology. *Journal of Child Psychology and Psychiatry, 37*(1), 51–87.

Phillips, W., Baron-Cohen, S., & Rutter, M. (1992). The role of eye contact in goal detection: Evidence from normal infants and children with autism or mental handicap. *Development and Psychopathology, 4*(3), 375–383.

Piaget, J. (1951). *Play, dreams and imitation in childhood.* New York: Norton.

Povinelli, D. (1993). Reconstructing the evolution of mind. *American Psychologist, 48,* 493–509.

Prior, M. R. (1979). Cognitive abilities and disabilities in infantile autism: A review. *Journal of Abnormal Child Psychology, 7,* 357–380.

Ricks, D. M., & Wing, L. (1975). Language, communication, and the use of symbols in normal and autistic children. *Journal of Autism and Childhood Schizophrenia, 5,* 191–221.

Rimland, B. (1964). *Infantile autism.* New York: Appleton, Century Crofts.

Rodrigue, J. R., Morgan, S. B., & Geffken, G. R. (1991). A comparative evaluation of adaptive behavior in children and adolescents with autism, Down Syndrome, and normal development. *Journal of Autism and Developmental Disabilities, 21,* 187–196.

Rogers, S. (2000). Interventions that facilitate socialization in children with autism. *Journal of Autism and Developmental Disorders, 30,* 399–409.

Rogers, S. (2004). Developmental regression in autism spectrum disorders. *Mental Retardation and Developmental Disabilities Research Reviews, 10,* 139–143.

Rogers, S., Hepburn, S. L., Stackhouse, T., & Wehner, E. (2003). Imitation performance in toddlers with autism and those with other developmental disorders. *Journal of Child Psychology, Psychiatry and Allied Disciplines, 44*(5), 763–781.

Rogers, S., Ozonoff, S., & Maslin-Cole, C. (1991). A comparative study of attachment behavior in young children with autism or other psychiatric disorders. *Journal of Child and Adolescent Psychiatry, 30,* 483–488.

Rogers, S., Ozonoff, S., & Maslin-Cole, C. (1993). Developmental aspects of attachment behavior in young children with pervasive developmental disorder. *Journal of Child and Adolescent Psychiatry, 32,* 1274–1282.

Rumsey, J. M., Rapoport, J. L., & Sceery, W. R. (1985). Autistic children as adults: Psychiatric, social, and behavioral outcomes. *Journal of the American Academy of Child Psychiatry, 24,* 465–473.

Rutgers, A. H., Bakermans-Kranenburg, M. J., van Ijzendoorn, M. H., & van Berckelaer-Onnes, I. A. (2004). *Journal of Child Psychology and Psychiatry, 45*(6), 1123–1134.

Rutherford, M. D., & Rogers, S. J. (2003). Cognitive underpinnings of pretend play in autism. *Journal of Autism and Developmental Disorders, 33*(3), 289–302.

Rutter, M. (1970). Autistic children: Infancy to adulthood. *Seminars in Psychiatry, 2,* 435–450.

Rutter, M. (1978). Diagnosis and definition. In M. Rutter & E. Schopler (Eds.), *Autism: A reappraisal of concepts and treatment.* New York: Plenum Press.

Rutter, M. (1981). *Maternal deprivation reassessed* (2nd ed.). New York: Penguin.

Rutter, M. (1983). Cognitive deficits in the pathogenesis of autism. *Journal of Child Psychology and Psychiatry, 24,* 513–531.

Schaffer, R. (1984). *The child's entry into a social world.* London: Academic Press.

Schopler, E., & Mesibov, G. (Eds.). (1983). *Autism in Adolescents and Adults.* New York: Plenum Press.

Seifer, R., & Schiller, M. (1995). The role of parenting sensitivity, infant temperament, and dyadic interaction in attachment theory and assessment. *Monographs of the Society for Research in Child Development, 60*(Serial no. 244), 146–174.

Seltzer, M. M., Krauss, M. W., Shattuck, P., Orsmond, G. I., Swe, A., & Lord, C. (2003). Changes in the symptoms of autism in adolescence and adulthood. *Journal of Autism and Developmental Disorders, 33,* 565–581.

Senju, A., Tojo, Y., Dairoku, H., & Hasegawa, T. (2004). Reflexive orienting in response to eye gaze and an arrow in children with and without autism. *Journal of Child Psychology and Psychiatry, 45*(3), 445–458.

Sheinkopf, S. J., Mundy, P., Oller, D., & Steffens, M. (2000). Vocal atypicalities of preverbal autistic children. *Journal of Autism and Developmental Disorders, 30*(4), 345–354.

Sherman, M., Shapiro, T., & Glassman, M. (1983). Play and language in developmentally disordered preschoolers: A new approach to classification. *Journal of the American Academy of Child Psychiatry, 22,* 511–524.

Siegel, B., Pliner, C., Eschler, J., & Elliott, G. R. (1988). How children with autism are diagnosed: Difficulties in identification of children with multiple developmental delays. *Developmental and Behavioral Pediatrics, 9,* 199–204.

Siegel, B., Vukicevic, J., Elliott, G. R., & Kraemer, H. C. (1989). The use of signal detection theory to assess DSM-III-R criteria. *Journal of the American Academy of Child and Adolescent Psychiatry, 28,* 542–548.

Sigman, M. D., Kasari, C., Kwon, J. H., & Yirmiya, N. (1992). Responses to the negative emotions of others by autistic, mentally retarded, and normal children. *Child Development, 63,* 796–807.

Sigman, M., & Mundy, P. (1989). Social attachments in autistic children. *Journal of Child Psychiatry, 28,* 74–81.

Sigman, M., Mundy, P., Sherman, T., & Ungerer, J. (1986). Social interactions of autistic, mentally retarded, and normal children and their caregivers. *Journal of Child Psychology and Psychiatry, 27,* 647–656.

Sigman, M., & Ruskin, E. (1999). Continuity and change in the social competence of children with autism, Down syndrome, and developmental delays. *Monographs of the Society for Research in Child Development, 64*(1, Serial No. 256).

Sigman, M., & Ungerer, J. (1984a). Attachment behaviors in autistic children. *Journal of Autism and Developmental Disorders, 14,* 231–244.

Sigman, M., & Ungerer, J. A. (1984b). Cognitive and language skills in autistic, mentally retarded, and normal children. *Developmental Psychology, 20,* 293–302.

Siller, M., & Sigman, M. (2002). The behaviors of parents of children with autism predict the subsequent development of their children's communication. *Journal of Autism and Developmental Disorders, 32*(2), 77–89.

Singer, J. (1996). Cognitive and affective implications of imaginative play in childhood. In M. Lewis (Ed.), *Child and adolescent psychiatry: A comprehensive textbook* (2nd ed., pp. 202–210). Baltimore: Williams & Wilkins.

Smith, I. M., & Bryson, S. E. (1994). Imitation and action in autism: A critical review. Psychological Bulletin, 116(2), 259–273.

Snow, M. E., Hertzig, M. E., & Shapiro, T. (1987). Expression of emotion in young autistic children. *Journal of the American Academy of Child and Adolescent Psychiatry, 26*(6), 836–838.

Sparrow, S., Balla, D., & Cicchetti, D. (1984). *Vineland Adaptive Behavior Scales. Circle Pines,* Minnesota: American Guidance Service.

Spiker, D., Lotspeich, L. J., Dimiceli, S., Myers, R. M., & Risch, N. (2002). Behavioral phenotypic variation in autism multiplex families: Evidence for a continuous severity gradient. *American Journal of Medical Genetics, 114*(2), 129–136.

Spitz, R. (1965). *The first year of life.* New York: International Universities Press.

Stern, D. (1987). *The interpersonal world of the human infant.* New York: Basic Books.

Stone, W. L., & Caro-Martinez, L. (1990). Naturalistic observations of spontaneous communication in autistic children. *Journal of Autism and Developmental Disorders, 20,* 437–454.

Stone, W. L., Hoffman, E. L., Lewis, S. E., & Ousley, O. Y. (1994). Early recognition of autism: Parental reports vs. clinical observation. *Archives of Pediatrics and Adolescent Medicine, 148*(2), 174–179.

Stone, W. L., & Lemanek, K. L. (1990). Parental report of social behaviors in autistic preschoolers. *Journal of Autism and Developmental Disorders, 20*(4), 513–522.

Stone, W. L., Lemanek, K. L., Fishel, P. T., Fermandez, M. C., & Altemeier, W. A. (1990). Play and imitation skills in the diagnosis of autism in young children. *Pediatrics, 86,* 267–272.

Stone, W. L., Ousley, O. Y., Hepburn, S. L., Hogan, K. L., & Brown, C. S. (1999). Patterns of adaptive behavior in very young children with autism. *American Journal of Mental Retardation, 104*(2), 187–199.

Stone, W. L., Ousley, O. Y., & Littleford, C. (1995, March). *A comparison of elicited imitation in young children with autism and developmental delay.* Poster session presented at the annual Gatlinburg Conference on Research and Theory in Mental Retardation and Developmental Disabilities.

Stone, W. L., Ousley, O. Y., & Littleford, C. D. (1997). Motor imitation in young children with autism: What's the object? *Journal of Abnormal Child Psychology, 25,* 475–485.

Stone, W. L., & Rosenbaum, J. L. (1988). A comparison of teacher and parent views of autism. *Journal of Autism and Developmental Disorders, 18,* 403–414.

Szatmari, P., Bryson, S. E., Streiner, D. L., Wilson, F., Archer, L., & Ryerse C. (2000). Two-year outcome of preschool children with autism or

Asperger's syndrome. *American Journal of Psychiatry, 157*(12), 1980–1987.

Terpstra, J. E., Higgins, K., & Pierce, T. (2002). Can I play? Classroom-based interventions for teaching play skills to children with autism. *Focus on Autism and Other Developmental Disabilities, 17.*

Teunisse, J.-P., & de Gelder, B. (1994). Do autistics have a generalized face processing deficit? *International Journal of Neuroscience, 77*(1–2), 1–10.

Thompson, R. A. (1996). Attachment theory and research. In M. Lewis (Ed.), *Child and adolescent psychiatry: A comprehensive textbook* (2nd ed., pp. 126–133). Baltimore: Williams & Wilkins.

Tomasello, M., Kruger, A., & Ratner, H. H. (1993). *Cultural learning. Behavioral and Brain Sciences, 16,* 495–552.

Trevarthen, C., & Aitken, K. J. (2001). Infant intersubjectivity: Research, theory, and clinical applications. *Journal of Child Psychology, Psychiatry and Allied Disciplines, 42*(1), 3–48.

Volkmar, F. R. (1987a). Diagnostic issues in the pervasive developmental disorders. *Journal of Child Psychology and Psychiatry, 28*(3), 365–369.

Volkmar, F. R. (1987b). Social development. In D. Cohen & A. Donnellan (Eds.), *Handbook of autism and pervasive developmental disorders* (p. 4160). New York: Wiley.

Volkmar, F. R., Carter, A., Sparrow, S. S., & Cicchetti, D. V. (1993). Quantifying social development in autism. *Journal of Child and Adolescent Psychiatry, 32,* 627–632.

Volkmar, F. R., & Cohen, D. J. (1985). A first person account of the experience of infantile autism by Tony W. *Journal of Autism and Developmental Disorders, 15,* 47–54.

Volkmar, F. R., Cohen, D. J., & Paul, R. (1986). An evaluation of DSM-III criteria for infantile autism. *Journal of the American Academy of Child Psychiatry, 25,* 190–197.

Volkmar, F. R., Klin, A., Schultz, R., Chawarska, K., & Jones, W. (2003). The social brain in autism. In M. Brune, H. Ribbert, & Wulf Schienfenhovel (Eds.), *The social brain: Evolution and pathology* (pp. 167–196). New York: Wiley.

Volkmar, F. R., Klin, A., Siegel, B., Szatmari, P., Lord, C., Campbell, M., et al. (1994). Field trial for autistic disorder in DSM-IV. *American Journal of Psychiatry, 151*(9), 1361–1367.

Volkmar, F. R., Lord, C., Bailey, A., Schultz, R. T., & Klin, A. J. (2004). Autism and Pervasive Developmental Disorders. *Journal of Child Psychology and Psychiatry, 45*(1), 135–170.

Volkmar, F. R., & Mayes, L. C. (1990). Gaze behavior in autism. *Developmental Psychopathology, 2,* 61–70.

Volkmar, F. R., Sparrow, S. A., Goudreau, D., Cicchetti, D. V., Paul, R., & Cohen, D. J. (1987). Social deficits in autism: An operational approach using the Vineland Adaptive Behavior Scales. *Journal of the American Academy of Child and Adolescent Psychiatry, 26,* 156–161.

Volkmar, F. R., Sparrow, S. S., Rende, R. D., & Cohen, D. J. (1989). Facial perception in autism. *Journal of Child Psychology and Psychiatry and Allied Disciplines, 30*(4), 591–598.

Werner, H., & Kaplan, B. (1963). *Symbol formation.* New York: Wiley.

Wetherby, A. M., Prizant, B. M., & Hutchinson, T. (1998). Communicative, social-affective, and symbolic profiles of young children with autism and pervasive developmental disorder. *American Journal of Speech-Language Pathology, 7,* 79–91.

Wing, L. (1976) *Early childhood autism.* New York: Pergamon Press.

Wing, L., & Gould, J. (1979). Severe impairments of social interaction and associated abnormalities in children: Epidemiology and classification. *Journal of Autism and Developmental Disorders, 9,* 11–29.

Wing, L., Gould, J., Yeates, S. R., & Brierley, L. M. (1977). Symbolic play in severely mentally retarded and in autistic children. *Journal of Child Psychology and Psychiatry, 18*(2), 167–178.

World Health Organization. (1993). *International Classification of Diseases* (ICD-10, 10th edition). Diagnostic Criteria for Research. Geneva, Switzerland: WHO.

Yirmiya, N., Kasari, C., Sigman, M., & Mundy, P. (1989). Facial expressions of affect in autistic, mentally retarded, and normal children. *Journal of Child Psychology and Psychiatry, 30,* 725–735.

CHAPTER 12

Language and Communication in Autism

HELEN TAGER-FLUSBERG, RHEA PAUL, AND CATHERINE LORD

Knowledge about human communication is central to theory and clinical practice in the field of autism. Milestones in language and communication play major roles at almost every point in development in understanding autism. Most parents of autistic children first begin to be concerned that something is not quite right in their child's development because of early delays or regressions in the development of speech (Short & Schopler, 1988). Functional language use by school age has been shown to be related to better long-term outcomes in autism (DeMyer et al., 1973; Paul & Cohen, 1984a). Fluency and flexibility of expressive language are dimensions underlying the distinction between "high-functioning" and "low functioning" autism in school age or adolescence. A history of language delay can be particularly crucial in differentiating autism from other psychiatric disorders in high-functioning adults (Lord & Venter, 1992).

Even though autism is often first recognized because of slow or unusual patterns of speech development, many early aspects of the language deficit associated with it overlap with other disorders (Beitchman & Inglis, 1991; Bishop & Adams, 1989). Thus, though skill in language is important to the functioning of people with autism, delays in expressive language in the early preschool years are not specific to autism (Cantwell, Baker, & Mattison, 1980). When there is a good description of a child's early social history and use of objects, the diagnosis of autism can often be made without reference to language delay at all (Cohen, Sudhalter, Landon-Jimenez, & Keogh, 1993; Lord, Storoschuk, Rutter, & Pickles, 1993; Siegel, Vukicevic, Elliott, & Kraemer, 1989). Although expressive language level at age 5 was an important discriminator of higher versus lower functioning older children and adults with autism (Rutter, 1970), simple characterization of language history did not add predictive power for outcome within a high-functioning group of adults (Howlin, Goode, Hutton, & Rutter, 2004). Asperger syndrome (AS) is an autism spectrum disorder (ASD) characterized by lack of general delays in language and cognition but by marked social deficits. Its existence suggests that, even though abnormalities in communication are a core feature of pervasive developmental disorders, slower language acquisition is not necessary or sufficient for a diagnosis within the spectrum of disorders associated with autism.

In addition, evidence from numerous sources suggests that the social and linguistic environments of autistic children, most of whom have active, loving, and determined parents and teachers, can be quite different from those of other children. Thus, initial deficits in language acquisition and in social or cognitive factors affecting language may be compounded by experiential differences (Konstantareas, Zajdemann, Homatidis, & McCabe, 1988; Siller & Sigman, 2002). The root of this difference is thought to be the limited nature of the social and linguistic opportunities that these youngsters provide to others (Doussard-Roosevelt, Joe, Bazhenova, & Porges, 2003; Lord, Merrin, Vest, & Kelly, 1983).

The history of autism has included waxing and waning of interest in language and communication, from interpreting language abnormalities as secondary to deficits in social-emotional functioning (Kanner, 1943), to the view that autism impairments are the result of primary linguistic disorder (Rutter, 1970), to an exclusive focus on pragmatic impairments (Baltaxe, 1977), to interest in using language to study other behaviors, particularly higher order cognitive abilities, such as theory of mind (Baron-Cohen, 1993). It is now recognized that language in autism is extremely variable and that there are likely to be subgroups of individuals within the autism spectrum that have distinct language profiles, some of which are similar to those found in other developmental language disorders.

Tager-Flusberg and Joseph (2003) identified two language phenotypes among verbal children with autism: children with normal linguistic abilities (phonological skills, vocabulary, syntax, and morphology) and children with autism and impaired language that is similar to the phenotype found in specific language impairment. There may also be other subgroups on the autism spectrum that reflect different kinds of language disorder. For example, a significant number of children with autism never acquire speech. It is unlikely that all these children remain mute for the same reason, especially since recent reports suggest that the proportion of nonspeakers within the autistic population is decreasing as early intervention becomes more prevalent (Goldstein, 2002). One potential subgroup within nonspeakers, for instance, may experience *verbal apraxia* or *apraxia of speech,* a neuromotor deficit that affects the ability to produce speech sounds, sound sequences, and prosodic features (Darley, Aronson, & Brown, 1975). If this subgroup exists, however, it is likely to account for a small minority of nonspeakers with ASD (Rogers, 2004). Since little is known about language capacities in nonspeaking children with autism, due to a dearth of communication research on these children without functional language, the causes of failure to acquire speech are primarily speculation at this time. Nonetheless, it is likely that subgroups

exist within both the speaking and nonspeaking autistic populations.

THE STUDY OF LANGUAGE DEVELOPMENT IN TYPICAL POPULATIONS

In order to provide a context in which we can evaluate the impairments in language and communication that characterize autism spectrum disorders, we begin with a brief overview of language acquisition in typically developing children.

Early Communicative Intent

Parents often recognize the absence of early communication in their young children with autism sometime during the second year, when the majority of children the same age begin to have established vocabularies of numerous words (Short & Schopler, 1988). However, nonhandicapped infants show communicative behaviors even from the first weeks and months of life, including recognizing their mothers' voice, synchronizing their patterns of eye gaze, movements, facial expressions of affect, as well as vocal turn taking (Fernald, 1992).

Infants typically exhibit a variety of communicative behaviors by the end of their first year that, to a knowing observer, are not usually seen in autism. These nonverbal communication patterns have been found to express the same intentions for which words will be used in the coming months, such as requesting objects, rejecting offered actions, calling attention to objects or events, and commenting on their appearance (Bates, 1976; Carpenter, Nagell, & Tomasello, 1998). These intents are expressed first with simple gestures, such as reaching to indicate a request or pushing away to indicate rejection, then by more complex gestures, such as pointing to request or shaking the head to mean "no," and then gradually accompanied by and, in some cases, replaced by vocalization and speech (Acredolo & Goodwyn, 1988; Adamson & Bakeman, 1991; Bloom, 1993).

Another achievement that normally occurs toward the end of the first year is the beginning of the understanding of words. At first, a few words associated with games such as pat-a-cake or so big will be recognized. Infants gradually become more active responders to these routines (Bruner, 1975). By 12 months, merely saying the words ("Let's play pat-a-cake!" or "Show me your nose") in a familiar context will often elicit a spontaneous action, such as clapping or touching the nose, from the child.

First Words

Conventional use of language begins around 12 months (see Table 12.1), when toddlers usually say their first recognizable words. At this age, children also show clear evidence of understanding some words or even simple phrases, responding appropriately to specific words outside the context of routine games (Huttenlocher, 1974; Tomasello & Kruger, 1992). During the 12- to 18-month period, there is a gradual increase in both receptive and expressive vocabulary. The words children learn in this period name objects and people, usually those on which the child acts (e.g., daddy, mommy, cookie, ball) and describe relationships among objects (e.g., "all gone," "more"; Fenson et al., 1994). Children also learn social words to be used in rituals such as greetings. Much like early gestures, first words are often used to express ideas, such as appearance ("Uh-oh"), disappearance ("All gone"), and recurrence ("More"), related to the child's developing notions of object permanence (Bloom & Lahey, 1978; Gopnik & Meltzoff, 1987).

By the age of 18 months, expressive vocabulary size reaches an average of about 50 to 100 words (Fenson et al., 1994; Nelson, 1973), and the "word explosion" begins. This period may be punctuated by many requests from children for adults to label things in the world around them, and words are now learned very quickly, often after only a single exposure without any explicit instruction. This stage marks an important turning point as children are no longer learning via association; instead, they understand the referential nature of words (Nazzi & Bertoninci, 2003) and are able now to use words to get new information about the world (Halliday, 1975). By 16 to 19 months, infants are able to use nonverbal cues, such as an adult's eye gaze, to make fine distinctions between an object that an adult is naming and another object

that happens to be present (Baldwin, 1991), suggesting that they can now understand the intentions of others within language contexts. Similar findings for learning words to describe actions have been reported for 2-year-olds (Tomasello & Kruger, 1992).

Prior to age 2, most children begin combining words to form two-word "telegraphic" sentences (Brown, 1973), encoding a small set of meanings. Children talk about objects by naming them and by discussing their locations or attributes, who owns them, and who is doing things to them. They also talk about other people, their actions, their locations, their own actions on objects, and so forth. Objects, people, actions, and their interrelationships preoccupy the young typically developing child. Thus, early language development, from gestures to single words to beginning sentences, is in many ways a remarkably organized process that reflects both how young children think about the world (e.g., recognition of the coming and going of things and people) and what is important to them (e.g., things that they can act on, interesting events such as going outside or wiping up a spill). Individual differences exist among typically developing children, but language acquisition is not a random process. There are generally clear links between forms (i.e., gesture, words, syntax) and functions (e.g., why the child is trying to communicate) over time.

Toddlers often appear to understand everything they hear; however, studies of early language comprehension in highly structured settings have suggested that young children do not understand many more words than they are able to say (Bloom, 1974). When parents are asked to report the kinds of words and instructions that their young children are able to understand, they typically give much higher estimates than is observed during formal testing. Using a standard questionnaire (Fenson et al., 1994), parents estimated that their 8-month-olds understood an average of 6 phrases and about 20 words, increasing to an average of 23 phrases and 169 words by 16 months. Comprehension in ordinary situations may be achieved by a variety of nonlinguistic strategies that allow children to respond to what their parents say, when in fact they are responding to what their parents do or what they know about the way things usually happen

TABLE 12.1 A Summary of Milestones in Typical Language Development

	12 to 15 months	18 months	24 to 36 months	3 to 4 years	4 to 7 years
Semantics	Average expressive vocabulary size at 15 months: 10 words Average receptive vocabulary size at 15 months: 50 words Comprehension strategies include attending to objects named, and doing what is usually done	Average expressive vocabulary size at 18 months: 100 words (±105) Average receptive vocabulary size at 18 months: 300 words Comprehension strategies include acting on objects in the way mentioned, interpreting sentences as requests for child action	Average expressive vocabulary size at 24 months: 300 words (±75) Average receptive vocabulary size at 24 months: 900 words Comprehension strategies include interpreting sentences according to knowledge of probable events	Average expressive vocabulary size at 3 years: 900 words Comprehension strategies include supplying most probable information in answer to difficult questions	Average expressive vocabulary size at 6 years: 2,500 words Average receptive vocabulary size at 6 years: 8,000 words Comprehension strategies include overreliance on word order to process sentences that use unusual word order, such as passives
Syntax	First productions are single-word *holophrases*; one word carries the force of a whole sentence	Average age of first word combinations: 18 months (normal range: 14 to 24 months) First word combinations express basic semantic relations with consistent word order	Average MLU at 24 months: 1.92 (±0.5) Average MLU at 30 months: 2.54 (±0.6) Average MLU at 36 months: 3.16 (±0.7)	Average MLU at 4 years: 4.4 (±0.9) Grammatical morphemes become more consistent Mature forms of negatives and questions develop	Average MLU at 5 years: 5.6 (±1.2) Use of complex sentences increases from less than 10% to more than 20% of all utterances
Phonology	Most productions have CV or CVCV (consonant vowel/consonant vowel consonant vowel combinations, e.g., "ba" or "mama") form Front stops and nasals are most frequent consonants	Back stops, fricatives, and glides are added to the consonant inventory CVC syllable shapes begin to be used 50% of consonants are produced correctly	9 to 10 different consonants are used in initial position; 5 to 6 in final; stops at all places of articulation are used; liquids appear Two-syllable words and initial consonant clusters are used by a majority of children 70% of consonants are correct; speech is 50% intelligible	Most sounds are produced correctly Consonant blends are used Some phonological simplification processes may persist Speech is nearly 100% intelligible	Almost all sounds are produced correctly Phonological processes are no longer used; a few distortions on difficult sounds (/s/, /l/, /r/) may persist Phonological analysis skills are learned for reading and spelling

Pragmatics	Average rate of communications: 1 per minute Requests and comments are used; communication is accomplished by combining gestures with speechlike vocalizations	Average rate of communications: 2 per minute Requests and comments are used; words predominate; gestural/vocal communication decreases	Average rate of communications: 5 per minute Requests and comments are used; children begin to ask questions and convey new information; word combinations predominate	Talk about past and future events increases More options for politeness are acquired New communicative functions (projecting, narrating, imagining, etc.) are expressed	Language is used to predict, reason, negotiate
Play	Conventional, functional play	Symbolic play using self as actor	Pretend play involving others and using multiple schemes	Sequences of events are played out (preparing food, setting table, eating) Child engages in dialogues, talking for all characters	Fantasy themes are played out Child or doll can take multiple roles Elaboration of planning and narrative story lines included in play

MLU = mean length of utterance
CV = consonant vowel
CVCV = consonant vowel consonant vowel

(Chapman, 1978). Such strategies include a child looking at whatever his or her parent is looking at ("See the balloon!"), doing whatever is usually done in this situation ("Brush your hair"), and interpreting sentences as a request for the child to do something. Few parents truly test their children's language comprehension by asking them to do things completely out of context (e.g., asking a child to go get Mommy's keys from the bedroom during a family meal).

The period of 18 to 24 months is also a time of important developments in conversational ability. Children now begin to understand the "conversational obligation" to answer speech with speech (Chapman, 1981). They reliably ask *and* answer routine questions ("Where's the doggy?" "What's this?" "What does the cow say?") and can now genuinely take their own part in a back-and-forth linguistic exchange.

The Acquisition of Linguistic Structures

The preschool period (from 2 to 5 years) is the time during which the child's language evolves from simple telegraphic utterances to fully grammatical forms. In addition to rapidly acquiring new vocabulary, the child goes through a process of approximating more and more closely the grammar of the language spoken in the home. There is evidence of the child's active role as a hypothesis-generator in the frequent occurrence of overgeneralized forms, such as "goed," "comed," and "mouses" (Cazden, 1968; Pinker, 1999). These errors are taken as evidence that the child is indeed acquiring a rule-governed system, rather than learning these inflections by imitation or on a word-by-word basis.

As the child's grammar becomes more complex, sentence length increases (Brown, 1973; Loban, 1976; Miller & Chapman, 1981), and children begin to use a variety of sentence forms including statements, negation, and questions. As structures in simple sentences approach the adult model, complex sentences using embedded clauses ("Whoever wins can go first") and conjoined clauses ("Then it broke and we didn't have it any more") emerge (Paul, Chapman, & Wanska, 1980). The abilities to encode ideas grammatically ("Daddy's shoe" versus "Daddy shoe") and to relate

ideas within one utterance ("I'll go get it if you give me a bite of your candy") free the child's language from dependence on nonlinguistic contexts for interpretation. Whereas an adult had to use knowledge of the child and the situation to interpret "Daddy shoe" (The shoe that belongs to Daddy? Daddy put on the shoe?), the morphologically marked "Daddy's shoe" is unambiguous and interpretable by anyone.

In addition to changing their use of grammatical form, children between 3 and 5 years of age also change the ideas that they express in their sentences. Earlier utterances generally described actions and objects that were immediately present. During later preschool years, sentence content expands to allow for reference to events that are remote in time and space. Children begin to use their language in more diverse ways (Dore, 1978) to include imaginative, nonliteral, interpretive, and logical functions.

At this time, a variety of more advanced conversational and other discourse skills also emerge and become refined. Children increase their ability to maintain and add new information to the conversational topic, to clarify and request clarification of misunderstood utterances, to make their requests or comments using polite or indirect forms, and to choose the appropriate speech style on the basis of the speaker's role and the listener's status (Bates, 1976). Children also begin to engage in different types of discourse including storytelling, recounting events, and personal narratives, all of which follow cultural conventions for these diverse genres of linguistic reporting.

The Elaboration of Language

Although children have acquired most of the sentence structure of their language by age 5, syntactic development continues into the school years as children learn devices for elaborating their utterances, expressing coreference relations using pronouns (e.g., "When Mom wakes up, she'll help me dress"), and condensing more information into each sentence by increasing the proportion of dependent clauses (Loban, 1976). Children also gradually learn to use and to comprehend the more complex, optional sentence types in their language, such as passives

("The boy was hit by the car"; Lempert, 1978). They learn to use syntactic cues not only to decode semantic relations within sentences but also to identify the connections between sentence elements and those given previously in the discourse (Paul, 1985). Semantic and conversational abilities continue to develop during the school years. Vocabulary size is still increasing, and new words are now being learned from reading as well as from conversation. School-age children gradually acquire the ability to communicate with precision, to take the listener's viewpoint into account in formulating an utterance (Asher, 1978), and to tell more complex, well-structured narratives.

Issues from the Study of Language Development in Typical Children

Several issues arise in determining how to fit the different patterns of language development seen in autism into models of normal language acquisition. One source of confusion to parents and professionals is the question of consistency. Both children with autism and, on occasion, typically developing children may use a new word for a few days but then fail to continue to use this word in appropriate contexts. Are these "real" words? Does the child have them stored somewhere in the brain to be used if sufficiently motivated? Two questions arise: (1) How do we set standards for what is a reasonable level of consistency? (2) How broad do the contexts have to be in which we can reliably expect a behavior? For example, we might expect a 10-month-old to understand "bubbles" only in the bathtub, but by 18 months, the child should be able to say and understand the same word in a variety of different situations. The development of these sorts of standards may be particularly helpful for parents and primary care professionals trying to evaluate the seriousness of a possible communication delay in a very young child.

Another source of confusion is that if a person does not have a reasonable level of knowledge about the breadth and depth of typical language development, it is fairly easy to fail to notice its absence in autism. For example, a child who occasionally says five words but does so without clear communicative intent is very different from another child who also has only five different words but uses them to express a range of different meanings (as described earlier) marked in a number of different ways (gesture, words, simple syntax, intonation) throughout each day. There is variability within the normal range in the development of expressive language (Rutter & Lord, 1987) though, on close inspection, individual differences within the normal range do not resemble the kinds of patterns of communication delay seen in autism. It is important that recognition of individual differences does not lead to underestimating communication delays usually seen in autism.

COMMUNICATION AND DEVELOPMENT IN AUTISM

In this section, we explore the unique characteristics of the development of language in children with autism, in comparison to typical development, and the corresponding implications for language research.

Course and Developmental Change

As noted earlier, there is enormous variation in the timing and patterns of acquisition of language among children with autism. A minority of children, usually diagnosed with AS, do not show any significant delays in the onset of language milestones. In contrast, most individuals with autism begin to speak late and develop speech at a significantly slower rate than typically developing children (Le Couteur, Bailey, Rutter, & Gottesman, 1989). Because autism is not usually diagnosed until age 3 or 4, there is relatively little information about language in very young children with autism. Various retrospective studies using parent report and videotapes collected during infancy and the toddler years suggest that by the second year of life, the communication of most children with autism is different from other children (Dahlgren & Gillberg, 1989). Several studies have found that, as early as 1 year of age, very young children with autism are less responsive to their names or to someone speaking compared to other children (Lord, 1995; Osterling & Dawson, 1994), and they are less responsive to the sound of their mother's voice (Klin, 1991). In one study (Lord, Pickles, DiLavore,

& Shulman, 1996), 2-year-old children judged very likely to have autism had mean expressive and receptive language ages of less than 9 months, in contrast to other skills falling between 16 and 21 months. Not only was their language severely delayed at 2, but also their expressive skills continued to develop at a slower rate through age 5 compared to nonautistic children with developmental delays at similar nonverbal levels.

About 25% of children with autism are described by their parents as having some words at 12 or 18 months and then losing them (Kurita, 1985). A recent large-scale systematic longitudinal study of toddlers by Lord, Shulman, and DiLavore (2004) found that this kind of "language regression" after a pattern of normal language onset was unique to autism and not found among children with other developmental delays. Generally, the regression is a gradual process in which the children do not learn new words and fail to engage in communicative routines in which they may have participated before. Language loss occurred in these children when they still had relatively small expressive vocabularies and before the word explosion. Lord and her colleagues found that children who experienced loss of words also lost some social skills, supporting the findings from Goldberg and her colleagues (Goldberg et al., 2003), and that similar losses of social skills occurred in a smaller group of children with autism who had not yet used words at the time of loss (Luyster et al., in press). This phenomenon is quite different from the regression that is associated with disintegrative disorder (see Chapter 4, this volume), which typically occurs at a later time and involves loss of advanced linguistic skills and communication to no speech. Though the skills children with autism may have had before the regression are often minimal, it is still confusing and heartbreaking for parents to watch their children lose any component of communicative skill, fleeting though it may have been. Studies have demonstrated only a minimal relationship between language regression in autism and later prognosis or outcome, with children who had regressions having, on average, slightly lower verbal IQ scores at school age than children with no history of loss (Richler et al., in press).

To gauge the developmental timing of language milestones for children with autism, we are generally dependent on parental report. Most diagnostic interviews, such as the Autism Diagnostic Interview-Revised (ADI-R; Rutter, Le Couteur, & Lord, 2003), include questions about the age of first words and phrases. (See Lord et al., 2004, for examples of regression questions from a modified ADI for toddlers.) Lord and her colleagues have found that repeated administrations of the ADI-R revealed that the ages that parents reported these language milestones increased with the age of the child at the time of the interview (Lord, Risi, & Pickles, 2004; Taylor, 2004). This systematic "telescoping" means that parents of older children with autism are more likely to recall their children's language as being even more delayed than they did when their children were younger.

Both within and across categories of children with ASDs, there is significant variability in the rate at which language progresses among those children who do acquire some functional language (Lord et al., 2004). In the preschool period and beyond, certain nonverbal skills, especially the frequency of initiating joint attention, and imitation, are strong predictors of language acquisition for children with autism (Charman et al., 2003; Rogers, Hepburn, Stackhouse, & Wehner, 2003; Sigman & Ruskin, 1999). There is also a significant correlation between IQ and language outcomes, although higher levels of nonverbal IQ are not always associated with higher level language skills (Howlin, Goode, Hutton, & Rutter, 2004; Kjelgaard & Tager-Flusberg, 2001). Although few longitudinal studies of language acquisition among verbal children with autism have been conducted, the research suggests that during the preschool years, progress within each domain of language (e.g., vocabulary, syntax) follows similar pathways as has been found for typically developing children (e.g., Tager-Flusberg & Calkins, 1990). Individuals with autism continue to make progress in language and related developmental domains well beyond the preschool years. Paul, Cohen, and Caparulo (1983), in a longitudinal study of children with aphasic and autistic disorders, showed that comprehension ability at early ages was related to degree of improvement in social relations in late adolescence and early adulthood. Paul and Cohen (1984a) suggested that both comprehension and expressive abilities continue to improve in these populations through adolescence and adulthood, although expressive skills show greater rates of improvement. This pattern may occur because speech is more accessible than comprehension and is more often a direct target of remedial efforts. In another series of follow-up studies in Britain, almost all of the participants with autism or developmental language disorders showed substantial improvements in formal aspects of language into adulthood (Cantwell & Baker, 1989). However, the group with autism, who had serious receptive language deficits in early childhood, remained more severely language delayed as a whole (Rutter, Mawhood, & Howlin, 1992). They had more severe behavioral limitations compared to the nonautistic language-disordered group, who had a much broader range of outcome, from total independence and good language skill to severe psychiatric disorder and continued expressive language problems.

Some children with autism never acquire functional language; many of these children have very low nonverbal IQ scores. Epidemiological studies indicate that about half the population remains nonverbal by middle childhood (Bryson, Clark, & Smith, 1988); however, recent longitudinal studies of children referred for possible autism at early ages have suggested that the proportion of children with ASD who do not use words to speak is less than 20% (Lord et al., 2004). Such a statistic is clearly affected by variation in who is studied: What age are the participants with autism? Are they recruited from special education services or clinics or from broader populations? What about the effect of education and treatment? The statistic is also affected by how useful speech is defined: Are single words enough? Simple sentences? How spontaneous do they have to be? How often do they have to be used? How intelligible must they be?

There is some optimism that with more children receiving earlier diagnoses and thus better access to early intensive interventions, especially for language and communication skills, the proportion of children with autism who fail to acquire functional language is diminishing. Nevertheless, as the prevalence

rates for ASDs increase, it is not easy to disentangle improvements in language skills across the autism spectrum from an increase in the diagnosis among higher functioning, more verbal individuals.

Articulation

Among children with autism who speak, articulation is often normal or even precocious (Kjelgaard & Tager-Flusberg, 2001; Pierce & Bartolucci, 1977). However, Bartak and colleagues (Bartak, Rutter, & Cox, 1975) found articulation development to be somewhat slower than normal. These delays were more transient in a group of high-functioning boys with autism than in language-level-matched nonautistic boys with severe receptive-expressive delays in middle childhood (Rutter et al., 1992) and may be the result of later onset of language milestones. Still, Shriberg et al. (2001) reported that one-third of speakers with high-functioning autism (HFA) and with AS retained residual speech distortion errors on sounds such as /r/, /l/, and /s/ into adulthood, whereas the rate of these errors in the general population is 1%.

Bartolucci, Pierce, Streiner, and Tolkin-Eppel (1976) showed that phoneme frequency distribution and the distribution of phonological error types in a small group of children with autism was similar to that of mentally handicapped and typical children matched for nonverbal mental age. The less frequent the phoneme's use in the language, the greater was the number of errors. Phonological perception among the groups also was similar. These findings indicate that the developmental trajectory for phonological development in autism follows the same path as in other groups of children, although a higher rate of distortion errors is seen in adult speakers.

Two caveats should be noted. First, difficulties in articulation are relatively common in nonautistic children with intellectual handicaps. Thus, the fact that there is no difference between autistic and IQ-matched children with mental handicaps does not mean that no children with autism have articulation difficulties. Second, there are a relatively small number of autistic children who are identified as high functioning on the basis of nonverbal tests during preschool but who have extraordinary difficulties in producing intelligible speech. These children are not likely to be included in many studies of language because they are relatively rare. By the time they are 10 or 12 years old, fluent language often becomes an implicit criteria for the category of "high functioning." Little is known about either the existence or phenomenology of this pattern of development.

Word Use

Word use in autism can be observed by asking two rather different questions: (1) Do children with autism use and understand words as belonging to the same categories as other people? and (2) Is there anything unusual about how individuals with autism use words? The answer to both questions is *yes*. In the first case, studies have shown that verbal children with autism use semantic groupings (e.g., bird, boat, food) in very similar ways to categorize and to retrieve words (Boucher, 1988; Minshew & Goldstein, 1993; Tager-Flusberg, 1985). High-functioning children and adolescents with autism can score well on standardized vocabulary tests, indicating an unusually rich knowledge of words (Fein & Waterhouse, 1979; Jarrold, Boucher, & Russell, 1997; Kjelgaard & Tager-Flusberg, 2001) and an area of relative strength for some individuals with autism. At the same time, Tager-Flusberg (1991) found that children with autism often fail to use their knowledge of words in a normal way to facilitate performance on retrieval or organizational tasks.

At the same time, it appears that certain classes of words may be underrepresented in the vocabularies of children with autism. For example, Tager-Flusberg (1992) found that the children participating in a longitudinal language study used hardly any mental state terms, particularly terms for cognitive states (e.g., *know, think, remember, pretend*). These findings were replicated in research including older children with autism (Storoschuk, Lord, & Jaedicke, 1995; Tager-Flusberg & Sullivan, 1994). Other studies suggest that children with autism have particular difficulties understanding social-emotional terms as measured on vocabulary tests such as the Peabody Picture Vocabulary Test (Eskes, Bryson, & McCormick, 1990; Hobson & Lee, 1989; Van Lancker, Cornelius, &

Needleman, 1991). Thus, while overall lexical knowledge may be a relative strength in autism, the acquisition of words that map onto mental state concepts may be specifically impaired in this disorder.

Abnormal use of words and phrases has been described in autism for many years (Rutter, 1970). In samples of high-functioning adolescents and adults, a significant minority has been shown to use words with special meanings (Rumsey, Rapoport, & Sceery, 1985; Volden & Lord, 1991) or "metaphorical language" use, as Kanner (1946) described this unusual phenomenon. In most cases, these words or phrases were modifications of ordinary word roots or phrases that produced slightly odd sounding, but comprehensible, terms such as "commendment" for praise or "cuts and bluesers" for cuts and bruises. These terms were not radically different from those used occasionally by mentally handicapped or younger, nonhandicapped children matched on expressive language level, except that they were more frequent in the autistic population. Only subjects with autism produced neologisms or odd phrases for which the root was not fairly obvious, though these, too, were relatively rare (Volden & Lord, 1991). Increased language ability was associated with increased (proportions as well as absolute numbers) peculiarities and perseveration in individuals with autism. Conversely, in a nonautistic mentally handicapped group, oddities decreased steadily as expressive language ability improved (Volden & Lord, 1991). Rutter (1987) suggests that these abnormal uses of words may be functionally similar to the kinds of early word meaning errors made by young typically developing children. It is their persistence in autism that defines them as abnormal, and they may reflect the fact that children with autism are not sensitive, because of their social impairments, to the corrective feedback provided by their parents.

Pedantic speech and being overly precise in a rather concrete way are also descriptors frequently used with individuals with HFA or AS (Ghaziuddin, Tsai, & Ghaziuddin, 1992), though these qualities can be very difficult to quantify. Wing (1981) commented on the language of people with AS as having a "bookish" quality exemplified by the use of obscure words. She considered pedantic speech to be one of the main clinical features of this disorder (Burgoine & Wing, 1983). Mayes, Volkmar, Hooks, and Cicchetti (1993) found that the presence of peculiar language patterns was one of the best discriminators of pervasive developmental disorder from language disability.

Syntax and Morphology

Relatively few studies have systematically investigated grammatical aspects of language acquisition in autism. The longitudinal study of six autistic boys conducted by Tager-Flusberg and her colleagues found that these children followed the same developmental path as an age-matched comparison group of children with Down syndrome who were part of the study and to normally developing children drawn from the extant literature (Tager-Flusberg et al., 1990). The children with autism and Down syndrome showed similar growth curves in their Mean Length of Utterance (MLU), which is usually taken as a hallmark measure of grammatical development. At the same time, in a follow-up study using the same language samples, Scarborough, Rescorla, Tager-Flusberg, Fowler, and Sudhalter (1991) compared the relationship between MLU and scores on a different index of grammatical development, which charts the emergence of a wide range of grammatical constructions: the Index of Productive Syntax (IPSyn). The main findings were that at higher MLU levels, MLU tended to significantly overestimate IPSyn scores for the subjects with autism, suggesting that for the children with autism, the relatively limited growth in IPSyn reflects the tendency to make use of a narrower range of constructions and to ask fewer questions, which accounts for a significant portion of the IPSyn score.

Several studies of English-speaking children with autism investigated the acquisition of grammatical morphology, based on data from spontaneous speech samples. Some of these studies must be interpreted with caution as they included very small numbers of children who varied widely in age, mental age, and language ability. Two cross-sectional studies found differences between children with autism and a comparison group of typical chil-

dren or children with mental retardation in the mastery of certain grammatical morphemes (Bartolucci, Pierce, & Streiner, 1980; Howlin, 1984). Bartolucci et al. (1980) found that children with autism were more likely to omit certain morphemes, particularly articles (a, the), auxiliary and copula verbs, past tense, third-person present tense, and present progressive. Tager-Flusberg (1989) also found that children with autism were significantly less likely to mark past tense than were matched controls with Down syndrome. Bartolucci and Albers (1974) compared children with autism to controls in performance on a task designed to elicit production of present progressive -ing and past tense -ed for different verbs. The children with autism performed well on the present progressive form, as did the controls. The children with autism were, however, significantly impaired on the past tense elicitation trials. This finding was replicated in a recent study of over 60 children with autism who were given tasks to elicit both the past tense and the third-person present tense (Roberts, Rice, & Tager-Flusberg, 2004). The sample was divided into those who had scores within the normal range on standardized language tests and those who were significantly below the mean. Only those with impaired language scores performed poorly on the tense tasks. Across these studies, then, marking tense was impaired among children with autism. Roberts et al. (2004) interpret their findings as evidence that a subgroup of children with autism have grammatical deficits that are similar to those reported among children with specific language impairment (cf. Rice, 2004).

Studies of other sentence forms in spontaneous language have generally indicated that children with autism are similar to mental-age-matched youngsters in terms of the acquisition of rule-governed syntactic systems (Bartak et al., 1975; Pierce & Bartolucci, 1977). Children with autism, mental handicap, or developmental language disorders lag in language development relative to nonverbal mental age. It seems very likely that syntactic development in children with autism is more similar than dissimilar to normal development. It often proceeds at a slower pace and is related to developmental level more than to chronological age, although it may not keep pace with other areas of development (Tager-Flusberg, 1981a).

Studies of adults with autism (Paul & Cohen, 1984a) suggest that this development eventually reaches a plateau in at least some individuals with autism. Adults with autism did significantly more poorly on measures of syntactic production in free speech than adults with mental handicap matched for nonverbal IQ. The lags shown by children and adolescents with autism are often more severe than those of other children with comparable delays earlier in childhood. In research, these delays are often less obvious because children with autism who are not delayed on nonverbal tests are generally grouped with children with autism who are more severely delayed. Moreover, it is now clear that among children with autism, there are different subgroups, some of whom have impaired language while others have normal language, as measured on standardized tests (Tager-Flusberg, 2003). The entire autism group is erroneously compared to a more homogeneous control group of nonautistic children with mental handicap (Lord & Pickles, 1996). These concerns highlight the need for more studies that are longitudinal in design, providing follow-up into late adolescence or adulthood, with a focus on individual variation among participants with ASDs.

Echolalia

One of the most salient aspects of deviant speech in autism is the occurrence of echolalia. Echolalia is the repetition, with similar intonation, of words or phrases that someone else has said. It can be immediate; for example, a child repeats back her teacher's greeting, "Hi, Susie," exactly as it was said to her. It can be delayed, as in the case of a child who approaches his father and says, "It's time to tickle you!" as a signal that he wants to be tickled, repeating a phrase he has heard his parents say in the past.

Echolalia was once viewed as an undesirable, nonfunctional behavior (Lovaas, 1977). However, other clinicians, beginning with Fay (1969) and elaborated by Prizant and colleagues (see Chapter 36, this *Handbook,* Volume 2), have emphasized that often echolalia serves specific functions for the child. Prizant and Duchan (1981) highlighted six communicative functions that they found were served by immediate echolalia: turn taking, assertions, affirmative answers, requests, rehearsal to aid processing, and self-regulation. Delayed echoes can be used communicatively to request re-creations of the scenes with which the remarks were originally associated, such as a child saying, "You're okay" in a sympathetic tone of voice if he falls down. They can serve other functions as well. Baltaxe and Simmons (1977) showed that the bedtime soliloquies of an 8-year-old autistic child contained frequent examples of delayed echolalia, which they suggested the child used as a base for analyzing linguistic forms that she was in the process of acquiring, as found among some nonautistic children (Weir, 1962).

Although echolalia is one of the most classic symptoms of autism (Kanner, 1946), not all children with autism echo, nor is echoing seen only in autism. Echoing—particularly immediate repetition—occurs in blind children, in children with other language impairments, in older people with dementia, and, perhaps most importantly, in some normally developing children as well (Yule & Rutter, 1987). McEvoy, Loveland, and Landry (1988) found that immediate echolalia was most frequent in children with autism who had minimal expressive language but was not closely associated with chronological or nonverbal mental age. Shapiro (1977) and Carr, Schreibman, and Lovaas (1975) found that children with autism were most likely to echo immediately questions and commands that they did not understand or for which they did not know the appropriate response.

A substantial minority, but not all, of verbal autistic adolescents and adults are described by their parents as having engaged in delayed echolalia at some point in their development (Le Couteur et al., 1989). Echolalia has been offered as evidence of "gestalt" processing in autism (Frith, 1989). Prizant (1983) proposed that children with autism are especially dependent on the gestalt approach to acquiring language (cf. Peters, 1983) and that this is evident in their reliance on echolalia. Tager-Flusberg and Calkins (1990) investigated whether variations in echolalia were tied to differences in the process by which grammar was acquired in autism, when compared to language-matched groups of typically developing children and young children with Down syndrome. As predicted, the children with autism at the early stages of language development produced the most echolalic and formulaic speech. For all children, echolalia declined rapidly over the course of development. To investigate whether children with autism used echolalia as a means for acquiring new grammatical knowledge, Tager-Flusberg and Calkins compared echolalic and nonecholalic spontaneous speech drawn from the same language sample for length of utterances using MLU and for the complexity of grammatical constructions using IPSyn. If imitation is important in the acquisition of grammatical knowledge, then length and grammatical complexity should be more advanced in echolalic than in spontaneous speech produced at the same developmental point. This hypothesis was not confirmed for any of the children in this study. On the contrary, across all language samples, spontaneous utterances were significantly longer and included more advanced grammatical constructions. These findings suggest that echolalia is not an important process in facilitating grammatical development in autism, though it clearly reflects a different conversational style and plays an important role in children's communication with others, especially when they have very limited linguistic knowledge.

In summary, although immediate and delayed echolalia are salient features of autistic speech, they are neither synonymous with nor unique to this syndrome. Although some echolalia in autism may appear to be nonfunctional or self-stimulatory, both immediate and delayed echolalia can serve communicative purposes for the speaker.

Use of Deictic Terms

Confusion of personal pronouns (e.g., when a child asks for a drink by saying, "Do you want a drink of water?") is another frequently mentioned atypical language behavior associated with autism. As with other aspects of deviant language, pronoun reversal sometimes occurs in children with language disorders other than autism or in blind children (Fraiberg, 1977), and it may even be present briefly in the language of some normally developing children (Chiat, 1982). As with echolalia, pronoun reversal errors may not occur in all children with

autism, but they are more common in individuals with autism than in any other population (Le Couteur et al., 1989; Lee, Hobson, & Chiat, 1994). It is interesting that Tager-Flusberg (1994) found that among small groups of young children with autism, all of them went through a stage of reversing pronouns, though as they got older, the more linguistically advanced children stopped making these errors. The majority of the time, children used pronouns correctly; reversal errors averaged only 13% of all pronouns produced.

Kanner (1943) originally attributed pronoun reversals to echolalia. Some examples, such as the child who says, "Carry you!" seem to reflect this relationship. Other accounts have considered the linguistic or information-processing demands in having to shift and mark reference (Rice et al., 1994). Within autism, difficulty using pronouns is generally viewed as part of a more general difficulty with deixis, the aspect of language that codes shifting reference between the speaker and the listener. For example, in labeling a person by name (e.g., "James"), the label remains the same without regard to who is speaking whereas, for pronouns, whether James is referred to as "I" or "you" depends on whether he is the speaker or the listener during a particular conversation. Deixis is marked not only by pronouns but also in various ways in different languages. In English, these include various determiners (e.g., whether a speaker uses "this" or "that" depending on previous reference or location of an object) or the selection of verbs (e.g., "come" and "go") and verb tense.

Most current interpretations of pronoun errors in autism view them as a reflection of the difficulties that children with autism have in conceptualizing notions of self and other as they are embedded in shifting discourse role between speaker and listener (Lee et al., 1994; Tager-Flusberg, 1993). Their difficulty understanding discourse roles is related to impaired social communicative functioning, specifically conceptual perspective-taking (Loveland, 1984), and may be related to their broader social deficits (see Chapter 12, this volume).

Suprasegmental Aspects of Language

Paralinguistic features such as vocal quality, intonation, and stress patterns are another frequently noted speech characteristic of individuals with ASDs (Rutter et al., 1992). Odd intonation patterns associated with autism seem to be one of the most immediately recognizable clinical signs of the disorder. However, defining what constitutes autism-related paralinguistic abnormalities so that clinicians can make reliable judgments about them has been quite challenging (Lord, Rutter, & Le Couteur, 1994; Lord et al., 2000; Volkmar et al., 1994), in part, perhaps because of the number of different ways in which language can sound unusual.

There are several levels of prosodic function: grammatical, pragmatic, and affective (Merewether & Alpert, 1990). Grammatical prosody includes cues to the type of utterance (e.g., questions end with rising pitch) and different stress patterns used to distinguish different parts of speech (e.g., marking the word *present* with stress on the first syllable if used as a noun). Pragmatic stress may highlight new information or draw the listener's attention to the significance of the message expressed (e.g., "Are *you* the writer of this note?" versus "Are you the writer of this note?"). Affective prosody conveys the speaker's feelings or attitudes and may include variations in vocal tone and speech rate. Failure to use and appreciate intonational cues, then, will likely not only affect the emotional tone of a verbal exchange but also hamper its comprehensibility.

Intonational peculiarities frequently are associated with ASDs. The most frequently cited is monotony (see Fay & Schuler, 1980). These patterns were formerly attributed to emotional states thought to be present (or absent) in autistic individuals and were originally thought to reflect flat affect, the failure to express personality, or repressed anger (see Lord & Rutter, 1994). Fay and Schuler (1980) also describe a subset of autistic individuals who used a singsong rather than flat pattern. Goldfarb, Braunstein, and Lorge (1956) and Pronovost, Wakstein, and Wakstein (1966) found unusually high fundamental frequency levels in autistic speakers. Other voice disorders, such as hoarseness, harshness, and hypernasality, have been identified (Pronovost et al., 1966). Our own clinical observations detected hyponasality in some children with autism. Poor control of volume, with unexplained fluctuations, has also been reported (Pronovost et al., 1966). Fay (1969) reported frequent whispering among children who echo.

Research on AS suggests that these abnormalities in intonation and prosody are even more prevalent for children and adults with AS than for individuals with autism who had acquired language. Eisenmajer and his colleagues (Eisenmajer et al., 1996) compared the clinical behaviors of children with autism and children with AS using in-depth interviews conducted with their parents. The children with AS were more likely to be described by their parents as having an unusual tone of voice such as flat or monotonous quality. The most systematic direct investigation of prosodic features in AS was conducted by Shriberg et al. (2001). They analyzed speech samples collected during a diagnostic interview, the Autism Diagnostic Observation Schedule (ADOS), which was conducted with the adolescent and adult participants with autism or AS. The main findings were that about one-third of the participants with AS had distorted speech and articulation problems, and two-thirds expressed prosodic abnormalities at grammatical, pragmatic, or affective levels. Like Asperger's case studies (Asperger, 1991), quite a number of the study participants had loud, high voices with a nasal tone. Koning and Magill-Evans (2001) investigated whether adolescents with AS were able to use nonverbal cues, including facial expression, body gestures, and prosody, to interpret the feelings of people acting in videotaped scenes. They found that the adolescents with AS were significantly worse than controls in interpreting the emotions and relied least on prosodic information. These findings suggest that people with AS not only are impaired in expressive prosody but also have difficulty comprehending prosodic information expressed by others. The reasons behind these deficits in suprasegmental features remain obscure. Frith (1969) showed that like typically developing children, children with autism recalled stressed words better than unstressed ones, especially when the stress was placed on content words. On the other hand, children with autism seemed less able than typical children to take advantage of stress cues for meaning (see also Baltaxe, 1984). Thurber and Tager-Flusberg (1993) found autistic children produced fewer nongrammatical pauses than controls matched on verbal mental age when telling a story from a wordless picture book. There was no difference in grammatical pauses (i.e., those between phrases). Deviance in intonation seems unlikely to be due solely to simple perceptual or motor deficits. More fundamental aspects of the autistic syndrome reflected in higher level language and communicative behaviors, such as understanding of other persons, related social cognitive deficits, and/or ability to plan and execute a complex action, may contribute to how autistic children learn to use intonation and other paralinguistic features.

There seems no doubt that there is something different about the way in which the stream of sound associated with speech is produced in many persons with autism. Ricks and Wing (1976) carried out one of the first studies in this area. They studied parents' identification of the meaning of the prelinguistic vocalizations of autistic children and found that parents of children with autism were unable to understand the preverbal vocalizations of other children with autism, even though they could understand their own child's messages. In contrast, parents of typically developing children could understand vocalizations of typical children who were not their own, as well as those of their own child. These findings were not replicated in a later study by Elliott (1993).

Historically, autistic children have been described as babbling less frequently than other children during early childhood. However, Elliott (1993) found no difference in the frequency with which preverbal, developmentally delayed 2-year-olds, preverbal typically developing 10- to 12-month-olds, and 2-year-olds with autism produced vocalizations in situations that were intended to engage the children socially (e.g., watching a balloon fly around the room); however, a smaller proportion of the children with autism vocalized than in the comparison groups. Moreover, the vocalizations the children with autism did produce were less likely to be paired with other nonverbal communication, such as shifts in gaze or gesture or changes in facial expression than they were for the other children (Hellreigel, Tao, DiLavore, & Lord, 1995). Sheinkopf and his colleagues conducted a detailed examination of the vocal behavior of young preverbal children with autism and a group of comparison children with developmental delays (Sheinkopf, Mundy, Oller, & Steffens, 2000). Although the children with autism did not have difficulty with the expression of well-formed syllables (i.e., canonical babbling), they did display significant impairments in vocal quality (i.e., atypical phonation). Specifically, autistic children produced a greater proportion of syllables with atypical phonation than did comparison children. The atypicalities in the vocal behavior of children with autism were, however, unrelated to individual differences in joint attention skill, suggesting that a multiple process model may be needed to describe early social-communication impairments in children with autism.

Taken together, these findings suggest that the source of the difference between the vocalizations of the young children with autism and those of other young, nonverbal children was not just in social intent, but also in a more basic aspect of the form of the vocalization beginning very early in development.

Language Comprehension in Autism

Most research on the language of individuals with autism centers on their productive capacities. In contrast, less attention has been focused on their comprehension skills. This is unfortunate because early response to language, a likely precursor to comprehension, is one of the strongest indicators of autism in very young children (Dahlgren & Gillberg, 1989; Lord, 1995). Charman and his colleagues collected data on early language development from a large group of preschool-age children with autism using a parent report measure: the MacArthur Communicative Development Inventory (Charman, Drew, Baird, & Baird, 2003). They found that comprehension of words was delayed relative to production, though, like typically developing children, in absolute terms the children with autism understood more words than they produced. The continuation of significant delays in comprehension is also one of the strongest differentiators of HFA from specific language disorders (Rutter et al., 1992).

Bartak et al. (1975) and Paul and Cohen (1984a) showed that individuals with autism performed more poorly on standardized measures of language comprehension than participants with aphasic or mental handicap at similar nonverbal mental age levels. Studies of very young children (Paul, Chawarska, Klin, & Volkmar, 2004) suggest that comprehension skills are depressed relative to production in the second year of life, while the gap tends to narrow, with receptive skills moving closer to expressive levels, in the third to fourth year. Studies that have compared receptive and expressive language skills among somewhat older children with autism using standardized tests have found that receptive skills as measured by standard scores tend to be comparable to expressive on vocabulary tests as well as tests of higher order language processing (Jarrold et al., 1997; Kjelgaard & Tager-Flusberg, 2001). Yet, there is a clear clinical impression that among verbal children with autism, comprehension is more significantly impaired (Tager-Flusberg, 1981a).

More insight into the mechanisms that underlie the impression of impaired language comprehension in autism comes from experimental studies. Sigman and Ungerer (1981) looked at language comprehension and sensorimotor performance in children with autism with mental ages of about 2 years. They found sophisticated performance on object permanence tasks but poor performance on receptive language measures. They suggested that sensorimotor skills play a small role in the acquisition of language. Play skills, on the other hand, were highly related to receptive language level, particularly those forms of play that were directed outward toward dolls. Thus, the more social aspects of cognition, those involving the imaginary creation of a scene with dolls and interactions between people, appear to be more related to the understanding of language than are those involving knowledge about objects, which can be learned with very little social interaction. Tager-Flusberg (1981b) investigated sentence comprehension using experimental tasks that assessed the use of different strategies. Children with autism performed at the same level as typical controls in their use of a word order strategy for processing sentences (interpreting noun-verb-noun sequences as agent-action-object); however, they were less likely to use a semantically based probable event strategy, interpreting sentences based on

their likelihood of occurring in the real world (e.g., knowing that a mother is more likely to pick up a baby than a baby pick up a mother). Tager-Flusberg (1981b) concluded that children with autism have difficulty applying their knowledge about the probabilities of occurrence of events in the world to the task of understanding sentences.

In a partial replication of this study, Gaddes (1984) showed that children with autism were much less consistent in identifying probable events that involved relationships between people (e.g., the mother feeds the baby) than were very young normally developing children with lower or equivalent expressive abilities. This occurred when the relationships were acted out by dolls, even when no comprehension of language was required. Thus, the difficulties may lie in comprehending the situation and what is probable in it, as well as comprehending the word order that depicts the situation. Paul, Fischer, and Cohen (1988) found that although children with autism used similar strategies in sentence comprehension as other children, they always performed less competently. Together, these findings suggest that children not only may have limited ability to integrate linguistic input with real-world knowledge but also, in some cases, may lack knowledge about social events used by normally developing children to buttress emerging language skills and to acquire increasingly advanced linguistic structures (Lord, 1985).

Another source of difficulty in comprehending language in everyday situations rather than in standardized testing situations may be the ability to integrate nonverbal cues to help interpret linguistic input. Examples include noticing the smile on another's face, the way in which another person touches you, the tone of his or her voice, as well as the words, to determine whether someone is being affectionate, teasing, or being aggressive (Loveland, 1991; Ozonoff, Pennington, & Rogers, 1990; St. James & Tager-Flusberg, 1994).

Paul and Cohen (1985) looked at the ability of matched groups of participants with autism and mental handicap to understand indirect requests for action (e.g., "Can you color this circle blue?") of varying syntactic complexity. The two groups, with IQs in the mildly to moderately retarded range, performed similarly in a context in which the request intent of the utterance was made explicit (e.g., "I'm going to tell you to do some things. Can you . . ."). However, the autism group performed significantly worse when the same requests were presented in an unstructured context with no prefacing cue as to the intention of the utterance. The authors concluded that the individuals with autism are impaired in the ability to determine the speaker's intention without explicit cuing over and above any syntactic comprehension deficit that might be present. This pattern may be an example of why, in their follow-up of HFA individuals, Rutter et al. (1992) found a strong relationship between language comprehension and social functioning in adulthood, with no similar finding for adults identified as having specific receptive and expressive language impairment as children.

For individuals with autism, understanding language in conversational and other discourse contexts remains a significant challenge because semantic and pragmatic aspects of language are so closely linked to nonverbal social communication and other aspects of social adaptation.

Language Use

Language use or the pragmatic aspects of language in autism has been studied from a variety of perspectives. This domain has been the focus of research for the past several decades because problems have been found across all individuals with ASDs. Studies on language use including specific, unusual aspects of language use such as delayed echolalia and neologisms, as well as language used to describe particular phenomena such as mental states or emotions, are discussed elsewhere in the chapter; this section focuses on research on speech acts, referential communication, discourse, and narration.

One of the most interesting characteristics of language use in autism is that it has aspects that are constant across development and aspects that change. As with the development of social behavior (Lord, 1995), some of the changes occur because children improve in their communicative abilities; other changes occur because situational demands for communication are different for children of different ages and for adults and vary with the contexts

in which individuals find themselves. Thus, in considering deficits in language use, factors such as what individuals are expected to do, what they are given the opportunity to do, and what they usually do all must be considered. Stone and Caro-Martinez (1990), in an observational study of the spontaneous communication of children with autism of varying abilities placed in special classrooms, found differences in the functions about which the children communicated. These differences were related to chronological age, nonverbal IQ, and whether the children's primary mode of communication was through speech or motor acts. Children who did not talk engaged in more social routines than verbal children. Children with speech were more likely to use language to offer new information. They communicated to a greater number of different people (rather than just the teacher) and were more likely to address communications to peers as well as adults than children without speech. McHale, Simeonsson, Marcus, and Olley (1980) showed that autistic students communicated more in the presence of their teachers than in their absence and directed their communication only to adults, not to peers.

Across different language levels, children with autism also share important similarities. Despite deficits in spontaneous speech, most children on the autism spectrum do attempt to use their language to communicate even if only in limited ways. Bernard-Opitz (1982) showed that communicative performance of one child with autism varied with different interlocutors and in different settings, indicating some social awareness in his use of language. However, rate of initiation of spontaneous communications in autism is often described as very low. In the study by Stone and Caro-Martinez (1990), the modal frequency in school was two or three spontaneous communicative acts per child per hour. Only half of the children ever directed a communication to a peer across multiple observations. Several other investigators have shown autistic children to have less frequent and less varied speech acts in free play or more open-ended situations, even when their responses to highly structured situations were similar to those of control groups (Landry & Loveland, 1989; Mermelstein, 1983; Wetherby & Prutting, 1984). General studies of younger children with autism find that they rarely use language for comments, showing off, acknowledging the listener, initiating social interaction, or requesting information. Even among older higher functioning children, language is rarely used to explain or describe events in a conversational context (Ziatas, Durkin, & Pratt, 2003). The speech acts that are missing or rarely used in the conversations of children with autism all have in common an emphasis on social rather than regulatory uses of language (Wetherby, 1986). There are also similarities in abnormalities in language use across verbal individuals with autism who show a range of expressive language abilities. Difficulties in listening, talking to self, problems in following rules of politeness, and making irrelevant remarks occur in many children and adults with autism (Baltaxe, 1977; Rumsey, Rapoport, & Sceery, 1985).

Difficulties in social uses of language, especially in conversations and other discourse contexts, have also been widely noted for people with both HFA and AS by clinicians and researchers (e.g., Klin & Volkmar, 1997; see Landa, 2000, for review). Chuba, Paul, Miles, Klin, and Volkmar (2003) reported on conversational behaviors in 30 adolescents with either HFA or AS who were engaged in semistructured conversational interviews with clinicians. Findings revealed that for both diagnoses, conversational errors were *inconsistent,* rather than constant. Nonetheless, it was possible to distinguish teenagers with ASD from those with typical development (TD) in terms of the quantity of conversational errors. No TD subject made more than five errors within a 30-minute sample, whereas all subjects with HFA and AS made more than eight errors. The most robust differences observed were in the areas of gaze and intonation, while remaining differences centered on ability to share topics and infer others' informational state. Similarly, Paul and Feldman (1984) reported in a case series presentation that highly verbal adolescents and adults with autism showed difficulties in identifying the topic initiated by the conversational partner and in providing a relevant comment. They had difficulty judging, on the basis of cues in the conversation and on the basis of general knowledge about what listeners could reasonably be expected already to have in their knowledge store, how much information was

the right amount to include in an utterance (Lord et al., 1989). For example, when asked the question, "Did you and your sister do anything besides rake leaves over the weekend?" a participant responded, "Yes." This answer, although correct in a strictly syntactic sense, fails to appreciate the listener's real purpose in asking the question. It fails to provide the socially appropriate amount of information in response. On the other hand, another adolescent with autism, when asked how his day had gone, began the account with a description of the exact time when he awakened, the bathroom where he washed his face, and the color of his toothbrush. Similar findings were reported by Surian and his colleagues using a structured experimental task (Surian, Baron-Cohen, & Van der Lely, 1996).

Few differences have been reported between subjects with HFA and AS, although Shriberg et al. (2001) found that young adults with AS were significantly more garrulous than those with HFA. Ghaziuddin and Gerstein (1996) included monologue speech as part of their definition of pedantic speech style, which suggests that people with AS do not engage much in turn taking during reciprocal conversations with other people and may also talk too much. Ramberg, Ehlers, Nyden, Johansson, and Gillberg (1996) found that children with AS were impaired in taking turns during dyadic conversations, providing some support for this view.

Adams, Green, Gilchrist, and Cox (2002) compared conversational samples collected from adolescents with AS and a group of age- and IQ-matched children with severe conduct disorder. Although there were no overall significant group differences in verbosity, the adolescents with AS tended to talk more during conversational contexts that focused on emotional topics. A few participants with AS were extremely verbose. The groups were similar in their ability to respond to questions and comments offered by their conversational partner, but a qualitative analysis of responses revealed that the participants with AS had more pragmatic problems such as providing an inadequate or tangential response especially when discussing an unusual event or personal narrative.

Children and adolescents with autism perform less well on tasks of referential communication (Loveland, Tunali, McEvoy, & Kelley, 1989), although many can identify another person's visual perspective (Baron-Cohen, 1989; Hobson, 1984). More social and/or more complex aspects of referential communication, such as those that affect narration and discourse, are particularly affected (Hemphill, Picardi, & Tager-Flusberg, 1991). Children with autism often have difficulty dealing with new information (Tager-Flusberg & Anderson, 1991). They produce more noncontingent utterances, with patterns similar to those of language-impaired children but with proportionately more errors (Baltaxe & D'Angiola, 1992). Hurtig, Ensrud, and Tomblin (1980) reported that persistent and perseverative questioning generally did not serve the purpose of requesting information in autistic children but was communicative, often functioning as a means of initiating interaction or getting attention.

Bishop, Hartley, and Weir (1994) studied a group of children with semantic-pragmatic disorder who had some social and communicative behaviors that overlap with autism and pervasive developmental disorder. They found that, in these more verbally fluent children, there was a higher proportion of utterances that were initiations rather than responses. This finding seemed to account for how language-impaired children, including some with autism, could be considered talkative, even though the total amount of language they produce is not higher than that of other children.

Paul and Cohen (1984b) studied responses to requests for clarification in adults with autism or mental retardation matched for nonverbal IQ. They found that although the participants with autism were just as likely to respond to requests for clarification, their answers were less specific than those of the nonautistic participants. They were also less likely to add information that might be of help to the listener, suggesting that they had difficulty judging what piece of information was relevant.

Chuba et al. (2003) used conversational probes and role playing to examine the pragmatic abilities of adolescents with HFA and AS. In these more structured conversational situations, as in more naturalistic interviews discussed earlier, subjects with ASD had significantly more difficulty than controls with TD in responding to topics introduced by others and in making comments contingent on the

interlocutor's remark. They also had difficulty gracefully terminating topics. In role-playing situations that required the subject to lead the conversation, teenagers with ASD generally were unable to take assertive conversational roles. Paradoxically, then, adolescents with ASD showed difficulty in responding contingently to others' conversational input *and* in appropriately guiding conversations to elicit remarks from an interlocutor. Taken together, these results suggest a basic difficulty in establishing and maintaining reciprocity in conversation—in the ability to engage in mutual, cooperative social dialogue.

Studies of the ability of individuals with autism to produce narrative discourse have also provided information about the ways in which persons with autism organize and convey their thoughts to others. In general, studies have found that, commensurate with their language ability, children and adults with autism are able to narrate stories and follow simple scripts for common social events, such as a birthday party. Particular difficulties in making causal statements were found in one study (Tager-Flusberg, 1995), but these findings were not replicated in a later study (Capps, Losh, & Thurber, 2000). Loveland and her colleagues asked individuals with autism or Down syndrome, matched on chronological and verbal mental age, to retell the story they were shown in the form of a puppet show or video sketch (Loveland, McEvoy, Tunali, & Kelley, 1990). Compared to the controls, the children with autism were more likely to exhibit pragmatic violations including bizarre or inappropriate utterances and were less able to take into consideration the listener's needs. Some of the participants with autism in this study even failed to understand the story as a representation of meaningful events, suggesting that they lacked a cultural perspective underlying narrative (Bruner & Feldman, 1993; Loveland & Tunali, 1993). Norbury and Bishop (2003), however, found few differences between narrative skills of children with ASD and those with specific language impairment, suggesting that difficulties with stories may be common to children with communication impairments.

Taken together, these studies of pragmatic skills in verbal autistic individuals echo the suggestions of studies of nonverbal communication in young autistic children. Although basic intention to communicate often exists, the autistic person has impaired skill in participating in communicative activities involving joint reference or shared topics. This is particularly true in supplying new information relevant to a listener's purposes. The strategies used by an individual with autism to maintain conversation are less advanced than syntactic ability would predict, as is the ability to infer the interlocutor's implicit intentions.

One difference between individuals with autism and other populations with language impairments has been that, in most groups with language impairment, the more a child talks, the less likely it is that the language will have unusual characteristics. In contrast, two studies with autistic children and adolescents showed that subjects' unusual aspects of language and lack of cohesiveness increased with the amount of speech (Caplan, Guthrie, Shields, & Yudovin, 1994; Volden & Lord, 1991). In autism, difficulties in explaining and predicting behavior seem to be related both to general language deficits and to deficits in specific cognitive functions, such as metarepresentation and using the information at hand (Tager-Flusberg & Sullivan, 1994). Because most, though not all, individuals with autism have significant delays as well as deviance in language, they are doubly handicapped in communication.

Reading

Many children with autism have an early interest in letters and numbers, and some learn to read words without any direct instruction (Loveland & Tunali-Kotoski, 1997). Decoding, or pronouncing written words, and spelling tend to be relative strengths for many individuals with ASD. These strengths are especially noteworthy when children with autism are compared to other individuals with histories of language delay, who tend to do especially poorly in reading and writing. Children with autism typically show literacy skills that are on par with their overall developmental level (Loveland & Tunali-Kotoski, 1997; Myles et al., 2002) and can understand simple reading passages at grade level (Ventner, Lord, & Schopler, 1992). Written material has been shown in a variety of studies to provide a helpful medium of intervention for these children.

Written scripts, social stories, graphic organizers, reminder cards, and lists are useful in increasing social and communicative behavior for individuals with autism who read (e.g., Gray, 2000; Krantz & McClannahan, 1998). Nonetheless, these individuals can have relative deficits in comprehension, particularly when longer, more complex texts, such as narratives, are involved (Walhberg & Magliano, 2004).

While developmental level-appropriate literacy skills are the norm in autism, there is a subset of children with ASD who show remarkable decoding ability (Grigorenko, Klin, & Volkmar, 2003). These children are often referred to as *hyperlexic*. They usually begin reading words before they get to school and are obsessive in their interest in letters, writing, and reading (Nation, 1999). However, Grigorenko et al. (2003) point out that hyperlexia is not synonymous with autism. Their review reveals that only 5% to 10% of children with autism show hyperlexia, although this rate is much higher than that which occurs in otherwise normal development. Moreover, hyperlexia is not specific to autism; it is also seen in a variety of other disabilities including Turner syndrome, Tourette's syndrome, and mental retardation. Although hyperlexia is more prevalent in autism than in these disorders, it can occur in conjunction with nonautistic disabilities. The hallmarks of hyperlexia are advanced word recognition in children who otherwise have significant cognitive, linguistic, or social handicaps; a compulsive preoccupation with reading, letters, or writing; and a significant discrepancy between strong word recognition and weak comprehension of what has been read. Children with autism who show hyperlexia are often baffling to families, because their independent, early acquisition of word recognition contrasts so sharply with their severe handicaps in social communication and learning in other areas. Hyperlexia is, to some extent, a "savant" skill, like other special abilities occasionally seen in children with autism (e.g., drawing, calculation, music, calendar calculation), which fails to connect to general intellectual and functional abilities. Like other savant skills, hyperlexia can be used as a starting point for teaching other, more functional behaviors, but direct instruction and intensive practice will be necessary to move from the unprocessed "word calling" that is characteristic of this syndrome to more purposeful and communicative uses of reading.

Theories of Origin

Recently, increasingly sophisticated neuroimaging and neurophysiological measures have offered a promise for autism of eventual documentation of anatomical and functional differences in the brain. Although a replicable, consistent, meaningful neuroanatomic or neurophysiological basis for autism has not yet been identified (Bailey, Phillips, & Rutter, 1996), there have been some small-scale studies that have investigated structural brain abnormalities related to language using magnetic resonance imaging (MRI).

In the normal population, left cortical regions, especially in key language areas (perisylvian region, planum temporale, and Heschel's gyrus), are enlarged relative to the size of those regions in the right hemisphere. Herbert and her colleagues compared 16 boys with autism (all with normal nonverbal IQ scores) to 15 age-, sex-, and handedness-matched typically developing controls (Herbert et al., 2002). Their main findings were that the boys with autism had significant *reversal* of asymmetry in the inferior lateral frontal cortex, which was 27% larger in the right hemisphere compared to 17% larger in the left hemisphere for the normal controls. There were also significant differences between the autism and control groups in the asymmetry patterns in the planum temporale. While both groups showed a left hemisphere asymmetry, this was more extreme in the autistic boys (25% leftward asymmetry for autism compared to only 5% in the controls). These findings for the planum temporale were not replicated in a study comparing adults with autism and age-matched normal controls (Rojas, Bawn, Benkers, Reite, & Rogers, 2002). Rojas and his colleagues found that their adults with autism had significantly reduced left hemisphere planum temporale volumes and no hemispheric asymmetry in this important language region. Perhaps methodological differences can explain these conflicting findings. Rojas et al. studied adults rather than children, included women in their sample, and their groups were not matched for IQ.

Functional magnetic resonance imaging (fMRI) is beginning to be used, as well, to investigate online language processing in autism. Just, Cherkassky, Keller, and Minshew (2004) investigated brain activation during sentence comprehension. Reliable differences were found between subjects with HFA and TD in activation in the basic language areas of the cortex. Subjects with HFA showed higher activation in Wernicke's (left laterosuperior temporal) region, which is traditionally associated with language comprehension (particularly, understanding words), and lower activity in Broca's area (left inferior frontal gyrus), usually associated with production and grammar. Functional connectivity between cortical regions also appeared lower in the subjects with HFA.

New discoveries about brain structure and function are also being incorporated into thinking about origins of autistic language difficulties. For example, Rogers (2004) has noted research showing the presence of "mirror neurons" (Bekkering, 2002), which are activated both when a movement is seen and when it is made. This "resonance" may facilitate imitation of motor activities. Rogers speculates that specific mirror neurons for sights and sounds associated with speech may exist that could impact the ability to imitate and learn from language input. Children with ASDs, who are known to have special difficulties with vocal imitation (Stone, Lemanek, Fishel, Fernandez, & Altemeier, 1990), may be impacted by deficits in these mirror neuron systems, which might provide one element of etiology of speech delays and deviance in these syndromes. Further studies are clearly needed to explore the structural abnormalities in brain regions subserving language in both children and adults with autism. Although research exploring the neurobiology of language impairment in autism is still in the early stages, together with advances in molecular genetics, the likelihood is that, in the long term, neurobiological approaches will contribute significantly to our understanding and treatment of language and communication in autism.

Any robust theoretical model for communication abnormalities in autism must have several characteristics. It needs to describe a course that goes awry very early in development and that has a range of consequences, from severe language disability involving no representational-communication system, to more circumscribed abnormalities primarily affecting the pragmatics of connected discourse. It needs to be related to other social and cognitive functions, but not completely accounted for by other factors. That is, there are children and adults without apparent syntactic and semantic difficulties who share the social difficulties seen in autism (as in AS), and there are children and adults with severe to profound mental handicap or with specific language disorders who make substantial improvements in social areas and/or nonverbal cognitive functioning but who remain significantly impaired in spoken language. Thus, it appears that, although outcome and severity of social and cognitive deficits in autism are related to language level, these factors are also independent to some degree.

A complete theoretical account of language impairment ultimately needs to delineate the underlying mechanisms that explain these very different patterns of language acquisition and impairment in autism. It is likely that across different children, different mechanisms may be impaired. For some, communicative deficits are related most closely to social impairments in decoding nonverbal cues and understanding other minds. For other children, these social-cognitive impairments may be more severe, leading to the inability to understand language as an intentional symbolic system, which may impede them from even entering the linguistic system as marked by the absence of rudimentary comprehension skills and severe joint attention deficits. Additional mechanisms that may be directly or indirectly linked to language acquisition in children with autism include oral motor skills, imitation, and auditory processing and attentional systems. We are still at the early stages of developing theoretical accounts to explain the individual variation in language outcomes in ASDs that encompass all levels of analysis from genetics to neuropathology to cognition and behavior.

CONCLUSION

Many questions remain to be answered about communication in autism. For example, how is odd intonation related to deficits in communication and social cognition? How do linguistic comprehension deficits relate to the various aspects of deviant language seen in the syndrome? What triggers the initial failure of social cognition and joint attention that seems to be associated with such pervasive communicative difficulties? Like so many other questions about autism, the answers to these are likely to be neither simple nor universally true. A wide and heterogeneous range of communicative behaviors and function is seen in the syndrome. Whatever the biological explanation, communication disorders in autism are most likely affected by deficits in the ability to process information about social situations and how people behave when interacting with each other at every point in development. This deficit must be addressed in any attempt to remediate autistic communicative disorders. In addition, although they are integrally tied to broader cognitive and social deficits, delays in the ability to understand and produce words and sentences may have an even greater effect on the lives of individuals with autism than they do on persons with other handicaps. The double handicap of delay and deviance in autism means that we cannot assume that either individuals with autism or those who provide their linguistic environments can naturally compensate for these deficits without carefully considered intervention. This intervention must include understanding of how these deficits are manifested in particular children or adults and the communicative contexts in which each individual needs to function.

Cross-References

Aspects of classification and diagnosis are discussed in Chapters 1 to 7; developmental changes in autism, in Chapters 8 through 15; and language intervention, in Chapters 36 through 38.

REFERENCES

Acredolo, L. P., & Goodwyn, S. (1988). Symbolic gesturing in normal infants. *Child Development, 59*(2), 450–466.

Adams, C., Green, J., Gilchrist, A., & Cox, A. (2002). Conversational behaviour of children with Asperger syndrome and conduct disorder.

Journal of Child Psychology and Psychiatry, 43, 679–690.

Adamson, L. B., & Bakeman, R. (1991). The development of shared attention during infancy. *Annals of Child Development, 8,* 1–41.

Asher, S. R. (1978). Referential communication. In G. J. Whitehurst & B. J. Simmerman (Eds.), *The functions of language and cognition.* New York: Academic Press.

Asperger, H. (1991). "Autistic psychopathy" in childhood. In U. Frith (Ed.), *Autism and Asperger syndrome* (pp. 37–91). Cambridge: Cambridge University Press. (Original work published 1944)

Bailey, A., Phillips, W., & Rutter, M. (1996). Autism: Towards an integration of clinical, genetic, neuropsychological, and neurobiological perspectives. *Journal of Child Psychology and Psychiatry, 37,* 89–126.

Baldwin, D. A. (1991). Infants' contribution to the achievement of joint reference. *Child Development, 62,* 875–890.

Baltaxe, C. (1977). Pragmatic deficits in the language of autistic adolescents. *Journal of Pediatric Psychology, 2,* 176–180.

Baltaxe, C. (1984). Use of contrastive stress in normal, aphasic and autistic children. *Journal of Speech and Hearing Research, 24,* 97–105.

Baltaxe, C., & D'Angiola, N. (1992). Cohesion in the discourse interaction of autistic, specific language-impaired, and normal children. *Journal of Autism and Developmental Disorders, 22,* 1–22.

Baltaxe, C. A. M., & Simmons, J. Q. (1977). Bedtime soliloquies and linguistic competence in autism. *Journal of Speech and Hearing Disorder, 42,* 376–393.

Baron-Cohen, S. (1989). Perceptual role-taking and protodeclarative pointing in autism. *British Journal of Developmental Psychology, 7,* 113–127.

Baron-Cohen, S. (1993). From attention-goal psychology to belief-desire psychology: The development of a theory of mind, and its dysfunction. In S. Baron-Cohen, H. Tager-Flusberg, & D. Cohen (Eds.), *Understanding other minds: Perspectives from autism* (pp. 59–82). Oxford, England: Oxford University Press.

Bartak, L., Rutter, M., & Cox, A. (1975). A comparative study of infantile autism and specific developmental receptive language disorder: I. The children. *British Journal of Psychiatry, 126,* 127–145.

Bartolucci, G., & Albers, R. J. (1974). Deictic categories in the language of autistic children. *Journal of Autism and Childhood Schizophrenia, 4,* 131–141.

Bartolucci, G., Pierce, S. J., & Streiner, D. (1980). Cross-sectional studies of grammatical morphemes in autistic and mentally retarded children. *Journal of Autism and Developmental Disorders, 10,* 39–50.

Bartolucci, G., Pierce, S., Streiner, D., & Tolkin-Eppel, P. (1976). Phonological investigation of verbal autistic and mentally retarded subjects. *Journal of Autism and Childhood Schizophrenia, 6,* 303–315.

Bates, E. (1976). *Language in context.* New York: Academic Press.

Beitchman, J. H., & Inglis, A. (1991). The continuum of linguistic dysfunction from pervasive developmental disorders to dyslexia. *Psychiatric Clinics of North America, 14,* 95–111.

Bekkering, H. (2002). Common mechanisms in the observation and execution of finger and mouth movements. In A. Meltzoff & W. Prinz (Eds.), *The imitative mind: Development, evolution, and brain basis* (pp. 163–182). Cambridge: Cambridge University Press.

Bernard-Opitz, V. (1982). Pragmatic analysis of the communicative behavior of an autistic child. *Journal of Speech and Hearing Disorders, 47,* 99–109.

Bishop, D. V., & Adams, C. (1989). Conversational characteristics of children with semantic-pragmatic disorder: II. What features lead to a judgment of inappropriacy? *British Journal of Disorders of Communication, 24*(3), 241–263.

Bishop, D., Hartley, J., & Weir, F. (1994). Why and when do some language-impaired children seem talkative? A study of initiation in conversations of children with semantic-pragmatic disorder. *Journal of Autism and Developmental Disorders, 24*(2), 177–197.

Bloom, L. (1974). Talking, understanding and thinking. In R. C. Scheifelbusch & L. L. Lloyd (Eds.), *Language perspectives: Acquisition, retardation and intervention* (pp. 285–311). Baltimore: University Park Press.

Bloom, L. (1993). *The transition from infancy to language: Acquiring the power of expression.* Cambridge, England Cambridge University Press.

Bloom, L., & Lahey, M. (1978). *Language development and language disorders.* New York: Wiley.

Boucher, J. (1988). Word fluency in high-functioning autistic children. *Journal of Autism and Developmental Disorders, 18,* 637–645.

Brown, R. (1973). *A first language.* Cambridge: Harvard University Press.

Bruner, J. (1975). The ontogenesis of speech acts. *Journal of Child Language, 2*(1), 1–19.

Bruner, J., & Feldman, C. (1993). Theories of mind and the problem of autism. In S. Baron-Cohen,

H. Tager-Flusberg, & D. J. Cohen (Eds.), *Understanding other minds: Perspectives from autism*. Oxford, England: Oxford University Press.

Bryson, S. E., Clark, B. S., & Smith, T. M. (1988). First report of a Canadian epidemiological study of autistic syndromes. *Journal of Child Psychology and Psychiatry, 29,* 433–445.

Burgoine, E., & Wing, L. (1983). Identical triplets with Asperger's syndrome. *British Journal of Psychiatry, 143,* 261.

Cantwell, D. P., & Baker, L. (1989). Infantile autism and developmental receptive dysphasia: A comparative follow-up into middle childhood. *Journal of Autism and Developmental Disorders, 19,* 19–30.

Cantwell, D. P., Baker, L., & Mattison, R. E. (1980). Psychiatric disorders in children with speech and language retardation. *Archives of General Psychiatry, 37,* 423–426.

Caplan, R., Guthrie, D., Shields, W. D., & Yudovin, S. (1994). Communication deficits in pediatric complex partial seizure disorders and schizophrenia. *Development and Psychopathology, 6,* 499–517.

Capps, L., Losh, M., & Thurber, C. (2000). "The frog ate the bug and made his mouth sad": Narrative competence in children with autism. *Journal of Abnormal Child Psychology, 28,* 193–204.

Carpenter, M., Nagell, K., & Tomasello, M. (1998). Social cognition, joint attention, and communicative competence from 9 to 15 months of age. *Monographs of the Society for Research in Child Development, 63*(4), 176.

Carr, E., Schreibman, L., & Lovaas, O. L. (1975). Control of echolalic speech in psychotic children. *Journal of Abnormal Child Psychology, 3,* 331–351.

Cazden, C. (1968). The acquisition of noun and verb inflections. *Child Development, 39,* 443–448.

Chapman, R. (1978). Comprehension strategies in children. In J. F. Kavanagh & W. Strange (Eds.), *Speech and language in the laboratory, school and clinic* (pp. 308–327). Cambridge, MA: MIT Press.

Chapman, R. (1981). Exploring children's communicative intents. In J. Miller (Ed.), *Assessing language production in children: Experimental procedures.* Baltimore: University Park Press.

Charman, T., Baron-Cohen, S., Swettenham, J., Baird, G., Drew, A., & Cox, A. (2003). Predicting language outcome in infants with autism and pervasive developmental disorder. *International Journal of Language and Communication Disorders, 38,* 265–285.

Charman, T., Drew, A., Baird, C., & Baird, G. (2003). Measuring early language development in preschool children with autism spectrum disorder using the MacArthur Communicative Development Inventory (Infant Form). *Journal of Child Language, 30,* 213–236.

Chiat, S. (1982). If I were you and you were me: The analysis of pronouns in a pronoun-reversing child. *Journal of Child Language, 9,* 359–379.

Chuba, H., Paul, R., Miles, S., Klin, A., & Volkmar, F. (2003, November). *Assessing pragmatic skills in individuals with autism spectrum disorders.* Presentation at the National Convention of the American Speech-Language-Hearing Association, Chicago.

Cohen, I. L., Sudhalter, V., Landon-Jimenez, D., & Keogh, M. (1993). A neural network approach to the classification of autism. *Journal of Autism and Developmental Disorders, 23,* 443–466.

Dahlgren, S. O., & Gillberg, C. (1989). Symptoms in the first two years of life: A preliminary population study of infantile autism. *European Archives of Psychiatric and Neurological Science, 283,* 169–174.

Darley, F., Aronson, A., & Brown, J. (1975). *Motor speech disorders.* Philadelphia: Saunders.

DeMyer, M. K., Barton, S., DeMyer, W. E., Norton, J. A., Allen, J., & Steel, R. (1973). Prognosis in autism: A follow-up study. *Journal of Autism and Childhood Schizophrenia, 3,* 199–245.

Dore, J. (1978). Requestive systems in nursery school conversations: Analysis of talk in its social context. In R. Campbell & P. Smith (Eds.), *Recent advances in the psychology of language.* New York: Plenum Press.

Doussard-Roosevelt, J., Joe, C., Bazhenova, O., & Porges, S. (2003). Mother-child interaction in autistic and nonautistic children: Characteristics of maternal approach behaviors and child social responses. *Development and Psychopathology, 15,* 277–295.

Eisenmajer, R., Prior, M., Leekam, S., Wing, L., Gould, J., Welham, M., et al. (1996). Comparison of clinical symptoms in autism and Asperger's disorder. *Journal of the American Academy of Child Adolescent Psychiatry, 35*(11), 1523–1531.

Elliott, M. J. (1993). *Prelinguistic vocalizations in autistic, developmentally delayed, and normally developing children.* Unpublished master's thesis, University of North Carolina, Greensboro.

Eskes, G. A., Bryson, S. E., & McCormick, T. A. (1990). Comprehension of concrete and abstract words in autistic children. *Journal of Autism and Developmental Disorders, 20,* 61–73.

Fay, W. (1969). On the basis of autistic echolalia. *Journal of Communication Disorders, 2,* 38–47.

Fay, W., & Schuler, A. L. (1980). *Emerging language in autistic children.* Baltimore: University Park Press.

Fein, D., & Waterhouse, L. (1979). *Autism is not a disorder of language.* Paper presented at the meeting of the New England Child Language Association, Boston.

Fenson, L., Dale, P., Reznick, J., Bates, E., Thal, D., & Pethick, S. (1994). Variability in early communicative development. *Monographs of the Society for Research in Child Development, 59*(5, Serial No. 242).

Fernald, A. (1992). Human maternal vocalizations to infants as biologically relevant signals: An evolutionary perspective. In J. H. Barkow & L. Cosmides (Eds.), *Adapted mind: Evolutionary psychology and the generation of culture* (pp. 391–428). London: Oxford University Press.

Fraiberg, S. (1977). *Insights from the Blind.* New York: Basic Books.

Frith, U. (1969). Emphasis and meaning in recall in normal and autistic children. *Language and Speech, 2,* 29–38.

Frith, U. (1989). *Autism: Explaining the enigma.* New York: Blackwell.

Gaddes, J. (1984). *Probable events and sentence comprehension in autistic children.* Unpublished senior honors thesis, University of Alberta, Edmonton, Alberta.

Ghaziuddin, M., & Gerstein, L. (1996). Pedantic speaking style differentiates Asperger syndrome from high-functioning autism. *Journal of Autism and Developmental Disorders, 26,* 585–595.

Ghaziuddin, M., Tsai, L., & Ghaziuddin, N. (1992). Brief report: A comparison of the diagnostic criteria for Asperger syndrome. *Journal of Autism and Developmental Disorders, 22,* 643–649.

Goldberg, W., Osann, K., Filipek, P., Laulhere, T., Jarvis, K., Modahl, C., et al. (2003). Language and other regression: Assessment and timing. *Journal of Autism and Developmental Disorders, 33,* 607–616.

Goldfarb, W., Braunstein, P., & Lorge, I. (1956). A study of speech patterns in a group of schizophrenic children. *American Journal of Orthopsychiatry, 26,* 544–555.

Goldstein, H. (2002). Communication Intervention for children with autism: A review of treatment efficacy. *Journal of Autism and Developmental Disorders, 32,* 373–396.

Gopnik, A., & Meltzoff, A. (1987). The development of categorization in the second year and its relation to other cognitive and linguistic developments. *Child Development, 58,* 1523–1531.

Gray, C. (2000). *The new social story book.* Arlington, TX: Future Horizons.

Grigorenko, E., Klin, A., & Volkmar, F. (2003). Hyperlexia: Disability or superability? *Journal of Child Psychology and Psychiatry, 44,* 1079–1091.

Halliday, M. A. K. (1975). *Learning how to mean: Exploration in the development of language.* London: Edward Arnold.

Hellreigel, C., Tao, L., DiLavore, P., & Lord, C. (1995). *The effect of context on nonverbal social behaviors of very young autistic children.* Paper presented at the biannual meetings of the Society for Research in Child Development, Indianapolis, IN.

Hemphill, L., Picardi, N., & Tager-Flusberg, H. (1991). Narrative as an index of communicative competence in mildly mentally retarded children. *Applied Psycholinguistics, 12,* 263–279.

Herbert, M. R., Harris, G. J., Adrien, K. T., Makris, N., Kennedy, D. N., Lange, N. T., et al. (2002). Abnormal asymmetry in language association cortex in autism. *Annals of Neurology, 52,* 588–596.

Hobson, R. P. (1984). Early childhood autism and the question of egocentrism. *Journal of Autism and Developmental Disorders, 14,* 85–104.

Hobson, R. P., & Lee, A. (1989). Emotion-related and abstract concepts in autistic people: Evidence from the British Picture Vocabulary Scale. *Journal of Autism and Developmental Disorders, 19,* 601–623.

Howlin, P. (1984). The acquisition of grammatical morphemes in autistic children: A critique and replication of the findings of Bartolucci, Pierce, and Streiner, 1980. *Journal of Autism and Developmental Disorders, 14,* 127–136.

Howlin, P., Goode, S., Hutton, J., & Rutter, M. (2004). Adult outcome for children with autism. *Journal of Child Psychology and Psychiatry, 45,* 212–229.

Hurtig, R., Ensrud, S., & Tomblin, J. B. (1980). *Question production in autistic children: A linguistic pragmatic perspective.* Paper presented at the University of Wisconsin Symposium on Research in Child Language Disorders, Madison, WI.

Huttenlocher, J. (1974). The origins of language comprehension. In R. L. Solso (Ed.), *Theories in cognitive psychology* (pp. 331–368). Hillsdale, NJ: Erlbaum.

Jarrold, C., Boucher, J., & Russell, J. (1997). Language profiles in children with autism: Theoretical and methodological implications. *Autism: Journal of Research and Practice, 1,* 57–76.

Just, M., Cherkassky, V., Keller, T., & Minshew, N. (2004). Cortical activation and synchronization during sentence comprehension in high-functioning autism: Evidence of under-connectivity. *Brain, 10,* 1093–2003.

Kanner, L. (1943). Autistic disturbances of affective contact. *Nervous Child, 2,* 217–250.

Kanner, L. (1946). Irrelevant and metaphorical language. *American Journal of Psychiatry, 103,* 242–246.

Kjelgaard, M., & Tager-Flusberg, H. (2001). An investigation of language impairment in autism: Implications for genetic subgroups. *Language and Cognitive Processes, 16,* 287–308.

Klin, A. (1991). Young autistic children's listening preferences in regard to speech: A possible characterization of the symptom of social withdrawal. *Journal of Autism and Developmental Disorders, 21,* 29–42.

Klin, A., & Volkmar, F. (1997). Asperger's syndrome. In D. J. Cohen & F. R. Volkmar (Eds.), *Handbook of autism and pervasive developmental disorders* (pp. 94–122). New York: Wiley.

Koning, C., & Magill-Evans, J. (2001). Social and language skills in adolescent boys with Asperger syndrome. *Autism: Journal of Research and Practice, 5*(1), 23–36.

Konstantareas, M., Zajdemann, H., Homatidis, S., & McCabe, A. (1988). Maternal speech to verbal and higher functioning versus nonverbal and lower functioning autistic children. *Journal of Autism and Developmental Disorders, 18,* 647–656.

Krantz, P. J., & McClannahan, L. E. (1998). Social interaction skills for children with autism: A script-fading procedure for beginning readers. *Journal of Applied Behavior Analysis, 31,* 191–202.

Kurita, H. (1985). Infantile autism with speech loss before the age of 30 months. *Journal of the American Academy of Child Psychiatry, 24,* 191–196.

Landa, R. (2000). Social language use in Asperger syndrome and high-functioning autism. In A. Klin, F. Volkmar, & S. Sparrow (Eds.), *Asperger syndrome* (pp. 125–155). New York: Guilford Press.

Landry, S. H., & Loveland, K. A. (1989). The effect of social context on the functional communication skills of autistic children. *Journal of Autism and Developmental Disorders, 19*(2), 283–299.

Le Couteur, A., Bailey, A., Rutter, M., & Gottesman, I. (1989, August 3–5). *Epidemiologically based twin study of autism.* Paper presented at the First World Congress on Psychiatric Genetics, Churchill College, Cambridge, England.

Lee, A., Hobson, R. P., & Chiat, S. (1994). I, you, me and autism: An experimental study. *Journal of Autism and Developmental Disorders, 24,* 155–176.

Lempert, H. (1978). Extrasyntactic factors affecting passive sentence comprehension in young children. *Child Development, 49,* 694–699.

Loban, W. (1976). *Language development: Kindergarten through grade 12.* Urbana, IL: National Council of Teachers of English.

Lord, C. (1985). Autism and the comprehension of language. In E. Schopler & G. Mesibov (Eds.), *Communication problems in autism* (pp. 257–281). New York: Plenum Press.

Lord, C. (1995). Follow-up of two year-olds referred for possible autism. *Journal of Child Psychology and Psychiatry, 36*(8), 1365–1382.

Lord, C., Merrin, D. J., Vest, L., & Kelly, K. M. (1983). Communicative behavior of adults with an autistic four-year-old boy and his nonhandicapped twin brother. *Journal of Autism and Developmental Disorders, 13,* 1–17.

Lord, C., & Pickles, A. (1996). The relationship between expressive language level and nonverbal social communication in autism. *Journal of the American Academy of Child and Adolescent Psychiatry, 35*(11), 1542–1550.

Lord, C., Pickles, A., DiLavore, P. C., & Shulman, C. (1996). *Longitudinal studies of young children referred for possible autism.* Paper presented at the biannual meetings of the International Society for Research in Child and Adolescent Psychopathology, Barcelona, Spain.

Lord, C., Risi, S., Lambrecht, L., Cook, E., Leventhal, B., DiLavore, P., et al. (2000). The Autism Diagnostic Observation Schedule—Generic: A standard measure of social and communication deficits associated with the spectrum of autism. *Journal of Autism and Developmental Disorders, 30,* 205–223.

Lord, C., Risi, S., & Pickles, A. (2004). Trajectory of language development in autism spectrum disorders. In M. Rice & S. Warren (Eds.), *Developmental language disorders: From phenotypes to etiologies* (pp. 7–29). Mahwah, NJ: Lawrence Earlbaum.

Lord, C., & Rutter, M. (1994). Autism and pervasive developmental disorders. In M. Rutter, L. Hersov, & E. Taylor (Eds.), *Child and adolescent psychiatry: Modern approaches* (3rd ed., pp. 569–593). Oxford, England: Blackwell.

Lord, C., Rutter, M., Goode, S., Heemsbergen, J., Jordan, H., Mawhood, L., et al. (1989). Autism Diagnostic Observation Schedule: A standardized observation of communicative and social behavior. *Journal of Autism and Developmental Disorders, 19,* 185–212.

Lord, C., Rutter, M., & Le Couteur, A. (1994). Autism Diagnostic Interview—Revised: A revised version of a diagnostic interview for caregivers of individuals with possible pervasive developmental disorders. *Journal of Autism and Developmental Disorders, 24,* 659–685.

Lord, C., Shulman, C., & DiLavore, P. (2004). Regression and word loss in autistic spectrum disorders. *Journal of Child Psychology and Psychiatry, 45,* 936–955.

Lord, C., Storoschuk, S., Rutter, M., & Pickles, A. (1993). Using the ADI-R to diagnose autism in preschool children. *Infant Mental Health Journal, 14,* 234–252.

Lord, C., & Venter, A. (1992). Outcome and follow-up studies of high-functioning autistic individuals. In E. Schopler & G. Mesibov (Eds.), *High-functioning individuals with autism* (pp. 187–199). New York: Plenum Press.

Lovaas, O. I. (1977). *The autistic child.* New York: Irvington.

Loveland, K. (1984). Learning about points of view: Spatial perspective and the acquisition of "I/you." *Journal of Child Language, 11,* 535–556.

Loveland, K. (1991). Social affordances and interaction: II. Autism and the affordances of the human environment. *Ecological Psychology, 3,* 99–119.

Loveland, K., McEvoy, R. E., Tunali, B., & Kelley, M. L. (1990). Narrative story telling in autism and Down syndrome. *British Journal of Developmental Psychology, 8,* 9–23.

Loveland, K., & Tunali, B. (1993). Narrative language in autism and the theory of mind hypothesis: A wider perspective. In S. Baron-Cohen, H. Tager-Flusberg, & D. J. Cohen (Eds.), *Understanding other minds: Perspectives from autism.* Oxford, England: Oxford University Press.

Loveland, K., Tunali, B., McEvoy, R. E., & Kelley, M. L. (1989). Referential communication and response adequacy in autism and Down's syndrome. *Applied Psycholinguistics, 10,* 301–313.

Loveland, K., & Tunali-Kotoski, B. (1997). The school-age child with autism. In D. Cohen & F. Volkmar (Eds.), *Handbook of autism and pervasive developmental disorders* (pp. 283–308). New York: Wiley.

Luyster, R., Richler, J., Hsu, W. L., Dawson, G., Bernier, R., Dunn, M., et al. (in press). Early regression in social communication in autistic spectrum disorders. *Developmental Neuropsychology.*

Mayes, L., Volkmar, F., Hooks, M., & Cicchetti, D. (1993). Differentiating Pervasive Developmental Disorder-Not Otherwise Specified from autism and language disorders. *Journal of Autism and Developmental Disorders, 23,* 79–90.

McEvoy, R. E., Loveland, K. A., & Landry, S. H. (1988). The functions of immediate echolalia in autistic children: A developmental perspective. *Journal of Autism and Developmental Disorders, 18,* 657–668.

McHale, S., Simeonsson, R. J., Marcus, L. M., & Olley, J. G. (1980). The social and symbolic quality of autistic children's communication. *Journal of Autism and Developmental Disorders, 10,* 299–310.

Merewether, F. C., & Alpert, M. (1990). The components and neuroanatomic bases of prosody. *Journal of Communication Disorders, 23,* 325–336.

Mermelstein, R. (1983). *The relationship between syntactic and pragmatic development in autistic, retarded, and normal children.* Paper presented to the Eighth Annual Boston University Conference on Language Development, Boston.

Miller, J., & Chapman, R. S. (1981). The relation between age and mean length of utterance in morphemes. *Journal of Speech and Hearing Research, 24,* 154–162.

Minshew, N. J., & Goldstein, G. (1993). Is autism an amnesic disorder? Evidence from the California Verbal Learning Test. *Neuropsychology, 7,* 209–216.

Myles, B., Hilgenfeld, T., Barnhill, G., Griswold, D., Hagiwara, T., Simpson, R. (2002). Analysis of reading skills in individuals with Asperger syndrome. *Focus on Autism and Other Developmental Disabilities, 17,* 1088–3576.

Nation, K. (1999). Reading skills in hyperlexia: A developmental perspective. *Psychological Bulletin, 125*(3), 338–355.

Nazzi, T., & Bertoninci, J. (2003). Before and after the vocabulary spurt: Two modes of word acquisition. *Developmental Science, 6,* 136–142.

Nelson, K. (1973). Structure and strategy in learning to talk. *Monographs of the Society for Research in Children Development, 38*(1–2, Serial no. 149).

Norbury, C., & Bishop, D. V. M. (2003). Narrative skills of children with communication impairments. *International Journal of Language and Communication Disorders, 38,* 287–314.

Osterling, J., & Dawson, G. (1994). Early recognition of children with autism: A study of first birthday home videotapes. *Journal of Autism and Developmental Disorders, 24,* 247–258.

Ozonoff, S., Pennington, B. F., & Rogers, S. J. (1990). Are there emotion perception deficits in young autistic children? *Journal of Child Psychology and Psychiatry, 31,* 343–362.

Paul, R. (1985). The emergence of pragmatic comprehension: A study of children's understanding of sentence-structure cues to given/new information. *Journal of Child Language, 12,* 161–179.

Paul, R., Chapman, R. S., & Wanska, S. (1980). *The development of complex sentence use.* Paper presented at the meeting of the American Speech and Hearing Association, Detroit, MI.

Paul, R., Chawarska, K., Klin, A., & Volkmar, F. (2004, July). *Profiles of communication in toddlers with autism spectrum disorders.* Invited paper presented at the American Psychological Association, Honolulu, HI.

Paul, R., & Cohen, D. J. (1984a). Outcomes of severe disorders of language acquisition. *Journal of Autism and Developmental Disorders, 14,* 405–422.

Paul, R., & Cohen, D. J. (1984b). Responses to contingent queries in adults with mental retardation and pervasive developmental disorders. *Applied Psycholinguistics,* 349–357.

Paul, R., & Cohen, D. J. (1985). Comprehension of indirect requests in adults with mental retardation and pervasive developmental disorders. *Journal of Speech and Hearing Research, 28,* 475–479.

Paul, R., Cohen, D. J., & Caparulo, B. K. (1983). A longitudinal study of patients with severe developmental disorders of language learning. *Journal of the American Academy of Child Psychiatry, 22,* 525–534.

Paul, R., & Feldman, C. (1984). *Communication deficits in autism.* Paper presented at the Institute for Communication Deficits in Autistic Youth, Columbia University, New York.

Paul, R., Fischer, M. L., & Cohen, D. (1988). Sentence comprehension strategies in children with autism and specific language disorders. *Journal of Autism and Developmental Disorders, 18,* 669–680.

Peters, A. (1983). *The units of language acquisition.* New York: Cambridge University Press.

Pierce, S., & Bartolucci, G. (1977). A syntactic investigation of verbal autistic, mentally retarded, and normal children. *Journal of Autism and Childhood Schizophrenia, 7,* 121–134.

Pinker, S. (1999). How the mind works. *Annals of the New York Academy of Sciences, 882,* 119–127.

Prizant, B. (1983). Echolalia in autism: Assessment and intervention. *Seminars in Speech and Language, 4,* 63–77.

Prizant, B., & Duchan, J. (1981). The functions of immediate echolalia in autistic children. *Journal of Speech and Hearing Disorders, 46,* 241–249.

Pronovost, W., Wakstein, M., & Wakstein, D. (1966). A longitudinal study of speech behavior and language comprehension in fourteen children diagnosed as atypical or autistic. *Exceptional Children, 33,* 19–26.

Ramberg, C., Ehlers, S., Nyden, A., Johansson, M., & Gillberg, C. (1996). Language and pragmatic functions in school-age children on the autism spectrum. *European Journal of Disorders of Communication, 31*(4), 387–413.

Rice, M. L. (2004). Growth models of developmental language disorders. In M. L. Rice & S. F. Warren (Eds.), *Developmental language disorders: From phenotypes to etiologies* (pp. 207–240). Mahwah, NJ: Lawrence Erlbaum.

Rice, M. L., Oetting, J. B., & Marquis, J. (1994). Frequency of input effects on word comprehension of children with specific language impairment. *Journal of Speech and Hearing Research, 37*(1), 106–121.

Richler, J., Luyster, R., Risi, S., Hsu, W. L., Dawson, G., Bernier, R., et al. (in press). Is there a regressive "phenotype" of autism spectrum disorder associated with the measles-mumps-rubella vaccine? A CPEA study. *Journal of Autism & Developmental Disorders.*

Ricks, D. M., & Wing, L. (1976). Language, communication and use of symbols. In L. Wing (Ed.), *Early childhood autism* (pp. 93–134). Oxford, England: Pergamon Press.

Roberts, J., Rice, M., & Tager-Flusberg, H. (2004). Tense marking in children with autism. *Applied Psycholinguistics, 25,* 429–448.

Rogers, S. (2004). Evidence-based intervention for language development in young children with autism. In T. Charman & W. Stone (Eds.), *Efficacy of intervention for autism.* New York: Guilford.

Rogers, S., Hepburn, S., Stackhouse, T., & Wehner, E. (2003). Imitation performance in toddlers with autism and those with other developmental disorders. *Journal of Child Psychology and Psychiatry, 44,* 763–781.

Rojas, D., Bawn, S., Benkers, T., Reite, M., & Rogers, S. (2002). Smaller left hemisphere planum temporale in adults with autistic disorder. *Neuroscience Letters, 328,* 237–240.

Rumsey, J. M., Rapoport, M. D., & Sceery, W. R. (1985). Autistic children as adults: Psychiatric, social, and behavioral outcomes. *Journal of the American Academy of Child Psychiatry, 24,* 465–473.

Rutter, M. (1970). Autistic children: Infancy to adulthood. *Seminars in Psychiatry, 2,* 435–450.

Rutter, M. (1987). The "what" and "how" of language development: A note on some outstanding issues and questions. In W. Yule & M. Rutter (Eds.), *Language development and disorders* (pp. 159–170). London: MacKeith Press.

Rutter, M., Le Couteur, A., & Lord, C. (2003). *Autism Diagnostic Interview-Revised* (ADI-R). Los Angeles: Western Psychological Services.

Rutter, M., & Lord, C. (1987). Language impairment associated with psychiatric disorder. In W. Yule, M. Rutter, & M. Bax (Eds.), *Language development and disorders: Clinic in developmental medicine, 101/102* (pp. 206–233). London: Simp/Seineman.

Rutter, M., Mawhood, L., & Howlin, P. (1992). Language delay and social development. In P. Fletcher & D. Hall (Eds.), *Specific speech and language disorders in children: Correlates, characteristics and outcomes* (pp. 63–78). London: Whurr.

Scarborough, H. S., Rescorla, L., Tager-Flusberg, H., Fowler, A. E., & Sudhalter, V. (1991). The relation of utterance length to grammatical complexity in normal and language-disordered groups. *Applied Psycholinguistics, 12,* 23–45.

Shapiro, T. (1977). The quest for a linguistic model to study the speech of autistic children: Studies of echoing. *Journal of the American Academy of Child Psychiatry, 16,* 608–619.

Sheinkopf, S., Mundy, P., Oller, K., & Steffens, M. (2000). Vocal atypicalities of preverbal autistic children. *Journal of Autism and Developmental Disorders, 30,* 345–354.

Short, C. B., & Schopler, E. (1988). Factors relating to age of onset in autism. *Journal of Autism and Developmental Disorders, 18,* 207–216.

Shriberg, L., Paul, R., McSweeney, J., Klin, A., Cohen, D., & Volkmar, F. (2001). Speech and prosody characteristics of adolescents and adults with high-functioning autism and Asperger syndrome. *Journal of Speech, Language, and Hearing Research, 44,* 1097–1115.

Siegel, B., Vukicevic, J., Elliott, G., & Kraemer, H. (1989). The use of signal detection theory to assess *DSM-III-R* criteria for autistic disorder. *Journal of the American Academy of Child and Adolescent Psychiatry, 28,* 542–548.

Sigman, M., & Ruskin, E. (1999). Continuity and change in the social competence of children with autism, Down syndrome and developmental delays. *Monographs of the Society for Research in Child Development, 64,* Serial No. 256.

Sigman, M., & Ungerer, J. (1981). Sensorimotor skills and language comprehension in autistic children. *Journal of Abnormal Child Psychology, 9,* 149–166.

Siller, M., & Sigman, M. (2002). The behaviors of parents of children with autism predict the subsequent development of their children's communication. *Journal of Autism and Developmental Disorders, 32,* 77–89.

St. James, P. J., & Tager-Flusberg, H. (1994). An observational study of humor in autism and Down syndrome. *Journal of Autism and Developmental Disorders, 24,* 603–617.

Stone, W. L., & Caro-Martinez, L. M. (1990). Naturalistic observations of spontaneous communication in autistic children. *Journal of Autism and Developmental Disorders, 20,* 437–453.

Stone, W., Lemanek, K., Fishel, P., Fernandez, M., & Altemeier, W. (1990). Play and imitation skills in the diagnosis of autism in young children. *Pediatrics, 86,* 267–272.

Storoschuk, S., Lord, C., & Jaedicke, S. (1995). *Autism and the use of mental verbs.* Paper presented at the Society for Research in child Development, Indianapolis, IN.

Surian, L., Baron-Cohen, S., & Van der Lely, H. (1996). Are children with autism deaf to Gricean maxims? *Cognitive Neuropsychiatry, 1,* 55–72.

Tager-Flusberg, H. (1981a). On the nature of linguistic functioning in early infantile autism. *Journal of Autism and Developmental Disorders, 11,* 45–56.

Tager-Flusberg, H. (1981b). Sentence comprehension in autistic children. *Applied Psycholinguistics, 2,* 5–24.

Tager-Flusberg, H. (1985). The conceptual basis for referential word meaning in children with autism. *Child Development, 56,* 1167–1178.

Tager-Flusberg, H. (1989). A psycholinguistic perspective on language development in the autistic child. In G. Dawson (Ed.), *Autism: New directions in diagnosis, nature and treatment* (pp. 92–115). New York: Guilford Press.

Tager-Flusberg, H. (1991). Semantic processing in the free recall of autistic children: Further evidence for a cognitive deficit. *British Journal of Developmental Psychology, 9,* 417–430.

Tager-Flusberg, H. (1992). Autistic children's talk about psychological states: Deficits in the early acquisition of a theory of mind. *Child Development, 63,* 161–172.

Tager-Flusberg, H. (1993). What language reveals about the understanding of minds in children with autism. In S. Baron-Cohen, H. Tager-Flusberg, & D. J. Cohen (Eds.), *Understanding other minds: Perspectives from autism* (pp. 138–157). Oxford, England: Oxford University Press.

Tager-Flusberg, H. (1994). Dissociations in form and function in the acquisition of language by autistic children. In H. Tager-Flusberg (Ed.), *Constraints on language acquisition: Studies of atypical children* (pp. 175–194). Hillsdale, NJ: Erlbaum.

Tager-Flusberg, H. (1995). "Once upon a ribbit": Stories narrated by autistic children. *British Journal of Developmental Psychology, 13,* 45–59.

Tager-Flusberg, H. (2003). Language impairments in children with complex neurodevelopmental disorders: The case of autism. In Y. Levy & J. Schaeffer (Eds.), *Language competence across populations: Toward a definition of specific language impairment* (pp. 297–321). Mahwah, NJ: Erlbaum.

Tager-Flusberg, H., & Anderson, M. (1991). The development of contingent discourse ability in autistic children. *Journal of Child Psychology and Psychiatry, 32,* 1123–1134.

Tager-Flusberg, H., & Calkins, S. (1990). Does imitation facilitate the acquisition of grammar? Evidence from a study of autistic, Down syndrome and normal children. *Journal of Child Language, 17,* 591–606.

Tager-Flusberg, H., Calkins, S., Noin, I., Baumberger, T., Anderson, M., & Chadwick-Denis, A. (1990). A longitudinal study of language acquisition in autistic and Down Syndrome children. *Journal of Autism and Developmental Disorders, 20,* 1–22.

Tager-Flusberg, H., & Joseph, R. M. (2003). Identifying neurocognitive phenotypes in autism. *Philosophical Transactions of the Royal Society, Series, B, 358,* 303–314.

Tager-Flusberg, H., & Sullivan, K. (1994). A second look at second-order belief attribution in autism. *Journal of Autism and Developmental Disorders, 24,* 577–586.

Taylor, A. (2004). *Telescoping in parent reports on milestones in autism.* Unpublished master's thesis, University of Chicago, Chicago, IL.

Thurber, C., & Tager-Flusberg, H. (1993). Pauses in the narratives produced by autistic, mentally retarded, and normal children as an index of cognitive demand. *Journal of Autism and Developmental Disorders.*

Tomasello, M., & Kruger, A. C. (1992). Joint attention on actions: Acquiring verbs in ostensive and non-ostensive contests. *Journal of Child Language, 19,* 311–333.

Van Lancker, D., Cornelius, C., & Needleman, R. (1991). Comprehension of verbal terms for emotions in normal, autistic, and schizophrenic children. *Developmental Neuropsychology, 7,* 1–18.

Ventner, A., Lord, C., & Schopler, D. (1992). A follow-up study of high-functioning autistic children. *Journal of Child Psychology and Psychiatry, 33,* 489–507.

Volden, J., & Lord, C. (1991). Neologisms and idiosyncratic language in autistic speakers. *Journal of Autism and Developmental Disorders, 21,* 109–130.

Volkmar, F. R., Klin, A., Siegal, B., Szatmari, P., Lord, C., Campbell, M., et al. (1994). Field trial for autistic disorder in *DSM-IV. American Journal of Psychiatry, 151,* 1361–1367.

Wahlberg, T., & Magliano, J. P. (2004). The ability of high function individuals with autism to comprehend written discourse. *Discourse Processes, 38*(1), 119–144.

Weir, R. (1962). *Language in the crib.* The Hague, The Netherlands: Mouton.

Wetherby, A. (1986). Ontogeny of communication functions in autism. *Journal of Autism and Developmental Disorders, 16,* 295–316.

Wetherby, A. M., & Prutting, C. A. (1984). Profiles of communicative and cognitive-social abilities in autistic children. *Journal of Speech and Hearing Research, 27,* 364–377.

Wing, L. (1981). Asperger's syndrome: A clinical account. *Journal of Autism and Developmental Disorders, 9,* 11–29.

Yule, W., & Rutter, M. (1987). *Language development and disorders.* London: MacKeith.

Ziatas, K., Durkin, K., & Pratt, C. (2003). Differences in assertive speech acts produced by children with autism, Asperger syndrome, specific language impairment, and normal development. *Development and Psychopathology, 15,* 73–94.

CHAPTER 13

Neuropsychological Characteristics in Autism and Related Conditions

KATHERINE D. TSATSANIS

Autism represents the paradigmatic pervasive developmental disorder (PDD) but is itself characterized by considerable clinical variability. Symptoms and signs typify this psychiatric syndrome (as well as others) rather than etiologies; in the face of substantial phenotypic heterogeneity, the identification of core psychological markers can be helpful toward studies of pathogenesis. There are numerous competing theories to account for pathways of development in autism. In the literature on the psychological and developmental aspects of the disorder, specific social-cognitive as well as general perceptual cognitive and learning mechanisms have been examined (Volkmar, Lord, Bailey, Schultz, & Klin, 2004). Within each of these divisions, there are specific skills and processes proposed to have causal explanatory value, including joint attention and face processing skills on the one hand, and sensory perception, attention, memory, and executive functions on the other.

An approach to understanding autism that puts faith in the explanatory power of a single construct is highly suspect. At the very least, the complexity and variability of expression of the syndrome argues against a unitary cause. Moreover, the proposed constructs are themselves neither unitary nor fully explicated. Although individual researchers may emphasize different components of functioning and use a distinct language, they are alike in fundamental ways. Each of their theories represents an attempt to characterize how individuals with autism acquire and process information and in turn form an internal representation of the world. Core deficits in regulation, integration, and flexibility are represented in these models.

OVERVIEW

Autism and related spectrum conditions are neurodevelopmental disorders that primarily involve disruptions of social development, impaired verbal and nonverbal communication, and behavioral disturbances. Reviewing neuropsychological factors in autism and PDD presents several challenges as the literature is expansive and diverse. Psychological models that currently dominate the field include theory of mind, central coherence, and executive functions, with related research findings interpreted and integrated into these specific constructs. Because these models are reviewed elsewhere in this *Handbook,* they will not be critically evaluated here. Social-cognitive mechanisms and language development also fall within the domain of neuropsychological function, but each is addressed in a separate chapter. In this chapter, focus is placed on specific cognitive learning mechanisms later positioned in the context of a broader discussion of relevant issues in the field.

Despite the noted quantity of research, methodological issues present a special challenge in this review because they render findings among studies equivocal and limit general conclusions. A major source of variability lies in subject selection, which includes age, level of functioning, choice of control groups, and number of subjects. The possibility of clinical heterogeneity between groups of individuals with autism is a crucial concern that highlights the need for a well-characterized sample and appropriate controls. In addition, a more clearly systematic approach to the investigation of these domains of functioning will advance understanding.

One unequivocal characteristic of PDD is clinical variability; children with various forms of PDD may share many core features, but their individual pathways to learning or cognitive profiles have unique characteristics. Treatment approaches are enhanced when the core areas of strength and vulnerability for individuals with autism are identified and evaluated across stages of development. In the current discussion, the specific assets and deficits identified are in most cases neither specific to nor characteristic of all individuals with autism. They do, however, represent meaningful areas for clinical consideration and recognize significant programs of research.

SENSORY PERCEPTION

In early emerging cognitive theories of autism, sensory disturbances are well documented and viewed as a primary area of deficit. Ornitz and Ritvo (1968b) detailed the range of hypo- and hypersensitivities affecting each of the senses in over 150 cases of autism. Based on their observations, they postulated that an inability to adequately modulate sensory input in children with autism manifests itself in alternating states of excitement (e.g., spinning, hand flapping, hypersensitivity to stimuli) and inhibition (e.g., nonresponsiveness) and that this state of dysregulation, or homeostatic imbalance, in turn leads to perceptual inconstancy. From this account, inadequate modulation of sensory input in autism produces inconsistent and disordered perceptions of external events. The (lack of) coherence of these children's perceptions is considered to impact on early developmental achievements including social relating and communication (Ornitz, 1974, 1983; Ornitz & Ritvo, 1968a, 1968b, 1976).

Descriptions of unusual responses to sensory stimuli are readily found in first-person accounts of autism. For example, Temple Grandin (1992) makes note of her profound hypersensitivity to touch and sound. The repetitive behaviors that are manifest in autism also often appear to involve a sensory stimulatory component (e.g., visual fascination with spinning wheels, fans, string), and it is argued that disturbances of movement, such as hand flapping and whirling, may in fact provide wanted sensory input through visual and proprioceptive channels (Ornitz, 1983). Variability of response to sensory input may also be linked to the individual's state of arousal. Grandin (1995) makes a connection between her own problems in sensory reactivity and her unresponsive affect (or shutting down) and fearful states.

In current research, autistic children's unusual responsivity to sensory stimuli and unusual patterns of behavior are understudied relative to other symptom areas, such as social, language, and cognitive deficits. Yet, an abnormal response to sensory stimulation is consistently found to differentiate between children with autism and developmentally matched controls in studies of early behavioral characteristics (Adrien et al., 1992; Dahlgren & Gillberg, 1989; Osterling & Dawson, 1994; Stone, 1997). This cluster of behaviors includes: empty gaze; visual fascination with patterns and movements; failure to react to sounds/appearing deaf; hyposensitivity to pain, cold, or heat; hypersensitivity to taste; and inappropriate use of objects (e.g., interest in the sensory aspects of objects, such as licking/mouthing, peering, or interest in texture). Abnormal sensory reactivity appears to differentiate children with autism from typical and mixed developmentally delayed groups by $2\frac{1}{2}$ years of age, although children with fragile X syndrome also show increased sensory symptoms (Rogers, Hepburn, & Wehner, 2003).

Studies using parent questionnaires also report more severe or more frequent sensory symptoms in young (3 through 6 years of age; Watling, Deitz, & White, 2001) and school-age children with autism (Kientz & Dunn, 1997) as well as children with Asperger syndrome (AS; Dunn, Myles, & Orr, 2002), with the need for external validation using clinical assessment methods. A significant association was not found when the relationship between sensory symptom severity and severity of autism symptomotology was examined (Kientz & Dunn, 1997; Rogers et al., 2003), but degree of abnormal sensory responsivity and impairments in adaptive behavior were related

(Rogers et al., 2003). The sensory qualities associated with autism do not appear to be specific to the disorder, nor is there evidence of a direct relationship between these disturbances and the central social and communicative impairments, but there is sufficient evidence to indicate that unusual responses to sensory stimuli are a significant feature.

The sensory features in autism merit further clinical and research attention. One approach to the presence of these sensory disturbances has been to appreciate more fully their connection with levels of arousal, attention, emotional regulation, and action or adaptive goal-directed behavior (Anzalone & Williamson, 2000; Laurent & Rubin, 2004). Ornitz and Ritvo (1968a; Ornitz, 1983, 1988) also proposed neurological substrates for a disturbance in the modulation of sensory input in autism. Their earlier writings pointed to the reticular activating system and vestibular system. More recently, Ornitz (1988) has also emphasized a role for the thalamus. In their seminal paper, Damasio and Maurer (1978) concluded that multiple brain regions are involved in autism, including the mesial frontal lobes, mesial temporal lobes, basal ganglia, and thalamus (specifically, dorsomedial and anterior nuclear groups). The thalamus has traditionally been referred to as the sensory gateway of the cortex, but a current perspective of this structure suggests that it is involved in multiple processes that permit the transmission, tuning, and integrated processing of information in the brain. A magnetic resonance imaging (MRI) study of the thalamus in individuals with autism indicated that despite increases in cortical size, the thalamus does not appear to develop to the expected degree in individuals with autism (Tsatsanis et al., 2003).

The early emphasis on the role of sensory modulation systems was later supplanted by an emphasis on attentional systems. The focus moved away from response to sensory input to the processes involved in the identification and selection of relevant information in general. This was reflected in deficit terminology such as stimulus overselectivity, directed attention, and attentional shifts. In addition, at least one group of researchers (Courchesne, 1995; Courchesne, Saitoh, et al., 1994; Courchesne, Townsend,

et al., 1994) proposed that attention was a central deficit in autism and that the neocerebellum was an important structure in the coordination of attention and arousal systems, presenting evidence for its abnormal development in autism (Courchesne, Saitoh, et al., 1994; Courchesne, Yeung-Courchesne, Press, Hesselink, & Jernigan, 1988; Murakami, Courchesne, Press, Yeung-Courchesne, Hesselink, 1989).

ATTENTION

Specific behavioral observations as well as programs of research give emphasis to impairments in attention in individuals with autism. Attention is a core capacity that is central to the processes of information reduction, response selection, and preparation for eventual action. New information arrives in the form of a continuous flow of both internal and external stimuli, and individuals develop an increasing capacity to override the impulse to attend to what is most striking or novel or desired in order to anticipate, direct, or guide attention based on prior knowledge and internal goals. Behavioral qualities of individuals with autism often include an intense focus on unusual features of objects and repetitive activities, attention to nonsalient aspects of the environment, and difficulty shifting focus or transitioning from one activity to the next. The preliminary research on attention in autism points to potential areas of relative function and dysfunction, with the early emphasis on the role of sensory modulation systems in autism supplanted in this literature by an emphasis on attentional systems.

Sustained attention for simple repetitive visual information is generally intact in individuals with autism compared to developmentally matched controls, as measured by continuous performance tasks (Buchsbaum et al., 1992; Casey, Gordon, Mannheim, & Rumsey, 1993; Garretson, Fein, & Waterhouse, 1990; Goldstein, Johnson, & Minshew, 2001; Minshew, Goldstein, & Siegel, 1997; Pascualvaca, Fantie, Papageorgiou, & Mirsky, 1998), whereas a preliminary study of attention in Asperger syndrome (AS) was suggestive of an attention deficit, specifically manifest in an inconsistent or variable response pattern to stimuli in a sustained visual attention task (Schatz, Weimer, & Trauner, 2002). Deficits in attention in autism are typically reported for more complex tasks requiring filtering, selective attention, and shifts in attentional focus. On a target discrimination task, low-functioning individuals with autism were found to benefit from the presentation of a target location cue, but were more susceptible to nontarget distracters than their developmentally matched counterparts (Burack, 1994). Ciesielski, Courchesne, and Elmasian (1990) compared high-functioning adults with autism to age-matched controls on a divided-attention task involving two modalities—vision and audition. The adults with autism showed significantly higher false alarm rates on this task, indicating greater difficulty ignoring the competing stimuli. This result was also interpreted as perseverative behavior or a failure to shift from one response modality to the other. The findings from other studies support the notion that individuals with autism may have difficulty shifting attention both within and between modalities (Casey et al., 1993; Courchesne, Townsend, et al., 1994; Townsend, Harris, & Courchesne, 1996; Wainwright-Sharp & Bryson, 1996). The two important variables identified in these studies were speed and expectancy, suggesting that individuals with autism have specific difficulty making rapid changes in their expectations. Researchers who place this deficit at a higher order level suggest that it is part of a more general difficulty with executive control originating from frontal lobe dysfunction, as evidenced by specific deficits on measures of attention that require cognitive flexibility or shifting between categories, sets, or rules (Goldstein et al., 2001; Ozonoff et al., 2004; Pascualvaca et al., 1998). Others find evidence for a more basic deficiency in broadening the spread of visual attention (e.g., the attentional spotlight) and difficulty moving from local to global processing in support of the theory of weak central coherence (Mann & Walker, 2003). Burack, Enns, Stauder, Mottron, and Randolf (1997) in their review originally emphasized a deficit in voluntary control over appropriate sizing of attentional gaze to allow for efficient task performance or focus on what is relevant in the context of ignoring what is extraneous.

The evidence from behavioral research points to the importance of clarifying these mechanisms in future research. Individuals with autism and AS show deficiencies with regard to processing the most essential or salient information from stimulus-rich environments (Klin, Jones, Schultz, & Volkmar, 2003) and attending to meaningful or shared aspects of a learning situation, namely, those not explicitly stated (Klin, 2000), both of which are of great relevance to the daily lives of individuals with autism. Developmentally, a related concept is that of joint attention. Joint attention skills, acts of coordinating attention between interactive social partners and environmental stimuli, are a distinguishing deficit area for children with autism (considered in more depth in Chapter 25). Orienting to the social overtures of others requires that specific information is registered, attended to, and has meaning. The findings of attentional limitations in both the social and cognitive arenas reflect two theoretical perspectives that have historically dominated the literature. The first asserts that social impairments in individuals with autism are a secondary effect of a primary deficit in cognitive functioning (e.g., Courchesne, Townsend, et al., 1994; DeLong, 1992; Hughes, Russell, & Robbins, 1994; Ozonoff, 1995; Ozonoff, Pennington, & Rogers, 1991; Ozonoff, Strayer, McMahon, & Filloux, 1994). In the second, social impairment, and specifically social cognition, is considered to be the primary deficit in autism (e.g., Baron-Cohen, Leslie, & Frith, 1985; Happe & Frith, 1995).

The pattern of relative strengths in attention, namely, the ability to sustain attention to simple repetitive visual information (i.e., static visual cues) versus relative vulnerabilities in attention such as determining salient aspects of the environment and shifting attention, has significant implications for educational programming. Therapists and educators can, for example, introduce consistent and static visual supports in the environment and within specific activities to enhance attention to salient pieces of information and to the need to shift to a new piece of information when relevant. For young children with autism who are at a prelinguistic or emerging language level, social orienting and joint attention are relevant programmatic goals. As infants begin to coordinate their attention to objects and people, they also begin to direct the attention of others to their objects of desire or interest (initiate joint attention). They further monitor others' focus of attention (respond to joint attention bids), deriving vast amounts of information about interests and dangers in the environment, and begin their participation in social learning opportunities (Adamson, 1995; Mundy & Gomes, 1998; Mundy, Sigman, & Kasari, 1994; Mundy, Sigman, Ungerer, & Sherman, 1986; Tomasello, Kruger, & Ratner, 1993; Ulvund & Smith, 1996). There is evidence further to support the relationship between these early developmental processes and language development in autism (Charman et al., 2001, 2003; Lord & Schopler, 1989; Mundy, Sigman, & Kasari, 1990; Mundy et al., 1994). Establishing early intentional behaviors and a consistent means for expressing intent appear to have a pivotal role in other aspects of development in individuals with autism.

MEMORY

It is well to understand the role of memory in autism because very few aspects of higher cognitive function and learning could operate successfully without some memory contribution. Memory is often treated as a unitary construct but should be recognized as comprising multiple interrelated systems. Both the behavioral and neuropsychological research evidence suggests the usefulness of considering different aspects of memory in autism. Some such individuals show extraordinary memory for discrete domains of knowledge. At the same time, they are observed to have tremendous difficulty navigating their daily environment, such as remembering where objects and belongings are located and remembering their schedule of classes and activities or morning routine. Further, the capacity of higher functioning individuals to provide a reliable account of the day's activities or to recollect personal experiences is more limited than might be predicted based on level of language or cognitive functioning alone. In the context of these observations, provisional conclusions that can be drawn from studies of memory function in autism and AS are considered next.

Clinical observations suggest that individuals with autism typically achieve learning through rote memory, classical conditioning (e.g., stimulus-response learning), and procedural mechanisms, but show a more limited capacity for flexibility, abstraction, and generalization. It is consistently found that individuals with autism show intact digit span and intact immediate recall for semantically unrelated lists of words relative to ability-matched and, in some cases, normal controls (Bennetto, Pennington, & Rogers, 1996; Goldstein et al., 2001; Lincoln, Allen, & Kilman, 1995). There is also evidence to suggest well-developed associative learning mechanisms (Boucher & Warrington, 1976; Minshew & Goldstein, 2001; Minshew, Goldstein, Muenz, & Payton, 1992). However, overall performance on the immediate recall of semantically *related* lists of words was impaired for autistic subjects relative to ability-matched and normal controls (Boucher & Warrington, 1976; Tager-Flusberg, 1991). When a cued recall paradigm was used, the autistic subjects benefited from the provision of semantic cues, suggesting a deficit in retrieval versus encoding processes. Individuals with autism may equally encode the meanings of the words presented but be deficient in their ability to employ a strategic search to assist their retrieval of the unrecalled semantically related words. The results of similar list learning tasks also offer some support for inefficiency in the ability to actively organize information during learning and retrieval for individuals with autism, reflected, for example, in an impaired serial position effect or failure to group words into conceptual categories (Bennetto et al., 1996; Minshew & Goldstein, 1993; Minshew et al., 1992; Renner, Klinger, & Klinger, 2000). This last effect was also found in adults with AS (Bowler, Matthews, & Gardiner, 1997). Tasks requiring a greater level of semantic organization also appear to impact the memory performance of autistic subjects, which may reflect a more general deficiency related to complexity of the material to be remembered (Fein et al., 1996; Minshew & Goldstein, 2001).

Organization has a role in memory as do other executive control processes. Working memory tasks require the ability to simultaneously attend to, recall, and act on information held in an online state. This aspect of memory function is often considered in the domain of executive function and is needed for completion of many such problem-solving tasks. Although deficits in working memory may be found in autism, they do not appear to be specific to this disorder. In a recent study (Russell, Jarrold, & Henry, 1996), when presented with working memory capacity tasks, both children with autism and children with moderate learning difficulties performed significantly more poorly than the normal controls on all three tasks. There was no difference, however, in the performance between the two comparison groups. The authors concluded that working memory deficits are not specific to autism but are likely related to a general deficit in information processing (marked by level of intellectual functioning). Ozonoff and Strayer (2001) also reported no autism-specific impairments in working memory in the context of a significant association between IQ, age, and performance on working memory tasks. Bennetto et al. (1996) ostensibly found a different set of results, but a careful consideration of the tasks used in their study is more suggestive of an evaluation of episodic versus working memory processes (see later discussion).

Most memory tasks comprise both implicit and explicit learning components. *Explicit memory,* also referred to as *declarative memory,* is considered with reference to two subsystems defined by Tulving (1972) as episodic and semantic memory. *Episodic* memory refers to the system involved in recollecting particular experiences, whereas *semantic* memory refers to factual knowledge or knowledge of the world. Bowler and colleagues examined episodic memory function in adults with AS in a series of studies and reported impairments in source memory as well as greater reliance on *knowing* and less reliance on *remembering* relative to controls (e.g., Bowler, Gardiner, & Grice, 2000; Gardiner, Bowler, & Grice, 2003). Episodic memory function has also been examined in autistic subjects, although often not the stated focus of study. Boucher (1981a) compared the performance of autistic children and ability-matched controls on a test of immediate recall of a series of word lists. There was no significant difference between the total recall scores of the two groups; however, there was a significant difference between their primacy and recency scores. The

children with autism showed significantly poorer recall of the first three words of the lists (primacy effect) but comparable recall of the last three words (recency effect). It is proposed that the last three words in the list are maintained in the articulatory loop of the working memory system. This account is consistent with the results of Russell et al.'s (1996) study indicating that the articulatory loop is intact in individuals with autism. In contrast, recall of the first three words of the study episode requires the individual to consciously recollect and reexamine the study list, thereby drawing on episodic memory.

Boucher (1981b) also examined memory for recent events in three groups of children who ranged in age from 10 to 16 years. They included children with autism, mentally retarded children, and normal controls. The children were present for a 1- to 2-hour session, during which they participated in a variety of activities. At the end of the session, the materials were cleared away and the children were asked to recall the session's events. Single-word responses and gestures were acceptable. Boucher reported a significant difference among the recall scores of all three groups. The children with autism recalled significantly fewer events relative to both comparison groups. In addition, the performance of the mentally retarded children was poorer than that of the normal controls. It is argued that this type of task also assesses episodic memory because it requires the children to think back to and reexperience a prior subjective event. Notably, Boucher (1981b) observed that the autistic children's recall improved when they were provided with cueing strategies. Again, the deficit appears to lie in retrieval (e.g., making use of context-dependent cues) versus encoding processes.

The results of a second related study appear to support this interpretation (Boucher & Lewis, 1989). In this case, children were asked to recall activities that they had taken part in several months earlier. The performance of children with autism was compared to learning-disabled controls under free recall (e.g., open questions) and cued recall (e.g., leading questions) conditions. Whereas the free recall scores differed significantly, the cued recall scores were not significantly different between the two groups. Although the children with autism engaged in little self-cueing, they were able to benefit from cues provided by the examiner.

Bennetto et al. (1996) examined whether individuals with autism display a pattern of deficits that is similar to patients with frontal lesions. Measures of temporal order memory, source memory, and working memory were administered. The subjects consisted of high-functioning autistic (HFA) children and children with learning disabilities. A comparison of the performance of the two groups showed that the children with autism were significantly impaired on all tasks. Notably, the autistic group also displayed significantly more intrusion errors on a list-learning task, which was interpreted as a deficit in source memory. Bennetto et al. observed that the children with autism in their study displayed a pattern of memory function that is similar to that of patients with frontal lesions and interpreted their findings in terms of a general deficit in working memory. However, the tasks that they employed in their study appeared more consistent with a usual approach to the assessment of episodic memory. On the Sentence and Counting Span tasks, subjects were required to process information, but they were not asked to simultaneously store that information. Rather, the subjects were asked to recall their responses at the end of the task. Wheeler, Stuss, and Tulving (1997) identified three types of tests that assess episodic memory. One approach is to assess aspects of the learning episode that are not central to the target information. The Sentence and Counting span tasks appear to fulfill this requirement. The items requested for recall on these tasks would be recoverable only through a conscious recollection of the study episode. In addition, Wheeler et al. identified tests of memory for source and memory for temporal order, specifically Corsi's task, as measures of episodic memory. Again, these appear to be precisely the kinds of instruments employed in the Bennetto et al. study.

In contrast to episodic memory, implicit memory does not require conscious or intentional recollection of experiences although they are shown to have an effect on current performance. When perceptual processing tasks have been used to examine implicit memory in autism and AS, no evidence of impairment has

been found (Bowler et al., 1997; Gardiner et al., 2003; Renner et al., 2000). Whereas age and level of intellectual ability are more strongly associated with performance on explicit memory tasks, task complexity (e.g., level of conceptual analysis or semantic organization) is likely to be a strong factor in both. Atypical patterns of results on list learning tasks (e.g., with manipulations to examine the effect of variables such as levels of processing, associative value, and redundancy) also suggest that it is the relation between semantic memory and episodic memory that explains impairment on explicit memory tasks (Beversdorf et al., 2000; Toichi & Kamio, 2002, 2003). There may not be a problem in semantic memory per se (but rather effective retrieval from semantic memory), but the question remains whether the organization of semantic memory in individuals with autism is similar to that of typically developing individuals.

There are a small number of researchers who have speculated that at least some of the characteristics of autism could be explained in terms of a memory deficit. Boucher (1981a; Boucher & Warrington, 1976) suggested that the pattern of memory performance of autistic individuals is similar to that of patients with medial temporal lobe amnesic disorder; however, the cumulative research evidence does not support this proposal. DeLong (1992) postulated that autism is the developmental syndrome of hippocampal dysfunction in the young child and proposed that individuals with autism are not able to benefit from experiential learning (i.e., integrating past and present experiences to create a structure of meaning), which may account for a typically rote or rigid manner when engaged in events and interactions and the need for explicit preparation when entering a novel context or social situation. Powell and Jordan (1993) discuss a role for episodic memory and its implications for teaching autistic individuals how to learn. There is also some support for abnormalities in brain regions identified as central to memory functions. Notably, the pathophysiology of autism implicates regions including the hippocampal formation, amygdala, and cerebellum (Abell et al., 1999; Aylward et al., 1999; Bachevalier, 1994; Bachevalier & Merjanian, 1994; Bauman & Kemper, 1994; Courchesne et al., 1988; Kemper & Bauman, 1993; Schultz, Romanski, & Tsatsanis, 2000). Clinical (e.g., executive function) studies support a role for frontal lobe dysfunction in autism. Bennetto et al. (1996) observed that the autistic children in their study displayed a pattern of memory function that is similar to that of patients with frontal lesions. Evidence from PET studies indicates that episodic retrieval is associated with increased blood flow in the right prefrontal cortex. In addition, episodic encoding has been consistently associated with activation in the region of the left prefrontal cortex (reviewed by Cabeza & Nyberg, 2000).

EXECUTIVE FUNCTION

Although there is some overlap with the domains of attention and memory, distinct measures, concepts, and neuroanatomical regions characterize this literature, especially pertaining to function in the prefrontal cortex and measures developed to assess such function. Several behavioral characteristics of individuals with autism are reminiscent of the kinds of impairments seen in patients with prefrontal cortical damage. These characteristics include response perseveration, disinhibition, narrow range of interests, failure to plan, difficulty taking the perspective of others, and lack of self-monitoring. A failure to generalize newly learned concepts is also ascribed to deficits in higher cognitive functioning. This led at least one group of researchers (e.g., Ozonoff and colleagues) to have proposed a primary role for executive function deficits in autism and implicate frontal regions in its expression.

Executive function corresponds to the ability to maintain an appropriate problem-solving set to guide future (goal-directed) behavior. It is composed of a set of abilities including inhibition, set shifting, planning, memory, and self-monitoring. From studies of traditional executive function tasks, such as the Wisconsin Card Sorting Test, it is observed that for individuals with autism, the capacity to deal with complex information or new situations is limited by deficits in cognitive flexibility and/or an incomplete understanding of novel/abstract concepts (Bennetto et al., 1996; Goldstein et al., 2001; Minshew, Meyer, & Goldstein, 2002; Ozonoff & McEvoy, 1994; Ozonoff, Pennington, et al., 1991; Ozonoff &

Strayer, 1997; Ozonoff et al., 1994; Rumsey & Hamburger, 1990; Szatmari, Tuff, Finlayson, & Bartolucci, 1990). Conceptual flexibility versus perceptual or attentional flexibility (or simple inhibitory control) appears to be the predominant deficit in higher functioning individuals (Goldstein et al., 2001; Ozonoff et al., 1994, 2004; Ozonoff & Strayer, 1997). Additionally, rule learning and shifting within a rule or category are within the range of normal function (Berger, Aerts, van Spaendonck, Cools, & Teunisse, 2003; Minshew et al., 2002; Ozonoff et al., 2004). Higher functioning individuals with autism show some capacity to learn rules and procedures as well as identify concepts but are challenged to abstract information to attain concepts or develop flexible strategies for problem solving, which may be evidenced most directly by perseverative errors or persisting in a strategy even when it is not successful.

Strong group differences in performance have also been found on the Tower of Hanoi and modified versions of this task (Bennetto et al., 1996; Hughes et al., 1994; Ozonoff et al., 1991, 1994, 2004; Szatmari et al., 1990). Ozonoff et al. (1991) reported that the Tower of Hanoi provided the highest discriminatory power between groups of high-functioning children with autism and matched controls, relative to other measures (e.g., theory of mind, memory, emotion perception, and visual spatial tasks). This finding was particularly interesting because the control group consisted of children who might also be expected to show executive function deficits (e.g., 25% of the control sample met criteria for attention deficit/hyperactivity disorder [ADHD]). Deficits were found at both lower and higher levels of IQ in individuals with autism on a related task (Stockings of Cambridge), and the expected age-related improvement in planning efficiency was not observed in the autistic group, indicating that these impairments may be most severe in adolescence (Ozonoff et al., 2004). This may explain failures to find group differences in younger children with autism on executive function tasks (e.g., Griffith, Pennington, Wehner, & Rogers, 1999).

These tests are commonly used measures of executive function that require the individual to solve a problem by planning before acting and identifying the subgoals needed to reach a target goal. The task also typically taps rule following and procedural learning. It is proposed that the challenge for higher functioning individuals with autism is related to planning efficiency (Ozonoff et al., 2004) and resolving goal-subgoal conflicts (Goldstein et al., 2001). When children with HFA and ADHD were compared on a range of tasks involving executive functions, the HFA group showed broad-based deficits but were distinguished by more significant difficulties with planning and cognitive flexibility, whereas the ADHD group showed deficits in inhibiting a prepotent response and verbal fluency (Geurts, Verté, Oosterlaan, Roeyers, & Sergeant, 2004). Parent ratings of the behavior in these groups of children also yield a range of elevations on executive function scales although, again, the autism group is distinguishable by deficits in flexibility whereas the ADHD (combined) group exhibits more severe inhibitory deficits when compared (Gioia, Isquith, Kenworthy, & Barton, 2002).

Individuals with AS also show deficits in executive functioning and may perform equally poorly as individuals with HFA (Manjiviona & Prior, 1999; Miller & Ozonoff, 2000; Ozonoff, Rogers, & Pennington, 1991; Szatmari et al., 1990). From Goldman-Rakic (1987), the function of the prefrontal cortex is to guide behavior by internal representations of the outside world, without direct stimulation from the environment. These deficits can be related more generally to an inability to disengage from immediate environmental cues and be guided by internal rules or mental representations. Indeed, a preliminary study of individuals with AS revealed a significant deficit in spatial working memory but no impairment in strategy formation on a spatial task (Morris et al., 1999). The authors suggested that individuals with AS may have more general difficulty in accessing different types of visual and spatial representations to guide behavior, which may also account for difficulties on problem-solving tasks.

Ozonoff (1995) and others (Hughes, 2001; Russell, 1997) have argued for the contributions of executive functions in understanding the range of impairments in autism. Frontal lobe abnormalities in autism are also hypothesized, by reason that executive function is mediated by regions of the frontal lobes. Two

regions in the prefrontal cortex are distinguished: Damage to dorsolateral regions is associated with impairment in high-level cognitive ability, whereas damage to orbital regions is associated with disturbances in social and affective behavior (e.g., Damasio, 1985). Ozonoff notes that because the frontal cortex is central to the regulation of both higher cognitive and social emotional behavior and individuals with autism display deficits in both of these domains, then frontal lobe dysfunction may be able to account for the impairments seen in autism. Recent results of neuroimaging studies do offer preliminary support for frontal lobe involvement in autism (Baron-Cohen et al., 1999; Luna et al., 2002; Minshew, Luna, & Sweeney, 1999; Zilbovicius et al., 1995). Notably, however, tasks designed to tap cognitive function associated with frontal and medial temporal regions of the brain were more strongly related to communication symptoms (Joseph & Tager-Flusberg, 2004) and adaptive behavior (Ozonoff et al., 2004) than to autism severity or specific autism symptoms related to social interaction and repetitive behavior. In their sample of verbal, school-age children, executive control abilities did not explain theory of mind performance when nonverbal ability and language level were controlled, with the exception of a task that required the combined capacity of inhibitory control and working memory (Joseph & Tager-Flusberg, 2004). The latter task did not have similar explanatory power for autism symptoms; rather, the higher order cognitive task (Tower test) did contribute to communication symptoms. This may be related to a more general deficit in planning and organization in the context of online discourse (Joseph & Tager-Flusberg, 2004).

Concrete thinking and limited abstraction abilities have long been observed in individuals with autism (Adams & Sheslow, 1983; Rutter, 1978; Tsai, 1992) and can be related to overall developmental or intellectual level. However, another relevant dichotomy when thinking about concrete versus abstract/conceptual ability is that of internally controlled processes or generative demands and externally generated problem-solving strategies and external structures (e.g., the solution is inherent in or constrained by the problem). This latter question is reminiscent of Klin et al.'s

(2003) discussion of "open domain" and "closed domain" tasks in the context of social environment as well as research suggesting intact rule categorization in the face of impaired formation of prototypic mental representations when a concrete rule is not available on cognitive tasks (e.g., Klinger & Dawson, 2001). In both instances, individuals with autism appear to be more capable of knowing through a set of rules versus knowing through learning formed from repeated experience. It is not surprising, then, that intervention approaches emphasize consistency, routine, and predictability, through the use of visual and verbal supports for planning events across the day, preparing for challenging situations, making the implicit rules of engagement explicit, as well as teaching generalization (e.g., applying the rules in naturalistic situations).

COGNITIVE PROFILES

Level of cognitive functioning for individuals with a PDD spans the entire range, from profound mental retardation to superior intellect. The terms *low-functioning* (IQ < 70) and *high-functioning* (IQ > 70) autism are often used in the literature to denote subgroups based on differences in level of intellectual ability. This distinction has also been applied to the children described by Kanner (1943) and Asperger (1944). Whereas Kanner's description is consistent with the classically autistic or lower functioning child with autism, Asperger's description has been associated with the less impaired, more verbal, and older child with autism (Klin & Volkmar, 1997).

The intellectual profiles of individuals with autism have been reviewed extensively, and it is typically found that visual and visual spatial processing are well preserved and frequently a strength relative to verbal abilities (e.g., Ghaziuddin & Mountain-Kimchi, 2004; and Barnhill, Hagiwara, Myles, & Simpson, 2000; Lincoln et al., 1995; Mayes & Calhoun, 2003, for a review). This finding is consistent with the observations of Temple Grandin (1992), a high-functioning individual with autism, who emphasizes her own visually mediated approach to learning and making sense of the world. Selected verbal subtests, such as Comprehension (assessing understanding or common sense reasoning and social judgment),

on the Wechsler scales are typically significantly impaired relative to strengths on subtests involving visual perceptual or spatial analysis and integration, such as Block Design and Object Assembly. The discrepancy between verbal and nonverbal abilities in autism also needs to be examined in the context of factors such as age and overall level of ability.

Whereas the Wechsler scales are recommended for more able and verbally proficient children with autism, the Leiter International Performance Scale Revised (Leiter-R) is valuable for the larger group of children with autism who have more profound communication, attentional, and behavioral difficulties. In a group of children who presented with significant language limitations and obtained a Vineland Expressive Communication age-equivalent score at or below 3 years of age, Leiter-R scores indicated higher nonverbal IQ scores with strengths on subtests drawing primarily on visualization skills and particularly spatial reasoning (Tsatsanis et al., 2003). Using the WISC-III, Mayes and Calhoun (2003) found strengths in lexical knowledge relative to verbal reasoning in both high- and low-IQ groups of older children, but a selective strength in visual spatial ability in their low-IQ group. Within the younger age group, assessed using the Stanford-Binet, IV, relative strengths in visual processing were found for both IQ groups, as well as a strength in rote memory. The disparity between verbal and nonverbal abilities observed in the younger group was not obtained in the group of older children, representing an increase in verbal IQ (VIQ) versus change in nonverbal ability. Ghaziuddin and Mountain-Kimchi (2004) also found no difference in WISC-III VIQ and performance IQ (PIQ) scores overall in their sample of subjects with HFA (mean age 12.42 years). Current knowledge regarding cognitive abilities in individuals with autism is at minimum consistent for a scattered profile; cognitive function may not be well integrated, yielding isolated strengths and a broad range of deficits. Longitudinal studies are needed to test evidence of continuity and discontinuity pertaining to cognitive profiles over time and whether specific performance profiles (versus overall level of ability) on measures of cognitive functioning predict outcome on measures of autistic symptomatology or social ability and disability.

The intellectual profiles of individuals with AS point to a pattern of better verbal relative to poorer perceptual organizational skills overall (Ehlers et al., 1997; Ghaziuddin & Mountain-Kimchi, 2004; Lincoln, Courchesne, Allen, Hanson, & Ene, 1998; Ozonoff, South, & Miller, 2000), with notable exceptions (e.g., Szatmari et al., 1990). Intragroup analyses indicate significantly higher global IQ scores and a significant split between VIQ and PIQ with VIQ > PIQ on average for AS as a group relative to HFA. In consideration of these findings, a particular neuropsychological model, nonverbal learning disability (NLD; Rourke, 1989), has been proposed as a source of external validity for AS (Klin & Volkmar, 1997; Klin, Volkmar, Sparrow, Cicchetti, & Rourke, 1995). In brief, the NLD profile involves a pattern of functioning of better developed verbal relative to visual, tactile, and complex motor skills as well as better reading and spelling skills relative to arithmetic. Klin et al. (1995) reported that deficits that were predictive of AS were fine motor skills, visual motor integration, visual spatial perception, nonverbal concept formation, gross motor skills, and visual memory. Deficits that were identified as not predictive of AS included articulation, verbal output, auditory perception, vocabulary, and verbal memory. This finding was also reflected more generally in the pattern of IQ scores in the two groups as the AS group showed a significant and unusually large verbal-performance discrepancy (higher VIQ compared to PIQ score), whereas no such discrepancy was exhibited by the HFA group. Preserved verbal memory skills, relative to individuals with HFA and relative to their own abilities, have been reported by others (e.g., Gunter, Ghaziuddin, & Ellis, 2002; Ozonoff et al., 1991). In addition, better reading/decoding relative to mechanical arithmetic skills is found (Griswold, Barnhill, Myles, Hagiwara, & Simpson, 2002). These results have important implications for intervention, suggesting that one treatment modality may be preferred for children and adolescents with AS (e.g., verbally mediated strategies), relative to children with HFA (e.g., visual supports; Volkmar, Klin, Schultz, Rubin, & Bronen, 2000). This is an area of ongoing debate complicated by differences in diagnostic approaches that make it difficult to compare studies (Klin & Volkmar, 2003), especially in the context of variability in the cognitive profiles within each group. Additionally, the restrictive onset criteria for AS relative to HFA (leading to differences in early language abilities) is considered by some to represent another confound.

CONCLUSION

Although autism is a syndrome that is defined primarily in behavioral terms, there has been considerable research devoted to the various cognitive impairments that characterize individuals with this disorder. In association with these findings, competing theories have arisen concerning the primacy of a specific deficit in explaining the disorder. The complexity and clinical heterogeneity that is typical of the PDDs is reflected not only in these accounts but also in differences in subject characteristics. With fundamental disparities in subject selection and diagnostic assignment, questions remain regarding the neuropsychological phenotype in autism, including aspects of the phenotype that are specific to the disorder, how the phenotype changes with development, and how these constructs might explain the fundamental social and adaptive impairments as well as any response to treatment in this population. It is reasonable to expect that if a psychological process is causatively linked to the pathogenesis of autism, then levels of disruption in the given area should hold a quantified and proportional relationship to levels of, for example, social competence in daily life (Volkmar et al., 2004). To date, few studies have attempted to measure this predictive relationship (Dawson et al., 2002; Klin, Jones, Schultz, Volkmar, & Cohen, 2002).

The questions of phenotypic boundaries and diagnostic categorization are far from resolved but are well to be considered from a developmental perspective. Cross-sectional studies predominately compare clinical characteristics between groups and, in some cases, examine the validity of categorical diagnostic distinctions using independent external markers. As noted, however, these studies tend to yield equivocal findings, limited by the fact that results on the dependent measures are impacted by the ways in which subjects were assigned to groups in the first place. A related and powerful approach to the nosologic question is to consider mediators of outcome through longitudinal associations and the mapping of developmental trajectories from the earliest stages of development using the simultaneous examination of social and neuropsychological processes. This serves not only to identify diagnostic pathways but also to study fundamental mechanisms of social development and their relationship to cognitive and neurobiological factors. Such studies are limited in number and have tended to rely on restricted measures of early and later processes.

Another more recent line of research has been to identify specific aspects of the broader autism phenotype, such as measurable components not detected by the unaided eye that might fall along the pathway between disease and distal genotype (e.g., endophenotypes; Gottesman & Gould, 2003). Reciprocally, identification of the genes involved in the disorder may also help to define the phenotype. This latter approach places a stronger emphasis on dimensionality and the measurement of continuously distributed traits. The challenge has been to identify and develop such measures. Innovative behavioral and neurofunctional methodologies have been used to assess salient social constructs and suggest that dimensionality can be achieved if we focus on processes that are very early emerging (Klin et al., 2003; Volkmar et al., 2004).

The development of more effective methods of measurement to expand our understanding of the neuropsychological characteristics of autism should encompass at least two approaches. Because of the amount of inherent structure available in the clinical or research framework, subtle impairments in problem solving, organization, and behavioral activation may not be easily revealed. Yet, the fundamental deficit for individuals with autism is that of initiating complex behavior in unstructured settings. This investigative focus requires a movement away from externally controlled or constrained tasks toward gaining access to internally controlled, experientially driven mechanisms. Acknowledgment of autism as a complex heterogeneous disorder signifies that understanding will be increased through multiple levels of analysis as well as the integration of tools and information from other disciplines (e.g., genetic and brain research).

Global features of brain function are far more likely to be bound up in the coordination and relation among things (cooperating to form coherent patterns) than they are to be revealed in an approach where one level of analysis has priority over any other.

Cross-References

Aspects of executive functioning are addressed in Chapter 22; theory of mind and central coherence theories of autism are addressed in Chapters 23 and 24, respectively. Joint attention is discussed in Chapter 25; the enactive mind model of autism is addressed in Chapter 26.

REFERENCES

Abell, F., Krams, M., Ashburner, J., Passingham, R., Friston, K., Frackowiak, R., et al. (1999). The neuroanatomy of autism: A voxel-based whole brain analysis of structural scans. *NeuroReport, 10,* 1647–1651.

Adams, A. V., & Sheslow, B. V. (1983). A developmental perspective of adolescence. In E. Schopler & G. B. Mesibov (Eds.), *Autism in adolescents and adults* (pp. 11–36). New York: Plenum Press.

Adamson, L. B. (1995). *Communication development in infancy.* Boulder, CO: Westview Press.

Adrien, J. L., Barthelemy, C., Perrot, A., Roux, S., Lenoir, P., Hameury, L., et al. (1992). Validity and reliability of the Infant Behavioral Summarized Evaluation (IBSE): A rating scale for the assessment of young children with autism and developmental disorders. *Journal of Autism and Developmental Disorders, 22,* 375–394.

Anzalone, M. E., & Williamson, G. G. (2000). Sensory processing and motor performance in autism spectrum disorders. In A. M. Wetherby & B. M. Prizant (Eds.), *Autism spectrum disorders: A transactional developmental perspective.* Baltimore: Paul H. Brookes Publishing.

Asperger, H. (1944). Die "Autistischen Psychopathen" im kindersalter. *Archive fur Psychiatrie und Nervenkrankheiten, 117,* 76–136.

Aylward, E. H., Minshew, N. J., Goldstein, G., Honeycutt, N. A., Augustine, A. M., Yates, K. O., et al. (1999). MRI volumes of amygdala and hippocampus in non-mentally retarded autistic adolescents and adults. *Neurology, 53,* 2145–2150.

Bachevalier, J. (1994). Medial temporal lobe structures and autism: A review of clinical and experimental findings. *Neuropsychologia, 32,* 627–648.

Bachevalier, J., & Merjanian, P. (1994). The contribution of medial temporal lobe structures in infantile autism: A neurobehavioral study in primates. In M. L. Bauman & T. L. Kemper (Eds.), *The neurobiology of autism* (pp. 146–169). Baltimore: Johns Hopkins University Press.

Barnhill, G., Hagiwara, T., Myles, B. S., & Simpson, R. L. (2000). Asperger syndrome: A study of the cognitive profiles of 37 children and adolescents. *Focus on Autism and Other Developmental Disabilities, 15,* 146–153.

Baron-Cohen, S., Leslie, A. M., & Frith, U. (1985). Does the autistic child have a "theory of mind?" *Cognition, 21,* 37–46.

Baron-Cohen, S., Ring, H., Wheelwright, S., Bullmore, E., Brammer, M., Simmons, A., et al. (1999). Social intelligence in the normal and autistic brain: A fMRI study. *European Journal of Neuroscience, 11,* 1891–1898.

Bauman, M. L., & Kemper, T. L. (1994). Neuroanatomic observations of the brain in autism. In M L. Bauman & T. L. Kemper (Eds.), *The neurobiology of autism* (pp. 119–145). Baltimore: Johns Hopkins University Press.

Bennetto, L., Pennington, B. F., & Rogers, S. J. (1996). Intact and impaired memory functions in autism. *Child Development, 67,* 1816–1835.

Berger, H. J. C., Aerts, F. H. T. M., van Spaendonck, K. P. M., Cools, A. R., & Teunisse, J. P. (2003). Central coherence and cognitive shifting in relation to social improvement in high-functioning young adults with autism. *Journal of Clinical and Experimental Neuropsychology, 25,* 502–511.

Beversdorf, D. Q., Smith, B. W., Crucian, G. P., Anderson, J. M., Keillor, J. M., Barrett, A. M., et al. (2000). Increased discrimination of "false memories" in autism spectrum disorder. *Proceedings of the National Academy of Sciences of the United States of America, 97,* 8734–8737.

Boucher, J. (1981a). Immediate free recall in early childhood autism: Another point of behavioral similarity with the amnesic syndrome. *British Journal of Psychology, 72,* 211–215.

Boucher, J. (1981b). Memory for recent events in autistic children. *Journal of Autism and Developmental Disorders, 11,* 293–301.

Boucher, J., & Lewis, V. (1989). Memory impairments and communication in relatively able autistic children. *Journal of Child Psychology and Psychiatry, 30,* 99–122.

Boucher, J., & Warrington, E. K. (1976). Memory deficits in early infantile autism: Some similarities to the amnesic syndrome. *British Journal of Psychology, 67,* 73–87.

Bowler, D. M., Gardiner, J. M., & Grice, S. J. (2000). Episodic memory and remembering in adults with Asperger syndrome. *Journal of Autism and Developmental Disorders, 30*(4), 295–304.

Bowler, D. M., Matthews, N. J., & Gardiner, J. M. (1997). Asperger's syndrome and memory: Similarity to autism but not amnesia. *Neuropsychologia, 35,* 65–70.

Buchsbaum, M. S., Siegel, B. V., Jr., Wu, J. C., Hazlett, E., Sicotte, N., & Haier, R. (1992). Brief report: Attention performance in autism and regional brain metabolic rate assessed by positron emission tomography. *Journal of Autism and Developmental Disorders, 22,* 115–125.

Burack, J. A. (1994). Selective attention deficits in persons with autism: Preliminary evidence of an inefficient attentional lens. *Journal of Abnormal Psychology, 103,* 535–543.

Burack, J. A., Enns, J. T., Stauder, J. E. A., Mottron, L., & Randolf, B. (1997). Attention and autism: Behavioral and electrophysiological evidence. In D. J. Cohen & F. R. Volkmar (Eds.), *Handbook of autism and pervasive developmental disorders* (pp. 226–247). New York: Wiley.

Cabeza, R., & Nyberg, L. (2000). Imaging cognition II: An empirical review of 275 PET and fMRI studies. *Journal of Cognitive Neuroscience, 12,* 1–47.

Casey, B. J., Gordon, C. T., Mannheim, G. B., & Rumsey, J. M. (1993). Dysfunctional attention in autistic savants. *Journal of Clinical and Experimental Neuropsychology, 15,* 933–946.

Charman, T., Baron-Cohen, S., Swettenham, J., Baird, G., Cox, A., & Drew, A. (2001). Testing joint attention, imitation, and play as infancy precursors to language and theory of mind. *Cognitive Development, 15*(4), 481–498.

Charman, T., Baron-Cohen, S., Swettenham, J., Baird, G., Drew, A., & Cox, A. (2003). Predicting language outcome in infants with autism and pervasive developmental disorder. *International Journal of Language and Communication Disorders, 38*(3), 265–285.

Ciesielski, K. T., Courchesne, E., & Elmasian, R. (1990). Effects of focused selective attention tasks on event-related potentials in autistic and normal individuals. *Electroencephalography and Clinical Neurophysiology, 75,* 207–220.

Courchesne, E. (1995). New evidence of cerebellar and brainstem hypoplasia in autistic infants, children, and adolescents: The MR imaging study by Hashimoto and colleagues. *Journal of Autism and Developmental Disorders, 25,* 19–22.

Courchesne, E., Saitoh, O., Yeung-Courchesne, R., Press, G. A., Lincoln, A. J., Haas, R. H., et al. (1994). Abnormality of cerebellar vermian lobules, VI & VII in patients with infantile autism: Identification of hypoplastic and hyperplastic subgroups with MR imaging. *American Journal of Roentgenology, 162,* 123–130.

Courchesne, E., Townsend, J., Akshoomoff, N. A., Saitoh, O., Yeung-Courchesne, R., Murakami, A., et al. (1994). Impairment in shifting attention in autistic and cerebellar patients. *Behavioral Neuroscience, 108,* 848–865.

Courchesne, E., Yeung-Courchesne, R., Press, G. A., Hesselink, J. R., & Jernigan, T. L. (1988). Hypoplasia of cerebellar vermal lobules VI & VII in autism. *New England Journal of Medicine, 318,* 1349–1354.

Dahlgren, S. O., & Gillberg, C. (1989). Symptoms in the first two years of life: A preliminary population study of infantile autism. *European Archives of Psychiatry and Neurological Sciences, 238,* 169–174.

Damasio, A. R. (1985). The frontal lobes. In K. M. Heilman & E. Valenstein (Eds.), *Clinical neuropsychology* (2nd ed., pp. 339–375). New York: Oxford University Press.

Damasio, A. R., & Maurer, R. G. (1978). A neurological model for childhood autism. *Archives of Neurology, 35,* 777–786.

Dawson, G., Munson, J., Estes, A., Osterling, J., McPartland, J., Toth, K., et al. (2002). Neurocognitive function and joint attention abilities in young children with autism spectrum disorder versus developmental delay. *Child Development, 73,* 345–358.

DeLong, G. R. (1992). Autism, amnesia, hippocampus, and learning. *Neuroscience and Biobehavioral Reviews, 16,* 63–70.

Dunn, W., Myles, B. S., & Orr, S. (2002). Sensory processing issues associated with Asperger syndrome: A preliminary investigation. *American Journal of Occupational Therapy, 56*(1), 97–102.

Ehlers, S., Nyden, A., Gillberg, C., Dahlgren-Sandberg, A., Dahlgren, S.-O., Hjelmquist, E., et al. (1997). Asperger syndrome, autism, and attention disorders: A comparative study of the cognitive profiles of 120 children. *Journal of Child Psychology and Psychiatry, 38,* 207–217.

Fein, D., Dunn, M. A., Allen, D. M., Aram, R., Hall, N., Morris, R., et al. (1996). Neuropsychological and language data. In I. Rapin (Ed.), *Preschool children with inadequate communication: Developmental language disorder, autism, low IQ* (pp. 123–154). London: Mac Keith Press.

Gardiner, J. M., Bowler, D. M., & Grice, S. J. (2003). Further evidence for preserved priming and impaired recall in adults with Asperger syndrome. *Journal of Autism and Developmental Disorders, 33,* 259–269.

Garretson, H. B., Fein, D., & Waterhouse, L. (1990). Sustained attention in children with autism. *Journal of Autism and Developmental Disorders, 20,* 101–114.

Geurts, H. M., Verté, S., Oosterlaan, J., Roeyers, H., & Sergeant, J. A. (2004). How specific are executive functioning deficits in attention deficit hyperactivity disorder and autism? *Journal of Child Psychology and Psychiatry, 45,* 836–854.

Ghaziuddin, M., & Mountain-Kimchi, K. (2004). Defining the intellectual profile of Asperger syndrome: Comparison with high-functioning autism. *Journal of Autism and Developmental Disorders, 34,* 279–284.

Gioia, G. A., Isquith, P. K., Kenworthy, L., & Barton, R. M. (2002). Profiles of everyday executive function in acquired and developmental disorders. *Child Neuropsychology, 8,* 121–137.

Goldman-Rakic, P. S. (1987). Circuitry of primate prefrontal cortex and regulation of behavior by representational memory. In V. B. Mountcastle, F. Plum, & S. R. Geiger (Eds.), *Handbook of physiology: The nervous system* (pp. 373–417). Bethesda: American Physiological Society.

Goldstein, G., Johnson, C. R., & Minshew, N. J. (2001). Attentional processes in autism. *Journal of Autism and Developmental Disorders, 31,* 433–440.

Gottesman, I., & Gould, T. D. (2003). The endophenotype concept in psychiatry: Etymology and strategic intentions. *American Journal of Psychiatry, 160,* 636–645.

Grandin, T. (1992). An inside view of autism. In E. Schopler & G. B. Mesibov (Eds.), *High functioning individuals with autism* (pp. 105–126). New York: Plenum Press.

Grandin, T. (1995). How people with autism think. In E. Schopler & G. B. Mesibov (Eds.), *Learning and cognition in autism* (pp. 137–156). New York: Plenum Press.

Griffith, E. M., Pennington, B. F., Wehner, E. A., & Rogers, S. J. (1999). Executive functions in young children with autism. *Child Development, 70,* 817–832.

Griswold, D. E., Barnhill, G. P., Myles, B. S., Hagiwara, T., & Simpson, R. L. (2002). Asperger syndrome and academic achievement. *Focus on Autism and Other Developmental Disabilities, 17,* 94–102.

Gunter, H. L., Ghaziuddin, M., & Ellis, H. D. (2002). Asperger syndrome: Tests of right hemisphere functioning and interhemispheric communication. *Journal of Autism and Developmental Disorders, 32,* 263–281.

Happé, F. G. E., & Frith, U. (1995). Theory of mind in autism. In E. Schopler & G. B. Mesibov (Eds.), *Learning and cognition in autism* (pp. 177–198). New York: Plenum Press.

Hughes, C. (2001). Executive dysfunction in autism: Its nature and implications for everyday problems experienced by individuals with autism. In J. Burack, T. Charman, N. Yirmiya, & P. Zelazo (Eds.), *The development of autism: Perspectives from theory and research* (pp. 255–275). Mahwah, NJ: Erlbaum.

Hughes, C., Russell, J., & Robbins, T. W. (1994). Evidence for executive dysfunction in autism. *Neuropsychologia, 32,* 477–492.

Joseph, R. M., & Tager-Flusberg, H. (2004). The relationship between theory of mind and executive functions to symptom type and severity in children with autism. *Development and Psychopathology, 16,* 137–155.

Kanner, L. (1943). Autistic disturbances of affective contact. *Nervous Child, 2,* 217–250.

Kemper, T. L., & Bauman, M. L. (1993). The contribution of neuropathologic studies of the understanding of autism. *Neurologic Clinics, 11,* 175–186.

Kientz, M. A., & Dunn, W. (1997). A comparison of the performance of children with and without autism on the Sensory Profile. *American Journal of Occupational Therapy, 51*(7), 530–537.

Klin, A. (2000). Attributing social meaning to ambiguous visual stimuli in higher functioning autism and Asperger syndrome: The Social Attribution Task. *Journal of Child Psychology, Psychiatry and Allied Disciplines, 33,* 763–769.

Klin, A., Jones, W., Schultz, R. T., & Volkmar, F. R. (2003). The enactive mind: From actions to cognition: Lessons from autism. *Philosophical Transactions of the Royal Society, Biological Sciences, 358,* 345–360.

Klin, A., Jones, W., Schultz, R., Volkmar, F. R., & Cohen, D. (2002). Visual fixation patterns during viewing of naturalistic social situations as predictors of social competence in individuals with autism. *Archives of General Psychiatry, 59*(9), 809–816.

Klin, A., & Volkmar, F. R. (1997). Asperger's syndrome. In D. J. Cohen & F. R. Volkmar (Eds.), *Handbook of autism and pervasive developmental disorders* (2nd ed., pp. 94–122). New York: Wiley.

Klin, A., & Volkmar, F. R. (2003). Asperger syndrome: Diagnosis and external validity. *Child and Adolescent Psychiatric Clinics of North America, 12,* 1–13.

Klin, A., Volkmar, F. R., Sparrow, S. S., Cicchetti, D. V., & Rourke, B. P. (1995). Validity and neuropsychological characterization of Asperger syndrome. *Journal of Child Psychology, Psychiatry, and Allied Disciplines, 36,* 1127–1140.

Klinger, L. G., & Dawson, G. (2001). Prototype formation in autism. *Development and Psychopathology, 13*(1), 111–124.

Laurent, A. C., & Rubin, E. (2004). Challenges in emotional regulation in Asperger syndrome and high-functioning autism. *Topics in Language Disorders, 24*(4), 286–297.

Lincoln, A. J., Allen, M. H., & Kilman, A. (1995). The assessment and interpretation of intellectual abilities in people with autism. In E. Schopler & G. B. Mesibov (Eds.), *Learning and cognition in autism* (pp. 89–117). New York: Plenum Press.

Lincoln, A., Courchesne, E., Allen, M., Hanson, E., & Ene, M. (1998). Neurobiology of Asperger syndrome: Seven case studies and quantitative magnetic resonance imaging findings. In E. Schopler & G. B. Mesibov (Eds.), *Asperger syndrome or high-functioning autism? Current issues in autism* (pp. 145–163). New York: Plenum Press.

Lord, C., & Schopler, E. (1989). The role of age at assessment, developmental level, and test in the stability of intelligence scores in young autistic children. *Journal of Autism and Developmental Disorders, 19,* 483–499.

Luna, B., Minshew, N. J., Garver, K. E., Lazar, N. A., Thulborn, K. R., Eddy, W. F., et al. (2002). Neocortical system abnormalities in autism: An fMRI study of spatial working memory. *Neurology, 59,* 834–840.

Manjiviona, J., & Prior, M. (1999). Neuropsychological profiles of children with Asperger syndrome and autism. *Autism, 3,* 327–356.

Mayes, S. D., & Calhoun, S. L. (2003). Analysis of WISC-III, Stanford-Binet, IV, & academic achievement test scores in children with autism. *Journal of Autism and Developmental Disorders, 33,* 329–341.

Miller, J. N., & Ozonoff, S. (2000). The external validity of Asperger disorder: Lack of evidence from the domain of neuropsychology. *Journal of Abnormal Psychology, 109,* 227–238.

Minshew, N. J., & Goldstein, G. (1993). Is autism an amnesic disorder? Evidence from the California Verbal Learning Test. *Neuropsychology, 7,* 209–216.

Minshew, N. J., & Goldstein, G. (2001). The pattern of intact and impaired memory functions in autism. *Journal of Child Psychology and Psychiatry and Allied Disciplines, 42,* 1095–1101.

Minshew, N. J., Goldstein, G., Muenz, L. R., & Payton, J. B. (1992). Neuropsychological functioning in nonmentally retarded autistic individuals. *Journal of Clinical and Experimental Neuropsychology, 14,* 749–761.

Minshew, N. J., Goldstein, G., & Siegel, D. J. (1997). Neuropsychologic functioning in autism: Profile of a complex information processing disorder. *Journal of the International Neuropsychological Society, 3,* 303–316.

Minshew, N. J., Luna, B., & Sweeney, J. A. (1999). Oculomotor evidence neocortical systems but no cerebellar dysfunction in autism. *Neurology, 52,* 917–922.

Minshew, N. J., Meyer, J., & Goldstein, G. (2002). Abstract reasoning in autism: A dissociation between concept formation and concept identification. *Neuropsychology, 16,* 327–334.

Morris, R. G., Rowe, A., Fox, N., Feigenbaum, J. D., Miotto, E. C., & Howlin, P. (1999). Spatial working memory in Asperger's syndrome and in patients with focal frontal and temporal lobe lesions. *Brain and Cognition, 41,* 9–26.

Mundy, P., & Gomes, A. (1998). Individual differences in joint attention skill development in the second year of life. *Infant Behavior and Development, 21,* 469–482.

Mundy, P., Sigman, M., & Kasari, C. (1990). A longitudinal study of joint attention and language development in autistic children. *Journal of Autism and Developmental Disorders, 20,* 115–128.

Mundy, P., Sigman, M., & Kasari, C. (1994). Joint attention, developmental level, and symptom presentation in autism. *Development and Psychopathology, 6,* 389–401.

Mundy, P., Sigman, M., Ungerer, J., & Sherman, T. (1986). Defining social deficits of autism: The contribution of nonverbal communication measures. *Journal of Child Psychology and Psychiatry, 27,* 657–659.

Murakami, J. W., Courchesne, E., Press, G. A., Yeung-Courchesne, R., & Hesselink, J. R. (1989). Reduced cerebellar hemisphere size and its relationship to vermal hypoplasia in autism. *Archives of Neurology, 46,* 689–694.

Ornitz, E. M. (1974). The modulation of sensory input and motor output in autistic children. *Journal of Autism and Childhood Schizophrenia, 4,* 197–215.

Ornitz, E. M. (1983). The functional neuroanatomy of infantile autism. *International Journal of Neuroscience, 19,* 85–124.

Ornitz, E. M. (1988). Autism: A disorder of directed attention. *Brain Dysfunction, 1,* 309–322.

Ornitz, E. M., & Ritvo, E. R. (1968a). Neurophysiological mechanisms underlying perceptual inconstancy in autistic and schizophrenic children. *Archives of General Psychiatry, 19,* 22–27.

Ornitz, E. M., & Ritvo, E. R. (1968b). Perceptual inconstancy in early infantile autism: The syndrome of early infant autism and its variants including certain cases of childhood schizophrenia. *Archives of General Psychiatry, 18,* 76–98.

Ornitz, E. M., & Ritvo, E. R. (1976). The syndrome of autism: A critical review. *American Journal of Psychiatry, 133,* 609–622.

Osterling, J., & Dawson, G. (1994). Early recognition of children with autism: A study of first-birthday home videotapes. *Journal of Autism and Developmental Disorders, 24,* 247–257.

Ozonoff, S. (1995). Executive functions in autism. In E. Schopler & G. B. Mesibov (Eds.), *Learning and cognition in autism* (pp. 199–219). New York: Plenum Press.

Ozonoff, S., Cook, I., Coon, H., Dawson, G., Joseph, R. M., Klin, A., et al. (2004). Performance on Cambridge Neuropsychological Test Automated Battery subtests sensitive to frontal lobe function in people with autistic disorder: Evidence from the Collaborative Programs of Excellence in Autism Network. *Journal of Autism and Developmental Disorders, 34,* 139–150.

Ozonoff, S., & McEvoy, R. E. (1994). A longitudinal study of executive function and theory of mind development in autism. *Development and Psychopathology, 6,* 415–431.

Ozonoff, S., Pennington, B. F., & Rogers, S. J. (1991). Executive function deficits in high-functioning autistic individuals: Relationship to theory of mind. *Journal of Child Psychology and Psychiatry, 32,* 1081–1105.

Ozonoff, S., Rogers, S., & Pennington, B. (1991). Asperger's syndrome: Evidence of an empirical distinction. *Journal of Child Psychology and Psychiatry, 32,* 1107–1122.

Ozonoff, S., South, M., & Miller, J. N. (2000). *DSM-IV*-defined Asperger syndrome: Cognitive, behavioral and early history differentiation from high-functioning autism. *Autism, 4,* 29–46.

Ozonoff, S., & Strayer, D. L. (1997). Inhibitory function in nonretarded children with autism. *Journal of Autism and Developmental Disorders, 27,* 59–77.

Ozonoff, S., & Strayer, D. L. (2001). Further evidence of intact working memory in autism. *Journal of Autism and Developmental Disorders, 31,* 257–263.

Ozonoff, S., Strayer, D. L., McMahon, W. M., & Filloux, F. (1994). Executive function abilities in autism and Tourette syndrome: An information processing approach. *Journal of Child Psychology and Psychiatry, 35,* 1015–1032.

Pascualvaca, D. M., Fantie, B. D., Papageorgiou, M., & Mirsky, A. F. (1998). Attentional capacities in children with autism: Is there a general deficit in shifting focus? *Journal of Autism and Developmental Disorders, 28,* 467–478.

Powell, S. D., & Jordan, R. R. (1993). Being subjective about autistic thinking and learning to learn. *Educational Psychology, 13,* 359–370.

Renner, P., Klinger, L. G., & Klinger, M. R. (2000). Implicit and explicit memory in autism: Is autism an amnesic disorder? *Journal of Autism and Developmental Disorders, 30,* 3–14.

Rogers, S., Hepburn, S., & Wehner, E. (2003). Parent reports of sensory symptoms in toddlers with autism and those with other developmental disorders. *Journal of Autism and Developmental Disorders, 33*(6), 631–642.

Rourke, B. P. (1989). *Nonverbal learning disabilities: The syndrome and the model.* New York: Guilford Press.

Rumsey, J. M., & Hamburger, S. D. (1990). Neuropsychological divergence of high-level autism and severe dyslexia. *Journal of Autism and Developmental Disorders, 20,* 155–168.

Russell, J. (1997). How executive disorders can bring about an inadequate "theory of mind." In J. Russell (Ed.), *Autism as an executive disorder* (pp. 256–304). Oxford, England: Oxford University Press.

Russell, J., Jarrold, C., & Henry, L. (1996). Working memory in children with autism and with moderate learning difficulties. *Journal of Child Psychology, Psychiatry, and Allied Disciplines, 37,* 673–686.

Rutter, M. (1978). Diagnosis and definitions of childhood autism. *Journal of Autism and Childhood Schizophrenia, 8,* 139–161.

Schatz, A. M., Weimer, A. K., & Trauner, D. A. (2002). Brief report: Attention differences in Asperger syndrome. *Journal of Autism and Developmental Disorders, 32,* 333–336.

Schultz, R. T., Romanski, L. M., & Tsatsanis, K. D. (2000). Neurofunctional models of Autistic Disorder and Asperger syndrome: Clues from neuroimaging. In A. Klin, F. R. Volkmar, & S. S. Sparrow (Eds.), *Asperger syndrome.* New York: Guilford Press.

Stone, W. L. (1997). Autism in infancy and early childhood. In D. J. Cohen & F. R. Volkmar (Eds.), *Handbook of autism and pervasive developmental disorders* (2nd ed., pp. 266–282). New York: Wiley.

Szatmari, P., Tuff, L., Finlayson, M. A. J., & Bartolucci, G. (1990). Asperger's syndrome and autism: Neurocognitive aspects. *Journal of the American Academy of Child and Adolescent Psychiatry, 29,* 130–136.

Tager-Flusberg, H. (1991). Semantic processing in the free recall of autistic children: Further evidence for a cognitive deficit. *British Journal of Developmental Psychology, 9,* 417–430.

Toichi, M., & Kamio, Y. (2002). Long-term memory and levels-of-processing in autism. *Neuropsychologia, 40,* 964–969.

Toichi, M., & Kamio, Y. (2003). Long-term memory in high-functioning autism: Controversy

on episodic memory in autism reconsidered. *Journal of Autism and Developmental Disorders, 33,* 151–161.

Tomasello, M., Kruger, A., & Ratner, H. H. (1993). Cultural learning. *Behavioral and Brain Sciences, 16,* 495–552.

Townsend, J., Harris, N. S., & Courchesne, E. (1996). Visual attention abnormalities in autism: Delayed orienting to location. *Journal of the International Neuropsychological Society, 2,* 541–550.

Tsai, L. Y. (1992). Diagnostic issues in high-functioning autism. In E. Schopler & G. B. Mesibov (Eds.), *High-functioning individuals with autism* (pp. 11–40). New York: Plenum Press.

Tsatsanis, K. D., Dartnall, N., Cicchetti, D., Sparrow, S., Klin, A., & Volkmar, F. R. (2003). A comparison of performance on the Leiter and Leiter-R in low-functioning children with autism. *Journal of Autism and Developmental Disorders, 33*(1), 23–30.

Tulving, E. (1972). Episodic and semantic memory. In E. Tulving & W. Donaldson (Eds.), *Organization of memory.* New York: Academic Press.

Ulvund, S., & Smith, L. (1996). The predictive validity of nonverbal communication skills in infants with perinatal hazards. *Infant Behavior and Development, 19,* 441–449.

Volkmar, F. R., Klin, A., Schultz, R., Rubin, E., & Bronen, R. (2000). Clinical case conference: Asperger's disorder. *American Journal of Psychiatry, 2*(157), 262–267.

Volkmar, F. R., Lord, C., Bailey, A., Schultz, R. T., & Klin, A. (2004). Autism and pervasive developmental disorders. *Journal of Child Psychology and Psychiatry, 45,* 135–170.

Wainwright-Sharp, J. A., & Bryson, S. E. (1996). Visual-spatial orienting in autism. *Journal of Autism and Developmental Disorders, 26,* 423–438.

Watling, R. L., Deitz, J., & White, O. (2001). Comparison of Sensory Profile score of young children with and without autism spectrum disorders. *American Journal of Occupational Therapy, 55*(4), 416–423.

Wheeler, M. A., Stuss, D. T., & Tulving, E. (1997). Toward a theory of episodic memory: The frontal lobes and autonoetic consciousness. *Psychological Bulletin, 121,* 331–354.

Zilbovicius, M., Garreau, B., Samson, Y., Remy, P., Barthelemy, C., Syrota, A., et al. (1995). Delayed maturation of the frontal cortex in childhood autism. *American Journal of Psychiatry, 152,* 248–252.

CHAPTER 14

Imitation and Play in Autism

SALLY J. ROGERS, IAN COOK, AND ADRIENNE MERYL

Over the past 20 years, the developmental aspects of autism have been a central focus of research activities. This developmental lens for viewing autism focuses attention on the evolving symptoms of autism, influenced by the interplay of biology and experience. This interactive, developmental framework has several implications that strongly affect current research ideas: (1) There is some plasticity in the evolution of the symptoms, (2) individual differences in course and outcomes will be affected by an individual's experiences as well as the individual biology of the disorder, and (3) early developmental course will have a substantially greater impact on outcomes than later events. In contrast to research in the period between 1960 and 1980 and in response to this developmental orientation, the past 20 years have seen much more emphasis on understanding autism as early in life as possible and searching for autism-specific deviations in the early developmental processes that lead to language, social, and cognitive development, both to understand the developmental processes involved in the disorder and to conceptualize treatment strategies for maximizing outcomes.

Strongly influenced by Piaget's model of cognitive development, the developmental studies of autism of the past 20 years have carefully dissected early development. In the first major papers reflecting this approach, Marian Sigman and her colleagues (Sigman & Ungerer, 1984; Ungerer & Sigman, 1981) found that of the multiple areas of sensorimotor development that

Piaget delineated, children with autism showed syndrome-specific impairments in only two: imitation and play. Furthermore, Piaget (1962) suggested that symbolic play developed from imitation, particularly deferred imitation, as children developed the ability to represent mentally events they had experienced and reproduce them at a later time. This theoretical linkage between imitation and pretend play gains support from the symptom pattern seen in early autism, and this chapter focuses on research findings in these two areas.

Thus, this chapter reviews what is currently known about imitative abilities and play characteristics that distinguish autism from other disorders. We also examine the nature of individual differences in play and imitation skills among children with autism. Finally, we consider the proposed mechanisms thought to underlie the autism impairments in imitation and play. For the purposes of this chapter, *play* is defined as play with objects, rather than social play with people.

IMITATION

Roles of Imitation in Development

In normal infant and early childhood development, imitative ability is considered to be a key mechanism for cultural transmission of skills and knowledge, serving an apprenticeship, or learning function, helping young children learn complex, goal-directed behavior patterns from others (Baldwin, 1906; Bruner, 1972; Piaget,

The authors were partially supported by NICHD U19 HD35468. Dr. Rogers also received support from NIDCD R21 05574. The help of Debbie Schilling and Huanh Meyer is gratefully acknowledged.

1962; Rogoff, Mistry, Goncu, & Mosier, 1993; Tomasello, Kruger, & Ratner, 1993; Uzgiris, 1999). A less emphasized function of imitation involves social interpersonal communication. Imitation of body movements and postures, facial expressions, and vocal behavior permeate social and emotional exchanges, providing a key mechanism for emotional synchrony and communication between social partners, from early infancy throughout the lifespan (Gopnik & Meltzoff, 1994; Hatfield, Cacioppo, & Rapson, 1994; Uzgiris, 1981).

How imitation is defined is crucial when reviewing imitative studies, since there are many nonimitative ways in which behavior acquisition can be socially influenced. The research on social behavior acquisition in animals has delineated these processes in the following way (see Byrne & Russon, 1998; Heyes & Galef, 1996; Tomasello et al., 1993; Want & Harris, 2002): *Stimulus enhancement* is the tendency to pay attention to or aim responses toward a particular object or place after observing a conspecific's actions. In the case of stimulus enhancement, the observer's actions on the object are generated through trial and error learning as opposed to reenacting the model's behavior, but the chance that the trial and error learning will take place with the object is elevated as a result of the model's behavior. *Emulation* is a process in which the goal of the other is made overt as a result of the other's actions and that goal becomes a goal for the observer also. The observer then attempts to reproduce the completed goal by whatever means he or she comes up with from his or her own behavioral repertoire. While the preceding processes do not reflect direct acquisition of another's behavior through observation and thus are not truly imitative, *response facilitation* is an increase in the frequency of a behavior already in an individual's repertoire as a result of seeing it performed by another. This kind of performance is considered to reflect imitation by most infant researchers. *Action level imitation* occurs when the observer fully demonstrates the behavior of another, including novel acts, and acts that match the minor details and the style of the model's action. There is disagreement in the field about whether this should involve a reproduction of the goals of the model, as well as the behav-

ioral means, or whether "mimicry" of body movements by themselves should be considered imitation (see Tomasello et al., 1993). Given the definition of imitation that pervades the autism studies, we define *imitation* as the purposeful reproduction of another's body movements, whether novel or familiar.

While the view of imitation as a powerful tool for learning instrumental actions from others has been present in developmental psychology for many years, Meltzoff and Moore's (1977) discovery of oral imitation in infants in the first days and weeks of life required considerable revision of the view of the role of imitation in development. While the evolutionary utility of imitation in older infants and children as a powerful learning tool is clear (Rogoff et al., 1993), what might the evolutionary role of neonatal oral imitations serve? Uzgiris (1981) was the first to suggest that in early infancy, imitation may primarily serve social communication and interpersonal development. Trevarthen, Kokkinaki, and Fiamenghi (1999) have extended this view, suggesting that the core function of human imitation is the sharing of motives or intentions, which is at the heart of its other functions, including but not limited to sharing emotional states, instrumental learning, and continuing interactions.

Rogers and Pennington (1991), following Stern's (1985) model of interpersonal development, suggested that early deficits in imitation could lead to impaired metarepresentation abilities characteristic of children with autism. Meltzoff and Gopnik (1993) took this idea further, suggesting that imitation serves social development by providing a mechanism for acquiring mental state understanding. Gopnik and Meltzoff (1994) proposed that early imitation initially provides the infant with shared experiences of interpersonal connectedness via bodies and movements. In the next few months of life, imitation of facial expressions leads to a shared experience of emotional expressions and inner sensations, and then to a shared sense of motives and intentions underlying communication in the 9- to 12-month period, thus laying the groundwork for intersubjectivity and developing theory of minds.

Is there supportive evidence for the role of early imitation in social relations? In line with Gopnik and Meltzoff (1994), Kugiumutzakis

(1999) suggested that the crucial social element in early imitation is sharing affect via facial, vocal, and physical matchings. Heimann and colleagues have provided the only longitudinal data that address this hypothesis. Their findings demonstrate: (1) relationships between neonatal imitative ability and social responses to the mother in 3-month-olds and (2) positive relationships between 3-month-old imitation and 12-month-old imitation (Heimann, 1998; Heimann & Ullstadius, 1999). Nor is this limited to infancy. The research on emotional contagion has provided a body of evidence on the role of facial and postural imitation in rapid sharing of emotional states between people across the lifespan (as reviewed in Hatfield et al., 1994).

Imitation Performance in Autism

Difficulty imitating other people's movements has been reported in autism in a variety of studies across the past 30 years. The studies reviewed all involve autism versus matched clinical comparison groups in order to examine the question of specificity of the imitation problem in autism. These studies used a variety of imitative tasks: actions on objects, imitation of body movements, and imitation of facial movements.

Actions on Objects

Studies in this area provide the most mixed findings and the strongest developmental relations of the three areas. An investigation of the youngest sample of children with autism documented an autism-specific deficit in imitation of simple actions on objects (Charman et al., 1997). The 20-month-old subjects with autism performed significantly worse than a matched clinical comparison group on tasks involving imitation of simple actions on familiar objects. Several other comparative studies of preschoolers with autism have demonstrated object imitation deficits, using both conventional and nonconventional acts (Dawson, Meltzoff, Osterling, & Rinaldi, 1998; DeMyer et al., 1972; Rogers, Stackhouse, Hepburn, & Wehner, 2003; Stone, Ousley, & Littleford, 1997). In contrast, several other groups have not identified such difficulties. McDonough, Stahmer, Schreibman, and Thompson (1997) failed to

find significant group differences in performance on tasks of both immediate and deferred imitation of familiar actions with realistic objects in a sample with a mean age just under 5 years old. In a sample of older children (mean age 8.1 years), Hammes and Langdell (1981) found that although imitation of actions with imaginary objects (pantomime) and imitation of actions with a counterconventional object (e.g., using a cup as a hat) distinguished the children with autism from children with mental retardation matched on language abilities, performance on the imitation of actions with real objects did not differentiate the two groups. In a sample of adolescents, Hobson and Lee (1999) did not find an autism-specific deficit in imitation when movements were analyzed in terms of functional actions on objects, This difference in the performance of older and younger age groups may be due to maturing imitative abilities in autism or to methodological issues involving coding systems or choices of tasks that are too simple, resulting in ceiling effects (as seen in a study by Charman and Baron-Cohen in 1994, which used a task designed for 7-month-old infants with subjects with a mean chronological age [CA] close to 12 years).

Imitation of Body Movements (Intransitive Acts)

An autism-specific deficit in imitating body movements has been consistently, but not universally supported. Of all the tasks analyzed in the first study of imitation in autism (De-Myer et al., 1972), imitation of body movements generated the most robust effects of all the imitation tasks. Ohta (1987) found significant differences between high functioning children with autism and nonverbal IQ-matched typical preschoolers on imitation of simple hand movements. Rogers, Bennetto, McEvoy, and Pennington (1996) found an autism-specific deficit on single and sequential non-meaningful hand movements in high-functioning adolescents. Dawson et al. (1998) found an autism deficit relative to developmentally delayed and typical control children on familiar and novel hand movements. Aldridge, Stone, Sweeney, and Bower (2000) found an autism deficit in gestural imitation in a sample of 2- to 4-year-olds relative to cognitively matched normally developing infants. Smith and Bryson

(1998) found an autism deficit on single hand postures for high-functioning children with autism. Bennetto (1999) also found body imitation deficits among a group of high-functioning older children compared to clinical controls and isolated the difficulty to the kinesthetic reproductions of limb postures. Two comparative studies that did not find any autism-specific deficits used very infantile tasks and had ceiling effects that may have accounted for their null results (see Charman & Baron-Cohen, 1994; Morgan, Cutrer, Coplin, & Rodrigue, 1989). In summary, in contrast to the findings on imitation of actions on objects, studies of imitation of body movements have repeatedly yielded autism-specific deficits across a wide range of IQ and language levels and across all ages studied. (While it may seem counterintuitive, the presence of echolalia does not indicate preserved imitative abilities. Curcio [1978] found that children with echolalia could produce almost no abstract forms of pantomime. Rogers and Pennington [1991] suggested that echolalia was part of the auditory rehearsal loop, a distinct system from the motor processes involved in action imitations. Thus, echolalia should not be considered an example of motor imitation.)

Oral-Facial Imitations

Like body movements, oral-motor movements are consistently reported to be severely affected in autism, though this area has been much less well studied. Rogers et al. (2003) found that oral-motor imitation was more impaired than imitation of body movements in toddlers with autism compared to clinical and typical controls. Rapin (1996) reported greater oral-motor impairment in both high- and lower functioning children with autism than with clinical comparison groups. In a small comparative study, Adams (1998) reported a greater level of oral-motor difficulty in children with autism than in the CA-matched typical comparison group. Rogers et al. (1996) found an overall deficit in facial imitation for their high-functioning adolescent subjects with autism relative to a CA- and verbal IQ VIQ-matched clinical control group, as did Dawson et al. (1998) with a much younger sample. Loveland, Tunali-Kotoski, Pearson, and Brelsford (1994) found that although their subjects with autism

did not differ significantly in the number of identifiable imitations of emotional facial expressions, the autism group made significantly more unusual and mechanical expressions than the control group. Given the consistency of the findings in the literature, oral-facial imitation appears to be specifically impaired in autism.

While it is well established that a significant percentage of people with autism do not acquire speech, we have few explanations for this phenomenon (see Rodier, 2000, for a model based on brain differences affecting cranial nerve function). Lord and colleagues have demonstrated that level of retardation does not fully explain the lack of speech in autism (Lord & Pickles, 1996). The consistently replicated finding of autism-specific difficulties with oral-facial imitation (see also Rogers et al., 2003; Sigman & Ungerer, 1984) and the strong relationship of oral-facial imitation to speech (both in autism and in typical development) have led to the suggestion that a specific oral-motor or speech dyspraxia might underlie lack of speech development for a subgroup of children with autism (DeMyer, Hingtgen, & Jackson, 1981; Page & Boucher, 1998; Rogers, 1999; Rogers et al., 1996).

Relations among the Three Kinds of Tasks

Is imitation across the three kinds of tasks a unitary phenomenon? So far the evidence is contradictory. While Stone and colleagues (1997) reported a dissociation between imitation of actions on objects and imitation of body/facial actions in young children with autism, Rogers et al. (1996, 2003) found all three different types of imitations to be significantly related in toddlers with autism, and they found hand and face imitations to be significantly related in adults (no object imitations were tested in that study). However, the correlations are in the .40 to .70 range, demonstrating that these are not totally overlapping phenomena.

Developmental Correlates of Imitation

Several studies of normal development in infancy have specifically linked early infant motor imitation skills to later social responsivity to a parent. As reported earlier, Heimann and Ullstadius (1999) reported relationships between frequency of imitation in newborns and frequency of gaze aversion to the other three months later. Furthermore, the same authors reported consistencies between facial imitation in 3-month-olds and both manual and vocal imitation at 12 months. Finally, Forman and Kochanska (2001) reported a longitudinal study of toddlers seen at 14 and 22 months that demonstrated stability between imitation of the mother and cooperation with her requests both concurrently and predictively. There is also evidence of concurrent relationships between imitation skills and social responsivity. Uzgiris (1999) reported a study demonstrating relationships between 12-month-olds' amount of affective imitation with their mothers and the emotionally congruent expressions shared with other people. The research of Asendorpf and Baudonniere (1993) and Nadel and Peze (1993) have demonstrated toddlers' use of synchronous imitations as a main vehicle for reciprocal peer interactions, demonstrated in complex rounds of nonverbal imitations. Thus, several different findings attest to the social impact of infant imitation.

In Autism

While the directionality of the effects from imitation to social engagement are clearly laid out in theories of typical development, it is less clear in developmental theories of autism. Rogers (1999) has hypothesized the same directionality in autism: That early imitation problems contribute to impaired social development in autism. However, Hobson (1989), among others, has suggested that a more general early social impairment leads to lessened imitation of other people.

While directionality is not yet established, relationships between imitation and delayed or disordered development of several social and communicative abilities have been described. In one of the earliest studies of imitation, Curcio (1978) reported concurrent relationships between imitation and social communication in a group of nonverbal children with autism. This relationship has been reported by others as well (Dawson & Galpert, 1990; Rogers et al., 2003; Sigman & Ungerer, 1984; Stone et al., 1997). Stone and Yoder (2001) found that, after controlling for language skills, at age 2, only motor

imitation and speech therapy hours predicted language ability at age 4 whereas SES, age 2 play skills, and joint attention did not.

Only one study has directly tested the effects of imitation on social responsivity in autism. Dawson and Adams (1984) demonstrated that imitation differentially facilitated other kinds of social engagement for more severely impaired young children with autism, but this did not hold true for young, higher functioning children. Two longitudinal studies also support the hypothesis that imitation affects social functioning in autism. Stone et al. (1997) reported that early imitation predicted later language development and play abilities. Rogers and colleagues (2003) found that early imitation was a better predictor of outcomes in language, IQ, and social skills than dyadic social behavior.

Delay versus Deviance

Though some have proposed that the imitation deficit in autism marks a delayed as opposed to deviant course of development (Stone et al., 1997), Carpenter, Pennington, and Rogers (2002) found that children with autism differ from typically developing children in terms of the sequence in which imitation and other social cognitive skills develop across the infancy period. Whereas joint engagement and attention following skills emerged prior to imitative learning in the developmentally delayed group (a pattern also seen in normal development), imitative learning preceded the development of the other social-cognitive skills for the subjects with autism. Their results suggest that the role of imitation in the development of social-communicative abilities differs in autism and that the course of development diverges from the normal path around the interaction of joint attention and imitation. Carpenter et al. suggested that the use of imitation without joint attention (or with diminished joint attention skills) may explain the atypical linguistic features observed in autism such as echolalia, "metaphorical speech," pronoun reversal, and the abnormal use of questioning intonation for statements. In addition to these findings, the previously reviewed reports of continuing imitation impairments in high-functioning adolescents and adults with autism support deviance, rather than delay, in imitative development in autism.

Possible Mechanisms Underlying the Imitation Problem

Praxis and Body Mapping

The idea that the imitation problem in autism might be due to dyspraxia was first suggested by DeMyer et al. (1981). They suggested that dyspraxia in autism was of sufficient severity to prevent the child with autism from participating in everyday nonverbal communication, contributing to the inability to learn the meaning and use of nonverbal communicative acts. *Dyspraxia* and its adult counterpart, *apraxia,* refer to impairments in the ability to plan and execute movements in the absence of other motor symptoms (Ayres, 2000). The dyspraxia hypothesis in autism has been suggested by others as well, both to explain autism-specific difficulties with imitation and pantomime tasks (Bennetto, 1999; Jones & Prior, 1985; Rogers et al., 1996) and to explain nonimitative problems with motor planning and sequencing (Hill & Leary, 1993; Hughes, 1996; Minshew, Goldstein, & Siegel, 1997). Clinicians have long suggested that children with autism have poor body awareness, which might contribute to their difficulties with praxis in terms of planning and executing an imitative movement (Hill & Leary, 1993). The findings of the Rogers et al. (1996) study involved widespread deficits in imitation and pantomime, classic tests of praxis.

Bennetto (1999) examined several aspects of praxis in autism, including body mapping, visual representation of the movement, and motor execution. Examining high-functioning older children with autism and well-matched clinical controls, she found no group differences in the ability to map locations onto the body and no differences in visual recognition memory for the movements, even after delay. The group differences in this study involved one specific aspect of motor execution: limb postures. She also demonstrated that performance on a standard motor test revealed significant group differences and accounted for much, but not all, of the variability in imitation performance in the subjects with autism, findings also reported by Smith and Bryson

(1998). Thus, while problems in praxis have been supported in autism studies, they appear confounded with general motor problems.

Motor Problems in Autism

Motor problems have frequently been reported in autism. Damasio and Maurer (1978) carefully described the many motor symptoms seen in autism in an early report. Kohen-Raz, Volkmar, and Cohen (1992) reported striking differences in children with autism on tasks involving standing balance on unstable surfaces. Lack of typical hand dominance has been demonstrated (Hauck & Dewey, 2001). Manjiviona and Prior (1995) reported clinically significant levels of general motor impairments in a majority of children with diagnoses of autism or Asperger syndrome compared to test norms. Rapin (1996) reported that hypotonia, limb dyspraxia, and stereotypies were all more frequent in a group of children with autism than those with other communication problems. In some of the most intriguing reports, home video studies of infants later diagnosed with autism suggest that some motor differences may be present in autism before the first birthday (Baranek, 1999; Osterling, Dawson, & Munson, 2002; Teitelbaum, Teitelbaum, Ney, Fryman, & Maurer, 1998).

However, in a direct test of the dyspraxia hypothesis, no autism-specific motor difficulties were found by Rogers et al. (2003) on fine motor, gross motor, and nonimitative praxis performance in a comparative study of a group of toddlers with autism compared to both developmentally matched clinical controls and typically developing children. Yet, the children with autism demonstrated an imitation deficit. Thus, even though motor functioning accounted for a significant amount of the variance in imitation scores in this study (a finding also reported by Bennetto, 1999, and Smith & Bryson, 1998), the evidence did not support a generalized dyspraxia as the main mechanism underlying overall imitation deficits in autism.

The age and functioning level of the subjects appear to influence findings of motor deficits in groups with autism. Comparative studies that report autism-specific motor differences have involved high-functioning children with autism compared to clinical controls (Bennetto, 1999; Smith & Bryson, 1998). However, when younger or lower functioning subjects are examined, different findings emerge. Several studies have compared children with autism to a group with mental retardation matched on CA and mental age (MA) (Hauck & Dewey, 2001; Kohen-Raz et al., 1992; Rapin, 1996; Rogers et al., 2003), and all have reported essentially *equivalent* levels of motor performance (though in Hauck & Dewey, 2001, the groups differed on established handedness preference). Thus, the general motor problem in autism may not differ in kind or severity from that seen in other groups with motor difficulties, such as children with retardation. If a nonspecific praxis deficit reflects a generalized central nervous system impairment rather than an autism-specific motor problem, then it cannot explain the imitation impairment in autism.

Executive Functions: Sequencing and Working Memory

Rogers and Pennington (1991) proposed that an executive function deficit might lead to problems with imitation, given that imitation may have a working memory component. The neurological literature has demonstrated that patients with frontal lesions have motor sequencing deficits (Kimberg & Farah, 1993). An executive function deficit has been consistently reported in studies of older children and adults with autism (Bennetto, Pennington, & Rogers, 1996; Ozonoff & McEvoy, 1994; Ozonoff, Pennington, & Rogers, 1991; Prior & Hoffman, 1990; Rumsey & Hamburger, 1988; Russell, 1997). However, the evidence for an executive function component in imitation problems is mixed. Rogers et al. (1996) demonstrated that imitating manual sequences was more impaired for the group with autism than a clinical comparison group. However, autism-specific deficits in single movements appear to be as marked as deficits in sequential movements. Smith and Bryson (1998) and Bennetto (1999) also reported that adding the sequencing element to the nonmeaningful hand imitation task did not lead to a decline in the autism group's performance. Finally, several studies have explicitly examined working memory for the stimuli (Bennetto, 1999; Rogers et al., 1996; Smith & Bryson, 1998). No study has reported any group difference involving the

ability of subjects with autism to remember the tasks correctly over time.

Dawson et al. (1998) demonstrated significant correlations between executive function tasks and infant imitation tasks in preschoolers with autism. However, the size of the correlations revealed that much of the variability in imitation scores was not accounted for by executive function performance. The executive function hypothesis lacks some face validity in explaining difficulty with imitation in young children with autism as several recent published studies have demonstrated unimpaired executive function performance in young children with autism compared to controls (Dawson et al., 2002; Griffith, Pennington, Wehner, & Rogers, 1999). Thus, while executive functions may play some role in imitative skill, the evidence does not support this as a primary mechanism for explaining the imitation difficulties in autism.

Symbolic Content

In a study by Rogers and colleagues (1996) in which actions with symbolic content were compared with nonmeaningful actions, subjects with autism never performed differentially worse on the meaningful conditions. Of four significant group differences found on the hand and face tasks, only one was on a meaningful task whereas three were found on nonmeaningful tasks. Furthermore, autism-specific differences on nonsymbolic tasks have been reported from several studies (Bennetto, 1999; Smith & Bryson, 1998). Thus, difficulties with symbolic content do not appear to explain the imitation deficit in autism.

Kinesthesia

Perceptual-motor studies by Hermelin and O'Connor (1970) led to the suggestion that children with autism may express abnormalities in the integration of visual and kinesthetic input, which could certainly impair imitation of body movements. One method for highlighting the role of kinesthesia in imitation is to prevent the subject from viewing his or her movements. Studies that have manipulated the imitator's view of his or her movement copying attempts have found that the nonvisible gesture imitation items tend to differentiate autism and control groups more than any other kind of task

(Roeyers, Van Oost, & Bothuyne, 1998). However, nonvisible presentations increase the error rate in typical and developmentally delayed participants as well as individuals with autism (Smith & Bryson, 1998). Bennetto (1999) identified reproduction of limb postures—kinesthesia—as the most affected component of imitation in her subjects with autism. Convergence of these findings makes kinesthesia an area that should be investigated further.

Cross-Modal Matching and Body Mapping

Difficulties with cross-modal matching and body mapping might impair imitative ability but have been examined in only one imitation study. Bennetto (1999) tested this explicitly using a task that examined body awareness. The group with autism showed no differences from comparison subjects in accurately identifying specific locations on their own bodies in response to a line drawing of a body profile with certain locations highlighted (also see Hobson, Ouston, & Lee, 1989). This is an understudied area that should be investigated further, but thus far, we have no evidence that cross-modal transfer is the impaired function responsible for imitation impairments in autism.

Neural Mechanisms

The information processing models of imitation underlying several of the preceding studies have been severely challenged by the discovery of specialized neurons in the superior temporal sulcus (STS) of monkeys that appear to be dedicated to the processing of visual information about the actions of others (Rizzolatti, Fadiga, Fogassi, & Gallese, 2003). Some of these neurons appear to code basic postures of the face, limbs, or whole body, whereas others appear to be involved in coding the movement of body parts in relation to objects or goals. A subset of these neurons, identified in the prefrontal cortex in monkeys, fires when a specific action (such as reach and grasp) has been performed by the monkey as well as when the monkey observes another monkey performing the same specific action. These neurons have been labeled "mirror neurons" and are located in Brodmann area 44, which corresponds to Broca's area in the human brain. This finding suggests potential connections among observations of another's acts, imitation, and communication of meaning, with critical links to language (Rizzolatti & Arbib, 1998).

Recent functional imaging studies in humans have identified parallel networks of cells in frontal regions of humans that fire during observation of finger movements and fire more rapidly when the observation is accompanied by performance of the same action by the observer (Rizzolatti et al., 2003). Observation of hand actions has been shown to result in activity in the premotor cortex and Broca's area in humans (Iacoboni et al., 1999). This area of premotor cortex has shown some evidence of mirror neuron activity and has been implicated in reading facial emotion in a normal population (Nakamura et al., 1999). J. H. Williams, Whiten, Suddendorf, and Perrett (2001) propose that mirror neurons may facilitate understanding of others' actions and intentions and that they may be involved in the development of language, executive function, and theory of mind abilities. Failure to develop an intact mirror neuron system (or alternatively, failure to develop the mechanisms necessary for proper regulation of such a system) could impair the development of these capabilities in humans. Williams and colleagues suggest this as a model for autism.

Two studies have examined mirror neuron functioning in autism. Individuals with autism showed less involvement in this mirror neuron region during emotional interpretation (Nakamura et al., 1999). A very small study of imitation in Asperger syndrome did not reveal group differences, but power problems may have been present (Avikainen, Kulomaki, & Hari, 1999). Mirror neurons have also been suggested as the neural mechanism by which we understand the intent of others' actions. Several studies of intentionality in autism have demonstrated that children with autism do not show difficulties on a simple intentionality task (Aldridge et al., 2000; Carpenter, Pennington, & Rogers, 2001) although mechanisms other than reading intentionality may underlie this task (see Huang, Heyes, & Charman, 2002). Thus, the existence of this mirror neuron system and its role in facilitating imitation (and other synchronous behaviors between people) may provide us with new understanding of brain-behavior relations involved in imitation, but this line of research is in its infancy and needs to be fully explored in both typical and atypical groups.

Methodological Issues

Methodological issues may underlie the discrepancies in findings across imitation studies, which have occurred most often on tasks involving actions on objects and in studies assessing older and higher functioning subjects. Task characteristics that appear to influence results include the novelty, difficulty level, and conventionality of the movement. One difficulty in many of the methods used in these studies has to do with task affordances and conventional actions. When people are asked to imitate conventional actions on common objects that tap specific affordances of the object (rolling a car, marking with a pen, hitting a drum with a stick, etc.), you must question to what extent imitation of the precise movements of the model is required. A simpler and nonimitative process, such as stimulus enhancement or repetition of previously learned and automatic actions, could suffice. To control for other interpretations, it is important that object imitation tasks involve novel acts that are not directly elicited by the object's unique features.

The effect of the type of task chosen for imitation of actions on objects was illustrated by Roeyers et al. (1998). The group of 18 young children with autism in their study performed significantly worse than a well-matched group of children with retardation on imitation of gestures and on imitation of actions on objects, with the imitation of gestures more impaired than imitation of actions on objects. However, the causal effect of the action on the object seemed to have an impact on the magnitude of the difference in group performance. The action task that best served to discriminate the two groups involved an object that did not produce a sensorimotor effect. This brings up a related methodological issue: How do we begin to examine the different functions of imitation? While on the surface, all imitation tasks seem inherently social, Tomasello (1998) has argued that, in an instrumental, goal-directed, and object-oriented act, the focus of the imitative behavior may be on the means-ends relations inherent in the act, rather than

on imitating the other person as a person. The observer may reproduce the model's actions because the actions invoke a representation of an outcome in the environment, creating an intention in the imitator to carry out the intended act, rather than to imitate the model's motor movements. Tomasello's distinction between *emulation learning* and *cultural learning* may be relevant here. In emulation learning, the individual's goal is to create a specific result in the environment. In cultural learning, the observer not only directs attention to the other's activity and to the objects involved but also attempts to be like the other person, to perceive the situation the way the other sees it.

How can these be teased apart? Hobson, Lee, and Brown (1999) provide a helpful example. The tasks given to the subjects had both an instrumental function and an affective quality to them, and the accuracy of the instrumental function and the stylistic quality were rated separately. Both the participants with autism and those with other developmental disorders could perform the instrumental aspects of the tasks accurately. However, those with autism were much poorer than the controls at imitating the affective quality of the movement. The authors proposed that what distinguished their subjects with autism from the clinical comparison group was not so much their inability to imitate *the actions* modeled but rather their deficiency in their attempts to imitate *the person* who modeled them. They suggested further that in typically developing infants, it may be these goal-irrelevant aspects of imitation such as the imitation of affective tone and body language that contribute to establishing the intersubjective contact, or the "like me" experience with others (Meltzoff & Gopnik, 1993). To understand the imitation problems in autism, we must tend to these distinctions.

A final methodological issue concerns scoring practices. Those studies that have reported differences on body imitations in older and higher functioning persons have tended to use more detailed scoring systems that involve analysis of the movements on videotape. However, the typical scoring system used in many studies involves live ratings of "correct, partial, or fail." While the differences among younger subjects may be extensive enough to be captured in live ratings, such scoring systems may not be sensitive to imitation differences in older and higher functioning persons, which may be more subtle and require a more fine-grained analysis.

Summary of Imitation

The imitation studies in autism appear to have established that imitation is specifically impaired in autism, from the earliest time at which autism can be diagnosed, persisting into adulthood, in both higher functioning and lower functioning groups. More than most other neuropsychological areas of impairment in autism, imitation thus appears to meet the four criteria for a primary psychological deficit in autism: universality, specificity, precedence, and persistence (Pennington & Ozonoff, 1991). Several mechanisms hypothesized to account for the imitation deficit in autism, such as symbolic content, visual representation, cross-modal transfer, and working memory, have been examined and rejected. The mechanism with the greatest support is motor planning/execution, which accounts for some, but not all, of the variance in imitation performance in autism. However, general motor problems do not appear to be specific to autism, as similar levels of motor impairment are also found in children with mental retardation who do not have autism. Thus, motor difficulties (or dyspraxia) certainly contribute to the imitation problems in autism, but are not necessarily a primary mechanism underlying imitation problems in autism. An exception to this may involve oral imitation. For the few studies that have specifically examined oral-facial movements, there is consistent evidence of dysfunction and deviation from typical patterns. Furthermore, the relationships between oral-facial imitations and speech development have been repeatedly found to be large and significant. Thus, a specific oral-motor dysfunction may be involved in autism, leading directly in its severe form to impairments in speech development specific to autism and perhaps to imitation of facial expressions as well.

Neither the various types of imitation nor the various functions of imitation may be uniformly affected in autism. Functions involving instrumental learning of meaningful actions on objects may be less affected than the function of imitation in facilitating social interactions. Oral-facial and body imitation may particularly subserve the social aspect, while imitations of acts on objects may particularly serve the instrumental aspect. There has been little examination of relationships between imitative ability and social behavior in autism. In addition to continued investigation into possible mechanisms underlying the imitation deficit and brain-behavior relations related to imitative behavior, future research should consider the possibility that different functions of imitation may be differentially affected in autism.

PLAY IN AUTISM

For the purposes of this chapter, *play* is defined as the purposeful manipulation of objects in which exploration and practice of effects appear to be the child's goals. Play is considered a powerful means by which the young of many species master skills that will eventually be important for their development and survival (Bruner, 1972). Piaget (1962) considered play to be an intrinsically motivated activity, in which carrying out the activity is pleasurable. He distinguished between sensorimotor play, involving object manipulation as a means for practice and mastery of action schemas, and symbolic, or pretend play, which grows out of the child's developing ability for mental representation and provides a means of practicing and understanding the events of the social world.

Symbolic play is generally defined as play in which absent elements are represented through objects, gestures, and language in the play. This may take the form of animating the play characters or by representing absent objects through object substitution or pantomime (pantomime would seem to play a very important role in bridging between imitation and symbolic play, since pantomime fuses the concepts of deferred imitation and pretending). Pretend play generally appears in a toddler's repertoire by 18 months and becomes increasingly elaborated over the preschool period (McCune-Nicholich, 1977).

Autism-Specific Findings in Pretend Play

In 1975, Ricks and Wing reviewed what was known about communication, conceptual development, and play in autism. "The central problem, present in even the most mildly handicapped autistic people, appears to be a specific difficulty in handling symbols, which affects language, nonverbal communication, and many other aspects of cognitive and social activity" (p. 214). Lack of symbolic play was considered to be one of the main symptoms of this inner lack of symbolic capacity. In 1977, Wing, Gould, Yeates, and Brierley published the first major research paper on symbolic play in autism. The group documented two original findings that would stand the test of time: (1) There is a paucity of spontaneous symbolic play in children with autism whose developmental functioning level appears mature enough to support symbolic play; and (2) for those who demonstrated symbolic play acts, their play appeared repetitive and stereotypic, lacking the typical variety of differing play acts seen in comparison groups of similar mental ages.

This paper was followed in 1981 by two important comparative papers that used adult scaffolded conditions to stimulate symbolic play. Hammes and Langdell (1981) compared pretend play acts using increasingly abstract props imitated from video models of eight children with autism who had little or no language and eight children with mental retardation, matched for mental and chronological age. They reported that children with autism imitated the play acts with real objects similarly to comparison children, but differed in their lack of use of pantomimed or symbolically transformed acts. In contrast to Wing et al.'s (1977) view, they suggested that the children's difficulty was *not* due to a problem with symbol formation, but rather with flexible manipulation of symbols. Riguet, Taylor, Benaroya, and Klein (1981) compared three groups of children in free play and modeling conditions, with the findings of better performance of all children in scaffolded conditions and poorer imitation and lower levels of symbolic play in scaffolded conditions for children with autism than language-matched clinical or typical controls. In these early papers arises another theme that reoccurs throughout the symbolic play literature in autism—the improved ability of children with autism to carry out pretend play in scaffolded conditions. These two papers, examined together, highlight issues that are not yet resolved: (1) methodological issues concerning appropriate methods for eliciting symbolic play in children with autism and (2) conceptual concerns involving the cognitive processes involved in imitating and spontaneously producing symbolic play schemas.

A number of papers in the 1980s replicated findings from these two papers, with increasing attention to methodological issues involved in administration and rating of play schemas, as well as matching of clinical populations. Sigman and Ungerer (1984) and Mundy, Sigman, Ungerer, and Sherman (1986) replicated Wing's earlier findings of autism-specific deficits in three related areas: frequency of spontaneous pretend play acts, frequency and complexity of symbolic sequences, and frequency of different symbolic acts. These findings were obtained for both spontaneous play acts and for play that occurred in response to an adult model. However, in a finding that has come to have large repercussions, these authors also reported that the children's nonsymbolic play was similarly affected. Under spontaneous play conditions, children with autism demonstrated fewer functional and sensorimotor play acts and fewer *different* play acts. However, unlike their symbolic play, adult modeling and prompting resulted in normalizing the frequency of functional play. These studies continued to emphasize symbolic deficits as a core part of the autism picture.

Symbolic Play as Metarepresentation

There were conceptual problems with this early view of autism as a problem of symbolic abilities. From the Piagetian standpoint, while symbolic play and symbolic language involve mental representation, so do stage 6 object permanence, means end relations, and spatial relations, which also require the child to operate from internalized, mental models of the world (Piaget, 1962), and which do not present special problems for children with autism (Morgan et al., 1989; Sigman & Ungerer, 1984).

Alan Leslie's (1987) landmark paper provided a new interpretation of pretend play. He suggested that, unlike other acts that require representational thought, pretend play involves a more complex representational stance. The child needs to simultaneously hold two representations in mind: the primary, or veridical representation, and the newly assigned pretend identity (a state of *double knowledge;* McCune-Nicholich, 1981), both during his or her own play and when faced with pretend play of others. The child decouples the representations from his or her real-world roles and assigns his or her new pretend identities, representing the pretend world alongside the real world. Leslie suggested that aspects of pretend representations were similar to those seen in mental state representations in that reference, truth, and existence relations among primary representations are suspended. Defining pretend play as a metarepresentational act drew parallels between the cognitive processes involved in theory of mind tasks and those involved in pretend play. Leslie suggested that the poor performance of children with autism on both tasks was due to a difficulty in cognitive decoupling necessary for metarepresentation.

Building on Leslie's theory, Baron-Cohen (1987) reported a very carefully constructed study of spontaneous play, in which he set out to correct earlier methodological inconsistencies, laid out a clear rationale for matching groups, and suggested tight definitions of symbolic and functional play. He also pointed out the problems of using adult modeling and the resulting confusion between imitation and symbolic acts in previous studies. In a study of completely spontaneous play using junk props, miniatures, and dolls, he compared 10 verbal children with autism, 10 with mental retardation, and 10 typical children, all matched for verbal ability of 4 years. This study thus involved higher functioning children with autism than had been previously reported on. The children with autism produced much less symbolic play than comparison groups, but no differences in functional play. Supporting Leslie's hypothesis, Baron-Cohen suggested the symbolic play deficit in autism reflected an impairment in metarepresentation, which he believed to be the primary psychological impairment in autism.

Challenges to the Metarepresentational Account

While the metarepresentational account of symbolic play problems in autism was theoretically satisfying, several challenges to this interpretation arose out of findings over the next decade, involving: (1) new evidence of symbolic play abilities in autism, (2) evidence of problems with nonsymbolic play in autism, and (3) symbolic immaturities in typical children.

Evidence of Intact Symbolic Abilities

The uniformity of findings in symbolic play deficits in autism was severely challenged when Lewis and Boucher (1988) published a paper demonstrating equivalent performance of children with autism and controls under conditions that involved no modeling. In an effort to isolate the cognitive deficit underlying children with autism's performance problems in symbolic play, these authors developed a method for separating symbolic play competence from performance. The task involved dolls and cars, miniature objects, and junk objects in two conditions: spontaneous and elicited. Unlike other studies, in the elicited condition, the symbolic idea was verbally suggested, but not modeled, by the adult, who asked the children, "Show me how you would make a . . ."

Using the strict definitions of symbolic play suggested by Leslie and measures of quantity, quality, and duration, the authors demonstrated that there was the expected autism-specific problem in the *spontaneous* condition. However, there was no autism difference in the use of substitute or imaginary objects in the *elicited* condition, which the authors interpreted as suggesting that children with autism did not have a problem with the representational aspects of play, but rather with generation of play ideas—an executive problem involving generativity rather than a representational problem.

This paper created great controversy, but the several replications that followed (Charman & Baron-Cohen, 1997; Jarrold, Boucher, & Smith, 1996; Lewis & Boucher, 1995; McDonough et al., 1997) all supported the initial findings. Additionally, Lewis and Boucher's replication specifically put in a direct test of generativity: a condition that examined the number of different ideas a child could generate in a specific time period. They found autism-specific differences in the generativity task, but not in the elicited play condition—findings they interpreted as supporting the idea that the symbolic play problem in autism is a *production* problem stemming from (1) a lack of generativity of ideas and (2) difficulty shifting attention from a current behavior to a new behavior.

Other papers published in the 1990s also demonstrated intact skills in children with autism in certain kinds of symbolic play tasks. Kavanaugh and Harris (1994) tested Leslie's (1987) suggestion that understanding another's pretend play required the same metarepresentational decoupling that production required another way of separating competence from performance. Children were shown pretend acts with six different small animals (e.g., the experimenter held a teapot over the animal and said he or she was pretending to pour tea on it). Children were then asked, "How does the . . . look now?" and were asked to select one of three pictures showing the animal in various physical states, including the real state, the pretend state, and another transformed state. The children with autism performed *better* than the comparison group on these tasks, which were also completed by typically developing children age 30 months. The authors interpreted the findings as supporting the idea that the symbolic play problem is one of production, not one of understanding, as supported also by treatment studies in autism that have demonstrated improved symbolic play after modeling (Goldstein, Wickstrom, Hoyson, Jamieson, & Odom, 1988; Rogers & Lewis, 1989; Thorp, Stahmer, & Schreibman, 1995). While a replication of this study also demonstrated no group differences (Jarrold, Smith, Boucher, & Harris, 1994), floor effects for both groups made further interpretation of results difficult. Finally, Jarrold et al. demonstrated that children with autism were as able to use ambiguous and counterconventional props to enact pretend sequences as well as comparison groups. Furthermore, the children with autism did not have trouble switching sets from the real to the pretend identity of these objects.

These various studies of symbolic play demonstrated that children with autism could form and manipulate symbols associated with play acts when the symbol was suggested by another. They could represent absent objects in play, assign new identities to existing objects, and ignore the salience of the object's true identity while representing a different identity. These findings of preserved function and the competence/performance contrast thus challenged Leslie's metarepresentational account of the symbolic play problem in autism.

Evidence of Impaired Sensorimotor and Functional Play

A second crucial challenge to the metarepresentational explanation of play deficits in autism concerns autism-specific differences in play that had no symbolic aspects to it. Nonsymbolic play can be categorized as *sensorimotor* or *functional*. Sensorimotor play involves manipulation of the objects for their sensorimotor properties, and functional play involves combining objects and forming play acts in ways that reflect social conventions—using objects in the way they are typically used (eating and drinking from plates, cups, and utensils) or combining objects in socially conventional ways (placing cups on saucers).

The findings about nonsymbolic play differences in autism are somewhat mixed. Baron-Cohen (1987) reported that 8-year-old children with autism did not differ from carefully matched comparison groups in their functional play. Sigman and Ruskin (1999) similarly reported no autism-specific differences in functional play skills in their sample of 70 preschoolers with autism.

However, the majority of studies examining functional and sensorimotor play have reported group differences. Tilton and Ottinger (1964) found that children with autism differed from mentally retarded and normal children in their organization of play behaviors. Using very careful definitions of play, Sigman and Ungerer (1984) reported that in spontaneous play conditions, young children with autism with low verbal mental ages produced fewer functional play acts, especially with dolls, fewer different functional play acts, and fewer sequences than a comparison group of children with mental retardation. However, in an adult modeling and prompting condition, the group differences were no longer present. Similar findings have been reported by Mundy et al. (1986), Lewis and Boucher (1988), Blanc et al. (2000), and

McDonough et al. (1997). E. Williams, Reddy, and Costall (2001) found striking qualitative differences in both functional and sensorimotor play of children with autism, In addition to abnormalities in rates and levels of sensorimotor and functional play, the proportion of immature to more mature play appears affected in autism. Sigman and Ungerer and Libby et al. documented that children with autism spent equivalent amounts of time playing in immature types of play as well as more mature types of play, while comparison children spent the majority of their play time in more mature play.

Thus, there is considerable evidence that children with autism exhibit qualitative differences compared to typically developing, developmentally delayed, and other clinical populations in their nonsymbolic play skills and that the differences somewhat mirror the differences seen in their symbolic play: more repetition, less novelty, and less diversity of play schemas, with immature patterns predominating. These differences are not well accounted for by the metarepresentational model.

Symbolic Difficulties in Typical Children

The final challenge to the metarepresentational theory of pretend play covered here comes from other cognitive theorists. There is a basic developmental problem in the metarepresentational account. How can pretend play, which is developing in 18-month-olds, involve the same metarepresentational abilities as theory of mind, which in typical development, does not develop until age 4? Several theorists suggest that early pretend play can be accounted for by simpler processes than metarepresentation. Piaget (1962), distinguishing between mental representations and the mental manipulation of symbols, suggested that neither early words nor early pretend play was synonymous with symbol use. He believed that early words, early pretend play, and deferred imitation all demonstrated the formation and use of mental representations of previous experiences. He suggested that manipulation of symbols in thought was a later accomplishment of the 2- to 4-year-old preoperational period.

Other theorists share somewhat similar views. Perner (1991) suggests that the onset of pretend play, object permanence, language, and the other representational milestones in the toddler period demonstrates the infant's new ability to generate multiple representations of reality. The infant can use multiple models to substitute for each other and, in doing so, represent past events, coming events, and as-if events. To Perner, acting as-if does not require metarepresentation. Substitution of representations does not require metarepresentation; it instead requires the use of multiple models, which young children mark in their play. The capacity for metarepresentation develops slowly across the preschool period and is later reflected by much more advanced pretend play, especially role play, with others.

Perner's view is nicely supported by work of Tomasello, Striano, and Rochat (1999), who also question the symbolic interpretation of early pretend play, both from their own and DeLoache's (1995) findings concerning young preschoolers' difficulties in understanding what miniatures represent. In two studies of 18- to 35-month-old children's understanding and production of symbols as representations of an absent object, Tomasello and his colleagues found that this ability *gradually* developed over this age period, *virtually absent at 18 months,* well developed and integrated at 35 months, and spotty in 26-month-olds. The authors suggest that early pretend play of the sort seen in 18- to 24-month-olds and older is heavily scaffolded by either adult language or through deferred imitation of previously seen events. Only gradually can children go on to use symbols that are socially acquired, as well as newly invented, in individually creative ways.

Development of the Generativity Hypothesis

The preceding findings represent powerful challenges to the metarepresentational hypothesis and led Christopher Jarrold and colleagues to focus on the competence/performance question. In a 1996 paper, they reported three experiments, each exploring one or more dimensions of symbolic understanding of children with autism. Two of these, replications of Kavanaugh and Harris (1994) and of Lewis and Boucher (1988), have already been described (Jarrold et al., 1996). The third experiment examined generativity. The children were first asked to generate as many pretend acts as they could, first without props, then with props (a ruler, a scarf, candle, etc.). In both conditions, children with autism generated fewer pretend acts than controls in both conditions.

In an integration of the findings of competences and difficulties of children with autism in pretend play studies, Jarrold considered problems both with inhibition and with generativity as possible obstacles to pretend play for children with autism (Jarrold, 1997; Jarrold et al., 1996). A problem with inhibition could impair symbolic play by making it difficult to inhibit the true nature of an object and shift to a hypothetical identity (Harris, 1993). From the empirical evidence, Jarrold concluded that there was little support for the idea that children with autism had difficulty inhibiting the real use of a prop in order to assign a substitute use. In contrast, difficulties with generativity of play ideas had considerable support across studies. He suggested that this generativity deficit occurred in many areas of functioning, citing research by others in word fluency, free recall, and drawing studies that demonstrated parallel results. In a detailed analysis of the kinds of executive problems seen in autism, Jarrold suggests that difficulties generating new behavior and difficulties in maintaining goals in working memory could account for both the patterns of reduced generativity and impulsive behavior seen in children with autism in their play and in many other situations (Jarrold, 1997; see also Harris & Leevers, 2000).

Tests of the Executive Function/Generativity Hypothesis

Very few studies have examined relations between any executive function measures and symbolic play abilities. Rutherford and Rogers (in press) examined the relationship among play maturity, joint attention, and executive function in a study of 28 very young children with autism and both delayed and typical comparison groups. Two executive function tasks were used: spatial reversal, which tests set shifting, and a generativity task, which examined number of different play acts generated to single toys without any particular function. Children with autism were equivalent to both comparison groups on both executive function tasks. However, for the entire group of children, both executive function tasks were strongly associ-

ated with pretend play but not with sensorimotor play. Generativity accounted for 27% of the variance in pretend play scores in the total group and correlated significantly with sensorimotor play scores, even when verbal ability was partialled out. (See Blanc et al., 2000 for a similar report on a small *n* study.)

However, in a somewhat contradictory finding, Dawson and colleagues (Dawson et al., 1998) used both a spontaneous and an elicited paradigm to stimulate pretend play in a group of 20 preschoolers with autism and with clinical and typical comparisons. While the expected symbolic play deficit was present in the children with autism, symbolic play scores did not correlate with performance on an executive function measure tapping working memory and inhibition—the delayed response task. Instead, it correlated at .72 with scores from a measure of orbital prefrontal cortex—the delayed nonmatch to sample (DNMS) task, which taps primary medial temporal lobe functions.

While the arguments supporting the executive function/generativity hypothesis are well reasoned and databased, the field has just begun to examine relationships between generativity (or, more broadly, executive functions) and performance on symbolic play tasks. The usefulness of this theory will be determined by the findings of additional studies that directly explore these relationships.

Specificity of Symbolic Play Deficits to Autism

Wing et al.'s (1977) study suggested that symbolic play problems were unique to autism. As seen from the review thus far, this finding has been universally supported among studies of *spontaneous* symbolic play. While it has been suggested that blind children have similar kinds of difficulties developing symbolic play (Fraiberg, 1977), there is evidence that symbolic play may develop better than was initially expected in blind children. Rogers and Puchalski (1984) documented the presence of pretend play acts in a group of blind children at age 25 months and found expected associations with language development and sensorimotor abilities. Hobson et al. (1999) compared the symbolic play of a group of blind children and a group of children with autism, matched on age and language level. The blind children demonstrated many more symbolic play acts than the children with autism, though the play was not complex. Thus, the current data suggest that the degree of difficulty that children with autism have producing symbolic play is unique.

Brain Behavior Correlates

We have no neuroimaging studies of pretend play, or even pantomime, at this time and very few neuropsychological models of pretend play. While the preceding generativity theory would emphasize frontal lobe contributions, Dawson et al. (1998) demonstrated a correlation between symbolic play and medial temporal lobe tasks rather than executive function tasks. This area is in great need of attention.

Individual Differences and Developmental Correlates of Symbolic Play in Autism

There are clearly large differences in performances of individual children with autism on both functional and pretend play tasks. IQ and language level (which are themselves closely related in autism) demonstrate associations with symbolic play skills. Baron-Cohen (1987) reported that children with autism who could demonstrate pretend play acts had significantly higher verbal and nonverbal IQs than nonpretenders. Sigman and Ungerer (1984) also reported correlations between language development and pretend play in autism, though not with sensorimotor play. However, Sigman and Ruskin (1999) reported that both functional play and symbolic play were related to concurrent language abilities. They also reported significant correlations between play and joint attention behavior in preschoolers with autism, but these were mediated by general developmental age, a precursor of language development, or with attention switching, which has implications for executive function.

However, two groups studying very young children with autism report an absence of correlations between pretend play and verbal language. Charman (2003) reported no relationship between play and language either concurrently or predictively from age 20 to age 42 months. Similarly, Rutherford and Rogers (2003) reported no relationship between either verbal or

nonverbal mental ages and elicited pretend play skills in a sample of 2-year-olds with autism, 90% of which had not yet developed speech. The absence of relationships between language and play in these two studies may be due to the very young ages and essentially nonverbal status of these toddlers with autism (the children with other diagnoses the same age and language level shared the expected relations).

The relationship of pretend play to language development is interesting in light of the varying theories concerning the nature of the pretend play problem. It was the presence of both play and language problems in autism that led to the early symbolic deficit hypothesis. Mind theory would also expect language and play to be related, given that a main purpose of language is sharing of mental states and learning language requires awareness of the contents of the speaker's mind. However, the generativity hypothesis would not necessarily predict that language and symbolic play should be related. This is further complicated by the studies that raise questions about how "symbolic" early pretend play really is (or, for that matter, how symbolic early language is). It is important to remember the modeling or imitation procedure used in most of the symbolic play procedures. Imitation is correlated with various developmental skills, including language development in autism and in normal development. Thus, it is possible that the relationships between symbolic play and language may be mediated by the imitation skills in play studies that provide play models for the children to imitate. The nature of the relationship between pretend play and language development in autism needs further study.

Delay versus Deficit

As Libby and colleagues pointed out (1998), the relationships between symbolic play development and language development in autism would suggest that symbolic play is delayed but eventually develops in those children with the cognitive abilities to acquire it. However, the unusual pattern of differences in symbolic and functional play—the lack of fluency, the repetitiveness of the play, the continuing use of very immature sensorimotor patterns as well as higher level patterns, and other aberrations in the expression of play—indicates that play is qualitatively different in autism, a deficit as well as a delay.

Experiential Effects on Pretend Play and the Ecological Model of Autism

In addition to developmental maturity, childhood experiences affect symbolic play development in typically developing children. While the tendency of developmentalists is to view symbolic play as a universal developmental accomplishment, cross-cultural studies do not support this view. Symbolic play as defined here seems to be to some extent a phenomenon of middle-class Western cultures. In other cultures, there may be much rough and tumble play or practice play, and there may be role play in which the children act out adult roles but without symbolic transformation (Feitelson, 1977; Feitelson & Ross, 1973). In addition, the play of Western children who are severely socioeconomically deprived is marked by continued sensorimotor practice play qualities (Murphy, 1972). Western preschoolers from rural settings also demonstrate a paucity of symbolic play transformations compared to their middle class suburban peers (Feitelson & Ross, 1973). Thus, symbolic play is to some extent a cultural phenomenon, supported by adult provision of play materials and play space, as well as by adult psychological support through active participation and modeling of pretend play and encouragement and respect for children's pretend play activities.

While adults often think of children's pretend play as involving fantastic images and deeply imaginative and creative activities, the reality of early pretend play is that it involves a replaying of daily life events (and again reflects the fuzzy boundaries between deferred imitation and early pretend play). Young children play out their lives: bedtime routines; mealtime routines; family dramas; and trips to the doctor, zoo, vet, and MacDonald's; using real objects, miniatures, and neutral objects, as well as verbal scripts associated with these activities. The learning mechanism appears to involve deferred imitation or social learning. And this leads to the final hypothesis concerning the nature of pretend play deficits

in autism—the impairment of social learning mechanisms in autism.

Earlier, this chapter reviewed what is currently known about problems of imitation in autism. Given the early reliance of pretend play on deferred imitation, you would expect that these two skills are related, both in typical development and in autism. To our knowledge, there are currently no published data on the relationships between deferred imitation and symbolic play.

Second, reenacting life events requires that children attend to social events and be oriented to others, their actions on objects, and their interactions. As Sigman and Ungerer suggested in 1984, lack of typical pretend play early in life in autism may reflect the lack of social learning on the part of the young child with autism or lack of pleasure in the social routines of life. Note that lack of social learning would affect functional play, which also involves the expression of socially conventional ways of acting on objects, as well as symbolic play. Relationships between play skills and social engagement have been described by Sigman and Ruskin (1999) in a large longitudinal study in which preschool functional and symbolic play skills predicted adolescent peer engagement, but not language development, in a large group of children with autism. The sociocultural aspects of pretend play have been eloquently summarized by Tomasello et al. (1999): ". . . the process of symbolic play development, as other cultural skills such as language development, may be seen as a delicate interplay between children's emerging skills to interact with the world in culturally conventional ways, and their emerging skills to use these cultural conventions in individually creative ways" (p. 583).

Finally, this kind of "acculturation" theory is congruent with the already described relationships between language and symbolic play, since both rely heavily on acculturation, or social learning and imitation, in the toddler period. Given the autism-specific effects on early social orienting documented by Osterling and Dawson (1994); Baranek (1999); Werner, Dawson, Osterling, and Dinno (2000); and others in infant video studies, there is every reason to believe that this would result in a diminished behavioral repertoire early enough to affect both functional and symbolic play (see Loveland, 2001, for a compelling description of this ecological model of autism). Whether the lack of social modeling, social learning, and experiential differences can fully account for the difficulties in spontaneous production of functional and symbolic play is unclear (Harris, 2000).

While we currently have no studies that describe relationships among symbolic play and social interest, social orientation, and imitation in early autism, the intervention evidence is useful here. A number of studies have documented improvements in children with autism's pretend play through a variety of focused treatment interventions, both behavioral and relational. These studies have demonstrated increases in frequency and complexity of symbolic play after treatment and corollary increases in social and communicative interactions with others. This treatment literature provides some indirect support for the hypothesis that there is an experiential aspect to the symbolic play difficulties seen in autism and that interventions focused on increasing children's experience and motivation for such play has effects on play complexity, play frequency, and increased social engagement.

The social hypothesis may present us with an independent explanation for the symbolic play difficulties in autism, or it may be intertwined with the generativity hypothesis, in that when social engagement and social learning are not providing new play content and ideas, children are left to the mercy of their own immature and meager repertoire of sensory motor acts to create play schemas.

Methodological Issues

A variety of methodological problems pervade the studies of pretend play in autism and have been well discussed by Baron-Cohen (1987) and Jarrold et al. (1993). While the more recent studies demonstrate improved methods, both researchers and readers of research must be sensitive to the design challenges involved. Selection of comparison groups is an ongoing challenge in autism studies. The question of autism-specific differences requires an age-matched clinical comparison group, rather than a typical group matched for developmental level (although the typical group is a very useful third group in these studies, since it provides a point of comparison for the data from the clinical comparison group). Because symbolic play has been found to have relationships with language abilities in some studies, it is crucial that groups are matched for expressive language skill rather than nonverbal or overall IQ or MA. Some researchers have argued that this needs to include a measure of expressive language complexity rather than a measure of picture naming vocabulary only, since picture naming may overestimate the language skills of children with autism.

In terms of tasks, a pervasive problem has been in the inconsistent definition of pretend play. Acts to self, acts to dolls, and use of miniatures have been classified as symbolic acts in some studies and as functional play acts in others. Baron-Cohen (1987) has suggested a clear definition of symbolic play, and Libby et al. (1998) have provided an excellent classification system for discriminating sensorimotor play from functional play, as well as clear definitions of symbolic play in line with Baron-Cohen's. While both of these systems classify doll play as functional (even when the doll is exhibiting agency), the unique and specific problems that children with autism have with doll play may illustrate that doll play involves symbolic rather than functional play and should be empirically examined.

Moving to the issue of task administration, the state of the science in this area requires that experimenters examine children's competence separate from their performance of pretend play. Having adults model pretend play acts and then scoring the child's productions as symbolic acts confounds imitation with symbolic production and impedes interpretation of findings, as nicely discussed by Libby, Powell, Messer, and Jordan (1997). Data have been most typically coded as frequency counts from videotape. There are some tools in the literature that provide developmental play age equivalents (e.g., Fewell, 1992), which can be useful in examining developmental correlates. However, if such tools are used, it is critical that the definitions of pretend play in those tests be examined to make sure that symbolic play is being classified according to the principles described earlier. Finally, what frequency variables are gathered and analyzed has significant effect on the interpretation of group differences. As the studies from Sigman's lab have illustrated, examining total number of play acts in a category can give quite a different picture than examining number of novel play acts or maturity of play acts. Qualitative differences may be missed when more fine-grained aspects of the play are not considered. Finally, both ceiling and floor effects have arisen in some of the symbolic play studies. Making sure that all the groups in a study are appropriately challenged by the task is crucial for identifying autism-specific differences or lack of differences.

Summary of Play

The work in symbolic play in autism seems poised at the edge of new developments. The increasing evidence that typically developing children are not actually using symbols as such until ages 3 to 4 requires us to view these early pretend play schemas as something other than symbolism per se. Metarepresentational theory is not a persuasive explanation for these deficits due to the timing of the deficits, the lack of symbolic ability of typically developing children in the early stages of pretend play, and the parallel impairments between pretend play and simpler types of play. Executive dysfunction theories capture several aspects of the play problems in autism: the predominance of repetitive, simple play behavior, both in sensorimotor schemes and in symbolic schemes; the ability to demonstrate understanding and production of symbolic transformations under various conditions; and the lack of fluency in spontaneously generating schemas. Yet, we do not currently have convincing data of early executive function differences in autism, nor do we have data that clearly links play difficulties with other executive function variables. The ecological, or social learning theory, is attractive, but it needs to be developed and tested.

Symbolic play research would benefit from refinement of our methods. We need straightforward procedures that are consistently used across studies so that data can be compared more easily. In each new study, we need to examine relations with other developmental skills, with neuropsychological correlates, and with social and environmental variables. The question of brain-behavior relations has only begun to be mentioned. Finally, we need to explore the theorized relations among immediate imitation, deferred imitation, pantomime, and symbolic play. Such efforts will most likely have a great payoff, for studying the primary symptoms of autism comparatively and at multiple levels of analysis have taken us far in understanding autism and have broadened considerably our understanding of normal development.

CONCLUSION

The research literature in imitation and symbolic play clearly demonstrates the severity with which autism affects these skills. The early appearance of these two skills in normal development and their seeming importance in human social, communicative, and cognitive development indicate that their impairment in autism may have powerful roles in determining outcomes in autism. From the work that has been done in imitation, it appears that there is a fundamental difficulty with imitation of other people's actions in autism that permeates many different kinds of tasks and performance across both highly scaffolded and natural settings. In contrast, performance of functional and symbolic play varies according to setting, with normalized levels of play demonstrated in certain types of scaffolded situations and the most impaired performance demonstrated in spontaneous or free play situations. This competence-performance distinction in symbolic play appears to indicate that mediating variables are at work, and the area of executive dysfunctions, particularly generativity deficits, is a prime candidate. Thus, the current literature leads us to consider that imitation may be the more primary of the autism deficits, with play abnormalities reflecting effects of intellectual impairment, executive dysfunction, possible experiential deficits, and imitation decrements. Developmental theory links imitation and symbolic play, a hypothesis that has not yet been tested. If this is indeed the case, these two areas of difficulty may in fact represent one core impairment in autism. We await studies that examine performance in these two skill areas to other levels of analysis, in autism and in other developmental groups, while at the same time examining the role of experience and environment, to understand the meaning of these skill deficits in the development of the behavioral phenotype in autism.

Cross-References

Developmental aspects of autism are addressed in Chapters 8 to 10, social development in autism is reviewed in Chapter 11 and communicative development in Chapter 12, affective aspects of autism are reviewed in Chapter 15, and theoretical perspectives are reviewed in Chapters 21 through 26.

REFERENCES

Adams, L. (1998). Oral-motor and motor-speech characteristics of children with autism. *Focus on Autism and Other Developmental Disabilities, 13,* 108–112.

Aldridge, M. A., Stone, K. R., Sweeney, M. H., & Bower, T. G. (2000). Preverbal children with autism understand intentions of others. *Developmental Science, 3,* 294–301.

Asendorpf, J. B., & Baudonniere, P. (1993). Self-awareness and other-awareness: Mirror self-recognition and synchronic imitation among unfamiliar peers. *Developmental Psychology, 29,* 88–95.

Avikainen, S., Kulomaki, T., & Hari, R. (1999). Normal movement reading in Asperger subjects. *Neuroreport, 10,* 3467–3470.

Ayres, A. J. (2000). *Developmental dyspraxia and adult onset apraxia.* Torrance, CA: Sensory Integration International.

Baldwin, J. M. (1906). *Social and ethical interpretations in mental development.* New York: Macmillan.

Baranek, G. (1999). Autism during infancy: A retrospective video analysis of sensory-motor and social behaviors at 9–12 months of age. *Journal of Autism and Developmental Disorders, 29,* 213–224.

Baron-Cohen, S. (1987). Autism and symbolic play. *British Journal of Developmental Psychology, 5,* 139–148.

Bennetto, L. (1999). A componential approach to imitation and movement deficits in autism. *Dissertation Abstracts International, 60*(2-B), 819.

Bennetto, L., Pennington, B. F., & Rogers, S. J. (1996). Intact and impaired memory functions in autism. *Child Development, 67,* 1816–1835.

Blanc, R., Tourrette, C., Delatang, N., Roux, S., Barthelemy, C., & Adrien, J. L. (2000). Regulation of symbolic activity and development of communication in children with autistic disorder. *European Review of Applied Psychology, 50,* 369–381.

Bruner, J. S. (1972). Nature and uses of immaturity. *American Psychologist, 27,* 687–708.

Byrne, R. W., & Russon, A. E. (1998). Learning by imitation: A hierarchical approach. *Behavioral and Brain Sciences, 21,* 667–721.

Carpenter, M., Pennington, B. F., & Rogers, S. J. (2001). Understanding of others' intentions in children with autism. *Journal of Autism and Developmental Disorders, 31,* 589–599.

Carpenter, M., Pennington, B. F., & Rogers, S. J. (2002). Interrelations among social-cognitive skills in young children with autism. *Journal of Autism and Developmental Disorders, 32,* 91–106.

Charman, T. (2003). Why is joint attention a pivotal skill in autism? *Philosophical Transactions of the Royal Society, 358,* 315–324.

Charman, T., & Baron-Cohen, S. (1994). Another look at imitation in autism. *Development and Psychopathology, 6,* 403–413.

Charman, T., & Baron-Cohen, S. (1997). Brief report: Prompted pretend play in autism. *Journal of Autism and Developmental Disorders, 27,* 321–328.

Charman, T., Swettenham, J., Baron-Cohen, S., Cox, A., Baird, G., & Drew, A. (1997). Infants with autism: An investigation of empathy, pretend play, joint attention, and imitation. *Developmental Psychology, 33,* 781–789.

Curcio, F. (1978). Sensorimotor functioning and communication in mute autistic children. *Journal of Autism and Childhood Schizophrenia, 8,* 281–292.

Damasio, A. R., & Maurer, R. G. (1978). A neurological model for childhood autism. *Archives of Neurology, 35,* 777–786.

Dawson, G., & Adams, A. (1984). Imitation and social responsiveness in autistic children. *Journal of Abnormal Child Psychology, 12,* 209–226.

Dawson, G., & Galpert, L. (1990). Mothers' use of imitative play for facilitating social responsiveness and toy play in young autistic children. *Development and Psychopathology, 2,* 151–162.

Dawson, G., Meltzoff, A., Osterling, J., & Rinaldi, J. (1998). Neuropsychological correlates of early symptoms of autism. *Child Development, 69,* 1276–1285.

Dawson, G., Munson, J., Estes, A., Osterling, J., McPartland, J., Toth, K., et al. (2002). Neurocognitive function and joint attention ability in young children with autism spectrum disorder versus developmental delay. *Child Development, 73,* 345–358.

DeLoache, J. S. (1995). Early symbol understanding and use. In D. Medin (Ed.), *The psychology of learning and motivation* (pp. 65–114). New York: Academic Press.

DeMyer, M. K., Alpern, G. D., Barton, S., DeMyer, W. E., Churchill, D. W., Hingtgen, J. N., et al. (1972). Imitation in autistic, early schizophrenic, and nonpsychotic subnormal children. *Journal of Autism and Childhood Schizophrenia, 2,* 264–287.

DeMyer, M. K., Hingtgen, J. N., & Jackson, R. K. (1981). Infantile autism reviewed: A decade of research. *Schizophrenia Bulletin, 7,* 388–451.

Feitelson, D. (1977). Cross-cultural studies of representational play. In B. Tizard & D. Harvey (Eds.), *Biology at play* (pp. 6–14). Philadelphia: Lippincott.

Feitelson, D., & Ross, G. S. (1973). The neglected factor—play. *Human Development, 11,* 291–296.

Fewell, R. R. (1992). *Play Assessment Scale* (5th rev.). (Available from University of Miami, Mailman Center for Child Development, P.O. Box 014621, Miami FL 33101)

Forman, D. R., & Kochanska, G. (2001). Viewing imitation as child responsiveness: A link between teaching and discipline domains of socialization. *Developmental Psychology, 37,* 198–206.

Fraiberg, S. (1977). *Insights from the blind: Comparative studies of blind and sighted infants.* New York: New American Library.

Goldstein, H., Wickstrom, S., Hoyson, M., Jamieson, B., & Odom, S. L. (1988). Effects of sociodramatic play training on social and communicative interaction. *Education and Treatment of Children, 11,* 97–117.

Gopnik, A., & Meltzoff, A. N. (1994). Minds, bodies, and persons: Young children's understanding of the self and others as reflected in imitation and theory of mind research. In S. T. Parker, R. W. Mitchell, & M. L. Bocchia (Eds.), *Self-awareness in animals and human* (pp. 166–186). New York: Cambridge University Press.

Griffith, E. M., Pennington, B. F., Wehner, E. A., & Rogers, S. J. (1999). Executive functions in young children with autism. *Child Development, 70,* 817–832.

Hammes, J. G. W., & Langdell, T. (1981). Precursors of symbol formation and childhood autism. *Journal of Autism and Developmental Disorders, 11,* 331–346.

Harris, P. (1993). Pretending and planning. In S. Baron-Cohen, H. Tager-Flusberg, & D. Cohen (Eds.), *Understanding other minds: Perspectives from autism* (pp. 182–202). Oxford, England: Oxford University Press.

Harris, P., & Leevers, H. J. (2000). Pretending, imagery, and self-awareness in autism. In S. Baron-Cohen, H. Tager-Flusberg, & D. J. Cohen (Eds.), *Understanding other minds: Perspectives from developmental cognitive neuroscience* (2nd ed., pp. 182–202). Oxford, England: Oxford University Press.

Hatfield, E., Cacioppo, J. T., & Rapson, R. L. (1994). *Emotional contagion.* New York: Cambridge University Press.

Hauck, J. A., & Dewey, D. (2001). Hand preference and motor functioning in children with autism. *Journal of Autism and Developmental Disorders, 31,* 265–278.

Heimann, M. (1998). Imitation in neonates, in older infants and in children with autism: Feedback to theory. In S. Braten (Ed.), *Intersubjective communication and emotion in early ontogeny* (de la Maison des Science de l'homme ed., pp. 89–104). Cambridge, NY: Cambridge University Press.

Heimann, M., & Ullstadius, E. (1999). Neonatal imitation and imitation among children with autism and Down's syndrome. In J. Nadel & G. Butterworth (Eds.), *Imitation in infancy* (pp. 235–253). Cambridge, England: Cambridge University Press.

Hermelin, B., & O'Connor, N. (1970). *Psychological experiments with autistic children.* New York: Pergamon Press.

Heyes, C. M., & Galef, B. G. (Eds.). (1996). *Social learning in animals: The roots of culture.* San Diego, CA: Academic Press.

Hill, D. A., & Leary, M. R. (1993). *Movement disturbance: A clue to hidden competencies in persons diagnosed with autism and other developmental disabilities.* Madison, WI: DRI Press.

Hobson, R. P. (1989). Beyond cognition: A theory of autism. In G. Dawson (Ed.), *Autism: Nature, diagnosis and treatment* (pp. 22–48). New York: Guilford Press.

Hobson, R. P., & Lee, A. (1999). Imitation and identification in autism. *Journal of Child Psychology and Psychiatry, 40,* 649–660.

Hobson, R. P., Lee, A., & Brown, R. (1999). Autism and congenital blindness. *Journal of Autism and Developmental Disorders, 29,* 45–56.

Hobson, R. P., Ouston, J., & Lee, A. (1989). Naming emotion in faces and voices: Abilities and disabilities in autism and mental retardation. *British Journal of Developmental Psychology, 7,* 237–250.

Huang, C. T., Heyes, C., & Charman, T. (2002). Infants' behavioral reenactment of "Failed

Attempts": Exploring the roles of emulation learning, stimulus enhancement, and understanding of intentions. *Developmental Psychology, 38,* 840–855.

Hughes, C. (1996). Planning problems in autism at the level of motor control. *Journal of Autism and Developmental Disorders, 26,* 99–109.

Iacoboni, M., Woods, R. P., Brass, M., Bekkering, H., Mazziotta, J. C., & Rizzolatti, G. (1999). Cortical mechanisms of human imitation. *Science, 286,* 2526–2528.

Jarrold, C. (1997). Pretend play in autism: Executive explanations. In J. Russell (Ed.), *Autism as an executive disorder* (pp. 101–133). Oxford, England: Oxford University Press.

Jarrold, C., Boucher, J., & Smith, P. (1993). Symbolic play in autism: A review. *Journal of Autism and Developmental Disorders, 23,* 281–307.

Jarrold, C., Boucher, J., & Smith, P. K. (1996). Generativity deficits in pretend play in autism. *British Journal of Developmental Psychology, 14,* 275–300.

Jarrold, C., Smith, P. K., Boucher, J., & Harris, P. (1994). Comprehension of pretense in children with autism. *Journal of Autism and Developmental Disorders, 24,* 433–455.

Jones, V., & Prior, M. (1985). Motor imitation abilities and neurological signs in autistic children. *Journal of Autism and Developmental Disorders, 15,* 37–46.

Kavanaugh, R. D., & Harris, P. L. (1994). Imagining the outcome of pretend transformations: Assessing the competence of normal children and children with autism. *Developmental Psychology, 30,* 847–854.

Kimberg, D. Y., & Farah, M. J. (1993). A unified account of cognitive impairments following frontal lobe damage: The role of working memory in complex, organized behavior. *Journal of Experimental Psychology, 122,* 411–428.

Kohen-Raz, R., Volkmar, F. R., & Cohen, D. J. (1992). Postural control in children with autism. *Journal of Autism and Developmental Disorders, 22,* 419–432.

Kugiumutzakis, G. (1999). Genesis and development of early infant mimesis to facial and vocal models. In J. Nadel & G. Butterworth (Eds.), *Imitation in infancy* (pp. 36–59). Cambridge, England: Cambridge University Press.

Leslie, A. (1987). Pretense and representation: The origins of "Theory of Mind." *Psychological Review, 94,* 412–426.

Lewis, V., & Boucher, J. (1988). Spontaneous, instructed and elicited play in relatively able autistic children. *British Journal of Developmental Psychology, 6,* 325–339.

Lewis, V., & Boucher, J. (1995). Generativity in the play of young people with autism. *Journal of Autism and Developmental Disorders, 25,* 105–122.

Libby, S., Powell, S., Messer, D., & Jordan, R. (1997). Imitation of pretend play acts by children with autism and Down syndrome. *Journal of Autism and Developmental Disorders, 27,* 365–383.

Libby, S., Powell, S., Messer, D., & Jordan, R. (1998). Spontaneous play in children with autism: A reappraisal. *Journal of Autism and Developmental Disorders, 28,* 487–497.

Lord, C., & Pickles, A. (1996). Language level and nonverbal social-communicative behaviors in autistic and language-delayed children. *Journal of the Academy of Child and Adolescent Psychiatry, 35,* 1542–1550.

Loveland, K. A. (2001). Toward an ecological theory of autism. In J. A. Burack, T. Charman, N. Yirmiya, & P. R. Zelazo (Eds.), *The development of autism: Perspective from theory and research* (pp. 17–37). Mahwah, NJ: Erlbaum.

Loveland, K. A., Tunali-Kotoski, B., Pearson, D. A., & Brelsford, K. A. (1994). Imitation and expression of facial affect in autism. *Development and Psychopathology, 6,* 433–444.

Manjiviona, J., & Prior, M. (1995). Comparison of Asperger syndrome and high-functioning autistic children on a test of motor impairment. *Journal of Autism and Developmental Disorders, 25,* 23–40.

McCune-Nicholich, L. (1977). Beyond sensorimotor intelligence: Assessment of symbolic maturity through analysis of pretend play. *Merrill-Palmer Quarterly, 23,* 89–99.

McCune-Nicholich, L. (1981). Toward symbolic functioning: Structure of early pretend games and potential parallels with language. *Child Development, 52,* 785–797.

McDonough, L., Stahmer, A., Schreibman, L., & Thompson, S. J. (1997). Deficits, delays, and distractions: An evaluation of symbolic play and memory in children with autism. *Development and Psychopathology, 9,* 17–41.

Meltzoff, A., & Gopnik, A. (1993). The role of imitation in understanding persons and developing a theory of mind. In S. Baron-Cohen, H. Tager-Flusberg, & D. J. Cohen (Eds.), *Understanding other minds: Perspectives from autism* (pp. 335–366). Oxford, England: Oxford University Press.

Meltzoff, A., & Moore, M. K. (1977). Imitation of facial and manual gestures by human neonates. *Science, 198,* 75–78.

Minshew, N. J., Goldstein, G., & Siegel, D. J. (1997). Neuropsychologic functioning in autism: Profile of a complex information processing disorder. *Journal of the International Neuropsychological Society, 3,* 303–316.

Morgan, S. B., Cutrer, P. S., Coplin, J. W., & Rodrigue, J. R. (1989). Do autistic children differ from retarded and normal children in Piagetian sensorimotor functioning? *Journal of Child Psychology and Psychiatry, 30,* 857–864.

Mundy, P., Sigman, M., Ungerer, J., & Sherman, T. (1986). Defining the social deficits of autism: The contribution of non-verbal communication measures. *Journal of Child Psychology and Psychiatry, 27,* 657–669.

Murphy, L. B. (1972). Infants' play and cognitive development. In M. W. Piers (Ed.), *Play and development* (pp. 119–126). New York: Norton.

Nadel, J., & Peze, A. (1993). What makes immediate imitation communicative in toddlers and autistic children. In J. Nadel & L. Camaioni (Eds.), *New perspectives in early communication development* (pp. 139–156). London: Routledge.

Nakamura, K., Kawashima, R., Ito, K., Sugiura, M., Kato, T., Nakamura, A., et al. (1999). Activation of the right inferior frontal cortex during assessment of facial emotion. *Journal of Neurophysiology, 82,* 1610–1614.

Ohta, M. (1987). Cognitive disorders of infantile autism: A study employing the WISC, spatial relationships, conceptualization, and gestural imitation. *Journal of Autism and Developmental Disorders, 17,* 45–62.

Osterling, J., & Dawson, G. (1994). Early recognition of children with autism: A study of first birthday home videotapes. *Journal of Autism and Developmental Disorders, 24,* 247–257.

Osterling, J., Dawson, G., & Munson, J. (2002). Early recognition of one-year old infants with autism spectrum disorder versus mental retardation. *Development and Psychopathology, 14,* 239–251.

Ozonoff, S., & McEvoy, R. E. (1994). A longitudinal study of executive function and theory of mind development in autism. *Development and Psychopathology, 6,* 415–431.

Ozonoff, S., Pennington, B. F., & Rogers, S. J. (1991). Executive function deficits in high-functioning autistic children: Relationship to theory of mind. *Journal of Child Psychology and Psychiatry, 32,* 1081–1105.

Page, J., & Boucher, J. (1998). Motor impairments in children with autistic disorder. *Child Language Teaching and Therapy, 14,* 233–259.

Pennington, B. F., & Ozonoff, S. (1991). A neuroscientific perspective on continuity and discontinuity in developmental psychopathology. In D. Cicchetti & S. L. Toth (Eds.), *Rochester symposium on developmental psychopathology:*

Vol. 3. Models and integrations (pp. 117–159). Rochester, NY: University of Rochester Press.

Perner, J. (1991). *Understanding the representational mind.* Cambridge, MA: MIT Press.

Piaget, J. (1962). *Play, dreams, and imitation in childhood.* New York: Norton.

Prior, M., & Hoffman, W. (1990). Brief report: Neuropsychological testing of autistic children through an exploration with frontal lobe tests. *Journal of Autism and Developmental Disorders, 20,* 581–590.

Rapin, I. (1996). *Preschool children with inadequate communication: Developmental language disorder.* London: Mac Keith Press.

Ricks, D. M., & Wing, L. (1975). Language, communication, and the use of symbols in normal and autistic children. *Journal of Autism and Childhood Schizophrenia, 5,* 191–221.

Riguet, C. B., Taylor, N. D., Benaroya, S., & Klein, L. S. (1981). Symbolic play in autistic, Down's, and normal children of equivalent mental age. *Journal of Autism and Developmental Disorders, 11,* 439–448.

Rizzolatti, G., & Arbib, M. A. (1998). Language within our grasp. *Trends in Neuroscience, 21,* 188–194.

Rizzolatti, G., Fadiga, L., Fogassi, L., & Gallese, V. (2003). From mirror neurons to imitation: Facts and speculations. In A. Meltzoff & W. Prinz (Eds.), *The imitative mind: Development, evolution, and brain bases* (pp. 247–266). Cambridge, England: Cambridge University Press.

Rodier, P. M. (2000). The early origins of autism. *Scientific American, 282,* 56–63.

Roeyers, H., Van Oost, P., & Bothuyne, S. (1998). Immediate imitation and joint attention in young children with autism. *Development and Psychopathology, 10,* 441–450.

Rogers, S. J. (1999). An examination of the imitation deficit in autism. In J. Nadel & G. Butterworth (Eds.), *Imitation in infancy* (pp. 254–283). Cambridge, England: Cambridge University Press.

Rogers, S. J., Bennetto, L., McEvoy, R. E., & Pennington, B. F. (1996). Imitation and pantomime in high functioning adolescents with autism spectrum disorders. *Child Development, 67,* 2060–2073.

Rogers, S. J., & Lewis, H. (1989). An effective day treatment model for young children with pervasive developmental disorders. *Journal of the American Academy of Child and Adolescent Psychiatry, 28,* 207–214.

Rogers, S. J., & Pennington, B. F. (1991). A theoretical approach to the deficits in infantile autism. *Development and Psychopathology, 3,* 137–162.

Rogers, S. J., & Puchalski, C. (1984). Development of symbolic play in visually impaired infants. *Topics in Early Childhood Special Education, 3,* 57–64.

Rogers, S. J., Stackhouse, T., Hepburn, S. L., & Wehner, E. A. (2003). Imitation performance in toddlers with autism and those with other developmental disorders. *Journal of Child Psychology and Psychiatry and Allied Disciplines.*

Rogoff, B., Mistry, J., Goncu, A., & Mosier, C. (1993). Guided participation in cultural activity by toddlers and caregivers. *Monographs of the Society for Research in Child Development, 58,* 1–161.

Rumsey, J., & Hamburger, S. D. (1988). Neuropsychological findings in high-functioning men with infantile autism, residual state. *Journal of Clinical and Experimental Neuropsychology, 10,* 201–221.

Russell, J. (1997). *Executive functioning in autism.* Oxford, England: Oxford University Press.

Rutherford, M. D., & Rogers, S. J. (in press). The cognitive underpinnings of pretend play. *Journal of Autism and Developmental Disorders.*

Sigman, M., & Ruskin, E. (1999). Continuity and change in the social competence of children with autism, Down syndrome, and developmental delays. *Monographs of the Society for Research inn Child Development, 64,* 1–114.

Sigman, M., & Ungerer, J. (1984). Cognitive and language skills in autistic, mentally retarded, and normal children. *Developmental Psychology, 20,* 293–302.

Smith, I. M., & Bryson, S. E. (1998). Gesture imitation in autism: I. Nonsymbolic postures and sequences. *Cognitive Neuropsychology, 15,* 747–770.

Stern, D. N. (1985). *The interpersonal world of the human infant.* New York: Basic Books.

Stone, W. L., Ousley, O. Y., & Littleford, C. D. (1997). Motor imitation in young children with autism: What's the object? *Journal of Abnormal Child Psychology, 25,* 475–485.

Stone, W. L., & Yoder, P. J. (2001). Predicting spoken language level in children with autism spectrum disorders. *Autism, 5,* 341–361.

Teitelbaum, P., Teitelbaum, O., Ney, J., Fryman, J., & Maurer, R. G. (1998). Movement analysis in infancy may be useful for early diagnosis of autism. *Proceedings of the National Academy of Sciences, USA, 95,* 13982–13987.

Thorp, D. M., Stahmer, A. C., & Schreibman, L. (1995). Effects of sociodramatic play training on children with autism. *Journal of Autism and Developmental Disorders, 25,* 265–282.

Tilton, J. R., & Ottinger, D. R. (1964). Comparison of the toy play behavior of autistic, retarded, and normal children. *Psychological Reports,* 967–975.

Tomasello, M. (1998). Intending that others jointly attend. *Pragmatics and Cognition, 6,* 1998, 229–243.

Tomasello, M., Kruger, A. C., & Ratner, H. H. (1993). Cultural learning. *Behavioral and Brain Sciences, 16,* 495–552.

Tomasello, M., Striano, T., & Rochat, P. (1999). Do young children use objects as symbols? *British Journal of Developmental Psychology, 17,* 563–584.

Trevarthen, C., Kokkinaki, T., & Fiamenghi, G. A. (1999). What infant's imitations communicate. In J. Nadel & G. Butterworth (Eds.), *Imitation in infancy* (pp. 127–185). Cambridge, England: Cambridge University Press.

Ungerer, J., & Sigman, M. (1981). Symbolic play and language comprehension in autistic children. *Journal of the American Academy of Child Psychiatry, 20,* 318–337.

Uzgiris, I. C. (1981). Two functions of imitation during infancy. *International Journal of Behavioral Development, 4,* 1–12.

Uzgiris, I. C. (1999). Imitation as activity: Its developmental aspects. In J. Nadel & G. Butterworth (Eds.), *Imitation in infancy* (pp. 186–206). Cambridge, England: Cambridge University Press.

Want, S. C., & Harris, P. L. (2002). Social learning: Compounding some problems and dissolving others. *Developmental Science, 5,* 39–41.

Werner, E., Dawson, G., Osterling, J., & Dinno, N. (2000). Brief report: Recognition of autism spectrum disorder before one year of age: A retrospective study based on home videotapes. *Journal of Autism and Developmental Disorders, 30,* 157–162.

Williams, E., Reddy, V., & Costall, A. (2001). Taking a closer look at functional play in children with autism. *Journal of Autism and Developmental Disorders, 31,* 67–77.

Williams, J. H., Whiten, A., Suddendorf, T., & Perrett, D. I. (2001). Imitation, mirror neurons and autism. *Neuroscience and Biobehavioral Review, 25,* 287–295.

Wing, L., Gould, J., Yeates, S., & Brierley, L. (1977). Symbolic play in severely mentally retarded and in autistic children. *Journal of Child Psychology and Psychiatry, 18,* 167–178.

CHAPTER 15

Autism and Emotion

PETER HOBSON

The characteristic of autism that most impressed Kanner (1943) about his 11 cases of children with "autistic disturbances of affective contact" was their "inability to relate themselves in the ordinary way to people and situations from the beginning of life" (p. 242). In the course of his case histories, Kanner recorded a variety of clinical features that reflected the children's seeming unawareness of the people around them and their imperviousness to the human significance of the surrounding world. He concluded: ". . . further study of our children may help to furnish concrete criteria regarding the still diffuse notions about the constitutional components of emotional reactivity" (p. 250).

It has taken several decades to disentangle Kanner's original take on autism from another and quite separate thesis about the disorder: that it might be caused by cold or otherwise pathological mothering. For a long time, it seemed that only by positing a primary linguistic or cognitive disorder could you reject the suggestion that this is a psychogenic disturbance or avoid the implication that the children's characteristic and severely restricting limitations in creative and context-sensitive thinking are somehow incidental or of secondary importance. Now freed from this constraint, we can acknowledge that social-affective engagement may be disrupted by constitutional abnormalities that have potentially far-reaching developmental repercussions.

This change brings fresh grounds for unease, however. Is there really going to be a *test* of whether perceptual, cognitive, motivational, or affective deficits are primary in the

pathogenesis of the syndrome? Is any one of these theoretical options likely to lead to a satisfactory explanation of autism? Or are we framing our questions in the wrong way?

CONCEPTUAL ISSUES

Kanner (1943) did not restrict himself to commenting on the children's limited affective engagement with people, pivotal though this seemed. He also referred to their ways of relating to things, for example, by showing repetitive and often highly restricted interests. One aspect of this disorder that has attracted much attention in the subsequent literature is the way in which children with autism have a paucity of symbolic play; another is their relative inflexibility in adjusting language to the context in which it is used and, especially, according to meanings that depend on the psychological orientations of speakers and listeners. Such impairments are *not* considered to be emotional for obvious reasons. If children with autism are unable to engage in creative, symbolic play, even when they seem to be trying their best to use play materials, you hardly want to say that they are prevented by emotional or motivational factors; if they are simply at a loss when trying to communicate, it would be wrong (not to say perverse) to attribute this to their feelings about the situation.

And yet these apparently clear examples may lead us to become overconfident about the conceptual boundaries that separate cognitive, conative, and affective domains of psychological functioning. There is not only the deep philosophical issue about what (if not some-

406

thing like feelings or experiences) connects us humans and our thoughts with what those thoughts are "about"—the representations of a computer are *not* like thoughts, because they do not have this natural aboutness and have to be interpreted by humans—but also the developmental issue of what thoughts, feelings, and motivations develop *out of*. It is at least plausible that certain qualities of our thinking (for example, some of the ways we discriminate this from that, or generalize from one object or situation or event to another) are dependent on the ways that things affect us or lend themselves to actions that have meaning because of accompanying feelings. In this sense, at least, there are emotional bases for thinking. Or again, there are forms of "feeling perception": To see a smile as a smile *is* to have a propensity to react with feelings, and it may be only because we have the capacity to perceive and relate to others' expressions in this way that we come to understand smiles as expressive of inner states and ultimately come to comprehend the nature of people with minds (Hobson, 1993a, 1993b). More radically still, if one person can share experiences with someone else only because of affective coordination between the two and if sharing of this kind is required for a range of transactions that occur *between* people—for example, an adult pointing out things to a child or negotiating those forms of symbolic meaning embodied in language and creative play—then the cognitive implications of supposedly "emotion-specific" impairments are wide-ranging indeed (Hobson, 2002).

Therefore, once you adopt a developmental perspective, you can no longer assume that psychological categories that seem to function fairly well when applied to adults are also applicable to earlier phases of development. What have become paradigmatic cases of *thinking* or *willing* or *perceiving* in adults, and seemingly separable from feelings, may have originated in infantile states that implicated each of these functions as inseparable aspects of the infant's relations with the world. If so, the challenge may become one of distinguishing among different modes of infant relatedness. In this case, we need to respect how *intersubjective* modes of relatedness that occur between infants and other people, sometimes in

relation to a shared world, are not only heavily imbued with affect and motivational force (especially through the "pull" of other people's attitudes) but also transformational for the growing child's ability to achieve a kind of mental space required for symbolic thinking.

Given that there are a number of things we want to know about the role of emotion in the pathogenesis and expression of autism, it is not surprising that methods have evolved to investigate the domain from various standpoints. Each method has its own strengths and limitations, and each its own standards for methodological adequacy. There are important insights to be gained from individual case descriptions, clinical accounts of groups of children, systematic observational studies, interviews with informants such as parents, quasi-experimental investigations, more strictly controlled experiments on specific aspects of the disorder, and family and related studies elucidating the role of genetic and environmental factors in pathogenesis. As discussed later, there is also value in studying atypical forms of autism, and neurofunctional studies will undoubtedly bring new insights. Some of these studies yield results that increase our knowledge of what is or is not characteristic of autism, some are more concerned with the degree to which given deficits are specific to the emotional domain, and others again point to alternative pathways of abnormal development. In the following discussion, a less than comprehensive sample of studies from the voluminous and increasingly convergent literature is presented.

Case descriptions comprise the most difficult part of that literature to summarize. The following excerpt from Kanner (1943) illustrates just how much we stand to gain by paying close attention to clinical detail. It concerns 6-year-old Frederick attending Kanner's clinic for the first time:

He was led into the psychiatrist's office by a nurse, who left the room immediately afterward. His facial expression was tense, somewhat apprehensive, and gave the impression of intelligence. He wandered aimlessly about for a few moments, showing no sign of awareness of the three adults present. He then sat down on the couch, ejaculating unintelligible sounds, and then abruptly lay down, wearing throughout a dreamy-like smile. . . . Objects absorbed him easily and he showed good attention and perseverance in playing with them. He seemed to regard people as unwelcome intruders to whom he paid as little attention as they would permit. When forced to respond, he did so briefly and returned to his absorption in things. When a hand was held out before him so that he could not possibly ignore it, he played with it briefly as if it were a detached object. (p. 224)

Allow this vivid portrayal to linger in your mind, as we turn to systematic controlled studies of socioemotional impairments in children and adolescents with autism.

SYSTEMATIC STUDIES OF THE EARLY YEARS

In considering what is basic to autism, special importance is attached to determining those features that characterize the earliest phases of development.

Parental Reports

Parental reports afford an important perspective on the early clinical features of autism. For example, Dahlgren and Gillberg (1989) asked mothers of a population sample of matched individuals with and without autism, then between 7 and 22 years of age, to complete a 130-item questionnaire on the child's behavior in the first two years of life. Among the features that discriminated the children with autism were their isolation, their lack of play, their failure to attract attention to their own activity, their lack of smiling at times when you might expect it, and their empty gaze (cf. Wing, 1969, whose study included several control groups; and Stone & Lemanek, 1990; Vostanis et al., 1998). Even in such a condensed summary of results from a less than sensitive measure, we sense the emotional implications of what is being reported.

A more in-depth approach adopted by Wimpory and colleagues (Wimpory, Hobson, Williams, & Nash, 2000) was to interview parents of very young children who were referred to a child development center with difficulties in relating to and communicating with others. At the time of interview, the undiagnosed children were between 32 and 48 months old, and it was only subsequently that 10 children diagnosed with autism were compared with 10 children, matched for age and developmental level, who did not have autism. This meant that when parents were asked about the children's behavior in the first two years of life, they were recalling events from only 6 to 24 months previously, and their memories were not distorted by knowledge of autism.

The parents' reports indicated that as infants, those with autism had a number of abnormalities in the area of person-to-person nonverbal communication and interpersonal contact. Not one of the infants with autism had shown frequent and intense eye contact, engaged in turn taking with adults, or used noises communicatively, whereas half of the control children were reported to show each of these kinds of behavior. There were also fewer infants with autism who greeted or waved to their parents, raised their arms to be picked up, directed feelings of anger and distress toward people, were sociable in play, or enjoyed and participated in lap games. In each of these respects, there were clear limitations in their affective engagement with others. Lord, Storoschuk, Rutter, and Pickles (1993) also reported that parents of young children with autism gave accounts of abnormalities across a range of socioemotional and communicative behavior, including socially directed babble.

In addition, the interviews of Wimpory et al. (2000) revealed group differences in the infants' ways of relating to other people with reference to objects and events in the environment. For example, not one of the infants with autism, but at least half the infants in the control group, was reported to offer or give objects to others in the first two years of life. The same was true of pointing at objects or following others' points. Few children with autism were said to show objects to others, and not one was said to have looked between an object of interest and an adult, for example, when the infant wanted something out of reach. Here we seem to be moving beyond what is paradigmatically emotional—and yet, do we suppose that the behavior just described lacks emotional underpinnings? The evidence clearly suggests that the children's lack of interpersonal engagement extends to circumstances in which they might share experiences of the world with other people. They appear to be not only less connected with other people for their own sake but also less connected with or able to share others' affective attitudes to a shared world (Kasari, Sigman, Mundy, & Yirmiya, 1990).

Observational and Experimental Studies

Some studies have employed diagnostic instruments alongside direct observations of young children with autism. For example, Stone, Hoffman, Lewis, and Ousley (1994) supplemented parental interviews to gather information on the current behavior of 2- to 4-year-old children with autism, with systematic clinical observations. They reported that there were deficits in imitation, nonverbal communication (including expressions of interest in things through eye contact or pointing), responsiveness to others, and social and imaginative play. Lord (1995) assessed 30 2-year-old children referred for possible autism using a modified version of the Autism Diagnostic Interview along with a rating scale for direct observations and reassessed them one year later to ascertain which children received a diagnosis of autism at this later stage. On reexamining the data from the earlier assessment, she concluded that the 2-year-olds with autism differed from the other children with developmental disorders in specific aspects of (1) communicative behavior: their lack of response to another person's voice, absence of pointing, and failure to understand gesture; (2) social reciprocity: lack of seeking to share their enjoyment, failure to greet, unusual use of others' bodies, lack of initiative in directing visual attention, and lack of interest in children; and (3) restricted, repetitive behavior: hand and finger mannerisms and unusual sensory behavior.

Therefore, there are firm indications that, from an early age, socioemotional engagement is a distinctive domain of abnormality in children with autism. The following controlled studies begin to tease out some of the characteristics of this disability.

INTERPERSONAL COORDINATION OF AFFECT

Kasari et al. (1990) employed videotapes of semistructured child-experimenter interactions to assess how matched autistic and nonautistic developmentally delayed 3- to 6-year-olds and mental age-matched typically developing children with a mean age of 2 years expressed affect toward the experimenter in the contexts of joint attention and requesting. Subjects' facial expressions were coded second by second for a total of 8 minutes, using a standardized coding instrument (the Maximally Discriminative Movement Coding System designed by Izard [1979]). Although the autistic children showed uniformly low levels of positive affect toward the adult, they diverged most markedly in their decreased level of positive feeling during situations of joint attention. These were the situations in which the typically developing children smiled most of all, sharing their feelings with the other person.

This evidence of autism-specific abnormality in face-to-face affective coordination is supported by two further studies. In the first, Snow, Hertzig, and Shapiro (1987) videotaped 10 autistic children between 2½ and 4 years and 10 age- and nonverbal mental age-matched developmentally delayed children as they interacted with the mother, a child psychiatrist, and a nursery school teacher who were told to behave "just as they normally would" in a comfortable room stocked with toys. Twenty 15-second intervals of child interaction with each partner were coded using a checklist of emotionally expressive actions such as smiles and laughter. Whereas almost all the positive affect of the nonautistic children was expressed toward the other person, the autistic children's less frequent displays of affect were as likely to occur at seemingly random, self-absorbed moments as in the context of social interaction.

In the second study, Dawson, Hill, Spencer, Galpert, and Watson (1990), videotaped 16 autistic children ages 2 to 6 years and 16 typically developing children matched for receptive language interacting with their mothers in three different contexts: free play, a more structured situation in which the mother asked the child to help her put away some toys, and a face-to-face situation over snack time. (This kind of comparison with nonretarded children leaves some uncertainty whether differences in the autistic children's behavior might reflect mental retardation rather than autism per se.)

The findings were interesting not only for the group differences that emerged but also for the fact that there were no significant differences in the autistic children's frequency or duration of gaze at the mother's face, nor differences in the frequency or duration of smiles in the face-to-face interaction over a snack. However, children with autism were much less likely than typically developing children to combine their smiles with eye contact in a single act that seemed to convey an intent to communicate feelings. In addition, whereas 10 of 14 typically developing children with codable data smiled in response to their mother's smile, only 3 of 15 autistic subjects ever did so. It was also observed that the mothers of the children with autism were less likely to smile in response to their children's smiles, which were rarely combined with sustained eye contact. You might question how much sharing or coordination of affective states was taking place between the mothers and children.

Further studies from the UCLA group (Sigman, Kasari, Kwon, & Yirmiya, 1992) have examined other forms of interpersonal coordination of affect. Participants were 30 young autistic children with a mean age of under 4 years and closely matched nonautistic retarded and typically developing children. The technique was to code these children's behavior when an adult pretended to hurt herself by hitting her finger with a hammer, simulated fear toward a remote-controlled robot, and pretended to be ill by lying down on a couch for a minute, feigning discomfort. In each of these situations, children with autism were unusual in rarely looking at or relating to the adult. When the adult pretended to be hurt, for example, children with autism often appeared unconcerned and continued to play with toys. When a small remote-controlled robot moved toward the child and stopped about four feet away, the parent and the experimenter, who were both seated nearby, made fearful facial expressions, gestures, and vocalizations for 30 seconds. Almost all of the nonautistic children looked at an adult at some point during this procedure, but fewer than half of the children with autism did so and then only briefly. The children with autism not only were less hesitant than the mentally retarded children in playing with the robot but also played with it for substantially longer periods of time. It

seemed that they were less influenced by the fearful attitudes of those around them. Again, we find evidence that autistic children are relatively unengaged, not only in one-to-one interpersonal-affective transactions but also with another person's emotional attitudes toward objects and events in the world.

These studies have inspired more recent investigations of 20-month-olds by Charman et al. (1997). Children's videotaped reactions to an investigator's feigned hurt revealed that only 4 of 10 children with autism but every one of the nonautistic children looked at the investigator's pained face. When a potentially anxiety-provoking toy (e.g., a robot) was placed on the floor a short distance from the child, the children with autism very rarely switched their gaze between toy and adult to check out the toy (see also Bacon, Fein, Morris, Waterhouse, & Allen, 1998, for related results with somewhat older children). In each respect, these very young children seemed unconnected with the feelings of others.

The preceding research illustrates how children with autism have characteristic abnormalities in reciprocal and mutual social engagement and shared affective relatedness with the surrounding world. Although there is much to be said for studying such interpersonal relations in context, it has also proved instructive to analyze the expression and perception of emotion in experimental settings that allow for more precise definition of specific profiles of impairment.

EMOTIONAL EXPRESSIVENESS

Ricks (1975, 1979) tape-recorded six 3- and 4-year-old nonverbal autistic children, six nonverbal nonautistic retarded children of the same age, and six typically developing infants between 8 and 11 months old in four situations. The first was a "request" situation, when the child was hungry and his favorite meal was prepared and shown to him; the second was an occasion of frustration, when the meal was withheld for a few moments; the third was one of greeting, when the child saw his mother on waking in the morning or when she returned to the room after an absence; and in the fourth, involving pleased surprise, the child was presented with a novel and interesting stimulus, the blowing up of a balloon, or the lighting of a sparkler firework. The recordings of the children's vocalizations in each of these situations were edited and played back to the mothers of the children. The mother's task was to identify (1) in which context each vocalization had been recorded, (2) her own child, and (3) the nonautistic child. The second set of recordings comprised the request vocalizations of all six autistic children, and the task was for the mother to identify her own child.

When this kind of procedure was conducted with recordings of typically developing infants' vocalizations, the mothers could easily identify the "message" of each signal of every infant but found difficulty in identifying which signals came from their own child. When the tapes of the autistic and nonautistic retarded subjects were presented to the autistic children's mothers, these mothers, too, could recognize the contexts from which their own autistic child's vocalizations had been derived, and they could also identify the signals of the one nonautistic child on tape (often explaining that the child "sounded normal"). What they were unable to do was to recognize the contexts associated with the vocalizations of autistic children other than their own. Each of these children's signals seemed to be idiosyncratic. Correspondingly, and in contrast with the parents of normal children, they could readily and unerringly identify their own child from the various vocalizations. Ricks concluded that whereas typically developing infants seem to have an unlearned set of emotionally communicative vocalizations, autistic children either do not develop these signals or, having reached the age of 3 to 5, they no longer use them. However, their idiosyncratic signals do have emotional meanings.

Yirmiya, Kasari, Sigman, and Mundy (1989) studied videotapes of semistructured child-experimenter interactions involving activated toys, a song-and-tickle social game, a turn-taking activity, and a balloon-blowing episode. The children's facial expressions were coded second by second, using the anatomically based scheme of Izard (1979). The principal findings were that children with autism were more flat or neutral in affective expressions than were control children, but more important, they

displayed a variety of unique and ambiguous expressions that were not displayed by any of the other children. Although the authors described these in terms of negative and incongruous "blends" of expression, for example, of fear with anger or anger with joy, it is uncertain whether what might normally serve as reliable indices of fear, anger, and so on had the same meanings here. The evidence suggests that for autistic children, the intrapersonal coordination of expressions might be abnormal, with obvious implications for the patterning of the children's personal and interpersonal affective experiences.

LATER CHILDHOOD AND ADOLESCENCE

Lee and Hobson (1998) videotaped children and adolescents greeting an unfamiliar person and later taking their leave. Compared with matched, mentally retarded control children, only half as many of the children and adolescents with autism gave spontaneous expressions of greeting, and many failed to respond even after prompting. All the young people without autism made eye contact, but a third of those with autism failed to do so; no fewer than 17 of the former group smiled, but only six of those with autism smiled. In the farewell episode, half the individuals without autism, but only three of those with autism, made eye contact and said a goodbye. Not only were there fewer than half as many autistic as nonautistic individuals who waved in response to a final prompt, but their waves were strangely uncoordinated and limp.

Another study of emotionally expressive gestures takes a rather different form. Attwood, Frith, and Hermelin (1988) observed adolescents with both autism and Down syndrome interacting with their peers for a total of twenty 30-second periods in the playground and at the dinner table. All 15 Down subjects interacted socially during the period of observation, but only 11 of the 18 autistic children did so. Although the mean number of gestures per interaction did not distinguish the groups, there were differences in the kinds of gestures employed. Both groups used simple pointing gestures and gestures to prompt behavior, such as those to indicate "Come here" or "Be quiet"; but whereas

10 of 15 individuals with Down syndrome used at least one expressive gesture such as giving a hug of consolation, making a thumbs-up sign, or covering the face in embarrassment, not one such gesture was seen in the autistic group.

Such observations of spontaneous social engagement are complemented by the work of investigators who have asked autistic individuals to pose emotionally expressive faces and voices. Thus, in an experiment conducted by Langdell (1981), judges rated children's attempts to make happy and sad faces as more inappropriate than those of nonautistic retarded children. In a more elaborate study by Macdonald et al. (1989), raters judged that high-functioning autistic subjects' posed facial and vocal expressions were more "odd" than those of control subjects, and the (photographed) faces were also less easily classified with respect to the emotions expressed. When Loveland et al. (1994) tested children's ability to imitate as well as produce expressions of facial affect on instruction, the children with autism not only found difficulty but also produced more bizarre and mechanical expressions. In deliberate as well as spontaneous expressions of emotion, therefore, the evidence points to qualitative as well as quantitative abnormalities in individuals with autism.

I have already remarked how in the realm of interpersonal relations, perception of people and their expressiveness is only partly dissociable from the emotional experience that such perception engenders in the heart (and the "I") of the beholder. Correspondingly, investigations of emotion perception are not divorced from the other studies we have been considering.

There is now a substantial body of experimental research to suggest that not only are children with autism abnormal in the ways they express emotion, but also there are autism-specific deficits in emotion perception and understanding. Some of the most persuasive evidence for autism-specific deficits has come from studies that have compared sizeable groups of closely matched autistic and nonautistic retarded subjects on tests that compare performance in judging emotion-related and emotion-unrelated materials, such as photographs, drawings, or videotape and audiotape recordings of people vis-à-vis nonpersonal objects (e.g., see Hobson, Ouston, & Lee,

1988b, for cross-modal matching of facial and vocal expressions vis-à-vis cross-modal matching of appearances and sounds of things and actions; Hobson, Ouston, & Lee, 1989 for naming emotions in faces and voices vis-à-vis naming photographs and sounds of nonemotional stimuli; and Hobson & Lee, 1989, for naming emotional vis-à-vis nonemotional pictures that appear in a standard IQ test). Novel research approaches are delineating abnormalities in specific aspects of social and emotion perception in autism, such as in the visual scanning of faces (Klin, Jones, Schultz, Volkmar, & Cohen, 2002; Pelphrey et al., 2002) and in compensatory strategies used to process emotional information (e.g., Grossman, Klin, Carter, & Volkmar, 2000).

Yet, controversy in this domain is far from over (e.g., Buitelaar, Van der Wees, Swaab-Barneveld, & Van der Gaag, 1999; Loveland et al., 1997). Two of the most serious sources of scientific contention about this body of research are that (1) often the group differences in the profiles of performance on index and control tasks have been quantitatively small, and (2) when emotion recognition abilities are adjudged *solely* with reference to subjects' levels of language ability, rather than with reference to performance on control tasks of appropriate difficulty, the differences sometimes disappear. Despite claims to the contrary, however, even when individuals are matched according to verbal ability, group differences are often substantial (see later examples). There remain outstanding issues to do with the specificity of *emotion* recognition in facial, vocal, and other expressions (e.g., Boucher, Lewis, & Collis, 1998; Klin, Sparrow, et al., 1999). Here, even if certain of the perceptual processing deficits extend beyond the emotional domain, their most significant developmental implications might arise through an impact on specifically socioemotional perception and the interpersonal relations for which such perception is needed.

Let us reexamine a little of the evidence. It is important to be clear on what these studies are aiming to achieve and the methods that are needed to address those aims (Hobson, 1991). It is not expected that experiments will provide a *quantitative* estimate of the size of real-life group differences in emotion perception for a number of reasons that include the effects of matching procedures (to match by verbal ability is to match by a partial index of social coordination, which may be emotion-dependent, thereby controlling out some of the group difference you are trying to examine), the artificiality of the test materials and test situation (which may be more manageable for children with autism than real-life emotional exchanges), and the possibility that successful judgments may be made with superficial understanding of emotion itself. For example, suppose some children with autism were to apply abnormal perceptual strategies and identify a smile as an upturned mouth (which is not the usual way to apprehend a smile). To be confident that you are testing the ability to register the subjective emotional meanings of expressions, you need to devise task materials that are difficult to interpret *unless* you perceive emotional meaning. In this respect, consider the study of Ozonoff, Pennington, and Rogers (1991), who tested a group of high-functioning autistic individuals and a heterogeneous control sample, matched for age and verbal IQ, on a battery of tests including one of "emotion perception." A photograph of a face displaying an emotional expression served as the target, and the subject was asked to choose one of four photographs that "felt the same way." Correct choices varied from the target in the identity of the model and the intensity of the expressed affect. There were 34 items, half of which contained distractor photographs that shared similar perceptual features with correct choices. For example, a face expressing fear was used as a distractor for the target emotion of surprise, since both emotions share the feature of an open mouth. Nine emotions were depicted: four "simple emotions" (happiness, sadness, anger, and fear) and five "complex emotions" (surprise, shame, disgust, interest, and contempt). The autistic group performed significantly less well than the control group in matching both simple and complex emotions and made a higher number of errors on items with an obvious perceptual foil. The authors considered that perhaps they were using a different, more perceptually driven matching strategy.

Such considerations determined the design adopted by Hobson, Ouston, and Lee (1988a; see also Celani, Battacchi, & Arcidiacono,

1999, for a related approach) to test whether individuals with autism who were matched for verbal ability with nonautistic people might be impaired in matching people's faces according to (1) happy, unhappy, angry, and afraid emotions and (2) identities. The subjects' task was to match emotions expressed by different individuals and to match people's identities although they were expressing different emotions. To explore the possibility that autistic children might perform well by applying some form of nonemotional perceptual analysis, we repeated the two forms of task with modifications: First, the faces on the cards to be sorted had blanked-out mouths, and second, they had blanked-out mouths and foreheads. Our intention was to retain the "feel" of the emotions even in these latter materials (to establish an advantage for emotion-sensitive subjects) while at the same time to reduce the availability of non-emotion-related cues (to thwart alternative strategies of sorting). In a final condition, the standard photographs and the full faces for sorting were each presented upside down to tilt the balance in the opposite direction in favor of participants with abnormal strategies of face perception.

The first result was that whereas on the identities task, the performance of the two groups showed a similar steady decline as the photographs became increasingly blanked out, on the emotions task, the performance of autistic subjects worsened more abruptly than that of control subjects as cues to emotion were progressively reduced. It seemed that the children with autism were relatively unable to use the "feel" in the faces to guide performance. In addition, correlations between individual subjects' scores on the identity and emotion tasks were higher for autistic than for nonautistic subjects, again suggesting that the participants with autism might have been sorting the expressive faces by nonemotional perceptual strategies. Second, whereas the performance of control participants slumped in sorting upside-down faces, the children with autism became significantly superior to the control group on matching both "identities" and "emotions" (see also Langdell, 1978).

A second approach to defeating "abnormal" perceptual strategies concerns judgments of gestural expressions of emotion

(Moore, Hobson, & Lee, 1997; see also Jennings, 1973; Weeks & Hobson, 1987, for equally strong evidence for group differences between language-matched groups in judging emotion in facial expressions). Here, children and adolescents with and without autism—again, matched for verbal ability as well as age and comparable in the productivity of what they said during the task—were shown videotape sequences of people's moving bodies depicted merely by dots of light attached to the trunk and limbs. As a stringent control task, we tested the children's abilities to judge actions such as digging or pushing. First, we presented separate 5-second sequences of the point-light person enacting in turn the gestures of surprise, sadness, fear, anger, and happiness. In the surprise sequence, for example, the person walked forward and suddenly checked his stride and jerked backward with his arms thrown out to the side and gave a sigh of relief; in the sad sequence, the person walked forward with a stooped posture, paused, and sighed, then raised his arms out slowly and allowed them to drop to his sides, and finally seated himself in a slumped manner and put his head in his hands. In each case, adults who saw the videotapes were 100% accurate in judging the expressions.

The children were told: "You're going to see some bits of film of a person moving. I want you to tell me about this person. Tell me what's happening." In response, all but one of the nonautistic children made a spontaneous comment about the person's emotional state for at least one presentation, and most referred to emotions on two or more of the five sequences. In contrast, 10 of the 13 children with autism *never* referred to emotional states, whether correctly or incorrectly. In the case of the children and adolescents with autism, it was the person's movements and actions rather than feelings that were reported. For example, the sad figure was described as "walking and sitting down on a chair," "walking and flapping arms and bent down," and "walking and waving his arms and kneeling down . . . hands to face." Almost none of the responses were wrong, but very few referred to feelings.

A final task was designed to explore how accurately the children and adolescents could name actions and emotions when explicitly asked to do so. We added five new emotionally expressive sequences to the five already described: These showed the point-light person in states of itchiness, boredom, tiredness, cold, and hurt. When these sequences were shown one by one, we said: "I want you to tell me what the person is feeling." Alongside this test involving emotions and other attitudes, there was a test for the recognition of nonemotional actions: lifting, chopping, hopping, kicking, jumping, pushing, digging, sitting, climbing, and running. Here the instructions were: "I want you to tell me what the person is doing." The tasks were adjusted to exclude items on which there were ceiling or floor effects and to equate tasks for level of difficulty. The participants with autism were not significantly different in their scores on the actions task (mean score 5 of 8 correct, compared with 6 of 8 for the control group); but on the emotions task, where once again the control group achieved a mean score of 6 of 8 correct, the children with autism had a mean score of only 2 of 8 correct. Here is striking evidence of a *specific* limitation in recognizing emotions in children carefully matched for verbal ability and linguistic productivity.

THE CASE OF SELF-CONSCIOUS EMOTIONS

Thus far, we have concentrated on so-called "simple" emotions that are often presumed to be less cognitively elaborated than feelings such as coyness, guilt, pride, or shame. One aspect of the latter emotions is that they appear to implicate self-consciousness, although it remains open to question how far such self-consciousness also assumes "primitive" forms in humans. Bosch (1970) remarked how the child with autism often seems to lack a sense of self-consciousness and shame and to be missing something of the " 'self-involvement,' the acting with, and the identification with the acting person" (p. 81). In my view, this process of identifying with others is critical in establishing the kinds of inward-facing attitudes that come to be experienced as guilt and other self-conscious emotions; also in my view, this is an area of basic impairment in autism. The crux is not that you need a certain cognitive architecture to feel guilt—rather, you need to have internalized attitudes to yourself through identifying with the attitudes of others. Then there is the additional matter of how individuals with autism reflect (self-consciously) on *all* of their feelings and other aspects of themselves, because self-reflection brings in emotional considerations concerning the route by which and the attitudes with which children come to reflect in this way. We may learn a lot from listening to what people with autism say about themselves and their emotional life and noting how they say it.

What, then, have controlled studies revealed about self-conscious feelings in individuals with autism? Young children with autism who are not severely cognitively impaired do remove rouge from their faces when they perceive themselves in a mirror (Dawson & McKissick, 1984; Neuman & Hill, 1978; Spiker & Ricks, 1984). What most do *not* show are the signs of coyness typical of young, typically developing and nonautistic, retarded children. Thus, autistic children can make use of their own reflection to register what it means to have their body marked, and they are likely to act accordingly in trying to remove the mark from their face. What is far less certain is whether such behavior is motivated by a concern with the way they "look" to other people and with the evaluative attitudes that others may entertain in seeing them marked in an unusual manner (Hobson, 1990).

This suggestion receives some support from a study conducted by Kasari, Sigman, Baumgartner, and Stipek (1993) with young autistic and nonautistic retarded subjects (mean age 42 months) and mental age-matched typically developing children (mean age 23 months). Each subject completed a puzzle, and the investigator and parent reacted neutrally; then the child completed a second puzzle, and after three seconds, both adults gave praise. Although children with autism were like mentally retarded and typically developing children in being inclined to smile when they succeeded with the puzzles, autistic children were less likely to draw attention to what they had done or to look up to an adult and less likely to show pleasure in being praised. Their pride assumed a strangely asocial form. In assessments of pride in high-functioning children and adolescents with autism (Capps, Yirmiya, & Sigman, 1992;

Kasari, Chamberlain, & Bauminger, 2001), the children could cite situations eliciting pride, but provided instances that were less personal and in some ways more stereotyped (e.g., finishing their homework or winning games) than was the case with control children.

Results were similar concerning guilt. Kasari et al. (2001) describe how high-IQ children with autism can report feeling guilt, but compared with control children they provide fewer self-evaluative statements and are more likely to describe situations in terms of rule breaking, disruptiveness, and damage to property, rather than those of causing physical or emotional harm to others. The researchers conclude that for children with autism, guilt appears to be defined in terms of memorizable rules and actions, such as taking toys from school, stealing cookies, running away, and so on, rather than in interpersonal, empathic terms.

Similar results emerge when the focus turns to embarrassment. According to Capps et al. (1992) and Kasari et al. (2001), children with autism are likely to give examples of embarrassing situations that are external and uncontrollable, whereas matched typically developing children often give more specific and personal examples that relate to controllable events. Especially frequent are reports of feeling embarrassment because of teasing by others, a relatively rare response from nonautistic children; but references to the presence of an audience are relatively infrequent.

These results are also supported and extended by recent studies by Chidambi (2003; Chidambi, Hobson, & Lee, 2003). He interviewed parents of children with autism ages 7 to 12 years, as well as parents of age- and ability-matched nonautistic children, to discover whether and in what ways the children manifested signs of a range of self-conscious emotions such as pride, guilt, shame, embarrassment, jealousy, envy, coyness, flirting, and pity, as well as "simple" emotions. The results were complex in that certain group differences emerged only when attention was given to the subtlety of the responses, but there were clear and significant group differences for feelings such as embarrassment, flirting, guilt, and shame. For example, flirtatious behavior was reported to be absent in all but one of 10 children with autism, but present in 9 children with learning disabilities; guilt was reported in only 2 of 10 children with autism (and here it seemed circumscribed), but 9 of 10 control children. Although pride was frequently reported in children with autism, it was generally restricted to scholastic achievements and seemed less personal in quality than in the nonautistic children.

There is accumulating evidence that children with autism neither manifest nor refer to these "complex" emotions with the quality of interpersonal engagement that characterizes children who do not have autism. What we need is a theoretical perspective that introduces order and understanding into these observations. We have already seen one example where evidence from autism promises to clarify and extend our thinking: Manifestations of pride appear to be of two distinct kinds, only one of which—the most interpersonal— is remarkable for its relative absence in autism. But there are other issues concerning which we have much to discover. What of jealousy, for example? In Chidambi's interview study previously mentioned, approximately half the parents of children with autism reported signs of jealousy, but there appeared to be limited contexts within which jealousy was shown and very restricted individuals (usually only the mother) toward whom jealousy was expressed. Bauminger (2004) reported that in two jealousy-eliciting conditions—one in which the child's parent praised another child's picture while ignoring his or her own child's and another in which the parent engaged in affectionate play exclusively with the other child—the majority of children with autism displayed clear indications of jealousy. There was not a group difference from control participants in this respect. The children with autism tended to express themselves by acting toward the parent, rather than looking at him or her. In separate tests, the children with autism were less proficient in recognizing jealousy in a picture, and only half could produce personal and affective (as opposed to social-cognitive) examples of jealousy, whereas all the control children could do so.

These latter findings of a difficulty encountered by children with autism in describing their own jealousy and (apparently) understanding the nature of jealousy are reminiscent of three other reports. In a study by Yirmiya, Sigman, Kasari, and Mundy (1992), high-functioning young adolescents with autism scored lower than control participants in reporting empathic feelings in response to videotapes of emotional scenarios, an ability correlated with full-scale IQ only for the group with autism. This suggested to the authors that the children might have been employing cognitive strategies in interpreting social situations. Lee and Hobson (1998) conducted "self-understanding interviews" and reported that children with autism not only were restricted in the feelings they expressed about themselves but also failed to mention friends or being members of a social group. Bauminger and Kasari (2000) described how children with autism spoke of loneliness but failed to refer to the more affective dimension of being left out of close intimate relationships. As Bauminger (2004) suggests, children with autism appear to have difficulty in considering interpersonal relationships when reflecting on their emotional experiences.

The upshot of all these studies is that we cannot *presume* which aspects of emotion, even "complex" emotion, are or are not absent in autism; and the patterning of the children's interpersonal behavior and reports of their experiences are very likely to elucidate in which respects there are dissociable aspects to emotional development in typical as well as atypical cases.

There is another setting that provides evidence of previously unforeseen (and relative) "normality" in the interpersonal relations of children with autism: the Strange Situation (Ainsworth, Blehar, Waters, & Wall, 1978) in which reactions to separations from and reunions with a parent can be studied. There are several published studies that indicate how young autistic children *do* respond to separation from and reunion with their caregivers, at least in the short term (Rogers, Ozonoff, & Maslin-Cole, 1991; Shapiro, Sherman, Calamari, & Koch, 1987; Sigman & Mundy, 1989; Sigman & Ungerer, 1984). Many (not all) 2- to 5-year-old autistic children are like matched nonautistic retarded children in showing somewhat variable reactions to the departure of the caregiver, sometimes showing behavioral and/or mood, changes such as fretting, and in responding to reunion by spending more time alongside the caregiver than the stranger. When allowance is made for their sometimes-idiosyncratic behavior, a substantial number of autistic children are rated as "securely attached" (Rogers et al., 1991; Shapiro et al., 1987). The children's relationship with their caregivers is clearly different from that with a stranger. It is still unclear how the quality and longer term implications of such attachments conform with those of nonautistic children (see also Rogers et al., 1991), and as we have seen, there are important respects in which children with autism do *not* relate to their parents normally.

Just as in the case of jealousy, there may turn out to be biologically based determinants of interpersonal *relationships* (and remember that goslings become attached, even though they do not have a highly sophisticated emotional life, as far as we know) that are dissociable from aspects of interpersonal *relatedness;* and we may yet have to revise some of our conventional ideas about which aspects of emotional relatedness do or do not require sophisticated cognitive underpinnings. Finally, but importantly, we must not neglect the fact that in many of the studies cited, there are a small but notable number of children with autism who do seem to register others' feelings, both toward themselves and toward a shared world, and who manifest a range of emotions, sometimes in interpersonal contexts—and this, too, needs investigation.

CONGENITALLY BLIND CHILDREN AND ROMANIAN ORPHANS

I have been presenting the case, as much by illustration as by logical argument, that there is developmental continuity between aspects of typically developing infants' emotional life and qualities of infants' subsequent social and cognitive relations that appear less obviously "emotional" in nature. I have also implied that some of these lines of development may be discerned through the specific profile of social and cognitive (and perceptual and motivational) impairments and limitations in individuals with autism. Especially important here is the idea that through emotional engagement with other people, typically developing infants are "moved" to assume the psychological

orientation of others. By means of this process of identification in the context of triadic person-person-world relations, they are lifted out of their one-track, inflexible perspective to apprehend things and events "according to the other." This process is not only critically disrupted in children with autism, but also critically important for the development of context-sensitive symbolic thinking (Hobson, 1993a, 1993b, 2002).

This theoretical perspective locates the "final common pathway" to autism in what fails to happen *between* people and in their mutual relations with the surroundings. Insofar as this perspective is valid, you might be led to investigate whether there are a variety of routes by which the critical experiences of identifying with (and being moved by) someone else's attitudes to a shared world could be impaired. In this context, studies of atypical autism may be especially revealing. Here I consider two such cases: congenital blindness and Romanian orphans.

When colleagues and I became intrigued by the social impairments of congenitally blind children, there were already clinical reports suggesting that both autistic features and the syndrome of autism might be more prevalent in children who suffered congenital blindness (e.g., Fraiberg, 1977; Keeler, 1958; Rogers & Newhart-Larson, 1989). It seemed to us that congenital blindness might deprive an infant of something essential in the domain of emotional relatedness: the ability to perceive, be moved by, and identify with the attitudes of someone else *as these are directed toward objects and events in a visually shared world.* Whereas sighted children with autism are not moved by others' feelings because they do not experience typical forms of "feeling perception" toward the expressions of others, so congenitally blind children are not only restricted in the expressions they perceive but also deprived of the insight that different attitudes may be directed to the same visually specified object or event—and, therefore, that objects and events may have multiple (context-sensitive, person-dependent, even symbolic) meanings. In other words, congenital blindness might predispose (but not predetermine) a child to develop autism, for the reason that blindness unhinges the very fulcrum of early development that is said to be lacking in sighted children with autism.

To establish whether the evidence was in keeping with this hypothesis, Brown, Hobson, Lee, and Stevenson (1997) tested children who had been totally or near-totally blind from birth, between 3 and 9 years of age, and with no identifiable disorder of the nervous system, available in six schools for visually impaired children. The children's behavior was rated over at least three periods of 20 minutes at free play, in the classroom during a lesson, and in a session of language testing, and the results were complemented by teacher reports. It turned out that no fewer than 10 of the 24 children satisfied the clinical criteria for autism—a proportion that is about 1,000 times as great as you would expect in sighted children. In a subsequent study (Hobson, Lee, & Brown, 1999), nine of the blind children who met the criteria for autism were compared with nine sighted children with autism matched for age and IQ. The two groups were similar in many respects, but there were indications that the blind children were not so impaired in their emotional expressions and that their relations with people were better. The majority gave the impression of being less severely autistic. In the clinical judgment of the child psychiatrist investigator, only two of the nine blind children displayed the *quality* of social impairment that was characteristic of the sighted but autistic children, a quality that involves the special feel you have of a lack of emotional contact. When children are blind from birth, they are predisposed to autism even if their social impairment is somewhat less profound than in sighted children with autism. Their lack of vision plays a role in causing the picture of autism, even when their intrinsic social disability is not so severe.

We also predicted that even in those whose social relations were less affected by blindness, there would be some indication of autistic-like problems. To test this prediction, we compared the children who were *not* autistic with sighted children from mainstream schools who were similar in age and IQ. Not one of the mainstream children showed any autistic-like behavior, whereas every one of the blind children did so. The two groups differed in several respects, including relating to people, responses to ob-

jects, communication of all kinds, motor coordination, and interactive play. Only the blind children had a tendency to echo back what other people said—arguably, a revealing index of their difficulty in identifying with a person-anchored linguistic perspective that shifts from person to person. In a separate study of such children, Minter, Hobson, and Bishop (1998) reported evidence of the children's difficulties on specially modified "theory of mind" tests of false belief and representational change.

The message from these studies of blind children is that there may be more than one way to develop autism because there may be more than one kind of barrier to experiencing personal relations toward other people—people with whose attitudes to a shared world an individual can identify.

Evidence that bears on this thesis comes from another, initially unexpected, quarter: studies by Michael Rutter and colleagues (1999) of 4- to 6-year-olds who had been placed in Romanian orphanages early in the first year of life and moved to the United Kingdom in their first or second year. In summary, about one in 16 of the children showed a picture that closely resembled that of autism, and a further one in 16 presented with milder autistic features. Severely affected children displayed problems with social relationships and impoverished reciprocal communication with others, lack of empathy toward others, poverty of eye-to-eye gaze and gestures in social exchanges, and limited language and to-and-fro conversation. A majority of the children had preoccupations with sensations and intense interests of unusual kinds. Yet, there was something atypical about the autism, for example, when the children made spontaneous efforts to communicate with sign language or other kinds of social approach.

It is too early to be confident what these studies mean. A picture emerges to suggest that particular forms of very severe deprivation of emotionally patterned interpersonal experience—whether this occurs through constitutional abnormalities in the child that restrict the effective social environment and weaken or deflect emotional pushes and pulls that occur between people, or through specific forms of perceptual handicap, or even through appalling privation of social input—may have autism-related social and cognitive implications. We may be drawing closer to an account that accords due weight to social-emotional factors in the pathogenesis of autism.

THE ESSENCE OF AUTISM

There are additional perspectives that are certain to shed further light on the nature and role of what we might broadly call *emotional* deficits in children with autism. One such perspective comes from effectiveness of interventions that facilitate emotional engagement between autistic children and others (e.g., Bauminger, 2002; Rogers, 2000). Another involves the study of related impairments in relatives of affected individuals (as reviewed in Bailey, Palferman, Heavey, & Le Couteur, 1998). Here we may discern attributes that, while they do not constitute grounds for the development of autism itself, nevertheless betray something of whatever genetic predisposition to social-affective impairment exists in a substantial proportion of individuals with autism. A third perspective comes from the burgeoning research on the neurofunctional correlates of emotional experience and even empathy, both in typically developing individuals (e.g., Decety & Chaminade, 2003) and in those with autism. Although it may be too soon to derive firm conclusions from functional brain scans about the status and specificity of reported abnormalities in neuronal activity during emotion-related tasks such as those involving the perception of emotion in faces (e.g., Baron-Cohen et al., 1999; Critchley et al., 2000; Schultz et al., 2000), it already seems likely that such investigations will demonstrate how neurological dysfunction underpins and reflects the behavioral and experiential abnormalities of people with autism described in this chapter—and in so doing, will highlight afresh the need to derive an adequate developmental story of mind-brain development in autism.

It remains to step back and reflect on autism and emotion—and to consider how reshaping our concepts of emotion may help us to understand autism and how investigations of autism may help us rethink emotion. We should not underestimate the value of clinical observations of autism for our understanding of typical early development because they alert us to the profound developmental significance of the coordination of subjective states between individuals; and we should not overestimate the decisive contribution of any particular methodological approach to determining the specific bases of autism, when the pathogenesis of autism appears to be complex and, to some extent, different in different children.

CONCLUSION

Any explanation of autism will need to trace the origins and repercussions of what Kanner (1943) called the children's abnormality in affective contact with others. We should pay special attention to the quality of emotional impairment in the interpersonal domain, for it would seem to be in the interpersonal domain—and specifically, in respect to sharing subjective states and coordinating attitudes with other people vis-à-vis the world, as in episodes of joint attention—that a critical abnormality is to be found. To be sure, nearly all children with autism have constitutional abnormalities, but these may be of diverse kinds and arise on the bases of diverse etiologies. Not all of these may be characterized as primarily emotional in nature, as the example of congenital blindness testifies. Yet, perhaps each cause operates through a final common pathway that implicates abnormality in the patterned coordination of affectively configured subjective states between the affected child and others. Affected children appear to have a restricted propensity to *identify with* other people, to move toward, and (in part) assimilate the other person's attitude and psychological orientation to the world.

It seems doubtful whether this essentially interpersonal abnormality will prove to be the result of some single perceptual or cognitive deficit, although as in the case of congenital blindness, lower level domain-general deficits play a pathogenic role in at least some cases. From a complementary perspective, it seems doubtful that we will arrive at an adequate theory of the syndrome of autism unless we accord this special form of interpersonal disorder—one that prevents or derails the coordination of subjective states involving feelings—a pivotal place within our multi-level explanatory scheme.

Cross-References

Developmental stages of autism are discussed in Chapters 8, 9, and 10. Social and communication development are discussed in Chapters 11 and 12. Joint attention is discussed in Chapter 25.

REFERENCES

Ainsworth, M. D. S., Blehar, M. C., Waters, E., & Wall, S. (1978). *Patterns of attachment.* Hillsdale, NJ: Erlbaum.

Attwood, A., Frith, U., & Hermelin, B. (1988). The understanding and use of interpersonal gestures by autistic and Down's syndrome children. *Journal of Autism and Developmental Disorders, 18,* 241–257.

Bacon, A. L., Fein, D., Morris, R., Waterhouse, L., & Allen, D. (1998). The responses of autistic children to the distress of others. *Journal of Autism and Developmental Disorders, 28,* 129–142.

Bailey, A., Palferman, S., Heavey, L., & Le Couteur, A. (1998). Autism: The phenotype in relatives. *Journal of Autism and Developmental Disorders, 28,* 369–392.

Baron-Cohen, S., Ring, H., Wheelwright, S., Bulmore, E., Brammer, M., Simmons, A., et al. (1999). Social intelligence in the normal and autistic brain: An fMRI study. *European Journal of Neuroscience, 11,* 1891–1898.

Bauminger, N. (2002). The facilitation of social-emotional understanding and social interaction in high-functioning children with autism: Intervention outcomes. *Journal of Autism and Developmental Disorders, 32,* 283–298.

Bauminger, N. (2004). The expression and understanding of jealousy in children with autism. *Development and Psychopathology, 16,* 157–177.

Bauminger, N., & Kasari, C. (2000). Loneliness and friendship in high-functioning children with autism. *Child Development, 71,* 447–456.

Bosch, G. (1970). *Infantile autism* (D. Jordan & I. Jordan, Trans.). New York: Springer-Verlag.

Boucher, J., Lewis, V., & Collis, G. (1998). Familiar face and voice matching and recognition in children with autism. *Journal of Child Psychology and Psychiatry, 39,* 171–181.

Brown, R., Hobson, R. P., Lee, A., & Stevenson, J. (1997). Are there "autistic-like" features in congenitally blind children? *Journal of Child Psychology and Psychiatry, 38,* 693–703.

Buitelaar, J. K., Van der Wees, M., Swaab-Barneveld, H., & Van Der Gaag, R. (1999). Theory of mind and emotion-recognition functioning in autistic spectrum disorders and psychiatric control and normal children. *Development and Psychopathology, 11,* 39–58.

Capps, L., Yirmiya, N., & Sigman, M. (1992). Understanding of simple and complex emotions in non-retarded children with autism. *Journal of Child Psychology and Psychiatry, 33,* 1169–1182.

Celani, G., Battacchi, M. W., & Arcidiacono, L. (1999). The understanding of the emotional meaning of facial expressions in people with autism. *Journal of Autism and Developmental Disorders, 29,* 57–66.

Charman, T., Baron-Cohen, S., Swettenham, J., Cox, A., Baird, G., & Drew, A. (1997). Infants with autism: An investigation of empathy, pretend play, joint attention, and imitation. *Developmental Psychology, 33,* 781–789.

Chidambi, G. (2003). *Autism and self-conscious emotions.* Unpublished doctoral dissertation, University College, London.

Chidambi, G., Hobson, R. P., & Lee, A. (2003, November). *A multifaceted investigation of pride, guilt, and shame in children with autism.* Poster presentation to the 7th International Autism Europe Congress.

Critchley, H., Daly, E., Bullmore, E., Williams, S., Van Amelsvoort, T., Robertson, D., et al. (2000). The functional anatomy of social behavior: Changes in cerebral blood flow when people with autistic disorder process facial expression. *Brain, 123,* 2203–2212.

Dahlgren, S. O., & Gillberg, C. (1989). Symptoms in the first two years of life: A preliminary population study of infantile autism. *European Archives of Psychiatry and Neurological Sciences, 238,* 169–174.

Dawson, G., Hill, D., Spencer, A., Galpert, L., & Watson, L. (1990). Affective exchanges between young autistic children and their mothers. *Journal of Abnormal Child Psychology, 18,* 335–345.

Dawson, G., & McKissick, F. C. (1984). Self-recognition in autistic children. *Journal of Autism and Development Disorders, 14,* 383–394.

Decety, J., & Chaminade, T. (2003). Neural correlates of feeling sympathy. *Neuropsychologia, 41,* 127–138.

Fraiberg, S. (1977). *Insights from the blind.* London: Souvenir Press.

Grossman, J. B., Klin, A., Carter, A. S., & Volkmar, F. R. (2000). Verbal bias in recognition of facial emotions in children with Asperger syndrome. *Journal of Child Psychology and Psychiatry, 41,* 369–379.

Hobson, R. P. (1990). On the origins of self and the case of autism. *Development and Psychopathology, 2,* 163–181.

Hobson, R. P. (1991). Methodological issues for experiments on autistic individuals' perception and understanding of emotion. *Journal of Child Psychology and Psychiatry, 32,* 1135–1158.

Hobson, R. P. (1993a). *Autism and the development of mind.* Hillsdale, NJ: Erlbaum.

Hobson, R. P. (1993b). The emotional origins of social understanding. *Philosophical Psychology, 6,* 227–249.

Hobson, R. P. (2002). *The cradle of thought.* London: Palgrave Macmillan.

Hobson, R. P., & Lee, A. (1989). Emotion-related and abstract concepts in autistic people: Evidence from the British Picture Vocabulary Scale. *Journal of Autism and Developmental Disorders, 19,* 601–623.

Hobson, R. P., Lee, A., & Brown, R. (1999). Autism and congenital blindness. *Journal of Autism and Developmental Disorders, 29,* 45–56.

Hobson, R. P., Ouston, J., & Lee, A. (1988a). Emotion recognition in autism: Coordinating faces and voices. *Psychological Medicine, 18,* 911–923.

Hobson, R. P., Ouston, J., & Lee, A. (1988b). What's in a face? The case of autism. *British Journal of Psychology, 79,* 441–453.

Hobson, R. P., Ouston, J., & Lee, A. (1989). Naming emotion in faces and voices: Abilities and disabilities in autism and mental retardation. *British Journal of Developmental Psychology, 7,* 237–250.

Izard, C. E. (1979). *The maximally discriminative facial movement coding system (MAX).* Newark: University of Delaware, Instructional Resources Center.

Jennings, W. B. (1973). *A study of the preference for affective cues in autistic children.* Unpublished doctoral dissertation, Memphis State University.

Kanner, L. (1943). Autistic disturbances of affective contact. *Nervous Child, 2,* 217–250.

Kasari, C., Chamberlain, B., & Bauminger, N. (2001). Social emotions and social relationships: Can children with autism compensate. In J. A. Burack, T. Charman, N. Yirmiya, & P. R. Zelazo (Eds.), *The development of autism* (pp. 309–323). Mahwah, NJ: Erlbaum.

Kasari, C., Sigman, M. D., Baumgartner, P., & Stipek, D. J. (1993). Pride and mastery in children with autism. *Journal of Child Psychology and Psychiatry, 34,* 352–362.

Kasari, C., Sigman, M. D., Mundy, P., & Yirmiya, N. (1990). Affective sharing in the context of joint attention interactions of normal, autistic and mentally retarded children. *Journal of Autism and Developmental Disorders, 20,* 87–100.

Keeler, W. R. (1958). Autistic patterns and defective communication in blind children with retrolental fibroplasias. In P. H. Hoch & J. Zubin (Eds.), *Psychopathology of communication* (pp. 64–83). New York: Grune & Stratton.

Klin, A., Jones, W., Schultz, R., Volkmar, F., & Cohen, D. (2002). Visual fixation patterns of naturalistic social situations as predictors of social competence in individuals with autism. *Archives of General Psychiatry, 59,* 809–816.

Klin, A., Sparrow, S. S., de Bildt, A., Cicchetti, D. V., Cohen, D. J., & Volkmar, F. R. (1999). A normed study of face recognition in autism and related disorders. *Journal of Autism and Developmental Disorders, 29,* 499–508.

Langdell, T. (1978). Recognition of faces: An approach to the study of autism. *Journal of Child Psychology and Psychiatry, 19,* 255–268.

Langdell, T. (1981). *Face perception: An approach to the study of autism.* Unpublished doctoral dissertation, University College, London.

Lee, A., & Hobson, R. P. (1998). On developing self-concepts: A controlled study of children and adolescents with autism. *Journal of Child Psychology and Psychiatry, 39,* 1131–1141.

Lord, C. (1995). Follow-up of two-year-olds referred for possible autism. *Journal of Child Psychology and Psychiatry, 36,* 1365–1382.

Lord, C., Storoschuk, S., Rutter, M., & Pickles, A. (1993). Using the ADI-R to diagnose autism in preschool children. *Infant Mental Health Journal, 14,* 234–252.

Loveland, K. A., Tunali-Kotoski, B., Chen, R., Ortegon, J., Pearson, D. A., Brelsford, K. A., et al. (1997). Emotion recognition in autism: Verbal and nonverbal information. *Development and Psychopathology, 9,* 579–593.

Loveland, K. A., Tunali-Kotoski, B., Pearson, D. A., Brelsford, K. A., Ortegon, J., & Chen, R. (1994). Imitation and expression of facial affect in autism. *Development and Psychopathology, 6,* 433–444.

Macdonald, H., Rutter, M., Howlin, P., Rios, P., Le Couteur, A., Evered, C., et al. (1989). Recognition and expression of emotional cues by autistic and normal adults. *Journal of Child Psychology and Psychiatry, 30,* 865–877.

Minter, M., Hobson, R. P., & Bishop, M. (1998). Congenital visual impairment and "theory of mind." *British Journal of Developmental Psychology, 16,* 183–196.

Moore, D., Hobson, R. P., & Lee, A. (1997). Components of person perception: An investigation with autistic, nonautistic retarded and normal children and adolescents. *British Journal of Developmental Psychology, 15,* 401–423.

Neuman, C. J., & Hill, S. D. (1978). Self-recognition and stimulus preference in autistic children. *Developmental Psychobiology, 11,* 571–578.

Ozonoff, S., Pennington, B. F., & Rogers, S. J. (1991). Executive function deficits in high-functioning autistic children: Relationship to theory of mind. *Journal of Child Psychology and Psychiatry, 32,* 1081–1105.

Pelphrey, K. A., Sasson, N. J., Reznick, J. S., Paul, G., Goldman, B. D., & Piven, J. (2002). Visual scanning of faces in autism. *Journal of Autism and Developmental Disorders, 32,* 249–261.

Ricks, D. M. (1975). Vocal communication in preverbal normal and autistic children. In N. O'-Connor (Ed.), *Language, cognitive deficits, and retardation* (pp. 75–80). London: Butterworth.

Ricks, D. M. (1979). Making sense of experience to make sensible sounds. In M. Bullowa (Ed.), *Before speech* (pp. 245–268). Cambridge, England: Cambridge University Press.

Rogers, S. J. (2000). Interventions that facilitate socialization in children with autism. *Journal of Autism and Developmental Disorders, 30,* 399–409.

Rogers, S. J., & Newhart-Larson, S. (1989). Characteristics of infantile autism in five children with Leber's congenital amaurosis. *Developmental Medicine and Child Neurology, 31,* 598–608.

Rogers, S. J., Ozonoff, S., & Maslin-Cole, C. (1991). A comparative study of attachment behaviour in young children with autism or other psychiatric disorders. *Journal of the American Academy of Child and Adolescent Psychiatry, 30,* 483–488.

Rutter, M., Andersen-Wood, L., Beckett, C., Bredenkamp, D., Castle, J., Groothues, C., et al. (1999). Quasi-autistic patterns following severe early global privation. *Journal of Child Psychology and Psychiatry, 40,* 537–549.

Schultz, R., Gauthier, I., Klin, A., Fulbright, A., Anderson, A., Volkmar, F., et al. (2000). Abnormal ventral temporal cortical activity during face discrimination among individuals with autism and Asperger syndrome. *Archives of General Psychiatry, 57,* 331–340.

Shapiro, T., Sherman, M., Calamari, G., & Koch, D. (1987). Attachment in autism and other developmental disorders. *Journal of the American Academy of Child and Adolescent Psychiatry, 26,* 485–490.

Sigman, M., Kasari, C., Kwon, J. H., & Yirmiya, N. (1992). Responses to the negative emotions of others by autistic, mentally retarded, and normal children. *Child Development, 63,* 796–807.

Sigman, M., & Mundy, P. (1989). Social attachments in autistic children. *Journal of the American Academy of Child and Adolescent Psychiatry, 28,* 74–81.

Sigman, M., & Ungerer, J. A. (1984). Attachment behaviors in autistic children. *Journal of Autism and Developmental Disorders, 14,* 231–243.

Snow, M. E., Hertzig, M. E., & Shapiro, T. (1987). Expression of emotion in autistic children. *Journal of the American Academy of Child and Adolescent Psychiatry, 26,* 836–838.

Spiker, D., & Ricks, M. (1984). Visual self-recognition in autistic children: Developmental relationships. *Child Development, 55,* 214–225.

Stone, W. L., Hoffman, E. L., Lewis, S. E., & Ousley, O. Y. (1994). Early recognition of autism: Parental reports vs clinical observation. *Archives of Pediatrics and Adolescent Medicine, 148,* 174–179.

Stone, W. L., & Lemanek, K. L. (1990). Parental report of social behaviors in autistic preschoolers. *Journal of Autism and Developmental Disorders, 20,* 513–522.

Vostanis, P., Smith, B., Corbett, J., Sungum-Paliwal, R., Edwards, A., Gingell, K., et al. (1998). Parental concerns of early development in children with autism and related disorders. *Autism, 2,* 229–242.

Weeks, S. J., & Hobson, R. P. (1987). The salience of facial expression for autistic children. *Journal of Child Psychology and Psychiatry, 28,* 137–152.

Wimpory, D. C., Hobson, R. P., Williams, J. M., & Nash, S. (2000). Are infants with autism socially engaged? A study of recent retrospective parental reports. *Journal of Autism and Developmental Disorders, 30,* 525–536.

Wing, L. (1969). The handicaps of autistic children: A comparative study. *Journal of Child Psychology and Psychiatry, 10,* 1–40.

Yirmiya, N., Kasari, C., Sigman, M., & Mundy, P. (1989). Facial expressions of affect in autistic, mentally retarded and normal children. *Journal of Child Psychology and Psychiatry, 30,* 725–735.

Yirmiya, N., Sigman, M., Kasari, C., & Mundy, P. (1992). Empathy and cognition in high-functioning children with autism. *Child Development, 63,* 150–160.

NEUROLOGICAL AND MEDICAL ISSUES

Autism and other pervasive developmental disorders are brought to clinical attention and are diagnosed on the basis of distinctive disturbances in behavior and development. There is broad consensus among clinicians and researchers, however, that autism and associated syndromes represent the *surface* or *phenotypic* manifestations of underlying neurobiological diatheses or biological genotypes. For this reason, these conditions are sometimes described as neuro-behavioral or neuropsychiatric disorders, to emphasize their neurobiological underpinnings. As more is learned, we will be able to trace the expression of the underlying neurobiological dysfunctions in autism and these other conditions through each level of brain and behavioral organization—-from the level of the gene(s) involved in brain formation and functioning, through the emergence and functioning of specific brain systems, to the appearance of symptoms and signs of the disorders during early childhood and the full picture of the clinical conditions.

Advances in molecular and behavioral genetics, neurochemistry, neuro-imaging, and other related fields in the neurosciences are providing a deeper understanding of the normal development of the central nervous system (CNS) and the integrated functioning of the CNS during complex tasks (such as thinking, imagining, reading, listening, inhibiting, or planning behavior). There are fascinating leads about what particular brain systems are involved in normal processes and may be implicated in neurological, psychiatric, and developmental disorders. We are only at the first stages of understanding how regulatory genes

guide the formation of brain structures, the mechanisms underlying the laying down and pruning of pathways, the sensitive timing of brain connections and the formation of synapses, the ways in which the templates for higher cognitive processes are programmed, and the many interactions between parallel systems that relate to behavioral regulation (such as the cortico-striatal-thalamo-cortical pathways). The biology of uniquely human functioning—abstract thinking, mature social relations—is at the cutting edge of research. Availability of newer methods for studying the functioning brain already are illuminating how the brain processes visual and auditory stimuli and the steps between physical sensation and conscious awareness, and about the parts of the brain that are activated during different mental tasks. The availability of postmortem brains will give new access to studying brain structure and function and integrating these findings with the functioning of the brain during life, using methods such as functional magnetic resonance imaging. We can look forward to being able to integrate these various neurobiological approaches with careful studies of behavior and development.

Far less is known about the functioning of the brain during the first years of life and during the course of early development. The understanding of normal development and the ways in which dysfunctions may arise during embryogenesis and postnatally will provide a framework for understanding the developmental disorders such as autism. Already, more than 1,000 forms of mental retardation are known and for many there are specific genetic

423

and biological findings that help clarify their etiology. The hope is that similar, rigorous studies will help clarify the causal pathways that lead to the clinical syndrome of autism and the other pervasive developmental disorders. We are still a long way from reaching this goal, but the advances in the neurosciences have been explosive and we can anticipate that these findings will have direct relevance to subgroups of individuals with pervasive disorders.

The following chapters highlight major domains of neuroscience research—genetics, neurology, neurochemistry, and neuroimaging—relating to autism and pervasive disorders. One chapter also describes the medical conditions that are sometimes associated with autism and similar disorders. Only through basic, neurobiological research will it be possible to provide firmly based genetic counseling, diagnose pervasive disorders in utero, offer highly ameliorative and hopefully curative therapies, and fundamentally alter the natural history of these conditions.

CHAPTER 16

Genetic Influences and Autism

MICHAEL RUTTER

When Kanner (1943) first described autism, he suggested that it resulted from an inborn defect of presumably constitutional origin. Nevertheless, over the next three decades, the possible role of genetic factors tended to be dismissed. In part, this was because the zeitgeist at that time was one of expecting environmental causes for all forms of psychopathology. This was the era of supposed "refrigerator" parents of autistic children and of "schizophrenogenic" mothers (see Rutter, 1999b). However, reviews by geneticists were equally dismissive (Hanson & Gottesman, 1976). The emphasis tended to be placed on the lack of vertical transmission (i.e., the rarity with which children with autism had parents with autism), the very low rate of autism in siblings, and the lack of identified chromosome anomalies associated with autism (Rutter, 1967).

QUANTITATIVE GENETICS

Twin Studies

An awareness that the logic of these arguments was faulty (Rutter, 1968) led Folstein and Rutter (1977a, 1977b) to undertake the first small scale ($N = 21$) twin study of autism. The earlier reasoning on genetic influences was false because follow-up studies had shown that few autistic people developed love relationships, and that it was very rare for them to have children, and hence vertical transmission would not be expected; also relative to the rate of autism in the general population (about 2 to 4 cases per 10,000 as defined at that time), the rate of autism in siblings (then estimated to be about 2%) was very high; furthermore, the cytogenetic techniques available in the 1960s were quite primitive so that the failure to show anomalies was essentially noncontributory.

There were two crucial findings from this first twin study. First, despite the small numbers, there was a significant monozygotic-dizygotic (MZ-DZ) difference in concordance. The fact that the population base rate of autism was so low implied a strong underlying genetic liability. Second, concordance within MZ pairs included a range of cognitive and social deficits and not just the seriously handicapping condition of autism itself. This implied that the genetic liability extended beyond autism proper. It also raised questions about the diagnostic boundaries of autism and led to an appreciation of a need to consider the likelihood of a broader phenotype of autism or of lesser variants of the same condition.

During the late 1980s and early 1990s, genetic research into autism advanced through further twin studies and genetic-family studies. Both the Scandinavian Twin Study (Steffenburg et al., 1989) and a further British twin study (Bailey et al., 1995) confirmed the great strength of genetic influences on the underlying liability for autism. The British study included four key design features. First, there was total population screening of the cases, with all clinics and special schools in the country contacted

I am greatly indebted to members of the International Molecular Genetic Study of Autism Consortium, and especially to Anthony Monaco, for much of my thinking on genetic issues. I am also most grateful to Anthony Bailey for helpful comments and suggestions on an earlier draft of this chapter.

and all twin registers examined. Second, systematic standardized methods of diagnosis using both parental interviews (Le Couteur et al., 1989) and observation of the child (Lord et al., 1989) were employed. Third, there was thorough screening for medical conditions and chromosomal abnormalities in order to focus on the study of genetic factors in idiopathic autism. Fourth, blood groups were used to test for zygosity. That was important because the marked behavioral differences associated with autism sometimes led parents and professionals to infer that the twins were nonidentical, whereas in fact they were identical.

Four main findings were particularly crucial:

1. The huge disparity in concordance rates for autism between monozygotic (MZ; $N = 25$) and dizygotic (DZ; $N = 20$) pairs (60% versus 5%—if the rate in siblings as well as DZ twins is used to estimate the figure, twins and DZ twins being genetically comparable) confirmed the earlier findings on the strength of the genetic influence. Quantitative analyses indicated a heritability in excess of 90%.
2. The exceedingly low rate of concordance in DZ pairs compared with that in MZ pairs pointed to the likelihood of epistatic effects involving synergistic interaction among several genes. The pattern was not compatible with a single gene Mendelian disorder. The fall-off rate from MZ to DZ twins, together with that from first-degree to second-degree relatives, was used by Pickles and colleagues (1995) to estimate the number of genes that were likely to be involved. The logic of this analysis is based on the fact that whereas MZ twins share 100% of their genes, and 100% of all combinations of their genes, the situation is quite different in DZ twins and siblings. On average, they share 50% of their segregating genes but this means that they will share only a quarter of two gene combinations, and an eighth of three gene combinations. The findings from the analysis by Pickles and colleagues (2000) suggested that three or four genes were most probable, but that any number between 2 and 10 genes was a possibility (depending on the relative strength of the effect of any one of these genes). However, Risch et al. (1999) sug-

gested that the number of susceptibility genes might be much higher than that. Uncertainties also remain on the likelihood that the susceptibility genes will involve relatively common allelic variations or rather rare variants reflecting a disease mutation (Pritchard, 2001).
3. The finding that the genetic liability for autism extended to include a broader phenotype was confirmed. Some 90% of MZ pairs were concordant for mixtures of social and cognitive deficits that were qualitatively similar to those found in traditional autism, but milder in degree (i.e., the broader phenotype). This applied, however, to only about 1 in 10 DZ pairs. Focusing on the 10 MZ and 20 DZ pairs' discordant for autism or autism-spectrum disorders, it was shown that there was a similar contrasting concordance for this broader phenotype, the difference being statistically significant (Bailey et al., 1995; Le Couteur et al., 1996). A follow-up of the original Folstein and Rutter sample also showed that this broader phenotype is associated with important deficits in social functioning that continued into adult life.
4. An examination of 16 MZ pairs concordant for autism or autism spectrum disorders showed that there was enormous clinical heterogeneity even when pairs shared exactly the same segregating genetic alleles. Surprisingly, individuals within MZ pairs were no more alike in IQ or symptomatology than were pairs selected at random from different twin pairs (Le Couteur et al., 1996).

Family Studies

Family-genetic studies were important in order to determine the rate of autism in siblings and in parents, to check family patterns of transmission in case there were single-gene Mendelian variants (this cannot be assessed from twin studies), and to better delineate the breadth and pattern of the possible broader phenotype. The Maudsley Hospital Study and the Johns Hopkins Study, initially planned together, provided the first systematic findings on sizable samples using standardized measures. Subsequent studies have added to the findings in important ways.

The Maudsley Hospital Family Study used measurement methods directly comparable with those in the British Twin Study and similarly excluded families in which the autism was associated with some known medical condition that was likely to be causal. The families of 99 individuals with autism were compared systematically with 36 families of individuals with Down syndrome using exactly the same methods of measurement (Bolton et al., 1994). There was direct assessment of all first-degree relatives, and systematic standardized reports on more distant relatives. The rate of autism in the siblings of autistic individuals was found to be 3%, with an additional 3% showing some form of, more broadly conceptualized, autism spectrum disorder. No cases of autism or autism spectrum disorder were found in the siblings of individuals with Down syndrome. As in the twin study, a broader phenotype of autism, comprising mixed patterns of cognitive and social deficits and repetitive stereotyped interest patterns, were even more frequent. Depending on how stringent a definition was used, the comparative rates of the broader phenotype as compared with Down syndrome families were about 12% versus 2%, or 20% versus 3%. The findings provided striking evidence that the broader phenotype might be much more common in the general population than previously considered.

Because some data on families (August, Stewart, & Tsai, 1981) had suggested that autism that was accompanied by profound mental retardation might be somewhat different from the rest of autism in which nonverbal IQs were above 50, the Maudsley Hospital group undertook a further family study to determine whether this might be the case (Pickles et al., 2000; Starr et al., 2001). However, in contrast with the earlier suggestion, the rate of autism and of the broader phenotype in the relatives was not significantly different from that found in the first family study. The only possible lead was the uncertain indication that cognitive problems in the relatives might be somewhat more common when autism was associated with profound retardation. What did emerge, from the combination of the two studies, was the finding that the linear association

between severity of autism and the level of family loading seemed to apply only to cases of autism in which there was some useful speech (Pickles et al., 2000). The implication is that when autism is associated with a very severe lack of language skills, it might be genetically different in some way. However, this remains only as a possibility to be further tested, rather than as an established fact.

The Johns Hopkins study was particularly important because of its evidence on the probable importance of pragmatic language problems (Landa, Wzorek, Piven, Folstein, & Isaacs, 1991; Landa et al., 1992), of social abnormalities (Piven et al., 1990, 1991), and of unusual personality features (Piven et al., 1994). The early findings had particularly emphasized the familial loading of language delay but, although this seemed to be part of the overall picture in some cases, the later findings from all studies have suggested the probably greater importance of social deficits (Bailey, Palferman, Heavey, & Le Couteur, 1998; Folstein & Piven, 1991; Piven, Palmer, Jacobi, Childress, & Arndt, 1997; Rutter, Bailey, Simonoff, & Pickles, 1997).

The family study by Szatmari and colleagues (2000) differed from the others in its strategy of comparing biological and nonbiological relatives (the latter being represented by stepparents and adoptive families). The finding that social, communicative, and repetitive behaviors were all more common in biological relatives supported the inference that the familial loading reflected a genetically mediated liability. They also found that the rate of broader phenotype in relatives was higher in multiplex than simplex families and was greater when the proband with autism had an IQ above 60.

As well as language deficits in the relatives of individuals with autism, the early findings had suggested that there might also be a familial loading for reading and spelling difficulties. However, that now seems not to be the case. Fombonne, Bolton, Prior, Jordan, and Rutter (1997) undertook a detailed analysis of cognitive patterns in relatives in the Maudsley Family Study. The findings showed that neither low IQ nor specific problems in reading or spelling showed an increased loading in the families of individuals with autism if these problems were not accompanied by other man-ifestations of the broader phenotype. In other words, although reading and spelling difficul-ties could constitute an important part of the broader phenotype, these specific cognitive deficits, when they occurred in isolation, did not seem to be indicators of a genetic liability to autism. Also, family data suggest that phonological processing deficits (in contrast to pragmatic deficits) are not part of the broad autism phenotype (Bishop et al., 2004). Simi-larly, language impairments do constitute an important part of the broader phenotype but ordinarily they do not appear to be genetically connected to autism if they occur without either social deficits or circumscribed interest patterns. Interestingly, both Fombonne et al. and Piven and Palmer (1997) found that the relatives of individuals with autism tended to show a cognitive pattern with verbal skills that were superior to visuospatial skills. This is the opposite of what is ordinarily found in autism. This unexpected finding requires confirmation from other studies but, if con-firmed, other research will be required to de-termine what it means.

Over the years, more and more clinical fea-tures, particularly including affective disorder and social anxiety (DeLong & Nohria, 1994; Smalley, McCracken, & Tanguay, 1995), came to be added to possible variations of the broader phenotype. The key question was whether these affective features reflected the same genetic li-ability that underlies autism, or whether it re-flected some other genetic or environmental mechanism. Bolton, Pickles, Murphy, and Rut-ter (1998) confirmed that the rates of clinically significant affective disorder were increased in the relatives of individuals with autism and Murphy et al. (2000), as in the Johns Hopkins study (Piven et al., 1994), found that the rela-tives of individuals with autism showed an in-crease in the traits of shyness and aloofness and also the traits of anxiety and oversensitivity. However, the meanings of these two sets of traits were somewhat different. The evidence suggested that shyness and aloofness were man-ifestations of the broader phenotype whereas anxiety and oversensitivity were related to anx-iety or depressive disorders, rather than to the broader phenotype of autism. Depression was associated with depression in other family members but it was not associated, at either the individual or the family level, with cognitive or social deficits. The cause of the increased rate of depression in the families of individuals with autism remains unclear but it does not seem to reflect a genetic liability to autism.

Retrospective studies of individuals with schizophrenia at one time led to the claim that, although not diagnosed at the time in childhood, schizophrenia had been preceded by an autism spectrum disorder. However, prospective stud-ies of individuals with autism have not found that autistic individuals have an increased rate of schizophrenia in adult life (Volkmar & Cohen, 1991). Family studies, similarly, have shown no increase in the familial loading for schizophrenia in the relatives of individuals with an autism spectrum disorder (Bolton et al., 1998). It is possible, however, that obsessive-compulsive disorder, which is somewhat more frequent in the relatives of individuals with autism, may index an underlying genetic liabil-ity to autism (Bolton et al., 1998).

The evidence on the reality, and relative frequency, of the broader phenotype of autism has been well demonstrated in numerous stud-ies and the concept is no longer controversial. Nevertheless, the precise boundaries of the broader phenotype have yet to be established and clear-cut criteria for differentiating the broader phenotype of autism from the many other varieties of social deficit have yet to be determined. Similarly, although it is apparent that the broader phenotype occurs in at least 10% to 20% of the first-degree relatives of in-dividuals with autism, it is not yet known whether it constitutes a common, but still a qualitatively distinct, category, or whether, in-stead, it constitutes a continuously distributed dimension.

There are two crucial differences, too, between the broader phenotype and autism as traditionally diagnosed. Unlike autism, the broader phenotype is not associated with men-tal retardation, and it is not associated with epilepsy. As yet, we do not know why that is so. Questions arise as to whether the broader phe-notype represents a lesser "dose" of genetic li-ability, a different pattern of susceptibility genes, or some kind of "two-hit" mechanism in which an additional risk factor is required to take individuals over the threshold from the broader phenotype into a more seriously handicapping disorder.

CHROMOSOMAL ABNORMALITIES AND GENETICALLY DETERMINED MEDICAL CONDITIONS

During the 1970s and 1980s, there was a range of medical studies of autism demonstrating positive findings (Rutter, 1999a). Gillberg (1992) claimed that 37% of cases of autism were associated with a diagnosable medical condition and, on this basis, argued that a wide range of intrusive medical investigations (including lumbar puncture, EEG, brain imaging, and metabolic studies) should be undertaken as a routine (Gillberg, 1990; Gillberg & Coleman, 1996). However, Rutter and colleagues (Rutter, Bailey, Bolton, & Le Couteur, 1994), putting together the evidence from several studies, concluded that the rate was probably more like 10%. Nevertheless, this figure is certainly sufficiently high to mean that all individuals suspected of having an autism spectrum disorder should have a careful medical assessment. The question of whether they should have invasive investigations is a rather separate matter. The key issue is how often the investigations lead to a diagnosis that cannot be obtained more straightforwardly through clinical history and examination. The answer seems to be that it is rare for the tests to reveal undiagnosed medical conditions; many of the supposedly abnormal laboratory findings have no unambiguous clinical implications; and the clinical value seems so slight as not to justify the distress inevitably caused to young children if such investigations are routinely undertaken. Rather, the recommendation is that a thorough clinical history and examination should be routine and that the decision as to whether to undertake systematic laboratory investigations should be decided on the basis of the clinical findings. Further investigations will be mandatory in some cases but they should not be undertaken routinely in a mindless fashion that ignores the need for clinical decision making.

Similar issues have arisen with respect to chromosomal abnormalities. Thus, the early reports on the fragile X anomaly led to claims that this was a very common cause of autism (Gillberg & Wahlstrom, 1985). Moreover, initial findings were often presented as providing a "minimum figure," failing to appreciate the dangers of relying on findings based on small samples. The ratio of false positives to true positives in a small sample is necessarily much greater than that in a large sample and the size of a difference between groups is no guide to the true strength of the association. To achieve statistical significance, the difference in a small sample is bound to be a large one, and the true difference will almost certainly be very much smaller (see Cohen, Cohen, & Brook, 1995; Pocock, 1983). With respect to the fragile X anomaly, there was the additional concern that, during the 1980s, this had to be diagnosed using problematic cell culture methods. The fragile X anomaly was initially often diagnosed on the basis of only 1% to 3% of X chromosomes showing a fragile site. Once DNA techniques were available, it became clear that this was an unwarranted inference (Gurling, Bolton, Vincent, Melmer, & Rutter, 1997). Available estimates indicate that fragile X anomalies are present in less than 5% of individuals with autism (Bailey et al., 1993; Dykens & Volkmar, 1997). This is still a meaningful association, the rate of which is well above that expected on the basis of the rates of both in the general population. In other words, it seems reasonable to assume that the fragile X anomaly can play a causal role in the etiology of autism, even though it does so only in a small proportion of cases. Nevertheless, it should be noted that although the fragile X anomaly constitutes an uncommon cause of autism, social abnormalities (of a kind that includes, but is not confined to autism) are frequently present in individuals with the fragile X anomaly (Reiss & Dant, 2003).

There are individual case reports of associations between autism and anomalies of one sort or another on almost all chromosomes (Gillberg, 1998; Yu et al., 2002); most of these are based on single cases, but a few have been replicated, and the meaning of many of the anomalies is quite unknown. Nevertheless, there is consistent evidence of chromosome 15 anomalies associated with autism (Buxbaum et al., 2002; Folstein & Rosen-Sheidley, 2001; Kim et al., 2002; Nurmi et al., 2003; Shao et al., 2003). Most involve interstitial duplications of maternal origin; the parental effect suggests the involvement of genomic imprinting. The mechanisms underlying the association between chromosome 15 anomalies and autism remain unclear but the reality of the association appears well established.

With respect to medical conditions, the association with autism is most firmly established in the case of tuberous sclerosis (Smalley, 1998). One percent to 4% of individuals with autism have tuberous sclerosis and the rate may be as high as 8% to 14% among the subgroup of those with a seizure disorder. Tuberous sclerosis is a wholly genetic Mendelian disorder associated with a gene on either chromosome 9 or chromosome 16. In about two-thirds of cases the mutations arise de novo, rather than being inherited. Opinions differ on whether an abnormal tuberous sclerosis gene directly influences the development of autism, or whether the association with autism comes about because a susceptibility gene for autism lies in close proximity to a tuberous sclerosis gene, or because the brain abnormalities resulting from tuberous sclerosis predispose toward autism. The last possibility is suggested by the evidence that the occurrence of autism is, in part, a function of epilepsy and low IQ, and in part a function of the size and location of the tubers occurring in the brain (Bolton & Griffiths, 1997; Bolton, Park, Higgins, Griffiths, & Pickles, 2002; Lauritsen & Ewald, 2001; Weber, Egelhoff, McKellop, & Franz, 2000).

It has also been claimed that autism is associated with neurofibromatosis (Gillberg & Forsell, 1984) but the reality and strength of the association remains somewhat uncertain (Folstein & Rosen-Sheidley, 2001). Early reports had suggested that autism might be associated with phenylketonuria, but it is not clear whether this was an important association because the findings on autism were not based on standardized measurement (Folstein & Rutter, 1988). In any case, it is no longer a relevant issue in most developed countries because newborn screening has meant that untreated phenylketonuria is extremely rare.

MOLECULAR GENETICS

Over the past dozen years or so, there have been important technical advances that have facilitated the search for susceptibility genes for psychiatric disorders, as well as for other multifactorial conditions (Maestrini, Marlow, Weeks, & Monaco, 1998; Rutter, 2000; Rutter, Silberg, O'Connor, & Simonoff, 1999). Most particularly, the combination of the development of robotic techniques and the availability of a very large number of polymorphic micro-satellite and single nucleotide genetic markers has made a total scan of the genome a practical possibility. In essence, there are two main approaches that may be followed—namely, linkage and association strategies. They work on a somewhat different principle and they involve a different mix of advantages and disadvantages.

Linkage studies examine co-inheritance—meaning inheritance within families in which there is a linkage between the gene locus being studied and the condition being investigated. Traditionally, this approach was mainly applied to very large families involving many individuals who were affected with the condition being studied. However, the approach required specification of the mode of inheritance involved and that is not known in the case of autism, any more than it is with most psychiatric conditions. Also, as a consequence of the relatively low frequency of autism, the collection of sizable samples of extended families with many affected members is not a practical proposition. A further disadvantage of the traditional family approach was that it was unclear how to deal with cases in which the diagnostic status was uncertain. Because of these features, most research groups have switched to the study of affected sib pairs, or affected relative pairs (Rutter, Silberg, et al., 1999). The strategy requires the collection of samples in which there are two or more affected individuals in the same family and it is necessary only to concentrate on those for whom the diagnosis is unambiguous. The analysis then determines whether the co-occurrence of particular gene loci coincides with the diagnosis to an extent that exceeds chance expectations. With this approach, it is not necessary to specify in advance where the locus is expected to be. Rather, there can be a scanning of the whole genome, using markers that are sufficiently close to one another to ensure that if there is a relevant susceptibility gene locus it will be picked up.

The strategy (which can be applied to large pedigrees as well as affected relative pairs; Davis, Schroeder, Goldin, & Weeks, 1996) has the huge advantage of involving a minimum of untestable assumptions but it has two considerable disadvantages. First, it will detect gene loci only when there are relatively strong effects. Second, even when a likely gene locus has been identified, the area of the chromosome within which the gene should be found in a complex genetic disorder is very large. This means that the area will include a very large number of possible genes. Accordingly, it will usually be necessary to combine linkage studies with association strategies.

Association studies are based on the quite different strategy of using linkage disequilibrium to search for differences between cases and controls in allelic patterns. They have the advantage of being better able than linkage strategies to detect very small genetic effects (Risch & Merikangas, 1996). The concern with association strategies derives from the fact that stratification bias may arise because cases and controls differ in their allelic patterns as a result of their ethnic origins, rather than for any reason to do with the disorder being studied. Opinions differ as to how big a problem this is if major ethnic differences have been taken into account (Ardlie, Lunetta, & Seielstad, 2002; Cardon & Palmer, 2003). Nevertheless, it is desirable to control for stratification biases and this is possible through the transmission disequilibrium test (TDT), which also tests for both association and linkage (Malhotra & Goldman, 1999; Spielman & Ewens, 1996). Ordinarily, it requires DNA samples on trios—meaning an affected child and both parents. A further limitation of association strategies, at least up to now, has been the fact that they rely on the availability of candidate genes, which are singularly lacking in the case of autism. It has been claimed that the technique of DNA pooling (in other words, combining DNA samples across cases and similarly across controls) provides a possible way forward (Barcellos et al., 1997; Daniels et al., 1998). There are three possible difficulties with the use of DNA pooling. First, the number of markers required would be very much greater than in linkage studies because the association strategies can produce positive findings only in relation to a susceptibility gene that is very close to the markers used, or is the trait marker itself. Second, there are statistical problems in determining the significance of case control differences when a very large number of gene markers have to be tested. Third, the pooling of all cases means that the groups are made up on the basis of the assumption that the susceptibility gene concerns the disorder, rather than the components of the disorder (see the discussion that follows).

Single Gene Major Mutations: The Case of Rett Syndrome

Rett syndrome is a progressive neurodevelopmental disorder with an incidence of about 1 in 10,000 in girls (Hagberg, 1985; Hagberg, Aircardi, Dias, & Ramos, 1983). Classically, the girls develop normally until 6 to 18 months of age, then gradually lose speech and purposeful hand use, developing microcephaly, seizures, social impairment, ataxia, intermittent hyperventilation, and stereotypic hand movements. Witt-Engerström and Gillberg (1987) noted that the majority of cases of Rett syndrome were initially suspected of having autism because of the social impairment. Gillberg (1989) went on to argue that the apparent symptomatic similarities might mirror common pathophysiological abnormalities at the brainstem level. However, although Rett syndrome may, in the past, have been misdiagnosed as autism, the social features of Rett syndrome and autism are somewhat different (Olsson & Rett, 1985, 1987). In 1999, Amir and colleagues showed, using a systematic gene screening method, that a mutation in the MECP2 gene was the cause of many cases of Rett syndrome. This has now been confirmed by numerous other investigators. Most crucially, it has been shown that mouse models of the MECP2 mutation causes a neurobehavioral syndrome that is closely similar to that found in humans (Guy, Hendrich, Holmes, Martin, & Bird, 2001; Shahbazian et al., 2002). The evidence is clear-cut that the genetic mutation constitutes a single gene disorder with the genetic abnormality providing a sufficient explanation for the clinical syndrome, without the need to invoke any other genetic or environmental factors.

However, as is usual with single gene disorders, it has been found that there are several different MECP2 mutations that have generally similar phenotypic consequences (Amir et al., 2000). Also, as is commonly the case with single gene mutations, it has been found that the clinical picture is more varied than was at first considered to be the case (Shahbazian et al., 2002). Because of this, several research groups have studied samples of patients with autism in order to determine whether mutations in the MECP2 gene might be present. Two of the studies (Beyer et al., 2002; Vourc'h et al., 2001) concluded that mutations in the coding region of MECP2 did not play a major role in autism susceptibility. However, a third study (Carney et al., 2003) reported that 2 out of 69 cases of autism did show the MECP2 mutation. Apparently, the affected individuals did not show an overall syndrome that was similar to Rett syndrome (although they did have some Rett syndrome features). The balance of evidence suggests that the MECP2 mutation invariably leads to a serious neurodevelopmental disorder, that in the great majority of cases this approximates to the clinical picture of Rett syndrome, but occasionally (but not often) the clinical picture may be somewhat different and, perhaps, uncommonly it may take the form of autism. It seems unlikely, however, that the MECP2 mutation has any broader significance in relation to autism. However, Zoghbi (2003) has argued that both autism and Rett syndrome could turn out to be similar disorders of synaptic modulation or maintenance.

Genome-Wide Screens of Sib Pair Samples

The discovery of the MECP2 mutation was important, but the evidence that autism is a multifactorial disorder and that multiple susceptibility genes are likely to be operative implies that it should be expected that, in most instances, these genes would be normal, common, allelic variations rather than rare pathological mutations, although the latter might also contribute to the liability (Pritchard, 2001; Rutter, 2004). Genome-wide scans of sib pair samples in order to detect susceptibility gene loci have been published by eight different groups (Auranen et al., 2002, 2003; Barrett et al., 1999; Buxbaum et al., 2001; Collaborative Linkage Study of Autism [CLSA], 1999; International Molecular Genetic Study of Autism Consortium [IMGSAC], 1998, 2001b; Liu et al., 2001; Philippe et al., 1999; Risch et al., 1999; Shao, Raiford, et al., 2002; Shao, Wolpert, et al., 2002; Yonan et al., 2003), of which the first was the International Molecular Genetic Study of Autism Consortium (1998, 2001b). The findings have been reviewed by Folstein and Rosen-Sheidley (2001), Gutknecht (2001), and Lamb, Moore, Bailey, and Monaco (2000; Lamb, Parr, Bailey, & Monaco, 2002). A locus on chromosome 7q has been found in four of the studies (IMGSAC, 1998, 2001a), the collaborative linkage study of autism—CLSA (1999; Ashley-Koch et al., 1999; Philippe et al., 1999; Shao, Wolpert, et al., 2002), and confirmed in a meta-analysis (Badner & Gershon, 2002). It is undoubtedly encouraging that several different groups have come up with comparable findings regarding a locus on chromosome 7. However, the peak of linkage is quite wide and the precise location has not been identical in all the studies. This is not necessarily a concern because simulation studies have shown that there is a large variation in peak location relative to actual disease-gene location (Roberts, MacLean, Neale, Eaves, & Kendler, 1999), the strength of the finding varies across studies. The postulated locus on chromosome 7q includes several key candidate genes. Thus, it is close to the location of the FOXP2 gene, which has been shown to be responsible for an unusual familial speech and language disorder (Lai, Fisher, Hurst, Vargha-Khadem, & Monaco, 2001). It was suggested that autism and severe language impairment might derive from the same gene in this area (Folstein & Mankoski, 2000) but the available evidence suggests that this is not likely to be the case (Newbury et al., 2002). The human reelin gene also maps to an area on 7q that is close to the peak of linkage found in relation to autism. The reelin protein plays an important role in neuronal migration during brain development and, hence, constitutes a plausible candidate gene in respect of autism. However, the evidence to date suggests that it probably does not play a major role in autism etiology (Bonora et al., 2003), although it is too early to conclude that it plays no role.

The strongest evidence for linkage in the International Molecular Genetic Study of Autism Consortium findings (IMGSAC, 2001b) was a susceptibility region on chromosome 2q. This was also the case in the findings of the Buxbaum and colleagues (2001) group, and of the Shao and colleagues group (Shao, Raiford, et al., 2002; Shao, Wolpert, et al., 2002). Again, the region of chromosome 2q includes a number of interesting genes that are potential candidates for a role in the etiology of autism.

Other positive linkage findings have been reported for chromosome 16p (IMGSAC, 2001b; Liu et al., 2001), chromosome 1p (Risch et al., 1999), chromosome 3 (Auranen et al., 2002, 2003; Shao, Raiford, et al., 2002, Shao, Wolpert, et al., 2002), chromosome 13q (CLSA, 1999), 5q (Liu et al., 2001), 5p (Yonan et al., 2003), 17q (IMGSAC, 2001b; Yonan et al., 2003), 19p and 19q (Liu et al., 2001), and Xq (Shao, Raiford, et al., 2002; Shao, Wolpert, et al., 2002).

Candidate Gene Strategies

The literature contains several positive findings with respect to candidate genes (Folstein & Rosen-Sheidley, 2001). They had been promising, for a variety of good reasons—including their role in neurotransmitters (such as serotonin, dopamine, and glutamate), because of connections with chromosome anomalies associated with autism, or because of their proximity to the locations derived from the genome screen linkage findings. However, the findings so far are contradictory and inconclusive with many failures to replicate. Although it is too early to rule out any of the candidate gene possibilities, the evidence that they do have an actual role in the liability to autism is so far unconvincing. A possible exception to the generally negative story may be provided by the report that mutations in two X-linked genes coding the neuroligands NLGN3 and LNNLGN4 are associated with autism spectrum disorders (Jamain, Betancur, et al., 2002). However, this finding has yet to be replicated.

Recently, two further claims have been made with regard to possible susceptibility genes for autism. Gharani et al. (2004), using a family-based association method with the Autism Genetic Resource Exchange (AGRE), found a significant association with two intronic markers of a cerebella patterning gene located on chromosome 7 (but no association with the flanking exons). Ramoz et al. (2004), using a partially overlapping data set, found association with common intronic polymorphisms in a gene located on chromosome 2 that is involved with mitochondrial aspartate/glutamate function. Both findings require replication before conclusions can be drawn, but it is of interest that the postulated genetic variants are common and that they are concerned with regulating functions rather than the production of polypeptides as such.

One of the striking findings with respect to autism concerns the marked male preponderance. Not surprisingly, therefore, attention has focused on the X chromosome in order to determine whether X linkage might be responsible. However, with the exception of Shao and colleagues (Shao, Raiford, et al., 2002; Shao, Wolpert, et al., 2002), the findings have been generally negative (Hallmayer et al., 1996; Yirmiya et al., 2002) and the evidence of father to son transmission of autism (which could not involve the X chromosome) indicates that it is unlikely that X linkage is responsible for the overall male preponderance (Hallmayer et al., 1996). Findings for the Y chromosome have also been negative (Jamain, Quach, et al., 2002). Skuse and his colleagues (Skuse, 2000; Skuse et al., 1997) put forward a somewhat different hypothesis. They found that in subjects with Turner syndrome (who have an XO karyotype), social interaction difficulties were much more prevalent in those who inherited the X chromosome from the mother as compared with those who inherited it from the father. It was argued that there might be an imprinted locus on the X chromosome that might serve to make males more susceptible because their X chromosome would have to have been inherited from the mother. By contrast, females would have an X chromosome from each parent, that from the father possibly providing some protection from a genetic liability to autism that derived from some other (presumably autosomal) locus. The hypothesis is intriguing and it has a certain amount of support within Skuse's Turner syndrome data set (Skuse, 2003). However, despite the fact that the hypothesis was first put forward over half a dozen years ago, no replications have been reported, apart from a single case report (Donnelly et al., 2000), which inevitably raises questions about the original findings.

EPIDEMIOLOGICAL FINDINGS

One of the most striking features of the findings on the rate of autism spectrum disorders in the general population is the enormous increase that has taken place over the past half century (Fombonne, 1999, 2003; Rutter, in press). The first study by Lotter (1966) suggested a rate of about four cases per 10,000. This contrasts starkly with the estimates from the best recent studies of between 30 and 60 cases per 10,000 (Baird et al., 2000; Chakrabarti & Fombonne, 2001). It is clear that this increase is largely a function of better ascertainment combined with a considerable broadening of the diagnostic criteria. Thus, for example, in recent studies, a high proportion of the children with autism spectrum disorders had a normal level of measured intelligence, whereas that applied to only a small minority in the early studies. However, whether or not this constitutes the whole story remains quite uncertain (Bock & Goode, 2003). It is possible that there has been a real rise in the incidence of autism and the available data neither confirm nor disconfirm the suggestion. If there has been a true rise, it would certainly have to involve the operation of environmental risk factors of some kind.

NONGENETIC RISK FACTORS

Monozygotic Twinning as a Risk Factor

There tends to be an assumption that the nongenetic factors involved in the etiology of autism must involve specific environmental risks. However, that is not necessarily the case (Jensen, 1997; Molenaar, Boomsma, & Dolan, 1993). Greenberg and colleagues (Greenberg, Hodge, Sowinski, & Nicoll, 2001), and also Betancur and colleagues (Betancur, Leboyer, & Gillberg, 2002) reported an apparent excess of twins among affected sibling pairs with autism

(but see Hodge, Greenberg, Betancur, & Gillberg, 2002; Visscher, 2002). If this finding were valid, it would suggest that being a twin constitutes a risk factor for autism. If that were the case, it might either reflect obstetric complications or the effect of developmental perturbations. Congenital anomalies have been found to be more common in individuals with autism and these probably index the ways in which development, which is probabilistically rather that deterministically programmed, may go awry (Vogel & Motulsky, 1997). Thus, congenital anomalies are more common in twins than in singletons and are more common in children born to older mothers (Myrianthopoulos & Melnick, 1977; Rutter et al., 1990). Thus, it could be that developmental perturbations enhance the adverse effects of a genetic liability to autism. However, it should be noted that congenital anomalies show an increased rate in a wide range of psychiatric disorders. Also, some skepticism is necessary with respect to the supposed finding that the rate of twinning is increased in autism. Ascertainment biases are likely to have played a major role and it is noteworthy that the most systematically ascertained twin sample of Bailey and colleagues (1995) did not include a significant excess of monozygotic twins; nor did Hallmayer and colleagues' (2002) Australian twin sample. It may be concluded that more evidence is needed on the postulated increased risk for autism associated with being a twin but, on the evidence available to date, it is not likely that being a monozygotic twin is a major risk factor.

Obstetric Complications

Numerous studies have shown a significant association between autism and obstetric complications (Tsai, 1987). Three very different hypotheses may be put forward to account for the finding: (1) It could be a secondary consequence of birth order effects; (2) it could reflect brain damage brought about by obstetric complications, however caused; or (3) it could reflect an epiphenomenon in which the obstetric complications derive from the presence of a genetically abnormal fetus. These possibilities were systematically examined by Bolton and colleagues (1997), who concluded that it was unlikely that the association reflected environmentally caused brain damage (because, among other things, the main excess of complications were mild, rather than severe), and that, rather, either the obstetric adversities represented an epiphenomenon or derived from some shared risk factors.

Measles-Mumps-Rubella Vaccination

In 1998, on the basis of totally inadequate evidence, Wakefield and colleagues suggested that autism might be caused by adverse effects stemming from measles-mumps-rubella (MMR) vaccination. The suggestion arose because of an observed temporal association between the timing of the MMR vaccination and the timing of the first manifestations of autism. Such an association would, of course, be expected by chance alone because the first manifestations are usually evident at about the age when it is recommended that MMR be given. Subsequently, it was suggested that the MMR vaccination was responsible for the major rise in the incidence of diagnosed autism that has occurred over time. The hypothesis has been examined in a number of different ways, all of which have produced findings that run counter to the hypothesis (Rutter, in press). First, the close temporal association has not been confirmed (Farrington, Miller, & Taylor, 2001; Taylor et al., 1999) and the rise in the rate of autism does not follow the pattern that would be expected on the basis of the MMR effect. Thus, the beginning of the rise began before the introduction of MMR; there was no stepwise increase in the rate of autism following the introduction of MMR; and the rate did not plateau during the period when MMR vaccination rates were both high and stable (Dales, Hammer, & Smith, 2001; Hillman, Kanafani, Takahashi, & Miles, 2000; Kaye, Melero-Montes, & Jick, 2001). Most crucially, too, the rate of autism in Japan continued to rise after MMR ceased to be used (Honda, Shimizu, & Rutter, in press). Case-control comparisons have been similarly negative (K. M. Madsen et al., 2002). It had been further suggested that the autism associated with MMR usually involved developmental regression and was accompanied by bowel abnormalities (Wakefield et al., 1998). However, the evidence runs counter to

these suggestions (Fombonne & Chakrabarti, 2001; Taylor et al., 2002; Uchiyama, Kurosawa, & Inaba, submitted). It may be concluded that it is quite implausible that MMR is generally associated with a substantially increased risk for autism. It is not possible to rule out the possibility that there may be occasional idiosyncratic responses to MMR that involve autism, but there is no good evidence that this happens.

Somewhat similar concerns have been expressed with respect to the possibility that Thimerosal, a vaccine preservative that contains ethyl mercury, might cause autism (Bernard, Enayati, Redwood, Roger, & Binstock, 2001). The question has biological plausibility in that it is known that mercury, in high dosage, can cause neurodevelopmental sequelae (Clarkson, 1997; Stratton, Gable, & McCormick, 2001). The opportunity to test this hypothesis arose in Denmark, where, from 1970 onward, the only Thimerosal-containing vaccine was the whole cell pertussis vaccine. Between April 1992, and January 1997, the same vaccine was used but without Thimerosal, and the vaccine was then replaced by an acellular pertussis vaccine. Data from the Danish Psychiatric Central Register was used to compare the rate of autism and autism-spectrum disorders in individuals who received only Thimerosal-free vaccinations and those containing Thimerosal. The Danish civil registration system allowed identification of the vaccinations used in each child and the number of doses given (thereby allowing calculation of the total Thimerosal dosage received). No difference in the rate of autism spectrum disorders was found between the groups that differed with respect to receipt of Thimerosal (Hviid, Stellfeld, Wohlfahrt, & Melbye, 2003). The causal hypothesis could also be tested by looking at time trends in the incidence of autism among children between 2 and 10 years of age, both before and after removal of Thimerosal from vaccines (K. E. Madsen et al., 2003). The findings showed that the discontinuation of Thimerosal-containing vaccines in 1992 was followed by an increase in the incidence of autism and not the predicted decrease (see Rutter, in press). The natural experiment provided by the removal of the postulated risk factor (Thimerosal) provided a good opportunity to test the causal hypothesis, with findings that were completely negative. The two-phase retrospective cohort study by Verstraeten et al. (2003), undertaken using a very large health records database in the United States similarly found no significant increased risk for autism associated with Thimerosal usage. There is no reason to suppose that Thimerosal is likely to be a general risk factor for autism spectrum disorders and certainly it cannot account for the rise in the rate of diagnosed autism in Denmark, as found also in other countries. As with MMR, the data do not allow testing of the different hypothesis of a rare, unusual, idiosyncratic response to Thimerosal in individual children, although there is no available evidence to indicate that such a response actually occurs. Moreover, the available evidence suggests that vaccines containing Thiomersal do not seem to raise blood concentration of mercury above safety levels (Pichichero, Cernichiari, Lopreiato, & Treanor, 2002), although this conclusion must be tentative in view of the paucity of evidence on what is a safe level.

Other Environmental Factors

Case reports and small scale studies have suggested a range of possible other environmental risk factors for autism (see Folstein & Rosen-Sheidley, 2001; Medical Research Council [MRC], 2001; Nelson, 1991; Rodier & Hyman, 1998). These include maternal hypothyroidisim, congenital hypothyroidism, maternal thalidomide use, maternal valproic acid use, maternal cocaine or alcohol use, and congenital cytomegalovirus infection. It is quite possible that these factors play at least a contributory causal role in individual cases but it seems unlikely that they constitute commonly operating risk factors for autism.

Probably the best evidence is that concerned with a possible causal link between congenital rubella and autism (Chess, 1977; Chess, Kern, & Fernandez, 1971). The findings derive from a systematically studied large sample of children with congenital rubella and the observations have been supported by other investigators. However, it is noteworthy that the follow-up showed that the course of apparent autism in these children tended, on the whole, to be rather different from that associated with idiopathic autism. In particular, although the

children remained markedly handicapped, the autistic features diminished as they grew older. In any case, the findings are of very limited contemporary relevance in view of the rarity of congenital rubella following vaccination programs.

Phenocopies

Over the past decade or so, evidence has accumulated on the existence of what appear to be phenocopies—meaning clinical features that look somewhat like autism but are not due to the same genetic liability. Thus, atypical syndromes of autism have been found to be associated with congenital blindness (Brown, Hobson, & Lee, 1997), with profound institutional privation (Rutter, Anderson-Wood, et al., 1999), and with a mixed bag of medical conditions all with profound mental retardation (Rutter et al., 1994). In each case, the clinical pictures are somewhat atypical and the implication is that the syndromes do not involve the same genetic liability that applies to ordinary idiopathic autism. However, although it seems highly likely that these atypical syndromes are distinct from the more usual varieties of idiopathic autism, that remains an inference rather than an established fact.

A further possible phenocopy concerns the marked social impairments that are associated with many cases of the severe developmental disorders of receptive language (Clegg, Hollis, Mawhood, & Rutter, in press; Howlin, Mawhood, & Rutter, 2000). Although the social impairments found in association with these severe cases of language delay differ from the syndrome of autism in many respects, it is nevertheless striking that the marked difficulties in social functioning persist into mid-adult life and are accompanied by considerable impairment. It is also noteworthy that there was a significant impairment on theory of mind tasks, albeit, not as severe as usually associated with autism.

GENETIC PARTITIONING OF AUTISM

Genetic findings throughout internal medicine have made it clear that, whether dealing with single gene conditions or multifactorial disorders, genetic heterogeneity must be expected. Accordingly, there have been various attempts to determine whether such heterogeneity can be indexed by clinical features.

Familial Clustering

Familial clustering could provide important clues in this connection. Le Couteur and colleagues (1996) used the strategy of comparing phenotypic variations within and between monozygotic pairs to examine the question. It was argued that variation within each monozygotic pair could not index genetic heterogeneity because both twins must share all of the same genes. By contrast, there is every reason to suppose that different pairs of monozygotic twins will vary genetically as much as any other population of individuals with autism. Variation within real monozygotic pairs was compared with the variation within pairs created statistically by having the pair made up of one twin from one pair and one twin from another, different, pair. The findings were striking, and surprising, in showing that, within the monozygotic pairs that were concordant for autism, there was as much variation in symptom severity and pattern and in cognitive level as that found within these pseudo-pairs that had been created statistically. For example, in one true monozygotic pair there was an IQ difference of over 50 points. It was evident that, even when the susceptibility genes were exactly the same, very wide phenotypic variation was still possible. The findings provided few clues on possible clinical indices of genetic heterogeneity.

Inevitably, the sample size was small and the same issues can be examined on much larger numbers by using affected sib pairs. Although it cannot necessarily be assumed that the susceptibility genes for autism will be the same in two pairs of siblings (whereas that could be assumed with monozygotic twin pairs), it is certainly likely that the genetic heterogeneity within affected sib pairs would be substantially less than that in the population as a whole. Relevant studies have been undertaken by Spiker and colleagues (1994), Silverman and colleagues (2002), and IMGSAC (Bailey, personal communication, 2004). The familial question was also studied by Szatmari and colleagues (1996, 2000). In the IMGSAC study, the strongest indication of familial clustering was for epilepsy; although the sample size was very small, this

also seemed a possibility in the Le Couteur and colleagues (1996) monozygotic twins study. However, there needs to be caution in the interpretation of this finding because of the peak age of onset of epilepsy in individuals with autism being late adolescence. This means, inevitably, that many younger children will be misclassified as not having epilepsy when, in reality, they are due to develop epilepsy when older. The similarity in age within pairs will influence clustering for epilepsy much more than it will for features that are manifest from the preschool years onward.

Epilepsy aside, the evidence on familial clustering has not been particularly informative on possible indices of genetic heterogeneity. The IMGSAC study (Bailey, personal communication, 2004) found no clustering for the degree of language delay (but this finding is inevitably influenced by inclusion/exclusion criteria used in the study). Nevertheless, the lack of clustering does cast doubt on any hypothesis that autism and Asperger syndrome are genetically distinct (because the diagnostic criteria usually employed specify a lack of significant language delay for the diagnosis of Asperger syndrome). However, although language delay as such does not seem to show any marked familial clustering, the sib pair studies have shown a significant (although not marked) tendency for sibs in each pair to be more similar on their degree of abnormalities on social reciprocity, communication, and repetitive behavior than are unrelated individuals with autism. Both verbal and performance IQ measures similarly showed some familial aggregation in the IMGSAC study (Bailey, personal communication, 2004), although not in the Spiker et al. (1994) study. The findings on repetitive stereotyped behavior were, however, somewhat different in that familial aggregation was not influenced by IQ or language-related measures whereas the other features were influenced by language levels.

In all the studies, the cases included have had to meet specified diagnostic criteria for autism or for a broader concept of autism spectrum disorder. Frequently, too, there has been exclusion of individuals with profound mental retardation. There are very good practical reasons for molecular genetic studies to adopt rigorous standardized diagnostic criteria for inclusion and exclusion but it is important to appreciate that this will have implications for findings on familial clustering. Thus, for example, if the genetic liability to autism represents a continuously distributed risk dimension, familial clustering would be more appropriately examined without exclusions. Equally, if autism associated with profound mental retardation is genetically different, familial clustering is likely to show this only if cases of autism across the whole IQ distribution are included. For the moment, it is difficult to go much beyond the rather general conclusion that there is some tendency for affected relatives in the same family to be more alike in their autistic features, and in their cognitive functioning, than unrelated individuals with autism, but neither the pattern nor the extent of clustering gives clear guidance on how autism spectrum disorders might better be subdivided.

Multiplex-Singleton Comparisons: Developmental Regression

Recently, strong claims have been made that use of the MMR vaccine leads to an unusual variety of autism that is especially characterized by developmental regression (Torrente et al., 2002; Wakefield et al., 2000, 2002). As already noted, the epidemiological evidence provides no support for this claim. However, it could still be the case that autism involving developmental regression might be etiologically distinct. As already noted in the findings from the IMGSAC study (Parr et al., poster, 2002), there was no familial loading for regression. Another approach to the question is provided by comparison between multiplex cases and singletons. The rationale is that in families in which there are two affected siblings the autism may have a stronger genetic component than cases in which there is only one affected family member. Parr and colleagues found that the rate of regression in the large IMGSAC sample of multiplex families was closely comparable with that reported in previous studies of singletons. The finding indicates that, in cases where strong genetic influences may be inferred, there is no reduced rate of regression. Thus, the hypothesis that cases of autism with regression represent an environmentally caused subgroup has no empirical support. However, two caveats are necessary. First, cases of de-

velopmental regression are almost certainly heterogeneous. At one extreme, there is the frequent phenomenon of children who gain just a few words of vocabulary and then subsequently lose this minimal amount of speech. In such cases, there are inevitable doubts about the reality of the developmental regression. At the other extreme, there are cases of children who gained substantial language and who then lost well-established language skills. The original version of the ADI-R (Lord, Rutter, & Le Couteur, 1994) provided a somewhat uncertain differentiation of patterns of developmental regression. The current version (Le Couteur, Lord, & Rutter, 2003; Rutter, Le Couteur, & Lord, 2003) provides much better assessment but it has been in use for too short a time to produce data on regression in large samples. Second, although comparisons of multiplex cases and singletons have often been used as a way of subdividing groups according to strength of genetic influence, it constitutes a methodologically weak approach (Rutter et al., 1990) particularly with a relatively uncommon disorder such as autism. When most nuclear families are quite small, there are bound to be many singleton cases that would have shown a familial loading if the families had been larger (Eaves, Kendler, & Schulz, 1986). Accordingly, although the conclusion clearly must be that there is no evidence that cases of autism with developmental regression are etiologically distinct, the inference is necessarily a relatively weak one.

Linkage Evidence

For obvious reasons, the starting point for most molecular genetic studies of psychiatric disorders has been the traditional diagnostic concept. However, it is entirely possible that individual genes will provide a susceptibility, not for the syndrome as a whole, but rather for some components of it. Thus, some findings suggested that this might be the case in relation to different components of dyslexia (Grigorenko et al., 1997) although subsequent research findings have raised queries (Fisher et al., 1999, 2002). In relation to autism, some studies have found stronger evidence for linkage in autism relative pairs with evidence of language delay or a family history of language delay (Alarcón et al., 2002; Bradford et al.,

2001; Buxbaum et al., 2001; Shao, Raiford, et al., 2002; Shao, Wolpert, et al., 2002), although this was not found in the IMGSAC study. Alarcón and colleagues (2002) applied nonparametric multipoint linkage analyses to the three main traits derived from the Autism Diagnostic Interview, and concluded that there may be separate quantitative trait loci for language and for stereotyped behavior—both on chromosome 7. At present, the evidence is far too fragmentary for any firm conclusions. Nevertheless, the general strategy of either determining whether the linkage evidence is stronger in relation to particular phenotypically different subgroups of individuals with autism, or looking for evidence of linkage in relation to particular dimensions or subcomponents of autism, remain worthwhile strategies (Folstein, Down, Mankoski, & Tadevosyan, 2003). It would be similarly worthwhile to use cognitive measures as a way of subdividing autism—for example, according to the presence or absence of severe mental retardation, or the presence or absence of unusual special talents or splinter skills.

Neurocognitive Endophenotypes

There has been increasing interest in the possibility of using cognitive findings to define endophenotypes that are not synonymous with the diagnostic symptoms pattern but which may constitute the relevant genetically influenced traits (Rutter, 2004). On this basis, Tager-Flusberg and Joseph (2003) presented evidence that there may be two different subtypes in autism—one based on language abilities and one based on IQ discrepancy scores. The language deficit group was found, using magnetic resonance imaging (MRI), to have a reversal of the usual brain asymmetry. The group with a discrepantly high nonverbal IQ was found to have a large head size and large brain volume, and more severe autism symptoms. The subgroupings would seem likely to be useful in genetic analyses.

Biological Findings

Two well-established biological correlates of autism are elevated platelet serotonin (Cook & Leventhal, 1996) and increased head circumference (Fombonne, Rogé, Claverie, Courty, &

Fremolle, 1999; Lainhart, Piven, Wzorek, & Landa, 1997; Woodhouse et al., 1996). The potential importance for subdividing cases of autism is provided by the fact that in both cases, although the correlate is a common one, it is far from universal. Accordingly, it would appear worthwhile to examine linkage findings separately according to the presence or absence of either of these features (Veenstra-VanderWeele et al., 2002). The situation is complicated, however, by the fact that in both cases there is evidence that the same biological features may also be elevated in other family members (Cook & Leventhal, 1996).

Minor congenital anomalies or dysmorphic features of one kind or another may well constitute another useful differentiating feature (Miles & Hillman, 2000). It appears that cases of autism without major or minor congenital anomalies have a much higher frequency of affected relatives and also show a much stronger male-female sex ratio.

Epigenetic Mechanisms

Baron-Cohen (2003) has suggested that high levels of prenatal testosterone may lead to an exaggeration of masculine features and that autism might constitute, in effect, an extreme of maleness (Baron-Cohen, 2002; Baron-Cohen, Richler, Bisarya, Gurunathan, & Wheelwright, 2003). The starting point for this suggestion was the marked male preponderance associated with autism. The suggestion that autism constitutes an extreme of maleness remains highly speculative. Autism is far from the only neurodevelopmental condition involving a male preponderance (Rutter, Caspi, & Moffitt, 2003). Attention deficit/hyperactivity disorder, dyslexia, and developmental language disorders all similarly show a male excess. Nevertheless, it is possible that sex hormone levels in the prenatal period affect gene expression in some manner, through epigenetic mechanisms. Although it is not at all likely that high levels of prenatal testosterone cause autism, it is possible that they might have a contributory role in conjunction with genetic risk determined in other ways.

There is a need to consider possible genomic imprinting; hence, possible loci for susceptibility genes need to be considered with respect to differential maternal and paternal transmission (Reik & Walter, 2001). Also, other epigenetic effects involving DNA methylation may turn out to be important means by which as yet to be identified environmental influences affect gene expression (Jaenisch & Bird, 2003; Robertson & Wolffe, 2000).

FUTURE DIRECTIONS

Quantitative Trait Loci (QTL) Approaches

As already noted, the finding that the broader phenotype of autism probably occurs in as many as one in five first-degree relatives of individuals with autism has raised the possibility that the susceptibility to autism may be based on a continuously distributed trait in the population that extends far beyond the syndrome of autism. Constantino and Todd (2003) reported that autistic features, as measured by their social responsiveness scale, were continuously distributed and were moderately to highly heritable as judged by twin sample findings. Spiker and colleagues (Spiker, Lotspeich, Dimiceli, Myers, & Risch, 2002), showed much the same (using the ADI-R) within a group of multiplex families with autism spectrum disorders. Several of the major autism research groups in the world are currently involved in developing measures of different facets of autism that can provide a differentiation of individuals who do not have the syndrome of autism as such. It is likely that QTL analyses may provide a useful additional strategy in molecular genetic studies. In that connection, as well as studying the distribution of autistic traits in all family members, there is something to be said for studying extremely discordant sib pairs in which one has the full syndrome of autism and the other completely lacks any autistic features (Risch & Zhang, 1995, 1996).

Leads for Candidate Genes

Three main approaches have been followed in selecting possible candidate genes for autism:

1. Attention has been paid to the location of chromosomal abnormalities. As noted earlier, the best evidence concerns the maternal duplications found on chromosome 15q11–13. However, the genome screens undertaken to date have failed to find any linkage in this region (Folstein & Rosen-Sheidley, 2001). Chromosome translocations of various kinds have also been reported on chromosome 7 (see references in Folstein & Rosen-Sheidley, 2001). However, most have not concerned the area in which linkage has been found, and, as with chromosome 15, they have not proved particularly useful as guides to candidate genes. The notion of using chromosome abnormalities as a lead is a reasonable one but it has not had much success to date.

2. The second approach is provided by genes that are concerned with one of the neurotransmitters that might plausibly be involved in autism (see Folstein & Rosen-Sheidley, 2001). Although there have been some positive findings, they have not been replicated and, again, leads have not proved as useful as was hoped.

3. The third approach has been to select candidate genes on the basis of the combination of their position near linkage signals that have been found on genome scans and functions that might plausibly be related to autism. Thus, this has applied to the reelin gene and the FOXP2 gene, among a variety of others (see Folstein & Rosen-Sheidley, 2001). The two genes known to be associated with tuberous sclerosis have also been thought to provide possible pointers.

Unfortunately, so far, none of these approaches has paid off in the case of autism, but the strategies remain potentially worthwhile.

Subdivisions within Autism

The potential value of considering molecular genetic strategies in relation to possibly meaningful subgroups within autism has already been noted in the section dealing with genetic dissection.

Animal Models and Studies of Postmortem Brain Tissues

Just as genetic findings can provide invaluable leads for other forms of biological investigation, so biological findings can provide useful leads for genetic research. This is most obviously the case with respect to evidence from animal models and from the study of postmortem brain tissues (see Bock & Goode, 2003). Both areas of research, in relation to autism, are in their infancy and no strong leads for candidate genes have yet emerged. However, as there is further progress in these areas, good leads may become available.

CLINICAL IMPLICATIONS

Initially, Kanner (1943) had postulated that autism was likely to be of constitutional origin. In the years that followed, however, many clinicians and researchers came to believe that autism was largely caused by "refrigerator parenting" and other types of maladaptive upbringing (see Rutter, 1999a). This concept of autism was later dropped—partly because of a lack of evidence in support of environmental causation and in part because of the growing evidence in favor of the view of autism as a neurodevelopmental disorder. The finding of strong genetic influences on autism also played a part in the demise of the refrigerator parent notions. But, more particularly, the genetic evidence led to an appreciation that the unusual personality features seen in some parents might represent genetically influenced traits rather than environmental causation of autism.

Clinical Assessment and Medical Investigations

The genetic findings have also been crucial in making a systematic medical assessment of individuals with autism standard practice. Thus, it would now be mandatory to examine all children suspected of autism for possible indications of tuberous sclerosis, followed by the appropriate medical investigations when there were positive findings from clinical examination. Although the fragile X anomaly accounts for only a very small proportion of cases of autism, it is important that the anomaly is identified when present because of its implications for family counseling. Accordingly, DNA methods need to be used in all cases to determine whether the fragile X anomaly is present. Possibly, the same may apply to the MECP2 gene for Rett syndrome, although in view of the

conflicting evidence, this remains more uncertain. Chromosome anomalies of one kind or another are found in some 5% to 10% of cases of autism. In most cases, the causal significance of these chromosome anomalies remains quite uncertain. Nevertheless, their potential importance is sufficient for karyotyping of chromosomes to be a routine investigation in all cases of suspected autism. Possibly, too, this should include a more detailed study of the imprinted region of chromosome 15 using Fluorescence In Situ Hybridization—(FISH).

Genetic Counseling

Given the strength of genetic influences on autism, it is clearly essential that genetic counseling be available to all families that want it (Simonoff, 1998; Simonoff & Rutter, 2002). The clinical issues involved are quite complex. As with any other form of genetic counseling (Simonoff, 2002), it is essential to make a careful diagnosis of the suspected autism spectrum disorder in the key individual whose problem led to the need for genetic counseling. In addition, however, it is essential to obtain a detailed and thorough family history followed, as necessary, by a detailed individual clinical assessment of the possibly affected family members. The main difficulty in this connection arises from the uncertainties as to exactly what should, and should not, be included in the broader phenotype. This means that, unlike the situation with the genetic counseling needed for Mendelian medical disorders, the counseling needs (at least in the first instance) to be provided by clinicians who are expert in the assessment of both autism spectrum disorders and the broader phenotype pictures with which they are associated.

The second issue is the need to help families understand the difference between the absolute risk and the relative risk of autism spectrum disorders and associated conditions. Thus, sticking with autism spectrum disorders, the available evidence suggests that the absolute rate in siblings is about 6%. In other words, the absolute likelihood of autism being present in a second child in the same family is quite low. This is so despite the fact that the risk relative to the general population is very high—some 20 to 50 times increased, the specific figure depending a bit on what assumptions are made about the general population base rate. Family members need to be helped to understand how this could happen as a result of autism developing as a consequence of the inheritance of several susceptibility genes, rather than the possession of one gene that leads fairly directly to autism. Thus, the counselor will need to explain how, although siblings share about half their segregating genes on average, the proportion of multiple gene combinations that they share is very much lower than that. In other words, other family members are quite likely to have one or another of the various susceptibility genes associated with autism but they may not have either enough of the susceptibility genes or the necessary pattern of susceptibility genes that leads to the syndrome as a whole. Two considerations complicate the advice that may be given. First, although the rate of autism in siblings is about 6% overall, the recurrence rate of autism (meaning the rate of autism in a second sibling following occurrence of autism in a previous sibling) may be somewhat higher—possibly about 8%. Second, the risk that another child in the same family will have some variety of the broader phenotype is very much higher than the expectation for the syndrome of autism. It is difficult to quantify in the absence of firm knowledge on the boundaries of the broader phenotype but it is likely to be in the region of 20% rather than 6%. The available evidence suggests that these broader phenotype abnormalities are functionally important (that is to say, they lead to difficulties in the children with them) but they are much less handicapping than autism as such.

These figures all refer to the average expectations in relation to idiopathic autism. Clearly, it is highly desirable to be able to individualize the expectations to provide much greater precision. This is straightforward enough in terms of the obvious prior need to rule out specific conditions such as the fragile X anomaly or tuberous sclerosis. However, it is much more difficult to individualize the expectations in cases of idiopathic autism. It is likely that if there are already two siblings in the family with autism, the recurrence risk in relation to a third child is likely to be well above 8% but the evidence is lacking to be more precise than that. On commonsense grounds, too, it must be pre-sumed that if there is a particularly heavy familial loading for either autism as such or for varieties of the broader phenotype, the recurrence risk is likely to be greater. However, the difficulties of being at all precise over the increase in risks stems from the inevitable unreliability of familial loading figures that are based on a relatively small number of relatives (Rutter et al., 1990) and uncertainties that derive from the difficulties in specifying just which social, communicative, and behavioral abnormalities in relatives are part of the broader phenotype of autism, rather than due to something else (Bailey et al., 1998). Conversely, if the autism is associated with some reasonably clear-cut environmental risk factor, it might be thought that the recurrence risk of autism should be lower than average in the general population. The difficulty here is in knowing what is a true environmental cause and effect. Thus, for example, if the autism is associated with particularly severe obstetric abnormalities that have been associated with neonatal problems, it would seem reasonable to infer the probability of some environmentally mediated causal influence. By contrast, however, the mere presence of obstetric complications or low birthweight or premature gestation would not be sufficient on its own.

The guidelines with respect to genetic counseling are, first, that the counselor should provide the family with as honest and well informed an account as is possible in the present state of knowledge. This should include as clear a statement as possible about what is reasonably definite with respect to what is said and what is much more uncertain (indicating why and how the uncertainty arises). Second, the counselor's job is to provide the family with the information that is necessary for them to come to their own decision on whatever issue is being considered. It is not acceptable for the counselor to attempt to push the family in one direction or another. Third, counseling must pay due attention to the ethical issues involved. For example, it is not at all uncommon for the parents of an autistic child to want advice on the risks that an unaffected sibling will have a child with autism. Unless the unaffected sibling (i.e., the parent or potential parent of the grandchild) is part of the consultation, it would be improper for advice to be given. Of course, it is entirely proper for grandparents to be concerned about the risks for one of their grandchildren but advice should not be given without the agreement and full involvement of the actual parents.

It is very common for families to ask whether or not there is some genetic test that could be done that would help particularize the recurrence risks that are involved. With the exception of the testing for the fragile X anomaly and the MECP2 gene (and testing for chromosome abnormalities), there are no applicable genetic tests. However, even when some susceptibility genes for idiopathic autism are found, there will still be marked limitations in what can be achieved by genetic screening. The point is that with a multifactorial disorder, the finding that someone has a susceptibility gene does not translate easily into a person-specific risk. That is because, unlike the situation with a Mendelian single gene disorder, the risks are probabilistic and may well vary according to other background genetic factors, as well as being possibly contingent on the co-occurrence of some important environmental risk factors. The findings on the APOE4 gene and Alzheimer's disease well illustrate the problem. The risk for Alzheimer's disease if someone is homozygous for the APOE4 allele is quite strong but it constitutes neither a necessary nor a sufficient cause (Liddell, Williams, & Owen, 2002). There are individuals with the APOE4 who will not develop Alzheimer's disease no matter how long they live and there are many individuals without the APOE4 gene who will nevertheless develop Alzheimer's disease. Also, for reasons that remain ill understood, the risk varies across ethnic groups (Kalaria, 2003). Whether or not the same will apply with susceptibility genes for autism remains quite unknown but it is important to be realistic that, even when susceptibility genes have been found, there will be considerable difficulties in translating the findings into a person-specific risk. That is particularly so when, at present, we know so little about environmental risk factors.

Neural Basis for Autism

The real potential value of genetic research in autism lies in the probability that it will provide invaluable leads for biological studies that will succeed eventually in identifying the neural basis of autism. Identification of the susceptibility genes will not, of course, do that on its own. Genes code for proteins and not for psychiatric disorders or behaviors (Rutter, 2004). Many areas of science will be needed in delineating the indirect pathways leading from susceptibility genes through effects on proteins and protein products, through physiological and neurochemical processes, and ultimately to the proximal pathway that leads to the syndrome of autism (Rutter, 2000). This wide-ranging program of research will need to consider how and why there is a transition in some individuals from the broader phenotype to the more seriously handicapping disorder of autism and why autism and autism spectrum disorders are so much more frequent in males than in females (Rutter, Caspi, et al., 2003). If the susceptibility genes are concerned, not with autism as such, but with continuously distributed risk characteristics or subcomponents of autism, there will be the further need to sort out why and how they come together to constitute the syndrome as a whole (Bock & Goode, 2003).

Prevention and Treatment

The ultimate goal, of course, is that this knowledge on the neural basis of autism, together with a parallel understanding of the mode of operation of identified environmental risk factors, will enable the development of new methods of prevention and intervention that will be much more effective than anything that we have available today. To what extent knowledge on the pathophysiology of autism will in fact lead to effective methods of prevention or intervention will, inevitably, depend on just what that pathophysiology comprises. Nevertheless, at the moment, it remains a puzzle that there is every reason to suppose that autism constitutes a systemwide disorder rather than being the result of some localized brain lesion, but yet neurochemical investigations have been so inconclusive and the results of pharmacological treatments so extremely disappointing.

CONCLUSION

At present, the clinical payoff from genetic research has been quite modest and it remains to be seen just what it will deliver, but there is every reason to suppose that susceptibility genes for autism will be identified during the next decade (probably much earlier than that) and that ultimately the biological understanding, which should follow from the studies to which this identification will give rise, will transform clinical practice in the field of autism spectrum disorders in ways that should be beneficial for children and their families.

Cross-References

Issues of diagnosis are discussed in Chapters 1 and 3 through 6, epidemiology is discussed in Chapter 2, other neurobiological issues are discussed in Chapters 17 through 20.

REFERENCES

Alarcón, M., Cantor, R. M., Liu, J., Gilliam, T. C., The Autism Genetic Resource Exchange Consortium, & Geschwind, D. (2002). Evidence for a language quantitative trait locus on chromosome 7q in multiplex autism families. *American Journal of Human Genetics, 70,* 60–71.

Amir, R. E., van den Veyver, I. B., Schultz, R., Malicki, D. M., Tran, C. Q., Dahle, E. J., et al. (2000). Influence of mutation type and X chromosome inactivation on Rett syndrome phenotypes. *Annals of Neurology, 47,* 670–679.

Amir, R. E., van den Veyver, I. B., Wan, M., Tran, C. Q., Francke, U., & Zoghbi, H. Y. (1999). Rett syndrome is caused by mutations in X-linked MECP2, encoding methyl-CpG-binding protein 2. *Nature Genetics, 23,* 185–188.

Ardlie, K. G., Lunetta, K. L., & Seielstad, M. (2002). Testing for population subdivision and association in four case control studies. *American Journal of Human Genetics, 71,* 304–311.

Ashley-Koch, A., Wolpert, C. M., Menold, M. M., Zaeem, L., Basu, S., Donnelly, S. L., et al. (1999). Genetic studies of autistic disorder and chromosome 7. *Genomics, 61,* 227–236.

August, G. J., Stewart, M. A., & Tsai, L. (1981). The incidence of cognitive disabilities in the siblings of autistic children. *British Journal of Psychiatry, 138,* 416–422.

Auranen, M., Vanhala, R., Varilo, T., Ayers, K., Kempas, E., Ylisaukko-Oja, T., et al. (2002). A genomewide screen for autism-spectrum disorders: Evidence for a major susceptibility locus on chromosome 3q25–27. *American Journal of Human Genetics, 71,* 777–790.

Auranen, M., Varilo, T., Alen, R., Vanhala, R., Ayers, K., Kempas, E., et al. (2003). Evidence for allelic association on chromosome 3q25–27 in families with autism spectrum disorders originating from a subisolate of Finland. *Molecular Psychiatry, 8,* 879–884.

Badner, J. A., & Gershon, E. S. (2002). Regional meta-analyses of published data supports linkage of autism with markers on chromosome 7. *Molecular Psychiatry, 7,* 56–66.

Bailey, A., Bolton, P., Butler, L., Le Couteur, A., Murphy, M., Scott, S., et al. (1993). Prevalence of the fragile X anomaly amongst autistic twins and singletons. *Journal of Child Psychology and Psychiatry, 34,* 673–688.

Bailey, A., Le Couteur, A., Gottesman, I., Bolton, P., Simonoff, E., Yuzda, F. Y., et al. (1995). Autism as a strongly genetic disorder: Evidence from a British twin study. *Psychological Medicine, 25,* 63–77.

Bailey, A., Palferman, S., Heavey, L., & Le Couteur, A. (1998). Autism: The phenotype in relatives. *Journal of Autism and Developmental Disorders, 28,* 369–392.

Baird, G., Charman, T., Baron-Cohen, S., Cox, A., Swettenham, J., Wheelwright, S., et al. (2000). A screening instrument for autism at 18 months of age: A 6-year follow-up study. *Journal of the American Academy of Child and Adolescent Psychiatry, 39,* 694–702.

Barcellos, L. F., Klitz, W., Field, L. L., Tobias, R., Bowcock, A. M., Wilson, R., et al. (1997). Association mapping of disease loci, by use of a pooled DNA genomic screen. *American Journal of Human Genetics, 61,* 734–747.

Baron-Cohen, S. (2002). The extreme male brain theory of autism. *Trends in Cognitive Sciences, 6,* 248–254.

Baron-Cohen, S. (2003). *The essential difference: Men, women and the extreme male brain.* London: Allen Lane.

Baron-Cohen, S., Richler, J., Bisarya, D., Gurunathan, N., & Wheelwright, S. (2003). The systemizing quotient: An investigation of adults with Asperger syndrome or high-functioning autism, and normal sex differences. *Philosophical Transactions of the Royal Society, London, B., 358,* 361–374.

Barrett, S., Beck, J. C., Bernier, R., Bisson, E., Braun, T. A., Casavant, T. L., et al. (1999). An autosomal genomic screen for autism: Collaborative linkage study of autism. *American Journal of Medical Genetics: Neuropsychiatric Genetics, 88,* 609–615.

Bernard, S., Enayati, A., Redwood, L., Roger, H., & Binstock, T. (2001). Autism: A novel form of mercury poisoning. *Medical Hypotheses, 56,* 462–471.

Betancur, C., Leboyer, M., & Gillberg, C. (2002). Increased rate of twins among affected sibling pairs with autism. *American Journal of Human Genetics, 70,* 1381–1383.

Beyer, K. S., Blasi, F., Bacchelli, E., Klauck, S. M., Maestrini, E., Poustka, A., et al. (2002). Mutation analysis of the coding sequence of the MECP2 gene in infantile autism. *Human Genetics, 111,* 305–309.

Bishop, D. V. M., Maybery, M., Wong, D., Maley, A., Hill, W., & Hallmayer, J. (2004). Are phonological processing deficits part of the broad autism phenotype? *American Journal of Medical Genetics: Neuropsychiatric Genetics, 1283,* 54–60.

Bock, G., & Goode, J. (Eds.). (2003). *Autism: Neural basis and treatment possibilities* (Novartis Foundation Symposium 251). Chichester, England: Wiley.

Bolton, P. F., & Griffiths, P. D. (1997). Association of tuberous sclerosis of temporal lobes with autism and atypical autism. *Lancet, 349,* 392–395.

Bolton, P. F., Macdonald, H., Pickles, A., Rios, P., Goode, S., Crowson, M., et al. (1994). A case-control family history study of autism. *Journal of Child Psychology and Psychiatry, 35,* 877–900.

Bolton, P. F., Murphy, M., Macdonald, H., Whitlock, B., Pickles, A., & Rutter, M. (1997). Obstetric complications in autism: Consequences or causes of the condition? *Journal of the American Academy of Child and Adolescent Psychiatry, 36,* 272–281.

Bolton, P. F., Park, R. J., Higgins, J. N., Griffiths, P. D., & Pickles, A. (2002). Neuro-epileptic determinants of autism spectrum disorders in tuberous sclerosis complex. *Brain, 125,* 1247–1255.

Bolton, P., Pickles, A., Murphy, M., & Rutter, M. (1998). Autistic, affective and other psychiatric disorders: Patterns of familial aggregation. *Psychological Medicine, 28,* 385–395.

Bonora, E., Beyer, K. S., Lamb, J. A., Parr, J. R., Klauck, S. M., Benner, A., et al. (2003). Analysis of reelin as a candidate gene for autism. *Molecular Psychiatry, 8,* 885–892.

Bradford, Y., Haines, J., Hutcheson, H., Gardiner, M., Braun, T., Sheffield, V., et al. (2001). Incorporating language phenotypes strengthens evidence of linkage to autism. *American Journal of Medical Genetics: Neuropsychiatric Genetics, 105,* 539–547.

Brown, R., Hobson, R. P., & Lee, A. (1997). Are there autistic-like features in congenitally blind children? *Journal of Child Psychology and Psychiatry, 38,* 693–703.

Buxbaum, J. D., Silverman, J. M., Smith, C. J., Greenberg, D. A., Kilifarski, M., Reichert, J., et al. (2002). Association between a GABRB3

polymorphism and autism. *Molecular Psychiatry, 7,* 311–316.

Buxbaum, J. D., Silverman, J. M., Smith, C. J., Kilifarski, M., Reichert, J., Hollander, E., et al. (2001). Evidence for a susceptibility gene for autism on chromosome 2 and for genetic heterogeneity. *American Journal of Human Genetics, 68,* 1514–1520.

Cardon, L. R., & Palmer, L. J. (2003). Population stratification and spurious allelic association. *Lancet, 361,* 598–604.

Carney, R. M., Wolpert, C. M., Ravan, S. A., Shahbazian, M., Ashley-Kioch, A., Cuccaro, M. L., et al. (2003). Identification of MECP2 mutations in a series of females with autistic disorder. *Pediatric Neurology, 28,* 205–211.

Chakrabarti, S., & Fombonne, E. (2001). Pervasive developmental disorders in preschool children. *Journal of the American Medical Association, 285,* 3093–3099.

Chess, S. (1977). Follow-up report on autism in congenital rubella. *Journal of Autism and Childhood Schizophrenia, 7,* 69–81.

Chess, S., Kern, S. J., & Fernandez, P. B. (1971). *Psychiatric disorders of children with congenital rubella.* New York: Brunner/Mazel.

Clarkson, T. W. (1997). The toxicology of mercury. *Critical Review of Clinical Laboratory Science, 34,* 369–403.

Clegg, J., Hollis, C., Mawhood, L., & Rutter, M. (in press). Developmental language disorders: A follow-up in later adult life: Cognitive, language and psychosocial outcomes. *Journal of Child Psychology and Psychiatry.*

Collaborative Linkage Study of Autism. (1999). An autosomal genomic screen for autism. *American Journal of Medical Genetics, 88,* 609–615.

Cohen, P., Cohen, J., & Brook, J. S. (1995). Bringing in the sheaves, or just gleaning? A methodological warning. *International Journal of Methods in Psychiatric Research, 5,* 263–266.

Constantino, J. N., & Todd, R. D. (2003). Autistic traits in the general population: A twin study. *Archives of General Psychiatry, 60,* 524–530.

Cook, E. H., & Leventhal, B. L. (1996). The serotonin system in autism. *Current Opinion in Pediatrics, 8,* 348–354.

Dales, L., Hammer, S. J., & Smith, N. J. (2001). Time trends in autism and in MMR immunization coverage in California. *Journal of the American Medical Association, 285,* 1183–1185.

Daniels, J., Holmans, J., Williams, N., Turic, D., McGuffin, P., Plomin, R., et al. (1998). A simple method for analyzing microsatellite allele image patterns generated from DNA pools and its application to allelic association studies.

American Journal of Human Genetics, 62, 1189–1197.

Davis, S., Schroeder, M., Goldin, L. R., & Weeks, D. E. (1996). Nonparametric simulation-based statistics for detecting linkage in general pedigrees. *American Journal of Human Genetics, 58,* 867–880.

DeLong, R., & Nohria, C. (1994). Psychiatric family history and neurological disease in autistic spectrum disorders. *Developmental Medicine and Child Neurology, 36,* 441–448.

Donnelly, S. L., Wolpert, C. M., Menold, M. M., Bass, M. P., Gilbert, J. R., Cuccaro, M. L., et al. (2000). Female with autistic disorder and monosomy X (Turner syndrome): Parent-of-origin effect of the X chromosome. *American Journal of Medical Genetics, 96,* 312–316.

Dykens, M., & Volkmar, F. (1997). Medical conditions associated with autism. In D. J. Cohen & F. R. Volkmar (Eds.), *Handbook of autism and pervasive developmental disorders* (2nd ed., pp. 388–410). New York: Wiley.

Eaves, L. J., Kendler, K. S., & Schulz, S. C. (1986). The familial-sporadic classification: Its power for the resolution of genetic and environmental etiologic factors. *Journal of Psychiatric Research, 20,* 115–130.

Farrington, C. P., Miller, E., & Taylor, B. (2001). MMR and autism: Further evidence against a causal association. *Vaccine, 19,* 3632–3635.

Fisher, S. E., Francks, C., Marlow, A. J., MacPhie, I. L., Newbury, D. F., Cardon, L. R., et al. (2002). Independent genome-wide scans identify a chromosome 18 quantitative-trait locus influencing dyslexia. *Nature Genetics, 30,* 86–91.

Fisher, S. E., Marlow, A. J., Lamb, J., Maestrini, E., Williams, D. F., Richardson, A. J., et al. (1999). A quantitative-trait locus on chromosome 6p influences different aspects of developmental dyslexia. *American Journal of Human Genetics, 64,* 146–156.

Folstein, S. E., Down, M., Mankoski, R., & Tadevosyan, O. (2003). How might genetic mechanisms operate in autism? In G. Bock & J. Goode (Eds.), *Autism: Neural basis and treatment possibilities* (Novartis Foundation Symposium 251, pp. 70–83). Chichester, England: Wiley.

Folstein, S. E., & Mankoski, R. E. (2000). Chromosome 7q: Where autism meets language disorder? *American Journal of Human Genetics, 67,* 278–281.

Folstein, S. E., & Piven, J. (1991). Etiology of autism: Genetic influences. *Pediatrics, 87,* 767–773.

Folstein, S. E., & Rosen-Sheidley, B. (2001). Genetics of autism: Complex aetiology for a heterogeneous disorder. *Nature Reviews: Genetics, 2,* 943–955.

Folstein, S. E., & Rutter, M. (1977a). Genetic influences and infantile autism. *Nature, 265,* 726–728.

Folstein, S. E., & Rutter, M. (1977b). Infantile autism: A genetic study of 21 pairs. *Journal of Child Psychology and Psychiatry, 18,* 297–321.

Folstein, S. E., & Rutter, M. (1988). Autism: Familial aggregation and genetic implications. *Journal of Autism and Developmental Disorders, 18,* 3–30.

Fombonne, E. (1999). The epidemiology of autism: A review. *Psychological Medicine, 29,* 769–786.

Fombonne, E. (2003). Epidemiological surveys of autism and other pervasive developmental disorders: An update. *Journal of Autism and Developmental Disorders, 33,* 365–382.

Fombonne, E., Bolton, P., Prior, J., Jordan, H., & Rutter, M. (1997). A family study of autism: Cognitive patterns and levels in parents and siblings. *Journal of Child Psychology and Psychiatry, 38,* 667–683.

Fombonne, E., & Chakrabarti, S. (2001). No evidence for a new variant of measles-mumps-rubella-induced autism. *Pediatrics, 108,* E58.

Fombonne, E., Rogé, B., Claverie, J., Courty, S., & Fremolle, J. (1999). Microcephaly and macrocephaly in autism. *Journal of Autism and Developmental Disorders, 29,* 113–119.

Gharani, N., Benayed, R., Mancuso, V., Brzustowicz, L. M., & Millonig, J. H. (2004). Association of the homeobox transcription factor, *ENGRAILED 2,* with autism spectrum disorder. *Molecular Psychiatry, 9,* 474–484.

Gillberg, C. (1989). The borderland of autism and Rett syndrome: Five case histories to highlight diagnostic difficulties. *Journal of Autism and Developmental Disorders, 19,* 545–559.

Gillberg, C. (1990). Medical work-up in children with autism and Asperger syndrome. *Brain Dysfunction, 3,* 249–260.

Gillberg, C. (1992). Autism and autism-like conditions: Sub-classes among disorders of empathy. *Journal of Child Psychology and Psychiatry, 33,* 813–842.

Gillberg, C. (1998). Chromosomal disorders and autism. *Journal of Autism and Developmental Disorders, 28,* 415–425.

Gillberg, C., & Coleman, M. (1996). Autism and medical disorders: A review of the literature. *Developmental Medicine and Child Neurology, 38,* 191–202.

Gillberg, C., & Forsell, C. (1984). Childhood psychosis and neurofibromatosis—more than a coincidence? *Journal of Autism and Developmental Disorders, 14,* 1–8.

Gillberg, C., & Wahlstrom, J. (1985). Chromosome abnormalities in infantile autism and other childhood psychoses: A population study of 66 cases. *Developmental Medicine and Child Neurology, 27,* 293–304.

Greenberg, D. A., Hodge, S. E., Sowinski, J., & Nicoll, D. (2001). Excess of twins among affected sibling pairs with autism: Implications for the etiology of autism. *American Journal of Human Genetics, 69,* 1062–1067.

Grigorenko, E. L., Wood, F. B., Meyer, M. S., Hart, L. A., Speed, W. C., Shuster, A., et al. (1997). Susceptibility loci for distinct components of developmental dyslexia on chromosomes 6 and 15. *American Journal of Human Genetics, 60,* 27–39.

Gurling, H. M. D., Bolton, P. F., Vincent, J., Melmer, G., & Rutter, M. (1997). Molecular and cytogenetic investigations of the fragile X region including the FRAX and FRAX E CGG trinucleotide repeat sequences in families multiplex for autism and related phenotypes. *Human Heredity, 47,* 254–262.

Gutknecht, L. (2001). Full-genome scans with autistic disorder: A review. *Behavior Genetics, 31,* 113–123.

Guy, J., Hendrich, B., Holmes, M., Martin, J. E., & Bird, A. (2001). A mouse MECP2-null mutation causes neurological symptoms that mimic Rett syndrome. *Nature Genetics, 27,* 322–326.

Hagberg, B. (1985). Rett's syndrome: Prevalence and impact on progressive severe mental retardation in girls. *Acta Paediatrica Scandinavica, 74,* 405–408.

Hagberg, B., Aircardi, J., Dias, K., & Ramos, O. (1983). A progressive syndrome of autism, dementia, ataxia and loss of purposeful hand use in girls: Rett syndrome; report of 35 cases. *Annals of Neurology, 14,* 471–479.

Hallmayer, J., Glasson, E. J., Bower, C., Petterson, B., Croen, L., Grether, J., et al. (2002). On the twin risk in autism. *American Journal of Human Genetics, 71,* 941–946.

Hallmayer, J., Hebert, J. M., Spiker, D., Lotspeich, L., McMahon, W. M., Petersen, P. B., et al. (1996). Autism and the X chromosome: Multipoint sib-pair analysis. *Archives of General Psychiatry, 53,* 980–983.

Hanson, D. R., & Gottesman, I. (1976). The genetics, if any, of infantile autism and childhood schizophrenia. *Journal of Autism and Schizophrenia, 6,* 209–233.

Hillman, R. E., Kanafani, N., Takahashi, T. N., & Miles, J. H. (2000). Prevalence of autism in Missouri: Changing trends and the effect of a comprehensive state autism project. *Missouri Medicine, 97,* 159–163.

Hodge, S. E., Greenberg, D. A., Betancur, C., & Gillberg, C. (2002). Response to Visscher. *American Journal of Human Genetics, 71,* 996–999.

Honda, H., Shimizu, Y., & Rutter, M. (submitted) *No effect of MMR withdrawal on the incidence of autism: A total population study.*

Howlin, P., Mawhood, L., & Rutter, M. (2000). Autism and developmental receptive language disorder: A comparative follow-up in early adult life: II. Social behavioural, and psychiatric outcomes. *Journal of Child Psychology and Psychiatry, 41,* 561–578.

Hviid, A., Stellfeld, M., Wohlfahrt, J., & Melbye, M. (2003). Association between Thimerosal-containing vaccine and autism. *Journal of the American Medical Association, 290,* 1763–1766.

International Molecular Genetic Study of Autism Consortium. (1998). A full genome screen for autism with evidence for linkage to a region on chromosome 7q. *Human Molecular Genetics, 7,* 571–578.

International Molecular Genetic Study of Autism Consortium. (2001a). Further characterization of the autism susceptibility locus *AUTS1* on chromosome 7. *Human Molecular Genetics, 10,* 973–982.

International Molecular Genetic Study of Autism Consortium. (2001b). A genomewide screen for autism: Strong evidence for linkage to chromosomes 2q, 7q and 16p. *American Journal of Human Genetics, 69,* 570–581.

Jaenisch, R., & Bird, A. (2003). Epigenetic regulation of gene expression: How the genome integrates intrinsic and environmental signals. *Nature Genetics Supplement, 33,* 245–254.

Jamain, S., Betancur, C., Quach, H., Philippe, A., Fellous, M., Giros, B., et al. (2002). Linkage and association of the glutamate receptor 6 gene with autism. *Molecular Psychiatry, 7,* 302–310.

Jamain, S., Quach, H., Quintana-Murci, L., Betancur, C., Philippe, A., Gillberg, C., et al. (2002). Y chromosome haplogroups in autistic subjects. *Molecular Psychiatry, 7,* 217–219.

Jensen, A. R. (1997). The puzzle of nongenetic variance. In R. J. Sternberg & E. L. Grigorenko (Eds.), *Intelligence, heredity, and environment* (pp. 42–88). Cambridge, England: Cambridge University Press.

Kalaria, R. N. (2003). Dementia comes of age in the developing world. *Lancet, 361,* 888–889.

Kanner, L. (1943). Autistic disturbances of affective contact. *Nervous Child, 2,* 217–250.

Kaye, J. A., Melero-Montes, M., & Jick, H. (2001). Mumps, measles, and rubella vaccine and the incidence of autism recorded by general practitioners: A time trend analysis. *British Medical Journal, 322,* 460–463.

Kim, S.-J., Herzing, L. B. K., Veenstra-Vander-Weele, J., Lord, C., Couchesne, R., Leventhal, B. L., et al. (2002). Mutation screening and transmission disequilibrium study of ATP10C in autism. *American Journal of Medical Genetics: Neuropsychiatric Genetics, 114,* 137–143.

Lai, C. S., Fisher, S. E., Hurst, J. A., Vargha-Khadem, F., & Monaco, A. P. (2001). A forkhead-domain gene is mutated in a severe speech and language disorder. *Nature, 413,* 519–523.

Lainhart, J., Piven, J., Wzorek, M., & Landa, R. (1997). Macrocephaly in children and adults with autism. *Journal of the American Academy of Child and Adolescent Psychiatry, 36,* 282–290.

Lamb, J. A., Moore, J., Bailey, A., & Monaco, A. P. (2000). Autism: Recent molecular genetic advances. *Human Molecular Genetics, 9,* 861–868.

Lamb, J. A., Parr, J. R., Bailey, A. J., & Monaco, A. P. (2002). Autism: In search of susceptibility genes. *Neuromolecular Medicine, 2,* 11–28.

Landa, R., Piven, J., Wzorek, M., Gayle, J. O., Chase, G. A., & Folstein, S. E. (1992). Social language use in parents in autistic individuals. *Psychological Medicine, 22,* 245–254.

Landa, R., Wzorek, M., Piven, J., Folstein, S. E., & Isaacs, C. (1991). Spontaneous narrative discourse characteristics of parents of autistic individuals. *Journal of Speech and Hearing Research, 34,* 1339–1345.

Lauritsen, M., & Ewald, H. (2001). The genetics of autism. *Acta Paediatrica Scandinavica, 103,* 411–427.

Le Couteur, A., Bailey, A. J., Goode, S., Pickles, A., Robertson, S., Gottesman, I., et al. (1996). A broader phenotype of autism: The clinical spectrum in twins. *Journal of Child Psychology and Psychiatry, 37,* 785–801.

Le Couteur, A., Lord, C., & Rutter, M. (2003). *Autism Diagnostic Interview-Revised.* Los Angeles: Western Psychological Services.

Le Couteur, A., Rutter, M., Lord, C., Rios, P., Robertson, S., Holdgrafer, M., et al. (1989). Autism Diagnostic Interview: A standardized investigator-based interview. *Journal of Autism and Developmental Disorders, 19,* 363–387.

Liddell, M. B., Williams, J., & Owen, M. J. (2002). The dementias. In P. McGuffin, M. J. Owen, & I. I. Gottesman (Eds.), *Psychiatric genetics and genomics* (pp. 341–393). Oxford, England: Oxford University Press.

Liu, J., Nyholt, D. R., Magnussen, P., Parano, E., Pavone, P., Geschwind, D., et al. (2001). A genomewide screen for autism susceptibility

loci. *American Journal of Human Genetics, 69,* 327–340.

Lord, C., Rutter, M., Goode, S., Heemsbergen, J., Jordan, H., & Mawhood, L. (1989). Autism Diagnostic Observation Schedule: A standardized observation of communicative and social behavior. *Journal of Autism and Developmental Disorders, 19,* 185–212.

Lord, C., Rutter, M., & Le Couteur, A. (1994). Autism Diagnostic Interview–Revised: A revised version of a diagnostic interview for caregivers of individuals with possible pervasive developmental disorders. *Journal of Autism and Developmental Disorders, 24,* 659–685.

Lotter, V. (1966). Epidemiology of autistic conditions in young children: 1. Prevalence. *Social Psychiatry, 1,* 124–137.

Madsen, K. M., Hviid, A., Vestergaard, M., Schendel, D., Wohlfahrt, J., Thorsen, P., et al. (2002). A population-based study of measles, mumps, and rubella vaccination and autism. *New England Journal of Medicine, 347,* 1477–1482.

Madsen, K. E., Lauritsen, M. B., Pedersent, C. B., Thorsen, P., Plesner, A.-M., Andersen, P. H., et al. (2003). Thimerosal and the occurrence of autism: Negative ecological evidence from Danish population-based data. *Pediatrics, 112,* 604–606.

Maestrini, E., Marlow, A. J., Weeks, D. E., & Monaco, A. P. (1998). Molecular genetic studies of autism. *Journal of Autism and Developmental Disorders, 28,* 427–437.

Malhotra, A. K., & Goldman, D. (1999). Benefits and pitfalls encountered in psychiatric genetic association studies. *Biological Psychiatry, 45,* 544–550.

Medical Research Council. (2001). *MRC review of autism research: Epidemiology and causes.* London: Author.

Miles, J. H., & Hillman, R. E. (2000). Value of a clinical morphology examination in autism. *American Journal of Medical Genetics, 91,* 245–253.

Molenaar, P. C. M., Boomsma, D. I., & Dolan, C. V. (1993). A third source of developmental differences. *Behavior Genetics, 23,* 519–524.

Murphy, M., Bolton, P., Pickles, A., Fombonne, E., Piven, J., & Rutter, M. (2000). Personality traits in the relatives of autistic probands. *Psychological Medicine, 30,* 1411–1424.

Myrianthopoulos, N. C., & Melnick, M. (1977). Malformations in monozygotic twins: A possible source of environmental influence on the developmental genetic clock. In E. Inouye & H. Nishimusa (Eds.), *Gene-environment interactions in common diseases* (pp. 206–220). Baltimore: University Park Press.

Nelson, K. B. (1991). Prenatal and perinatal factors in the etiology of autism. *Pediatrics, 87,* 761–766.

Newbury, D. F., Bonora, E., Lamb, J. A., Fisher, S. E., Lai, C. S. L., Baird, G., et al. (2002). FOXP2 is not a major susceptibility gene for autism or specific language impairment. *American Journal of Human Genetics, 70,* 1318–1327.

Nurmi, E. L., Amin, T., Olson, L. M., Jacobs, M. M., McCauley, J. L., Lam, A. Y., et al. (2003). Dense linkage disequilibrium mapping in the 15q11-q13 maternal expression domain yields evidence for association in autism. *Molecular Psychiatry, 8,* 624–634.

Olsson, B., & Rett, A. (1985). Behavioural observations concerning differential diagnosis between the Rett's syndrome and autism. *Brain and Development, 7,* 281–289.

Olsson, B., & Rett, A. (1987). Autism and Rett syndrome: Behavioural investigations and differential diagnosis. *Developmental Medicine and Child Neurology, 29,* 429–441.

Parr, J. R., Baird, G., Le Couteur, A., Rutter, M., Fombonne, E., Bailey, A. J., et al. (poster) *Autism regression in a genetically related sample.*

Philippe, A., Martinez, M., Guilloud-Bataille, M., Gillberg, C., Rastam, M., Sponheim, E., et al. (1999). Genome-wide scan for autism susceptibility genes. *Human Molecular Genetics, 8,* 805–812.

Pichichero, M. E., Cernichiari, E., Lopreiato, J., & Treanor, J. (2002). Mercury concentrations and metabolism in infants receiving vaccines containing Thiomersal: A descriptive study. *Lancet, 360,* 1737–1741.

Pickles, A., Bolton, P., Macdonald, H., Bailey, A., Le Couteur, A., Sim, L., et al. (1995). Latent class analysis of recurrence risk for complex phenotypes with selection and measurement error: A twin and family history study of autism. *American Journal of Human Genetics, 57,* 717–726.

Pickles, A., Starr, E., Kazak, S., Bolton, P., Papanikolau, K., Bailey, A. J., et al. (2000). Variable expression of the autism broader phenotype: Findings from extended pedigrees. *Journal of Child Psychology and Psychiatry, 41,* 491–502.

Piven, J., Chase, G. A., Landa, R., Wzorek, M., Gayle, J., Cloud, D., et al. (1991). Psychiatric disorders in the parents of autistic individuals. *Journal of the American Academy of Child and Adolescent Psychiatry, 30,* 471–478.

Piven, J., Gayle, J., Chase, J., Fink, B., Landa, R., Wrozek, M., et al. (1990). A family history study of neuropsychiatric disorders in the adult siblings of autistic individuals. *Journal of the American Academy of Child and Adolescent Psychiatry, 29,* 177–183.

Piven, J., & Palmer, P. (1997). Cognitive deficits in parents from multiple-incidence autism families. *Journal of Child Psychology and Psychiatry, 38,* 1011–1022.

Piven, J., Palmer, P., Jacobi, D., Childress, D., & Arndt, S. (1997). The broader autism phenotype: Evidence from a family study of multiple-incidence autism families. *American Journal of Psychiatry, 154,* 185–190.

Piven, J., Wzorek, M., Landa, R., Lainhart, J., Bolton, P., Chase, G. A., et al. (1994). Personality characteristics of the parents of autistic individuals. *Psychological Medicine, 24,* 783–795.

Pocock, S. J. (1983). *Clinical trials: A practical approach.* Chichester, England: Wiley.

Pritchard, J. K. (2001). Are rare variants responsible for susceptibility to complex diseases? *American Journal of Human Genetics, 69,* 124–137.

Ramoz, N., Reichert, J. G., Smith, C. J., Silverman, J. M., Bespalova, I. N., Davis, K. L., et al. (2004). Linkage and association of the mitochondrial aspartate/glutamate carrier SLC25A12 gene with autism. *American Journal of Psychiatry, 161,* 662–669.

Reik, W., & Walter, J. (2001). Genomic imprinting: Parental influence on the genome. *Nature Reviews: Genetics, 2,* 21–32.

Reiss, A. L., & Dant, C. C. (2003). The behavioral neurogenetics of fragile X syndrome: Analyzing gene-brain-behavior relationships in child developmental psychopathologies. *Development and Psychopathology, 15,* 927–968.

Risch, N., & Merikangas, K. (1996). The future of genetic studies of complex human diseases. *Science, 273,* 1516–1517.

Risch, N., Spiker, D., Lotspeich, L., Nouri, N., Hinds, D., Hallmayer, J., et al. (1999). A genomic screen of autism: Evidence for a multilocus etiology. *American Journal of Human Genetics, 65,* 493–507.

Risch, N., & Zhang, H. (1995). Extreme discordant sib pairs for mapping quantitative trait loci in humans. *Science, 268,* 1584–1589.

Risch, N., & Zhang, H. (1996). Mapping quantitative trait loci with extreme discordant sib pairs: Sampling considerations. *American Journal of Human Genetics, 58,* 836–843.

Roberts, S. B., MacLean, C. J., Neale, M. C., Eaves, L. J., & Kendler, K. S. (1999). Replication of linkage studies of complex traits: An examination of variation in location estimates. *American Journal of Human Genetics, 65,* 876–884.

Robertson, K. D., & Wolffe, A. P. (2000). DNA methylation in health and disease. *Nature Reviews: Genetics, 1,* 11–19.

Rodier, P., & Hyman, S. (1998). Early environmental factors in autism. *Mental Retardation and Developmental Disorders Research Review, 4,* 121–128.

Rutter, M. (1967). Psychotic disorders in early childhood. In A. J. Coppen & A. Walk (Eds.), *Recent developments in schizophrenia* (pp. 133–158). Ashford, Kent, England: Headley Bros/RMPA.

Rutter, M. (1968). Concepts of autism: A review of research. *Journal of Child Psychology and Psychiatry, 9,* 1–25.

Rutter, M. (1999a). The Emanuel Miller Memorial Lecture 1998. Autism: Two-way interplay between research and clinical work. *Journal of Child and Adolescent Psychiatry, 40,* 169–188.

Rutter, M. (1999b). Psychosocial adversity and child psychopathology. *British Journal of Psychiatry, 174,* 480–493.

Rutter, M. (2000). Genetic studies of autism: From the 1970s into the millennium. *Journal of Abnormal Child Psychology, 28,* 3–14.

Rutter, M. (2004). Pathways of genetic influences on psychopathology. *European Review, 12,* 19–33.

Rutter, M. (in press). *Autism research: Lessons from the past and prospects for the future.* Acta Paediatrica.

Rutter, M., Anderson-Wood, L., Beckett, C., Bredenkamp, D., Castle, J., Groothues, C., et al. (1999). Quasi-autistic patterns following severe early global privation. *Journal of Child Psychology and Psychiatry, 40,* 537–549.

Rutter, M., Bailey, A., Bolton, P., & Le Couteur, A. (1994). Autism and known medical conditions: Myth and substance. *Journal of Child Psychology and Psychiatry, 35,* 311–322.

Rutter, M., Bailey, A., Simonoff, E., & Pickles, A. (1997). Genetic influences and autism. In D. J. Cohen & F. R. Volkmar (Eds.), *Handbook of autism and pervasive developmental disorders* (2nd ed., pp. 370–387). New York: Wiley.

Rutter, M., Bolton, P., Harrington, R., Le Couteur, A., Macdonald, H., & Simonoff, E. (1990). Genetic factors in child psychiatric disorders: I. A review of research strategies. *Journal of Child Psychology and Psychiatry, 31,* 3–37.

Rutter, M., Caspi, A., & Moffitt, T. E. (2003). Making sense of sex differences in psychopathology: Unifying issues and research strategies. *Journal of Child Psychology and Psychiatry, 44,* 1092–1115.

Rutter, M., Le Couteur, A., & Lord, C. (2003). *ADI-R Autism Diagnostic Interview–Revised. Manual.* Los Angeles: Western Psychological Services.

Rutter, M., Silberg, J., O'Connor, T., & Simonoff, E. (1999). Genetics and Child psychiatry: I. Advances in quantitative and molecular genetics. *Journal of Child Psychology and Psychiatry, 40,* 3–18.

Shahbazian, M. D., Young, J. I., Yuva-Paylor, L. A., Spencer, C., Antalffy, B., Noebels, J., et al. (2002). Mice with truncated MeCP2 recapitulate many Rett syndrome features and display hyperacetylation of histone H3. *Neuron, 35,* 243–254.

Shao, Y. J., Cuccaro, M. L., Hauser, E. R., Raiford, K. L., Menold, M. M., Wolpert, C. M., et al. (2003). Fine mapping of autistic disorder to chromosome 15q11-q13 by use of phenotypic subtypes. *American Journal of Human Genetics, 72,* 539–548.

Shao, Y. J., Raiford, K. L., Wolpert, C. M., Cope, C. A., Ravan, S. A., Ashley-Koch, A. A., et al. (2002). Phenotypic homogeneity provides increased support for linkage on chromosome 2 in autistic disorder. *American Journal of Human Genetics, 70,* 1058–1061.

Shao, Y. J., Wolpert, C. M., Raiford, K. L., Menold, M. M., Donnelly, S. L., Ravan, S. A., et al. (2002). Genomic screen and follow-up analysis for autistic disorder. *American Journal of Medical Genetics, 114,* 99–105.

Silverman, J. M., Smith, C. J., Schmeidler, J., Hollander, E., Lawlor, B. A., Fitzgerald, M., et al. (2002). Symptom domains in autism and related conditions: Evidence for familiality. *American Journal of Medical Genetics: Neuropsychiatric Genetics, 114,* 64–73.

Simonoff, E. (1998). Genetic counseling in autism and pervasive developmental disorders. *Journal of Autism and Developmental Disorders, 28,* 447–456.

Simonoff, E. (2002). Genetic counseling. In M. Rutter & E. Taylor (Eds.), *Child and adolescent psychiatry* (4th ed., pp. 1101–1113). Oxford, England: Blackwell.

Simonoff, E., & Rutter, M. (2002). Autism and other behavioral disorders. In D. L. Rimoin, J. M. Connor, R. E. Pyeritz, & B. R. Korf (Eds.), *Emery and Rimoin's principles and practice of medical genetics* (4th ed., Vol. 3, pp. 2873–2893). London: Churchill Livingstone.

Skuse, D. H. (2000). Imprinting, the X chromosome, and the male brain: Explaining sex differences in the liability to autism. *Pediatric Research, 47,* 9–16.

Skuse, D. H. (2003). X-linked genes and the neural basis of social cognition. In G. Bock & J. Goode (Eds.) *Autism: Neural basis and treatment possibilities* (Novartis Foundation Symposium 251, pp. 84–108). Chichester, England: Wiley.

Skuse, D. H., James, R., Bishop, D., Coppihn, B., Dalton, P., Aamodt-Leeper, G., et al. (1997). Evidence from Turner's syndrome of an imprinted X-linked locus affective cognitive functioning. *Nature, 387,* 705–708.

Smalley, S. L. (1998). Autism and tuberous sclerosis. *Journal of Autism and Developmental Disorders, 28,* 407–414.

Smalley, S. L., McCracken, J. T., & Tanguay, P. E. (1995). Autism, affective disorders and social phobia. *American Journal of Medical Genetics, 60,* 19–26.

Spielman, R. S., & Ewens, W. J. (1996). Invited editorial: The TDT and other family-based tests for linkage disequilibrium and association. *American Journal of Human Genetics, 59,* 983–989.

Spiker, D., Lotspeich, L. J., Dimiceli, S., Myers, R. M., & Risch, N. (2002). Behavioral phenotypic variation in autism multiplex families: Evidence for a continuous severity gradient. *American Journal of Medical Genetics, 114,* 129–136.

Spiker, D., Lotspeich, L. J., Kraemer, H. C., Hallmayer, J., McMahon, W., Petersen, P. B., et al. (1994). Genetics of autism: Characteristics of affected and unaffected children from 37 multiplex families. *American Journal of Medical Genetics: Neuropsychiatric Genetics, 54,* 27–35.

Starr, E., Berument, S. K., Pickles, A., Tomlins, M., Bailey, A., Papanikolau, E., et al. (2001). A family genetic study of autism associated with profound mental retardation. *Journal of Autism and Developmental Disorders, 32,* 89–96.

Steffenburg, S., Gillberg, C., Hellgren, L., Andersson, L., Gillberg, I. C., Jakobsson, G., et al. (1989). A twin study of autism in Denmark, Finland, Iceland, Norway and Sweden. *Journal of Child Psychology and Psychiatry, 30,* 405–416.

Stratton, K., Gable, A., & McCormick, M. C. (Eds.). (2001). *Immunization safety review: Thimerosal-containing vaccines and neurodevelopmental disorders.* Washington, DC: National Academy Press.

Szatmari, P., Jones, M. B., Holden, J., Bryson, S. E., Mahoney, W. J., Tuff, L., et al. (1996). High phenotypic correlations among siblings with autism and pervasive development disorders. *American Journal of Medical Genetics: Neuropsychiatric Genetics, 67,* 354–360.

Szatmari, P., MacLean, J. E., Jones, M. B., Bryson, S. E., Zwaigenbaum, L., Bartolucci, G., et al. (2000). The familial aggregation of the lesser variant in biological and nonbiological relatives of PDD probands: A family history study. *Journal of Child Psychology and Psychiatry, 41,* 579–586.

Tager-Flusberg, H., & Joseph, R. M. (2003). Identifying neurocognitive phenotypes in autism. *Philosophical Transactions of the Royal Society, London, B., 358,* 303–314.

Taylor, B., Miller, E., Farrington, C. P., Petropoulos, M. C., Favot-Mayaud, I., Li, J., et al. (1999). Autism and measles, mumps, and rubella vaccine: No epidemiological evidence for a causal association. *Lancet, 353,* 2026–2029.

Taylor, B., Miller, E., Lingam, R., Andrews, N., Simmons, A., & Stowe, J. (2002). Measles, mumps, and rubella vaccination and bowel problems or developmental regression in children with autism: Population-based study. *British Medical Journal, 324,* 393–396.

Torrente, F., Ashwood, P., Day, R., Machado, N., Furlano, R. I., Anthony, A., et al. (2002). Small intestinal enteropathy with epithelial IgG and complement deposition in children with regressive autism. *Molecular Psychiatry, 7,* 375–382.

Tsai, L. (1987). Pre-, peri-, and neonatal factors in autism. In E. Schopler & G. B. Mesibov (Eds.), *Neurobiological issues in autism* (pp. 179–189). New York: Plenum Press.

Uchiyama, T., Kurosawa, M., & Inaba, Y. (submitted) *Does MMR vaccine cause so-called "regressive autism"?*

Veenstra-VanderWeele, J., Kim, S.-J., Lord, C., Courchesne, R., Akshoomoff, N., Leventhal, B. L., et al. (2002). Transmission disequilibrium studies of the serotonin 5-HT$_{2A}$ receptor gene (HTR2A) in autism. *American Journal of Medical Genetics (Neuropsychiatric Genetics), 114,* 277–283.

Verstraeten, T., Davis, R. L., DeStefano, F., Lieu, T. A., Rhodes, P. H., Black, S. B., et al. (2003). Safety of Thimerosal-containing vaccines: A two-phased study of computerized health maintenance organization databases. *Pediatrics, 112,* 1039–1048.

Visscher, P. M. (2002). Increased rate of twins among affected sib pairs. *American Journal of Human Genetics, 71,* 995–996.

Vogel, F., & Motulsky, A. G. (1997). *Human genetics: Problems and approaches* (3rd ed.). Berlin, Germany: Springer-Verlag.

Volkmar, F. R., & Cohen, D. J. (1991). Comorbid association of autism and schizophrenia. *American Journal of Psychiatry, 148,* 1704–1707.

Vourc'h, P., Bienvenu, T., Beldjord, C., Chelly, J., Barthélémy, C., Müh, J. P., et al. (2001). No mutations in the coding region of the Rett syndrome gene MECP2 in 59 autistic patients. *European Journal of Human Genetics, 9,* 556–558.

Wakefield, A. J., Anthony, A., Murch, S. H., Thomson, M., Montgomery, S. M., Davies, S., et al. (2000). Enterocolitis in children with developmental disorders. *American Journal of Gastroenterology, 95,* 2285–2295.

Wakefield, A. J., Murch, S. H., Anthony, A., Linnell, J., Casson, D. M., Malik, M., et al. (1998). Ileal-lymphoid-nodular hyperplasia, non-specific colitis, and pervasive developmental disorder in children. *Lancet, 351,* 637–641.

Wakefield, A. J., Puleston, J. M., Montgomery, S. M., Anthony, A., O'Leary, J. J., & Murch, S. H. (2002). Review article: The concept of enterocolonic encephalopathy, autism and opioid recepter ligands. *Alimentary Pharmacology Therapeutics, 16,* 663–674.

Weber, A. M., Egelhoff, J. C., McKellop, J. M., & Franz, D. N. (2000). Autism and the cerebellum: Evidence from tuberous sclerosis. *Journal of Autism and Developmental Disorders, 30,* 511–517.

Witt-Engerström, I., & Gillberg, C. (1987). Letter to the editor: Rett syndrome in Sweden. *Journal of Autism and Developmental Disorders, 17,* 149–150.

Woodhouse, W., Bailey, A., Rutter, M., Bolton, P., Baird, G., & Le Couteur, A. (1996). Head circumference in autism and other pervasive developmental disorders. *Journal of Child Psychology and Psychiatry, 37,* 785–801.

Yirmiya, N., Pilowsky, T., Tidhar, S., Nemanov, L., Altmark, L., & Ebstein, R. P. (2002). Family-based and population study of a functional promoter-region monoamine oxidase A polymorphism in autism: Possible association with, I. Q. *American Journal of Medical Genetics (Neuropsychiatric Genetics), 114,* 284–287.

Yonan, A. L., Alarcón, M., Cheng, R., Magnusson, P. K. E., Spence, S. J., Palmer, A. A., et al. (2003). A genomewide screen of 345 families for autism-susceptibility loci. *American Journal of Human Genetics, 73,* 886–897.

Yu, C.-E., Dawson, G., Munson, J., D'Souza, I., Osterling, J., Estes, A., et al. (2002). Presence of large deletions in kindreds with autism. *American Journal of Human Genetics, 71,* 100–115.

Zoghbi, H. Y. (2003). Postnatal neurodevelopmental disorders: Meeting at the synapse? *Science, 302,* 826–830.

CHAPTER 17

Neurochemical Studies of Autism

GEORGE M. ANDERSON AND YOSHIHIKO HOSHINO

The behavioral, emotional, and cognitive symptoms presented by autistic individuals clearly indicate that central nervous system (CNS) functioning is altered in autism. The early onset, pervasive nature, and chronicity of autism also point directly to brain abnormality. Furthermore, twin and family studies strongly suggest that autism has a genetic basis (Cook, 2001; Folstein & Piven, 1991; Lauritsen & Ewald, 2001; Lotspeich & Ciaranello, 1993; Rutter & Schopler, 1987; J. Young, Newcorn, & Leven, 1989; see Chapter 16).

Neurochemical studies of autistic individuals have been undertaken to examine processes related to neural transmission in the central and peripheral nervous systems. The search for neurochemical alterations and causes in autism is given impetus by the rapid advance of basic neuroscience and the success of neuropharmacology in the relatively specific treatment of a range of neurological and psychiatric disorders and symptoms. There is an increasing recognition that autism is polygenetic and heterogenetic, and that its neurobiology may be best approached by examining the component and continuous traits that combine in a particular individual to produce autism (Anderson & Cohen, 2002; Folstein & Rosen-Sheidley, 2001; McBride, Anderson, & Shapiro, 1996). Neurochemical and neuroendocrine measures offer promising endophenotypes for investigation.

A wide range of neurotransmitter and neuroendocrine systems have been examined. This examination, which we review in detail, has made its main goal the elucidation of etiology; but it also has been carried on in the hope that particular measures might have diagnostic and prognostic utility in the future. In this chapter, we deal primarily with neurochemical studies measuring levels of neurotransmitters; their metabolities; and associated enzymes in blood, urine, or cerebrospinal fluid (CSF). Separate sections on neurochemistry cover, in order, each of the three major central monoamine neurotransmitters: serotonin, dopamine, and norepinephrine. Following sections concern research on the hypothalamic-pituitary axis, the neuropeptides, amino acids, and acetylcholine, and the purines and related compounds.

Our review of these neurochemical and related neuroendocrine studies concentrates on recent findings and attempts to point out the more promising areas for research. A number of prior reviews have covered the biochemical research of autism either exclusively (Anderson, 1987, 2002; Anderson, Horne, Chatterjee, & Cohen, 1990; Cohen & Young, 1977; Cook, 1990; DeMyer et al., 1981; McBride, Anderson, & Mann, 1990; Ritvo, 1977; J. G. Young, Kavanagh, Anderson, Shaywitz, & Cohen, 1982; Yuwiler, Geller, & Ritvo, 1985) or as part of more general reviews (Anderson & Cohen, 2002).

SEROTONIN

Serotonin (5-hydroxytryptamine; 5-HT) is an important neurotransmitter in the central nervous system, where it is involved in controlling a number of important functions and behaviors, including sleep, mood, body temperature, appetite, and hormone release (Iverson & Iverson, 1981; Lucki, 1998). Cell bodies of most central neurons utilizing 5-HT as a neurotransmitter are located in the midbrain; however, the neurons make connections throughout the brain and spinal cord. Serotonin is synthesized from its amino acid precursor, tryptophan (TRP), by hydroxylation and decarboxylation, it is predominately metabolized to 5-hydroxyindoleacetic acid (5-HIAA), by the enzyme monoamine oxidase (MAO).

Serotonin is the neurotransmitter that has stimulated the most neurochemical research in autism. Initial interest in the possible role of 5-HT in autism arose from a consideration of its role in perception. The powerful effects of serotonergic hallucinogens, such as lysergic acid diethylamide (LSD), stimulated speculation around 5-HT and led to early studies of platelet 5-HT in autism (Schain & Freedman, 1961). Although much of the work has focused on the platelet hyperserotonemia of autism, a number of other observations have contributed to the increasing interest in 5-HT. Reports of a critical role for 5-HT during embryogenesis (Buznikov, 1984) and in the development of the central nervous system (Janusonis, Gluncic, & Rakic, 2004; Waage-Baudet et al., 2003; Whitaker-Azmitia, 2001; Whitaker-Azmitia, Druse, Walker, & Lauder, 1996; Zhou, Auerbach, & Azmitia, 1987) have made 5-HT of special interest in neurodevelopmental disorders.

Early studies of serotonergic drugs as possible therapeutic agents were not particularly promising. The 5-HT-releasing agent fenfluramine, despite initial enthusiasm, also has not been found to be of much use in treating autistic symptoms. However, a number of small treatment studies of 5-HT selective reuptake inhibitors—including clomipramine, fluvoxamine, and fluoxetine—have suggested that manipulation of the serotonergic system may be of some benefit (Posey & McDougle, 2000). Candidate gene studies and linkage analyses, while not definitive, have suggested that 5-HT-related genes, and especially the 5-HT transporter gene (*HTT*) may have some association with disorder risk or symptom expression (Cook, 2001).

To assess central and peripheral 5-HT function in autism, researchers have measured CSF and urine levels of the major metabolite of 5-HT, 5-HIAA, and blood and urine levels of 5-HT itself. Initial brain imaging studies have attempted to examine 5-HT synthesis rates in autism (Chugani et al., 1999); however methodological issues (Shoaf et al., 2000) make interpretation of reported differences difficult. Ongoing imaging studies of 5-HT receptor density in brain regions, as well as postmortem brain studies examining 5-HT-related neurochemistry, will provide valuable new perspectives on 5-HT neurobiology in autism. The neurochemical studies, along with those examining the metabolism as well as the behavioral and neuroendocrine effects of the 5-HT precursors, TRP and 5-hydroxytryptophan (5-HTP), are reviewed.

Blood 5-HT

The greatest number of 5-HT studies in autism concern the measurement of blood levels of 5-HT. A general consensus has been reached, dating from Schain and Freedman's original observation in 1961, that group mean levels of blood (platelet) 5-HT are increased in autism. Much of the 5-HT-related research in autism has been directed toward further characterizing the elevation and attempting to elucidate the causes. In a more recent study of a large and relatively homogenuous group, it was reported that platelet 5-HT is bimodally distributed in autism and Pervasive Developmental Disorder (PDD; Mulder et al., 2004). It now appears that *hyperserotonemia* can be rationally defined and that approximately half of individuals with PDD can be placed in this category. Careful examination of those hyperserotonmic individuals in the upper mode should facilitate research in this area.

A major line of research has focused on trying to identify the physiological mechanism of the elevation. Serotonin in blood derives from that synthesized in the wall of the gut; it is stored in platelets while circulating and is catabolized to 5-HIAA by monoamine oxidase (MAO) after uptake into lung, liver, and capillary endothelium (Anderson, Stevenson, & Cohen, 1987). These aspects of blood 5-HT, and the factor(s) that might cause the increase in autism, have been discussed in detail (Anderson, 2002; Anderson et al., 1990; Hanley, Stahl, & Freedman, 1977).

Research on the platelet storage of 5-HT has been extensive. At first it appeared that there might be differences between normal and autistic subjects in terms of the number of platelets (Ritvo et al., 1970) and in platelet efflux of 5-HT (Boullin et al., 1971). However, it appears that these platelet indices, as well as the number of platelet 5-HT uptake sites, are normal in autism (Anderson, Minderaa, van Bentem, Volkmar, & Cohen, 1984; Boullin et al., 1982; Yuwiler et al., 1975). A study of hyperserotonemic relatives of children with autism found some suggestive differences in platelet 5-HT uptake and the numbers of platelet 5-HT-type 2 receptors in subgroups of the relatives (Cook et al., 1993).

It should also be noted that no differences in platelet levels of the catabolic enzyme MAO have been found in autism (Giller et al., 1980; J. G. Young et al., 1982). Unfortunately, because 5-HT is principally metabolized by MAO-A rather than the form found in platelets, MAO-B, these studies of MAO are not definitive. Studies of 5-HT synthesis include those examining urine levels of 5-HIAA and 5-HT, and those in which TRP was administered.

Urine 5-HIAA and 5-HT

Because most 5-HT produced in the body is eventually metabolized to and excreted as 5-HIAA (Udenfriend, Titus, Weissbach, & Peterson, 1959), urine levels of 5-HIAA are a good indicator of the rate of 5-HT synthesis, at least as long as routes of metabolism and elimination are not altered significantly. There have been relatively few studies of urine 5-HIAA excretion in autistic subjects. One major study reported elevated levels (6.08 versus 3.23 mg/day) of 5-HIAA in autistic subjects compared to mentally retarded individuals (Hanley et al., 1977). In addition, a greater increase in 5-HIAA was seen for autistic subjects after a TRP load (12.95 versus 6.52 mg/day). Two previous studies (Partington, Tu, & Wong, 1973; Schain & Freedman, 1961) had not detected differences in urine 5-HIAA excretion between autistic and normal individuals, although in one of the studies hyperserotonemic autistic subjects did have elevated urine 5-HIAA levels. Urinary excretion of 5-HIAA in a group of individuals with autism who were not receiving medication was observed to be very similar to that seen in an age-matched control group

(Minderaa, Anderson, Volkmar, Akkerhuis, & Cohen, 1987). Furthermore, no correlation between urine 5-HIAA and whole blood 5-HT levels was observed in autistic or normal subjects, although hyperserotonemic autistic individuals may have had slightly higher urine levels of 5-HIAA compared to other autistic subjects or to normals. These data regarding 5-HIAA suggest that normal amounts of 5-HT are produced in autistic individuals. In a subsequent study, no differences in urinary excretion of 5-HT itself were seen between autistic and control subjects (Anderson, Minderaa, Cho, Volkmar, & Cohen, 1989), and in other related studies no group differences were seen for free plasma levels of 5-HT (Cook, Leventhal, & Freedman, 1988). Taken together, these observations indicate that the platelet of autistic individuals is exposed to normal levels of 5-HT. This in turn suggests that there is an alteration in the platelet's handling of 5-HT, at least in the hyperserotonemic subgroup.

Tryptophan Metabolism

Tryptophan, an essential amino acid, is the dietary precursor of 5-HT and of the vitamin nicotinic acid. It has been shown that the level of TRP in the brain is determined to some extent by plasma levels of free (nonprotein-bound) TRP. Hoshino, Yamamoto, et al. (1984) determined plasma free and total TRP levels and blood serotonin levels simultaneously and reported that both plasma free TRP and blood 5-HT levels were significantly higher in autistic children than in normal control subjects. In addition, there tended to be a significant correlation between the plasma free TRP level and several clinical rating scales in autistic children, although there was no correlation between blood 5-HT and free TRP levels in these children. In contrast, Anderson, Volkmar, et al. (1987) reported that whole blood TRP concentrations tended to be slightly (but not significantly) lower in unmedicated autistics compared to normal controls, while Takatsu, Onizawa, and Nakahato (1965) had previously reported that total plasma TRP was reduced in autism.

Several investigators have attempted to demonstrate metabolic alterations in the serotonin metabolism of autistic children by administering large oral doses of L-trypto-phan (L-TRP). Schain and Freedman (1961) performed TRP (one gram) loading tests in autistic and mildly retarded children but found no differences in blood 5-HT and urinary 5-HIAA concentration between the two groups. On the other hand, Hanley et al. (1977) reported that TRP (1g) loading raised urinary 5-HT levels in hyperserotonemic autistic children but lowered urinary 5-HT levels in mildly retarded children having normal levels of blood serotonin. In both groups the TRP load caused a slight decrease of blood 5-HT and a marked increase of urinary 5-HIAA excretion. In a more recent study (Cook et al., 1992) an oral TRP load was not observed to increase blood 5-HT levels in relatives of autistic individuals. However, depletion of plasma TRP by the use of an amino acid drink has been reported to exacerbate symptoms in autism (Mc-Dougle et al., 1996).

Neuroendocrine Studies of Serotonergic Functioning

Several groups (Hoshino, Tachibana, et al., 1984; Hoshino et al., 1983; Sverd, Kupretz, Winsberg, Hurwic, & Becker, 1978) have examined the effect of L-5-HTP on serotonin metabolism and hypothalamo-pituitary function in autistic children. Hoshino and colleagues administered L-5-HTP to autistic children and normal controls and measured chronological changes of blood serotonin, plasma human growth hormone (HGH), and prolactin (PRL). After loading, blood serotonin showed a smaller increase compared with normal controls, although the baseline levels of blood serotonin were significantly higher in autistic children. The levels of plasma HGH observed after 5-HTP-stimulated release were similar in the groups studied, as were baseline HGH concentrations. However, lower baseline levels of prolactin and a blunted prolactin response to 5-HTP were present in the autistic group (Hoshino, Tachibana, et al., 1984; Hoshino et al., 1983). These results might be explained on the basis of diminished central serotonergic functioning or enhanced activity of tuberoinfundibular dopamine neurons known to exert a powerful inhibitory control on prolactin release. In contrast, other researchers have found

normal baseline levels of plasma prolactin and have observed an apparently normal increase in prolactin after chronic treatment with dopamine blockers (Minderaa et al., 1989). In a detailed study of the neuroendocrine response to the serotonergic agent fenfluramine, McBride and colleagues (1989) found that autistic subjects had a blunted prolactin response (with normal baseline prolactin levels). This was interpreted to suggest that central 5-HT type-2 receptor functioning might be reduced on autism. Simultaneous studies of the responsivity of the platelet 5-HT type-2 receptor also showed a blunted response in the autistic subjects. Results from neuroimaging and postmortem brain studies of 5-HT type-2 receptors will be of special interest, given these reports.

CSF 5-HIAA

Levels of 5-HIAA and other monoamine metabolites have been widely measured in CSF in order to estimate brain turnover of the parent neurotransmitters (Garelis, Young, Lal, & Sourkes, 1974). Nearly all 5-HT is metabolized to 5-HIAA before elimination from the brain, and a substantial route for egress of brain 5-HIAA is through the CSF (Aizenstein & Korf, 1979; Meek & Neff, 1973). It is clear that certain drugs and treatments known to affect brain 5-HT turnover have corresponding effects on levels of CSF 5-HIAA (Kirwin et al., 1997; S. N. Young, Anderson, & Purdy, 1980), and it has been shown that CSF 5-HIAA is not contaminated with 5-HT or 5-HIAA arising elsewhere in the body. The close approach to the brain afforded by CSF measurements is attractive; however, the invasiveness of the lumbar puncture required has limited the number of studies carried out in autistic individuals.

Three studies have been performed using probenecid to block the transport of 5-HIAA and other acidic compounds out of CSF. In two of the studies, levels of 5-HIAA were observed to be similar (Cohen, Shaywitz, Johnson, & Bowers, 1974) or slightly lower (Cohen, Caparulo, Shaywitz, & Bowers, 1977) in autistic subjects compared to nonautistic psychotic children. In a third probenecid study, no control groups were used; however, a few of the autistic subjects did not show the expected increase in 5-HIAA after probenecid administration (Winsberg, Sverd, Castells, Hurwic, & Perel, 1980). In studies of baseline levels of CSF 5-HIAA, no significant differences have been observed between autistic and control subjects (Gillberg & Svennerholm, 1987; Gillberg, Svennerholm, & Hamilton-Hellberg, 1983; Narayan, Srinath, Anderson, & Meundi, 1993). In summary, the CSF studies suggest that if central 5-HT metabolism is altered in autism, the alteration does not involve a widespread or marked change in 5-HT turnover.

DOPAMINE

Most dopamine (DA) containing neurons lie in the midbrain. Dopaminergic neurons appear to be especially important in the control of motor function, in cognition, and in regulating hormone release. Dopamine is synthesized from the dietary amino acids, phenylalanine or tyrosine, by hydroxylation and decarboxylation. Dopamine can be subsequently converted to norepinephrine and epinephrine by the action of the enzymes dopamine-ß-hydroxylase and phenylethanolamine-N-methyltransferase. Once released from the neuron, DA is enzymatically degraded by MAO and catechol-O-methyltransferase (COMT) to homovanillic acid (HVA) and 3,4-dihydroxyphenylacetic acid (DOPAC).

The DA blockers (the neuroleptics or major tranquilizers) have been observed to be effective in treating some aspects of autism. This, and the fact that certain symptoms of autism—such as stereotypies and hyperactivity—can be induced in animals by increasing DA function, has suggested that central DA neurons may be overactive in autism. Central dopamine function has been assessed in humans by several methods, including postmortem measurements of DA, its metabolites, and receptors in brain tissue; positron emission tomography (PET scanning); CSF measurements of HVA and DOPAC; and blood or urine measures of DA, HVA, and DOPAC.

CSF Homovanillic Acid

Studies in humans and in animals have indicated that changes in central dopamine turnover are reflected to some extent in CSF levels of the principal dopamine metabolite, HVA (Garelis

et al., 1974). In previously discussed studies of CSF 5-HIAA in autistic individuals, measurements of HVA also were made. In two of the three studies using probenecid to block transport of the acid metabolites out of CSF (Cohen et al., 1974, 1977), no significant group differences were observed between autistic children and various comparison groups. Comparison groups included nonautistic psychotic (atypical), aphasic, motor disordered, and neurologically disordered (contrast) children. In both studies, CSF HVA did tend to be lower in autistic children compared to nonautistic psychotic children, and in one of the studies (Cohen et al., 1974), HVA values were reported to be lower in the more disturbed autistic individuals. A third study employing the probenecid technique did not include measurements made in comparison groups; however, the increases in CSF HVA seen after probenecid appeared normal (Winsberg et al., 1980).

In later CSF studies, probenecid was not administered. In a study carried out in Sweden, the baseline, unperturbed, concentrations of CSF HVA were observed to be elevated approximately 50% in the autistic group compared to an age- and sex-matched control group of neurologically disordered children (Gillberg & Svennerholm, 1987; Gillberg et al., 1983). However, two other studies of baseline CSF HVA in autism have not seen significant elevations in autistic individuals compared to controls (Narayan, Srinath, et al., 1993; Ross, Klykylo, & Anderson, 1985). This question of whether CSF levels are increased in autism has been the subject of debate (Gillberg, 1993; Narayan, Srinath, et al., 1993; Narayan, Srinath, & Anderson, 1993). Taken together, the CSF studies do not appear to provide strong support for the idea that central DA turnover is increased in autism. However, the discrepancies between the studies suggest that further research in this area is warranted.

Plasma and Urine Measures of Dopamine Function

Unfortunately, the relationship of peripheral measures of DA, HVA, and DOPAC to central DA function is unclear. Although at least some of the HVA found in blood and urine arises from the brain, the exact proportion has not been well established. It has been estimated that approximately 25% of blood or urine HVA is of central origin (Elchisak, Polinsky, Ebert, Powers, & Kopin, 1978; Maas, Hattox, Greene, & Landis, 1980). On the other hand, peripheral DA itself is known to arise almost completely from the adrenal, kidney, and the sympathetic nervous system, rather than from the brain.

In the one study of plasma HVA levels in autism, no differences were observed between unmedicated autistic subjects and normal controls (Minderaa et al., 1989). Slight, nonsignificant increases in plasma HVA were seen in autistics medicated with neuroleptics. In two studies examining baseline plasma levels of prolactin, a hormone under powerful tonic inhibitory control by dopaminergic tuberinfidibular neurons, no group differences have been seen (McBride et al., 1989; Minderaa et al., 1989).

Although several groups have reported that the urinary excretion of HVA is increased in autism, in a large study of urinary DA and HVA differences were not observed between autistic and control groups in the rate of urinary excretion of these compounds (Minderaa et al., 1989). Studies of the catabolic enzyme COMT, which along with MAO converts DA to HVA, have found similar activities in red blood cells of autistic and control subjects (Giller et al., 1980; O'Brien, Semenuk, & Spector, 1976). A study of CSF levels of one form of tetrahydrobiopterin, a cofactor in the synthesis of DA, has found lower levels in autistic subjects (Tani, Fernell, Watanbe, Kanai, & Langstrom, 1994).

Neuroendocrine Studies of Dopamine Functioning

Ritvo et al. (1971) designed a study to assess neurochemical, behavioral, and neuroendocrine effects of L-Dopa administration. Following a 17-day placebo period, four hospitalized autistic boys received the DA precursor, L-Dopa, for 6 months. Results indicated a significant decrease in blood 5-HT concentrations and a significant increase in platelet counts. Urinary excretion of 5-HIAA decreased significantly in one patient, and a similar trend was noted in others. However, no changes were observed in the clinical course of the disorder, the amount of motility disturbances (stereotypic behavior), percentages of REM sleep time, or in measures

of endocrine function (plasma LH and FSH levels). In a study of the effects of L-Dopa on the secretion of growth hormone (HGH), Realmuto and colleagues (Realmuto, Jensen, Reeve, & Garfinkel, 1990) found that, while autistic subjects had normal peak responses in plasma HGH, they had a delayed response compared to controls.

NOREPINEPHRINE

Norepinephrine (NE) is an important neurotransmitter in both the central nervous system (CNS) and in the peripheral sympathetic nervous system. Central and peripheral NE is produced from DA through the action of the enzyme dopamine-ß-hydroxylase. Upon release, most central NE is metabolized by MAO and COMT to 3-methoxy-4-hydroxyphenylglycol (MHPG), whereas peripheral NE is predominantly converted to vanillylmandelic acid (VMA).

Most central NE-containing neurons have their cell bodies localized in one section of the hindbrain, the locus coeruleus. These neurons project in a diffuse manner to many areas of the brain and spinal cord and are crucial in processes related to arousal, anxiety, stress responses, and memory. Drugs that lessen central NE function, such as clonidine, have been used to treat withdrawal symptoms (Redmond & Huang, 1979). Other agents that increase central noradrenergic functioning, such as yohimbine and desipramine, increase arousal or serve as antidepressants. Norepinephrine also serves as the major neurotransmitter in postganglionic sympathetic nervous neurons. These neurons serve to control autonomic functions and are balanced against cholinergic neurons that enervate the same organs. When sympathetic system activity predominates, the characteristic flight-or-fight response is elicited.

Activity of central NE neurons has been assessed by determining CSF levels of NE and MHPG. The CSF measures probably reflect NE activity in the spinal cord, as well as in the brain, and some small contribution of blood MHPG to CSF MHPG has been demonstrated (Kopin, Gordon, Jimerson, & Polinsky, 1983). Blood and urine levels of MHPG also have been measured in order to gauge central NE function; however, the proportion of MHPG in these fluids that originates in the CNS relative to that arising from NE released by sympathetic neurons is not clear (Maas & Leckman, 1983). Other NE metabolites, VMA and normetanephrine (NMN), along with MHPG, have been widely measured in urine and plasma to assess activity of the sympathetic nervous system.

The studies examining NE metabolism, other measures of noradrenergic and adrenergic functioning, and indices of hypothalamic-pituitary-adrenal (HPA) axis activity have produced a variety of results. However, as seen in Table 17.1, if the measures are grouped according to whether they reflect basal functioning of the stress response systems or their reactivity to acute stress, the results are actually quite consistent.

Overall, the CSF, plasma, and urine findings indicate that baseline sympathetic and adrenal function is probably not greatly altered in autism; however, there is some indication that in some autistic individuals the sympathetic nervous system may be hyper-responsive to stress. This notion is consistent with reports that clonidine may be of some benefit in treating patients with autism (Frankhauser, Karumanchi, German, Yales, & Karumanchi, 1992).

TABLE 17.1   Stress Response Systems in Autism: Sympathetic/Adrenomedullary and Hypothalamic-Pituitary-Adrenal Axis Function

Measure	Finding*	Reference
		Measures of Basal Functioning
Urine		
Norepinephrine	NC	Launay et al., 1987; Martineau et al., 1992; Minderaa et al., 1994.
	↓	J. G. Young et al., 1978
	↑	Barthelemy et al., 1988
Epinephrine	NC	Minderaa et al., 1994
MHPG	NC	Launay et al., 1987; Minderaa et al., 1994
	↓	Barthelemy et al., 1988; J. G. Young, Cohen, Hattox, et al., 1981
VMA	NC	Minderaa et al., 1994
Cortisol	NC	Richdale & Prior, 1992
Plasma/Serum		
MHPG	NC	Minderaa et al., 1994; J. G. Young, Cohen, Hattox, et al., 1981
DBH	NC	Lake et al., 1977; S. N. Young et al., 1980
Cortisol	NC	Tordjman et al., 1997; Nir et al., 1995; Sandman et al., 1990
	↓	Curin et al., 2003; Hoshino, Ohno, et al., 1984; Jensen et al., 1985
Cerebrospinal Fluid		
MHPG	NC	Gillberg & Svennerholm, 1987; J. G. Young, Cohen, Kavanaugh, et al., 1981
		Measures of Acute Response
Plasma		
Norepinephrine	↑	Lake et al.,1977; Leboyer et al., 1992; Leventhal et al., 1990
Adrenocorticotropin	↑	Tordjman et al.,1997
ß-Endorphin	↑	Tordjman et al.,1997
	NC	Herman, 1991; Weizman et al., 1988
Cardiovascular		
BP/heart rate	↑	Hirstein et al., 2001; Kootz & Cohen, 1981; S. Tordjman, personal comm., 2003

*Key: ↑ = Increased in autism; ↓ = Decreased in autism; DBH = Dopamine-ß-hyroxylase; MHPG = Methoxyhydroxyphenylethyleneglycol; NC = No change or difference in autism; VMA = Vanillylmandelic acid.

STUDIES OF THE HYPOTHALAMIC-PITUITARY-ADRENAL AXIS

Research examining hypothalamic-pituitary (HPA) function in autism can be divided into two main categories: a large number of studies have looked at HPA function in order to assess the stress response, in another avenue of research HPA function has been studied in hopes of determining the functioning of neurochemical systems that are involved in the regulation of neuroendocrine secretion. The hypothalamic-pituitary-adrenal axis plays a critical role in the stress response and is closely interrelated with the sympathetic nervous system.

Cortisol Secretion

The glucocorticoid cortisol is released from the adrenal cortex in response to stress; increased amounts also are normally released in the early morning. The secretion is under control of adrenocorticotropin hormone (ACTH) released from the pituitary; ACTH release is in turn under control of corticotropin-releasing factor (CRF) produced in the hypothalamus. Levels of cortisol or its metabolites in plasma, saliva and urine, and plasma levels of ACTH, have been measured to assess HPA function. Normally, cortisol inhibits its own release by suppressing CRF and ACTH release. The status of this feedback system has been studied extensively in depression using the dexamethasone suppression test (DST; Gwirtsman, Gerner, & Sternbach, 1982). Studies in autism have examined basal levels of ACTH and cortisol, diurnal variations, and the response to dexamethasone (a synthetic glucocorticoid) and other provocative agents.

The balance of the studies report either normal or elevated baseline secretion of cortisol, and a failure to suppress cortisol release after dexamethasone, in autistic subjects. Maher, Harper, Macleay, and King (1975) reported an increased release of cortisol in response to insulin in autistic children compared to retarded control subjects, whereas Yamazaki, Saito, Okada, Fujiede, and Yamashita (1975) found a normal increase in 11-hydroxycorticosteriods (11-OHCS) after pyrogen stress in autistic subjects. The latter investigators also reported abnormal diurnal variations in 11-OHCS levels in the autistic individuals.

Several groups have performed the dexamethasone suppression test (DST) in autistic subjects. Hoshino, Ohno, et al. (1984) reported that after DST low-functioning (IQ < 60) autistics examined were nonsuppressors, whereas high-functioning autistic subjects had nearly normal suppression of cortisol secretion. Similarly, in a group of 12 low-functioning autistic individuals (IQ < 30), Jensen, Realmuto, and Garfinkel (1985) found 10 were nonsuppressors. In both studies, baseline cortisol levels observed in the autistic group were similar to those seen in the control groups (Hoshino, Ohno, et al., 1984; Jensen et al., 1985). Hoshino and colleagues (1987) have also reported similar abnormalities with the DST when measuring cortisol levels in saliva. In other studies, normal levels of plasma cortisol (Sandman, Barron, Chicz-Demet, & Demet, 1990; Tordjman, Anderson, et al., 1997) or slightly elevated levels of urinary cortisol (Richdale & Prior, 1992) were seen in the autistic group.

On the whole, it would appear that baseline secretion of cortisol and ACTH are not greatly altered in autism (see Table 17.1). However, questions regarding possible abnormalities in the diurnal rhythm remain to be addressed. It does seem clear that lower IQ autistic subjects do not suppress cortisol secretion after dexamethasone to the same extent as normal or control subjects. Possible treatment effects of an ACTH analogue (Buitelaar, van Engeland, van Ree, & de Wied, 1990) added to the interest in this area, but have not led to definitive results.

Thyroid Hormone and TRH Test

Aspects of thyroid function in infantile autism and the efficacy of triiodothyronine (T3) treatment of autistic children have been studied by several investigators (Campbell, Small, et al., 1978; Sherwin, Flach, & Stokes, 1958). Kahn (1970) reported diminished values of T3 uptake in 45 of 62 autistic children. On the other hand, Abbassi, Linscheid, and Coleman (1978) and Cohen, Young, Lowe, and Harcherik (1980) have investigated T3, T4, and TSH (thyroid stimulating hormone, thyrotropin) concentrations in 13 autistic children and found no clinical evidence for hypothyroidism, reporting that all had levels within the normal range. Campbell, Small, et al. (1978) have conducted a placebo-controlled crossover study of behavioral effects of T3 in 30 young, clinically euthyroid autistic children and reported that T3 did not differ from placebo, although, as a group, the lower IQ autistic children responded to T3.

Campbell, Hollander, Ferris, and Greene (1978) performed the thyrotropin-releasing hormone (TRH) test in psychotic children. After administering synthetic TRH intravenously to 10 young psychotic children, plasma T3, TSH, and prolactin (PRL) were measured over time. In general, there was an elevated response to TSH and a delayed or blunted response of T3 in psychotic children. Suwa et al. (1984) examined hypothalamo-pituitary function by means of the TRH test in 4 children with autism. Hyperresponse of PRL to TRH was observed in one of the children with autism. Moreover, 3 of the 4 autistic children showed a hyperresponse of TSH to TRH. Similarly, Hoshino et al. (1983) reported that 6 autistic children showed an elevated response of TSH to TRH. Unlike Suwa et al., they found a blunted response of PRL to TRH. In contrast, Hashimoto and colleagues (1991) found a blunted TSH response to TRH in a large group ($N = 41$) of children with autism and others have observed normal hormone responses to TRH (P. A. McBride, personal communication). Congenital hypothyroidism has been described in a number of patients with autism (Gillberg & Coleman, 1992; Gillberg, Gillberg, & Koop, 1992; Ritvo et al., 1990). If the finding is not coincidental, this may indicate that hypothyroidism increases the risk for autism in vulnerable individuals.

Sex Hormones

So far, there have been no reports on the therapeutic effect in autism of sex-related hormones such as lutenizing hormone (LH) and follicle-stimulating hormone (FSH). However, Hoshino et al. (1983) have performed a LH-RH test in six autistic boys. They administered synthetic LH-RH intravenously and measured plasma release of LH and FSH; both LH and FSH exhibited a blunted response to LH-RH stimulation. In a study of plasma levels of the gonadal and the adrenal androgens, testosterone, and dehy-droepiandrosterone sulfate (DHEAS), Tordjman and colleagues (1995) found no differences between the autistic and control groups. The group similarities in the androgens were seen in both the pre- and postpubertal subjects. More recently, it has been suggested that differences in early androgen exposure may influence the expression of autism (Manning, Baron-Cohen, Wheelwright, & Sanders, 2001; Tordjman, Ferrari, Sulmont, Duyme, & Roubertoux, 1997) and the use of digit length ratios in assessing this has been suggested (Manning et al., 2001).

PEPTIDE RESEARCH

The important role of peptides in central neurotransmission and neuromodulation is well established. Neuropeptides have been shown to be crucial to processes related to emotion, appetite, pain perception, and sexual behavior. Measurement of CSF, plasma, and urine levels of specific or uncharacterized peptides in schizophrenia and depression has not clearly indicated whether peptides have etiological significance in these disorders. In autism, the work can be divided into studies of specific opioid peptides and more general studies of peptide excretion patterns.

Opioid peptides, such as the enkephalins and the endorphins, appear to be endogenous ligands for receptors activated by morphine and related compounds. Several investigators have theorized that the opioid peptides are involved in producing at least some of the symptoms of autism (Colette, 1978; Panksepp, 1979; Sandman, 1991, 1992). In particular, similarities between behaviors seen in opiate-injected animals and those displayed in autistic subjects (decreased pain perception, behavioral persistence, self-injurious behavior, poor social relations) have suggested that the opioid peptides are hyperfunctional in autism. The hypothesis has been tested by measuring levels of opioids in plasma and CSF, and by administering the opiate antagonist, naloxone, to self-injurious and autistic subjects.

Previous research on the plasma opioids yielded somewhat inconsistent results, with some investigators finding elevations in autism, while others have found little difference between groups (Barrett, Feinstein, & Hold, 1989; Bernstein, Hughes, Mitchell, &

Thompson, 1987; Coid, Allolio, & Rees, 1983; Leboyer, Bouvard, & Dupes, 1988; Sandman et al., 1990; Tordjman, Anderson, et al., 1997; Weizman et al., 1984). A study examining ß-endorphin fragments in plasma has reported an extreme elevation in C-terminal fragments in autistic individuals (Leboyer et al., 1994); further work on this aspect is warranted. Studies of CSF opioids have reported increased levels of met-enkephalin (Gillberg, Terenius, & Lonnerholm, 1985; Ross, Klykylo, & Hitzeman, 1987) and increased or unaltered (Nagamitsu, 1993) ß-endorphin in autistic subjects. While CSF opioids are presumably derived from central sources, plasma ß-endorphin has a peripheral origin. In fact, ß-endorphin appears to be released along with ACTH and probably should be considered a human stress hormone.

Initial tests of the effect of naloxone on self-injurious behavior in mentally retarded individuals were promising (Sandman et al., 1983). This result supported the idea of a hyperfunctional opioid system, at least with respect to this one dimension of behavior. However, further studies of naloxone's effects did not tend to demonstrate clear clinical effects of the opioid antagonists in treating autism (Campbell et al., 1990; Herman, 1991; Leboyer et al., 1992).

The urinary excretion of unidentified peptides and peptide complexes in autism has been described in a qualitative manner in several reports (Gillberg, Trygstad, & Foss, 1982; Isarangkun, Newman, Patel, Duruibe, & Abou-Issa, 1986; Reichelt, Saelid, Lindback, & Boler, 1986; Reichelt et al., 1981). Distinctive patterns of urinary peptides have been reported to occur in several childhood neuropsychiatric illnesses, including autism. Although there have been a number of reports of differences between autistic and control subjects in terms of their patterns of peptide excretion the studies are far from definitive. The relatively nonspecific nature of the analytical separations and detection processes employed and the nonquantitative aspect of the studies hinder interpretation. In a collaborative study (Le Couteur, Trygstad, Evered, Gillberg, & Rutter, 1988), researchers did not find reproducible differences between autistic and control subjects' excretion of peptides. Although differences in peptide handling are still hypothesized to be in-

volved in autism (Reichelt & Knivsberg, 2003), any further research should be directed toward establishing which specific peptide species are increased or decreased in autistic subjects. Subsequent identification of the specific peptides which might be abnormal in autism would be desirable in order to determine the etiological significance of the possible abnormalities. Recent research along these lines that has found differences in peptides in neonatal blood spots of autistic children is questionable given the lack of disorder specificity and the failure to replicate (Nelson et al., 2001). Similarly, reported differences in plasma oxytocin processing (Green et al., 2001), although interesting from a theoretical perspective (Insel, O'Brien, & Leckman, 1999), need careful replication.

AMINO ACIDS AND ACETYLCHOLINE

A number of inborn errors of amino acid metabolism have been identified, and several of these disorders, such as phenylketonuria, histidinemia, and homocystinuria affect the central nervous system and have severe behavioral consequences (Scriver & Rosenberg, 1973).

Sylvester, Jorgensen, Mellerup, and Rafaelsen (1970) surveyed amino acid excretion in 178 children suffering from different psychiatric disorders, including psychosis, neurosis, character disorder, mental deficiency, and other functional disturbances. In no case was a specific hyperaminoaciduria found. Johnson, Wiersema, and Kraft (1974) analyzed amino acid composition of hair protein and found no significant differences between autistic and control children. In 1978, T. L. Perry, Hansen, and Christie measured amino compounds and organic acids in CSF, plasma, and urine of autistic and control children. Similar levels of most compounds were observed in the two groups; however, the mean concentration of ethanolamine in CSF was significantly higher in autistic children than in control subjects. Based on this finding, they suggested that a subgroup of autistic children possibly may have a brain disorder involving ethanolamine metabolism.

Kotsopoulos and Kutty (1979) and Rutter and Bartak (1971) have reported cases showing features of infantile autism who exhibited histidinemia, with histidine blood levels several times higher than normal. It is not clear whether coexistence of autism and histidinemia is coincidental, if not histidinemia may have constituted a necessary but not sufficient factor leading to the clinical condition of autism.

An association between phenylketonceria and autism has been noted (Friedman, 1969). In a subsequent study, Lowe, Tanaka, Seashore, Young, and Cohen (1980) surveyed 65 children with pervasive developmental disturbance (autism and atypical childhood psychosis) using standard urinary amino acid screening methods and found three children exhibiting PKU. The children were treated with low phenylalanine diets and showed improvement in functioning and developmental level after treatment. The study underlined the relevance of urinary amino acid screening for children being evaluated for serious developmental disturbances of childhood. Other work on aromatic amino acid precursors of the catecholamines (phenylalanine) and the indoleamines (TRP) found that autistic subjects had reduced intestinal absorption of the compounds (Naruse, Hayashi, Takesada, Nakane, & Yamazaki, 1989). Although an attempt was made to relate these peripheral findings to some central alteration in monoamine metabolism, this relationship is not at all clear.

Abnormalities in plasma glutamate and gamma-aminobutyric acid (GABA) have been reported in autism (Aldred, Moore, Fitzgerald, & Waring, 2003; Dhossche et al., 2002), and recent postmortem brain studies have observed differences in hippocampal GABA receptor density and alterations in the synthetic enzyme (glutamic acid decarboxylase) that converts glutamate to GABA (Blatt et al., 2001; Fatemi et al., 2002). The neurochemical findings, as well as apparent association of GABA receptor genes with autism risk, indicate that further research in this area is warranted.

The general area of cholinergic mechanisms in autism has been relatively neglected due to difficulties in assessing central and peripheral cholinergic metabolism and functioning. However, recent striking findings of altered cholinergic receptors in cortical regions of postmortem brain specimens obtained from patients with autism (Lee et al., 2002; E. K. Perry et al., 2001), along with reported alterations in vivo brain choline levels using nuclear resonance spectroscopy (Sokol,

Dunn, Edwards-Brown, & Feinberg, 2002), have stimulated considerable interest in this area. Further neurobiological research is clearly called for and some consideration has been given to the possible utility of cholinergic agents in the treatment of autism.

PURINES AND RELATED COMPOUNDS

A good deal of attention has been paid to the role of cyclic AMP (adenosine-3', 5'-cyclic monophosphate) as a second messenger in the mechanism of neural transmission. The enzymes involved in brain synthesis (adenylate cyclase) and decomposition (phosphodiesterase) of cyclic AMP are more active in the brain than in other body organs. Norepinephrine, among other neurotransmitters, elevates intracellular cyclic AMP after interacting with membrane receptors; the elevation of cyclic AMP appears crucial to the subsequent neuronal firing. Cyclic GMP (guanosine-3', 5'-cyclic monophosphate) is a nucleotide related to cyclic AMP and also has second messenger properties.

Winsberg et al. (1980) measured cyclic AMP in CSF of autistic children and reported that levels were increased in all by probenecid administration; however, no comparison to control groups was made. Hoshino et al. (1980) determined plasma cyclic AMP levels in psychiatric diseases of children, such as early infantile autism, hyperkinetic mental retardation, attention deficit disorder, and Down's syndrome. The plasma cyclic AMP levels were higher in autistic and hyperkinetic mentally retarded children compared to normal children and were positively correlated with the hyperactivity score. In children with attention deficit disorder, the plasma cyclic AMP level was significantly lower than in normal children and was not correlated with the hyperactivity score.

Goldberg, Hattab, Meir, Ebstein, and Belmaker (1984) reported that an examination of plasma cyclic AMP and cyclic GMP in 18 patients with childhood autism, 7 patients with pervasive developmental disorder, and 12 age- and sex-matched healthy controls revealed that plasma cyclic AMP was significantly elevated by over 100% in both groups of patients with childhood-onset psychoses compared with controls, although plasma cyclic GMP was not elevated. They did not examine the correlation between plasma cyclic AMP, GMP, and clinical symptoms, including hyperkinesis. The origin of plasma cyclic AMP remains unclear; the compound has been assumed to be derived from peripheral organs, such as the liver, kidneys, lungs, and adrenals, as well as the brain.

Sankar (1971) determined red blood cell (erythrocyte) ATPase activity before and after lysing of the cells and reported that the level of ATPase in lyzate was significantly higher in autistic-like schizophrenic children compared to normal controls. The addition of magnesium ions to the lyzate further increased the ATPase activity especially in the case of schizophrenic children. Based on this result, he suggested that red cell membranes of schizophrenic children display either decreased permeability to ATP or to some other factor(s) necessary for ATPase activity in the cell.

Uric acid is the final end-product of all purine pathways and hyperuricosuria (increased urinary excretion of uric acid) has been reported to occur in up to a quarter of the autistic children studied in the United States and France (Page & Coleman, 2000; Rosenberger-Diesse & Coleman, 1986). These observations warrant further investigation, given the high proportion of patients suggested to be so affected (though elevated rates of gout have not been reported in autism). A more specific form of uric acid alteration has been reported to be present in a 3-year-old boy with unusual autistic behavior, who was shown to have an excessive rate of uric acid synthesis due to an increase in the purine enzyme phosphoribosylpyrophosphate sythetase in his fibroblasts (Becker, Raivio, Bakay, Adams, & Nyhan, 1980). Other children with this enzyme abnormality have now been reported (Christen, Hanfeld, Duley, & Simmonds, 1992; Simmonds, Webster, Lingham, & Wilson, 1985). Jaeken and Van den Berghe (1984) reported that succinyladenosine and succinylaminoimidazole carboxamide riboside were found in body fluids (CSF, plasma, and urine) in three children with severe infantile autism. Their presence indicates a deficiency of the enzyme adenylosuccinase, which is involved in both de novo synthesis of purines and the formation of adenosine monophosphate from inosine monophosphate. Moreover, according to their report, assays in one patient revealed markedly decreased adenylosuccinase activity in the liver and absence of activity in the kidney. They suggested that the accumulation of both succinylpurines in the CSF implies that there is also a deficiency of this enzyme in the brain and that this may be the basic defect in a subgroup of children with autism. This work was followed up with a study of autistic siblings having a markedly lowered Vmax of adenylosuccinase (Barshop, Alberts, & Gruber, 1989). The molecular basis of the three cases of severe retardation with autistic features has been identified; the affected children are homozygous for a point mutation while their family members are heterozygous (Stone et al., 1992). The point mutation in the purine nucleotide biosynthetic enzme, adenylosuccinate lyase, thus segregates with the disorder.

CONCLUSION

On surveying the field of neurochemical research in autism, it is notable how few replicated differences have been found between autistic and normal subjects. The studies reporting similarities between autistic and normal subjects should not be considered negative studies because they have served to narrow the field of investigation. The relatively few differences that have been reported tend to stand out. Most robust and well replicated is the increase in whole blood 5-HT seen in autism. However, abnormalities also have been reported in peptide excretion and in neuroendocrine and HPA functioning, in amino acid levels, uric acid excretion, and central cholinergic and gabaergic receptors.

Certainly an elucidation of the factor(s) causing the elevation of blood 5-HT would be of interest. Additional studies of peptide excretion, hormone release, amino acid, and purine metabolism seem warranted, given the reported abnormalities, their possible relevance to central neurotransmitter function, and the compounds' physiological importance. Finally, the diurnal rhythms of, and the effects of stress on, NE, epinephrine (adrenaline), and cortisol appear to be potentially fruitful areas of research.

The direction of future research on the biochemical basis of autism no doubt will be influenced by advances in the basic neurosciences and by parallel studies in the biological psychiatry of other mental disorders. In general, the availability of postmortem tissue should greatly enhance assessment of central neurochemistry in autism. In the future, a greater consensus should be reached as to just which aspects of neurochemical functioning are abnormal in autism. The application of improved techniques of neurochemical assessment also should allow a more complete picture to be drawn.

Cross-References

Neurologic and genetic aspects of autism are discussed in Chapters 16, 18, and 19; psychopharmacology is reviewed in Chapter 44.

REFERENCES

Abbassi, V., Linscheid, T., & Coleman, M. (1978). Triiodothyronine (T3) concentration and therapy in autistic children. *Journal of Autism and Childhood Schizophrenia, 8,* 383–387.

Aizenstein, M. L., & Korf, J. (1979). On the elimination of centrally formed 5-hydroxy-indoleacetic acid by cerebrospinal fluid and urine. *Journal of Neurochemistry, 32,* 1227–1233.

Aldred, S., Moore, K. M., Fitzgerald, M., & Waring, R. H. (2003). Plasma amino acid levels in children with autism and their families. *Journal of Autism and Developmental Disorders, 33,* 93–97.

Anderson, G. M. (1987). Monoamines in autism: An update of neurochemical research of a pervasive developmental disorder. *Medical Biology, 65,* 67–74.

Anderson, G. M. (2002). Genetics of childhood disorders: XLV. Autism: Part 4. Serotonin in autism. *Journal of the American Academy of Child and Adolescent Psychiatry, 41,* 1513–1516.

Anderson, G. M., & Cohen, D. J. (2002). Neurochemistry of childhood psychiatric disorders. In M. Lewis (Ed.), *Child and adolescent psychiatry: A comprehensive textbook* (3rd ed., pp. 47–60). Baltimore: Williams & Wilkins.

Anderson, G. M., Horne, W. C., Chatterjee, D., & Cohen, D. J. (1990). The hyperserotonemia of autism. *Annals of the New York Academy of Sciences, 600,* 333.

Anderson, G. M., Minderaa, R. B., Cho, S. C., Volkmar, F. R., & Cohen, D. J. (1989). The issue of hyperserotonemia and platelet serotonin exposure: A preliminary study. *Journal of Autism and Developmental Disorders, 19,* 349–351.

Anderson, G. M., Minderaa, R. B., van Bentem, P.-P. G., Volkmar, F. R., & Cohen, D. J. (1984). Platelet imipramine binding in autistic subjects. *Psychiatry Research, 11,* 133–141.

Anderson, G. M., Stevenson, J. M., & Cohen, D. J. (1987). Steady-state model for plasma free and platelet serotonin in man. *Life Sciences, 41,* 1777–1785.

Anderson, G. M., Volkmar, F. R., Hoder, E. L., McPhedran, P., Minderaa, R. B., Young, J. G., et al. (1987). Whole blood serotonin in autistic and normal subjects. *Journal of Child Psychiatry and Psychology, 28,* 885–900.

Barrett, P. R., Feinstein, C., & Hole, W. T. (1989). Effects of naloxone and naltrexone on self-injury: A double-blind placebo-controlled analysis. *American Journal of Mental Retardation, 93,* 644–651.

Barshop, B. A., Alberts, A. S., & Gruber, H. E. (1989). Kinetic studies of mutant human adenylosuccinase. *Biochemica et Biophysica Acta, 999,* 19–23.

Barthelemy, C., Bruneau, N., Cottet-Eymard, J. M., Domenech-Jouve, J., Garreau, B., Lelord, G., et al. (1988). Urinary free and conjugated catecholamines and metabolites in autistic children. *Journal of Autism and Developmental Disorders, 18,* 583–591.

Becker, M. A., Raivio, K. O., Bakay, B., Adams, W. B., & Nyhan, W. L. (1980). Variant human phosphoribosylpyrophosphate synthetase altered in regulatory and catalytic functions. *Journal of Clinical Investigations, 65,* 109–120.

Bernstein, G. A., Hughes, J. R., Mitchell, J. E., & Thompson, T. (1987). Effects of narcotic antagonist on self-injurious behavior: A single case study. *Journal of the American Academy of Child and Adolescent Psychiatry, 26,* 886–889.

Blatt, G. J., Fitzgerald, C. M., Guptill, J. T., Booker, A. B., Kemper, T. L., & Bauman, M. L. (2001). Density and distribution of hippocampal neurotransmitter receptors in autism: An autoradiographic study. *Journal of Autism and Developmental Disorders, 31,* 537–543.

Boullin, D. J., Coleman, M., O'Brien, R. A., & Rimland, B. (1971). Laboratory predictions of infantile autism based on 5-hydroxytryptamine efflux from blood platelets and their correlation with the Rimland E-2 score. *Journal of Autism and Childhood Schizophrenia, 1,* 63–71.

Boullin, D. J., Freeman, B. J., Geller, E., Ritvo, E. R., Rutter, M., & Yuwiler, A. (1982). Toward the resolution of conflicting findings. *Journal of Autism and Developmental Disorders, 12,* 97–98.

Buitelaar, J. K., van Engeland, H., van Ree, J. M., & de Wied, D. (1990). Behavioral effects of

Org 2766, a synthetic analog of the adrenocorticotrophic hormone (4–9), in 14 outpatient autistic children. *Journal of Autism and Developmental Disorders, 20,* 467–478.

Buznikov, G. A. (1984). The action of neurotransmitters and related substances on early embryogenesis. *Pharmacology and Therapeutics, 25,* 23–59.

Campbell, M., Anderson, L. T., Small, A. M., Locascio, J. J., Lynch, N. S., & Choroco, M. C. (1990). Naltrexone in autistic children: A double-blind and placebo controlled study. *Psychopharmacology Bulletin, 26,* 130–135.

Campbell, M., Hollander, C. S., Ferris, S., & Greene, L. W. (1978). Response to thyrotropin-releasing hormone stimulation in young psychotic children: A pilot study. *Psychoneuroendocrinology, 3,* 195–201.

Campbell, M., Small, A. M., Hollander, C. S., Korein, J., Cohen, I. L., Kalmijn, M., et al. (1978). A controlled crossover study of triiodothyronine in autistic children. *Journal of Autism and Childhood Schizophrenia, 8,* 371–381.

Christen, H. J., Hanfeld, F., Duley, J. A., & Simmonds, H. A. (1992). Distinct neurological syndrome in two brothers with hyperuricaemia. *Lancet, 340,* 1167–1168.

Chugani, D. C., Muzik, O., Behen, M. E., Rothermal, R., Lee, J., Chugani, H. T. (1999). Developmental changes in brain serotonin synthesis capacity in autistic and non-autistic children. *Annals of Neurology, 45,* 287–295.

Cohen, D. J., Caparulo, B. K., Shaywitz, B. A., & Bowers, M. B., Jr. (1977). Dopamine and serotonin metabolism in neuropsychiatrically disturbed children: CSF homovanillic acid and 5-hydroxyindoleacetic acid. *Archives of General Psychiatry, 34,* 545–550.

Cohen, D. J., Shaywitz, B. A., Johnson, W. T., & Bowers, M. B., Jr. (1974). Biogenic amines in autistic and atypical children: Cerebrospinal fluid measures of homovanillic acid and 5-hydroxyindoleacetic acid. *Archives of General Psychiatry, 31,* 845–853.

Cohen, D. J., & Young, J. G. (1977). Neurochemistry and child psychiatry. *Journal of the American Academy of Child Psychiatry, 16,* 353–411.

Cohen, D. J., Young, J. G., Lowe, T. L., & Harcherik, D. (1980). Thyroid hormone in autistic children. *Journal of Autism and Developmental Disorders, 10,* 445–450.

Coid, J., Allolio, B., & Rees, L. H. (1983). Raised plasma metenkephlin in patients who habitually mutilate themselves. *Lancet, 2,* 545.

Colette, J. W. (1978). Speculation on similarities between autism and opiate addiction. *Journal*

of Autism and Childhood Schizophrenia, 8, 477–479.

Cook, E. H. (1990). Autism: Review of neurochemical investigation [Review]. *Synapse, 6,* 292–308.

Cook, E. H. (2001). Genetics of autism. *Child and Adolescent Psychiatric Clinics of North America, 10,* 333–350.

Cook, E. H., Anderson, G. M., Heninger, G. R., Fletcher, K. E., Freedman, D. X., & Leventhal, B. L. (1992). Tryptophan loading in hyperserotonemic and normoserotonemic adults. *Biological Psychiatry, 31,* 525–528.

Cook, E. H., Arora, R. C., Anderson, G. M., Berry-Kravis, E. M., Yan, S., Yeoh, H. C., et al. (1993). Platelet serotonin in hyperserotonemic relatives of children with autistic disorder. *Life Sciences, 52,* 2005–2015.

Cook, E. H., Leventhal, B. L., & Freedman, D. X. (1988). Free serotonin in plasma: Autistic children and their first degree relatives. *Biological Psychiatry, 24,* 488–491.

Curin, J. M., Terzic, J., Petkovic, Z. B., Zekan, L., Terzic, I. M., & Susnjara, I. M. (2003). Lower cortisol and higher ACTH levels in individuals with autism. *Journal of Autism and Developmental Disorders, 33,* 443–448.

DeMyer, M. K., Hingtgen, J. N., & Jackson, R. K. (1981). Infantile autism reviewed: A decade of research. *Schizophrenia Bulletin, 7,* 388–451.

Dhossche, D., Applegate, H., Abraham, A., Maertens, P., Bland, L., Bencsath, A., et al. (2002). Elevated plasma gamma-aminobutyric acid (GABA) levels in autistic youngsters: Stimulus for a GABA hypothesis of autism. *Medical Science Monitor, 8,* PR1–6.

Elchisak, M. A., Polinsky, R. J., Ebert, M. H., Powers, J., & Kopin, I. J. (1978). Contribution of plasma homovanillic acid (HVA) to urine and CSF HVA in the monkey and its pharmacokinetic disposition. *Life Sciences, 23,* 2339–2348.

Fatemi, S. H., Halt, A. R., Stary, J. M., Kanodia, R., Schulz, S. C., & Realmuto, G. R. (2002). Glutamic acid decarboxylase 65 and 67 kDa proteins are reduced in autistic parietal and cerebellar cortices. *Biological Psychiatry, 52,* 805–810.

Folstein, S. E., & Piven, J. (1991). Etiology of autism: Genetic influences. *Pediatrics, 87*(Suppl.), 767–773.

Folstein, S. E., & Rosen-Sheidley, B. (2001). Genetics of autism: Complex aetiology for a heterogeneous disorder. *Nature Reviews: Genetics, 2,* 943–955.

Frankhauser, M. P., Karumanchi, V. C., German, M. L., Yales, A., & Karumanchi, S. D. (1992). A double-blind, placebo-controlled study of the efficacy of transdermal clonidine in autism. *Journal of Clinical Psychiatry, 53,* 77–82.

Friedman, E. (1969). The "autistic syndrome" and phenylketonuria. *Schizophrenia, 1,* 249–261.

Garelis, E., Young, S. N., Lal, S., & Sourkes, T. L. (1974). Monoamine metabolites in lumbar CSF: The question of their origin in relation to clinical studies. *Brain Research, 79,* 1–8.

Gillberg, C. (1993). Comment on CSF HVA. *Biological Psychiatry, 34,* 746.

Gillberg, C., & Coleman, M. (1992). *The biology of the autistic syndromes* (2nd ed., p. 131). London: Mac Keith Press.

Gillberg, C., & Svennerholm, L. (1987). CSF monoamines in autistic syndromes and other pervasive developmental disorders of early childhood. *British Journal of Psychiatry, 151,* 89–94.

Gillberg, C., Svennerholm, L., & Hamilton-Hellberg, C. (1983). Childhood psychosis and monoamine metabolites in spinal fluid. *Journal of Autism and Developmental Disorders, 13,* 38–96.

Gillberg, C., Terenius, L., & Lonnerholm, G. (1985). Endorphin activity in childhood psychosis. *Archives of General Psychiatry, 42,* 780–783.

Gillberg, C., Trygstad, O., & Foss, J. (1982). Childhood psychosis and urinary excretion of peptides and protein-associated peptide complexes. *Journal of Autism and Developmental Disorders, 12,* 229–241.

Gillberg, I. C., Gillberg, C., & Koop, S. (1992). Hypothyroidsim and autism spectrum disorders. *Journal of Child Psychology and Psychiatry and Allied Disciplines, 33,* 531–542.

Giller, E. L., Young, J. G., Breakefield, X. O., Carbonari, C., Braverman, M., & Cohen, D. J. (1980). Monoamine oxidase and catechol-O-methyltransferase activities in cultured fibroblasts and blood cells from children with autism and the Gilles de la Tourette syndrome. *Psychiatry Research, 2,* 187–197.

Goldberg, M., Hattab, J., Meir, D., Ebstein, R. P., & Belmaker, R. H. (1984). Plasma cyclic AMP and cyclic GMP in childhood-onset psychoses. *Journal of Autism and Developmental Disorders, 14,* 159–164.

Green, L., Fein, D., Modahl, C., Feinstein, C., Waterhouse, L., & Morris, M. (2001). Oxytocin and autistic disorder: Alterations in peptide forms. *Biological Psychiatry, 50,* 609–613.

Guthrie, R. D., & Wyatt, R. J. (1975). Biochemistry and schizophrenia: III. A review of childhood psychosis. *Schizophrenia Bulletin, 12,* 18–32.

Gwirtsman, H., Gerner, R. H., & Sternbach, H. (1982). The overnight dexamethasone suppression test: Clinical and theoretical review. *Journal of Clinical Psychiatry, 48,* 321–327.

Hanley, H. G., Stahl, S. M., & Freedman, D. X. (1977). Hyperserotonemia and amine metabolites in autistic and retarded children. *Archives of General Psychiatry, 34,* 521–531.

Hashimoto, T., Aihara, R., Tayama, M., Miyazaki, M., Shirakawa, Y., & Kuroda, Y. (1991). Reduced thyroid-stimulating hormone response to thyrotropin-releasing hormone in autistic boys. *Developmental Medicine and Child Neurology, 33,* 313–319.

Herman, B. H. (1991). Effects of opioid receptor antagonists on the treatment of autism and self-injurious behavior. In J. J. Ratey (Ed.), *Mental retardation: Developing pharmacotherapies progress in psychiatry* (Vol. 32, pp. 107–137). Washington, DC: American Psychiatric Press.

Hill, S. D., Wagner, E. A., Shedlorski, J. G., & Sears, S. P. (1977). Diurnal cortisol and temperature variation of normal and autistic children. *Developmental Psychobiology, 10,* 579–583.

Hirstein, W., Iversen, P., & Ramachandran, V. S. (2001). Autonomic responses of autistic children to people and objects. *Proceedings of the Royal Society of London. Series B Biological Sciences, 268,* 1883–1888.

Hoshino, Y., Kumashiro, H., Yashima, Y., Kaneko, M., Numato, Y., Oshima, N., et al. (1980). Plasma cyclic AMP level in psychiatric diseases of childhood. *Folia Psychiatrica et Neurologica Japonica, 34,* 9–16.

Hoshino, Y., Ohno, Y., Yamamoto, T., Tachibana, R., Murata, S., Yokoyama, F., et al. (1984). Dexamethasone suppression test in autistic children. *Japanese Journal of Clinical Psychiatry, 26,* 100–102.

Hoshino, Y., Tachibana, R., Watanabe, M., Murata, S., Yokoyama, F., Kaneko, M., et al. (1984). Serotonin metabolism and hypothalamic-pituitary function in children with infantile autism and minimal brain dysfunction. *Japanese Journal of Clinical Psychiatry, 26,* 937–945.

Hoshino, Y., Watanabe, M., Tachibana, R., Murata, S., Kaneko, M., Yashima, Y., et al. (1983). A study of the hypothalamus-pituitary function in autistic children by the loading test of 5HTP, TRH and LH-RH. *Japanese Journal of Brain Research, 9,* 94–95.

Hoshino, Y., Yamamoto, T., Kaneko, M., Tachibana, R., Watanabe, M., Ohno, Y., et al. (1984). Blood serotonin and free tryptophan concentration in autistic children. *Neuropsychobiology, 11,* 22–27.

Hoshino, Y., Yokoyama, F., Watanabe, M., Murata, S., Kaneko, M., & Kumashiro, H. (1987). The diurnal variation and response to dexamethasone suppression test of saliva cortisol level in autistic children. *Japanese Journal of Psychiatry and Neurology, 41,* 227–235.

Insel, T. R., O'Brien, D. J., & Leckman, J. F. (1999). Oxytocin, vasopressin, and autism: Is there a connection? *Biological Psychiatry, 45*(2), 145–157.

Isarangkun, P. P., Newman, H. A., Patel, S. T., Duruibe, V. A., & Abou-Issa, H. (1986). Potential biochemical markers for infantile autism. *Neurochemical Pathology, 5,* 51–70.

Iverson, S. D., & Iverson, L. L. (1981). *Behavioral pharmacology* (2nd ed.). New York: Oxford University Press.

Jaeken, J., & Van den Berghe, G. (1984). An infantile autistic syndrome characterized by the presence of succinylpurines in body fluids. *Lancet, 2,* 1058–1061.

Janusonis, S., Gluncic, V., & Rakic, P. (2004). Early serotonergic projections to Cajal-Retzius cells: Relevance for cortical development. *Journal of Neuroscience, 7,* 1652–1659.

Jensen, J. B., Realmuto, G. M., & Garfinkel, B. D. (1985). The dexamethasone suppression test in infantile autism. *Journal of the American Academy of Child Psychiatry, 24,* 263–265.

Johnson, R. J., Wiersema, V., & Kraft, I. A. (1974). Hair amino acids in childhood autism. *Journal of Autism and Childhood Schizophrenia, 4,* 187–188.

Kahn, A. A. (1970). Thyroid dysfunction. *British Medical Journal, 4,* 495.

Kirwin, P. D., Anderson, G. M., Chappell, P. D., Saberski, L., Leckman, J. F., Geracioti, T. D., et al. (1997). Assessment of diurnal variation of cerebrospinal fluid tryptophan and 5-hydrxyindoleacetic acid in healthy human females. *Life Sciences, 60,* 899–907.

Kopin, I. J., Gordon, E. K., Jimerson, D. C., & Polinsky, R. J. (1983). Relationship between plasma and cerebrospinal fluid levels of 3-methoxy-4-hydroxyphenylglycol. *Science, 219,* 73–75.

Kotsopoulos, S., & Kutty, K. M. (1979). Histidinemia and infantile autism. *Journal of Autism and Developmental Disorders, 9,* 55–60.

Lake, R., Ziegler, M. G., & Murphy, D. L. (1977). Increased norepinephrine levels and decreased DBH activity in primary autism. *Archives of General Psychiatry, 35,* 553–556.

Launay, J. M., Bursztejn, C., Ferrari, P., Dreux, C., Braconnier, A., Zarifian E., et al. (1987). Catecholamines metabolism in infantile autism: A controlled study of 22 autistic children. *Journal of Autism and Developmental Disorders, 17,* 333–347.

Lauritsen, M. B., & Ewald, H. (2001). The genetics of autism. *Acta Psychiatrica Scandinavica, 103,* 411–427.

Leboyer, M., Bouvard, M. P., & Dupes, M. (1988). Effects of naltrexone on infantile autism. *Lancet, 1,* 715.

Leboyer, M., Bouvard, M. P., Launay, J. M., Tableau, F., Waller, D., Kerdelhue, B., et al. (1992). Brief report: A double-blind study of naltrexone on infantile autism. *Journal of Autism and Developmental Disorders, 22,* 309–319.

Leboyer, M., Bouvard, M. P., Recasens, C., Philippe, A., Guilloud-Bataille, M., Bondoux, D., et al. (1994). Differences between plasma N- and C-terminally directed ß-endorphin immunoreactivity in infantile autism. *American Journal of Psychiatry, 151,* 1797–1801.

Le Couteur, A., Trygstad, O., Evered, C., Gillberg, C., & Rutter, M. (1988). Infantile autism and urinary excretion of peptides and protein-associated peptide complexes. *Journal of Autism and Developmental Disorders, 18,* 181–190.

Lee, M., Martin-Ruiz, C., Graham, A., Court, J., Jaros, E., Perry, R., et al. (2002). Nicotinic receptor abnormalities in the cerebellar cortex in autism. *Brain, 125,* 1483–1495.

Leventhal, B. L., Cook, E. H., Jr., Morford, M., Ravitz, A., & Freedman, D. X. (1990). Relationships of whole blood serotonin and plasma norepinephrine within families. *Journal of Autism & Developmental Disorders, 20,* 499–511.

Lotspeich, L. J., & Ciaranello, R. D. (1993). The neurobiology and genetics of infantile autism. *International Review of Neurobiology, 35,* 87–129.

Lowe, T. L., Tanaka, K., Seashore, M. R., Young, J. G., & Cohen, D. J. (1980). Detection of phenylketonuria in autistic and psychotic children. *Journal of the American Medical Association, 243,* 126–128.

Lucki, I. (1998). The spectrum of behaviors influenced by serotonin. *Biological Psychiatry, 44,* 151–162.

Maas, J. W., Hattox, S. E., Greene, N. M., & Landis, B. H. (1980). Estimates of dopamine and serotonin synthesis by the awake human brain. *Journal of Neurochemistry, 34,* 1547–1549.

Maas, J. W., & Leckman, J. F. (1983). Relationships between CNS noradrenergic function and plasma and urine MHPG and other norepinephrine metabolites. In J. W. Maas (Ed.), *MHPG: Basal mechanisms and psychopathology* (pp. 33–43). New York: Academic Press.

Maher, K. R., Harper, J. F., Macleay, A., & King, M. G. (1975). Peculiarities in the endocrine response to insulin stress in early infantile autism. *Journal of Nervous and Mental Diseases, 161,* 180–184.

Manning, J. T., Baron-Cohen, S., Wheelwright, S., & Sanders, G. (2001). The 2nd to 4th digit ratio and autism. *Developmental Medicine and Child Neurology, 43,* 160–164.

Martineau, J., Barthelemy, C., Jouve, J., Muh, J. P., & Lelord, G. (1992). Monoamines (serotonin and catecholamines) and their derivatives in infantile autism: Age-related changes and drug effects. *Developmental Medicine & Child Neurology, 34,* 593–603.

McBride, P. A., Anderson, G. M., Hertzig, M. E., Sweeney, J. A., Kream, J., Cohen, D. J., et al. (1989). Serotonergic responsivity in male young adults with autistic disorder. *Archives of General Psychiatry, 46,* 213–221.

McBride, P. A., Anderson, G. M., & Mann, J. J. (1990). Serotonin in autism. In E. F. Coccaro & D. L. Murphy (Eds.), *Serotonin in major psychiatric disorders* (pp. 47–68). Washington, DC: American Psychiatric Press.

McBride, P. A., Anderson, G. M., & Shapiro, T. (1996). Autism research: Bringing together approaches to pull apart the disorder. *Archives of General Psychiatry, 53,* 980–983.

McDougle, C. J., Naylor, S. T., Cohen, D. J., Aghajanian, G. K., Heninger, G. R., & Price, L. H. (1996). Effects of tryptophan depletion in drug-free adults with autistic disorder. *Archives of General Psychiatry, 53,* 993–1000.

Meek, J. L., & Neff, N. H. (1973). Is cerebrospinal fluid the major avenue for the removal of 5-hydroxyindoleacetic acid from the brain? *Neuropharmacology, 12,* 497–499.

Minderaa, R. B., Anderson, G. M., Volkmar, F. R., Akkerhuis, G. W., & Cohen, D. J. (1987). Urinary 5-HIAA and whole blood 5-HT and tryptophan in autism and normal subjects. *Biological Psychiatry, 22,* 933–940.

Minderaa, R. B., Anderson, G. M., Volkmar, F. R., Akkerhuis, G. W., & Cohen, D. J. (1994). Noradrenergic and adrenergic functioning in autism. *Biological Psychiatry, 36,* 237–241.

Minderaa, R. B., Anderson, G. M., Volkmar, F. R., Harcherik, D., Akkerhuis, G. W., & Cohen, D. J. (1989). Neurochemical study of dopamine functioning in autistic and normal subjects. *Journal of the American Academy of Child and Adolescent Psychiatry, 28,* 200–206.

Mulder, E. J., Anderson, G. M., Kema, I. P., de Bildt, A., van Lange, N. D. J., et al. (2004). Platelet serotonin levels in pervasive developmental disorders and mental retardation: Diagnostic group differences, within group distribution and behavioral correlates. *Journal of the American*

Academy of Child and Adolescent Psychiatry, 43, 491–499.

Nagamitsu, S. (1993). CSF ß-endorphin levels in pediatric neurologic disorders. *Kurume Medical Journal, 40,* 223–241.

Narayan, M., Srinath, S., & Anderson, G. M. (1993). CSF HVA in autism (in reply). *Biological Psychiatry, 34,* 746–747.

Narayan, M., Srinath, S., Anderson, G. M., & Meundi, D. B. (1993). Cerebrospinal fluid levels of homovanillic acid and 5-hydroxyindoleacetic acid in autism. *Biological Psychiatry, 33,* 630–635.

Naruse, H., Hayashi, T., Takesada, M., Nakane, A., & Yamazaki, K. (1989). Metabolic changes in aromatic amino acids and monoamines in infantile autism and development of new treatment related to the finding. *No to Hattatsu [Brain and Development], 21,* 181–189.

Nelson, K. B., Grether, J. K., Croen, L. A., Dambrosia, J. M., Dickens, B. F., Jelliffe, L. L., et al. (2001). Neuropeptides and neurotrophins in neonatal blood of children with autism or mental retardation. *Annals of Neurology, 49,* 597–606.

Nir, I., Meir, D., Zilber, N., Knobler, H., Hadjez, J., & Lerner, Y. (1995). Brief report: Circadian melatonin, thyroid-stimulating hormone, prolactin, and cortisol levels in serum of young adults with autism. *Journal of Autism and Developmental Disorders, 25*(6), 641–654.

O'Brien, R. A., Semenuk, G., & Spector, S. (1976). Catechol-O-methyltransferase activity in erythrocytes of children with autism. In E. Coleman (Ed.), *The autistic syndromes* (pp. 43–49). Amsterdam: North Holland.

Page, T., & Coleman, M. (2000). Purine metabolism abnormalities in a hyperuricosuric subclass of autism. *Biochimica et Biophysica Acta, 1500,* 291–296.

Panksepp, J. (1979). A neurochemical theory of autism. *Trends in Neuroscience, 2,* 174–177.

Partington, M. W., Tu, J. B., & Wong, C. Y. (1973). Blood serotonin levels in severe mental retardation. *Developmental Medicine and Child Neurology, 15,* 616–627.

Perry, E. K., Lee, M. L., Martin-Ruiz, C. M., Court, J. A., Volsen, S. G., Merrit, J., et al. (2001). Cholinergic activity in autism: Abnormalities in the cerebral cortex and basal forebrain. *American Journal of Psychiatry, 158,* 1058–1066.

Perry, T. L., Hansen, S., & Christie, R. G. (1978). Amino compounds and organic acids in CSF, plasma, and urine of autistic children. *Biological Psychiatry, 13,* 575–586.

Posey, D. J., McDougle, C. J. (2000). The pharmacotherapy of target symptoms associated with autistic disorder and other pervasive developmental disorders. *Harvard Review of Psychiatry, 8,* 45–63.

Realmuto, G. M., Jensen, J. B., Reeve, E., & Garfinkel, B. D. (1990). Growth hormone response to L-dopa and clonidine in autistic children. *Journal of Autism and Developmental Disorders, 20,* 455–465.

Redmond, D. E., Jr., & Huang, Y. W. (1979). New evidence for a locus coeruleus-norepinephrine connection with anxiety. *Life Sciences, 25,* 2149–2162.

Reichelt, K. L., Hole, K., Hamberger, A., Saelid, G., Edminson, P. D., Braestrup, C. B., et al. (1981). Biologically active peptide-containing fractions in schizophrenia and childhood autism. *Advances in Biochemistry and Psychopharmacology, 28,* 627–643.

Reichelt, K. L., & Knivsberg, A. M. (2003). Can the pathophysiology of autism be explained by the nature of the discovered urine peptides? *Nutritional Neuroscience, 6,* 19–28.

Reichelt, K. L., Saelid, G., Lindback, T., & Boler, J. B. (1986). Childhood autism: A complex disorder. *Biological Psychiatry, 21,* 1279–1290.

Richdale, A. L., & Prior, M. R. (1992). Urinary cortisol circadian rhythm in a group of high-functioning children with autism. *Journal of Autism and Developmental Disorders, 22,* 433–446.

Ritvo, E. R. (1977). Biochemical studies of children with the syndromes of autism, childhood schizophrenia and related developmental disabilities: A review. *Journal of Child Psychology and Psychiatry, 13,* 373–379.

Ritvo, E. R., Mason-Brothers, A., Freeman, B. J., Pingree, C., Jenson, W. R., McMahon, W. M., et al. (1990). The UCLA–University of Utah epidemiologic survey of autism: The etiologic role of rare diseases. *American Journal of Psychiatry, 147,* 1614–1621.

Ritvo, E. R., Yuwiler, A., Geller, E., Kales, A. Rashkis, S., Schicor, A., et al. (1971). Effects of L-dopa in autism. *Journal of Autism and Childhood Schizophrenia, 1,* 190–205.

Ritvo, E. R., Yuwiler, A., Geller, E., Ornitz, E. M., Saeger, K., & Plotkin, S. (1970). Increased blood serotonin and platelets in early infantile autism. *Archives of General Psychiatry, 23,* 566–572.

Rosenberger-Diesse, J., & Coleman, M. (1986). Brief report: Preliminary evidence for multiple etiologies in autism. *Journal of Autism and Developmental Disorders, 16,* 385–392.

Ross, D. L., Klykylo, W. M., & Anderson, G. M. (1985). Cerebrospinal fluid indoleamine and monoamine effects in fenfluramine treatment of autism. *Annals of Neurology, 18,* 394.

Ross, D. L., Klykylo, W. M., & Hitzeman, R. (1987). Reduction of elevated CSF ß-endorphin by fenfluramine in infantile autism. *Pediatric Neurology, 3,* 83–86.

Rutter, M., & Bartak, L. (1971). Causes of infantile autism: Some considerations from recent research. *Journal of Autism and Childhood Schizophrenia, 1,* 20–32.

Rutter, M., & Schopler, E. (1987). Autism and pervasive developmental disorders: Concepts and diagnostic issues. *Journal of Autism and Developmental Disorders, 17,* 159–186.

Sandman, C. A. (1991). The opiate hypothesis in autism and self-injury. *Journal of Child and Adolescent Psychopharmacology, 1,* 237–248.

Sandman, C. A. (1992). Various endogenous opioids and autistic behavior: A response to Gillberg. *Journal of Autism and Developmental Disorders, 22,* 132–133.

Sandman, C. A., Barron, J. L., Chicz-Demet, A., & Demet, E. M. (1990). Plasma ß-endorphin and cortisol levels in autism. *American Journal of Mental Retardation, 95,* 84–92.

Sandman, C. A., Patta, P. C., Banon, J., Hoehler, F. K., Williams, C., Williams, C., et al. (1983). Naloxone attenuates self-abusive behavior in developmentally disabled clients. *Applied Research in Mental Retardation, 4,* 5–11.

Sankar, D. V. S. (1971). Studies on blood platelets, blood enzymes, and leukocyte chromosome breakage in childhood schizophrenia. *Behavioral Neuropsychiatry, 2,* 2–10.

Schain, R. J., & Freedman, D. X. (1961). Studies on 5-hydroxyindole metabolism in autistic and other mentally retarded children. *Journal of Pediatrics, 58,* 315–320.

Scriver, C. R., & Rosenberg, L. E. (1973). *Amino acid metabolism and its disorders.* Philadelphia: Saunders.

Sherwin, A. C., Flach, F. F., & Stokes, P. E. (1958). Treatment of psychoses in early childhood with triiodothyronine. *American Journal of Psychiatry, 115,* 166–167.

Shoaf, S. E., Carson, R. E., Hommer, D., Williams, W. A., Higley, J. D., Schmall, B., et al. (2000). The suitability of 11C-alpha-methyl-L-tryptophan as a tracer for serotonin synthesis. *Journal of Cerebral Blood Flow and Metabolism, 20,* 244–252.

Simmonds, H. A., Webster, D. R., Lingham, S., & Wilson, J. (1985). An inborn error of purine metabolism, deafness and neurodevelopmental abnormality. *Neuropediatrics, 16,* 106–108.

Sokol, D. K., Dunn, D. W., Edwards-Brown, M., & Feinberg, J. (2002). Hydrogen proton magnetic resonance spectroscopy in autism: Preliminary evidence of elevated choline/creatine ratio. *Journal of Child Neurology, 17,* 245–249.

Stone, R. L., Aimi, J., Barshop, B. A., Jaeken, J., Van den Berghe, G., Zalkin, H., et al. (1992). A mutation in adenylosuccinate lyase associated with mental retardation and autistic features. *Nature Genetics, 1,* 59–63.

Suwa, S., Naruse, H., Ohura, T., Tsuruhara, T., Takesada, M., Yamazaki, K., et al. (1984). Influence of pimozide on hypothalamo-pituitary function in children with behavioral disorders. *Psychoneuroendocrinology, 9,* 37–44.

Sverd, J., Kupretz, S. S., Winsberg, B. G., Hurwic, M. J., & Becker, L. (1978). Effect of L-5-hydroxytryptophan in autistic children. *Journal of Autism and Childhood Schizophrenia, 8,* 171–180.

Sylvester, O., Jorgensen, E., Mellerup, T., & Rafaelsen, O. J. (1970). Amino acid excretion in urine of children with various psychiatric diseases. *Danish Medical Bulletin, 17,* 166–170.

Takatsu, T., Onizawa, J., & Nakahato, M. (1965). Tryptophan metabolism disorder and therapeutic diet in children with infantile autism. *Amino Acids, 5,* 13–14.

Tani, Y., Fernell, E., Watanbe, Y., Kanai, T., & Langstrom, B. (1994). Decrease in 6R-5, 6, 7, 8-tetrahydrobiopterin content in cerebrospinal fluid of autistic patients. *Neuroscience Letters, 181,* 169–172.

Tordjman, S., Anderson, G. M., McBride, P. A. Hall, L. M., Ferrari, P., & Cohen, D. J. (1995). Plasma androgens in autism. *Journal of Autism and Developmental Disorders, 25,* 295–304.

Tordjman, S., Anderson, G. M., McBride, P. A., Hertzig, M. E., Snow, M. E., Hall, L. M., et al. (1997). Plasma ß-endorphin, adrenocorticotropin hormone, and cortisol in autism. *Journal of Child Psychology and Psychiatry, 38,* 705–715.

Tordjman, S., Ferrari, P., Sulmont, V., Duyme, M., & Roubertoux, P. (1997). Androgenic activity in autism. *American Journal of Psychiatry, 154,* 1626–1627.

Udenfriend, S., Titus, E., Weissbach, H., & Peterson, R. E. (1959). Biogenesis and metabolism of 5-hydroxyindole compounds. *Journal of Biological Chemistry, 219,* 335–344.

Waage-Baudet, H., Lauder, J. M., Dehart, D. B., Kluckman, K., Hiller, S., Tint, G. S., et al. (2003). Abnormal serotonergic development in a mouse model for the Smith-Lemli-Opitz syndrome: Implications for autism. *International Journal of Developmental Neuroscience, 21*(8), 451–459.

Weizman, R., Weizman, A., Tyrano, S., Szekely, B., Weissman, B. A., & Sarne, Y. (1984). Humoral-endorphin blood levels in autistic, schizophrenic and healthy subjects. *Psychopharmacology, 82,* 368–370.

Whitaker-Azmitia, P. M. (2001). Serotonin and brain development: Role in human developmental diseases. *Brain Research Bulletin, 56,* 479–485.

Whitaker-Azmitia, P. M., Druse, M., Walker, P., & Lauder, J. M. (1996). Serotonin as a developmental signal. *Behavioural Brain Research, 73,* 19–29.

Winsberg, B. G., Sverd, J., Castells, S., Hurwic, M., & Perel, J. M. (1980). Estimation of monoamine and cyclic-AMP turnover and amino acid concentrations of spinal fluid in autistic children. *Neuropediatrics, 11,* 250–255.

Yamazaki, K., Saito, Y., Okada, F., Fujiede, T., & Yamashita, I. (1975). An application of neuroendocrinological studies in autistic children and Heller's syndrome. *Journal of Autism and Childhood Schizophrenia, 5,* 323–332.

Young, J. G., Cohen, D. J., Brown, S. L., & Caparulo, B. K. (1978). Decreased urinary free catecholamines in childhood autism. *Journal of the American Academy of Child Psychiatry, 17,* 671–678.

Young, J. G., Cohen, D. J., Hattox, S. E., Kavanagh, M. E., Anderson, G. M., Shaywitz, B. A., et al. (1981). Plasma free MHPG and neuroendocrine responses to challenge doses of clonidine in Tourette's syndrome: Preliminary report. *Life Sciences, 29,* 1467–1475.

Young, J. G., Cohen, D. J., Kavanagh, M. E., Landis, H. D., Shaywitz, B. A., & Maas, J. W. (1981). Cerebrospinal fluid, plasma, and urinary MHPG in children. *Life Sciences, 28,* 2837–2845.

Young, J. G., Kavanagh, M. E., Anderson, G. M., Shaywitz, B. A., & Cohen, D. J. (1982). Clinical neurochemistry of autism and associated disorders. *Journal of Autism and Developmental Disorders, 12,* 147–165.

Young, J. G., Newcorn, J. H., & Leven, L. I. (1989). Pervasive developmental disorders. In H. I. Kaplan & B. J. Saddock (Eds.), *Comprehensive textbook of psychiatry* (pp. 1772–1787). Baltimore: Williams & Wilkins.

Young, S. N., Anderson, G. M., & Purdy, W. C. (1980). Indoleamine metabolism in rat brain studied through measurements of tryptophan, 5-hydroxyindoleactic acid and indoleactetic acid in cerebrospinal fluid. *Journal of Neurochemistry, 34,* 309–315.

Yuwiler, A., Geller, A., & Ritvo, E. R. (1985). Biochemical studies of autism. In E. Lajtha (Ed.),

Handbook of Neurochemistry (pp. 671–691). New York: Plenum Press.

Yuwiler, A., Ritvo, E. R., Geller, E., Glousman, R., Schneiderman, G., & Matsuno, D. (1975). Uptake and efflux of serotonin from platelets of autistic and nonautistic children. *Journal of Autism and Childhood Schizophrenia, 5,* 83–98.

Zhou, E. C., Auerbach, S., & Azmitia, E. C. (1987). Denervation of serotonergic fibers in the hippocampus induced a trophic factor which enhance the maturation of transplanted serotonergic neurons but not norepinephrine neurons. *Journal of Neuroscience Research, 17,* 235–246.

CHAPTER 18

Neurologic Aspects of Autism

NANCY J. MINSHEW, JOHN A. SWEENEY, MARGARET L. BAUMAN, and SARA JANE WEBB

Autism is now widely accepted as being a disorder of brain development and, hence, of neurologic origin. Histopathologic abnormalities of multiple brain structures and alterations in brain weight were described 2 decades ago, providing definitive evidence of a brain basis for this disorder. Recently, structural imaging studies have provided evidence of early abnormalities in brain growth that coincide with, if not predate, the onset of clinically recognized symptoms. Functional imaging studies have provided evidence of underconnectivity of neocortical neural systems for social, communication, and reasoning abilities related to the core symptoms of autism. From a neuropathologic perspective, the onset of the neurodevelopmental events appears to be no later than 28 to 30 weeks, based on the limited available autopsy material. Neuropathologic and neuroimaging studies suggest abnormalities in the elaboration of dendritic and axonal ramifications, the establishment of synaptic connections, the selective elimination of neuronal processes, and the development of white matter tracts. However, most of the developmental neurobiology of autism remains speculative and unconfirmed. Autism is a sporadic disorder, the core features of which are faithfully reproduced both neuropathologically and clinically from case to case, suggesting a common pathophysiology that originates at the level of DNA or its transcription for brain development.

Geneticists have calculated a heritability index of .90 or above for autism. The rapid drop-off in cases from first- to second- and third-degree relatives supports a polygenetic mode of inheritance. Each case is suspected to reflect the influence of several autism susceptibility genes, but not the same genes in each case. Geneticists hypothesize that there are 10 to 20, if not more, autism susceptibility genes. Several phenotypic findings are thought to be linked to autism susceptibility genes, in particular the prominent incidence of affective disorder in first-degree relatives, the expression of characteristics of the clinical syndrome in first-degree relatives, and macrocephaly.

The frequent co-occurrence of autistic symptomatology with tuberous sclerosis, a disorder also characterized by overgrowth of cerebral white matter, may also provide a link to the genetics and neurobiology of autism. Identification of the genes involved in affective disorder and tuberous sclerosis may identify regions of DNA with increased likelihood for containing genes related to neurodevelopmental errors in autism and the impairments exhibited by less affected relatives. Genetic studies are vigorously attempting to identify the susceptibility genes for autism. Interesting

This work was supported by a NICHD Collaborative Program of Excellence in Autism grant U19 HD35469, Nancy Minshew, MD, director. We gratefully acknowledge the participation of individuals with autism and control subjects in all research studies. We also appreciate the work of Sara Eddy, who helped with the research and writing of sections of this chapter and the final formatting assistance of Kelsey Woods, Rosie Christ, and Bernadette MacDonald, who provided secretarial assistance.

473

findings have included the serotonin transporter gene and linkage to chromosome 17 (Cook et al., 1997); the linkage between the absence of language in autism and chromosome 7 and, more recently, 2q (mitochondrial aspartate/glutamate carrier gene; Ramoz et al., 2004); and the association with the homeobox transcription factor Engrailed 2 (Gharani, Benayed, Mancuso, Brzustowicz, & Millonig, 2004). While none of these have been confirmed yet, the results attest to the progress being made and the likelihood of success in the future in finding the genes for autism.

Substantial progress has also been made in the past 2 decades in defining the behavioral neurology of autism, that is, the cognitive and brain basis for the behavior. Over the past 10 years, the capability for characterizing autism has improved substantially as a result of advances in research diagnostic methods and criteria used to define autism and the evolution in technology for the in vivo study of central nervous system (CNS) function and structure. The introduction of magnetic resonance imaging (MRI) made studies of children and repeated studies feasible, and the development of functional MRI (fMRI) is leading to further understanding of the brain basis of cognitive impairments and intact or enhanced abilities in autism. Structural studies have provided evidence of increased supratentorial total brain and white matter volumes, increased brain weight, and above-average head circumference on the one hand and, on the other, truncation of the dendritic tree development of neurons in limbic structures and decreased neuronal number in the cerebellum. Functional studies are revealing evidence of underconnectivity in the distributed networks of cortical centers that subserve the core symptoms of autism, including social, language, and reasoning. Areas of intact or superior abilities appear to have enhanced local connectivity. This constellation of structural and functional findings has defined two intriguing "paradoxes": (1) the dissociation between the CNS localizations of some structural and functional findings and (2) the contrast between "too much brain" in some regions and "too little brain" in other regions. These paradoxes are starting to resolve with the recent histologic findings of Casanova, Buxhoeveden, Switala, and Roy (2002) in minicolumns in the cerebral cortex and the emerging perspective of autism as a distributed neural systems disorder rather than a focal brain disorder.

Neurologic conceptualizations or models proposed for autism have altered in accordance with the changing structural and functional characterization of autism. Current neurobiologic theories postulate single or multiple deficits in complex or higher order cognitive abilities, dysfunction at the neural systems level of brain organization, and a central role for cerebral cortex in the final common pathophysiology of the clinical manifestations. Such theories represent a closer approximation of the pathophysiology of autism, but certainly not the final step. The goal of research underway is to define with precision the cognitive and neural basis of all of the features of the clinical syndrome, the developmental neurobiology of the structural and functional abnormalities of the brain, the genes involved in the developmental neurobiology, and other etiologies that might trigger the disruption in brain development. This knowledge will result in a substantial improvement in diagnosis and in all phases of intervention and will pave the way for the development of definitive neurobiologic interventions designed to ameliorate the brain abnormalities underlying autism.

CENTRAL NERVOUS SYSTEM FUNCTION IN AUTISM

The neurophysiologic integrity of neural pathways in the brain can be investigated with several methods, most commonly through studies of evoked potentials and oculomotor physiology. These methods provide information about neural pathways at multiple levels of the neuraxis and about selected aspects of sensory, motor, and cognitive function. Both evoked potentials and oculomotor physiology were originally applied to autism shortly after their introduction to medical science. Subsequently, two types of scientific pursuits were undertaken: neurophysiological studies and neuropsychological studies. Neurophysiologic studies typically assess functional integrity of the nervous system. Neuropsychological studies investigate brain function at an integrative level beyond the more basic functions assessed with neurophysiologic methods and thus potentially provide an intermediate step between basic laboratory findings and clinical symptom expression. The first era of this research in autism, ending in the early to mid-1980s, largely documented results of clinical studies that had been conducted with problematic experimental designs. Research studies since 1980 have defined a neurophysiologic profile in autism that is characterized by abnormalities in cognitive processing and neocortical circuitry, with intact early information processing, simple cognitive abilities, and very subtle disturbances in posterior fossa circuitry (e.g., brainstem and cerebellum).

Findings using both neurophysiological and neuropsychological methods are dependent on the cognitive abilities and cooperation of high-functioning autistic individuals. These individuals provide the opportunity to define the qualitative features of the deficits and preserved abilities and to study the disorder in the absence of mental retardation in order to determine abnormalities solely related to autism. These findings have major implications for the neurobiology of autism as a whole since high-functioning individuals have the same disorder as low-functioning individuals.

Evoked Potentials: Sensory and Cognitive Processing

Evoked potentials (EPs) are recordings from an array of scalp electrodes of the neural response to a sensory stimulus or cognitive challenge task. The EPs or event-related potentials (ERPs) originate from a population of synchronous firing neurons in the brain, are time-locked to stimulus presentation, and can be averaged to distinguish them from background electroencephalographic activity. Stimuli, such as a visual image or a tone, trigger electrical activity within the brain within a millisecond time course, and simple sensory stimuli can evoke a prototypical response at many locations in the brain. For "higher" perceptual and cognitive processes, scalp EPs likely reflect the activity and contributions of many different neural systems that overlap in time and spatial distribution. Given that EP recordings reflect the activation of neural circuitry, the resulting waveform is composed of multiple

potentials, each with a characteristic latency range and spatial distribution. Amplitude of EPs varies with the characteristics of the stimulus or cognitive task and, in the case of the cognitive potentials, with subject characteristics. Some potentials also have a developmental trajectory, which adds yet another dimension to experimental design and data interpretation.

EPs are typically classified as either exogenous (evoked by perception of an external stimuli) or endogenous (evoked by mental processes or behavior). Exogenous potentials occur within the first 40 milliseconds of the stimulus and are typically an obligatory response of brain neurons to a sensory stimulus. Their amplitude and latency are influenced by the physical properties of the stimulus, specifically its intensity, duration, and frequency. These potentials are affected by the auditory or visual acuity of the subject but are minimally affected by attention, motivation, and level of consciousness. Exogenous potentials are often used to test perception of the stimulus in the visual or auditory modality.

Endogenous potentials are elicited by stimulus paradigms that require the subject to perform a perceptual analysis of a stimulus such as distinguishing one tone from another. These potentials occur between 30 milliseconds and 1 second following the stimulus and depend primarily on the setting in which the stimulus occurs. They are relatively independent of the physical properties of the stimulus but are influenced by subject attention, comprehension of the task, past experience with the task, importance of task performance to the subject, and the subject's ability level and knowledge. Thus, all the various sources of influence on human perception may have an influence on endogenous potentials.

EPs can be recorded during both passive and active tasks. In passive tasks, subjects are not required to make a verbal or behavioral response, and these tasks are appropriate for younger children and low-functioning individuals. With few exceptions, EP research in autism to date has been confined to the study of auditory (exogenous) brainstem potentials, auditory (endogenous) potentials during attentional control and modulation, and, to a very limited extent, the visual (endogenous) potentials during passive viewing or low demand tasks (e.g., target detection). Notable for their relative absence from the neurophysiologic literature in autism are studies of the social, language, and reasoning deficits inherent to the definition of this disorder. This bias is likely due to the fact that these tasks require understanding of verbal directions or selective behavioral responses and are often difficult to modify to fit the event-related nature of EP methodology. A second major research limitation of EPs is the degree to which scalp-recorded EPs can be localized to generators within the brain. This limitation reflects methodological constraints, as very few studies have used high-density recording arrays, making it difficult to employ source localization algorithms; thus, little is known of the precise localization of EP abnormalities.

Auditory Brainstem Evoked Potentials (Exogenous)

These potentials are generated within the first 10 milliseconds following a click stimulus and reflect early neural activity in the auditory pathway. Waves I and II represent activity in the eighth cranial nerve and are commonly used to assess hearing in infants and noncooperative children. Wave III is thought to result from activity in the lower pons and in the area of the superior olive, and wave V from activity in the upper pons and area of the inferior colliculus. Waves I, III, and V are the most reliable waveforms. At lower stimulus intensities or higher stimulation rates, only wave V remains clinically reliable (Courchesne, Courchesne, Hicks, & Lincoln, 1985; Galambos & Hecox, 1978; Starr, Sohmer, & Celesia, 1978; Stockard, Stockard, & Sharbrough, 1978). Waves II and IV are often not measured because of lack of established clinical utility (Chiappa & Gladstone, 1978; Rumsey, Grimes, Pikus, Duara, & Ismond, 1984).

The most reliable measurements are the latencies of the waves, particularly wave V, and the interpeak intervals between waves I, III, and V, which are used to assess the integrity of the brainstem auditory pathway, thalamocortical pathway, and auditory nerve. In healthy individuals, the latencies of waves I and V achieve adult values by 2 years of age. The maturation of the I-V interpeak latency (IPL) exhibits two phases, one completed by 1 year

of age and the second by 3 years, which may reflect different aspects of brainstem maturation (Aminoff, 1992; Zimmerman, Morgan, & Dubno, 1987). Gender also impacts the norms for these potentials, with females generally having shorter latencies with higher amplitudes and shorter I-V and III-V intervals compared to males. Middle ear, cochlear, eighth nerve, and brainstem pathology involving or immediately adjacent to the auditory pathways may cause abnormalities in these potentials.

The first study of brainstem auditory evoked potentials (BAEPs) in autism reported normal results (Ornitz, Mo, & Olson, 1980; Ornitz & Walter, 1975) but was followed by a number of studies emphasizing abnormalities (Gillberg, Rosenthal, & Johansson, 1983; Rosenblum et al., 1980; Skoff, Mirsky, & Turner, 1980; Student & Sohmer, 1978, 1979; Tanguay & Edwards, 1982; Tanguay, Edwards, Buchwald, Schwafel, & Allen, 1982; Taylor, Rosenblatt, & Linschoten, 1982; Thivierge, Bedard, Cote, & Maziade, 1990; Wong & Wong, 1991). The latter studies reported abnormalities consisting of moderate to severe abnormalities or absence of wave I (sensorineural deafness) and delays in brainstem transmission time in 20% to 60% of the autistic subjects. Over time, the abnormalities described in these studies were traced to various methodological limitations. The abnormalities reported by Student and Sohmer (1978) were found to be secondary to equipment error and were retracted (Student & Sohmer, 1979). Several abnormal findings from other studies were traced to limitations in subject selection or ERP methodology. Subject selection procedures often failed to exclude autistic subjects with causes of brain damage other than autism, to assess audiologic function, to exclude individuals with hearing loss, and to match autistic and healthy subjects on age and gender. Technical limitations of these early studies included the failure to consider the impact of age and gender on measurements, to differentiate between brainstem transmission times that were too short and too long when determining the incidence of abnormalities, to assess measurement reliability, and to use reliable EP measurements or procedures. The largest well controlled of these early studies (Tanguay & Edwards, 1982; Tanguay et al.,

1982) emphasized abnormalities but actually found very few abnormal brainstem transmission values except at the lowest stimulus intensity, and these abnormal values were in both directions. When the autistic and control groups in this study were matched on both age and gender, no statistically significant abnormalities were found.

These various design and methodological issues were rigorously addressed in the studies of Rumsey et al. (1984) and Courchesne, Courchesne, et al. (1985). In a study of 25 children and adults with a wide range of autism severity, Rumsey et al. (1984) found prolonged brainstem transmission (>3 SD of laboratory norms) in one autistic subject and one normal control. Three autistic subjects were found to have shortened brainstem transmission times, which accounted for the few group differences observed. Based on the review of prior work and the results of their study, Rumsey and colleagues (1984) concluded: "Reports of prolonged transmission times in a substantial percentage of autistic children may be attributable to concomitant identifiable neurological disease and peripheral hearing impairments, inadequately matched control groups, high artifact levels, and poor reliability of measurements."

In 1985, Courchesne, Courchesne, et al. evaluated the BAEP of 14 high-functioning (PIQ > 70) and 14 normal control adolescents and young adults at slow, medium, and fast rates of stimulation; soft, medium, and loud stimulus intensities; right and left ear stimulation; and rarefaction and compression clicks. The authors also controlled for body temperature. In a follow-up study, they further emphasized the limitations of using small numbers of normal subjects to represent population norms (Grillon, Courchesne, & Akshoomoff, 1989). This study found no group differences in the auditory brainstem EPs among autistic subjects, normal controls, and clinical norms under any of the stimulus conditions. Examination of the individual cases further revealed that every autistic subject in the study had normal auditory EPs.

Courchesne, Courchesne, et al. (1985) concluded that there was unlikely to be an abnormality in autism in the brainstem auditory pathways that generate early ERPs and that

abnormalities in the brainstem auditory ERPs were neither necessary nor sufficient to produce autism. These authors further emphasized that the previously demonstrated abnormalities in longer latency sensory and cognitive EPs in these autistic subjects (Courchesne, Kilman, Galambos, & Lincoln, 1984) were not the downstream consequence of abnormalities in brainstem auditory pathways but rather the result of an abnormality in higher auditory processing.

In the early 1990s, reports of abnormal BAEP reemerged (McClelland, Eyre, Watson, Calvert, & Sherrard, 1992; Thivierge et al., 1990; Wong & Wong, 1991). However, it was again difficult to interpret the significance of those findings for autism because of the inclusion of individuals with tuberous sclerosis, fetal cytomegalovirus, Rett syndrome, and fragile X syndrome (Wong & Wong, 1991) and the use of idiosyncratic methodology with unclear physiologic significance for brainstem potentials (Thivierge et al., 1990). McClelland et al. (1992) reported normal BAEPs in all autistic subjects under age 14 years and in all high-functioning autistic subjects. However, the autism group failed to show brainstem auditory potential latency decreases after 14 years of age; this is in contrast to the decreases found in the normal control group ($n = 54$). Since age effects on these potentials are largely confined to the first 3 years of life, the difference between autistic and control subjects after 14 years of age may be related more to subject factors, such as how representative the control group was of normative values, rather than to diagnosis. Although the investigators interpreted their data as evidence of a delay in brainstem myelination, myelination of the brainstem is a very early developmental event that is complete within the first year of life. Abnormal brainstem myelination would result in abnormalities in BAEPs prior to age 14 in the autism group; these results seem inconsistent with delayed myelination as an explanation. Alternatively, this pattern of findings, if demonstrated to be valid, might reflect the observations of Bauman and Kemper of the persistence of a fetal pattern in inferior olivary circuits, which they suggested may be vulnerable to deterioration during the teens.

In a more recent study, Maziade et al. (2000) investigated the BAEP in autistic individuals and their unaffected relatives. Compared to the control group, the autistic participants had prolonged I-III IPLs. Some of the unaffected first-degree relatives also showed this same prolongation of the early brain-auditory evoked response. However, in about 50% of the families, neither the autistic participants nor the parents showed a significant IPL prolongation. Therefore, the authors concluded that prolongation of the IPL is not a necessary or sufficient cause in the development of autism (Maziade et al., 2000). Maziade et al. also found cases where the parents had prolonged IPL, but their autistic child did not, and the opposite pattern where the parents did not have prolonged IPL, but the autistic child did. Nagy and Loveland (2002) proposed that it might be beneficial to subdivide the impaired and nonimpaired subjects into separate groups. This finding and its familial pattern require further investigation.

Two additional studies have recently been conducted on BAEP with inconsistent results. Rosenhall, Nordin, Brantberg, and Gillberg (2003) found the III-V IPL was significantly prolonged in male and female autistic individuals with normal hearing. There were, however, no significant differences in the latencies for wave III or the I-V IPL. These findings are inconsistent with the results of a study by Chen et al. (2003), which found that a group of children with autism had longer latencies than a control group in waves III and V as well as longer IPLs in wave I-II and I-V.

Given the inconsistent results of the various BAEP studies, it is apparent that further research is needed to determine whether a solid relationship exists between prolonged auditory brainstem transmission times and autism.

Auditory Middle Latency Potentials

The middle latency auditory potentials occur 10 to 50 milliseconds following a click stimulus and consist of several positive and negative components: (1) Na (10 to 25 milliseconds), (2) Pa (25 to 40 milliseconds), (3) Nb (40 to 50 milliseconds), and (4) P1 (50 to 65 milliseconds). These potentials are thought to represent activity in the thalamus, thalamocortical radiations, and primary auditory cortex. Only two studies have investigated middle latency potentials in autism and then only in small numbers of subjects (Buchwald et al., 1992; Grillon et al., 1989). Grillon et al. found no abnormalities in Na, Pa, and Nb latencies and Wave Na-Pa and Pa-Nb amplitudes in their study of eight autistic young adults and age-, gender-, and performance IQ-matched normal controls. Buchwald et al. studied Pa and P1 in 11 high-functioning autistic subjects and reported normal Pa amplitude and latency. In contrast, P1 in the autistic subjects was reported to be smaller in amplitude and did not habituate with increasing stimulus rate. The failure of habituation was interpreted as evidence of a disturbance in the input of the brainstem ascending reticular activating system cholinergic neurons to the thalamus. However, it is equally plausible, given the data in this study, that the failure of P1 to habituate represents diminished thalamic and auditory cortical feedback inhibition on P1 generators. Additional data are required to differentiate between these two possibilities.

To date, there is one study investigating the P50 gating response. The P50 gating response reflects the decline of the amplitude of the P50 component of the AEP to the second of a pair of clicks and is thought to measure stimulus filtering or inhibitory mechanisms. Children with autism spectrum disorder have been described as both hypersensitive and hyposensitive to auditory sound and it has been suggested that people with autism may have difficulty filtering sensory input (Kootz, Marinelli, & Cohen, 1982). Kemner, Oranje, Verbaten, and van Engeland (2002) found that children between 7 and 13 years of age with autism and controls both demonstrated P50 suppression. The authors suggest that children with autism demonstrate normal excitability of the neuronal substrate related to P50 gating. While these results are consistent with Ornitz and colleagues (1993) who found normal stimulus filtering using a measure of prepulse inhibition of the acoustic startle response (Ornitz, Lane, Sugyama, & de Traversay, 1993), further work is needed on larger as well as younger samples.

Long Latency Auditory Potentials

The long latency potentials to a frequent stimulus occur after 50 milliseconds and consist of a large negative (N1)-positive (P2) complex, which is maximal in amplitude at the vertex

(Goodin, 1992). The generators of these potentials are unknown. At least part of this activity is from neural areas that can be activated by more than one sensory modality. Like the early and middle latency potentials, this complex is a stimulus-related response; thus the amplitude and latency of these potentials are related to stimulus intensity and frequency and are relatively independent of subject attention. The long latency potentials to the frequent stimulus reach adult levels by 5 to 6 years if not before (Courchesne, 1978; Finley, Faux, Hutcheson, & Amstutz, 1985; Goodin, Squires, & Starr, 1978; Kurtzberg et al., 1984; Polich & Starr, 1984). In the midteens to early 20s, the P2 latency begins to increase linearly with age. Gender also has a significant impact on these potentials (Stockard et al., 1978).

The auditory N1 and P2 potentials to frequent tones have been examined in autism in only a few studies. Courchesne and colleagues (Courchesne, Courchesne, et al., 1985; Courchesne, Lincoln, Kilman, & Galambos, 1985; Courchesne, Lincoln, Yeung-Courchesne, Elmasian, & Grillon, 1989) did not find any differences in N1 or P2 amplitude or latency between autistic subjects and normal controls to a listening task and a two-tone task. Ferri et al. (2003) found that the N1 latency was significantly shorter and that amplitude was not significantly different in the autistic group using 1000 Hz tones. Contrary to these results, Seri, Cerquiglini, Pisani, and Curatolo (1999) found the N1 response in tuberous sclerosis patients with autistic behaviors to have prolonged latencies with lower amplitudes. However, while this indicates a deficit in auditory sensory processing, due to the tuberous sclerosis, these results cannot be viewed as characteristic of autism alone.

Bruneau, Roux, Adrien, and Barthélémy (1999) investigated auditory processing at the cortical level using late auditory EPs (N1 wave-T complex) to pure tones in 4- to 8-year-old autistic children with mental retardation. Bruneau et al. (1999) specifically looked at two negative peaks, the N1b and the N1c, which peak around 140 ms and 170 ms, respectively. The N1b component is thought to have cortical generators on the superior temporal plane; this component appears to be within the typical range in terms of latency in children with autism (Bruneau et al., 1999; Lincoln, Courchesne, Harms, & Allen, 1995; Novick, Vaughan, Kurtzberg, & Simson, 1980, but see Oades, Walker, Geffen, & Stern, 1988). The N1c component is thought to be generated within the auditory association cortex (lateral surface of the superior temporal gyrus). In contrast to the N1b, the N1c wave showed the most significant differences between the subjects with autism and the two control groups (normal control group and mentally retarded subjects without autistic symptoms). At bilateral temporal sites, the autism group's N1c wave had a smaller amplitude and longer latency than either of the other groups (Bruneau et al., 1999). Additionally, the N1c wave of the autism group showed a hemispheric difference. While the left and right hemispheres of the control groups showed an increase in the N1c peak amplitude with increasing stimulus intensity, the autism group failed to show this effect on the left side.

Similar results were found (Bruneau, Bonnet-Brilhault, Gomot, Adrien, & Barthélémy, 2003) when these authors investigated N1c wave and the verbal and nonverbal abilities in children with autism. The N1c wave was found to have both smaller amplitude and a longer latency in the autistic group when 750-Hz tones of varying intensity were presented. The amplitude of the N1c wave also increased with increasing stimulus intensity in both the healthy control group and the group with autism, but again the effect was not seen on the left side for the autism participants, suggesting a lateralized disturbance in early cortical sensory processing in the left hemisphere. In a contrasting report, the N1c was found to not be delayed in 7- to 11-year-old children with autism with normal mental functioning during passive listening but was delayed in the same children when the task involved selective attention or word classification (Dunn, Vaughan, Kreuzer, & Kurtzer, 1999).

Auditory Cognitive Potentials

The long latency response to a rare auditory stimulus is considerably different from the response to the frequent stimulus, consisting of a negative (N1)-positive (apparent P2)-negative (N2)-positive (P3) complex (Goodin, 1992).

The apparent P2 is so named because it represents the sum of the stimulus-related P2 and the event-related P165. The P3 component has a latency of 300 to 400 milliseconds after a rare "odd-ball" stimulus, and its amplitude is maximal in the midline over the central and parietal scalp regions. The P3 peak can be further resolved into two components referred to as P3a and P3b. The P3a subcomponent appears to be constant regardless of subject attention, whereas the P3b component appears to be sensitive to task requirements (Squires, Squires, & Hillyard, 1975). These long-latency ERPs can be recorded to stimuli in any of the sensory modalities and can be recorded in response to the unexpected omission of an anticipated stimulus. These potentials are relatively insensitive to stimulus intensity but are very sensitive to change in the ease with which targets can be distinguished from nontargets, by alterations in the ratio of target to nontarget stimuli, or by fluctuations in subject attention to the stimulus. The N2 and P3 components are markedly prolonged in young children and decrease in latency with increasing age until reaching adult values in adolescence and young adulthood. Thereafter, there is a gradual increase in latency with increasing age. Gender does not impact latency, but P3 amplitude tends to be larger in females.

Numerous papers have reported abnormalities in auditory cognitive potentials in autism. In selective attention paradigms, unexpected, rare, or novel auditory (or visual) probes are inserted into a sequence of attended, standard, or expected sounds. This can be conducted during a passive task, in which the subject simply listens to the sequence of sounds or during an active task in which the subject presses a button when a target sound occurs. Abnormal auditory P300 potentials to rare tones and stimulus omissions in autism were first reported by Novick et al. (Novick, Kurtzberg, & Vaughan, 1979; Novick et al., 1980) and then replicated by Courchesne and colleagues (1984; Courchesne, Lincoln, et al., 1985). In general, the autism group did perceive the novel information as being novel; that is, the novel unexpected sounds evoked a different EP response, but the autism group compared to controls exhibited smaller P3 amplitudes to the novel probes suggestive of "less" processing. Lincoln, Courchesne, Harms, and Allen (1993) also reported decreased amplitudes of P3b responses to auditory stimuli in young nonretarded autistic children, indicating difficulty in modifying expectancies to contextually relevant sequences of auditory information and perhaps a general disturbance in habituation processes that interfere with the discrimination of novel information. The reaction times of responses to oddball or rare stimuli by the autistic children in this study were normal, indicating intact sensory processing and task compliance. Similar findings of decreased P3b amplitude have been reported by other investigators during visual/audio divided attention tasks (Ciesielski, Courchesne, & Elmasian, 1990; Courchesne et al., 1989) and have been linked to deficits in language function (Dawson, Finley, Phillips, Galpert, & Lewy, 1988).

Of note, a subsequent study of children with pervasive developmental disorder, using a similar auditory detection task, has partially failed to replicate these results. Kemner et al. (1995) replicated Courchesne et al. (1984, 1985) with respect to decreased A/Pcz/300 potentials in children with autism ages 8 to 13 years who were matched to children with typical development, ADHD, and dyslexia. However, no differences were found to the mismatch negativity, N1, and P3 components, and the lateralization of components. Unexpectedly in an auditory task, the authors also found P3 differences at the occipital midline lead, which was suggested as reflecting abnormal cortical organization to auditory input (Kemner, Verbaten, Cuperus, Camfferman, & Van Engeland, 1995). Further, in an easy and hard auditory detection task with a secondary passive visual task, all subjects demonstrated increased amplitude to the auditory stimuli with increased task difficulty. However, children (and to a lesser extent adolescents) with pervasive developmental disorder failed to demonstrate a decrease in P3 amplitude to the irrelevant visual probes with increased auditory task difficulty. The authors suggested that this might reflect a failure to allocate processing resources (Hoeksma, Kemner, Verbaten, & van Engeland, 2004).

The P3 has also been used to assess responses to affective and nonaffective prosodic language discrimination. Erwin et al. (1991) reported normal P3 responses in adult autistic individuals of normal intelligence during prosodic discriminations (Erwin et al., 1991). From a language standpoint, the tasks used in this study were of low difficulty, and the prosodic discriminations were well within the abilities of adults with autism of normal IQ, whose most prominent impairments are in higher order prosodic discriminations related to satire and innuendo. One study (Strandburg et al., 1993) reported *increased* P3 responses to oddball stimuli in a visual continuous performance task and a visually presented idiom recognition task. In contrast to the simple prosodic discriminations of the Erwin study, idiomatic language is a well-documented element of the deficits in higher order language abilities in high-functioning individuals with autism. The Strandburg finding could indicate a modality effect with different P3 effects to some auditory and visual stimuli or an indication that there may be some situations where autistic individuals may have a greater allocation of attention to some tasks to compensate for dysfunction in cognitive processes that would otherwise interfere with performance.

Two additional automatic components of auditory ERPs, the mismatch negativity (MMN) and the P3a wave, have been investigated in relation to autism. The MMN is an index of auditory processing that occurs due to a deviation in repetitive auditory stimulation (Uther, Jansen, Huotilainen, Ilmoniemi, & Näätänen, 2003). The "mismatch" occurs when the expected standardized auditory stimulus is replaced with an unexpected stimulus. It is considered to be automatic because even when the stimulus is not being attended to, the MMN still appears when an atypical stimulus is presented (Uther et al., 2003). In cases where the deviant or novel stimulus is largely different from the frequent and expected standard stimulus, a P3a wave is exhibited just after the MMN (Friedman, Cycowicz, & Gaeta, 2001). The P3a wave (or novelty P3) is a component of the P3 that is said to engage the frontal lobe in response to novel stimuli. It is thought that the P3a is a late stage of novelty processing most likely related to the evaluative aspects of the orienting response (Friedman et al., 2001). So while the MMN represents the detection of a deviant stimulus, the P3a is thought to deal with the events that will ultimately result in a behavioral response due to that unexpected stimulus.

Only a few studies have looked at the MMN and/or the P3a wave in relation to autism, and the results remain inconclusive. Seri et al. (1999) investigated autism in individuals with tuberous sclerosis and found that MMN was present in all of the subjects but that the MMN latency was significantly longer in the subjects with autistic behavior. In a study done by Ferri et al. (2003), the amplitude of the MMN in low-functioning autistic individuals to the deviant stimuli (1300 Hz sinusoidal tone rather than the standard 1000 Hz) was significantly larger than in the normal control group. Ferri et al. (2003) suggested that their results may indicate problems with auditory sensory processing at early stages in the temporal cortex. Additionally, the MMN latencies for the autistic group tended to be shorter (Ferri et al., 2003; Gomot, Giard, Adrien, Barthelemy, & Bruneau, 2002). Gomot et al. suggested that the shortened MMN latencies may be the result of heightened cerebral reactivity to auditory change, which allows autistic individuals to detect variations in auditory inputs more quickly than controls. However, Kemner et al. (1995), with children with autism compared to 3 control groups matched on age found no differences in the MMN (also see Ceponiene et al., 2003) and P3.

There has been one study that has measured MMN in relation to speech processing in young children. In children aged 3 to 4 with autism, Kuhl and colleagues (2005) found that the children with autism did not show MMN responses to changes in speech syllables while typical children matched on mental age or chronological age did. In addition, as a group, the children with autism also failed to show a listening preference for human speech over non-speech. When the autism group was divided based on their preference for human speech versus nonhuman speech, the group that preferred human speech did show a MMN that was similar to the typical children; the group that preferred nonspeech did not. The authors suggest that the lack of MMN in some of the children with autism suggests central auditory deficits although additional work would be needed to determine if the lack of MMN was reflective of a failure to differentiate complex auditory signals or specific to speech (Kuhl, Coffey-Corina, Padden, & Dawson, 2005).

In Ferri et al.'s (2003) study, the P3a wave also revealed significant differences between the autistic group and the control group. The P3a amplitude increased with age in the control group, but in the autistic group, the opposite pattern was found: Larger amplitudes were seen in childhood with decreasing amplitudes in early adulthood (Ferri et al., 2003). Since the P3a is thought to be an automatic and involuntary response that represents a later stage of novelty processing (Friedman et al., 2001), Ferri et al. (2003) proposed that autistic individuals may be better at shifting their attention to novel stimuli in childhood than in adulthood. Ceponiene et al. (2003) looked at the P3a and how it was affected when changes in simple tones, complex tones, and vowels were presented using standard and deviant stimuli. High-functioning autistic participants showed normal P3a responses for changes in both simple and complex tones, but no P3a was present for changes in the vowel. Given that the complex tones were similar to the speech sounds in complexity, it seems that the "speechness" of the vowel sounds acted as a limiting factor in the autistic group's orienting abilities, which may indicate a deficit in vowel exclusive attention that could hinder verbal communication in autistic individuals (Ceponiene et al., 2003).

A fifth potential, the Nc, has been the subject of more recent investigation in autism (Courchesne, Elmasian, & Yeung-Courchesne, 1987; Courchesne et al., 1989). Nc is the earliest endogenous component to appear developmentally and is elicitable in infants. In general, the Nc is thought to reflect an obligatory attentional response and is elicited by both auditory and visual stimuli; it is known to vary based on frequency of stimulus presentation, familiarity with the stimulus, and habituation (Nelson, 1994). Nc has an onset at around 100 to 200 milliseconds with a peak amplitude at about 350 to 450 milliseconds and is maximal in amplitude over the front of the scalp.

Nc abnormalities also appear to be a prominent cognitive potential finding in autism. Courchesne et al. (1987, 1989) have reported

Nc to be small and often absent to auditory and visual stimuli and to the omission of auditory and visual stimuli. P3b was also documented to be small, demonstrating the coexistence of abnormalities in these two cognitive potentials. When Kemner, van der Gaag, Verbaten, and van Engeland (1999) had participants perform a visual task with an oddball stimulus component, they were not able to replicate Courchesne et al.'s (1987, 1989) findings that the Nc is smaller in autistic children, suggesting that the effect may be modality specific.

Last, the N4 component is a negative component that peaks at approximately 400 milliseconds after stimulus presentation and is thought to be related to semantic processing and varies based on the expectation of the association between words. For example, the amplitude of the N4 is related to the degree to which a word is related to the semantic context, with incongruent words resulting in greater amplitude and longer latencies (Kutas, Lindamood, & Hillyard, 1984). In children 7 to 11 years of age with autism and nonverbal IQ-matched typical children, Dunn and colleagues (1999) found that the autism group failed to show differential N4 amplitude for targets (expected animal word) and nontargets (incongruent nonanimal word). The typical group did show a differential response between the two categories. The authors interpreted this finding as a failure of the children with autism to develop an expectancy for the within category words, possibly suggestive of abnormal lexical organization. In addition, as reported earlier, children with autism also showed increased latencies for the N1 and P2 components.

Visual and Somatosensory Cognitive Potentials

Fewer EP studies have been conducted with visual than auditory stimuli. Some data suggest that late visual evoked responses (P3b) to novel stimuli are abnormal (Novick et al., 1979; Verbaten, Roelofs, van Engeland, Kenemans, & Slangen, 1991), but they may be less impaired than auditory responses (Courchesne et al., 1989; Courchesne, Lincoln, et al., 1985). Studies of somatosensory ERPs in autism also have demonstrated abnormal P3 responses (Kemner, Verbaten, Cuperus, Camfferman, & van Engeland, 1994).

Townsend et al. (2001) studied visuospatial processing in a group of high-functioning autistic individuals, specifically looking at the late positive complex (LPC), which is said to consist of three main components: an early fronto-centrally maximal response, a parietally maximal P3b, and a posterior positive slow wave. In the autistic group, a delay was found in the early frontal LPC responses as well as smaller amplitude for the parietal maximal LPC responses. Autistic participants also had accuracy difficulties when targets were displayed in the visual periphery. These findings may indicate impairments in spatial orienting and/or encoding of spatial information (Townsend et al., 2001).

Both early and late EP components of visual processing have been studied during face and object perception and memory in children and adults with autism. In typical adults, faces evoke a specific ERP component that is negative going and peaks at approximately 170 milliseconds. This N170 is more negative in the right than left hemisphere to faces; more negative to eyes, inverted faces, and upright faces than other stimuli; and faster to upright faces than other face parts and other stimuli (e.g., Bentin, Allison, Puce, Perez, & McCarthy, 1996). This component is thought to reflect early stage processing of faces and has been hypothesized to be indicative of configural processing. The N170 undergoes a prolonged developmental course with decreases in amplitude and latency from 4 to 14 years of age (Taylor, McCarthy, Saliba, & Degiovanni, 1999). In addition to early stage processing of faces, face and object memory differentially evoke later stage components such as the Nc, P400, and slow wave in children. These components are influenced by stimulus familiarity, repetition, and task directions.

Individuals with autism use atypical behavioral strategies for processing faces and have impaired face and emotion memory (Dawson, Webb, & McPartland, 2005). McPartland, Dawson, Webb, Carver, and Panagiotides (2004) found that high-functioning adolescents and adults with autism show delayed N170 latencies to faces compared to nonface stimuli (e.g., furniture) and fail to show a temporal benefit for the processing of upright compared to inverted faces; age- and IQ-matched typical

individuals show faster N170 latencies to faces compared to nonface stimuli and show faster activation to upright compared to inverted faces. Three- to 4-year-old and 6-year-old children with autism spectrum disorder (ASD) also fail to show a temporal benefit to processing faces in comparison to typical developing and developmental-delayed control groups (Webb, Bernier, Panagiotides, Paul, & Dawson, 2003; Webb, Bernier, Shook, Paul, & Dawson, 2004; Webb, Dawson, Bernier, & Panagiotides, 2004). These results were interpreted as reflecting aberrant neural circuitry resulting in less efficient processing strategies (Dawson et al., 2005).

As to later stage visual processing EPs, Dawson et al. (2002) evaluated children with ASD to evaluate face and object recognition ability in comparison to children with delayed development (DD) and children with typical development (TD). Participants (ages 3 to 4 years) were shown a picture of their mother (familiar face), a picture of an unfamiliar female face, a picture of a familiar object (favorite toy), and a picture of an unfamiliar toy. They found that unlike the TD and DD children, children with ASD did not show amplitude differences in P400 or Nc when viewing the familiar face versus the unfamiliar face. However, similar to the TD and DD children, ASD children did show amplitude differences in both P400 and Nc when they were looking at a picture of a familiar object (a favorite toy) versus an unfamiliar one. This is of interest because while the ASD children showed differential brain activity for objects, they did not show this pattern for faces, indicating a social processing deficit (Dawson et al., 2002). This finding agrees with those found in related studies, such as one by Pelphrey et al. (2002), which investigated how individuals with autism scan human faces. The autistic participants spent less time fixating on feature areas of the face, such as the eyes, mouth, and nose, than did the control group (Pelphrey et al., 2002).

Oculomotor Physiology: Motor and Cognitive Physiology

As with the EP literature in autism, eye movement studies in the 1960s and 1970s reported abnormalities involving postrotatory nystagmus and nystagmus during REM sleep (Ornitz, Brown, Mason, & Putnam, 1974; Ornitz, Forsythe, & de la Pena, 1973; Ornitz & Ritvo, 1968a; Ornitz et al., 1968; Ornitz et al., 1969; Ritvo et al., 1969). However, these investigators subsequently concluded that their early findings were the result of idiosyncratic methods, and a repetition of these studies using current methodology revealed only one statistically significant result (Ornitz, Atwell, Kaplan, & Westlake, 1985). Only a few other studies have been added to this literature.

To assess vestibular function, eye movement responses to caloric challenge, or rotation of the head or body, can be assessed by measuring the duration and amplitude of the procedure-induced nystagmus as well as the velocity of the slow phase component. Eye movement studies also can provide important information about the well-characterized cortical and subcortical regions that control eye movement activity. Such eye movement studies can be viewed as complementary to sensory-evoked responses, in that they provide information primarily about the motor system and sensorimotor integration rather than about sensory information processing. For quantitative eye movement studies, patients are typically taken to a dark room, their heads are comfortably restrained so that head and eye movements are not confounded, and various eye movement tasks are performed. Eye movements can be recorded noninvasively by electrooculography (EOG) procedures (similar to those used in EEG studies to identify eye movement "artifacts"), camera-based recording systems, or direct monitoring of the reflection of an infrared light source from the corneal-scleral margin.

Responses to lights moving abruptly from one point to another can be measured (latency, accuracy, peak velocity) to assess the integrity of saccadic eye movements, and the tracking of slowly but steadily moving targets can be evaluated to assess smooth pursuit eye movements (Leigh & Zee, 1991). These procedures approximate those used in neurological examinations but are conducted under controlled conditions and in ways that are amenable to quantitative analysis. Examining reflexive saccadic responses to unpredictable lights can be informative about the integrity of subcortical regions involved in basic oculomotor control. By varying saccadic eye movement tasks in different ways, such as by instructing subjects to look away from lights, requiring delayed responses to locations that need to be remembered for brief periods of time, and cueing locations where targets will be presented, various cortical visual attention systems can be evaluated.

Eye movement studies of autism have included analysis of the oculomotor effects of vestibular challenge that bear on the functional integrity of the cerebellum (Minshew, Furman, Goldstein, & Payton, 1990; Ornitz et al., 1985); saccadic and pursuit responses to visual stimuli that assess the functional integrity of the brainstem, cerebellum, and neocortex (Minshew et al., 1990; Rosenhall, Johansson, & Gillberg, 1988); and volitional saccadic eye movement subserved by frontal and parietal cortex (Minshew, Luna, & Sweeney, 1999).

Ornitz et al. (1985) tested 22 autistic patients and reported slightly prolonged postrotary nystagmus, though there was no disturbance in gain of the slow component. These equivocal findings are difficult to interpret because the study was performed in the dark, and there can be considerable subject variability in performance in this situation based on idiosyncratic factors such as whether subjects imagine a visual stimulus moving with them or a stimulus that is stationary (Leigh & Zee, 1991). In addition, the statistically significant difference was confined to one parameter, the vestibulo-ocular reflex (VOR) time constant, and appeared to be the result of two outliers in the data rather than a trend for the group as a whole. Goldberg, Landa, Lasker, Cooper, and Zee (2000) performed a VOR experiment measuring the duration of vestibular responses and tilt-suppression of postrotatory nystagmus and found that tilt-suppression of the VOR was not impaired in children with autism, nor were there any differences in the vestibular responses during the rotation, which suggests that the cerebellar nodulus, the uvula, and the vestibular system are not dysfunctional. Rosenhall et al. (1988) reported hypometric horizontal visually guided saccades to unpredictable targets in 6 of 11 low-IQ autistic children. Pursuit eye movements were described as normal. However, some patients were taking CNS-active medications that affect eye movements, cooperation was frequently a problem, and the healthy subjects had normal IQ in comparison to the high rates of mental retardation in the autistic subjects.

In a study of voluntary saccadic eye movements known to be subserved by discrete regions in frontal and parietal cortex, Minshew et al. (1999) found significant abnormalities in cortically controlled eye movements in 26 autistic subjects compared to 26 age, IQ and gender-matched controls. The autistic subjects demonstrated significant impairments both in the ability to willfully suppress saccades to unpredictable targets and to shift gaze to remembered target locations. These findings, together with findings of intact visually guided saccades in the same cases, indicate a disturbance in the cortical connectivity required for volitional control of saccadic eye movements. Recently, Goldberg et al. (2002) recorded eye movements of high-functioning autistic individuals on antisaccade, memory-guided saccade (MGS), predictive saccade, and gap/overlap tasks. In comparison to normal subjects, high-functioning individuals with autism had greater difficulty voluntarily suppressing eye movements to visual targets, replicating the Minshew et al. (1999) findings. Koczat, Rogers, Pennington, and Ross (2002) performed a study to determine whether this deficit in memory-guided saccades is also found in the parents of individuals with autism. Using a similar oculomotor delayed response task, they found similar deficits in unaffected family members.

To further define the circuitry underlying spatial working memory in autism, Luna et al. (2002) completed an fMRI study using this same task. This study demonstrated significantly less activation in dorsolateral prefrontal cortex and posterior cingulate in the 11 high-functioning autistic subjects compared to 6 healthy controls during the performance of this task.

Kemner, Verbaten, Cuperus, Camfferman, and van Engeland (1998) found that autistic children make more saccades during and between stimulus presentations than the healthy individuals and children with attention deficit disorder, regardless of the type of stimulus shown. The abnormally high number of sac-

cades may be due to attentional difficulties in autism and was further explored by van der Geest, Kemner, Cammfferman, Verbaten, and van Engeland (2001) using a gap-overlap paradigm. In both conditions, subjects fixated on a cross in the center of the screen, while waiting to look at a square that was to appear on the right or left side of the cross. In the overlap condition, the cross remained on the screen when the square appeared, but in the gap condition, the cross disappeared 200 milliseconds before the appearance of the square.

In comparison to the control group, the autistic group in this study showed no differences in performance on the gap or overlap conditions (van der Geest et al., 2001). This suggests a deficiency in attentional engagement, which may be related to dysfunction in several areas of the brain, including the frontal eye fields, the superior colliculus, and/or parietal cortex.

Postural Physiology

Studies of postural function are another method for providing direct and specific evidence of the physiologic integrity of the vestibular system including the cerebellum. Although posterior fossa circuitry contributes significantly to postural function, contributions from more widespread regions are also important. Kohen-Raz, Volkmar, and Cohen (1992) conducted a study of 91 autistic children and adolescents ages 6 to 20 years chronologically and 8 months to 7 years in mental age using a computerized posturographic procedure that evaluated the effects of various stresses to this system. These children were compared to 166 normal 4- to 11-year-old children, 18 mentally retarded children (7 to 16 years chronologically), and 20 normal adults with vestibular disease. Postural sway was recorded as changes in weight distribution as subjects stood on plates, one for the heel and toe of each foot. The autistic subjects and the mentally retarded nonautistic subjects had significantly lower postural stability than the control subjects, performing at the level of preschool children even as adolescents. The autism group showed paradoxically better stability when vision was occluded or somatosensory input restricted by standing on pads. They also exhibited unusual monopodal or tripodal stances. The latter two findings were not seen in the mentally retarded nonautistic subjects. In this study, the postural impairment of the autistic subjects was comparable to that of the small group of mentally retarded nonautistic subjects; it was only the paradoxical improvement in stability with visual occlusion and somatosensory restriction that distinguished them from the mentally retarded nonautistic subjects. There were also some limitations to this study, as roughly a third of the sample was taking neuroleptic medications, and many were unable to maintain cooperation through all procedures.

In Gepner, Mestre, Masson, and de Schonen (1995) studied five mentally retarded autistic children ages 4 to 7 years and 12 normal controls. The subjects stood on a force platform with three strain gauges measuring shifts in their center of gravity. The mentally retarded children with autism had impaired postural stability compared to the normal children under eyes closed and static visual conditions but were more stable to visually perceived environmental motion than controls. It was not clear whether this was due to general lack of attention to surrounding motion or to a deficit in motion processing.

More recently, Molloy, Dietrich, and Bhattacharya (2003) investigated the postural stability of 8 children with ASD ages 5 to 12 years of age with a receptive language level of at least 4 years. The participants stood on a firm or foam platform with their eyes opened or closed. This study measured both sway area and sway length over a 30-second time period for each of the four conditions. ASD children were, in general, found to have an increased sway area. Contrary to Kohen-Raz et al.'s (1992) findings, this study found that when the visual cues, somatosensory cues, or both were modified, the sway area increased; that is, they were less stable, not more stable. Based on these findings, children with ASD exhibited a deficit in the capacity of afferent systems to coordinate postural stability. In others words, their postural instability was the result of a deficit in sensory integration.

Minshew, Sung, Jones, and Furman (2004) tested the postural stability of 79 nonretarded high-functioning autistic individuals ages 5 to 52 years compared to 61 healthy controls matched in age, IQ, and gender using dynamic posturography. Autistic individuals with associated neurologic, genetic, infectious, metabolic, or seizure disorders, as well as those taking any medication known to affect the measurements under investigation, were excluded from the study. Compared to previous studies, this is the only one that coupled floor and/or visual surround motion to postural sway. Autistic subjects were found to have reduced postural stability and delayed development of postural stability. Postural stability was reduced under all conditions but was only clinically significant when somatosensory input was disrupted alone or in combination with other sensory challenges. Postural control did not begin to improve in the autistic subjects until 12 years of age and never achieved adult levels, whereas in normal controls it improved steadily from age 5 years to 15 to 20 years when it reached adult levels. There were no abnormalities in the adaptation ratios, measurements primarily dependent on motor control. Rather, the abnormalities in postural control were indicative of deficits in sensorimotor integration, which is dependent on a widely distributed multineuronal system that typically involves the basal ganglia, supplementary motor cortex, anterior cingulate cortex, and subcortical connections more generally.

The decreased postural stability found in this study is part of a more pervasive impairment in movement that ranges from fine and gross motor apraxia to the planning and execution of skilled motor sequences. The evidence that deficits in motor sequences and now sensory integration are integral parts of the autism syndrome suggests that the neural abnormalities responsible for autism are not restricted to the neural systems involved in social, language, and reasoning abilities. Rather, the motor and sensory deficits suggest more general involvement of neural circuitry related to a cytoarchitectural feature of brain organization required for higher levels of integration of information.

Neuropsychologic Profile

Comprehensive studies of neuropsychologic functioning in autism are relatively recent, having awaited a consensus on the diagnostic criteria and research methods for defining autism in verbal individuals with IQs in the normal and near-normal range. Studies of multiple domains of function within the same individuals with autism remain few, as the tendency of most studies has been to focus on a single area of function. The rationale for studies of multiple domains, from a neurologic perspective, is to determine the common feature of impairments and common feature of intact abilities, as common features may provide clues to the essential aspects of the neural basis of autism.

The first such study in 1988 reported a pattern of neuropsychologic functioning characterized by the predominance of deficits in abstraction and conceptual reasoning, relative sparing of memory and language, and intact visuospatial, sensoriperceptual, and motor abilities in 10 autistic men with average full-scale and verbal IQ scores (Rumsey & Hamburger, 1988, 1990). Several other laboratories confirmed this general profile of relative deficits and strengths (Minshew, Goldstein, Muenz, & Payton, 1992; Ozonoff, Pennington, & Rogers, 1991; Prior & Hoffman, 1990).

In a more detailed investigation of each neuropsychologic domain and both the auditory and visual modalities, Minshew, Goldstein, and Siegel (1997) reported evidence in 33 autistic individuals of deficits in complex tasks across all domains involving both the visual and auditory modalities and preserved function on tests of simpler abilities in these same domains (see Table 18.1).

Thus, deficits were found in concept formation and problem solving, higher order interpretative language abilities, memory for complex material, skilled motor abilities or praxis, and higher cortical sensory perception. Auditory and visual modalities appeared equally involved. This pattern of widespread deficits in complex or higher order abilities

was not that of a general deficit syndrome or mental retardation, since autistic subjects did as well or better than age- and IQ-matched controls in preserved areas and substantially below expectations based on age and IQ in deficit areas.

The profile of neuropsychologic functioning in autism is one of deficits in complex or higher order cognitive and neurologic abilities as defined relative to age and IQ expectations and intact or enhanced simpler abilities relative to age and IQ expectations. This profile has been replicated in a second sample of adults with high-functioning autism (Minshew, unpublished data) and in children 8 to 15 years of age with high-functioning autism (Minshew, unpublished data).

A subsequent fMRI study demonstrated an analogous pattern of brain activation with enhanced activation in Wernicke's area for word processing and diminished activation in Broca's area for sentence processing. In addition, there was reduced synchronization among cortical regions indicating reduced functional connectivity (Just, Cherkassky, Keller, & Minshew, 2004). Other unpublished studies from this laboratory have demonstrated a similar profile with an executive function task and a social cognitive task as well as a task requiring the transfer of information from the language area to the visual imagery area. In other words, there is generalized underdevelopment of the functional connectivity of higher order neural systems underlying the core symptoms of autism. Thus, there is a reduction in information processing capacity that particulary affects integrative circuitry and integrative functions. Documenting this profile moves us one large step closer to understanding the cognitive and brain basis of the behaviors that define autism.

This profile is furthermore the key to behavioral intervention. Normal or typical individuals function, interact, and communicate on the basis of skills on the right half of Table 18.1, which are areas of deficits for individuals with high-functioning autism and Asperger disorder. However, intact abilities as indicated on the left-hand side of Table 18.1 mislead many into thinking that individuals with autism have intact skills on the right hand side of the table. Individuals with high-functioning autism and Asperger disorder frequently do

TABLE 18.1   Intact or Enhanced Abilities and Deficits

Intact or Enhanced	Cognitive Weaknesses
Attention	
Sensory perception	
Elementary motor	Complex motor
Simple memory	Complex memory
Formal language	Complex lanuage
Rule learning	Concept formation
Visuospatial processing	

not respond to or understand fully reasoning, concepts, insight, and complex language (right hand side of the table skills). In contrast, they do respond to facts and details (left hand side of the table skills). This has lead to a mismatch between the intervention (right hand side of the table skills) and the affected individual (left hand side of the table skills).

CENTRAL NERVOUS SYSTEM STRUCTURE IN AUTISM

The structure of the brain in autism has been investigated with a small number of anatomic studies and a growing number of neuroimaging studies. Most of the neuroanatomic studies have involved examinations of structures and cells and only recently has work begun on neuronal architecture and synaptic number. Neuroimaging studies have a long history but actual contributions began with magnetic resonance imaging.

Neuropathology

Our understanding of the neuroanatomical abnormalities in the autistic brain has been hampered by the limited availability of suitable autopsy material and the lack of an animal model. The few autopsy studies reported by the mid-1970s showed a paucity of findings. In the absence of hard data, a number of brain regions were hypothesized as possible sites of abnormality based on clinical features of the disorder and evidence obtained from neurophysiologic studies (Boucher & Warrington, 1976; Coleman, 1979; Damasio & Maurer, 1978; Delong, 1978; Maurer & Damasio, 1982; Ornitz & Ritvo, 1968b; Vilensky, Demasio, & Maurer, 1981).

In 1984, the results of a systematic analysis of the brain of a 29-year-old man with well-documented autism studied by means of whole brain serial section, in comparison with an identically processed age- and sex-matched control, was reported (Bauman & Kemper, 1984). A more detailed description was published the following year (Bauman & Kemper, 1985). Since that initial report, eight additional cases have been similarly studied (Bauman & Kemper, 1994). All nine brains demonstrated abnormalities in the limbic system as well as

in the cerebellum and related inferior olive. When compared with controls, the autistic subjects showed reduced neuronal size and increased cell packing density in the hippocampus, amygdala, mammillary body, anterior cingulate gyrus, and medial nucleus of the septum. All of these regions are known to be related to one another by interconnecting circuits and comprise a major portion of the limbic system of the brain.

Studies of the CA1 and CA4 pyramidal neurons of the hippocampus, using the rapid Golgi technique, have demonstrated reduced complexity and extent of dendritic arbors in these cells (Raymond, Bauman, & Kemper, 1996). Although small cell size and increased cell packing density was found in the medial septal nucleus (MSN) in the autistic brains, a different pattern of abnormality was observed in the nucleus of the diagonal band of Broca (NDB). In this nucleus, enlarged but otherwise normal-appearing neurons were found in the NDB of all autistic subjects under the age of 13 years. In contrast, these same neurons were noted to be small in size and markedly reduced in number in all of the autistic subjects over the age of 22 years (Bauman & Kemper, 1994).

A systematic survey of the remainder of the forebrain in these nine autistic cases showed no abnormalities in the striatum, pallidum, thalamus, hypothalamus, basal forebrain, and bed nucleus of the stria terminalis (Kemper, unpublished data). The only other abnormality noted in these brains was a minor malformation of the orbitofrontal cortex in one hemisphere. Bailey et al. (1998), however, noted neocortical malformations in four of the six brains he examined. These included irregular laminar patterns, areas of increased neuronal density, abnormally oriented pyramidal cells, areas of cortical thickening, and increased numbers of neurons in layer I. More recently, Casanova, Buxhoeveden, Switala, and Roy (2002) observed that, in comparison to controls, neocortical minicolumns were smaller, less compact, and more numerous in the three areas studied. The authors suggested that, since inhibitory GABAergic double bouquet cells define the microcolumnar organization, they might be a site of abnormality.

Outside the forebrain, additional abnormalities have been reported in the cerebellum and related inferior olive. A significant reduction in the number of Purkinje cells has been demonstrated throughout the cerebellar hemispheres, most prominently in the posteriolateral neocerebellar cortex and adjacent archicerebellar cortex (Arin, Bauman, & Kemper, 1991; Ritvo et al., 1986). In contrast to the findings in the hemispheres, detailed quantitative analysis of Purkinje cell number in the vermis has shown no statistically significant differences when compared with age- and sex-matched controls (Bauman & Kemper, 1996). In addition to these cerebellar cortical findings, abnormalities have been noted in the fastigial, globose, and emboliform nuclei in the roof of the cerebellum, which, like the findings in the NDB of the septum, appear to differ with the age of the patient. As in the NDB, small pale neurons, which are reduced in number, characterize these cerebellar nuclei in all of the adult subjects. In all of the younger brains, however, these same neurons as well as those of the dentate nucleus are enlarged and present in adequate numbers (Bauman & Kemper, 1994).

No evidence of retrograde cell loss or atrophy has been found in the principal olivary nucleus of the brainstem in any of the autistic brains, areas which are known to be related to the abnormal regions of the cerebellar cortex (Holmes & Stewart, 1988). In human pathology, neuronal cell loss and atrophy of the inferior olive have been invariably observed following perinatal and postnatal Purkinje cell loss (Greenfield, 1954; Norman, 1940). This cell loss is presumably due to the close relationship of the olivary climbing fiber axons to the Purkinje cell dendrites (Eccles, Iro, & Szentagothai, 1967). In the adult autistic brain, despite the markedly reduced numbers of cerebellar Purkinje cells, the olivary neurons have been found to be present in adequate numbers but small in size. In contrast, the olivary neurons in the younger brains were significantly enlarged but otherwise normal in appearance and number (Kemper & Bauman, 1998). Of interest is a single case report of an autistic individual with Mobius syndrome describing decreased numbers of neurons in the facial nucleus and superior olive and shortening of the distance between the trapezoid body and the inferior olive (Rodier, Ingram, Tisdale, Nelson, & Roman, 1996). Additional abnormalities have also been reported in the brainstem by Bailey et al. (1998), which have included a dysplastic configuration of the lamella of the inferior olive and the presence of ectopic neurons lateral to the inferior olive.

To date, postmortem studies of the brain in autism have failed to show any abnormalities of gross brain structure. Myelination has been found to be comparable to controls in all cases, both microscopically and by MRI (Bauman & Kemper, 1994). However, in 1993, Bailey, Luthert, Bolton, Le Couteur, and Rutter reported that three of four autopsied brains from autistic subjects were heavier than expected for age and sex. Since that time, it has become apparent that although most autistic children are born with normal head circumferences, the trajectory of head growth in these children tends to significantly accelerate during the preschool years (Lainhart et al., 1997). This observation has been supported by MRI studies in which the brain volume was observed to increase most markedly between 2 and 4.5 years of age, followed by deceleration of brain growth in older autistic children (Courchesne et al., 2001). Although both gray and white matter volumes were found to be increased, the major changes involved the cerebral and cerebellar white matter. Subsequently, Carper, Moses, Tigue, and Courchesne (2002) observed that, although several brain regions showed increased gray and white matter enlargement in 2- to 3-year-old autistic children, the greatest volumetric increase was found in the frontal lobe, with the occipital lobe being virtually unaffected. More recently, Herbert et al. (2004) observed that the white matter increase in both autism and children with developmental language disorders (DLD) appeared to primarily involve the radiate white matter, which myelinates later than the deep white matter, a concept that appears to be consistent with the unusual postnatal head growth reported in autism.

Coincident with the reports of increased brain volume in childhood autism has been the observation of increased brain weight in this same age group. In a review of 19 postmortem cases obtained from autistic subjects less than 13 years of age, brain weight was found to be heavier than expected for age and sex by 100 to 200 grams, and this difference was statistically significant when compared with controls (Bauman & Kemper, 1997). In contrast, brains from adult autistic subjects, over the age of 21 years, were noted to be lighter in weight than expected for age and sex. The pathogenesis of this brain enlargement is as yet unknown. It has been hypothesized, however, that this unusual early brain growth may reflect the presence of increased numbers of neurons and/or glia, premature and accelerated proliferation of synapses, axonal and dendritic arbors, and/or increased myelination. Given the presence of atypical information processing, which has been characteristically observed clinically and with fMRI in autistic individuals, it seems reasonable to consider the possibility that abnormalities in the composition and structure of components of cortical neurons and/or of the myelin sheath might significantly contribute to both the increased brain size and cognitive impairment observed in this disorder. Whatever the underlying cause or causes, the differences in brain weight and brain volume, combined with microscopic changes with age, suggest that, although the disorder appears to begin before birth, autism is also associated with a postnatal ongoing process.

While the defining of neuroanatomic abnormalities of the autistic brain will continue to be an important line of investigation, it will be equally important to expand our understanding of the underlying neurochemical profile in these same regions. To date, Chugani et al. (1997) have reported decreased serotonin synthesis in the dentatothalamocortical pathway in seven autistic boys using positron emission tomography (PET). Fatemi, Stary, Halt, and Realmuto (2001) have described decreased amounts of reelin and Bcl-2 proteins in 44% of the autistic cerebella studied. Reelin is important for brain development and appears to play a role in the process of synapse elimination, and Bcl-2 is important for programmed cell death. Blatt at el. (2001), studying neurotransmitter receptors in the autistic hippocampus, have documented reduced binding of GABAa receptors but no change in serotonin, cholinergic, or kainate receptors. Several studies have also investigated cholinergic activity in the autistic brain. A decrease in nicotinic and M1 receptors has been reported in the parietal cortex. The frontal cortex also showed a decrease

in nicotinic receptors and an increase in brain-derived neurotrophic factor (BDNF) in the basal forebrain but no M1 abnormalities (Perry et al., 2001). In a more recent study, Lee et al. (2002) noted that three of four nicotinic receptors were found to be decreased in the cerebellar cortex. No significant changes were noted in M1 and M2 receptors or in choline acetyltransferase activity. In 2004, Martin-Ruiz et al., using complementary measures of receptor expression, found that reduced gene expression of the a4b2 nicotinic receptor in the cerebral cortex was a major feature of the neurochemical pathology of autism, while post-transcriptional abnormalities of both a4b2 and a7 subtype were evident in the cerebellum. The authors concluded that dendritic and/or synaptic nicotinic receptor abnormalities may be involved in the disruption of the development of cerebral and cerebellar circuitry in autism.

Theories of Pathogenesis

What can be learned from the neuroanatomic evidence acquired to date? The pattern of small neuronal cell size and increased call packing density, which characterizes much of the limbic system of the autistic brain, suggests a curtailment of development in this circuitry. Studies in human and nonhuman primates support the role of the limbic system structures in learning, memory, behavior, and emotion. In the cerebellum, because of the known tight relationship between the Purkinje cells and the cells of the inferior olivary nucleus, reduced numbers of Purkinje cells in the face of preserved olivary neurons strongly suggest that the process that resulted in these abnormalities had its onset before birth. In addition, there is growing evidence that the cerebellum may be important for the mediation and modulation of some aspects of language, learning, attention, and affective behavior.

Although much progress has been made in autism research over the past 20 years, many questions remain before we can truly understand the neural mechanisms that result in the clinical features of autism. Given the continued short supply of suitable autopsy material, research would be aided significantly by the availability of an animal model for anatomic, neurochemical, and neurophysiologic study.

Neurochemical analysis of blood, urine, and spinal fluid have shown inconsistent findings, and related neuropharmacological research has been discouraging in many cases. Neurochemical analysis of brain tissue is beginning to emerge but is hampered by small samples and quality of tissue available for study. However, with a more concerted effort to obtain autopsy material, combined with rapidly improving technology, it is likely that significant advances in these areas can be expected within the next 5 to 10 years.

In the future, it will be important for neuroanatomic research in autism to focus more intensely on a systematic correlation between location and degree of histoanatomic abnormality and the clinical characteristics of the patient, thereby expanding our knowledge of site-specific developmental brain dysfunction and behavior. Further, what is now known about the brain in autism should not only serve as a guide for research questions in genetics, immunology, neurophysiology, and neurochemistry, but also provide the defining yardstick against which possible etiologic hypotheses and related biological investigations in both animals and humans can be measured.

Structural Brain Imaging

The neuroanatomy of autism can also be investigated with imaging methods. Because imaging can be performed in living subjects, it provides a much more accessible window into the brain in autism. The types of information it can provide are different. In some ways, it is more limited with regard to structural information but in other ways it provides a broader picture because of the larger number of subjects that can be surveyed and the capacity to measure the relative size of structures and their developmental dynamics. Functional imaging also provides information about the status of the brain that neuropathologic information cannot. (Functional Imaging in Autism is the subject of a separate chapter in this *Handbook.*) Likewise diffusion tensor imaging and tracking methods are opening entirely new and valuable views of white matter connectivity in autism that promise exciting insights into the pathophysiology. The first era of neuroimaging in autism began with pneumoencephalograms

(PEG) and then computerized axial tomography (CT). The second era began with MRI and an appreciation of the importance of excluding autistic subjects who had underlying causes for their autism so that abnormalities found on imaging could be linked solely to autism.

Clinical Imaging

After several decades of research reviewed in the previous version of this chapter, it was determined that in the absence of an associated disorder such as tuberous sclerosis or fetal rubella, the most common neuroradiologic finding in autism was one of normal neuroanatomy. As mentioned in the next section, Research Imaging, a minority of autistic individuals have ventricular enlargement not related to increased intracranial pressure or to autism severity, and thus it has no diagnostic or treatment implications. Very rarely, other findings such as an arachnoid cyst may be present. In the absence of clinical manifestations referable to this focal abnormality, management and treatment are unchanged. Such focal abnormalities are not etiologic of autism, which from all available data is the result of a bilateral, largely symmetric neurologic abnormality involving multiple levels of the neuraxis. Thus, in the absence of an unusual clinical course, such as focal findings, the late appearance of symptoms or a progressive or fluctuating course (Volkmar, 1992, 1994), or evidence on history or examination of an associated disorder, such as tuberous sclerosis or focal neurologic findings, clinical imaging is unlikely to be useful and should not be a routine part of the neurologic evaluation of autistic children (Filipek et al., 1999; Rapin, 1991).

Research Imaging

As with EPs and eye movements, the first era of imaging research in autism from the 1960s through the early 1980s largely demonstrated the relationship of gross anatomic abnormalities to causes of brain damage other than autism (see Minshew & Dombrowski, 1994, for detailed review of early literature). Several reports have provided excellent reviews of recent literature (Brambilla et al., 2003; Cody, Pelphrey, & Piven, 2002; Nicolson & Szatmari, 2003; Palmen & van Engeland, 2004).

The first imaging studies to employ rigorous screening procedures were those of M. S. Campbell et al. (1982) and Rosenbloom, Campbell, and George (1984). With the exception of a low incidence of ventricular enlargement, the CT scans of these 58 autistic children were normal. Mild to moderate ventricular enlargement was present in 25% of the 45 subjects in the study of M. S. Campbell et al. (1982) and 15% of the 13 autistic subjects in the Rosenbloom et al. (1984) study. In both studies, ventricular size was unrelated to all clinical indices examined, and thus its relationship to the pathophysiology was unknown. These two studies were followed by the negative report of Prior, Tress, Hoffman, and Boldt (1984); Harcherik et al. (1985); and Creasey et al. (1986), concluding that autistic individuals without other neurologic conditions were "very unlikely to have detectable CT abnormalities" (Harcherik et al., 1985) and that the "cerebral defect in autism was likely to be microscopic without major gross anatomic correlate" (Creasey et al., 1986). These conclusions were consistent with the neuropathologic findings of Bauman and Kemper (1985), consisting of abnormalities at the microscopic level but no gross structural abnormalities other than a 100 to 200 gm increase in brain weight. These findings and those that followed became the basis for current clinical recommendations that imaging not be a routine part of the evaluation of children with ASD (see *Practice Parameter,* Filipek et al., 1999).

The current era of imaging research began with the introduction of MRI technology and morphometric methodology for deriving volumetric measurements of brain structures. The advantage of this method, especially for children and adolescents, is the absence of radiation, making studies of them and repeated studies feasible and safe. The other great strengths of MRI are its other applications, including fMRI, diffusion tensor imaging, diffusion tensor fiber tracking, and magnetic resonance spectroscopy.

The limitations of MRI research studies in autism over the past 15 years have been inadequate sample sizes and the inability to add samples across research sites to define the status of structures across the age and severity range in autism. An additional need is for a representative normative database of brain measurements, which considers all relevant influences on brain structure size, specifically age, gender, IQ, height, and possibly socioeconomic status.

Thus far, no studies are available that provide a comprehensive analysis of the whole brain and its component structures in even medium-size samples. Such an integrated perspective is essential to understanding the neuroanatomy of autism, as this is a neural systems disorder and the structures are interconnected and a developmental disorder in which the developmental dynamics of brain growth are differentially disturbed.

Total Brain Volume and Growth

In 1992, Piven and colleagues reported an increase in the midsagittal, supratentorial brain area in 15 high-functioning autistic men compared to well-matched control groups (Piven et al., 1992). Subsequently, Piven and colleagues reported an increase in the total brain volume of the cerebral hemispheres down to the lower boundary of the brainstem in 22 autistic male adolescents and young adults (Piven et al., 1995). The increase in cerebral volume involved both brain parenchyma and the lateral ventricles, but the increase was not accounted for by the increase in ventricular volume. This sample was subsequently expanded to 35 autistic adolescents and adults with the same increase in total brain volume. The latter study also found that the increase in brain volume involved the occipital, parietal, and temporal lobes but not the frontal lobes. Similar findings were reported by Filipek and colleagues (1992) in 9 high-functioning and 13 low-functioning autistic children (*n* = 22) between 6 and 10 years of age. They found an increase in total brain volume localized to the same occipital, parietal, and temporal regions but found that it was largely the result of increased white matter volume.

Recent studies have expanded on this early finding. Courchesne and colleagues (2001) studied 60 autistic and 50 normal boys between 2 and 16 years. Thirty of these autistic children were scanned between 2 and 4 years of age, and 90% were found to have larger than normal brain volumes, indicating increased early brain growth. One-third of these or 10 children met criteria for macrencephaly. Cerebral gray matter was increased by 12% and cerebral white matter by 18% compared to controls. The other 30 children were scanned between 5 and 16 years of age and demonstrated that brain growth decelerated with brain volume normalizing in autism by later childhood. In a second study, Sparks et al. (2002) examined brain volume in forty-five 3- to 4-year-old children with ASD and found an increase in total brain volume. At 6 to 7 years of age, brain volume was no longer increased in this group of children. In a third study of 67 nonretarded children, adolescents and adults with autism and 83 healthy controls ages 8 to 46 years, Aylward, Minshew, Field, Sparks, and Singh (2002) found an increase in total brain volume in those ages 8 to 12 years but not in those older than 12 years of age. It is interesting that both the children, adolescents, and adults had enlarged head circumferences, suggesting that even the adults had had enlarged brain volumes as children. A very recent study of 21 7- to 15-year-old high-functioning ASD children and adolescents revealed proportionate increases (6%) in total brain volume and proportionate increases in cerebral gray matter but not white matter compared to controls (Palmen et al., in press). Unlike some other studies, the cortical gray matter was evenly affected in all lobes. A fourth important study was that of Herbert et al. (2004) of 13 autistic children, which reported that the source of the brain enlargement was the outer zone of radiate white matter. This white matter consists of connections between immediately adjacent cortical regions and longer distant intrahemispheric connections. Herbert et al. (2003) also did an interesting factor analysis of intercorrelations between the sizes of brain structures. The volumes of cerebral cortex, cerebral white matter, and amygdala-hippocampus were significantly different from controls after adjustment for total brain size but not basal ganglia, brainstem, or cerebellum. Based on the factor analysis, the structures fell into three groups based on intercorrelations in their sizes. One factor was cerebral white matter, which showed a trend toward being disproportionately larger. A second factor was cerebral cortex-hippocampus-amygdala, which showed trends toward being disproportionately smaller. The third factor was central white matter-gray matter consisting of globus pallidus-putamen, caudate, putamen, diencephalon, brainstem,

and cerebellum, which, with the exception of caudate, showed significantly larger volumes. The investigators proposed: "These differences in volumes and proportions suggest that autistic brains have nonuniform differences in scaling as compared to controls: it appears that the first group of regions is scaled comparably to controls, the second is scaled somewhat smaller and the third is scaled larger." These findings are intriguing and represent a different way of viewing the brain in autism, more akin to a systems approach.

One other interesting study of the cerebral cortex in autism pertains to the gyral pattern. Hardan, Jou, Keshavan, Varma, and Minshew (2004) examined the gyrification index, the ratio of total to outer cortical contour, to measure the cerebral folding pattern on a frontal coronal slice in 30 non-mentally retarded autistic individuals and 32 matched normal controls. They found that cortical folding was increased on the left in children and adolescents but not adults with autism. They also found that cortical folding decreased bilaterally with age in autism but not in controls. Since the amount of cortical folding may be a reflection of cortical volume, this is an intriguing finding and an important measurement that needs to be pursued in multiple brain regions and a larger sample.

In summary, the data thus far appear consistent in indicating an early acceleration in brain growth leading to increased brain volume in early childhood, which several studies found normalizes in mid-childhood (Aylward et al., 2002; Courchesne et al., 2001). Other studies have supported this developmental profile indirectly by failing to find differences in brain volume in adolescents or adults (McAlonan et al., 2002; Murphy et al., 2002; Rojas, Bawn, Benkers, Reite, & Rogers, 2002; Townsend et al., 2001). However, Piven, Arndt, Bailey, and Andreasen (1996) and Hardan, Minshew, Mallikarjuhn, and Keshavan (2001) reported increased brain volume in adolescents and adults with autism and a recent study of 21 high-functioning adolescents and adults with ASD also found increased total brain volume (Palmen et al., 2004). This study found a proportionate diffuse increase in cerebral gray matter but not white matter. Thus, it is not clear what the status is of brain volume in adolescence and adulthood in autism. The statistical significance or lack of in older individuals may depend on sample size and on the presence of a few autistic individuals in the sample with megalencephaly, e.g., outliers. There are clearly autistic adults with megalencephaly. Thus, there are likely to be two perhaps interrelated phenomena. One is the early acceleration in brain growth that appears to coincide with the presentation if not the onset of symptoms. The second and third are the increase in the mean head circumference for the autism group as a whole and the 20% that have megalencephaly, which may both represent the consequences of overgrowth and the right shift of the curve for the autism group as a whole, a continuous phenomenon, or it could represent two separate phenomenon with those having persistent megalencephaly being a separate subgroup and separate biologic phenomenon from the early overgrowth. Since parents can have large heads without having autism, this physical feature may represent a susceptibility gene that acts in concert with other genes to produce a case of autism. Consistent with this is the recent observed co-occurrence of the G allele of the HoxA1 gene with macrocephaly in autism (Conciatori et al., 2004). It is clear that white matter is an important contributor to the increase in brain volume and that it is probably the outer radiate zone related to intrahemispheric and corticocortical connectivity that matures postnatally that is involved in autism. The increase in white matter as the major source of the increase in brain volume is consistent with the increase in brain weight in autism and the density of myelin. Gray matter volume may also be affected but data are sparse on this. Also, several studies have suggested that it is the early maturing posterior regions of cerebral cortex that are increased in volume, not the late maturing frontal cortex, but again there are little data on this and some conflicting evidence. The difference between the gray-white matter volume results of the Herbert et al. studies and those of the Palmen et al. studies may relate to the methods of image analysis which segmented tissue into gray versus white matter. Finally, the recent factor analysis of brain structure volumes of Herbert et al. (2003) suggests that there are systems differences in the dysregulation of brain growth in autism that are likely to provide insight into the understanding of the developmental neurobiology of autism.

Corpus Callosum

Because neural connectivity is a central issue in autism, the corpus callosum as the major white matter structure connecting the two hemispheres has become of particular interest. It is interesting that only cortical layer III contributes axons that cross in the corpus callosum. The corpus callosum is typically segmented into regions for measurement that correspond to the cortical origin of their fibers. The Witelson method involves seven regions, but some studies in autism have used three or five segments. The most recent study has used voxel-based morphometry (Chung, Dalton, Alexander, & Davidson, 2004). Ten studies of the corpus callosum have been carried out in autism. With the exception of two that employed 0.5 Tesla scanners (Elia et al., 2000; Gaffney, Kuperman, Tsai, Minchin, & Hassanein, 1987) and one that found no differences (Herbert et al., 2004), seven have reported a reduction in the size of the corpus callosum (Chung et al., 2004; Egaas, Courchesne, & Saitoh, 1995; Filipek et al., 1992; Hardan, Minshew, & Keshavan, 2000; Manes et al., 1999; Piven, Bailey, Ranson, & Arndt, 1997; Saitoh, Courchesne, Egaas, Lincoln, & Schreibman, 1995). In some cases, the size of the corpus callosum was only disproportionately small relative to total brain volume and was not reduced in size independent of brain volume. Of the ones reporting a reduction in the size of the corpus callosum, all reported a decrease in the body and posterior regions except one (Hardan et al., 2000), which reported a reduction in the anterior region corresponding to frontal cortices in the sample of nonretarded autistic subjects. The most recent study (Chung et al., 2004) of 16 high-functioning autistic adolescents and young adults reported a reduction in the white matter concentration in the genu, rostrum, and splenium and demonstrated that this was the result of hypoplasia and not atrophy, something that prior studies had not been able to do. A preliminary study using tensor-based methods reported a reduction in the genu, spenium, and midbody in 15 autistic children (Vidal et al., 2003). However, in some studies it appears that the reduction was the result of a few subjects rather than a reduction of the size of the corpus callosum in all subjects. It is therefore important that future studies begin to examine individual subject data and not just group differences.

In summary, numerous structural imaging studies have provided evidence of reduced size of the corpus callosum and, hence, reduced interhemispheric connectivity. In some cases, the reduction has been relative to total brain volume, which was increased in autism, and in other cases the reduction was absolute, for example, with and without correction for total brain volume. The reductions have primarily affected the body and/or posterior regions. It is notable that the reductions in the corpus callosum do not appear to be entirely consistent with the regions of the cortex that are dysfunctional, particularly in the case of frontal dysfunction. Executive dysfunction is a pervasive problem in autism, and you would expect a consistent reduction across studies in the corresponding callosal segments; yet, only one study found this to be the case. This raises the issue of whether an increase or decrease in brain tissue corresponds to improved or impaired function. It is therefore critical that future structural studies pair structural measurements with functional measurements. Although total brain volume is increased early in brain development in autism, this coincides with presentation of symptoms and brain dysfunction. Thus, too much brain is not good in this case. In the case of the corpus callosum, there has been only one paper purported to investigate interhemispheric cognitive abilities and reported impairments (Nydén, Carlsson, Carlsson, & Gillberg, 2004). However, the measures used were not true measures of interhemispheric communication so it is not clear if there is impaired interhemispheric function in autism. In addition, if only a small subset of autistic subjects have reduced corpus callosum area then such measures would need to be compared to those who clearly have and do not have reduced area to shed light on structural-functional correlations.

Cortical Language Areas

The left planum temporale is involved in receptive speech and is commonly referred to as Wernicke's area. It is larger on the left than

the right in 78% of normal people. Rojas et al. (2002) measured the volume of the gray matter in the left and right planum temporale and in Heschl's gyrus in 15 autistic adults and 15 normal controls. In the control subjects, the left planum temporale was larger than the right, but in the autistic subjects the structures were essentially the same size in the two hemispheres, reflecting a lack of the normal specialization and hypertrophy of the left planum temporale. Heschl's gyrus was larger on the left than the right in both the control and autistic subjects, demonstrating that the lack of specialization in the planum temporale was not a generalized left hemisphere phenomenon. Of note, the normal controls in this study had substantially higher IQ scores than the autistic subjects, though total brain volume and left and right hemisphere volumes were not different across groups. In contrast, in a study of 7- to 11-year-old children, Herbert et al. (2002) found more extreme left asymmetry in the planum temporale in the autism group ($n = 16$) compared to the control group ($n = 15$) all with IQ scores over 80. In a third study, De Fossé and colleagues (2004) reported exaggerated leftward asymmetry of the planum temporale in language impaired autistic children (6 to 13 years with mean VIQ 75) and children with specific language impairment, but not in non language impaired children with autism (mean VIQ 97) or typically developing control children.

The left inferior prefrontal gyrus or Broca's area has also been reported to be abnormal in autism in a few studies. Abell and colleagues (1999) reported a decrease in the gray matter density in this cortical region using voxel based morphometry. Herbert and colleagues (2002) also found a right ward asymmetry in 7- to 11-year old children with autism. The study of Fosse and colleagues (2004) similarly found a right ward asymmetry in the frontal language cortex (reversal of the normal asymmetry) but only in the autism group with language impairment and in the specific language impairment group but not in the autism group without current language impairment.

These reports of abnormalities in the symmetry patterns of the language cortex are supported by reports of increased left-handedness and ambidextrousness in autism, another reflection of the lack of the normal left hemisphere specialization (Escalante-Mead, Minshew, & Sweeney, 2003). In a similar vein, there was a small series of CT studies in the 1980s in autism that proposed abnormalities in hemispheric specialization. The studies were inconsistent and the issue was dropped (see Minshew & Dombrowski, 1994, for review), but there is a recent reemergence of studies suggesting a failure of the normal developmental specialization of function and structure in the brain. Thus, this study is probably the first of many to demonstrate the developmental failure of regional specialization in the brain in autism.

Cingulate Cortex

The anterior cingulate gyrus was investigated in one study (Haznedar et al., 1997) in seven autistic subjects and seven controls, which found the right anterior cingulate to be significantly smaller when corrected for total brain volume in the autism group. There was also less activation of this structure during a verbal learning task. This sample was expanded to 17 subjects with ASD and 17 controls with replication of this finding (Haznedar et al., 2000). In addition, the expanded study reported hypometabolism in both the anterior and posterior cinguli. In an fMRI study of spatial working memory, Luna et al. (2002) found reduced activity in posterior cingulate cortex and dorsolateral prefrontal cortex in 11 high-functioning autistic subjects compared to 6 healthy controls. These few studies reporting evidence of structural and functional abnormalities of the cingulate cortex are consistent with the increased cell packing density reported by Bauman and Kemper (1994) in neuropathological studies. Further studies are obviously needed, though, before any conclusions can be made about the volume of this structure in autism.

Hippocampus

The hippocampus is involved in associative memory and linking multiple inputs, allowing for representations of the relations between elements of scenes or events (Cohen et al., 1999). Like many other brain structures, structural imaging abnormalities have been inconsistent in the hippocampus in autism. Four of eight studies reported no differences in hippocampal volume in autism compared to control groups. Three found hippocampal volume to be

smaller, and one reported increased hippocampal volume.

Two of the five studies of autistic children found no differences in hippocampal volume. In 1995, Saitoh et al. measured the posterior hippocampal formation (CA1-CA4, dentate gyrus, subiculum) in one single oblique coronal slice. They found no difference between 33 autistic children (12 with mental retardation and 30 males) and 23 control children (19 males), whether the autistic subjects were retarded or whether they had a history of seizures. Piven, Bailey, Ranson, and Arndt replicated these findings in 1998, comparing the hippocampal volumes of 35 autistic subjects (26 males) and 36 controls (20 males), both before and after adjusting for gender, performance IQ, and total brain volume.

Herbert et al. (2003) and Saitoh, Karns, and Courchesne (2001) both reported smaller hippocampal volumes in children with autism. Herbert et al. reported smaller hippocampal volume only after correction for total brain volume in 15 boys with high-functioning autism compared to 17 control boys. In this study, however, the combined volumes of the amygdala and hippocampus were measured, and no separate measurement of the hippocampus was made. In 2001, Saitoh et al. found smaller area dentata (dentate gyrus and CA4) both before and after correction for total brain volume in 59 autistic children (52 males) compared to 51 controls (40 males). Only cross-sectional areas, not volumes, were measured, however.

The only study that has reported increased hippocampal volume, Sparks et al. (2002), used 45 subjects (38 males) between the ages of 3 and 4 compared with 26 age-matched controls (18 males). Increased hippocampal volume, proportional to the increase in total brain volume, was found. The hippocampus was no longer enlarged in these children at age 6 to 7 years, nor was their total brain volume. It has been suggested that increased hippocampal volume might be seen only in younger subjects, and individuals with autism might exhibit arrested growth or perhaps increased apoptosis over time.

In the adult studies, Haznedar et al. (2000) investigated the hippocampal volume of 17 adults with ASD and 17 age- and sex-matched controls and did not find any significant difference. Howard et al.'s (2000) study of 10 male adults with high-functioning autism and 10 age-, sex-, and verbal IQ-matched controls reported similar results; however, a trend toward a smaller hippocampus was found in the autism group. Aylward et al. (1999) studied hippocampal volume in 14 male adolescents and adults with high-functioning autism and 14 male controls matched on age, IQ, height, weight, and socioeconomic status. Hippocampal volume was found to be smaller in autistic subjects only after correction for total brain volume, which was larger in autistic subjects.

In summary, studies of the hippocampus have reported diverse results. The growth of this structure is dynamic in autism and so are abnormalities. To define the structural pathology, it will be essential to control for age, gender, and IQ differences between groups and to define changes over the age span and in relation to total brain volume and the cerebral cortex and other structures to which it is heavily connected.

Amygdala

The amygdala is associated with social behavior and cognition (Adolphs, 2001, 2002; Adolphs, Baron-Cohen, & Tranel, 2002). Since social impairment is one of the main symptoms of autism, the amygdala has often been thought to be abnormal in autism and the subject of considerable structural and functional investigation. Three of seven studies investigating amygdala volume in autism have reported increased volume, three have reported decreased volume, and one study found no difference between the amygdala volumes in the autism and control group.

Among the five studies investigating amygdala volumes of adults, two reported increased volume, two reported decreased volume, and one reported no difference between the autistic and control groups. Abell et al. (1999) investigated the amygdala volumes of 15 high-functioning autistic adults (12 males) compared with 15 IQ-matched controls (12 males). Increased gray matter was found in the amygdala and periamygdaloid cortex. Howard et al. (2000) found bilateral increased amygdala volumes in 10 high-functioning autistic males compared to 10 age-, sex-, and verbal IQ-matched controls. Aylward et al. (1999) studied 14 male adolescents and adults with high-

functioning autism and 14 age-, sex-, IQ-, height-, weight-, and socioeconomic status-matched controls. Amygdala volumes were found to be significantly smaller in the autism group both before and after correction for total brain volume. Pierce, Muller, Ambrose, Allen, and Courchesne (2001) reported bilateral decrease in amygdala volume in seven male adults and eight male controls matched on age, sex, and handedness. In 2000, Haznedar et al. studied 17 adults with ASD (15 males) and 17 adult age- and sex-matched controls (15 males). When the subject group was divided into autism and Asperger syndrome categories, the subjects with Asperger syndrome had a significantly larger left amygdala than the subjects with autism.

The two studies investigating child subjects had contradictory results. Sparks et al. (2002) found bilateral increased amygdala volume in 45 children (38 males) with ASD between the ages of 3 and 4, as compared to 26 age-matched controls (18 males). They found the increase in amygdala volume to be proportional to the increase in total brain volume. However, in the most severely affected children (the core autism group), amygdala enlargement was present even without correction for total brain volume, suggesting a positive correlation between amygdala volume and the severity of symptoms. The increase in amygdala volume continued to be present at 6 to 7 years of age in this group when total brain volume was not different from controls. Contrary to these findings, Herbert et al. (2003) found decreased amygdala volume in 15 male children with high-functioning autism, compared to 17 control boys, but only after correction for total brain volume. This study also used the combined volumes of the hippocampus and amygdala, with no separate measurements.

In summary, the studies of the amygdala are contradictory at all ages. A limitation is the inability to add data across sites to achieve a large sample size. This is a critical structure to understand in light of the social and emotional impairments in autism. It is hoped that studies will overcome this obstacle over the next 5 years.

Basal Ganglia

The caudate nucleus, putamen, and globus pallidus, which together make up the basal ganglia, are believed to be involved in stereotypic and repetitive behavior in autism and perhaps other aspects of the motor problems. Sears et al. (1999) reported increased caudate nucleus volume, proportional to the increase in total brain volume, in 35 high-functioning autistic adults compared to 36 adult controls of comparable age, sex, and IQ. The authors replicated their findings in another 13 autistic subjects and 25 controls. The size of this structure correlated with repetitive behavior in these subjects. In 2003, Herbert et al. reported an increase in the globus pallidus-putamen proportional to the increase in brain volume, but no differences in the caudate nucleus in 15 high-functioning autistic boys compared to 17 control boys. In a study of 40 high-functioning autistic individuals between 8 and 45 years of age and 41 healthy controls, Hardan, Kilpatrick, Keshavan, and Minshew (2003) found no differences in the volumes of the caudate and putamen when controlling for total brain volume. They were not able to achieve satisfactory intraclass correlation coefficients for the globus pallidus and thus did not report measurements for this structure. They also reported impaired motor performance primarily involving praxis and reduced grip strength in the autistic subjects. The reduction in grip strength is consistent with functional abnormalities in the basal ganglia whereas the abnormalities in praxis are more consistent with cerebral cortical dysfunction. Thus, studies of the basal ganglia have been few and the data inconclusive about the status of this structure in autism.

Thalamus

The thalamus has reciprocal connections with nearly all major brain structures and is particularly interesting with regard to synchronization of information processing and the sensory symptoms in autism. There has been only one reported study of thalamic volume in 12 high-functioning adolescents and adults compared to 12 matched healthy controls (Tsatsanis et al., 2003). There were no differences in thalamic volume before adjustment for total brain volume. In the control group, there was a positive correlative between thalamic volume and total brain volume but only when the groups were divided using a split median procedure to yield high and low brain volume groups. The investigators interpreted these findings to mean there

was underdevelopment of connections between cortical and subcortical regions in the autism group. This is an interesting finding but a tentative one in need of much further investigation before any conclusions can be drawn about this structure in autism.

Cerebellum

There has been considerable imaging attention focused on the cerebellum in autism, initially because the vermis was accessible to measurement on mid-*sagittal* sections. Rather quickly there ensued a controversy in the literature about the presence or absence of vermal hypoplasia. For a while, it was even argued that the vermis was the seat of autism in the brain largely on the basis of unproven hypotheses that it was the site of a cognitive deficit in shifting attention. Subsequently, neuropsychologic and neurophysiologic tests using multiple different methods demonstrated that the deficit in shifting attention was related to the frontal lobe and executive processes, not the cerebellum and elementary attentional processes (Minshew et al., 1999; Ozonoff, Strayer, McMahon, & Filloux, 1994; Pascualvaca, Fantie, Papageorgiou, & Mirsky, 1998). The initial imaging reports of vermal hypoplasia were never independently replicated. Ultimately, the finding to be replicated was increased volume of the cerebellar hemispheres proportionate to total brain volume.

Cerebellar Hemispheres

Several studies have reported an increase in overall cerebellar volume in children (Herbert et al., 2003; Sparks et al., 2002) and adults (Hardan et al., 2001; Piven et al., 1997) with autism. These studies involved a total of 60 children with autism or ASD and 43 matched controls and 51 adults with autism and 55 controls. The increase in cerebellar volume was generally proportionate to the increase in total brain volume. Other studies evaluated cerebellar volume (Allen & Courchesne, 2003) and did not find differences in subject populations that also did not have increases in total brain volume. Thus, it appears that cerebellar volume is increased proportionately to total brain volume in autism in most studies. This finding is in contrast to neuropathologic reports of reduced Purkinje cells. However, the increase in volume, both total cerebellar and total brain volume, measured in imaging studies appears to be the result of increased white matter and not the result of changes in neuronal populations. A few studies have reported a disproportionate increase in the volume of the cerebellum on the order of a 40% increase relative to the increase in the volume of the cerebrum (Courchesne et al., 2001; Palmen et al., in press; Palmen, 2004).

Cerebellar Vermis

In a series of publications since 1988, Courchesne and colleagues reported a decrease in the midsagittal area of vermal lobules VI and VII (Ciesielski et al., 1990; Courchesne, Yeung-Courchesne, Press, Hesselink, & Jernigan, 1988; Murakami, Courchesne, Press, Yeung-Courchesne, & Hesselink, 1989; Saitoh et al., 1995) in the absence of an alteration in the midsagittal area of the pons (Hsu, Yeung-Courchesne, Courchesne, & Press, 1991) and suggested an intrinsic abnormality of neocerebellar vermis. Subsequently, Courchesne and colleagues reported both a selective hypoplasia and hyperplasia of the neocerebellar vermis (Courchesne et al., 1994). However, these studies failed to control for IQ. Numerous studies that have collectively examined vermal size in a wide age and IQ range of autistic subjects have failed to replicate these findings when autistic and control subjects were well matched on age, gender, and IQ (Filipek, 1999; Filipek et al., 1992; Garber & Ritvo, 1992; Garber et al., 1989; Hardan et al., 2001; Hashimoto, Murakawa, Miyazaki, Tayama, & Kuroda, 1992; Hashimoto, Tayama, Miyazaki, Murakawa, & Kuroda, 1993; Holttum, Minshew, Sanders, & Phillips, 1992; Kleiman, Neff, & Rosman, 1992; Levitt et al., 1999; Manes et al., 1999; Nowell, Hackney, Muraki, & Coleman, 1990; Piven et al., 1992, 1997; Ritvo & Garber, 1988). In summary, although much was made about early reports of vermal hypo- and hyperplasia of lobules VI and VII, these MRI findings appear to be related to lack of matching between the autism and control groups on IQ (Filipek, 1999; Filipek et al., 1992; Palmen & van Engeland, 2004; Piven et al., 1992, 1997) and were never confirmed.

Brainstem

The brainstem has been reported to be decreased in area in a few studies, but these stud-ies often compared mentally retarded autistic subjects to non-mentally retarded controls or failed to control for total brain size (Gaffney, Kuperman, Tsai, & Minchin, 1988; Hashimoto et al., 1989, 1992, 1993, 1995). Other studies found no abnormalities of the brainstem (Elia et al., 2000; Garber & Ritvo, 1992; Hardan et al., 2001; Hsu et al., 1991; Piven et al., 1992). Histologic studies of the brainstem have not revealed cell loss and thus do not provide an anatomic correlate for imaging studies reporting a reduction in size. In summary, the studies of the brainstem are inadequate to date because they have primarily measured midsagittal areas and most have failed to control for the effects of IQ and total brain size. Those that have adequately controlled for key variables have failed to document structural abnormalities of the brainstem in autism.

Ventricles

Although early CT studies reported clinically apparent lateral ventricular enlargement, sometimes asymmetric, in up to 15% of autistic subjects, this has not been investigated to any degree by MRI research studies since. Lateral ventricular size has been reported to be increased in one study (Howard et al., 2000) but not in two other studies (Hardan et al., 2001; Piven et al., 1995). This needs further study in a large sample. In early studies, lateral ventricular enlargement was not related to any of the clinical parameters investigated. However, regression as a mode of presentation was not considered as a possible factor and should be. Palmen et al. have reported a 40% increase in the lateral and third ventricular volumes in 21 medication naïve high-functioning autistic children aged 7 to 15 years compared to controls, in the context of a 6% increase in total brain volume. In a sample of 21 adolescents with PDD and 21 controls, a similar increase in ventricular volumes was also increased (Palmen et al., 2004).

In a study of 16 high-functioning autistic (HFA) adults and 19 healthy controls, Hardan et al. (2001) reported an increase in the volume of the third ventricle after adjustment for intracranial volume. The significance of this finding, as with other findings related to the ventricles in autism, is that it might reflect reduction in the size of the brain structure that surrounds it, for example, the thalamus.

Enlargement of the fourth ventricle has been reported in a single study but not in seven other studies (see Brambilla et al., 2003, for a review).

CLINICAL NEUROLOGY

This section encompasses certain aspects of the neurologic examination not considered in the standard assessment of autism. Thus, although behavioral child neurologists would also assess social function, language, and repetitive behavior these are not discussed here. Instead, this section covers long tract signs, motor signs, head circumference, minor physical anomalies, the electroencephalogram and epilepsy from a clinical perspective.

The Neurologic Examination

The neurologic examination in autism is remarkable for the absence of findings, other than the manifestations of autism, and for above-average head circumference in some but not all individuals (Bailey et al., 1993, 1995). Microcephaly is not part of this syndrome if subjects are screened for associated disorders. The presence of microcephaly should suggest the presence of fetal infection with rubella or cytomegalovirus, Rett syndrome, or a chromosomal anomaly. Cranial nerve examination is normal except for the facial nerve. Most individuals with autism have a "sober" or masked facial expression during interactions, although they exhibit expression or animation in response to internally experienced emotion. Their attempts at imitation of facial emotion typically result in stilted expressions as a result of problems with praxis and perhaps weakness. Czapinski and Bryson (2003) have reported evidence of reduced and weak muscle movements in the eye and mouth regions but not the brow region and suggested this was evidence of abnormalities of the vii cranial nerve nucleus. There are many interesting studies of facial movement ongoing, both expression and the capacity of autistic individuals to detect expression, and it will be interesting to see their results. Oral-motor apraxia or dyspraxia may also become apparent on examination of cranial nerves. Muscle tone is subtly decreased. Joints tend to be hypermobile. Deep

tendon reflexes are variable. In some children, they are markedly diminished; in others, they are normal or increased. Babinski signs are down going. Toe walking is not uncommon. Gait lacks the normal fluidity reflecting diminished postural balance, incoordination, and motor planning problems. Motor apraxia is nearly universal. Stereotypies are present in about one-third of children. Complaints of sensory sensitivity to sound, light, and texture are frequent, but objective sensory signs are not, with the exception of errors on fingertip number writing (see Chapter 32, this *Handbook, Volume 2,* for further information about the motor and sensory abnormalities in autism).

Head Circumference

In Kanner's original description of autism, 5 of the 11 children had large heads (Kanner, 1943). Studies since then have determined that 20% of individuals with idiopathic autism have macrocephaly, for example, a head circumference > 97 percentile or >2 *SD* above the mean (Fombonne, Roge, Claverie, Coury, & Fremolle, 1999; Lainhart, 2003). The increase in head circumference is typically disproportionate to height. A large but normal size head (>50 percentile but <97%) is even more common. The mean head circumference for the autism population is at the 60 to 70 percentile for the standardization sample. Macrocephaly in autism is usually not present at birth, though it is on occasion. It appears to develop in the first or second year of life, though head circumference data documenting this are very limited. It has also been documented to develop as late as 4 years of age (Lainhart et al., 1997; Mason-Brothers et al., 1987). One retrospective study of head circumference measurements suggested that the onset of macrocephaly in most autistic children was between birth and 6 to 14 months of age when head circumference was increased by 1.67 *SD*s to the 84th percentile (Courchesne, Carper, & Akshoomoff, 2003), although such early changes in head circumference were not found by Lainhart and collaborators in the multi-site data from the Collaborative Programs of Excellence in Autism. The increase in head circumference in autism corresponds to an increase in brain volume, which plateaus

academic performance including arithmetic, reading, and spelling (Aarts, Binnie, Smit, & Wilkins, 1984; Binnie, 1993; Kasteleijn-Nolst Trenite et al., 1988; Shewmon & Erwin, 1988a, 1988b; Siebelink, Bakker, Binnie, Kasteleijn-Nolst Trenite, 1988). Such episodes may be exhibited in good performance on a class assignment punctuated by transient unexplained errors that the child does not recall later, followed by immediate resumption of good performance. This same performance phenomenon can occur in the context of any task.

Electroencephalograms in Autism

Epileptiform abnormalities on EEG are even more frequent than epilepsy in the autism population. The frequency of such abnormalities increases with the number of EEGs obtained, the inclusion of sleep in the recording, and the duration of the recording. In one study in which the mean number of recordings was four and all recordings included sleep, 60.8% of the individuals with ASD had epileptiform activity (Kawasaki et al., 1997). If only the individuals with ASD without clinical epilepsy were considered, then only 31% had an epileptiform EEG. A lower prevalence of 21% epileptiform EEGs was found in individuals with ASD in recordings that included sleep, but the EEGs varied in quality and number (Tuchman & Rapin, 1997). This 21% included individuals with clinical epilepsy. It is also notable in this study that only 59% of the children with clinical epilepsy had epileptiform EEGs. It is not clear what treatment, if any, is appropriate for individuals with epileptiform EEGs and no evidence of clinical seizure activity.

One particular issue with regard to epilepsy, EEG abnormalities, and autism has been in the context of regression. Tuchman and Rapin (1997) found no significant difference in the occurrence of epilepsy between ASD children presenting with regression and those presenting with developmental delays. Using 23-hour telemetry recordings, Tuchman, Jayakar, Yaylali, and Villalobos (1997) observed that 46% of ASD children presenting with regression had an epileptiform EEG. It has been suggested that some children with ASD and regression have Landau Kleffner syndrome or epileptic aphasia, despite clear differences between these two syndromes. The onset of re-

gression in Landau Kleffner syndrome is typically later than in autism, and the regression is limited to language (an epileptic aphasia) and is not associated with social or behavioral symptoms. In addition, the spike activity is typically frequent and temporal rather than infrequent and centro-temporal. On the basis of this analogy, however, the use of steroids and other aggressive treatments for regression and epileptiform activity was proposed in autism (Lewine et al., 1999; Stefanos, Grover, & Geller, 1995). However, there have been little data to support the efficacy of steroids in ASD associated with regression and epileptiform EEGs and not much more for depakote or other anticonvulsants (Nass & Petrucha, 1990; Plioplys, 1994; Tuchman, 2000). Certainly radical treatments such as subpial resection are not recommended.

Other Potential Neurologic Conditions

There are other aspects of brain function such as sleep that have been relatively untouched by research but deserve careful attention. Sleep disorders are pervasive in ASD and are not confined to early childhood (Honomichl, Goodlin-Jones, Burnham, Gaylor, & Anders, 2002). They lead to considerable stress among the children, parents, and siblings; yet we know little about the neurobiologic and medical causes of this problem.

CONCLUSION

Autism is a fascinating neurologic disorder that appears to primarily affect neuronal organization events and to have a currently estimated onset in brain development no later than 30 weeks gestation. Based on current data, it furthermore appears to be a neural systems disorder that constrains information processing, in particular integrative processing and circuitry. Imaging studies have demonstrated a reduction in functional connectivity when challenging social, language, and problem solving tasks are employed and intact connectivity when simpler tasks in areas of intact function are employed. Structural imaging studies have demonstrated an increase in total brain volume suggesting a premature acceleration in brain growth coinciding with the onset of symptoms. This increase appears largely to arise from the outer zone of white matter that contain fibers connecting adjacent regions of cortex as well longer intra-hemispheric connections. Head circumference studies have been the largest source of data about brain growth as imaging studies remain limited by cost, subject recruitment and cooperation. FMRI studies though provide evidence of altered activation in gray matter suggesting that it is a disorder of both cortical gray matter and its white matter projections. Abnormalities documented in sensorimotor integration in studies of postural physiology and the essentially universal abnormalities in praxis suggest that the neurobiologic abnormality is pervasive and broadly involves brain functions that require a high degree of integration. Clinical symptoms are most apparent in those domains that place the highest demand on information integration (e.g., the social, communication, and information processing domains). The measurement of other brain structures has largely been fraught with controversial results due to small sample sizes across the wide age and severity spectrum of autism. The presence of minor physical anomalies suggests the possibily of an early onset in brain development than the third trimester, though none of the identified brain abnormalities found are typical of such an early time. The identification of susceptibility genes for autism will greatly aide in the progress in understanding the pathophysiology of autism as it has done in Rett syndrome. Such advances await the accrual of a pooled sample of accurately diagnosed and characterized multiplex families and thus families willing to participate.

Cross-References

Other aspects of the neurobiology of autism are discussed in Chapters 16, 17, 19, and 20. Pharmacological treatments are addressed in Chapter 44.

REFERENCES

Aarts, J. P., Binnie, C. D., Smit, A. M., & Wilkins, A. J. (1984). Selective Cognitive Impairment During Focal and Generalized Epileptiform EEG Activity. *Brain, 107,* 293–308.

Abell, F., Krams, M., Ashburner, J., Passingham, R., Friston, K., Frackowiak, R., et al. (1999). The neuroanatomy of autism: A voxel-based whole brain analysis of structural scans. *Neuro-Report, 10,* 1647–1651.

Adolphs, R. (2001). The neurobiology of social cognition. *Current Opinion in Neurobiology, 11,* 231–239.

Adolphs, R. (2002). Neural systems for recognizing emotion. *Current Opinion in Neurobiology, 12,* 169–177.

Adolphs, R., Baron-Cohen, S., & Tranel, D. (2002). Impaired recognition of social emotions following amygdala damage. *Journal of Cognitive Neuroscience, 14,* 1264–1274.

Allen, G., & Courchesne, E. (2003). Differential effects of developmental cerebellar abnormality on cognitive and motor functions in the cerebellum: An fMRI study of autism. *American Journal of Psychiatry, 160,* 262–273.

Aminoff, M. J. (1992). *Electrodiagnosis in clinical neurology.* New York: Churchill Livingston.

Arin, D. M., Bauman, M. L., & Kemper, T. L. (1991). The distribution of Purkinje cell loss in the cerebellum in autism [Abstract]. *Neurology, 41,* 307.

Aylward, E. H., Minshew, N. J., Field, K., Sparks, B. F., & Singh, N. (2002). Effects of age on brain volume and head circumference in autism. *Neurology, 59,* 175–183.

Aylward, E. H., Minshew, N. J., Goldstein, G., Honeycutt, N. A., Augustine, A. M., Yates, K. O., et al. (1999). MRI volumes of amygdala and hippocampus in non-mentally retarded autistic adolescents and adults. *Neurology, 53,* 2145–2150.

Bailey, A., Le Couteur, A., Gottesman, I., Bolton, P., Simonoff, E., Yuzda, E., et al. (1995). Autism as a strongly genetic disorder: Evidence from a British twin study. *Psychological Medicine, 25,* 63–78.

Bailey, A., Luthert, P., Bolton, P., Le Couteur, A., & Rutter, M. (1993). Autism and megalencephaly. *Lancet, 34,* 1225–1226.

Bailey, A., Luthert, P., Dean, A., Harding, B., Janota, I., Montgomery, M., et al. (1998). A clinicopathologic study of autism. *Brain, 121,* 889–905.

Bauman, M. L., & Kemper, T. L. (1984). The brain in infantile autism: A histoanatomic report. *Neurology, 34,* 275. [abstract].

Bauman, M. L., & Kemper, T. L. (1985). Histoanatomic observations of the brain in early infantile autism. *Neurology, 35,* 866–874.

Bauman, M. L., & Kemper, T. L. (1994). Neuroanatomic observations of the brain in autism. In M. L. Bauman & T. L. Kemper (Eds.), *The neurobiology of autism* (pp. 119–145). Baltimore: Johns Hopkins Press.

Bauman, M. L., & Kemper, T. L. (1996). Observations on the Purkinje cells in the cerebellar vermis in autism. *Journal of Neuropathology and Experimental Neurology, 55,* 613.

Bauman, M. L., & Kemper, T. L. (1997). Is autism a progressive process? *Neurology, 48* (Suppl. 2), A285.

Bentin, S., Allison, T., Puce, A., Perez, E., & McCarthy, G. (1996). Electrophysiological studies of face perception in humans. *Journal of Cognitive Neuroscience, 8,* 551–565.

Binnie, C. D. (1993). Significance and management of transitory cognitive impairment due to subclinical EEG discharges in children. *Brain Development, 15,* 23–30.

Blatt, G. I., Fitzgerald, C. M., Guptill, J. T., Booker, A. B., Kemper, T. L., & Bauman, M. L. (2001). Density and distribution of hippocampal neurotransmitter receptors in autism. *Journal of Autism and Developmental Disorders, 31,* 537–543.

Boucher, J., & Warrington, E. K. (1976). Memory deficits in early infantile autism: Some similarities to the amnestic syndrome. *British Journal of Psychology, 67,* 73–87.

Brambilla, P., Stanley, J. A., Sassi, R. B., Nicoletti, M. A., Mallinger, A. G., Keshavan, M. S., et al. (2003). In vivo effects of lithium in dorso-lateral prefrontal cortex in healthy human subjects: A ^{1}H-MRS study. *Bipolar Disorders* (Suppl. 5), 35.

Bruneau, N., Bonnet-Brilhault, F., Gomot, M., Adrien, J. L., & Barthélémy, C. (2003). Cortical auditory processing and communication in children with autism: Electrophysiological/behavioral relations. *International Journal of Psychophysiology, 51,* 17–25.

Bruneau, N., Roux, S., Adrien, J. L., & Barthélémy, C. (1999). Auditory associative cortex dysfunction in children with autism: Evidence from late auditory evoked potentials (N1 wave-T complex). *Clinical Neuropsychology, 110,* 1927–1934.

Buchwald, J. S., Erwin, R., van Lancker, D., Guthrie, D., Schwafel, J., & Tanguay, P. (1992). Midlatency auditory evoked responses: P1 abnormalities in adult autistic subjects. *Electroencephalography and Clinical Neurophysiology, 84,* 164–171.

Campbell, M. B., Geller, B., Small, A. M., Petti, T. A., & Ferris, S. H. (1978). Minor physical anomalies in young psychotic children. *American Journal of Psychiatry, 135,* 573–575.

Campbell, M. S., Rosenbloom, S., Perry, R., George, A. E., Kricheff, I. I., Anderson, L., et al. (1982). Computerized axial tomography in young autistic children. *American Journal of Psychiatry, 139,* 510–512.

Carper, R. A., Moses, P., Tigue, Z. D., & Courchesne, E. (2002). Cerebral lobes in autism: Early hyperplasia and abnormal age effects. *Neuroimage, 16,* 1038–1051.

Casanova, M. F., Buxhoeveden, D. P., Switala, A. E., & Roy, E. (2002). Minicolumnar pathology in autism. *Neurology, 58,* 428–432.

Ceponiene, R., Lepistö, T., Shestakova, A., Vanhala, R., Alku, P., Näätänen R, et al. (2003). Speech-sound selective auditory impairment in children with autism: They can perceive but do not attend. *Proceedings of the National Academy of Sciences, 100,* 5567–5572.

Chen, W., Chen, Y., Chen, D., Chen, J., Yin, X., & Lin, Q. (2003). Brainstem auditory evoked potentials in children with autistic disorder [Abstract] *Chinese Mental Health Journal, 17,* 24–26.

Chiappa, K., & Gladstone, K. (1978). The limits of normal variations in waves I through VII of the human brainstem auditory response. *Neurology, 28,* 402.

Chugani, D. C., Muzik, O., Rothermel, R., Behen, M., Chakraborty, P., Mangner, T., et al. (1997). Altered serotonin synthesis in the dentatothalamocortical pathway in autistic boys. *Annals of Neurology, 42,* 666–669.

Chung, M. K., Dalton, K. M., Alexander, A. L., & Davidson, R. J. (2004). Less white matter concentration in autism: 2D voxel based morphometry. *Neuroimage, 23,* 242–251.

Ciesielski, K. T., Allen, P. S., Sinclair, B. D., Pabst, H. F., Yanossky, R., & Ludwig, R. (1990). Hypoplasia of cerebellar vermis in autism and childhood leukemia [Abstract]. *Proceedings of the 5th International Child Neurology Congress, Tokyo, Japan,* 650.

Ciesielski, K. T., Courchesne, E., & Elmasian, R. (1990). Effects of focused selective attention tasks on event-related potentials in autistic and normal individuals. *Electroencephalography and Clinical Neurophysiology, 75,* 207–220.

Cody, H., Pelphrey, K., & Piven, J. (2002). Structural and functional magnetic resonance imaging of autism. *International Journal of Developmental Neuroscience, 20,* 421–431.

Cohen, N. J., Ryan, E., Hunt, C., Romine, L., Wszalek, T., & Nash, C. (1999). Hippocampal system and declarative (relational) memory: Summarizing the data from functional neuroimaging studies. *Hippocampus, 9,* 83–98.

Coleman, M. (1979). Studies of the autistic syndromes. In R. Katzman (Ed.), *Congenital and acquired cognitive disorders* (pp. 265–303). New York: Raven Press.

Conciatori, M., Stodgell, C. J., Hyman, S. L., O'Bara, M., Militerni, R., Bravaccio, C., et al. (2004). Association between the HOXA1 A218G polymorphism and increased head circumference in patients with autism. *Biological Psychiatry, 55,* 413–419.

Cook, E. H., Lindgren, V., Leventhal, B. I., Courchesne, R., Lincoln, A., Shulman, C., et al. (1997). Autism or atypical autism in maternally but not paternally derived proximal 15q duplication. *American Journal of Human Genetics, 60,* 928–934.

Courchesne, E. (1978). Neurophysiological correlates of cognitive development: Changes in long-latency event-related potentials from childhood to adulthood. *Electroencephalography and Clinical Neurophysiology, 45,* 468–482.

Courchesne, E., Carper, R., & Akshoomoff, N. (2003). Evidence of brain overgrowth in the first year of life in autism. *Journal of the American Medical Association, 290,* 337–344.

Courchesne, E., Courchesne, R. Y., Hicks, G., & Lincoln, A. J. (1985). Functioning of the brain-stem auditory pathway in non-retarded autistic individuals. *Electroencephalography and Clinical Neurophysiology, 61,* 491–501.

Courchesne, E., Elmasian, R., & Yeung-Courchesne, R. (1987). Electrophysiological correlates of cognitive processing: P3b and Nc, basic, clinical, and developmental research. In A. M. Halliday, S. R. Butler, & R. Paul (Eds.), *A textbook of clinical neurophysiology* (pp. 645–676). New York: Wiley.

Courchesne, E., Karns, C. M., Davis, H. R., Ziccardi, R., Carper, R. A., Tigue, Z. D., et al. (2001). Unusual brain growth patterns in early life in patients with autistic disorder. *Neurology, 57,* 245–254.

Courchesne, E., Kilman, B. A., Galambos, R., & Lincoln, A. J. (1984). Autism: Processing of novel auditory information assessed by event-related brain potentials. *Electroencephalog-raphy and Clinical Neurophysiology, 59,* 238–248.

Courchesne, E., Lincoln, A. J., Kilman, B. A., & Galambos, R. (1985). Event-related brain potential correlates of the processing of novel visual and auditory information in autism. *Journal of Autism and Developmental Disorders, 15,* 55–76.

Courchesne, E., Lincoln, A. J., Yeung-Courchesne, R., Elmasian, R., & Grillon, C. (1989). Pathophysiologic findings in non-retarded autism and receptive developmental language disorders. *Journal of Autism and Developmental Disorders, 19,* 1–17.

Courchesne, E., Saitoh, O., Yeung-Courchesne, R., Press, G. A., Lincoln, A. J., Haas, R. H., et al.

(1994). Abnormality of cerebellar vermian lobules VI and VII in patients with infantile autism: Identification of hypoplastic and hyperplastic subgroups with M. R. Imaging. *American Journal of Roentgenology, 162,* 123–130.

Courchesne, E., Yeung-Courchesne, R., Press, G. A., Hesselink, J. R., & Jernigan, T. L. (1988). Hypoplasia of cerebellar vermal lobules VI and VII in autism. *New England Journal of Medicine, 318,* 1349–1354.

Creasey, J., Rumsey, J. M., Schwartz, M., Duara, R., Rapoport, J. L., & Rapoport, S. I. (1986). Brain morphometry in autistic men as measured by volumetric computed tomography. *Archives of Neurology, 32,* 669–672.

Czapinski, P., & Bryson, S. E. (2003). Reduced facial muscle movements in autism: Evidence for dysfunction in the neuromuscular pathway? [Abstract]. *Brain and Cognition, 51,* 177–179.

Damasio, A. R., & Maurer, R. G. (1978). A Neurological model for childhood autism. *Archives of Neurology, 35,* 777–786.

Dawson, G., Carver, L., Meltzoff, A., Panagiotides, H., McPartland, J., & Webb, S. (2002). Neural correlates of face and object recognition in young children with autism spectrum disorder, developmental delay, and typical development. *Child Development, 73,* 700–717.

Dawson, G., Finley, C., Phillips, S., Galpert, L., & Lewy, A. (1988). Reduced P3 amplitude of the event-related brain potential: Its relationship to language ability in autism. *Journal of Autism and Developmental Disorders, 18,* 493–504.

Dawson, G., Webb, S. J., & McPartland, J. (2005). Electrophysiological and behavioral studies of face processing in autism: Understanding the nature of face processing impairments in autism. *Developmental Neuropsychology.* 27:3.

De Fossé, L., Hodge, S. M., Makris, N., Kennedy, D., Caviness, V., McGrath, L., et al. (2004). Language-association cortex asymmetry in autism and specific language impairment. *Annals of Neurology, 56,* 757–766.

Delong, G. R. (1978). A neuropsychological interpretation of infantile autism. In M. Rutter & E. Schopler (Eds.), *Autism* (pp. 207–218). New York: Plenum Press.

Dunn, M., Vaughan, H., Kreuzer, J., & Kurtzer, D. (1999). Electrophysiological correlates of semantic classification in autistic and normal children. *Developmental Neuropsychology, 16,* 79–99.

Eccles, J. C., Iro, M., & Szentagothai, J. (1967). *The cerebellum as a neuronal machine.* New York: Springer.

Egaas, B., Courchesne, E., & Saitoh, O. (1995). Reduced-size of corpus-callosum in autism. *Archives of Neurology, 52,* 794–801.

Elia, M., Ferri, R., Musumeci, S. A., Panerai, S., Bottitta, M., & Scuderi, C. (2000). Clinical correlates of brain morphometric features of subjects with low-functioning autistic disorder. *Journal of Child Neurology, 15,* 504–508.

Erwin, R., van Lancker, D., Guthrie, D., Schwafel, J., Tanguay, P., & Buchwald, J. S. (1991). P3 responses to prosodic stimuli in adult autistic subjects. *Electroencephalography and Clinical Neurophysiology, 80,* 561–571.

Fecoleau Mead, F. R., Minshew, N. J., & Sweeney, J. A. (2003). Abnormal brain lateralization in high-functioning autism. *Journal of Autism and Developmental Disorders, 33,* 539–543.

Fatemi, S. H., Stary, J. M., Halt, A. R., & Realmuto, G. R. (2001). Dysregulation of reelin and Bcl-2 proteins in autistic cerebellum. *Journal of Autism and Developmental Disorders, 31,* 529–535.

Ferri, R., Elia, M., Agarwal, N., Lanuzza, B., Musumeci, S., & Pennisi, G. (2003). The mismatch negativity and the P3a components of the auditory event-related potentials in autistic low-functioning subjects. *Clinical Neurophysiology, 114,* 1671–1680.

Filipek, P. A. (1999). Neuroimaging in the developmental disorders: The state of the science. *Journal of Child Psychology and Psychiatry and Allied Disciplines, 40,* 113–128.

Filipek, P. A., Accardo, P. J., Baranek, G. T., Cook, E. H., Dawson, G., Gordon, B. et al. (1999). The Screening and Diagnosis of Autistic Spectrum Disorders. *Journal of Autism and Developmental Disorders, 29,* 437–482.

Filipek, P. A., Richelme, C., Kennedy, D. N., Rademacher, J., Pitcher, D. A., Zidel, S., et al. (1992). Morphometric analysis of the brain in developmental language disorders and autism [Abstract]. *Annals of Neurology, 32,* 475.

Finley, W. W., Faux, S. F., Hutcheson, J., & Amstutz, L. (1985). Long-latency event-related potentials in the evaluation of cognitive function in children. *Neurology, 35,* 323–327.

Fombonne, E., Roge, B., Claverie, J., Coury, S., & Fremolle, J. (1999). Microcephaly and macrocephaly in autism. *Journal of Autism and Developmental Disorders, 29,* 113–119.

Friedman, D., Cycowicz, Y., & Gaeta, H. (2001). The novelty P3: An event related brain potential (ERP) sign of the brain's evaluation of novelty. *Neuroscience and Behavioral Reviews, 25,* 355–373.

Gaffney, G. R., Kuperman, S., Tsai, L. Y., & Minchin, S. (1988). Morphological evidence for brainstem involvement in infantile autism. *Biological Psychiatry, 24,* 578–586.

Gaffney, G. R., Kuperman, S., Tsai, L. Y., Minchin, S., & Hassanein, K. M. (1987). Midsagittal magnetic resonance imaging of autism. *British Journal of Psychiatry, 151,* 831–833.

Galambos, R., & Hecox, K. E. (1978). Clinical applications of the auditory brain stem response. *Otolaryngological Clinics of North America, 11,* 709–722.

Garber, H. J., & Ritvo, E. R. (1992). Magnetic resonance imaging of the posterior fossa in autistic adults. *American Journal of Psychiatry, 149,* 245–247.

Garber, H. J., Ritvo, E. R., Chui, L. C., Griswold, V. J., Kashanian, A., & Oldendorf, W. H. (1989). A magnetic resonance imaging study of autism: Normal fourth ventricle size and absence of pathology. *American Journal of Psychiatry, 146,* 532–535.

Gepner, B., Mestre, D., Masson, G., & de Schonen, S. (1995). Postural effects of motion vision in young autistic children. *NeuroReport, 6,* 1211–1214.

Gharani, N., Benayed, R., Mancuso, V., Brzustowicz, L. M., & Millonig, J. H. (2004). Association of the homeobox transcription factor, ENGRAILED 2, 3, with autism spectrum disorder. *Molecular Psychiatry, 9,* 474–484.

Gillberg, C. (1991). The treatment of epilepsy in autism. *Journal of Autism and Developmental Disorders, 21,* 61–67.

Gillberg, C., Rosenthal, U., & Johansson, E. (1983). Auditory brainstem responses in childhood psychosis. *Journal of Autism and Developmental Disorders, 13,* 181–195.

Gillberg, C., & Schaumann, H. (1983). Epilepsy presenting as infantile autism? Two case studies. *Neuropaediatrics, 14,* 206–212.

Goldberg, M., Landa, R., Lasker, A., Cooper, L., & Zee, D. S. (2000). Evidence of normal cerebellar control of the vestibulo-ocular reflex (VOR) in children with high-functioning autism. *Journal of Autism and Developmental Disorders, 30,* 519–524.

Goldberg, M., Lasker, A., Zee, D., Garth, E., Tien, A., & Landa, R. (2002). Deficits in the initiation of eye movements in the absence of a visual target in adolescents with high functioning autism. *Neuropsychologia, 40,* 2039–2049.

Gomot, M., Giard, M., Adrien, J., Barthelemy, C., & Bruneau, N. (2002). Hypersensitivity to acoustic change in children with autism: Electrophysiological evidence of left frontal cortex dysfunctioning. *Psychophysiology, 39,* 548–577.

Goodin, D. S. (1992). Event-related (endogenous) potentials. In M. J. Aminoff (Ed.), *Electrodiagnosis in clinical neurology* (pp. 627–648). New York: Churchill Livingstone.

Goodin, D. S., Squires, K., & Starr, A. (1978). Long latency event-related components of the auditory evoked potential in dementia. *Brain, 101,* 635–648.

Greenfield, J. G. (1954). *The spino-cerebellar degenerations.* Springfield, Il: Charles C Thomas.

Grillon, C., Courchesne, E., & Akshoomoff, N. (1989). Brainstem and middle latency auditory evoked potentials in autism and developmental language disorder. *Journal of Autism and Developmental Disorders, 19,* 255–269.

Gualtieri, C. T., & Adams, A. (1982). Minor physical anomalies in alcoholic and schizophrenic adults and hyperactive and autistic children. *American Journal of Psychiatry, 139,* 640–643.

Harcherik, D. F., Cohen, D. J., Ort, S., Paul, R., Shaywitz, B. A., Volkmar, F. R., et al. (1985). Computed tomographic brain scanning in four neuropsychiatric disorders of childhood. *American Journal of Psychiatry, 142,* 731–734.

Hardan, A. Y., Jou, R. J., Keshavan, M. S., Varma, R., & Minshew, N. J. (2004). Increased frontal cortical folding in autism: A preliminary MRI study. *Psychiatry Research: Neuroimaging, 131,* 263–268.

Hardan, A. Y., Kilpatrick, M., Keshavan, M. S., & Minshew, N. J. (2003). Motor performance and anatomic magnetic resonance imaging (MRI) of the basal ganglia in autism. *Journal of Child Neurology, 18,* 317–324.

Hardan, A. Y., Minshew, N. J., & Keshavan, M. S. (2000). Corpus callosum size in autism. *Neurology, 55,* 1033–1036.

Hardan, A. Y., Minshew, N. J., Mallikarjuhn, M., & Keshavan, M. S. (2001). Brain volume in autism. *Journal of Child Neurology, 16,* 421–424.

Hashimoto, T., Murakawa, K., Miyazaki, M., Tayama, M., & Kuroda, Y. (1992). Magnetic-Resonance-Imaging of the Brain Structures in the Posterior-Fossa in Retarded Autistic-Children. *Acta Paediatrica, 81,* 1030–1034.

Hashimoto, T., Tayama, M., Fujino, M. K., Miyazaki, M., & Kuroda, Y. (1989). Magnetic resonance imaging in autism: Preliminary report. *Neuropediatrics, 20,* 142–146.

Hashimoto, T., Tayama, M., Miyazaki, M., Murakawa, K., & Kuroda, Y. (1993). Brainstem and cerebellar vermis involvement in autistic children. *Journal of Child Neurology, 8,* 149–153.

Hashimoto, T., Tayama, M., Murakawa, K., Yoshimoto, T., Miyazaki, M., Harada, M., et al. (1995). Development of the brainstem and cerebellum in autistic patients. *Journal of Autism and Developmental Disorders, 25,* 1–18.

Haznedar, M. M., Buchsbaum, M. S., Luu, C., Hazlett, E. A., Siegel, B. V., Lohr, J., et al. (1997). Decreased anterior cingulate gyrus metabolic rate in schizophrenia. *American Journal of Psychiatry, 154,* 682–684.

Haznedar, M. M., Buchsbaum, M. S., Wei, T. C., Hof, P. R., Cartwright, C., Bienstock, C. A., et al. (2000). Limbic circuitry in patients with autism spectrum disorders studied with positron emission tomography and magnetic resonance imaging. *American Journal of Psychiatry, 157,* 1994–2001.

Herbert, M. R., Ziegler, D. A., Deutsch, C. K., O'Brien, L. M., Lange, N., Bakardjiev, A., et al. (2003). Dissociations of cerebral cortex, subcortical and cerebral white matter volumes in autistic boys. *Brain, 126,* 1182–1192.

Herbert, M. R., Ziegler, D. A., Makris, N., Filipek, P. A., Kemper, T. L., Normandin, J. J., et al. (2004). Localization of white matter volume increase in Autism and Developmental Language Disorder. *Annals of Neurology, 55,* 530–540.

Hoeksma, M., Kemner, C., Verbaten, M., van Engeland, H. (2004). Processing capacity in children and adolescents with pervasive developmental disorders. *Journal of Autism and Developmental Disorders, 34*(3), 341–354.

Holmes, G., & Stewart, T. G. (1988). On the connection of the inferior olives to the cerebellum in man. *Brain, 31,* 125–137.

Holttum, J. R., Minshew, N. J., Sanders, R. S., & Phillips, N. E. (1992). Magnetic resonance imaging of the posterior fossa in autism. *Biological Psychiatry, 32,* 1091–1101.

Honomichl, R. D., Goodlin-Jones, B. L., Burnham, M., Gaylor, E., & Anders, T. F. (2002). Sleep patterns of children with pervasive developmental disorders. *Journal of Autism and Developmental Disorders, 32,* 553–561.

Howard, M. A., Cowell, P. E., Boucher, J., Broks, P., Mayes, A., Farrant, A., et al. (2000). Convergent neuroanatomical and behavioural evidence of an amygdala hypothesis of autism. *NeuroReport, 11,* 2931–2935.

Hsu, M., Yeung-Courchesne, R., Courchesne, E., & Press, G. A. (1991). Absence of pontine abnormality in infantile autism. *Archives of Neurology, 48,* 1160–1163.

Just, M. A., Cherkassky, V. L., Keller, T. A., & Minshew, N. J. (2004). Cortical activation and synchronization during sentences comprehension in high-functioning autism: Evidence of underconnectivity. *Brain, 127,* 1811–1821.

Kanner, L. (1943). Autistic disturbances of affective contact. *Nervous Child, 2,* 217–250.

Kasteleijn-Nolst Trenite, D. G. (1988). Reflex seizures induced by intermittent light stimulation. *Advances in Neurology, 75,* 99–121.

Kawasaki, Y., Yokota, K., Shinomiya, M., Simizu, Y., & Niwa, S. (1997). Brief report: Electroencephalographic paroxysmal activities in the frontal area emerged in middle childhood and during adolescence in a followup study of autism. *Journal of Autism and Developmental Disorders, 27,* 605–620.

Kemner, C., Oranje, B., Verbaten, M., van Engeland, H. (2002). Normal P50 gating in children with autism. *Journal of Child Psychiatry, 63,* 214–217.

Kemner, C., van der Gaag, R., Verbaten, M., & van Engeland, H. (1999). ERP differences among subtypes of pervasive developmental disorders. *Biological Psychiatry, 46,* 781–789.

Kemner, C., Verbaten, M. N., Cuperus, J. M., Camfferman, G., & van Engeland, H. (1994). Visual and somatosensory event-related brain potentials in autistic children and three different control groups. *Electroencephalography and Clinical Neurophysiology, 92,* 225–237.

Kemner, C., Verbaten, M. N., Cuperus, J. M., Camfferman, G., & van Engeland, H. (1995). Auditory event related brain potentials in autistic children and three different control groups. *Biological Psychiatry, 38,* 150–165.

Kemner, C., Verbaten, M. N., Cuperus, J. M., Camfferman, G., & van Engeland, H. (1998). Abnormal saccadic eye movements in autistic children. *Journal of Autism and Developmental Disorders, 28,* 61–67.

Kemper, T. L., & Bauman, M. L. (1998). Neuropathology of infantile autism. *Journal of Neuropathology and Experimental Neurology, 57,* 645–652.

Kleiman, M. D., Neff, S., & Rosman, N. P. (1992). The brain in infantile autism: Is the cerebellum really abnormal? *Neurology, 2,* 753–760.

Koczat, D., Rogers, S., Pennington, B., & Ross, R. (2002). Eye movement abnormality suggestive of a spatial working memory deficit present in parents of autistic probands. *Journal of Autism and Developmental Disorders, 32,* 513–518.

Kohen-Raz, R., Volkmar, F. R., & Cohen, D. J. (1992). Postural control in children with autism. *Journal of Autism and Developmental Disorders, 22,* 419–432.

Kootz, J. P., Marinelli, B., & Cohen, D. J. (1982). Modulation of response to environmental stimulation in autistic children. *Journal of Autism and Developmental Disorders, 12,* 185–193.

Kuhl, P., Coffey-Corina, S., Padden, S., Dawson, G. (2005). Links between social and linguistic processing of speech in preschool children with autism: behavioral and electrophysiological measures. *Developmental Science, 8,* 1.

Kurtzberg, D., Vaughan, H. G., Jr., Courchesne, E., Friedman, D., Harter, M. R., & Putnam, L. E. (1984). Brain and information: Event-related potentials. *Annals of the New York Academy of Science, 425,* 300.

Kutas, M., Lindamood, T., & Hillyard, S. (1984). Word expectancy and event related brain potentials during sentence processing. In S. Kornblum & J. Requin (Eds.), *Preparatory states and processes* (pp. 217–238). Hillsdale, NJ: Erlbaum.

Lainhart, J. E. (2003). Increased Rate of Head Growth During Infancy in Autism. *Journal of the American Medical Association, 290,* 393–394.

Lainhart, J. E., Piven, J., Wzorek, M., Landa, R., Santangelo, S. L., Coon, H., et al. (1997). Macrocephaly in Children and Adults With Autism. *Journal of the American Academy of Child and Adolescent Psychiatry, 36,* 282–290.

Lee, M., Martin-Ruiz, C., Graham, A., Court, J., Jaros, E., Perry, R., et al. (2002). Nicotinic receptor abnormalities in the cerebellar cortex in autism. *Brain, 125,* 1483–1495.

Leigh, R. J., & Zee, D. S. (1991). *The neurology of eye movements* (2nd ed.). Philadelphia: F. A. Davis.

Levitt, J. G., Blanton, R., Capetillo-Cunliffe, L., Guthrie, D., Toga, A., & McCracken, J. T. (1999). Cerebellar vermis lobules VIII-X in autism. *Progress in Neuro-Psychopharmacology and Biological Psychiatry, 23,* 625–633.

Lewine, J. D., Andrews, R., Chez, M., Patil, A. A., Devinsky, O., Smith, M., et al. (1999). Magnetoencephalographic patterns of epileptiform activity in children with regressive autism spectrum disorders. *Pediatrics, 104,* 405–418.

Lincoln, A. J., Courchesne, E., Harms, L., & Allen, M. (1993). Contextual probability evaluation autistic, receptive developmental language disorder, and control children: Event-related brain potential evidence. *Journal of Autism and Developmental Disorders, 23,* 37–58.

Lincoln, A. J., Courchesne, E., Harms, L., & Allen, M. (1995). Sensory modulation of auditory stimuli in children with autism and receptive developmental language disorder: Event-related brain potential evidence. *Journal of Autism and Developmental Disorders, 25,* 521–539.

Links, P. S., Stokwell, M., Abichandani, F., & Simeon, J. (1980). Minor physical anomalies in childhood autism: I. Their relationship to pre- and perinatal complications. *Journal of Autism and Developmental Disorders, 10,* 228–273.

Luna, B., Minshew, N. J., Garver, B. A., Lazar, N. A., Thulborn, K. R., Eddy, W. F., et al. (2002). Neocortical system abnormalities in autism: An fMRI study of spatial working memory. *Neurology, 59,* 834–840.

Manes, F., Piven, J., Vrancic, D., Nanclares, V., Plebst, C., & Starkstein, S. E. (1999). An MRI study of the corpus callosum and cerebellum in mentally retarded autistic individuals. *Journal of Neuropsychiatry and Clinical Neurosciences, 11,* 470–474.

Martin-Ruiz, C. M., Lee, M., Perry, R. H., Bauman, M., Court, J. A., & Perry, E. K. (2004). Molecular analysis of nicotinic receptor expression in autism. *Molecular Brain Research, 123,* 81–90.

Mason-Brothers, A., Ritvo, E. R., Guze, B., Mo, A., Freeman, B. J., Funderburk, S. J., et al. (1987). PC: Pre-, peri-, and postnatal factors in 181 autistic patients from single and multiple incidence families. *Journal of the American Academy of Child and Adolescent Psychiatry, 20,* 39–42.

Maurer, R. G., & Demasio, A. R. (1982). Childhood autism from the point of view of behavioral neurology. *Journal of Autism and Developmental Disorders, 12,* 195–205.

Maziade, M., Merette, C., Cayer, M., Roy, M., Szatmari, P., Cote, R., et al. (2000). Prolongation of brainstem auditory-evoked responses in autistic probands and their unaffected relatives. *Archives of General Psychiatry, 57,* 1077–1083.

McAlonan, G. M., Daly, E., Kumari, V., Critchley, H. D., van Amelsvoort, T., Suckling, J., et al. (2002). Brain anatomy and sensorimotor gating in Asperger's syndrome. *Brain, 125,* 1594–1606.

McClelland, R. J., Eyre, D. G., Watson, D., Calvert, G. J., & Sherrard, E. (1992). Central conduction time in childhood autism. *British Journal of Psychiatry, 160,* 659–663.

McPartland, J., Dawson, G., Webb, S. J., Carver, L., & Panagiotides, H. (2004). Event-related brain potentials reveal anomalies in temporal processing of faces in autism. *Journal of Child Psychology and Psychiatry and Allied Disciplines 45*(7), 1235–1245.

Miles, J. H., Hadden, L. L., Takahashi, T. N., & Hillman, R. E. (2000). Head Circumference Is an Independent Clinical Finding Associated With Autism. *American Journal of Genetics, 95,* 339–350.

Miles, J. H., & Hillman, R. E. (2000). Value of a clinical morphology examination in autism. *American Journal of Genetics, 91,* 245–253.

Minshew, N. J., & Dombrowski, S. M. (1994). In vivo neuroanatomy of autism: Imaging studies. In M. Bauman & T. L. Kemper (Eds.), *The neurobiology of autism* (pp. 66–85). Baltimore: Johns Hopkins University Press.

Minshew, N. J., Furman, J. M., Goldstein, G., & Payton, J. B. (1990). The cerebellum in autism: A central role or an epiphenomenon? [Abstract]. *Neurology, 40,* 14.

Minshew, N. J., Goldstein, G., Muenz, L. R., & Payton, J. B. (1992). Neuropsychological functioning in non-mentally retarded autistic individuals. *Journal of Clinical and Experimental Neuropsychology, 14,* 749–761.

Minshew, N. J., Goldstein, G., & Siegel, D. J. (1997). Neuropsychologic functioning in autism: Profile of a complex information processing disorder. *Journal of the International Neuropsychological Society, 3,* 303–316.

Minshew, N. J., Luna, B., & Sweeney, J. (1999). Oculomotor evidence for neocortical systems but cerebellar dysfunction in autism. *Neurology, 52,* 917–922.

Minshew, N. J., Sung, K., Jones, B. L., & Furman, J. M. (2004). Underdevelopment of the postural control system in autism. *Neurology, 63,* 2056–2061.

Molloy, C., Dietrich, K., & Bhattacharya, A. (2003). Postural stability in children with autistic spectrum disorder. *Journal of Autism and Developmental Disorders, 33,* 643–652.

Murakami, J. W., Courchesne, E., Press, G. A., Yeung-Courchesne, R., & Hesselink, J. R. (1989). Reduced cerebellar hemisphere size and its relationship to vermal hypoplasia in autism. *Archives of Neurology, 46,* 689–694.

Murphy, D. G. M., Critchley, H. D., Schmitz, N., McAlonan, G., van Amelsvoort, T., Robertson, D., et al. (2002). Asperger syndrome—A proton magnetic resonance spectroscopy study of brain. *Archives of General Psychiatry, 59,* 885–891.

Nagy, E., & Loveland, K. (2002). Prolonged brainstem auditory evoked potentials: An autism-specific or non-specific marker. *Archives of General Psychiatry, 59,* 228–290.

Nass, R., & Petrucha, D. (1990). Acquired aphasia with convulsive disorder: A pervasive developmental disorder variant. *Journal of Child Neurology, 5,* 327–328.

Nelson, C. A. (1994). Neural correlates of recognition memory in the first postnatal year of life. In G. Dawson & K. Fischer (Eds.), *Human behavior and the developing brain* (pp. 269–313). New York: Guilford Press.

Nicolson, K., & Szatmari, P. (2003). Genetic and neurodevelopmental influences in autistic disorder. *Canadian Journal of Psychiatry, 48,* 526–537.

Norman, R. M. (1940). Cerebellar atrophy associated with etat marbre of the basal ganglia. *Journal of Neurological Psychiatry, 3,* 311–318.

Novick, B., Kurtzberg, A., & Vaughan, H. G., Jr. (1979). An electrophysiologic indication of defective information storage in childhood autism. *Psychiatry Research, 1,* 101–108.

Novick, B., Vaughan, H. G., Jr., Kurtzberg, D., & Simson, R. (1980). An electrophysiologic indication of auditory processing defects in autism. *Psychiatry Research, 3,* 107–114.

Nowell, M. A., Hackney, D. B., Muraki, A. S., & Coleman, M. (1990). Varied MR appearance of autism: Fifty-three pediatric patients having the full autistic syndrome. *Magnetic Resonance Imaging, 8,* 811–816.

Nydén, A., Carlsson, M., Carlsson, A., & Gillberg, C. (2004). Interhemispheric transfer in high-functioning children and adolescents with autism spectrum disorders: A controlled pilot study. *Developmental Medicine and Child Neurology, 46,* 448–454.

Oades, R., Walker, M., Geffen, L., & Stern, L. (1988). Event related potentials in autistic and healthy children on an auditory choice reaction time task. *International Journal of Psychophysiology, 6,* 25–37.

Ornitz, E. M., Atwell, C. W., Kaplan, A. R., & Westlake, J. R. (1985). Brain-stem dysfunction in autism. *Archives of General Psychiatry, 42,* 1018–1025.

Ornitz, E. M., Brown, M. B., Mason, A., & Putnam, N. H. (1974). Effect of visual input on vestibular nystagmus in autistic children. *Archives of General Psychiatry, 31,* 369–375.

Ornitz, E. M., Forsythe, A. B., & de la Pena, A. (1973). The effect of vestibular and auditory stimulation on the rapid eye movements of REM sleep in normal children. *Electroencephalography and Clinical Neurophysiology, 34,* 379–390.

Ornitz, E., Lane, S., Sugiyama, T., & de Traversay, J. (1993). Startle modulation studies in autism. *Journal of Autism and Developmental Disorders, 23,* 619–637.

Ornitz, E. M., Mo, A., & Olson, S. T. (1980). Influence of click sound pressure direction on brainstem responses in children. *Audiology, 19,* 245–254.

Ornitz, E. M., & Ritvo, E. R. (1968a). Neurophysiologic mechanisms underlying perceptual inconstancy in autistic and schizophrenic children. *Archives of General Psychiatry, 19,* 22–27.

Ornitz, E. M., & Ritvo, E. R. (1968b). Perceptual inconstancy in early infantile autism. *Archives of General Psychiatry, 18,* 76–98.

Ornitz, E., Ritvo, E. R., Brown, M., La Franchi, S., Parmelee, T., & Walter, R. (1969). The EEG and rapid eye movements during REM sleep in autistic and normal children. *Electroencephalography and Clinical Neurophysiology, 26,* 167–175.

Ornitz, E. M., Ritvo, E. R., Panman, L. E., Lee, Y. H., Carr, E. M., & Walker, R. D. (1968). The auditory evoked response in normal and autistic children during sleep. *Electroencephalography and Clinical Neurophysiology, 25,* 221–230.

Ornitz, E. M., & Walter, D. O. (1975). The effect of sound pressure waveform on human brainstem auditory evoked responses. *Brain Research, 92,* 490–498.

Ozonoff, S., Pennington, B. F., & Rogers, S. J. (1991). Executive function deficits in high-functioning autistic individuals: Relationship to theory of mind. *Journal of Child Psychology and Psychiatry, 32,* 1081–1105.

Ozonoff, S., Strayer, D. L., McMahon, W. M., & Filloux, F. (1994). Executive function abilities in autism and Tourette syndrome: An information-processing approach. *Journal of Child Psychology and Psychiatry and Allied Disciplines, 35,* 1015–1032.

Palmen, S. J. M. C., Hulshoff Pol, H. E., Kemner, C., Schnack, H. G., Durston, S., Lahuis, B. E., et al. (in press). Increased gray matter volume in medication naïve high-functioning children with autism spectrum disorder. *Psychological Medicine.*

Palmen, S. J. M. C., Hulshoff Pol, H. E., Kemner, C., Schnack, H. G., Janssen, J., Kahn, R. S., et al. (2004). Larger brains in medication naïve high-functioning subjects with Pervasive Developmental Disorder. *Journal of Autism and Developmental Disorders.*

Palmen, S. J. M. C., & van Engeland, H. (2004). Review on structural neuroimaging findings in autism. *Journal of Neural Transmission, 111,* 903–929.

Pascualvaca, D. M., Fantie, B. D., Papageorgiou, M., & Mirsky, A. F. (1998). Attentional capacities in children with autism: Is there a general deficit in shifting focus? *Journal of Autism and Developmental Disorders, 28,* 467–478.

Pelphrey, K., Sasson, N., Reznick, J., Paul, G., Goldman, B., & Piven, J. (2002). Visual scanning of faces in autism. *Journal of Autism and Developmental Disorders, 32,* 249–261.

Perry, E. K., Lee, M. L. W., Martin-Ruiz, C. M., Court, J. A., Volsen, S. G., Merrit, J., et al. (2001). Cholinergic activity in autism:

Abnormalities in the cerebral cortex and basal forebrain. *American Journal of Psychiatry, 158,* 1058–1066.

Pierce, K., Muller, R. A., Ambrose, J., Allen, G., & Courchesne, E. (2001). Face processing occurs outside the fusiform "face area" in autism: Evidence from functional MRI. *Brain, 124,* 2059–2073.

Piven, J., Arndt, S., Bailey, N., & Andreasen, N. (1996). Regional brain enlargement in autism: A magnetic resonance imaging study. *Journal of the American Academy of Child and Adolescent Psychiatry, 35,* 530–536.

Piven, J., Arndt, S., Bailey, J., Havercamp, S., Andreasen, N. C., & Palmer, P. (1995). An MRI study of brain size in autism. *American Journal of Psychiatry, 152,* 1145–1149.

Piven, J., Bailey, J., Ranson, B. J., & Arndt, S. (1997). An MRI study of the corpus callosum in autism. *American Journal of Psychiatry, 154,* 1051–1056.

Piven, J., Bailey, J., Ranson, B. J., & Arndt, S. (1998). No difference in hippocampus volume detected on magnetic resonance imaging in autistic individuals. *Journal of Autism and Developmental Disorders, 28,* 105–110.

Piven, J., Nehme, E., Simon, J., Barta, P., Pearlson, G., & Folstein, S. E. (1992). Magnetic resonance imaging in autism: Measurement of the cerebellum, pons, and fourth ventricle. *Biological Psychiatry, 31,* 491–504.

Plioplys, A. V. (1994). Autism: Electroencephalogram abnormalities and clinical improvement with valproic acid. *Archives of Pediatric and Adolescent Medicine, 148,* 220–222.

Polich, J., & Starr, A. (1984). Evoked potentials in aging. In M. L. Albert (Ed.), *Clinical neurology of aging* (p. 149). New York: Oxford University Press.

Prior, M., & Hoffmann, W. (1990). Brief report: Neuropsychological testing of autistic children through an exploration with frontal lobe tests. *Journal of Autism and Developmental Disorders, 4,* 581–590.

Prior, M. R., Tress, B., Hoffman, W. L., & Boldt, D. (1984). Computed tomographic study of children with classic autism. *Archives of Neurology, 41,* 482–484.

Ramoz, N., Reichert, J. G., Smith, C. J., Silverman, J. M., Bespalova, I. N., Davis, K. L., et al. (2004). Linkage and association of the mitochondrial aspartate/glutamate carrier SLC25A12 gene with autism. *American Journal of Psychiatry, 16,* 662–669.

Rapin, I. (1991). Autistic children: Diagnostic and clinical features. *Pediatrics, 87,* (Suppl.), 751–760.

Raymond, G., Bauman, M. L., & Kemper, T. L. (1996). Hippocampus in autism: A Golgi analysis. *Acta Neuropathologica, 91,* 117–119.

Ritvo, E. R., Freeman, B. J., Scheibel, A., Duong, T., Robinson, H., Guthrie, D., et al. (1986). Lower Purkinje cell counts in the cerebella of four autistic subjects: Initial finding of the UCLA-NSAC Autopsy Research report. *American Journal of Psychiatry, 143,* 862–866.

Ritvo, E. R., & Garber, H. J. (1988). Cerebellar hypoplasia and autism [Letter]. *New England Journal of Medicine, 319,* 1152.

Ritvo, E. R., Ornitz, E. M., Eviatar, A., Markham, C. H., Brown, M. B., & Mason, A. (1969). Decreased postrotatory nystagmus in early infantile autism. *Neurology, 19,* 653–658.

Rodier, P. M., Bryson, S. E., & Welch, J. P. (1997). Minor malformation and physical measurements in autism: Data from Nova Scotia. *Teratology, 55,* 319–325.

Rodier, P. M., Ingram, J. L., Tisdale, B., Nelson, S., & Roman, J. (1996). Embryological origins for autism: Developmental anomalies of the cranial nerve nuclei. *Journal of Comparative Neurology, 36,* 351–356.

Rojas, D. C., Bawn, S. D., Benkers, T. L., Reite, M. L., & Rogers, S. J. (2002). Smaller left hemisphere planum temporale in adults with autistic disorder. *Neuroscience Letters, 328,* 237–240.

Rosenbloom, S., Campbell, M., & George, A. E. (1984). High resolution CT scanning in infantile autism: A quantitative approach. *Journal of the American Academy of Child Psychiatry, 23,* 72–77.

Rosenblum, S. M., Arick, J. R., Krug, D. A., Stubbs, E. G., Young, N. B., & Pelson, R. O. (1980). Auditory brainstem evoked responses in autistic children. *Journal of Autism and Developmental Disorders, 10,* 215–225.

Rosenhall, U., Johansson, E., & Gillberg, C. (1988). Oculomotor findings in autistic children. *Journal of Laryngology and Otology, 102,* 435–439.

Rosenhall, U., Nordin, V., Brantberg, K., & Gillberg, C. (2003). Autism and auditory brain stem responses. *Ear and Hearing, 24,* 206–214.

Rossi, F. G., Okun, M., Yachnis, A., Quisling, R., & Triggs, W. (2002). Corticosteroid treatment of mitochondrial encephalomyopathies. *Neurologist, 8,* 313–315.

Rossi, P. G., Parmeggiani, A., Bach, V., Santucci, M., & Visconti, P. (1995). EEG features and epilepsy in patients with autism. *Brain and Development, 17,* 169–174.

Rumsey, J. M., Grimes, A. M., Pikus, A. M., Duara, R., & Ismond, D. R. (1984). Auditory brainstem responses in pervasive developmental disorders. *Biological Psychiatry, 19,* 1403–1418.

Rumsey, J. M., & Hamburger, S. D. (1988). Neuropsychological findings in high-functioning men with infantile autism, residual state. *Journal of Clinical and Experimental Neuropsychology, 10,* 201–221.

Rumsey, J. M., & Hamburger, S. D. (1990). Neuropsychological divergence of high-level autism and severe dyslexia. *Journal of Autism and Developmental Disorders, 20,* 155–168.

Saitoh, O., Courchesne, E., Egaas, B., Lincoln, A. J., & Schreibman, L. (1995). Cross-sectional area of the posterior hippocampus in autistic patients with cerebellar and corpus callosum abnormalities. *Neurology, 45,* 317–324.

Saitoh, O., Karns, C. M., & Courchesne, E. (2001). Development of the hippocampal formation from 2 to 42 years—MRI evidence of smaller area dentata in autism. *Brain, 124,* 1317–1324.

Sears, L. L., Vest, C., Mohamed, S., Bailey, J., Ranson, B. J., & Piven, J. (1999). An MRI study of the basal ganglia in autism. *Progress in Neuro-Psychopharmacology and Biological Psychiatry, 23,* 613–624.

Seri, S., Cerquiglini, A., Pisani, F., & Curatolo, P. (1999). Autism in tuberous sclerosis: Evoked potential evidence for a deficit in auditory sensory processing. *Clinical Neurophysiology, 110,* 1825–1830.

Shewmon, D. A., & Erwin, R. J. (1988a). The effect of focal interictal spikes on perception and reaction time. I: General considerations. *Electroencephalography and Clinical Neurophysiology, 69,* 319–337.

Shewmon, D. A., & Erwin, R. J. (1988b). The effect of focal interictal spikes on perception and reaction time. II: Neuroanatomic specificity. *Electroencephalography and Clinical Neurophysiology, 69,* 319–337.

Siebelink, B. M., Bakker, D. J., Binnie, C. D., & Kasteleijn-Nolst Trenite, D. G. A. (1988). Psychological effects of subclinical epileptiform EEG discharges in children. II: General intelligence tests. *Epilepsy Research, 2,* 117–121.

Skoff, B. F., Mirsky, A. F., & Turner, D. (1980). Prolonged brainstem transmission time in autism. *Psychiatric Research, 2,* 157–166.

Sparks, B. F., Friedman, S. D., Shaw, D. W., Aylward, E. H., Echelard, D., Artru, A. A., et al. (2002). Brain structural abnormalities in young children with autism spectrum disorder. *Neurology, 59,* 184–192.

Squires, N., Squires, K., & Hillyard, S. A. (1975). Two varieties of long-latency positive waves evoked by unpredictable auditory stimuli in man. *Electroencephalography and Clinical Neurophysiology, 38,* 387–401.

Starr, A., Sohmer, H., & Celesia, G. G. (1978). Some applications of evoked potentials to patients with neurological and sensory impairment. In E. Callaway, P. Tueting, & S. H. Koslow (Eds.), *Event-related brain potentials in man* (pp. 155–196). San Francisco: Academic Press.

Stefanos, G. A., Grover, W., & Geller, E. (1995). Case study: Corticosteroid treatment of language regression in pervasive developmental disorder. *Journal of the American Academy of Child and Adolescent Psychiatry, 34,* 1107–1111.

Steg, J. P., & Rapoport, J. L. (1975). Minor physical anomalies in normal, neurotic, learning disabled, and severely disturbed children. *Journal of Autism and Childhood Schizophrenia, 5,* 299–307.

Stevenson, R. E., Schroer, R. J., Skinner, C., Fender, D., & Simensen, R. J. (1997). Autism and macrocephaly. *Lancet, 349,* 1744–1745.

Stockard, J. J., Stockard, J. E., & Sharbrough, F. W. (1978). Nonpathologic factors influencing brainstem auditory evoked potentials. *American Journal of EEG Technology, 18,* 177–209.

Strandburg, R. J., Marsh, J. T., Brown, W. S., Asarnow, R. F., Guthrie, D., & Higa, J. (1993). Event-related potentials in high-functioning adult autistics: Linguistic and nonlinguistic visual information processing tasks. *Neuropsychologia, 31,* 413–434.

Student, M., & Sohmer, H. (1978). Evidence from auditory nerve and brainstem evoked responses for an organic brain lesion in children with autistic traits. *Journal of Autism and Childhood Schizophrenia, 8,* 13–20.

Student, M., & Sohmer, H. (1979). Erratum. *Journal of Autism and Developmental Disorders, 9,* 309.

Tanguay, P. E., & Edwards, R. (1982). Electrophysiological studies of autism: The whisper of the bang. *Journal of Autism and Developmental Disorders, 12,* 177–184.

Tanguay, P. E., Edwards, R. M., Buchwald, J., Schwafel, J., & Allen, V. (1982). Auditory brainstem responses in autistic children. *Archives of General Psychiatry, 39,* 174–180.

Taylor, M., McCarthy, G., Saliba, E., & Degiovanni, E. (1999). ERP evidence of developmental changes in processing of faces. *Clinical Neurophysiology, 110,* 910–915.

Taylor, M. J., Rosenblatt, B., & Linschoten, L. (1982). Electrophysiological study of the auditory system in autistic children. In A. Rothenberger (Ed.), *Event-related potentials in children* (pp. 23–38). Amsterdam: Elsevier.

Thivierge, J., Bedard, C., Cote, R., & Maziade, M. (1990). Brainstem auditory evoked response and subcortical abnormalities in autism. *American Journal of Psychiatry, 12,* 1609–1613.

Townsend, J., Westerfield, M., Leaver, E., Makeig, S., Jung, T., Pierce, K., et al. (2001). Event-related brain response abnormalities in autism: Evidence for impaired cerebello-frontal spatial attention networks. *Cognitive Brain Research, 11,* 137–145.

Tsatsanis, K. D., Rourke, B. P., Klin, A., Volkmar, F. R., Cicchetti, D., & Schultz, R. T. (2003). Reduced thalamic volume in high-functioning individuals with autism. *Biological Psychiatry, 53,* 121–129.

Tuchman, R. (2000). Treatment of seizure disorders and EEG abnormalities in children with autism spectrum disorders. *Journal of Autism and Developmental Disorders, 30,* 485–489.

Tuchman, R. F., Jayakar, P., Yaylali, I., & Villalobos, R. (1997). Seizures and EEG findings in children with autism spectrum disorders. *CNS Spectrums, 3,* 61–70.

Tuchman, R. F., & Rapin, I. (1997). Regression in pervasive developmental disorders: Seizures and epileptiform electroencephalogram correlates. *Pediatrics, 99,* 560–566.

Tuchman, R. F., & Rapin, I. (2002). Epilepsy in autism. *Neurology, 1,* 352–358.

Tuchman, R. F., Rapin, I., & Shinnar, S. (1991a). Autistic and Dysphasic Children. I. Clinical Characteristics. *Pediatrics, 88,* 1211–1218.

Tuchman, R. F., Rapin, I., & Shinnar, S. (1991b). Autistic and Dysphasic Children. II: Epilepsy. *Pediatrics, 88,* 1219–1225.

Uther, M., Jansen, D. H. J., Huotilainen, M., Ilmoniemi, R. J., & Näätänen, R. (2003). Mismatch negativity indexes auditory temporal resolution: Evidence from event-related potential (ERP) and event-related field (ERF) recordings. *Cognitive Brain Research, 17,* 685–691.

van der Geest, J. N., Kemner, C., Cammfferman, G., Verbaten, M. N., & van Engeland, H. (2001). Eye movements, visual attention, and autism: A saccadic reaction time study using the gap and overlap paradigm. *Biological Psychiatry, 50,* 614–619.

Verbaten, M. N., Roelofs, J. W., van Engeland, H., Kenemans, J. K., & Slangen, J. L. (1991). Abnormal visual event-related potentials of autistic children. *Journal of Autism and Developmental Disorders, 21,* 449–470.

Vidal, C. N., DeVito, T. J., Hayashi, K. M., Drost, D. J., Williamson, P. C., Craven-Thuss, B., et al. (2003). Detection and visualization of corpus callosum deficits in autistic children using novel anatomical mapping algorithms. *Proceedings of the International Society for Magnetic Resonance in Medicine.* Toronto, Canada, May 10–16.

Vilensky, J. A., Demasio, A. R., & Maurer, R. G. (1981). Gait disturbances in patients with autistic behavior. *Archives of Neurology, 38,* 646–649.

Volkmar, F. R. (1992). Childhood disintegrative disorder: Issues for *DSM-IV. Journal of Autism and Developmental Disorders, 22,* 625–642.

Volkmar, F. R. (1994). Childhood disintegrative disorder. *Child and Adolescent Psychiatric Clinics of North America, 3,* 119–129.

Walker, H. A. (1977). Incidence of minor physical anomaly in autism: Epilepsy. *Journal of Autism and Childhood Schizophrenia, 7,* 165–176.

Webb, S. J., Bernier, R., Panagiotides, H., Paul, M., & Dawson, G. (2003, April). *Further evidence for an abnormality in the temporal processing of faces in autism.* Poster presented at the Society for Research in Child Development, Tampa, FL.

Webb, S. J., Bernier, R., Shook, J., Paul, M., & Dawson, G. (2004, May). *Electrophysiological evidence of delayed neural processing of faces in children with autism.* Paper presented at the International Meeting for Autism Research, Sacramento, CA.

Webb, S. J., Dawson, G., Bernier, R., & Panagiotides, H. (2004). *ERP evidence of atypical face processing in young children with autism.* Manuscript in preparation.

Wong, V., & Wong, S. N. (1991). Brainstem auditory evoked potential study in children with autistic disorder. *Journal of Autism and Developmental Disorders, 21,* 329–340.

Zimmerman, M. C., Morgan, D. E., & Dubno, J. R. (1987). Auditory brainstem evoked response characteristics in developing infants. *Annals of Otology, Rhinolology, and Laryngology, 96,* 291.

CHAPTER 19

Functional Neuroimaging Studies of Autism Spectrum Disorders

ROBERT T. SCHULTZ AND DIANA L. ROBINS

As reviewed in Chapter 18 ("Neurologic Aspects of Autism"), there is a large and growing body of evidence characterizing the pathophysiology of the autism spectrum disorders (ASDs). This chapter reviews the research literature that uses functional neuroimaging techniques to study the brain bases of the ASDs. Autism is defined on the basis of a select set of behavioral disturbances that more or less map onto specific functional systems of the brain. The difficulties with social reciprocity, communication, and restricted and repetitive behaviors and interests that occur with autism suggest that the syndrome affects a functionally diverse and widely distributed set of neural systems. However, at the same time, not all brain systems are affected, and thus it would be a mistake to consider autism as a disorder of general brain function. There can be many areas of spared function in autism, for example, basic visual perceptual skills, as well as certain cognitive skills. In fact, autism is not incompatible with superior IQ; there are many very bright but very severely affected persons with autism, indicating that general intellectual functions need not

be impaired for classic autistic symptoms to be present. Although there may be deficits in complex cognitive functions in many persons with autism, those deficits are probably mediated by deficits in general intelligence, such that it is difficult to see evidence for these complex cognitive deficits in persons with autism who are average or above average in general intelligence. It remains a puzzle why autism is generally associated with impaired intellectual functioning (i.e., why as many as 70% of cases have some degree of mental retardation), and solving this puzzle may well shed light on the basic mechanisms causing autism.

All the evidence points to autism being a highly heritable but complex genetic disorder, with locus and allelic heterogeneity (Rutter, 2000; Veenstra-VanderWeele, Christian, & Cook, 2004; Yonan et al., 2003). This genetic heterogeneity, coupled with the gene-gene and gene-environment interaction effects on brain development, makes the autism phenotype inherently heterogeneous. Even where a set of susceptibility genes is completely shared in common by two individuals, we should expect differences, sometimes marked, in phenotypic

This work was supported by grants from the National Institute of Child Health and Human Development (grants PO1 HD 03008, PO1 HD/DC35482 and U54 MH066494-01) and by a grant from the James S. McDonnell Foundation to the Perceptual Expertise. Ideas presented in this chapter are based in part on many helpful discussions with our colleagues James Tanaka, Mathew State, Isabel Gauthier, Tom James, Cheryl Klaiman, Ami Klin, and Fred Volkmar. Portions of this work appear in R. T. Schultz (in press), "Developmental Deficits in Social Perception in Autism: The Role of the Amygdala and Fusiform Face Area," *International Journal of Developmental Neuroscience*.

expression for the two individuals. It is important to note that whereas the same genes can give rise to different phenotypic outcomes, phenotypic variation must be completely mediated by variation at the level of brain functioning (i.e., the endophenotype), and there exists a very direct mapping of behavior to brain functioning. Too much variation in the behavioral phenotype of a study sample can complicate a neuroimaging study, where the goal is to define a common set of brain characteristics that can be linked to a set of cardinal features for the disorder. Yet, from a genetic point of view, it is probably unwise to place restrictions on the sample variability in the phenotype because doing so risks obfuscating what might be important and common genetic mechanisms. However, in neuroimaging research more generally, and in this particular review of neural systems that mediate autistic symptoms, we chose to restrict our focus to those core features that are invariably present across the otherwise heterogeneous population.

Functional neuroimaging procedures such as ^{15}O-water positron emission tomography (PET) and functional magnetic resonance imaging (fMRI) are ideally suited for studying in detail the separate neural systems that govern select sensory and cognitive domains in relative isolation from other brain systems. Both techniques rely on the fact that when specific brain areas are engaged (more active relative to some baseline set of circumstances), there is an increase in blood flow to those neural regions. Both ^{15}O-water PET and fMRI techniques measure neural activity indirectly through the increased blood flow that is the brain's response to local neural activity. Whereas conventional MRI and computed tomography (CT) allow imaging of the structure of the brain and its components, functional techniques allow dynamic interrogation of the brain at work and allow specifying which systems are aberrant in autism and what circumstances (e.g., types of processing load) modulate these aberrations when compared to typically developing persons. Chapter 18 (this *Handbook,* this volume) reviews the literature on brain structure using MRI as well as postmortem work; thus, this work is not reviewed here in any detail and is mentioned only in passing insofar as sometimes it provides the

context necessary to appreciate a set of functional findings. Moreover, computer-averaged electroencephalography (EEG), as is done for event-related potential (ERP) recordings, might properly be considered a functional technique, but because EEG is a technique closely affiliated with the topic of neurological findings that is central to Chapter 18, its derivative, ERPs, is also contained in that chapter. A newer technique, magnetoencephalography (MEG), is not covered in Chapter 18 or in this chapter because it has rarely been used in studies of autism (though the interested reader should see the work of Timothy P. Roberts and colleagues from the University of Toronto for some promising first studies using MEG to study the auditory system in autism).

fMRI is far and away the most popular functional technique for investigating the processing capacities of discrete brain areas and distributed brain systems. Compared to other techniques, such as ^{15}O-water PET and MEG, the equipment and expertise needed to perform fMRI studies are widely available; nearly every academic medical center in the United States and many other developed countries throughout the world have the basic equipment to perform these studies. However, while this practicality is important, fMRI also has several other attributes that contribute to its popularity. Unlike PET, fMRI is noninvasive and involves only minimal risk. ^{15}O-water PET requires the use of a radioactive tracer to map brain blood flow (via the tagged water in blood) and hence the neural systems involved in specific processes. PET can also use a radioactive tag on other ligands instead of water to map glucose metabolism or to map aspects of neurotransmitter systems. This ability is its great advantage compared to fMRI, which can measure only the hemodynamic response to localized neural activity, not metabolism or receptor density. Because most countries do not allow exposing children to radioactivity purely for research purposes, even though the levels are small, PET is not available on a research basis for use with minors. This is one reason that it has been used less frequently for the study of autism. fMRI also offers a slight advantage in spatial resolution compared to PET—the smallest elements that can be resolved with fMRI are about 1 mm^3, though in practice, most studies employ a voxel resolution of at least 3 mm^3. fMRI is predicated on the fact that the oxygenated and deoxygenated states of hemoglobin in the blood have different magnetic properties. The hemodynamic response to local neural activity results in an increase in the local concentration of oxyhemoglobin relative to deoxyhemoglobin. This is detected with fMRI because deoxyhemoglobin causes a local magnetic susceptibility that dampens the magnitude of signal in that region; thus, active brain tissue provides locally stronger MRI signal values than less active regions. The fMRI signal is referred to as the *blood oxygen level dependent* (BOLD) signal.

This review is organized around the core features of ASDs, namely, studies of (1) language and communication dysfunction, (2) social dysfunction, and (3) repetitive behaviors and stereotypes, and, to a lesser extent, some ancillary features of autism. Although there have been some structural MRI (sMRI) studies that correlated magnitude of repetitive behaviors with volumetric measures of select brain parts, there have been no fMRI studies that have explored this third component of the autism triad. Thus, we dispense with that aspect of the review at the outset. And although studies of language are relatively common in the normative fMRI and PET literature, there has been surprisingly little work done in this area in autism, so our review here is necessarily short. The social deficits in autism, however, have been studied rather frequently with functional neuroimaging approaches, which is probably a testament to the prevailing view that these deficits are the core of autism (Schultz, in press). This chapter, therefore, is devoted largely to reviewing the research on the social-cognitive and social-perceptual processes in ASDs.

STUDIES OF COMMUNICATION AND LANGUAGE

Even though behavioral studies of language and communication abilities in ASDs are rather common, there have been only five published fMRI or PET studies focusing on language abilities in persons with an ASD. Müller and colleagues (1999) studied five high-functioning persons with autism during a series of auditory and verbal tasks using ^{15}O-water PET. The persons with an ASD showed significantly less left lateralization compared to controls in the perisylvian language areas when listening to sentences. This finding has now been replicated by Boddaert et al. (2003), who used ^{15}O-water PET in five autistic adults and eight comparison subjects while listening to speechlike sounds and during a rest condition. As in the study by Müller and colleagues, the persons with an ASD showed less left lateralization for the speechlike sounds. Both studies point to deficiencies in the left temporal language regions as likely reasons underlying the language difficulties found in autism. These studies are also consistent with one recent sMRI study that showed reversed left-right tissue asymmetry in language related cortices (Herbert et al., 2002).

More recently, Gervais et al. (2004) used fMRI to study five persons with an ASD compared to eight healthy controls. The ASD group failed to activate superior temporal sulcus (STS) voice-selective regions in response to vocal sounds compared to nonvocal sounds. The STS, however, showed normal activation patterns to nonvocal sounds, suggesting that some more basic auditory processing deficit was not responsible for the finding. They did not report the abnormal hemispheric lateralization found in prior studies, and their discussion of the significance of these findings emphasized the difficulties that persons with an ASD have in processing socially relevant auditory information. The ASD group appeared to attend less to the vocal sounds, as after the fMRI they were able to recall significantly fewer of the vocal sounds (but not the nonvocal sounds) compared to the controls. Thus, the STS activation failure may be a simple failure to attend to the voices, something that was rather automatic among the controls. It is not clear whether these differences might also be modulated by the group differences in general intelligence, which were presumably large (the mean *global IQ* for the five ASD cases was 81, and they had significantly fewer years of education compared to the controls).

Just, Cherkassky, Keller, and Minshew (2004) used fMRI to compare sentence comprehension in a group of 17 persons with high-functioning autism (HFA) compared to a verbal IQ-matched control group (gender distribution for each group was not specified). The task was a two-choice sentence comprehension task (e.g., "The cook thanked the father. Who was thanked? Cook—Father"). The ASD group showed significantly more activation in the posterior left superior temporal gyrus (Wernicke's area) and less activation in the left inferior frontal gyrus (Broca's area) compared to the control group. The authors speculated that this pattern of results might mean that the autistic group engaged in more extensive analyses of the meanings of individual words (via computations in Wernicke's area) and less integration of the meanings of individual words into a coherent whole statement (in Broca's area) and that this pattern is consistent with their tendency toward hyperlexia with poorer conceptual comprehension. They did not find a significant difference in lateralization of activation between the two groups. In a somewhat related study, Turkeltaub et al. (2004) studied the neural basis of hyperlexia in a 9-year-old boy with pervasive developmental disorder-not otherwise specified (PDD-NOS) who was reading at a 15-year-old level and found greater left Broca's and left Wernicke's activation compared to age and reading level control groups. This boy did not demonstrate the frontal-posterior imbalance shown by the group studied by Just and colleagues. However, a different finding might have been expected because the task differed (covert reading without a comprehension query). The difference might also reflect something specific to hyperlexia.

In addition, Just and colleagues (2004) explored the correlation between the fMRI time series data for select pairs of regions of interest, for example, between the average time course for Broca's and Wernicke's areas. These types of correlations have been used in the literature as an index of "functional connectivity" (Friston, Frith, Liddle, & Frackowiak, 1993). Just and colleagues describe the correlations as suggesting "synchronization" between brain areas. Prior work with ^{15}O-water PET in two studies has suggested that persons with autism have reduced synchronization during a theory of mind (ToM) task (Castelli, Frith, Happe, & Frith, 2002) and during rest (Horwitz, Rumsey, Grady, &

Rapoport, 1988). Just and colleagues confirmed these observations in the most extensive testing of this hypothesis to date. Across 186 regions of interest (ROI) pairings, the autism group had a reliable lower functional connectivity measurement (0.58 versus 0.61); in 79% of the ROI pairs, the average correlation in the autism group was less than that of the control group. Ten of these ROI pairs were significantly different between the groups, and in each case the autism group showed significantly less connectivity. These data and those of Castelli et al. and Horwitz et al. are consistent in pointing to deficits in synchronized brain activity.

The measurement approach used by Just and colleagues (2004) cannot make any strong statements about the meaning of these correlations. It is possible that any pair of nodes may be more or less synchronized in their BOLD signal across time because of a host of common influences on them, with the possibility of no direct relationship between them. Friston et al. (1997) distinguished this type of functional connectivity from what they term *effective connectivity*, which is a stronger form of the hypothesis that the regions have a direct influence on each other. One means of assessing effective connectivity is to look for significant increases or decreases in the magnitude of the correlation between two brain areas due to a change in task demands. Friston and colleagues have called this correlation a *psychophysical interaction* (PPI), such that during one type of processing task the correlation is greater than during another. When someone tests for a PPI between two nodes that are known to be involved in a specific function and finds a task-related modulation of that function, this is believed to be a stronger argument for a direct functional relationship between the nodes (see Pasley, Mayes, & Schultz, 2004, for an example concerning face perception).

It will be important to confirm these observations suggestive of reduced functional connectivity with additional data and with tests employing task-dependent modulation of the magnitude of the correlation in a hypothesized direction. Nevertheless, the existing fMRI and PET data provide exciting models of the nature of the dysfunction in the autistic brain. Moreover, these functional findings are consistent with the sMRI data pointing to aberrations in the volume of the cerebral white matter across development. This topic is covered more extensively in Chapter 18, but briefly, recent data suggest a possible overgrowth of white matter during the first years of life in autism (Courchesne et al., 2001; Herbert et al., 2003) that is followed by a selective reduction in specific white matter tracks by later adolescence and adulthood (Berthier, Bayes, & Tolosa, 1993; Egass, Courchesne, & Saitoh, 1995; Hardan, Minshew, & Keshavan, 2000; Manes et al., 1999; Piven, Saliba, Bailey, & Arndt, 1997). This all might make particular sense in the context of the overall increase in brain size found in autism, especially at the youngest ages. We have argued elsewhere (Schultz, Romanski, et al., 2000) that one consequence of an increased brain size in the ASDs will be a reduction of interconnectivity because theoretic models of brain size growth suggest that the degree of tissue connectivity must be reduced with increasing brain size (Ringo, 1991). Such a reduction in neural integration would also be consistent with one influential theory that attributes autistic symptoms to a lack of "central coherence" (Frith, 1989), a cognitive processing style that makes integration of parts into wholes problematic. It will be interesting to see the result of the many diffusion tensor-imaging studies currently underway at autism neuroimaging labs in several places throughout the United States and Europe. Diffusion tensor imaging should add important information on the nature of the white matter and possibly on the nature of specific fiber tracks within the autistic brain.

STUDIES OF SOCIAL PERCEPTION AND SOCIAL COGNITION

Current conceptualization of the social deficits as embodied by the nomenclature of the *Diagnostic and Statistical Manual of Mental Disorders,* fourth edition (*DSM-IV;* American Psychiatric Association, 1994) entails an emphasis on absent or deficient behaviors important for social relatedness. The diagnostic criteria of *DSM-IV* describe social behavioral deficits in several areas. Persons with autism fail to develop peer relationships appropriate to their developmental level; have poor eye contact; have abnormal emotional intonations in their voice and speech; have marked impairment in the use of multiple nonverbal behaviors such as eye-to-eye gaze, facial expression, body postures, and gestures to regulate social interaction; and do not spontaneously seek to share enjoyment, interests, or achievements with other people (e.g., by a lack of showing, bringing, or pointing out objects of interest).

From a neuropsychological perspective, the prevailing belief is that these aberrant social behaviors are due to deficits in (1) social perception, for example, reading facial expressions; (2) social cognition, for example, perspective taking and ToM; and (3) social motivation. Thus, functional brain imaging studies seek to study these underlying processes because they are thought to directly mediate the aberrant or absent behaviors that define autism. This section reviews fMRI and PET studies that relate to this set of impairments, as well as some of the lesion literature that supports the functional imaging data.

Face Perception Deficits

Face perception can be subdivided into two general types: (1) recognition of person identity via the structural features of the face and (2) recognition of internal affective state of another individual, independent of his or her identity, via the shape of individual features and changes in their relative distance from one another during the expression. Both sets of skills are necessary for successful functioning within a social group; it is important to be able to quickly differentiate friends, enemies, and potential mates prior to any interpersonal encounter. Moreover, for the development and maintenance of social relationships, it is essential to successfully perceive and comprehend the changes in facial countenance that reflect the internal state of others. These two sets of skills, while related, nonetheless appear to be mediated by somewhat different neural systems.

Individuals with an ASD are selectively impaired in their ability to recognize face identity (Boucher & Lewis, 1992; Braverman, Fein, Lucci, & Waterhouse, 1989; Davies, Bishop, Manstead, & Tantam, 1994; de Gelder, Vroomen, & Van der Heide, 1991;

Deruelle, Rondan, Gepner, & Tardif, 2004; Grelotti, Gauthier, & Schultz, 2002; Hauck, Fein, & Maltby, 1999; Hobson, 1986a, 1986b; Hobson, Ouston, & Lee, 1988b; Joseph & Tanaka, 2002; Klin, Jones, Schultz, Volkmar, & Cohen, 2002; Klin et al., 1999; Langdell, 1978; Tantam, Monaghan, Nicholson, & Stirling, 1989; Weeks & Hobson, 1987). Although faces may appear to be quite different from one another, features of the face and their placement are remarkably uniform compared to those of other common objects, and thus our skill in discriminating faces is more precisely developed than for other types of object perception (Diamond & Carey, 1986). The impairment in face perception among those with autism is specific to faces because they are not impaired with other types of complex objects such as buildings or furniture (Grelotti et al., 2002; Schultz, in press). We have hypothesized that persons with an ASD fail to develop the same level of expertise for faces as typically developing persons because of inadequately motivated attention to faces across development, which leads to less actual experience with faces (Grelotti et al., 2002; Schultz, in press; Schultz, Gauthier, et al., 2000; Schultz, Romanski, & Tsatsanis, 2000). Persons with an ASD are also impaired in their ability to perceive, label, and show comprehension of facially expressed emotions (Capps, Yirmiya, & Sigman, 1992; Dawson, Hill, Spencer, Galpert, & Watson, 1990; Fein, Lucci, Braverman, & Waterhouse, 1992; Hobson, 1986a, 1986b; Hobson & Lee, 1989; Hobson, Ouston, & Lee, 1988a, 1988b; Jaedicke, Storoschuk, & Lord, 1994; MacDonald et al., 1989; McGee, Feldman, & Chernin, 1991; Snow, Hertzig, & Shapiro, 1987; Yirmiya, Sigman, Kasari, & Mundy, 1992). On the surface, deficits in facial expression perception might appear to have the most relevance for the social deficits in autism. This may indeed prove to be true, but, at this time, deficits in person identity from the face are better understood, especially concerning the functional neuroanatomy of autism. Because this literature is too large to cover adequately in detail in this chapter on neuroimaging, the interested reader is referred to several of the most recent papers and reviews on face perception and autism (e.g., Deruelle et al., 2004; Grelotti et al., 2002; Klin et al., 2002; Schultz, in press).

Functional Neuroimaging Studies of Social Perception

In the past 5 to 10 years, there has been a sharp increase in interest in using functional neuroimaging to understand the neural systems that mediate social perception and social cognition in normative as well as autistic populations. Of these areas, person identity via the face is probably best understood and probably engages the most restricted set of neural tissue.

A small region on the underside of the temporal lobe, along the lateral extent of the middle portion of the fusiform gyrus (FG), shows selectivity (i.e., enhanced activation) for faces compared to other complex objects (Kanwisher, McDermott, & Chun, 1997; Kanwisher & Wojciulik, 2000; Puce, Allison, Gore, & McCarthy, 1995); this area has been termed the *fusiform face area* (FFA; Kanwisher et al., 1997). Anatomically, the middle portion of the FG is split along its rostral-caudal extent by a shallow, midfusiform sulcus. In fMRI, the center of activation in face perception tasks is typically offset toward the lateral aspect of the FG, in the right hemisphere (Haxby et al., 1999). Group composites show right hemisphere activations to be larger than left; in fact, individual subjects may or may not show left FG activation during face perception tasks. It is not completely clear what special computations are carried out in this region compared to neighboring tissue such as the medial FG, lingual gyrus, inferior temporal gyrus, and the lateral occipital gyrus. Most accounts, however, hypothesize that the FFA is particularly tuned to holistic and configural processing, but attempts to demonstrate this have not always been successful (Yovel & Kanwisher, 2004).

The FFA is one of the two primary social perceptual areas. The other is the STS, a brain area known to be important for interpreting dynamic social signals, such as direction of eye gaze, gestures, facial expression, and other "changeable" aspects of the face and body (Adolphs, 2003; Allison, Puce, & McCarthy, 2000; Haxby, Hoffman, & Gobbini, 2000). There are no published fMRI studies of social perception implicating the STS in autism, though there have been a number of conference presentations suggesting that this region is clearly underactive during social perceptual tasks (e.g., Robins, Hunyadi, & Schultz, 2004). There are, however, published reports of the morphology of the STS being altered in autism (Boddaert et al., 2004; Waiter et al., 2004); thus, it seems clear that this region will have an important role in developing models of the autistic deficits in the "social brain."

In the first functional neuroimaging study of face perception among people with an ASD, we showed that the FFA was hypoactive in a mixed group of 14 persons with autism and Asperger syndrome compared to two independent samples of 14 control participants (Schultz, Gauthier, et al., 2000). Because a typical set of fMRI data for a single person will have more than 50,000 individual data points (image voxels), comparing fMRI data between people and between groups is statistically complicated because multiple comparisons greatly inflate the risk of falsely identifying voxels as significantly different between data sets by chance. This problem has long been recognized and is a very active area of research (see Jezzard, Matthews, & Smith, 2001, for a complete discussion of this topic). To deal with this problem, we employed a strategy of first identifying the FFA region in one sample of controls and then using that FFA definition in an independent sample of 14 controls compared to our group of 14 persons with an ASD. We also reversed this process and defined the FFA in the second control group and then used that definition in a comparison of ASD and the first control group. In this way we were able to show selective underactivity of the FFA region, which differed somewhat between control samples in its precise location and extent; if this hypoactivation were a spurious finding, we would not expect it to be significant in both analyses. We also showed compensatory overactivity of the neighboring tissue in the inferior temporal gyrus, an area that was selectively active during the object differentiation task.

Hadjikhani, Chabris, et al. (2004) used fMRI to study the organization of the early visual cortex in autism and found it to be intact, with a normal ratio between central and peripheral visual field representation. Although requiring replication, this finding suggests that the differences in higher-level perception, such as face perception, more likely arise from top-down processes than bottom-up processes.

Hypoactivity of the FFA has now been replicated by nine other labs (Aylward, Bernier, Field, Grimme, & Dawson, 2004; Critchley et al., 2000a; Curby, Schyns, Gosselin, & Guthier, 2003; Davidson et al., 2004; Hall, Szechtman, & Nahmias, 2003; Hubl et al., 2003; Pierce, Müller, Ambrose, Allen, & Courchesne, 2001; Piggot et al., 2004; Wang, Dapretto, Hariri, Sigman, & Bokheimer, 2004). The compensatory activation of object selective areas during face perception among persons with an ASD has only clearly been replicated once (Hubl et al., 2003), and our own replication work (Schultz, 2004), with a sample size three times larger than any other study, also fails to find reliable differences in that region. Critchley and colleagues demonstrated hypoactivation of the FFA in a group of nine adult males with a clinical diagnosis of either autism ($n = 2$) or Asperger syndrome ($n = 7$), using an active face perception task requiring the participants to categorize faces as expressive or neutral. Pierce and colleagues also used an active perceptual task involving gender discrimination of neutral faces in a sample of six adults with autism. Hubl et al. showed FFA hypoactivation in seven adult males with autism using both a gender discrimination and a neutral versus expressive discrimination task. Aylward et al. examined FFA activation to familiar and unfamiliar faces in a group of 11 persons with an ASD as compared to 10 healthy controls; the FFA was hypoactive to only the unfamiliar faces. Hall and colleagues used ^{15}O-water PET in a group of eight high-functioning males with autism as compared to eight healthy male controls during an emotion recognition task and showed hypoactivation of the FFA, as well as other deficits. Wang and colleagues used two tasks in a group of 12 males. In one task, participants had to select the facial expression that matched the facial expression of the target face from two alternatives. In the second task, participants had to pair a verbal label with a facial expression. Hypoactivation of the FFA was found only in the purely perceptual task, perhaps because of the overall increase in the face perceptual load in that condition relative to the verbal labeling condition. Piggot and colleagues were the first to use a sample of all children, 14 boys with an ASD. This was a companion to the Wang et al. study in that both used the same task methodology, and it is interesting that both found hypoactivation only under task conditions devoid of verbal stimulation. It is impossible to know without simultaneous eye tracking data how the verbal labels may have affected attention and FFA activation, but it is significant that both studies were sensitive to the hypoactivation of the FFA effect in ASDs only under the pure face condition. Attentional effects were explicitly examined by Davidson et al. (2004), who showed hypoactivation of the FFA across two samples of males with an ASD (n's = 14 and 17), compared to samples of controls of an equal size. However, posterior regions of the FG showed strong attentional effects, in that activation was increased significantly when participants focused on the eye region as opposed to other aspects of the display.

Grelotti et al. (2005) studied an 11-year-old boy with autism who was expert at distinguishing a novel class of objects known as *Digimon* (digital monsters), cartoon characters of Japanese origin. This Digimon "expert" was compared to another boy with autism and a healthy control during several tasks involving Digimon discrimination as well as face and common object discrimination. Both boys with autism showed hypoactivation of their FFA to faces, but the Digimon expert showed enhanced activation to the Digimon images, supporting an expertise model of FFA functions.

In their detailed case study of face perception in a young adult with ASD, Curby and colleagues (2003) used fMRI to map out FFA responses to different spatial frequency ranges. Any visible object can be described in terms of its different spatial frequency components. The high spatial frequencies (HSFs), that is, the sharp changes in brightness (the edges), are especially important for individual feature identification. Low spatial frequencies (LSFs) capture information about the spatial configuration of the features. Curby and colleagues showed that this individual had the expected hypoactivation of the FFA to broad spatial frequency faces (i.e., unfiltered images). However, consistent with the literature on deficits in holistic processing and a bias toward features (see Schultz, in press, for a current review), he showed greater than normal FFA activation to HSF faces and hypoactivation to LSF faces.

Finally, using active face discrimination tasks in two new samples of persons with an ASD (total ASD $n = 44$), we have replicated the FFA hypoactivation effect using neutral face pictures in one study and expressive faces in the second (Schultz et al., under review). Importantly, we showed in both samples a significant correlation to degree of face expertise, such that those with better scores on a standardized test of face perception outside the magnet showed more FFA activation during fMRI, regardless of group membership (i.e., ASD or controls). Moreover, degree of social impairment as measured by the Autism Diagnostic Observation Schedule (ADOS) social domain also correlated with degree of FFA hypoactivation, such that the more socially impaired participants had less FFA activation to faces.

Counting our two new samples, the two case studies, and the two samples included within Davidson et al. (2004), there are now 15 reports of FFA hypoactivation with a total sample size of 157 persons with an ASD and a combined control sample of 167. There are also now two reported failures to find hypoactivation of the FFA in ASD. Pierce, Haist, Sedaghat, and Courchesne (2004) used familiar and unfamiliar faces in an fMRI study of 8 adult males with autism and 10 healthy control males. Like Aylward et al. (2004) and Grelotti et al. (in press), Pierce et al. found significantly greater activation to familiar as compared to unfamiliar faces in the autism sample. Whereas controls showed more FFA activation to unfamiliar faces than did the males with autism, this difference failed to reach statistical significance. It is not clear why this study failed to confirm the group difference in FFA engagement to unfamiliar faces, but it is noteworthy that the means were in the direction reported by other studies, and thus the results of this study might simply be due to insufficient statistical power (especially because the study used an event-related design, which is much lower in statistical power than the block designs used by other studies; Birn, Cox, & Bandettini, 2002). However, it is also noteworthy that the fMRI task employed in this study did not demand person identification processes, but rather entailed a button press to each occurrence of a female face. As Grill-Spector, Knouf, and Kanwisher (2004) have nicely demonstrated, the FFA is involved in both person detection (e.g., the gender task of Pierce et al.) and person identification (i.e., differentiating unique individuals), and this latter process may significantly bolster FFA activation above and beyond levels achieved with simple person or gender detection. Moreover, it may be the FFA's contributions to person identification processes that are important for differentiating controls and those with an ASD. Another interesting contribution of the study by Pierce and colleagues is the demonstration that personally meaningful faces (friends and family) modulate FFA engagement; this is consistent with the argument that inputs from the amygdala on affective salience are critical for amplifying FFA activation and engendering proficient face perceptual processes (Schultz, in press; Vuilleumier, Richardson, Armony, Driver, & Dolan, 2004).

The second report failing to show hypoactivation of the FFA in ASD was by Hadjikhani, Joseph, and colleagues (2004). They studied 11 adult males with an ASD (six autism, four Asperger, and one PDD-NOS) compared to 10 adult males; notably, the control sample was significantly younger (mean age of 26 years versus 36 years for the participants with an ASD). This failure to find hypoactivation of the FFA might be attributable to the particulars of this study, including the use of a passive viewing of faces as the "task" during fMRI recording (all other studies to date used an active task to monitor attention and ensure that all participants were actively processing the faces), a sample that was much older than those of the other studies, a slice thickness that varied between participants, and, probably most important, a sample of patients who were, on average, less socially impaired compared to samples from other studies. Given that we have reported a significant relationship between degree of FFA activation and degree of social impairment, this seems to be the most likely factor contributing to the reported activations (Schultz, 2004; Schultz et al., under review). However, Hadjikhani et al. also used pictures of faces that subtended 20 degrees of visual angle; this is much larger than

any prior study (note that not all studies report image size) and is about four times larger than face pictures that we have employed in our studies. Images greater than about 3 to 5 degrees of visual angle cannot be viewed in their entirety (foveated) without eye movements. Moreover, smaller images effectively emphasize LSFs because details will be blurred. Recalling that Curby et al. (2003) found greater FFA activation to HSF faces in their case study, the relative emphasis on HSFs might also have been an important influence to the results of Hadjikhani and colleagues. This possibility is especially intriguing.

In light of the majority of findings indicating that the FG has some specific role in ASDs, studies are now beginning to appear examining its morphology by way of high-resolution sMRI. Waiter and colleagues (2004) studied 16 males with an ASD between the ages of 12 and 20 and compared their brain structure to a group of 16 healthy controls using an automated procedure known as *voxel brain morphology* (VBM). They found about a dozen brain areas that were specifically enlarged in the ASD group, consistent with the findings of overall brain enlargement that have been reported multiple times (see Chapter 18, this *Handbook,* this volume). Their second strongest finding involved a specific enlargement of the right FG, with the location of the peak size difference consistent with peak coordinates found in fMRI studies of the FFA. Moreover, we have now measured the structure of the FG in a sample of 110 males with an ASD compared to 103 male controls, with a large age range (from age 5 to 55 years) with a mean of about 17 years for the two groups combined. We find bilateral enlargement of the fusiform, as well as overall brain enlargement (Schultz et al., in preparation). In the entire group, the fusiform enlargement is not significant after accounting for the whole brain enlargement; however, when the two groups are divided at the median age of 14.9 years of age, we find significant enlargement in the older group of ASD versus the controls, even when controlling for overall brain size, and a positive correlation with age only in the ASD group. This suggests some aberrant growth process extending into later adolescence and early adulthood. Thus, the functional abnormalities of the FFA may have demonstrable structural underpinnings and longer-term causal influences on the structure of the brain itself.

Functional Neuroimaging Studies of Social Cognition

Data emerging over the past several years from neuroimaging studies, human lesion studies, and animal studies suggest a working model of the social brain composed of a diverse set of frontal, limbic, and temporal lobe circuitry. In addition to its primary role in social perception, the FFA appears to be involved in select aspects of social cognition. Three studies employing visual ToM type of tasks have now shown the FFA to be active during social judgments in the absence of any presentation of a face or facelike object (Castelli, Happe, Frith, & Frith, 2000; Martin & Weisberg, 2003; Schultz, Klin, Grelotti, Herrington, & Volkmar, 2003). One interpretation of the FG's activity during social-cognitive tasks is that it actively codes and stores social semantic knowledge (Schultz, Grelotti, et al., 2003). In this context, the FFA's low activity level during face perception in individuals with an ASD may then in part reflect a paucity of social ideation, as well as deficits in face perception, both of which would have adverse consequences for social interactions (Schultz, in press; Schultz, Grelotti, et al., 2003). Consistent with the proposed role for the FG in social cognition, Kriegstein and Giraud (2004) showed FG activation (at coordinates typical of activation during face perception) during a familiar voice recognition task. This might suggest some involuntary/automatic activation of social semantic content stored in this region when forced to identify persons by their voices alone, or it may have been driven by visual imagery of the person heard speaking.

In addition to these social perceptual processing nodes, the brain areas most often implicated by functional neuroimaging and lesion studies as important to social functions include the amygdala, aspects of the orbital prefrontal cortex (PFC), the medial PFC (outside the cingulate region), and the temporal poles (see Adolphs, 2003; Schultz, Grelotti, et al., 2003, for recent reviews). In addition, aspects of the inferior frontal convexity may have a specific role in empathy (Leslie, Johnson-Frey, & Grafton, 2004) and imitation learning (Rizzolatti & Craighero, 2004), both of which would be relevant to the deficits found in autism. Indeed, the involvement of the frontal and temporal lobe cortices seems very likely, as a number of resting blood flow studies have shown that these lobes are hypoactive in autism (reviewed in Boddaert & Zilbovicius, 2002). These functional findings are consistent with the structural findings in children showing the frontal and temporal lobes to be the most deviant in terms of abnormal enlargement (Carper, Moses, Tigue, & Courchesne, 2002). Moreover, there are a number of case studies of temporal lobe lesions causing autisticlike sequelae (Gillberg, 1986, 1991; Hoon & Reiss, 1992) and one report suggesting that tuberous sclerosis preferentially results in autism when the lesions cluster in the temporal lobes (Bolton & Griffiths, 1997).

Within the frontal lobes, the orbital and medial PFCs are most often implicated in social functions (Bechara, Tranel, Damasio, & Damasio, 1996; Brothers, 1990; Damasio, 1996). The orbital and medial PFCs have dense reciprocal connections with medial temporal areas, forming a system for regulating emotional processes (Carmichael & Price, 1995; Price, Carmichael, & Drevets, 1996). Nonhuman primate studies have documented abnormal social responsivity and loss of social position within the group following lesions to orbital and medial PFCs (Bachevalier & Mishkin, 1986; Butter, McDonald, & Snyder, 1969). Involvement of orbital and medial PFCs in social cognition is also consistent with findings of ToM task deficits among neurological patients with bilateral orbital and medial PFC lesions (Stone, Baron-Cohen, & Knight, 1998).

Functional imaging studies have repeatedly suggested that dorsomedial prefrontal cortex (DMPFC) is a critical substrate for "social cognition," that is, for thinking about others' thoughts, feelings, and intentions (Adolphs, 2003; Castelli et al., 2002; Schultz, Grelotti, et al., 2003). Function of this prefrontal region appears to be disturbed in persons with an ASD. A PET study, for example, reported reduced dopaminergic activity in the DMPFC of autistic subjects (Ernst, Zametkin, Matochik, Pascualvaca, & Cohen, 1997). Reduced glucose metabolism has also been reported in a subdivision of the anterior cingulate gyrus in persons with autism engaged in a verbal memory task (Haznedar et al., 2000). A pilot ^{15}O-water PET study of Asperger syndrome using a ToM task showed specific engagement of the medial PFC, except that the center of activation was displaced below and anterior in patients compared with controls (Happé et al., 1996). More recently, Castelli et al. (2002) showed reduced dorsomedial PFC activation in ASDs during an adaptation of Heider and Simmel's (1944) social attribution task, involving ToM skills.

Frontal Lobe Findings Concerning Cognitive and Motor Systems

The dorsal-lateral PFC is critical for working memory and executive functioning. One recent fMRI study of 11 high-functioning autistic subjects compared to 6 healthy controls showed that subjects with autism had significantly less task-related activation in dorsolateral PFC (Brodmann area 9/46) in comparison with healthy subjects during a spatial working memory task (Luna et al., 2002). These data support the neuropsychological literature that finds deficits in executive function in the ASDs (see Chapter 22, this *Handbook,* this volume).

Müller and colleagues have studied the motor system in autism with fMRI. Most recently, they (Müller, Kleinhans, Kemmosu, Pierce, & Courchesne, 2003) reported, in a sample of eight male autistic patients and eight comparison subjects, variable and scattered representation along the lateral convexity of the frontal and parietal lobes during a visually cued motor sequencing task. They suggest that this representation could be caused by an early-onset disturbance in the cerebello-thalamo-cortical pathways in autism. Allen, Müller, and Courchesne (2004) and Allen and Courchesne (2003) conducted two fMRI studies targeting cerebellar functions in autism. Both employed a sample of eight autistic participants and eight matched control participants during different motor and attention tasks. Results suggest abnormal increases in cerebellar activity during the motor tasks but not during the attention tasks.

The Role of the Amygdala

Of the specific brain systems implicated in the pathobiology of autism, none has attracted more attention than the limbic system, especially the amygdala and functionally related cortical regions (e.g., Baron-Cohen et al., 1999, 2000; Schultz, in press; Schultz, Romanski, et al., 2000). A number of findings using different measurement approaches implicate limbic dysfunction in ASDs, including postmortem examination of the cytoarchitechtonics of limbic tissue of persons who were on the autism spectrum, lesion studies in humans and animals, and functional neuroimaging studies of healthy controls as well as persons with an ASD.

The amygdaloid complex is a small, almond-shaped structure located deep in the medial temporal lobe. Although initially the amygdala was conceptualized as a single anatomical structure, it is actually composed of more than a dozen nuclei, each with its own afferent and efferent connections, neurochemical makeup, and cytoarchitecture (Amaral & Price, 1984; Amaral, Price, Pitkanen, & Carmichael, 1992). Afferents to the lateral nucleus of the amygdala include frontal, cingulate, insular, and temporal neocortex as well as subcortical regions, such as nuclei of the thalamus. The lateral nucleus acts as the *sensory interface* for the amygdala (Amaral et al., 1992; LeDoux, Cicchetti, Xagoraris, & Romanski, 1990). Cortical projections from the amygdala target virtually all regions of the temporal and occipital lobes important for visual processing (Amaral & Price, 1984), as well as multiple regions of the PFC, most notably the orbital PFC and the medial wall of the PFC, including the anterior cingulate (Carmichael & Price, 1995; Price et al., 1996). Thus, the amygdala has a reciprocal set of connections with the temporal cortex as well as orbital and medial PFCs. In this way, the amygdala is centrally positioned and capable of modulating and interpreting the emotional significance of data processed in the perceptual cortices as well as assisting with the integration of emotion and cognition for decision making and action in the frontal cortices (Adolphs, 2003; Allison et al., 2000; Hoffman & Haxby, 2000; Vuilleumier et al., 2004).

The healthy amygdala supports the automatic processing of emotional information, and it can be engaged independently of attention (Pasley et al., 2004, but see Pessoa, McKenna, Gutierrez, & Ungerleider, 2002) below the level of conscious awareness in an obligatory fashion. In this way it may normally activate social schemas (Heberelein & Adolphs, 2004; Schultz, Grelotti, et al., 2003). The amygdala plays a critical role in emotional arousal, assigning significance to environmental stimuli and mediating emotional learning (Gaffan, Gaffan, & Harrison, 1988; LeDoux, 1996). Damage to the amygdala causes impairment in recognizing facial expression (Adolphs, 1999; Calder et al., 1996), detecting social faux pas (Stone, Baron-Cohen, Young, Calder, & Keane, 2003), judging trustworthiness (Adolphs et al., 1998), and attributing social intentions (Heberelein & Adolphs, 2004).

Postmortem examination of the brains of persons with autism finds consistent evidence for abnormalities in size, density, and dendritic arborization of neurons in the limbic system, including the amygdala, hippocampus, septum, anterior cingulate, and mammillary bodies (Bauman & Kemper, 1994; Kemper & Bauman, 1998). Findings indicate a stunting of neuronal processes and increased neuronal packing density, suggesting a curtailment of normal development.

Several studies have now found hypoactivation of the amygdala in autism during tasks involving the perception of facial expressions and during ToM-type tasks (Baron-Cohen et al., 1999; Castelli et al., 2002; Critchley et al., 2000b; Pierce et al., 2001; Wang et al., 2004). New data suggest that the amygdala's role in these social-cognitive and perceptual processes might largely be one of mediating physiological arousal (e.g., see Anderson & Sobel, 2003). Thus, hypoactivation of the amygdala in autism may reflect nonspecific task effects, such as less interest in or reduced emotional arousal by task stimuli. This view is consistent with social motivation hypotheses of autism (e.g., Dawson, Meltzoff, Osterling, & Rinaldi, 1998; Klin, Jones, Schultz, & Volkmar, 2003). MRI studies of amygdala volume, however, have produced many conflicting results (for a review, see Sweeten, Posey, Shekhar, & McDougle, 2002). Most recently,

Schumann et al. (2004) suggested an interaction between age and amygdala volume in individuals with an ASD, such that at the earliest ages, the amygdala is larger than typical, but its growth plateaus prematurely and by adolescence there is not significant size difference compared to healthy controls.

Animal models using nonhuman primates suggest that abnormalities in the development of the amygdala may play a particularly important role in the development of autistic symptomatology. Bilateral damage of the amygdala shortly after birth can produce patterns of behavior similar to those seen in autism, such as social isolation, lack of eye contact, impaired facial expression, and motor stereotypes (Bachevalier, 1994). However, similar lesions made in adulthood fail to produce these behaviors (Emery et al., 2001). It is most interesting that the early postnatal lesions do not produce autistic characteristics immediately; rather, these features emerge with age and experience, suggesting that lesion impacts the animal's ability to learn, perhaps by altering their behavior in such a way that they obtain different experiences. Over the first years of development, faulty early social and emotional learning appears to culminate in the presentation of autistic-like symptoms, a developmental course not dissimilar from autism. Bachevalier's monkeys also showed signs of frontal lobe abnormalities later in life (Bertolino et al., 1997; Saunders, Kolachana, Bachevalier, & Weinberger, 1998). While an attractive model, one recent attempt to replicate these findings with three neonatally lesioned macaque monkeys failed to recreate the autistic type of behaviors found by Bachevalier and colleagues (Prather et al., 2001). At age 8 to 9 months, the monkeys were attentive to social communications but nevertheless showed a complex pattern of changed social behaviors that included increased fear during dyadic social interactions (Amaral et al., 2003; Prather et al., 2001). Current speculation about these disparate results centers on methodological differences (Amaral et al., 2003; Prather et al., 2001). This area is clearly very important, and more studies, with larger samples, are now needed to clarify the effects of early amygdala damage.

CONCLUSION

Functional neuroimaging studies, particularly fMRI studies of social cognition, emotion, and social perception, hold great promise in defining the neural systems most aberrant in autism. Since the last edition of the *Handbook of Autism,* there has been a dramatic upswing of research activity in this area, and judging from the large number of studies out this year on social perception and social cognition, this area of research promises to provide a great deal of important data for understanding autism in the years to come. Studies using persons with an ASD are still relatively uncommon, and existing studies continue to grapple with experimental designs and issues particular to studying children and adults with, on average, lower cognitive ability and reduced ability to comply with what can be a somewhat difficult study environment.

Studies to date are making progress in understanding the language and social skill deficits that are defining features of the ASDs. In particular, there has been substantial progress from research studying aspects of face perception, which highlights a role for the FG, amygdala, and select aspects of the STS in autism. More work needs to be done on social cognition, including empathy and ToM skills, but preliminary data implicate orbital and medial PFCs, as well as the amygdala. There is an expectation in the research community that mirror neuron networks in the lateral-inferior frontal cortex will prove to be highly relevant to understanding autism, but work here is just beginning. There have been just a few studies on language functioning, with mixed results. However, abnormalities in hemispheric laterality and in the relative workload of frontal and temporal-parietal language areas appear to be likely.

FMRI studies will have to be augmented and integrated with other types of approaches, including sMRI, diffusion tensor imaging, and electrophysiological approaches. Multimodal and systems level investigations, including studies of effective connectivity, are clearly the way of future research, and these approaches will undoubtedly yield a much greater understanding of pathobiology of this complex disorder. Already, abnormalities in cerebral white matter volume are being related to fMRI data suggesting decreased functional connectivity. This type of integration across types of data is essential in the near future, else the field risks being overwhelmed by isolated findings and information that cannot easily be integrated into a functional model of the brain bases of the ASDs.

Cross-References

Other aspects of the neurobiology of autism are discussed in Chapters 16, 17, and 18. Associated medical conditions and pharmacological treatments are addressed in Chapters 20 and 44, respectively, and related issues in communication and neuropsychology, in Chapters 12, 32, and 22 through 25.

REFERENCES

Adolphs, R. (1999). Social cognition and the human brain. *Trends in Cognitive Science, 3,* 469–479.

Adolphs, R. (2003). Cognitive neuroscience of human social behaviour. *Nature Reviews, 4,* 165–178.

Adolphs, R., Tranel, D., & Damasio, A. R. (1998). The human amygdala in social judgment. *Nature, 393*(6684), 470–474.

Allen, G., & Courchesne, E. (2003). Differential effects of developmental cerebellar abnormality on cognitive and motor functions in the cerebellum: An fMRI study of autism. *American Journal of Psychiatry, 160,* 262–273.

Allen, G., Müller, R. A., & Courchesne, E. (2004). Cerebellar function in autism: Functional magnetic resonance image activation during a simple motor task. *Biological Psychiatry, 56*(4), 269–278.

Allison, T., Puce, A., & McCarthy, G. (2000). Social perception from visual cues: Role of the STS region. *Trends in Cognitive Sciences, 4*(7), 267–278.

Amaral, D. G., Bauman, M. D., Capitanio, J. P., Lavenex, P., Mason, W. A., Mauldin-Jourdain, M. L., et al. (2003). The amygdala: Is it an essential component of the neural network for social cognition? *Neuropsychologia, 41*(4), 517–522.

Amaral, D. G., & Price, J. L. (1984). Amygdalo-cortical projections in the monkey (Macaca fascicularis). *Journal of Comparative Neurology, 230,* 465–496.

Amaral, D. G., Price, J. L., Pitkanen, A., & Carmichael, S. T. (1992). Anatomical organization of the primate amygdaloid complex. In J. Aggleton (Ed.), *The amygdala: Neurobiological aspects of emotion, memory and mental dysfunction* (pp. 1–66). New York: Wiley-Liss.

American Psychiatric Association. (1994). *Diagnostic and statistical manual of mental disorders* (4th ed.). Washington, DC: Author.

Anderson, A. K., & Sobel, N. (2003). Dissociating intensity from valence as sensory inputs to emotion. *Neuron, 39*(4), 581–583.

Aylward, E., Bernier, R., Field, K., Grimme, A., & Dawson, G. (2004). Normal activation of fusiform gyrus in adolescents and adults with autism during viewing of familiar, but not unfamiliar, faces. *Paper presented at the CPEA/STAART annual meeting,* Bethesda, Maryland.

Bachevalier, J. (1994). Medial temporal lobe structures and autism: A review of clinical and experimental findings. *Neuropsychologia, 32,* 627–648.

Bachevalier, J., & Mishkin, M. (1986). Visual recognition impairment follows ventromedial but not dorsolateral prefrontal lesions in monkeys. *Behavioural Brain Research, 20*(3), 249–261.

Baron-Cohen, S., Ring, H. A., Bullmore, E. T., Wheelwright, S., Ashwin, C., & Williams, S. C. R. (2000). The amygdala theory of autism. *Neuroscience and Biobehavioral Reviews, 24,* 355–364.

Baron-Cohen, S., Ring, H. A., Wheelwright, S., Bullmore, E. T., Brammer, M. J., Simmons, A., et al. (1999). Social intelligence in the normal and autistic brain: An fMRI study. *European Journal of Neuroscience, 11,* 1891–1898.

Bauman, M. L., & Kemper, T. L. (1994). Neuroanatomic observations of the brain in autism. In M. L. Bauman & T. L. Kemper (Eds.), *The neurobiology of autism* (pp. 119–145). Baltimore: Johns Hopkins Press.

Bechara, A., Tranel, D., Damasio, H., & Damasio, A. R. (1996). Failure to respond autonomically to anticipated future outcomes following damage to prefrontal cortex. *Cerebral Cortex, 6,* 215–225.

Berthier, M. L., Bayes, A., & Tolosa, E. S. (1993). Magnetic resonance imaging in patients with concurrent Tourette's disorder and Asperger's syndrome. *Journal of the American Academy of Child and Adolescent Psychiatry, 32,* 633–639.

Bertolino, A., Saunders, R. C., Mattay, V. S., Bachevalier, J., Frank, J. A., & Weinberger, D. R. (1997). Altered development of prefrontal neurons in rhesus monkeys with neonatal mesial temporo-limbic lesions: a proton magnetic resonance spectroscopic imaging study. *Cerebral Cortex, 7,* 740–748.

Birn, R., Cox, R., & Bandettini, P. (2002). Detection versus Estimation in Event-Related fMRI: Choosing the Optimal Stimulus Timing. *Neuroimage, 15,* 252–264.

Boddaert, N., Belin, P., Chabane, N., Poline, J. B., Barthélémy, C., Mouren-Simeoni, M. C., et al. (2003). Perception of complex sounds: Abnormal pattern of cortical activation in autism. *American Journal of Psychiatry, 160,* 2057–2060.

Boddaert, N., Chabane, N., Gervais, H., Good, C. D., Bourgeois, M., Plumet, M. H., et al. (2004). Superior temporal sulcus anatomical abnormalities in childhood autism: A voxel-based morphometry MRI study. *Neuroimage, 23*(1), 364–369.

Boddaert, N., & Zilbovicius, M. (2002). Functional neuroimaging and childhood autism. *Pediatric Radiology, 23,* 1–7.

Bolton, P. F., & Griffiths, P. D. (1997). Association of tuberous sclerosis of temporal lobes with autism and atypical autism. *Lancet, 349,* 392–395.

Boucher, J., & Lewis, V. (1992). Unfamiliar face recognition in relatively able autistic children. *Journal of Child Psychology and Psychiatry, 33*(5), 843–859.

Braverman, M., Fein, D., Lucci, D., & Waterhouse, L. (1989). Affect comprehension in children with pervasive developmental disorders. *Journal of Autism and Developmental Disorders, 19,* 301–316.

Brothers, L. (1990). The social brain: A project for integrating primate behavior and neurophysiology in a new domain. *Concepts Neuroscience, 1,* 27–151.

Butter, C. M., McDonald, J. A., & Snyder, D. R. (1969). Orality, preference behavior, and reinforcement value of nonfood object in monkeys with orbital frontal lesions. *Science, 164,* 1306–1307.

Calder, A. J., Young, A. W., Rowland, D., Perrett, D. I., Hodges, J. R., & Etcoff, N. L. (1996). Facial emotion recognition after bilateral amygdala damage: Differentially severe impairment of fear. *Cognitive Neuropsycology, 13,* 699–745.

Capps, L., Yirmiya, N., & Sigman, M. (1992). Understanding of simple and complex emotions in nonretarded children with autism. *Journal of Child Psychology and Psychiatry, 33,* 1169–1182.

Carmichael, S. T., & Price, J. L. (1995). Limbic connections of the orbital and medial prefrontal cortex in macaque monkeys. *Journal of Comparative Neurology, 363,* 615–641.

Carper, R. A., Moses, P., Tigue, Z. D., & Courchesne, E. (2002). Cerebral lobes in autism: Early hyperplasia and abnormal age effects. *Neuroimage, 16,* 1038–1051.

Castelli, F., Frith, C., Happe, F., & Frith U. (2002). Autism, Asperger's syndrome and brain mechanisms for the attribution of mental states to animated shapes. *Brain, 125,* 1839–1849.

Castelli, F., Happe, F., Frith, U., & Frith, C. (2000). Movement and mind: A functional imaging study of perception and interpretation of complex intentional movement patterns. *Neuroimage, 12,* 314–325.

Courchesne, E., Karns, C. M., Davis, H. R., Ziccardi, R., Carper, R. A., Tigue, Z. D., et al. (2001). Unusual brain growth patterns in early life in patients with autistic disorder. *Neurology, 57,* 245–254.

Critchley, H. D., Daly, E. M., Bullmore, E. T., Williams, S. C., Van Amelsvoort, T., Robertson, D. M., et al. (2000). The functional neuroanatomy of social behaviour: Changes in cerebral blood flow when people with autistic disorder process facial expressions. *Brain, 123,* 2203–2212.

Critchley, H., Daly, E., Phillips, M., Brammer, M., Bullmore, E., Williams, S., et al. (2000). Explicit and implicit neural mechanisms for processing of social information from facial expressions: A functional magnetic resonance imaging study. *Human Brain Mapping, 9*(2), 93–105.

Curby, K. M., Schyns, P. G., Gosselin, F., & Gauthier, I. (2003). *Face-selective fusiform activation in Asperger's syndrome: A matter of tuning to the right (spatial) frequency.* Poster presented at Cognitive Neuroscience, New York.

Damasio, A. R. (1996). The somatic marker hypothesis and the possible functions of the prefrontal cortex. *Proceedings of the Royal Society of London. Series B, Biological Sciences, 351,* 1413–1420.

Davidson, R., Dalton, K. M., Nacewicz, B. M., Alexander, A. L., Gernsbacher, A. M., & Goldsmith, H. H. (2004, May). *Functional and structural substrates of affective processing in autism: Reframing the origins of fusiform hypoactivation.* Paper presented at the third annual meeting of the International Meeting for Autism Research (IMFAR), Sacramento, CA.

Davies, S., Bishop, D., Manstead, A. S. R., & Tantam, D. (1994). Face perception in children with autism and Asperger's syndrome. *Journal of Child Psychology and Psychiatry, 35*(6), 1033–1057.

Dawson, G., Hill, D., Spencer, A., Galpert, L., & Watson, L. (1990). Affective exchanges between young autistic children and their mothers. *Journal of Abnormal Child Psychology, 18,* 335–345.

Dawson, G., Meltzoff, A. N., Osterling, J., & Rinaldi, J. (1998). Neuropsychological correlates of early symptoms of autism. *Child Development, 69*(5), 1276–1285.

de Gelder, B., Vroomen, J., & Van der Heide, L. (1991). Face recognition and lip reading in autism. *European Journal of Cognitive Psychology, 3,* 69–86.

Deruelle, C., Rondan, C., Gepner, B. & Tardif, C. (2004). Spatial frequency and face processing in children with Autism and Asperger syndrome. *Journal of Autism and Developmental Disorders, 34*(2), 199–210.

Diamond, R., & Carey, S. (1986). Why faces are and are not special: An effect of expertise. *Journal of Experimental Psychology: General, 115,* 107–117.

Egaas, B., Courchesne, E., & Saitoh, O. (1995). Reduced-Size of Corpus-Callosum in Autism. *Archives of Neurology, 52,* 794–801.

Emery, N. J., Capitanio, J. P., Mason, W. A., Machado, C. J., Mendoza, S. P., & Amaral, D. G. (2001). The effects of bilateral lesions of the amygdala on dyadic social interactions in rhesus monkeys (*Macaca mulatta*). *Behavioral Neuroscience, 115,* 515–544.

Ernst, M., Zametkin, A. J., Matochik, J. A., Pascualvaca, D., & Cohen, R. M. (1997). Reduced medial prefrontal dopaminergic activity in autistic children. *Lancet, 350,* 638.

Fein, D., Lucci, D., Braverman, M., & Waterhouse, L. (1992). Comprehension of affect in context in children with pervasive developmental disorders. *Journal of Child Psychology and Psychiatry, 33,* 1157–1167.

Friston, K. J., Buechel, C., Fink, G. R., Morris, J., Rolls, E., & Dolan, R. J. (1997). Psychophysiological and modulatory interactions in neuroimaging. *Neuroimage, 6,* 218–229.

Friston, K. J., Frith, C. D., Liddle, P. F., & Frackowiak, R. S. (1993). Functional connectivity: The principal-component analysis of large (PET) data sets. *Journal of Cerebral Blood Flow and Metabolism, 13*(1), 5–14.

Frith, U. (1989). *Autism: Explaining the enigma.* Oxford, England: Blackwell.

Gaffan, E. A., Gaffan, D., & Harrison, S. (1988). Disconnection of the amygdala from visual association cortex impairs visual-reward association learning in monkeys. *Journal of Neuroscience, 8,* 3144–3150.

Gervais, H., Belin, P., Boddaert, N., Leboyer, M., Coez, A., Sfaello, I., et al. (2004). Abnormal cortical voice processing in autism. *Nature Neuroscience, 7*(8), 801–802.

Gillberg, C. (1986). Onset at age 14 of a typical autistic syndrome: A case report of a girl with herpes simplex encephalitis. *Journal of Autism and Developmental Disorders, 16,* 369–375.

Gillberg, C. (1991). The treatment of epilepsy in autism. *Journal of Autism and Developmental Disorders, 21,* 61–67.

Grelotti, D., Gauthier, I., & Schultz, R. T. (2002). Social interest and the development of cortical face specialization: What autism teaches us about face processing. *Developmental Psychobiology, 40,* 213–225.

Grelotti, D., Klin, A. J., Gauthier, I., Skudlarski, P., Cohen, D. J., Gore, J. C., et al. (2005). fMRI activation of the fusiform gyrus and amygdala to cartoon characters but not to faces in a boy with autism. *Neuropsychologia, 43*(5), 373–385.

Grill-Spector, K., Knouf, N., & Kanwisher, N. (2004). The fusiform face area subserves face perception, not generic within-category identification. *Nature Neuroscience, 7*(5), 555–562.

Hadjikhani, N., Chabris, C. F., Joseph, R. M., Clark, J., McGrath, L., Aharon, I., et al. (2004). Early visual cortex organization in autism: An fMRI study. *NeuroReport, 15*(2), 267–270.

Hadjikhani, N., Joseph, R. M., Snyder, J., Chabris, C. F., Clark, J., Steele, S., et al. (2004). Activation of the fusiform gyrus when individuals with autism spectrum disorder view faces. *Neuroimage, 22,* 1141–1150.

Hall, G. B. C., Szechtman, H., & Nahmias, C. (2003). Enhanced salience and emotion recognition in autism: A PET Study. *American Journal of Psychiatry, 160,* 1439–1441.

Happé, F., Ehlers, S., Fletcher, P., Frith, U., Johansson, M., Gillberg, C., et al. (1996). 'Theory of mind' in the brain: Evidence from a PET scan Study of Asperger's syndrome. *NeuroReport, 8,* 197–201.

Hardan, A. Y., Minshew, N. J., & Keshavan, M. S. (2000). Corpus callosum size in autism. *Neurology, 55,* 1033–1036.

Hauck, M., Fein, D., & Maltby, N. (1999). Memory for faces in children with autism. *Child Neuropsychology, 4,* 187–198.

Haxby, J. V., Hoffman, E. A., & Gobbini, M. I. (2000). The distributed human neural system for face perception. *Trends in Cognitive Science, 4,* 223–233.

Haxby, J. V., Ungerleider, L. G., Clark, V. P., Schouten, J. L., Hoffman, E. A., & Martin, A. (1999). The effect of face inversion on activity in human neural systems for face and object perception. *Neuron, 22*(1), 189–199.

Haznedar, M. M., Buchsbaum, M. S., Wei, T. C., Hof, P. R., Cartwright, C., Bienstock, C. A., et al. (2000). Limbic circuitry in patients with autism spectrum disorders studied with positron emission tomography and magnetic resonance imaging. *American Journal of Psychiatry, 157,* 1994–2001.

Heberlein, A. S., & Adolphs, R. (2004). Impaired spontaneous anthropomorphizing despite intact perception and social knowledge. *Proceedings of the National Academy of Sciences of the United States of America, 101*(19), 7487–7491.

Heider, F., & Simmel, M. (1944). An experimental study of apparent behavior. *American Journal of Psychology, 57*(2), 243–259.

Herbert, M. R., Harris, G. J., Adrien, K. T., Ziegler, D. A., Makris, N., Kennedy, D., et al. (2002). Abnormal asymmetry in language association cortex in autism. *Annals of Neurology, 52,* 588–596.

Herbert, M. R., Ziegler, D. A., Deutsch, C. K., O'Brien, L. M., Lange, N., Bakardjiev, A., et al. (2003). Dissociations of cerebral cortex, subcortical and cerebral white matter volumes in autistic boys. *Brain, 126,* 1182–1192.

Hobson, R. P. (1986a). The autistic child's appraisal of expressions of emotion: A further study. *Journal of Child Psychology and Psychiatry, 2,* 671–680.

Hobson, R. P. (1986b). The autistic child's appraisal of expressions of emotion. *Journal of Child Psychology and Psychiatry, 27,* 321–342.

Hobson, R. P., & Lee, A. (1989). Emotion-related and abstract concepts in autistic people: Evidence from the British Picture Vocabulary Scale. *Journal of Autism and Developmental Disorders, 19,* 601–623.

Hobson, R. P., Ouston, J., & Lee, A. (1988a). Emotion recognition in autism: Coordinating faces and voices. *Psychological Medicine, 18,* 911–923.

Hobson, R. P., Ouston, J., & Lee, A. (1988b). What's in a face? The case of autism. *British Journal of Psychology, 79,* 441–453.

Hoffman, E. A., & Haxby, J. V. (2000). Distinct representations of eye gaze and identity in the distributed human neural system for face perception. *Nature Neuroscience, 3*(1), 80–84.

Hoon, A. H., & Reiss, A. L. (1992). The mesial-temporal lobe and autism: Case report and review. *Developmental Medicine and Child Neurology, 34,* 252–259.

Horwitz, B., Rumsey, J. M., Grady, C. L., & Rapoport, S. I. (1988). The cerebral metabolic landscape in autism: Intercorrelations of regional glucose utilization. *Archives of Neurology, 45,* 749–755.

Hubl, D., Bolte, S., Feineis-Matthews, S., Lanfermann, H., Federspiel, A., Strik, W., et al. (2003). Functional imbalance of visual pathways indicates alternative face processing strategies in autism. *Neurology, 61*(9), 1232–1237.

Jaedicke, S., Storoschuk, S., & Lord, C. (1994). Subjective experience and causes of affect in high-functioning children and adolescents with autism. *Development and Psychopathology, 6,* 273–284.

Jezzard, P., Matthews, P. M., & Smith, S. M. (2001). *Functional MRI: An introduction to methods.* Oxford, England: Oxford University Press.

Joseph, R. M., & Tanaka, J. R. (2002). Holistic and part-based face recognition in children with autism. *Journal of Child Psychology and Psychiatry, 44,* 529–542.

Just, M. A., Cherkassky, V. L., Keller, T. A., & Minshew, N. J. (2004). Cortical activation and synchronization during sentences comprehension in high-functioning autism: Evidence of underconnectivity. *Brain, 127,* 1811–1821.

Kanwisher, N., McDermott, J., & Chun, M. M. (1997). The fusiform face area: A module in human extrastriate cortex specialized for the perception of faces. *Journal of Neuroscience, 17,* 4302–4311.

Kanwisher, N., & Wojciulik, E. (2000). Visual attention: Insights from brain imaging. *Nature Reviews Neuroscience, 1*(2), 91–100.

Kemper, T. L., & Bauman, M. L. (1998). Neuropathology of infantile autism. *Journal of Neuropathology and Experimental Neurology, 57,* 645–652.

Klin, A., Jones, W., Schultz, R., & Volkmar, F. R. (2003). The enactive mind: From actions to cognition: Lessons from autism. *Philosophical Transactions of the Royal Society, Series, B., 358,* 345–360.

Klin, A., Jones, W., Schultz, R. T., Volkmar, F., & Cohen, D. J. (2002). Visual fixation patterns during viewing of naturalistic social situations as predictors of social competence in individuals with autism. *Archives of General Psychiatry, 59,* 809–816.

Klin, A., Sparrow, S. S., de Bildt, A., Cicchetti, D. V., Cohen, D. J., & Volkmar, F. R. (1999). A normed study of face recognition in autism and related disorders. *Journal of Autism and Developmental Disorders, 29,* 499–508.

Kriegstein, K. V., & Giraud, A. L. (2004). Distinct functional substrates along the right superior temporal sulcus for the processing of voices. *Neuroimage, 22*(2), 948–955.

Langdell, T. (1978). Recognition of faces: An approach to the study of autism. *Journal of Child Psychology and Psychiatry, 19,* 255–268.

LeDoux, J. E. (1996). *The emotional brain.* New York: Simon & Shuster.

LeDoux, J. E., Cicchetti, P., Xagoraris, A., & Romanski, L. M. (1990). The lateral amygdaloid nucleus: Sensory interface of the amygdala in fear conditioning. *Journal of Neuroscience, 10,* 1062–1069.

Leslie, K. R., Johnson-Frey, S. H., & Grafton, S. T. (2004). Functional imaging of face and hand imitation: Towards a motor theory of empathy. *Neuroimage, 21*(2), 601–607.

Luna, B., Minshew, N. J., Garver, B. A., Lazar, N. A., Thulborn, K. R., Eddy, W. F., et al. (2002). Neocortical system abnormalities in autism: An fMRI study of spatial working memory. *Neurology, 59,* 834–840.

Macdonald, H., Rutter, M., Howlin, P., Rios, P., Le Conteur, A., Evered, C., et al. (1989). Recognition and expression of emotional cues by autistic and normal adults. *Journal of Child Psychology and Psychiatry, 30,* 865–877.

Manes, F., Piven, J., Vrancic, D., Nanclares, V., Plebst, C., & Starkstein, S. E. (1999). An MRI study of the corpus callosum and cerebellum in mentally retarded autistic individuals. *Journal of Neuropsychiatry and Clinical Neurosciences, 11,* 470–474.

Martin, A., & Weisberg, J. (2003). Neural foundations for understanding social and mechanical concepts. *Cognitive Neuropsychology, 20,* 575–587.

McGee, G. G., Feldman, R. S., & Chernin, L. (1991). A comparison of emotional facial display by children with autism and typical preschoolers. *Journal of Early Intervention, 15,* 237–245.

Müller, R. A., Behen, M. E., Rothermel, R. D., Chugani, D. C., Muzik, O., Mangner, T. J., et al. (1999). Brain mapping of language and auditory perception in high-functioning autistic adults: A PET study. *Journal of Autism and Developmental Disorders, 29*(1), 19–31.

Müller, R. A., Kleinhans, N., Kemmotsu, N., Pierce, K., & Courchesne, E. (2003). Abnormal variability and distribution of functional maps in autism: An FMRI study of visuomotor learning. *American Journal of Psychiatry, 160*(10), 1847–1862.

Pasley, B. N., Mayes, L. C., & Schultz, R. T. (2004). Subcortical discrimination of unperceived objects during binocular rivalry. *Neuron, 42,* 163–172.

Pessoa, L., McKenna, M., Gutierrez, E., & Ungerleider, L. G. (2002). Neural processing of emotional faces requires attention. *Proceedings of the National Academy of Science, 99,* 11458–11463.

Pierce, K., Haist, F., Sedaghat, F., & Courchesne, E. (2004). The brain response to personally familiar faces in autism: Findings of fusiform activity and beyond. *Brain, 127,* 2703–2716.

Pierce, K., Müller, R. A., Ambrose, J., Allen, G., & Courchesne, E. (2001). Face processing occurs outside the fusiform "face area" in autism: Evidence from functional MRI. *Brain, 124,* 2059–2073.

Piggot, J., Kwon, H., Mobbs, D., Blasey, C., Lotspeich, L., Menon, V., et al. (2004). Emotional attribution in high-functioning individuals with autistic spectrum disorder: A functional imaging study. *Journal of the American Academy of Child and Adolescent Psychiatry, 43*(4), 473–480.

Piven, J., Saliba, K., Bailey, J., & Arndt, S. (1997). An MRI study of autism: The cerebellum revisited. *Neurology, 49,* 546–551.

Prather, M. D., Lavenex, P., Mauldin-Jourdain, M. L., Mason, W. A., Capitanio, J. P., Mendoza, S. P., et al. (2001). Increased social fear and decreased fear of objects in monkeys with neonatal amygdala lesions. *Neuroscience, 106*(4), 653–658.

Price, J. L., Carmichael, S. T., & Drevets, W. C. (1996). Networks related to the orbital and medial prefrontal cortex; a substrate for emotional behavior? *Progress in Brain Research, 107,* 523–536.

Puce, A., Allison, T., Gore, J. C., & McCarthy, G. (1995). Face-sensitive regions in human extrastriate cortex studied by functional MRI. *Journal of Neurophysiology, 74,* 1192–1199.

Ringo, J. L. (1991). Neuronal interconnection as a function of brain size. *Brain, Behavior, and Evolution, 38,* 1–6.

Rizzolatti, G., & Craighero, L. (2004). The mirror-neuron system. *Annual Review of Neuroscience, 27,* 169–192.

Robins, D. L., Hunyadi, E. T., & Schultz, R. T. (2004, May). *Unique brain activations to integration of audio-visual emotional cues.* Paper presented at the 3rd annual meeting of the International Meeting for Autism Research (IMFAR), Sacramento, CA.

Rutter, M. (2000). Genetic studies of autism: From the 1970s into the millennium. *Journal of Abnormal Child Psychology, 28,* 3–14.

Saunders, R. C., Kolachana, B. S., Bachevalier, J., & Weinberger, D. R. (1998). Neonatal lesions of the medial temporal lobe disrupt prefrontal cortical regulation of striatal dopamine. *Nature, 393,* 169–171.

Schultz, R. T. (2004). *Functional brain imaging in autism.* Paper presented at the annual CPEA/STAART meeting, Bethesda, Maryland.

Schultz, R. T. (in press). Developmental deficits in social perception in autism: The role of the amygdala and fusiform face area. *International Journal of Developmental Neuroscience.*

Schultz, R. T., Gauthier, I., Klin A., Fulbright, R., Anderson, A., Volkmar, F., et al. (2000). Abnormal ventral temporal cortical activity during face discrimination among individuals with autism and Asperger's syndrome. *Archives of General Psychiatry, 57,* 331–340.

Schultz, R. T., Grelotti, D. J., Hunyadi, E., Herrington, J. B., Klin, A., Klaiman, C., et al. (under review). *Toward an understanding of fusiform face area activation in autism spectrum conditions.*

Schultz, R. T., Grelotti, D. J., Klin, A., Kleinman, J., Van der Gaag, C., Marois, R., et al. (2003). The role of the fusiform face area in social cognition: Implications for the pathobiology of autism. *Philosophical Transactions of the Royal Society, Series, B., 358,* 415–427.

Schultz, R. T., Klin, A., Grelotti, D. J., Herrington, J., & Volkmar, F. (2003, October). *fMRI studies of the fusiform face area in autism spectrum disorders.* Paper presented at the annual meeting of the Society for Psychophysical Research, Chicago, IL.

Schultz, R. T., Romanski, L., & Tsatsanis, K. (2000). Neurofunctional models of autistic disorder and Asperger's syndrome: Clues from neuroimaging. In A. Klin, F. R. Volkmar, & S. S. Sparrow (Eds.), *Asperger's syndrome* (pp. 179–209). New York: Plenum Press.

Schultz, R. T., Win, L., Jackowski, A., Klin, A., Staib, L., Papademetris, X., et al. (in preparation). *Brain morphology in autism spectrum disorders: An MRI study.*

Schumann, C. M., Hamstra, J., Goodlin-Jones, B. L., Lotspeich, L. J., Kwon, H., Buonocore, M. H., et al. (2004). The amygdala is enlarged in children, but not adolescents, with autism; the hippocampus is enlarged at all ages. *Journal of Neuroscience, 24,* 6392–6401.

Snow, M. E., Hertzig, M. E., & Shapiro, T. (1987). Expression of emotion in young autistic children. *Journal of the American Academy of Child and Adolescent Psychiatry, 26,* 836–838.

Stone, V. E., Baron-Cohen, S., & Knight, R. T. (1998). Frontal lobe contributions to theory of mind. *Journal of Cognitive Neuroscience, 10*(5), 640–656.

Stone, V. E., Baron-Cohen, S., Young, A. W., Calder, A. J., & Keane, J. (2003). Acquired theory of mind impairments in patients with bilateral amygdala lesions. *Neuropsychologia, 41,* 209–220.

Sweeten, T. L., Posey, D. J., Shekhar, A., & McDougle, C. J. (2002). The amygdala and related structures in the pathophysiology of autism. *Pharmacology, Biochemistry and Behavior, 71,* 449–455.

Tantam, D., Monaghan, L., Nicholson, H., & Stirling, J. (1989). Autistic children's ability to interpret faces: A research note. *Journal of Child Psychology and Psychiatry, 30,* 623–630.

Turkeltaub, P. E., Flowers, L., Verbalis, A., Miranda, M., Gareau, L., & Eden, G. F. (2004). The neural basis of hyperlexic reading: An fMRI Case Study. *Neuron, 41,* 11–25.

Veenstra-VanderWeele, J., Christian, S. L., & Cook, E. H. (2004). Autism as a paradigmatic complex genetic disorder. *Annual Review of Genomics and Human Genetics, 5,* 379–405.

Vuilleumier, P., Richardson, M. P., Armony, J. L., Driver, J., & Dolan, R. J. (2004). Distant influences of amygdala lesion on visual cortical activation during emotional face processing. *Nature Neuroscience, 7*(11), 1271–1278.

Waiter, G. D., Williams, J. H., Murray, A. D., Gilchrist, A., Perrett, D. I., & Whiten, A.

(2004). A voxel-based investigation of brain structure in male adolescents with autistic spectrum disorder. *Neuroimage, 22*(2), 619–625.

Wang, T. A., Dapretto, M., Hariri, A. R., Sigman, M., & Bookheimer, S. Y. (2004). Neural correlates of facial affect processing in children and adolescents with autism spectrum disorder. *Journal of the American Academy of Child and Adolescent Psychiatry, 43*(4), 481–490.

Weeks, S., & Hobson, R. (1987). The salience of facial expression for autistic children. *Journal of Child Psychology and Psychiatry, 28,* 137–151.

Yirmiya, N., Sigman, M. D., Kasari, C., & Mundy, P. (1992). Empathy and cognition in high-functioning children with autism. *Child Development, 63,* 150–160.

Yonan, A. L., Palmer, A. A., Smith, K. C., Feldman, I., Lee, H. K., Yonan, J., et al. (2003). Bioinformatic analysis of autism positional candidate genes using biological databases and computational gene network prediction. *Genes, Brain, and Behavior, 2,* 303–320.

Yovel, G., & Kanwisher, N. (2004). Face perception: Domain specific, not process specific. *Neuron, 44*(5), 889–898.

CHAPTER 20

Medical Aspects of Autism

PAULINE A. FILIPEK

It is now unequivocal that neurobiological dysfunction is causative in autism. Although a number of disorders have been potentially associated with autism, the extent and nature of these associations have traditionally been the subject of much debate (Rutter, 1996). Wing and Gould (1979) found relatively lower rates of known medical problems in their autistic sample relative to nonautistic subjects (17% versus 71%, respectively). Further, disorders such as phenylketonuria (PKU) and tuberous sclerosis were found only in the nonautistic group. Tuchman, Rapin, and Shinnar (1991) compared groups of children with autism to those with developmental language disorder and found similar rates of medical conditions, about 5%, across groups. Similarly, Fombonne and du Mazaubrun (1992) noted that autistic children and those with special educational needs did not differ in the frequency of most medical conditions, including congenital rubella or chromosomal abnormalities. Of note, the autistic group was significantly less likely to have Down syndrome or cerebral palsy, and all cases of neurofibromatosis and PKU were found in the nonautistic group.

In a series of studies, Bolton et al. (1991) and Rutter, Bailey, Bolton, and Le Couteur (1993) conducted extensive evaluations on 151 individuals with autism and found that 8.1% of these cases showed medical conditions that were

likely to be causal factors of autism, including fragile X syndrome (FXS), bilateral deafness, cerebral palsy, multiple congenital abnormalities, and chromosomal anomalies. About 3.8% had other medical concerns that were considered less likely to be etiologic factors. The overall rate of medical conditions, 11.9%, is similar to the rate found in a study of medical conditions in twins with autism (12.9%; A. Bailey et al., 1991). Although some found that IQ is not related to medical risk (Steffenburg, 1991), others found more medical conditions among autistic persons at lower IQ levels. For example, in an epidemiologic study of autism, Ritvo et al. (1990) demonstrated that medical conditions were more frequent in persons with severe mental retardation, which is consistent with other reports (Rutter, Bailey, Bolton, & Le Couteur, 1994; Wing & Gould, 1979). The possibility of finding any associated medical condition rises with increasing degrees of mental retardation—approaching 50% among persons at the severe and profound levels of cognitive dysfunction (Scott, 1994). More recent studies corroborate the findings of these earlier studies (Barton & Volkmar, 1998; Challman, Barbaresi, Katusic, & Weaver, 2003; Fombonne, du Mazaubrun, Cans, & Grandjean, 1997; C. Gillberg & Billstedt, 2000; Kielinen, Rantala, Timonen, Linna, & Moilanen, 2004; Lauritsen, Mors, Mortensen, & Ewald, 2002;

This work was funded by grants from the National Institutes of Health, Bethesda, MD (RO1 HD 26554, PO1 HD 35458, and RO1 NS 35896) and from the Children and Families Commission of Orange County, CA. The author wishes to specifically thank Joseph H. Donnelly, MD; Jenifer Juranek, PhD; J. Jay Gargus, MD, PhD; Teri M. Book, MSN, CPNP; and Laurie Ann Lennon, MS-CCC, for their insightful reviews and comments. This chapter is dedicated to the memory of Doris A. Allen, EdD.

Shevell, Majnemer, Rosenbaum, & Abraham-owicz, 2001; Skjeldal, Sponheim, Ganes, Jellum, & Bakke, 1998).

In summary, traditional studies have found variable rates of medical conditions in autism, ranging from 5% to 33%. The first edition of this text (1987) reviewed associated medical conditions in the chapter titled, "Neurologic Functioning" (pp. 133–147). The accompanying table (p. 138) listed almost 40 disorders that had been reported in only "one or more" (p. 137) cases of autism, but the text detailed, very briefly, less than a dozen of these, including then-newly described Rett syndrome (Hagberg, Aicardi, Dias, & Ramos, 1983). In contrast, the second edition (1997) included a chapter dedicated to associated medical conditions (pp. 388–407), which selectively focused on only four syndromes, two commonly co-occurring with autism (FXS and tuberous sclerosis complex [TSC]) and two with seemingly uncommon associations with autism (Down and Williams syndromes).

AUTISM AND MEDICAL CONDITIONS: VIEWING THE RELATIONSHIP FROM BOTH SIDES OF A SEMANTIC COIN

It would appear, at first glance, that this corresponding chapter in this third edition could be titled either "Medical Conditions Associated with Autism" or "Autism Associated with Medical Conditions." *Medical conditions* can refer either to broader classes of medical signs and symptoms or to specific disorders and syndromes. Additionally, the term *medical condition* does not specify the presumed population under study, for example, a cohort with a specific medical disorder or a cohort with autism. The premise traditionally used for significant "associated medical conditions" has been of *specific disorders or syndromes* occurring *within populations of autistic individuals.*

Since the first edition was published in 1987, a wealth of information about autism has emerged, much of it initially anecdotal (e.g., case reports) but increasingly empirical. Concurrently, the concept of autism is evolving from the singular *autistic disorder* into the pleural *autistic spectrum disorders* (ASDs). As a result of this ongoing ontogeny, in tandem with rapid genetic progress, more and more disorders and syndromes are now recognized to be behaviorally on the autistic spectrum. As specific genotypes are identified within the spectrum of autism and related conditions, it is likely that many, if not most, cases will be related to a specific medical (genetic) disorder or syndrome.

The original chapter title, "Medical Conditions Associated with Autism," must now be revised to include both vantage points. It has therefore been updated to "Medical Aspects of Autism" and is addressed as two, now complementary, topics: (1) medical signs and symptoms in children presenting with autism and (2) comorbid autism in children presenting with specific disorders or syndromes.

This seemingly unconventional approach incorporates presumably rarer disorders whose prevalence may be marginal within an autistic population; for example, many children presenting with TSC are autistic, but few children presenting with autism have comorbid TSC. Particularly in medical settings where experience with ASDs is less common, there has been a tendency for medical specialists to focus less on behavior and more on specific signs and symptoms. As a result, many children with the classic hallmarks of autism in addition to their other medical diagnoses may not be correctly diagnosed and thereby served. For example, Howlin, Wing, and Gould (1995) eloquently championed the importance of recognizing autism specifically in children with Down syndrome. Although autism diagnoses are typically made in the preschool years, they noted much later ages of autistic diagnoses in Down syndrome cases, as well as in all cases of Down reported in the literature (range from 7 years to adulthood). This "diagnostic overshadowing" of sorts creates unnecessary stress for families and prevents them from using supports and interventions available to families with an autistic child. Even though most of the following disorders and syndromes are uncommon in samples of individuals with autism, they should always be considered in the range of diagnostic possibilities.

This chapter begins with a brief outline of the appropriate medical evaluation for individuals with an ASD, then discusses the medical symptoms commonly seen in autism and the specific disorders presenting with an autistic behavioral phenotype. A resource list for parents and professionals is provided at the end of the chapter.

THE MEDICAL EVALUATION IN AUTISM*

The medical evaluation in autism consists of a careful physical and neurologic examination with selected laboratory testing.

Physical and Neurologic Examination

The *head circumference* in autistic children is larger than is found in typically developing children (Aylward, Minshew, Field, Sparks, & Singh, 2002; A. Bailey et al., 1995; Bolton et al., 1994; Courchesne, Carper, & Akshoomoff, 2003; Davidovitch, Patterson, & Gartside, 1996; Fidler, Bailey, & Smalley, 2000; Fombonne, Roge, Claverie, Courty, & Fremolle, 1999; Ghaziuddin, Zaccagnini, Tsai, & Elardo, 1999; C. Gillberg & de Souza, 2002; Lainhart et al., 1997; Miles, Hadden, Takahashi, & Hillman, 2000; Woodhouse et al., 1996). The same has been noted with postmortem brain weights (A. Bailey et al., 1993, 1998; Bauman, 1992, 1996; Bauman & Kemper, 1994, 1997). Only a small proportion of autistic children have frank macrocephaly/megalencephaly, but the distribution of the measures is clearly shifted upward with the large majority falling above the 50 percentile with the mean approximately at the 75 percentile (A. Bailey et al., 1995; Bolton et al., 1994; Courchesne et al., 2003; Davidovitch et al., 1996; Filipek, Richelme, et al., 1992; Lainhart, 2003; Lainhart et al., 1997; Rapin, 1996b; Woodhouse et al., 1996). Some investigators have noted that the large head circumference correlates with higher IQ (Filipek, Richelme, et al., 1992; Miles et al., 2000). The large head circumference is not necessarily present at birth but may appear in early to mid-childhood with increased rates of growth (Lainhart et al., 1997; Mason-Brothers et al., 1987; Mason-Brothers et al., 1990). It also appears that the head circumference is normal by adolescence and adulthood (Aylward et al., 2002), as is postmortem brain

weight by adulthood (Bauman & Kemper, 1997). *This phenomenon of large head size in autistic children is readily acknowledged, and barring lateralizing signs on the remainder of the examination, routine neuroimaging work-up for the finding of a large head alone in autism is not warranted.* Several reports also show a higher prevalence of microcephaly in autism, which is associated with abnormal physical morphology, medical disorders, lower IQ, and seizures (e.g., Fombonne et al., 1999; Miles et al., 2000).

Sensorimotor function is commonly problematic in autistic individuals and most severe in those with lower cognitive function (Noterdaeme, Mildenberger, Minow, & Amorosa, 2002; Rapin, 1996b; S. J. Rogers, Bennetto, McEvoy, & Pennington, 1996). Sensory issues are very common, particularly sensory seeking, oral sensitivity, and low endurance (Baranek, 1999; Baranek, Foster, & Berkson, 1997; Bernabei, Fenton, Fabrizi, Camaioni, & Perucchini, 2003; Watling, Deitz, & White, 2001). Sensory-processing abilities are aberrant in 42% to 88% of autistic individuals and include preoccupation with sensory features of objects, over- or under-responsiveness to environmental stimuli, or paradoxical responses to sensory stimuli (Kientz & Dunn, 1997). Hypotonia was noted in about 25% of 176 autistic children and in 33% of 110 nonautistic mentally retarded children, while spasticity was found in less than 5% of either group (exclusionary criteria for this sample included the presence of lateralizing gross motor findings; Rapin, 1996b). Motor apraxia was noted in almost 30% of autistic children with normal cognitive function, in 75% of retarded autistic children, and in 56% of a nonautistic retarded control group (Mari, Castiello, Marks, Marraffa, & Prior, 2003; Rapin, 1996b; J. H. Williams, Whiten, & Singh, 2004). The presence of *observed* motor stereotypies was noted in over 40% of autistic children (in contrast to a much higher prevalence by parental report) and in over 60% of those with low IQ, but in only 13% of the nonautistic control group (Rapin, 1996b). Hand or finger mannerisms, body rocking, or unusual posturing is reported

---

* Portions of this section are taken with permission from Filipek et al. (1999, 2000).

in 37% to 95% of individuals and often manifests during the preschool years (Lord, 1995; Rapin, 1996b; S. J. Rogers et al., 1996).

In a large longitudinal study of autistic children, over 6% also had a sibling with autism (Rapin, 1996a). The overall *recurrence risk estimate* for ideopathic autism—the percent chance that a younger sibling will also develop the disorder—varies from about 3% to 7% (A. Bailey, Phillips, & Rutter, 1996; Bolton et al., 1994; Piven et al., 1990; Ritvo, Jorde, et al., 1989; Smalley, Asarnow, & Spence, 1989). However, there are gender differences to this risk estimate: If the first autistic child is male, the recurrence risk estimate ranges from about 4% to 7%, but if female, the recurrence risk estimate ranges from 7% to 14.5% (Jorde et al., 1991; Ritvo, Jorde, et al., 1989). The risk of having a second autistic child, therefore, is approximately 50-fold higher than in the general population. These risk estimates are based on the older prevalence rates of approximately 4 per 10,000 and, therefore, cannot reflect the fact that many families choose not to have more natural children subsequent to receiving a diagnosis of autism. Regardless, it is the physician's responsibility to inform parents of this recurrence risk when a child is diagnosed with autism.

Definitive Hearing Test

Every child presenting with a receptive language deficit should receive a definitive hearing test. Audiologic assessment should occur early in the differential diagnostic process and use a battery of tests including behavioral audiometric measures, assessment of middle ear function, and electrophysiologic procedures (American Speech-Language-Hearing Association, 1991). If audiology cannot be performed adequately, brainstem-evoked responses should be performed (Filipek, Accardo, et al., 2000; Filipek et al., 1999).

Lead Level

Children with developmental delays who spend an extended period in the oral-motor stage of play (where everything goes into their mouths) are at increased risk for lead toxicity, especially in certain environments. The prevalence of pica in this group can result in high rates of substantial and often recurrent exposure to lead and, possibly, other metals (Shannon & Graef, 1997). Several studies report the neurobehavioral effects and behavioral toxicity of lead and its potential clinical relevance in patients with autism. Mean blood lead concentration was notably higher in 18 children with autism than in 16 nonautistic children or in 10 normal siblings; 44% of the autistic and psychotic children had blood lead levels greater than two standard deviations above the mean for normal controls (Cohen, Johnson, & Caparulo, 1976). In three of six reported cases of lead poisoning in children with autism, developmental deviance seemed to have been present before the possible impact of lead toxicity, while in two, the lead poisoning may have contributed to the onset or acceleration of developmental symptomatology (Accardo, Whitman, Caul, & Rolfe, 1988). A more recent chart review found that 17 children with autism were treated for plumbism over a 6-year period from 1987 to 1992. When compared with a randomly selected group of 30 children without autism who were treated during the same interval, the children with autism were significantly older at diagnosis and had a longer period of elevated blood lead levels during treatment; 75% were subsequently reexposed despite close monitoring, environmental inspection, and either lead hazard reduction or alternative housing (Shannon & Graef, 1997). Therefore, all children with delays or who are at risk for autism should have a periodic lead screen until the pica disappears (Centers for Disease Control and Prevention, 1997; Shannon & Graef, 1997).

Karyotype and DNA Analysis for Fragile X

The newer cytogenetic methods of karyotyping and molecular analyses for FXS and the implications of a cytogenetic or molecular diagnosis for other family members justify their routine inclusion in the diagnostic evaluation of a child with autism (American College of Medical Genetics: Policy Statement, 1994; A. Bailey, 1994; Bauer, 1995; Dykens & Volkmar, 1997; Rutter, Bailey, Simonoff, & Pickles, 1997; Rutter et al., 1994; Schaefer & Bodensteiner, 1992).

Metabolic Testing

A wide range of biochemical determinations have been performed in urine, blood, and cerebrospinal fluid in an attempt to identify a specific metabolic abnormality in individuals with autism. Included are studies of inborn errors in amino acid, carbohydrate, purine, peptide, and mitochondrial metabolism, as well as toxicological studies. The reported co-occurrence of autistic-like symptoms in individuals with inborn errors of metabolism has led to consideration of screening tests as part of the routine assessment of patients with severe developmental impairment (Steffenburg, 1991). However, the percentage of children with autism who prove to have an identifiable metabolic disorder is probably less than 5% (Dykens & Volkmar, 1997; Rutter et al., 1994, 1997). Most of the biochemical analyses are useful at present *only as research tools* in the ongoing effort to understand the biology of autism.

Metabolic testing or consultation clearly is indicated by a history of lethargy, cyclic vomiting, early seizures, dysmorphic or coarse features, mental retardation, or, if mental retardation cannot be excluded, questionable newborn screening or birth out of the United States because of the potential absence of newborn screening and maternal public health measures. As recommended by the American College of Medical Genetics, selective metabolic testing should be initiated only in the presence of suggestive clinical and physical findings (Curry et al., 1997). However, as described later in the section titled Mitochondrial Disorders, recent findings may ultimately lead to future recommendations for screenings of lactate, pyruvate, ammonia, and free and total carnitine (Filipek, Juranek, Nguyen, Cummings, & Gargus, in press).

Electroencephalography

The association among electroencephalogram (EEG) abnormalities, seizures, and developmental regression is described in Chapter 18 (this *Handbook,* this volume). An adequate EEG should be performed *with prolonged sleep to Stages III and IV* in any child who presents with suspicion of developmental regression (Dykens & Volkmar, 1997; Tuchman, 1995; Tuchman & Rapin, 1997; Tuchman, Rapin, &

Shinnar, 1991). However, some neurologists are routinely performing sleep EEGs on autistic children at diagnosis and are finding subtle abnormalities in many, often localized to the temporal lobes. It is unclear whether the children with the abnormalities are those who would eventually develop clinical seizures, and these findings along with the potential benefits of valproate therapy need to be systematically evaluated.

Neuroimaging Studies

A review of the many neuroimaging reports in autism noted a very low prevalence of focal lesions or other abnormalities, none of which localized consistently to be more than coincidental findings (Filipek, Kennedy, & Caviness, 1992). In a subsequent study using magnetic resonance imaging (MRI), the prevalence of lesions in autistic children was equal to that in the normal control volunteers (Filipek, Richelme, et al., 1992). However, cortical migration malformations have been reported on MRI in *a small number of* high-functioning autistic or Asperger subjects, including polymicrogyria, schizencephaly, and macrogyria, without collective preference for a particular lobe or hemisphere (Berthier, 1994; Berthier, Starkstein, & Leiguarda, 1990; Piven et al., 1990). It is unclear whether these findings of cortical dysplasias are more prevalent in autism than is currently recognized, as another study of 63 developmentally disabled children did not note dysplasias (Filipek, Richelme, et al., 1992). Regardless, unless lateralized findings are present on neurological examination, conventional clinical computed tomography (CT) or MRI scans are not indicated in the routine diagnostic evaluation of autism or any of the developmental disorders. Positron emission tomography (PET) and single photon emission computerized tomography (SPECT) are presently used only as research tools and are not indicated in the diagnostic evaluation of autism.

Tests of Unproven Value

There is inadequate evidence to support routine clinical testing of individuals with autism for hair analysis for trace elements (Gentile, Trentalange, Zamichek, & Coleman, 1983;

Shearer, Larson, Neuschwander, & Gedney, 1982; Wecker, Miller, Cochran, Dugger, & Johnson, 1985), celiac antibodies (Pavone, Fiumara, Bottaro, Mazzone, & Coleman, 1997), allergies (in particular, food allergies for gluten, casein, candida and other molds; Lucarelli et al., 1995), immunological or neurochemical abnormalities (Cook, Perry, Dawson, Wainwright, & Leventhal, 1993; Singh, Warren, Averett, & Ghaziuddin, 1997; Yuwiler et al., 1992), micronutrients such as vitamin levels (Findling et al., 1997; LaPerchia, 1987; Tolbert, Haigler, Waits, & Dennis, 1993), intestinal permeability studies (D'Eufemia et al., 1996), stool analysis, urinary peptides (Le Couteur, Trygstad, Evered, Gillberg, & Rutter, 1988), thyroid function (Cohen, Young, Lowe, & Harcherik, 1980; T. Hashimoto et al., 1991), or erythrocyte glutathione peroxidase (Michelson, 1998).

MEDICAL SIGNS AND SYMPTOMS ASSOCIATED WITH AUTISM

The more common signs and symptoms associated with autism include perinatal factors, hearing loss, food and gastrointestinal problems, immunologic abnormalities and sleep disorders.

Perinatal Factors

Early studies indicated that autism may be associated with increased but mild obstetrical risk factors (Bryson, Smith, & Eastwood, 1988; Deykin & MacMahon, 1980; Finegan & Quarrington, 1979; Folstein & Rutter, 1977a, 1977b; C. Gillberg & Gillberg, 1983; Levy, Zoltak, & Saelens, 1988; Lord, Mulloy, Wendelboe, & Schopler, 1991; Mason-Brothers et al., 1987, 1990; Nelson, 1991; Piven et al., 1993; Tsai, 1987). However, the strong influence of maternal parity/reproductive stoppage accounted for differences in at least two of these studies (Lord et al., 1991; Piven et al., 1993) and was not necessarily appropriately considered in the others. Subsequently, Zambrino, Balottin, Bettaglio, Gerardo, and Lanzi (1995) found that the obstetrical optimality score was lower only in those autistic children with central nervous system (CNS) damage; and Bolton, Murphy, Macdonald, Whitlock, Pickles, et al. (1997) noted an increase of only

mild obstetrical complications independent of maternal age or parity, which makes a causal relationship unlikely. Specifically, no associations were found between autism and maternal factors, such as vaginal bleeding, infection, diabetes, toxemia, use of pitocin, age, or prior abortions (Bolton, Murphy, Macdonald, Whitlock, Pickles, et al., 1997; Cryan, Byrne, O'Donovan, & O'Callaghan, 1996; Fein et al., 1997; Gale, Ozonoff, & Lainhart, 2003; Ghaziuddin, Shakal, & Tsai, 1995; Piven et al., 1993; Rapin, 1996a). There were also no associations noted between autism and gestational age, forceps or caesarian delivery, neonatal depression, need for intensive care or mechanical ventilation, neonatal seizures, or prolonged neonatal hospitalization (Bolton, Murphy, Macdonald, & Whitlock, 1997; Piven et al., 1993; Rapin, 1996a).

More recent studies simply add more conflicting data to the debate. Juul-Dam, Townsend, and Courchesne (2001) noted that their autism cohort had a higher incidence of uterine bleeding, a lower incidence of maternal vaginal infection, and less maternal use of contraceptives when compared with the general population; the pervasive developmental disorder–not otherwise specified (PDD-NOS) cohort showed a higher incidence of hyperbilirubinemia. The authors concluded that interpretation of these data "is difficult, as the specific complications with the highest risk of autism represented various forms of pathologic processes with no presently apparent unifying feature" (p. E63). Wilkerson, Volpe, Dean, and Titus (2002) noted that different perinatal factors and maternal medical conditions contributed to the risk of autism: prescriptions during pregnancy, length of labor, viral infection, abnormal presentation at delivery, low birthweight, maternal urinary infection, high temperatures, and depression. In a population study in Sweden, Hultman, Sparen, and Cnattingius (2002) reported yet additional factors as being associated with the risk of autism: daily cigarette smoking, maternal birth outside Europe or North America, caesarean delivery, being small for gestational age, Apgar scores below 7, and congenital malformations. In contrast, Klug, Burd, Kerbeshian, Benz, and Martsolf (2003) examined parental, prenatal, and perinatal risk factors and found that the cohort with autism was quantitatively less influenced by 15 specific risk markers than were fetal alcohol and sudden infant death syndromes; only low-magnitude risk markers (low birthweight, child malformations, and low level of maternal education) were mildly but significantly elevated for autism, producing odds ratios of less than 2.4. Again, differing diagnostic methods for autism and differing risk factor assessments can account for at least some of the discrepancies noted.

Only one report has examined the incidence of autism in survivors of neonatal intensive care units (NICU; Matsuishi et al., 1999). In this study, 90% of almost 6,000 NICU survivors born between 1983 and 1987 were followed neurodevelopmentally at 2 to 3 and 5 years of age. Eighteen were diagnosed with *Diagnostic and Statistical Manual of Mental Disorders,* third edition, revised (*DSM-III-R;* American Psychiatric Association, 1987) autistic disorder. The only risk factor identified of the 28 factors examined was meconium aspiration syndrome. The mean incidence for autism in the NICU survivors was 34 per 10,000, which is more than twice that found in two previous studies in the same geographic region in Japan (Matsuishi et al., 1987; Ohtaki et al., 1992). However, note that these referenced epidemiological studies were performed more than 15 years ago, during the same time frame as those performed by Ritvo, Freeman, et al. (1989) and do not reflect current prevalence rates.

Hearing Loss

Many children diagnosed with autism are first described by parents as acting "as if deaf." However, the vast majority of children with autism are found to have normal hearing function. Rosenhall, Nordin, Sandstrom, Ahlsen, and Gillberg (1999) performed audiological evaluations on 199 children and adolescents with autism and found that pronounced to profound bilateral hearing loss or deafness was present in 3.5% of all cases, a prevalence greater than that seen in the general population but similar to that seen in individuals with mental retardation. However, the rate of hearing loss in this study was equivalent across all levels of cognitive functioning. In contrast, hyperacusis was commonly found and affected almost 20% of the autistic sample. As recom-

mended by the practice parameters for screening and diagnosing autism (Filipek, Accardo, et al., 2000; Filipek et al., 1999), audiological evaluations or evoked potentials should be performed on all children with autism so that, if indicated, appropriate referrals can be made for aural habilitation.

Feeding Disturbances and Gastrointestinal Problems

Feeding habits and food preferences of children with autism are traditionally unconventional and were even at one time considered as part of the diagnostic indicators (Ahearn, Castine, Nault, & Green, 2001; Ritvo & Freeman, 1978). However, this specific aspect of the constellation of atypical behaviors has not received much formal study. Ahearn et al. (2001) studied 30 children with autism using the procedures developed by Munk and Repp (1994) for classifying feeding problems in the developmentally disabled. Just over half of the sample lived at home with their parents, the remainder lived in community group homes for the disabled, and all attended the same private educational and treatment program. More than half showed low levels of food acceptance, with 13% refusing all foods presented to them. However, the authors acknowledged caution in interpreting these results, as there were no comparison groups of either typically developing children or those with other developmental disabilities. Field, Garland, and Williams (2003) also noted food selectivity by type (62%) and by texture (31%); all three children with food refusal (12%) also had gastroesophageal reflux. Food selectivity "by type" was significantly higher for children with autism, and food refusal and oral motor problems were significantly lower than found in children with other developmental disorders. Bowers (2002) performed an audit of referrals of autistic children to a dietetic service over a 3-month period and found that, despite selective food preferences in 46%, the majority of children had intakes that met or exceeded dietary reference values.

Although there have been reports of gastrointestinal (GI) complaints in children with autism dating back more than 30 years (e.g., Goodwin, Cowen, & Goodwin, 1971; Walker-Smith & Andrews, 1972), such problems have become a significant focus of study in recent years. Lightdale, Siegel, and Heyman (2001) surveyed 500 parents of autistic children; almost 50% reported loose stools or frequent diarrhea. In an epidemiologic study, Fombonne and Chakrabarti (2001) found that 19% of children with autism reported GI symptoms, with constipation identified in 9%. Molloy and Manning-Courtney (2003) found that, of 137 children with autism diagnosed with the Autism Diagnostic Observation Schedule-Generic (ADOS-G; Lord et al., 2000), 24% had a history of at least one chronic GI symptom and 17% had diarrhea; they found no association between GI symptoms and autistic regression.

Some reports from gastroenterologists have stated that GI symptoms occur in 46% to 84% of children with autism (Horvath, Papadimitriou, Rabsztyn, Drachenberg, & Tildon, 1999; Horvath & Perman, 2002a, 2002b). However, in these studies, most of the autistic samples had been referred to the gastroenterologists for preexisting GI complaints, thus limiting the generalizability of the data. Afzal et al. (2003) noted moderate or severe constipation to be more frequent in the autistic group referred for GI symptoms than in control subjects with abdominal pain (36% versus 10%); over 50% had moderate to severe recto-sigmoid loading than did controls (24%). Milk consumption was the strongest predictor of constipation in the autistic group; stool frequency, gluten consumption, soiling, and abdominal pain were *not* predictive of constipation.

Sandler et al. (2000) hypothesized that, in children with "regressive"-onset autism who had antecedent antibiotic exposure followed by diarrhea, endogenous intestinal microflora might be disrupted by neurotoxin-producing bacteria. Eleven children received a trial of vancomycin, leading to only short-term improvement of autistic symptomatology in 8 of the 10 children. There was no control group in this study, and the raters were *not* blinded as to the hypotheses being tested. Finegold et al. (2002) went on to investigate intestinal microflora and found a higher prevalence of clostridia in the stools of children with autism than in control children, all of whom were presumably referred for GI procedures.

Kuddo and Nelson (2003) reviewed the literature and noted that the frequency of GI symptoms in autistic children is not as common as the GI literature might suggest. Taylor et al. (2002) noted an 8% rate of chronic constipation, which is similar to that estimated for the general childhood population (Loening-Baucke, 1998). Black, Kaye, and Jick (2002) performed a nested case-control study in the United Kingdom and found that both 9% of children with autism and 9% of children without autism had a history of GI complaints, producing an odds ratio of 1.0 (no effect) for autism with GI complaints. Peltola et al. (1998) also noted no association of ASD and GI symptoms over a 14-year period in Finland. DeFelice et al. (2003) found no relationship between autism and GI immune dysregulation by investigating intestinal cytokines; in fact, intestinal levels of interleukin (IL)-6 and IL-8 were lower in patients with ASD than in age-matched controls. Whiteley (2004, p. 9) also noted that "only a minority" of participants with autism in their study showed some bowel problems.

A. J. Wakefield et al. (1998) first reported an apparent link among GI disease, developmental regression, and the measles-mumps-rubella (MMR) vaccine *in 10 autistic children*. These authors published over a dozen additional studies apparently supporting their initial report (Ashwood et al., 2003; Furlano et al., 2001; Kawashima et al., 2000; O'Leary, Uhlmann, & Wakefield, 2000; Torrente et al., 2002; A. J. Wakefield, 1999, 2002, 2003; A. J. Wakefield & Montgomery, 1999; A. J. Wakefield et al., 2000, 2002; J. Wakefield, 2002). While the ensuing international controversy and the direct effect of these studies on the drop in the rates of immunization of children is beyond the scope of this chapter, it should be noted that the majority of these authors have recently retracted their initial interpretation that there is a causal connection between the onset of autistic symptoms and the MMR vaccine (Murch et al., 2004).

It was of great interest when a case series claimed that three autistic patients with GI complaints had dramatic improvement in the core symptoms of autism after receiving the hormone secretin as part of a diagnostic endoscopy (Horvath et al., 1998; Larsen, 1998). Subjective improvement was noticed, particularly in areas of eye contact, alertness, and language capacities. Subsequently, 15 empiric studies were performed and found no positive effects of either porcine or human recombinant secretin on autistic symptomatology (Carey et al., 2002; Chez et al., 2000; Coniglio et al., 2001; Corbett et al., 2001; Dunn-Geier et al., 2000; Kern, Van Miller, Evans, & Trivedi, 2002; Levy et al., 2003; Lightdale, Hayer, et al., 2001; Molloy et al., 2002; Owley et al., 2001; Roberts et al., 2001; Robinson, 2001; Sponheim, Oftedal, & Helverschou, 2002; Unis et al., 2002); in fact, in one study, autistic symptoms worsened (Robinson, 2001).

Immune Factors

Interest in the potential relationship between the immune system and autism arises given the various cases reported in which infections (and possibly altered immune response) are associated with the development of autism (Marchetti, Scifo, Batticane, & Scapagnini, 1990; Menage et al., 1992; Singh, Warren, Odell, Warren, & Cole, 1993; Warren, Margaretten, Pace, & Foster, 1986). However, the few studies conducted have yielded inconsistent or contradictory findings and are discussed in recent review articles (Hornig & Lipkin, 2001; Korvatska, Van de Water, Anders, & Gershwin, 2002; Krause, He, Gershwin, & Shoenfeld, 2002).

Sleep Disturbances

Sleep disturbances have been a recognized feature of autism for over 25 years, particularly abnormalities in sleep-wake cycles (Hoshino, Watanabe, Yashima, Kaneko, & Kumashiro, 1984; Inanuma, 1984; Ornitz, 1985; Tanguay, Ornitz, Forsythe, & Ritvo, 1976; see also Didde & Sigafoos, 2001; Richdale, 1999; and Stores & Wiggs, 1998, for reviews). Studies find that the majority of children with autism have sleep problems, often severe, and usually involving extreme sleep latencies, lengthy nighttime awakenings, shortened night sleep, and early morning awakenings (Honomichl, Goodlin-Jones, Burnham, Gaylor, & Anders, 2002; Patzold, Richdale, & Tonge, 1998; Richdale & Prior, 1995; Schreck & Mulick, 2000; Wiggs & Stores, 2004). Children with autism also have more unusual and obligatory bedtime routines, for example, re-

quiring that parents hold them, lie down with them, or sit beside their bed; all family members go to bed at the same time; or curtains or bedclothes be positioned in a certain way. If these routines are not performed exactly, the result is usually a tantrum or other angry outburst. As might be expected, only the autistic children studied *always* followed their bedtime routine (Patzold et al., 1998), and the presence of sleep problems was significantly associated with parental stress (Richdale, Francis, Gavidia-Payne, & Cotton, 2000). Schreck, Mulick, and Smith (2004) suggested that both the quantity and quality of sleep per night predicted overall autism scores, as measured by the Gilliam Autism Rating Scale (GARS; Gilliam, 1995), social skills deficits, and stereotypic behaviors. According to Wiggs and Stores (1996), it is uncertain whether sleep disorders in children with autism cause daytime maladaptive behaviors, simply allow them to continue, or worsen preexisting problems.

Hering, Epstein, Elroy, Iancu, and Zelnik (1999) compared the results of parental questionnaires with electronic movement activity recordings (actigraphy) in three groups of children: Group 1: autistic children whose parents reported sleep difficulties, Group 2: autistic children whose parents did not report sleep difficulties, and Group 3: typically developing children. The initial questionnaires showed that 50% of children in Group 1 had sleep disorders versus only 20% in Group 2 and none in Group 3. When sleep was quantified using actigraphy, there were no differences in patterns of sleep between Groups 1 and 2 except for more early morning awakenings in Group 1. These findings support the need for objective study methodologies in these samples.

Diomedi et al. (1999) compared polysomnograph parameters in adult autistic individuals, who demonstrated a significant reduction of rapid eye movement (REM) sleep, increased interspersed wakefulness, and increased number of awakenings with reduction of sleep efficiency relative to normal controls (see Harvey & Kennedy, 2002, for a comprehensive review of polysomnography in autism and other developmental disabilities). Elia et al. (2000) noted that the total time in bed and total sleep time were significantly lower in autistic individuals, who also had a higher density of muscle twitches, which correlated with some psychological indices of autism from the Psychoeducational Profile-Revised (Schopler, Reichler, Bashford, Lansing, & Marcus, 1990) and the Childhood Autism Rating Scale (CARS; Schopler, Reichler, & Rochen-Renner, 1988).

Thirumalai, Shubin, and Robinson (2002) identified REM sleep behavior disorder in almost half of 11 autistic children studied. Usually seen in elderly males, the diagnostic criteria include movements of the body or limbs associated with dreaming (REM), potentially harmful sleep behavior, dreams that appear to be acted out, and sleep behavior that disrupts sleep continuity (American Sleep Disorders Association, 1997, pp. 177–180). Additional studies on this topic are needed because pharmacologic treatment may ameliorate some of the effects of this specific sleep disorder.

AUTISM ASSOCIATED WITH SPECIFIC DISORDERS OR SYNDROMES

Autism is now associated with many more specific disorders or syndromes than previously known, many more than the traditionally recognized tuberous sclerosis and fragile X syndrome (Table 20.1).

Tuberous Sclerosis Complex

TSC is a neurocutaneous disorder that affects as many as 1 in 6,000 to 10,000 individuals and is characterized by benign tumors (hamartomas) and nongrowing lesions (hamartias) in the brain and in many other organs such as the skin, kidneys, eyes, heart, and lungs (Curatolo, Verdecchia, & Bombardieri, 2002; Kandt, 2003). Depigmented macules (shaped like an ash leaf; Fitzpatrick, 1991) are usually the first sign of the disease, which are often visualized only with the use of an ultraviolet Wood light. Facial angiofibroma, formerly called adenoma sebaceum, and shagreen patches over the lower back are also characteristic but often do not appear until late childhood or early adolescence (Webb, Clarke, Fryer, & Osborne, 1996). The major intracerebral lesions are the tubers, which consist of histogenic malformations of both neuronal and glial elements with giant heterotopic cells, characteristically lo-

cated in the subependymal regions and in the cortex (Braffman & Naidich, 1994; Harrison & Bolton, 1997; Truhan & Filipek, 1993). These tumors are variably expressed, resulting in a phenotype that ranges from only mild skin manifestations to severe mental retardation and intractable epilepsy (Curatolo et al., 2002; Kandt, 2003; Short, Richardson, Haines, & Kwiatkowski, 1995). Between 50% and 60% of affected individuals are mentally retarded and 80% have seizures; those with mental retardation invariably have seizures (Gomez, Sampson, & Whittemore, 1999).

TSC is an autosomal dominant disorder caused by mutations in either of two genes: TSC1 on chromosome 9q34 producing hamartin and TCS2 on chromosome 16p13.3 producing tuberin (Curatolo et al., 2002; OMIM™, 2000). It has been puzzling that two separate genotypes could be associated with apparently identical phenotypes. It is now known that hamartin and tuberin must bind together into a protein complex to regulate mTOR (mammalian *t*arget *o*f *r*apamycin) in a critical signaling pathway to control cell size and proliferation (Lewis, Thomas, Murphy, & Sampson, 2004; McManus & Alessi, 2002; for a review, see Kwiatkowski, 2003).

The phenotypes of TSC1 and TSC2 have been considered to be identical in character. However, recent studies indicate that there may be differences in severity between the two genotypes. TSC1 accounts for 85% to 90% of familial cases, while TSC2 is responsible for 70% of sporadic cases. It also appears that individuals with TSC2 may more likely be mentally retarded than those with TSC1 (P. J. de Vries & Bolton, 2000; A. C. Jones et al., 1997, 1999; van Slegtenhorst et al., 1999; Zhang et al., 1999) and, therefore, more likely to have severe seizures. Lewis et al. (2004) noted that the presence of a TSC2 mutation carried a significantly higher risk of low IQ, autistic disorder, and infantile spasms than a TSC1 mutation. The odds ratio of low IQ in TSC2 has been reported as 2.44 (P. J. de Vries & Bolton, 2000) and 3.5 (Lewis et al., 2004), the latter adjusted for a history of infantile spasms. It would make sense, therefore, that individuals with TSC1 with a potentially milder phenotype would be more likely to reproduce and contribute to familial lines of

Table 20.1   Other Syndromic Associations

47, XYY		Abrams & Pergament, 1971
		Nielsen, Christensen, Friedrich, Zeuthen, & Ostergaard, 1973
		Nicolson, Bhalerao, & Sloman, 1998
		Weidmer-Mikhail et al., 1998
CHARGE association (coloboma, heart defect, choanal atresia, retarded growth and development, genital hypoplasia, ear anomalies		Fernell et al., 1999
Chromosome 2q37 deletion syndrome		Ghaziuddin & Burmeister, 1999
		Smith et al., 2001
Chromosome 13 deletion syndrome		Steele, Al-Adeimi, Siu, & Fan, 2001
		Smith et al., 2002
Chromosome 22q13 terminal deletion syndrome		Prasad et al., 2000
Cohen syndrome		Chandler, Moffett, Clayton-Smith, & Baker, 2003
Cornelia de Lang syndrome		Berney, Ireland, & Burn, 1999
Pediatric epilepsy syndromes		Besag, 2004
Infantile spasms/West syndrome		Askalan et al., 2003
Aristaless-related homeobox gene (ARX) syndrome		Stromme, Mangelsdorf, Scheffer, & Gecz, 2002
		Sherr, 2003
Fetal alcohol syndrome		Aronson, Hagberg, & Gillberg, 1997
FG syndrome (mental retardation, large head, imperforate anus, congenital hypotonia, and partial agenesis of corpus callosum)		Ozonoff, Williams, Rauch, & Opitz, 2000
Goldenhar syndrome		Landgren, Gillberg, & Stromland, 1992
Histidinemia		Kotsopoulos & Kutty, 1979
Hypomelanosis of Ito		Akefeldt & Gillberg, 1991
		Zappella, 1993
		Pascual-Castroviejo et al., 1998
Infections	Congenital	Chess, 1971
		Stubbs, 1978
		Yamashita, Fujimoto, Nakajima, Isagai, & Matsuishi, 2003
	Acquired	Ghaziuddin, Al-Khouri, & Ghaziuddin, 2002
		Ghaziuddin, Tsai, Eilers, & Ghaziuddin, 1992
		C. Gillberg, 1991
		C. Gillberg, 1986
		Domachowske et al., 1996
Joubert syndrome		Ozonoff, Williams, Gale, & Miller, 1999
		Raynes, Shanske, Goldberg, Burde, & Rapin, 1999
Kleinfelter's syndrome		Kielinen et al., 2004
Lesch-Nyhan syndrome		Nyhan, James, Teberg, Sweetman, & Nelson, 1969
Neurofibromatosis Type 1		C. Gillberg & Forsell, 1984
		P. G. Williams & Hersh, 1998
		Fombonne et al., 1997
Smith-Lemli-Opitz syndrome		Tierney et al., 2001
		Goldenberg, Chevy, Bernard, Wolf, & Cormier-Daire, 2003
Thalidomide embryopathy		Stromland, Nordin, Miller, Akerstrom, & Gillberg, 1994
		Stromland, Philipson, & Andersson Gronlund, 2002
Turner syndrome		Skuse et al., 1997
		El Abd, Patton, Turk, Hoey, & Howlin, 1999
		Donnelly et al., 2000

TSC (A. C. Jones et al., 1997; Lewis et al., 2004). However, the jury is still out with respect to differential representation of autism in the TSC1 and TSC2 genotypes.

Autistic symptoms were first described in patients with TSC a decade before Kanner's classic delineation of infantile autism (Critchley & Earl, 1932). These early noted symptoms included stereotypies, absent or abnormal speech, withdrawal, and impaired social interactions. TSC has since been strongly associated with autism, and estimates range from 17% to over 65% of individuals with TSC who are also autistic, identified more frequently in those with mental retardation, most commonly with epilepsy (Curatolo et al., 1991; I. Gillberg, Gillberg, & Ahlsen, 1994; Gutierrez, Smalley, & Tanguay, 1998; Harrison & Bolton, 1997; Hunt & Shepherd, 1993; Kandt, 2003; Riikonen & Simell, 1990). The reverse, the number of autistic individuals with TSC, has been estimated between 0.4% and 4% in epidemiological studies (C. Gillberg, Steffenburg, & Schaumann, 1991; Lotter, 1967; Ritvo et al., 1990; Smalley, Tanguay, Smith, & Gutierrez, 1992). This rate increases to 8% to 14% in autistic subjects with epilepsy (C. Gillberg, 1991; Riikonen & Amnell, 1981).

Fragile X

As the most common inherited cause of mental retardation, FXS is second only to Down syndrome in terms of a known chromosomal cause of mental retardation. FXS is characterized by macroorchidism, large protruding ears, and moderate to severe mental retardation (for recent reviews, see Hagerman, 2002; Kooy, Willemsen, & Oostra, 2000; and Willemsen, Oostra, Bassell, & Dictenberg, 2004). In over 99% of the cases, this syndrome is caused by an unstable amplification (excessive triplet repetition) of cytosine (C) and guanine (G) within the FMR1 gene on chromosome Xq27.3 (Verkerk et al., 1991). The range of ~5 to ~44 CGG triplet repeats is considered to be a normal finding, ~45 to 54 repeats is considered the intermediate "gray zone," and ~55 to 200 repeats is considered the premutation state producing carriers who may or may not be affected. Above a threshold of approximately 200 to 230 repeats with an abnormal methyla-tion pattern, no FXS protein (FMRP) is produced and people are fully affected with FXS (Maddalena et al., 2001). Prevalence of the full syndrome is 2.4 per 10,000 in males and 1.6 per 10,000 in females; prevalence of the premutation carrier status is 12.3 per 10,000 in males and 38.6 per 10,000 in females (Dombrowski et al., 2002).

FXS is associated with numerous distinctive neuropsychological deficits, which are not analogous with the overall cognitive impairment (Bennetto & Pennington, 2002; Loesch, Huggins, & Hagerman, 2004). Loesch et al. (2004) reviewed the correlations between FMRP depletion and deficits of cognitive and executive function on both genders with FXS using the Wechsler Adult Intelligence Scale-III (WISC-III, Wechsler, 1997). The Digit Span and Symbol Search subtests in both sexes and Picture Arrangement subtest in females showed that subjects were particularly affected by FMRP depletion, suggesting deficits in the cognitive constructs of processing speed, short-term memory, and attention. Although females are usually less affected than males because of the presence of the second unaffected X chromosome (Loesch et al., 2004), 50% to 70%, nonetheless, demonstrated significant cognitive deficits (B. B. de Vries et al., 1996), which correlated with the ratio of cells in which the normal X chromosome is activated (B. B. de Vries et al., 1996; Riddle et al., 1998; Tassone et al., 2000) and FMRP levels (Mazzocco, Kates, Baumgardner, Freund, & Reiss, 1997).

Premutation carriers, both male and female, have traditionally been thought to be entirely unaffected. It is surprising, however, that a premutation phenotype has recently been recognized. Hagerman et al. (2001) and Jacquemont et al. (2003, 2004) reported a syndrome of progressive intention tremor, cerebellar ataxia, executive function deficits, and brain atrophy (FXTAS) in asymptomatic older males with the FXS premutation status. Additional documented signs include short-term memory loss, cognitive decline, parkinsonism, peripheral neuropathy, proximal muscle weakness, and autonomic dysfunction. The late onset of this syndrome is due to an age-related penetrance, giving such carriers an age-adjusted 13-fold increased risk of combined intention tremor and gait ataxia (Jacquemont et al., 2004). Most recently, Hagerman et al. (2004) reported five female premutation carriers with symptoms of FXTAS, but none demonstrated the dementia noted in the males with FXTAS. In addition, females with the premutation had an increased (~20%) incidence of premature ovarian failure and early menopause, which has not been reported in females with the full FXS mutation (Murray, 2000; Sherman, 2000).

The early descriptions of FXS focused on fully affected males and their many autistic features. These features included poor eye contact; language delay, perseveration, and echolalia; self-injurious behaviors; motor stereotypies (e.g., hand flapping and body rocking); hypersensitivity to auditory stimuli or environmental change; tactile defensiveness; preoccupations with a narrow range of stimuli; and poor social relating (August & Lockhart, 1988; Borghgraef, Fryns, Dielkens, Pyck, & Van den Berghe, 1987; Fryns, Jacobs, Kleczkowska, & Van den Berghe, 1984; C. Gillberg, Persson, & Wahlstrom, 1986; Hagerman, Jackson, Levitas, Rimland, & Braden, 1986; Meryash, Szymanski, & Gerald, 1982). In the previous edition of this text (1997), over 30 studies were noted describing the prevalence of autism in FXS and vice versa (Dykens & Volkmar, 1997). The prevalence rates for FXS in autistic samples ranged from 0 to 16%, with a median of about 4%, while the prevalence rates of autism in fragile XFXS samples varied considerably, from 5% to 60%. Some researchers asserted that their prevalence rates of FXS and autism—16% to 20%—far exceeded the 4.5% to 7% of severely and mildly retarded males with FXS, concluding that FXS was strongly associated with autism (Blomquist et al., 1985; Fisch, Cohen, Jenkins, & Brown, 1988; C. Gillberg & Wahlstrom, 1985). In contrast, others claimed that their ~3% to 5% prevalence rates of autism and fragile XFXS were no higher than the rate of FXS among mentally retarded males (Payton, Steele, Wenger, & Minshew, 1989; Watson et al., 1984); therefore, the argument was that FXS should not increase the risk of autism above and beyond the risk associated with mental retardation. Subsequent work supported this latter position. A. Bailey et al. (1993) found that only 1.6% of their autistic

population had FXS, and Einfeld, Molony, and Hall (1989) found comparable rates of autism in appropriately matched groups of FXS and non-fragile XFXS males. Summarizing data across 40 studies, Fisch (1992) found virtually identical pooled proportions of FXS in autistic males and in mentally retarded males in general. These studies suggested that autism and FXS indeed may co-occur, but the prevalence of these cases is much lower than originally thought, and that FXS is not a major etiologic factor in autism.

The debate continues, with data that support both sides of the argument. O. Hashimoto, Shimizu, and Kawasaki (1993) noted no association between FXS and autism in their cohort. Klauck et al. (1997) found that 139 of 141 patients with autism were negative for the full syndrome. Only one multiplex family accounted for the positive FXS testing in their cohort: the mother with a premutation, one female autistic child who was heterozygous, and two male children with full mutations—one autistic with mental retardation and one with normal cognition and mild learning disabilities. Maes, Fryns, Van Walleghem, and Van den Berghe (1993) described males with FXS as having stereotypic movements, disturbing language patterns, social avoidance reactions, and eccentric peculiarities, but also showing social openness and sensitivity; however, there was no difference in the general levels of autistic behaviors between the mentally retarded males with and without FXS. Turk and Graham (1997) reported that their FXS cohort also did not demonstrate more autism than the comparison group with idiopathic mental retardation; however, both groups demonstrated more autism diagnoses (~70% to 80%) than did a second comparison group with Down syndrome (~30%). They concluded that FXS demonstrates a characteristic autistic-like phenotype of communication and stereotypic disturbances with delayed echolalia, repetitive speech, and hand flapping.

D. B. Bailey, Hatton, Mesibov, Ament, and Skinner (2000), using the CARS (Schopler et al., 1988), reported that FXS boys without autism showed a relatively flat developmental profile in contrast to the varied, uneven profiles and more severe cognitive difficulties seen in FXS with autism; FXS without autism also demonstrated more social competence and temperaments that were similar to typically developing children. They subsequently noted that the expression of the FXS protein (FMRP) accounted for less variance in developmental level in FXS than did the comorbidity of autism, suggesting that autism in FXS may come from a second hit predisposing to autism (D. B. Bailey, Hatton, Skinner, & Mesibov, 2001; also postulated by Feinstein & Reiss, 1998).

S. J. Rogers, Wehner, and Hagerman (2001) used the Autism Diagnostic Interview-Revised (ADI-R; Lord, Rutter, & Le Couteur, 1994) and the ADOS-G (Lord et al., 2000) to evaluate FXS in comparison to non-FXS autistic and other developmentally disabled children and reported two FXS subgroups: One-third of the FXS group met the stringent criteria for autism and were very similar to the non-FXS autistic cohort, while the remaining two-thirds of the FXS group were not autistic and were very similar to the group with other developmental disabilities. Philofsky, Hepburn, Hayes, Hagerman, and Rogers (2004), also using the ADOS and ADI for autism diagnosis, reported that the FXS/autism cohort was more impaired in nonverbal cognition and receptive and expressive language relative to the FXS children; receptive language function was similarly poor in children with autism, regardless of FXS status. Kau et al. (2004), again using the ADI, noted that the FXS/autism cohort was more cognitively impaired and demonstrated more aberrant behaviors but, notwithstanding, was less impaired in the reciprocal social domain than the autistic cohort without FXS. The authors proposed a Social Behavior Profile (SBP) as a distinct subphenotype of FXS, which may share mechanisms with autism.

The extent of association of autism and FXS is still unknown. As stated by Mazzocco et al. (1998):

... despite the specificity of autistic behavior among fragile X males and females, these behaviors (a) are not seen in all children with the disorder, (b) range in severity across individuals with the disorder, and (c) may be seen among individuals with fragile X regardless of whether they meet *DSM* criteria for autistic disorder. (p. 326)

This issue may be resolved with current studies that are using the gold standard autism diagnostic instruments (ADOS-G and ADI-R)

so that variability in mode of diagnosis should no longer be a confounding factor in this debate.

Down Syndrome

Down syndrome is the most common chromosomal cause of mental retardation, originally occurring in approximately 1 in 800 live births (Hook, 1982); more recently, with available options for prenatal diagnosis and elective termination, it has decreased to approximately 1 in 1,000 live births (Bell, Rankin, & Donaldson, 2003; Iliyasu, Gilmour, & Stone, 2002; Olsen, Cross, & Gensburg, 2003). Although once considered implausible, the comorbidity of autism and Down syndrome is not rare (Bregman & Volkmar, 1988; Ghaziuddin, 1997, 2000; Ghaziuddin, Tsai, & Ghaziuddin, 1992; Howlin et al., 1995; Wakabayashi, 1979; Wing & Gould, 1979). In fact, Down's original phenotypic description (Down, 1887/1990, pp. 6–7) of Mongolism certainly gives credence to the concept that comorbidity of Down syndrome and autism has always existed:

These children have always great power of imitation and become extremely good mimics . . . I have known a ventriloquist to be convulsed with laughter between the first and second parts of his entertainment on seeing a Mongolian patient mount the platform, and hearing him grotesquely imitate the performance with which the audience had been entertained. They have a strong sense of the ridiculous; this is indicated by their humorous remarks and the laughter with which they hail accidental falls, even of those to whom they are most attached. Another feature is their great obstinacy—they can only be guided by consummate tact. No amount of coercion will induce them to do that which they have made up their minds not to do. Sometimes they initiate a struggle for mastery, and the day previous will determine what they will or will not do on the next day. Often they will talk to themselves, and they may be heard rehearsing the disputes which they think will be the feature of the following day. They in fact, go through a play in which the patient, doctor, governess, and nurses are the *dramatis personae*—a play in which the patient is represented as defying and contravening the wishes of those in authority.

In epidemiological studies, the prevalence of Down syndrome in individuals with autism ranges from none to 16.7% (see Fombonne, 2003, for review). Large-scale studies that screened samples with Down syndrome for autism found relatively low rates of autism, ranging from 1.0% to 2.2%. However, other series have reported that as many as 10% of subjects with Down syndrome also meet criteria for autism (Ghaziuddin, 1997; Ghaziuddin et al., 1992; C. Gillberg et al., 1986; Lund, 1988; Wing & Gould, 1979).

Howlin et al. (1995) eloquently championed the importance of recognizing autism in children with Down syndrome. Although autism diagnoses are typically made in the preschool years, they noted later ages of autistic diagnoses in all cases reported in the literature (range from 7 years to adulthood). This singular diagnostic view creates unnecessary stress for families and prevents them from using supports and interventions available to families with an autistic child.

Reasons for the lack of recognition of autistic signs in Down syndrome are unclear. The stereotyped personality of individuals with Down syndrome is outgoing, affectionate, easygoing, placid, cheerful, highly social, and verbal—like "Prince Charming" (Gibbs & Thorpe, 1983; Menolascino, 1965). Some mothers describe their children with Down syndrome with a wide range of personality features (C. Rogers, 1987; Wishart & Johnston, 1990). While some children are easygoing, others are more active and distractible, with difficult temperaments (see Ganiban, Wagner, & Cicchetti, 1990, for a review). Yet, children with comorbid Down syndrome and autism are very different from other children with Down syndrome, demonstrating classic deficits in sociability, immediate and delayed echolalia, poor developmental progress in communication skills, motor stereotypies and ritualistic behaviors or interests, and adaptive behaviors. Even though autism may not be common in Down syndrome, it should be considered in the range of diagnostic possibilities for all individuals with this syndrome.

Rates of other psychiatric disorders are low for persons with Down syndrome, even as compared to groups with other types of developmental delay (Collacott, Cooper, & Mc-Grother, 1992; Grizenko, Cvejic, Vida, & Sayegh, 1991; Myers & Pueschel, 1991). Some children, however, may be prone to attentional difficulties, overactivity, oppositionality, and anxiety (Gath & Gumley, 1986; Myers & Pueschel, 1991; Pueschel, Bernier, & Pezzullo, 1991). Further, adults with Down syndrome are particularly vulnerable to Alzheimer-type dementia (Bush & Beail, 2004).

Williams-Beuren Syndrome

Williams-Beuren syndrome (WBS) is a rare disorder first described over 40 years ago (Beuren, Apitz, & Harmjanz, 1962; J. C. Williams, Barratt-Boyes, & Lowe, 1961) and caused by a microdeletion on chromosome 7q11.23 that includes the gene for elastin (OMIM™, 2000). Persons with WBS often show a distinctive cognitive profile, hyperacusis, supravalvular aortic stenosis, hypercalcemia, and characteristic facial features described as "elfin-like" (Bellugi, Lichtenberger, Mills, Galaburda, & Korenberg, 1999; Osborn, Harnsberger, Smoker, & Boyer, 1990; Pober & Dykens, 1996). Although WBS is thought to affect about 1 in 20,000 people (Pober & Dykens, 1996), the most recent epidemiological study in Finland noted a prevalence of 1 in 7,500 individuals (Stromme, Bjornstad, & Ramstad, 2002). The association between WBS and autism has not yet been widely studied, and there are only a few cases of comorbidity formally reported in the literature (C. Gillberg & Rasmussen, 1994; Reiss, Feinstein, Rosenbaum, Borengasser-Caruso, & Goldsmith, 1985). Individuals with WBS were almost twice as likely to be diagnosed with a psychiatric disorder characterized by anxiety, preoccupations, wandering, being overaffectionate, and seeking attention, and having difficulty with interpersonal interactions, with sleep disorders, and hyperacusis, than were controls who were matched for degree of cognitive deficit (Einfeld, Tonge, & Florio, 1997).

WBS and autism have traditionally been thought to show opposing patterns of cognitive strength and weakness. By definition, individuals with autism have poor verbal and nonverbal communication skills (see Chapter 12, this *Handbook,* this volume). In contrast, despite significant early language delay, many individuals with WBS have been described as showing relative sparing of expressive language and linguistic functioning, including high-level syntax and semantics (Bellugi, Marks, Bihrle, & Sabo, 1988), storytelling and narrative enrichment strategies involving affective prosody and a sense of drama (Reilly, Klima, & Bellugi, 1990), and a reliance on stereotypic, adult phrases (Udwin & Yule, 1990). However, nonverbal, perceptual skills are typically weak in WBS, often with marked difficulties in visual-spatial processing, especially integrating details into a whole. Yet, certain visual-spatial skills seem well preserved even within this area of deficit. In particular, persons with WBS generally excel on facial perception and recognition tasks (Bellugi, Wang, & Jernigan, 1994; Udwin & Yule, 1991). They often look intently at the faces of both strangers and familiar people (Bellugi, Bihrle, Neville, Doherty, & Jernigan, 1992; Bertrand, Mervis, Rice, & Adamson, 1993), although they solve face-processing tasks by different cognitive processes (Grice et al., 2001). (For reviews, see Bellugi, Lichtenberger, Jones, Lai, & St. George, 2000; and W. Jones et al., 2000.)

Recently, investigators have more specifically characterized atypical language development in WBS. Mervis (1999) noted that referential language precedes referential pointing in WBS, and the developmental vocabulary spurt occurs prior to spontaneous exhaustive sorting, the opposite of what is seen in typical language development. Toddlers with WBS also do not spontaneously use the pointing gesture in free-play situations. Laing et al. (2002) reported that despite superficially good social skills, children with WBS were deficient at both initiating and responding to triadic interactions (e.g., child-interlocutor-object), which are essential for instrumental and declarative joint attention and for referential uses of language; they did show proficiency at dyadic interactions (e.g., face to face), however. It has been suggested that children with WBS may be less interested in objects and more interested in faces than typical children (Bertrand et al., 1993). The WBS group was also impaired on the comprehension and production of referential pointing, despite vocabulary levels higher than those of typically developing children of the same mental age, which could not be explained on the basis of fine motor impairments (Laing et al., 2002). The authors thereby challenged the published claims that individuals with WBS have "preserved linguistic and social skills."

Tager-Flusberg and Sullivan (2000) reported on the dissociation of the social-cognitive and social-perceptual components of theory of mind in WBS, with relative sparing of the latter. Children with WBS did poorly on false-belief understanding (social-cognition) tasks but were able to provide mental-age-appropriate explanations for another person's behaviors and to discriminate and match facial expressions of emotion (social-perceptual tasks). Laws and Bishop (2004) demonstrated that children with WBS indeed have difficulties with social relationships and a semantic-pragmatic language disorder (described by some as "loquaciousness"), particularly with inappropriate initiation of conversation and the use of stereotyped conversation. They produce less coherent narratives and conversation despite having syntactic abilities equivalent to normal controls, and they score low for conversation rapport. They also have a restricted range of interests, specialized factual knowledge, and usual vocabulary. The authors (2004, p. 45) even suggested that:

Far from representing the polar opposite of autism, as suggested by some researchers, Williams syndrome would seem to share many of the characteristics of autistic disorder.

Further research in WBS will elucidate whether the extent of shared characteristics would enable official inclusion on the autistic spectrum.

Mitochondrial Disorders

Coleman and Blass (1985) first reported an association of lactic acidosis with autism over 20 years ago, which was corroborated by Laszlo, Horvath, Eck, and Fekete (1994). Lombard (1998) postulated a mitochondrial etiology for autism based on, among other things, his unpublished anecdotal observations of carnitine deficiency. Functional neuroimaging methodologies have also related autism and deficient energy metabolism in the brain (Chugani, Sundram, Behen, Lee, & Moore, 1999; Levitt et al., 2003; Minshew, Goldstein, Dombrowski, Panchalingam, & Pettegrew,

1993). Graf et al. (2000) reported a family with a group of neurologic disorders associated with the mitochondrial DNA G8363A transfer ribonucleic acid (RNA)[Lys] mutation; of four family members affected, one child was also severely autistic. Ramoz et al. (2004) reported linkage and association of the mitochondrial aspartate/glutamate carrier SLC25A12 gene with autism. Filiano, Goldenthal, Rhodes, and Marin-Garcia (2002) reported a group of 12 children presenting with hypotonia, intractable epilepsy, autism, and developmental delay (HEADD syndrome), who demonstrated reduced levels in specific mitochondrial respiratory activities encoded by mitochondrial DNA, with a majority also showing mitochondrial structural abnormalities. Pons et al. (2004) recently reported five patients with autism who had concurrent A3243G mitochondrial (mt)DNA mutations and mtDNA depletion syndromes. This mutation typically causes mitochondrial encephalopathy, lactic acidosis, seizures, hearing loss, and strokes (MELAS syndrome) with ragged red fibers in skeletal muscle. Four of these five patients were ascertained because a maternal relative was identified with the mutation, not because they presented with symptoms consistent with a mitochondrial disorder. Clark-Taylor and Clark-Taylor (2004) reported a child with autism who also had an abnormal acyl-carnitine profile with elevations of unsaturated fatty-acid metabolites C14:1 and C14:2 and ammonia and alterations of tricarboxylic acid cycle energy production. Filipek et al. (in press) reported that free and total carnitine and pyruvate were significantly reduced while ammonia, lactate, and alanine levels were considerably elevated in 100 autistic children. The relative carnitine deficiency in these patients, accompanied by slight elevations in lactate and significant elevations in alanine and ammonia levels, is suggestive of mild mitochondrial dysfunction, and the authors hypothesized that a mitochondrial defect might be the origin of the carnitine deficiency in these autistic children.

Lerman-Sagie, Leshinsky-Silver, Watemberg, and Lev (2004) reviewed the literature on the association of autism and mitochondrial disorders:

Mitochondrial diseases are probably a rare and insignificant cause of pure autism; however, evidence is accumulating that . . . mitochondrial disorders can present with autistic features. Most patients will present with multisystem abnormalities (especially neurologic) associated with autistic behavior. (p. 381)

Nevertheless, because our knowledge of mitochondrial function and dysfunction is presently expanding exponentially and concurrently with our knowledge of the neurobiology and genetics of autism, further research is indicated to elucidate the validity and extent of mitochondrial dysfunction in individuals with autism.

Isodicentric Chromosome 15q Syndrome

A chromosomal duplication syndrome found in autism involves the proximal long arm of chromosome 15q11-q13 (IDIC 15). The duplication is usually maternally inherited and involves the area roughly corresponding to the Prader-Willi/Angelman critical region (PWACR) of approximately four million base pairs. The additional genetic material may be interstitial (within one chromosome 15, producing 46,XY) and may or may not be inverted, producing a trisomy (three copies) of 15q11-q13. Or, the additional material may form a separate marker chromosome (47,XY), producing a tetrasomy (four copies) of this region. Although the prevalence of duplications of the PWACR is estimated to be similar to that of deletions in this region, 1:15,000 (Mohandas et al., 1999), the phenotype of the duplication syndrome has become appreciated only within the past 8 to 10 years.

This syndrome is one of the most frequent of the currently identifiable chromosomal disorders associated with autism, occurring in between 1% and 4% of autistic individuals (Browne et al., 1997; Konstantareas & Homatidis, 1999; Schroer et al., 1998). The clinical phenotype in autism is highly variable, ranging from profound psychomotor retardation to normal nonverbal cognitive scores (Filipek, Smith, et al., 2000). Rineer, Finucane, and Simon (1998) noted that, of 29 individuals with IDIC 15, 20 met criteria for autism using the GARS (Gilliam, 1995); those autistic IDIC

15 differed from the GARS autistic norming group only on having better social function as measured by the social interaction subscale, which corresponds to the anecdotal experience of this author and other investigators (Catherine Lord, personal communication). More than 100 individuals with autism and this chromosomal anomaly have been reported in the literature to date (Baker, Piven, Schwartz, & Patil, 1994; Battaglia et al., 1997; Bolton et al., 2001; Borgatti et al., 2001; Bundey, Hardy, Vickers, Kilpatrick, & Corbett, 1994; Cheng, Spinner, Zackai, & Knoll, 1994; Cook et al., 1997; Estecio, Fett-Conte, Varella-Garcia, Fridman, & Silva, 2002; Fantes et al., 2002; Flejter et al., 1996; C. Gillberg, Steffenburg, Wahlstrom, et al., 1991; Gurrieri et al., 1999; Hotopf & Bolton, 1995; Hou & Wang, 1998; Keller et al., 2003; Konstantareas & Homatidis, 1999; Lauritsen, Mors, Mortensen, & Ewald, 1999; Ludowese, Thompson, Sekhon, & Pauli, 1991; Mann et al., 2004; Mao & Jalal, 2000; Moeschler, Mohandas, Hawk, & Noll, 2002; Rausch & Nevin, 1991; Repetto, White, Bader, Johnson, & Knoll, 1998; Rineer et al., 1998; Sabry & Farag, 1998; Schroer et al., 1998; Silva, Vayego-Lourenco, Fett-Conte, Goloni-Bertollo, & Varella-Garcia, 2002; Ungaro et al., 2001; Webb et al., 1998; Weidmer-Mikhail, Sheldon, & Ghaziuddin, 1998; Wisniewski, Hassold, Heffelfinger, & Higgins, 1979; Wolpert et al., 2000; Woods, Robinson, Gardiner, & Roussounis, 1997; Yardin et al., 2002).

Filipek et al. (2003) reported mitochondrial dysfunction in two autistic children with isodicentric 15q syndrome. Both had uneventful perinatal courses, normal EEGs and MRI scans, moderate motor delay, pronounced lethargy when ill, severe hypotonia, and modest lactic acidosis. On muscle mitochondrial enzyme assays, each had pronounced mitochondrial hyperproliferation and a partial respiratory chain block most parsimoniously placed at the level of complex III, suggesting candidate gene loci for autism within the PWACR that affect pathways influencing mitochondrial function.

Some investigators have recently questioned whether fluorescent in situ hybridization (FISH) studies should be performed in addition to high-resolution karyotype in all cases of autism to detect duplication of 15q (Keller et al., 2003; Yardin et al., 2002). In addition to its association with autism, Longo et al. (2004) reported isodicentric 15q11-q13 duplications in 3 of 63 (4.7%) patients with Rett syndrome in addition to the MECP2 deletions.

Angelman/Prader-Willi Syndromes

Described as "sister imprinting disorders" (Cassidy, Dykens, & Williams, 2000), Angelman and Prader-Willi (PWS) syndromes are each the result of either a deletion or uniparental disomy (UPD) in the PWACR of chromosome 15 (see Clayton-Smith & Laan, 2003, for a review). Angelman syndrome, coined the "happy puppet syndrome" (Bower & Jeavons, 1967), presents with severe motor and intellectual retardation, ataxia, hypotonia, epilepsy, absence of speech, and unusual "happy" facies (OMIM™, 2000). Evidence is strong that the gene for Angelman syndrome is the E6-associated protein ubiquitin-protein ligase gene (UBE3A), which suggests that Angelman syndrome is the first recognized example of a genetic disorder of the ubiquitin-dependent proteolytic pathway in humans (Kishino, Lalande, & Wagstaff, 1997; OMIM™, 2000). Steffenburg, Gillberg, Steffenburg, and Kyllerman (1996) reported that all four children with Angelman syndrome ascertained in a population study met behavioral criteria for autism. Trillingsgaard and Stergaard (2004) found that 13 of 16 children with Angelman met ADOS-G (Lord et al., 2000) criteria for an ASD; however, the authors noted that autism might have been overdiagnosed in their sample because of the extremely low cognitive levels of the children with Angelman. C. A. Williams, Lossie, and Driscoll (2001) noted that some children with ASD may be misdiagnosed with Angelman, particularly with negative genetic testing for Angelman. Thompson and Bolton (2003) reported one case of Angelman syndrome and paternal UPD and described the milder Angelman symptomatology associated with UPD as including a lack of autistic features.

PWS is characterized by obesity, muscular hypotonia, mental retardation, short stature, hypogonadotropic hypogonadism, and small hands and feet. It appears that PWS results from UPD or deletion of the paternal copies of the imprinted small nuclear ribonucleoprotein polypeptide N (SNRPN) and necdin genes and possibly others as well (OMIM™, 2000). Veltman et al. (2004) found that maternal UPD cases of PWS would be more likely to exhibit ASD than would cases with deletions in the PWACR. Therefore, the extent of the associations of Angelman and PWS with autism remains unclear, particularly the differential effects of UPD as compared with deletions of the responsible genes.

Velocardiofacial Syndrome

Shprintzen, Goldberg, Young, and Wolford (1981) first described velocardiofacial syndrome (VCFS), which is characterized by cleft palate, cardiac malformations (usually a ventricular septal defect), typical facies (tubular nose, narrow palpebral fissures, and retruded jaw), learning disabilities and/or mental retardation, microcephaly, short stature, CNS vascular malformations, and seizures (Coppola, Sciscio, Russo, Caliendo, & Pascotto, 2001; OMIM™, 2000; Perez & Sullivan, 2002; Roubertie et al., 2001). VCFS is now known to be caused by a microdeletion on chromosome 22q11.2. It is also known as CATCH 22 and chromosome 22q11 deletion syndromes, and its prevalence is estimated at 1 per 4,000 (Bassett & Chow, 1999).

There is an extremely high prevalence of neuropsychiatric disorders in VCFS involving over 50% of the reported cases. Gothelf and colleagues reported that 16% to 25% will develop psychotic disorder by adolescence; the prevalence of schizophrenia in VCFS is 25 times that of the general population (Gothelf & Lombroso, 2001; Gothelf, Presburger, Levy, et al., 2004; Gothelf, Presburger, Zohar, et al., 2004). Up to 40% meet criteria for attention deficit/hyperactivity disorder, and 33% for obsessive-compulsive disorder. Over half of the cases in some series were mentally retarded (Niklasson, Rasmussen, Oskarsdottir, & Gillberg, 2001).

The most characteristic behavioral phenotype is that of a nonverbal learning disorder, with verbal IQ scores significantly greater

than nonverbal, despite almost universal severe early language delay (Bearden et al., 2001; Niklasson et al., 2001; Wang, Woodin, Kreps-Falk, & Moss, 2000; Woodin et al., 2001). A marked deficit in visuospatial memory has been documented in these children, producing the described mathematics disabilities. In addition to the selective deficit in visuospatial memory, Bearden et al. (2001) found a dissociation between visuospatial and object memory and noted the similarity of the VCFS cognitive profile with WBS (Bearden, Wang, & Simon, 2002).

Kozma (1998) was the first to report comorbid autism in VCFS, with associated severe mental retardation. Niklasson et al. (2001; Niklasson, Rasmussen, Oskarsdottir, & Gillberg, 2002) found that more than 30% of their VCFS subjects were also autistic, 50% had "autistic traits," and more than 50% had mental retardation; only 6% of their sample had a normal IQ and were free of neuropsychiatric disorders. Scherer, D'Antonio, and Rodgers (2001) noted a sparse vocabulary and pattern of sound types and very low mean babbling length relative to other communication measures, differing qualitatively and quantitatively from that found in Down syndrome. Glaser et al. (2002) noted uniquely lower receptive language function relative to expressive language ability; they also found parent-of-origin effects, with those with a deletion of paternal origin scoring higher on language measures than those with a deletion of maternal origin.

Möbius Syndrome

Möbius syndrome maps to chromosome 13q12.2-q13 and is characterized by brainstem maldevelopment resulting in congenital unilateral or bilateral paresis of the facial (7th) cranial nerve. There is variable involvement of other cranial nerves, usually the abducens (6th), but also possibly the trigeminal (5th), glossopharyngeal (9th), or hypoglossal (12th). There is associated mental retardation, orofacial and limb malformations, and musculoskeletal defects (Möbius, 1888; OMIM™, 2000).

Several reports noted the co-occurrence of autism and Möbius syndrome (C. Gillberg &

Winnergard, 1984; Larrandaburu, Schuler, Ehlers, Reis, & Silveira, 1999; Ornitz, Guthrie, & Farley, 1977), while others described difficulties in communication, social interactions, and maladaptive behaviors without specific diagnoses of autism (Giannini, Tamulonis, Giannini, Loiselle, & Spirtos, 1984; Meyerson & Foushee, 1978). In an early report, C. Gillberg and Steffenberg (1989) noted autistic behaviors in about 40% of individuals with Möbius syndrome. One autistic child, whose brainstem neuropathology noted virtual absence of neurons in the facial nerve nucleus, was also described as having little facial expression and may have also had Möbius or a similar syndrome (Rodier, Ingram, Tisdale, Nelson, & Romano, 1996).

Johansson et al. (2001) found an ASD in 40% of their cohort with Möbius syndrome, using the ADI-R (Lord et al., 1994), with mental retardation in one-third of the subjects. Bandim, Ventura, Miller, Almeida, and Costa (2003) used the CARS (Schopler et al., 1988) to diagnose autism in one-third of their cohort; the average CARS score for the autistic individuals was 40.4, in the severe range, while the average for the nonautistic individuals was 18.4. Stromland et al. (2002) reported comorbid autism in 24% of their cohort with Möbius, using the ADI-R (Lord et al., 1994).

Although Möbius syndrome has an identified genetic locus, there have been reports of an association of Möbius after in utero exposure to misoprostol, a prostaglandin analogue used to prevent and treat GI ulceration from nonsteroidal anti-inflammatory medications (Pastuszak et al., 1998); misoprostol is also available over the counter in some countries and used to self-induce abortions (Gonzalez et al., 1998).

Phenylketonuria

Autism has been associated with several inborn errors of metabolism, primarily PKU (Folstein & Rutter, 1988; Friedman, 1969; Miladi, Larnaout, Kaabachi, Helayem, & Ben Hamida, 1992; R. S. Williams, Hauser, Purpura, DeLong, & Swisher, 1980). Almost half of one cohort with PKU had autistic symptomatology (Bliumina, 1975), and 2% to 5% of autistic children in two other cohorts were found to have untreated PKU (Lowe, Tanaka, Seashore, Young, & Cohen, 1980; Moreno et al., 1992). In contrast, other studies have found essentially no significant abnormalities in metabolic tests in autistic individuals (Johnson, Wiersema, & Kraft, 1974; Perry, Hansen, & Christie, 1978; Pueschel, Herman, & Groden, 1985). In the study by Lowe et al. (1980), the autistic symptoms in the children with PKU improved after initiation of dietary therapy.

Rutter et al. (1997) stated that because untreated PKU is very rare, it must be an even rarer cause of autism. However, reliance on newborn screening programs alone may give a false sense of security, particularly in regions with large immigrant populations. A 4-year-old child, born in the Middle East and diagnosed with autism by both a child psychiatrist and child neurologist in the United States, presented with undiagnosed PKU after her newborn brother was identified on routine newborn screen (Gargus & Filipek, n.d.). In addition, despite extremely strict dietary control of his PKU and frequent normal serum phenylalanine levels when followed in metabolic clinic, the younger child also met *Diagnostic and Statistical Manual of Mental Disorders,* fourth edition (*DSM-IV;* American Psychiatric Association, 1994), criteria for Asperger syndrome (Filipek, unpublished observation). Baieli, Pavone, Meli, Fiumara, and Coleman (2003) reported that 2 of 35 individuals with classic PKU who were diagnosed late in infancy (before newborn screening became common) met criteria for autism, using the ADI-R (Lord et al., 1994) and the CARS (Schopler et al., 1988); none of the 62 children identified by newborn screening and on dietary treatment met criteria for autism. In addition, in the group of 144 with mild hyperphenylalanemia due to causes other than classic PKU, one boy had Asperger syndrome with normal IQ, and one retarded child with tetrahydropterin deficiency met criteria for autism. Again, in a sample of individuals with autism, finding undiagnosed and untreated PKU is rare; however, in a sample of individuals with PKU, up to 5% may be autistic.

Congenital Blindness and Deafness

Autistic symptomatology has been anecdotally associated with congenital blindness (CB) for decades; in some studies, up to 30% of children with CB were also described as being autistic (Chase, 1972; Fraiberg, 1977; Fraiberg & Freedman, 1964; Keeler, 1958; Norris, Spaulding, & Bordie, 1957; Wing, 1969; as cited in reviews by Cass, 1998; Hobson & Bishop, 2003; Hobson, Lee, & Brown, 1999). S. J. Rogers and Newhart-Larson (1989) reported a diagnosis of autism in all five boys studied with Leber's congenital amaurosis. Ek, Fernell, Jacobson, and Gillberg (1998) found that 56% of premature babies with retinopathy of prematurity (ROP) had both autistic disorder and mental retardation, and, of those, one-third had coexistent cerebral palsy. In comparison, only 14% of those with hereditary retinal disease had autistic disorder. Janson (1993) postulated that, in blind children with ROP, a behavior pattern of unresponsivity and stereotypic object manipulation emerges between 12 and 30 months to distinguish autistic and nonautistic children with CB. Msall et al. (2004) followed children with ROP at ages 5 and 8 years and found that 23% had epilepsy; 39%, cerebral palsy; and 44%, learning disabilities. Of the children with no or minimal light perception or totally detached retinas bilaterally, 9% were autistic, as compared with only 1% of those with more favorable visual status.

Cass, Sonksen, and McConachie (1994) reported that, of an entire sample of over 600 congenitally blind children of differing etiologies, only 17% demonstrated no evidence of additional disabilities and were developing normally at age 16 months when first studied. Subsequently, 31% had a regression in their development at between 16 and 27 months of age; children who regressed tended to have disorders of CNS/optic nerve/retina while children who did not regress had a purely optical cause for their blindness (e.g., congenital cataracts or glaucoma). The more "central" pathophysiology of the blindness in the regression cohort was subsequently confirmed by neuroimaging studies; the children with developmental regression had more CNS lesions than those who did not regress (Waugh, Chong, & Sonksen, 1998).

Brown, Hobson, Lee, and Stevenson (1997) reported that almost half of their sample with CB met criteria for autism and that, even in CB without autism, there were significantly more "autistic features" than seen in matched, sighted children. Brown et al. (1997) and Hobson et al. (1999) compared congenitally blind (of various etiologies) and sighted autistic children and noted remarkably similar clinical features. The mean CARS score (Schopler et al., 1988) was 27.8 (without Item VII, visual responsiveness, scored) for the CB children with autism. The authors' clinical impression was that blind autistic children were less severely impaired than sighted autistic children; none were abnormal in listening response (Item VIII), but most were markedly abnormal in body (IV) and object use (V). Therefore, they noted the close similarities and possible subtle distinctions between the two autistic groups. Hobson and Bishop (2003) went on to evaluate 18 CB children between 4 and 8 years of age who did not meet *DSM-IV* (American Psychiatric Association, 1994) criteria for autism and had an IQ > 55; teacher impressions were used to divide the sample into "more social" (MS, $N = 9$) and "less social" (LS, $N = 9$) groups. In the MS group, the highest CARS score was 15.5 (lowest possible score is 14 without rating Item VII), and no individual item was rated higher than 0.5 above normal. In contrast, in the LS group, the CARS scores ranged from 17.5 to 27.5 (mean 22.3 + 3.6). Four of the subjects had Leber's congenital amaurosis and were all placed into the LS group; almost half of the subjects had ROP and were spread across both groups.

The comorbidity of autism and congenital blindness has received relatively meager attention in the autism research literature. Diagnosis of autism in children with CB is particularly difficult. As Cass (1998) asked:

. . . distinguishing normal from abnormal social-communication development in children with visual impairment is an even more complex problem. Is it possible to use diagnostic tools more firmly rooted in *ICD-10* criteria such as the Autism Diagnostic Interview (ADI) and the Autism Diagnostic Observation Schedule (ADOS; Le Couteur et al., 1989; Lord, 1991)? Again, there are major problems with this approach since these instruments focus (entirely appropriately for diagnosis in the sighted) on highly visual dependent behaviors such as referential eye gaze, eye gaze for social purposes, protodeclarative pointing and symbolic play, all of which are either delayed or absent in normally developing children with visual impairment. (p. 129)

Gense and Gense (1994) tried to develop guidelines, using an educational approach, for children with CB and autism, but to date no pragmatic approach to autistic children with CB has been developed. Hobson et al. (1999) proposed several theoretical questions that need to be addressed on a larger scale to formally investigate the associations between autism and CB:

(a) Is the syndrome of autism in blind children to be clearly demarcated from autism-like clinical manifestations in nonautistic blind children, given that there appears to be a gradation in the number, quality, and severity of abnormalities shown by different children? (b) How far is it appropriate to consider each of the clinical manifestations as autistic-like, when such abnormalities might arise on the basis of quite different psychopathological mechanisms? (c) When blind children present with a constellation of clinical features and a picture that approximates to the syndrome of early childhood autism, is this picture distinguishable from that of autism in sighted children? If it is, might the distinguishing features afford insight into the developmental psychopathology of autism itself? (p. 46)

The incidence and prevalence of hearing impairment in children is 11 to 12 per 10,000 (Boyle et al., 1996; Kubba, MacAndie, Ritchie, & MacFarlane, 2004), and the rate steadily increases with age (Boyle et al., 1996). The comorbidity of hearing impairment and autism may be higher than expected (Gordon, 1991; Jure, Rapin, & Tuchman, 1991). Jure et al. (1991) performed a chart review of 46 children diagnosed as deaf and autistic; nearly 20% had normal or near-normal nonverbal cognitive function, and only 20% had severe mental retardation. The severity of the autistic behaviors correlated with the level of cognitive impairment but not to the level of hearing loss. In almost 24%, the diagnosis of comorbid autism did not occur for over 4 years after the diagnosis of deafness; and in another 22%, the diagnosis of hearing impairment was delayed for many years after the diagnosis of autism. Because the diagnosis of the comorbid condition (e.g., autism in the deaf or deafness in the

autistic) is often delayed, remediation is often suboptimal and ineffective.

Roper, Arnold, and Monteiro (2003) evaluated deaf autistic, deaf learning disabled, and hearing autistic children. There were no differences across the groups in the age at which parents first suspected a developmental or hearing problem or when the hearing deficit was diagnosed. However, the deaf autistic children were first diagnosed with deafness at a mean of 1 year of age (range 6 months to 2½ years), but not diagnosed with autism until a mean of 15 years of age (range 5 to 16 years) despite parental suspicions averaging 7 months of age (range 2 to 18 months). In contrast, the hearing autistic children were diagnosed at a mean of 7½ years of age (range 4 to 11 years), albeit late since their parents' suspicions averaged 18 months of age (range 3 months to 5 years). There were no differences in the current levels of autistic behaviors demonstrated by the deaf or hearing autistic groups, which is consistent with the previous findings of Garreau, Barthelemy, and Sauvage (1984). The authors also noted no discriminating characteristics of the deaf autistic individuals that would have facilitated earlier recognition of the autistic symptoms. Therefore, early recognition of hearing impairment in autistic children and of autism in deaf children is essential for the provision of an appropriate intervention strategy for these children (Ewing & Jones, 2003).

Fetal Anticonvulsant/Valproate Syndrome

Although the syndrome was described earlier (Chessa & Iannetti, 1986; DiLiberti, Farndon, Dennis, & Curry, 1984; Paulson & Paulson, 1981), Ardinger et al. (1988) confirmed that the multiple congenital anomalies and developmental delay noted in infants exposed to valproic acid (VPA) in utero represented a definitive *fetal valproate syndrome* (FVS). The clinical features include craniofacial, cardiovascular, urinary tract, genital, digital, and respiratory anomalies, and meningomyelocele. Up to 90% have developmental delay.

Several subsequent papers reported autism in children with FVS (Bescoby-Chambers, Forster, & Bates, 2001; Christianson, Chesler, & Kromberg, 1994; Moore et al.,

2000; Samren, van Duijn, Christiaens, Hofman, & Lindhout, 1999; G. Williams et al., 2001; P. G. Williams & Hersh, 1997). Christianson et al. (1994) first reported FVS in two sibling pairs. In the first family, the dose of valproate was halved when the first pregnancy was confirmed and phenytoin was added; in the second pregnancy, valproate was continued at the mother's usual dose. Although both children demonstrated many of the classic dysmorphic findings associated with fetal anticonvulsant syndrome (epicanthal folds, synophrys, upturned nasal tip with anteverted nares, and long philtrum), the older child was developmentally normal while the younger child was classically autistic with additional craniofacial anomalies. The authors suggested that there may be a valproate dosage effect in FVS, which was corroborated by Samren et al. (1999).

Four of the 57 children with fetal anticonvulsant syndromes reported by Moore et al. (2000) were reported to have autism (two exposed to VPA alone, one to VPA and phenytoin, and one to carbamazepine and diazepam). Two additional children were diagnosed with Asperger syndrome (one exposed to VPA and one to VPA, phenytoin, and a benzodiazepine). Eight additional cases were reported (Bescoby-Chambers et al., 2001; G. Williams et al., 2001; P. G. Williams & Hersh, 1997), one with Asperger syndrome and seven who met *DSM-IV* or *International Classification of Diseases (ICD-10)* criteria for autistic disorder.

CONCLUSION

Studies of relatively strictly defined autistic disorder have generally revealed low rates of medical conditions that might be associated with autism; the broadened view of ASDs forces us to revisit this issue. This chapter provided a summary of the medical aspects of this complex disorder from complementary perspectives, reinforcing the complexity of the ASDs and strengthening the bridge between evidence-based medicine and clinical application. Providers and investigators in all clinical and research disciplines should become familiar with the medical aspects of autism. When a child with an ASD is seen, providers need to consider all potential associated medical disorders and syndromes, both relatively common and rare. They also need to consider associated signs and symptoms that the family will confront, such as sleeping and feeding disturbances. In addition, when a provider sees a child with a rare syndrome or disorder, the child's behavioral phenotype must be considered: Does this child have autism or another neurobehavioral disorder? These deliberations will improve the recognition of autism and the role of associated medical factors and ultimately best serve the children and their families.

Cross-References

Issues of diagnosis are addressed in Chapters 1 to 6; genetic factors are discussed in Chapter 16; neurobiological aspects of the disorder are discussed in Chapter 18.

RECOMMENDED READING LIST FOR PARENTS AND PROFESSIONALS*

Batshaw, Mark, M. D. (2002). *Children with disabilities* (5th ed.). Baltimore: Paul H. Brookes.

A very well-written medical book on developmental disabilities.

Durand, V. M. (1998). *Sleep better! A guide to improving sleep for children with special needs.* Baltimore: Paul H. Brookes.

Provides practical strategies for encouraging children with special needs to sleep.

Filipek, P. A., Accardo, P. J., Baranek, G. T., Cook Jr., E. H., Dawson, G., Gordon, B., et al. (1999). The screening and diagnosis of autistic spectrum disorders. *Journal of Autism and Developmental Disorders, 29,* 437–482.

Filipek, P. A., Accardo, P. J., Ashwal, S., Baranek, G. T., Cook, Jr., E. H., Dawson, G., et al. (2000). Practice parameter: Screening and diagnosis of autism: Report of the Quality Standards Subcommittee of the American Academy of Neurology and the Child Neurology Society. *Neurology, 55*(4), 468–479.

Background paper and current recommendations for physicians and other professionals for screening, diagnosis, and the medical evaluation of autism.

---

*Portions of this section were taken with permission from Volkmar & Wiesner (2004).

Available to download at www.forockids.org/en
/forockids.php?page=12.

Freeman, J., Vining, E. P. J., & Pillas, D. J. (2002).
Seizures and Epilepsy in Childhood: A Guide.
Baltimore: Johns Hopkins University Press.

A parent-oriented guide to seizure disorders.

Immunization Safety Review Committee. (2001).
*Immunization Safety Review: Measles-Mumps-
Rubella Vaccine and Autism.* Institute of Medi-
cine. Washington, DC: National Academy Press.

Immunization Safety Review Committee. (2001).
*Immunization Safety Review: Thimerosal Con-
taining Vaccines and Neurodevelopmental Disorders.* Institute of Medicine. Washington,
DC: National Academy Press.

Immunization Safety Review Committee. (2004).
*Immunization Safety Review: Vaccines and
Autism.* Institute of Medicine. Washington,
DC: National Academy Press.

Reviews the evidence on MMR and mercury-
containing vaccines and autism. Available from
www.nap.edu.

National Academy of Science. (2001). *Report of the
Committee on Educational Interventions for
Autistic Children.* Washington, DC: National
Academies Press.

An excellent source of information on recommended educational interventions for children with
autism, including language, physical/occupational,
and social cognition therapies.

Powers, M. D. (2000). *Children with Autism: A Parent's Guide* (2nd ed.). Bethesda, MD: Woodbine House.

An excellent resource for parents, full of useful information on a range of issues.

Volkmar, F. R., Cook, E. H. J., Pomeroy, J., Realmuto, G., & Tanguay, P. (1999). Practice parameters for autism and pervasive developmental
disorders. *Journal of the American Academy of
Child and Adolescent Psychiatry, 38*(Suppl.
12), 32S–54S.

Professional guidelines for psychiatric assessment
of autism.

Volkmar, F. R., & Wiesner, L. A. (2004). *Health-
care for Children on the Autism Spectrum: A
Guide to Medical, Nutritional, and Behavioral
Issues.* Bethesda, MD: Woodbine House.

A very well-written and highly informative book
for parents and professionals.

Weber, J. D. (2000). *Children with Fragile X Syndrome: A Parent's Guide.* Bethesda, MD:
Woodbine House.

A well-written introduction to fragile X syndrome,
written for parents and families.

REFERENCES

Abrams, N., & Pergament, E. (1971). Childhood
psychosis combined with XYY abnormalities.
*Journal of Genetic Psychology; Child Behav-
ior, Animal Behavior, and Comparative Psychology, 118,* 13–16.

Accardo, P., Whitman, B., Caul, J., & Rolfe, U.
(1988). Autism and plumbism. A possible association. *Clinical Pediatrics, 27*(1), 41–44.

Afzal, N., Murch, S., Thirrupathy, K., Berger, L.,
Fagbemi, A., & Heuschkel, R. (2003). Constipation with acquired megarectum in children
with autism. *Pediatrics, 112*(4), 939–942.

Ahearn, W. H., Castine, T., Nault, K., & Green, G.
(2001). An assessment of food acceptance in
children with autism or pervasive developmental disorder-not otherwise specified. *Journal
of Autism and Developmental Disorders, 31*(5),
505–511.

Akefeldt, A., & Gillberg, C. (1991). Hypomelanosis of Ito in three cases with autism and
autistic-like conditions. *Developmental Medicine and Child Neurology, 33*(8), 737–743.

American College of Medical Genetics: Policy
Statement. (1994). Fragile X Syndrome: Diag-
nostic and carrier testing. *American Journal of
Medical Genetics, 53,* 380–381.

American Psychiatric Association. (1987). *Diagnostic and statistical manual of mental disorders* (3rd ed., rev.). Washington, DC: Author.

American Psychiatric Association. (1994). *Diagnostic and statistical manual of mental disorders* (4th ed.). Washington, DC: Author.

American Sleep Disorders Association. (1997). *International classification of sleep disorders,
revised: Diagnostic and coding manual.*
Rochester, MN: American Sleep Disorders
Association.

American Speech-Language-Hearing Association.
(1991). Guidelines for the audiologic assessment of children from birth through 36 months
of age. (Committee on Infant Hearing.) *American Speech-Language-Hearing Association,
33*(Suppl. 5), 37–43.

Ardinger, H. H., Atkin, J. F., Blackston, R. D.,
Elsas, L. J., Clarren, S. K., Livingstone, S.,
et al. (1988). Verification of the fetal valproate syndrome phenotype. *American Journal
of Medical Genetics, 29*(1), 171–185.

Aronson, M., Hagberg, B., & Gillberg, C. (1997).
Attention deficits and autistic spectrum problems in children exposed to alcohol during

gestation: A follow-up study. *Developmental Medicine and Child Neurology, 39*(9), 583–587.

Ashwood, P., Anthony, A., Pellicer, A. A., Torrente, F., Walker-Smith, J. A., & Wakefield, A. J. (2003). Intestinal lymphocyte populations in children with regressive autism: Evidence for extensive mucosal immunopathology. *Journal of Clinical Immunology, 23*(6), 504–517.

Askalan, R., Mackay, M., Brian, J., Otsubo, H., McDermott, C., Bryson, S., et al. (2003). Prospective preliminary analysis of the development of autism and epilepsy in children with infantile spasms. *Journal of Child Neurology, 18*(3), 165–170.

August, G., & Lockhart, L. (1988). Familial autism and the fragile-X chromosome. *Journal of Autism and Developmental Disorders, 14*(2), 197–204.

Aylward, E. H., Minshew, N. J., Field, K., Sparks, B. F., & Singh, N. (2002). Effects of age on brain volume and head circumference in autism. *Neurology, 59*(2), 175–183.

Baieli, S., Pavone, L., Meli, C., Fiumara, A., & Coleman, M. (2003). Autism and phenylketonuria. *Journal of Autism and Developmental Disorders, 33*(2), 201–204.

Bailey, A. (1994). Physical examination and medical investigation. In M. Rutter, E. Taylor, & L. Hersov (Eds.), *Child and adolescent psychiatry: Modern approaches* (3rd ed., pp. 79–93). Oxford, England: Blackwell Press.

Bailey, A., Bolton, P., Butler, L., Le Couteur, A., Murphy, M., Scott, S., et al. (1993). Prevalence of the fragile X anomaly amongst autistic twins and singletons. *Journal of Child Psychology and Psychiatry, 34*, 673–688.

Bailey, A., Le Couteur, A., Gottesman, I., Bolton, P., Simonoff, E., Yuzda, E., et al. (1995). Autism as a strongly genetic disorder: Evidence from a British twin study. *Psychological Medicine, 25*, 63–77.

Bailey, A., Le Couteur, A., Rutter, M., Pickles, A., Yuzda, E., Schmidt, D., et al. (1991). Obstetric and neurodevelopmental data from the British Twin Study of Autism. *Psychiatric Genetics, 2*, S7A/1.

Bailey, A., Luthert, P., Bolton, P., Le Couteur, A., Rutter, M., & Harding, B. (1993). Autism and megalencephaly. *Lancet, 341*, 1225–1226.

Bailey, A., Luthert, P., Dean, A., Harding, B., Janota, I., Montgomery, M., et al. (1998). A clinicopathological study of autism. *Brain, 121*, 899–905.

Bailey, A., Phillips, W., & Rutter, M. (1996). Autism: Towards an integration of clinical, genetic, neuropsychological, and neurobiological perspectives. *Journal of Child Psychology and Psychiatry, 37*, 89–126.

Bailey, D. B., Jr., Hatton, D. D., Mesibov, G., Ament, N., & Skinner, M. (2000). Early development, temperament, and functional impairment in autism and fragile X syndrome. *Journal of Autism and Developmental Disorders, 30*(1), 49–59.

Bailey, D. B., Jr., Hatton, D. D., Skinner, M., & Mesibov, G. (2001). Autistic behavior, FMR1 protein, and developmental trajectories in young males with fragile X syndrome. *Journal of Autism and Developmental Disorders, 31*(2), 165–174.

Baker, P., Piven, J., Schwartz, S., & Patil, S. (1994). Duplication of chromosome 15q11–13 in two individuals with autistic disorder. *Journal of Autism and Developmental Disorders, 24*(4), 529–535.

Bandim, J. M., Ventura, L. O., Miller, M. T., Almeida, H. C., & Costa, A. E. (2003). Autism and Mobius sequence: An exploratory study of children in northeastern Brazil. *Arquivos de Neuro-Psiquiatria, 61*(2A), 181–185.

Baranek, G. T. (1999). Autism during infancy: A retrospective video analysis of sensory-motor and social behaviors at 9–12 months of age. *Journal of Autism and Developmental Disorders, 29*, 213–224.

Baranek, G. T., Foster, L. G., & Berkson, G. (1997). Tactile defensiveness and stereotyped behaviors. *American Journal of Occupational Therapy, 51*, 91–95.

Barton, M., & Volkmar, F. (1998). How commonly are known medical conditions associated with autism? *Journal of Autism and Developmental Disorders, 28*(4), 273–278.

Bassett, A. S., & Chow, E. W. (1999). 22q11 deletion syndrome: A genetic subtype of schizophrenia. *Biological Psychiatry, 46*(7), 882–891.

Battaglia, A., Gurrieri, F., Bertini, E., Bellacosa, A., Pomponi, M. G., Paravatou-Petsotas, M., et al. (1997). The inv dup(15) syndrome: A clinically recognizable syndrome with altered behavior, mental retardation, and epilepsy. *Neurology, 48*(4), 1081–1086.

Bauer, S. (1995). Autism and the pervasive developmental disorders: Part 1. *Pediatrics in Review, 16*(4), 130–136.

Bauman, M. L. (1992). Neuropathology of autism. In A. B. Joseph & R. R. Young (Eds.), *Movement disorders in neurology and psychiatry* (pp. 664–668). Boston: Blackwell Scientific Publications.

Bauman, M. L. (1996). Brief report—Neuroanatomic observations of the brain in pervasive developmental disorders. *Journal of Autism and Developmental Disorders, 26*(2), 199–203.

Bauman, M. L., & Kemper, T. L. (1994). Neuroanatomic observations of the brain in autism. In M. L. Bauman & T. L. Kemper (Eds.), *The neurobiology of autism* (pp. 119–145). Baltimore: Johns Hopkins University Press.

Bauman, M. L., & Kemper, T. L. (1997). Is autism a progressive process? *Neurology, 48*(Suppl.), A285.

Bearden, C. E., Woodin, M. F., Wang, P. P., Moss, E., McDonald-McGinn, D., Zackai, E., et al. (2001). The neurocognitive phenotype of the 22q11.2 deletion syndrome: Selective deficit in visual-spatial memory. *Journal of Clinical and Experimental Neuropsychology, 23*(4), 447–464.

Bell, R., Rankin, J., & Donaldson, L. J. (2003). Down's syndrome: Occurrence and outcome in the north of England, 1985–99. *Paediatric Perinatal Epidemiology, 17*(1), 33–39.

Bellugi, U., Bihrle, A., Neville, H., Doherty, S., & Jernigan, T. (1992). Language, cognition, and brain organization in a neurodevelopmental disorder. In M. R. Gunnar & C. A. Nelson (Eds.), *Developmental behavioral neuroscience. The Minnesota symposia on child psychology* (Vol. 24, pp. 201–232). Hillsdale, NJ: Erlbaum.

Bellugi, U., Lichtenberger, L., Jones, W., Lai, Z., & St. George, M. (2000). The neurocognitive profile of Williams syndrome: A complex pattern of strengths and weaknesses [Special issue]. *Journal of Cognitive Neuroscience, 12*(Suppl. 1), 7–29.

Bellugi, U., Lichtenberger, L., Mills, D., Galaburda, A., & Korenberg, J. R. (1999). Bridging cognition, the brain and molecular genetics: Evidence from Williams syndrome. *Trends in Neurosciences, 22*(5), 197–207.

Bellugi, U., Marks, S., Bihrle, A., & Sabo, H. (1988). Dissociation between language and cognitive functions in Williams syndrome. In D. Bishop & K. Mogfont (Eds.), *Language development in exceptional circumstances* (pp. 177–189). London: Churchill Livingstone.

Bellugi, U., Wang, P. P., & Jernigan, T. L. (1994). Williams syndrome: An unusual neuropsychological profile. In S. H. Broman & J. Grafman (Eds.), *Atypical cognitive deficits in developmental disorders: Implications for brain function* (pp. 23–56). Hillsdale, NJ: Erlbaum.

Bennetto, L., & Pennington, B. F. (2002). Neuropsychology. In R. J. Hagerman & P. J. Hagerman (Eds.), *Fragile X syndrome: Diagnosis, treatment and research* (pp. 3–109). Baltimore: Johns Hopkins University Press.

Bernabei, P., Fenton, G., Fabrizi, A., Camaioni, L., & Perucchini, P. (2003). Profiles of sensorimotor development in children with autism and with developmental delay. *Perceptual & Motor Skills, 96*(3, Pt. 2), 1107–1116.

Berney, T. P., Ireland, M., & Burn, J. (1999). Behavioural phenotype of Cornelia de Lange syndrome. *Archives of Disease in Childhood, 81*(4), 333–336.

Berthier, M. L. (1994). Corticocallosal anomalies in Asperger's syndrome [Letter]. *American Journal of Roentgenology, 162,* 236–237.

Berthier, M. L., Starkstein, S. E., & Leiguarda, R. (1990). Developmental cortical anomalies in Asperger's syndrome: Neuroradiological findings in two patients. *Journal of Neuropsychiatry and Clinical Neurosciences, 2,* 197–201.

Bertrand, J., Mervis, C. B., Rice, C. E., & Adamson, L. (1993). *Development of joint attention by a toddler with Williams syndrome.* Paper presented at the Gatlinburg Conference on Research and Theory in Mental Retardation and Developmental Disabilities, Gatlinburg, TN.

Besag, F. M. (2004). Behavioral aspects of pediatric epilepsy syndromes. *Epilepsy & Behavior, 5*(Suppl. 1), S3–S13.

Bescoby-Chambers, N., Forster, P., & Bates, G. (2001). Foetal valproate syndrome and autism: Additional evidence of an association. *Developmental Medicine and Child Neurology, 43*(12), 847.

Beuren, A. J., Apitz, J., & Harmjanz, D. (1962). Supravalvular aortic stenosis in association with mental retardation and a certain facial appearance. *Circulation, 26,* 1235–1240.

Black, C., Kaye, J. A., & Jick, H. (2002). Relation of childhood gastrointestinal disorders to autism: Nested case-control study using data from the U. K. General Practice Research Database. *British Medical Journal, 325*(7361), 419–421.

Bliumina, M. G. (1975). A schizophrenia-like variant of phenylketonuria. *Zhurnal nevopatologii i psikhiatrii, 75*(10), 1525–1529.

Blomquist, H., Bohman, M., Edvinsson, S., Gillberg, C., Gustavson, K., Holmgren, G., et al. (1985). Frequency of the fragile X syndrome in infantile autism. A Swedish multicenter study. *Clinical Genetics, 27*(2), 113–117.

Bolton, P., Dennis, N. R., Browne, C. E., Thomas, N. S., Veltman, M. W., Thompson, R. J., et al. (2001). The phenotypic manifestations of interstitial duplications of proximal 15q with special reference to the autistic spectrum disorders. *American Journal of Medical Genetics, 105*(8), 675–685.

Bolton, P., Macdonald, H., Murphy, M., Scott, S., Yuzda, E., Whitlock, B., et al. (1991). Genetic findings and heterogeneity in autism. *Psychiatric Genetics, 2,* S7A/2.

Bolton, P., Macdonald, H., Pickles, A., Rios, P., Goode, S., Crowson, M., et al. (1994). A case-control family history study of autism. *Journal of Child Psychology and Psychiatry, 35*(5), 877–900.

Bolton, P., Murphy, M., Macdonald, H., & Whitlock, B. (1997). Obstetric complications in autism: Consequences or causes of the condition? *Journal of the American Academy of Child and Adolescent Psychiatry, 36*(2), 272–281.

Bolton, P., Murphy, M., Macdonald, H., Whitlock, B., Pickles, A., & Rutter, M. (1997). Obstetric complications in autism: Consequences or causes of the condition? *Journal of the American Academy of Child and Adolescent Psychiatry, 36,* 272–281.

Borgatti, R., Piccinelli, P., Passoni, D., Dalpra, L., Miozzo, M., Micheli, R., et al. (2001). Relationship between clinical and genetic features in "inverted duplicated chromosome 15" patients. *Pediatric Neurology, 24*(2), 111–116.

Borghgraef, M., Fryns, J., Dielkens, A., Pyck, K., & Van den Berghe, H. (1987). Fragile (X) syndrome: A study of the psychological profile in 23 prepubertal patients. *Clinical Genetics, 32*(3), 179–186.

Bower, B. D., & Jeavons, P. M. (1967). The "happy puppet" syndrome. *Archives of Diseases in Childhood, 42*(223), 298–302.

Bowers, L. (2002). An audit of referrals of children with autistic spectrum disorder to the dietetic service. *Journal of Human Nutrition and Diet, 15*(2), 141–144.

Boyle, C. A., Yeargin-Allsopp, M., Doernberg, N. S., Holmgreen, P., Murphy, C. C., & Schendel, D. E. (1996). Prevalence of selected developmental disabilities in children 3–10 years of age: The Metropolitan Atlanta Developmental Disabilities Surveillance Program, 1991. *MMWR Surveillance Summaries, 45*(SS-2), 1–14.

Braffman, B., & Naidich, T. P. (1994). The phakomatoses: Part I. Neurofibromatosis and tuberous sclerosis. *Neuroimaging Clinics of North America, 4,* 299–324.

Bregman, J., & Volkmar, F. (1988). Autistic social dysfunction and Down syndrome. *Journal of the American Academy of Child and Adolescent Psychiatry, 18*(3), 343–354.

Brown, R., Hobson, R. P., Lee, A., & Stevenson, J. (1997). Are there "autistic-like" features in congenitally blind children? *Journal of Child Psychology and Psychiatry, 38*(6), 693–703.

Browne, C. E., Dennis, N. R., Maher, E., Long, F. L., Nicholson, J. C., Sillibourne, J., et al. (1997). Inherited interstitial duplications of proximal 15q: Genotype-phenotype correlations. *American Journal of Human Genetics, 61*(6), 1342–1352.

Bryson, S. E., Smith, I. M., & Eastwood, D. (1988). Obstetrical suboptimality in autistic children. *Journal of the American Academy of Child and Adolescent Psychiatry, 27,* 418–422.

Bundey, S., Hardy, C., Vickers, S., Kilpatrick, M. W., & Corbett, J. A. (1994). Duplication of the 15q11–13 region in a patient with autism, epilepsy and ataxia. *Developmental Medicine and Child Neurology, 36,* 736–742.

Bush, A., & Beail, N. (2004). Risk factors for dementia in people with down syndrome: Issues in assessment and diagnosis. *American Journal of Mental Retardation, 109*(2), 83–97.

Carey, T., Ratliff-Schaub, K., Funk, J., Weinle, C., Myers, M., & Jenks, J. (2002). Double-blind placebo-controlled trial of secretin: Effects on aberrant behavior in children with autism. *Journal of Autism and Developmental Disorders, 32*(3), 161–167.

Cass, H. (1998). Visual impairment and autism. *Autism: Journal of Research and Practice, 2*(2), 117–138.

Cass, H., Sonksen, P. M., & McConachie, H. R. (1994). Developmental setback in severe visual impairment. *Archives of Diseases in Childhood, 70*(3), 192–196.

Cassidy, S. B., Dykens, E., & Williams, C. A. (2000). Prader-Willi and Angelman syndromes: Sister imprinted disorders. *American Journal of Medical Genetics, 97*(2), 136–146.

Centers for Disease Control and Prevention. (1997, November). *Screening young children for lead poisoning: Guidance for state and local public health officials.* Atlanta, GA: Centers for Disease Control and Prevention-National Center for Environmental Health.

Challman, T. D., Barbaresi, W. J., Katusic, S. K., & Weaver, A. (2003). The yield of the medical evaluation of children with pervasive developmental disorders. *Journal of Autism and Developmental Disorders, 33*(2), 187–192.

Chandler, K. E., Moffett, M., Clayton-Smith, J., & Baker, G. A. (2003). Neuropsychological assessment of a group of UK patients with Cohen syndrome. *Neuropediatrics, 34*(1), 7–13.

Chase, J. (1972). *Retrolental fibroplasia and autistic symptomatology.* New York: American Foundation for the Blind.

Cheng, S. D., Spinner, N. B., Zackai, E. H., & Knoll, J. H. (1994). Cytogenetic and molecular characterization of inverted duplicated chromosomes 15 from 11 patients. *American Journal of Human Genetics, 55*(4), 753–759.

Chess, S. (1971). Autism in children with congenital rubella. *Journal of Autism and Childhood Schizophrenia, 1*(1), 33–47.

Chessa, L., & Iannetti, P. (1986). Fetal valproate syndrome. *American Journal of Medical Genetics, 24*(2), 381–382.

Chez, M. G., Buchanan, C. P., Bagan, B. T., Hammer, M. S., McCarthy, K. S., Ovrutskaya, I., et al. (2000). Secretin and autism: A two-part clinical investigation. *Journal of Autism and Developmental Disorders, 30*(2), 87–94.

Christianson, A. L., Chesler, N., & Kromberg, J. G. (1994). Fetal valproate syndrome: Clinical and neuro-developmental features in two sibling pairs. *Developmental Medicine and Child Neurology, 36*(4), 361–369.

Chugani, D. C., Sundram, B. S., Behen, M., Lee, M. L., & Moore, G. J. (1999). Evidence of altered energy metabolism in autistic children. *Progress in Neuro-Psychopharmacology and Biological Psychiatry, 23*(4), 635–641.

Clark-Taylor, T., & Clark-Taylor, B. E. (2004). Is autism a disorder of fatty acid metabolism? Possible dysfunction of mitochondrial beta-oxidation by long chain acyl-CoA dehydrogenase. *Medical Hypotheses, 62*(6), 970–975.

Clayton-Smith, J., & Laan, L. (2003). Angelman syndrome: A review of the clinical and genetic aspects. *Journal of Medical Genetics, 40*(2), 87–95.

Cohen, D. J., Donnellan, A. M., & Paul, R. (1987). *Handbook of autism and pervasive developmental disorders.* Oxford, England: Wiley.

Cohen, D. J., Johnson, W. T., & Caparulo, B. K. (1976). Pica and elevated blood lead level in autistic and atypical children. *American Journal of Diseases of Children, 130,* 47–48.

Cohen, D. J., & Volkmar, F. R. (1997). *Handbook of Autism and Pervasive Developmental Disorders* (2nd ed.). New York: Wiley.

Cohen, D. J., Young, J. G., Lowe, T. L., & Harcherik, D. (1980). Thyroid hormone in autistic children. *Journal of Autism and Developmental Disorders, 10*(4), 445–450.

Coleman, M., & Blass, J. P. (1985). Autism and lactic acidosis. *Journal of Autism and Developmental Disorders, 15*(1), 1–8.

Collacott, R., Cooper, S., & McGrother, C. (1992). Differential rates of psychiatric disorders in adults with Down's syndrome compared with other mentally handicapped adults. *British Journal of Psychiatry, 161,* 671–674.

Coniglio, S. J., Lewis, J. D., Lang, C., Burns, T. G., Subhani-Siddique, R., Weintraub, A., et al. (2001). A randomized, double-blind, placebo-controlled trial of single-dose intravenous secretin as treatment for children with autism. *Journal of Pediatrics, 138*(5), 649–655.

Cook, E. H., Jr., Lindgren, V., Leventhal, B. L., Courchesne, R., Lincoln, A., Shulman, C., et al. (1997). Autism or atypical autism in maternally but not paternally derived proximal 15q duplication. *American Journal of Human Genetics, 60,* 928–934.

Cook, E. H., Jr., Perry, B. D., Dawson, G., Wainwright, M. S., & Leventhal, B. L. (1993). Receptor inhibition by immunoglobulins: Specific inhibition by autistic children, their relatives, and control subjects. *Journal of Autism and Developmental Disorders, 23,* 67–78.

Coppola, G., Sciscio, N., Russo, F., Caliendo, G., & Pascotto, A. (2001). Benign idiopathic partial seizures in the velocardiofacial syndrome: Report of two cases. *American Journal of Medical Genetics, 103*(2), 172–175.

Corbett, B., Khan, K., Czapansky-Beilman, D., Brady, N., Dropik, P., Goldman, D. Z., et al. (2001). A double-blind, placebo-controlled crossover study investigating the effect of porcine secretin in children with autism. *Clinical Pediatrics, 40*(6), 327–331.

Courchesne, E., Carper, R., & Akshoomoff, N. (2003). Evidence of brain overgrowth in the first year of life in autism. *Journal of the American Medical Association, 290*(3), 337–344.

Critchley, M., & Earl, C. J. (1932). Tuberous sclerosis and allied conditions. *Brain, 55,* 311–346.

Cryan, E., Byrne, M., O'Donovan, A., & O'Callaghan, E. (1996). A case-control study of obstetric complications and later autistic disorder. *Journal of Autism and Developmental Disorders, 26,* 453–460.

Curatolo, P., Cusmai, R., Cortesi, F., Chiron, C., Jambaque, I., & Dulac, O. (1991). Neuropsychiatric aspects of tuberous sclerosis. *Annals of the New York Academy of Sciences, 615,* 8–16.

Curatolo, P., Verdecchia, M., & Bombardieri, R. (2002). Tuberous sclerosis complex: A review of neurological aspects. *European Journal of Paediatric Neurology, 6*(1), 15–23.

Curry, C. J., Stevenson, R. E., Aughton, D., Byrne, J., Carey, J. C., Cassidy, S., et al. (1997). Evaluation of mental retardation: Recommendations of a Consensus Conference: American College of Medical Genetics. *American Journal of Medical Genetics, 72*(4), 468–477.

Davidovitch, M., Patterson, B., & Gartside, P. (1996). Head circumference measurements in children with autism. *Journal of Child Neurology, 11,* 389–393.

DeFelice, M. L., Ruchelli, E. D., Markowitz, J. E., Strogatz, M., Reddy, K. P., Kadivar, K., et al. (2003). Intestinal cytokines in children with pervasive developmental disorders. *American Journal of Gastroenterology, 98*(8), 1777–1782.

D'Eufemia, P., Celli, M., Finocchiaro, R., Pacifico, L., Viozzi, L., Zaccagnini, M., et al. (1996). Abnormal intestinal permeability in children with autism. *Acta Paediatricaica, 85*(9), 1076–1079.

de Vries, B. B., Wiegers, A. M., Smits, A. P., Mohkamsing, S., Duivenvoorden, H. J., Fryns, J. P., et al. (1996). Mental status of females with an FMR1 gene full mutation. *American Journal of Human Genetics, 58*(5), 1025–1032.

de Vries, P. J., & Bolton, P. F. (2000). Genotype-phenotype correlations in tuberous sclerosis. *Journal of Medical Genetics, 37*(5), E3.

Deykin, E. Y., & MacMahon, B. (1980). Pregnancy, delivery, and neonatal complications among autistic children. *American Journal of Diseases of Children, 134*(9), 860–864.

Didde, R., & Sigafoos, J. (2001). A review of the nature and treatment of sleep disorders in individuals with developmental disabilities. *Research in Developmental Disabilities, 22*(4), 255–272.

DiLiberti, J. H., Farndon, P. A., Dennis, N. R., & Curry, C. J. (1984). The fetal valproate syndrome. *American Journal of Medical Genetics, 19*(3), 473–481.

Diomedi, M., Curatolo, P., Scalise, A., Placidi, F., Caretto, F., & Gigli, G. L. (1999). Sleep abnormalities in mentally retarded autistic subjects: Down's syndrome with mental retardation and normal subjects. *Brain and Development, 21*(8), 548–553.

Domachowske, J. B., Cunningham, C. K., Cummings, D. L., Crosley, C. J., Hannan, W. P., & Weiner, L. B. (1996). Acute manifestations and neurologic sequelae of Epstein-Barr virus encephalitis in children [see comments]. *Journal of Pediatric Infectious Disease, 15*(10), 871–875.

Dombrowski, C., Levesque, S., Morel, M. L., Rouillard, P., Morgan, K., & Rousseau, F. (2002). Premutation and intermediate-size FMR1 alleles in 10572 males from the general population: Loss of an AGG interruption is a late event in the generation of fragile X syndrome alleles. *Human Molecular Genetics, 11*(4), 371–378.

Donnelly, S. L., Wolpert, C. M., Menold, M. M., Bass, M. P., Gilbert, J. R., Cuccaro, M. L., et al. (2000). Female with autistic disorder and monosomy X (Turner syndrome): Parent-of-origin effect of the X chromosome. *American Journal of Medical Genetics, 96*(3), 312–316.

Down, J. L. (1990). *On some of the mental affectations of childhood and youth.* Oxford, England: MacKeith Press. (Original work published 1887)

Dunn-Geier, J., Ho, H. H., Auersperg, E., Doyle, D., Eaves, L., Matsuba, C., et al. (2000). Effect of secretin on children with autism: A randomized controlled trial. *Developmental Medicine and Child Neurology, 42*(12), 796–802.

Dykens, E. M., & Volkmar, F. R. (1997). Medical conditions associated with autism. In D. J. Cohen & F. R. Volkmar (Eds.), *Handbook of autism and pervasive developmental disorders* (2nd ed., pp. 388–410). New York: Wiley.

Einfeld, S., Molony, H., & Hall, W. (1989). Autism is not associated with the fragile X syndrome. *American Journal of Medical Genetics, 34*(2), 187–193.

Einfeld, S., Tonge, B. J., & Florio, T. (1997). Behavioral and emotional disturbance in individuals with Williams syndrome. *American Journal on Mental Retardation, 102*(1), 45–53.

Ek, U., Fernell, E., Jacobson, L., & Gillberg, C. (1998). Relation between blindness due to retinopathy of prematurity and autistic spectrum disorders: A population-based study. *Developmental Medicine and Child Neurology, 40*(5), 297–301.

El Abd, S., Patton, M. A., Turk, J., Hoey, H., & Howlin, P. (1999). Social, communicational, and behavioral deficits associated with ring X turner syndrome. *American Journal of Medical Genetics, 88*(5), 510–516.

Elia, M., Ferri, R., Musumeci, S. A., Del Gracco, S., Bottitta, M., Scuderi, C., et al. (2000). Sleep in subjects with autistic disorder: A neurophysiological and psychological study. *Brain and Development, 22*(2), 88–92.

Estecio, M. R. H., Fett-Conte, A. C., Varella-Garcia, M., Fridman, C., & Silva, E. (2002). Molecular and cytogenetic analyses on Brazilian youths with pervasive developmental disorders. *Journal of Autism and Developmental Disorders, 32*(1), 35–41.

Ewing, K. M., & Jones, T. W. (2003). An educational rationale for deaf students with multiple disabilities. *American Annals of the Deaf, 148*(3), 267–271.

Fantes, J. A., Mewborn, S. K., Lese, C. M., Hedrick, J., Brown, R. L., Dyomin, V., et al. (2002). Organisation of the pericentromeric region of chromosome 15: At least four partial gene copies are amplified in patients with a proximal duplication of 15q. *Journal of Medical Genetics, 39*(3), 170–177.

Fein, D., Allen, D., Dunn, M., Feinstein, C., Green, L., Morris, R., et al. (1997). Pitocin induction and autism. *American Journal of Psychiatry, 154,* 438–439.

Feinstein, C., & Reiss, A. L. (1998). Autism: The point of view from fragile X studies. *Journal of Autism and Developmental Disorders, 28*(5), 393–405.

Fernell, E., Olsson, V. A., Karlgren-Leitner, C., Norlin, B., Hagberg, B., & Gillberg, C. (1999). Autistic disorders in children with CHARGE association. *Developmental Medicine and Child Neurology, 41*(4), 270–272.

Fidler, D. J., Bailey, J. N., & Smalley, S. L. (2000) Macrocephaly in autism and other pervasive developmental disorders. *Developmental Medicine and Child Neurology, 42*(11), 737–740.

Field, D., Garland, M., & Williams, K. (2003). Correlates of specific childhood feeding problems. *Journal of Paediatrics and Child Health, 39*(4), 299–304.

Filiano, J. J., Goldenthal, M. J., Rhodes, H., & Marin-Garcia, J. (2002). Mitochondrial dysfunction in patients with hypotonia, epilepsy, autism and developmental delay: HEADD Syndrome. *Journal of Child Neurology, 17,* 435–439.

Filipek, P. A., Accardo, P. J., Ashwal, S., Baranek, G. T., Cook Jr, E. H., Dawson, G., et al. (2000). Practice parameter: Screening and diagnosis of autism: Report of the Quality Standards Subcommittee of the American Academy of Neurology and the Child Neurology Society. *Neurology, 55*(4), 468–479.

Filipek, P. A., Accardo, P. J., Baranek, G. T., Cook Jr, E. H., Dawson, G., Gordon, B., et al. (1999). The screening and diagnosis of autistic spectrum disorders. *Journal of Autism and Developmental Disorders, 29,* 437–482.

Filipek, P. A., Juranek, J., Nguyen, M. T., Cummings, C., & Gargus, J. J. (in press). Relative carnitine deficiency in autism. *Journal of Autism and Developmental Disorders.*

Filipek, P. A., Juranek, J., Smith, M., Mays, L. Z., Ramos, E. R., Bocian, M., et al. (2003). Mitochondrial dysfunction in autistic patients with 15q inverted duplication. *Annals of Neurology, 53*(6), 801–804.

Filipek, P. A., Kennedy, D. N., & Caviness, V. S., Jr. (1992). Neuroimaging in child neuropsychology. In I. Rapin & S. Segalowitz (Eds.), *Handbook of neuropsychology: Vol. 6 Child neuropsychology* (pp. 301–329). Amsterdam: Elsevier Science.

Filipek, P. A., Richelme, C., Kennedy, D. N., Rademacher, J., Pitcher, D. A., Zidel, S. Y.,

et al. (1992). Morphometric analysis of the brain in developmental language disorders and autism. *Annals of Neurology, 32,* 475.

Filipek, P. A., Smith, M., Gargus, J. J., Bocian, M., Masser-Frye, D. S., & Spence, M. A. (2000). Evidence of mitochondrial dysfunction in autistic patients with 15q inv dup [Abstract]. *Annals of Neurology, 48,* 542.

Findling, R. L., Maxwell, K., Scotese-Wojtila, L., Huang, J., Yamashita, T., & Wiznitzer, M. (1997). High-dose pyridoxine and magnesium administration in children with autistic disorder: An absence of salutary effects in a double-blind, placebo-controlled study. *Journal of Autism and Developmental Disorders, 27*(4), 467–478.

Finegan, J.-A., & Quarrington, B. (1979). Pre-, peri- and neonatal factors and infantile autism. *Journal of Child Psychology and Psychiatry, 20,* 119–128.

Finegold, S. M., Molitoris, D., Song, Y., Liu, C., Vaisanen, M. L., Bolte, E., et al. (2002). Gastrointestinal microflora studies in late-onset autism. *Clinical Infection and Disease, 35*(Suppl. 1), S6–S16.

Fisch, G. (1992). Is autism associated with the fragile X syndrome? *American Journal of Medical Genetics, 43*(1/2), 47–55.

Fisch, G., Cohen, I., Jenkins, E., & Brown, W. (1988). Screening developmentally disabled male populations for fragile X: The effect of sample size. *American Journal of Medical Genetics, 30*(1/2), 655–663.

Fitzpatrick, T. B. (1991). History and significance of white macules, earliest visible sign of tuberous sclerosis. *Annals of the New York Academy of Science, 615,* 26.

Flejter, W. L., Bennett-Baker, P. E., Ghaziuddin, M., McDonald, M., Sheldon, S., & Gorski, J. L. (1996). Cytogenetic and molecular analysis of inv dup(15) chromosomes observed in two patients with autistic disorder and mental retardation. *American Journal of Medical Genetics, 61,* 182–187.

Folstein, S., & Rutter, M. (1977a). Genetic influences and infantile autism. *Nature, 265*(5596), 726–728.

Folstein, S., & Rutter, M. (1977b). Infantile autism: A genetic study of 21 twin pairs. *Journal of Child Psychology and Psychiatry, 18*(4), 297–321.

Folstein, S., & Rutter, M. (1988). Autism: Familial aggregation and genetic implications. *Journal of Autism and Developmental Disorders, 18*(1), 3–30.

Fombonne, E. (2003). Epidemiological surveys of autism and other pervasive developmental disorders: An update. *Journal of Autism and Developmental Disorders, 33*(4), 365–382.

Fombonne, E., & Chakrabarti, S. (2001). No evidence for a new variant of measles-mumps-rubella-induced autism. *Pediatrics, 108*(4), E58.

Fombonne, E., & du Mazaubrun, C. (1992). Prevalence of infantile autism in four French regions. *Social Psychiatry and Psychiatric Epidemiology, 27*(4), 203–210.

Fombonne, E., du Mazaubrun, C., Cans, C., & Grandjean, H. (1997). Autism and associated medical disorders in a French epidemiological survey. *Journal of the American Academy of Child and Adolescent Psychiatry, 36*(11), 1561–1569.

Fombonne, E., Roge, B., Claverie, J., Courty, S., & Fremolle, J. (1999). Microcephaly and macrocephaly in autism. *Journal of Autism and Developmental Disorders, 29*(2), 113–119.

Fraiberg, S. (1977). *Insights from the blind.* London: Souvenir.

Fraiberg, S., & Freedman, D. (1964). Studies in the ego development of the congenitally blind. *Psychoanalytic Study of the Child, 19,* 113–169.

Friedman, E. (1969). The "autistic syndrome" and phenylketonuria. *Schizophrenia, 1,* 249–261.

Fryns, J., Jacobs, J., Kleczkowska, A., & Van den Berghe, H. (1984). The psychological profile of the fragile X syndrome. *Clinical Genetics, 25*(2), 131–134.

Furlano, R. I., Anthony, A., Day, R., Brown, A., McGarvey, L., Thomson, M. A., et al. (2001). Colonic CD8 and gamma delta T-cell infiltration with epithelial damage in children with autism. *Journal of Pediatrics, 138*(3), 366–372.

Gale, S., Ozonoff, S., & Lainhart, J. (2003). Brief report: Pitocin induction in autistic and nonautistic individuals. *Journal of Autism and Developmental Disorders, 33*(2), 205–208.

Ganiban, J. M., Wagner, S., & Cicchetti, D. (1990). Temperament and Down syndrome. In D. Cicchetti & M. Beeghly (Eds.), *Children with Down syndrome: A developmental perspective* (pp. 63–100). New York: Cambridge University Press.

Gargus, J. J., & Filipek, P. A. (n.d.). Diagnosis of PKU in a young autistic child secondary to routine screening of a newborn sibling. Unpublished observation.

Garreau, B., Barthelemy, C., & Sauvage, D. (1984). A comparison of autistic symptoms with and without associated neurological problems. *Journal of Autism and Developmental Disorders, 14,* 105–111.

Gath, A., & Gumley, D. (1986). Behaviour problems in retarded children with special reference to Down's syndrome. *British Journal of Psychiatry, 149,* 156–161.

Gense, M. H., & Gense, D. J. (1994). Identifying autism in children with blindness and visual impairments. *Review, 26*(2), 55–62.

Gentile, P. S., Trentalange, M. J., Zamichek, W., & Coleman, M. (1983). Brief report: Trace elements in the hair of autistic and control children. *Journal of Autism and Developmental Disorders, 13*(2), 205–206.

Ghaziuddin, M. (1997). Autism in Down's syndrome: Family history correlates. *Journal of Intellectual Disability Research, 41*(Pt. 1), 87–91.

Ghaziuddin, M. (2000). Autism in Down's syndrome: A family history study. *Journal of Intellectual Disability Research, 44*(Pt. 5), 562–566.

Ghaziuddin, M., Al-Khouri, I., & Ghaziuddin, N. (2002). Autistic symptoms following herpes encephalitis. *European Child & Adolescent Psychiatry, 11*(3), 142–146.

Ghaziuddin, M., & Burmeister, M. (1999). Deletion of chromosome 2q37 and autism: A distinct subtype? *Journal of Autism and Developmental Disorders, 29*(3), 259–263.

Ghaziuddin, M., Shakal, J., & Tsai, L. (1995). Obstetric factors in Asperger syndrome: Comparison with high-functioning autism. *Journal of Intellectual Disability Research, 39*(Pt. 6), 538–543.

Ghaziuddin, M., Tsai, L. Y., Eilers, L., & Ghaziuddin, N. (1992). Brief report: Autism and herpes simplex encephalitis. *Journal of Autism and Developmental Disorders, 22*(1), 107–113.

Ghaziuddin, M., Tsai, L., & Ghaziuddin, N. (1992). Autism in Down's syndrome: Presentation and diagnosis. *Journal of Intellectual Disability Research, 36*(5), 449–456.

Ghaziuddin, M., Zaccagnini, J., Tsai, L., & Elardo, S. (1999). Is megalencephaly specific to autism? *Journal of Intellectual Disability Research, 43*(Pt. 4), 279–282.

Giannini, A. J., Tamulonis, D., Giannini, M. C., Loiselle, R. H., & Spirtos, G. (1984). Defective response to social cues in Mobius' syndrome. *Journal of Nervous Mental Disorders, 172*(3), 174–175.

Gibbs, M., & Thorpe, J. (1983). Personality stereotype of noninstitutionalized Down syndrome children. *American Journal of Mental Deficiency, 87*(6), 601–605.

Gillberg, C. (1986). Onset at age 14 of a typical autistic syndrome. A case report of a girl with herpes simplex encephalitis. *Journal of Autism and Developmental Disorders, 16*(3), 369–375.

Gillberg, C. (1991). The treatment of epilepsy in autism. *Journal of Autism and Developmental Disorders, 21*(1), 61–77.

Gillberg, C., & Billstedt, E. (2000). Autism and Asperger syndrome: Coexistence with other clinical disorders. *Acta Psychiatrica Scandinavica, 102*(5), 321–330.

Gillberg, C., & de Souza, L. (2002). Head circumference in autism, Asperger syndrome, and ADHD: A comparative study. *Developmental Medicine and Child Neurology, 44*(5), 296–300.

Gillberg, C., & Forsell, C. (1984). Childhood psychosis and neurofibromatosis: More than a coincidence? *Journal of Autism and Developmental Disorders, 14*(1), 1–8.

Gillberg, C., & Gillberg, I. C. (1983). Infantile autism: A total population study of reduced optimality in the pre-, peri-, and neonatal period. *Journal of Autism and Developmental Disorders, 13,* 153–166.

Gillberg, C., Persson, E., & Wahlstrom, J. (1986). The autism-fragile-X syndrome (AFRAX): A population-based study of ten boys. *Journal of Mental Deficiency Research, 30*(Pt. 1), 27–39.

Gillberg, C., & Rasmussen, P. (1994). Brief report: Four case histories and a literature review of Williams syndrome and autistic behavior. *Journal of Autism and Developmental Disorders, 24*(3), 381–393.

Gillberg, C., & Steffenburg, S. (1989). Autistic behaviour in Moebius syndrome. *Acta Paediatricaica Scandinavica, 78*(2), 314–316.

Gillberg, C., Steffenburg, S., & Schaumann, H. (1991). Is autism more common now than ten years ago? *British Journal of Psychiatry, 158,* 403–409.

Gillberg, C., Steffenburg, S., Wahlstrom, J., Gillberg, I. C., Sjostedt, A., Martinsson, T., et al. (1991). Autism associated with marker chromosome. *Journal of the American Academy of Child and Adolescent Psychiatry, 30*(3), 489–494.

Gillberg, C., & Wahlstrom, J. (1985). Chromosome abnormalities in infantile autism and other childhood psychoses: A population study of 66 cases. *Developmental Medicine and Child Neurology, 27*(3), 293–304.

Gillberg, C., & Winnergard, I. (1984). Childhood psychosis in a case of Moebius syndrome. *Neuropediatrics, 15*(3), 147–149.

Gillberg, I., Gillberg, C., & Ahlsen, G. (1994). Autistic behaviour and attention deficits in tuberous sclerosis: A population-based study. *Developmental Medicine and Child Neurology, 36*(1), 50–56.

Gilliam, J. E. (1995). *Gilliam Autism Rating Scale (GARS).* Austin, TX: ProEd.

Glaser, B., Mumme, D. L., Blasey, C., Morris, M. A., Dahoun, S. P., Antonarakis, S. E., et al. (2002). Language skills in children with velo-cardiofacial syndrome (deletion 22q11.2). *Journal of Pediatrics, 140*(6), 753–758.

Goldenberg, A., Chevy, F., Bernard, C., Wolf, C., & Cormier-Daire, V. (2003). Clinical characteristics and diagnosis of Smith-Lemli-Opitz syndrome and tentative phenotype-genotype correlation: Report of 45 cases. *Archives of Pediatrics, 10*(1), 4–10.

Gomez, M. R., Sampson, J., & Whittemore, V. (1999). *The tuberous sclerosis complex.* Oxford, England: Oxford University Press.

Gonzalez, C. H., Marques-Dias, M. J., Kim, C. A., Sugayama, S. M., Da Paz, J. A., Huson, S. M., et al. (1998). Congenital abnormalities in Brazilian children associated with misoprostol misuse in first trimester of pregnancy. *Lancet, 351*(9116), 1624–1627.

Goodwin, M. S., Cowen, M. A., & Goodwin, T. C. (1971). Malabsorption and cerebral dysfunction: A multivariate and comparative study of autistic children. *Journal of Autism and Childhood Schizophrenia, 1*(1), 48–62.

Gordon, A. G. (1991). Co-occurrence of deafness and infantile autism. *American Journal of Psychiatry, 148*(11), 1615.

Gothelf, D., & Lombroso, P. J. (2001). Genetics of childhood disorders: XXV. Velocardiofacial syndrome. *Journal of the American Academy of Child and Adolescent Psychiatry, 40*(4), 489–491.

Gothelf, D., Presburger, G., Levy, D., Nahmani, A., Burg, M., Berant, M., et al. (2004). Genetic, developmental, and physical factors associated with attention deficit hyperactivity disorder in patients with velocardiofacial syndrome. *American Journal of Medical Genetics, 126B*(1), 116–121.

Gothelf, D., Presburger, G., Zohar, A. H., Burg, M., Nahmani, A., Frydman, M., et al. (2004). Obsessive-compulsive disorder in patients with velocardiofacial (22q11 deletion) syndrome. *American Journal of Medical Genetics, 126B*(1), 99–105.

Graf, W. D., Marin-Garcia, J., Gao, H. G., Pizzo, S., Naviaux, R. K., Markusic, D., et al. (2000). Autism associated with the mitochondrial DNA G8363A transfer RNA(Lys) mutation. *Journal of Child Neurology, 15*(6), 357–361.

Grice, S. J., Spratling, M. W., Karmiloff-Smith, A., Halit, H., Csibra, G., de Haan, M., et al. (2001). Disordered visual processing and oscillatory brain activity in autism and Williams syndrome. *Neuroreport: For Rapid Communication of Neuroscience Research, 12*(12), 2697–2700.

Grizenko, N., Cvejic, H., Vida, S., & Sayegh, L. (1991). Behaviour problems of the mentally retarded. *Canadian Journal of Psychiatry, 36*(10), 712–717.

Gurrieri, F., Battaglia, A., Torrisi, L., Tancredi, R., Cavallaro, C., Sangiorgi, E., et al. (1999). Pervasive developmental disorder and epilepsy due to maternally derived duplication of 15q11-q13. *Neurology, 52*(8), 1694–1697.

Gutierrez, G. C., Smalley, S. L., & Tanguay, P. E. (1998). Autism in tuberous sclerosis complex. *Journal of Autism and Developmental Disorders, 28*(2), 97–103.

Hagberg, B., Aicardi, J., Dias, K., & Ramos, O. (1983). A progressive syndrome of autism, dementia, ataxia, and loss of purposeful hand use in girls: Rett's syndrome: Report of 35 cases. *Annals of Neurology, 14*(4), 471–479.

Hagerman, R. (2002). The physical and behavioral phenotype. In R. J. Hagerman & P. J. Hagerman (Eds.), *Fragile X syndrome: Diagnosis, treatment and research* (pp. 3–109). Baltimore: Johns Hopkins University Press.

Hagerman, R., Jackson, A., Levitas, A., Rimland, B., & Braden, M. (1986). An analysis of autism in fifty males with the fragile X syndrome. *American Journal of Medical Genetics, 23*(1/2), 359–374.

Hagerman, R., Leavitt, B. R., Farzin, F., Jacquemont, S., Greco, C. M., Brunberg, J. A., et al. (2004). Fragile-X-associated tremor/ataxia syndrome (FXTAS) in females with the FMR1 premutation. *American Journal of Human Genetics, 74*(5), 1051–1056.

Hagerman, R., Leehey, M., Heinrichs, W., Tassone, F., Wilson, R., Hills, J., et al. (2001). Intention tremor, parkinsonism, and generalized brain atrophy in male carriers of fragile X. *Neurology, 57*(1), 127–130.

Harrison, J. E., & Bolton, P. F. (1997). Annotation: Tuberous sclerosis. *Journal of Child Psychology and Psychiatry, 38*, 603–614.

Harvey, M. T., & Kennedy, C. H. (2002). Polysomnographic phenotypes in developmental disabilities [Special issue]. *International Journal of Developmental Neuroscience, 20*(3/5), 443–448.

Hashimoto, O., Shimizu, Y., & Kawasaki, Y. (1993). Brief report: Low frequency of the fragile X syndrome among Japanese autistic subjects. *Journal of Autism and Developmental Disorders, 23*, 201–209.

Hashimoto, T., Aihara, R., Tayama, M., Miyazaki, M., Shirakawa, Y., & Kuroda, Y. (1991). Reduced thyroid-stimulating hormone response to thyrotropin-releasing hormone in autistic boys. *Developmental Medicine and Child Neurology, 33*(4), 313–319.

Hering, E., Epstein, R., Elroy, S., Iancu, D. R., & Zelnik, N. (1999). Sleep patterns in autistic children. *Journal of Autism and Developmental Disorders, 29*(2), 143–147.

Hobson, R. P., & Bishop, M. (2003). The pathogenesis of autism: Insights from congenital blindness. *Philosophical transactions of the Royal Society of London. Series B, Biological sciences, 358*(1430), 335–344.

Hobson, R. P., Lee, A., & Brown, R. (1999). Autism and congenital blindness. *Journal of Autism and Developmental Disorders, 29*(1), 45–56.

Honomichl, R. D., Goodlin-Jones, B. L., Burnham, M., Gaylor, E., & Anders, T. F. (2002). Sleep patterns of children with pervasive developmental disorders. *Journal of Autism and Developmental Disorders, 32*(6), 553–561.

Hook, E. (1982). The epidemiology of Down syndrome. In S. M. Pueschel & J. Rynders (Eds.), *Down syndrome: Advances in biomedicine and the behavioral sciences.* Cambridge, MA: Ware Press.

Hornig, M., & Lipkin, W. I. (2001). Infectious and immune factors in the pathogenesis of neurodevelopmental disorders: Epidemiology, hypotheses, and animal models. *Mental Retardation and Developmental Disabilities Research Review, 7*(3), 200–210.

Horvath, K., Papadimitriou, J. C., Rabsztyn, A., Drachenberg, C., & Tildon, J. T. (1999). Gastrointestinal abnormalities in children with autistic disorder. *Journal of Pediatrics, 135*(5), 559–563.

Horvath, K., & Perman, J. A. (2002a). Autism and gastrointestinal symptoms. *Current Gastroenterology Reports, 4*(3), 251–258.

Horvath, K., & Perman, J. A. (2002b). Autistic disorder and gastrointestinal disease. *Current Opinion in Pediatrics, 14*(5), 583–587.

Horvath, K., Stefanatos, G., Sokolski, K. N., Wachtel, R., Nabors, L., & Tildon, J. T. (1998). Improved social and language skills after secretin administration in patients with autistic spectrum disorders. *Journal of the Association of Academic Minority Physicians, 9*(1), 9–15.

Hoshino, Y., Watanabe, H., Yashima, Y., Kaneko, M., & Kumashiro, H. (1984). An investigation on sleep disturbance of autistic children. *Folia psychiatrica et neurologica japonica, 38*(1), 45–51.

Hotopf, M., & Bolton, P. (1995). A case of autism associated with partial tetrasomy 15. *Journal of Autism and Developmental Disorders, 25*, 41–49.

Hou, J. W., & Wang, T. R. (1998). Unusual features in children with inv dup(15) supernumerary marker: A study of genotype-phenotype correlation in Taiwan. *European Journal of Pediatrics, 157*(2), 122–127.

Howlin, P., Wing, L., & Gould, J. (1995). The recognition of autism in children with Down syndrome—implications for intervention and some speculations about pathology. *Developmental Medicine and Child Neurology, 37,* 406–414.

Hultman, C. M., Sparen, P., & Cnattingius, S. (2002). Perinatal risk factors for infantile autism. *Epidemiology, 13*(4), 417–423.

Hunt, A., & Shepherd, C. (1993). A prevalence study of autism in tuberous sclerosis. *Journal of Autism and Developmental Disorders, 23,* 323–339.

Iliyasu, Z., Gilmour, W. H., & Stone, D. H. (2002). Prevalence of Down syndrome in Glasgow, 1980–96—The growing impact of prenatal diagnosis on younger mothers. *Health Bull, 60*(1), 20–26.

Inanuma, K. (1984). Sleep-wake patterns in autistic children (Summary in English). *Japanese Journal of Child and Adolescent Psychiatry, 25,* 205–217.

Jacquemont, S., Hagerman, R. J., Leehey, M., Grigsby, J., Zhang, L., Brunberg, J. A., et al. (2003). Fragile X premutation tremor/ataxia syndrome: Molecular, clinical, and neuroimaging correlates. *American Journal of Human Genetics, 72*(4), 869–878.

Jacquemont, S., Hagerman, R. J., Leehey, M. A., Hall, D. A., Levine, R. A., Brunberg, J. A., et al. (2004). Penetrance of the fragile X-associated tremor/ataxia syndrome in a premutation carrier population. *Journal of the American Medical Association, 291*(4), 460–469.

Janson, U. (1993). Normal and deviant behavior in blind children with ROP. *Acta Ophthalmologica* (Suppl. 210), 20–26.

Johansson, M., Wentz, E., Fernell, E., Stromland, K., Miller, M. T., & Gillberg, C. (2001). Autistic spectrum disorders in Mobius sequence: A comprehensive study of 25 individuals. *Developmental Medicine and Child Neurology, 43*(5), 338–345.

Johnson, R. J., Wiersema, V., & Kraft, I. A. (1974). Hair amino acids in childhood autism. *Journal of Autism and Childhood Schizophrenia, 4*(2), 187–188.

Jones, A. C., Daniells, C. E., Snell, R. G., Tachataki, M., Idziaszczyk, S. A., Krawczak, M., et al. (1997). Molecular genetic and phenotypic analysis reveals differences between TSC1 and TSC2 associated familial and sporadic tuberous sclerosis. *Human Molecular Genetics, 6,* 2155–2161.

Jones, A. C., Shyamsundar, M. M., Thomas, M. W., Maynard, J., Idziaszczyk, S., Tomkins, S., et al. (1999). Comprehensive mutation analysis of TSC1 and TSC2-and phenotypic correlations in 150 families with tuberous sclerosis. *American Journal of Human Genetics, 64*(5), 1305–1315.

Jones, W., Bellugi, U., Lai, Z., Chiles, M., Reilly, J., Lincoln, A., et al. (2000). II. Hypersociability in Williams syndrome [Special issue]. *Journal of Cognitive Neuroscience, 12*(Suppl. 1), 30–46.

Jorde, L. B., Hasstedt, S. J., Ritvo, E. R., Mason-Brothers, A., Freeman, B. J., Pingree, C., et al. (1991). Complex segregation analysis of autism. *American Journal of Human Genetics, 49,* 932–938.

Jure, R., Rapin, I., & Tuchman, R. F. (1991). Hearing-impaired autistic children. *Developmental Medicine and Child Neurology, 33*(12), 1062–1072.

Juul-Dam, N., Townsend, J., & Courchesne, E. (2001). Prenatal, perinatal, and neonatal factors in autism, pervasive developmental disorder-not otherwise specified, and the general population. *Pediatrics, 107*(4), E63.

Kandt, R. S. (2003). Tuberous sclerosis complex and neurofibromatosis type 1: The two most common neurocutaneous diseases. *Neurologic Clinics, 21,* 983–1004.

Kau, A. S., Tierney, E., Bukelis, I., Stump, M. H., Kates, W. R., Trescher, W. H., et al. (2004). Social behavior profile in young males with fragile X syndrome: Characteristics and specificity. *American Journal of Medical Genetics, 126A*(1), 9–17.

Kawashima, H., Mori, T., Kashiwagi, Y., Takekuma, K., Hoshika, A., & Wakefield, A. (2000). Detection and sequencing of measles virus from peripheral mononuclear cells from patients with inflammatory bowel disease and autism. *Digestive Diseases and Sciences, 45*(4), 723–729.

Keeler, W. R. (1958). Autistic patterns and defective communication in blind children with retrolental fibroplasia. In H. P. Hoch & J. Zubin (Eds.), *Psychopathology of communication* (pp. 64–83). New York: Rune and Stratton.

Keller, K., Williams, C., Wharton, P., Paulk, M., Bent-Williams, A., Gray, B., et al. (2003). Routine cytogenetic and FISH studies for 17p11/15q11 duplications and subtelomeric rearrangement studies in children with autism spectrum disorders. *American Journal of Medical Genetics, 117A*(2), 105–111.

Kern, J. K., Van Miller, S., Evans, P. A., & Trivedi, M. H. (2002). Efficacy of porcine secretin in children with autism and pervasive developmental disorder. *Journal of Autism and Developmental Disorders, 32*(3), 153–160.

Kielinen, M., Rantala, H., Timonen, E., Linna, S. L., & Moilanen, I. (2004). Associated medical disorders and disabilities in children with autistic disorder: A population-based study. *Autism: Journal of Research and Practice, 8*(1), 49–60.

Kientz, M. A., & Dunn, W. (1997). A comparison of the performance of children with and without autism on the Sensory Profile. *American Journal of Occupational Therapy, 51,* 530–537.

Kishino, T., Lalande, M., & Wagstaff, J. (1997). UBE3A/E6-AP mutations cause Angelman's syndrome. *Nature Genetics, 15,* 70–73.

Klauck, S. M., Munstermann, E., Bieber-Martig, B., Ruhl, D., Lisch, S., Schmotzer, G., et al. (1997). Molecular genetic analysis of the FMR-1 gene in a large collection of autistic patients. *Human Genetics, 100*(2), 224–229.

Klug, M. G., Burd, L., Kerbeshian, J., Benz, B., & Martsolf, J. T. (2003). A comparison of the effects of parental risk markers on pre- and perinatal variables in multiple patient cohorts with fetal alcohol syndrome, autism, Tourette syndrome, and sudden infant death syndrome: An enviromic analysis. *Neurotoxicol Teratol, 25*(6), 707–717.

Konstantareas, M. M., & Homatidis, S. (1999). Chromosomal abnormalities in a series of children with autistic disorder. *Journal of Autism and Developmental Disorders, 29*(4), 275–285.

Kooy, R. F., Willemsen, R., & Oostra, B. A. (2000). Fragile X syndrome at the turn of the century. *Molecular Medicine Today, 6*(5), 193–198.

Korvatska, E., Van de Water, J., Anders, T. F., & Gershwin, M. E. (2002). Genetic and immunologic considerations in autism. *Neurobiology of Disease, 9*(2), 107–125.

Kotsopoulos, S., & Kutty, K. M. (1979). Histidinemia and infantile autism. *Journal of Autism and Developmental Disorders, 9*(1), 55–60.

Kozma, C. (1998). On cognitive variability in velo-cardiofacial syndrome: Profound mental retardation and autism. *American Journal of Medical Genetics, 81*(3), 269–270.

Krause, I., He, X. S., Gershwin, M. E., & Shoenfeld, Y. (2002). Brief report: Immune factors in autism: A critical review. *Journal of Autism and Developmental Disorders, 32*(4), 337–345.

Kubba, H., MacAndie, C., Ritchie, K., & MacFarlane, M. (2004). Is deafness a disease of poverty? The association between socioeconomic deprivation and congenital hearing impairment. *International Journal of Audiology, 43*(3), 123–125.

Kuddo, T., & Nelson, K. B. (2003). How common are gastrointestinal disorders in children with autism? *Current Opinion in Pediatrics, 15*(3), 339–343.

Kwiatkowski, D. J. (2003). Tuberous sclerosis: From tubers to mTOR. *Annals of Human Genetics, 67*(Pt. 1), 87–96.

Laing, E., Butterworth, G., Ansari, D., Gsodl, M., Longhi, E., Panagiotaki, G., et al. (2002). Atypical development of language and social communication in toddlers with Williams syndrome. *Developmental Science, 5*(2), 233–246.

Lainhart, J. E. (2003). Increased rate of head growth during infancy in autism. *Journal of the American Medical Association, 290*(3), 393–394.

Lainhart, J. E., Piven, J., Wzorek, M., Landa, R., Santangelo, S. L., Coon, H., et al. (1997). Macrocephaly in children and adults with autism. *Journal of the American Academy of Child and Adolescent Psychiatry, 36,* 282–290.

Landgren, M., Gillberg, C., & Stromland, K. (1992). Goldenhar syndrome and autistic behaviour. *Developmental Medicine and Child Neurology, 34*(11), 999–1005.

LaPerchia, P. (1987). Behavioral disorders, learning disabilities and megavitamin therapy. *Adolescence, 22*(87), 729–738.

Larrandaburu, M., Schuler, L., Ehlers, J. A., Reis, A. M., & Silveira, E. L. (1999). The occurrence of Poland and Poland-Moebius syndromes in the same family: Further evidence of their genetic component. *Clinical Dysmorphology, 8*(2), 93–99.

Larsen, J. (1998, October 7). Could new therapy cure autism? [Segment in television series.] *Dateline,* NBC Television.

Laszlo, A., Horvath, E., Eck, E., & Fekete, M. (1994). Serum serotonin, lactate and pyruvate levels in infantile autistic children [Letter]. *Clinical Chimica Acta, 229*(1/2), 205–207.

Lauritsen, M., Mors, O., Mortensen, P. B., & Ewald, H. (1999). Infantile autism and associated autosomal chromosome abnormalities: A register-based study and a literature survey. *Journal of Child Psychology and Psychiatry, 40*(3), 335–345.

Lauritsen, M., Mors, O., Mortensen, P. B., & Ewald, H. (2002). Medical disorders among inpatients with autism in Denmark according to *ICD-8:* a nationwide register-based study. *Journal of Autism and Developmental Disorders, 32*(2), 115–119.

Laws, G., & Bishop, D. (2004). Pragmatic language impairment and social deficits in Williams syndrome: A comparison with Down's syndrome and specific language impairment. *In-*

ternational Journal of Language and Communications Disorders, 39(1), 45–64.

Le Couteur, A., Rutter, M., Lord, C., Rios, P., Robertson, S., Holdgrafer, M., et al. (1989). Autism diagnostic interview: A standardized investigator-based instrument. *Journal of Autism and Developmental Disorders, 19,* 363–387.

Le Couteur, A., Trygstad, O., Evered, C., Gillberg, C., & Rutter, M. (1988). Infantile autism and urinary excretion of peptides and protein-associated peptide complexes. *Journal of Autism and Developmental Disorders, 18*(2), 181–190.

Lerman-Sagie, T., Leshinsky-Silver, E., Watemberg, N., & Lev, D. (2004). Should autistic children be evaluated for mitochondrial disorders? *Journal of Child Neurology, 19*(5), 379–381.

Levitt, J. G., O'Neill, J., Blanton, R. E., Smalley, S., Fadale, D., McCracken, J. T., et al. (2003). Proton magnetic resonance spectroscopic imaging of the brain in childhood autism. *Biological Psychiatry, 54*(12), 1355–1366.

Levy, S., Souders, M. C., Wray, J., Jawad, A. F., Gallagher, P. R., Coplan, J., et al. (2003). Children with autistic spectrum disorders. I: Comparison of placebo and single dose of human synthetic secretin. *Archives of Disease in Childhood, 88*(8), 731–736.

Levy, S., Zoltak, B., & Saelens, T. (1988). A comparison of obstetrical records of autistic and nonautistic referrals for psychoeducational evaluations. *Journal of Autism and Developmental Disorders, 18*(4), 573–581.

Lewis, J. C., Thomas, H. V., Murphy, K. C., & Sampson, J. R. (2004). Genotype and psychological phenotype in tuberous sclerosis. *Journal of Medical Genetics, 41*(3), 203–207.

Lightdale, J. R., Hayer, C., Duer, A., Lind-White, C., Jenkins, S., Siegel, B., et al. (2001). Effects of intravenous secretin on language and behavior of children with autism and gastrointestinal symptoms: A single-blinded, open-label pilot study. *Pediatrics, 108*(5), E90.

Lightdale, J. R., Siegel, B., & Heyman, M. B. (2001). Gastrointestinal symptoms in autistic children. *Clinical Perspectives in Gastroenterology, 1,* 56–58.

Loening-Baucke, V. (1998). Constipation in children. *New England Journal of Medicine, 339*(16), 1155–1156.

Loesch, D. Z., Huggins, R. M., Bui, Q. M., Taylor, A. K., Pratt, C., Epstein, J., et al. (2003). Effect of fragile X status categories and FMRP deficits on cognitive profiles estimated by robust pedigree analysis. *American Journal of Medical Genetics, 122A*(1), 13–23.

Loesch, D. Z., Huggins, R. M., & Hagerman, R. J. (2004). Phenotypic variation and FMRP levels in fragile X. *Mental Retardation and Developmental Disabilities Research Review, 10*(1), 31–41.

Lombard, J. (1998). Autism: A mitochondrial disorder? *Medical Hypotheses, 50*(6), 497–500.

Longo, I., Russo, L., Meloni, I., Ricci, I., Ariani, F., Pescucci, C., et al. (2004). Three Rett patients with both MECP2 mutation and 15q11–13 rearrangements. *European Journal of Human Genetics, 12*(8), 682–685.

Lord, C. (1991). Methods and measures of behavior in the diagnosis of autism and related disorders. *Psychiatric Clinics of North America, 14,* 69–80.

Lord, C. (1995). Follow-up of two-year-olds referred for possible autism. *Journal of Child Psychology and Psychiatry, 36,* 1365–1382.

Lord, C., Mulloy, C., Wendelboe, M., & Schopler, E. (1991). Pre- and perinatal factors in high-functioning females and males with autism. *Journal of Autism and Developmental Disorders, 21*(2), 197–209.

Lord, C., Risi, S., Lambrecht, L., Cook, E. H., Jr., Leventhal, B. L., DiLavore, P. C., et al. (2000). The Autism Diagnostic Observation Schedule-Generic: A standard measure of social and communication deficits associated with the spectrum of autism. *Journal of Autism and Developmental Disorders, 30*(3), 205–223.

Lord, C., Rutter, M., & Le Couteur, A. (1994). Autism Diagnostic Interview-Revised: A revised version of a diagnostic interview for caregivers of individuals with possible pervasive developmental disorders. *Journal of Autism and Developmental Disorders, 24,* 659–685.

Lotter, V. (1967). Epidemiology of autistic conditions in young children: Some characteristics of the children and their parents. *Social Psychiatry, 1,* 163–173.

Lowe, T. L., Tanaka, K., Seashore, M. R., Young, J. G., & Cohen, D. J. (1980). Detection of phenylketonuria in autistic and psychotic children. *Journal of the American Medical Association, 243*(2), 126–128.

Lucarelli, S., Frediani, T., Zingoni, A. M., Ferruzzi, F., Giardini, O., Quintieri, F., et al. (1995). Food allergy and infantile autism. *Panminerva Medica, 37,* 137–141.

Ludowese, C. J., Thompson, K. J., Sekhon, G. S., & Pauli, R. M. (1991). Absence of predictable phenotypic expression in proximal 15q duplications. *Clinical Genetics, 40*(3), 194–201.

Lund, J. (1988). Psychiatric aspects of Down's syndrome. *Acta Psychiatrica Scandinavica, 78*(3), 369–374.

Maddalena, A., Richards, C. S., McGinniss, M. J., Brothman, A., Desnick, R. J., Grier, R. E., et al. (2001). Technical standards and guidelines for fragile X: The first of a series of disease-specific supplements to the Standards and Guidelines for Clinical Genetics Laboratories of the American College of Medical Genetics. (Quality Assurance Subcommittee of the Laboratory Practice Committee) *Genetics in Medicine, 3*(3), 200–205.

Maes, B., Fryns, J. P., Van Walleghem, M., & Van den Berghe, H. (1993). Fragile-X syndrome and autism: A prevalent association or a misinterpreted connection? *Genetic Counseling, 4,* 245–263.

Mann, S. M., Wang, N. J., Liu, D. H., Wang, L., Schultz, R. A., Dorrani, N., et al. (2004). Supernumerary tricentric derivative chromosome 15 in two boys with intractable epilepsy: Another mechanism for partial hexasomy. *Human Genetics,115*(2), 104–111.

Mao, R., & Jalal, S. M. (2000). Characteristics of two cases with dup(15)(q11.2-q12): One of maternal and one of paternal origin. *General Medicine Journal, 2*(2), 131–135.

Marchetti, B., Scifo, R., Batticane, N., & Scapagnini, U. (1990). Immunological significance of opiod peptide dysfunction in infantile autism. *Brain Dysfunction, 3*(5/6), 346–354.

Mari, M., Castiello, U., Marks, D., Marraffa, C., & Prior, M. (2003). The reach-to-grasp movement in children with autism spectrum disorder. *Philosophical transactions of the Royal Society of London. Series B, Biological sciences, 358*(1430), 393–403.

Mason-Brothers, A., Ritvo, E. R., Guze, B., Mo, A., Freeman, B. J., Funderburk, S. J., et al. (1987). Pre-, peri-, and postnatal factors in 181 autistic patients from single and multiple incidence families. *Journal of the American Academy of Child and Adolescent Psychiatry, 26*(1), 39–42.

Mason-Brothers, A., Ritvo, E. R., Pingree, C., Petersen, P. B., Jenson, W. R., McMahon, W. M., et al. (1990). The UCLA-University of Utah epidemiologic survey of autism: Prenatal, perinatal, and postnatal factors. *Pediatrics, 86*(4), 514–519.

Matsuishi, T., Shiotsuki, Y., Yoshimura, K., Shoji, H., Imuta, F., & Yamashita, F. (1987). High prevalence of infantile autism in Kurume City, Japan. *Journal of Child Neurology, 2*(4), 268–271.

Matsuishi, T., Yamashita, Y., Ohtani, Y., Ornitz, E., Kuriya, N., Murakami, Y., et al. (1999). Brief report: Incidence of and risk factors for autistic disorder in neonatal intensive care unit survivors. *Journal of Autism and Developmental Disorders, 29*(2), 161–166.

Mazzocco, M. M., Kates, W. R., Baumgardner, T. L., Freund, L. S., & Reiss, A. L. (1997). Autistic behaviors among girls with fragile X syndrome. *Journal of Autism and Developmental Disorders, 27*(4), 415–435.

Mazzocco, M. M., Pulsifer, M., Fiumara, A., Cocuzza, M., Nigro, F., Incorpora, G., et al. (1998). Autistic behaviors among children with fragile X or Rett syndrome: Implications for the classification of pervasive developmental disorder. *Journal of Autism and Developmental Disorders, 28*(4), 321–328.

McManus, E. J., & Alessi, D. R. (2002). TSC1-TSC2: A complex tale of PKB-mediated S6K regulation. *Nature Cell Biology, 4*(9), E214–216.

Menage, P., Thibault, G., Martineau, J., Herault, J., Muh, J., Barthelemy, C., et al. (1992). An IgE mechanism in autistic hypersensitivity. *Biological Psychiatry, 31*(2), 210–212.

Menolascino, F. (1965). Psychiatric aspects of mongolism. *American Journal of Mental Deficiency, 69,* 653–660.

Mervis, C. B. (1999). The Williams syndrome cognitive profile: Strengths, weaknesses, and interrelations among auditory short-term memory, language, and visuospatial constructive cognition. In E. Winograd & R. Fivush (Eds.), *Ecological approaches to cognition: Essays in honor of Ulric Neisser* (pp. 193–227). Mahwah, NJ: Erlbaum.

Meryash, D., Szymanski, L., & Gerald, P. (1982). Infantile autism associated with the fragile-X syndrome. *Journal of Autism and Developmental Disorders, 12*(3), 295–301.

Meyerson, M. D., & Foushee, D. R. (1978). Speech, language and hearing in Moebius syndrome: A study of 22 patients. *Developmental Medicine and Child Neurology, 20*(3), 357–365.

Michelson, A. M. (1998). Selenium glutathione peroxidase: Some aspects in man. *Journal of Environmental Pathology, Toxicology, and Oncology, 17*(3/4), 233–239.

Miladi, N., Larnaout, A., Kaabachi, N., Helayem, M., & Ben Hamida, M. (1992). Phenylketonuria: An underlying etiology of autistic syndrome. A case report. *Journal of Child Neurology, 7*(1), 22–23.

Miles, J. H., Hadden, L. L., Takahashi, T. N., & Hillman, R. E. (2000). Head circumference is an independent clinical finding associated with autism. *American Journal of Medical Genetics, 95*(4), 339–350.

Minshew, N. J., Goldstein, G., Dombrowski, S. M., Panchalingam, K., & Pettegrew, J. W. (1993). A preliminary 31P MRS study of autism: Evidence for undersynthesis and increased degradation of brain membranes. *Biological Psychiatry, 33,* 762–773.

Möbius, P. J. (1888). Über Angeborenen doppelseitige Abducens-Facialis-Lähmung. *Münchener Medizinische Wochenschrift, 35,* 91–94, 108–111.

Moeschler, J. B., Mohandas, T. K., Hawk, A. B., & Noll, W. W. (2002). Estimate of prevalence of proximal 15q duplication syndrome. *American Journal of Medical Genetics, 111*(4), 440–442.

Mohandas, T. K., Park, J. P., Spellman, R. A., Filiano, J. J., Mamourian, A. C., Hawk, A. B., et al. (1999). Paternally derived de novo interstitial duplication of proximal 15q in a patient with developmental delay. *American Journal of Medical Genetics, 82*(4), 294–300.

Molloy, C. A., & Manning-Courtney, P. (2003). Prevalence of chronic gastrointestinal symptoms in children with autism and autistic spectrum disorders. *Autism: Journal of Research and Practice, 7*(2), 165–171.

Molloy, C. A., Manning-Courtney, P., Swayne, S., Bean, J., Brown, J. M., Murray, D. S., et al. (2002). Lack of benefit of intravenous synthetic human secretin in the treatment of autism. *Journal of Autism and Developmental Disorders, 32*(6), 545–551.

Moore, S. J., Turnpenny, P., Quinn, A., Glover, S., Lloyd, D. J., Montgomery, T., et al. (2000). A clinical study of 57 children with fetal anticonvulsant syndromes. *Journal of Medical Genetics, 37*(7), 489–497.

Moreno, H., Borjas, L., Arrieta, A., Saez, L., Prassad, A., Estevez, J., et al. (1992). Clinical heterogeneity of the autistic syndrome: A study of 60 families. *Investigacion Clinica, 33*(1), 13–31.

Msall, M. E., Phelps, D. L., Hardy, R. J., Dobson, V., Quinn, G. E., Summers, C. G., et al. (2004). Educational and social competencies at 8 years in children with threshold retinopathy of prematurity in the CRYO-ROP multicenter study. *Pediatrics, 113*(4), 790–799.

Munk, D. D., & Repp, A. C. (1994). Behavioral assessment of feeding problems of individuals with severe disabilities. *Journal of Applied Behavior Analysis, 27*(2), 241–250.

Murch, S. H., Anthony, A., Casson, D. H., Malik, M., Berelowitz, M., Dhillon, A. P., et al. (2004). Retraction of an interpretation. *Lancet, 363*(9411), 750.

Murray, A. (2000). Premature ovarian failure and the FMR1 gene. *Seminars in Reproductive Medicine, 18*(1), 59–66.

Myers, B., & Pueschel, S. (1991). Psychiatric disorders in persons with Down syndrome. *Journal of Nervous and Mental Diseases, 179*(10), 609–613.

Nelson, K. B. (1991). Prenatal and perinatal factors in the etiology of autism. *Pediatrics, 87*(5, Pt. 2), 761–766.

Nicolson, R., Bhalerao, S., & Sloman, L. (1998). 47,XYY karyotypes and pervasive developmental disorders. *Canadian Journal of Psychiatry, 43*(6), 619–622.

Nielsen, J., Christensen, K. R., Friedrich, U., Zeuthen, E., & Ostergaard, O. (1973). Childhood of males with the XYY syndrome. *Journal of Autism and Childhood Schizophrenia, 3*(1), 5–26.

Niklasson, L., Rasmussen, P., Oskarsdottir, S., & Gillberg, C. (2001). Neuropsychiatric disorders in the 22q11 deletion syndrome. *General Medicine Journal, 3*(1), 79–84.

Niklasson, L., Rasmussen, P., Oskarsdottir, S., & Gillberg, C. (2002). Chromosome 22q11 deletion syndrome (CATCH 22): Neuropsychiatric and neuropsychological aspects. *Developmental Medicine and Child Neurology, 44*(1), 44–50.

Norris, M., Spaulding, P., & Bordie, F. (1957). *Blindness in children.* Chicago: University of Chicago Press.

Noterdaeme, M., Mildenberger, K., Minow, F., & Amorosa, H. (2002). Evaluation of neuromotor deficits in children with autism and children with a specific speech and language disorder. *European Child and Adolescent Psychiatry, 11*(5), 219–225.

Nyhan, W. L., James, J. A., Teberg, A. J., Sweetman, L., & Nelson, L. G. (1969). A new disorder of purine metabolism with behavioral manifestations. *Journal of Pediatrics, 74*(1), 20–27.

Ohtaki, E., Kawano, Y., Urabe, F., Komori, H., Horikawa, M., Yamashita, Y., et al. (1992). The prevalence of Rett syndrome and infantile autism in Chikugo District, the southwestern area of Fukuoka prefecture, Japan. *Journal of Autism and Developmental Disorders, 22*(3), 452–454.

O'Leary, J. J., Uhlmann, V., & Wakefield, A. J. (2000). Measles virus and autism. *Lancet, 356*(9231), 772.

Olsen, C. L., Cross, P. K., & Gensburg, L. J. (2003). Down syndrome: Interaction between culture, demography, and biology in determining the prevalence of a genetic trait. *Human Biology, 75*(4), 503–520.

OMIM™. (2000). *Online Mendelian Inheritance in Man—OMIMJ* . Baltimore: McKusick-Nathans Institute for Genetic Medicine, Johns Hopkins University, Bethesda, MD: National Center for Biotechnology Information, National Library of Medicine. Available from http://www.ncbi.nlm.nih.gov/omim.

Ornitz, E. M. (1985). Neurophysiology of infantile autism. *Journal of the American Academy of Child Psychiatry, 24*(3), 251–262.

Ornitz, E. M., Guthrie, D., & Farley, A. H. (1977). The early development of autistic children. *Journal of Autism and Childhood Schizophrenia, 7,* 207–229.

Osborn, A. G., Harnsberger, H. R., Smoker, W. R., & Boyer, R. S. (1990). Multiple sclerosis in adolescents: CT and MR findings. *American Journal of Roentgenology, 155,* 385–390.

Owley, T., McMahon, W., Cook, E. H., Laulhere, T., South, M., Mays, L. Z., et al. (2001). Multisite, double-blind, placebo-controlled trial of porcine secretin in autism. *Journal of the American Academy of Child and Adolescent Psychiatry, 40*(11), 1293–1299.

Ozonoff, S., Williams, B. J., Gale, S., & Miller, J. N. (1999). Autism and autistic behavior in Joubert syndrome. *Journal of Child Neurology, 14*(10), 636–641.

Ozonoff, S., Williams, B. J., Rauch, A. M., & Opitz, J. O. (2000). Behavior phenotype of FG syndrome: Cognition, personality, and behavior in eleven affected boys. *American Journal of Medical Genetics, 97*(2), 112–118.

Pascual-Castroviejo, I., Roche, C., Martinez-Bermejo, A., Arcas, J., Lopez-Martin, V., Tendero, A., et al. (1998). Hypomelanosis of ITO: A study of 76 infantile cases. *Brain and Development, 20*(1), 36–43.

Pastuszak, A. L., Schuler, L., Speck-Martins, C. E., Coelho, K. E., Cordello, S. M., Vargas, F., et al. (1998). Use of misoprostol during pregnancy and Mobius' syndrome in infants. *New England Journal of Medicine, 338*(26), 1881–1885.

Patzold, L. M., Richdale, A. L., & Tonge, B. J. (1998). An investigation into sleep characteristics of children with autism and Asperger's Disorder. *Journal of Paediatrics and Child Health, 34*(6), 528–533.

Paulson, G. W., & Paulson, R. B. (1981). Teratogenic effects of anticonvulsants. *Archives of Neurology, 38*(3), 140–143.

Pavone, L., Fiumara, A., Bottaro, G., Mazzone, D., & Coleman, M. (1997). Autism and celiac disease: Failure to validate the hypothesis that a link might exist. *Biological Psychiatry, 42*(1), 72–75.

Payton, J., Steele, M., Wenger, S., & Minshew, N. (1989). The fragile X marker and autism in perspective. *Journal of the American Academy of Child and Adolescent Psychiatry, 28*(3), 417–421.

Peltola, H., Patja, A., Leinikki, P., Valle, M., Davidkin, I., & Paunio, M. (1998). No evidence for measles, mumps, and rubella vaccine-associated inflammatory bowel disease or autism in a 14-year prospective study [Letter]. *Lancet, 351*(9112), 1327–1328.

Perez, E., & Sullivan, K. E. (2002). Chromosome 22q11.2 deletion syndrome: DiGeorge and velocardiofacial syndromes. *Current Opinion in Pediatrics, 14*(6), 678–683.

Perry, T. L., Hansen, S., & Christie, R. G. (1978). Amino compounds and organic acids in CSF, plasma, and urine of autistic children. *Biological Psychiatry, 13*(5), 575–586.

Philofsky, A., Hepburn, S. L., Hayes, A., Hagerman, R., & Rogers, S. J. (2004). Linguistic and cognitive functioning and autism symptoms in young children with fragile X syndrome. *American Journal of Mental Retardation, 109*(3), 208–218.

Piven, J., Berthier, M. L., Starkstein, S. E., Nehme, E., Pearlson, G., & Folstein, S. E. (1990). Magnetic resonance imaging evidence for a defect of cerebral cortical development in autism. *American Journal of Psychiatry, 147,* 734–739.

Piven, J., Gayle, J., Chase, G. A., Fink, B., Landa, R., Wzorek, M. M., et al. (1990). A family history study of neuropsychiatric disorders in the adult siblings of autistic individuals. *Journal of the American Academy of Child and Adolescent Psychiatry, 29*(2), 177–183.

Piven, J., Simon, J., Chase, G. A., Wzorek, M., Landa, R., Gayle, J., et al. (1993). The etiology of autism: Pre-, peri- and neonatal factors. *Journal of the American Academy of Child and Adolescent Psychiatry, 32,* 1256–1263.

Pober, B. R., & Dykens, E. M. (1996). Williams syndrome: An overview of medical, cognitive, and behavioral features. *Child and Adolescent Psychiatric Clinics of North America, 5*(4), 929–943.

Pons, R., Andreu, A. L., Checcarelli, N., Vila, M. R., Engelstad, K., Sue, C. M., et al. (2004). Mitochondrial DNA abnormalities and autistic spectrum disorders. *Journal of Pediatrics, 144,* 81–85.

Prasad, C., Prasad, A. N., Chodirker, B. N., Lee, C., Dawson, A. K., Jocelyn, L. J., et al. (2000). Genetic evaluation of pervasive developmental disorders: The terminal 22q13 deletion syndrome may represent a recognizable phenotype. *Clinical Genetics, 57*(2), 103–109.

Pueschel, S., Bernier, J., & Pezzullo, J. (1991). Behavioural observations in children with Down's syndrome. *Journal of Mental Deficiency Research, 35*(6), 502–511.

Pueschel, S., Herman, R., & Groden, G. (1985). Brief report: Screening children with autism for fragile-X syndrome and phenylketonuria. *Journal of Autism and Developmental Disorders, 15*(3), 335–338.

Ramoz, N., Reichert, J. G., Smith, C. J., Silverman, J. M., Bespalova, I. N., Davis, K. L., et al. (2004). Linkage and association of the mitochondrial aspartate/glutamate carrier SLC25A12 gene with autism. *American Journal of Psychiatry, 161*(4), 662–669.

Rapin, I. (1996a). Historical data. In I. Rapin (Ed.), *Preschool children with inadequate communication: Developmental language disorder, autism, low IQ* (pp. 58–97). London: MacKeith Press.

Rapin, I. (1996b). Neurological examination. In I. Rapin (Ed.), *Preschool children with inadequate communication: Developmental language disorder, autism, low IQ* (pp. 98–122). London: MacKeith Press.

Rausch, L. A., & Nevin, N. C. (1991). Duplication of 15q11.2–15q13 in five cases with different phenotypes. *Journal of Medical Genetics, 28,* 573–574.

Raynes, H. R., Shanske, A., Goldberg, S., Burde, R., & Rapin, I. (1999). Joubert syndrome: Monozygotic twins with discordant phenotypes. *Journal of Child Neurology, 14*(10), 649–654.

Reilly, J., Klima, E. S., & Bellugi, U. (1990). Once more with feeling: Affect and language in atypical populations. *Development and Psychopathology, 2*(4), 367–391.

Reiss, A. L., Feinstein, C., Rosenbaum, K. N., Borengasser-Caruso, M. A., & Goldsmith, B. M. (1985). Autism associated with Williams syndrome. *Journal of Pediatrics, 106*(2), 247–249.

Repetto, G. M., White, L. M., Bader, P. J., Johnson, D., & Knoll, J. H. (1998). Interstitial duplications of chromosome region 15q11q13: Clinical and molecular characterization. *American Journal of Medical Genetics, 79*(2), 82–89.

Richdale, A. (1999). Sleep problems in autism: Prevalence, cause, and intervention. *Developmental Medicine and Child Neurology, 41*(1), 60–66.

Richdale, A., Francis, A., Gavidia-Payne, S., & Cotton, S. (2000). Stress, behaviour, and sleep problems in children with intellectual disability. *Journal of Intellectual and Developmental Disability, 25,* 147–161.

Richdale, A., & Prior, M. R. (1995). The sleep/wake rhythm in children with autism. *European Child and Adolescent Psychiatry, 4,* 175–186.

Riddle, J. E., Cheema, A., Sobesky, W. E., Gardner, S. C., Taylor, A. K., Pennington, B. F., et al. (1998). Phenotypic involvement in females with the FMR1 gene mutation. *American Journal of Mental Retardation, 102*(6), 590–601.

Riikonen, R., & Amnell, G. (1981). Psychiatric disorders in children with earlier infantile spasms. *Developmental Medicine and Child Neurology, 23*(6), 747–760.

Riikonen, R., & Simell, O. (1990). Tuberous sclerosis and infantile spasms. *Developmental Medicine and Child Neurology, 32*(3), 203–209.

Rineer, S., Finucane, B., & Simon, E. W. (1998). Autistic symptoms among children and young adults with isodicentric chromosome 15. *American Journal of Medical Genetics, 81*(5), 428–433.

Ritvo, E., & Freeman, B. J. (1978). National society for autistic children definition of the syndrome of autism. *Journal of Autism and Childhood Schizophrenia, 8,* 162–167.

Ritvo, E., Freeman, B. J., Pingree, C., Mason-Brothers, A., Jorde, L., Jenson, W. R., et al. (1989). The UCLA-University of Utah epidemiologic survey of autism: Prevalence. *American Journal of Psychiatry, 146*(2), 194–199.

Ritvo, E., Jorde, L. B., Mason-Brothers, A., Freeman, B. J., Pingree, C., Jones, M. B., et al. (1989). The UCLA-University of Utah epidemiologic survey of autism: Recurrence risk estimates and genetic counseling. *American Journal of Psychiatry, 146*(8), 1032–1036.

Ritvo, E., Mason-Brothers, A., Freeman, B., Pingree, C., Jenson, W., McMahon, W., et al. (1990). The UCLA-University of Utah epidemiologic survey of autism: The etiologic role of rare diseases. *American Journal of Psychiatry, 147*(12), 1614–1621.

Roberts, W., Weaver, L., Brian, J., Bryson, S., Emelianova, S., Griffiths, A. M., et al. (2001). Repeated doses of porcine secretin in the treatment of autism: A randomized, placebo-controlled trial. *Pediatrics, 107*(5), E71.

Robinson, T. W. (2001). Homeopathic Secretin in autism: A clinical pilot study. *British Homeopathic Journal, 90*(2), 86–91.

Rodier, P. M., Ingram, J. L., Tisdale, B., Nelson, S., & Romano, J. (1996). Embryological origin for autism: Developmental anomalies of the cranial nerve motor nuclei. *Journal of Comparative Neurology, 370,* 247–261.

Rogers, C. (1987). Maternal support for the Down's syndrome stereotype: The effect of direct experience on the condition. *Journal of Mental Deficiency Research, 31,* 271–278.

Rogers, S. J., Bennetto, L., McEvoy, R., & Pennington, B. F. (1996). Imitation and pantomime in high-functioning adolescents with autism spectrum disorders. *Child Development, 67,* 2060–2073.

Rogers, S. J., & Newhart-Larson, S. (1989). Characteristics of infantile autism in five children with Leber's congenital amaurosis. *Developmental Medicine and Child Neurology, 31*(5), 598–608.

Rogers, S. J., Wehner, E. A., & Hagerman, R. (2001). The behavioral phenotype in fragile X: Symptoms of autism in very young children with fragile X syndrome, idiopathic autism, and other developmental disorders. *Journal of Developmental and Behavioral Pediatrics, 22*(6), 409–417.

Roper, L., Arnold, P., & Monteiro, B. (2003). Co-occurrence of autism and deafness: Diagnostic considerations. *Autism: Journal of Research and Practice, 7*(3), 245–253.

Rosenhall, U., Nordin, V., Sandstrom, M., Ahlsen, G., & Gillberg, C. (1999). Autism and hearing loss. *Journal of Autism and Developmental Disorders, 29*(5), 349–357.

Roubertie, A., Semprino, M., Chaze, A. M., Rivier, F., Humbertclaude, V., Cheminal, R., et al. (2001). Neurological presentation of three patients with 22q11 deletion: CATCH 22 syndrome. *Brain Development, 23*(8), 810–814.

Rutter, M. (1996). Autism research: Prospects and priorities. *Journal of Autism and Developmental Disorders, 26*(2), 257–275.

Rutter, M., Bailey, A., Bolton, P., & Le Couteur, A. (1993). Autism: Syndrome of definition and possible genetic mechanisms. In R. Plomin & G. E. McLearn (Eds.), *Nature, nurture and psychology.* Washington, DC: American Psychological Association.

Rutter, M., Bailey, A., Bolton, P., & Le Couteur, A. (1994). Autism and known medical conditions: Myth and substance. *Journal of Child Psychology and Psychiatry, 35,* 311–322.

Rutter, M., Bailey, A., Simonoff, E., & Pickles, A. (1997). Genetic influences and autism. In D. J. Cohen & F. R. Volkmar (Eds.), *Handbook of autism and pervasive developmental disorders* (2nd ed., pp. 370–387). New York: Wiley.

Sabry, M. A., & Farag, T. I. (1998). Chromosome 15q11–13 region and the autistic disorder [Letter]. *Journal of Intellectual Disability Research, 42*(Pt. 3), 259.

Samren, E. B., van Duijn, C. M., Christiaens, G. C., Hofman, A., & Lindhout, D. (1999). Antiepileptic drug regimens and major congenital abnormalities in the offspring. *Annals of Neurology, 46*(5), 739–746.

Sandler, R. H., Finegold, S. M., Bolte, E. R., Buchanan, C. P., Maxwell, A. P., Vaisanen, M. L., et al. (2000). Short-term benefit from oral vancomycin treatment of regressive-onset autism. *Journal of Child Neurology, 15*(7), 429–435.

Schaefer, G. B., & Bodensteiner, J. B. (1992). Evaluation of the child with idiopathic mental retardation. *Pediatric Clinics of North America, 39*(4), 929–943.

Scherer, N. J., D'Antonio, L. L., & Rodgers, J. R. (2001). Profiles of communication disorder in children with velocardiofacial syndrome: Comparison to children with Down syndrome. *General Medicine Journal, 3*(1), 72–78.

Schopler, E., Reichler, R., Bashford, A., Lansing, M. D., & Marcus, L. M. (1990). *Individualized assessment and treatment for autistic and developmentally disabled children: Vol. 1. Psychoeducational Profile Revised.* Austin, TX: ProEd.

Schopler, E., Reichler, R., & Rochen-Renner, B. (1988). *The Childhood Autism Rating Scale (CARS).* Los Angeles: Western Psychological Services.

Schreck, K. A., & Mulick, J. A. (2000). Parental report of sleep problems in children with autism. *Journal of Autism and Developmental Disorders, 30*(2), 127–135.

Schreck, K. A., Mulick, J. A., & Smith, A. F. (2004). Sleep problems as possible predictors of intensified symptoms of autism. *Research in Developmental Disabilities, 25*(1), 57–66.

Schroer, R. J., Phelan, M. C., Michaelis, R. C., Crawford, E. C., Skinner, S. A., Cuccaro, M., et al. (1998). Autism and maternally derived aberrations of chromosome 15q. *American Journal of Medical Genetics, 76,* 327–336.

Scott, S. (1994). Mental retardation. In M. Rutter, E. Taylor, & L. Hersov (Eds.), *Child and adolescent psychiatry: Modern approaches* (3rd ed., pp. 618–646). Oxford, England: Blackwell Scientific Publications.

Shannon, M., & Graef, J. W. (1997). Lead intoxication in children with pervasive developmental disorders. *Journal of Toxicology-Clinical Toxicology, 34,* 177–182.

Shearer, T. R., Larson, K., Neuschwander, J., & Gedney, B. (1982). Minerals in the hair and nutrient intake of autistic children. *Journal of Autism and Developmental Disorders, 12*(1), 25–34.

Sherman, S. L. (2000). Premature ovarian failure in the fragile X syndrome. *American Journal of Medical Genetics, 97*(3), 189–194.

Sherr, E. H. (2003). The ARX story (epilepsy, mental retardation, autism, and cerebral malformations): One gene leads to many phenotypes. *Current Opinions in Pediatrics, 15*(6), 567–571.

Shevell, M. I., Majnemer, A., Rosenbaum, P., & Abrahamowicz, M. (2001). Etiologic yield of autistic spectrum disorders: A prospective study. *Journal of Child Neurology, 16*(7), 509–512.

Short, M., Richardson, E., Haines, J., & Kwiatkowski, D. (1995). Clinical, neuropathological and genetic aspects of the tuberous sclerosis complex. *Brain Pathology, 5*(2), 173–179.

Shprintzen, R. J., Goldberg, R. B., Young, D., & Wolford, L. (1981). The velo-cardio-facial syndrome: A clinical and genetic analysis. *Pediatrics, 67*(2), 167–172.

Silva, A. E., Vayego-Lourenco, S. A., Fett-Conte, A. C., Goloni-Bertollo, E. M., & Varella-Garcia, M. (2002). Tetrasomy 15q11-q13 identified by fluorescence in situ hybridization in a patient with autistic disorder. *Arquivos de neuro-psiquiatria, 60*(2-A), 290–294.

Singh, V., Warren, R., Averett, R., & Ghaziuddin, M. (1997). Circulating autoantibodies to neuronal and glial filament proteins in autism. *Pediatric Neurology, 17*(1), 88–90.

Singh, V., Warren, R., Odell, J., Warren, W., & Cole, P. (1993). Antibodies to myelin basic protein in children with autistic behavior. *Brain, Behavior, and Immunity, 7*(1), 97–103.

Skjeldal, O. H., Sponheim, E., Ganes, T., Jellum, E., & Bakke, S. (1998). Childhood autism: The need for physical investigations. *Brain and Development, 20*(4), 227–233.

Skuse, D. H., James, R. S., Bishop, D. V., Coppin, B., Dalton, P., Aamodt-Leeper, G., et al. (1997). Evidence from Turner's syndrome of an imprinted X-linked locus affecting cognitive function. *Nature, 387*(6634), 705–708.

Smalley, S., Asarnow, R., & Spence, M. A. (1989). Autism and genetics: A decade of research. *Archives of General Psychiatry, 45*, 953–961.

Smalley, S., Tanguay, P., Smith, M., & Gutierrez, G. (1992). Autism and tuberous sclerosis. *Journal of Autism and Developmental Disorders, 22*(3), 339–355.

Smith, M., Escamilla, J. R., Filipek, P., Bocian, M. E., Modahl, C., Flodman, P., et al. (2001). Molecular genetic delineation of 2q37.3 deletion in autism and osteodystrophy: Report of a case and of new markers for deletion screening by PCR. *Cytogenetics and Cell Genetics, 94*(1/2), 15–22.

Smith, M., Woodroffe, A., Smith, R., Holguin, S., Martinez, J., Filipek, P. A., et al. (2002). Molecular genetic delineation of a deletion of chromosome 13q12:>q13 in a patient with autism and auditory processing deficits. *Cytogenetic and Genome Research, 98*(4), 233–239.

Sponheim, E., Oftedal, G., & Helverschou, S. B. (2002). Multiple doses of secretin in the treatment of autism: A controlled study. *Acta Paediatrica, 91*(5), 540–545.

Steele, M. M., Al-Adeimi, M., Siu, V. M., & Fan, Y. S. (2001). Brief report: A case of autism with interstitial deletion of chromosome 13. *Journal of Autism and Developmental Disorders, 31*(2), 231–234.

Steffenburg, S. (1991). Neuropsychiatric assessment of children with autism: A population-based study. *Developmental Medicine and Child Neurology, 33*(6), 495–511.

Steffenburg, S., Gillberg, C. L., Steffenburg, U., & Kyllerman, M. (1996). Autism in Angelman syndrome: A population-based study. *Pediatric Neurology, 14*, 131–136.

Stores, G., & Wiggs, L. (1998). Abnormal sleep patterns associated with autism. *Autism: Journal of Research and Practice, 2*, 157–169.

Stromland, K., Nordin, V., Miller, M., Akerstrom, B., & Gillberg, C. (1994). Autism in thalidomide embryopathy: A population study. *Developmental Medicine and Child Neurology, 36*(4), 351–356.

Stromland, K., Philipson, E., & Andersson Gronlund, M. (2002). Offspring of male and female parents with thalidomide embryopathy: Birth defects and functional anomalies. *Teratology, 66*(3), 115–121.

Stromland, K., Sjogreen, L., Miller, M., Gillberg, C., Wentz, E., Johansson, M., et al. (2002). Mobius sequence—a Swedish multidiscipline study. *European Journal of Paediatric Neurology, 6*(1), 35–45.

Stromme, P., Bjornstad, P. G., & Ramstad, K. (2002). Prevalence estimation of Williams syndrome. *Journal of Child Neurology, 17*(4), 269–271.

Stromme, P., Mangelsdorf, M. E., Scheffer, I. E., & Gecz, J. (2002). Infantile spasms, dystonia, and other X-linked phenotypes caused by mutations in Aristaless related homeobox gene, ARX. *Brain and Development, 24*(5), 266–268.

Stubbs, E. G. (1978). Autistic symptoms in a child with congenital cytomegalovirus infection. *Journal of Autism and Childhood Schizophrenia, 8*(1), 37–43.

Tager-Flusberg, H., & Sullivan, K. (2000). A componential view of theory of mind: Evidence from Williams syndrome. *Cognition, 76*(1), 59–89.

Tanguay, P. E., Ornitz, E. M., Forsythe, A. B., & Ritvo, E. R. (1976). Rapid eye movement

(REM) activity in normal and autistic children during REM sleep. *Journal of Autism and Childhood Schizophrenia, 6*(3), 275–288.

Tassone, F., Hagerman, R. J., Taylor, A. K., Mills, J. B., Harris, S. W., Gane, L. W., et al. (2000). Clinical involvement and protein expression in individuals with the FMR1 premutation. *American Journal of Medical Genetics, 91*(2), 144–152.

Taylor, B., Miller, E., Lingam, R., Andrews, N., Simmons, A., & Stowe, J. (2002). Measles, mumps, and rubella vaccination and bowel problems or developmental regression in children with autism: Population study. *British Medical Journal, 324*(7334), 393–396.

Thirumalai, S. S., Shubin, R. A., & Robinson, R. (2002). Rapid eye movement sleep behavior disorder in children with autism. *Journal of Child Neurology, 17*(3), 173–178.

Thompson, R. J., & Bolton, P. F. (2003). Case report: Angelman syndrome in an individual with a small SMC(15) and paternal uniparental disomy: A case report with reference to the assessment of cognitive functioning and autistic symptomatology. *Journal of Autism and Developmental Disorders, 33*(2), 171–176.

Tierney, E., Nwokoro, N. A., Porter, F. D., Freund, L. S., Ghuman, J. K., & Kelley, R. I. (2001). Behavior phenotype in the RSH/Smith-Lemli-Opitz syndrome. *American Journal of Medical Genetics, 98*(2), 191–200.

Tolbert, L., Haigler, T., Waits, M. M., & Dennis, T. (1993). Brief report: Lack of response in an autistic population to a low dose clinical trial of pyridoxine plus magnesium. *Journal of Autism and Developmental Disorders, 23,* 193–199.

Torrente, F., Ashwood, P., Day, R., Machado, N., Furlano, R. I., Anthony, A., et al. (2002). Small intestinal enteropathy with epithelial IgG and complement deposition in children with regressive autism. *Molecular Psychiatry, 7*(4), 375–382, 334.

Trillingsgaard, A., & Stergaard, O. (2004). Autism in Angelman syndrome: An exploration of co-morbidity. *Autism: Journal of Research and Practice, 8*(2), 163–174.

Truhan, A. P., & Filipek, P. A. (1993). Magnetic resonance imaging: Its role in the neuroradiologic evaluation of neurofibromatosis, tuberous sclerosis, and Sturge-Weber syndrome. *Archives of Dermatology, 129,* 219–226.

Tsai, L. Y. (1987). Pre-, peri- and neonatal factors in autism. In E. Schopler & G. B. Mesibov (Eds.), *Neurobiological issues in autism: Current issues in autism* (pp. 179–189). New York: Plenum Press.

Tuchman, R. (1995). Regression in pervasive developmental disorders: Is there a relationship with Landau-Kleffner Syndrome? *Annals of Neurology, 38,* 526.

Tuchman, R., & Rapin, I. (1997). Regression in pervasive developmental disorders: Seizures and epileptiform electroencephalogram correlates. *Pediatrics, 99,* 560–566.

Tuchman, R., Rapin, I., & Shinnar, S. (1991). Autistic and dysphasic children. II: Epilepsy. *Pediatrics, 88*(6), 1219–1225.

Turk, J., & Graham, P. (1997). Fragile X syndrome, autism and autistic features. *Autism: Journal of Research and Practice, 1,* 175–197.

Udwin, O., & Yule, W. (1990). Expressive language of children with Williams syndrome. *American Journal of Medical Genetics* (Suppl. 6), 108–114.

Udwin, O., & Yule, W. (1991). A cognitive and behavioural phenotype in Williams syndrome. *Journal of Clinical and Experimental Neuropsychology, 13*(2), 232–244.

Ungaro, P., Christian, S. L., Fantes, J. A., Mutirangura, A., Black, S., Reynolds, J., et al. (2001). Molecular characterisation of four cases of intrachromosomal triplication of chromosome 15q11-q14. *Journal of Medical Genetics, 38*(1), 26–34.

Unis, A. S., Munson, J. A., Rogers, S. J., Goldson, E., Osterling, J., Gabriels, R., et al. (2002). A randomized, double-blind, placebo-controlled trial of porcine versus synthetic secretin for reducing symptoms of autism. *Journal of the American Academy of Child and Adolescent Psychiatry, 41*(11), 1315–1321.

van Slegtenhorst, M., Verhoef, S., Tempelaars, A., Bakker, L., Wang, Q., Wessels, M., et al. (1999). Mutational spectrum of the TSC1 gene in a cohort of 225 tuberous sclerosis complex patients: No evidence for genotype-phenotype correlation. *Journal of Medical Genetics, 36*(4), 285–289.

Veltman, M. W., Thompson, R. J., Roberts, S. E., Thomas, N. S., Whittington, J., & Bolton, P. F. (2004). Prader-Willi syndrome—a study comparing deletion and uniparental disomy cases with reference to autism spectrum disorders. *European Child and Adolescent Psychiatry, 13*(1), 42–50.

Verkerk, A. J., Pieretti, M., Sutcliffe, J. S., Fu, Y. H., Kuhl, D. P., Pizzuti, A., et al. (1991). Identification of a gene (FMR-1) containing a CGG repeat coincident with a breakpoint cluster region exhibiting length variation in fragile X syndrome. *Cell, 65*(5), 905–914.

Volkmar, F. R., & Weisner, L. A. (2004). *Healthcare for Children on the Autism Spectrum: A Guide to Medical, Nutritional, and Behavioral*

Issues (pp. 348–362). Bethesda, MD: Woodbine House.

Wakabayashi, S. (1979). A case of infantile autism associated with Down's syndrome. *Journal of Autism and Developmental Disorders, 9*(1), 31–36.

Wakefield, A. J. (1999). MMR vaccination and autism. *Lancet, 354*(9182), 949–950.

Wakefield, A. J. (2002). Enterocolitis, autism and measles virus. *Molecular Psychiatry, 7*(Suppl. 2), S44–S46.

Wakefield, A. J. (2003). Measles, mumps, and rubella vaccination and autism. *New England Journal of Medicine, 348*(10), 951–954.

Wakefield, A. J., Anthony, A., Murch, S. H., Thomson, M., Montgomery, S. M., Davies, S., et al. (2000). Enterocolitis in children with developmental disorders. *American Journal of Gastroenterology, 95*(9), 2285–2295.

Wakefield, A. J., & Montgomery, S. M. (1999). Autism, viral infection and measles-mumps-rubella vaccination. *The Israel Medical Association Journal, 1*(3), 183–187. .

Wakefield, A. J., Murch, S. H., Anthony, A., Linnell, J., Casson, D. M., Malik, M., et al. (1998). Ileal-lymphoid-nodular hyperplasia, non-specific colitis, and pervasive developmental disorder in children. *Lancet, 351*(9103), 637–641.

Wakefield, A. J., Puleston, J. M., Montgomery, S. M., Anthony, A., O'Leary, J. J., & Murch, S. H. (2002). Review article: The concept of entero-colonic encephalopathy, autism and opioid receptor ligands. *Alimentary Pharmacology Therapeutics, 16*(4), 663–674.

Wakefield, J. (2002). New centers to focus on autism and other developmental disorders. *Environmental Health Perspectives, 110*(1), A20–A21.

Walker-Smith, J., & Andrews, J. (1972). Alpha-1-antitrypsin, autism, and coeliac disease. *Lancet, 2*(7782), 883–884.

Wang, P. P., Woodin, M. F., Kreps-Falk, R., & Moss, E. M. (2000). Research on behavioral phenotypes: Velocardiofacial syndrome: Deletion 22q11.2. *Developmental Medicine and Child Neurology, 42*(6), 422–427.

Warren, R. P., Margaretten, N. C., Pace, N. C., & Foster, A. (1986). Immune abnormalities in patients with autism. *Journal of Autism and Developmental Disorders, 16*(2), 189–197.

Watling, R. L., Deitz, J., & White, O. (2001). Comparison of Sensory Profile scores of young children with and without autism spectrum disorders. *American Journal of Occupational Therapy, 55*(4), 416–423.

Watson, M., Leckman, J., Annex, B., Breg, W., Boles, D., Volkmar, F., et al. (1984). Fragile X

in a survey of 75 autistic males. *New England Journal of Medicine, 310*(22), 1462.

Waugh, M. C., Chong, W. K., & Sonksen, P. (1998). Neuroimaging in children with congenital disorders of the peripheral visual system. *Developmental Medicine and Child Neurology, 40*(12), 812–819.

Webb, D. W., Clarke, A., Fryer, A., & Osborne, J. P. (1996). The cutaneous features of tuberous sclerosis: A population study. *British Journal of Dermatology, 135*(1), 1–5.

Webb, T., Hardy, C. A., King, M., Watkiss, E., Mitchell, C., & Cole, T. (1998). A clinical, cytogenetic and molecular study of ten probands with supernumerary inv dup (15) marker chromosomes. *Clinical Genetics, 53*(1), 34–43.

Wechsler, D. (1997). *Wechsler Adult Intelligence Scale-III (WAIS-III)*. San Antonio, TX: Psychological Corporation.

Wecker, L., Miller, S. B., Cochran, S. R., Dugger, D. L., & Johnson, W. D. (1985). Trace element concentrations in hair from autistic children. *Journal of Mental Deficiency Research, 29*(Pt. 1), 15–22.

Weidmer-Mikhail, E., Sheldon, S., & Ghaziuddin, M. (1998). Chromosomes in autism and related pervasive developmental disorders: A cytogenetic study. *Journal of Intellectual Disability Research, 42*(Pt. 1), 8–12.

Whiteley, P. (2004). Developmental, behavioural and somatic factors in pervasive developmental disorders: Preliminary analysis. *Child: Care, Health, and Development, 30*(1), 5–11.

Wiggs, L., & Stores, G. (1996). Severe sleep disturbance and daytime challenging behaviour in children with severe learning disabilities. *Journal of Intellectual Disability Research, 40* (Pt. 6), 518–528.

Wiggs, L., & Stores, G. (2004). Sleep patterns and sleep disorders in children with autistic spectrum disorders: Insights using parent report and actigraphy. *Developmental Medicine and Child Neurology, 46*(6), 372–380.

Wilkerson, D. S., Volpe, A. G., Dean, R. S., & Titus, J. B. (2002). Perinatal complications as predictors of infantile autism. *International Journal of Neuroscience, 112*(9), 1085–1098.

Willemsen, R., Oostra, B. A., Bassell, G. J., & Dictenberg, J. (2004). The fragile X syndrome: From molecular genetics to neurobiology. *Mental Retardation and Developmental Disabilities Research Review, 10*(1), 60–67.

Williams, C. A., Lossie, A., & Driscoll, D. (2001). Angelman syndrome: Mimicking conditions and phenotypes. *American Journal of Medical Genetics, 101*(1), 59–64.

Williams, G., King, J., Cunningham, M., Stephan, M., Kerr, B., & Hersh, J. H. (2001). Fetal valproate syndrome and autism: Additional evidence of an association. *Developmental Medicine and Child Neurology, 43*(3), 202–206.

Williams, J. C., Barratt-Boyes, B. G., & Lowe, J. B. (1961). Supravalvular aortic stenosis. *Circulation, 24,* 1311–1318.

Williams, J. H., Whiten, A., & Singh, T. (2004). A systematic review of action imitation in autistic spectrum disorder. *Journal of Autism and Developmental Disorders, 34*(3), 285–299.

Williams, P. G., & Hersh, J. H. (1997). A male with fetal valproate syndrome and autism. *Developmental Medicine and Child Neurology, 39*(9), 632–634.

Williams, P. G., & Hersh, J. H. (1998). Brief report: The association of neurofibromatosis type 1 and autism. *Journal of Autism and Developmental Disorders, 28*(6), 567–571.

Williams, R. S., Hauser, S. L., Purpura, D. P., DeLong, G. R., & Swisher, C. N. (1980). Autism and mental retardation: Neuropathologic studies performed in four retarded persons with autistic behavior. *Archives of Neurology, 37,* 749–753.

Wing, L. (1969). The handicaps of autistic children—a comparative study. *Journal of Child Psychology and Psychiatry, 10*(1), 1–40.

Wing, L., & Gould, J. (1979). Severe impairments of social interaction and associated abnormalities in children: Epidemiology and classification. *Journal of Autism and Developmental Disorders, 9*(1), 11–29.

Wishart, J., & Johnston, F. (1990). The effects of experience on attribution of a stereotyped personality to children with Down's syndrome. *Journal of Mental Deficiency Research, 34*(5), 409–420.

Wisniewski, L., Hassold, T., Heffelfinger, J., & Higgins, J. V. (1979). Cytogenetic and clinical studies in five cases of inv dup(15). *Human Genetics, 50*(3), 259–270.

Wolpert, C. M., Menold, M. M., Bass, M. P., Qumsiyeh, M. B., Donnelly, S. L., Ravan, S. A., et al. (2000). Three probands with autistic disorder and isodicentric chromosome 15. *American Journal of Medical Genetics, 96*(3), 365–372.

Woodhouse, W., Bailey, A., Rutter, M., Bolton, P., Baird, G., & Le Couteur, A. (1996). Head circumference in autism and other pervasive developmental disorders. *Journal of Child Psychology and Psychiatry, 37,* 665–671.

Woodin, M., Wang, P. P., Aleman, D., McDonald-McGinn, D., Zackai, E., & Moss, E. (2001). Neuropsychological profile of children and adolescents with the 22q11.2 microdeletion. *General Medicine Journal, 3*(1), 34–39.

Woods, C. G., Robinson, M., Gardiner, C., & Roussounis, T. (1997). Four cases of the condition described by Bundey with autism and a maternal 15q11–13 duplication [Abstract]. *American Journal of Human Genetics, 61,* A117.

Yamashita, Y., Fujimoto, C., Nakajima, E., Isagai, T., & Matsuishi, T. (2003). Possible association between congenital cytomegalovirus infection and autistic disorder. *Journal of Autism and Developmental Disorders, 33*(4), 455–459.

Yardin, C., Esclaire, F., Laroche, C., Terro, F., Barthe, D., Bonnefont, J. P., et al. (2002). Should the chromosome region 15q11q13 be tested systematically by FISH in the case of an autistic-like syndrome? *Clinical Genetics, 61*(4), 310–313.

Yuwiler, A., Shih, J. C., Chen, C. H., Ritvo, E. R., Hanna, G., Ellison, G. W., et al. (1992). Hyperserotoninemia and antiserotonin antibodies in autism and other disorders. *Journal of Autism and Developmental Disorders, 22*(1), 33–45.

Zambrino, C. A., Balottin, U., Bettaglio, E., Gerardo, A., & Lanzi, G. (1995). Obstetrical suboptimality in children with autism: An Italian sample [Letter]. *Journal of Autism and Developmental Disorders, 25,* 553–555.

Zappella, M. (1993). Autism and hypomelanosis of Ito in twins. *Developmental Medicine and Child Neurology, 35*(9), 826–832.

Zhang, H., Nanba, E., Yamamoto, T., Ninomiya, H., Ohno, K., Mizuguchi, M., et al. (1999). Mutational analysis of TSC1 and TSC2 genes in Japanese patients with tuberous sclerosis complex. *Journal of Human Genetics, 44*(6), 391–396.

THEORETICAL PERSPECTIVES

Theory is an attempt to understand and integrate observable phenomena. In turn, theories focus the attention of researchers and clinicians on particular types of data. New methodologies generate new data, and challenge theories; in turn, intellectual curiosity and theoretical questions lead investigators to perform new studies and create new methods. Autism has been a testing ground for theories regarding every aspect of human behavior, including language, social interaction, and affective development. In turn, studies of autism have led to new observations that require new or amended theories about the preconditions and course of normal development. The major domains of behavioral and psychological difficulties of individuals with autism and similar conditions have been recognized throughout the world since the time of Kanner's original descriptions. These include a particular profile of cognitive functioning with relative sparing of some areas that call on visual-perceptual abilities (exemplified by the Block Design tests of the Wechsler intelligence batteries) and profound difficulties with activities that require social judgment (as shown in difficulties in understanding the plot line of the Picture Arrangement tasks in the same scales). The presence of specific neuropsychological profiles has motivated a major stream of research and provides a rich source of theoretical speculation about the underlying basis of autism. In general, the difficulties of individuals with autism are most apparent when they are called upon to understand implicit motives and intentions in social situations, to use abstract reasoning and apply concepts to

novel situations, or to intuitively understand what the other person knows, wants, and expects from a query or social action. However intellectually gifted an individual with autism may be, there are difficulties in spontaneous, novel, and naturalistic social interactions. Such individuals may be stymied by subtle humor; by when and how to repair the common breakdowns, ambiguities, and miscommunications of ordinary discourse; and by the complex subplots of typical social relationships. Gifted as they may be in work with computers or explicit sciences, for individuals with autism the intuitive algebra of belief, knowledge, desire, and intent may remain wholly or in part elusive. And the perplexity and confusion that they feel in regard to the internal lives of others are mirrored to a great extent in similarly baffling feelings in regard to their minds. Early in the life of a child with autism, the parents become aware, sometimes gradually and then with a sense of shock, that something is going wrong at the heart of social relations. They initially may think their child is deaf or may worry about her language skills; they then sense and can describe that she is not socially present in the way that other children are. Children's social abilities and interests are represented in the most subtle and moving ways: calming down in the parents' arms; anticipating and enjoying the approach, touch, and hug of someone offering affection; paying attention to what interests another and hoping to focus the other's attention on something wished for or especially attractive; playing and working alongside a peer; expressing dislike, annoyance, and anger in ways that make the point without harming self or others; coping with depression and anxiety, often with the help of others; falling in love with parents and then with others, and, as happens, falling out of love, mourning a loss, and making new friendships. The developmental line from first relations to mature relationships is the personal novel written by each individual, with fewer or more subplots. For individuals with autism, this saga is markedly more restricted than for most typically developing persons. The task of theory is to understand at what point, and for what reasons, the developmental pathway from being cared for to becoming capable of passionate love is disrupted. Other behavioral processes that are dysfunctional in autism include the capacity to engage in imaginative and creative play, to find pleasure in diverse activities, to be able to move from one topic (interest, activity, hobby) to another, over time and in different situations, to be able to appreciate that others may not share one's passionate interest or preoccupation. Thus, individuals with autism tend to be narrow in their interests and focus and to be obsessively preoccupied by details or their own hobbies (train schedules, sports statistics, historical events). Their perceptual abilities, perseverance in the face of obstacles, and single-mindedness may lead to personal achievements (such as remarkable mastery of a body of knowledge) and vocational advancement (in fields that call for hard work, care, honesty, memory, detail, and predictability, while being suited to the individual's intellectual level), but often isolate them from other people.

Of course, there are broad variations and blurring between "normal" and "atypical." Traits such as obsessiveness and preoccupation with one's favorite sports team or historical epoch are not restricted to individuals with autism; on the other hand, there are individuals with autism spectrum disorders who have wonderful and genuine talents (including artistic talents) that reveal imagination and creativity, a special way of seeing the world and conveying it to others. Theories are needed to explain the etiological relations that exist between difficulties in imagination and restriction of interest and other areas of difficulty, including the modulation of affect and the formation of flexible relations and areas of ability. All these psychological functions are closely tied in with basic intellectual competence in complex manners. A developmental approach to understanding the more sophisticated mental difficulties shown by individuals with autism must start with consideration of IQ, mental age, or underlying cognitive capacity. These intellectual abilities may be conceptualized as a single, basic, general level of intelligence (as in classical formulations of a g factor in intelligence) or as multiple, only partially correlated types of intelligences. From whatever theoretical perspective, it is important to recognize that some aspects of the psychological problems of individuals with autism are shared with other individuals with cognitive and adaptive problems (those with mental retardation) while others seem distinctive. Thus, patterns or subtypes of social-behavioral functioning (e.g., Wing and Gould, 1979) may, in part, be related to general intellectual level (Volkmar, Cohen, Bregman, Hooks, & Stevenson, 1989). However, IQ alone does not predict the full range of impairments or the specific pattern of impairment or competence. The most distinctively human competence is the ability to use language—to ask for things; to plan; to fantasize; to engage in abstract thinking; to share thoughts and feelings in speech; to read, write, and translate; to argue, compromise, deceive, seduce, and insult; to record our histories in mind and on paper. Babies in utero hear their mothers' voices and respond to sounds. From the very first months of life, children engage in communication that will eventually be encoded by language. They understand words and phrases and soon have a small vocabulary; around 18 months or so, they begin to spout words like weeds and become active language users. From then on, language and communication through speech affects every domain of mental and behavioral life. Standing back from all that is known about autism, surely the most salient fact would be that up to 30% to 40% of individuals with strictly defined autism are mute. Those that do speak exhibit a range of communication difficulties, in prosody, narrative skills, and the social use of language. Some of these communicative difficulties were already apparent to Kanner; others have been clearly defined over the past decades. Since communication is so deeply encoded biologically and so relevant to all aspects of social functioning, it is natural to place heavy emphasis on communication in the pathogenesis of autism. Are these, however, at the core? Do they reflect some deeper or more proximal disturbance in socialization? In the history of theories in the field of autism, there has been a tendency to highlight one domain at the expense of others. Of course, in science, theories are generally meant to explain only a circumscribed set of data, and one should not ask too much of a good theory. In the field of autism, the breadth of data is enormous. There are many domains of functioning that are impaired, and there are areas that are relatively intact; behavior and psychological functioning change over the course of development; there is enormous heterogeneity in clinical severity, intelligence, adaptive functioning, and presumably in etiology. One should not expect any single theory to do justice to all of this. A useful theory, such as one that relates aspects of autistic social dysfunction to impairments in acquisition of a theory of how the mind of others operates, can be pushed beyond its limits if asked to explain why the majority of individuals with autism suffer from intellectual disability. For example, a theory aimed at problems in communication may, or may not, have any relevance to understanding stereotypies, motor clumsiness, or executive dysfunction. Eventually, there will be further clarification of the neurobiological templates underlying domains of behavior, and the interconnections among systems that lead to emerging social, intellectual, and communicative competencies. The rapid technological and theoretical advances of many biomedical and behavioral fields—developmental neuroscience, neuro-imaging of the brain function, cognitive sciences, to name a few—will surely lead to new data concerning normal development and impairments in autism and associated disorders. These data will generate new theories and, we hope, provide increasingly comprehensive and useful understanding of development in autism including the connections across domains of function and sensitive points for therapeutic intervention.

REFERENCES

Volkmar, F. R., Cohen, D. J., Bregman, J. D., Hooks, M. Y., & Stevenson, J. M. (1989). An examination of social typologies in autism. *Journal of the American Academy of Child and Adolescent Psychiatry, 28*(1), 82–86.

Wing, L., & Gould, J. (1979). Severe impairments of social interaction and associated abnormalities in children: epidemiology and classification. *Journal of Autism and Developmental Disorders, 9*(1), 11–29.

CHAPTER 21

Problems of Categorical Classification Systems

LORNA WING

Some system of classification of developmental and behavioral disorders is essential for clinical work and research. The problem besetting all attempts to produce reliable and valid diagnostic categories for autism and related disorders is the continuing lack of any independent biological or psychological markers. In the absence of such markers, classification systems have used various aspects of clinical history, patterns of behavior, and psychological functions. Each of these is comprised of many different elements, manifested in many different ways, partially or completely independent of each other. It is not surprising that the categories suggested have a number of drawbacks.

This chapter examines the weaknesses of the categorical systems for diagnostic classification published to date. It also proposes a classification based on multiple dimensions. The steps in the argument will be as follows: First, the history of the development of concepts of autism is described. Second, the classification problems caused by the frequent co-occurrence of autistic conditions with other developmental disorders is outlined. Third, the many anomalies of the past and present international systems of classification are considered. Finally, a dimensional approach to classification that is being used in clinical work and in research is presented.

THE HISTORY OF CONCEPTS OF AUTISM

There have been many attempts to define specific diagnostic subgroups among autism and related conditions. The difficulty of the task is

shown in the way that the ideas put forward have tended to appear, disappear, and sometimes reappear in a different form, still without a final resolution.

Before the Twentieth Century

There are a few detailed accounts, written before the twentieth century, of individuals with behavior closely resembling that seen in autistic spectrum disorders (Frith, 1989; Houston & Frith, 2000; Lane, 1977; Wing, 1997a). As far as can be ascertained, no one suggested any connection between such individuals with strange behavior until Henry Maudsley (1867) made what was perhaps the first step toward a classification. He grouped children with bizarre, disturbed behavior under the label "insane." He suggested a number of subgroups but his descriptions are couched in such theoretical terms that it is difficult or impossible to relate them to observable clinical pictures. There are hints that some of the children he discussed had autistic spectrum disorders, particularly those in the subgroup he labeled "instinctive insanity." Maudsley also described children with catatonic features, which he referred to as "cataleptoid insanity."

The 1900s to 1950s

In the first half of the twentieth century, a number of authors attempted to define syndromes among children regarded as having psychoses. De Sanctis (1906) and Heller (see Hulse, 1954) described children who seemed to develop normally for up to 3 or 4 years and then lost language, social, and other skills. De Sanctis (1908) also wrote about children he referred to as having *dementia precoccissima catatonica*. Earl (1934) used the term catatonia with reference to adolescents with bizarre patterns of movement in an institution for those with mental retardation. Much of the behavior he described was characteristic of children with severe autism. Mahler (1952) was concerned with children with a pattern of behavior she called *symbiotic psychosis*. They clung to their caregivers without real feeling and had other disturbances of communication and behavior. These authors are rarely referred to now. However, echoes of their descriptions of the children they studied, including the similarities between autistic behavior and catatonic features, can be found in more recent writings on subgrouping of autistic spectrum disorders, to be discussed later in this chapter.

The two writers among this group who did eventually become recognized internationally were Kanner (1943) and Asperger (1944, 1991). Kanner wrote vivid descriptions of children with an unusual pattern of behavior he labeled *early infantile autism*. These children, from birth or very early in life, (1) were aloof and indifferent to other people; (2) were mute or had echolalic, repetitive speech they did not use for communication; (3) had an "anxiously obsessive desire for the maintenance of sameness" in their own repetitive routines; (4) were fascinated with objects that they did not use for the purposes for which they were designed; and (5) had "good cognitive potential" shown in performance tests or unusual rote memory. Kanner and Eisenberg (1956) considered that social aloofness and resistance to change in repetitive routines that were *elaborate* in form were the essential diagnostic criteria. If these two were present, they believed that the rest would also be found. In their experience, this clinical picture began from birth or became manifest during the first 2 years of life. Later, Rutter (1978) argued against the use of Kanner and Eisenberg's two criteria, particularly because language impairments were not mentioned. He suggested three criteria for autism: (1) impaired social relationships; (2) impairment of language and prelanguage skills; and (3) insistence on sameness, by which was meant a variety of stereotyped behaviors and routines.

Rutter gave detailed descriptions of each of these criteria. (See Chapter 16, by M. Rutter, this volume.)

Asperger (1944, 1991) described children with a behavior pattern he called *autistic psychopathy*. The main characteristics were (1) social approaches that were inappropriate, one-sided, egocentric; (2) a narrow, limited range of special interests pursued with intensity; (3) good expressive language used mainly to engage in monologues on their special interests; (4) poor motor coordination; and (5) a marked lack of common sense. Despite the differences from Kanner's group, careful reading of Asperger's lengthy descriptions shows that many of the features found in early infantile autism were also present in Asperger's group (Wing, 1981a, 1991, 2000). Asperger's ideas, originally published in German, did not become well known in English-speaking countries until the 1980s (Frith, 1991; Wing, 1981a). Wing suggested the term *Asperger's syndrome* in preference to autistic psychopathy.

Some writers used the term *childhood schizophrenia* for conditions that were closely similar to those given the various labels mentioned above (Bender, 1947; Despert, 1938; Goldfarb, 1974). Bleuler (1911) coined the label *schizophrenia* for a disorder in adults. He used the term *autism* to refer to the turning away from the external environment into a world of fantasy. He considered this was the result of the emotional flattening and the thought disorder characteristic of schizophrenia. Kanner borrowed the terms autism and autistic for his group of socially aloof children, though he acknowledged that there were differences between the social problems in the two conditions (Kanner, 1965). At first he believed that early infantile autism was "a unique and separate condition" (Kanner, 1943). Later, however, Kanner (1949) quoted from a letter Despert wrote to him. She argued that social withdrawal was the crucial feature of schizophrenia regardless of the age when it began. She suggested that communication impairment, insistence on sameness, fear of noise, and so on, as seen in early infantile autism, were all symptoms of schizophrenic social withdrawal. This letter made Kanner lean toward the view that early infantile autism probably was the earliest form of childhood schizophrenia, though he later expressed doubts about this formulation as being too simplistic (Kanner, 1965).

Anthony (1958) discussed the ideas on childhood psychosis put forward during this period of time. He pointed out that these syndromes, named after their authors, overlapped to such an extent that they could not properly be differentiated.

The 1960s

A more scientific approach to the study of childhood psychoses began to emerge in the 1960s (Wing, 1997a) when a group of psychiatrists, psychologists, and pediatricians met under the chairmanship of Creak (1964). Their original remit was to clarify the diagnosis of childhood psychosis, but they eventually decided to label the clinical picture they were defining *schizophrenic syndrome of childhood.* They agreed on a list of nine diagnostic points for this condition. In effect, the nine points covered virtually the same clinical features as Kanner's description of early infantile autism, except they did not specify age of onset. It is worth noting that, under the heading of "distortion in motility patterns" they included "immobility as in katatonia" (i.e., catatonia). Although unsatisfactory in many ways, the list of nine points was the first attempt to lay down specific criteria for diagnosing psychosis in young children.

Among others, Despert (1938), Bender (1947), and Anthony (1958) had, in previous decades, identified three groups among children with psychoses. They classified them by age of onset: (1) very early onset, (2) onset between 3 and 5 years, and (3) onset in middle or late childhood. The different authors gave different names to these three subgroups depending on their theoretical orientation. Kolvin and his colleagues were the first workers to undertake systematic research into the correlates of age of onset (Kolvin, 1971; Kolvin, Ounsted, Humphrey, & McNay, 1971). They studied 80 children admitted to hospital as inpatients, during the course of the 1960s, for intensive assessment of their psychoses. Forty-seven had an onset before 3 years, and 33 had an onset between 5 to 15 years. (The authors found only three children with onset between 3 and 5 years. One had a progressive degenera-

tive disorder and one had clear-cut organic features. Because so few children with this age of onset were found, this subgroup was not included in the study.) There were significant differences between the early and late onset groups, not only in their clinical pictures but also in their cognitive abilities and family, genetic, and social factors. The early onset group most clearly resembled Kanner's early infantile autism. The late onset group had the features and family histories similar to that of schizophrenia in adults.

This study was influential in the move toward using the term *autism* for the early onset group and away from the diagnosis of childhood schizophrenia. Rutter (1972) noted the confusion previously surrounding the diagnosis of childhood schizophrenia. He concluded that, in the way it had been used in the past, this diagnosis had ceased to have any scientific meaning or communicative value. Rutter used the term *schizophrenic psychosis in childhood* to refer to the adult-type condition beginning in middle or late childhood. He differentiated this from infantile autism beginning in the first 3 years of life.

Another important event in this decade was that Lotter (1966) completed the first epidemiological study of autism in the former English county of Middlesex. He identified, in a series of increasingly stringent screening steps, those children who had Kanner and Eisenberg's (1956) main criteria of social aloofness and elaborate repetitive routines.

The 1970s

During the 1970s, Wing and Gould (1979) carried out an epidemiological study among children known to have any kind of special needs living in the former London borough of Camberwell, in the United Kingdom. The aim of the study was to identify children under 15 years of age on December 31, 1970, who had any of the features described as occurring in autism. In contrast to Lotter, Wing and Gould did not begin with preset diagnostic criteria. They were concerned to discover how the individual features found in autistic disorders were manifested and distributed among the population of children they studied and how they related to each other. They found that impairments of social interaction, communication, and imagination were very likely to occur together and to be associated with a narrow repetitive range of activities and/or interests. This was referred to as the *triad of impairments*. Their more innovative (and controversial) finding was that each of these features could occur in a wide range of manifestations, of which those in Kanner's autism formed only a small proportion. In particular, they found that impairment of social interaction could be shown in the following ways: (1) aloofness and indifference to others, (2) passive acceptance of approaches from others, and (3) active-but-odd approaches to others. The findings led to the development of the concept of the *autistic spectrum of disorders*. (This was originally referred to as the *autistic continuum;* Wing, 1988; Wing & Gould, 1979). The word *spectrum* is preferred because, unlike continuum, it does not imply a smooth transition from one end to the other. By analogy with the color spectrum, it does imply a range of clinical pictures that differ from each other but have an underlying unity. The spectrum included the most severe to the subtlest manifestations of the triad.

Support for the concept of a wide spectrum of autistic disorders has appeared, for example, in a genetic study of families by Rutter and his colleagues (Bolton et al., 1994). They provided evidence for broadening the phenotypic definition beyond the criteria for autism and other pervasive developmental disorders. C. Gillberg (1992) suggested that autism be regarded as a subclass among a very wide group of disorders of empathy. He considered that this approach would have value for both research and clinical work. The implications of these findings for classification are discussed later in this chapter.

The 1980s Onward

In the 1980s, attention turned to disorders in the wider autistic spectrum. Asperger (1944, 1991) did not lay down specific criteria for his syndrome but, subsequently, others have done so (Ehlers & Gillberg, 1993; C. Gillberg, Gillberg, Rastam, & Wentz, 2001; Szatmari, Brenner, & Nagy, 1989; Tantam, 1988). Although details differed, they all included so-

cial impairments, and peculiarities of verbal and nonverbal communication, despite adequate expressive speech. Gillberg and his colleagues, and Tantam also included narrow and intense interests, and clumsiness.

Wolff (1995) described her series of studies, beginning in the 1960s, of a group of children she originally suggested had *schizoid personality disorder of childhood*. She now believes that they represent the most able end of Asperger's syndrome.

Rourke and Tsatsanis (2000) discussed nonverbal learning disabilities, also known as developmental learning disabilities of the right hemisphere. These authors noted the considerable overlap with Asperger's syndrome. They emphasized the need for further research to clarify the nature of the relationship between these disorders.

Rapin and Allen (1983) suggested that disorder of semantic and pragmatic aspects of language, although an integral ¬art of autism and related disorders, could occur without the rest of the autistic picture. Bishop (2000) argued that children with this disorder could fall between the diagnostic boundaries of autistic spectrum disorders and developmental language disorders. Wing and Gould (1979) had previously described children who were chatty, but whose speech was inappropriate in the social context. These authors placed the children in the autistic spectrum and referred to them as "active-but-odd" in social interaction (see later in this chapter). The close relationship between semantic pragmatic disorder and autism was emphasized by Lister Brook and Bowler (1992).

In 1983, Newson introduced her concept of a pattern of behavior she referred to as *pathological demand avoidance syndrome* (PDA) (Newson, 1983; Newson, Le Maréchal, & David, 2003). She emphasized the children's resistance to carrying out the ordinary functions of everyday life, such as dressing oneself, or obeying direct commands to complete tasks. They sometimes reacted to such demands with rage and panic. Newson described their inappropriate social interaction, which tended to be "ill-judged, labile, ambiguous, without depth." They could slip from loving to violent behavior for no apparent reason. Other features listed were marked passivity in infancy, poor motor coordination, apparent lack of awareness of their own social identity, acting out being another person, real or fictional, with complete conviction, retelling fantasies as if they were true, obsessive interest in another person, and blaming other people if anything went wrong. Much of the behavior of these children was destructive or harmful to others, including harassment of individuals. The children seemed to enjoy other people's distress. Possibly, they found extremes of emotional response easier to read than the usual more subtle nonverbal aspects of communication. Newson considered this disorder to be a pervasive developmental disorder but not part of the autistic spectrum, despite the finding that the prevalence of autism among the siblings was as high as in typical autistic disorder. A few of the active-but-odd children in Wing and Gould's (1979) study showed the same characteristics. There are also similarities to Mahler's (1952) description of the clinical picture she referred to as "symbiotic psychosis." Newson found that her syndrome was more commonly seen in girls. Wolff and McGuire (1995) followed up girls they had diagnosed as schizoid personality disorder of childhood and noted that they were more likely than the boys to be antisocial and delinquent. One of the case descriptions was particularly reminiscent of Newson's syndrome.

Cohen, Paul, and Volkmar (1986) discussed children with disorders that appeared to be on a spectrum between pervasive developmental disorder and specific developmental disorder. They coined the term *multiplex developmental disorder*. They suggested three major diagnostic features: (1) impairment in regulation of affective state and anxiety, (2) impairment of social behavior and social sensitivity, and (3) impaired cognitive processing, including confusion between reality and fantasy, paranoid preoccupations and over engagement with fantasy figures. There are obvious similarities to Newson's pathological demand-avoidance syndrome.

ASSOCIATED CONDITIONS CAUSING DIAGNOSTIC PROBLEMS

The borderlines that separate the autistic spectrum, other developmental disorders, some psychiatric conditions, and even eccentric normality are not clearly demarcated. Some disorders cause particular diagnostic problems because they share features with the autistic spectrum. Autistic spectrum disorders and an associated condition may co-exist but only the latter be recognized. Alternatively, an autistic spectrum disorder may be the only condition present but can be misdiagnosed as one of the associated conditions. It can be difficult to decide the most appropriate diagnostic formulation.

Disorders Beginning in Childhood

All the disorders that begin in childhood can co-exist with each other and with an autistic spectrum disorder. The disorders likely to cause diagnostic problems and the reasons for confusion among these disorders are discussed next.

Generalized Mental Retardation

Retardation of cognitive, language, and motor skills from any cause can occur with or without autism. Down's syndrome is usually associated with appropriate sociability and good nonverbal communication, but an autistic spectrum disorder can occur even in association with this condition (Howlin, Wing, & Gould, 1995; Wakabayashi, 1979; Wing & Gould, 1979).

Accurate diagnosis may be a problem if a person's mental age is too low for pretend play to have developed—that is, below 20 months (Wing, Gould, Yeates, & Brierley, 1977). People at this mental level often have simple stereotypies, such as body rocking or finger flicking, but when their social responsiveness is observed, a differential diagnosis can be made even at this level of function. The diagnosis is worth making because it has practical implications for treatment and management. Some simple stereotypies can occur in young children with mental retardation whose mental age is above 20 months. If the children do not have autism, these behaviors do not dominate their activity pattern, and social responses and pretend play appropriate to their mental age will be evidenced.

Developmental Language Disorders

Disorders that affect receptive and/or expressive language can occur alone or with other disorders, including the autistic spectrum conditions. To differentiate developmental language disorders from autism and related conditions, clinicians must observe the social relationships, imaginative activities, and the desire to communicate as shown in the use of gesture and other nonverbal methods (Wing, 1969). Rutter and his colleagues (Bartak, Rutter, & Cox, 1975, 1977; Cox, Rutter, Newman, & Bartak, 1975) studied young children with severe developmental language disorder (SDLD) including impairment of receptive language, and compared them with children with autism. Both groups had nonverbal IQs of 70 or above. They found clear differences between the groups on the variables mentioned earlier, and they noted the presence of deviant as well as delayed language in the group with autism. There was, however, some overlapping of the clinical symptoms, and there were a small number of children with features of both groups. Cantwell, Baker, Rutter, and Mawhood (1989) followed the children into middle childhood and Rutter, Mawhood, and Howlin (1992) extended the study into early adult life. In these follow-up studies, marked differences between the groups remained. However, those with SDLD tended to have limited social relationships and this lasted into early adult life, despite improvement in the individual's conversational language. A further follow-up at age 23 to 24 (Mawhood, Howlin, & Rutter, 2000) showed continuing social and language difficulties in the SDLD group and more overlap with the group with autism.

Developmental Coordination Disorder

Some children are particularly clumsy in gross or fine motor movements or both. This problem is characteristic of the subgroups described by Asperger (1944, 1991) and by Newson (1983; Newson et al., 2003). However, such clumsiness can occur alone or in association with other developmental disorders (Green et al., 2002). The diagnosis of an associated autistic spectrum disorder has to be made on the developmental history and observation of the pattern of behavior, especially the quality of the social interaction.

Attention Deficit/Hyperactivity Disorder

Many children with autistic spectrum disorders are restless and distractible, though typically they are able to concentrate on the repetitive activities of their own choosing. Conversely, children diagnosed as having attention deficit/hyperactivity disorder (ADHD) often have features of autistic spectrum disorders (Clark, Feehan, Tinline, & Vostanis, 1999). The two disorders can occur together and accurate diagnostic formulation can be difficult.

Deficits of Attention, Motor Control, and Perception

C. Gillberg, Rasmussen, Carlström, Svenson, and Waldenström (1982), in an epidemiological study of 6-year-old children in Gothenborg, Sweden, identified a group of 14 children (1.2% of the population not mentally retarded) who had a combination of severe motor clumsiness and attention deficit disorder. In later papers, this condition was referred to as *deficits of attention, motor control and perception* (the DAMP syndrome). I. C. Gillberg and Gillberg (1989) found that 8 of the 14 children had autistic-like traits. One of the eight had autistic disorder (*DSM-III-R* definition), three met the criteria for Asperger's syndrome as defined by the authors, based on Asperger's (1944, 1991) original description, and four had many of the features of this syndrome.

When deficits of attention, motor control, and perception are present, they can mask an associated autistic spectrum disorder. Therefore, careful assessment of the total behavior pattern is essential so that all the elements are detected.

Tourette's Syndrome

The tics, compulsive shouting and swearing, and the echoing of words, sounds and actions that can occur in *Tourette's Syndrome* (Shapiro, Shapiro, Brown, & Sweet, 1978) resemble the same phenomena occurring in autism. This disorder can occur together with autistic spectrum disorders (Kerbeshian & Burd, 1986; Realmuto & Main, 1982).

Hearing Impairments

Hearing loss is often suspected in young children who exhibit speech delay associated with autistic spectrum disorders. Rutter and Lockyer (1967) noted that this concern had been present for one-third of their sample of children with autism. The presence of the triad of impairments (Wing & Gould, 1979), especially the lack of nonspoken methods of communication, points to a diagnosis of an autistic spectrum disorder. However, hearing impairments can occur along with autistic disorders. They can be difficult to diagnose because individuals with autism commonly ignore some sounds, especially speech that they cannot comprehend. Careful investigation is important because poor hearing can exacerbate social and communication problems in children with autism.

Visual Impairments

Impairments of social interaction, communication, and imagination and stereotypies including eye poking, rocking, and hand-flapping have been described in a substantial minority of children with severe congenital visual impairments. This pattern of behavior sometimes occurs as part of a developmental setback in the second or third year of life in some children with severe visual impairments who were initially thought to be of normal cognitive potential (Cass, 1998; Cass, Sonksen, & McConachie, 1994). These authors noted that the developmental impairments were strongly associated with the severity of the visual loss. The most severe congenital visual impairments are known to be associated with central nervous system disorders, such as congenital rubella. It is often difficult to estimate how much of the developmental problem is due to the visual impairment and how much to the neuropathology. Chess (1971), in a study of children with congenital rubella, found a strikingly high prevalence of autism, using Kanner's strict criteria, and of "partial autism." On follow-up at 8 to 9 years of age, Chess (1977) found, among those with autism or partial autism diagnosed at 2.5 to 5 years, some had recovered, some improved, and some remained autistic. Three children had become autistic and one partially autistic since first seen. The results strongly suggested that the autistic behavior followed from the effects of the virus on the central nervous system rather than the sensory impairments. The relationship of such impairments to autistic conditions is of considerable interest. Some visually impaired children experience a period of apparent normality before a setback, and the timing of this setback is very similar to that described in some

children with autistic spectrum disorders (Cass, 1998).

Neuropsychiatric Conditions in Adults

Any of the psychiatric conditions that usually begin in adult life can occur along with autistic spectrum disorders. The commonest of these are the affective disorders, especially anxiety and depression (Wright, 1982). Some clinical features found in certain psychiatric conditions resemble those found in autism. These conditions can pose problems of differential diagnosis.

Catatonia

Acute catatonia is diagnosed on the combination of (1) mutism, (2) absence of voluntary movement, and (3) maintenance of imposed postures. However, a number of authors have described a range of clinical phenomena they consider to be catatonic features (Bush, Fink, Petrides, Dowling, & Francis, 1996; Joseph, 1992; Rogers, 1992). A large number of these features (for example, stereotyped movements, tiptoe walking, echolalia, echopraxia, odd hand postures) are also seen in autistic disorders, especially in younger and more severely disabled children. A severe exacerbation of catatonic features, sufficient to cause major problems with carrying out everyday activities, can occur in some people with autistic spectrum disorders. Motor problems seen in Parkinsonism, such as freezing in the course of an action, or hesitation in crossing a threshold, are frequently part of the same picture (Realmuto & August, 1991). Wing and Shah (2000) found that 17% of people with autistic spectrum disorders age 15 and over when referred to a diagnostic center had marked catatonic and Parkinsonian features. They also found a significant association between passivity in social interaction and the later development of catatonic features.

The occurrence of catatonic phenomena has probably added to the confusion between autistic spectrum disorders and schizophrenia. Although it can occur in schizophrenia, catatonia can also be associated with a variety of neurological and psychiatric conditions (Rogers, 1992). It is particularly characteristic of postencephalitic states, as described in considerable detail by Sacks (1982). The diagnosis of associated autistic spectrum disorder has to be made on the developmental history and the complete clinical picture.

Obsessive-Compulsive Disorder

Some of the phenomena seen in obsessive-compulsive disorder, or in obsessive-compulsive personality disorder, including the urge to count and manipulate numbers, to carry out the same action over and over again, or fearfully to avoid particular situations, have obvious similarities to the repetitive routines of people with autism (Bejerot, Nylander, & Lindstrom, 2001). Baron-Cohen (1989) discussed the use of the term *obsessions* to describe the repetitive behavior typical of autistic disorders. He considered the term inappropriate because the subjective phenomena of resistance to the repetitive activities could not be discerned in autism. Overlap of the features of obsessive-compulsive disorder and autistic spectrum disorders, especially in high-functioning adults with autism, can obscure the diagnosis of an autistic spectrum disorder unless a detailed developmental history of the person is obtained (Szatmari, 1991; Szatmari, Bartolucci, Bremner, Bond, & Rich, 1989; Thomsen, 1994).

The similarities and differences among autism, catatonia, obsessional disorders, Parkinson's disease, Tourette's syndrome, and encephalitic encephalopathy raise interesting questions concerning the possible site and nature of the neuropathology and neurochemistry (Damasio & Maurer, 1978).

Anorexia Nervosa

Severe eating problems are common in children with autistic spectrum disorders. Among 371 children and adults with autistic spectrum disorders seen at the British National Autistic Society's diagnostic and assessment center, whose records were analyzed, one-third had a history of bizarre food fads causing a severely restricted diet (unpublished data). C. Gillberg and Rastam (1992) found that a minority among 51 teenagers with anorexia nervosa had autistic-like conditions. Wentz (2000) followed up this group for 10 years and confirmed that 16% had persistent impairment of social interaction and obsessive-compulsive

behaviors dating from childhood. This subgroup tended to have a very poor outcome. The results suggested that they required the type of therapeutic approach that is appropriate for an autistic spectrum disorder.

Schizoid Personality Disorder and Schizotypal Personality Disorder

There is a marked overlap among the *DSM-IV* criteria for these disorders and those for Asperger's syndrome. Unlike the labels schizoid or schizotypal personality, the diagnosis of autistic spectrum disorder is useful because it helps the individual, the parents, and others involved to understand the underlying impairments. Furthermore, it has implications for education and treatment and the voluntary autism societies provide reference groups for parents and for the individuals concerned.

Schizophrenia

The reasons for separating autistic spectrum disorders from schizophrenia of the adult type occurring in childhood were discussed previously. The social impairment and odd speech and behavior that are characteristic of autistic spectrum disorders have been (and still are) sometimes confused with adult schizophrenia (Nylander & Gillberg, 2001). This is most likely to happen if the person concerned is referred to psychiatric services for the first time in adolescence or adult life, especially if a detailed developmental history is not available.

Among the 371 people seen at the British National Autistic Society's diagnostic and assessment center whose records have been analyzed (unpublished data) there were 78 adolescents and adults with autistic spectrum disorders (over 15 years old with enough expressive speech to describe symptoms). Of these, only one had had an episode of typical schizophrenic delusions and auditory hallucinations. In addition, 6% had had episodes of bizarre behavior, in some cases accompanied by visual hallucinations of a concrete kind, such as a bus emerging from the bathroom wall or a freight train running across the floor. These episodes were in response to stress and resolved when the stress was removed. As mentioned, the association of autistic disorders with catatonia has also caused confusion with schizophrenia.

Psychosocial Deprivation

Children deprived from the earliest years of social interaction and opportunities for learning can be withdrawn, may be delayed in developing speech, and may show stereotyped movements. If the deprivation is gross and prolonged, they may function as severely retarded. If they are of potentially normal cognitive ability, recovery tends to be rapid once the environment is improved (Clarke & Clarke, 1976; Koluchova, 1972, 1976). A child who is autistic may have the added disadvantage of a poor environment, but the coincidence should not be taken to imply a causal connection.

Rutter et al. (1999) studied children adopted into U.K. families from extremely physically and emotionally deprived environments in Roumanian orphanages. These authors found that, at 4 years old, 6% had autistic-like patterns of behavior and a further 6% had isolated autistic features. There were differences from typical autism, especially the improvement in the adopted children seen at follow-up at 6 years of age, so the authors used the term "quasi-autism" for this clinical picture. The relationship with typical autism remains to be explored.

Borderlines of Normality

The normal variation of human behavior encompasses people who collect objects, people who have circumscribed interests, and people who are not particularly sociable or adept in social interaction. As pointed out by Asperger (1944, 1991), artists and scientists need a capacity to lose themselves at times in their own special fields to the exclusion of all else. The borderlines of normality and the autistic spectrum overlap, sometimes blurring the edge where normal variation ends and pathology begins. The theoretical issues are of great interest but, in practice, differential diagnosis is of importance only when the individuals concerned, or their families, experience problems and need help.

INTERNATIONAL SYSTEMS OF CLASSIFICATION

Successive editions of the World Health Organization's *International Classification of Diseases* (*ICD*) and the American Psychiatric Association's *Diagnostic and Statistical Manual of Mental Disorders* (*DSM*), have reflected changing ideas of autism and related disorders. The evolution of these systems illustrates both the advances in understanding that have occurred in the past three decades and the confusions and conflicts of concepts that remain.

The chapter on mental disorders in *ICD-8* (World Health Organization [WHO], 1967) mentioned only infantile autism—and this only as an atypical form of schizophrenia. No diagnostic criteria were given.

Ten years later, this same chapter in *ICD-9* (World Health Organization, 1977) included a section titled "Psychoses with Origins Specific to Childhood." In a notable change from the eighth edition, schizophrenia of adult type occurring in childhood was specifically excluded from the list of so-called childhood psychoses.

Three years after *ICD-9*, the third edition of the *DSM*, referred to as *DSM-III* (American Psychiatric Association, 1980) was published, This introduced the term pervasive developmental disorders (PDD) as a general category, thus acknowledging the shift in the concept of autism from a psychiatric to a developmental disorder. There were two main subgroups; (1) infantile autism with onset before 30 months and (2) childhood onset pervasive developmental disorder with onset after 30 months but before 12 years. A category of infantile autism, residual state was also included for those with a history of infantile autism but who no longer met the full criteria. The criteria for infantile autism were, in brief: (1) social impairment, (2) language impairment, (3) resistance to change or attachments to objects, and (4) absence of symptoms of schizophrenia (delusions, hallucinations, etc.).

Denckla (1986) chaired a working party that considered possible revisions of the *DSM-III* criteria. The report emphasized that the generally accepted criteria for autism and related disorders, namely social and communication impairment and repetitive, stereotyped activities, could occur in widely varying degrees of severity. The working party recommended that the subtlest forms of social and communication impairments and verbal and abstract repetitive routines should be recognized as part of the range of pervasive developmental disorders. Age of onset was excluded as a defining feature. The revised version of *DSM-III*, known as *DSM-III-R* (American Psychiatric Association, 1987) was influenced by these views (Waterhouse, Wing, Spitzer, & Siegal, 1992). This revision kept the general category of PDD but the subgroups were labeled autistic disorder and pervasive developmental disorder not otherwise specified (PDD-NOS). The main criteria for autistic disorder were the same as those for *DSM-III* infantile autism, but age of onset and absence of schizophrenic symptoms were no longer included. For each main criterion, a list of different manifestations, with clinical examples, was given, adding up to 16 items in total. A minimum number and distribution of items had to be present for diagnosis of each of the two subgroups. The list of manifestations for each criterion was arranged in order so that those more likely to be seen in younger or more disabled people were earlier in each list. This version was criticised for being over-inclusive (Volkmar, Cicchetti, & Bregman, 1992). It was found that more children who were severely or profoundly mentally retarded were diagnosed as having autism than when *ICD-10* criteria were used. This was considered by the critics to be inappropriate on the grounds that the social impairment and other features of autism in many severely or profoundly retarded children was not "true autism." Since there are no objective criteria for true autism, it could be argued that, regardless of etiology, there are good clinical reasons for grouping together all those with the triad of impairments. The arrangement of the *DSM-III-R* diagnostic criteria in developmental order could have facilitated studies of how different clinical patterns were related to cognitive ability.

The fourth version, *DSM-IV* (American Psychiatric Association, 1994) also retained the overall category of PDD but introduced new subgroups, in effect moving away from the concept of the autistic spectrum. These were (1) autistic disorder, (2) Rett's disorder, (3) childhood disintegrative disorder, (4) Asperger's disorder, and (5) pervasive developmental disorder not otherwise specified (PDD NOS). The three main behavioral criteria for autistic dis-

order were the same as for *DSM-III-R* infantile autism. Lists of manifestations were also given. There were 12 of these, four for each main criterion. The content of these overlapped with those in *DSM-III-R* but differed in detail and no clinical examples were given. The arrangement in developmental order in *DSM-III-R* was also lost in *DSM-IV,* though no reason was given. In contrast to *DSM-III-R,* age of onset for autistic disorder was included again, this time being under 3 years. The tenth revision of the *International Classification of Diseases, ICD-10* (WHO, 1993) had closely similar subgroups and research criteria but included atypical autism. This would be classified with PDD-NOS in *DSM-IV.* Both systems allowed PDD-NOS/atypical autism to be diagnosed if social *or* communication impairment *or* repetitive activities were present. Social impairment was not obligatory. *ICD-10* also included a subgroup labeled overactive disorder associated with mental retardation and stereotyped movements, for which one of the criteria was *absence* of social impairment of the autistic type.

The American Psychiatric Association (2000) published *DSM-IV-Text Revision (TR)* in which the descriptive texts accompanying the diagnostic criteria were revised but the criteria were left unaltered apart from one small but significant change to the criteria for *PDD-NOS.* Instead of the criteria being social impairment *or* communication impairment *or* stereotyped behavior as in *DSM-IV,* the first *or* in this list was changed to *and.* This meant that social impairment was now necessary for the diagnosis of all of the subgroups of pervasive developmental disorders in *DSM-IV-TR,* thus making it similar to the concept of the autistic spectrum. At the time of writing, *ICD-10* still has the *or . . . or* format in the criteria for atypical autism.

Problems of the *DSM-IV/ICD-10* System of Classifications

This brief history indicates that the authors of the two international classification systems have responded to research findings differentiating autism from schizophrenia (Anthony, 1958; Kolvin, 1971; Kolvin et al., 1971; Rutter, 1972). They have recognized the appropriateness of regarding autism as one of a wider range of developmental disorders. It is less clear that the changes between editions have represented advances in the specifying of diagnostic categories within the pervasive developmental disorders. The bases for distinguishing categories have included age of onset, type of onset, etiology, level of ability, and current clinical picture. The advantages and disadvantages of grouping in each of these categories are now considered.

Age of Onset

Age of onset as a diagnostic criterion for autistic disorder has progressed through the different editions of *DSM* and *ICD* from before 30 months to before 3 years, being temporarily discarded on the way. As discussed above, Kolvin and his colleagues demonstrated that age of onset was very closely associated with the clinical picture. However, the correlation was not absolute and there was some blurring of the borderlines between subgroups. Specifying a limited age range within which onset can occur leads to various problems. Volkmar, Stier, and Cohen (1985) pointed out that the term *age of recognition* was more appropriate than age of onset because the early signs of abnormal development may not be detected by parents. Identifying age of onset for those seen for the first time as adolescents or adults can be difficult. Parents may not remember or may be unavailable. There are occasional cases of typically autistic behavior beginning well after 3 years due, for example, to a virus encephalitis (Ghaziuddin, Tsai, Eilers, & Ghaziuddin, 1992; C. Gillberg, 1986, 1991). Parents, at least those in the United Kingdom, are puzzled and dissatisfied if their child is diagnosed as having PDD-NOS or atypical autism (or worse still, "autistic features") especially since, in some educational districts, such diagnoses may make a child ineligible for the type of education he or she requires.

The criteria for Asperger's disorder demand typical development of various skills, including language and curiosity, up to 3 years of age. However, some older children, adolescents and adults with the behavior pattern described by Asperger (1944, 1991) have histories dating from infancy that are identical to those with typical autistic disorder (Leekam, Libby, Wing, Gould, & Gillberg,

2000; Wing, 1981a, 1991, 2000). In effect, the *DSM-IV* and *ICD-10* criteria for Asperger's disorder are the same as for autistic disorder apart from the criteria relating to language, early development and cognitive ability. This does not accord with the way the diagnosis is used in clinical practice, which is more in line with Asperger's own descriptions of his syndrome (Eisenmajer et al., 1996). There may be justification for defining a subgroup with social impairment but with typical development of language and adaptive skills up to 3 years of age (though none has yet been published), but this should not be called Asperger's syndrome.

Since, in clinical work, the clinical picture is of prime importance, there is a strong case to be made for dropping age of onset as a criterion. In the international classification systems the close but by no means absolute link between age of onset and clinical picture can be noted. The importance of careful investigation where age of onset is different from the usual pattern can be emphasised, without making age of onset a criterion.

Type of Onset

In childhood disintegrative disorder both age of onset and type of onset are included among the *DSM-IV* and *ICD-10* criteria. Catastrophic loss of at least two adaptive skills has to have occurred after a period of normal development lasting at least 2 years. This picture is rare (Fombonne & Chakrabarti, 2001). In a small minority of cases of this kind, it becomes apparent over time that the cause is a progressive neurological disorder (Corbett, Harris, Taylor, & Trimble, 1977). In the majority, no further deterioration occurs after the initial loss of skills and the clinical picture from then on is like that in autistic disorder in children of similar levels of ability. Volkmar (1992) concluded from a case review that there was some support for the validity of this diagnostic concept on grounds of onset, course, and prognosis. Volkmar also mentioned clinical features as differentiating the two disorders but, in the light of his description, it is difficult to see why. He did note that there could be problems of differential diagnosis. From the parents' point of view, the term *disintegrative* suggests a continuing deterioration, with all that implies for the child's future care. This did not occur in most of the children who had been given this diagnosis and who were reviewed by Volkmar.

Etiology

In the great majority of cases, the exact cause of an autistic spectrum disorder is unknown, although there is good evidence for the importance of genetic factors (Bolton et al., 1994). Only one subgroup of the pervasive developmental disorders in *DSM-IV* and *ICD-10* is based on etiology—that is Rett's syndrome (Hagberg, Aicardi, Dias, & Ramos, 1983). Children with this neurological condition may go through a stage in early childhood when they meet diagnostic criteria for autism (C. Gillberg, 1989; Tsai, 1992). After a few years, some of these become sociable and affectionate. There are a variety of other conditions that are sometimes or often associated autistic spectrum disorders, such as tuberose sclerosis (Hunt & Dennis, 1987; Hunt & Shepherd, 1993), infantile spasms (Taft & Cohen, 1971), the Fragile X anomaly (Bailey et al., 1993; Meryash, Szymanski, & Park, 1982), and Williams' syndrome (C. Gillberg & Rasmussen, 1994; Udwin, Yule, & Martin, 1987). It is not at all clear why Rett's syndrome should be selected as a subgroup while the rest are excluded.

Level of Ability

Absence of delay in cognitive development is one of the criteria for Asperger's disorder. This is despite the fact that Asperger noted the clinical picture he described could be found in individuals with cognitive ability in the mildly or even severely retarded range (Asperger, 1944, 1991; Frith, 1991). The subgroup that is found only in *ICD-10,* overactive disorder associated with mental retardation and stereotyped movements, has IQ of less than 50 as one of its criteria. As mentioned previously, another criterion is the absence of social impairment of the autistic type, so it is difficult to understand why this subgroup was included in the category of pervasive developmental disorders.

Bartak and Rutter (1976) compared children with autism who had intelligence quotients (IQs) of 69 and below (low functioning) with those with IQs of 70 and above (high functioning). The greatest difference was in prognosis in adult life, which was significantly

better in the high-functioning group. The authors discussed the possibility of differences in etiology between these two IQ groups but the question is still unresolved. Lotter (1974), Wing and Gould (1979), and Wing (1981b) found that the severity of the impairment of social interaction was related to IQ. These findings point to the importance of IQ as one of the factors in diagnostic formulations, though not as a diagnostic criterion, for individuals with autistic spectrum disorders.

Current Clinical Picture

As noted, for clinical work, the clinical picture is the most important aspect of a diagnostic formulation. *DSM-IV* and *ICD-10* give detailed clinical criteria for various subgroups. However, the use of the varied mixture of age of onset, type of onset, etiology, level of ability together with clinical picture as the basis for classification has produced many anomalies.

A MULTIDIMENSIONAL DIAGNOSTIC FORMULATION

The precise relationship between the overt clinical picture and the underlying neuropsychology and neuropathology is as yet unknown. It is therefore more logical to classify the clinical picture separately from other features such as level of ability and physical etiology if known. In this section of the chapter, a multidimensional diagnostic formulation that the author and colleagues have found useful in clinical practice is described. Its value is that it communicates to other professionals, and the families involved, the essentials of the clinical picture and the needs of the child or adult concerned.

A semi-structured interview schedule, the Diagnostic Interview Schedule for Social and Communication Disorders (DISCO) has been designed to collect information, systematically, concerning developmental history and present clinical picture. It is completed, in association with psychological observation and testing, for the clinical assessment of individuals with autistic spectrum disorders and other developmental conditions. The present author and colleagues have used it in the assessment of over 700 children and adults. An analysis of the data from 200 of these has been published (Leekam, Libby, Wing, Gould, & Taylor, 2002; Wing, Leekam, Libby, Gould, & Larcombe, 2002). From this clinical experience, it has become obvious that the multidimensional approach to classification is much more in line with clinical reality than is any categorical system.

The first step is to establish, from the developmental history and pattern of behavior, whether the person concerned has the triad of impairments, especially impairment of social interaction. Then the diagnostic formulation includes the following dimensions:

1. Type of social impairment (aloof, passive, active-but-odd)
2. Pattern of skills and disabilities (verbal, performance, self-care, motor, forward planning ability, and level of independence)
3. Etiology, if known
4. Co-existing conditions, such as epilepsy, ADHD, and so on
5. The social situation of the family and the individual

Only one clinical feature is included—that is, the quality of the impaired social interaction. Why should this one feature be selected as the key when there are so many other features to be found in autistic spectrum disorders? It would be theoretically possible to subgroup on, for example, language problems, or reactions to sensory stimuli, or motor coordination, or types of stereotyped activities, or any other aspect or combination that can be defined. Such subgroups would overlap in their clinical features but would not be identical. Any of them might be of interest for research. The quality of social interaction was chosen for purely pragmatic reasons. Impairment in this aspect of behavior is associated with impairments of communication and imagination. It has particularly marked effects on the whole life of the individuals concerned.

No claim is made that this subgrouping has validity in terms of the neuropathology, or that it is the only or best system possible. In the author's experience, however, it has proved useful in planning education, management, and the provision of services. Impairments of two-way social interaction and nonverbal communication can be detected even in the first year of a child's life, if the condition is manifested at that stage (Klin, Volkmar, & Sparrow, 1992; Osterling & Dawson, 1994; Ricks, 1975, 1979; Ricks & Wing, 1975).

Research into theory of mind and its relationship to skill in social interaction also emphasizes the importance of social impairment in autistic spectrum disorders (Bowler, 1994; Frith, 1989; Happé, 1999). Klin, Jones, Schultz, Volkmar, and Cohen (2002) discussed the need for a more precise characterization and quantification of the social disorder, which they considered to be the core impairment in autism.

As Szatmari (1992) pointed out, at this stage, the issue regarding classification within the autistic spectrum may be its value for clinical practice, education, and research rather than any absolute concept of validity. The usefulness of Wing and Gould's (1979) division of social interaction into the aloof, passive, and active-but-odd subgroups has received some support from studies by Castelloe and Dawson (1993), Borden and Ollendick (1994), Eaves, Ho, and Eaves (1994), C. Gillberg (1992), and Volkmar, Cohen, Bregman, Hooks, and Stevenson (1989) even though the studies varied in the degree to which each of the three groups differed from the others. Each subgroup tends to be associated with particular kinds of clinical pictures. These are described next, with the variations associated with different levels of cognitive ability and the relationships to the *DSM-IV* classification.

Wing and Gould (1979) found approximately half of the fully mobile children with IQs under 70 that they studied were aloof at the time of interview, one quarter were passive and one quarter active-but-odd. From experience with clinic referrals, the proportions of passive and active-but-odd would have been much higher if children with IQs of 70 and above had been included, but no exact figures are available.

The Aloof Group

This group corresponds most closely to the popular image of autism, so the diagnosis is less likely to be missed than in the other subgroups. It comprises children and adults who are most cut off from social contact. They may become agitated when in close proximity to others. They usually reject unsolicited physical or social contact, although they may, for a brief time, enjoy rough physical play. Some individuals in this group approach other persons to obtain food or other needs. They may seek the physical comfort of sitting on a lap or being cuddled. Once satisfied, they move away abruptly and without a backward glance. They tend to avoid eye contact, though brief glances are common and intense staring may occur occasionally. Their social aloofness is particularly marked with age peers. It tends to be less obvious with well-known people, especially parents. However, at least in the early years, the signs of normal attachment behavior are minimal or absent (Churchill & Bryson, 1972; Wing, 1969; Wolff & Chess, 1964).

Understanding and use of both verbal and nonverbal communication are severely impaired; in the most disabled of this group, they can be virtually absent. Those who do speak often show immediate and delayed echolalia, pronoun reversal, and/or idiosyncratic use of words or phrases as described by Kanner (1946).

There is little or no evidence of the development of imagination. Play tends to be confined to the manipulation of objects. Repetitive behavior may be seen in simple or complex motor stereotypies, fascination with simple sensory stimuli, lining up objects, insisting on complex routines for particular activities such as preparing to go to bed or following precisely the same route to familiar places.

In their early years, their tendency to walk on tiptoe, their springy gait, and their rapid movements may make the aloof children appear graceful. As adolescence approaches, posture and gait tend to become more obviously ill coordinated and odd. Unusual reactions to sensory stimuli may also be seen, especially in the early years. These include ignoring, being distressed by, or becoming unusually fascinated with, sound, light, heat, cold, touch, pain, vibration, or kinesthetic sensations, including self-spinning or watching things that spin. Lack of response to pain can lead to diagnostic problems in physical illness. It may also be a factor in repetitive self-injury that may be seen in some aloof severely retarded children. Responses to sensory stimuli may be paradoxical—for example, covering of the eyes on hearing a loud sound.

Inappropriate or socially embarrassing behavior is very common. This includes temper tantrums, aggression, destructiveness, restlessness, and screaming. These may occur in response to interference with repetitive routines. The underlying problem is lack of understanding of instructions and of the rules of social behavior. Those who can speak may repeatedly make inappropriate, even obscene, remarks in a loud voice in public as well as at home. Some, whether or not they have speech, may grunt, bellow, or otherwise vocalize in socially unacceptable ways.

On standardized psychological tests, visuospatial skills tend to be better than verbal skills (Wing, 1981b). Wing and Gould (1979) found that 78% of the aloof children in their study had nonverbal IQs under 50 and 92% had language comprehension ages under 20 months. A small minority of people who are aloof in social interaction have a special skill in, for example, drawing, fitting and assembling tasks, or arithmetical calculations. They may show surprisingly good rote memory for visual or verbal material or music. Some perform at such a high level in their special skill in contrast to their severe retardation in other areas that the term *autistic savant* has been applied to them (Hermelin, 2001; O'Connor & Hermelin, 1988; Rimland, 1965; Treffert, 1989). Aloof children with higher levels of ability are those most likely to show elaborate repetitive routines and therefore to fit Kanner and Eisenberg's (1956) two essential criteria. This classic picture is rare because aloofness is significantly associated with severe or profound retardation. In contrast, elaborate repetitive routines with objects are much more likely to be seen in children with moderate or mild levels of mental retardation.

Aloofness and indifference to others are most likely to persist throughout childhood and into adult life in those who are severely or profoundly mentally retarded. The clinical picture in children who are aloof in their early years but have higher levels of ability may change in middle or later childhood to become identical with that described by Asperger. They may become passive or even active-but-odd in social interaction. However, there are some people of good ability who become independent and high achievers as adults but remain aloof all their lives.

An associated identifiable neuropathology is more often found in the history or present state of severely or profoundly retarded aloof people than in those who have higher levels of ability (Wing & Gould, 1979).

Those in the aloof group may fit the *DSM-IV* categories of autistic disorder, PDD-NOS, or childhood disintegrative disorder. Asperger's disorder is a less likely diagnosis.

The Passive Group

Children in this subgroup may not be diagnosed in their early years. The main signs of impairment in children are absence of spontaneous social interaction and poor nonverbal communication, rather than indifference to others and overtly strange and difficult behavior, which are so noticeable in the aloof group. Children and adults in this group do not make spontaneous social approaches, except to obtain their needs. However, they accept other's approaches without protest and even with some appearance of enjoyment. They can be led to join in games and activities organized by others although they typically take a passive role, such as that of the baby in the game of mothers and fathers. They are able to copy other people's actions, but without full understanding. Their eye contact is usually poor.

Speech is often better developed than in the aloof group, but there is usually poor intonation and the characteristic lack of interpersonal communication for pleasure. Some have abnormalities of speech as in the aloof group. Others have large vocabularies and even good grammar although the content is mostly repetitive and confined within a narrow range of subjects. Passive individuals have little appreciation of subtle verbal jokes, but they may enjoy slapstick humor, and simple childish play on words. Understanding and use of nonverbal communication is equally impaired.

Imaginative play may be absent, or they may simply copy other children's activities—for example, bathing and feeding dolls. This play lacks spontaneity and inventiveness, and remains repetitive and limited in form. Occasionally, a passive person will show echopraxia of gestures equivalent to echolalia of speech (Attwood, 1984).

Passive individuals have repetitive routines but, compared to the aloof group, they usually show less intense resistance to interference. Some have elaborate routines, including elaborate repetitive activities with objects. In the more able passive persons, routines may take the form of circumscribed interests that require rote memorization of masses of facts about a chosen subject, though with little understanding of the real meaning. Some copy actions of characters from books or the television, perhaps enacting lengthy scenarios with amazing accuracy but little or no understanding of their meaning. This can be mistaken for pretend play, but careful observation shows that the activity is mostly solitary, derivative, and repetitive.

Other characteristics of the aloof group, including stereotyped movements and odd responses to sensory stimuli, may be found in passive children. These features are usually less marked or absent, especially after the early years. Some are poorly coordinated in gross motor skills. Passive children are likely to be the best behaved and the most easily managed of all the autistic groups.

They tend to have higher levels of ability than the aloof group and some are in the average or superior range. The majority perform better on visuospatial skills than on verbal skills, but some have higher scores on language tests. Some have one or more special skills at a very high level, meriting the label of autistic savant.

The prognosis in adult life for the passive group tends, overall, to be better than for the aloof children. By later childhood or adolescence, some have become active-but-odd in behavior. Despite the generally more amenable behavior in childhood, some of those in the passive group may become very difficult in periods of stress or pressure, especially in adolescence. This change is sometimes dramatic and long lasting. Another problem that is significantly more likely to occur in the passive group in adolescence or early adult life is the exacerbation of catatonic features (Wing & Shah, 2000). These features sometimes remit but can remain a problem over many years. However, the most able people in the passive group may adapt to the demands of adult life. Some may even become high achievers in areas related to their special skills. Level of ability, as in all autistic spectrum disorders, is of major importance in relation to outcome.

They are less likely than the aloof group to have an associated identifiable neuropathology (Wing & Gould, 1979).

Among the *DSM-IV* diagnostic categories, those in the passive group could fit the categories of autistic disorder, PDD-NOS, or Asperger's disorder. They are unlikely to fit the criteria for childhood disintegrative disorder.

The Active-but-Odd Group

Children and adults who make spontaneous approaches to others, but in a peculiar, naive, and one-sided fashion, comprise the active-but-odd group. These individuals seek to indulge their circumscribed interests by talking *at* another person or by asking questions but not for the pleasure of reciprocal social interaction. The active approaches may be so persistent—perhaps accompanied by physical clinging—that these people are boring, unwelcome, or even distressing to their unwilling listeners. Diagnosis and classification are particularly difficult for this group. In some cases, the autistic features are fairly obvious, despite the active social approaches. In others, different aspects of behavior, such as poor motor coordination, inappropriate use of language, or high anxiety, may capture attention, so that the autistic characteristics are overlooked.

Compared to the aloof and passive groups, speech tends to be greater in quantity but, at least in the early years, may be characterized by delay and by the same abnormalities as previously described. Some individuals, however, have no delay in speech development and can use correct grammar and employ large vocabularies even at a young age. Repetitiveness, long-windedness, and lack of ease with colloquial turns of phrase are characteristic of even the best speakers in the group. Hurtig, Ensrud, and Tomblin (1982), examining the conversations of active-but-odd children with adults, described how the children used questions as conversational openers without prefacing their inquiries with social conventions, such as a greeting. This behavior generally seemed very odd to the conversational partner.

Active-but-odd individuals also have impairments in the nonverbal aspects of communication. Vocal intonation is monotonous or has strange inflections and poor volume control.

They may not use gestures, especially those indicating feeling and emotions (Attwood, 1984) but some in this group make exaggerated and inappropriate movements of face and limbs when speaking. Their eye contact is also inappropriate, staring too hard at times but looking away when it would be socially correct to meet the gaze of the conversational partner. People in this group have, in particularly marked form, the impairment of the pragmatic aspects of communication that are common to all autistic spectrum disorders (Lister Brook & Bowler, 1992).

Like some passive children, many in this group have repetitive, stereotyped pseudo-pretend play. They build and rebuild the same imaginary system of roads and bridges, or they pretend to be the same animal or the same inanimate object such as a train (Wing et al., 1977). Some children act out scenes from their favorite videos, which they watch repetitively. Their re-enactment is remarkable for the accuracy with which they copy the fragments chosen, the repetitiveness and absence of any imaginative embroidery, and the lack of comprehension or even interest in the meaning. Some invent their own imaginary worlds, which may be very elaborate but have the characteristic rigidity and repetitiveness.

As in the other two groups, some active-but-odd children have repetitive routines involving objects. Others have more abstract circumscribed interests, including time-tables, calendars, genealogy of royal families, physics, astronomy, particular birds or animals or even specific people. Repetitive asking of the same series of questions, regardless of the answers received, is also characteristic.

In their early years, some display motor stereotypies and unusual responses to sensory stimuli. These may fade with increasing age. Children in this group frequently have problems of motor coordination and have an odd, immature gait and posture. Some have been described as puppet-like in their movements. Unlike children in the aloof group, those who are active-but-odd in social interaction tend to be wary of balancing and climbing.

Behavior problems are common. Irrelevant remarks and repetitive questioning can include socially inappropriate themes such as physical abnormalities, details of other people's personal lives, or sex and violence. Odd approaches to others easily turn to pestering and then to temper tantrums and physical aggression. They may show oversensitivity to any perceived criticism. A small minority get into trouble with the law (Wing, 1981a, 1997b) because they lack understanding of social rules. Asperger (1944, 1991) described one small subgroup of people with his syndrome, who would fit into the active-but-odd group, who appeared to take delight in malicious acts against others. Newson's group with pathological demand avoidance syndrome also shows this type of behavior.

Most but not all members of this group have higher levels of skill than those who are aloof, and some are in the average or superior range. Some active-but-odd people have verbal scores that are equal to or higher than their performance scores on Wechsler IQ batteries, but the subtests on which they do well depend more on rote memory than on reasoning ability.

Prognosis is varied. Some make good progress and become more appropriate in social interaction as adults. As with the passive group, the most able of those who as children were active-but-odd in social interaction may adapt to the demands of adult life and some become high achievers in their own special fields of interest. Most difficulties of adaptation occur in those whose social behavior is inappropriate, especially if they have the characteristics of the pathological demand avoidance group described by Newson.

In their study, Wing and Gould (1979) found that, of the three groups, the active-but-odd were least likely to have an associated identifiable neuropathology.

Among the diagnostic categories in *DSM-IV* and *ICD-10,* the active-but-odd group would be most likely to show the criteria for Asperger's disorder or PDD-NOS. Some possibly might meet the criteria for autistic disorder.

The Need for Flexibility

This classification of the impairments of social interaction found in the spectrum of autistic disorders should not be regarded as rigid. The borderlines between the groups are ill defined, lending weight to the view that they are part of a spectrum of related conditions. One person can show the behavior of different groups in different environments (Lord, 1984) and at different ages. Wing (1988) found in an epidemiological study that 14% of the 42 fully mobile children with autistic spectrum disorders, who were aloof in their early years had, by later childhood or adolescence, become passive or active-but-odd. However, among the 37 fully mobile children who were passive or active-but-odd in their early years, 14% became socially aloof as they grew older. Almost all the children in this study had varying degrees of mental retardation. In contrast, 39 (65%) of 60 children and adults referred to a clinic, who had overall IQs of 70 or above and who had been aloof in early childhood, had become passive or active-but-odd with increasing age. None of the 70 referrals with this level of ability who had been passive or active-but-odd had become aloof (unpublished data). Diagnostic formulations for individuals need to change over time in response to changes in the person concerned.

CONCLUSION

The so-called syndromes into which autistic spectrum disorders have been divided are not unique and separate conditions. They are best understood in the context of the full range of developmental disorders right up to the borderline of normality.

There are major problems with the past and current classification systems based on categories, which to a large extent overlap with each other. No objective measures have been found to test the validity of the diagnostic categories used in existing classification systems. The categories have not proved helpful in prescribing type of education, behavior management, medication, or other treatment. They are useful in comparative research only if their reliability is enhanced by increasing the details of the specifications, thereby narrowing the categories, and by training the workers involved (Le Couteur et al., 1989). But, however necessary this is for comparing the results of different studies, it has the effect of excluding those who do not fit neatly into the categories. Thus, it artificially endorses the categories used.

The multidimensional approach suggested groups together clinical pictures that have in common the triad of impairments whatever the underlying cause. The justification for this is on the clinical grounds that the presence of the triad is the most important factor determining an individual's needs, whatever other condition is present (Wing, 2001). The lumping together for a clinical diagnostic formulation does not prevent researchers from splitting off special groups they want to investigate, as long as they give clear descriptions of the group they select. In any case, stating only, for example, that the children being studied have *DSM-IV* autistic disorder is not sufficient information to allow comparison with other studies.

A multidimensional approach of this kind is a practical way to cope with the current incomplete state of knowledge concerning autistic spectrum disorders and the difficulties of defining the borderlines with other developmental and neuropsychiatric conditions. It has to be acknowledged that it would be difficult to incorporate into a standardized method of classification such as *DSM-IV* or *ICD-10*. Categories are much easier to deal with in a theoretical system. The problem is that, in the real world of clinical practice, when trying to help people with autistic spectrum disorders, neatly defined categories are of very little use. There may come a time when the relationship between neuropathology, psychology, and overt behavior is fully understood. Until then, it is likely that problems of classification will continue unresolved.

Cross-References

Approaches to categorical classification are discussed in Chapters 1 through 7; assessment issues are addressed in Chapters 27 through 33; Chapter 47 discusses cross-cultural issues of classification as does Chapter 48.

REFERENCES

American Psychiatric Association. (1980). *Diagnostic and statistical manual* (3rd ed.). Washington, DC: Author.

American Psychiatric Association. (1987). *Diagnostic and statistical manual of mental disorders* (3rd ed., rev.). Washington, DC: Author.

American Psychiatric Association. (1994). *Diagnostic and statistical manual of mental disorders* (4th ed.). Washington, DC: Author.

American Psychiatric Association. (2000). *Diagnostic and statistical manual of mental disorders* (4th ed., text rev.). Washington, DC: Author.

Anthony, E. J. (1958). An experimental approach to the psychopathology of childhood autism. *British Journal of Medical Psychology, 21,* 211–225.

Asperger, H. (1944). Die "autistischen psychopathen" im kindersalter [Autistic psychopathy in childhood]. *Archives fur Psychiatrie und Nervenkrankheiten, 117,* 76–136.

Asperger, H. (1991). Autistic psychopathy in childhood. In U. Frith (Ed. & Trans.), *Autism and Asperger syndrome* (pp. 37–92). Cambridge, England: Cambridge University Press.

Attwood, A. (1984). *The gestures of autistic children.* Unpublished doctoral dissertation, University of London, London, England.

Bailey, A., Bolton, P., Butler, L., Le Couteur, A., Murphy, M., Scott, S., et al. (1993). Prevalence of the Fragile X anomaly amongst autistic twins and singletons. *Journal of Child Psychology and Psychiatry, 34,* 673–688.

Baron-Cohen, S. (1989). Do autistic children have obsessions and compulsions? *British Journal of Clinical Psychology, 28,* 193–200.

Bartak, L., & Rutter, M. (1976). Differences between mentally retarded and normally intelligent autistic children. *Journal of Autism and Childhood Schizophrenia, 6,* 109–120.

Bartak, L., Rutter, M., & Cox, A. (1975). A comparative study of infantile autism and specific developmental receptive language disorder: I. The children. *British Journal of Psychiatry, 126,* 127–145.

Bartak, L., Rutter, M., & Cox, A. (1977). A comparative study of infantile autism and specific developmental receptive language disorder: III. Discriminant function analysis. *Journal of Autism and Childhood Schizophrenia, 7,* 297–302.

Bejerot, S., Nylander, L., & Lindstrom, E. (2001). Autistic traits in obsessive-compulsive disorder. *Nordic Journal of Psychiatry, 55,* 169–176.

Bender, L. (1947). Childhood schizophrenia: A clinical study of 100 schizophrenic children. *American Journal of Orthopsychiatry, 17,* 40–56.

Bishop, D. (2000). What's so special about Asperger syndrome? The need for further exploration of the borderlands of autism. In A. Klin, F. R. Volkmar, & S. S. Sparrow (Eds.), *Asperger syndrome* (pp. 231–253). New York: Guilford Press.

Bleuler, E. (1911). *Dementia praecox or the group of schizophrenias* (J. Zinkin, Trans.). New York: International Universities Press.

Bolton, P., Macdonald, H., Pickles, A., Rios, P., Goode, S., Crowson, M., et al. (1994). A case-control family history study of autism. *Journal of Child Psychology and Psychiatry, 35,* 877–900.

Borden, M., & Ollendick, T. (1994). An examination of the validity of social subtypes in autism. *Journal of Autism and Developmental Disorders, 24,* 23–38.

Bowler, D. (1994). "Theory of mind" in Asperger's syndrome. *Journal of Child Psychology and Psychiatry, 33,* 877–894.

Bush, G., Fink, M., Petrides, G., Dowling, F., & Francis, A. (1996). Catatonia: I. Rating scale and standardised examination. *Acta Psychiatrica Scandinavica, 93,* 129–136.

Cantwell, D., Baker, L., Rutter, M., & Mawhood, L. (1989). Infantile autism and developmental receptive dysphasia: A comparative follow-up into middle childhood. *Journal of Autism and Developmental Disorders, 19,* 19–32.

Cass, H. (1998). Visual impairment and autism: Current questions and future research. *Autism: International Journal of Research and Practice, 2,* 117–138.

Cass, H., Sonksen, P., & McConachie, H. (1994). Developmental setback in severe visual impairment. *Archives of Diseases in Childhood, 70,* 192–196.

Castelloe, P., & Dawson, G. (1993). Subclassification of children with autism and pervasive developmental disorder: A questionnaire based on Wing's subgrouping scheme. *Journal of Autism and Developmental Disorders, 23,* 229–242.

Chess, S. (1971). Autism in children with congenital rubella. *Journal of Autism and Childhood Schizophrenia, 1,* 33–47.

Chess, S. (1977). Follow-up report on autism in congenital rubella. *Journal of Autism and Childhood Schizophrenia, 7,* 69–81.

Churchill, D., & Bryson, C. Q. (1972). Looking and approach behavior of psychotic and normal children as a function of adult attention or preoccupation. *Comprehensive Psychiatry, 13,* 171–177.

Clark, T., Feehan, C., Tinline, C., & Vostanis, P. (1999). Autistic symptoms in children with attention deficit-hyperactivity disorder. *European Child and Adolescent Psychiatry, 8,* 50–55.

Clarke, A. M., & Clarke, A. D. B. (1976). *Early experience: Myth and evidence.* London: Open Books.

Cohen, D. J., Paul, R., & Volkman, F. R. (1986). Issues in the classification of pervasive and other developmental disorders: Toward *DSM-IV. Journal of the American Academy of Child Psychiatry, 25*(2), 213–220.

Corbett, J., Harris, R., Taylor, E., & Trimble, M. (1977). Progressive disintegrative psychosis of childhood. *Journal of Child Psychology and Psychiatry, 17,* 211–219.

Cox, A., Rutter, M., Newman, S., & Bartak, L. (1975). A comparative study of infantile autism and specific developmental receptive language disorder: II. Parental characteristics. *British Journal of Psychiatry, 126,* 146–159.

Creak, E. M. (1964). Schizophrenic syndrome in childhood: Further progress report of a working party. *Developmental Medicine and Child Neurology, 6,* 530–535.

Damasio, A. R., & Maurer, R. G. (1978). A neurological model for childhood autism. *Archives of Neurology, 35,* 777–786.

Denckla, M. B. (1986). New diagnostic criteria for autism and related behavior disorders: Guidelines for research protocols. *Journal of the American Academy of Child and Adolescent Psychiatry, 25,* 221–224,

De Sanctis, S. (1906). Sopra alcune varieta della demenza precoce [Concening various kinds of precocious dementia]. *Rivista Sperimentale di Freniatria e di Medicina Legale, 32,* 141–165.

De Sanctis, S. (1908). Dementia praecocissima catatonica oder katatonie des fruheren kindersalters? [Catatonic dementia praecox or catatonia of early childhood?]. *Folia Neurobiologica, 2,* 9–12.

Despert, J. C. (1938). Schizophrenia in children. *Psychiatric Quarterly, 12,* 366–371.

Earl, C. J. C. (1934). The primitive catatonic psychosis of idiocy. *British Journal of Medical Psychology, 14,* 230–253.

Eaves, L., Ho, H., & Eaves, D. (1994). Subtypes of autism by cluster analysis. *Journal of Autism and Developmental Disorders, 24,* 3–22.

Ehlers, S., & Gillberg, C. (1993). The epidemiology of Asperger syndrome: A total population study. *Journal of Child Psychology and Psychiatry, 34,* 1327–1350.

Eisenmajer, R., Prior, M. R., Leekam, S., Wing, L., Gould, J., Welham, M., et al. (1996). Comparison of clinical symptoms in autism and Asperger's disorder. *Journal of the American Academy of Child and Adolescent Psychiatry, 35,* 1523–1531.

Fombonne, E., & Chakrabarti, S. (2001). No evidence for a new variant of measles-mumps-rubella-induced autism. *Pediatrics, 108,* e56.

Frith, U. (1989). *Autism: Explaining the enigma.* Oxford, England: Blackwell.

Frith U. (Ed.). (1991). *Autism and Asperger syndrome.* Cambridge, England: Cambridge University Press.

Ghaziuddin, M., Tsai, L., Eilers, L., & Ghaziuddin, N. (1992). Autism and herpes simplex encephalitis. *Journal of Autism and Developmental Disorders, 22,* 107–114.

Gillberg, C. (1986). Onset at age 14 of a typical autistic syndrome: A case report of a girl with herpes simplex encephalitis. *Journal of Autism and Developmental Disorders, 16,* 369–376.

Gillberg, C. (1989). The borderland of autism and Rett syndrome: Five case histories to highlight diagnostic difficulties. *Journal of Autism and Developmental Disorders, 19,* 545–560.

Gillberg, C. (1991). Autistic syndrome with the onset at age 31 years: Herpes encephalitis as a possible model for childhood autism. *Developmental Medicine and Child Neurology, 33,* 920–924.

Gillberg, C. (1992). Autism and autistic-like conditions: Subclasses among disorders of empathy (The Emmanuel Miller Memorial Lecture 1991). *Journal of Child Psychology and Psychiatry, 33,* 813–842.

Gillberg, C., Gillberg, C., Rastam, M., & Wentz, E. (2001). Asperger syndrome (and high-functioning autism) Diagnostic Interview (ASDI): A preliminary study of a new structured clinical interview. *Autism: International Journal of Research and Practice, 5,* 57–66.

Gillberg, C., & Rasmussen, P. (1994). Four case histories and a literature review of Williams' syndrome and autistic behavior. *Journal of Autism and Developmental Disorders, 24,* 381–393.

Gillberg, C., Rasmussen, P., Carlström, G., Svenson, B., & Waldenström, E. (1982). Perceptual, motor and attentional deficits in six-year-old children. *Journal of Child Psychology and Psychiatry, 23,* 131–144.

Gillberg, C., & Rastam, M. (1992). Do some cases of anorexia nervosa reflect underlying autistic-like conditions? *Behavioural Neurology, 5,* 27–32.

Gillberg, I. C., & Gillberg, C. (1989). Asperger syndrome: Some epidemiological considerations. *Journal of Child Psychology and Psychiatry, 30,* 631–638.

Goldfarb, W. (1974). *Growth and change of schizophrenic children.* New York: Wiley.

Green, D., Baird, G., Barnett, A., Henderson, L., Huber, J., & Henderson, S. (2002). The severity and nature of motor impairment in Asperger's syndrome: A comparison with specific developmental disorder of motor function. *Journal of Child Psychology and Psychiatry, 43,* 655–668.

Hagberg, B., Aicardi, J., Dias, K., & Ramos, O. (1983). A progressive syndrome of autism, dementia, ataxia, and loss of purposeful hand use in girls: Rett's syndrome. A report of 35 cases. *Annals of Neurology, 14,* 471–479.

Happé, F. (1999). Theory of mind and self consciousness: What is it like to be autistic? *Mind and Language, 14,* 82–89.

Hermelin, B. (2001). *Bright splinters of the mind.* London: Jessica Kingsley.

Houston, R., & Frith, U. (2000). *Autism in history.* Oxford, England: Blackwell.

Howlin, P., Wing, L., & Gould, J. (1995). The recognition of autism in children with Down syndrome: Implications for intervention and some speculations about pathology. *Developmental Medicine and Child Neurology, 37,* 406–414.

Hulse, W. C. (1954). Dementia infantilis. *Journal of Nervous and Mental Diseases, 119,* 471–477.

Hunt, A., & Dennis, J. (1987). Psychiatric disorder among children with tuberous sclerosis. *Developmental Medicine and Child Neurology, 29,* 190–198.

Hunt, A., & Shepherd, C. (1993). A prevalence study of autism in tuberous sclerosis. *Journal of Autism and Developmental Disorders, 23,* 323–340.

Hurtig, R., Ensrud, S., & Tomblin, J. B. (1982). The communicative function of question production in autistic children. *Journal of Autism and Developmental Disorders, 12,* 57–69.

Joseph, A. (1992). Catatonia. In A. Joseph & R. Young (Eds.), *Movement disorders in neurology and neuropsychiatry* (pp. 342–345). Oxford, England: Blackwell.

Kanner, L. (1943). Autistic disturbances of affective contact. *Nervous Child, 2,* 217–250.

Kanner, L. (1946). Irrelevant and metaphorical language in early childhood autism. *American Journal of Psychiatry, 103,* 242–246.

Kanner, L. (1949). Problems of nosology and psychodynamics in early infantile autism. *American Journal of Orthopsychiatry, 19,* 416–426.

Kanner, L. (1965). Infantile autism and the schizophrenias. *Behavioural Science, 10,* 412–420.

Kanner, L., & Eisenberg, L. (1956). Early infantile autism, 1943–1955. *American Journal of Orthopsychiatry, 26,* 55–65.

Kerbeshian, J., & Burd, L. (1986). Asperger's syndrome and Tourette syndrome. *British Journal of Psychiatry, 148,* 731–735.

Klin, A., Jones, W., Schultz, R., Volkmar, F., & Cohen, D. (2002). Defining and quantifying the social phenotype in autism. *American Journal of Psychiatry, 159,* 895–908.

Klin, A., Volkmar, F., & Sparrow, S. (1992). Autistic social dysfunction: Some limitations of the theory of mind hypothesis. *Journal of Child Psychology and Psychiatry, 33,* 861–876.

Koluchova, J. (1972). Severe deprivation in twins: A case study. *Journal of Child Psychology and Psychiatry, 13,* 107–114.

Koluchova, J. (1976). A report on the further development of twins after severe and prolonged deprivation. In A. M. Clarke & A. D. B. Clarke (Eds.), *Early experience: Myth and evidence* (pp. 56–66). London: Open Books.

Kolvin, I. (1971). Studies in the childhood psychoses: I. Diagnostic criteria and classification. *British Journal of Psychiatry, 118,* 381–384.

Kolvin, I., Ounsted, C., Humphrey, M., & McNay, A. (1971). Studies in the childhood psychoses: II. The phenomenology of childhood psychoses. *British Journal of Psychiatry, 118,* 385–395.

Lane, H. (1977). *The wild boy of Aveyron.* London: Allen & Unwin.

Le Couteur, A., Rutter, M., Lord, C., Rios, P., Robertson, S., Holdgrafer, M., et al. (1989). Autism diagnostic interview: A standardized investigator instrument. *Journal of Autism and Developmental Disorders, 19,* 363–387.

Leekam, S., Libby, S., Wing, L., Gould, J., & Gillberg, G. (2000). Comparison of *ICD-10* and Gillberg's criteria for Asperger syndrome. *Autism: International Journal of Research and Practice, 4,* 11–28.

Leekam, S., Libby, S., Wing, L., Gould, J., & Taylor, C. (2002). The Diagnostic Interview for Social and Communication Disorders: Algorithms for *ICD-10* childhood autism, and Wing and Gould autistic spectrum disorder. *Journal of Child Psychology and Psychiatry, 43,* 327–342.

Lister Brook, S., & Bowler, D. (1992). Autism by another name? Semantic and pragmatic impairments in children. *Journal of Autism and Developmental Disorders, 22,* 61–82.

Lord, C. (1984). The development of peer relations in children with autism. In F. J. Morrison, C. Lord, & D. P. Keating (Eds.), *Applied developmental psychology* (pp. 165–229). New York: Academic Press.

Lotter, V. (1966). Epidemiology of autistic conditions in young children: I. prevalence. *Social Psychiatry, 1,* 124–137.

Lotter, V. (1974). Factors related to outcome in autistic children. *Journal of Autism and Childhood Schizophrenia, 4,* 263–277.

Mahler, M. S. (1952). On child psychoses and schizophrenia: Autistic and symbiotic infantile psychoses. *Psychoanalytic Study of the Child, 7,* 286–305.

Maudsley, H. (1867). Insanity of early life. In H. Maudsley (Ed.), *The physiology and pathology of the mind* (pp. 259–386). New York: Appleton.

Mawhood, I., Howlin, P., & Rutter, M. (2000). Autism and developmental receptive language disorder—a comparative follow-up in early adult life: I. Cognitive and language outcomes. *Journal of Child Psychology and Psychiatry, 41,* 547–559.

Meryash, D. L., Szymanski, L. S., & Park, G. S. (1982). Infantile autism associated with the Fragile-X syndrome. *Journal of Autism and Developmental Disorders, 12,* 295–302.

Newson, E. (1983). Pathological demand-avoidance syndrome: *Communication, 17,* 3–8.

Newson, E., Le Maréchal, K., & David, C. (2003). Pathological demand avoidance syndrome: A necessary distinction within the pervasive developmental disorders. *Archives of Diseases of Childhood, 88,* 595–600.

Nylander, L., & Gillberg, C. (2001). Screening for autism spectrum disorders in adult psychiatric out-patients: A preliminary report. *Acta Psychiatrica Scandinavica, 103,* 428–434.

O'Connor, N., & Hermelin, B. (1988). Low intelligence and special abilities. *Journal of Child Psychology and Psychiatry, 29,* 391–396.

Osterling, J., & Dawson, G. (1994). Early recognition of children with autism: A study of first birthday home videotapes. *Journal of Autism and Developmental Disorders, 24,* 247–258.

Rapin, I., & Allen, D. A. (1983). Developmental language disorders: Nosologic considerations. In U. Kirk (Ed.), *Neuropsychology of language, reading and spelling* (pp. 155–184). New York: Academic Press.

Realmuto, G. M., & August, G. J. (1991). Catatonia in autistic disorder: A sign of co-morbidity or variable expression? *Journal of Autism and Developmental Disorders, 21,* 517–528.

Realmuto, G. M., & Main, B. (1982). Coincidence of Tourette's disorder and infantile autism. *Journal of Autism and Developmental Disorders, 12,* 367–372.

Ricks, D. M. (1975). Vocal communication in pre-verbal normal and autistic children. In N. O'Connor (Ed.), *Language, cognitive deficits and retardation* (pp. 75–80). London: Butterworths.

Ricks, D. M. (1979). Making sense of experience to make sensible sounds. In M. Bullowa (Ed.), *Before speech: The beginning of interpersonal communication* (pp. 245–268). Cambridge: Cambridge University Press.

Ricks, D. M., & Wing, L. (1975). Language, communication and the use of symbols in normal and autistic children. *Journal of Autism and Childhood Schizophrenia, 5,* 191–221.

Rimland, B. (1965). *Infantile autism.* London: Methuen.

Rogers, D. (1992). *Motor disorder in psychiatry: Towards a neurological psychiatry.* Chichester, England: Wiley.

Rourke, B., & Tsatsanis, K. (2000). Non-verbal learning disabilities and Asperger syndrome. In A. Klin, F. R. Volkmar, & S. S. Sparrow (Eds.), *Asperger syndrome* (pp. 231–253). New York: Guilford Press.

Rutter, M. (1972). Childhood schizophrenia reconsidered. *Journal of Autism and Childhood Schizophrenia, 2,* 315–337.

Rutter, M. (1978). Diagnosis and definition. In M. Rutter & E. Schopler (Eds.), *Autism: A reappraisal of concepts and treatment* (pp. 1–25). New York: Plenum Press.

Rutter, M., Anderson-Wood, L., Beckett, C., Bredenkamp, D., Castle, J., Groothues, C., et al. (1999). Quasi-autistic patterns following severe early global privation. *Journal of Child Psychology and Psychiatry, 40,* 537–550.

Rutter, M., & Lockyer, L. (1967). A five to fifteen year follow-up study of infantile psychosis: I. Description of the sample. *British Journal of Psychiatry, 113,* 1169–1182.

Rutter, M., Mawhood, L., & Howlin, P. (1992). Language delay and social development. In P. Fletcher & D. Hall (Eds.), *Specific speech and language disorders in children* (pp. 63–78). London: Whurr.

Sacks, O. (1982). *Awakenings* (Rev. ed.). London: Pan Books.

Shapiro, A. K., Shapiro, E. S., Brown, R. D., & Sweet, R. D. (1978). *Gilles de la Tourette syndrome.* New York: Raven Press.

Szatmari, P. (1991). Asperger's syndrome: Diagnosis, treatment, and outcome. *Psychiatric Clinics of North America, 14,* 81–93.

Szatmari, P. (1992). The validity of autistic spectrum disorders: A literature review. *Journal of Autism and Developmental Disorders, 22,* 583–600.

Szatmari, P., Bartolucci, G., Bremner, R. S., Bond, S., & Rich, S. (1989). A follow-up study of high functioning autistic children. *Journal of Autism and Developmental Disorders, 19,* 213–226.

Szatmari, P., Brenner, R., & Nagy, J. (1989). Asperger syndrome: A review of clinical features. *Canadian Journal of Psychiatry, 34,* 554–560.

Taft, L. T., & Cohen, H. J. (1971). Hypsarrhythmia and childhood autism: A clinical report. *Journal of Autism and Childhood Schizophrenia, 1,* 327–336.

Tantam, D. (1988). Asperger's syndrome. *Journal of Child Psychology and Psychiatry, 29,* 245–255.

Thomsen, P. (1994). Obsessive-compulsive disorder in children and adolescents. A review of the literature. *European Child and Adolescent Psychiatry, 3,* 138–158.

Treffert, D. (1989). *Extraordinary people.* New York: Bantam Books.

Tsai, L. (1992). Is Rett syndrome a subtype of pervasive developmental disorders? *Journal of Autism and Developmental Disorders, 22,* 551–562.

Udwin, O., Yule, W., & Martin, N. (1987). Cognitive abilities and behavioral characteristics of children with idiopathic infantile hypercalcemia. *Journal of Child Psychology and Psychiatry, 28,* 297–310.

Volkmar, F. (1992). Childhood disintegrative disorder: Issues for *DSM-IV. Journal of Autism and Developmental Disorders, 22,* 625–642.

Volkmar, F., Cicchetti, D., & Bregman, J. (1992). Three diagnostic systems for autism: *DSM-III, DSM-III-R* and *ICD-10. Journal of Autism and Developmental Disorders, 22,* 483–492.

Volkmar, F., Cohen, D., Bregman, J., Hooks, M., & Stevenson, J. (1989). An examination of social subtypologies in autism. *Journal of the American Academy of Child and Adolescent Psychology, 28,* 82–86.

Volkmar, F., Stier, D., & Cohen, D. (1985). Age of recognition of pervasive developmental disorder. *American Journal of Psychiatry, 142,* 1450–1452.

Wakabayashi, S. (1979). A case of infantile autism associated with Down's syndrome. *Journal of Autism and Developmental Disorders, 9,* 31–36.

Waterhouse, L., Wing, L., Spitzer, R., & Siegal, B. (1992). Pervasive developmental disorders: From *DSM-III* to *DSM-III R. Journal of Autism and Developmental Disorders, 22,* 525–550.

Wentz, E. (2000). *Ten-year outcome of anorexia nervosa with teen-age onset.* Gothenberg: Gothenberg University, Sweden.

Wing, L. (1969). The handicaps of autistic children: A comparative study. *Journal of Child Psychology and Psychiatry, 10,* 1–40.

Wing, L. (1981a). Asperger's syndrome: A clinical account. *Psychological Medicine, 11,* 115–129.

Wing, L. (1981b). Language, social and cognitive impairments in autism and severe mental retardation. *Journal of Autism and Developmental Disorders, 11,* 31–44.

Wing, L. (1988). The continuum of autistic characteristics. In E. Schopler & G. Mesibov (Eds.), *Diagnosis and assessment in autism* (pp. 91–110). New York: Plenum Press.

Wing, L. (1991). Asperger syndrome and Kanner's autism. In U. Frith (Ed. & Trans.), *Autism and Asperger syndrome* (pp. 93–121). Cambridge England: Cambridge University Press.

Wing, L. (1997a). Asperger's syndrome: Management requires diagnosis. *Journal of Forensic Psychiatry, 8,* 253–257.

Wing, L. (1997b). The history of ideas on autism: Legends, myths and reality. *Autism: International Journal of Research and Practice, 1,* 13–23.

Wing, L. (2000). Past and future research on Asperger syndrome. In A. Klin, F. R. Volkmar, & S. S. Sparrow (Eds.), *Asperger syndrome* (pp. 418–432). New York: Guilford Press.

Wing, L. (2001). *The autistic spectrum* (pp. 45–56). Berkeley, CA: Ulysses.

Wing, L., & Gould, J. (1979). Severe impairments of social interaction and associated abnormalities in children: Epidemiology and classification. *Journal of Autism and Developmental Disorders, 9,* 11–29.

Wing, L., Gould, J., Yeates, S., & Brierley, L. (1977). Symbolic play in severely mentally retarded and in autistic children. *Journal of Child Psychology and Psychiatry, 18,* 167–178.

Wing, L., Leekam, S. R., Libby, S. J., Gould, J., & Larcombe, M. (2002). The Diagnostic Interview for Social and Communication disorders: Background, inter-rater reliability and clinical use. *Journal of Child Psychology and Psychiatry, 43,* 307–325.

Wing, L., & Shah, A. (2000). Catatonia in autistic spectrum disorders. *British Journal of Psychiatry, 176,* 357–362.

Wolff, S. (1995). *Loners: The life path of unusual children.* London: Routledge.

Wolff, S., & Chess, S. (1964). A behavioral study of schizophrenic children. *Acta Psychiatrica Scandinavica, 40,* 438–466.

Wolff, S., & McGuire, R. J. (1995). Schizoid personality in girls: A follow-up study. What are the links with Asperger's syndrome? *Journal of Child Psychology and Psychiatry, 36,* 793–818.

World Health Organization. (1967). *Manual of the international statistical classification of diseases, injuries and causes of death* (8th ed., Vol. 1). Geneva, Switzerland: Author.

World Health Organization. (1977). *Manual of the international statistical classification of diseases, injuries and causes of death* (9th ed., Vol. 1). Geneva, Switzerland: Author.

World Health Organization. (1993). *The ICD-10 classification of mental and behavioral disorders: Diagnostic criteria for research.* Geneva, Switzerland: Author.

Wright, E. C. (1982). The presentation of mental illness in mentally retarded adults. *British Journal of Psychiatry, 141,* 496–502.

CHAPTER 22

Executive Functions

SALLY OZONOFF, MIKLE SOUTH, AND SHERRI PROVENCAL

Executive function (EF) is the cognitive construct used to describe goal-directed, future-
oriented behaviors thought to be mediated
by the frontal lobes (Duncan, 1986), including
planning, inhibition of prepotent responses,
flexibility, organized search, self-monitoring,
and use of working memory (Baddeley, 1986;
Goldman-Rakic, 1987; Pennington, 1994). Executive dysfunction has been found in both
individuals with autism and their family members, across many ages and functioning levels,
on many different instruments purported to
measure executive function. This chapter summarizes this still growing literature. We explore a number of issues that have emerged in
the EF literature as the field has matured, including the developmental trajectory of EF,
its relation to other cognitive abilities and features of autism, and its association with other
neurodevelopmental disorders. We conclude the
chapter with thoughts about future research directions, including new findings that executive
dysfunction may be familial, and suggestions
for remediation.

EXECUTIVE FUNCTIONS IN AUTISM:
A LITERATURE REVIEW

Executive difficulties have been found in empirical investigations of people with autism
for as long as EF tasks have been included in
studies. Initial investigations were published
two decades ago and the domain continues to
be actively studied today. In this section, we
first review early studies of EF in autism and
then present new issues that have emerged in
more recent investigations.

Initial Studies

The first empirical investigation of the EFs
of people with autism was done by Rumsey
(1985), who administered the Wisconsin Card
Sorting Test (WCST), a measure of cognitive
flexibility, to adult men with high-functioning
autism. Relative to a sample of typical adults
matched on age, individuals with autism
demonstrated significant perseveration, sorting by previously correct rules, despite feedback that their strategies were incorrect. In a
later study, Rumsey and Hamburger (1990)
demonstrated that this perseveration was not a
general consequence of learning or developmental disorders, as WCST impairment was
specific to an adult sample with autism and
was not apparent in matched controls with severe dyslexia.

Prior and Hoffmann (1990) were the first research team to administer the WCST to a pediatric sample with autism. Like adults with
autism, the children in this study made significantly more perseverative errors than matched
controls. They also performed significantly less
well than controls on the Milner Maze Test,
demonstrating deficits in planning and difficulty learning from mistakes. The authors noted
that the autistic group "perseverated with maladaptive strategies, made the same mistakes repeatedly, and seemed unable to conceive of a
strategy to overcome their difficulties" (p. 588).

The results of another study using the
WCST with individuals with high-functioning
autism were particularly interesting because
deficits were found relative to a control group
with attention-deficit/hyperactivity disorder
(ADHD) and conduct disorder (Szatmari, Tuff,

than tasks in other cognitive domains to predict social understanding and social competence in high-functioning adolescents and adults with autism.

Working Memory

Another component of EF that has been explored in people with autism is working memory. This term refers to the ability to maintain information in an activated, online state to guide cognitive processing (Baddeley, 1986). Initial interest in working memory in autism was driven by studies of performance on Tower tasks (Tower of Hanoi, Tower of London), which, as reviewed earlier, is typically poor in individuals with autism. Tower tasks are thought to measure planning and, thus, at least intuitively, should require working memory (e.g., maintaining a representation of a potential move online while considering its consequences). Bennetto, Pennington, and Rogers (1996) found that adolescents and adults with high-functioning autism were significantly impaired relative to age- and IQ-matched controls on several tests of verbal working memory (counting and sentence span tasks), while they performed similarly to controls on tests of declarative memory function, such as rote short-term, verbal long-term, and recognition memory.

In contrast, other studies have failed to find working memory deficits in autism. In an investigation by Russell and colleagues, a group with both autism and mental retardation did not differ from matched controls on three measures of verbal working memory capacity, a dice-counting task, an odd-man-out task, and a sentence span test (Russell et al., 1996). Similarly, a case report of an individual with autism and mental retardation demonstrated deficits in flexibility but normal working memory (Mottron, Peretz, Belleville, & Rouleau, 1999). And no group differences were found in a higher functioning sample, relative to matched comparison groups with Tourette's syndrome and typical development, on three tasks of working memory in a third study (Ozonoff & Strayer, 2001). One hypothesis of this study was that performance would be more impaired on a task of verbal working memory (an n-back task, in which participants had to identify whether the digit on the computer screen was the same as or

different from the digit of either one or two previous trials) than on tasks of nonverbal working memory (a box search task, with penalties for returning to locations that had already been examined, and a spatial span task). This prediction was not borne out, and the group with autism performed as well as both comparison groups on all tasks, despite having a nonsignificant but still substantial IQ disadvantage of approximately two thirds of a standard deviation.

Thus, there is mixed evidence for working memory as an impaired component of EF. This has prompted some reconsideration of Tower tasks as measures of working memory. A task analysis performed by Goel and Grafman (1995) suggests that Tower tasks measure planning functions less than they might appear, but are instead primary measures of the ability to resolve goal-subgoal conflicts. Tower tasks often require participants to perform moves that appear, at a superficial level, to be incorrect or opposite the goal state. Failure to appreciate this results in poorer task performance and lower planning efficiency scores, but for reasons more conceptually related to flexibility than to working memory. It is not currently clear whether working memory is a specific difficulty for people with autism, and more research is needed.

Section Summary

This body of research begins to clarify the nature of executive dysfunction in autism. While tasks employed in initial research, such as the WCST, suggested impairments in flexibility, they were relatively imprecise measures that confounded a number of executive processes. Further work has refined our ability to examine specific executive components and their respective associations with autism. This work suggests that inhibitory control and possibly working memory are relatively spared functions, while mental flexibility of a variety of types (set shifting, attention shifting) appears compromised (Hill & Russell, 2002; Hughes, 2002; Ozonoff & Jensen, 1999). As the affected components of EF in autism have been clarified, a number of additional interesting issues have emerged from the EF literature in recent years.

EMERGING ISSUES

As the study of EF in autism has continued, several new issues have arisen, suggesting that the story is not as simple as it first appeared.

Developmental Course of Executive Dysfunction

An important question related to the contribution of executive processes to autism centers on *when* deficits emerge. Historically, based primarily on work with adult patients, the frontal lobes were assumed to become functionally mature only in adolescence; however, both developmental research and animal models have shown that this brain region is operational, remarkably capable, and adaptable throughout development (Duncan, 2001; Hughes & Graham, 2002). EF research on children and animals necessarily requires adapting tasks to appropriate levels; the resulting creativity and simplicity have been very beneficial for component process research (Dawson et al., 2002; Diamond, Prevor, Callender, & Druin, 1997; Hughes & Graham, 2002).

Two research groups have tested age-related EF development in very young children with autism. The first investigation to examine EFs in preschool-age children with autism was conducted by McEvoy, Rogers, and Pennington (1993). They used several developmentally simple measures of prefrontal function that were first designed for use with nonhuman primates and human infants (Diamond & Goldman-Rakic, 1986). Their sample included young children with autism (mean age = 5 years, 4 months) and matched developmentally delayed and typically developing control groups. In the spatial reversal task, an object was hidden in one of two identical wells outside the subject's vision. The side of hiding remained the same until the subject successfully located the object on four consecutive trials, after which the side of hiding was changed to the other well. Thus, successful search behavior required flexibility and set shifting. Significant group differences were found, with the children with autism making more perseverative errors than children in either the mental- or chronological-age-matched groups. However, no group differences were evident on three other EF measures. It was

suggested that these tasks may have been less developmentally appropriate for the sample.

However, in another investigation by the same research team (Griffith, Pennington, Wehner, & Rogers, 1999), studying even younger children with autism (mean age = 4 years, 3 months), there were no differences in performance on any of eight executive tasks (including the spatial reversal task), compared to a developmentally delayed group matched on chronological age and both verbal and nonverbal mental age. Based on limited normative data (Diamond et al., 1997), both groups performed at levels lower than expected for their mental age, suggesting that EF impairment at this age may not be autism-specific, but rather a function of general developmental delay. Likewise, in a larger study (*n* = 72) of even younger children with autism (mean age = 3 years, 8 months), Dawson et al. (2002) reported no significant differences on six EF tasks (again including spatial reversal), relative to developmentally delayed and typically developing control groups matched on mental age.

This work raises the possibility that differential EF deficits emerge with age and are not present (at least relative to other samples with delayed development) early in the preschool range. Whether this is because of a general deficit, common to developmental delay, or whether there is no delay in autism early on is not certain. Since EFs are just beginning to develop during the early preschool period in all children, a relative lack of variance across groups may explain this apparent developmental discontinuity. Differences in the way EF is measured at different ages may also contribute to this finding. The executive tests that have been administered to very young children with autism do not require the same use of arbitrary rules that those given to older individuals do. If arbitrary rule use is central to the EF performance deficits of autism (Biro & Russell, 2001), the discontinuity between earlier and later development may be due simply to measurement differences.

Further work, particularly longitudinal research, is needed to examine when during development specific executive difficulties emerge and what their developmental precursors may be. It has been argued, for example, that executive dysfunction is secondary to (and thus driven by) other earlier appearing symptoms, a topic to which we turn next. This timing argument has at times been used to determine which cognitive or psychological processes are core or "primary" to autism. Emergence early in development does not necessarily indicate primacy, nor must development of an impairment over time imply that it is secondary. If autism is a disorder with multiple core deficits, as many researchers suspect, then it is plausible that different impairments may come online at different points in development.

Relationship to Other Cognitive Impairments and Symptoms of Autism

The relationship among EFs, other cognitive and social-cognitive processes, and the development of autism is complex and has been explored in several recent studies. The explanatory power of executive dysfunction to autism would be greatest if individual differences in EF predicted variations in other impairments or in symptoms of autism. In this section, we discuss the relationships among EFs, social-cognitive processes, language, intelligence, and autistic symptoms.

Executive Function and Social Processes

Prefrontal cortex appears to be involved not only in EF performance but also in the regulation of social behavior, emotional reactions, and social discourse (Dennis, 1991; Grattan, Bloomer, Archambault, & Eslinger, 1990; Price, Daffner, Stowe, & Mesulam, 1990; Stuss, 1992), so relationships among these skills are not unexpected. Bennetto et al. (1996) provide a coherent model of how executive deficits could lead to social difficulties in autism, as effective social interaction depends on the ability to hold a variable stream of context-specific information in mind, including subtle verbal and nonverbal cues, then plan and respond to this ever-changing stream appropriately and flexibly. As mentioned earlier, significant correlations between performance on set-shifting tasks and social understanding tasks have been found (Berger et al., 2003), as have relationships between EF and adaptive behavior (Gilotty, Kenworthy, Sirian, Black, & Wagner, 2002).

One of the first studies to document a relationship between social and executive processes was conducted by McEvoy et al. (1993), who reported that performance on executive tasks was significantly correlated with measures of social interaction, including joint attention, in preschool-age autism and control groups. This was an intriguing finding, as joint attention intuitively would appear to require rapid attention shifting and, by extension, intact EF. In fact, an EEG study indicated that activity in the left frontal region was associated with the initiation of joint attention in typical infants (Mundy, Card, & Fox, 2000). Also examining very young children with autism, Griffith et al. (1999) replicated the finding of significant correlations between joint attention and EFs. In contrast, Dawson, Meltzoff, Osterling, and Rinaldi (1998; Dawson et al., 2002) did not find a relationship between joint attention and executive performance in their young sample of children with autism, but instead found an association with a memory task, the delayed nonmatch to sample task. And Swettenham et al. (1998) found that young children with autism have more difficulty shifting attention between social than nonsocial stimuli, suggesting that the impairment is not simply in the shifting process, but interacts with the nature of the stimulus.

The relationship between executive dysfunction and theory of mind impairment has also been studied. Ozonoff et al. (1991) found significant correlations between performance on EF and false belief tasks, and this finding has since been replicated several times (see Perner & Lang, 1999, for a review). Several explanations for this association have been proposed: (1) the deficits are independent modular cognitive operations that are parallel central impairments of autism, (2) one ability is a prerequisite for the other, so that deficits in one cause deficits in the other, (3) both are driven by a third shared impairment, or (4) both share similar neural underpinnings (Hughes, 2001; Ozonoff, 1995; Rutter & Bailey, 1993).

One way to examine these possibilities is to experimentally manipulate task requirements to see which ability contributes more to success or failure on the task. An early study of this type was performed by Russell and colleagues, using a task originally designed to examine strategic deception ability (Russell, Mauthner, Sharpe, & Tidswell, 1991). Children with autism were taught to play a game in which they competed with an experimenter for a piece of candy. The candy was placed in one of two boxes with windows that revealed the contents of the box to subjects, but not to the experimenter. The objective of the task was to "fool" the experimenter into looking for the candy in the empty box. It was explained that the strategy of pointing to the empty box would be successful in winning the candy, whereas pointing to the box that contained the chocolate would result in losing it. Even after many trials, however, the participants with autism were unable to point to the empty box, despite the consequences of this strategy. Russell et al. first attributed these results to a perspective-taking deficit that caused an inability to engage in deception. In a follow-up study, however, Hughes and Russell (1993) demonstrated that significant group differences remained even after the element of deception was removed from the task. Subjects were simply instructed to point to the empty box to get the candy. Even with no opponent present, the children with autism persisted in using the inappropriate strategy. Hughes and Russell attributed this pattern of performance to a deficit in disengaging from the object and using internal rules to guide behavior. This behavior is similar to the perseveration, inappropriate strategy use, and stimulus overselectivity documented on the WCST and other tasks.

The work of Russell and Hughes led the way for several other studies that explored the hypothesis that some degree of executive control is necessary for successful performance on theory of mind tasks and, by extension, for the development of theory of mind (Moses, 2001; Russell, Saltmarsh, et al., 1999). In one of the most recent studies of this kind, Perner and Lang (2002) reported a pair of large studies of typically developing preschool children in which the executive account of false belief was explicitly tested. As in previous studies, the false belief performance was strongly correlated ($r = .65$) with performance on a simple card sorting task. However, against explicit predictions from the executive theory, the card sorting task was just as strongly correlated ($r = .65$) with a verbal explanation task that was *not* dependent on executive abilities. Perner and colleagues also found intact theory of mind, but deficient EFs, in young children at risk of ADHD, arguing against the theory that later theory of mind development is a consequence of improvements in executive control (Perner, Kain, & Barchfeld, 2002). Perner and Lang (2002), having, in their minds, discounted the strictly executive account of false belief and other mentalizing skills, concluded that there was still no clear explanation to account for the remarkably strong relationship between theory of mind and executive tasks.

Indeed, the story was not so simple and the opposite hypothesis, that some level of social awareness is necessary for EF, has also received support. In the WCST, for example, feedback is provided by the examiner after each card is sorted; successful set shifting requires using this feedback to alter behavior. If, however, feedback supplied in a social context is less salient or more difficult to process for people with autism, they may perform poorly on EF tasks for primarily social reasons. A few studies have contrasted performance on executive tests when they are administered in the traditional manner—by human examiners—to performance when they are administered by computer. Ozonoff (1995) reported that the WCST was significantly easier for individuals with autism when it was given by computer, with group differences considerably smaller in the computer administration than the human administration conditions. In the group with autism, the number of perseverations was cut in half on the computerized version of the task, while performance did not differ across conditions in the typically developing control group (Ozonoff, 1995). Two other research teams have found similar facilitation of performance on computer-administered executive tasks relative to standard (human) administration (Griffith, 2002; Pascualvaca, Fantie, Papageorgiou, & Mirsky, 1998). This suggests that the format of the executive task, particularly the nature of the feedback (social versus nonsocial), may have a much greater impact on performance for people with autism than has previously been appreciated. This may even help explain the apparent developmental discontinuity of performance on executive tests discussed earlier. In the tasks used with very young children with autism (Griffith et al., 1999), feedback is supplied by the apparatus itself (e.g., a tangible reward under a cup or in a well) and not by a human. However, other studies have found executive deficits in individuals with autism when the task was fully computerized and all feedback was provided by machine, with no social interaction required, as in the CANTAB studies reported earlier (Ozonoff et al., 2004). And computerized tasks, in constraining the problem space, reduce the opportunity for rule violations and thus may be less sensitive to particular types of executive deficits (Brophy, Taylor, & Hughes, 2002). Thus, it has been difficult to tease apart the relative primacy of EF and mentalizing or other social deficits in the chain of cognitive impairments that are involved in autism.

Another hypothesis is that EF and theory of mind abilities share similar cognitive underpinnings, and impairments in this basic cognitive function drive both deficits. At a superficial level of analysis, EF and theory of mind appear rather dissimilar. Focusing on the content of the domains may, however, obscure similarities that exist at a process level of analysis. Several writers have suggested that the operations involved in successful EF and theory of mind task performance are similar (Carlson, Moses, & Breton, 2002; Hughes, 1998; Perner & Lang, 1999).

The Smarties task is a standard false-belief measure (Perner, Frith, Leslie, & Leekam, 1989). Subjects are shown a box of Smarties (similar to M&M's) and asked what it contains. After a response is given, the box is opened to reveal that it holds a pencil. Subjects are then asked to predict what the next subject, who has never seen the box, will think it contains. A pass is scored if the subject responds, "Candy." An analysis of this task (following Frye, Zelazo, & Palfai, 1995) suggests that successful performance requires consideration of two mental perspectives and two types of cognitive judgments. The subject must attend to two different perspectives about the contents of the box—his or her own perspective and that of the other person—and must also make two types of judgments—what *is thought to be* in the box and *what is really* in the box. As Frye et al. explain, subjects must employ two recursive if-then rules to solve the problem correctly. Using only one or the other rule will result in an incorrect answer. Successful performance requires that the rules be considered in an embedded and sequential manner, for ex-

ample, "If the question is about me, and if it is asking what the contents really are, then the answer is a pencil" versus "If the question is about someone else, and if it is asking what the contents are thought to be, then the answer is candy." Thus, a critical skill to successful solution of this false-belief task is *embedded use of if-then rules* (Frye et al., 1995).

The Tower of Hanoi is a standard EF measure in which subjects must sequentially move disks among pegs to duplicate a goal state determined by the experimenter. To receive a high score on this task, subjects must predict intermediate disk configurations produced by different potential moves, consider their implications for future disk configurations, and evaluate their utility toward eventual attainment of the goal state (Harris, 1993). Embedded rules, applied recursively, must again be used, for example, "If I move the blue disk to peg 3, then it will leave peg 1 open for the yellow disk, thus freeing up the red disk." This component process analysis suggests that Tower tasks are primary measures of rule-based reasoning and recursive rule use, as much as or more than they are measures of working memory (Goel & Grafman, 1995). Furthermore, this analysis suggests that theory of mind and EF tasks, which appear rather different at the content level, may be similar at the process level. Tasks in both domains appear to require recursive or sequential analysis of information and embedded rule use (Frye et al., 1995; Hughes & Russell, 1993). The focus is not on *what type* of information is processed but on *how* it is processed. Other impairments of autism that appear different at the macroanalytic, surface, or content level may be related at the microanalytic or process level.

The last hypothesis regarding the relationship between EF and theory of mind is that both abilities are subserved by neural networks in the same brain regions (Ozonoff et al., 1991). Imaging studies have, in fact, provided support for this hypothesis, both confirming the role of frontal cortex in EFs (Baker et al., 1996; Dias et al., 1996) and demonstrating the involvement of frontal cortex in networks that are activated during social-cognition tasks (Baron-Cohen et al., 1999; Fletcher et al., 1995; Happé et al., 1996; Stone, Baron-Cohen, & Knight, 1998). Component process research has to date been very useful for suggesting and disproving theories and should continue to be fruitful over the next decade, particularly in combination with the new possibilities afforded by functional imaging techniques.

Relation to Language and Intelligence

The contribution of language development to EF ability has also received significant research attention. Hughes (1996) reported a simple set-shifting deficit in preschool children with autism, who had significant difficulty imitating a simple hand gesture after being primed with a different hand movement. She suggested that the deficit arose from a failure to use language to control thoughts and behavior. Russell, Jarrold, and Hood (1999) explored this idea by devising an EF task that had no arbitrary or novel rules to follow and another that required only verbal response. There were no differences in performance between groups with autism, mixed developmental delay, and typical development. The authors theorized that the deficient performance on EF tests of people with autism arises primarily from failure to verbally encode rules and use them to drive behavior. When no such ability was required, performance was predicted to be unimpaired.

Liss et al. (2001) gave a battery of EF tests to children with high-functioning autism and a control group of children with developmental language disorders. The only group difference, more perserverative errors on the WCST by the autism group, disappeared when verbal IQ (VIQ) was statistically controlled. Likewise, significant relationships between EF performance and measures of autism symptom severity and adaptive behavior disappeared when controlling for IQ. Liss et al. concluded that EF deficits, while common in autism, are likely a function of more general cognitive impairments and should not be considered causal. Ozonoff has also identified significant contributions of IQ to EF performance in people with autism (Miller & Ozonoff, 2000; Ozonoff & McEvoy, 1994; Ozonoff & Strayer, 2001).

Relation to Repetitive Behavior

Turner (1997, 1999) has suggested that executive dysfunction (e.g., perseveration, deficient inhibitory control, impaired generativity) may be responsible for the stereotyped, repetitive behaviors of autism spectrum disorders. Further, she hypothesized that different components of EF would be associated with different types of repetitive behavior. In support of this, she reported that perseveration on a set-shifting task was correlated with more primitive stereotyped behaviors, such as hand flapping, while impoverished generativity was correlated with higher level repetitive behaviors such as circumscribed interests. In contrast, South, Ozonoff, and McMahon (under review) found no significant correlations between any category of repetitive behavior and any EF variable. For example, the correlations between the number of perseverations on the WCST and various forms of repetitive behavior ranged from a low of $r = -.03$ for lifetime history of circumscribed interests to a high of $r = .16$ for lifetime history of unusual obsessions with objects. This sample was significantly older (mean age = 14 years) and more intellectually capable (mean VIQ = 111) than Turner's sample, so direct comparisons are difficult and further research is clearly needed.

Specificity to Autism

No review of the EF hypothesis would be complete without discussion of the so-called "discriminant validity" problem (Pennington, Bennetto, McAleer, & Roberts, 1996). For a causal mechanism to have explanatory power, it should be relatively specific to the disorder it is intended to explain (Pennington & Ozonoff, 1991). Yet, difficulties in EF are seen in a wide variety of disorders, including ADHD (Chelune et al., 1986), conduct disorder (Lueger & Gill, 1990), early treated phenylketonuria (Welsh, Pennington, Ozonoff, Rouse, & McCabe, 1990), obsessive-compulsive disorder (OCD; Head, Bolton, & Hymas, 1989), Tourette's syndrome (Bornstein, 1990), and schizophrenia (Axelrod, Goldman, Tompkins, & Jiron, 1994; Beatty, Jocic, Monson, & Katzung, 1994). If deficits in EF generally distinguish "normal" from "abnormal," but are not specific indicators that distinguish one syndrome from another, their explanatory power is diminished.

The discriminant validity problem may be "more apparent than real" (Hughes, 2001), however. Once the large construct of EF is parsed into more unitary and functionally independent cognitive operations through component process analyses, it appears that different neurodevelopmental disorders are associated with different profiles of strength and weakness in EF. For example, as discussed earlier, evidence suggests that inhibitory function may be intact in individuals with autism (Ozonoff & Strayer, 1997). In contrast, performance on inhibition paradigms such as the Negative Priming and Stop-Signal tasks is deficient in both adults with schizophrenia and children with attention problems (Beech, Powell, McWilliam, & Claridge, 1989; Schachar & Logan, 1990). Other dissociations are apparent in the domain of attention. The ability to sustain attention appears intact in autism, with several studies finding unimpaired performance on the Continuous Performance Test (Buchsbaum et al., 1992; Casey et al., 1993; Garretson, Fein, & Waterhouse, 1990). Deficits in sustained attention are a cardinal feature of ADHD (Douglas & Peters, 1979) and are also prominent in Tourette's syndrome (Comings & Comings, 1987), schizophrenia (Bellak, 1994; Cornblatt & Keilp, 1994), and other disorders. Autism does appear to involve difficulty shifting attention, while this skill appears unimpaired in children with ADHD. Studies using Posner's (1980) paradigm have demonstrated difficulties in the disengage and move operations in children with autism (Casey et al., 1993; Courchesne et al., 1994; Wainwright-Sharp & Bryson, 1993), but not children with ADHD (Swanson et al., 1991). Finally, selective associations of executive deficits with specific disorders have been demonstrated using CANTAB. On this battery's tower task, the Stockings of Cambridge, individuals with autism show clearly deficient performance (Ozonoff et al., 2004), while medicated children with ADHD (Kempton, Vance, Luk, Costin, & Pantelis, 1999) and adults with OCD (Purcell, Maruff, Kyrios, & Pantelis, 1998) perform comparably to typical controls. Thus, considering EF as a multidimensional rather than a unitary construct has helped obtain more precision in the nature of the dysfunction associated with autism and has provided preliminary dissociations and evidence of distinct EF profiles in autism and other neurodevelopmental disorders.

Section Summary

Although there remain many important questions to be answered, research on the component processes of executive dysfunction in autism has made many gains since the publication of the previous edition of this *Handbook*. Robust findings of EF deficits in older children and adults with autism, relative to appropriate clinical and normal controls, have been tempered by the discovery of more complex patterns of EF development in very young children with autism. It is likely that some important turning point is missed by children with autism sometime during the late preschool age; nonetheless, the specifics of this developmental milestone are not yet elucidated. There are indications of significant correlations between EF abilities and core symptoms of autism, beginning with very early social impairments and continuing throughout childhood and adulthood, but the causal directions and specific nature of these relationships are unknown. This section also reviewed associations between EF and other important characteristics of autism, including metacognitive mentalizing ability (e.g., theory of mind), IQ, language, and repetitive behaviors.

FUTURE DIRECTIONS

In the next section, we explore exciting future directions for research on EF and autism.

Executive Function and Families: Are Executive Function Deficits Part of the Broader Autism Phenotype?

Evidence exists that autism is inherited in a complex polygenic fashion, with up to a dozen genes possibly involved (Pickles et al., 1995; Risch et al., 1999). There is much interest in identifying the multiple susceptibility loci involved in causing the disorder. Research suggests that what is inherited is not autism itself, but an extended set of difficulties that are milder than but qualitatively similar to autism (Bailey et al., 1998; Piven & Palmer, 1997).

This broader autism phenotype, as it has come to be known, has been found in 15% to 45% of family members of people with autism in different samples (Bailey et al., 1998). New research, summarized in this section, suggests that cognitive difficulties, including executive dysfunction, may be part of the broader autism phenotype. It is hoped that specification of intermediate phenotypes may one day assist in gene localization efforts (Piven, 2001). Examining the profiles of cognitive strengths and weaknesses in first-degree relatives of individuals with autism also provides an alternative strategy for identifying the core cognitive impairments of autism (Hughes, 2001).

Ozonoff, Rogers, Farnham, and Pennington (1993) found that siblings of probands with autism performed significantly less well than siblings of children with reading disabilities on the Tower of Hanoi, while the two groups performed equally on theory of mind tasks. Hughes, Plumet, and Leboyer (1999) found deficient extradimensional shifting on CANTAB's ID/ED task in siblings of children with autism but not siblings of children with either delayed or typical development. The siblings of children with autism also performed more poorly than the comparison siblings on CANTAB's tower task once their significantly better performance on a spatial working memory subtest was statistically controlled.

Similar deficits in EF have been reported for parents of children with autism, using tasks of set shifting and planning (Hughes, Leboyer, & Bouvard, 1997; Piven & Palmer, 1997), although there are complex relationships with sex and clinical diagnosis. In one study, executive performance in the autism parent group was significantly positively correlated with pretest clinical impressions of social oddity (Hughes et al., 1997), consistent with findings discussed earlier of significant correlations between set shifting and social behavior.

Other cognitive difficulties have also been reported in family members, including weak central coherence (Happé, Briskman, & Frith, 2001) and impaired theory of mind (Baron-Cohen & Hammer, 1997). One study examined a variety of neuropsychological functions in children diagnosed with either autism or dyslexia and all their parents and siblings (Ozonoff, McMahon, Coon, & Lainhart, 2002). Probands

with autism demonstrated weaknesses in EF and memory but strengths in phonological decoding and visual-spatial function relative to probands with dyslexia. The very same cognitive profiles were found in both parents and siblings of the probands, with family members of children with autism demonstrating significantly inferior executive and memory functions, but significantly superior reading and visual-spatial skills, relative to the family members of children with dyslexia. Only 6% of the dyslexia families included at least one member with executive dysfunction, while 94% of the autism families did. Thus, while executive dysfunction is not the only cognitive difficulty that appears to be part of the inherited phenotype and that may be useful in gene localization efforts, its clear presence in family members, across multiple studies and laboratories, highlights its centrality to autism.

Remediation of Executive Function

Another new direction in EF research is intervention. The component process approach to identifying relationships between specific cognitive deficits and behavioral symptoms of autism has clear implications for treatment. Almost no empirical work has been done on remediation of executive deficits in autism, but there is a large literature on cognitive remediation of other disorders that may prove relevant to autism. Defined broadly, cognitive remediation is a systematic approach to teaching individuals to overcome cognitive deficits arising from brain dysfunction (Task Force on Head Injury, 1984). It involves the identification of specific neuropsychological deficits and the design and implementation of a treatment program to retrain and/or compensate for deficits. Typically, cognitive remediation is only part of a more comprehensive program that includes other treatment modalities such as psychotherapy and organized social activities (Butler, 1998). Typical targets of cognitive remediation are memory, attention, motivation, language, and EFs. In this section, we describe the potential of cognitive remediation to address the executive deficits of autism described in the literature and highlight some key issues that will need to be addressed before this approach will be of utility for persons with autism.

Cognitive Remediation in Pediatric Populations

Much of what we know about the effectiveness of cognitive remediation is based on studies of adults with acquired brain injury or schizophrenia (Bell, Bryson, Greig, Corcoran, & Wexler, 2001; Butler & Namerow, 1988; Gianutsos, 1991; Glisky & Schacter, 1989; Kurtz, Moberg, Gur, & Gur, 2001; Levine et al., 2000; Parente & Anderson-Parente, 1991; Pilling et al., 2002; Wehman et al., 1989; Wood & Eames, 1989). One of the more widely utilized approaches is the Attention Process Training (APT) program (Sohlberg & Mateer, 1986). APT was originally developed for adults with brain injury. It contains modules for improving focused attention (the ability to respond to specific sensory information in the environment), sustained attention (the ability to maintain a behavioral response over time), selective attention (the ability to maintain a response in the presence of distracting or competing stimuli), alternating attention (the ability to shift focus of attention and demonstrate mental flexibility), and divided attention (the ability to respond simultaneously to more than one task or stimulus). The efficacy of APT has been demonstrated in adults with brain injury (Mateer, 1992; Mateer, Sohlberg, & Youngman, 1990; Sohlberg & Mateer, 1987) and schizophrenia (Kurtz et al., 2001).

The clinical application of cognitive remediation techniques to pediatric populations is fairly new. Several investigators have used the APT training package with some success with children with ADHD (Semrud-Clikeman, Teeter, Parle, & Conner, 1995; Stevenson, Whitmont, Bornholt, Livesey, & Stevenson, 2002; Williams, 1989) and traumatic brain injury (Thomson, 1994). Theoretical approaches underlying adult rehabilitation programs, however, may not fully apply to pediatric remediation efforts (Parente & Herrmann, 1996). The developing brain is not as well understood as the adult brain, and developmental neuroscientists are just beginning to uncover relationships between brain structure and function in the typically developing brain.

Recognizing the need to address both developmental issues and the limited awareness and compromised reasoning skills of children with brain dysfunction, Kerns, Eso, and Thomson (1999) modified APT to start at a more basic level and make tasks more child-friendly. Materials were made more interesting and engaging, and stimuli were changed from abstract symbols to more familiar concepts, such as human features (hair, sex, clothing), family relationships (siblings, grandparents), and household items. In a small study of the efficacy of this program—called *Pay Attention!*—children with ADHD in the treatment group performed significantly better than matched controls on several measures of attention and academic performance.

Butler and Copeland (2002) developed a comprehensive cognitive rehabilitation program to remediate attention and executive processes in children suffering neurological impairments secondary to treatment for cancer (e.g., cranial irradiation). Their 20 session program included APT, training in metacognitive strategies, individual cognitive-behavioral therapy focused on self-monitoring and self-coaching skills, and games and activities to promote generalization of new skills. A pilot study found that children in the treatment group improved their performance on measures of attention significantly more than no-treatment controls (Butler & Copeland, 2002). No group differences were found on academic tests, however, suggesting generalization to other cognitive skills was not obtained. Nevertheless, this comprehensive therapeutic approach may be helpful in other populations of cognitively impaired children, including children and adolescents with autism spectrum disorders.

Cognitive Remediation and Autism

At first glance, the literature on the cognitive remediation of autism appears sparse. However, many comprehensive early treatment models, including applied behavioral analysis and Treatment and Education of Autistic and Related Communication-handicapped CHildren (TEACCH) programs, fit into the broadest category of cognitive remediation. These approaches aim to improve skills within specific cognitive domains (e.g., expressive and receptive language, visual-spatial abilities) by breaking down complex behaviors into basic components through a component process task analysis. Skill components are then taught in a hierarchical manner, with repeated practice. The TEACCH program also places much emphasis on the development of compensatory strategies, such as visual schedules, to address cognitive deficits, which is another hallmark of cognitive remediation programs.

There are, however, few papers specifically addressing EF remediation for people with autism (Ozonoff, 1998). Bock (1994) reported an intervention that trained four children with autism on a tridimensional sorting task. Participants learned to sort the same set of objects into three different categories (color, shape, number). This required shifting cognitive set from one attribute of an object to another and is thus analogous to the WCST and the ID/ED subtest of CANTAB. After training, children were tested using a different set of objects (cans of food) that they were asked to sort into new categorical sets (brand, size, food type). The study found that training on the categorization task increased sorting ability on the untrained item set and that gains were maintained two months postintervention (Bock, 1994).

A report of a program called REHABIT suggested it may have efficacy for children with autism (Jepsen & von Thaden, 2002). This program was developed to teach a variety of cognitive skills, including EFs, attention, memory, language, and academic achievement. Adolescents with mixed diagnoses, including autism, other developmental delays, and acquired neurological insults, were matched in a pairwise fashion on diagnosis, age, sex, and IQ and randomly assigned to either the REHABIT treatment group or the education-as-usual group. Pre- or posttest comparisons suggested significant group by time interaction effects, with adolescents in the treatment group demonstrating significantly more improvement than controls in planning, simultaneous processing, reading, and adaptive behavior (e.g., independent functioning, prevocational skills, self-direction, responsibility). While small sample size precluded diagnosis-specific analyses, the authors state that significant gains were made across diagnostic categories. Thus, it appears that the subgroup of children with autism who participated in this study benefited from this type of cognitive (including executive) remediation (Jepsen & von Thaden, 2002).

Cognitive remediation of autism is faced with many of the same challenges that are common to other pediatric populations, including the poor fit that results from application of adult rehabilitation models to children, as noted earlier. Other challenges may be unique to autism spectrum disorders. Functional organization in the brain of individuals with a developmental disorder may be dissimilar from that of the typically developing brain. And most cognitive remediation programs have only a small component devoted to the particular cognitive difficulties of autism (e.g., shifting and divided attention, EFs), suggesting that any efforts to use these packages with autism will require substantial modification or tailoring. Most cognitive rehabilitation programs are based on the assumption that the cognitive processes being trained were previously established and then damaged. Techniques are aimed at "retraining" and strengthening neural connections through massed practice in order to restore mental functions and processing speed. This assumption likely does not apply to a developmental disorder like autism, and its impact on the efficacy of the approach is not known. Another issue is the problem of generalization of learned skills; as Butler and Copeland (2002) found, lack of generalization is not unique to children with autism. This imposes serious challenges to professionals developing and implementing cognitive remediation programs for individuals with autism spectrum disorders, who often have severe problems generalizing gains to other settings, materials, and teachers. Many cognitive remediation programs include some form of individual psychotherapy, usually focused on increasing awareness of deficits and teaching self-monitoring and compensatory strategies. Due to the limited self-awareness and insight of most people with autism spectrum disorders, however, the role that psychotherapy should play in the cognitive remediation of autism is not clear. In summary, cognitive remediation approaches may eventually prove useful in improving the EFs of people with autism, but they will require modifications and careful thought to develop techniques appropriate for this population. This is an exciting new direction for future EF research.

CONCLUSION

In this chapter, we reviewed the empirical literature on EF in autism, from initial studies finding large group differences to more recent work specifying the nature of the affected component processes. An eventual goal of this research is to identify the executive profile or fingerprint of autism, which may someday assist in diagnosis, contribute to gene localization efforts, and improve remediation techniques. We also explored issues that have emerged as EF research has matured. With new studies have come new questions, most still unanswered, about the developmental course of executive dysfunction and its relationship to other symptoms of autism and to other neurodevelopmental disorders. Finally, this chapter presented new research on the familiality of executive dysfunction and the promise of newly developed remediation techniques. In the years since the previous edition of this *Handbook*, we have learned a great deal, only to find out how much more there is yet to know about this complex disorder and its many manifestations.

Cross-References

Other aspects of development and behavior are reviewed in Chapters 8 to 15; psychological assessment is discussed in Chapter 29, and other theoretical perspectives on autism are provided in Chapters 21 and 23 through 26.

REFERENCES

Anderson, J. R., & Bower, G. H. (1973). *Human associative memory*. Hillsdale, NJ: Erlbaum.

Axelrod, B. N., Goldman, R. S., Tompkins, L. M., & Jiron, C. C. (1994). Poor differential performance on the Wisconsin Card Sorting Test in schizophrenia, mood disorder, and traumatic brain injury. *Neuropsychiatry, Neuropsychology, and Behavioral Neurology, 7,* 20–24.

Baddeley, A. D. (1986). *Working memory*. Oxford, England: Clarendon Press.

Bailey, A., Luthert, P., Dean, A., Harding, B., Janota, I., Montgomery, M., et al. (1998). A clinicopathological study of autism. *Brain, 121,* 889–905.

Baker, S. C., Rogers, R. D., Owen, A. M., Frith, C. D., Dolan, R. J., Frackowiak, R. S. J., et al. (1996). Neural systems engaged by planning: A PET study of the Tower of London task. *Neuropsychologia, 34,* 515–526.

Baron-Cohen, S., & Hammer, J. (1997). Parents of children with Asperger syndrome: What is the cognitive phenotype? *Journal of Cognitive Neuroscience, 9,* 548–554.

Baron-Cohen, S., Ring, H., Wheelwright, S., Bullmore, E., Brammer, M., Simmons, A., et al. (1999). Social intelligence in the normal and autistic brain: An fMRI study. *European Journal of Neuroscience, 11,* 1891–1898.

Beatty, W. W., Jocic, Z., Monson, N., & Katzung, V. M. (1994). Problem solving by schizophrenic and schizoaffective patients on the Wisconsin and California Card Sorting Tests. *Neuropsychology, 8,* 49–54.

Beech, A., Powell, T., McWilliam, J., & Claridge, G. (1989). Evidence of reduced "cognitive inhibition" in schizophrenia. *British Journal of Clinical Psychology, 28,* 109–116.

Bell, M., Bryson, G., Greig, T., Corcoran, C., & Wexler, B. E. (2001). Neurocognitive enhancement therapy with work therapy: Effects on neuropsychological test performance. *Archives of General Psychiatry, 58,* 763–768.

Bellak, L. (1994). The schizophrenic syndrome and attention deficit disorder: Thesis, antithesis, and synthesis? *American Psychologist, 49,* 25–29.

Bennetto, L., Pennington, B. F., & Rogers, S. J. (1996). Intact and impaired memory functions in autism. *Child Development, 67,* 1816–1835.

Berger, H. J. C., Aerts, F. H. T. M., van Spaendonck, K. P. M., Cools, A. R., & Teunisse, J. P. (2003). Central coherence and cognitive shifting in relation to social improvement in high-functioning young adults with autism. *Journal of Clinical and Experimental Neuropsychology, 25,* 502–511.

Biro, S., & Russell, J. (2001). The execution of arbitrary procedures by children with autism. *Development and Psychopathology, 13,* 97–110.

Bock, M. A. (1994). Acquisition, maintenance, and generalization of a categorization strategy by children with autism. *Journal of Autism and Developmental Disorders, 24,* 39–51.

Bond, J. A., & Buchtel, H. A. (1984). Comparison of the Wisconsin card sorting test and the Halstead category test. *Journal of Clinical Psychology, 40,* 1251–1255.

Bornstein, R. A. (1990). Neuropsychological performance in children with Tourette's syndrome. *Psychiatry Research, 33,* 73–81.

Brian, J. A., Tipper, S., Weaver, B., & Bryson, S. (2003). Inhibitory mechanisms in autism spectrum disorders: Typical selective inhibition of location versus facilitated perceptual processing. *Journal of Child Psychology and Psychiatry, 44,* 552–560.

Brophy, M., Taylor, E., & Hughes, C. (2002). To go or not to go: Inhibitory control in "hard to manage" children. *Infant and Child Development, 11,* 125–140.

Buchsbaum, M. S., Siegel, B. V., Wu, J. C., Hazlett, E., Sicotte, N., Haier, R., et al. (1992). Attention performance in autism and regional brain metabolic rate assessed by positron emission tomography. *Journal of Autism and Developmental Disorders, 22,* 115–125.

Butler, R. W. (1998). Attentional processes and their remediation in childhood cancer. *Medical and Pediatric Oncology, 1,* 75–78.

Butler, R. W., & Copeland, D. R. (2002). Attentional processes and their remediation in children treated for cancer: A literature review and the development of a therapeutic approach. *Journal of the International Neuropsychological Society, 8,* 115–124.

Butler, R. W., & Namerow, N. S. (1988). Cognitive retraining in brain injury rehabilitation: A critical review. *Journal of NeuroRehabilitation and Neural Repair, 2,* B1–B5.

Carlson, S. M., Moses, L. J., & Breton, C. (2002). How specific is the relation between executive function and theory of mind? Contributions of inhibitory control and working memory. *Infant and Child Development, 11,* 73–92.

Casey, B. J., Gordon, C. T., Mannheim, G. B., & Rumsey, J. M. (1993). Dysfunctional attention in autistic savants. *Journal of Clinical and Experimental Neuropsychology, 15,* 933–946.

Chelune, G. J., Ferguson, W., Koon, R., & Dickey, T. O. (1986). Frontal lobe disinhibition in Attention Deficit Disorder. *Child Psychiatry and Human Development, 16,* 221–234.

Comings, D. E., & Comings, B. G. (1987). A controlled study of Tourette syndrome: Attention deficit disorders, learning disorders, and school problems. *American Journal of Human Genetics, 41,* 701–741.

Cornblatt, B. A., & Keilp, J. G. (1994). Impaired attention, genetics, and the pathophysiology of schizophrenia. *Schizophrenia Bulletin, 20,* 31–46.

Courchesne, E., Akshoomoff, N. A., & Ciesielski, K. (1990). Shifting attention abnormalities in autism: ERP and performance evidence. *Journal of Clinical and Experimental Neuropsychology, 12,* 77.

Courchesne, E., Townsend, J. P., Akshoomoff, N. A., Yeung-Courchesne, R., Press, G. A., Murakami, J. W., et al. (1994). A new finding in autism: Impairment in shifting attention. In S. H. Broman & J. Grafman (Eds.), *Atypical cognitive deficits in developmental disorders: Implications for brain function* (pp. 101–137). Hillsdale, NJ: Erlbaum.

Dawson, G., Meltzoff, A. N., Osterling, J., & Rinaldi, J. (1998). Neuropsychological correlates of early symptoms in autism. *Child Development, 69,* 1276–1285.

Dawson, G., Munson, J., Estes, A., Osterling, J., McPartland, J., Toth, K., et al. (2002). Neurocognitive function and joint attention ability in young children with autism spectrum disorder versus developmental delay. *Child Development, 73,* 345–358.

Dehaene, S., & Changeux, J. P. (1991). The Wisconsin Card Sorting Test: Theoretical analysis and modeling in a neuronal network. *Cerebral Cortex, 1,* 62–79.

Dennis, M. (1991). Frontal lobe function in childhood and adolescence: A heuristic for assessing attention regulation, executive control, and the intentional states important for social discourse. *Developmental Neuropsychology, 7,* 327–358.

Diamond, A., & Goldman-Rakic, P. S. (1986). Comparative development in human infants and infant rhesus monkeys on cognitive functions that depend on prefrontal cortex. *Society of Neuroscience Abstracts, 12,* 742.

Diamond, A., Prevor, M. B., Callender, G., & Druin, D. P. (1997). Prefrontal cortex cognitive deficits in children treated early and continuously for PKU. *Monographs of the Society for Research in Child Development, 62,* 1–205.

Dias, R., Robbins, T. W., & Roberts, A. C. (1996). Dissociation in prefrontal cortex of attentional and affective shifts. *Nature, 380,* 69–72.

Douglas, V. I., & Peters, K. G. (1979). Toward a clearer definition of the attentional deficit of hyperactive children. In G. A. Hale & M. Lewis (Eds.), *Attention and cognitive development* (pp. 173–247). New York: Plenum Press.

Duncan, J. (1986). Disorganization of behaviour after frontal lobe damage. *Cognitive Neuropsychology, 3,* 271–290.

Duncan, J. (2001). Frontal lobe function and the control of visual attention. In J. Braun & C. Koch (Eds.), *Visual attention and cortical circuits* (pp. 69–88). Cambridge, MA: MIT Press.

Farah, M. J. (1984). The neurological basis of mental imagery: A componential analysis. *Cognition, 18,* 245–272.

Fletcher, P. C., Happé, F., Frith, U., Baker, S. C., Dolan, R. J., & Frackowiak, R. (1995). Other minds in the brain: A functional imaging study of theory of mind in story comprehension. *Cognition, 57*(2), 109–128.

Friedrich, F., & Rader, S. (1996). Component process analysis in experimental and clinical neuropsychology. In M. Marirish & J. Moses (Eds.), *Theoretical foundations of clinical neuropsychology for clinical practitioners* (pp. 59–79). Hillsdale, NJ: Erlbaum.

Frye, D., Zelazo, P. D., & Palfai, T. (1995). Theory of mind and rule-based reasoning. *Cognitive Development, 10,* 483–527.

Garretson, H. B., Fein, D., & Waterhouse, L. (1990). Sustained attention in children with autism. *Journal of Autism and Developmental Disorders, 20,* 101–114.

Gianutsos, R. (1991). Cognitive rehabilitation: A neuropsychological specialty comes of age. *Brain Injury, 5,* 353–368.

Gilotty, L., Kenworthy, L., Sirian, L., Black, D. O., & Wagner, A. E. (2002). Adaptive skills and executive function in autism spectrum disorders. *Child Neuropsychology, 8,* 241–248.

Glisky, E. L., & Schacter, D. L. (1989). Extending the limits of complex learning in organic amnesia: Computer training in a vocational domain. *Neuropsychologia, 27,* 107–120.

Goel, V., & Grafman, J. (1995). Are the frontal lobes implicated in planning functions? Interpreting data from the Tower of Hanoi. *Neuropsychologia, 33,* 623–642.

Goldman-Rakic, P. S. (1987). Circuitry of primate prefrontal cortex and regulation of behavior by representational memory. In V. B. Mountcastle, F. Plum, & S. R. Geiger (Eds.), *Handbook of physiology: The nervous system* (pp. 373–417). Bethesda, MD: American Physiological Society.

Grattan, L. M., Bloomer, R., Archambault, F. X., & Eslinger, P. J. (1990). Cognitive and neural underpinnings of empathy. *Clinical Neuropsychologist, 4,* 279.

Griffith, E. M. (2002). *Manipulating feedback normalizes perseveration in individuals with autism.* Unpublished doctoral dissertation, University of Denver, Colorado.

Griffith, E. M., Pennington, B. F., Wehner, E. A., & Rogers, S. J. (1999). Executive functions in young children with autism. *Child Development, 70,* 817–832.

Happé, F., Briskman, J., & Frith, U. (2001). Exploring the cognitive phenotype of autism: Weak "central coherence" in parents and siblings of children with autism: I. Experimental tests. *Journal of Child Psychology and Psychiatry, 42,* 299–307.

Happé, F., Ehlers, S., Fletcher, P., Frith, U., Johansson, M., Gillberg, C., et al. (1996). Theory of mind in the brain: Evidence from a PET scan study of Asperger syndrome. *NeuroReport, 8,* 197–201.

Harris, P. (1993). Pretending and planning. In S. Baron-Cohen, H. Tager-Flusberg, & D. J. Cohen (Eds.), *Understanding other minds: Perspectives from autism* (pp. 228–246). Oxford, England: Oxford University Press.

Head, D., Bolton, D., & Hymas, N. (1989). Deficit in cognitive shifting ability in patients with obsessive-compulsive disorder. *Biological Psychiatry, 25,* 929–937.

Hill, E. L., & Russell, J. (2002). Action memory and self-monitoring in children with autism:

Self versus other. *Infant and Child Development, 11,* 159–170.

Hughes, C. (1996). Planning problems in autism at the level of motor control. *Journal of Autism and Developmental Disorders, 26,* 99–107.

Hughes, C. (1998). Executive function in preschoolers: Links with theory of mind and verbal ability. *British Journal of Developmental Psychology, 16,* 233–253.

Hughes, C. (2001). Executive dysfunction in autism: Its nature and implications for the everyday problems experienced by individuals with autism. In J. A. Burack, T. Charman, N. Yirmiya, & P. R. Zelazo (Eds.), *The development of autism: Perspectives from theory and research* (pp. 255–275). Mahwah, NJ: Erlbaum.

Hughes, C. (2002). Executive functions and development: Emerging themes. *Infant and Child Development, 11,* 201–209.

Hughes, C., & Graham, A. (2002). Measuring executive functions in childhood: Problems and solutions? *Child and Adolescent Mental Health, 7,* 131–142.

Hughes, C., Leboyer, M. H., & Bouvard, M. (1997). Executive function in parents of children with autism. *Psychological Medicine, 27,* 209–220.

Hughes, C., Plumet, M.-H., & Leboyer, M. (1999). Towards a cognitive phenotype for autism: Increased prevalence of executive dysfunction and superior spatial span amongst siblings of children with autism. *Journal of Child Psychology and Psychiatry, 40,* 705–718.

Hughes, C., & Russell, J. (1993). Autistic children's difficulty with mental disengagement from an object: Its implications for theories of autism. *Developmental Psychology, 29,* 498–510.

Hughes, C., Russell, J., & Robbins, T. W. (1994). Evidence for executive dysfunction in autism. *Neuropsychologia, 32,* 477–492.

Ingram, R. E. (1989). Information processing as a theoretical framework for child and adolescent psychiatry. In M. H. Schmidt & H. Remschmidt (Eds.), *Needs and prospects of child and adolescent psychiatry* (pp. 25–36). Cambridge, MA: Hogrefe & Huber.

Jepsen, R. H., & von Thaden, K. (2002). The effect of cognitive education on the performance of students with neurological developmental disabilities. *NeuroRehabilitation, 17,* 201–209.

Kempton, S., Vance, A., Luk, E., Costin, J., & Pantelis, C. (1999). Executive function and attention deficit hyperactivity disorder: Stimulant medication and better executive function performance in children. *Psychological Medicine, 29,* 527–538.

Kerns, K. A., Eso, K., & Thomson, J. (1999). Investigation of a direct intervention for improving attention in young children with ADHD. *Developmental Neuropsychology, 16,* 273–295.

Kurtz, M. M., Moberg, P. J., Gur, R. C., & Gur, R. E. (2001). Approaches to cognitive remediation of neuropsychological deficits in schizophrenia: A review and meta-analysis. *Neuropsychology Review, 11,* 197–210.

Levine, B., Robertson, I. H., Claire, L., Carter, G., Hong, J., Wilson, B. A., et al. (2000). Rehabilitation of executive functioning: An experimental-clinical validation of Goal Management Training. *Journal of the International Neuropsychological Society, 6,* 299–312.

Liss, M., Fein, D., Allen, D., Dunn, M., Feinstein, C., Morris, R., et al. (2001). Executive functioning in high-functioning children with autism. *Journal of Child Psychology and Psychiatry, 42,* 261–270.

Logan, G. D. (1994). On the ability to inhibit thought and action: A user's guide to the stop-signal paradigm. In D. Dagenbach & T. H. Carr (Eds.), *Inhibitory processes in attention, memory and language* (pp. 189–239). San Diego, CA: Academic Press.

Logan, G. D., Cowan, W. B., & Davis, K. A. (1984). On the ability to inhibit simple and choice reaction time responses: A model and a method. *Journal of Experimental Psychology Human Perception and Performance, 10,* 276–291.

Lueger, R. J., & Gill, K. J. (1990). Frontal-lobe cognitive dysfunction in conduct disorder adolescents. *Journal of Clinical Psychology, 46,* 696–706.

Luria, A. R. (1966). *The higher cortical functions in man.* New York: Basic Books.

Mateer, C. A. (1992). Systems of care for post-concussive syndrome. In L. J. Horn & N. D. Zasler (Eds.), *Rehabilitation of post-concussive disorders* (pp. 143–160). Philadelphia: Hanley & Belfus.

Mateer, C. A., Sohlberg, M. M., & Youngman, P. (1990). The management of acquired attention and memory disorders following mild closed head injury. In R. Wood (Ed.), *Cognitive rehabilitation in perspective* (pp. 68–96). London: Taylor & Francis.

McEvoy, R. E., Rogers, S. J., & Pennington, B. F. (1993). Executive function and social communication deficits in young autistic children. *Journal of Child Psychology and Psychiatry, 34,* 563–578.

Miller, J. N., & Ozonoff, S. (2000). The external validity of Asperger disorder: Lack of evidence from the domain of neuropsychology. *Journal of Abnormal Psychology, 109,* 227–238.

Moses, L. J. (2001). Executive accounts of theory-of-mind development. *Child Development, 72,* 688–690.

Mottron, L., Peretz, I., Belleville, S., & Rouleau, N. (1999). Absolute pitch in autism: A case study. *Neurocase, 5,* 485–501.

Mundy, P., Card, J., & Fox, N. (2000). EEG correlates of the development of infant joint attention skills. *Developmental Psychobiology, 36,* 325–338.

Neill, W. T., Lissner, L. S., & Beck, J. L. (1990). Negative priming in same-different matching: Further evidence for a central locus of inhibition. *Perception and Psychophysics, 48,* 398–400.

Ozonoff, S. (1995). Executive functions in autism. In E. Schopler & G. B. Mesibov (Eds.), *Learning and cognition in autism* (pp. 199–219). New York: Plenum Press.

Ozonoff, S. (1997). Components of executive function in autism and other disorders. In J. Russell (Ed.), *Autism as an executive disorder* (pp. 179–211). New York: Oxford University Press.

Ozonoff, S. (1998). Assessment and remediation of executive dysfunction in autism and Asperger syndrome. In E. Schopler, G. B. Mesibov, & L. Kunce (Eds.), *Asperger syndrome and high-functioning autism* (pp. 263–289). New York: Plenum Press.

Ozonoff, S., Coon, H., Dawson, G., Joseph, R., Klin, A., McMahon, W. M., et al. (2004). Performance on CANTAB subtests sensitive to frontal lobe function in people with autistic disorder: Evidence from the CPEA network. *Journal of Autism and Developmental Disorders, 34,* 139–150.

Ozonoff, S., & Jensen, J. (1999). Specific executive function profiles in three neurodevelopmental disorders. *Journal of Autism and Developmental Disorders, 29,* 171–177.

Ozonoff, S., & McEvoy, R. E. (1994). A longitudinal study of executive function and theory of mind development in autism. *Development and Psychopathology, 6,* 415–431.

Ozonoff, S., McMahon, W. M., Coon, H., & Lainhart, J. (2002). *Neuropsychological profiles of autism and dyslexia families.* Paper presented at the annual meeting of the American Academy of Child and Adolescent Psychiatry, San Francisco.

Ozonoff, S., Pennington, B. F., & Rogers, S. J. (1991). Executive function deficits in high-functioning autistic individuals: Relationship to theory of mind. *Journal of Child Psychology and Psychiatry, 32,* 1081–1105.

Ozonoff, S., Rogers, S. J., Farnham, J. M., & Pennington, B. F. (1993). Can standard measures identify subclinical markers of autism? *Journal of Autism and Developmental Disorders, 23,* 429–441.

Ozonoff, S., & Strayer, D. L. (1997). Inhibitory function in nonretarded children with autism. *Journal of Autism and Developmental Disorders, 27,* 59–77.

Ozonoff, S., & Strayer, D. L. (2001). Further evidence of intact working memory in autism. *Journal of Autism and Developmental Disorders, 31,* 257–263.

Parente, R., & Anderson-Parente, J. (1991). *Retraining memory: Techniques and applications.* Houston, TX: CSY Publishing.

Parente, R., & Herrmann, D. (1996). *Retraining cognition: Techniques and applications.* Gaithersburg, MD. Aspen Press.

Pascualvaca, D. M., Fantie, B. D., Papageorgiou, M., & Mirsky, A. F. (1998). Attentional capacities in children with autism: Is there a general deficit in shifting focus? *Journal of Autism and Developmental Disorders, 28,* 467–478.

Pennington, B. F. (1994). The working memory function of the prefrontal cortices: Implications for developmental and individual differences in cognition. In M. M. Haith, J. Benson, R. Roberts, & B. F. Pennington (Eds.), *Future-oriented processes in development* (pp. 243–289). Chicago: University of Chicago Press.

Pennington, B. F., Bennetto, L., McAleer, O., & Roberts, R. J. (1996). Executive functions and working memory: Theoretical and measurement issues. In G. R. Lyon & N. A. Krasnegor (Eds.), *Attention, memory, and executive function* (pp. 327–348). Baltimore: Paul H. Brookes.

Pennington, B. F., & Ozonoff, S. (1991). A neuro-scientific perspective on continuity and discontinuity in developmental psychopathology. In D. Cicchetti & S. L. Toth (Eds.), *Rochester symposium on developmental psychopathology: Volume III. Models and integrations* (pp. 117–159). Rochester, NY: University of Rochester Press.

Pennington, B. F., & Ozonoff, S. (1996). Executive functions and developmental psychopathologies. *Journal of Child Psychology and Psychiatry, 37,* 51–87.

Perner, J., Frith, U., Leslie, A. M., & Leekam, S. R. (1989). Exploration of the autistic child's theory of mind: Knowledge, belief, and communication. *Child Development, 60,* 689–700.

Perner, J., Kain, W., & Barchfeld, P. (2002). Executive control and higher-order theory of mind in children at risk of ADHD. *Infant and Child Development, 11,* 141–158.

Perner, J., & Lang, B. (1999). Development of theory of mind and executive control. *Trends in Cognitive Sciences, 3,* 337–334.

Perner, J., & Lang, B. (2002). What causes 3-year-olds' difficulty on the dimensional change card sorting task? *Infant and Child Development, 11,* 93–105.

Perrine, K. (1993). Differential aspects of conceptual processing in the Category Test and Wisconsin Card Sorting Test. *Journal of Clinical and Experimental Neuropsychology, 15,* 461–473.

Pickles, A., Bolton, P. F., Macdonald, H., Bailey, A., Le Couteur, A., Sim, C. H., et al. (1995). Latent-class analysis of recurrence risks for complex phenotypes with selection and measurement error: A twin and family history study of autism. *American Journal of Human Genetics, 57, 717–726.*

Pilling, S., Bebbington, P., Kuipers, E., Garety, P., Geddes, J., Martindale, B., et al. (2002). Psychological treatments in schizophrenia: II. Meta-analyses of randomized controlled trails of social skills training and cognitive remediation. *Psychological Medicine, 32,* 783–791.

Piven, J. (2001). The broad autism phenotype: A complementary strategy for molecular genetic studies of autism. *American Journal of Medical Genetics, 8,* 34–35.

Piven, J., & Palmer, P. (1997). Cognitive deficits in parents from multiple-incidence autism families. *Journal of Child Psychology and Psychiatry, 38,* 1011–1021.

Posner, M. I. (1980). Orienting of attention. *Quarterly Journal of Experimental Psychology, 32,* 3–25.

Price, B. H., Daffner, K. R., Stowe, R. M., & Mesulam, M. M. (1990). The comportmental learning disabilities of early frontal lobe damage. *Brain, 113,* 1383–1393.

Prior, M. R., & Hoffmann, W. (1990). Neuropsychological testing of autistic children through an exploration with frontal lobe tests. *Journal of Autism and Developmental Disorders, 20,* 581–590.

Purcell, R., Maruff, P., Kyrios, M., & Pantelis, C. (1998). Neuropsychological deficits in obsessive-compulsive disorder: A comparison with unipolar depression, panic disorder, and normal controls. *Archives of General Psychiatry, 55,* 415–423.

Rinehart, N. J., Bradshaw, J. L., Moss, S. A., Brereton, A. V., & Tonge, B. J. (2001). A deficit in shifting attention present in high-functioning autism but not Asperger's disorder. *Autism: Journal of Research and Practice, 5,* 67–80.

Risch, N., Spiker, D., Lotspeich, L., Nouri, N., Hinds, D., Hallmayer, J., et al. (1999). A genomic screen of autism: Evidence for a multilocus etiology. *American Journal of Human Genetics, 65,* 493–507.

Robbins, T. W., James, M., Owen, A. M., Sahakian, B. J., Lawrence, A. D., McInnes, L., et al. (1998). A study of performance on tests from the CANTAB battery sensitive to frontal lobe dysfunction in a large sample of normal volunteers: Implications for theories of executive functioning and cognitive aging. *Journal of the International Neuropsychological Society, 4,* 474–490.

Rumsey, J. M. (1985). Conceptual problem-solving in highly verbal, nonretarded autistic men. *Journal of Autism and Developmental Disorders, 15,* 23–36.

Rumsey, J. M., & Hamburger, S. D. (1990). Neuropsychological divergence of high-level autism and severe dyslexia. *Journal of Autism and Developmental Disorders, 20,* 155–168.

Russell, J., Jarrold, C., & Henry, L. (1996). Working memory in children with autism and with moderate learning difficulties. *Journal of Child Psychology and Psychiatry, 37,* 673–686.

Russell, J., Jarrold, C., & Hood, B. (1999). Two intact executive capacities in children with autism: Implications for the core executive dysfunctions in the disorder. *Journal of Autism and Developmental Disorders, 29,* 103–112.

Russell, J., Mauthner, N., Sharpe, S., & Tidswell, T. (1991). The "windows task" as a measure of strategic deception in preschoolers and autistic subjects. *British Journal of Developmental Psychology, 9,* 331–349.

Russell, J., Saltmarsh, R., & Hill, E. (1999). What do executive factors contribute to the failure on false belief tasks by children with autism? *Journal of Child Psychology and Psychiatry, 40,* 859–868.

Rutter, M., & Bailey, A. (1993). Thinking and relationships: Mind and brain (some reflections on theory of mind and autism). In S. Baron-Cohen, H. Tager-Flusberg, & D. J. Cohen (Eds.), *Understanding other minds: Perspectives from autism* (pp. 481–504). Oxford, England: Oxford University Press.

Sandson, J., & Albert, M. L. (1984). Varieties of perseveration. *Neuropsychologia, 22,* 715–732.

Schachar, R., & Logan, G. D. (1990). Impulsivity and inhibitory control in normal development and childhood psychopathology. *Developmental Psychology, 26,* 710–720.

Semrud-Clikeman, M., Teeter, P. A., Parle, N., & Conner, R. T. (1995). *Innovative approaches for working with children with ADHD.* Paper presented at the annual conference of the American Educational Research Association, San Francisco.

Shu, B. C., Lung, F. W., Tien, A. Y., & Chen, B. C. (2001). Executive function deficits in non-retarded autistic children. *Autism: Journal of Research and Practice, 5,* 165–174.

Sohlberg, M. M., & Mateer, C. A. (1986). *Attention process training (APT).* Puyallup: Washington Association for Neuropsychological Research and Development.

Sohlberg, M. M., & Mateer, C. A. (1987). Effectiveness of an attention training program. *Journal of Clinical and Experimental Neuropsychology, 9,* 117–130.

South, M., Ozonoff, S., & McMahon, W. M. (under review). *Repetitive behavior in the high-functioning autism spectrum: Phenotypic characterization and relationship to cognitive functioning.*

Stevenson, C. S., Whitmont, S., Bornholt, L., Livesey, D., & Stevenson, R. J. (2002). A cognitive remediation programme for adults with attention deficit hyperactivity disorder. *Australian and New Zealand Journal of Psychiatry, 36,* 610–616.

Stone, V. E., Baron-Cohen, S., & Knight, R. T. (1998). Frontal lobe contributions to theory of mind. *Journal of Cognitive Neuroscience, 10,* 640–656.

Stuss, D. T. (1992). Biological and psychological development of executive functions. *Brain and Cognition, 20,* 8–23.

Swanson, J. M., Posner, M., Potkin, S. G., Bonforte, S., Youpa, D., Fiore, C., et al. (1991). Activating tasks for the study of visual-spatial attention in ADHD children: A cognitive anatomic approach. *Journal of Child Neurology, 6,* S119–S127.

Swettenham, J., Baron-Cohen, S., Charman, T., Cox, A., Baird, G., Drew, A., et al. (1998). The frequency and distribution of spontaneous attention shifts between social and nonsocial stimuli in autistic, typically developing, and nonautistic developmentally delayed infants. *Journal of Child Psychology and Psychiatry, 39,* 747–753.

Szatmari, P., Tuff, L., Finlayson, A. J., & Bartolucci, G. (1990). Asperger's Syndrome and autism: Neurocognitive aspects. *Journal of the American Academy of Child and Adolescent Psychiatry, 29,* 130–136.

Task Force on Head Injury. (1984). *Standards for cognitive rehabilitation.* Erie, PA: American Congress of Rehabilitation Medicine.

Thomson, J. (1994). Rehabilitation of high school-aged individuals with traumatic brain injury through utilization of an attention training program. *Journal of the International Neuropsychological Society, 1,* 149.

Tipper, S. P. (1985). The negative priming effect: Inhibitory priming by ignored objects. *Quar-*

terly Journal of Experimental Psychology, 37, 571–590.

Turner, M. (1997). Towards an executive dysfunction account of repetitive behavior in autism. In J. Russell (Ed.), *Autism as an executive disorder* (pp. 57–100). New York: Oxford University Press.

Turner, M. (1999). Repetitive behavior in autism: A review of psychological research. *Journal of Child Psychology and Psychiatry, 40,* 839–849.

van der Does, A. W., & van den Bosch, R. J. (1992). What determines Wisconsin Card Sorting performance in schizophrenia? *Clinical Psychology Review, 12,* 567–583.

Wainwright-Sharp, J. A., & Bryson, S. E. (1993). Visual orienting deficits in high-functioning people with autism. *Journal of Autism and Developmental Disorders, 23,* 1–13.

Wehman, P., Kreutzer, J., Sale, P., West, M., Morton, M., & Diambra, J. (1989). Cognitive impairment and remediation: Implications for employment following traumatic brain injury. *Journal of Head Trauma Rehabilitation, 4,* 66–75.

Welsh, M. C., Pennington, B. F., Ozonoff, S., Rouse, B., & McCabe, E. R. B. (1990). Neuropsychology of early-treated phenylketonuria: Specific executive function deficits. *Child Development, 61,* 1697–1713.

Williams, D. J. (1989). *A process-specific training program in the treatment of attention deficits in children.* Unpublished doctoral dissertation, University of Washington, Seattle.

Wood, R. L., & Fussy, L. (1990). *Cognitive rehabilitation in perspective.* London: Taylor & Francis.

CHAPTER 23

Empathizing and Systemizing in Autism Spectrum Conditions

SIMON BARON-COHEN, SALLY WHEELWRIGHT, JOHN LAWSON, RICHARD GRIFFIN, CHRIS ASHWIN, JAC BILLINGTON, AND BHISMADEV CHAKRABARTI

Autism is diagnosed when a child or adult has abnormalities in a triad of behavioral domains: social development, communication, and repetitive behavior/obsessive interests (American Psychological Association [APA], 1994; World Health Organization [WHO], 1994). In the 1960s and 1970s, many of the children with autism who were studied by cognitive developmentalists also had comorbid learning difficulties (i.e., below-average intelligence) and language delay (Frith, 1970; Hermelin & O'Connor, 1970; Wing, 1976). An average IQ of 60 was not uncommon in samples studied during that period.

AUTISM SPECTRUM CONDITIONS: LOW, MEDIUM, AND HIGH-FUNCTIONING SUBGROUPS

In the 1980s, cognitive developmentalists began to focus on what was then called *high-functioning autism* (Baron-Cohen, Leslie, & Frith, 1985, 1986). Such children might be better described as *medium-functioning* because although they had IQs within the average range, their IQ fell within two standard deviations from the population mean of 100. Because one standard deviation is 15 points, anyone with an IQ above 70 would still have been included in this band. An IQ of 71 is by statistical definition average but is hardly high functioning.

By the 1990s, interest had shifted to studying the truly high-functioning strata of the autistic spectrum: those whose IQs were close to 100 or above. This strata would have included those with *superior IQ,* that is, those whose IQ was higher than 2 standard deviations above the population mean (Baron-Cohen, Jolliffe, Mortimore, & Robertson, 1997; Frith, 1991; Jolliffe & Baron-Cohen, 1997; Klin, Volkmar, Sparrow, Cicchetti, & Rourke, 1995; Szatmari, Tuff, Finlayson, & Bartolucci, 1990). Since we know that IQ is a strong predictor of outcome in autism (Rutter, 1978), it is important to take IQ into account.

Asperger syndrome (AS) was first described by Asperger (1944). The descriptions of the children he documented overlapped considerably with the accounts of childhood autism (Kanner, 1943). Little was published on AS in English until relatively recently (Frith, 1991; Wing, 1981). Current diagnostic practice recognizes people with AS as meeting the same criteria as for high-functioning autism (HFA) but with no history of language delay and no cognitive delay. That is, as a toddler, the individual was speaking on time (i.e., single words by age 2 and/or phrase speech by 3 years old) and has had a mental age in line

We are grateful for support from the MRC (United Kingdom), the James S. McDonnell Foundation, and the Isaac Newton Trust during the period of this work. Parts of this chapter are reprinted from elsewhere (Baron-Cohen, Wheelwright, Griffin, Lawson, & Hill, 2002).

with his or her chronological age (i.e., an IQ in the normal range). Although some studies have claimed a distinction between AS and HFA (Klin et al., 1995), the majority of studies have not demonstrated many, if any, significant differences.

This background into autism and intelligence is important because it reveals that over the past 40 years, there has been a major shift in research strategy. When studying the cognitive development of autism, one strategy (and one we focus on here) is to identify the deficits or talents that are present in all three subgroups (low, medium, and high functioning). In this way, we can characterize necessary, core characteristics of people on the autism spectrum and test whether a cognitive theory can account for such core features. At the same time, we can clarify those associated characteristics that may occur more frequently than chance but may not lie in this core. The list of *associated* (but not universal) characteristics is very long and includes the following: language delay, learning disability, self-injury, clumsiness, attention deficit/hyperactivity disorder (ADHD), epilepsy, gastrointestinal inflammation, hyperlexia, and nonright-handedness. We suggest that the *core characteristics* comprise two triads:

> *Triad A:* Social difficulties, communication difficulties, and difficulties in imagining other people's minds
>
> *Triad B:* Strong, narrow obsessional interests, repetitive behavior, and "islets of ability"

This new view builds on the concept of the triad but extends it into two triads (Wing & Gould, 1979). In the next sections, we look at some different cognitive theories to see how well they can account for these two triads of characteristics.

THE MINDBLINDNESS/EMPATHIZING THEORY

The mindblindness theory of autism (Baron-Cohen, 1995) and its extension into empathizing theory (Baron-Cohen, 2002) propose that in autism spectrum conditions, there are deficits in the normal process of empathizing,

relative to mental age. These deficits can occur by degrees. The term *empathizing* encompasses the following earlier terms: *theory of mind, mind reading,* and taking the *intentional stance* (Dennett, 1987).

Empathizing involves two major elements: (1) the ability to attribute mental states to self and others as a natural way to understand agents (Baron-Cohen, 1994a; Leslie, 1995; Premack, 1990) and (2) having an emotional reaction that is appropriate to the other person's mental state. In this sense, it includes what is normally meant by the term *theory of mind* (the attributional component), but it goes beyond to include having some affective reaction (e.g., sympathy).

The first of these elements, the mental state attribution component, has been widely discussed in terms of being an evolved ability, given that the universe can be broadly divided into two kinds of entities: those that possess intentionality and those that do not (Brentano, 1970). The mental state attribution component is effectively judging whether this is the sort of entity that might possess intentionality. *Intentionality* is defined as the capacity of something to refer or point to things other than itself. A rock cannot point to anything. It just is. In contrast, a mouse can "look" at a piece of cheese, it can "want" the piece of cheese, it can "think" that this is a piece of cheese, and so on. Essentially, agents have intentionality, whereas nonagents do not.

This means that when we observe agents and nonagents move, we construe their motion as having different causes (Csibra, Gergely, Biro, Koos, & Brockbanck, 1999; Gelman & Hirschfield, 1994). Agents can move by self-propulsion, which we naturally interpret as driven by their goals and desires, while nonagents can reliably be expected not to move unless acted on by another object (e.g., following a collision). Note that mental state attribution is quite broad, because it includes not just attribution of beliefs, desires, intentions, thoughts, and knowledge, but also perceptual or attentional states and all of the emotions (Baron-Cohen, Wheelwright, Hill, & Golan, submitted; Griffin & Baron-Cohen, 2002).

The second empathizing element, the affective reaction component, is closer to what we ordinarily refer to with the English word *empathy*. Thus, we not only attribute a mental state to the agent in front of us (e.g., the man "thinks" the cake is made of soft, creamy chocolate) but also anticipate his or her emotional state (the man will be disappointed when he bites into it and discovers it is hard and stale), and we react to his or her emotional state with an appropriate emotion ourselves (we feel sorry for him). Empathizing thus essentially allows us to make sense of the behavior of other agents we are observing and predict what they might do next and how they might feel. And it allows us to feel connected to other agents' experience and respond appropriately to them.

The Normal Development of Empathizing

Empathizing develops from human infancy (Johnson, 2000). In the infancy period, it includes:

- Being able to judge whether something is an agent (Premack, 1990)
- Being able to judge whether another agent is looking at you (Baron-Cohen, 1994b)
- Being able to judge whether an agent is expressing a basic emotion (Ekman, 1992) and, if so, what type
- Engaging in shared attention, for example, by following gaze or pointing gestures (Mundy & Crowson, 1997; Scaife & Bruner, 1975; Tomasello, 1988)
- Showing concern or basic empathy at another's distress or responding appropriately to another's basic emotional state (Yirmiya, Sigman, Kasari, & Mundy, 1992)
- Being able to judge an agent's goal or basic intention (Premack, 1990)

Empathizing can be identified and studied from at least 12 months of age (Baron-Cohen, 1994a; Premack, 1990). Thus, infants show dishabituation to actions of agents who appear to violate goal directedness (Gergely, Nadasdy, Gergely, & Biro, 1995; Rochat, Morgan, & Carpenter, 1997). They also expect agents to emote (express emotion), and they expect consistency across modalities (between face and voice; Walker, 1982). They are also highly sensitive to where another person is looking and, by 14 months, strive to establish joint attention (Butterworth, 1991; Hood, Willen, & Driver, 1997; Scaife & Bruner, 1975). By 14 months, they also start to produce and understand pretense (Bates, Benigni, Bretherton, Camaioni, & Volterra, 1979; Leslie, 1987). By 18 months, they begin to show concern at the distress of others (Yirmiya et al., 1992). By 2 years old, they begin to use mental state words in their speech (Wellman & Bartsch, 1988).

Empathizing develops beyond early childhood and continues to develop throughout the life span. These later developments include:

- Attribution of the range of mental states to self and others, including pretense, deception, and belief (Leslie & Keeble, 1987)
- Recognizing and responding appropriately to complex emotions, not just basic ones (Harris, Johnson, Hutton, Andrews, & Cooke, 1989)
- Linking mental states to action, including language, and, therefore, understanding and producing pragmatically appropriate language (Tager-Flusberg, 1993)
- Making sense of others' behavior, predicting it, and even manipulating it (Whiten, 1991)
- Judging what is appropriate in different social contexts, based on what others will think of our own behavior
- Communicating an empathic understanding of another mind

Thus, by 3 years old, children can understand relationships between mental states such as "seeing leads to knowing" (Pratt & Bryant, 1990). By 4 years old, they can understand that people can hold false beliefs (Wimmer & Perner, 1983). By 5 to 6 years old, they can understand that people can hold beliefs about beliefs (Perner & Wimmer, 1985). By 7 years old, they begin to understand what *not* to say to avoid offending others (Baron-Cohen, O'Riordan, Jones, Stone, & Plaisted, 1999). With age, mental state attribution becomes increasingly more complex (Baron-Cohen, Jolliffe, et al., 1997; Happé, 1993). The little cross-cultural evidence that exists suggests a similar picture in very different cultures (Avis & Harris, 1991).

These developmental data have been interpreted in terms of an innate module being part of the infant cognitive architecture. This has been dubbed a theory of mind mechanism (ToMM; Leslie, 1995). But as we have suggested, empathizing also encompasses the skills that are needed for normal reciprocal social relationships (including intimate ones) and in sensitive communication. Empathizing is a narrowly defined domain, namely, *understanding and responding to people's minds.* Deficits in empathizing are referred to as degrees of mindblindness.

Empathizing in Autism Spectrum Conditions

Since the first test of mindblindness in children with autism (Baron-Cohen et al., 1985), there have been more than 30 experimental tests. The vast majority of these have revealed profound impairments in the development of their empathizing ability. These tests are reviewed elsewhere (Baron-Cohen, 1995; Baron-Cohen, Tager-Flusberg, & Cohen, 1993) but include deficits in the following:

- Joint attention (Baron-Cohen, 1989c)
- Use of mental state terms in language (Tager-Flusberg, 1993)
- Production and comprehension of pretense (Baron-Cohen, 1987; Wing & Gould, 1979)
- Understanding that "seeing leads to knowing" (Baron-Cohen & Goodhart, 1994; Leslie & Frith, 1988)
- Distinguishing mental from physical entities (Baron-Cohen, 1989a; Ozonoff, Pennington, & Rogers, 1990)
- Making the appearance-reality distinction (Baron-Cohen, 1989a)
- Understanding false belief (Baron-Cohen et al., 1985)
- Understanding beliefs about beliefs (Baron-Cohen, 1989b)
- Understanding complex emotions (Baron-Cohen, 1991)
- Showing concern at another's pain (Yirmiya et al., 1992)

Some children and adults with AS show their empathizing deficits only on age-appropriate adult tests (Baron-Cohen, Jolliffe, et al., 1997;

Baron-Cohen, Wheelwright, Hill, Raste, & Plumb, 2001; Baron-Cohen, Wheelwright, & Jolliffe, 1997) or on age-appropriate screening instruments such as the Empathy Quotient (EQ; Baron-Cohen, Richler, Bisarya, Gurunathan, & Wheelwright, 2003; Baron-Cohen & Wheelwright, 2004) or the Friendship and Relationship Quotient (FQ; Baron-Cohen & Wheelwright, 2003).

THE EMPATHIZING-SYSTEMIZING THEORY

A deficit in empathizing might account for Triad A—the social and communication abnormalities that are diagnostic of autism—and it could even account for difficulties in *imagining* other people's mental states. However, such a deficit has little if anything to contribute to our understanding of Triad B—repetitive behavior, obsessions, and the islets of ability. Thus, our view of autism is now broader and suggests that alongside empathizing deficits, a different process is *intact or even superior.* This process is what we call *systemizing* (Baron-Cohen et al., 2003).

Systemizing

Whereas we think of empathizing as the drive to identify and respond affectively to agents' mental states to understand and predict the behavior of that agent, we think of systemizing as the drive to analyze and build systems to understand and predict the behavior of nonagentive events. Systems are all around us in our environment and fall into at least six classes:

1. *Technical* (e.g., machines and tools)
2. *Natural* (e.g., biological and geographical phenomena)
3. *Abstract* (e.g., mathematics or computer programs)
4. *Social* (e.g., a business or a football league)
5. *Motoric* (e.g., a juggling technique or a Frisbee throw)
6. *Organizable* (e.g., a collection, a taxonomy, or a list)

The way we make sense of any of these systems is not in terms of mental states, but rather in terms of underlying rules and regularities.

Systemizing involves an initial analysis of the system down to its lowest level of detail to identify potentially relevant *parameters* that may play a causal role in the behavior of the system. These parameters are then systematically observed or manipulated one by one, and their effects on the whole system are noted. That is, systemizing entails an analysis of input-operation-output relationships. Once the operations on inputs are identified and checked, the output of the system becomes totally predictable.

Systemizing in Autism Spectrum Conditions

Are people with autism intact or even superior at systemizing? We know from clinical descriptions of children with autism that they are typically fascinated by machines (the paragon of nonintentional systems). Parents' accounts (Hart, 1989; Lovell, 1978; Park, 1967) are a rich source of such descriptions. Typical examples include extreme fascinations with electricity pylons, burglar alarms, vacuum cleaners, washing machines, video players, trains, planes, and clocks. Sometimes, the machine that is the object of the child's obsession is quite simple (e.g., the workings of drainpipes or the design of windows). Our survey of obsessions in children with autism substantiated this clinical observation that their preoccupations tend to cluster in the area of systems (Baron-Cohen & Wheelwright, 1999).

Children with an autism spectrum condition who have enough language, such as is seen in children with AS, may be described as holding forth, like a "little professor," on their favorite subject or area of expertise, often failing to detect that their listener may have long since become bored of hearing more on the subject. The apparently precocious systematic understanding, while being relatively oblivious to their listener's level of interest, suggests that their systemizing might be outstripping their empathizing skills in development. The anecdotal evidence includes an obsession with not just machines (technical systems) but also other kinds of systems. Examples of their interest in natural systems include obsessions with the weather (meteorology), the formation of mountains (geography),

motion of the planets (astronomy), and classification of lizards (taxonomy).

Experimental studies converge on the same conclusion: Children with autism have not only an intact intuitive physics but also an accelerated or superior development in this domain (relative to their empathizing and relative to their mental age, both verbal and nonverbal). For example, using a picture-sequencing paradigm, children with autism performed significantly better than mental age-matched controls in sequencing physical-causal stories (Baron-Cohen et al., 1986). Two studies found children with autism showed superior understanding of a camera (Leekam & Perner, 1991; Leslie & Thaiss, 1992). In two direct tests of intuitive physics in children and adults with AS (Baron-Cohen, Wheelwright, Hill, et al., 2001; Lawson, Baron-Cohen, & Wheelwright, 2004), people with AS were found to be functioning at a normal or even superior level relative to controls. Finally, using the Systemizing Quotient (SQ), it was found that adults with AS scored higher than controls (Baron-Cohen et al., 2003).

Family Studies of Empathizing and Systemizing

Family studies add to this picture. Parents of children with AS also show mild but significant deficits on an adult mind-reading task (on the adult version of the Reading the Mind in the Eyes test). This task mirrors the deficit in empathizing seen in patients with autism or AS (Baron-Cohen & Hammer, 1997b; Baron-Cohen, Wheelwright, Hill, et al., 2001). This familial resemblance at the cognitive level is assumed to reflect genetic factors, since autism and AS appear to have a strong heritable component (Bailey et al., 1995; Bolton et al., 1994; Folstein & Rutter, 1977; Le Couteur et al., 1996).

We should also expect that parents of children with autism or AS would be overrepresented in occupations in which possession of superior systemizing is an advantage, while a deficit in empathizing would not necessarily be a disadvantage. A clear occupation for such a cognitive profile is engineering. A study of 1,000 families found that fathers and grandfathers (patri- and matrilineal) of children with autism or AS were more than twice as likely to work in the field of engineering, compared to fathers and grandfathers of children with other disabilities (Baron-Cohen, Wheelwright, Stott, Bolton, & Goodyer, 1997). Indeed, 28.4% of children with autism or AS had at least one relative (father and/or grandfather) who was an engineer. Related evidence comes from a survey of students at Cambridge University, studying either sciences (physics, engineering, or mathematics) or humanities (English or French literature). When asked about family history of a range of psychiatric conditions (schizophrenia, anorexia, autism, Down syndrome, or manic depression), the students in the science group showed a sixfold increase in the rate of autism in their families, and this increase was specific to autism (Baron-Cohen et al., 1998).

Plotting Empathizing and Systemizing

If empathizing and systemizing are independent dimensions, it is possible to plot on orthogonal axes possible scores from possible tests assessing these two abilities. Figures 23.1 and 23.2 provides a visual representation of this model of the relationship between empathizing and systemizing. It suggests appropriate labels for different possible patterns of scores. The axes show number of standard de-

viations from the mean. The scale of the diagram is less important than the principle underlying it.

We have used the terms *Brain Type B (Balanced), Brain Type E (Empathizing), Brain Type S (Systemizing),* to describe the three basic brain types that are generated from this model. These all fall within two standard deviations from the mean on both dimensions. We have also shown on the graph the *extremes* of Brain Types S and E. The terms describe the discrepancy between the empathizing score and the systemizing score. In the Balanced Brain, there is no difference between scores (i.e., E = S). In Brain Type E, empathizing is one or two standard deviations higher than systemizing (i.e., E > S). In the Extreme Brain Type E, this discrepancy is greater than two standard deviations (i.e., E >> S). In Brain Type S, systemizing is one or two standard deviations higher than empathizing (i.e., S > E). For the Extreme Brain Type S, this discrepancy is greater than two standard deviations (i.e., S >> E).

The key point is the discrepancy between the scores rather than the absolute scores themselves. For example, someone could score two standard deviations above the mean on empathizing (a very high score), but if the score was three standard deviations above the mean on systemizing, he or she would be

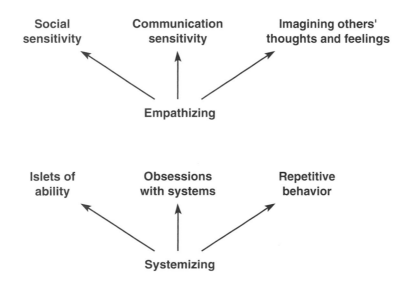

Figure 23.1 Explaining the core characteristics of autism spectrum conditions in terms of empathizing and systemizing.

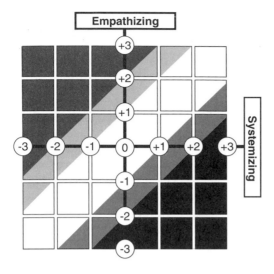

Figure 23.2 Empathizing and systemizing associations. *Note:* Axes show standard deviations from the mean.

described as having Brain Type S. Thus, the key issue is possible asymmetries of ability.

Evidence from sex difference research (Kimura, 1992) suggests that Brain Type S is more commonly found in males, while Brain Type E is more frequent in females. For this reason, we can also use the terminology *Female Brain* and *Male Brain* types as synonyms for Brain Types E and S, respectively. One result that is consistent with this idea is that human neonates, 1 day old, show a sex difference: Female babies look longer at a human face than a mechanical mobile, while male babies show the opposite pattern of preferences (Connellan, Baron-Cohen, Wheelwright, Ba'tki, & Ahluwalia, 2001).

THE EXTREME MALE BRAIN THEORY

Autism has been described as the extreme of the male brain (Asperger, 1944; Baron-Cohen, 2002; Baron-Cohen & Hammer, 1997a). A number of pieces of evidence are consistent with the extreme male brain (EMB) theory of autism. First, regarding empathizing measures, females score higher than males on tests of understanding faux pas, and people with AS score even lower than unaffected boys (Baron-Cohen, Wheelwright, Stone, & Rutherford, 1999; Lawson et al., 2004). Second, girls make more eye contact than boys (Lutchmaya, Baron-Cohen, & Raggett, 2002), and children with autism make even less eye contact than unaffected boys (Swettenham et al., 1998). Third, girls tend to pass false belief tests slightly earlier than boys (Happé, 1995), and children with autism are even later to pass false belief tests. Finally, women score slightly higher than men on the Reading the Mind in the Eyes test, and adults with AS or high-functioning autism score even lower than unaffected men (Baron-Cohen, Jolliffe, Mortimore, & Robertson, 1997). There are also established sex differences in systemizing, males tending to score higher on tests of folk physics, map use, and mental rotation, for example (Kimura, 1999), and people with autism being at least intact if not superior on these tasks (Baron-Cohen, Wheelwright, Scahill, Lawson, & Spong, 2001; Baron-Cohen et al., 2003; Lawson et al., 2004).

This model of the independence of empathizing and systemizing also predicts the existence of very high-functioning individuals with AS, who may be extreme high achievers in domains such as mathematics and physics—equivalent to Nobel Prize winners even—but who have deficits in empathizing. Some case studies are beginning to identify such very high-functioning individuals (Baron-Cohen, Wheelwright, et al., 1999).

OTHER MODELS OF COGNITIVE DEVELOPMENT IN AUTISM

In this final section, we briefly summarize some other cognitive developmental theories of autism because they are important alternatives against which to consider the empathizing-systemizing theory.

Executive Function Theory

People with autism spectrum conditions show repetitive behavior, a strong desire for routines, and a need for sameness. The only cognitive account that has attempted to explain this aspect of the syndrome is the executive dysfunction theory (Ozonoff, Rogers, Farnham, & Pennington, 1994; Pennington et al., 1997; Russell, 1997b). This theory paints an essentially negative view of this repetitive behavior, assuming that it is a form of frontal lobe perseveration or inability to shift attention.

We recognize that some forms of repetitive behavior in autism such as *stereotypies* (e.g., twiddling the fingers rapidly in peripheral vision) are likely to be due to executive deficits. Moreover, we recognize that, as people with autism who have additional learning disabilities are tested, executive deficits are more likely to be found (Russell, 1997a). But the fact that it is possible for people with AS to have no demonstrable executive dysfunction while still having deficits in empathizing and talents in systemizing suggests that executive dysfunction cannot be a core feature of autism spectrum conditions.

The executive account has also traditionally ignored the *content* of repetitive behavior. The emphasizing-systemizing (E-S) theory, in contrast, draws attention to the fact that much repetitive behavior involves the child's obsessional or strong interests with mechanical systems (e.g., light switches or water faucets) or other systems that can be understood in terms of rules and regularities. Rather than these behaviors being a sign of executive dysfunction, they may reflect the child's intact or even superior development of his or her systemizing. The child's obsession with machines and systems and what is often described as his or her "need for sameness" in attempting to hold the environment constant might be signs that the child is a superior systemizer. The child might be conducting mini-experiments in his or her surroundings in an attempt to identify physical-causal or other systematic principles underlying events.

One possibility is that the strong drive to systemize seen in autism spectrum conditions may underlie the Triad B features (repetitive behavior, obsessional or narrow interests, and the islets of ability).

Central Coherence Theory

It could be argued that good systemizing skills are simply an expression of an anomaly previously documented, namely, weak central coherence (Frith, 1989; Happé, 1996). *Weak central coherence* refers to the individual's preference for local detail over global processing. This has been demonstrated in terms of an autistic superiority on the Embedded Figures Task (EFT) and the Block Design Subtest (Jolliffe & Baron-Cohen, 1997; Shah & Frith, 1983, 1993). It has also been demonstrated in terms of an autistic deficit in integrating fragments of objects and integrating sentences within a paragraph (Jolliffe & Baron-Cohen, 2001a; Jolliffe & Baron-Cohen, 2001b). The faster and more accurate performance on the EFT and Block Design subtest has been interpreted as evidence of good segmentation skills and superior attention to detail. The latter has also been demonstrated on visual search tasks (Plaisted, O'Riordan, & Baron-Cohen, 1998a, 1998b).

Our view of systemizing certainly embraces aspects of the central coherence (CC) theory. For example, systemizing requires as a first stage an excellent attention to detail, identifying parameters that may then be tested for their role in the behavior of the system under examination. So, both the E-S theory and the CC theory predict excellent attention to detail. However, the E-S and CC theories also make opposite predictions when it comes to an individual with autism being able to understand a whole system. The E-S theory predicts that people with autism, faced with a new system to learn, will learn it faster than someone without autism, as long as there are underlying rules and regularities that can be discovered. Moreover, they will readily grasp that a change of one parameter in one part of the system may have distant effects on another part of the system. Thus, if the task is a constructional one (e.g., building a model plane), they will be able to grasp that changing the thickness of the wings may cause the plane to land at a steeper angle. This kind of reasoning clearly involves good central coherence of the system. What is being understood is the *relationship* between one parameter and one distal outcome. In contrast, the CC theory should predict that they should fail to understand whole (global) systems or the relationships between parts of a system. This has not been tested.

SUMMARY

This chapter has reviewed both the early mind-blindness theory of autism and the more recent extensions of the empathizing-systemizing theory and the extreme male brain theory of autism. The first of these extensions addresses a problem that the early theory had, namely, the need to also account for the obsessional features of autism. The second of these may help explain the marked sex ratio in autism and throw light on the biological basis of autism (Lutchmaya & Baron-Cohen, 2002). Both of these extensions lead to new predictions when contrasted with other cognitive developmental theories of this condition and illustrate some of the progress that is being made in this part of the field of developmental psychopathology.

Cross-References

Aspects of social development are discussed in Chapters 11 and 26; attention and perception are discussed in Chapter 13. Issues of emotional developmental are discussed in Chapter 15.

REFERENCES

American Psychiatric Association. (1994). *Diagnostic and statistical manual of mental disorders* (4th ed.). Washington, DC: Author.

Asperger, H. (1944). Die "Autistischen Psychopathen" im Kindesalter. *Archiv fur Psychiatrie und Nervenkrankheiten, 117*, 76–136.

Avis, J., & Harris, P. (1991). Belief-desire reasoning among Baka children: Evidence for a universal conception of mind. *Child Development, 62*, 460–467.

Bailey, A., Le Couteur, A., Gottesman, I., Bolton, P., Simmonoff, E., Yuzda, E., et al. (1995). Autism as a strongly genetic disorder: Evidence from a British twin study. *Psychological Medicine, 25*, 63–77.

Baron-Cohen, S. (1987). Perception in autistic children. In D. Cohen (Ed.), *Handbook of autism and pervasive developmental disorders*. New York: Wiley.

Baron-Cohen, S. (1989a). Are autistic children behaviourists? An examination of their mental-physical and appearance-reality distinctions. *Journal of Autism and Developmental Disorders, 19*, 579–600.

Baron-Cohen, S. (1989b). The autistic child's theory of mind: A case of specific developmental delay. *Journal of Child Psychology and Psychiatry, 30*, 285–298.

Baron-Cohen, S. (1989c). Perceptual role-taking and protodeclarative pointing in autism. *British Journal of Developmental Psychology, 7*, 113–127.

Baron-Cohen, S. (1991). Do people with autism understand what causes emotion? *Child Development, 62*, 385–395.

Baron-Cohen, S. (1994a). How to build a baby that can read minds: Cognitive mechanisms in mindreading. *Cahiers de Psychologie Cognitive/Current Psychology of Cognition, 13*, 513–552.

Baron-Cohen, S. (1994b). The mindreading system: New directions for research. *Current Psychology of Cognition, 13*, 724–750.

Baron-Cohen, S. (1995). *Mindblindness: An essay on autism and theory of mind*. Boston: MIT Press/Bradford Books.

Baron-Cohen, S. (2002). The extreme male brain theory of autism. *Trends in Cognitive Sciences, 6*, 248–254.

Baron-Cohen, S., Bolton, P., Wheelwright, S., Short, L., Mead, G., Smith, A., et al. (1998). Does autism occur more often in families of physicists, engineers, and mathematicians? *Autism, 2*, 296–301.

Baron-Cohen, S., & Goodhart, F. (1994). The "seeing leads to knowing" deficit in autism: The Pratt and Bryant probe. *British Journal of Developmental Psychology, 12*, 397–402.

Baron-Cohen, S., & Hammer, J. (1997a). Is autism an extreme form of the male brain? *Advances in Infancy Research, 11*, 193–217.

Baron-Cohen, S., & Hammer, J. (1997b). Parents of children with Asperger syndrome: What is the cognitive phenotype? *Journal of Cognitive Neuroscience, 9*, 548–554.

Baron-Cohen, S., Jolliffe, T., Mortimore, C., & Robertson, M. (1997). Another advanced test of theory of mind: Evidence from very high functioning adults with autism or Asperger Syndrome. *Journal of Child Psychology and Psychiatry, 38*, 813–822.

Baron-Cohen, S., Leslie, A. M., & Frith, U. (1985). Does the autistic child have a "theory of mind"? *Cognition, 21*, 37–46.

Baron-Cohen, S., Leslie, A. M., & Frith, U. (1986). Mechanical, behavioural and intentional understanding of picture stories in autistic children. *British Journal of Developmental Psychology, 4*, 113–125.

Baron-Cohen, S., O'Riordan, M., Jones, R., Stone, V., & Plaisted, K. (1999). A new test of social sensitivity: Detection of faux pas in normal children and children with Asperger syndrome. *Journal of Autism and Developmental Disorders, 29,* 407–418.

Baron-Cohen, S., Richler, J., Bisarya, D., Gurunathan, N., & Wheelwright, S. (2003). The Systemising Quotient (SQ): An investigation of adults with Asperger Syndrome or High Functioning Autism and normal sex differences. *Philosophical Transactions of the Royal Society, Series B [Special issue], 358,* 361–374.

Baron-Cohen, S., Tager-Flusberg, H., & Cohen, D. (Eds.). (1993). *Understanding other minds: Perspectives from autism:* Oxford University Press.

Baron-Cohen, S., & Wheelwright, S. (1999). Obsessions in children with autism or Asperger syndrome: A content analysis in terms of core domains of cognition. *British Journal of Psychiatry, 175,* 484–490.

Baron-Cohen, S., & Wheelwright, S. (2003). The Friendship Questionnaire (FQ): An investigation of adults with Asperger Syndrome or High Functioning Autism, and normal sex differences. *Journal of Autism and Developmental Disorders, 33,* 509–517.

Baron-Cohen, S., & Wheelwright, S. (2004). The Empathy Quotient (EQ). An investigation of adults with Asperger Syndrome or High Functioning Autism, and normal sex differences. *Journal of Autism and Developmental Disorders, 34,* 163–175.

Baron-Cohen, S., Wheelwright, S., Griffin, R., Lawson, J., & Hill, J. (2002). The exact mind: Empathising and systemising in autism spectrum conditions. In U. Goswami (Ed.), *Handbook of cognitive development:* Blackwells.

Baron-Cohen, S., Wheelwright, S., Hill, J., & Golan, O. (submitted). A Taxonomy of Human Emotions.

Baron-Cohen, S., Wheelwright, S., Hill, J., Raste, Y., & Plumb, I. (2001). The "Reading the Mind in the Eyes" test revised version: A study with normal adults, and adults with Asperger Syndrome or High-Functioning autism. *Journal of Child Psychology and Psychiatry, 42,* 241–252.

Baron-Cohen, S., Wheelwright, S., & Jolliffe, T. (1997). Is there a "language of the eyes"? Evidence from normal adults and adults with autism or Asperger syndrome. *Visual Cognition, 4,* 311–331.

Baron-Cohen, S., Wheelwright, S., Scahill, V., Lawson, J., & Spong, A. (2001). Are intuitive physics and intuitive psychology independent? *Journal of Developmental and Learning Disorders, 5,* 47–78.

Baron-Cohen, S., Wheelwright, S., Stone, V., & Rutherford, M. (1999). A mathematician, a physicist, and a computer scientist with Asperger syndrome: Performance on folk psychology and folk physics test. *Neurocase, 5,* 475–483.

Baron-Cohen, S., Wheelwright, S., Stott, C., Bolton, P., & Goodyer, I. (1997). Is there a link between engineering and autism? *Autism: An International Journal of Research and Practice, 1,* 153–163.

Bates, E., Benigni, L., Bretherton, I., Camaioni, L., & Volterra, V. (1979). Cognition and communication from 0 12 months. Correlational findings. In E. Bates (Ed.), *The emergence of symbols: Cognition and communication in infancy.* New York: Academic Press.

Bolton, P., MacDonald, H., Pickles, A., Rios, P., Goode, S., Crowson, M., et al. (1994). A case-control family history study of autism. *Journal of Child Psychology and Psychiatry, 35,* 877–900.

Brentano, F. (1970). *Psychology from an empirical standpoint.* London: Routledge, and Kegan Paul.

Butterworth, G. (1991). The ontogeny and phylogeny of joint visual attention. In A. Whilen (Ed.), *Natural theories of mind.* Oxford, England.

Connellan, J., Baron-Cohen, S., Wheelwright, S., Ba'tki, A., & Ahluwalia, J. (2001). Sex differences in human neonatal social perception. *Infant Behavior and Development, 23,* 113–118.

Csibra, G., Gergely, G., Biro, S., Koos, O., & Brockbanck, M. (1999). Goal attribution without agency cues: The perception of "pure reason" in infancy. *Cognition, 72,* 253–284.

Dennett, D. (1987). *The intentional stance.* Cambridge, MA: MIT Press/Bradford Books.

Ekman, P. (1992). Facial expressions of emotion: An old controversy and new findings. In V. Bruce, A. Cowey, et al. (Eds.), *Processing the facial image.* New York: Clarendon Press/Oxford University Press.

Folstein, S., & Rutter, M. (1977). Infantile autism: A genetic study of 21 twin pairs. *Journal of Child Psycholology and Psychiatry, 18,* 297–321.

Frith, U. (1970). Studies in pattern detection in normal and autistic children: I. Immediate recall of auditory sequences. *Journal of Abnormal Psychology, 76,* 413–420.

Frith, U. (1989). *Autism: Explaining the enigma.* Oxford, England: Basil Blackwell.

Frith, U. (1991). *Autism and Asperger's syndrome.* Cambridge: Cambridge University Press.

Gelman, S., & Hirschfield, L. (1994). *Mapping the mind.* Cambridge: Press Syndicate, University of Cambridge.

Gergely, G., Nadasdy, Z., Gergely, C., & Biro, S. (1995). Taking the intentional stance at 12 months of age. *Cognition, 56,* 165–193.

Griffin, R., & Baron-Cohen, S. (2002). The intentional stance: Developmental and neurocognitive perspectives. In A. Brook & D. Ross (Eds.), *Dennett beyond philosophy:* Cambridge University Press.

Happé, F. (1993). Communicative competence and theory of mind in autism: A test of Relevance Theory. *Cognition, 48,* 101–119.

Happé, F. (1995). The role of age and verbal ability in the theory of mind task performance of subjects with autism. *Child Development, 66,* 843–855.

Happé, F. (1996). Studying weak central coherence at low levels: Children with autism do not succumb to visual illusions: A research note. *Journal of Child Psychology and Psychiatry, 37,* 873–877.

Harris, P., Johnson, C. N., Hutton, D., Andrews, G., & Cooke, T. (1989). Young children's theory of mind and emotion. *Cognition and Emotion, 3,* 379–400.

Hart, C. (1989). *Without reason.* New York: Harper & Row.

Hermelin, B., & O'Connor, N. (1970). *Psychological experiments with autistic children.* London: Pergamon Press.

Hood, B., Willen, J., & Driver, J. (1997). *An eye-direction detector triggers shifts of visual attention in human infants.* Unpublished manuscript, Harvard University.

Johnson, S. (2000). The recognition of mentalistic agents in infancy. *Trends in Cognitive Sciences, 4,* 22–28.

Jolliffe, T., & Baron-Cohen, S. (1997). Are people with autism or Asperger's syndrome faster than normal on the Embedded Figures Task? *Journal of Child Psychology and Psychiatry, 38,* 527–534.

Jolliffe, T., & Baron-Cohen, S. (2001a). A test of central coherence theory: Can adults with high-functioning autism or Asperger Syndrome integrate fragments of an object. *Cognitive Neuropsychiatry, 6,* 193–216.

Jolliffe, T., & Baron-Cohen, S. (2001b). A test of central coherence theory: Can adults with high-functioning autism or Asperger syndrome integrate objects in context? *Visual Cognition, 8,* 67–101.

Kanner, L. (1943). Autistic disturbance of affective contact. *Nervous Child, 2,* 217–250.

Kimura, D. (1992, September). Sex differences in the brain. *Scientific American,* 119–125.

Kimura, D. (1999). *Sex and cognition.* Cambridge, MA: MIT Press.

Klin, A., Volkmar, F., Sparrow, S., Cicchetti, D., & Rourke, B. (1995). Validity and neuropsychological characterization of Asperger syndrome: Convergence with nonverbal learning disabilities syndrome. *Journal of Child Psychology and Psychiatry, 36,* 1127–1140.

Lawson, J., Baron-Cohen, S., & Wheelwright, S. (2004). Empathising and systemising in adults with and without Asperger Syndrome. *Journal of Autism and Developmental Disorders, 34,* 301–310.

Le Couteur, A., Bailey, A., Goode, S., Pickles, A., Robertson, S., Gottesman, I., et al. (1996). A broader phenotype of autism: The clinical spectrum in twins. *Journal of Child Psychology and Psychiatry, 37,* 785–801.

Leekam, S., & Perner, J. (1991). Does the autistic child have a metarepresentational deficit? *Cognition, 40,* 203–218.

Leslie, A. (1987). Pretence and representation: The origins of "theory of mind." *Psychological Review, 94,* 412–426.

Leslie, A. (1995). ToMM, ToBy, and agency: Core architecture and domain specificity. In L. Hirschfeld & S. Gelman (Eds.), *Domain specificity in cognition and culture.* New York: Cambridge University Press.

Leslie, A., & Frith, U. (1988). Autistic children's understanding of seeing, knowing, and believing. *British Journal of Developmental Psychology, 6,* 315–324.

Leslie, A., & Keeble, S. (1987). Do six-month old infants perceive causality? *Cognition, 25,* 265–288.

Leslie, A., & Thaiss, L. (1992). Domain specificity in conceptual development: Evidence from autism. *Cognition, 43,* 225–251.

Lovell, A. (1978). *In a summer garment.* London: Secker and Warburg.

Lutchmaya, S., & Baron-Cohen, S. (2002). Human sex differences in social and non-social looking preferences at 12 months of age. *Infant Behaviour and Development, 25,* 319–325.

Lutchmaya, S., Baron-Cohen, S., & Raggett, P. (2002). Foetal testosterone and eye contact in 12 month old infants. *Infant Behavior and Development, 25,* 327–335.

Mundy, P., & Crowson, M. (1997). Joint attention and early social communication. *Journal of Autism and Developmental Disorders, 27,* 653–676.

Ozonoff, S., Pennington, B., & Rogers, S. (1990). Are there emotion perception deficits in young autistic children? *Journal of Child Psychology and Psychiatry, 31,* 343–363.

Ozonoff, S., Rogers, S., Farnham, J., & Pennington, B. (1994). Can standard measures identify subclinical markers of autism? *Journal of Autism and Developmental Disorders.*

Park, C. (1967). *The siege.* London: Hutchinson.

Pennington, B., Rogers, S., Bennetto, L., Griffith, E., Reed, D., & Shyu, V. (1997). Validity test of the executive dysfunction hypothesis of autism. In J. Russell (Ed.), *Executive functioning in autism.* Oxford, England: Oxford University Press.

Perner, J., & Wimmer, H. (1985). "John thinks that Mary thinks that . . . " Attribution of second-order beliefs by 5–10 year old children. *Journal of Experimental Child Psychology, 39,* 437–471.

Plaisted, K., O'Riordan, M., & Baron-Cohen, S. (1998a). Enhanced discrimination of novel, highly similar stimuli by adults with autism during a perceptual learning task. *Journal of Child Psychology and Psychiatry, 39,* 765–775.

Plaisted, K., O'Riordan, M., & Baron-Cohen, S. (1998b). Enhanced visual search for a conjunctive target in autism: A research note. *Journal of Child Psychology and Psychiatry, 39,* 777–783.

Pratt, C., & Bryant, P. (1990). Young children understand that looking leads to knowing (so long as they are looking into a single barrel). *Child Development, 61,* 973–983.

Premack, D. (1990). The infant's theory of self-propelled objects. *Cognition, 36,* 1–16.

Rochat, P., Morgan, R., & Carpenter, M. (1997). Young infants' sensitivity to movement information specifying social causality. *Cognitive Development, 12,* 537–561.

Russell, J. (Ed.). (1997a). *Autism as an executive disorder.* Oxford, England: Oxford University Press.

Russell, J. (1997b). How executive disorders can bring about an inadequate theory of mind. In J. Russell (Ed.), *Autism as an executive disorder.* Oxford, England: Oxford University Press.

Rutter, M. (1978). Language disorder and infantile autism. In M. Rutter & E. Schopler (Eds.), *Autism: A reappraisal of concepts and treatment.* New York: Plenum Press.

Scaife, M., & Bruner, J. (1975). The capacity for joint visual attention in the infant. *Nature, 253,* 265–266.

Shah, A., & Frith, U. (1983). An islet of ability in autism: A research note. *Journal of Child Psychology and Psychiatry, 24,* 613–620.

Shah, A., & Frith, U. (1993). Why do autistic individuals show superior performance on the block design test? *Journal of Child Psychology and Psychiatry, 34,* 1351–1364.

Swettenham, J., Baron-Cohen, S., Charman, T., Cox, A., Baird, G., Drew, A., et al. (1998). The frequency and distribution of spontaneous attention shifts between social and non-social stimuli in autistic, typically developing, and non-autistic developmentally delayed infants. *Journal of Child Psychology and Psychiatry, 9,* 747–753.

Szatmari, P., Tuff, L., Finlayson, M., & Bartolucci, G. (1990). Asperger's syndrome and autism: Neurocognitive aspects. *Journal of the American Academy of Child and Adolescent Psychiatry, 29,* 130–136.

Tager Flusberg, H. (1993). What language reveals about the understanding of minds in children with autism. In S. Baron-Cohen, H. Tager-Flusberg, & D. J. Cohen (Eds.), *Understanding other minds: Perspectives from autism.* Oxford, England: Oxford University Press.

Tomasello, M. (1988). The role of joint-attentional processes in early language acquisition. *Language Sciences, 10,* 69–88.

Walker, A. S. (1982). Intermodal perception of expressive behaviours by human infants. *Journal of Experimental Child Psychology, 33,* 514–535.

Wellman, H., & Bartsch, K. (1988). Young children's reasoning about beliefs. *Cognition, 30,* 239–277.

Whiten, A. (1991). *Natural theories of mind.* Oxford, England: Basil Blackwell.

Wimmer, H., & Perner, J. (1983). Beliefs about beliefs: Representation and constraining function of wrong beliefs in young children's understanding of deception. *Cognition, 13,* 103–128.

Wing, L. (1976). *Early childhood autism.* Oxford: Pergamon Press.

Wing, L. (1981). Asperger syndrome: A clinical account. *Psychological Medicine, 11,* 115–130.

Wing, L., & Gould, J. (1979). Severe impairments of social interaction and associated abnormalities in children: Epidemiology and classification. *Journal of Autism and Developmental Disorders, 9,* 11–29.

World Health Organization. (1992). *The ICD-10 classification of mental and behavioral disorders: Clinical descriptions and diagnostic guidelines.* Geneva, Switzerland: Author.

Yirmiya, N., Sigman, M., Kasari, C., & Mundy, P. (1992). Empathy and cognition in high functioning children with autism. *Child Development, 63,* 150–160.

CHAPTER 24

The Weak Central Coherence Account of Autism

FRANCESCA HAPPÉ

Many of the chapters in this volume offer accounts of the core deficits that characterize autism spectrum disorders. The social and communicative difficulties and the rigid pattern of behavior and interests are the focus of current theories postulating deficits in "theory of mind," executive functions, and so forth. What such deficit accounts fail to explain, however, is why people with autism show not only deficits but also striking assets in certain areas. Savant skills, in recognized areas such as music, art, calculation, and memory, are 10 times more common in people with autism than in others with intellectual disabilities, occurring in approximately 1 in 10 individuals with autism (Miller, 1999). If skills outside these areas are included, such as doing jigsaw puzzles remarkably well, the great majority of people with autism might be said to have a specific and surprising talent. Even the child who is extremely distressed by minute changes to a familiar room (undetectable to most people) shows an unusual skill, albeit with upsetting results. How can we account for these assets, which current deficit theories of autism appear unable to explain?

One current theory of autism proposes a different, rather than merely deficient, mind at the center of autism. Frith (1989), prompted by a strong belief that assets and deficits in autism might have one and the same origin, proposed that autism is characterized by weak "central coherence." Central coherence is the term she coined for the everyday tendency to process incoming information in context for gist—pulling information together for higher level meaning, often at the expense of memory for detail. For example, as Bartlett's classic work showed, the gist of a story is easily recalled, while the surface form is effortful to retain and quickly lost (Bartlett, 1932). Global processing also predominates over local processing in at least some aspects of perception; we see the whole rather than the parts (Kimchi, 1992; Navon, 1977). The preference for integration and global processing also characterizes young typically developing children and individuals with (nonautistic) intellectual disability—who (unlike those with autism) show an advantage recalling organized versus jumbled material (Hermelin & O'Connor, 1967). Indeed, research suggests that global processing may predominate even in infants as young as 3 months (Bhatt, Rovee-Collier, & Shyi, 1994; Freedland & Dannemiller, 1996).

Frith suggested that this aspect of human information processing is disturbed in autism and that people with autism show detail-focused processing in which features are perceived and retained at the expense of global configuration and higher level meaning. Clinically, children and adults with autism often show a preoccupation with details and parts, while failing to extract gist or see "the big

I would like to thank the people with autism spectrum disorders, their families, and caregivers who have helped us with our research. The ideas presented here were developed with Uta Frith and my research team at the SGDP Research Centre and have been discussed in part in Happé (1999).

picture." Kanner, in his original writings on autism, commented on the tendency for fragmentary processing in relation to the children's characteristic resistance to change: ". . . a situation, a performance, a sentence is not regarded as complete if it is not made up of exactly the same elements that were present at the time the child was first confronted with it" (Kanner, 1943). Indeed, Kanner saw as a universal feature of autism the "inability to experience wholes without full attention to the constituent parts," a description akin to Frith's notion of weak central coherence.

One of the most positive aspects of Frith's notion of central coherence is the ability to explain patterns of excellent and poor performance with one cognitive postulate. Weak central coherence predicts relatively good performance where attention to local information (i.e., relatively piecemeal processing) is advantageous, but poor performance on tasks requiring the recognition of global meaning or integration of stimuli in context. The central coherence account of autism, then, is better characterized in terms of cognitive *style* than cognitive deficit.

WEAK CENTRAL COHERENCE: EVIDENCE AT THREE LEVELS OF PROCESSING

In recent years, the notion that children with autism show weak central coherence has received increasing interest and prompted a rapidly growing number of studies. Detail-focused processing has been demonstrated at several levels (reviewed later). The division into verbal-semantic, visuo-spatial constructional, and perceptual levels for the purpose of this review is largely for convenience. An interesting issue for future research concerns possible high-level or top-down effects on even apparently peripheral perceptual processes (Coren & Enns, 1993).

Verbal-Semantic Coherence

Some of the earliest empirical evidence that influenced Frith's notion of weak central coherence came from the groundbreaking studies by Hermelin and O'Connor (1967), who showed that people with autism do not derive

the usual benefit from meaning in memory tests. Thus, while control subjects recalled sentences far better than unconnected word strings, this advantage was greatly diminished in the autism group. This work and subsequent replications (Tager-Flusberg, 1991; but see Lopez & Leekam, 2003) suggest that people with autism do not make use of either semantic relations (same category versus assorted words) or grammatical relations (sentences versus word lists) in memory. Weak coherence is also demonstrated by good verbatim but poor gist memory for story material (Scheuffgen, 1998) and poor inference, disambiguation, and construction of narrative (Dennis, Lazenby, & Lockyer, 2001; Jolliffe, 1998; Jolliffe & Baron-Cohen, 1999; Norbury & Bishop, 2002).

Frith and Snowling (1983) used homographs (words with one spelling, two meanings, and two pronunciations) to examine use of preceding sentence context to derive meaning and determine pronunciation; for example, "In her eye there was a big tear," "In her dress there was a big tear." If people with autism have weak central coherence at this level, then reading a sentence may, for them, be akin to reading a list of unconnected words, and sentence context will not be built up to allow meaning-driven disambiguation. In the original studies and subsequent replications with high-functioning children and adults (Happé, 1997; Jolliffe & Baron-Cohen, 1999), individuals with autism spectrum disorder failed to use preceding sentence context to determine the pronunciation of homographs. These findings bring to mind Kanner's description of his original cases: ". . . the children read monotonously, and a story . . . is experienced in unrelated portions rather than in its coherent totality" (Kanner, 1943). This finding is particularly interesting, in that people with autism (at these levels of intelligence) clearly are able to read for meaning when explicitly required to do so. Indeed, when instructed in reading for meaning, group differences on the homograph task disappeared (Snowling & Frith, 1986). It seems, then, that weak central coherence characterizes the spontaneous approach or automatic processing preference of people with autism and is thus a cognitive "style" best captured in open-ended tasks.

Visuo-Spatial Constructional Coherence

An elegant demonstration of weak coherence was given by Shah and Frith (1993), who showed that the well-documented facility of people with autism on the standard Wechsler Block Design task is due specifically to segmentation abilities. A sizable advantage was gained from presegmentation of designs for typically developing and intellectually impaired groups but was not observed in individuals with autism, suggesting that the latter processed the design in terms of its constituent blocks. Individuals with autism, both low- and high-functioning, also excel at the Embedded Figures Test (EFT), in which a small shape must be found within a larger design (Jolliffe & Baron-Cohen, 1997; Shah & Frith, 1983). Autistic weak coherence has also been demonstrated in studies showing good recognition of objects from detail despite poor integration of object parts (Jolliffe & Baron-Cohen, 2001) and detail-by-detail drawing style (Booth, Charlton, Hughes, & Happé, in press; Mottron & Belleville, 1993) with facility for copying even globally incoherent ("impossible") figures (Mottron, Belleville, & Ménard, 1999).

Perceptual Coherence

In recent years, there has been a renewal of interest in perceptual processes in autism. In particular, Plaisted and colleagues have suggested that the mechanism underlying weak coherence effects may operate at the perceptual level and specifically lies in enhanced discrimination and reduced generalization (see Plaisted, 2001). Plaisted hypothesizes that people with autism process features held in common between objects relatively poorly and process features unique to an object (those that discriminate items) relatively well. This is thought to underlie the pattern of superior visual search (O'Riordan, Plaisted, Driver, & Baron-Cohen, 2001), superior discrimination learning of highly confusable patterns (Plaisted, O'Riordan, & Baron-Cohen, 1998), and poor prototype extraction (Plaisted, O'Riordan, Aitken, & Killcross, submitted; but see also Klinger & Dawson, 2001), demonstrated by Plaisted, O'Riordan, and their colleagues in an elegant series of studies.

Mottron and colleagues also situate the mechanism for weak coherence effects at the level of perception. Their "enhanced perceptual functioning framework" posits overdeveloped low-level perception and atypical relationships between low- and high-level processing (see Mottron & Burack, 2001). They cite in favor of their proposal, but also compatible with Plaisted et al.'s account, the finding that people with autism show enhanced local processing and intact global processing of musical stimuli (Heaton, 2003; Heaton, Hermelin, & Pring, 1998; Mottron, Peretz, & Menard, 2000). While such findings may be at odds with the original description of weak coherence, they are in keeping with the suggestion (see preceding discussion of homograph reading) that weak coherence is a cognitive style or bias; that is, that global processing is possible for people with autism, but local processing is preferred in open-ended tasks.

Other evidence of good feature processing or local bias at the perceptual level includes reduced benefit from canonical pattern in dot counting (Jarrold & Russell, 1997), unusually high occurrence of absolute pitch (Heaton, Hermelin, & Pring, 1998), reduced susceptibility to visually induced motion (Gepner, Mestre, Masson, & de Schonen, 1995), a reduced McGurk effect (i.e., less influence from visual to auditory speech perception; DeGelder, Vroomen, & Van der Heide, 1991), and mixed findings regarding susceptibility to visual illusions (Happé, 1996; Ropar & Mitchell, 1999). It is notable that autobiographical accounts of autism often describe fragmented perception (Gerland, 1997).

Negative Findings

In general, then, people with autism are distinguished from age- and ability-matched comparison groups in showing relative attention to parts and relative inattention to wholes. People with autism *do* appear to integrate the properties of a single object (e.g., color and form in a visual search task; Plaisted et al., 1998) and to process the meaning of individual words (in Stroop tasks; Eskes, Bryson, & McCormick, 1990; Frith & Snowling, 1983) and objects (in memory tasks; Ameli, Courchesne, Lincoln, Kaufman, & Grillon, 1988; Pring & Hermelin,

1993). It seems to be in connecting words or objects that coherence is weak, although Lopez and Leekam (2003) have shown that straightforward priming from a word or scene (or perhaps local elements of the scene) does occur in autism. There have also been findings directly counter to those predicted by the weak coherence hypothesis. Ozonoff, Strayer, McMahon, and Filloux (1994) and Mottron, Burack, Stauder, and Robaey (1999) failed to find the predicted local advantage using the well-known Navon (1977) hierarchical figures; asked to report about large letters composed of smaller letters, people with autism showed the normal tendency to process the global form first and with greater interference from global to local levels. However, this paradigm is known to be sensitive to small changes of methodology (Kimchi, 1992); more recently, Plaisted, Swettenham, and Rees (1999) have found evidence of local advantage and interference from local to global stimuli in a condition where participants with autism were required to divide attention between local and global levels but not in a selective attention task. Another counterfinding comes from Brian and Bryson (1996), who found normal effects of meaning in a modified EFT, although they failed to find the well-replicated superiority on standard EFT, and it is unclear whether different results would have been obtained with groups matched on IQ. Overall, the evidence to date would appear to support the notion that processing of details and features is somewhat superior in autism, while the data on impairments of global or configural processing are less clear. What is certain is that the notion of central coherence requires further refinement and can only benefit from the alternative accounts and suggestions for underlying mechanisms now emerging in the field.

CENTRAL COHERENCE AND DEFICIT ACCOUNTS

There are relatively few studies of the relation between coherence and those key abilities thought to be impaired in autism, such as theory of mind or executive function. Central coherence was at first proposed to account for the theory of mind impairment as well as for nonsocial assets and deficits (Frith, 1989).

Deficits in theory of mind were considered just one consequence of weak central coherence: Understanding social interaction, and extracting the higher level representation of thoughts underlying behavior, was seen as the pinnacle of coherent processing and gist extraction. On this account, people with autism were socially impaired because they were unable to derive high-level meaning, necessary for development and use of theory of mind. Subsequently, Frith and Happé (1994) modified this view and proposed as a working hypothesis that weak central coherence and impaired theory of mind were independent facets of autism (for discussion, see Happé, 2000). However, it is likely that these two aspects of autism interact, and failure to integrate information in context may contribute to everyday life social difficulties. Featural processing may play a part in certain social impairments: Piecemeal processing of faces, for example (as reflected in reduced decrement from inversion in face recognition tests; Hobson, Ouston, & Lee, 1988), may hamper emotion recognition (McKelvie, 1995).

There is evidence that some people with autism who pass false belief tests still show weak central coherence. For example, theory of mind task performance is related to performance on the Comprehension subtest of the Wechsler scales (commonly thought to require pragmatic and social skill) but not to performance on the Block Design subtest (Happé, 1994), thought to be a marker of central coherence. Weak coherence seems to characterize people with autism regardless of their theory of mind ability in studies using perceptual (visual illusions; Happé, 1996) and verbal tasks (homograph reading; Happé, 1997). Jarrold, Butler, Cottington, and Jimenez (2000), however, found evidence of an inverse relation between ability to ascribe mental states to faces (interpreted as tapping theory of mind) and segmentation ability (interpreted as evidence of weak coherence; Shah & Frith, 1983). They found that performance on Baron-Cohen's "Eyes task" and speed on the EFT were significantly negatively correlated in a sample of undergraduates. In addition, in a group of children with autism, false belief task performance was negatively correlated with EFT performance, with the correlation reaching significance once verbal mental age was partialled out. Longitudinal studies would be necessary, however, to establish possible developmental causal relations between coherence and theory of mind (for further discussion, see Happé, 2001).

There have been two investigations of the possible relation between coherence and executive functions. Teunisse, Cools, van Spaendonck, Aerts, and Berger (2001) tested coherence and shifting ability in high-functioning adolescents with autism. They found weak coherence and poor shifting to be more common in the autism group than among comparison typically developing participants, but neither was universal. Performance on the two types of measure was unrelated and did not correlate with symptom severity or social ability. Booth et al. (2003) examined directly the possible role of one executive function, planning, on global/local processing in a drawing task. They compared boys with autism spectrum disorders and boys with attention-deficit/hyperactivity disorder (ADHD), as well as a typically developing comparison group, all matched on age and IQ. A drawing task requiring planning ahead (to add a requested internal element), showed the predicted planning deficits in both clinical groups, while analysis of drawing style showed that piecemeal drawing (e.g., starting with features, drawing detail to detail) was characteristic of the autism group only. Performance on the executive function and central coherence elements of the task did not correlate in the clinical groups, and the authors conclude that weak coherence is not common to all groups with executive dysfunction and that poor planning cannot explain detail focus in autism.

COHERENCE AND SAVANT SKILLS

Weak central coherence, then, may be a cognitive style capable of explaining autistic assets, as well as deficits, in experimental tasks. It may also be able to explain the high rate of savant skills among people with autism (but for an alternative account, see Mottron & Burack, 2001). In the area of musical talent, Heaton et al. (1998) have shown that musically naive children with autism are significantly better than matched controls at learning labels for individual pitches—the ability underlying ab-

solute pitch. Takeuchi and Hulse (1993) conclude from a review of the research on typical development that absolute pitch could be learned by most children before about 6 years of age, after which "a general developmental shift from perceiving individual features to perceiving relations among features makes [absolute pitch] difficult or impossible to acquire" (p. 345). If people with autism show a pervasive and persistent local processing bias, this would explain the high frequency of absolute pitch and the superior ability to learn note-name mappings at later ages.

In the domain of graphic talent, it also appears that the extraordinary skill of some individuals with autism may reflect a detail-focused processing style. Mottron and Belleville (1993) present a case study of an artist with autism whose productions are characterized by proceeding from one contiguous detail to the next, rather than the more usual sketching of outline followed by details. On a number of tasks (e.g., copying of impossible figures), this man showed fragmented perception and a bias toward local processing. Pring, Hermelin, and Heavey (1995), who tested part-whole processing (using modified Block Design tasks) in children with autism and normally developing children with and without artistic talent, conclude that there is "a facility in autism for seeing wholes in terms of their parts, rather than as unified gestalts" (p. 1073), and that this ability may be a general characteristic of individuals with an aptitude for drawing, with or without autism. Thus, a natural focus on features may be a predisposing factor for talent in both music and art.

CENTRAL COHERENCE AND NORMAL VARIATION IN COGNITIVE STYLE

Since weak central coherence gives both advantages and disadvantages, it is possible to think of this balance (between preference for parts versus wholes) as akin to a cognitive style—a style that may vary in the normal population. There may be a normal distribution of cognitive style from "weak" central coherence (preferential processing of parts, e.g., good proofreading), to "strong" (preferential processing of wholes, e.g., good gist memory). There is some disparate evidence of normal individual differences in local-global processing from infancy (Stoecker, Colombo, Frick, & Allen, 1998), through childhood (Chynn, Garrod, Demick, & DeVos, 1991), and in adulthood (Marendaz, 1985). Sex differences have been reported on tasks thought to tap local-global processing (Kramer, Ellenberg, Leonard, & Share, 1996), although studies have typically confounded type (local/global) and domain (visuo-spatial/ verbal) of processing. The possibility of sex differences in coherence is intriguing in relation to autism, which shows a very high male to female ratio especially at the high ability end of the spectrum. Might the normal distribution of coherence in males be shifted toward weak coherence and featural processing? At the extreme weak coherence end of the continuum may lie an area of increased risk for autism—individuals who fall at this extreme end of the continuum of cognitive style may be predisposed to develop autism if unlucky enough to suffer the additional deficits (e.g., impaired theory of mind, executive dysfunctions) apparent in this disorder.

CENTRAL COHERENCE AND THE EXTENDED PHENOTYPE OF AUTISM

As a cognitive style, rather than deficit, weak central coherence is an interesting contender for an aspect of autism that is transmitted genetically and characterizes the relatives of individuals with autism. We compared cognitive style in parents of boys with autism, with dyslexia, or without developmental disorder (Happé, Briskman, & Frith, 2001). The parents, and especially fathers, of the children with autism showed significantly superior performance on tasks favoring local processing: They excelled at the EFT, at (unsegmented) block design, and at accurately judging visual illusions. They were also more likely than other fathers to give local completions to sentence stems such as, "The sea tastes of salt and . . . ?," "pepper." In all these respects, they resembled individuals with autism, but for these fathers their detail-focused cognitive style was an asset, not a deficit. Performance on the tests of coherence also related strongly to self-ratings of everyday preferences and abilities in detail-focused areas but not to self-ratings of social skills and interests (Briskman, Happé, & Frith, 2001). These

results fit with work by Baron-Cohen and colleagues, showing that fathers of children with autism are fast at the EFT (Baron-Cohen & Hammer, 1997) and overrepresented in professions such as engineering (Baron-Cohen, Wheelwright, Stott, Bolton, & Goodyer, 1997; but see counterargument by Jarrold & Routh, 1998). However, while Baron-Cohen et al. explain their results in terms of superior "folk physics" (intuitive understanding of physical systems) or, more recently, superior "systemizing" (Baron-Cohen, 2002), the hypothesis of weak central coherence predicts that people with autism and their relatives will be characterized by expertise only with those mechanical (and nonmechanical) systems where detail focus is an advantage. Weak central coherence also stretches beyond the visuo-spatial domain and predicts piecemeal processing in verbal tasks (see earlier discussion), not easily accounted for by superior folk physics or systemizing.

CONCLUSION

Many challenges remain to the central coherence account, not least to specify the cognitive and neural mechanisms for coherence. Should we think of a single, central mechanism integrating information from diverse modules/ systems for higher level meaning/configuration? Or should coherence be thought of as a property of each subsystem, a setting for the relative precedence of global versus local processing, repeated throughout the brain? We are currently exploring individual differences in coherence across and within a number of domains to establish whether, for example, degree of coherence in a verbal task predicts degree of coherence in a visuo-spatial task.

Neuropsychological lesion and brain imaging studies may also give clues to the unitary or distributed basis of central coherence. The right hemisphere has long been implicated in global, integrative, and context-sensitive processing. Individuals with acquired right hemisphere damage show deficits on visuo-spatial constructional tasks, maintaining details but missing global configuration (Robertson & Lamb, 1991). Discourse also becomes piecemeal in such patients, with difficulties in integrating verbal information and extracting gist

(Benowitz, Moya, & Levine, 1990). Functional imaging work, too, suggests a role for right hemisphere regions in configural processing. Fink et al. (1997), using fMRI, found right lingual gyrus activation during attention to global aspects of a hierarchical figure (e.g., an H made up of Ss) and left inferior occipital activation during local focus. Electrophysiological (ERP) studies, too, suggest right hemisphere activity during global versus local tasks (Heinze, Hinrichs, Scholz, Burchert, & Mangun, 1998). Since people with autism show piecemeal processing, as well as repetitive stereotyped behavior (normally suppressed by regions in the right hemisphere; Brugger, Monsch, & Johnson, 1996), it is tempting to look for the origins of autism in right hemisphere anomalies. However, there is relatively little conclusive evidence of localized and specific structural damage. At least one brain imaging study to date has found right hemisphere abnormalities in (three) individuals with a high-functioning form of autism, Asperger syndrome (McKelvey, Lambert, Mottron, & Shevell, 1995). However, evidence of damage in limbic, frontal, and cerebellar regions has also been reported, and it is by no means clear which anomalies are specific and universal to autism.

It is unlikely, however, that autism will prove to be the result of damage confined to one brain region, and the very notion of central coherence suggests diffuse differences in brain organization. One intriguing finding, in this respect, is that some individuals with autism have larger or heavier brains than do comparison groups, with increased cell packing in several areas (Aylward, Minshew, Field, Sparks, & Singh, 2002; Piven et al., 1995). Recent work suggests an early, transient period of brain overgrowth, due perhaps to an abnormal acceleration of postnatal growth processes or failure of the usual pruning (Courchesne, Carper, & Akshoomoff, 2003). This brain growth dysregulation appears to result in reduced functional connectivity (e.g., Just, Cherkassky, Keller, & Minshew, in press). Processing with excess neurons may result in a failure to process information for gist: If there is the capacity for registering and recalling each exemplar, perhaps there would be no drive to extract prototypes or make generalizations. Cohen (1994) has presented a computational model of autism, in which lack of generalization results from an increase in units—an intriguing example of how computational analyses may interact with neuroanatomical data and psychological theory to help solve the puzzle of autism. It is intriguing to think that the cognitive style of weak coherence in autism, with its attendant assets and deficits, might result from an "embarrassment of riches" at the neural level.

Cross-References

Other theoretical perspectives are provided in Chapters 21 to 23 and 25 to 26; developmental aspects of autism are addressed in Chapters 8 to 10.

REFERENCES

Ameli, R., Courchesne, E., Lincoln, A., Kaufman, A. S., & Grillon, C. (1988). Visual memory processes in high-functioning individuals with autism. *Journal of Autism and Developmental Disorders, 18,* 601–615.

Aylward, E. H., Minshew, N. J., Field, K., Sparks, B. F., & Singh, N. (2002). Effects of age on brain volume and head circumference in autism. *Neurology, 59,* 175–183.

Baron-Cohen, S. (2002). The extreme male brain theory of autism. *Trends in Cognitive Sciences, 6,* 248–254.

Baron-Cohen, S., & Hammer, J. (1997). Parents of children with Asperger syndrome: What is the cognitive phenotype? *Journal of Cognitive Neuroscience, 9,* 548–554.

Baron-Cohen, S., Wheelwright, S., Stott, C., Bolton, P., & Goodyer, I. (1997). Is there a link between engineering and autism? *Autism: Journal of Research and Practice, 1,* 101–109.

Bartlett, F. C. (1932). *Remembering: A study in experimental and social psychology.* Cambridge, England: Cambridge University Press.

Benowitz, L. I., Moya, K. L., & Levine, D. N. (1990). Impaired verbal reasoning and constructional apraxia in subjects with right hemisphere damage. *Neuropsychologia, 23,* 231–241.

Bhatt, R. S., Rovee-Collier, C., & Shyi, G. C. W. (1994). Global and local processing of incidental information and memory retrieval at 6 months. *Journal of Experimental Child Psychology, 57,* 141–162.

Booth, R., Charlton, R., Hughes, C., & Happé, F. (2003). Disentangling weak coherence and executive dysfunction: Planning drawing in Autism and ADHD. *Philosophical Transactions of the Royal Society, 358*(1430), 387–392.

Brian, J. A., & Bryson, S. E. (1996). Disembedding performance and recognition memory in autism/PDD, *Journal of Child Psychology and Psychiatry, 37,* 865–872.

Briskman, J., Happé, F., & Frith, U. (2001). Exploring the cognitive phenotype of autism: Weak "central coherence" in parents and siblings of children with autism. II. Real-life skills and preferences. *Journal of Child Psychology and Psychiatry, 42,* 309–316.

Brugger, P., Monsch, A. U., & Johnson, S. A. (1996). Repetitive behavior and repetition avoidance: The role of the right hemisphere. *Journal of Psychiatry and Neuroscience, 21,* 53–56.

Chynn, E. W., Garrod, A., Demick, J., & DeVos, E. (1991). Correlations among field dependence-independence, sex, sex-role stereotype, and age of preschoolers. *Perceptual and Motor Skills, 73,* 747–756.

Cohen, I. L. (1994). An artificial neural network analogue of learning in autism. *Biological Psychiatry, 36,* 5–20.

Coren, S., & Enns, J. T. (1993). Size contrast as a function of conceptual similarity between test and inducers. *Perception and Psychophysics, 54,* 579–588.

Courchesne, E., Carper, R., & Akshoomoff, N. (2003). Evidence of brain overgrowth in the first year of life in autism. *Journal of the American Medical Association, 290,* 337–344.

DeGelder, B., Vroomen, J., & Van der Heide, L. (1991). Face recognition and lip-reading in autism. *European Journal of Cognitive Psychology, 3,* 69–86.

Dennis, M., Lazenby, A. L., & Lockyer, L. (2001). Inferential language in high-functioning children with autism. *Journal of Autism and Developmental Disorders, 31,* 47–54.

Eskes, G. A., Bryson, S. E., & McCormick, T. A. (1990). Comprehension of concrete and abstract words in autistic children. *Journal of Autism and Developmental Disorders, 20,* 61–73.

Fink, G. R., Halligan, P. W., Marshall, J. C., Frith, C. D., Frackowiak, R. S. J., & Dolan, R. J. (1997). Neural mechanisms involved in the processing of global and local aspects of hierarchically organized visual stimuli. *Brain, 120,* 1779–1791.

Freedland, R. L., & Dannemiller, J. L. (1996). Nonlinear pattern vision processes in early infancy. *Infant Behavior and Development, 19,* 21–32.

Frith, U. (1989). *Autism: Explaining the enigma.* Oxford: Blackwell.

Frith, U., & Happé, F. (1994). Autism: Beyond "theory of mind." *Cognition, 50,* 115–132.

Frith, U., & Snowling, M. (1983). Reading for meaning and reading for sound in autistic and dyslexic children. *Journal of Developmental Psychology, 1,* 329–342.

Gepner, B., Mestre, D., Masson, G., & de Schonen, S. (1995). Postural effects of motion vision in young autistic children. *NeuroReport, 6,* 1211–1214.

Gerland, G. (1997). *A real person: Life on the outside* (J. Tate, Trans.). London: Souvenir Press.

Happé, F. G. E. (1994). Wechsler IQ profile and theory of mind in autism: A research note. *Journal of Child Psychology and Psychiatry, 35,* 1461–1471.

Happé, F. G. E. (1996). Studying weak central coherence at low levels: Children with autism do not succumb to visual illusions, a research note. *Journal of Child Psychology and Psychiatry, 37,* 873–877.

Happé, F. G. E. (1997). Central coherence and theory of mind in autism: Reading homographs in context. *British Journal of Developmental Psychology, 15,* 1–12.

Happé, F. G. E. (1999). Autism: Cognitive deficit or cognitive style? *Trends in Cognitive Sciences, 3,* 216–222.

Happé, F. G. E. (2000). Parts and wholes, meaning and minds: Central coherence and its relation to theory of mind. In S. Baron-Cohen, H. Tager-Flusberg, & D. Cohen (Eds.), *Understanding other minds: Perspectives from autism and developmental cognitive neuroscience* (pp. 203–221). Oxford, England: Oxford University Press.

Happé, F. G. E. (2001). Social and non-social development in autism: Where are the links. In J. A. Burack, T. Charman, N. Yirmiya, & P. R. Zelazo (Eds.), *Perspectives on development in autism* (pp. 237–253). Hillsdale, NJ: Erlbaum.

Happé, F. G. E., Briskman, J., & Frith, U. (2001). Exploring the cognitive phenotype of autism: Weak "central coherence" in parents and siblings of children with autism: I. Experimental tests. *Journal of Child Psychology and Psychiatry, 42,* 299–307.

Heaton, P. (2003). Pitch memory, labelling and disembedding in autism. *Journal of Child Psychology and Psychiatry, 44,* 543–551.

Heaton, P., Hermelin, B., & Pring, L. (1998). Autism and pitch processing: A precursor for savant musical ability. *Music Perception, 15,* 291–305.

Heinze, H. J., Hinrichs, H., Scholz, M., Burchert, W., & Mangun, G. R. (1998). Neural mechanisms of global and local processing: A combined PET and ERP study. *Journal of Cognitive Neuroscience, 10,* 485–498.

Hermelin, B., & O'Connor, N. (1967). Remembering of words by psychotic and subnormal children. *British Journal of Psychology, 58,* 213–218.

Hobson, R. P., Ouston, J., & Lee, T. (1988, November). What's in a face? The case of autism. *British Journal of Psychology, 79*(4), 441–453.

Jarrold, C., Butler, D. W., Cottington, E. M., & Jimenez, F. (2000). Linking theory of mind and central coherence bias in autism and in the general population. *Developmental Psychology, 36,* 126–138.

Jarrold, C., & Routh, D. A. (1998). Is there really a link between engineering and autism? A reply to Baron-Cohen et al., Autism, 1997 1(1), 101–109. *Autism: Journal of Research and Practice, 2,* 281–289.

Jarrold, C., & Russell, J. (1997). Counting abilities in autism: Possible implications for central coherence theory. *Journal of Autism and Developmental Disorders, 27,* 25–37.

Jolliffe, T. (1997). Central coherence dysfunction in autistic spectrum disorder. Unpublished doctoral dissertation, University of Cambridge.

Jolliffe, T., & Baron-Cohen, S. (1997). Are people with autism and Asperger syndrome faster than normal on the Embedded Figures Test? *Journal of Child Psychology and Psychiatry, 38,* 527–534.

Jolliffe, T., & Baron-Cohen, S. (1999). A test of central coherence theory; linguistic processing in high-functioning adults with autism or Asperger's syndrome: Is local coherence impaired? *Cognition, 71,* 149–185.

Jolliffe, T., & Baron-Cohen, S. (2001). A test of central coherence theory: Can adults with high-functioning autism or Asperger's syndrome integrate fragments of an object? *Cognitive Neuropsychiatry, 6,* 193–216.

Just, M. A., Cherkassky, V. L., Keller, T. A., & Minshew, N. J. (in press). Cortical activation and synchronization during sentence comprehension in high-functioning autism: Evidence of underconnectivity. *Brain.*

Kanner, L. (1943). Autistic disturbances of affective contact. *Nervous Child, 2,* 217–250.

Kimchi, R. (1992). Primacy of wholistic processing and the global/local paradigm: A critical review. *Psychological Bulletin, 112,* 24–38.

Klinger, L. G., & Dawson, G. (2001). Prototype formation in autism. *Development & Psychopathology, 13,* 111–124.

Kramer, J. H., Ellenberg, L., Leonard, J., & Share, L. J. (1996). Developmental sex differences in global-local perceptual bias. *Neuropsychology, 10,* 402–407.

Lopez, B., & Leekam, S. R. (2003). Do children with autism fail to process information in context? *Journal of Child Psychology and Psychiatry, 44,* 285–300.

Marendaz, C. (1985). Global precedence and field dependence: Visual routines? *Cahiers de Psychologie Cognitive, 5,* 727–745.

McKelvey, J. R., Lambert, R., Mottron, L., & Shevell, M. I. (1995). Right-hemisphere dysfunction in Asperger's syndrome. *Journal of Child Neurology, 10,* 310–314.

McKelvie, S. J. (1995). Emotional expression in upside-down faces: Evidence for configurational and componential processing. *British Journal of Social Psychology, 34,* 325–334.

Miller, L. K. (1999). The savant syndrome: Intellectual impairment and exceptional skill. *Psychological Bulletin, 125,* 31–46.

Mottron, L., & Belleville, S. (1993). A study of perceptual analysis in a high-level autistic subject with exceptional graphic abilities. *Brain and Cognition, 23,* 279–309.

Mottron, L., Belleville, S., & Ménard, A. (1999). Local bias in autistic subjects as evidenced by graphic tasks: Perceptual hierarchization or working memory deficit? *Journal of Child Psychology and Psychiatry, 40,* 743–755.

Mottron, L., & Burack, J. A. (2001). Enhanced perceptual functioning in the development of autism. In J. A. Burack, T. Charman, N. Yirmiya, & P. R. Zelazo (Eds.), *The development of autism: Perspectives from theory and research* (pp. 131–148). Hillsdale, NJ: Erlbaum.

Mottron, L., Burack, J. A., Stauder, J. E. A., & Robaey, P. (1999). Perceptual processing among high-functioning persons with autism. *Journal of Child Psychology and Psychiatry, 40,* 203–211.

Mottron, L., Peretz, I., & Menard, E. (2000). Local and global processing of music in high-functioning persons with autism: Beyond central coherence? *Journal of Child Psychology and Psychiatry, 41,* 1057–1065.

Navon, D. (1977). Forest before trees: The precedence of global features in visual perception. *Cognitive Psychology, 9,* 353–383.

Norbury, C. F., & Bishop, D. M. V. (2002). Inferential processing and story recall in children with communication problems: A comparison of specific language impairment, pragmatic language impairment and high-functioning autism. *International Journal of Language and Communication Disorders, 37,* 227–251.

1a.   1b.

Figure 25.1 Examples of (a) responding to joint attention bids, (b) initiating joint attention with a point, and (c) initiating joint attention with alternating gaze. *Source:* "A Preliminary Manual for the Abridged Early Social Communication Scales (ESCS)", by P. Mundy, A. Hogan, and P. Doehring, 1996, available from http://yin.psy.miami.edu:80/Child/Pmundy/manual.html; and "Assessing Interactional Competencies: The Early Social Communication Scales," by J. M. Seibert, A. E. Hogan, and P. C. Mundy, 1982, *Infant Mental Health Journal, 3,* pp. 244–245.

tal theory suggests that a large part of early ontology hinges on experience, including the experiences children create for themselves through their own actions (Cicchetti & Tucker, 1994; Gottlieb & Halpern, 2002; Piaget, 1952). More recently, theory also has begun to suggest that not only do infants play a role in creating critical experiences for themselves, but also a failure to create these self-generated social experiences may contribute to suboptimal neurodevelopmental outcomes (cf. Greenough, Black, & Wallace, 1987). We have attempted to incorporate some of these important ideas into our own efforts to understand the significance of joint attention disturbance in autism. The result is a coactive model of development (Gottlieb & Halpern, 2002) that suggests there may be a complex interplay between early behavior disturbance (i.e., symptoms of autism) and subsequent neurodevelopmental pathology in autism. In particular, joint attention distur-

bance may be viewed as associated with a robust disturbance in the early tendency of young children with autism to initiate social-orienting and sharing with others (Dawson, Meltzoff, Osterling, Rinaldi, & Brown, 1998; Mundy, 1995). This behavioral disturbance reduces the flow of social information to the child to such an extent that it contributes to subsequent disorganization in the neural, as well as behavioral, development of these children (Dawson, Webb, et al., 2002; Klin, Warren, Schultz, & Volkmar, 2003; Mundy & Crowson, 1997; Mundy & Neal, 2001). We review elements of this coactive model of the neurodevelopmental disturbance of autism later in this chapter.

The observation that autism is characterized by a deficit in the *initiation of joint attention* with others may also be especially important as we attempt to understand the brain systems that play a role in this syndrome. Currently, much of the brain-behavior research and theory on the social impairments of autism emphasizes the study of the perception of social behavior rather than systems involved in the initiation of social behavior (Baron-Cohen et al., 2000; Carver & Dawson, in press; Critchley et al., 2000). This emphasis is not necessarily misplaced because individuals with autism display deficits in social perception (e.g., Baron-Cohen et al., 1999; Hobson, 1993; Langdell, 1978; Sigman, Kasari, Kwon, & Yirmiya, 1992). Moreover, the interpretation of research on the neurodevelopment of social perception in autism is supported by a rich corpus of data on the brain systems that are involved in the perception of social behaviors in primates and humans (Adolphs, 2001; Brothers, 1990; Elgar & Cambell, 2001; LeDoux, 1989). However, as noted earlier, autism is marked not only by social-perceptual or social-information processing difficulties but also by impairments in the spontaneous generation and expression of social behaviors and cognition (U. Frith, 1989; Klin et al., 2003; Leslie, 1987; Minshew et al., 2002; Mundy, 1995). Therefore, in addition to research on the neural systems involved in social perception, neurodevelopmental studies of the systems involved in the self-initiation of social behavior may be of great importance for research on autism.

It may be instructive to recognize that the brain systems involved in *initiating* social behavior may not be identical to those involved in the *perception* of social behavior. For example, several papers have emphasized the importance of ventral "social brain" brain systems in perception of social behaviors and the social pathology of autism. These brain systems include the orbitofrontal cortex, temporal cortical areas including the superior temporal sulcus (STS) and superior temporal gyrus (STG), and subcortical areas such as the amygdala (Adolphs, 2001; Bachvalier, 1994; Baron-Cohen et al., 2000; Brothers, 1990). In contrast, when the tendency to initiate social behaviors, such as joint attention bids or social-cognitive problem solving is studied, research suggests that a more dorsal, medial-frontal cortical (DMFC) system may be involved in autism (U. Frith & Frith, 1999, 2001; Mundy, 2003). Thus, understanding the functional neurodevelopment of dorsal sys-

tems for the self-initiation of social behaviors and cognition and how these dorsal systems relate to ventral social-perceptual systems constitutes a goal of the highest order in the current field of research on autism (cf. Frith & Frith, 1999, 2001). Indeed, it is important to recognize that we do not yet clearly understand the degree to which the initiation of social behaviors serves to organize social perception (or vice versa). Detailed knowledge of this topic may be critical to understanding the atypical neurodevelopment of autism.

In this chapter, we take a small step in this direction by reviewing research that links joint attention development and its disturbance in autism to the DMFC system. We also provide a discussion of the potential links between research on the DMFC and brain systems involved in social perception. Finally, we attempt to link the coactive model of the neurodevelopmental disturbance of autism and research on the DMFC. To provide a foundation for these discussions, we begin with a brief overview of joint attention disturbance in autism.

JOINT ATTENTION AND SOCIAL IMPAIRMENT IN AUTISM

As is well known, Kanner (1943/1973) first noted that the pathognomonic feature of autism was the "children's inability to relate themselves in the ordinary way to people and situations" because "these children have come into the world with an innate inability to form the usual biologically provided affective contact with people, just as other children come into the world with innate physical or intellectual handicaps" (Kanner, 1943/1973, pp. 42–43). It is less well known that in the three decades following Kanner's and Asperger's (1944) identification of the syndrome, very little empirical or theoretical work was devoted to defining the nature of the fundamental social impairments that afflict these children (Howlin, 1978). One result of this paucity of information was a relatively impoverished diagnostic system. The statement that children with autism display "a pervasive lack of responsiveness to others" (e.g., American Psychiatric Association, 1980) was the only descriptor of the social deficits associated with autism until the late 1980s (e.g., American Psychiatric Association, 1987). This descriptor painted a broad but inaccurate picture of the social behavior of these children. It described only the most aloof subgroup of children with autism and contributed substantially to an underestimation of the prevalence of autism (see Wing & Potter, 2002, for a related discussion). Indeed, it was only with the publication of the most recent nosology (e.g., American Psychiatric Association, 1994) that there are sufficiently well-articulated diagnostic criteria to *begin* to provide a clear and comprehensive description of the social impairments of autism.

The observation that early social-communication disturbance in autism is exemplified by a robust failure to adequately develop joint attention skills (Curcio, 1978; Loveland & Landry, 1986; Mundy, Sigman, Ungerer, & Sherman, 1986; Wetherby & Prutting, 1984) has contributed to the improved description of the social deficits of autism (Mundy & Crowson, 1997; Ozonoff & South, 2001). As noted previously, the term *joint attention skills* refers to the capacity of individuals to coordinate or share attention with a social partner regarding an object or event. This capacity in infancy may involve only the social coordination of overt aspects of visual attention, as when a toddler shows a toy to a parent (Carpenter, Nagell, & Tomasello, 1998; Rheingold, Hay, & West, 1976). However, with development, joint attention skills in older children and adults also play a role in the social coordination of covert aspects of attention, as when social partners coordinate attention vis-à-vis psychological phenomena, such as ideas, intentions, or emotions (Bretherton, McNew, & Beeghly-Smith, 1981; Tomasello, 1999). Thus, the regulation and sharing of overt visual attention in early development is thought to contribute (in a manner we do not yet fully understand) to the subsequent development of the capacity to socially share aspects of cognition later in development.

Joint attention skill deficits in children with autism involve a robust and early-onset disturbance in the tendency to share or coordinate overt visual attention with a social partner. It is manifest in an attenuation of the functional use of eye contact, affect, and gestures for the sharing experiences with others (Kasari, Sigman, Mundy, & Yirmiya, 1990; Mundy et al., 1986). In previous work, we argued that joint attention disturbance in autism was central to what Kanner described as the "children's inability to relate themselves in the ordinary way to people and situations" (Mundy & Sigman, 1989).

The capacity for joint attention begins to emerge by 6 months of age (Scaife & Bruner, 1975) and takes several different forms, each of which may be reliably measured in infants and young children. One behavior involves infants' ability to follow the direction of gaze, head turn, and/or pointing gesture of another person (Scaife & Bruner, 1975). This behavior is called *responding to joint attention skill* (RJA; Mundy et al., 2003; Seibert, Hogan, & Mundy, 1982). Another type of skill involves infants' use of eye contact and/or deictic gestures (e.g., pointing or showing) to spontaneously initiate coordinated attention with a social partner. This type of protodeclarative act (Bates, 1976) is referred to as *initiating joint attention* (IJA; Mundy et al., 2003; Seibert et al., 1982). These behaviors, especially IJA, appear to serve social functions as the goal, and reinforcement for these behaviors seems to relate simply to the value of sharing experience with others (Bates, 1976; Mundy, 1995). Social attention coordination may also be used for imperative purposes (Bates, 1976). Infants and young children may use eye contact and gestures to initiate attention coordination with another person to elicit aid in obtaining an object or event. This may be referred to as a proto-imperative act (Bates, 1976) or *initiating behavior requests* (IBR; Mundy et al., 2003). This type of attention coordination serves a less social function, insofar as it is employed as part of an instrumental goal of obtaining a desired object or event (Bates, 1976; Mundy, 1995).

Joint attention skill acquisition is a major milestone of early development (Bakeman & Adamson, 1984), in part, because these skills assist infants in organizing social information to facilitate their own learning and development. In language learning, for example, parents do not sit with their infants in structured situations to teach vocabulary word by word. Rather, much of early language acquisition takes place in unstructured or incidental social-learning situations where: (1) the parent provides a learning opportunity by referring to a new object or event in the environment, but (2) the infant may need to discriminate among a number of stimuli in the environment in order to focus on the correct object/event and acquire the new word-object-event association. Thus, the infant is confronted with the possibility of committing a referential mapping error or focusing on the wrong stimuli during incidental word learning opportunities (Baldwin, 1995). To resolve this problem, the infant may attend to and process the direction of gaze of the parent (i.e., use RJA skill) to limit the number of potential stimuli they need to attend to, thereby increasing the likelihood of a correct word learning experience (Baldwin, 1995). Similarly, when the infant initiates a bid for joint attention, the responsive caregiver may follow the child's line of regard and take advantage of the child's focus of attention to provide a new word in a context that maximizes the learning opportunity (cf. Tomasello, 1995). Joint attention skills assist infants in organizing social information input and avoiding referential mapping errors in these situations (Baldwin, 1995). Hence, joint attention may be regarded as an early developing *self-organizing facility* that is critical to much of subsequent social and cognitive development (e.g., Baldwin, 1995; Bruner, 1975; Mundy & Neal, 2001).

Children with autism, unfortunately, display robust levels of impairments in the tendency to initiate and respond to joint attention bids. This impairment contributes to a significant deficit in the capacity for early social learning. Observations suggest that joint attention disturbance may be manifest in children with autism as early as between 12 and 18 months of age (Osterling & Dawson, 1994; Swettenham et al., 1998). Theoretically, from early in development, children with autism display deficits in types of social behaviors that ordinarily serve to organize and facilitate subsequent social and communicative development. It is interesting, though, that this deficit in early social-communication skill is not pervasive as children with autism display only modest evidence of IBR impairments on measures of social attention coordination for instrumental purposes (see Charman, 1998; Leekam & Moore, 2001; Mundy & Crowson, 1997, for reviews).

The self-organizing function of joint attention in autism may be illustrated with findings from a recent important study by Bono and Sigman (in press). In this study, 29 children with autism were followed longitudinally between approximately 4 and 5 years of age. Data on the amount of time per week children were in structured interventions were collected, as were data on joint attention abilities using the Early Social-Communication Scales (ESCS; Mundy et al., 2003) and data from standardized language assessments. The results revealed that across this 1-year period, both IJA and RJA were significantly related to language gains. Alternatively, amount of intervention was only weakly related to language gains across the 1-year interval. However, significant conditional intervention effects were observed such that more time in structured intervention was associated with significant language gains for children with better-developed RJA skills. Thus, measures of joint attention may be a marker of individual differences in intervention responsivity among children with autism. One possible interpretation of this finding is that differences in RJA skills reflected differences in the ability of children with autism to self-organize information in social learning situations and that this skill contributes to their capacity to benefit from early intervention.

In addition to reflecting a self-organizing disturbance, joint attention deficits in autism may reflect impairments in the social-cognitive capacity to represent another person's perspectives (Leslie & Happé, 1989), as well as a disturbance in the social motivation to approach or orient to social partners (Mundy, 1995). Joint attention deficits in children with autism, however, should not be confused with processes associated with attachment because children with autism display atypical, but clear, signs of attachment (Sigman & Mundy, 1989; see also Pierce, Frank, Farshad, & Courchesne, 2001). Moreover, attachment does not appear to be strongly related to joint attention skills in children with autism or typical development (Capps, Sigman, & Mundy, 1994; Crowson, Mundy, Neal, & Meyer, 2003).

Although young children with autism display deficits in both IJA and RJA skills, the impairment in RJA appears to remit to a significant degree with development (Leekam & Moore, 2001; Mundy, Sigman, & Kasari, 1994). The impairment in IJA, however, remains in older children (Baron-Cohen, 1995). Research also suggests that symptom intensity (Mundy et al., 1994) and symptom course, such as the tendency to initiate interaction with peers in later childhood and adolescence (Lord, Floody, Anderson, & Pickles, 2003; Sigman & Ruskin, 1999), are related to individual differences in IJA, but not RJA impairment among young children with autism. A dissociated pattern of IJA and RJA development is also observed in typical development and may occur because IJA and RJA reflect different integrations of neurodevelopmental, social-cognitive, and social-emotional processes (Mundy, Card, & Fox, 2000; Mundy & Willoughby, 1998).

IJA reflects the tendency to spontaneously initiate social attention coordination behavior, whereas RJA is a measure of the tendency to respond to another person's signal to shift attention. Hence, IJA may be more affected by executive and social-motivation processes involved in the generation and self-initiation of behavioral goals than RJA (Mundy, 1995; Mundy & Willoughby, 1998; Mundy et al., 2000). In particular, IJA appears to involve the tendency to spontaneously initiate episodes of sharing the affective experience of an object or event with a social partner (Mundy, Kasari, & Sigman, 1992). Indeed, a significant component of IJA disturbance in autism may be explained in terms of an attenuation of the tendency to initiate episodes of shared positive affect with a social partner (Kasari et al., 1990). However, a recent report has failed to replicate this finding, suggesting the need for more research on this important topic (Plousia, 2002).

This literature has led to the instantiation of joint attention disturbance, and especially IJA disturbance, as a cardinal symptom of autism. For example, a "lack of spontaneous seeking to share enjoyment, interests, or achievements with other people (e.g., by a lack of showing, bringing or pointing out objects of interest)" is now one of four symptoms of the

social impairment of autism in a current nosology (American Psychiatric Association, 2000, p. 75). Thus, many of the current autism diagnostic and screening instruments include measures of joint attention (Baron-Cohen et al., 1996; Charman, 1998; Lord et al., 1999; Stone, Coonrod, & Ousley, 2000). The gold standard Autism Diagnostic Observation Schedule (Lord et al., 1999) even reflects the notion of a developmental dissociation in joint attention. Measures used for diagnosis with the youngest children (Module 1) include both IJA and RJA assessments, while Module 2 designed for developmentally more advanced children includes only the IJA measures in the diagnostic scores.

JOINT ATTENTION, SOCIAL ORIENTING, AND AUTISM

Given its central role in the phenotype of autism, it is not surprising that considerable effort over the past 20 years has been directed toward understanding the development of joint attention. Most models of joint attention disturbance, indeed most models of autism, approach the social symptoms of the syndrome from a relatively linear and deterministic perspective. These models view behavioral symptoms of the syndrome, such as joint attention disturbance, as the end point of a unidirectional process. This process starts with some form of genotypic atypicality that leads directly to neurodevelopmental anomalies, which, in turn, are unerringly expressed as abnormal social behavior (Minshew, Johnson, & Luna, 2001). For example, social behavior disturbance in autism has been viewed as an end-point outcome of "core" neurodevelopmental deficits in a social-cognitive module (Baron-Cohen, 1995; Leslie & Happé, 1989), executive functions (McEvoy, Rogers, & Pennington, 1993), or cerebellar contributions to attention control (Courchesne et al., 1994). However, an understanding of atypical, as well as typical development, may benefit from a less linear and deterministic perspective (Cicchetti & Tucker, 1994). "Epigenetic," "relational," or "coactive" models of causality suggest that biological and environmental experience *interact over time and maturation* to yield developmental disturbance (Gottlieb &

Halpern, 2002). Moreover, "experience" as a causal influence on development includes not only external sources of stimulation but also forms of stimulation that the individual actively generates through self-initiated interactions with the world (Piaget, 1952; Scarr, 1992). Thus, rather than end points in pathological process, it may be especially important to understand how the early onset of impairments in major milestones of social development potentially contributes to the subsequent unfolding of the full syndrome of autism across the first years of life. It may be especially instructive to consider the potential developmental impact of an early disturbance of the self-organizing functions of joint attention.

To understand this developmental impact, consider the notion that joint attention disturbance may be part of a broader social-orienting impairment in autism. The term *social-orienting impairment* has been introduced to the field by the seminal work of Dawson et al. (1998), who observed that children with autism may display a more robust orienting deficit to social rather than nonsocial sounds. However, the notion that children with autism display a deficit in orienting to social stimuli has a long history in research on autism. For example, it can be discerned in various forms in models of autism that emphasize impairments in the first year of life in cerebellar processes (Courchesne et al., 1994) or in the biological reward mechanisms that serve to promote social behavior (Mundy, 1995; Panksepp, 1979). The latter impairments may be related to a disturbance in the early onset of orbital and/or more dorsal medial-frontal contributions to orienting and learning (Dawson, Munson, et al., 2002; Mundy, 2003; Mundy et al., 2000), as well as problems in the perception or processing of affect and behavioral contingencies (Dawson & Lewy, 1989; Hobson, 1993). All these models embrace the supposition that a social-orienting impairment may reflect an initial or core aspect of pathology that has ramifications for the subsequent development of social, cognitive, and even neurological disturbance in autism.

Our own version of social-orienting impairment in autism is based in part on the assumption that in the first year of life, there are predispositions that guide attention deployment to relevant aspects of the environment (Bahrick & Lickliter, 1999; Karmiloff-Smith, 1995). These predispositions provide a "preparedness with which human infants come to the task of learning" (Tomasello, 1999, p. 305) and a starting point around which subsequent brain and behavior development organizes. In particular, infants may display a predisposition toward social information processing (Blass, 1999; Cummins & Cummins, 1999). A disturbance of such a bias in autism may result from imbalances in general aspects of early perception and information processing (Mottron & Burack, 2001) or aspects of perception that are specific to social information processing (e.g., Adolphs, 2001). In any event, a critical assumption of our social-orienting model has been that joint attention skill deficits in children with autism reflect a disturbance in the predilection to spontaneously orient to and process social information that is normally manifest in the first years of life (Mundy, 1995; Mundy & Sigman, 1989).

Results of several studies suggest social-orienting and joint attention skills are related and that impairments in these domains may be manifest very early in children with autism. For example, 20-month-old infants who were subsequently diagnosed with autism at 42 months have been observed to display far less social orienting, or spontaneous gaze shifts between objects and people, than did control infants (Swettenham et al., 1998). Measuring spontaneously alternating gaze between an object and a person is also a core component of the assessment of IJA skill. In fact, it was the type of behavior that best discriminated children with autism from comparison children in our original joint attention study (Mundy et al., 1986).

Other research also speaks to the commonality and very early onset of social-orienting and joint attention disturbance in autism. The literature on normal development indicates that forms of social-orienting and joint attention skill development emerge between 6 and 12 months of age (Morales, Mundy, & Rojas, 1998; see Moore & Dunham, 1995, for review). In research on autism, studies of family videotape records suggest that by 12 months of age, children with autism may display evidence of a disturbance in joint attention and social orienting (Osterling & Dawson, 1994). Measures of joint attention skills have also contributed to the very early identification of autism at 18 months of age in a sample of 16,000 children (Baron-Cohen et al., 1996). Even earlier social-orienting measures such as parent reports of eye contact, showing interest in others, reacting when spoken to, and laughing to others may serve to facilitate early identification as early as 14 months (Willensen-Swinkel et al., 2002).

Several other studies provide further evidence for a basic social-orienting disturbance in autism. Klin (1991) has reported that the typical preference for speech and speech-like sounds, usually displayed by infants in the first months of life, was not present in any of the children with autism observed by him. It was, however, present in all of the developmentally delayed matched controls observed in this study. As noted earlier, Dawson et al. (1998) examined the degree to which children with autism, Down syndrome, or normal development oriented (displayed a head turn) toward social stimuli (clapping hands or calling the child's name) and to nonsocial stimuli (playing a musical jack-in-the-box or shaking a rattle). The results indicated that the children with autism displayed deficits in orienting to both types of stimuli. Their failure to orient to social stimuli, however, was significantly more impaired than their orienting to nonsocial stimuli. Furthermore, individual differences in difficulty with social orienting, but not object-orienting, were significantly related to a measure of joint attention among the children with autism. Additional efforts from this group have also shown that joint attention is directly related to language acquisition, and social-orienting measures are indirectly related to language through their association with joint attention development in 3- to 4-year-old children with autism (Dawson et al., 2004). Research also suggests that a social-orienting factor may reflect a symptom cluster assessed with the Childhood Autism Rating Scale (CARS; Stella, Mundy, & Tuchman, 1999). Processes involved in individual differences in joint attention measures of social orienting have displayed long-term continuity with processes involved in adaptive outcomes. Individual differences in early joint attention predict the social and cognitive outcomes of adolescent children with autism (Sigman & Ruskin, 1999), as well as how well children with autism process nonverbal social-affective information (Dissanayake, Sigman, & Kasari, 1996).

NEURAL PLASTICITY, SOCIAL ORIENTING, AND JOINT ATTENTION

How do joint attention and related early social-orienting impairments play a role in the etiology of autistic developmental pathology? The microgenetic theory of pathology suggests that understanding the developmental nature and timing of symptoms may be of critical importance if the complete basis of pathology is to be understood (Brown, 1994). This may be the case with respect to the developmental nature and timing of joint attention and social-orienting disturbance in autism. Thus, another critical feature of our model is based on theory that suggests early experience drives a substantial portion of postnatal brain development.

Several researchers have suggested that since the normal environment reliably provides species members with certain invariable types of stimulation and experience, many mammalian species have evolved neural mechanisms that take advantage of the consistency of experience to shape and organize neural development (e.g., Brown, 1994; Changeux & Danchin, 1976; Goldman-Rakic, 1987; Gottlieb & Halpern, 2002; Greenough et al., 1987). One research group has described this process as *experience-expectant* neural development (Greenough et al., 1987). Experience-expectant process in neural development involves a "readiness of the brain" to receive specific types of information from the environment (Black, Jones, Nelson, & Greenough, 1998). This assumption parallels the notion in developmental research and theory that there are predispositions that guide attention and learning early in infancy (Bahrick & Lickliter, 1999; Karmiloff-Smith, 1995; Tomasello, 1999). One aspect of this readiness is an initial overproduction of potential neural connections in the brain. Research on cortical development suggests that the number of synaptic connections between neurons increases dramatically for several years postnatally, especially in the first 12 to 24 months of life. Subsequently, average brain volume, as measured in terms of synaptic density, gradually decreases (see Huttenlocher, 1994, for review). This decrease in brain volume involves the process of culling the early proliferation of synaptic neural connections through the effects of experience into a more efficient and functional system of connections (Brown, 1994; Changeux & Danchin, 1976; Gottlieb & Halpern, 2002; Greenough et al., 1987; Huttenlocher, 1994). Distinctive aspects of environmental stimulation encountered by each member of a species (e.g., patterned visual stimulation, speech sounds, social-affective exchanges) may promote species-specific functional neurodevelopment during early sensitive periods of development (Black et al., 1998). Many of these sensitive periods are thought to occur in the first few years of life (Greenough et al., 1987). Typically, activated or functional synapses are retained, while those that are not activated by stimulation degenerate. Consequently, variation in the environment and stimulus input during an early sensitive period of neural plasticity may lead to fundamental effects on physiological, morphological, and functional aspects of central nervous system development that lay a foundation for future typical or atypical neurobehavioral development (Black et al., 1998; Greenough et al., 1987).

If there is a robust failure of early information input into developing neural subsystems, then a decrease in synapse elimination may occur, leaving a persistent and abnormal organization of neural structure (Greenough et al., 1987). For example, Huttenlocher (1994, pp. 139–141) reviewed studies that suggested that the early blockade of neuromuscular activity in animals, through curare administration or forelimb restraint, leads to significantly more (albeit less usefully organized) synaptic connections in the motor cortex. Thus, early in development, a significant impairment in the input to and/or output from brain systems may result in a stable, diffuse, and overabundant pattern of connections that renders the system functionally atypical. Consequently, the development of behaviors based on this diffuse and overabundant system may be substantially less than optimal.

Greenough et al. (1987) also noted that, while evidence of experience-expectant

processes in neurological development currently stems almost exclusively from research on sensory development, it is likely that other aspects of human neurobehavioral development are also affected by experience-expectant processes. In this aspect of their discussion, Greenough et al. make two comments that are potentially relevant to understanding the impact of a joint attention/social-orienting impairment in autism. They suggested that some early experience-expectant effects may involve self-organizing processes whereby "some types of 'expected' experience may rely largely on the infant to produce them" (p. 545). They also suggested that infant preverbal social communication interactions may provide an example of the "active participation of the infant in acquiring and organizing experience" that provides necessary and critical experience-expectant information in early stages of human development (Greenough et al., 1987, p. 553; see Gottlieb & Halpern, 2002; McWhinney, 1998, for related discussions). Infants' tendency for early social orienting and to ultimately engage in numerous episodes of social attention coordination, or joint attention, may make a contribution that is critical to experience-expectant processes that serve to organize social neurodevelopment (Mundy & Neal, 2001). Moreover, in children with autism, a disruption of social orienting and joint attention may lead to an impoverishment of critical forms of social information input that exacerbates atypical social neurodevelopment through an attenuation of the typical experience-expectant process (Mundy & Crowson, 1997; Mundy & Neal, 2001; see Figure 25.2).

In our initial discussion of this possibility (Mundy & Sigman, 1989), we noted that a failure of joint attention development may serve to isolate the infant with autism from the typical pattern of social exchange, contributing to something akin to a primate isolation effect (Kraemer, 1985). Primate isolation syndrome is a behavioral response to attenuated early social interactive opportunities that leads to some symptoms that have been observed in children with autism, such as stereotypies. We subsequently revised this notion to suggest that autism may be characterized by an initial neuropathological process (INP), which leads to

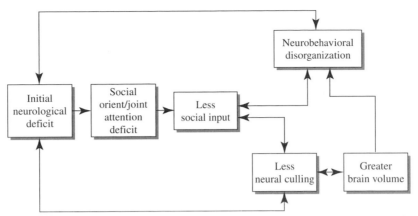

Figure 25.2 A coactive model of organism-environment interaction in the neurobehavioral development of autism in the first 6 years of life. Adapted from "Joint Attention and Early Communication: Implications for Intervention with Autism," by P. Mundy and M. Crowson, 1997, *Journal of Autism and Developmental Disorders, 27,* 653–675; and "Neural Plasticity, Joint Attention and a Transactional Social-Orienting Model of Autism," by P. Mundy and R. Neal, 2001, *International Review of Mental Retardation, 23,* pp. 139–168.

less than optimal social-orienting behavior in the first months of life (Mundy & Crowson, 1997). The INP may involve a deficit in neural systems that contribute to social reward sensitivity (Mundy, 1995; Panksepp, 1979) or other processes that may affect social orienting (e.g., Courchesne et al., 1994; Dawson & Lewy, 1989). *Indeed, the model is not about the cause of the INP. Rather, it raises the hypotheses that the social behavior symptoms caused by the INP may themselves contribute to the etiology of the subsequent neurodevelopmental pathology of autism.* Specifically, this model illustrated the possibility that a robust attenuation of social orienting in the first months of life could, in turn, contribute to secondary neurological disturbance (SND) in autism (Mundy & Crowson, 1997).

One assumption of this model is that social-orienting and joint attention behaviors create a vital and unique source of social information that is necessary for typical experience-expectant social neurodevelopment. In particular, episodes of joint attention, especially those initiated by the child, are thought to provide unique information for infants. This involves the integration of proprioceptive information on the actions and intentions of the self with exteroceptive information from observations of the actions and intentions of others, in reference to some third object or event (Mundy, Sigman, & Kasari,

1993). For example, during showing, infants have the opportunity to monitor their own experience of an object (e.g., enjoyment), while also observing the response of a social partner (e.g., their direction of gaze and affect) to both the object and their own behavior. Thus, self-initiated bids for joint attention provide a rich opportunity for infants to compare information about a social partner's awareness and responses to the displayed object with their own (Bates, 1976). This kind of self-other comparison of experience with respect to a third object or referent provides information that makes a vital contribution to the development of the capacity of infants to simulate the mental states of others. Simulation theory suggests that individuals use their awareness of their own current or past mental processes to analyze and estimate the intentions of others (Gallese & Goldman, 1998; Stich & Nichols, 1992). That is, developmentally, people learn to use self-knowledge, derived from context-specific self-monitoring, to extrapolate and make inferences about the covert psychological processes that contribute to the behaviors of other people in related contexts. In infancy, joint attention, as well as other behaviors such as imitation, provides fundamental opportunities to practice and develop the ability to simulate the mental states of others (Meltzoff & Gopnik, 1993; Mundy et al., 1993). Thus, an attenuation of joint attention deprives children with autism of the practice of self and other social information processing that may be critical to the stimulation of neural systems involved in social-cognitive development (Mundy, 1995, 2003; Mundy & Neal, 2001; Mundy et al., 1993).

Another assumption inherent to this model is that the contribution of the SND to the developmental processes involved in autism will be reduced to the degree early intervention increases the tendency of the young child with autism to process social information (see Mundy & Crowson, 1997, for discussion). Indeed, a model of autism that incorporates a disturbance of experience-expectant processes may assist in understanding intervention process and may assist us in understanding the common observation that earlier intervention may work better than later intervention and that more intervention may work better than less (Black et al., 1998).

The coactive component of the social-orienting model is not so much an alternative to other models of autism as it is a complement or extension of extant models. For example, it is possible that a social-orienting disturbance, and subsequent disruption of experience-expectant neural development, is an important part of the disturbance of the development of social-cognitive modules envisioned in the theory of mind (ToM) model of autism (Mundy, 1995). A basic notion of the latter is that there has been an evolution toward increasing specialization of central nervous systems to support complex social-cognitive and social-communication functions (Baron-Cohen, 1995; Brothers, 1990; Cosmides, 1989; Humphrey, 1976; Whiten & Byrne, 1988). If this notion is accurate, it is also plausible that there has been an evolution of experience-expectant neurodevelopmental processes that provide a foundation for modular social-cognitive development. Indeed, research with sensory-impaired children suggests that sufficient social input is required for typical ToM development, measured by false belief tasks (Peterson & Siegal, 1995). Thus, in the modular terms of the ToM model, a failure of early experience in social interactions may yield a disturbance of early information processing. This failure contributes to a disturbance in the neurological development of

dedicated systems necessary for the typical development and function of social-cognitive modules (Mundy, 1995). This presents a complementary but different view than typical ToM models, which emphasize critical errors within the specific functional parameters of one or another module but do not consider possible errors in the developmental processes that may give rise to the modules themselves.

THE SOCIAL-ORIENTING MODEL AND BRAIN VOLUME IN AUTISM

We have briefly reviewed theory and evidence on early neural plasticity that suggests that proliferation of *potential* synaptic connections between neurons leads to an increase in brain volume in the first 12 to 24 months followed by a gradual decrease in brain volume in part due to experience-expectant processes of culling understimulated or underutilized connections (Greenough et al., 1987; Huttenlocher, 1994). We have also suggested that an attenuation of social information processing and experience-expectant processes early in the life of children with autism may contribute to a disruption of this typical pattern of neural plasticity and development (Mundy & Neal, 2001).

One of the more interesting and consistent findings in neuroanatomical research is that many individuals with autism display larger than average brain volumes (Hardan, Minshew, Mallikarjuhn, & Keshavan, 2001; Piven et al., 1995), at least across the first 6 years of development (Aylward, Minshew, Field, Sparks, & Singh, 2002). Moreover, recent evidence suggests that level of impairment may be positively associated with brain volume in autism (Akshoomoff et al., 2004). However, the current neuroanatomical findings in research on autism are often inconsistent. Null findings and even decreased regional brain volumes among individuals with autism have also been noted in the literature (Aylward et al., 1999; Haznedar et al., 1997). Variations among studies complicate this type of research but may be expected because: (1) The power of these studies is often low due to small sample sizes, (2) consensus has yet to be reached on uniform imaging and data analysis methods to be used across studies, and (3) there is a need to con-

tion of the different cortical correlates of IJA and IBR appears unlikely. Instead, since IJA pointing and IBR pointing serve different social-communicative functions, it is reasonable to assume that the difference in EEG correlates of these infant behaviors also reflects differences in the neurodevelopmental substrates of these functions.

Another important aspect of the results of the Henderson et al. (2002) study is that they suggest baseline activity in *other* cortical areas such as dorsolateral, orbitofrontal, and temporal cortex may be involved in IJA. The latter observations are especially intriguing as they are consistent with the hypothesis that IJA development reflects an integration of dorsal-cortical functions with ventral "social brain" facilities noted in other research (Dawson, Munson et al., 2002). We return to the possible nature of this integrated activity later in this chapter.

The EEG methodology of the Mundy et al. (2000) and Henderson et al. (2002) studies were insufficiently precise to be indicative of the specific cortical systems involved in joint attention. Therefore, it is important to consider additional data on brain behavior correlates in social-cognitive development. Joint attention development has long been theoretically linked to subsequent ToM development in research on typical development (Bretherton et al., 1981), as well as in research on the nature of autism (Baron-Cohen, 1995; Mundy et al., 1993). Charman et al. (2000), for example, have observed that, after controlling for differences in typical 20-month-olds' IQ and language development, an IJA measure of alternating gaze at 20 months was a significant predictor of ToM performance at 44 months. This alternating gaze measure was the same measure that most readily identified autism in 20-month-olds (Swettenham et al., 1998) and was similar to the IJA measure that best discriminated autism and control samples in our initial studies (Mundy et al., 1986). Thus, data indicating that ToM skill development is associated with DMFC functioning would provide important indirect support for the hypothesis that the DMFC may contribute to joint attention development. This type of association between the DMFC and ToM have been reported

(C. Frith & Frith, 1999; U. Frith & Frith, 2001).

BRAIN-BEHAVIOR RESEARCH AND THEORY OF MIND

In one of the first studies of its kind, Fletcher et al. (1995) observed that the performance of six typical adult men on the ToM stories was associated with PET indices of increased blood flow in an area of the left medial-frontal gyrus corresponding to Brodmann's area 8 relative to their performance on the "physical stories." Goel, Grafman, Sadato, and Hallett (1995) also observed that only tasks involving inferences about other people's minds elicited PET activation of a distributed set of neural networks characterized by prominent activation of the left medial-frontal lobe and left medial-frontal gyrus. These authors concluded that, when inferential reasoning depends on constructing a mental model about the beliefs and intentions of others, activation of the DMFC is required. Goel, Gold, Kapur, and Houle (1997) also observed that while general inferential reasoning processes also seem to involve frontal activation, this activation may be centered on more dorsolateral areas of the frontal cortex (Brodmann's area 46) rather than the more dorsal-medial areas 8/9 associated with social cognition.

Since studies have often used stories, or verbal stimuli, language-related processes may have affected the functional localization of ToM skills in these studies. To address this possibility, Gallagher et al. (2000) used functional magnetic resonance imaging (fMRI) to examine brain activity in both verbal-ToM stories and nonverbally presented ToM tasks that involved the processing of visually presented cartoons. The results indicated that the bilateral brain activation correlates of both tasks displayed considerable overlap, specifically in the paracingulate area of the DMFC. The paracingulate area (Brodmann's area 32) refers to a subcortical frontal structure that forms the ventral border between the DMFC (Brodmann's area 8/9, superior and middle frontal gyri) and the AC of the limbic system (especially Brodmann's area 24). Schultz, Romanski, and Tsatsanis (2000) have also reported a study that employed nonverbal ToM task presentation called the Social Attribution Task (SAT; Klin, 2000). In this task, a brief sequence of geometric forms moving across a blank white background was presented to eight typical adult participants. People viewing the SAT tend to anthropomorphize the movement sequence of geometric forms and describe it in terms of intentional, animate behavior. Presumably, this is a fundamental component of ToM skill (Klin, 2000). Schultz et al. reported that processing of this task recruited bilateral activation of the DMFC (Brodmann's area 9) in their typical sample. Related research has demonstrated that people with autism spectrum disorders do not tend to anthropomorphize the movement sequence on the SAT (Klin, 2000).

An important control condition was also included in a study by Sabbagh and Taylor (2000). Using evoked response potentials (ERP) and a dense EEG electrode array (128 sites), they presented university students with a paradigm that compared false-belief ToM task performance with an analogous nonsocial task. The latter involves thinking about the contents held within a camera (i.e., picture) instead of the false belief held within someone's mind, as in a ToM task (see Leslie & Thaiss, 1992). Sabbagh and Taylor observed significantly greater ERP data from the left dorsolateral and dorsomedial cortex in the ToM false belief task (e.g., ERP from electrode sites approximately above BA 9/10/46), rather than in the nonsocial camera task in their sample.

Thus, although some imaging and case studies have observed associations between ToM performance and orbital activity, rather than dorsal medial-frontal activity (Bach, Happé, Fleminger, & Powell, 2000; Baron-Cohen et al., 1999), the link between ToM performance and the DMFC currently is the most consistent finding in the relevant literature (U. Frith & Frith, 2001). Moreover, in addition to basic studies, applied research with clinical samples points to the involvement of the DMFC in ToM performance.

In a PET study of autism spectrum disorders, Happé et al. (1996) reported that five adults with Asperger disorder did not display activity in the medial-frontal gyrus in the con-text of reading and solving ToM stories but did display activity in an immediately adjacent area. This pattern distinguished the people with Asperger disorder from controls. Somewhat different findings emerged in a related fMRI study by Baron-Cohen et al. (1999), which assessed the ability of groups to infer emotional states from pictures of eyes. This social-cognitive assessment method revealed that activity in part of the "social brain" network, involving orbitofrontal cortex, the STG, and the amygdala, was involved in ToM processing. Moreover, significant differences were found between the Asperger and typical samples in this pattern of task-related brain action. In addition, activation of the left and right DMFC was also observed to be a specific component of ToM task performance in this study. However, unlike the data from Happé et al. (1996), the Asperger sample did not differ from controls in task-related activation of this cortical area. It was apparent that the typical controls in Baron-Cohen et al. (1999) displayed evidence of bilateral medial-frontal activation on ToM tasks. Alternatively, the people with Asperger disorder displayed evidence of unilateral left medial-frontal activation, but no evidence of right medial-frontal activation in association with the ToM tasks (see Tables 3 and 4, Baron-Cohen et al., 1999). Thus, there may have been a medial-frontal group difference in this study that was not detected by the analyses provided.

Russell et al. (2000) have also employed a ToM measure known as the "eyes" task (Baron-Cohen et al., 1999) in an fMRI study that examined the neural metabolic activation patterns associated with ToM in individuals affected by schizophrenia. The schizophrenic participants made more errors on this measure of attributions of mental state than did the controls. Moreover, the controls displayed relatively more activity in the medial-frontal lobe (Brodmann's area 45/9) in association with ToM task performance relative to the individuals with schizophrenia. Again, though, the group differences were not limited to the DMFC, but also included ventral "social brain" components of the left inferior-frontal gyrus (Brodmann's areas 44/45/47) and the left middle- and superior-temporal gyri (Brodmann's areas 21/22).

Complementing these group comparison data are observations that suggest there may be dopaminergic activity in the DMFC of children with autism (Ernst, Zametkin, Matochik, Pascualvacae, & Cohen, 1997). A recent voxel-based morphometric study with 28 high-function children and adults with autism also indicated increased gray matter density in the AC and left superior frontal gyrus, as well as the left inferior parietal lobe and right frontal lobe subgyral regions (Hardan, Yorbik, Minshew, Diwadkar, & Keshavan, 2002). Recall that the first three of these brain regions correspond to the dorsal medial-frontal area (Brodmann's areas 8/9/24) that has been implicated in joint attention and social-cognitive processing.

There are also at least two individual difference studies that emphasize the potentially important role of the DMFC in autistic social symptom presentation. Ohnishi et al. (2000) used PET to examine the associations between regional cerebral blood flow (rCBF) and symptom presentation in children with autism and IQ-matched controls. Symptom presentation was measured using factor-based scale scores for the Impairments in Communication and Social Interaction scale and the Obsessive Desire for Sameness scale from the CARS (Schopler, Reichlet, DeVellis, & Daly, 1980). The results indicated that the children with autism displayed decreased baseline rCBF relative to controls in the superior temporal gyrus (BA 22), left inferior frontal gyrus (BA 45), and left medial prefrontal cortex (BA 9/10). Moreover, less activity in the latter area (DMFC, BA 9/10) was reportedly correlated with CARS factor scores indicative of more disturbance on the Impairments in Communication and Social Interaction factor-based scale. Alternatively, rCBF in the right hippocampus and the amygdala was reportedly correlated with the Obsessive Desire for Sameness factor-scaled score.

In another study, Haznedar et al. (2000) used PET and MRI coregistration to examine the hypothesis that the amygdala and hippocampus would display metabolic rate and morphometric differences in 17 high-functioning individuals with autism relative to typical controls. The results, however, revealed few differences in these areas. Alternatively, a consistent pattern of significant findings was revealed for areas of the AC (Brodmann's area 24 and 24'). Volumetric data indicated that the autism group displayed smaller brain volume in the right AC region, especially Brodmann's area 24' relative to the control sample. The autism sample also displayed hypometabolism in the right AC cortex relative to controls. The Asperger subsample displayed left AC hypometabolism relative to controls. This hypometabolism was not observed in more ventral portions of the AC (Brodmann's area 25). Finally, in the autism sample, metabolism in left Brodmann's area 24 was correlated with the social interaction, verbal communication, and nonverbal communication scores on the Autism Diagnostic Interview (ADI), and metabolism in Brodmann's area 24' was correlated with the ADI social interaction scores in the autism sample. Thus, consistent with the notion that the MFC/AC system may be integral to the development of joint attention and social cognition, these studies provide evidence that activity in this system may be related to social symptom presentation in autism.

In summary, theory suggests that infant joint attention and later social-cognitive measures may reflect common processes (e.g., Bretherton et al., 1981; Wellman, 1993) and sources of disturbance in autism (Baron-Cohen, 1995; Mundy et al., 1986). Recent research indicates that common neuropsychological functions of the DMFC/AC may play a role in IJA, ToM, and related social impairments in individuals with autism. At present, though, the functional resolution of the data is inexact, especially those from the joint attention studies. Thus, the degree to which this apparent commonality across tasks and measures actually involves the same functional units within the DMFC/AC system is not clear. Moreover, current data also raise the possibility that DMFC processes contribute to both joint attention and ToM skill in conjunction with processes associated with ventral "social brain" systems (e.g., Henderson et al., 2002; Russell et al., 2000) that may be involved in the perception and analysis of the social behaviors of others. An argument could also be made that other brain systems, such as cerebellar contributions to the attention regulation functions of the DMFC/AC, may also be involved (Courchesne et al., 1994). Ultimately, it may be necessary to adopt a complex systems approach (e.g., Bressler, 1995; Miller & Cohen, 2001) in attempts to fully understand the dynamic neural systems involved in these behavior domains. Prior to such an inclusive and dynamic level of analysis, a better understanding of the component processes involved in the system will be necessary. However, there has been little detailed recognition of what the DMFC/AC component may bring to such a system (e.g., Adolphs, 2001; Dawson, Munson, et al., 2002). This may be a gap in our collective research efforts with autism that requires reconsideration.

THE ROLE OF THE DORSAL MEDIAL-FRONTAL CORTEX IN SOCIAL AND NONSOCIAL BEHAVIOR

What processes and functions of the DMFC/AC complex may make it important to social development? How do these functions develop? Are they specific to social behavior? Is an impairment in DMFC/AC social functions integral to the pathogenesis of autism? Is there a primary developmental impairment of the DMFC/AC system in autism, or are functions in the DMFC/AC complex disrupted in autism secondary to neurodevelopmental deficits in "upstream" cerebellar mechanisms or ventral-brain mediated social information perception and processing? Does impairment of the DMFC lead to a critical organism-environment disturbance in autism (e.g., the early infancy tendency to initiate social orienting), and does such a disturbance contribute to subsequent neurobehavioral disturbance in autism?

These and related questions may occupy the efforts of many people over the next few years of research on autism. While definitive answers to these questions are not close at hand, a wealth of information is emerging on the functions of the DMFC and AC, which may guide inquiry in this arena. Moreover, several hypotheses concerning the specific social-cognitive, as well as nonsocial functions of the DMFC, have been generated, and these intersect with current theory on autism.

The DMFC and AC may play a central role in several processes that are related to an *executive system*. In particular, the DMFC/AC complex contributes to the planning and execution of self-initiated, goal-directed behavior. The DMFC/AC system also appears to play a role in the *self-monitoring of goal-directed behaviors*. Goal-directed behaviors refer to a range of activities, from control of overt behavior such as saccades in visual orienting, to the more covert mental activity involved in generating or operating on mental representations (cognition). Self-monitoring, in part, refers to the evaluation of whether goal-directed behavior does or does not lead to reward (e.g., Amador, Schlag-Rey, & Schlag, 2000; Busch, Luu, & Posner, 2000; Ferstl & von Cramon, 2001). Related to these facilities is the role the DMFC/AC complex plays in the maintenance of representations of multiple goals in working memory. The DMFC/AC is also involved in the capacity to flexibly switch between goal representations (e.g., Birrell & Brown, 2000; DiGirolamo et al., 2001; Koechlin, Basso, Peirini, Panzer, & Grafman, 1999), as well as the DMFC/AC role in the appraisal of the valence of stimuli and the generation or modulation of emotional responses to stimuli (e.g., Fox & Davidson, 1987; Lane, Fink, Chua, & Dolan, 1997; Teasdale et al., 1999).

The foregoing, in all likelihood, is a nonexhaustive list of DMFC/AC functions. Nevertheless, it is important to note that even in this constrained view, there are functional characteristics of the DMFC/AC system that may provide a unifying bridge between theories of autism that emphasize impairments in basic cognitive functions and those that emphasize specific social-cognitive or social-emotional impairments. For example, in their recent elegant work, Minshew et al. (2001) have argued that autism involves a selective disorder of complex information processing. This disorder of complex information processing is reportedly manifest, at least in higher functioning individuals, as a fundamental impairment in concept formation. This involves the capacity to spontaneously initiate a strategy for eliminating alternatives, and the strategy needs to be monitored and changed in accordance with experience of success or failure while processing the solution (Minshew et al., 2002). Given the current functional analysis of the DMFC briefly outlined earlier, it seems reasonable to suggest that the DMFC/AC system may play a role in this aspect of cognitive disturbance in autism. Moreover, it is interesting that Minshew et al. (2001) suggest that, at its most basic level, the disorder of complex information processing may be associated with impairments in neocortical systems involved in overt saccade and occulomotor control. Brodmann's area 8/9 of the DMFC/AC system includes portions of the frontal eye fields and is integral to saccadic and occulomotor control (Martin, 1996).

Another recently developed cognitive/perceptual model of autism revolves around the weak central coherence (WCC) hypothesis (U. Frith & Happé, 1994). Briefly, WCC in autism reflects a bias toward processing stimulus details. Alternatively, holistic stimulus processing, which involves integration of multiple dimensions of information (central coherence), is more difficult for people with autism. Hence, they often have difficulty with the types of gestalt, inferential, contextually bound information processing that is necessary to adaptive social information processing, such as in face processing or the processing of pragmatic aspects of communication. One indication of weak central coherence is the difficulty verbal children with autism have on homograph tasks that demand processing of the entire context of the sentence to interpret the correct meaning of a word, such as, "a *tear* in her eye" versus "a *tear* in her dress" (Burnette et al., in press; Happé, 1997). It is interesting that wholistic or inferential text interpretation has recently been observed to be associated with left medial-frontal activation in an MRI study (Ferstl & von Cramon, 2001). Indeed, Ferstl and von Cramon suggest that the "frontomedian area [of the cortex] has a function for the self-initiation of a cognitive process in the context of tasks that require the active utilization of the individual's background knowledge" (p. 338). This function described by Ferstl and von Cramon appears to have much in common with the nature of central coherence. Ferstl and von Cramon also relate this capacity for the self-initiation of background-dependent cognition directly to the capacity for successful performance on ToM measures. Indeed, in our own research, we have recently observed that poorer performance on a homographs task, indicative of WCC, was related to poor performance on the ToM task or evidenced greater social-cognitive

impairment among high-functioning children with autism (Burnette et al., in press). Hence, a better understanding of the relations among weak central coherence, DMFC functions, and social-cognitive disturbance in autism may be a useful and integrative goal for future studies.

The executive functions of the DMFC/AC may also play several *specific* roles in social and social-cognitive impairments in autism. Impairments in the DMFC/AC facility for self-monitoring, as well as maintaining multiple goals and representations (Birrell & Brown, 2000; DiGirolamo et al., 2001; Koechlin et al., 1999), may conceivably be essential to the representation decoupling and tagging mechanism that Leslie (1987) suggested underlies metarepresentational processes that may be impaired in autism. IJA may also involve the capacity to shift attention between social and nonsocial goals and representations (Mundy et al., 1986, 2000). Hence, impairment in this facility of the DMFC/AC may also be involved in joint attention disturbance in autism.

From another perspective, though, it may be useful to consider the proposition that, as part of early social development, some of the general executive facilities of the DMFC/AC become redescribed as specific "social-executive functions." These may arise, in part, from the self-monitoring and self-initiating facilities of the DMFC/AC. The hypothesis that the DMFC/AC plays an integral role in self-monitoring stems from several findings (Craik et al., 1999; C. Frith & Frith, 1999; U. Frith & Frith, 2001). Prominent here is research that has led to the observation that, when people make erroneous saccadic responses in an attention deployment task, there is a negative deflection in the stimulus and response locked ERP called the error-related negativity (ERN; Busch et al., 2000; Luu, Flaisch, & Tucker, 2000). Source location suggests the ERN emanates from an area proximal to the AC (e.g., Luu et al., 2000). Observations of the ERN suggest that there are specific cell groups within the DMFC/AC that are not only active in initiating a behavioral act, such as orienting to a stimulus, but also distinct cell groups involved in processing the positive or negative outcome of the response behavior (i.e., accuracy and reinforcement information; e.g., Busch et al., 2000; Stuphorn, Taylor, & Schall,

2000). Thus, cell groups within the DMFC/AC come to serve as part of a supervisory attention system (SAS; Norman & Shallice, 1986) that functions to guide behavior, especially attention deployment, depending on the motivational context of the task (Amador et al., 2000; Busch et al., 2000; Luu et al., 2000).

Robert Schultz and coworkers at Yale (Schultz et al., 2000) have begun to consider this functional role of the DMFC/AC in social behavior and its impairment in autism. In one scenario, Schultz et al. suggested that impaired information flow from the amygdala to the DMFC may attenuate the tendency for social stimuli to acquire their normal valence causing social processing difficulties. The nature of these social processing difficulties is not yet well defined, though this research team has suggested that they might include face processing disturbance in autism, which, in turn, contributes to impairments in the typical development of social-cognitive facilities (Grelotti, Gauthier, & Schultz, 2002).

Similar hypotheses were raised in attempts to understand the nature of joint attention and social-orienting disturbance in autism (Dawson et al., 1998; Dawson, Munson, et al., 2002; Mundy, 1995; Mundy & Neal, 2001). These researchers have suggested that: (1) frontal and temporal/amygdala circuits that mediate reinforcement and emotional/motivational goal guidance contribute to a bias to attend to social stimuli in infancy, and (2) a disturbance in this bias, from the neonatal period onward, plays a fundamental role in developmental disturbance of social behavior and social cognition in autism. As noted in earlier sections of this chapter, an early onset of this disturbance hypothetically leads to a robust disturbance in social orienting in autism and a robust attenuation of the flow of social information to the developing child. The resulting impoverishment of social information could be sufficiently severe to disrupt experience-expectant neurodevelopmental processes (see Greenough et al., 1987) and contribute to the subsequent disorganization and impairment of brain and behavior systems including those that subserve social-emotional and social-cognitive skill development (Dawson, 1994; Loveland, 2001; Mundy & Crowson, 1997; Mundy & Neal, 2001; Mundy & Sigman, 1989).

Previous theory and research on social reward sensitivity and social-orienting disturbance in autism (Dawson et al., 1998; Dawson, Munson, et al., 2002; Grelotti et al., 2002) have emphasized the possible contributions of the orbitofrontal cortex or subcortical structures such as the amygdala (e.g., de-Haan, Pascalis, & Johnson, 2002; Tremblay & Schultz, 1999; Wantanabe, 1999). The literature reviewed herein, though, suggests that it may be useful to expand this focus to include contributions from the DMFC/AC complex. The logic here is twofold. First, infant measures of IJA provide one operationalization of the tendency to spontaneously social orient to an interactive partner (Mundy & Neal, 2001), and there is now empirical evidence to directly link this tendency with DMFC activity (Henderson et al., 2002; Mundy et al., 2000). Second, and equally important, the areas of the DMFC associated with IJA (Brodmann's area 8/9) overlap aspects of the frontal eye fields and supplementary motor cortex. *These cortical areas may be important to consider in understanding processes that hamper the tendency of children with autism to look appropriately or sufficiently often at people because they are vital to regulating attention deployment through the active integration of the context in which reward occurs with the planning and control of saccades or visual orienting* (Amador et al., 2000; Luu et al., 2000; Stuphorn et al., 2000).

There is also some evidence that dopaminergic projections to the AC play a role in the mediation of reward-related activity (Allman, Hakeem, Erwin, Nimchinsky, & Hof, 2001). Moreover, Allman et al. note two characteristics of the AC that make this brain region of particular interest in understanding joint attention and pathology in autism. First, they present evidence to suggest that spindle cell formations in the AC may be a novel specialization of neural circuitry found only in great apes and humans. Interestingly, joint attention facilities and related social-cognitive ability may also be unique to apes and humans (Tomasello, 1999). Allman et al. also suggest that these spindle cells appear to emerge postnatally, at about 4 months of age, and their development may be affected by environmental factors (Allman et al., 2001, pp. 109–112). The timing of the emergence of spindle cell systems of the AC suggest they have the potential to be involved in experience-expectant, as well as experience-dependent, coactive neurodevelopmental process. A corollary is that this characteristic of the spindle cell system of the AC may be important to consider in exploring the type of coactive, organism environment interactive model of autistic pathology we have outlined here and elsewhere (Mundy & Neal, 2001).

One challenge to the notion that the DMFC/AC complex plays a role in the *early* onset of social-orienting disturbance in autism is that frontal occulomotor control of attention deployment may be relatively late to develop in infancy (Johnson, Posner, & Rothbart, 1991). However, recent research suggests that *by* 3 to 4 months, "the cortical eye fields are actively involved in the prospective control of saccades and visual attention" (Canfield & Kirkham, 2001, p. 207). Further inquiry into the mechanisms and early development of this system in relation to early social attention and information processing may hold a key to a deeper understanding of the pathogenesis of autism, as well as typical social development. Future studies may find the ERN paradigm to be useful in infant studies, as well as studies of the cortical control of attention to social and nonsocial stimuli in children affected by autism spectrum disorders. It may also be important to begin to explore the role that spindle cell formation may play in typical development, as well as in the atypical case of autism.

Another issue is that it is not completely clear if social orienting, in particular, is impaired in autism. Although a social-orienting disturbance may be a robust phenomenon in children with autism (Dawson et al., 1998; Klin, 1991), a more general impairment in orienting to nonsocial stimuli is apparent as well (Dawson et al., 1998; Townsend, Harris, & Courchesne, 1996). Moreover, some research suggests that social orienting and social-emotional processing disturbances in autism may not be as pervasive as theory would suggest (Pierce et al., 2001; Sigman et al., 1992; Warreyn & Roeyers, 2002). Instead, autism may be characterized by a general rather than socially specific orienting disturbance that arises from impairment in a complex cerebellar, parietal, and frontal axis of systems in-

volved in the development and control of attention (Carper & Courchesne, 2000; Townsend et al., 1996, 2001). Thus, a major goal of research on autism is to resolve this issue and examine the possible complex interplay among the DMFC/AC complex, orbitofrontal and amygdala functions, and cerebellar input in the development of attention regulation in people affected by this disorder (see Mundy, 2003; Vaughan & Mundy, in press, for related discussions).

In addition to its role in social attention impairment, the DMFC/AC may play another related and critical role in the social disturbance of autism. C. Frith and Frith (1999; U. Frith & Frith, 2001) have suggested that the supervisory attention system of the DMFC that engages in self-monitoring of attention deployment also develops the capacity to represent the actions, goals, intentions, and emotions of the self (see also Craik et al., 1999). Furthermore, Frith and Frith (1999; U. Frith & Frith, 2001) argue that, as the DMFC comes to participate in the development of representations of the self, it also integrates information from the ventral social brain perception system (e.g., STS) that provides information about the goal-directed behaviors and emotions of others. This integrative activity may be facilitated by the abundance of connections between the DMFC and the STS, as well as the orbitofrontal cortex in primates (Morecraft, Guela, & Mesulam, 1993). Moreover, it may be useful to think of this *facility for the integration of proprioceptive self-action information with exteroceptive information on the actions and behaviors of others* as another emergent social-executive facility of the DMFC/AC. Ultimately, this DMFC/AC social-executive function may serve to compare and integrate the actions of self and the actions of others (Frith & Frith, 2001), perhaps utilizing the DMFC/AC facility for the maintenance of representation of multiple goals in working memory. This integration gives rise to the capacity to infer the intentions of others by matching them with representations of self-initiated actions or intentions (cf. Leslie, 1987). Once this integration begins to occur in the DMFC/AC, a fully functional, adaptive human social-cognitive system emerges with experience (C. Frith & Frith, 1999; U. Frith &

Frith, 2001). Thus, it may be very important to better understand the developmental links between temporal systems involved in the perception of social behavior of others (e.g., Adolphs, 2001) and this more dorsal system for self-monitoring and self-other comparison (U. Frith & Frith, 2001). In terms of joint attention development and autism, it may be especially important to understand how information gleaned about others in RJA (presumably via the temporal/parietal other monitoring system) feeds into and affects the development of the DMFC self-other monitoring system putatively involved in IJA.

In a recent essay, we attempted to begin to address this topic by suggesting that the timely and early onset of RJA, and related behavior development, may be an important stimulant for typical IJA and DMFC social-executive development (Vaughan & Mundy, in press). Furthermore, as we noted earlier in this chapter, episodes of joint attention, especially those initiated by the child, provide a context for infants to integrate proprioceptive information on the actions and intentions of self with exteroceptive information on the actions and intentions of others, in reference to some third object or event (Mundy et al., 1993). Recall the example that, during the act of showing, infants have the opportunity to monitor their own experience (e.g., emotions) and their behavior directed toward an object, while observing the response of a social partner (e.g., their direction of gaze and affect) to both the object and the infant's behavior. This interaction provides an opportunity for the infant to process some information about a social partner's awareness and responses to the displayed object as well as the showing (sharing) behavior of the child (cf. Bates, 1976). Thus, self-initiated bids for joint attention may provide infants an important if not unique opportunity to learn about the internal psychological processes of the self and, perhaps, of others as well.

Theoretically, engagement in this process within joint attention episodes facilitates social-cognitive development, as well as social-emotional attunement in typical development (Mundy, Kasari, & Sigman, 1992, 1993; Mundy & Willoughby, 1998; Stern, 1985). A failure in the development of this fundamental and complex interactive skill, albeit through poorly understood processes, has been suggested as an essential component of the genesis of social-cognitive disturbance in autism (Hobson, 1993; Meltzoff & Gopnik, 1993; Mundy et al., 1993). Some have described this, and related phenomena, as a fundamental disturbance in the capacity for children with autism to engage in shared experience or intersubjectivity (Hobson, 1993; Mundy & Hogan, 1994). These observations, in conjunction with the theoretical analysis by C. Frith and Frith (1999; U. Frith & Frith, 2001), lead to the hypothesis that the activity of the DMFC/AC complex may well be integral to this function. Stated more forthrightly, although not yet well recognized in the relevant literature (e.g., Trevarthen & Aitken, 2001), it may well be that DMFC/AC complex may make an important contribution to the neuro-functional platform from which the essential human capacity for intersubjectivity springs.

C. Frith and Frith's (1999; U. Frith & Frith, 2001) model also has parallels with simulation theory as applied to social cognition (e.g., Stich & Nichols, 1992). As noted earlier, simulation theory suggests that individuals use their awareness (i.e., representations) of their own mental processes to simulate and analyze the intentions of others (Gallese & Goldman, 1998). Gallese and Goldman have also discussed the possible role of mirror neurons in the social-cognitive simulation facility of the DMFC/AC. Mirror neurons are a specific class of motor neurons that are activated both by particular actions performed by an individual and when the individual observes a similar action performed by another person. According to Gallese and Goldman, the motor and premotor cortex adjacent to or overlapping with the DMFC is rich in mirror neurons (see Rizzolatti & Arbib, 1998). Too little is yet known about the nature and distribution of mirror neurons to provide an extended discussion here. Nevertheless, further inquiry into the relations among mirror neurons, social cognition, and the DMFC may be useful (Gallese & Goldman, 1998). In particular, there may be a link between mirror neurons and imitative behavior. Since imitation constitutes a domain of impairment in autism that has been theoretically linked to social and social-cognitive disturbance in autism (Meltzoff & Gopnik, 1993; Rogers & Pennington, 1991), it may be judicious to explore the tripartite link among imitation, social cognition, and the functions of the DMFC/AC in research on the nature of autism.

There are many other important implications for research on autism to be drawn from the sagacious and potentially seminal synthesis provided by Uta and Chris Frith. One of these was alluded to at the beginning of this chapter. The basic idea is that a component of information that is necessary for adequate social-cognitive development derives from self-monitoring of *self-initiated actions* in social situations (C. Frith & Frith, 1999). Moreover, an impairment in the early tendency to initiate social behaviors may be especially problematic for the development of children with autism because it disrupts their capacity for social action, which ultimately is the foundation of social self-knowledge requisite to social-cognitive development (Mundy, 1995; Mundy & Neal, 2001). It may be useful to adopt something akin to a Piagetian view of development. Among his many brilliant contributions, Piaget (1952) helped us understand that early cognitive development derived in large part from the actions infants took on objects in their world. Indeed, a major component of cognitive development was explained in terms of the redescription of overt action (sensorimotor schemes) to covert mental representations of action in the sensorimotor period (i.e., in infancy). Unfortunately, Piaget did not speak as directly or as completely to social development as he did to cognition applied to solving object-related problems in the world. Nevertheless, his constructivist model of development may be equally applicable to social development. That is, it is plausible that the infant's capacity to initiate action in social interaction (e.g., in orienting to a social partner or showing a toy to a social partner) and to note social reactions to self-initiated action constitute a major early building block of social-cognitive development (see Braten, 1998). Hence, early difficulty in organizing and initiating social action may play as significant a role in the pathogenesis of autism (Mundy & Neal, 2001). Indeed, it may be useful to consider a common developmental path of impairment in autism that begins with the

early onset of difficulty in the self-initiation of action (e.g., in social orienting or IJA) in infancy and eventually is manifest in difficulty in the self-initiation of aspects of social cognition (Frith & Frith, 1999), as well as the self-initiation of aspects of nonsocial cognition (Minshew et al., 2001). Moreover, it may be useful to consider this conjecture in the context of the observation that one common goal of intervention protocols with people with autism seems to be to increase their tendency to self-initiate adaptive goal-directed action in social, as well as nonsocial, situations.

CONCLUSION

The study of autism presents an enormously complex puzzle. Unfortunately, several critical pieces of the puzzle seem to be missing. One of these pieces may involve the role of coactive organism-environment interactive processes wherein deficits in the early social behavior repertoire of children with autism contribute to a disturbance in social experience that is so robust as to compromise subsequent neurological and behavioral development. If so, our efforts may need to be redoubled with respect to the development of early identification and intervention methodologies. Another piece that may be missing in our attempt to attain a veridical view of the etiology of autism may involve the role of the DMFC/AC complex in cognitive and social-cognitive development. This role may be embodied in a fundamental disturbance in the capacity to self-initiate, organize, and monitor behavior and cognition. The DMFC/AC complex may be integral to social-orienting disturbance and the coactive organism-experience model of autism we have attempted to outline in this chapter. Moreover, a DMFC/AC system impairment may be central to difficulties that people with autism appear to display in intersubjectivity and social-cognitive development, as well as the development of other complex cognitive processes. Finally, it may be instructive to note that impairment of the DMFC/AC complex reportedly produces a symptom profile that includes apathy, inattention, dysregulation of autonomic functions, variability in pain sensitivity, akinetic mutism, and emotional instability (see Busch et al., 2000). This profile has obvious commonalities with characteristics of people affected by autism. The observation of related functional commonalities led to the proposal of an influential neurological model some 25 years ago, which also emphasized the role of the DMFC/AC complex in autism (Damasio & Maurer, 1978). When it was proposed, the model of Damasio and Maurer was not easily open to empirical investigation. Currently, though, the tools are at hand and inquiry into the neurodevelopmental role of the DMFC/AC complex in the pathogenesis of autism has once again become an important goal of future research.

Cross-References

Development of infants and young children with autism is discussed in Chapter 8, social development is addressed in Chapter 11, aspects of attention and perception are reviewed in Chapter 13. A convergent theoretical perspective is provided in Chapter 26.

REFERENCES

Adolphs, R. (2001). The neurobiology of social cognition. *Current Opinion in Neurobiology, 11,* 231–239.

Akshoomoff, N. A., Lord, C., Lincoln, A., Courchesne, R., Carper, R., Townsend, J. P., et al. (2004). Outcome classification of preschool children with autism spectrum disorders using MRI brain measures. *Journal of the American Academy of Child Psychiatry, 43,* 349–357.

Akshoomoff, N. A., Pierce, K., & Courchesne, E. (2002). The neurobiological basis of autism form a developmental perspective. *Development and Psychopathology, 14,* 613–634.

Allman, J., Hakeem, A., Erwin, J., Nimchinsky, E., & Hof, P. (2001). The anterior cingulate: The evolution of the interface between emotion and cognition. *Annals of the New York Academy of Sciences, 935,* 107–117.

Amador, N., Schlag-Rey, M., & Schlag, J. (2000). Reward predicting and reward detecting neuronal activity in the primate supplementary eye field. *Journal of Neurophysiology, 84,* 2166–2170.

American Psychiatric Association. (1980). *Diagnostic and statistical manual of mental disorders* (3rd ed.). Washington, DC: American Psychiatric Association.

American Psychiatric Association. (1987). *Diagnostic and statistical manual of mental disorders* (3rd ed., rev.). Washington, DC: American Pyschiatric Association.

American Psychiatric Association. (1994). *Diagnostic and statistical manual of mental disorders* (4th ed.). Washington, DC: American Psychiatric Association.

American Psychiatric Association. (2000). *Diagnostic and statistical manual of mental disorders* (4th ed., text rev.). Washington, DC: American Psychiatric Association.

Asperger, H. (1944). Die Autistischen psychopathen [Autistic psychopathy in childhood]. *Kindesalter: Archiv Für Psychiatrie und Nevenkrankheiten, 117,* 76–136.

Aylward, E. H., Minshew, N. J., Field, K., Sparks, B. F., & Singh, N. (2002). Effects of age on brain volume and head circumference in autism. *Neurology, 59,* 175–183.

Aylward, E. H., Minshew, N. J., Goldstein, G., Honeycutt, N., Augustine, A., Yates, K., et al. (1999). MRI volumes of amygdala and hippocampus in the non-mentally retarded autistic adolescents and adults. *Neurology, 53,* 2145–2150.

Bach, L., Happé, F., Fleminger, S., & Powell, J. (2000). Theory of mind: Independence of executive function and the role of the frontal cortex in acquired brain injury. *Cognitive-Neuropsychiatry, 5,* 175–192.

Bachvalier, J. (1994). Medial temporal lobe structures and autism: A review of clinical and experimental findings. *Neuropsychologia, 32,* 627–648.

Bahrick, L., & Lickliter, R. (1999). Intersensory redundancy guides attentional selectivity and perceptual learning in infancy. *Developmental Psychology, 36,* 190–201.

Bailey, A., Philips, W., & Rutter, M. (1996). Autism: Towards an integration of clinical, genetic, neuropsychological, and neurobiological perspectives. *Journal of Child Psychology and Psychiatry, 37,* 89–126.

Bakeman, R., & Adamson, L. (1984). Coordinating attention to people and objects in mother-infant and peer-infant interaction. *Child Development, 55,* 1278–1289.

Baldwin, D. A. (1995). Understanding the link between joint attention and language. In C. Moore & P. J. Dunham (Eds.), *Joint attention: Its origins and role in development* (pp. 131–158). Hillsdale, NJ: Erlbaum.

Baron-Cohen, S. (1995). *Mindblindness.* Cambridge, MA: MIT Press.

Baron-Cohen, S., Cox, A., Baird, G., Swettenham, J., Nightingale, N., Morgan, K., et al. (1996).

Psychological markers in the detection of autism in infancy in a large population. *British Journal of Psychiatry, 168,* 158–163.

Baron-Cohen, S., Ring, H., Bullmore, E., Wheelwright, S., Ashwin, C., & Williams, S. (2000). Social intelligence in the normal and autistic brain: An fMRI study. *Neuroscience and Biobehavioral Reviews, 24,* 355–364.

Baron-Cohen, S., Ring, H., Wheelwright, S., Bullmore, E., Brammer, M., Simmons, A., et al. (1999). Social intelligence in the normal and autistic brain: An fMRI study. *European Journal of Neuroscience, 11,* 1891–1898.

Bates, E. (1976). *Language and context: The acquisition of performatives.* New York: Academic Press.

Birrell, J., & Brown, V. (2000). Medial-frontal cortex mediates perceptual attention set shifting in the rat. *Journal of Neuroscience, 20,* 4320–4324.

Black, J., Jones, T., Nelson, C., & Greenough, W. (1998). Neuronal plasticity and the developing brain. In N. Alessi (Ed.), *The handbook of child and adolescent psychiatry: Vol. 4. Varieties of development* (pp. 31–53). New York: Wiley.

Blass, E. (1999). The ontogeny of human infant face recognition: Orogustatory, visual and social influences. In P. Rochat (Ed.), *Early social cognition: Understanding others in the first months of life* (pp. 35–66). Mahwah, NJ: Erlbaum.

Bono, M., & Sigman, M. (in press). Relations among joint attention, amount of intervention, and language gain in early autism. *Journal of Autism and Developmental Disorders.*

Braten, S. (1998). Infant learning by altercentric participation: The reverse of egocentric observation in autism. In S. Braton (Ed.), *Intersubjective communication and emotion in early ontogeny* (pp. 105–124). Cambridge, England: Cambridge University Press.

Bressler, S. (1995). Large scale cortical networks and cognition. *Brain Research Reviews, 20,* 288–304.

Bretherton, I., McNew, S., & Beeghly-Smith, M. (1981). Early person knowledge as expressed in gestural and verbal communication: When do infants acquire a theory of mind. In M. E. Lamb & L. R. Sherrod (Eds.), *Infant social cognition* (pp. 333–373). Hillsdale, NJ: Erlbaum.

Brothers, L. (1990). The social brain: A project for integrating primate behavior and neurophysiology in a new domain. *Concepts in Neuroscience, 1,* 27–51.

Brown, J. (1994). Morphogenesis and mental process. *Development and Psychopathology, 6,* 551–564.

Bruner, J. S. (1975). From communication to language: A psychological perspective. *Cognition, 3,* 255–287.

Burnette, C., Mundy, P., Meyer, J., Sutton, S., Vaughan, A., & Charak, D. (in press). Weak central coherence and its relation to theory of mind and anxiety in autism. *Journal of Autism and Related Disorders.*

Busch, G., Luu, P., & Posner, M. (2000). Cognitive and emotional influences in the anterior cingulate cortex. *Trends in Cognitive Science, 4,* 214–222.

Calder, A., Lawrence, A., Keane, J., Scott, S., Owen, A., Christoffels, I., et al. (2002). Reading the mind from eye gaze. *Neuropsychologia, 40,* 1129–1138.

Canfield, R., & Kirkham, N. (2001). Infant cortical development and the prospective control of saccadic eye movements. *Infancy, 2,* 197–211.

Caplan, R., Chugani, H., Messa, C., Guthrie, D., Sigman, M., Traversay, J., et al. (1993). Hemispherectomy for early onset intractable seizures: Presurgical cerebral glucose metabolism and postsurgical nonverbal communication patterns. *Developmental Medicine and Child Neurology, 35,* 582–592.

Capps, L., Sigman, M., & Mundy, P. (1994). Attachment security in children with autism. *Developmental Psychopathology, 6,* 29–261.

Carpenter, M., Nagell, K., & Tomasello, M. (1998). Social cognition, joint attention, and communicative competence from 9 to 15 months of age. *Monographs of the Society for Research in Child Development, 63*(4, Serial No. 255), 1–142.

Carper, R., & Courchesne, E. (2000). Inverse correlation between frontal lobe and cerebellum sizes in children with autism. *Brain, 123,* 836–844.

Carver, L., & Dawson, G. (in press). Development and neural basis of face recognition in autism. *Molecular Psychiatry.*

Changeux, J., & Danchin, A. (1976). Selective stabilization of developing synapses as a mechanism for specification of neuronal networks. *Nature, 264,* 705–712.

Charman, T. (1998). Specifying the nature and course of the joint attention impairment in autism in the preschool years: Implications for diagnosis and intervention. *Autism: International Journal of Research and Practice, 2,* 61–79.

Charman, T., Baron-Cohen, S., Swettenham, J., Baird, G., Cox, A., & Drew, A. (2000). Testing joint attention, imitation, and play infancy precursors to language and theory of mind. *Cognitive Development, 15,* 481–498.

Cicchetti, D., & Tucker, D. (1994). Development and self-regulatory structures of the mind. *Development and Psychopathology, 6,* 553–550.

Cosmides, L. (1989). The logic of social exchange: Has natural selection shaped how humans reason? Studies with the Wason selection task. *Cognition, 31,* 187–276.

Courchesne, E., Karns, C., Davis, H., Ziccardi, R., Carper, R., Tigue, Z., et al. (2001). Unusual brain growth patterns in early life in patients with autistic disorder: An MRI study. *Neurology, 57,* 245–254.

Courchesne, E., Townsend, J. P., Akshoomoff, N. A., Yeung-Courchesne, G., Murakami, J. W., Lincoln, A., et al. (1994). A new finding: Impairment in shifting attention in autistic and cerebellar patients. In E. Broman & E. Grafman (Eds.), *Atypical cognitive deficits in developmental disorder: Implications for brain function* (pp. 101–137). Hillsdale, NJ: Erlbaum.

Craik, F., Moroz, T., Moscovich, M., Stuss, D., Winocur, G., Tulving, E., et al. (1999). In search of the self: A positron emission tomography study. *Psychological Science, 10,* 26–34.

Critchley, H., Daly, E., Bullmore, E., Williams, S., Van Amelsvoort, T., Robertson, D., et al. (2000). The functional neuroanatomy of social behavior: Changes in the cerebral blood flow when people with autistic disorder process facial expressions. *Brain, 123,* 2203–2212.

Crowson, M., Mundy, P., Neal, R., & Meyer, J. (2003). *Joint attention and developmental vulnerability in infants with insecure attachment.* Manuscript submitted for publication.

Cummins, D., & Cummins, R. (1999). Biological preparedness and evolutionary explanation. *Cognition, 73,* B37–B53.

Curcio, F. (1978). Sensorimotor functioning and communication in mute autistic children. *Journal of Autism and Childhood Schizophrenia, 8,* 282–292.

Damasio, A., & Maurer, R. (1978). A neurological model for childhood autism. *Archive of Neurology, 35,* 777–786.

Dawson, G. (1994). Development of emotional expression and emotional regulation in infancy: Contributions of the frontal lobe. In G. Dawson & K. Fischer (Eds.), *Human behavior and the developing brain* (pp. 346–378). New York: Guilford Press.

Dawson, G., & Lewy, A. (1989). Arousal, attention, and the social-emotional impairments of individuals with autism. In G. Dawson (Ed.), *Autism, nature, diagnosis, and treatment* (pp. 49–74). New York: Guilford Press.

Dawson, G., Meltzoff, A. N., Osterling, J. A., Rinaldi, J., & Brown, E. (1998). Children with autism fail to orient to naturally-occurring social stimuli. *Journal of Autism and Developmental Disorder, 28,* 479–485.

Dawson, G., Munson, J. A., Estes, A., Osterling, J. A., McPartland, J., Toth, K., et al. (2002). Neurocognitive function and joint attention ability in young children with autism spectrum disorder versus developmental delay. *Child Development, 73,* 345–358.

Dawson, G., Toth, K., Abott, R., Osterling, J. A., Munson, J. A., Estes, A., et al. (2004). Early social attention impairments in autism: Social orienting, joint attention and attention to distress. *Developmental Psychology, 40,* 271–283.

Dawson, G., Webb, S., Schellenberg, G. D., Dager, S., Friedman, S., Aylward, E. H., et al. (2002). Defining the broader phenotype of autism: Genetic, brain, and behavioral perspectives. *Developmental Psychopathology, 14*(3), 581–611.

de-Haan, M., Pascalis, O., & Johnson, M. (2002). Specialization of neural mechanisms underlying face recognition in human infants. *Journal of Cognitive Neuroscience, 14,* 199–202.

DiGirolamo, G., Kramer, A., Barad, V., Cepeda, N., Weissman, D., Milham, M., et al. (2001). General and task specific frontal lobe recruitment in older adults during executive processes: A fMRI investigation of task-switching. *NeuroReport, 12,* 2065–2071.

Dissanayake, C., Sigman, M., & Kasari, C. (1996). Long-term stability of individual differences in the emotional responsiveness of children with autism. *Journal of Child Psychology and Psychiatry, 36,* 1–8.

Elgar, K., & Cambell, R. (2001). Annotation: The cognitive neuroscience of face recognition: Implications for developmental disorders. *Journal of Child Psychology and Psychiatry, 6,* 705–717.

Ernst, M., Zametkin, J., Matochik, J., Pascualvaca, D., & Cohen, R. (1997). Low medial prefrontal dopaminergic activity in autistic children. *Lancet, 350,* 638.

Ferstl, E., & von Cramon, D. Y. (2001). The role of coherence and cohesion in text comprehension: An event-related fMRI study. *Cognitive Brain Research, 11,* 325–340.

Fletcher, P., Happé, F., Frith, U., Baker, S., Dloan, R., Frackowiak, R., et al. (1995). Other minds in the brain: A functional imaging study of "theory of mind" in story comprehension. *Cognition, 57,* 109–128.

Fox, N. (1991). It's not left, it's right: Electroencephalograph asymmetry and the development of emotion. *American Psychologist, 46,* 863–872.

Fox, N., & Davidson, R. (1987). EEG asymmetry in ten-month-old infants in response to approach of a stranger and maternal separation. *Developmental Psychology, 23,* 233–240.

Frith, C., & Frith, U. (1999). Interacting minds: A biological basis. *Science, 286,* 1692–1695.

Frith, U. (1989). *Autism: Explaining the enigma.* Oxford, England: Blackwell.

Frith, U., & Frith, C. (2001). The biological basis of social interaction. *Current Directions in Psychological Science, 10,* 151–155.

Frith, U., & Happé, F. (1994). Autism: Beyond "theory of mind." *Cognition, 50,* 115–132.

Gallagher, H., Happé, F., Brunswick, P., Fletcher, P., Frith, U., & Frith, C. (2000). Reading the mind in cartoons and stories: An fMRI study of "theory of mind" in verbal and nonverbal tasks. *Neuropsychologia, 38,* 11–21.

Gallese, V., & Goldman, A. (1998). Mirror neurons and the simulation theory of mind-reading. *Trends in Cognitive Science, 2,* 493–501.

Goel, V., Gold, B., Kapur, S., & Houle, S. (1997). The seats of reason? An imaging study of deductive and inductive reasoning. *NeuroReport, 8,* 1305–1310.

Goel, V., Grafman, J., Sadato, N., & Hallett, M. (1995). Modeling other minds. *NeuroReport, 6,* 1741–1746.

Goldman-Rakic, P. (1987). Development of cortical circuitry and cognitive function. *Child Development, 58,* 601–622.

Gottlieb, G., & Halpern, C. (2002). A relational view of causality in normal and abnormal development. *Development and Psychopathology, 14,* 421–436.

Greenough, W., Black, J., & Wallace, C. (1987). Experience and brain development. *Child Development, 58,* 539–559.

Grelotti, D., Gauthier, I., & Schultz, R. (2002). Social interest and the development of cortical face specialization: What autism teaches us about face processing. *Developmental Psychobiology, 40,* 213–225.

Griffith, E., Pennington, B., Wehner, E., & Rogers, S. (1999). Executive functions in young children with autism. *Child Development, 70,* 817–832.

Hamano, K., Iwasaki, N., Kawashima, K., & Takita, H. (1990). Volumetric quantification of brain volume in children using sequential CT scans. *Neuroradiology, 32,* 300–303.

Happé, F. (1997). Central coherence and theory of mind in autism: Reading homographs in context. *British Journal of Developmental Psychology, 15,* 1–12.

Happé, F., Ehlers, S., Fletcher, P., Frith, U., Johansson, M., Gillberg, C., et al. (1996). "Theory of mind" in the brain: Evidence from a PET scan study of Asperger syndrome. *NeuroReport, 8,* 197–201.

Hardan, A., Minshew, N. J., Harenski, K., & Keshavan, M. (2001). Posterior fossa magnetic resonance imaging in autism. *Journal of the American Academy of Child and Adolescent Psychiatry, 40,* 666–672.

Hardan, A., Minshew, N. J., Mallikarjuhn, M., & Keshavan, M. (2001). Brain volume in autism. *Journal of Child Neurology, 16,* 421–424.

Hardan, A., Yorbik, O., Minshew, N. J., Diwadkar, V., & Keshavan, M. (2002, November). *A voxel based morphometry study of gray matter in autism.* Paper presented at the International Meeting for Autism Research (IMFAR), Orlando, FL.

Haznedar, M., Buchsbaum, M., Metzger, M., Solimando, A., Spiegle-Cohen, J., & Hollander, E. (1997). Anterior cingulate gurus volume and glucose metabolism in autistic disorder. *American Journal of Psychiatry, 154,* 1047–1050.

Haznedar, M., Buchsbaum, M., Wei, T., Hof, P., Cartwright, C., Bienstock, C., et al. (2000). Limbic circuitry in patients with autism spectrum disorders studied with positron emission tomography and magnetic resonance imaging. *American Journal of Psychiatry, 157,* 1994–2001.

Henderson, L., Yoder, P., Yale, M., & McDuffie, A. (2002). Getting the point: Electrophysiological correlates of protodeclarative pointing. *International Journal of Developmental Neuroscience, 20,* 449–458.

Hobson, R. P. (1993). *Autism and the development of mind.* Hillsdale, NJ: Erlbaum.

Hood, B. M., Willen, J. D., & Driver, J. (1998). Adult's eyes trigger shifts of visual attention in human infants. *Psychological Science, 9,* 131–134.

Howlin, P. (1978). The assessment of social behavior. In M. Rutter & E. Schopler (Ed.), *Autism: A reappraisal of concepts and treatment* (pp. 63–69). New York: Plenum Press.

Humphrey, N. (1976). The social function of intellect. In P. Bateson & R. Hinde (Eds.), *Growing points in ethology* (pp. 303–317). London: Cambridge University Press.

Huttenlocher, P. (1994). Synaptogenesis in the human cerebral cortex. In G. Dawson & K. Fischer (Eds.), *Human behavior and brain development* (pp. 137–152). New York: Guilford Press.

Jasper, H. (1958). The 1020 international electrode system. *EEG and Clinical Neurophysiology, 10,* 371–375.

Johnson, M., Posner, M., & Rothbart, M. (1991). Components of visual orienting in early infancy: Contingency learning, anticipatory looking, and disengaging. *Journal of Cognitive Neuroscience, 3,* 335–344.

Kanner, L. (1973). *Childhood psychosis: Initial studies and new insights.* New York: Wiley. (Original work published 1943)

Karmiloff-Smith, A. (1995). Annotation: The extraordinary cognitive journey from foetus through infancy. *Journal of Child Psychology and Psychiatry, 36,* 1293–1313.

Kasari, C., Sigman, M., Mundy, P., & Yirmiya, N. (1990). Affective sharing in the context of joint attention interactions of normal, autistic, and mentally retarded children. *Journal of Autism and Developmental Disorders, 20,* 87–100.

Kawashima, R., Sugiura, M., Kato, T., Nakamura, A., Hatano, K., Ito, K. et al. (1999). The human amygdala plays an important role in gaze monitoring: A PET Study. *Brain, 122,* 779–783.

Kingstone, A., Friesen, C. K., & Gazzaniga, M. (2000). Reflexive joint attention depends on lateralized cortical functions. *Psychological Science, 11,* 159–166.

Klin, A. (1991). Young autistic children's listening preferences in regard to speech: A possible characterization of the symptoms of social withdrawal. *Journal of Autism and Developmental Disorders, 21,* 29–42.

Klin, A. (2000). Attributing meaning to ambiguous visual stimuli in higher functioning autism and Asperger syndrome: The Social Attribution Task. *Journal of Child Psychology and Psychiatry, 41,* 831–846.

Klin, A., Warren, J., Schultz, R., & Volkmar, F. R. (2003). The enactive mind, or from actions to cognition: Lessons from autism. *Philosophical Transaction of the Royal Society of London, 10,* 1–16.

Koechlin, E., Basso, G., Peirini, P., Panzer, S., & Grafman, J. (1999). The role of the anterior prefrontal cortex in human cognition. *Nature, 399,* 148–151.

Kraemer, G. (1985). Effects of differences in early social experience on primate neurobiological-behavioral development. In M. Reite & T. Fields (Eds.), *The psychobiology of attachment and separation* (pp. 135–161). New York: Academic Press.

Lane, R., Fink, G., Chua, P., & Dolan, R. (1997). Neural activation during selective attention to subjective emotional responses. *NeuroReport, 8,* 3969–3972.

Langdell, T. (1978). Recognition of faces: An approach to the study of autism. *Journal of Child Psychology and Psychiatry, 19,* 255–268.

LeDoux, J. (1989). Cognitive-emotional interactions in the brain. *Cognition and emotion, 3,* 267–289.

Leekam, S., & Moore, C. (2001). The development of joint attention in children with autism. In J. Barack, T. Charman, N. Yirmiya, & P. Zelazo (Eds.), *The development of autism: Perspectives from theory and research* (pp. 105–130). Mahwah, NJ: Erlbaum.

Leslie, A. (1987). Pretense and representation: The origins of "theory of mind." *Psychological Review, 94,* 412–426.

Leslie, A., & Happé, E. F. (1989). Autism and ostensive communication: The relevance of metarepresentation. *Development and Psychopathology, 1,* 205–212.

Leslie, A., & Thaiss, L. (1992). Domain specificity in conceptual development: Neuropsychological evidence from autism. *Cognition, 43,* 225–251.

Lord, C., Floody, H., Anderson, D., & Pickles, A. (2003, April). *Social engagement in very young children with autism: Differences across contexts.* Poster presented at the Society for Research in Child Development, Tampa, FL.

Lord, C., Risi, S., Lambrecht, L., Cook, E., Leventhal, B., DiLavore, P., et al. (1999). The Autism Diagnostic Observations Schedule-Generic: A standard measure of social and communication deficits associated with autism spectrum disorder. *Journal of Autism and Developmental Disorders, 30,* 205–223.

Loveland, K. (2001). Toward an ecological model of autism. In J. Burack, T. Charman, N. Yirmiya, & P. Zelazao (Eds.), *The development of autism: Perspectives from theory and research* (p. 17–37). Mahwah, NJ: Erlbaum.

Loveland, K., & Landry, S. (1986). Joint attention and language in autism and developmental language delay. *Journal of Autism and Developmental Disorders, 16,* 335–349.

Luu, P., Flaisch, T., & Tucker, D. (2000). Medial-frontal cortex in action monitoring. *Journal of Neuroscience, 20,* 464–469.

Martin, J. (1996). *Neuroanatomy: Text and Atlas* (2nd ed.). New York: McGraw-Hill.

McEvoy, R., Rogers, S., & Pennington, R. (1993). Executive function and social communication deficits in young autistic children. *Journal of Child Psychology and Psychiatry, 34,* 563–578.

McWhinney, B. (1998). Models of the emergence of language. *Annual Review of Psychology, 49,* 199–227.

Meltzoff, A. N., & Gopnik, A. (1993). The role of imitation in understanding persons and developing a theory of mind. In S. Baron-Cohen, H. Tager-Flusberg, & D. Cohen (Eds.), *Understanding the minds of others: Perspectives from autism* (pp. 335–366). New York: Oxford University Press.

Miller, E., & Cohen, J. (2001). An integrative theory of prefrontal cortex functioning. *Annual Reviews of Neuroscience, 24,* 167–202.

Minshew, N. J., Johnson, C., & Luna, B. (2001). The cognitive and neural basis of autism: A disorder of complex information processing and dysfunction of neocortical systems. *International Review of Mental Retardation, 23,* 111–137.

Minshew, N. J., Meyer, J., & Goldstein, G. (2002). Abstract reasoning in autism: A dissociation between concept formation and concept identification. *Neuropsychology, 16,* 327–334.

Moore, C., & Dunham, D. (1995). *Joint attention: Its origins and role in development.* Hillsdale, NJ: Erlbaum.

Morales, M., Mundy, P., & Rojas, J. (1998). Following the direction of gaze and language development in six month olds. *Infant Behavior and Development, 21,* 373–377.

Morecraft, R., Guela, C., & Mesulam, M. (1993). Architecture of connectivity within the cingulo-frontal-parietal neurocognitive network for directed attention. *Archives of Neurology, 50,* 279–283.

Mottron, L., & Burack, J. (2001). Enhanced perceptual functioning in the development of autism. In J. Burack, T. Charman, N. Yirmiya, & P. Zelazo (Eds.), *The development of autism: Perspectives from theory and research* (pp. 131–148). Mahwah, NJ: Erlbaum.

Mundy, P. (1995). Joint attention and social-emotional approach behavior in children with autism. *Development and Psychopathology, 7,* 63–82.

Mundy, P. (2003). The neural basis of social impairments in autism: The role of the dorsal medial-frontal cortex and anterior cingulate system. *Journal of Child Psychology and Psychiatry, 44,* 793–809.

Mundy, P., Card, J., & Fox, N. (2000). EEG correlates of the development of infant joint attention skills. *Developmental Psychobiology, 36,* 325–338.

Mundy, P., & Crowson, M. (1997). Joint attention and early communication: Implications for intervention with autism. *Journal of Autism and Developmental Disorders, 27,* 653–675.

Mundy, P., Delgado, C., Block, J., Venezia, M., Hogan, A., & Seibert, J. (2003). *A Manual for the Abridged Early Social Communication Scales (ESCS).* (Available from the University of Miami Psychology Department, Coral Gables, Florida; pmundy@miami.edu)

Mundy, P., & Hogan, A. (1994). Intersubjectivity, joint attention and autistic developmental pathology. In D. Cicchetti & S. Toth (Eds.), *Rochester symposium of developmental psychopathology: Vol. 5. A developmental perspective on the self and its disorders* (pp. 1–30). Hillsdale, NJ: Erlbaum.

Mundy, P., Hogan, A., & Doehring, P. (1996). A preliminary manual for the abridged Early Social Communication Scales (ESCS). Available from http://yin.psy.miami.edu:80/Child/Pmundy/manual.html.

Mundy, P., Kasari, C., & Sigman, M. (1992). Joint attention, affective sharing, and intersubjectivity. *Infant Behavior and Development, 15,* 377–381.

Mundy, P., & Neal, R. (2001). Neural plasticity, joint attention and a transactional social-orienting model of autism. *International Review of Mental Retardation, 23,* 139–168.

Mundy, P., & Sigman, M. (1989). Specifying the nature of the social impairment in autism. In G. Dawson (Ed.), *Autism: New perspectives on diagnosis, nature, and treatment* (pp. 3–21). New York: Guilford Press.

Mundy, P., Sigman, M., & Kasari, C. (1990). A longitudinal study of joint attention and language development in autistic children. *Journal of Autism and Developmental Disorders, 20,* 115–128.

Mundy, P., Sigman, M., & Kasari, C. (1993). The theory of mind and joint attention deficits in autism. In S. Baron-Cohen, H. Tager-Flusberg, & D. Cohen (Eds.), *Understanding other minds: Perspectives from autism* (pp. 181–203). Oxford, England: Oxford University Press.

Mundy, P., Sigman, M., & Kasari, C. (1994). Joint attention, developmental level, and symptom presentation in young children with autism. *Development and Psychopathology, 6,* 389–401.

Mundy, P., Sigman, M., Ungerer, J., & Sherman, T. (1986). Defining the social deficits of autism: The contribution of nonverbal communication measures. *Journal of Child Psychology and Psychiatry, 27,* 657–669.

Mundy, P., & Willoughby, J. (1998). Nonverbal communication, affect, and social emotional development. In A. Wetherby, S. Warren, & J. Reichle (Eds.), *Transitions in prelinguistic communication: Preintentional to intentional and presymbolic to symbolic* (pp. 111–134). Baltimore: Paul H. Brookes.

Nichols, K., Fox, N., & Mundy, P. (in press). Neurocognitive functions of initiating joint attention in toddlers. *Infancy*.

Norman, D., & Shallice, T. (1986). Attention to action: Willed and automatic control of behavior. In R. Davidson, G. Schwartz, & D. Shapiro (Eds.), *Consciousness and self-regulation* (pp. 1–18). New York: Plenum Press.

Ohnishi, T., Matsuda, H., Hashimoto, T., Kunihiro, T., Nishikawa, M., Uema, T., et al. (2000). Abnormal regional cerebral blood flow in childhood autism. *Brain, 123,* 1838–1844.

Osterling, J. A., & Dawson, G. (1994). Early recognition of children with autism: A study of first birthday home videotapes. *Journal of Autism and Developmental Disorders, 24,* 247–257.

Ozonoff, S., & South, M. (2001). Early social development in young children with autism: Theoretical and clinical implications. In G. Bremmer & A. Fogel (Eds.), *Blackwell handbook of infant development* (pp. 565–588). Oxford, England: Blackwell.

Panksepp, J. (1979). A neurochemical theory of autism. *Trends in Neurosciences, 2,* 174–177.

Peterson, C., & Siegal, M. (1995). Deafness, conversation and theory of mind. *Journal of Child Psychology and Psychiatry, 36,* 459–474.

Piaget, J. (1952). *The origins of intelligence in children.* New York: Norton.

Pierce, K., Frank, H., Farshad, S., & Courchesne, E. (2001, November). *Brain activity to mother and other familiar faces: Evidence for socioemotional responding in autism.* Paper presented at the International Meeting for Autism Research (IMFAR), San Diego, CA.

Piven, J., Arndt, S., Bailey, J., & Andreasen, N. (1996). Regional brain enlargement in autism: A magnetic resonance imaging study. *Journal of the American Academy of Child and Adolescent Psychiatry, 35,* 530–536.

Piven, J., Arndt, S., Bailey, J., Havercamp, S., Andreasen, N., & Palmer, P. (1995). An MRI study of brain size in autism. *American Journal of Psychiatry, 152,* 1145–1149.

Piven, J., Saliba, K., Bailey, J., & Arndt, S. (1997). An MRI study of autism: The cerebellum revisited. *Neurology, 49,* 546–551.

Plousia, M. (2002). Affective expressions during joint attention interactions with an adult: The case of autism. *Journal of the Hellenic Psychological Society, 9,* 9–21.

Posner, M., & Petersen, S. (1990). The attention system of the human brain. *Annual Review of Neuroscience, 13,* 25–42.

Rheingold, H. L., Hay, D. F., & West, M. J. (1976). Sharing in the second year of life. *Child Development, 47,* 1148–1158.

Rizzolatti, G., & Arbib, M. (1998). Language within our grasp. *Trends in Neuroscience, 21,* 188–194.

Rogers, S., & Pennington, B. (1991). A theoretical approach to the deficits in infantile autism. *Developmental Psychopathology, 6,* 635–652.

Russell, T., Rubia, K., Bullmore, E., Soni, W., Suckling, J., Brammer, M., et al. (2000). Exploring the social brain in schizophrenia: Left prefrontal underactivation during mental state attribution. *American Journal of Psychiatry, 157,* 2040–2042.

Sabbagh, M., & Taylor, M. (2000). Neural correlates of theory of mind: An event related potential study. *Psychological Science, 11,* 46–50.

Scaife, M., & Bruner, J. (1975). The capacity for joint visual attention in the infant. *Nature, 253,* 265–266.

Scarr, S. (1992). Developmental theories for the 1990's: Development and individual differences. *Child Development, 63,* 1–19.

Schopler, E., Reichlet, R., DeVellis, R., & Daly, K. (1980). Toward objective classification of childhood autism: Childhood Autism Rating Scale (CARS). *Journal of Autism and Developmental Disorders, 10,* 91–103.

Schultz, R., Romanski, L., & Tsatsanis, K. (2000). Neurofunctional models of autistic disorder and Asperger syndrome: Clues from neuroimaging. In A. Klin, F. Volkmar, & S. Sparrow (Eds.), *Asperger syndrome* (pp. 172–209). New York: Guilford Press.

Sears, L., Cortney, V., Somaia, M., Bailey, J., Bonnie, J., & Piven, J. (1999). An MRI study of basal ganglia in autism. *Progress in Neuro-Psychopharmacology and Biological Psychiatry, 23,* 613–624.

Seibert, J. M., Hogan, A. E., & Mundy, P. C. (1982). Assessing interactional competencies: The Early Social Communication Scales. *Infant Mental Health Journal, 3,* 244–245.

Sigman, M., Kasari, C., Kwon, J., & Yirmiya, N. (1992). Responses to the negative emotions of others by autistic, mentally retarded and normal children. *Child Development, 63,* 796–807.

Sigman, M., & Mundy, P. (1989). Social attachments in autistic children. *Journal of the American Academy of Child and Adolescent Psychiatry, 28,* 74–81.

Sigman, M., & Ruskin, E. (1999). Continuity and change in the social competence of children with autism, down syndrome, and developmental delay. *Monographs of the Society for Research in Child Development, 64*(Serial No. 256), 1–108.

Stella, J., Mundy, P., & Tuchman, R. (1999). Social and non-social factors in the Childhood

Autism Rating Scales. *Journal of Autism and Developmental Disorders, 29,* 307–317.

Stern, D. (1985). *The interpersonal world of the infant.* New York: Basic Books.

Stich, S., & Nichols, S. (1992). Folk psychology: Simulation versus tacit theory. *Mind and Language, 7,* 29–65.

Stone, W., Coonrod, E., & Ousley, O. (2000). Brief report: Screening Tool for Autism in Two-years-olds (STAT): Development and preliminary data. *Journal of Autism and Developmental Disorders, 30,* 607–612.

Stuphorn, V., Taylor, T., & Schall, J. (2000). Performance monitoring by the supplementary eye field. *Nature, 408,* 857–860.

Swettenham, J., Baron-Cohen, S., Charman, T., Cox, A., Baird, G., Drew, A., et al. (1998). The frequency and distribution of spontaneous attention shifts between social and nonsocial stimuli in autistic, typically developing, and nonautistic developmentally delayed infants. *Journal of Child Psychology and Psychiatry, 39,* 747–753.

Teasdale, J., Howard, R., Cox, S., Ha, Y., Brammer, M., Williams, S., et al. (1999). Functional MRI of the cognitive generation of affect. *American Journal of Psychiatry, 156,* 209–215.

Tomasello, M. (1995). Joint attention as social cognition. In C. Moore & P. Dunham (Eds.), *Joint attention: Its origins and role in development* (pp. 103–130). Hillsdale, NJ: Erlbaum.

Tomasello, M. (1999). *The cultural origins of human cognition.* Cambridge, MA: Harvard University Press.

Townsend, J., Harris, N., & Courchesne, E. (1996). Visual attention abnormalities in autism: Delayed orienting to location. *Journal of the International Neuropsychological Society, 2,* 541–550.

Townsend, J., Westerfield, M., Leaver, E., Makeig, S., Tzyy-Ping, J., Pierce, K., et al. (2001). Event-related brain response abnormalities in autism: Evidence for impaired cerebello-frontal spatial attention networks. *Cognitive Brain Research, 11,* 127–145.

Tremblay, L., & Schultz, W. (1999). Relative reward preference in primate orbitofrontal cortex. *Nature, 398,* 704–708.

Trevarthen, C., & Aitken, K. (2001). Infant intersubjectivity: Research, theory and clinical applications. *Journal of Child Psychology and Psychiatry, 42,* 3–48.

Vaughan, A., & Mundy, P. (in press). Neural systems and the development of gaze following and related joint attention skills. In R. Flom, K. Lee, & D. Muir (Eds.), *The ontogeny of gaze processing in infants and children.* Mahwah, NJ: Erlbaum.

Volkmar, F. R., Lord, C., Bailey, A., Schultz, R., & Klin, A. (2004). Autism and pervasive developmental disorders. *Journal of Child Psychology and Psychiatry, 45,* 135–170.

Wantanabe, M. (1999). Neurobiology: Attraction is relative not absolute. *Nature, 398,* 661–663.

Warreyn, P., & Roeyers, H. (2002, November). *Joint attention, social referencing and requesting abilities in young children with autism spectrum disorder.* Paper presented at the International Meeting for Autism Research (IMFAR). Orlando, FL.

Wellman, H. (1993). Early understanding of mind: The normal case. In S. Baron-Cohen, H. Tager-Flusberg, & D. Cohen (Eds.), *Understanding other minds: Perspectives from autism* (pp. 40–58). Oxford, England: Oxford University Press.

Wetherby, A., & Prutting, C. (1984). Profiles of communicative and cognitive-social abilities in autistic children. *Journal of Speech and Hearing Research, 27,* 367–377.

Whiten, A., & Byrne, R. (1988). Tactical deception in primates. *Behavioral and Brain Sciences, 11,* 233–273.

Willensen-Swinkel, S., Dietz, F., Nober, E., van Daalen, H., van Engeland, H., & Buitlaar, J. (2002, October). *A population based study on early detection of autism at age 14 months in the Netherlands.* Paper presented at the International Meeting for Autism Research (IMFAR). Orlando, FL.

Wing, L., & Potter, D. (2002). The epidemiology of autistic spectrum disorders: Is the prevalence rising? *Mental Retardation and Developmental Disabilities Research Review, 8,* 151–161.

The Enactive Mind—From Actions to Cognition: Lessons from Autism

AMI KLIN, WARREN JONES, ROBERT T. SCHULTZ, AND FRED R. VOLKMAR

One of the most intriguing puzzles posed by individuals with autism is the great discrepancy between what they can do on explicit tasks of social reasoning (when all of the elements of a problem are verbally given to them) and what they fail to do in more naturalistic situations (when they need to spontaneously apply their social reasoning abilities to meet the moment-by-moment demands of their daily social life; Klin, Schultz, & Cohen, 2000). While even the most intellectually gifted individuals display deficits in some complex social reasoning problems (Baron-Cohen, Jolliffe, Mortimore, & Robertson, 1997; Happé, 1994), some, particularly those without cognitive deficits, can solve such problems at relatively high levels (Bowler, 1992; Dahlgren & Trillingsgaard, 1996) without showing commensurate levels of social adaptation. This discrepancy is troublesome because while it is possible to teach them better social reasoning skills, such new abilities may have little impact on their real-life social or communicative competence (Hadwin, Baron-Cohen, Howlin, & Hill, 1997; Ozonoff & Miller, 1995).

There has been little systematic research to investigate the magnitude of this discrepancy. Nevertheless, an indicator of its size can be derived from a sample of 40 older adolescents and adults with autism followed in our center.

Their full scale IQs are within the normative range, whereas their mean age equivalent score on the Interpersonal Relationships subdomain of the Vineland Adaptive Behavior Scales (Sparrow, Balla, & Cicchetti, 1984) is 4 years. These individuals have many cognitive, linguistic, knowledge-based, and potentially useful vocational assets, yet this social adaptive score would suggest that if left to their own devices in a challenging social situation, their social survival skills or street smarts might be equivalent to those of young children. Yet, many of these individuals are capable of a degree of self-sufficiency that is much higher than 4 years. It is possible, however, that they are able to achieve this level of independence despite significant social disabilities by choosing highly structured and regimented life routines that avoid novelty and the inherent unpredictability of typical social life. In other words, they may be able to constrain the inevitable complexity of social life by setting themselves a routine of rigid rules and habits, adhering very closely to this lifestyle in what is typically a very solitary life.

Some recent studies focused on responses to naturalistic social situations suggest that the discrepancy between performance on structured and naturalistic tasks may be even greater than hitherto thought possible. Con-

This chapter is reprinted by permission of Oxford University Press.

(*a*)   (*b*)

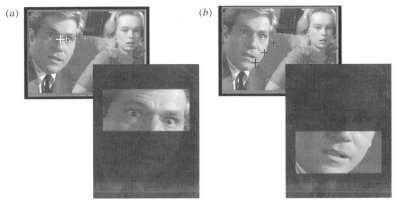

Figure 26.1   Focus on eyes versus mouth: Cut to shocked young man. (a) Focus on typically developing viewer. (b) Focus of viewer with autism.

sider the following two examples from eye-tracking studies of normative-IQ adolescents and adults with autism. In these experiments (Klin, Jones, Schultz, Volkmar, & Cohen, 2002a, 2002b), eye-tracking technology allows researchers to see and measure what a person is visually focusing on when viewing complex social situations. This paradigm allows for an appreciation of a person's spontaneous reactions to naturalistic demands inherent in seeking meaning in what is viewed. In real-life social situations, many crucial social cues occur very rapidly. Failure to notice may lead to a general failure in assessing the meaning of entire situations, thus precluding adaptive reactions to them. Figure 26.1 shows a still image of two characters from a movie: at left, a young man, and at right, a young woman. Overlaid on the image are crosses that mark, in green, the focus of a normative-IQ adult with autism and, in yellow, the focus of a typical adult viewer matched for gender and IQ. The boldest crosshairs mark each viewer's point of regard at the moment of this still, while the gradated crosses reveal the path of each viewer's focus over the preceding five frames. The image in this figure is a still from a shot immediately following an abrupt camera cut. In the preceding shot, a character smashes a bottle in the right half of the frame (where both viewers were focused). The camera cuts to show the reaction of the young man and woman, and both viewers respond immediately. While the typical viewer responds directly to the look of surprise and horror in the young man's wide eyes, the viewer with

autism is seen trying to gather information from the young man's mouth. The young man's mouth is slightly open but expressionless, and it provides few clues about what is happening in the scene.

This discrepancy in viewing patterns is also seen in group data. Figure 26.2 plots the focus of eight normative-IQ adults with autism (in red) and eight age-, IQ-, and gender-matched typical controls (in blue; this is a subsample from the data in Klin et al., 2002b) for one frame of this video sequence. This subsample is used here to visually illustrate the findings obtained for the entire sample summarized later. While typical viewers converge on the eye region, some individuals with autism converge on the mouth regions, whereas others' focus is peripheral to the face. When the visual fixation patterns were summarized for the

Figure 26.2   Group data (*N* = 16) illustrating focus on eyes versus mouth. Viewers with autism: black crosses; typically developing viewers: white crosses.

entire sample in this study ($N=30$, 15 participants in each group), individuals with autism, relative to controls, focused twice as much time on the mouth region of faces and 2½ times less on the eye region of faces when viewing dynamic social scenes. There was virtually no overlap in the distributions of visual fixation patterns across the two groups of participants. Figure 26.3 presents these data as a

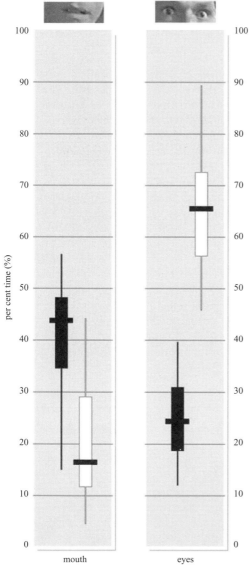

Figure 26.3 Group data ($N = 30$) summarizing visual fixation patterns on eyes versus mouth. Black bars: viewers with autism; white bars: typically developing viewers.

percentage of overall viewing time focused on eyes and mouths.

These results contrast markedly with another recent study of face scanning in autism (van der Geest, Kemner, Verbaten, & van Engeland, 2002), in which participants showed normative visual fixation patterns when viewing photographs of human faces relative to controls. The difference between the two studies was that while in the latter investigation participants were presented with static pictures of faces, in the former study participants were presented with dynamic (i.e., video) depictions of social interactions, coming perhaps closer to replicating a more naturalistic social situation (i.e., we almost never encounter static depictions of faces in our daily social interactions). In such more "spontaneous situations," the deviation from normative face-scanning patterns in autism seems to be magnified. And the magnitude of this deviation is put in context if we appreciate the fact that preferential looking at the eyes rather than at the mouths of an approaching person has been shown in infants as young as 3 months of age (Haith, Bergman, & Moore, 1979).

A second example from the same eye-tracking studies (Klin et al., 2002a) focuses on a developmental skill that emerges and is fully operational by the time a child is about 12 to 14 months of age. It involves the joint-attention skill of following a pointing gesture to the target indicated by the direction of pointing (Mundy & Neal, 2000). Pointing, like many other nonverbal social cues, can both modify and further specify what is said. For effective communication exchange, verbal and nonverbal cues need to be quickly integrated. Figure 26.4 shows a scene from a movie in which the young man inquires about a painting hanging on a distant wall. In doing so, he first points to a specific painting on the wall and then asks the older man (who lives in the house), "Who did the painting?" While the verbal request is more general (as there are several pictures on the wall), the act of pointing has already specified the painting in which the young man is interested. The figure shows the visual scanning paths of the adult viewer with autism (in green) and the typical viewer (in yellow). As shown in Figure 26.4 and more clearly in the schematic renditions underneath, the viewer

Figure 26.4 Scanning patterns in response to social visual versus verbal cues. Viewers with autism: black trace in (a) and (b); typically developing viewer: white trace in (a) and (c).

with autism does not follow the pointing gesture but instead waits until he hears the question and then appears to move from picture to picture without knowing which one the conversation is about. The typical viewer (in yellow) follows the young man's pointing immediately, ending up, very deliberately, on the correct (large) picture. Hearing the question, he then looks to the older man for a reply and back to the young man for his reaction. The visual path he follows clearly illustrates his ability to use the nonverbal gesture to immediately inspect the painting referenced by the young

man. In contrast, the viewer with autism uses primarily the verbal cue, neglecting the nonverbal gesture and, in doing so, resorts to a much more inefficient pursuit of the referenced painting. When the viewer with autism was later questioned in an explicit fashion about whether he knew what the pointing gesture meant, he had no difficulty defining the meaning of the gesture. Yet, he failed to apply this knowledge spontaneously when viewing the scene from the movie.

That normative-IQ adolescents and adults with autism fail to display normative reactions exhibited by typical young children does not mean that their ability to function in the world is at this very early stage of development. Rather, it raises the possibility that these individuals learn about the social world in a different manner. What is this developmental path is of both clinical and research importance. Collectively, the various examples presented here suggest a need to explain the discrepancy between performance on structured and explicit as against naturalistic and spontaneous tasks and, in so doing, to explore what might be a unique social developmental path evidenced in autism. This chapter contends that theories of the social dysfunction in autism need to address both of these phenomena. Traditionally, theories of social-cognitive development have relied on a framework delineated by computational models of the mind and of the brain (Gardner, 1985), which focus on abstracting problem-solving capacities necessary to function in the social environment. The methodologies used typically employ explicit and often verbally mediated tasks to probe whether a person has these capacities. In real life, however, social situations rarely present themselves in this fashion. Rather, the individual needs to go about defining a social task as such by paying attention to and identifying the relevant aspects of a social situation prior to having an opportunity to use his or her available social-cognitive problem-solving skills. Thus, to study more naturalistic social adaptation, there may be some utility in using an alternative theoretical framework that centers around a different set of social-cognitive phenomena such as people's predispositions to orient to salient social stimuli, to naturally seek to impose social meaning on what they see and hear, to differentiate what is relevant from what is not, and to be intrinsically motivated to solve a social problem once such a problem is identified. The framework presented in this chapter is called *enactive mind* (EM) to highlight the central role of motivational predispositions to respond to social stimuli and a developmental process in which social cognition results from social action.

The emphases of the EM framework differ from those in computational models in a number of ways:

- Instead of assuming a social environment that consists of a pregiven set of definitions and regularities and a perceiving social agent (e.g., a child) whose mind consists of a pregiven set of cognitive capacities that can solve problems as they are explicitly presented to it, this framework proposes an active mind that sets out to make sense of the social environment and that changes itself as a result of this interaction (Mead, 1924).

- Moving from a focus on abstracted competencies (what an organism can do), this framework focuses on the adaptive functions that are subserved by these competencies (i.e., how an agent engages in the process of acquiring such competencies in the first place; Klin et al., 2000).

- Moving away from a focus on cognition, this framework rekindles a once more prominent role given to affect and predispositional responses in the process of socialization (Damasio, 1999).

- It shifts the focus of investigation from what can be called *disembodied cognition,* or insular abstractions captured by computational cognition (e.g., algorithms in a digital computer) to *embodied cognition,* or cognitive traces left by the action of an organism on an environment defined by species-specific regularities and by a species-specific topology of differential salience (i.e., some things in the environment are more important than others).

Of particular importance in this framework is the premise that agents may vary in what they are seeking in the environment, resulting in highly disparate "mental representations" of the world that they are interacting with (Clark, 1999; Varela, Thompson, & Rosch, 1991). This process, in turn, leads to individual variation in neurofunctional specialization because more prominence is given in this framework to the notion of the brain as a repository of experiences (LeDoux, 2002); that is, our brain becomes who we are or experience repeatedly.

Specifically, the EM approach is offered as an avenue to conceptualize phenomena deemed essential for understanding social adaptation, and which are typically not emphasized in research based on computational models of the social mind. These phenomena include the need to consider the complexity of the social world, the very early-emerging nature of a multitude of social adaptive mechanisms, and how these mechanisms contextualize the emergence of social cognition, as well as important temporal constraints on social adaptation. Our formulation of the EM framework is primarily based on Mead's Darwinian account of the emergence of mind (Mead, 1924), the work of Searle (1980) and Bates (1976, 1979) as to the underlying functions of communication, the philosophy of perception of Merleau-Ponty (1962), and, particularly, on a framework for cognitive neuroscience outlined by Varela and colleagues (1991), from which the term *enactive mind* is borrowed. Excellent summaries of psychological and neurofunctional aspects of this framework have been provided by Clark (1999) and Iacoboni (2000a). Some of the views proposed here have long been part of discussions contrasting information processing and ecological approaches to every aspect of the mind, including attention and sensorimotor integration, memory and language, among other psychological faculties (e.g., Gibson, 1963; Neisser, 1997).

THE SOCIAL WORLD AS AN OPEN-DOMAIN TASK

In the EM approach, a fundamental difference between explicit and naturalistic social tasks is captured in the distinction between *closed domains* and *open domains* of operation (Winograd & Flores, 1986). Research paradigms based on computational models of the social mind often reduce the social word to a set of pregiven rules and regularities that can be symbolically represented in the mind of a young child. In other words, the social world is simplified into a closed-task domain, in which all essential elements to be studied can be fully represented and defined. This is justified in terms of the need to reduce the complexity of the social environment into a number of easily tested problem-solving tasks. In contrast, the EM approach embraces the open-ended nature of social adaptation. The social world as an open-task domain implies the need to con-

sider a multitude of elements that are more or less important depending on the context of the situation and the person's perceptions, desires, goals, and ongoing adjustment. Successful adaptation requires from a person a sense of relative salience of each element in a situation, preferential choices on the basis of priorities learned through experience, and further moment-by-moment adjustments. For example, if we were to represent the skills of driving a car successfully, we could define the *driving domain* as involving wheels, roads, traffic lights, and other cars, but this domain is hardly complete without encompassing a host of other factors including attention to pedestrians (sometimes but not always), driving regulations (but these can be overridden by safety factors), local customs (in some cities or countries more than others), variable weather conditions, signals from other drivers, and so on. This rich texture of elements defines the "background" of knowledge necessary to solve problems in the driving domain. Similarly, the social domain consists of people with age, gender, ethnic, and individual differences; facial and bodily gestures; language and voice/prosodic cues in all of their complexity and context-dependent nature; posture; physical settings and social props; situation-specific conventions, among a host of other factors. Successful driving or social adaptation would require more than knowing a set of rules—at times referred to as *knowing that*—it would rather require *knowing how,* or a learning process that is based on the accumulation of experiences in a vast number of cases that result in being able to navigate the background environment according to the relative salience of each of the multitude of elements of a situation and the moment-by-moment emerging patterns that result from the interaction of the various elements. In autism, one of the major limitations of available teaching strategies, including forms of social skills training (e.g., Howlin, Baron-Cohen, & Hadwin, 1999), is the difficulty in achieving generalization of skills or how to translate a problem-solving capacity learned in a closed-domain environment (e.g., therapeutic methods relying on explicit rules and drilling) into a skill that the person avails himself or herself of in an open-domain environment (e.g., a naturalistic social situation). This may also be the reason that individuals with autism have difficulty in spontaneously using whatever social-cognitive skills they may have learned through explicit teaching. Incidentally, driving is an equally challenging task to individuals with autism.

In the EM approach, the child "enacts the social world," perceiving it selectively in terms of what is immediately essential for social action, whereas mental representations of that individualized social world arise from repeated experiences resulting from such perceptually guided actions (Varela et al., 1991). In this way, the surrounding environment is reduced to perceptions that are relevant to social action, a great simplification if we are to consider the richness of what is constantly available for an agent to hear, see, and otherwise experience. Similarly, the mental representations (i.e., social cognition) available for the child to reason about the social environment are deeply embedded in the child's history of social actions, thus constituting a tool for social adaptation. Thus, there are two principles underlying the EM approach to naturalistic social situations as open-domain tasks. First, the vast complexity of the surrounding environment is greatly simplified in terms of a differential *topology of salience* that separates aspects of the environment that are irrelevant (e.g., light fixtures, a person turned away) from those that are crucially important (e.g., someone staring at you). Second, this topology of salience is established in terms of perceptually or cognitively guided actions subserving social adaptation.

These principles imply, however, that the surrounding environment will be enacted or recreated differently on the basis of differences in predispositions to respond in a certain way (Maturana & Varela, 1973). In autism, our eye-tracking illustrations are beginning to show what this social landscape may look like from the perspective of individuals with this condition. Consider, for example, the illustration in Figure 26.5, showing the point of regard (signaled by the white cross in the center of the green circle) of a normative-IQ adult with autism who is viewing a romantic scene. Rather than focusing on the actors in the foreground, he is foveating on the room's light switch on the left. In Figure 26.6, a 2-year-old boy with autism is viewing a popular American children's show. His point of regard on the video frame presented as well as his scanpath immediately before and after that frame (seen in green on the right corner of the picture) indicate that rather than focusing on the protagonists of the show and their actions, this child is visually inspecting inanimate details on the shelves. By enacting these scenes in this manner, it is likely that, from the perspective of the two viewers with autism, the scenes are no longer social scenes, however clear their social nature might be to a typical viewer. It is also likely that if these viewers were explicitly asked or prompted to observe the social scenes and perform a task about them, they might be able to fare much better. The fact that they did not orient to the essential elements in the scene, however, suggests that were they to be part of such a situation, their adjustment to the environmental demands (e.g., fit in the ongo-

Figure 26.5 Adult viewer with autism (white cross circled in black): Focus on nonessential inanimate details.

Figure 26.6 Toddler viewer with autism (white cross circled in white): Focus on nonessential inanimate details.

ing play taking place between the two child protagonists) would be greatly compromised.

DEVELOPMENTAL ELEMENTS IN THE EMERGENCE OF MENTAL REPRESENTATIONS

Computational models of the social mind make use of cognitive constructs that could help a child navigate successfully the social environment (e.g., Baron-Cohen, 1995). There is less emphasis on how these constructs emerge within a broader context of early social development, which is a justifiable way of modeling the more specific, targeted social-cognitive skills. In contrast, the EM approach depends on this broader discussion of early social predispositions to justify the need to consider complex social situations in terms of a differential topology of salience. In other words, why should some aspects of the environment be more salient than others? To address this question, we need to outline a set of early social reactions that may precede and accompany the emergence of social-cognitive skills.

In the EM approach, the perceptual makeup of typical human infants is seen as consisting of a specific set of somatosensory organs that are constantly seeking salient aspects of the world to focus on, particularly those that have survival value. To invoke the notion of survival value implies the notion of adjustment to or action on the environment. In this context, the gravitation toward and engagement of cospecifics is seen as one of the important survival functions. Thus, social stimuli are seen as having a higher degree of salience than competing inanimate stimuli (e.g., Bates, 1979; Klin et al., 2000). The possibility that in autism the relative salience of social stimuli might be diminished (e.g., Dawson, Meltzoff, Osterling, Rinaldi, & Brown, 1998; Klin, 1989) could be the basis for a cascade of developmental events in which a child with this condition fails to enact a relevant social world, thus failing to accrue the social experiences hypothesized in the EM approach to be the basis for social-cognitive development.

A large number of social predispositions have been documented in the child development literature, some of which appear to be greatly reduced in children with autism. To limit the discussion to early social orientation skills, we consider only infants' reactions to human sounds and faces. The human voice appears to be one of the earliest and most effective stimuli conducive of social engagement (Alegria & Noirot, 1978; Eimas, Siqueland, Jusczyk, & Vigorito, 1971; Eisenberg, 1979; Mills & Melhuish, 1974), a reaction that is not observed in autism (Adrien et al., 1991, 1993; Klin, 1991, 1992; Osterling & Dawson, 1994; Werner, Dawson, Osterling, & Dinno, 2000). In fact, the lack of orientation to human sounds (e.g., when the infant hears the voice of a nearby adult) has been found to be one of the most robust predictors of a later diagnosis of autism in children first seen at the age of 2 years (Lord, 1995). In the visual modality, human faces have been emphasized as one of the most potent facilitators of social engagement (Bryant, 1991). For example, 2-day-olds look at their mother rather than at another unknown woman (I. W. R. Bushnell, Sai, & Mullin, 1989), 3-month-olds focus on the more emotionally revealing eye regions of the face (Haith et al., 1979), and 5-month-olds are sensitive to very small deviations in eye gaze during social interactions (Symons, Hains, & Muir, 1998) and can match facial and vocal expressions on the basis of congruity (Walker, 1982). In autism, a large number of face perception studies have shown deficits and abnormalities in such basic visual social processing situations (Hobson, Ouston, & Lee, 1988; Klin et al., 1999; Langdell, 1978), which, incidentally, were not accompanied by failure in developmentally equivalent tasks in the physical (nonsocial) domain. For example, one study demonstrated adequate visual processing of buildings as against faces (Boucher & Lewis, 1992). Another study asked children with autism to sort people who varied in terms of age, sex, facial expressions of emotion, and the type of hat that they were wearing (Weeks & Hobson, 1987). In contrast to typical children who grouped pictures by emotional expressions, the participants with autism grouped the pictures by the type of hat the people were wearing. Such studies indicated not only abnormalities in face processing but also preferential orientation to inanimate objects, a finding corroborated in other studies (Dawson et al., 1998). In a more recent study (Dawson et al., 2002), children with autism failed to exhibit differential brain event-related potentials to familiar versus unfamiliar faces, but they did show differences relative to familiar versus unfamiliar objects.

While computational models of the social mind are often modular in nature (e.g., Leslie, 1987), that is, certain aspects of social functioning could be preserved while others were disrupted, the EM approach ascribes importance to early disruptions in sociability because of its central premise that normative social cognition is embedded in social perception and experience. This principle states that social perception is perceptually guided social action, and social-cognitive processes emerge only from recurrent sensorimotor patterns that allow action to be perceptually guided (hence the notion of *embodied cognition;* Varela et al., 1991). The radical assumption of this framework, therefore, is that it is not possible to disentangle cognition from actions and that if this happened (e.g., a child was taught to perform a social-cognitive task following an explicit drill rather than acquiring the skill as a result of repeated social engagement and actions), the given skill would represent a *disembodied cognition,* or a reasoning skill that would not retain its normative functional value in social adaptation (Markman & Dietrich, 2000). For example, an infant may be attracted to the face of his or her mother, seeking to act on it. In the context of acting on it, the infant learns a great deal about faces and mothers, although this knowledge is a function of the child's active experiences with that face, which may include learning of contingencies (e.g., vocal sounds and lip movements go together; certain voice inflections go with certain face configurations such as smiles and frowns) and that these contingencies have pleasurable value (thus leading to approach or an attempt at reenactment of the situation) or unpleasurable value (thus leading to withdrawal). Studies of infants' early social development have shown that they not only are sensitive to affective salience but also act on that salience through reactions that are appropriate to emotional signals (Haviland & Lelwica, 1987). They react negatively to their mothers' depressed affect (Tronick, Cohn, & Shea, 1986) and appropriately to the emotional content of praise or prohibition (Fernald, 1993). From very early on, they expect contingency between their actions and those of their partners (Tarabulsy, Tessier, & Kappas, 1996). Fewer developmental phenomena have demonstrated this effect more clearly than studies using the "still-face paradigm" (Tronick, Als, Adamson, Wise, & Brazelton, 1978). When mothers who have previously been stimulating their babies in a playful fashion withdraw the smiles and vocalization and assume a still face, infants as young as 2 to 3 months first make attempts to continue the interaction but then stop smiling, avert their gaze, and may protest vigorously (Field, Vega-Lahar, Scafidi, & Goldstein, 1986; Gusella, Muir, & Tronick, 1988). One study of the still-face effect involving children with autism has failed to document this normative pattern of response (Nadel et al., 2000).

In summary, in the EM approach early social predispositions are thought to create the basis and the impetus for the subsequent emergence of mental representations, which because of their inseparability from social action (i.e., they are embodied), retain their adaptive value. Infants do not build veridical models of the social world on the basis of universals or context-invariant representations. Rather, their models or expectations of the world follow their salience-guided actions on an ever-changing environment that needs to be coped with in an adaptive, moment-by-moment, and context-dependent manner (Engel, Fries, & Singer, 2001).

CONTEXTUAL ELEMENTS IN THE EMERGENCE OF MENTAL REPRESENTATIONS

The classical computation model in cognitive science assumes that cognitive processes are rule-based manipulations of symbols representing the outside environment (e.g., Newell, 1991). Similarly, computational models of the social mind build on the notion that to operate socially is to execute algorithms involving mental representations (e.g., Baron-Cohen, 1994). In contrast, the EM approach raises the nontrivial question of how a representation acquires meaning to a given child, the so-called mind-mind problem (Jackendoff, 1987). The question is: What is the relationship between computational states (e.g., manipulation of mental representations) and a person's experience of the real-life referent of the computational state? How do we go from having a representation of a person's intention to experiencing that intention by reacting to it in a certain way? In the computer world, we do know where the meaning of the computational algorithms comes from, namely, the programmer. But how do mental representations acquire meaning to a developing child? In autism, individuals often acquire a large number of symbols and symbolic computations that are devoid of shared meaning with others; that is, the symbols do not have the meaning to them that they have to typical children. Examples are hyperlexia (reading decoding skills go unaccompanied by reading comprehension; Grigorenko et al., 2002), echolalia and echopraxia (echoing of sounds or mimicry of movements; Prizant & Duchan, 1981; Rogers, 1999), metaphoric language (e.g., neologisms, words used in idiosyncratic ways; Lord & Paul, 1997), and prompt-dependent social gestures, routines, or scripts (e.g., waving bye-bye without eye contact, staring when requested to make eye contact), among many others. While it is difficult to conceive of a dissociation between knowing a symbol and acting on it (e.g., knowing the meaning of the pointing gesture and spontaneously turning the head when somebody is pointing somewhere), this actually happens in autism, as shown in Figure 26.3 and the other earlier examples. We know that children with autism can learn associatively (e.g., a symbol becomes paired with a referent). This happens, for example, in vocabulary instruction using simple behavioral techniques. But one of the big challenges for these children is often to pair a symbol with the adaptive action subsumed by the symbol (Wetherby, Prizant, & Schuler, 2000).

In the EM approach, symbols or cognition in general have meaning to the child using them because they are "embodied actions" (Clark, 1999; Johnson, 1987), meaning that "cognition depends upon the experiences that come from having a body with various sensorimotor capacities," and "perception and action are fundamentally inseparable in lived cognition" (Varela et al., 1991, p. 173). An artificial separation of cognition from the other elements would render the given cognitive construct a "mental ghost" once again. We can exemplify the inseparability of cognition and action through Held and Hein's (Held, 1965; Held & Hein, 1963) classic studies of perceptual guidance of action. They raised kittens in the dark and exposed them to light only under controlled conditions. One group of kittens was allowed to move around normally, but each of them was harnessed to a carriage that contained a second group of kittens. While the groups shared the same visual experience, the second group was entirely passive. When the kittens were released after a few weeks of this treatment, members of the first group (the one that moved around) behaved normally, whereas members of the second group (the one that was passively carried by the others) behaved as blind, bumping into objects and falling off edges. These experiments illustrate the point that meaningful cognition of objects (i.e., the way we see them and adjust to them) cannot be formed by means of visual extraction alone; rather, there is a need for perceptual processes to be actively linked with action to guide further action on these objects. Studies of adaptation of disarranged hand-eye coordination in humans (Held & Hein, 1958), tactile vision substitution in blind humans (Bach-y-Rita, 1983), and neural coding of body schema in primates (Iriki, Tanaka, & Iwamura, 1996), among others (see Iacoboni, 2000b), support this point. A striking example is provided in a study (Aglioti, Smania, Manfredi, & Berlucchi, 1996) of a patient with right brain damage who denied the ownership of her left hand and of objects that were worn by her left hand (e.g., rings). When the same objects were worn by the right hand, the patient recognized them as her own. In infancy research, a wide range of phenomena, from haptic and depth perception (E. W. Bushnell & Boudreau, 1993) to Piagetian milestones (Thelen, Schoener, Scheier, & Smith, 2001), have begun to characterize developmental skills as "perception-for-action" systems, while neuroimaging studies have shown over-lapping brain circuitry subserving action observation and action generation (Blakemore & Decety, 2001).

Perception-for-action systems are particularly relevant to a discussion of social adaptation. Consider the skill of imitation, one of the major deficits in autism (Rogers, 1999). It is interesting that while children with autism have great difficulty in learning through imitation, they do exhibit a great deal of mirroring or copying behaviors, both vocally (e.g., echoing what other people say) and motorically (e.g., making the same gesture as another person), which, however, are typically devoid of the function that these behaviors serve to typical people displaying them. One hypothesis derived from the EM approach would predict that this curious discrepancy originates from the aspect of the typical person's action that is most salient in the child's perception. Whereas typical children may see a waving gesture as a motion embedded in the act of communication or emotional exchange, children with autism may dissociate the motion from the social context, focusing on the salient physical facts and thus repeating the gesture in a mechanical fashion, not unlike what a typical child might do in a game of imitating meaningless gestures or what a neonate might do when protruding his or her tongue in response to seeing an adult doing so (Meltzoff & Moore, 1977). This hypothesis originates from the notion that while perception for action may occur in the absence of social engagement (e.g., in neonates), in typical infants sometime around the middle of their second year of life, imitation is much more likely to serve social engagement and social learning than to occur outside the realm of social interaction, as in autism. Supporting this hypothesis is a series of studies in which, for example, 18-month-old infants were exposed to a human or a mechanical device attempting to perform various actions. The children imitated the action when it was performed by the human model, but not when it was performed by the mechanical device (Meltzoff, 1995).

Perception-for-action systems are of particular interest in the context of survival abilities (e.g., responding to a threatening person or a lethal predator). A central example of such systems is the ability to perceive certain patterns of movement as biological motion. This system allows humans, as well as other species, to discern motion of biological forms from motion occurring in the inanimate environment. In the wild, an animal's survival would depend on its ability to detect approaching predators and predict their future actions. In humans, this system has been linked to the emergence of the capacity to attribute intentions to others (Frith & Frith, 1999). The study of biological motion has traditionally used Johansson's (1994) paradigm of human motion display. In his work, the motion of the living body is represented by a few bright spots describing the motions of the main joints. In this fashion, the motion pattern is dissociated from the form of people's bodies. The moving presentation of this set of bright spots evokes a compelling impression of basic human movements (e.g., walking, running, dancing) as well as of social movements (e.g., approaching, fighting, embracing). Figure 26.7 illustrates a series of static images of the human form rendered as point-light animations. The phenomenon studied by Johansson, however, can be fully appreciated only when the display is set in motion.

Using this paradigm, several studies have documented adults' abilities to attribute gender, emotions, and even personality features to these moving dots (Dittrich, Troscianko, Lea, & Morgan, 1996; Koslowski & Cutting, 1978). Even 3-month-old infants are able to discriminate between the moving dots depicting a walking person and the same dot display moving randomly (Fox & McDaniel, 1982). The presence of this ability at such a young age, as well as its presence in other species including monkeys (Oram & Perret, 1994) and birds (Regolin, Tommasi, & Vallortigara, 2000), and the demonstrated singularity of biological motion relative to other forms of motion from the perspective of the visual system (Neri,

Figure 26.7 Series of static images of the human form rendered as point-light displays.

Morrone, & Burr, 1998) suggest that this is a highly conserved and unique system that makes possible the recognition of movements of others in order to move toward or away from them. Several neuroimaging studies have singled out the superior temporal sulcus as an important structure involved in the perception of biological motion (Grezes et al., 2001; Grossman et al., 2000), a region also associated with basic survival reactions such as evaluating facial expressions and/or direction of eye gaze (Puce, Allison, Benton, Gore, & McCarthy, 1998). A PET study attempting to separate decontextualized human motions (point-light displays depicting a hand bringing a cup to a person's mouth) from what can be seen as a more naturalistic human motion (a person dancing) showed that the perception of the latter also implicated limbic structures such as the amygdala (Bonda, Petrides, Istry, & Evans, 1996). This finding is consistent with a perception-for-action system that not only perceives to act but also is embedded in an approach/withdrawal, affective-based context (Gaffan, Gaffan, & Harrison, 1988).

Given the fundamental and adaptive nature of perception of biological motion, we would expect this system to be intact in even very disabled children. One study has shown the system to be intact in children with profound spatial deficits and a degree of mental retardation (Jordan, Reiss, Hoffman, & Landau, 2002). In contrast, our own preliminary data suggest that this system may be compromised in young children with autism. We used Johansson point-light displays to depict a series of social approaches that are part of typical experiences of young children (e.g., an animated adult trying to attract the attention of a young toddler, "pat-a-cake," "peek-a-boo"). Scenes were presented in two formats simultaneously, one on each of the two horizontal halves of a computer screen. The scenes were identical except that one was right side up and the other was upside down. The child heard the corresponding sound effects of that social scene (e.g., the verbal approach of an adult). The experiment followed a visual preference paradigm in which the child looked at one of the two scenes presented. By requiring the child to choose between an upside-down and a right-

side-up animation matching the sound effects of the social interaction, we were able to test the child's ability to impose mental representations of human movement interactions on the ambiguous visual stimuli. This paradigm is illustrated in Figure 26.8. Our preliminary data for eleven 2-year-old toddlers, 5 with a diagnosis of autism and 6 typical children, are given in Figure 26.9. Overall, the typically developing toddlers demonstrated a marked preference for the right-side-up figure (83% of total

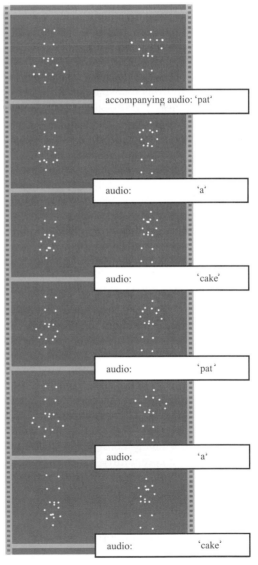

Figure 26.8 Cross-modal matching task with social animation stimuli.

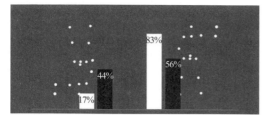

Figure 26.9 Percent of total viewing time spent on upright versus inverted figures. Black bars; toddlers with autism; white bars: typically developing toddlers.

viewing time versus 17% for the upside-down display), while the toddlers with autism showed a pattern closer to a random choice (56% versus 44%). We also analyzed initial fixations and final fixations (defined by the figure the child was focusing on at the end of the animation) as a rudimentary look at how understanding of the animation's content might progress during viewing and recorded the number of times the toddlers with autism shifted their focus from the upright to the inverted figure, relative to typically developing controls. These results are depicted graphically in Figure 26.10. While typically developing toddlers and toddlers with autism both exhibited initial fixations at chance or near-chance levels, the typically developing infants were focused on the upright figure at the end of more than three-fourths of all trials, while the toddlers with autism remained at chance level. Of similar interest are group differences in the pattern of shifting between the upright and inverted figures. Toddlers with autism shifted more frequently than typically developing toddlers, a trend suggestive of increased difficulty in adequately understanding either of the two displays. If corroborated in larger studies, this finding would point to a major disruption in a highly conserved skill that is thought to be a core ability underlying social engagement and, subsequently, the capacity to attribute intentionality to others.

TEMPORAL CONSTRAINTS ON MODELS OF SOCIAL ADAPTATION

Computational models of the mind place less emphasis on the temporal unfolding of the cognitive processes involved in a task (Newell,

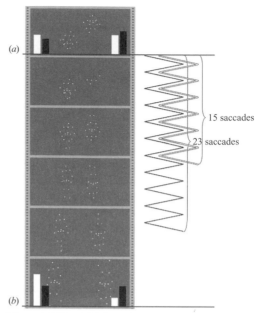

Figure 26.10 Initial and final fixation data and number of saccades between upright and inverted figures. (a) Initial fixation: toddlers with autism 40% upright, 60% inverted: typically developing toddlers 50% upright, 50% inverted. (b) Final fixation: toddlers with autism 50% upright, 50% inverted; typically developing toddlers 79% upright, 21% inverted. Number of saccades between upright and inverted figures; toddlers with autism 23 saccades min^{-1}, typically developing toddlers 15 saccades min^{-1}.

1991). This stance is justified when a given task is explicit and fully defined. However, in naturalistic situations, there are important temporal constraints in social adaptation because failure to detect an important but fleeting social cue or a failure to detect temporal relationships between two social cues may lead to partial or even misleading comprehension of the situation, which may in turn lead to ineffective adjustment to the situation. For example, if the viewer of a scene fails to monitor a nonspeaker in a social scene who is clearly embarrassed by what another person is saying, the viewer is unlikely to correctly identify the meaning of that situation (Klin et al., 2002a). In this way, the EM approach sees social adaptation along the same principles currently being considered in research of "embodied vision" (Churchland, Ramachandran, & Sejnowski, 1994). This view holds that the task of the visual system is not to generate exhaustive mental models of a veridical surrounding environment but to use visual information to perform real-time, real-life adaptive reactions. Rather than creating an inner mirror of the outside world to formulate problems and then to solve them ahead of acting on them, vision is seen as the active retrieval of useful information as it is needed from the constantly present and complex visual environment. From the organism's adaptive perspective, the topology of salience of this visual tapestry, from light reflections to carpet patterning, to furniture and clothing, to mouths and eyes, is far from flat. We would be overwhelmed and paralyzed by its richness if we were to start from a position of equal salience to every aspect of what is available to be visually inspected. Rather, we actively retrieve aspects of the visual environment that are essential for quick, adaptive actions by foveating on sequential locations where we expect to find them. These expectations are generated by a brain system dedicated to salience (a lion entering the room is more important than the light switch next to the door) and an ever more complex (going from infancy to adulthood) understanding of the context of the situation, the so-called top-down approach to vision (Engel et al., 2001).

A pertinent example of this view of vision is Clark's (1999, p. 346) analysis of a baseball game in which an outfielder positions himself or herself to catch a fly ball:

It used to be thought that this problem required complex calculations of the arc, acceleration and distance of the ball. More recent work, however, suggests a computationally simpler strategy (McBeath, Shaffer, & Kaiser, 1995). Put simply, the fielder continually adjusts his or her run so that the ball never seems to curve toward the ground, but instead appears to move in a straight line in his or her visual field. By maintaining this strategy, the fielder should be guaranteed to arrive in the right place at the right time to catch the ball. (p. 346)

Piaget (1973) provided similar examples from children's play, and Zajonc (1980) provided similar examples from intersubjective adaptation. Consistent with these examples, the EM approach considers the "social game" to be not unlike the outfielder's effort. A typical toddler entering a playroom pursues a sequence of so-

cial adaptive reactions to split-second environmental demands with moment-by-moment disregard of the vast majority of the available visual stimulation. Such a child is ready to play the social game. For individuals with autism, however, the topology of salience, defined as the "foveal elicitation" of socially relevant stimuli (as exemplified in our eye-tracking illustrations and in studies of preferential attention to social versus nonsocial entities; see earlier discussion), is much flatter. If viewed in this light, the social worlds enacted by individuals with autism and by their typical peers may be strikingly different.

SOCIAL COGNITION AS SOCIAL ACTION

The radical assumption made in the EM approach is that mental representations as described in computational models of the mind are proxies for the actions that generated them and for which they stand (Lakoff & Johnson, 1999; Thelen & Smith, 1994; Varela et al., 1991). This counterintuitive view can be traced back to Mead's (1924) account of the social origins of mind. Mead saw the emergence of mind as the capacity of an individual to make a "gesture" (e.g., bodily sign, vocal sound) that means to the other person seeing or hearing it the same as for the person making it. The meaning of the gesture, however, is in the reaction of the other. A gesture used in this way becomes a symbol, that is, something that stands for the predicted reaction of the other person. Once a child has such a symbolic gesture, he or she can then uphold it as a representation for the reaction of the social partner, thus being able to take a step back from the immediate experience and then to contemplate alternatives of action using such symbols as proxies for real actions. In the EM approach, the fact that the emergence and evolution of a symbol are tied to actions of adaptation, which in turn are immersed in a context of somatosensory experiences, salience, and perceptually guided actions, makes the symbol a proxy for these elements of the action. When we uphold and manipulate symbols in our mind, therefore, we are also evoking a network of experiences resulting from a life history of actions associated with that symbol.

This view connecting social cognition with social action is of help in our attempt to explore possible reasons that accomplishments in social reasoning in individuals with autism are not accompanied by commensurate success in social action. Consider an example from research on face perception. While face recognition deficits are very pronounced in young children with autism (Klin et al., 1999), the size of this deficit is much smaller in older and more cognitively able adolescents (Celani, Battacchi, & Arcidiacono, 1999). The possibility that older individuals might perform such tasks using atypical strategies relative to their peers was investigated in our recent fMRI study of face recognition in autism (Schultz et al., 2000) in which normative-IQ individuals with autism and controls were presented with face versus object recognition tasks. In contrast to controls for whom face processing was associated with fusiform gyrus (FG) activation, in individuals with autism, face processing was associated with activation in inferior temporal gyrus (ITG) structures, an activation pattern that was obtained for controls when they were processing objects. These results indicated that individuals with autism did not rely on the normal neural substrate during face perception (Kanwisher, McDermott, & Chun, 1997) but rather engaged brain areas that were more important to nonface, object processing (Haxby et al., 1999). In other words, they failed to treat faces as a special form of visual stimulus, treating them instead as ordinary objects.

It would be tempting from these results to hypothesize that a circumscribed area of the brain—namely, the FG—and the mechanism it represents—namely, perception of face identity—were causally related to autism. Given the centrality of face perception in interpersonal interactions, this would be a plausible theory of autism. However, other recent studies (Gauthier & Tarr, 1997; Gauthier, Tarr, Anderson, Skudlarski, & Gore, 1999) have suggested that the FG is not necessarily the brain site for face recognition, appearing instead to be a site associated with visual expertise, so that when a person becomes an expert on a given object category (e.g., Persian carpets), selective activation of the FG occurs when the person is looking at an instance of that object. This notion suggests a reinterpretation of our face recognition results in autism. The FG was not selectively activated when individuals with autism were looking at faces because they were not experts on faces. In contrast, typically developing individuals have a lifetime to develop this expertise, a result of a very large number of recurrent experiences of focusing on and acting on other people's faces beginning in very early infancy. As previously described, faces have little salience to young children with autism and would thus represent a much less frequent target of recurrent actions necessary to produce expertise.

If this interpretation is correct, were individuals with autism asked to perform a visual recognition task using stimuli on which they had expertise, we might observe FG activation. Preliminary results supportive of this suggestion were obtained in an fMRI study of an individual with autism whose expertise area is *Digimon* characters (a large series of cartoon figures; Grelotti et al., in press). Of interest, fMRI activations for *Digimon* characters in this individual with autism also included the amygdala, suggesting salience-driven rewards associated with the characters. Results such as these are beginning to delineate a developmental profile of functional brain maturation in autism in which hardwired social salience systems are derailed from very early on, following a path marked by seeking physical entities (not people) and repeatedly enacting them and thus neglecting social experiences (Klin et al., 2002a). This hypothesis is consistent with the notion of functional brain development as "an activity-dependent process" that emphasizes the infancy period as a window of maximal plasticity (Johnson, 2001). An interesting line of research supporting this hypothesis is the case of people with a period of visual deprivation early in postnatal life due to bilateral congenital cataracts. Although early surgical correction was associated with rapid improvement of visual acuity, deficits in configural processing of faces remained even after many years postsurgery (Le Grand, Mondloch, Maurer, & Brent, 2001; Maurer, Lewis, Brent, & Levin, 1999). Configural processing of a class of visual stimuli (e.g., faces) represents a developmental shift from processing an object from its parts to processing objects in a Gestalt manner (Tanaka, Kay, Grinnell, Stansfield, & Szechter, 1998), which, in turn, is a mark of the acquisition of perceptual expertise (Diamond & Carey, 1986; Gauthier & Nelson, 2001). Thus, studies of early visual deprivation seem to highlight the effects of reduced early visual enactment of a class of visual stimuli on later, automatic, and more efficient ways of processing that class of stimuli.

Returning to the fMRI example in which individuals with autism treated faces as objects (Schultz et al., 2000), it is of considerable interest that all participants could perform relatively well on the behavioral task of face recognition. They could correctly match faces, albeit using a strategy that differed markedly from controls. Thus, an analysis of results on the behavioral task by itself would have unveiled no significant differences between the two groups. Yet, we might consider the behavioral impact of failing to process faces as a special class of objects. Most people are able to recognize possibly thousands of faces very quickly, whereas their ability to recognize, for example, pieces of luggage is much more limited. Thus, some of us are likely to mistake our bags when coming to pick them up from a luggage carousel at the airport, but we are very unlikely to mistake our mother-in-law rushing to greet us from the surrounding crowd.

The point illustrated in this example is the importance of developmental and contextual aspects of social development in making social-cognitive accomplishments into tools of social action. Temporal constraints on social adaptation require skills to be displayed spontaneously and quickly, without the need for an explicit translation of the requirements to be met in a given social task. There is a need to seek socially relevant information and to maintain online, as it were, a continuous process of imposing social meaning to what is seen. This comes easily and effortlessly to typical individuals. In contrast, the most challenging task in the daily lives of individuals with autism involves the need to adjust to commonplace, naturalistic social situations. Consider, for example, an adolescent with autism entering a high school cafeteria. There is usually an array of interrelated social events taking place, each one consisting of a vast amount

of social cues including language exchange, voice/prosody cues, facial and bodily gestures, posture, and body movements, among many others. These cues are embedded in a complex visual and auditory setting, with some physical stimuli being relevant to the social events (i.e., representing specific social contexts—e.g., a cafeteria—or specific "props"—e.g., a costume worn by one of the students) and other physical stimuli being entirely irrelevant (e.g., light switches or fixtures, number of doors, detailing in the walls). Such situations are challenging because there is hardly any aspect of the social event that is explicitly defined. Faced with a highly complex and ambiguous social display that demands a reaction (e.g., where to sit down, how to insert themselves in an unfolding social event), they need to make sense of what they see and hear by imposing social meaning onto essential social aspects of the situation (e.g., facial expressions) while ignoring irrelevant stimuli (e.g., light fixtures).

To study how difficult it might be for individuals to make sense of such a situation, we can use an experimental metaphor that measures a person's spontaneous tendency to impose social meaning on ambiguous visual stimuli. More specifically, it measures how salient the social meaning of an array of ambiguous visual stimuli is to a viewer and how socially relevant the viewer's thinking is when making an effort to make sense of the presented visual stimuli. The paradigm involves the presentation of a classic animation in which geometric shapes move and act like humans (Heider & Simmel, 1944; Figure 26.11). Typical viewers immediately recognize the social nature of the cartoon and provide narratives

Figure 26.11 Screen shot showing cast of characters from Heider and Simmel's (1944) cartoon.

that include a number of social attributions involving relationships portrayed there (e.g., being a bully, being a friend), the meaning of specific actions (e.g., trapping, protecting), and attributions of mental states (e.g., being shy, thinking, being surprised) to the characters. In contrast, cognitively able adolescents and adults with autism have great difficulty in doing so. In one study (Klin, 2000), they were, on average, able to recognize only one-fourth of the social elements deemed essential to understanding the plot of the story. A large proportion of them limited their narratives to faithful descriptions of the geometric events depicted in the cartoon but without any social attributions. This was surprising considering that an inclusionary condition in this study required participants to pass a relatively advanced social reasoning task (a second-order theory of mind task; Tager-Flusberg & Sullivan, 1994). Thus, these individuals' ability to solve explicit social-cognitive problems was no assurance that they would use these skills spontaneously. Some were unable to make any social attribution at all. Yet, such spontaneous attributions of intentionality to these geometric cartoons have been documented in infants (Gergely, Nadasdy, Csibra, & Biro, 1995) and even primates (Uller & Nichols, 2000). Some of the individuals with autism did, however, make a meaningful effort to make sense of the cartoon, but in doing so provided entirely irrelevant attributions, explaining the movements of the geometric shapes in terms of physical meaning (e.g., magnetic forces), not social meaning. Translated into a task of social adjustment to a naturalistic setting like the high school cafeteria, the results of this study would suggest that some of these individuals might have no access to the social cues (not even noticing them), whereas others might search for causation relationships in the wrong domain, namely, physical rather than social.

To impose social meaning on an array of visual stimuli is an adaptive reaction displayed by typical children from infancy onward at an ever-increasing level of complexity. This spontaneous skill is cultivated in countless hours of recurrent social engagement. From discerning the meaning of facial expressions and detecting human motion and forms of human action, to attributing intentionality and elaborate

mental states to others, the act of adjusting to social demands imbues social-cognitive accomplishments with their functional value. It is in this light that the preceding examples suggest that in autism there is a breakdown in the process through which social-cognitive skills and social action become inseparable.

CONCLUSION

This chapter began with an intriguing puzzle posed by normative-IQ individuals with autism: How can they learn so much about the world yet still be unable to translate this knowledge into real-life, social adaptive actions? A framework different from the prevailing computational models of social-cognitive development was offered—enactive mind—as a way of exploring this puzzle. This framework is based on the emerging embodied cognitive neuroscience. EM views cognition as embedded in experiences resulting from a body's actions on salient aspects of its surrounding environment. Social cognition is seen as the experiences associated with a special form of action, namely, social interaction. These experiences are tools of social adaptation that can be abstracted in the form of symbols and used to reason about social phenomena, although they retain their direct connection to the composite of enactive experiences that originated and shaped them over the lifetime of the child.

In autism, the EM approach proposes the hypothesis that the preceding process is derailed from its incipience because the typical overriding salience of social stimuli is not present. In its place is a range of physical stimuli, which attracts the child's selective attention, leading into a path of ever-greater specialization in things rather than people. Individuals with autism are capable of acquiring language and concepts and even a vast body of information on people. But these tools of thought are acquired outside the realm of active social engagement and the embodied experiences predicated by them. In a way, they possess what is typically the rooftop of social development. However, this rooftop is freestanding. The constructs and definitions are there, but their foundational experiences are not. The EM approach contends that without the set of embodied social-cognitive tools required to produce moment-by-moment, social adaptive reactions in naturalistic social situations, social behavior becomes truncated, slow, and inefficient.

A corollary of this hypothesis is that individuals with autism learn about people in a way that departs from the normative processes of social development. The fact that cognitively able individuals with autism are able to demonstrate so much social-cognitive understanding in some situations is as interesting as the fact that they fail to make use of these skills in other situations. To study possible compensatory paths and the degrees to which they help these individuals to achieve more independence is as important a research endeavor as to document their social-cognitive failures. But to do so, there will be a need to go beyond results on explicit tasks. There will be a need to both explore more in depth the atypical processes used by these individuals to perform explicit tasks and increase our arsenal of methodologies capable of studying social adaptation in more naturalistic settings (Klin et al., 2002a).

Cross-References

A review of social development is provided in Chapter 11; relevant developmental concepts are reviewed in Chapters 12, 14, and 15; and related theoretical perspective is described in Chapters 22 to 25.

REFERENCES

Adrien, J., Faure, M., Perrot, A., Hameury, L., Garreau, B., Barthelemy, C., et al. (1991). Autism and family home movies: Preliminary findings. *Journal of Autism and Developmental Disorders, 21,* 43–49.

Adrien, J., Lenoir, P., Martineau, J., Perot, A., Hameury, L., Larmande, C., et al. (1993). *Journal of the American Academy of Child and Adolescent Psychiatry, 33,* 617–625.

Aglioti, S., Smania, N., Manfredi, M., & Berlucchi, G. (1996). Disownership of left hand and objects related to it in a patient with right brain damage. *NeuroReport, 8,* 293–296.

Alegria, J., & Noirot, E. (1978). Neonate orientation behavior towards human voice. *International Journal of Behavioral Development, 1,* 291–312.

Bach-y-Rita, P. (1983). Tactile vision substitution: Past and future. *International Journal of Neuroscience, 19,* 29–36.

Baron-Cohen, S. (1994). How to build a baby that can read minds: Cognitive mechanisms in mindreading. *Cahiers de Psychologie Cognitive, 13*(5), 513–552.

Baron-Cohen, S. (1995). *Mindblindness: An essay on autism and theory of mind.* Cambridge, MA: MIT Press.

Baron-Cohen, S., Jolliffe, T., Mortimore, C., & Robertson, M. (1997). Another advanced test of theory of mind: Evidence from very high functioning adults with autism or Asperger syndrome. *Journal of Child Psychology and Psychiatry, 38*(7), 813–822.

Bates, E. (1976). *Language and context: The acquisition of pragmatics.* New York: Academic Press.

Bates, E. (1979). On the evolution and development of symbols. In E. Bates (Ed.), *The emergence of symbols: Cognition and communication in infancy* (pp. 1–32). New York: Academic Press.

Blakemore, S.-J., & Decety, J. (2001). From the perception of action to the understanding of intention. *Nature Reviews Neuroscience, 2,* 561–567.

Bonda, E., Petrides, M., Ostry, D., & Evans, A. (1996). Specific involvement of human parietal systems and the amygdala in the perception of biological motion. *Journal of Neuroscience, 15*(1), 3737–3744.

Boucher, J., & Lewis, V. (1992). Unfamiliar face recognition in relatively able autistic children. *Journal of Child Psychology and Psychiatry, 33*(5), 843–859.

Bowler, D. M. (1992). "Theory of Mind" in Asperger's syndrome. *Journal of Child Psychology and Psychiatry, 33*(5), 877–893.

Bryant, P. E. (1991). Face to face with babies. *Nature, 354,* 19.

Bushnell, E. W., & Boudreau, J. P. (1993). Motor development and the mind: The potential role of motor abilities as a determinant of aspects of perceptual development. *Child Development, 64*(4), 1005–1021.

Bushnell, I. W. R., Sai, F., & Mullin, J. T. (1989). Neonatal recognition of the mother's face. *British Journal of Developmental Psychology, 7,* 3–15.

Celani, G., Battacchi, M. W., & Arcidiacono, L. (1999). The understanding of the emotional meaning of facial expressions in people with autism. *Journal of Autism and Developmental Disorders, 29,* 57–66.

Churchland, P. S., Ramachandran, V. S., & Sejnowski, T. J. (1994). A critique of pure vision. In C. Koch & J. L. Davis (Eds.), *Large-scale neuronal theories of the brain: Computational neuroscience* (pp. 23–60). Cambridge, MA: MIT Press.

Clark, A. (1999). An embodied cognitive science? *Trends in Cognitive Science, 3,* 345–351.

Dahlgren, S. O., & Trillingsgaard, A. (1996). Theory of mind in non-retarded children with autism and Asperger's syndrome. A research note. *Journal of Child Psychology and Psychiatry, 37,* 759–763.

Damasio, A. (1999). *The feeling of what happens: Body and emotion in the making of consciousness.* New York: Harcourt.

Dawson, G., Carver, L., Meltzoff, A. N., Panagiotides, H., McPartland, J., & Webb, S. J. (2002). Neural correlates of face and object recognition in young children with autism spectrum disorder, developmental delay and typical development. *Child Development, 73*(3), 700–717.

Dawson, G., Meltzoff, A. N., Osterling, J., Rinaldi, J., & Brown, E. (1998). Children with autism fail to orient to naturally occurring social stimuli. *Journal of Autism and Developmental Disorders, 28*(6), 479–485.

Diamond, R., & Carey, S. (1986). Why faces are and are not special: An effect of expertise. *Journal of Experimental Psychology, 115,* 107–117.

Dittrich, W. H., Troscianko, T., Lea, S. E., & Morgan, D. (1996). Perception of emotion from dynamic point-light displays represented in dance. *Perception, 25,* 727–738.

Eimas, P., Siqueland, E., Jusczyk, P., & Vigorito, J. (1971). Speech perception in infants. *Science, 171,* 303–306.

Eisenberg, R. (1979). Stimulus significance as a determinant of infant responses to sound. In E. B. Thomas (Ed.), *Origins of infant's social responsiveness.* Hillsdale, NJ: Erlbaum.

Engel, A. K., Fries, P., & Singer, W. (2001). Dynamic predictions: Oscillations and synchrony in top-down processing. *Nature Reviews Neuroscience, 2,* 704–716.

Fernald, A. (1993). Approval and disapproval: Infant responsiveness to vocal affect in familiar and unfamiliar languages. *Child Development, 64,* 657–674.

Field, T., Vega-Lahar, N., Scafidi, F., & Goldstein, S. (1986). Effects of maternal unavailability on motion-infant interactions. *Infant Behavior and Development, 9,* 473–478.

Fox, R., & McDaniel, C. (1982). The perception of biological motion by human infants. *Science, 218,* 486–487.

Frith, C. D., & Frith, U. (1999). Interacting minds: A biological basis. *Science, 286*(5445), 1692–1695.

Gaffan, E. A., Gaffan, D., & Harrison, S. (1988). Disconnection of the amygdala from visual association cortex impairs visual-reward association learning in monkeys. *Journal of Neuroscience, 8,* 3144–3150.

Gardner, H. (1985). *The mind's new science: A history of the cognitive revolution* (chapter 5). New York: Basic Books.

Gauthier, I., & Nelson, C. A. (2001). The development of face expertise. *Current Opinion in Neurobiology, 11*(2), 219–224.

Gauthier, I., & Tarr, M. (1997). Becoming a "greeble" expert: Exploring mechanisms for face recognition. *Vision Research, 37,* 1673–1681.

Gauthier, I., Tarr, M., Anderson, A., Skudlarski, P., & Gore, J. (1999). Activation of the middle fusiform face area increases with expertise in recognizing novel objects. *Nature Neuroscience, 2,* 568–573.

Gergely, G., Nadasdy, Z., Csibra, G., & Biro, S. (1995). Taking the intentional stance at 12 months of age. *Cognition, 56,* 165–193.

Gibson, J. J. (1963). The useful dimension of sensitivity. *American Psychologist, 18,* 1–15.

Grelotti, D. J., Klin, A., Volkmar, F. R., Gauthier, I., Skudlarski, P., Cohen, D. J., et al. (in press). FMRI activation of the fusiform gyrus and amygdala to cartoon characters but not faces in a boy with autism. *Neuropsychologia.*

Grezes, J., Fonlupt, P., Bertenthal, B., Delon-Martin, C., Segebarth, C., & Decety, J. (2001). Does perception of biological motion rely on specific brain regions? *Neuroimage, 13*(5), 775–785.

Grigorenko, E. L., Klin, A., Pauls, D. L., Senft, R., Hooper, C., & Volkmar, F. R. (2002). A descriptive study of hyperlexia in a clinically referred sample of children with developmental delays. *Journal of Autism and Developmental Disorders, 32*(1), 3–12.

Grossman, E., Donnelly, M., Price, R., Pickens, D., Morgan, V., Neighbor, G., et al. (2000). Brain areas involved in perception of biological motion. *Journal of Cognitive Neuroscience, 12*(5), 711–720.

Gusella, J. L., Muir, D. W., & Tronick, E. Z. (1988). The effect of manipulating maternal behavior during an interaction on 3- and 6-month olds' affect and attention. *Child Development, 59,* 1111–1124.

Hadwin, J., Baron-Cohen, S., Howlin, P., & Hill, K. (1997). Does teaching theory of mind have an effect on the ability to develop conversation in children with autism? *Journal of Autism and Developmental Disorders, 27*(5), 519–537.

Haith, M. M., Bergman, T., & Moore, M. J. (1979). Eye contact and face scanning in early infancy. *Science, 198*(4319), 853–855.

Happé, F. G. (1994). An advanced test of theory of mind: Understanding of story characters' thoughts and feelings by able autistic, mentally handicapped, and normal children and adults. *Journal of Autism and Developmental Disorders, 24*(2),: 129–154.

Haviland, J. M., & Lelwica, M. (1987). The induced affect response: 10-week-old infants' responses to three emotional expressions. *Developmental Psychology, 23,* 97–104.

Haxby, J., Ungerleider, L., Clark, V., Schouten, J., Hoffman, E., & Martin, A. (1999). The effect of face inversion on activity in human neural systems for face and object perception. *Neuron, 22*(1), 189–199.

Heider, F., & Simmel, M. (1944). An experimental study of apparent behavior. *American Journal of Psychology, 57*(2), 243–259.

Held, R. (1965). Plasticity in sensory-motor systems. *Scientific American, 213*(5), 84–94.

Held, R., & Hein, A. (1958). Adaptation of disarranged hand-eye coordination contingent upon re-afferent stimulation. *Perceptual and Motor Skills, 8,* 87–90.

Held, R., & Hein, A. (1963). Movement-produced stimulation in the development of visually guided behavior. *Journal of Comparative and Physiological Psychology, 56*(5), 872–876.

Hobson, R. P., Ouston, J., & Lee, A. (1988). What's in a face? The case of autism. *British Journal of Psychology, 79,* 441–453.

Howlin, P., Baron-Cohen, S., & Hadwin, J. (1999). *Teaching children with autism to mind-read.* New York: Wiley.

Iacoboni, M. (2000a). Attention and sensorimotor integration: Mapping the embodied mind. In A. W. Toga & J. C. Mazziotta (Eds.), *Brain mapping: The systems* (pp. 463–490). San Diego, CA: Academic Press.

Iacoboni, M. (2000b). Mapping human cognition: Thinking, numerical abilities, theory of mind, consciousness. In A. W. Toga & J. C. Mazziotta (Eds.), *Brain mapping: The systems* (pp. 523–534). San Diego, CA: Academic Press.

Iriki, A., Tanaka, M., & Iwamura, Y. (1996). Coding of modified body schema during tool use by macaque postcentral neurons. *NeuroReport, 7,* 2325–2330.

Jackendoff, R. (1987). *Consciousness and the computational mind.* Cambridge, MA: MIT Press.

Johansson, G. (1973). Visual perception of biological motion and a model for its analysis. *Perception and Psychophysics, 14,* 201–211.

Johnson, M. (1987). *The body in the mind: The bodily basis of meaning, imagination, and reason.* Chicago: University of Chicago Press.

Johnson, M. (2001). Functional brain development in humans. *Nature Reviews Neuroscience, 2,* 475–483.

Jordan, H., Reiss, J. E., Hoffman, J. E., & Landau, B. (2002). Intact perception of biological motion in the face of profound spatial deficits: Williams syndrome. *Psychological Science, 13*(2), 162–167.

Kanwisher, N., McDermott, J., & Chun, M. (1997). The fusiform face area: A module in human extrastriate cortex specialized for face perception. *Journal of Neuroscience, 17,* 4302–4311.

Klin, A. (1989). Understanding early infantile autism: An application of, G. H. Mead's theory of the emergence of mind. *L. S. E. Quarterly, 3*(4), 336–356.

Klin, A. (1991). Young autistic Children's listening preferences in regard to speech: A possible characterization of the symptom of social withdrawal. *Journal of Autism and Developmental Disorders, 21*(1), 29–42.

Klin, A. (1992). Listening preferences in regard to speech in four children with developmental disabilities. *Journal of Child Psychology and Psychiatry, 33*(4), 763–769.

Klin, A. (2000). Attributing social meaning to ambiguous visual stimuli in higher functioning autism and Asperger syndrome: The social attribution task. *Journal of Child Psychology and Psychiatry, 41,* 831–846.

Klin, A., Jones, W., Schultz, R., Volkmar, F., & Cohen, D. (2002a). Defining and quantifying the social phenotype in autism. *American Journal of Psychiatry, 159*(6), 895–908.

Klin, A., Jones, W., Schultz, R., Volkmar, F. R., & Cohen, D. J. (2002b). Visual fixation patterns during viewing of naturalistic social situations as predictors of social competence in individuals with autism. *Archives of General Psychiatry, 59*(9), 809–816.

Klin, A., Schultz, R., & Cohen, D. (2000). Theory of mind in action: Developmental perspectives on social neuroscience. In S. Baron-Cohen, H. Tager-Flusberg, & D. Cohen (Eds.), *Understanding other minds: Perspectives from developmental neuroscience* (2nd ed., pp. 357–388). Oxford, England: Oxford University Press.

Klin, A., Sparrow, S. S., de Bildt, A., Cicchetti, D. V., Cohen, D. J., & Volkmar, F. R. (1999). A normed study of face recognition in autism and related disorders. *Journal of Autism and Developmental Disorders, 29*(6), 497–507.

Koslowski, L. T., & Cutting, J. E. (1978). Recognizing the sex of a walker from point-lights mounted on ankles: Some second thoughts. *Perception and Psychophysics, 23,* 459.

Lakoff, G., & Johnson, M. (1999). *Philosophy in the flesh.* Cambridge, MA: MIT Press.

Langdell, T. (1978). Recognition of faces: An approach to the study of autism. *Journal of Child Psychology and Psychiatry, 19,* 255–268.

LeDoux, J. (2002). *Synaptic self: How our brains become who we are.* New York: Viking Penguin.

Le Grand, R., Mondloch, C. J., Maurer, D., & Brent, H. P. (2001). Early visual experience and face processing. *Nature, 410,* 890.

Leslie, A. (1987). Pretence and representation: The origins of "theory of mind." *Psychological Review, 94,* 412–426.

Lord, C. (1995). Follow-up of two-year olds referred for possible autism. *Journal of Child Psychology and Psychiatry, 36*(8), 1365–1382.

Lord, C., & Paul, R. (1997). Language and communication in autism. In D. Cohen & F. Volkmar (Eds.), *Handbook of autism and pervasive developmental disorders* (pp. 195–225). New York: Wiley.

Markman, A. N., & Dietrich, E. (2000). Extending the classical view of representation. *Trends in Cognitive Science, 4,* 470–475.

Maturana, H. R., & Varela, F. G. (1973). *De máquinas y seres vivos.* Santiago, Chile: Editorial Universitaria.

Maurer, D., Lewis, T. L., Brent, H. P., & Levin, A. V. (1999). Rapid improvement in the acuity of infants after visual input. *Science, 286,* 108–110.

McBeath, M., Shaffer, D., & Kaiser, M. (1995). How baseball outfielders determine where to run to catch fly balls. *Science, 268,* 569–573.

Mead, G. H. (1924). *Mind, self, and society.* Chicago: University of Chicago Press.

Meltzoff, A. N. (1995). Understanding the intention of others: Re-enactment of intended acts by 18-month-old children. *Developmental Psychology, 31,* 838–850.

Meltzoff, A. N., & Moore, M. K. (1977). Imitation of facial and manual gestures by human neonates. *Science, 198,* 75–78.

Merleau-Ponty, M. (1962). *Phenomenology of perception.* London: Routledge & K. Paul.

Mills, M., & Melhuish, E. (1974). Recognition of mother's voice in early infancy. *Nature, 252,* 123–124.

Mundy, P., & Neal, R. (2000). Neural plasticity, joint attention and autistic developmental pathology. In L. Glidden (Ed.), *International review of research in mental retardation* (Vols. 2–3, pp. 141–168). New York: Academic Press.

Mundy, P., & Sigman, M. (1989). The theoretical implications of joint attention deficits in autism. *Development and Psychopathology, 1,* 173–183.

Nadel, J., Croue, S., Mattlinger, M.-J., Canet, P., Hudelot, C., Lecuyer, C., et al. (2000). Do children with autism have expectancies about the social behavior of unfamiliar people? A pilot study using the still face paradigm. *Autism, 4*(2), 133–146.

Neisser, U. (1997). The future of cognitive science: An ecological approach. In D. M. Johnson & C. E. Erneling (Eds.), *The future of the cognitive revolution* (pp. 247–260). New York: Oxford University Press.

Neri, P., Morrone, M. C., & Burr, D. C. (1998). Seeing biological motion. *Nature, 395*(6705), 894–896.

Newell, A. (1991). *Unified theories of cognition.* Cambridge, MA: Harvard University Press.

Oram, M. W., & Perrett, D. I. (1994). Response of anterior superior temporal polysensory (STPa) neurons to "biological motion" stimuli. *Journal of Cognitive Neuroscience, 6*(2), 99–116.

Osterling, J., & Dawson, G. (1994). Early recognition of children with autism: A study of first birthday home video tapes. *Journal of Autism and Developmental Disorders, 24,* 247–257.

Ozonoff, S., & J. N. Miller. (1995). Teaching theory of mind: A new approach to social skills training for individuals with autism. *Journal of Autism and Developmental Disorders, 25*(4), 415–433.

Piaget, J. (1973). The affective unconscious and the cognitive unconscious. *Journal of the American Psychoanalytic Association, 21,* 249–261.

Prizant, B., & Duchan, J. (1981). The functions of immediate echolalia in autistic children. *Journal of Speech and Hearing Disorders, 46*(3), 241–249.

Puce, A., Allison, T., Bentin, S., Gore, J. C., & McCarthy, G. (1998). Temporal cortex activation in humans viewing eye and mouth movements. *Journal of Neuroscience, 18*(6), 2188–2199.

Regolin, L., Tommasi, L., & Vallortigara, G. (2000). Visual perception of biological motion in newly hatched chicks as revealed by an imprinting procedure. *Animal Cognition, 3*(1), 53–60.

Rogers, S. (1999). An examination of the imitation deficits in autism. In J. Nadel & G. Butterworth (Eds.), *Imitation in infancy: Cambridge studies in cognitive perceptual development* (pp. 254–283). New York: Cambridge University Press.

Schultz, R. T., Gauthier, I., Klin, A., Fulbright, R., Anderson, A., Volkmar, F. R., et al. (2000). Abnormal ventral temporal cortical activity among individuals with autism and Asperger syndrome during face discrimination. *Archives of General Psychiatry, 57,* 331–340.

Searle, J. (1980). *Speech act theory and pragmatics.* Boston: D. Reidel.

Sparrow, S., Balla, D., & Cicchetti, D. (1984). *Vineland adaptive behavior scales, expanded edition.* Circle Pines, MN: American Guidance Service.

Symons, L. A., Hains, S. M. J., & Muir, D. W. (1998). Look at me: Five-month-old infants' sensitivity to very small deviations in eye-gaze during social interactions. *Infant Behavior and Development, 21*(3), 531–536.

Tager-Flusberg, H., & Sullivan, K. (1994). A second look at second-order belief attribution in autism. *Journal of Autism and Developmental Disorders, 24*(5), 577–586.

Tanaka, J. W., Kay, J. B., Grinnell, E., Stansfield, B., & Szechter, L. (1998). Face recognition in young children: When the whole is greater than the sum of its parts. *Visual Cognition, 5*(4), 479–496.

Tarabulsy, G. M., Tessier, R., & Kappas, A. (1996). Contingency detection and the contingent organization of behavior in interactions: Implications for socioemotional development in infancy. *Psychological Bulletin, 120*(1), 25–41.

Thelen, E., Schoener, G., Scheier, C., & Smith, L. B. (2001). The dynamics of embodiment: A field theory of infant perseverative reaching. *Behavioral and Brain Sciences, 24*(1), 1–86.

Thelen, E., & Smith, L. (1994). *A dynamic systems approach to the development of cognition and action.* Cambridge, MA: MIT Press.

Tronick, E. Z., Als, H., Adamson, L., Wise, S., & Brazelton, T. B. (1978). The infant's response to entrapment between contradictory messages in face-to-face interaction. *Journal of the American Academy of Child and Adolescent Psychiatry, 17,* 1–13.

Tronick, E. Z., Cohn, J., & Shea, E. (1986). The transfer of affect between mothers and infants. In T. B. Brazelton & M. W. Yogman (Eds.), *Affective development in infancy* (pp. 11–25). Norwood, NL: Ablex.

Uller, C., & Nichols, S. (2000). Goal attribution in chimpanzees. *Cognition, 76,* B27–34.

Van der Geest, J. N., Kemner, C., Verbaten, M. N., & van Engeland, H. (2002). Gaze behavior of children with pervasive developmental disorder toward human faces: A fixation time study. *Journal of Child Psychology and Psychiatry, 43*(4), 1–11.

Varela, F., Thompson, E., & Rosch, E. (1991). *The embodied mind: Cognitive science and human experience.* Cambridge, MA: MIT Press.

Walker, A. S. (1982). Intermodal perception of expressive behaviors by human infants. *Journal of Experimental Child Psychology, 33,* 514–535.

Weeks, S., & Hobson, R. (1987). The salience of facial expression for autistic children. *Journal of Child Psychology and Psychiatry, 28*(1), 137–151.

Werner, E., Dawson, G., Osterling, J., & Dinno, H. (2000). Recognition of autism spectrum disorder before one year of age: A retrospective study based on home videotapes. *Journal of Autism and Developmental Disorders, 30*(2), 157–162.

Wetherby, A. M., Prizant, B. M., & Schuler, A. L. (2000). Understanding the nature of communication and language impairments. In A. M. Wetherby & B. M. Prizant (Eds.), *Autism spectrum disorders: A transactional developmental perspective* (pp. 109–142). Baltimore: Paul H. Brookes.

Winograd, T., & Flores, F. (1986). *Understanding computers and cognition.* Norwood, NJ: Ablex Publications.

Zajonc, R. (1980). Feeling and thinking: Preferences need no inferences. *American Psychologist, 35*(2), 151–175.

Author Index

Aamodt-Leeper, G., 433, 544
Aarts, J. P., 503
Abbassi, V., 460
Abbeduto, L., 961
Abe, T., 44, 47, 140
Abell, F., 371, 495, 497, 1305
Abichandani, F., 501
Abott, R., 657
Abou-Issa, H., 462
Abraham, A., 463
Abrahamowicz, M., 535
Abrams, M., 141
Abrams, N., 544
Abramson, R. K., 208, 269, 754
Accardo, P., 172, 187, 491, 492, 499, 537, 540, 708, 709, 712, 713, 724, 782, 841, 1124, 1139, 1310
Achenbach, T. M., 747, 748, 799
Ackerman, A. B., 1142
Ackerman, L., 252
Acredolo, L. P., 336
Adams, A., 233, 237, 238, 318, 320, 321, 386, 501, 934
Adams, A. N., 819, 821, 823
Adams, A. V., 373
Adams, C., 175, 335, 352
Adams, L., 385, 836, 847
Adams, M. J., 886, 1143
Adams, P., 189, 1102, 1104, 1112
Adams, P. B., 739, 1102, 1107
Adams, P. I., 189
Adams, T., 889
Adams, W. B., 464
Adamson, L., 235, 318, 319, 336, 369, 549, 653, 690
Adkins, W. N., 144
Adoh, T. O., 842
Adolphs, R., 250, 497, 520, 524, 525, 526, 652, 656, 668, 672

Adrien, J., 229, 232, 240, 366, 394, 479, 481, 689, 708, 712, 751, 134
Adrien, K. T., 355, 517
Aerts, F. H., 372, 610, 613, 644
Afzal, N., 541
Agarwal, N., 479, 481, 482
Aghajanian, G. K., 456
Aglioti, S., 691
Agran, M., 868, 912
Aharon, I., 521
Ahearn, W. H., 540
Ahlsen, G., 51, 185, 540, 545, 832
Ahluwalia, J., 634
Aicardi, J., 126, 135, 154, 535, 594
Aihara, R., 461, 539
Aimi, J., 464
Ainsworth, M. D. S., 416, 1223
Ainsworth, M. S., 238, 322
Aircardi, J., 431
Aisemberg, P., 27, 839, 847, 1107
Aitken, K., 319, 325, 673
Aitken, M. R. F., 642
Aizenstein, M. L., 456
Akefeldt, A., 544
Akerley, M. S., 1069
Akerstrom, B., 544
Akiskal, H. S., 266
Akkerhuis, G. W., 455, 456, 458, 459
Akshoomoff, N., 367, 368, 439, 477, 478, 500, 536, 610, 617, 646, 655, 656, 659, 660, 661, 668, 832, 889, 1014, 1305
Akyerli, C., 130
Al-Adeimi, M., 544
Alaghband-Rad, J., 181
Alar, N., 1013, 1022
Alarcón, M., 432, 433, 438, 439, 754
Albano, A. M., 181, 182
Albers, R. J., 345
Albert, M. L., 608

Alberto, P. A., 903, 907, 908, 913
Alberts, A. S., 464
Albin, R. W., 822, 824, 825, 903, 1124
Albus, K. F., 181
Aldred, S., 463
Aldridge, M. A., 384, 389
Alegria, J., 689
Aleman, D., 552
Alen, R., 432
Alessandri, M., 1004, 1030, 1089
Alessandri, S. M., 149
Alessi, D. R., 543
Alessi, N., 27, 189
Alexander, A. L., 494, 521, 522
Alexander, D., 1142
Alexiou, C., 1215, 1217
Alinsanski, S., 324
Al-Khouri, I., 544
Alkin, M. C., 1034
Alku, P., 481, 482
Allan, J., 204, 206, 215
Allard, A., 267
Allen, D., 30, 97, 325, 410, 539, 616, 1306
Allen, D. A., 30, 132, 169, 175, 586, 1307, 1310
Allen, D. M., 369
Allen, D. S., 251
Allen, G., 261, 497, 498, 521, 525, 526, 832, 1306
Allen, J., 227, 229, 288, 293, 335, 645, 713, 714, 741, 962, 1304
Allen, K., 967
Allen, L., 759
Allen, M., 24, 97, 103, 104, 107, 369, 374, 375, 479, 480
Allen, P. S., 499
Allen, V., 476
Allison, D. B., 900
Allison, T., 483, 520, 525, 693
Allman, J., 670
Allolio, B., 462
Almeida, H. C., 553

Almeida, M. C., 890, 1011, 1030, 1031, 1130
Almes, M. J., 136
Almond, P., 719, 731, 733, 741, 747, 750, 762, 1004, 1005, 1006, 1008, 1199
Almqvist, F., 1238
Alper, S., 868, 911
Alpern, D. G., 836
Alpern, G. D., 384, 1011
Alpern, M., 1126, 1127
Alpert, C. L., 883, 884, 890
Alpert, M., 348
Als, H., 690
Altemeier, W., 320, 321, 355, 707
Althaus, M., 177, 268
Althouse, R. B., 916
Altmark, L., 433
Amador, J., 668, 670
Aman, M., 189, 762, 838, 839, 1102, 1103, 1104, 1109, 1110, 1111, 1310
Amanullah, S., 324
Amaral, D. G., 525, 526, 732, 1306
Ambrose, J., 261, 497, 521, 526, 1306
Ambrosini, P., 762
Ameli, R., 642
Ament, N., 546
Ames, T., 1092
Amin, T., 429
Aminoff, M. J., 476
Amir, R. E., 21, 77, 78, 130, 136, 138, 431, 432
Amnell, G., 545
Amorosa, H., 177, 536
Amos, P., 151, 153
Amstutz, L., 479
Anastasi, A., 822
Anastasopoulos, G., 1215
Andelman, A. S., 904
Anders, T. F., 29, 503, 542, 1312
Andersen, P. H., 435
Andersen-Wood, L., 180, 418

Anderson, A., 419, 519, 520, 521, 525, 696, 697
Anderson, A. E., 885, 888
Anderson, A. K., 526
Anderson, A. W., 170, 191, 889
Anderson, C., 152, 824
Anderson, D., 655
Anderson, G. M., 453, 454, 455, 456, 457, 458, 459, 460, 461, 462, 1108, 1208
Anderson, I., 1283
Anderson, J. L., 1124
Anderson, J. M., 371
Anderson, J. R., 607
Anderson, L., 189, 462, 492, 1102, 1104, 1112
Anderson, M., 257, 258, 345, 353, 960
Anderson, S., 267, 899, 929, 936, 938, 949, 1036
Anderson, T., 1177
Anderson-Parente, J., 619
Anderson-Wood, L., 436, 591
Andersson, L., 425
Andersson Gronlund, M., 544, 553
Ando, H., 251, 252, 289, 317
Andrasik, F., 1143
Andreasen, N., 179, 492, 493, 499, 646, 660, 661
Andrellos, P. J., 845
Andresen, J., 144
Andretta, M., 1093
Andreu, A. L., 550
Andrews, C. E., 64
Andrews, G., 630
Andrews, J., 540
Andrews, N., 435, 541
Andrews, R., 503
Angrist, B., 838, 839, 847
Angus, J. W. S., 838, 848
Annell, A.-L., 1240
Anneren, G., 109
Annex, B., 546
Ansari, D., 549
Ansermet, F., 80, 82
Antalffy, B., 140, 431, 432
Anthony, A., 435, 438, 541
Anthony, E. J., 585, 592
Antolovich, M., 1058
Antonarakis, S. E., 552
Anvret, M., 130, 138
Anzalone, M., 367, 939, 980, 981, 983, 1310
Apitz, J., 548
Apolito, P. M., 906
Applebee, A., 813
Applegate, H., 463
Apter, A., 299
Aquaviva, C., 78
Aram, R., 369
Aras, T., 107
Arbelle, S., 171, 833, 1011
Arbib, M., 389, 673

Arcas, J., 544
Archambault, F. X., 613
Archer, L., 93, 95, 110, 213, 252, 317, 719, 734, 735, 736, 743, 845
Archer, P., 712
Arcidiacono, L., 413, 696
Arcus, D., 983
Ardinger, H. H., 555
Ardlie, K. G., 431
Ariani, F., 551
Arick, J., 476, 719, 731, 733, 741, 747, 750, 762, 1004, 1005, 1006, 1007, 1008, 1009, 1012, 1023, 1199
Arin, D. M., 489
Armenteros, J., 839, 1102, 1107
Armony, J. L., 523, 525
Armstrong, D., 139, 140, 143, 145
Arndt, S., 5, 107, 123, 214, 288, 289, 427, 492, 493, 494, 496, 498, 499, 519, 646, 660, 661, 741, 1076, 1077
Arnold, L. E., 762, 1102, 1103, 1104, 1109, 1110
Arnold, M., 953
Arnold, M. E., 27, 838
Arnold, M. S., 1036, 1044, 1045, 1132
Arnold, P., 555, 886
Arnold, S., 76, 79, 80, 82, 1312
Aron, M., 152
Aronson, A., 336
Aronson, M., 544
Arora, R. C., 455
Arora, T., 1034
Arrieta, A., 553
Artru, A. A., 170, 172, 493, 496, 497, 498, 501
Arvanitis, L. A., 1105
Arvidsson, T., 48, 62
Asano, E., 752
Asano, F., 47
Asarnow, R., 181, 183, 481, 537
Asendorpf, J. B., 386
Asgharian, A., 708, 724, 1056
Ashburner, J., 371, 495, 497, 1305
Ashden, B., 324
Ashenden, B., 288, 298
Asher, S. R., 341
Ashford, L., 31, 227, 232, 233, 707, 708, 721, 734
Ashley-Kioch, A., 432
Ashley-Koch, A., 32, 432, 433, 439, 754
Ashman, S. B., 709
Ashwal, S., 172, 187, 537, 540, 709, 841, 1124, 1139, 1310
Ashwin, C., 525, 652

Ashwood, P., 438, 541
Askalan, R., 544
Asperger, H., 8, 24, 89, 91, 93, 94, 95, 105, 108, 109, 118, 169, 186, 187, 209, 248, 298, 305, 348, 374, 584, 586, 588, 591, 593, 594, 599, 628, 634, 652, 981, 983, 1247, 1279, 1304, 1306
Assemany, A. E., 1061
Aston, M., 304
Atkin, J. F., 555
Attwood, A., 249, 250, 323, 411, 597, 598, 735
Attwood, T., 113, 761, 980, 981, 982, 983, 984
Atwell, C. W., 484
Audero, M. A., 1232
Auerbach, J. G., 183
Auerbach, S., 454
Auersperg, E., 542, 1112
Aughton, D., 538
August, G., 30, 427, 546, 589, 838
Augustine, A., 371, 497, 660
Auranen, M., 432, 433
Avdi, E., 1058
Averett, R., 539
Avikainen, S., 389
Avis, J., 630
Awad, S., 962
Axelrod, B. N., 616
Ayers, K., 432, 433
Ayllon, T., 1125
Aylward, E., 165, 170, 171, 172, 191, 371, 493, 496, 497, 498, 501, 521, 522, 536, 646, 651, 660, 755
Aylward, G. P., 709, 710, 711
Ayres, A. J., 387, 835, 836, 844, 890
Ayres, J. A., 1280, 1281
Azen, S. P., 849
Azmitia, E. C., 454
Azrin, N. H., 905, 1125, 1126, 1134

Babb, S., 208, 269
Bacchelli, E., 130, 432
Bach, L., 666
Bach, V., 502
Bachevalier, J., 371, 524, 526, 652
Bachmann-Andersen, L., 50
Bach-y-Rita, P., 691
Bacon, A. L., 325, 410
Baddeley, A. D., 606, 611
Bader, P. J., 551
Badner, J. A., 432
Baer, D., 823, 826, 883, 915, 950, 1006, 1130
Bagan, B. T., 542
Bagenholm, A., 1074
Bagnato, S. J., 713
Bagwell, C. L., 177
Bahrick, L., 656, 657

Baieli, S., 553
Bailey, A., 5, 7, 8, 14, 25, 26, 28, 51, 65, 76, 92, 93, 96, 107, 108, 170, 189, 210, 216, 239, 291, 293, 304, 325, 341, 346, 347, 355, 365, 375, 376, 419, 425, 426, 427, 429, 432, 434, 436, 437, 438, 439, 442, 488, 489, 500, 534, 536, 537, 538, 546, 553, 594, 613, 617, 618, 632, 650, 661, 722, 732, 740, 754, 763, 777, 834, 1305
Bailey, D., 932
Bailey, D. B., 1034, 1035, 1038
Bailey, D. B., Jr., 546, 547
Bailey, J., 123, 492, 494, 496, 498, 499, 519, 646, 660, 661
Bailey, J. N., 536
Bailey, J. S., 1126, 1127, 1128
Bailey, K. J., 249
Bailey, M. E., 130, 138
Bailey, N., 493
Bailey, V., 260
Baird, C., 342, 349, 947, 961
Baird, G., 31, 48, 52, 54, 57, 60, 105, 227, 229, 231, 232, 233, 234, 235, 237, 248, 266, 315, 320, 342, 349, 369, 384, 410, 432, 434, 438, 439, 536, 588, 613, 634, 652, 654, 655, 656, 657, 665, 707, 708, 709, 713, 714, 715, 716, 717, 730, 732, 733, 734, 741, 754, 755, 759, 760, 763, 832, 837, 847, 947, 961, 1307
Bakardjiev, A., 493, 494, 496, 497, 498, 519, 1305
Bakay, B., 464
Bakeman, R., 319, 336, 653
Baker, B., 962
Baker, G. A., 544
Baker, L., 9, 335, 343, 588
Baker, M. J., 254, 913
Baker, P., 551
Baker, S., 615, 665
Bakermans-Kranenburg, M. J., 322
Bakke, S., 535
Bakker, D. J., 503
Bakker, L., 543
Baldessarini, R. J., 1103
Baldwin, D. A., 236, 337, 650, 654
Baldwin, J. M., 382
Baldwin, S., 1244
Baldwin, V. L., 1076
Ball, J., 745, 750

Balla, D., 83, 225, 238, 315, 316, 682, 754, 755, 793, 800, 804, 845

Ballaban-Gil, K., 76, 79, 80, 82, 202, 204, 205, 206, 212, 213, 214, 288, 289, 290, 291, 292, 293, 296, 298, 299, 1312

Ballantyne, A. O., 100, 835, 836

Ballenger, J., 1282

Balottin, U., 539

Baltaxe, C., 256, 257, 336, 346, 348, 352, 353, 393, 962, 1306

Bambara, L., 929

Bandettini, P., 522

Bandim, J. M., 553

Bangs, T., 148

Banks, B., 1088

Banks, P. D., 1088

Bannerman, D. J., 1098

Banon, J., 462

Barad, V., 668, 669

Darak, Y., 1220

Barale, F., 1305

Baran, J. A., 844

Baranek, G., 172, 187, 226, 234, 236, 387, 398, 491, 492, 499, 536, 537, 540, 707, 708, 709, 712, 713, 724, 782, 831, 832, 833, 834, 837, 841, 843, 844, 848, 849, 870, 1124, 1139, 1310

Barbaresi, W. J., 534

Barber, M., 44

Barbetta, P., 991, 1032

Barbieri, F., 243

Barcellos, L. F., 431

Barchfeld, P., 614

Barcus, M. J., 1091, 1092

Barkley, R. A., 28, 1061, 1062

Barlow, A., 97

Barlow, D., 826

Barnard, L., 189

Barnes, T. R., 848

Barnett, A., 588

Barnett, C., 832, 833

Barnett, J. Y., 27, 839, 847, 1107

Barnhill, G., 354, 374, 375, 872, 876, 1018, 1020

Barnhill, L. J., 1105

Baroff, G., 291

Baron-Cohen, S., 27, 31, 48, 52, 54, 57, 60, 64, 88, 95, 101, 104, 105, 118, 185, 186, 190, 191, 227, 229, 231, 232, 233, 234, 235, 236, 237, 253, 254, 258, 259, 261, 266, 299, 318, 320, 325, 336, 342, 352, 353, 368, 369, 373, 384, 385, 393, 394, 397, 399, 410, 419, 434,

439, 461, 497, 524, 525, 526, 590, 613, 615, 618, 628, 629, 630, 631, 632, 633, 634, 635, 636, 641, 642, 645, 652, 654, 655, 656, 657, 660, 665, 666, 667, 682, 687, 689, 690, 707, 708, 709, 713, 714, 715, 716, 724, 730, 732, 733, 734, 739, 741, 754, 755, 763, 795, 832, 837, 838, 847, 872, 873, 947, 961, 1306, 1307, 1308

Barratt, P., 991

Barratt-Boyes, B. G., 548

Barrett, A. M., 371

Barrett, P. R., 461

Barrett, S., 432

Barretto, A., 904

Barron, J. L., 189, 459, 460, 462

Barry, L. M., 869

Barry, R. J., 268

Barshop, B. A., 464

Barta, P., 107, 492, 499, 768

Bartak, L., 8, 237, 256, 265, 292, 343, 345, 349, 462, 588, 594, 1201, 1244, 1306

Barth, A., 75, 77

Barthe, D., 551

Barthélémy , C., 229, 232, 366, 373, 394, 432, 459, 479, 481, 517, 542, 555, 689, 712, 751, 834, 1208

Bartlett, F. C., 640

Bartolucci, G., 77, 78, 92, 93, 94, 104, 109, 169, 170, 172, 173, 174, 183, 186, 187, 202, 203, 204, 206, 207, 210, 211, 256, 257, 258, 288, 295, 297, 298, 299, 343, 345, 372, 373, 375, 427, 437, 590, 606, 607, 628, 731, 734, 753, 754

Barton, L. E., 904

Barton, M., 229, 534, 713, 716, 717, 1306

Barton, R. M., 373

Barton, S., 204, 206, 215, 288, 293, 320, 335, 384, 835, 836, 962, 1011, 1304

Bartsch, K., 630

Bashe, P. R., 113

Bashford, A., 543, 757, 1055, 1060, 1064, 1069, 1176, 1178, 1216

Basile, V. C., 900

Bass, L., 1034

Bass, M. P., 434, 544, 551, 754

Bassell, G. J., 545

Bassett, A. S., 552

Basso, G., 668, 669

Basu, S., 432

Bates, E., 149, 224, 235, 320, 336, 337, 340, 630, 653, 659, 673, 687, 689, 800

Bates, G., 555, 556

Bates, P. E., 1092

Bat-Haee, M. A., 152

Ba'tki, A., 634

Battacchi, M. W., 413, 696

Battaglia, A., 551

Batticane, N., 542

Baudonniere, P., 386

Bauer, S., 537

Bauman, K. E., 825

Bauman, M. D., 526, 1306

Bauman, M. L., 371, 372, 463, 488, 489, 490, 492, 496, 526, 536, 832, 1014, 1108, 1282, 1305

Baumberger, T., 257, 345, 960

Baumeister, A., 1141, 1183

Baumgardner, T. L., 269, 545

Baumgartner, P., 324, 415

Bauminger, N., 323, 415, 416, 419, 1020, 1021, 1034

Bawn, S., 355, 493, 495

Baxter, M., 209, 295

Bayes, A., 108, 519

Bayley, N., 83, 791

Bazhenova, O., 336

Beadle-Brown, J., 214

Beail, N., 548

Bean, J., 542

Beard, C. M., 51

Bearden, C. E., 552

Beatty, W. W., 616

Beaty, T., 141

Beauchamp, K., 870

Beaumanoir, A., 80, 82, 175

Bebbington, P., 619

Bebko, J. M., 749, 903, 1072

Bechara, A., 524

Beck, J. C., 432

Beck, J. L., 609

Becker, L., 456

Becker, M. A., 464

Becker, W. C., 1126

Beckett, C., 180, 418, 436, 591

Bedair, H. S., 1103

Bedard, C., 476, 477

Bedrosian, J., 806

Beech, A., 617

Beeghly, M., 324

Beeghly-Smith, M., 653, 665, 667

Beery, K., 794, 844, 847

Beh, M. B., 1282

Behar, D., 266

Behen, M., 454, 490, 517, 549, 752

Behrmann, M., 956

Beidel, D. C., 181, 182

Beisler, J. M., 790

Beitchman, J. H., 335

Bejerot, S., 102, 590

Bekkering, H., 355, 389

Belcher, R., 207, 298, 302, 1078, 1091, 1093

Belchic, J. K., 1032, 1033

Beldjord, C., 77, 138, 432

Belfiore, P., 901

Belicohenko, P., 137

Belin, P., 517

Belin, T. R., 1108

Bell, M., 619

Bell, R., 547, 1061

Bellacosa, A., 551

Bellak, L., 617

Bellamy, G. T., 1095

Belleville, S., 611, 642, 644

Bellgrove, M. A., 104

Bellugi, U., 260, 548, 549

Belmaker, R. H., 463

Belsito, K. M., 1111

Bemporad, J., 183, 189, 324, 1015

Bemporad, M. L., 1281

Benaroya, S., 253, 392

Benavidez, D. A., 833

Benayed, R., 433, 474

Bence, R., 744

Bencsath, A., 463

Bender, L., 8, 167, 584, 585

Ben Hamida, M., 553

Ben-Hur, T., 255

Benigni, L., 149, 630

Benjamin, E., 1239

Benkers, T., 355, 493, 495

Benner, A., 433

Bennett-Baker, P. E., 551

Bennetto, L., 234, 237, 369, 370, 371, 372, 384, 385, 387, 388, 389, 536, 537, 545, 611, 613, 616, 635, 836, 837

Benowitz, L. I., 646

Bentin, S., 483, 693

Benton, D., 1112

Bent-Williams, A., 551

Benz, B., 539

Berant, M., 552

Berberich, J. P., 882, 883

Berelowitz, M., 541

Berg, C. J., 266

Berg, M., 129

Berg, W., 912, 916

Berger, H. J., 372, 610, 613, 644

Berger, L., 541

Berger, M., 1244

Bergman, T., 317, 684, 689

Bergstrom, T., 1023

Berinlinger, M., 184

Berk, R. A., 846

Berkell, D. E., 1091, 1093

Berker, M., 130

Berkson, G., 536, 833, 834

Berlin, I., 209

Berlucchi, G., 691

Bernabei, P., 536, 1221, 1223

Bernal, J., 299

Bernard, C., 544

Bernard, S., 435
Bernard-Opitz, V., 259, 351, 871, 873, 876, 902, 956
Berney, T. P., 544
Bernier, J., 548
Bernier, R., 342, 432, 483, 521, 522
Bernstein, D., 249
Bernstein, G. A., 461, 462
Berry-Kravis, E. M., 455
Berryman, J., 269, 914
Bertenthal, B., 693
Berthier, M. L., 107, 108, 519, 537, 538
Bertini, E., 551
Bertolino, A., 526
Bertoninci, J., 337
Bertrand, J., 49, 52, 57, 60, 185, 549
Berument, S. K., 427, 722, 763
Besag, F. M., 544
Besalel, V. A., 905
Bescoby-Chambers, N., 555, 556
Bespalova, I. N., 433, 474, 550
Betancur, C., 433, 434
Bettaglio, E., 539
Bettelheim, B., 256, 1089, 1195, 1243
Bettison, S., 832, 1200
Beuren, A. J., 548
Beversdorf, D. Q., 371
Beyer, J., 1182
Beyer, K. S., 130, 432, 433
Beyer, S., 207
Bezemer, M., 30, 183
Bhalerao, S., 544
Bhangoo, R. K., 181
Bhatt, R. S., 640
Bhattacharya, A., 486
Bhaumik, S., 1108
Bibby, P., 897, 1061, 1064
Bible, G. H., 1126
Bice, T. L., 251, 292, 294, 316
Bick, P., 189
Bieber-Martig, B., 546
Bieber Nielsen, J., 130, 132, 137, 138
Biederman, J., 28, 177, 183, 189, 208, 1109, 1111
Bienenstock, B., 29
Bienstock, C., 496, 497, 525, 667
Bienvenu, T., 78, 130, 138, 432
Bihrle, A., 549
Bijou, S. J., 823
Billingsly, F., 826
Billstedt, E., 534
Bilu, Y., 1185
Bimbela, A., 884, 1060, 1061
Binkoff, J. A., 885, 1089
Binnie, C. D., 503
Binstock, T., 435
Bird, A., 431, 440
Bird, H., 732, 762

Birmaher, B., 27, 189, 1110
Birn, R., 522
Birnbrauer, J. S., 1070
Biro, S., 612, 629, 630, 698
Birrell, J., 668, 669
Bisarya, D., 439, 631, 632, 634
Bishop, D., 353, 433, 519, 549, 586
Bishop, D. V., 32, 33, 169, 174, 175, 176, 335, 544
Bishop, D. V. M., 73, 80, 82, 97, 98, 353, 428, 641, 722, 740, 753, 759, 760, 810, 812, 813
Bishop, M., 32, 418, 554
Bishop, P., 1112
Bissette, G., 142
Bisson, E., 432
Bitsika, V., 1058, 1064, 1065, 1069
Björck, P. O., 46
Bjorevall, G. B., 1177
Bjornstad, P. G., 548
Black, A., 1076
Black, C., 541
Black, D. O., 613
Black, D. W., 212
Black, G., 130, 139
Black, J., 651, 657, 658, 660, 661, 670
Black, M., 321
Black, S., 436, 551
Blackston, R. D., 555
Blake, D. T., 1308
Blakemore, S.-J., 692
Blanc, R., 394
Bland, L., 463
Blanton, R., 499, 549, 1305
Blasey, C., 170, 185, 521, 552
Blasi, F., 130, 432
Blass, E., 656
Blass, J. P., 549
Blatt, G. J., 463, 490
Bleger, J., 1229
Blehar, M., 238, 322, 416, 1223
Bleuler, E., 7, 89, 584
Blew, P., 1030
Blischak, D., 802
Bliumina, M. G., 553
Block, J., 653, 654, 662
Blomquist, H., 546
Bloom, A. S., 267
Bloom, D., 183
Bloom, F. E., 183
Bloom, K., 317
Bloom, L., 336, 337
Bloomer, R., 613
Bober, S. J., 849
Bobrove, P., 1127, 1148
Bocian, M., 544, 550, 551
Bock, G., 434, 441, 443
Bock, M. A., 620
Boddaert, N., 517, 521, 524
Boddington, E., 1283
Bodensteiner, J. B., 537

Bodfish, J. W., 265, 267, 838, 839, 847, 848, 1112
Boggs, S. R., 1060, 1062
Bohman, I. L., 46, 1243
Bohman, M., 46, 546, 1243
Boiron, M., 751
Boksenbaum, N., 183
Boldt, D., 492
Boler, J. B., 462
Boles, D., 546
Bolhofner, K., 181
Bolick, T., 978, 981
Bolte, E., 541
Bölte, S., 294, 521
Bolton, D., 616
Bolton, P., 5, 8, 26, 28, 51, 57, 65, 76, 107, 108, 170, 171, 185, 208, 269, 295, 425, 426, 427, 428, 429, 430, 434, 436, 438, 439, 442, 489, 500, 524, 534, 536, 537, 538, 539, 543, 545, 546, 551, 552, 586, 594, 617, 632, 633, 645, 724, 1305
Bombardieri, R., 543
Bond, J. A., 607
Bond, S., 169, 186, 187, 202, 203, 204, 206, 207, 210, 211, 288, 295, 297, 298, 299, 590
Bonda, E., 693
Bondoux, D., 462
Bondy, A., 708, 885, 891, 929, 940, 955, 956, 1036
Bonforte, S., 617
Bonham, J. R., 145
Bonnefont, J. P., 551
Bonnet-Brilhault, F., 479
Bonnie, J., 661
Bono, M., 654
Bonora, E., 432, 433
Bonvillian, J., 836, 955
Booker, A. B., 463, 490
Bookheimer, S., 170, 173, 521, 526
Boomsma, D. I., 434
Boon, F., 1108
Booth, R., 642, 644
Boozer, H., 1126, 1128
Borden, M., 30, 595
Border, M., 1004
Bordie, F., 554
Borengasser-Caruso, M. A., 548
Borgatti, R., 551
Borghgraef, M., 546
Borjas, L., 553
Bornholt, L., 619
Bornstein, M. H., 236
Bornstein, R. A., 616
Borsook, T. K., 886
Bosch, G., 118, 414
Bosch, S., 870, 876
Bothuyne, S., 236, 237, 389, 390
Bottaro, G., 539

Botting, N., 759, 760
Bottitta, M., 494, 499, 542, 1307
Boucher, J., 237, 252, 254, 324, 344, 350, 369, 370, 371, 385, 393, 394, 395, 396, 399, 412, 488, 497, 499, 519, 689, 836, 847, 962, 1307
Boudreau, J. P., 691
Boullin, D. J., 455
Boulton, D., 27
Bourbeau, P. E., 1095
Bourgeois, M., 521
Bourland, G., 151
Bouvard, M., 189, 326, 459, 462, 618, 1112
Bove, F., 49, 52, 57, 60, 185
Bowcock, A. M., 431
Bower, B. D., 551
Bower, C., 127, 434
Bower, G. H., 607
Bower, T. G., 384, 389
Bowers, L., 540
Bowers, M. B., Jr., 456, 457, 1103
Bowlby, J., 322
Bowler, D., 105, 175, 186, 189, 325, 369, 370, 371, 586, 595, 598, 682, 1182
Bowman, E. P., 108
Bowman, L., 128, 908
Box, M., 951
Boyd, S. G., 144
Boyer, R. S., 548
Boyle, C., 49, 52, 57, 60, 63, 185, 555, 1070, 1123
Boyle, M. H., 24, 110, 174, 733
Braconnier, A., 459
Braddock, B. A., 150
Braddock, S. R., 150
Braden, M., 546
Bradford, Y., 438, 754
Bradshaw, J. L., 104, 610, 836, 1308
Brady, M., 901, 968
Brady, N., 542, 1112
Braestrup, C. B., 462
Braffman, B., 543
Brain, P. F., 1112
Brambilla, P., 491, 500, 1305
Brammer, M., 373, 419, 521, 525, 526, 615, 652, 666, 667, 668
Brandon, P. K., 901
Brandt, B. B., 870
Branford, D., 1108
Brannon, M. E., 1127, 1128
Brantberg, K., 478
Brase, D. A., 142
Brasic, J., 27, 762, 839, 847, 1107
Brask, B. H., 46, 52
Brass, M., 389
Braten, S., 673
Braun, T., 432, 438, 754

Braunstein, P., 348
Bravaccio, C., 80, 265, 266, 494
Braverman, M., 455, 458, 519, 520, 1306
Brawley, E. R., 1130
Brayne, C., 57, 185, 724
Brazelton, T. B., 690
Breakefield, X. O., 455, 458
Bréart, G., 61
Breaux, A. M., 1110
Bredenkamp, D., 180, 418, 436, 591
Breen, C. G., 904, 991, 1031
Breg, W., 546
Bregman, J., 16, 17, 18, 50, 177, 311, 300, 392, 595, 749, 1105
Brehm, S., 1067, 1177
Breinlinger, M., 46
Brelsford, K., 261, 324, 385, 412
Bremner, R., 92, 93, 94, 109, 169, 186, 187, 202, 203, 204, 206, 207, 210, 211, 256, 288, 295, 297, 298, 299, 590
Brendlinger, J., 908
Brenner, R., 586
Brent, H. P., 696
Brentano, F., 629
Brereton, A., 104, 610, 836, 1061, 1065, 1199
Bresnick, B., 712
Bressler, S., 668
Bretherton, I., 149, 324, 630, 653, 665, 667
Breton, C., 615
Brian, J., 542, 544, 609, 643
Bricker, D., 712, 1003
Bridge, J., 27, 189, 1110
Brierley, L., 46, 52, 321, 392, 396, 587, 598
Briesmeister, J. M., 1060, 1062, 1065
Brigance, A., 712
Brion-Meisels, S., 795
Briskman, J., 618, 645
Brissie, J., 31, 227, 232, 233, 707, 708, 721, 734
Bristol, M., 889, 926, 1061, 1064, 1068, 1070, 1074, 1075
Britten, K., 823, 887, 890
Britton, L. N., 908
Brockbank, M., 318, 629
Brodkin, E. S., 1107, 1108
Broks, P., 497, 499
Brondino, M. J., 1063
Bronen, R., 107, 108, 375, 977, 979, 982, 998
Bronicki, G. J., 1078, 1092, 1093
Bronkema, J., 1092
Brook, J. S., 429
Brook, S. L., 175

Brookner, F., 183
Brooks, C., 846
Brooks, R., 317
Brophy, M., 615
Brophy, S. L., 315
Brothers, L., 326, 524, 652, 660
Brotherson, M. J., 1092, 1093
Brothman, A., 545
Brough, S., 1058
Browder, D. M., 865, 866, 867, 868, 869, 877
Brown, A., 541
Brown, B., 145
Brown, C. S., 233, 238, 251, 316, 835
Brown, E., 234, 235, 236, 651, 656, 657, 670, 671, 689, 707, 799, 832
Brown, F., 900, 929, 941, 1004
Brown, J., 336, 657, 658
Brown, J. M., 542
Brown, J. R., 32, 1193
Brown, K. A., 819, 823
Brown, K. M., 1126, 1127
Brown, L., 818, 885, 1090
Brown, M., 484
Brown, R., 337, 340, 390, 396, 418, 436, 554, 555, 805
Brown, R. D., 588
Brown, R. L., 551
Brown, S., 236, 459
Brown, V., 668, 669
Brown, W., 546, 967, 968
Brown, W. H., 991
Brown, W. S., 481
Browne, C. E., 550, 551
Brubaker, J., 128
Brucke, T., 139, 141, 142
Bruggeman, R., 1103
Brugger, P., 646
Bruininks, R., 794, 835, 846
Brun, P., 260
Brunberg, J. A., 545, 546
Bruneau, N., 459, 479, 481
Bruner, J., 226, 236, 259, 260, 319, 337, 353, 382, 391, 630, 653, 654, 946, 1181
Brunswick, P., 665
Bruttini, M., 78, 130
Bryan, A. A., 235, 707
Bryan, R. N., 141
Bryant, P., 630, 689
Bryson, C. Q., 596
Bryson, G., 619
Bryson, S., 24, 31, 44, 47, 77, 78, 100, 101, 110, 170, 172, 173, 174, 184, 187, 190, 237, 268, 269, 291, 294, 295, 317, 320, 343, 344, 368, 384, 387, 388, 389, 427, 437, 500, 501, 539, 542, 544, 609, 610, 617,

642, 643, 719, 720, 731, 734, 735, 750, 753, 754, 832, 835, 836, 837, 1014
Brzustowicz, L. M., 433, 474
Bucci, J. P., 1108
Buchan, K. A., 886
Buchanan, C. P., 541, 542
Buchsbaum, M., 367, 496, 497, 525, 617, 660, 667
Buchtel, H. A., 607
Buchwald, J., 476, 478, 481
Buckley, J., 1076, 1094
Buckley, N. K., 1126
Budd, C. M., 911
Budd, on 131, 133, 142, 144, 147, 149
Buechel, C., 518
Buell, J., 967
Buervenich, S., 130, 138
Buffington, D., 959
Buggey, T., 871, 876, 886
Bui, Q. M., 569
Buican, B., 1109
Buitelaar, J., 5, 30, 166, 169, 171, 182, 183, 189, 190, 249, 269, 318, 319, 412, 460, 657, 662, 723, 1103, 1111
Bukelis, I., 547
Buktenica, N., 794, 844, 847
Bullmore, E., 373, 419, 521, 525, 526, 615, 652, 666, 667
Bullock, T. M., 1282
Bumin, G., 153
Bundey, S., 551
Bundy, A. C., 845
Buonocore, M. H., 108, 526
Burack, J., 206, 234, 238, 251, 317, 368, 642, 643, 644, 656, 1068, 1182
Burchert, W., 646
Burd, L., 27, 28, 46, 52, 55, 71, 75, 77, 101, 135, 539, 588, 838, 1111
Burde, R., 544
Burford, B., 127
Burg, M., 552, 1128
Burgio, L. D., 908
Burgoine, E., 108, 345
Burke, C., 1177
Burke, J. C., 821, 887, 890, 1055, 1160
Burke, M., 800
Burlew, S. B., 869
Burmeister, M., 544
Burn, J., 544
Burnette, C., 669
Burnham, M., 503, 542
Burns, T. G., 542, 1112
Burns, T. L., 212
Buron, K. D., 1016
Bursztejn, C., 459, 1208
Burt, D. B., 1088, 1093

Burton, D., 33, 95, 100, 110, 167, 290, 294, 295, 300, 303
Busch, G., 668, 669, 670, 673
Buschbacher, P., 932, 934, 940
Bush, A., 548
Bush, G., 589
Bushnell, E. W., 691
Bushnell, I. W. R., 689
Butera, G., 872
Butler, B., 255
Butler, C., 44
Butler, D. W., 643
Butler, E., 24, 120, 835, 846
Butler, I., 141, 142
Butler, L., 429, 536, 546, 594
Butler, R. W., 618, 619, 620
Butter, C. M., 524
Butterworth, G., 549, 630
Butterworth, J., 1092
Buxbaum, J. D., 429, 432, 433, 439, 753, 754
Buxhoeveden, D. P., 107, 474, 488, 1305
Buysse, A., 105, 177
Buysse, V., 1034, 1035, 1038
Buznikov, G. A., 454
Byl, N. N., 1308
Bymaster, F. P., 1105
Byrd, R., 289, 291, 296
Byrne, J., 538
Byrne, M., 539
Byrne, R., 383, 660
Bzoch, K., 83, 800

Cabeza, R., 372
Cacioppo, J. T., 383, 384, 836
Cain, D. H., 236
Cairns, R. B., 313
Caison, W., 758
Calamari, G., 251, 416, 417
Calamari, J. E., 905
Calder, A., 526, 663
Calhoun, S. L., 93, 294, 374
Caliendo, G., 552
Calkins, S., 256, 257, 342, 345, 346, 960
Callender, G., 612
Callesen, K., 105
Callias, M., 1059
Calligaro, D. O., 1105
Calvert, G. J., 477
Calzada, E., 177
Camaioni, L., 149, 536, 630
Camarata, M. N., 959
Camarata, S., 959, 1049
Cambell, R., 652
Cameron, K., 1243
Cameron, M. J., 902
Cameron, S., 909
Camfferman, G., 480, 481, 482, 485
Campbell, B., 902
Campbell, H. A., 747, 750
Campbell, J. O., 886

Campbell, M., 13, 18, 19, 45, 72, 93, 174, 175, 179, 184, 189, 212, 232, 233, 234, 248, 323, 348, 460, 461, 462, 492, 730, 732, 734, 739, 740, 750, 838, 839, 840, 847, 984, 1102, 1104, 1107, 1112, 1221
Campbell, M. B., 501
Campbell, M. S., 492
Campbell, P., 1133
Campbell, R., 236, 911
Campbell, S., 1036
Candela, P., 872
Candland, D. K., 6
Canet, P., 690
Canfield, R., 671
Cannon, B., 949
Cannon, M., 181
Cans, C., 47, 52, 61, 534, 544
Cantor, R. M., 438, 439, 754
Cantwell, D., 9, 168, 335, 343, 588
Caparulo, B. K., 342, 456, 457, 459, 537, 744
Capelle, P., 107
Capetillo-Cunliffe, L., 499
Capitanio, J. P., 526, 1306
Caplan, R., 183, 354, 662
Capps, L., 238, 258, 259, 260, 322, 353, 415, 520, 654
Capute, A., 800
Caputo, J. N., 905
Caputo, V., 758
Carbonari, C., 455, 458
Carbone, V., 964, 965
Card, J., 613, 655, 656, 662, 663, 664, 665, 669, 670
Cardon, L. R., 431, 438
Caretto, F., 542
Carey, J. C., 538
Carey, S., 520, 697
Carey, T., 542, 1112
Carlson, C. F., 1060
Carlson, D. C., 267, 1108
Carlson, J., 821, 897, 911, 916, 926
Carlson, M., 849
Carlson, S. M., 615
Carlsson, A., 495
Carlsson, M., 495
Carlström, G., 588
Carmichael, S. T., 524, 525
Carney, R. M., 432
Caro-Martinez, L., 237, 320, 351, 962
Caron, A. J., 317
Caron, M. J., 185
Caron, R. F., 317
Carpenter, M., 236, 336, 386, 389, 630, 653, 884, 885, 956, 978, 979
Carpentieri, S., 251

Carper, R., 489, 492, 493, 499, 500, 501, 519, 524, 536, 646, 660, 661, 671, 1305
Carr, E., 346
Carr, E. G., 819, 821, 822, 823, 824, 883, 885, 897, 898, 899, 902, 910, 911, 916, 926, 961, 966, 1030, 1033, 1088, 1089
Carr, E. M., 484
Carr, J., 819, 821, 823, 908, 1076, 1077
Carrie, A., 77, 130, 138
Carrington, S., 1013
Carrow-Woolfolk, E., 807
Carson, R. E., 454
Carson, W. H., 1106
Carswell, H. W., 849
Carter, A., 103, 106, 111, 170, 177, 238, 252, 294, 316, 412, 735, 772, 773, 782, 793, 800, 803
Carter, B., 1068
Carter, C., 254, 929, 930, 932, 934, 937, 940, 941, 952, 953, 954, 1005, 1006, 1049
Carter, G., 619
Cartwright, C., 496, 497, 525, 667, 1111
Caruso, M. A., 185
Carver, L., 171, 235, 483, 652, 690, 709
Casanova, M., 107, 142, 474, 488, 1305
Casat, C. D., 1110, 1111
Casavant, T. L., 432
Cascella, P., 799, 961
Casella, C., 243
Casey, B. J., 367, 368, 610, 617
Casey, F. G., 903, 904
Casey, S., 907
Caspi, A., 181, 439, 443
Cass, H., 127, 145, 554, 589
Cassanova, M. F., 140
Cassidy, S., 538, 551
Casson, D. H., 541
Casson, D. M., 435, 541
Castellani, P. J., 1089
Castelli, F., 518, 524, 525, 526
Castelloe, P., 30, 292, 595, 818, 820
Castells, S., 457, 463
Castiello, U., 536
Castine, T., 540
Castle, J., 180, 418, 436, 591
Catalano, R. A., 1312
Cataldo, M., 819, 825, 912
Cater, J., 1105
Cathcart, K., 264, 758, 890, 1050, 1061, 1064
Cattaneo, V., 243
Cattell, P., 147
Caul, J., 537
Caulfield, M., 903
Cautela, J., 269, 914, 1016

Cavallaro, C., 551
Cavallaro, M., 225, 234, 236, 243
Caviness, V., 495
Caviness, V., Jr., 538
Cayer, M., 31, 170, 172, 477, 478, 731, 735, 754
Cazden, C., 340
Celani, G., 413, 696
Celesia, G. G., 476
Celiberti, D. A., 890, 1089
Celli, M., 539
Cepeda, N., 668, 669
Ceponiene, R., 481, 482
Cernerud, L., 1057, 1074, 1076
Cernichiari, E., 436
Cerniglia, L., 883, 912, 1004, 1009
Cerquiglini, A., 479, 481
Cervetti, M., 871, 876, 886
Cesaroni, L., 831, 832, 1014, 1284
Cestone, V., 888
Chabane, N., 517, 521
Chabris, C. E., 521
Chabris, C. F., 521
Chadsey-Rusch, J., 1091
Chadwick-Denis, A., 345
Chadwick-Dias, A., 257, 960
Chakrabarti, S., 49, 52, 54, 55, 57, 60, 61, 64, 171, 175, 185, 204, 291, 434, 435, 541, 593, 740, 753
Chakraborty, P., 490
Challman, T. D., 534
Chamberlain, B., 250, 415
Chambers, C. T., 833, 834
Chambers, D., 747, 750
Chambers, W. W., 1282
Chambless, D. L., 1059
Chaminade, T., 419
Chance, P., 291
Chandler, K. E., 544
Chandler, L., 967, 968, 991, 1031
Changeux, J., 607, 657, 658
Channon, S., 1017
Chapman, M., 1176
Chapman, R., 340, 805, 806
Chapman, S., 909
Chapman, T. F., 181, 182
Chappell, P. B., 1111
Chappell, P. D., 456
Charak, D., 669
Charlop, M. H., 257, 819, 823, 886, 903, 904, 908, 950, 953, 995, 1004, 1009, 1061, 1129
Charlop-Christy, M. H., 871, 873, 884, 885, 887, 956
Charlton, R., 642, 644
Charman, T., 28, 31, 48, 52, 54, 57, 60, 105, 127, 227, 229, 231, 232, 233, 234, 235, 237, 248, 266, 315, 320, 342, 349, 369,

384, 385, 389, 393, 397, 410, 434, 613, 634, 650, 654, 655, 656, 665, 707, 708, 709, 713, 714, 715, 716, 717, 730, 732, 733, 734, 741, 754, 755, 832, 837, 847, 947, 961, 1011, 1017, 1068, 1307
Charney, D. S., 181
Charney, R., 256
Charnov, E. K., 147, 148
Chase, G., 170, 195, 197, 295, 427, 428, 537, 538, 539, 808, 809
Chase, J., 427, 554
Chatterjee, D., 453, 454
Chawarska, K., 31, 32, 224, 232, 233, 234, 317, 318, 319, 325, 326, 350, 773, 946, 960, 961
Chaze, A. M., 552
Cheadle, J. P., 130, 132
Checcarelli, N., 550
Cheema, A., 545
Chelly, J., 77, 138, 432
Chelune, G. J., 607, 616
Cheminal, R., 552
Chen, B. C., 607
Chen, C. H., 539
Chen, D., 478
Chen, J., 478
Chen, N. C., 1103
Chen, R., 64, 261, 324, 412
Chen, S. H. A., 902
Chen, W., 478
Chen, Y., 478
Cheng, R., 432, 433
Cheng, S. D., 551
Cherkassky, V., 355, 487, 517, 518, 646
Chernin, L., 324, 520
Chernoff, R., 1062
Cherro Aguerre, M., 1233
Cherry, K. E., 251, 267
Chesler, N., 555, 556
Chess, S., 7, 50, 436, 544, 589, 596
Chessa, L., 555
Chevy, F., 544
Chez, M., 503, 542
Chheda, R. L., 144
Chiappa, K., 476
Chiat, S., 256, 347
Chick, J., 97, 169, 178, 179, 184, 187
Chicz-Demet, A., 459, 460, 462
Chidambi, G., 415
Childress, D., 5, 107, 170, 173, 427
Childs, J., 234
Childs, K. E., 1032
Chiles, M., 260, 549
Chin, H. H., 259
Chin, H. Y., 873, 876
Chin, Y., 833, 834, 849
Chiron, C., 545
Cho, S. C., 455
Chock, P., 1138, 1141

Chodirker, B. N., 544
Chong, W. K., 554
Choroco, M. C., 462, 839, 840
Choudhury, M. S., 1105
Chouinard, S., 185
Chow, E. W., 552
Christen, H. J., 464
Christensen, K. R., 544
Christiaens, G. C., 556
Christian, L., 914, 1016
Christian, S. L., 515, 551
Christian, W. P., 1128
Christianson, A. L., 555, 556
Christie, R. G., 462, 553
Christodoulou, J., 126
Christoffels, I., 883
Christopher, B., 1089
Christopher, J. A., 241
Christopher, W., 1089
Christophersen, E. R., 1059
Chritodoulou, J., 143
Chua, P., 668
Chuba, H., 352, 353, 810, 962
Chugani, D. C., 454, 490, 517, 549, 752
Chugani, H., 140, 454, 662
Chui, L. C., 499
Chun, M., 520, 696
Chung, M. C., 1056, 1057
Chung, M. K., 494
Chung, S. Y., 209
Chung, Y. B., 900, 1183
Church, C., 324
Churchill, D., 384, 596, 836, 1011
Churchland, P. S., 694
Chynn, E. W., 645
Cialdella, P., 47, 52
Cianchetti, C., 1103
Ciaranello, R. D., 29, 453
Ciccehetti, D. V., 173
Cicchetti, D., xv, 16, 17, 18, 20, 24, 30, 33, 83, 96, 97, 103, 104, 170, 173, 177, 183, 225, 234, 238, 247, 251, 275, 315, 316, 326, 345, 367, 374, 375, 412, 498, 520, 548, 592, 628, 651, 655, 682, 689, 696, 719, 720, 736, 738, 749, 750, 754, 755, 777, 779, 783, 784, 789, 793, 800, 804, 845, 1062
Cicchetti, P., 525
Ciesielski, K., 268, 368, 480, 499, 610, 1014
Cimbis, M., 130
Cipani, E., 908
Cirignotta, F., 152
Cisar, C. L., 1032
Claire, L., 619
Clare, A. J., 151
Claridge, G., 617
Clark, A., 142, 145, 686, 687, 691, 695, 710, 711

Clark, B. S., 44, 47, 184, 343
Clark, F., 849
Clark, H. B., 1128
Clark, J., 267, 521
Clark, L., 84
Clark, M. L., 1064
Clark, P., 205
Clark, T., 268, 588
Clark, V., 520, 696
Clarke, A., 543
Clarke, A. D. B., 591
Clarke, A. M., 591
Clarke, D., 101, 209, 210, 265, 295
Clarke, S., 820, 1032
Clarkson, T. W., 435
Clark-Taylor, B. E., 550
Clark-Taylor, T., 550
Clarren, S. K., 555
Claverie, J., 439, 500, 501, 536
Clayton-Smith, J., 130, 139, 544, 551
Cleary, J., 759
Clegg, J., 436
Clement, S., 1064, 1065, 1075
Clements-Baartman, J., 958
Close, D., 181
Cloud, D., 197, 295, 427, 808, 809
Cnattingius, S., 539
Cobo, C., 1235
Cochran, S. R., 539
Cocuzza, M., 547
Cody, H., 491
Coe, D., 720, 745, 749, 751, 833, 1029, 1030
Coelho, K. E., 553
Coello, A. R., 868
Coez, A., 517
Coffey-Corina, S., 481, 482
Cohen, C., 205
Cohen, D., 17, 106, 191, 234, 236, 248, 249, 250, 275, 317, 343, 348, 350, 352, 375, 412, 593, 595, 631, 682, 683, 684, 686, 689, 696, 696, 699, 804, 813, 832, 839
Cohen, D. F., 750
Cohen, D. J., xv, xviii, xix, 8, 9, 15, 16, 17, 18, 21, 25, 27, 29, 30, 50, 71, 72, 73, 74, 75, 76, 79, 80, 93, 94, 101, 104, 108, 169, 170, 175, 178, 180, 181, 182, 185, 209, 210, 211, 223, 224, 238, 251, 256, 267, 293, 312, 315, 316, 318, 323, 324, 335, 342, 343, 346, 349, 350, 353, 387, 388, 412, 428, 453, 454, 455, 456, 457, 458, 459, 460, 461, 463, 478, 485, 486, 492, 520, 522,

537, 539, 553, 561, 580, 587, 689, 696, 707, 719, 720, 744, 749, 772, 782, 783, 789, 793, 820, 832, 961, 962, 984, 1107, 1108, 1121, 1224, 1225, 1281
Cohen, H. J., 594
Cohen, I., 30, 251, 335, 460, 461, 546, 646
Cohen, J., 429, 668
Cohen, M., 1095
Cohen, N. J., 496
Cohen, P., 182, 429
Cohen, R., 524, 525, 667
Cohen, S., 929
Cohen, Y., 1218, 1219
Cohn, A., 690
Coid, J., 462
Coker, S. B., 145
Colarusso, R. P., 844
Cole, C. L., 1030
Cole, P., 542
Cole, T., 551
Coleman, M., 26, 51, 127, 128, 130, 185, 212, 248, 249, 261, 429, 455, 460, 461, 464, 488, 499, 538, 539, 549, 553, 1055, 1212
Colette, J. W., 461
Collacott, R., 548
Collerton, D., 142
Collier-Crespin, A., 762, 1102, 1109, 1111
Collis, G., 412
Colman, H., 189
Colombo, J., 645
Comings, B. G., 617, 838
Comings, D. E., 136, 617, 838
Conciatori, M., 494
Condon, S. O., 183
Cone, J. D., 826
Coniglio, S. J., 542, 1112
Conley, R. W., 1094
Connellan, J., 634
Connelly, R., 64
Conner, R., 619, 912
Connor, R., 1034, 1112
Conroy, M., 967, 968, 991
Constantino, J., 32, 95, 315, 440, 746, 753, 754
Conti-Ramsden, G., 759, 760
Cook, C., 61, 316, 317
Cook, E., 45, 348, 655
Cook, E. H., 27, 228, 233, 439, 453, 454, 455, 456, 474, 491, 492, 499, 515, 542, 732, 752, 757, 762, 1112
Cook, E. H., Jr., 169, 170, 172, 187, 196, 326, 459, 537, 539, 540, 541, 547, 551, 708, 709, 712, 713, 724, 731, 739, 753, 754, 756, 757, 761, 782, 808, 841, 1055, 1059,

1060, 1107, 1124, 1134, 1139, 1310
Cook, I., 368, 372, 373
Cook, K. T., 872, 876, 1015, 1016, 1020
Cooke, T., 630
Cools, A. R., 372, 610, 613, 644
Coon, H., 73, 77, 78, 368, 372, 373, 489, 500, 501, 536, 609, 610, 615, 617, 618
Coonrod, E., 31, 227, 229, 232, 233, 655, 707, 708, 712, 717, 718, 721, 734
Cooper, J. O., 1004, 1009
Cooper, K. J., 868
Cooper, L., 484
Cooper, R., 151, 153
Cooper, S., 548
Cope, C. A., 432, 433, 439
Cope, H. A., 32, 754
Copeland, D. R., 619, 620
Coplan, J., 542, 800
Coplin, J. W., 234, 385, 392
Coppihn, B., 433, 544
Coppola, G., 552
Corbett, B., 542, 1112
Corbett, J., 75, 101, 210, 265, 266, 408, 551, 593
Corcoran, C., 619
Cordello, S. M., 553
Cordisco, L. K., 1035, 1045, 1047
Core, A. J., 849
Coren, S., 641
Corliss, M., 962
Cormier-Daire, V., 544
Cornblatt, B. A., 617
Cornelius, C., 344
Cornford, M. E., 140
Corona, R., 833, 1011
Cort, C., 967
Cortesi, F., 545
Cortney, V., 661
Cosmides, L., 660
Costa, A. E., 553
Costall, A., 253, 395, 833, 849
Coster, W., 841, 845
Costin, J., 617
Cote, R., 476, 477, 478
Cotgrove, A., 1283
Cottet-Eymard, J. M., 459
Cottington, E. M., 643
Cotton, S., 542
Cottrel, D., 1283
Couchesne, R., 429
Coulter, L., 958
Courchesne, E., 24, 31, 97, 104, 107, 141, 172, 261, 266, 268, 367, 368, 371, 375, 476, 477, 478, 479, 480, 482, 489, 492, 493, 494, 496, 497, 498, 499, 500, 501, 519, 521, 522, 524, 525, 526, 536, 539, 610,

Courchesne, E. *(Continued)*
617, 642, 646, 654,
655, 656, 659, 661,
668, 671, 832, 837,
889, 1014, 1282, 1305,
1306
Courchesne, R., 439, 474,
476, 477, 479, 480,
551, 660
Court, J., 463, 490
Courty, S., 439, 536
Courvoisie, H. E., 1105
Coury, S., 500, 501
Couvert, P., 77, 78, 130, 138
Couzin, J., 1283
Covington, C., 151
Cowan, C., 81
Cowan, W. B., 608
Cowdery, G. E., 819, 825,
907
Cowell, P. E., 497, 499
Cowen, M. A., 540
Cowen, P. S., 1063
Cox, A., 8, 31, 33, 48, 52,
54, 57, 60, 95, 100,
105, 110, 167, 213,
214, 227, 229, 231,
232, 233, 234, 235,
237, 266, 290, 292,
294, 295, 300, 303,
320, 342, 343, 345,
349, 352, 369, 384,
410, 434, 588, 613,
634, 652, 654, 655,
656, 657, 665, 707,
708, 709, 713, 714,
715, 716, 730, 732,
733, 734, 741, 754,
755, 763, 832, 837,
847, 947, 961, 1306,
1307
Cox, N. J., 733
Cox, R., 522, 720, 721,
741, 748, 749
Cox, S., 668
Coyle, J. T., 142
Coyne, P., 875, 1019, 1020,
1022, 1023
Craig, J., 253, 259
Craig, K. D., 833, 834
Craighero, L., 524
Craik, F., 669, 671
Craney, J. L., 181
Craven-Thuss, B., 494
Crawford, E. C., 550, 551
Crawford, S., 1017
Creak, E. M., 585, 1243
Creak, M., 201, 204
Creasey, J., 492
Creedon, M., 832
Crimmins, D. B., 824, 903,
910
Crispino, L., 1282
Critchley, H., 107, 419,
493, 521, 526, 652
Critchley, M., 545
Crites, D. L., 93
Crocker, W. T., 909
Croen, L., 44, 49, 59, 61,
63, 184, 291, 434, 462
Cronin, P., 189, 839, 872,
1310

Crosbie, J., 183
Crosland, K. A., 821
Crosley, C. J., 544
Cross, P. K., 547
Crossley, S. A., 322, 707,
1057
Croue, S., 690
Crowson, M., 170, 171,
236, 427, 536, 537,
586, 594, 630, 632,
650, 651, 653, 654,
658, 659, 660, 661,
670, 709, 1306
Crucian, G. P., 371
Cryan, E., 539
Csibra, G., 317, 549, 629,
698
Cuccara, M. L., 208
Cuccaro, M., 269, 429, 432,
434, 544, 550, 551,
753, 754
Cueva, J., 212, 839, 1107
Cullain, R. E., 269
Cummings, C., 538, 550
Cummings, D. L., 544
Cummins, D., 656
Cummins, R., 656
Cunningham, C. E., 1060,
1064
Cunningham, C. K., 544
Cunningham, L. J., 1064
Cunningham, M., 556
Cunningham, P. B., 1063
Cuperus, J. M., 177, 480,
481, 482, 485
Curatolo, P., 479, 481, 542,
543, 545
Curby, K. M., 521, 522,
523
Curcio, C., 909
Curcio, F., 236, 320, 385,
386, 653
Curen, E. L., 189
Curin, J. M., 459
Curran, C., 905
Curry, C. J., 538, 555
Curtis, M., 1016
Cusmai, R., 545
Cutler, B., 997, 998
Cutrer, P. S., 234, 385,
392
Cutting, J. E., 692
Cvejic, H., 548
Cycowicz, Y., 481, 482
Czapansky-Beilman, D.,
542, 1112
Czapinski, P., 500
Czarkowski, K. A., 1108

D'Adamo, P., 78
Dadds, M. R., 1060
Daffner, K. R., 613
Dager, S., 165, 171, 191,
651, 755
Daggett, J., 889
Dahl, E. K., 29, 182
Dahl, K., 9
Dahl, N., 109
Dahl, V., 212
Dahle, E. J., 138, 432
Dahlgren, S. O., 105, 227,
232, 234, 325, 329,

341, 349, 366, 375,
408, 682, 833, 834
Dahlgren-Sandberg, A.,
103, 375
Dahlin, G., 1243
Dahlstrom, B., 261
Dahoun, S. P., 552
Dairoku, H., 318
Dake, L., 963, 985, 996
Dale, P., 337, 800
Dales, L., 435
Daley, T., 1004
Dalpra, L., 551
Dalrymple, N., 267, 301,
916, 985, 996, 997,
1023
Dalton, K. M., 494, 521,
522
Dalton, P., 433, 544
Daly, E., 107, 419, 493,
521, 526, 652
Daly, K., 289, 667, 721,
744, 748
Daly, T., 799, 874, 875,
884, 885, 899, 929,
930, 932, 933, 934,
937, 939, 941, 950,
1035, 1036, 1045,
1046, 1132, 1133, 1140
Damasio, A., 367, 373,
387, 488, 524, 526,
590, 674, 686, 838,
839, 840
Damasio, H., 524
Dambrosia, J. M., 462
Damiani, V. B., 1076
Danchin, A., 657, 658
Daneshvar, S., 871, 873
D'Angiola, N., 257, 353
Daniells, C. E., 543, 545
Daniels, J., 431
Danielsson, B., 48, 62
Danko, C. D., 968, 990,
991, 1057, 1061, 1064,
1074
Dannals, R. F., 142
Dannemiller, J. L., 640
Dant, C. C., 429
D'Antonio, L. L., 552
D'Anuono, P., 80
Daoud, A. S., 130
Da Paz, J. A., 553
Dapretto, M., 170, 173,
521, 526
Darby, J. K., 84
Darcy, M., 1030, 1033
Darley, F., 336
Darling, R. B., 1060, 1064,
1068
Darrow, M. A., 916
Dartnall, N., 367, 374, 789
D'Ateno, P., 871
Dattilo, J., 890
Davanzo, P. A., 1108
Davey, M., 101
David, C., 586, 588
David, F. J., 833, 843
Davidkin, I., 541
Davidovitch, M., 49, 73, 80,
536, 1312
Davids, A., 744
Davidson, L., 142

Davidson, R., 494, 521,
522, 668
Davies, B., 961
Davies, S., 438, 519, 541
Davis, B., 953, 1044, 1132,
1141
Davis, C. A., 901
Davis, H., 489, 492, 493,
499, 501, 519, 661
Davis, J. M., 848
Davis, K. A., 608
Davis, K. L., 433, 474, 550
Davis, R. L., 436
Davis, S., 315, 431, 746,
753, 1073
Dawson, A. K., 544
Dawson, G., 5, 30, 31, 113,
165, 171, 172, 187,
191, 224, 225, 226,
233, 234, 235, 236,
237, 238, 251, 252,
268, 294, 316, 318,
319, 320, 321, 324,
326, 341, 342, 366,
368, 372, 373, 374,
375, 384, 385, 386,
387, 388, 396, 397,
398, 409, 415, 429,
480, 481, 482, 483,
491, 492, 499, 520,
521, 522, 526, 537,
539, 540, 595, 609,
610, 612, 613, 615,
617, 642, 651, 652,
654, 656, 657, 659,
662, 663, 665, 668,
670, 671, 689, 690,
707, 708, 709, 712,
713, 724, 755, 757,
782, 793, 799, 800,
818, 820, 832, 833,
834, 837, 841, 846,
934, 942, 946, 959,
962, 987, 998, 1003,
1004, 1008, 1078,
1124, 1139, 1310, 1311
Dawson, J. E., 267
Dawson, M., 109, 201, 203,
204, 206
Day, H. M., 821, 911
Day, J. R., 821
Day, R., 438, 541
Deal, A., 932
Dean, A., 488, 489, 536,
617, 618
Dean, R. S., 539
Deb, S., 100
Debbaudt, D., 299
de Bildt, A., 170, 412, 454,
520, 689, 696, 753,
789
DeBoer, M., 1004
DeCasper, A., 319
Decety, J., 419, 692, 693
de Chaffoy de Courcelles,
D., 1103
DeCoste, D., 801
Decoufle, P., 49, 52, 57,
60, 185
Deeney, T., 845
DeFelice, M. L., 541
De Fossé, L., 495

DeGangi, G. A., 846
Degangi, G. A., 980, 982
de Gelder, B., 324, 519
DeGelder, B., 324, 642
De Giacomo, A., 223, 227, 235, 1056, 1057
Degiovanni, E., 483
de Gomberoff, L., 670
de Haan, M., 549, 670
Dehaene, S., 607
Dehart, D. B., 454
Deibert, A. N., 1126
Deitz, J., 366, 536, 834, 843
De Jonge, R. C., 183
de Kogel, K., 249, 318, 319
Delaney, M. A., 1105
de la Pena, A., 484
Delatang, N., 394
Delbello, M. P., 181
DeLeon, I. G., 824
Delgado, C., 653, 654, 662
Del Gracco, S., 542, 1307
del Junco, D., 144, 145
Dellve, L., 1057, 1074, 1076
del Medico, V., 1110
Delmolino, L., 290, 297
DeLoache, J. S., 395
DeLong, G. R., 108, 270, 368, 371, 488, 553, 1107, 1305
DeLong, M. R., 142
DeLong, R., 428
Delon-Martin, C., 693
Delprato, D., 883, 884, 937, 951
Delquadri, J., 264, 991, 1032
Demasio, A. R., 488
DeMaso, D. R., 1108
Demchak, M., 1033
de Mendilaharsu, S. A., 1229
Demet, E. M., 459, 460, 462
Demeter, K., 146
Demick, J., 645
DeMyer, B., 962
DeMyer, M. K., 9, 204, 206, 215, 288, 293, 296, 301, 320, 321, 335, 384, 385, 387, 453, 835, 836, 839, 882, 1011, 1056, 1068, 1069, 1072, 1075, 1077, 1089, 1198, 1304
DeMyer, W., 204, 206, 215, 288, 293, 335, 384, 836, 962, 1011
Denckla, M. B., 98, 591, 839
Dennett, D., 629
Dennis, J., 594
Dennis, M., 613, 641
Dennis, N. R., 550, 551, 555
Dennis, T., 539
Denny, R., 968, 1030
Deno, S., 205

Denzler, B., 1176
Deonna, T., 80, 82
Depastas, G., 139, 145
de Plá, E. P., 1232
DeRaad, A., 916
Derby, K. M., 819, 823, 916
de Roux, N., 130, 138
Derrick, A., 32, 169, 173, 754, 755, 757
Deruelle, C., 261, 519, 520
De Sanctis, S., 583, 584, 1221
de Schonen, S., 486, 642
DesLauriers, A. M., 1060
Desnick, R. J., 545
Desombre, H., 751
de Souza, L., 536
Despert, J. C., 584, 585
Despert, J. L., 167
Desrochers, M. N., 915
Desser, P. R., 1018
DeStefano, F., 436
DeStefano, L., 1091, 1092
de Traversay, J., 478
Detweiler, J. B., 1182
D'Eufemia, P., 539
Deutsch, C. K., 493, 494, 496, 497, 498, 519, 1305
Deutsch, G. K., 1308
Devaney, J., 130, 138, 139, 148, 151
DeVellis, R., 289, 667, 721, 744, 748
DeVet, K. A., 1062
Devinsky, O., 503
DeVito, T. J., 494
DeVos, E., 645
de Vries, B. B., 78, 545
de Vries, H., 249, 318, 319
de Vries, P. J., 543
DeWeese, J., 1112
Dewey, D., 387, 388, 1057, 1074, 1077
Dewey, M., 1014, 1021
Dewey, W. L., 142
de Wied, D., 460
Deykin, E. Y., 51, 76, 539, 1305
Dharmani, C., 82
Dhillon, A. P., 541
Dhossche, D., 463
Diambra, J., 619
Diament, D. M., 1060
Diamond, A., 612
Diamond, R., 520, 697
Dias, K., 126, 154, 431, 535, 594
Dias, R., 609, 615
Dick, J., 1220
Dickens, B. F., 462
Dickey, T. O., 607, 616
Dickinson, H., 759
Dictenberg, J., 545
Didde, R., 542
Didden, R., 898
Didonato, R. M., 147, 148
Dielkens, A., 546
Dietrich, E., 690
Dietrich, K., 486
Dietz, C., 723

Dietz, F., 657, 662
Dietz, P. E., 299
Diggs, C. C., 149
DiGirolamo, G., 668, 669
DiLalla, D. L., 73, 75, 224, 225, 227, 721, 1051
DiLavore, P., 45, 110, 196, 214, 224, 228, 233, 248, 326, 341, 342, 343, 348, 349, 541, 547, 551, 655, 709, 712, 730, 731, 732, 734, 739, 740, 753, 756, 757, 780, 781, 808, 1124, 1143, 1216
DiLeo, D., 875
DiLiberti, J. H., 555
DiMarco, R., 956
Dimiceli, S., 170, 315, 440, 754
di Nemi, S. U., 1305
Dinh, E., 73, 77, 78
Dinno, H., 689
Dinno, N., 225, 398, 708
Dio Bleichmar, E., 1229
Diomedi, M., 542
Dion, Y. D., 834
Dirlich-Wilhelm, H., 888, 1058, 1129
DiSalvo, C. A., 870
Dissanayake, C., 174, 213, 251, 322, 657, 707, 833, 1057, 1199
Dissanayake, M., 1011
Dittrich, W. H., 692
Diwadkar, V., 667
Dix, T., 1057
Dixon, J. M., 909
Dixon, P., 716
Dixon, S. D., 81
Djukic, A., 82
Dloan, R., 665
Dobbin, A. R., 900
Dobson, V., 554
Dodds, J., 712
Dodman, T. N., 1281
Dodson, S., 148
Doehring, P., 315, 320, 651, 800
Doernberg, N., 57, 63, 555, 1070, 1123
Doherty, S., 549
Doke, L. A., 1154
Dolan, C. V., 434
Dolan, R., 518, 523, 525, 615, 646, 668
Dolgoff-Kaspar, R., 1111
Doll, E. A., 745
Domachowske, J. B., 544
Dombrowski, C., 545
Dombrowski, S. M., 491, 496, 549
Domenech-Jouve, J., 459
Domingue, B., 997, 998
Domino, E. F., 848
Donahoe, P. A., 1044, 1132, 1141
Donahue, P., 953
Donaldson, L. J., 547
Donnellan, A., xviii, xix, 149, 561, 866, 902, 903, 904, 905, 906, 907, 934, 966

Donnellan-Walsh, A., 1008
Donnelly, M., 693
Donnelly, S. L., 432, 433, 434, 439, 544, 551, 753, 754
Donovan, L., 1232
Dooley, J. M., 130
Dore, J., 340
Dorrani, N., 78, 551
Dorsey, M. F., 825
Doryon, Y. D., 834
Doss, S., 910
Dougherty, J. M., 1177
Douglas, V. I., 617
Doussard-Roosevelt, J., 336, 832
Dover, R., 734, 748, 749, 753
Dowd, M., 32, 731, 733, 754, 755
Dowling, F., 589
Down, J. L., 547
Down, M., 439
Doyle, D., 542, 1112
Doyle, S., 293, 804
Dozier, C. L., 819, 821, 823
Drachenberg, C., 541
Dragich, J., 78, 138
Drasgow, E., 967
Dratman, M. L., 744
Dreux, C., 459
Drevets, W. C., 524, 525
Drew, A., 105, 233, 234, 235, 237, 320, 342, 349, 369, 384, 410, 613, 634, 654, 656, 665, 708, 730, 732, 832, 837, 947, 961
Drinkwater, S., 1033
Driscoll, D., 551
Driver, J., 318, 523, 525, 630, 642, 663
Dropik, P., 542, 1112
Drost, D. J., 494
Druin, D. P., 612
Drury, I., 144
Druse, M., 454
D'Souza, I., 429
Duara, R., 476, 477, 492, 1015
Dubno, J. R., 476
Duchan, J., 255, 257, 346, 691, 961
Ducharme, J. M., 268, 907
Duer, A., 542
Duffy, K., 1088, 1278
Dugan, E., 251, 1030, 1032
Dugas, M., 189, 1112
Dugger, D. L., 539
Duivenvoorden, H. J., 545
Duker, P. C., 867, 898, 899, 903, 1127
Duku, E., 24, 110, 174
Dulac, O., 545
Duley, J. A., 464
du Mazaubrun, C., 47, 52, 61, 534, 544
Duncan, J., 606, 612
Dunham, D., 656
Dunlap, G., 264, 820, 823, 865, 866, 869, 899, 900, 906, 912, 916,

Dunlap, G. *(Continued)*
    932, 934, 940, 1003,
    1004, 1032, 1033,
    1058, 1060, 1092,
    1124, 1129
Dunn, D. W., 463
Dunn, J. K., 129, 139, 140,
    143
Dunn, L., 147, 790, 804
Dunn, M., 30, 169, 251,
    342, 369, 479, 482,
    539, 616, 1306, 1307,
    1311, 1313
Dunn, W., 268, 366, 536,
    832, 833, 834, 842,
    843, 981, 983
Dunn-Geier, J., 542, 1112
Dunst, C., 83, 932
Duong, T., 489
Dupes, M., 462
DuPre, E. P., 177
Durand, V., 819, 823, 824,
    903, 910, 911, 926
Durbach, M., 1034
Durkin, K., 105, 352
Durnik, M., 1177
Durston, S., 493, 499
Duruibe, V. A., 462
Dussault, W. L. E., 1125
Duvner, T., 102
Duyme, M., 459, 461
Dwyer, J. J., 270
Dwyer, J. T., 108
Dyer, K., 821, 823, 824,
    900, 910, 1128
Dyken, P., 76
Dykens, E., 187, 211, 551,
    719, 720, 750, 794
Dykens, E. D., 169, 182
Dykens, E. M., 26, 537,
    538, 546, 548, 1055
Dykens, M., 429
Dyomin, V., 551
Dyson, L. L., 1074
Dziurawiec, S., 317

Earl, C. J., 545, 584
Eastman, L. E., 909
Eastwood, D., 539
Eaves, D., 29, 595, 833
Eaves, L., 542, 595, 1112
Eaves, L. C., 29, 262, 288,
    290, 291, 833
Eaves, L. J., 432, 438
Eaves, R. C., 720, 746, 747,
    750
Ebert, M. H., 458
Ebstein, R. P., 433, 463
Eccles, J. C., 489
Echelard, D., 170, 172, 493,
    496, 497, 498, 501
Eck, E., 549
Ecker, C. L., 843
Eddy, M., 885, 1089
Eddy, W. F., 373, 485, 496,
    525
Edelson, S. M., 832
Eden, G. F., 518
Edminson, P. D., 462
Edvinsson, S., 546
Edwards, A., 48, 52, 54, 61,
    63, 266, 408

Edwards, D., 1060, 1062
Edwards, J. G., 1283
Edwards, M., 48, 52, 54,
    61, 63
Edwards, R., 476
Edwards, S., 804
Edwards-Brown, M., 463
Eeg-Olofsson, O., 130
Eens, A., 1103
Egaas, B., 494, 496, 499,
    519
Egel, A., 264, 820, 823,
    1030, 1037, 1126, 1138
Egelhoff, J. C., 430
Egger, J., 143
Ehlers, J. A., 553
Ehlers, S., 53, 102, 103,
    105, 227, 232, 234,
    329, 352, 375, 525,
    586, 615, 666, 724,
    834, 1244
Eikeseth, S., 239, 254, 870,
    874, 897, 1061, 1064
Eikseth, S., 984
Eilers, L., 544, 548, 593
Eimas, P., 689
Einfeld, S., 546, 548, 1197,
    1198, 1199
Eisenberg, L., 201, 204,
    215, 224, 293, 584,
    585, 596
Eisenberg, R., 689
Eisenberg, Z. W., 1102
Eisenmajer, R., 24, 93, 167,
    172, 348, 593
Ek, U., 554
Ekdahl, M. M., 901
Ekman, P., 630
El Abd, S., 544
Elardo, S., 536
Elbert, J. C., 863, 1181
Elchisak, M. A., 458
Eldevik, S., 239, 254, 870,
    874, 984
Elgar, K., 652
Elia, M., 479, 481, 482,
    494, 499, 542, 1307
Elizur, A., 1220
Ellaway, C., 126, 143
Ellenberg, L., 645
Elliot, G. R., 708
Elliott, C. D., 789
Elliott, G., 21, 31, 73, 314,
    317, 335
Elliott, M. J., 349
Elliott, R. O., Jr., 900
Ellis, D., 100, 968
Ellis, H., 97, 100, 317,
    375
Ellis, W., 207
Ellison, D., 1068, 1074
Ellison, G. W., 539
Elmasian, R., 24, 268, 368,
    479, 480, 482, 499
Elroy, S., 542
Elsas, L. J., 555
Elwin, B., 1243
Emelianova, S., 542
Emerson, E., 1245
Emery, N. J., 526
Emilsson, B., 1177
Enayati, A., 435

Endicott, J. E., 15
Ene, M., 97, 104, 107, 375
Eng, D., 141, 142
Engel, A. K., 690, 695
Engel, W., 138
Engelstad, K., 550
English, K., 969, 990, 991
Enns, J., 234, 368, 641
Ensrud, S., 257, 353, 598
Ephrimidis, B., 1058, 1069
Epperson, N., 1108
Epstein, J., 569
Epstein, R., 542
Erdem, E., 107
Erel, O., 1058
Erfanian, N., 914
Erickson, C., 267
Erickson, K., 154, 155,
    937, 941
Erikson, K., 802, 804
Eriksson, I., 76, 142
Ermer, J., 268, 833
Ernst, M., 189, 524, 525,
    667, 1112
Erwin, E. J., 941
Erwin, J., 670
Erwin, R., 478, 481, 503
Escalante-Mead, P. R., 496
Escamilla, J. R., 544
Eschler, J., 31, 73, 317, 708
Esclaire, F., 551
Eskes, G. A., 344, 642
Eskes, P. J., 613
Eso, K., 619
Espin, G., 205
Estecio, M. R. H., 551
Estes, A., 5, 31, 171, 233,
    234, 375, 388, 429,
    612, 613, 656, 657,
    662, 663, 665, 668,
    670
Estevez, J., 553
Estill, K., 902
Etcoff, N. L., 526
Etcoff, N. L., 526
Evans, A., 693
Evans, I. M., 820, 915, 916,
    1004
Evans, P. A., 542
Evans-Jones, L. G., 73
Everaard, T., 109
Everall, I. P., 101
Everard, M., 1014
Everard, T., 201, 203, 204,
    206
Evered, C., 107, 124, 412,
    462, 520, 539
Evered, C., 542
Eviatar, A., 484
Eviatar, Z., 260
Ewald, H., 185, 188, 430,
    453, 534, 551
Ewell, M. D., 1126, 1127
Ewens, W. J., 431
Ewing, K. M., 555
Exner, J. E., 794
Eyberg, S. M., 1060, 1062
Eyre, D. G., 477

Fabrizi, A., 536, 1221
Fabry, P. L., 1138
Facchinetti, F., 142, 143
Factor, D. C., 17, 749, 762
Fadale, D., 549

Fadiga, L., 255, 389
Fagbemi, A., 541
Fagen, J. A., 147
Faherty, C., 867
Fahey, K., 169, 181
Fahum, T., 299
Falco, C., 265, 266
Falco, R., 1004, 1005,
    1006, 1007, 1008,
    1009, 1012
Falcone, J. F., 1105
Falfai, T., 325
Fan, Y. S., 544
Fann, W. E., 848
Fantes, J. A., 551
Fantie, B. D., 367, 368,
    498, 614
Farag, T. I., 551
Farah, M. J., 388, 608
Faranda, N., 253
Faraone, S. V., 177, 183,
    208
Farbotko, M., 1064, 1065
Farley, A. H., 227, 316,
    553, 832, 834, 837
Farley, I., 142
Farmer-Dougan, V., 903
Farndon, P. A., 555
Farnham, J., 618, 634, 635
Farrant, A., 497, 499
Farrell, P., 205
Farrington, C. P., 48, 54,
    60, 519
Farroni, R., 317
Farroni, T., 318
Farshad, S., 654, 671
Faruque, F., 141
Farzin, F., 546
Fassbender, L. L., 149
Fatemi, S. H., 463, 490
Faure, M., 689, 834
Faux, S. F., 479
Favell, J. E., 819, 1130,
    1141, 1144, 1151,
    1183
Favot-Mayaud, I., 48, 54,
    60, 435
Faw, G. D., 913, 1126
Fay, W., 255, 256, 346,
    348, 961
Federspiel, A., 521
Fee, M., 914
Fee, V., 720, 745, 749, 751,
    1029, 1030
Feehan, C., 268, 588
Fehm, L., 181, 182
Feigenbaum, J. D., 373
Fein, D., 29, 30, 169, 229,
    238, 251, 323, 325,
    344, 367, 369, 410,
    462, 519, 520, 539,
    616, 617, 713, 716,
    717, 833, 1306, 1307
Fein, G. G., 795
Feinberg, E., 1182
Feinberg, J., 463
Feineis-Matthews, S., 521
Feinstein, C., 30, 169, 185,
    251, 323, 461, 462,
    539, 547, 548, 616,
    1306
Feitelson, D., 398

Fekete, M., 549
Felce, D., 904
Feldman, C., 259, 260, 352, 353
Feldman, H. M., 1110, 1111, 1112
Feldman, I., 515
Feldman, R. S., 324, 520, 890, 899, 953, 1011, 1030, 1031, 1130
Fellous, M., 433
Fender, D., 501
Fenske, E. C., 875, 1029
Fenson, L., 337, 800
Fenton, G., 536
Ferguson, W., 607, 616
Fermanian, J., 751
Fernald, A., 336, 690
Fernald, R. D., 326, 327
Fernandez, M., 320, 321, 355, 707
Fernandez, P., 7, 436
Fernell, E., 458, 544, 553, 554
Ferrante, L., 758
Ferrara, J. M., 916
Ferrari, M., 251, 818
Ferrari, P., 459, 461, 1208
Ferri, R., 479, 481, 482, 494, 499, 542, 1307
Ferris, S., 461, 501
Ferruzzi, F., 539
Ferster, C. B., 882, 1089
Ferstl, E., 668, 669
Fett-Conte, A. C., 551
Fewell, R. R., 399, 846
Fey, M., 959, 966
Fiamenghi, G. A., 383
Fico, C., 265, 266
Fidler, D. J., 536
Field, D., 540
Field, K., 493, 501, 521, 522, 536, 646, 660
Field, L. L., 431
Field, T., 253, 690
Fifer, W., 319
Figueroa, R. G., 905
Filiano, J. J., 550
Filipek, P., 172, 187, 342, 489, 491, 492, 493, 494, 499, 536, 537, 538, 540, 543, 544, 550, 551, 553, 708, 709, 712, 713, 722, 724, 752, 782, 841, 1124, 1139, 1305, 1307, 1310
Fill, C., 138
Filloux, F., 368, 372, 498, 643
Findling, R. L., 539, 1109
Fine, J., 256, 257, 258
Fine, M. J., 1060
Finegan, J.-A., 539
Finegold, S. M., 541
Finestack, L., 966
Fink, B., 170, 427, 537, 538
Fink, G., 518, 646, 668
Fink, M., 589
Finlayson, A. J., 174, 183, 606, 607

Finlayson, M., 104, 372, 373, 375, 628
Finley, C., 480
Finley, W. W., 479
Finocchiaro, R., 539
Finucane, B., 550, 551
Fiona, J. S., 185
Fiore, C., 617
Firestone, P., 1142
First, M., 10, 200
Fisch, G., 251, 546
Fischer, K. J., 870
Fischer, M. L., 350
Fish, B., 183
Fishel, P., 320, 321, 355, 707
Fisher, J. R., 1044, 1046
Fisher, M., 1034
Fisher, P., 762
Fisher, S. E., 432, 438, 1307
Fisher, W., 27, 28, 46, 52, 55, 71, 75, 128, 135, 152, 838, 907, 908, 909, 912, 1111
Fisman, S., 93, 95, 213, 252, 719, 734, 735, 736, 743, 845, 1068, 1074
Fitzgerald, C. M., 463, 490
Fitzgerald, M., 46, 437, 463, 754
Fitzgerald, P. M., 150
Fitzpatrick, T. B., 543
Fiumara, A., 539, 547, 553
Flach, F. F., 460
Flagler, S., 1069
Flaisch, T., 669, 670
Flannery, K. B., 823, 900
Flejter, W. L., 551
Fleming, J. E., 733
Fleming, N., 130, 132
Fleminger, S., 666
Fletcher, J., 260
Fletcher, K. E., 27, 456
Fletcher, P., 105, 525, 615, 665, 666, 804
Flodman, P., 544
Flood, W. A., 267
Floody, H., 655
Flores, F., 687
Florio, T., 548
Flowers, L., 518
Floyd, J., 904
Flynn, B. M., 1094
Fogassi, L., 255, 389
Foley, D., 886
Foley, S. M., 1092
Folio, M. R., 846
Folstein, S., 28, 107, 170, 195, 208, 270, 291, 427, 429, 430, 432, 433, 436, 439, 440, 453, 492, 499, 537, 538, 539, 553, 632, 754, 768
Fombonne, E., 27, 42, 43, 47, 49, 52, 53, 54, 55, 57, 58, 59, 60, 61, 75, 102, 171, 175, 185, 204, 223, 227, 235, 269, 291, 316, 317,

427, 428, 434, 435, 438, 439, 500, 501, 534, 536, 541, 544, 547, 593, 740, 741, 753, 773, 1056, 1057, 1175, 1308
Fonagy, P., 1283
Fong, L., 290, 1075, 1093
Fong, P. L., 257, 1089
Fonlupt, P., 693
Fontanesi, J., 147, 148
Foote, R., 1060, 1062
Ford, T., 49, 60
Forehand, R., 1060
Forman, D. R., 386
Forsberg, P., 48, 62
Forsell, C., 430, 544
Forster, P., 555, 556
Forsythe, A. B., 484, 542
Foshee, T. J., 1126, 1127
Foss, J., 462
Foster, A., 542
Foster, L. G., 536, 833, 834
Foster, S. L., 826
Foushee, D. R., 553
Fowler, A. E., 345
Fox, A., 1031
Fox, J., 968
Fox, L., 932, 934, 940, 1003, 1004
Fox, M., 1307
Fox, N., 373, 613, 655, 656, 662, 663, 664, 665, 668, 669, 670
Fox, R., 692
Fox, S., 905
Foxx, R. M., 910, 913, 915, 916, 1126, 1134
Frackowiak, R., 371, 495, 497, 518, 615, 646, 665, 1305
Fraiberg, S., 347, 396, 417, 554
Fraknoi, J., 744
Frances, A. J., 11
Francis, A., 542, 589
Francis, K., 951
Francke, U., 21, 77, 78, 130, 136, 431
Francks, C., 438
Frank, H., 654, 671
Frank, J. A., 526
Frankenburg, F. R., 1103
Frankenburg, W. K., 710, 711, 712
Frankhauser, M., 459, 1111
Franz, D. N., 430
Franzini, L. R., 1183
Fraser, W., 44, 48, 59, 62, 100, 177
Fratta, A., 1103
Frazier, J., 181, 208
Frea, W. D., 267, 886, 897, 911, 912, 913, 1033
Fredericks, H. D., 1076
Frediani, T., 539
Fredrika, M., 731, 750
Freed, J., 27, 189, 1110
Freedland, R. L., 640
Freedman, D., 554
Freedman, D. G., 322

Freedman, D. X., 454, 455, 456, 459, 1195
Freeman, B., 38, 47, 63, 184, 234, 251, 292, 294, 299, 316, 321, 455, 461, 489, 500, 534, 536, 537, 539, 540, 545, 724, 741, 745, 750, 751, 753, 755, 762, 872
Freeman, K. A., 871, 887
Freeman, N. L., 17, 749
Freeman, S. F. N., 1034
Freeman, S. K., 963, 985, 996
Freeman, T., 1068, 1074
Freidlander, B., 1093
Freitag, C. M., 754
Freitag, G., 249, 882
Fremolle, J., 439, 500, 501, 536
Freund, L. S., 269, 544, 545
Friberg, L., 140
Frick, J. E., 645
Fridman, C., 551
Fridman, C., 551
Friedman, D., 479, 481, 482
Friedman, E., 463, 553
Friedman, S., 165, 170, 171, 172, 191, 493, 496, 497, 498, 501, 651, 755
Friedrich, F., 608
Friedrich, U., 544
Fries, P., 690, 695
Friesen, C. K., 663
Friesen, D., 746
Friston, K., 371, 495, 497, 518, 1305
Frith, C., 171, 518, 524, 525, 526, 615, 646, 652, 665, 666, 669, 671, 672, 673, 692
Frith, J., 323
Frith, U., 88, 89, 105, 109, 169, 174, 186, 255, 259, 263, 265, 299, 326, 346, 348, 368, 411, 518, 519, 524, 525, 526, 583, 584, 594, 595, 615, 618, 628, 631, 632, 635, 640, 641, 642, 643, 645, 652, 665, 666, 669, 671, 672, 673, 692, 1016, 1244
Fritz, M. S., 44, 57, 61
Frolile, L. A., 1078
Frost, J. D., 144, 145
Frost, L., 708, 885, 891, 929, 940, 955, 956, 1036
Frydman, M., 552
Frye, D., 325, 615
Frye, V., 1006
Fryer, A., 543
Fryer, S. L., 108
Fryman, J., 387, 837
Fryns, J., 545, 546
Fu, Y. H., 545
Fueki, N., 140

Fuentes, F., 708, 949, 1004, 1032
Fujiede, T., 460
Fujikawa, H., 100
Fujimoto, C., 544
Fujino, M. K., 499
Fujita, T., 254
Fukuda, T., 138
Fukuyama, Y., 127
Fulbright, A., 419
Fulbright, R., 170, 191, 519, 520, 521, 525, 696, 697, 889
Fuller, K., 1034
Fuller, S. P., 1088, 1093
Fullerton, A., 875, 1022, 1023
Funderburk, S. J., 500, 536, 539
Funk, J., 542, 1112
Fuqua, R. W., 870, 876
Furlano, R. I., 438, 541
Furman, J. M., 484, 486
Furman, L., 961
Furniss, F., 269
Furukawa, H., 227, 834, 1224
Fussy, L., 619
Fyer, A. J., 181, 182

Gabbay, U., 1220
Gable, A., 435
Gabler-Halle, D., 900, 1183
Gabrielli, W. F., 1108
Gabriels, R., 542, 1112
Gaddes, J., 350
Gademan, P. J., 183
Gaeta, H., 481, 482
Gaffan, D., 526, 693
Gaffan, E. A., 526, 693
Gaffney, G. R., 494, 499
Gagnon, E., 907
Gajzago, C., 27
Galaburda, A., 548
Galambos, R., 476, 477, 479, 480, 482
Galant, K., 1003
Gale, S., 539, 544
Galef, B. G., 383
Gallagher, C., 958
Gallagher, H., 665
Gallagher, J. J., 1061, 1070
Gallagher, P. A., 1088
Gallagher, P. R., 542
Gallese, V., 255, 389, 659, 673
Galpert, L., 318, 324, 386, 409, 480, 520, 946
Gamache, T. B., 152, 155
Gane, L. W., 545
Ganes, T., 535
Ganiban, J. M., 548
Ganz, J. B., 869, 913
Gao, H. G., 550
Garand, J., 889, 985, 996
Garbarino, H., 1229
Garber, H. J., 499, 1107
Garber, M., 831, 832, 1014, 1284
Garcia, J., 251, 1030, 1031
Gardener, P., 871, 876, 886
Gardiner, C., 551

Gardiner, J. M., 369, 370, 371
Gardiner, M., 438, 754
Gardner, A., 1060
Gardner, H., 686, 1180
Gardner, J. M., 1126
Gardner, M. F., 844, 847
Gardner, Medwin, D., 145
Gardner, S. C., 545
Gareau, L., 518
Garelis, E., 456, 457
Garety, P., 619
Garfin, D., 720, 721, 741, 748, 749, 926, 978
Garfinkel, B. D., 458, 459, 460
Garfinkle, A. N., 889, 969, 1031
Gargus, J. J., 538, 550, 553
Garland, M., 540
Garman, M., 804
Garmezy, N., 14, 249
Garofalo, E., 144
Garreau, B., 373, 459, 555, 689, 751, 834
Garretson, H. B., 367, 617
Garrison, H. L., 991, 1031
Garrod, A., 645
Garth, E., 485
Gartside, P., 536
Garver, B. A., 485, 496, 525
Garver, K. E., 373
Garvey, J., 967
Gath, A., 548
Gauthier, I., 170, 191, 419, 519, 520, 521, 522, 523, 525, 670, 696, 697, 889
Gavidia-Payne, S., 542
Gaviria, P., 1231, 1232
Gayle, J., 170, 195, 197, 295, 427, 537, 538, 539, 808, 809
Gaylor, E., 503, 542
Gaylord-Ross, R., 904
Gazdag, G. E., 889
Gazzaniga, M., 663
Gecz, J., 544
Geddes, J., 189, 619
Gedney, B., 539
Geffen, L., 479
Geffken, G. R., 251, 316
Geller, A., 453
Geller, B., 181, 501
Geller, E., 455, 458, 503
Gelman, S., 629
Gena, A., 261
Genazzani, A., 142, 143
Gendrot, C., 78
Gensburg, L. J., 547
Gense, D. J., 555
Gense, M., 555, 1004, 1005, 1006
Gentile, P. S., 538
George, A. E., 492
Gepner, B., 261, 486, 519, 520, 642, 839
Geracioti, T. D., 456
Gerald, P., 546
Gerard, J. D., 912
Gerardo, A., 539
Gergely, C., 630

Gergely, G., 629, 630, 698
Gerhardt, P., 899, 1089, 1093, 1095
Gericke, G. S., 1103
Gerland, G., 201, 642
German, M., 459, 1111
Gerner, R. H., 460
Gernsbacher, A. M., 521, 522
Gernsbacher, M., 952
Gershon, B., 1032
Gershon, E. S., 432
Gershwin, M. E., 542, 1312
Gerstein, L., 24, 99, 352
Gervais, H., 517, 521
Geschwind, D., 432, 433, 438, 439, 754
Geurts, H. M., 373
Gharani, N., 433, 474
Ghaziuddin, M., 24, 27, 50, 91, 93, 97, 99, 100, 101, 102, 103, 120, 187, 209, 210, 295, 299, 344, 352, 374, 375, 536, 539, 544, 547, 548, 551, 593, 734, 835, 846
Ghaziuddin, N., 24, 27, 50, 91, 93, 100, 101, 102, 120, 209, 210, 295, 299, 344, 544, 547, 548, 593, 734
El-Ghoroury, N. H., 254
Ghuman, J. K., 544
Giannini, A. J., 553
Giannini, M. C., 553
Gianutsos, R., 619
Giard, M., 481
Giardini, O., 539
Gibbs, B., 1071
Gibbs, M., 258, 261, 548
Gibson, J. J., 687
Giedd, J., 181
Gigli, G. L., 542
Gigrand, K., 916
Gil-Ad, I., 1220
Gilbert, J. R., 434, 544
Gilchrist, A., 33, 95, 100, 110, 167, 213, 214, 290, 294, 295, 300, 303, 352, 521, 523
Gill, H., 130, 132
Gill, K. J., 607, 616
Gill, M. J., 1089
Gillam, R., 813
Gillberg, C., 11, 15, 18, 21, 24, 26, 28, 47, 48, 49, 51, 53, 54, 60, 62, 63, 76, 77, 92, 93, 94, 100, 101, 102, 103, 105, 107, 108, 109, 113, 127, 132, 134, 142, 143, 149, 165, 171, 177, 184, 185, 186, 187, 199, 202, 204, 205, 212, 213, 215, 227, 229, 232, 234, 248, 249, 261, 265, 270, 288, 289, 290, 291, 292, 293, 295, 296, 297, 299, 304, 329, 341, 349, 352,

366, 375, 408, 425, 429, 430, 431, 432, 433, 434, 457, 459, 461, 462, 476, 478, 484, 495, 502, 524, 525, 534, 536, 539, 540, 544, 545, 546, 548, 551, 552, 553, 554, 586, 588, 590, 593, 594, 595, 615, 666, 713, 714, 720, 724, 735, 736, 741, 743, 748, 749, 750, 751, 753, 756, 760, 832, 833, 834, 1055, 1074, 1212, 1243, 1244, 1305, 1306
Gillberg, G., 593
Gillberg, I., 28, 62, 92, 93, 94, 102, 107, 108, 113, 185, 425, 461, 539, 545, 551, 588
Giller, E. L., 455, 458
Gillham, J. E., 170, 238
Gillham, J. G., 316
Gilliam, J. E., 542, 550, 720, 721, 751, 752
Gilliam, T. C., 438, 439, 754
Gillies, S., 201, 204
Gillis, B., 1074
Gillott, A., 269
Gillum, H., 959
Gilmour, W. H., 547
Gilotty, L., 613
Gingell, K., 266, 408
Ginsberg, G., 256, 257, 258
Gioia, G. A., 373, 794
Giovanardi Rossi, P., 296
Girard, M., 77, 138
Girardi, M. A., 1112
Giraud, A. L., 524
Girolametto, L., 806, 958, 959
Giron, J., 130, 138, 139, 148
Giros, B., 433
Gispen-de Wied, C. C., 183
Givner, A., 1126
Glad, K. S., 250, 261
Gladstone, K., 476
Glahn, T. J., 1138, 1141
Glasberg, B., 290, 297, 1074, 1075
Glascoe, F. P., 710, 712
Glaser, B., 552
Glassman, M., 321
Glasson, E. J., 434
Glaze, D. G., 129, 139, 141, 142, 143, 144, 145, 150
Gleason, J. R., 800
Glennon, S., 801
Glennon, T. J., 842
Glenwick, D. S., 1055, 1057
Glesne, H., 886
Glick, L., 73, 80, 1312
Glick, M., 187, 211, 794
Glisky, E. L., 619
Glousman, R., 455
Glover, S., 555, 556

Gluncic, V., 454
Gobbini, M. I., 520
Göbel, D., 46, 184
Gochman, P., 183
Goel, V., 611, 615, 665
Goetz, L., 883, 884
Goh, H., 907
Golan, O., 629
Gold, B., 665
Gold, J. R., 744
Gold, M. W., 1095
Gold, N., 1074
Gold, V. J., 882
Goldberg, B., 296
Goldberg, J., 170, 173, 190
Goldberg, M., 463, 484, 485
Goldberg, P., 1075, 1077
Goldberg, R. B., 552
Goldberg, S., 544
Goldberg, T. E., 140, 263
Goldberg, W., 342
Golden, C. J., 844
Golden, F., 1126
Goldenberg, A., 544
Goldenthal, M. J., 550
Goldfarb, W., 348, 584
Goldfried, M. R., 1181
Goldin, L. R., 431
Goldman, A., 659, 673
Goldman, B., 412, 483
Goldman, D., 431, 542, 1112
Goldman, R. S., 616
Goldman-Rakic, P., 373, 606, 612, 657
Goldsmith, B., 185, 548
Goldsmith, H. H., 521, 522
Goldson, E., 542, 1112
Goldstein, G., 97, 103, 144, 257, 263, 264, 267, 268, 295, 344, 367, 368, 369, 371, 372, 373, 387, 484, 487, 497, 549, 652, 660, 668, 767, 835, 1306
Goldstein, H., 336, 394, 887, 947, 950, 951, 955, 967, 968, 969, 990, 991, 1004, 1011, 1030, 1031, 1032, 1033
Goldstein, J. M., 1105
Goldstein, M., 142
Goldstein, S., 690
Goloni-Bertollo, E. M., 551
Golse, B., 225, 234, 236
Gomberoff, M., 1230
Gomes, A., 369
Gomez, J., 320
Gomez, M. R., 51, 543
Gommeren, W., 1103
Gomot, M., 479, 481
Goncu, A., 383
Gonen, N., 1220
Gonzaga, A. M., 1112
Gonzalez, C. H., 553
Gonzalez, N. M., 189, 1112
Gonzalez-Lopez, A., 251, 1030, 1031
Good, A., 883, 912, 1004, 1009
Good, C. D., 521

Goode, J., 434, 441, 443
Goode, S., 100, 108, 170, 171, 202, 205, 206, 207, 210, 212, 215, 216, 288, 290, 292, 293, 295, 296, 297, 298, 299, 304, 335, 342, 352, 426, 427, 437, 536, 537, 586, 594, 632, 732, 733, 753, 754, 756, 820, 1088
Goodhart, F., 631
Goodin, D. S., 479
Goodlin-Jones, B. L., 108, 503, 526, 542
Goodman, R., 49, 60, 61
Goodman, W., 27, 178, 1034, 1107, 1111, 1282
Goodman, Y., 1185
Goodson, S., 31
Goodwin, M. S., 540
Goodwin, T. C., 540
Goodwyn, S., 336
Goodyer, I., 632, 645
Gopnik, A., 320, 337, 383, 390, 659, 672, 673, 836
Gordon, A. G., 555
Gordon, B., 301, 491, 492, 499, 537, 540, 708, 712, 713, 724, 782
Gordon, C. T., 27, 169, 181, 367, 368, 610, 617, 1106
Gordon, E. K., 458
Gordon, K. E., 130
Gordon, M., 953
Gordon, O. T., 267
Gordon, R., 708, 949, 1032, 1034, 1036, 1044, 1045, 1132
Gordon-Williamson, G., 1310
Gore, J., 520, 522, 693, 696
Gorman-Smith, D., 914
Gorski, J. L., 551
Gosling, A., 1110
Gossage, L., 966
Gosselin, F., 521, 522, 523
Gothelf, D., 552
Goto, T., 127
Gotoh, H., 141
Gottesman, I., 108, 170, 341, 346, 347, 376, 425, 426, 434, 437, 500, 536, 632, 754
Gottfries, J., 139
Gottlieb, D., 105
Gottlieb, G., 651, 655, 656, 657, 658, 661
Goudreau, D., 183, 238, 251, 315, 783, 793
Goudy, K., 1149
Goujard, J., 61
Gould, J., 16, 24, 28, 30, 33, 46, 49, 50, 52, 53, 93, 94, 102, 167, 172, 184, 214, 248, 249, 265, 313, 317, 321, 323, 324, 348, 392, 396, 534, 535, 547,

548, 580, 585, 586, 587, 589, 593, 594, 595, 596, 597, 598, 599, 629, 631, 734, 735, 736, 741, 743, 745, 749, 755, 756, 833, 1189, 1243, 1245, 1305, 1306
Gould, M., 9, 91, 165, 168, 732, 762
Gould, T. D., 376
Goulet, P., 258
Goutieres, F., 129, 135
Grace, A. A., 1306
Grady, C., 518, 1015
Graef, J. W., 537
Graf, W. D., 550
Graff, J. C., 1074
Grafman, J., 611, 615, 665, 668, 669
Grafton, S. T., 524
Graham, A., 463, 490, 612
Graham, J. M., 150
Graham, L., 1013
Graham, P., 79, 546
Grandin, T., 201, 261, 295, 366, 374, 832, 939, 1013, 1014, 1015, 1016, 1017, 1077, 1088, 1178, 1184, 1185, 1276, 1277, 1278, 1280, 1281, 1311
Grandjean, H., 47, 52, 61, 534, 544
Grant, J., 236
Grant, S. B., 148, 149, 152, 153
Grattan, L. M., 613
Graubard, P. S., 1126
Gray, B., 551
Gray, C., 354, 869, 889, 912, 985, 988, 995, 996, 998, 1021, 1022
Gray, D. E., 1057, 1058, 1059, 1068, 1075
Gray, K. M., 265, 266
Graziano, A. M., 1060
Greco, C. M., 546
Greden, J., 27, 100, 295
Green, D., 588
Green, G., 540, 891, 936, 987, 1003, 1005, 1006, 1007, 1008
Green, J., 33, 95, 100, 110, 167, 213, 214, 229, 290, 294, 295, 300, 303, 352, 713, 716, 717
Green, L., 462, 539
Greenberg, D. A., 429, 434
Greenberg, J., 958
Greene, B. F., 1126, 1128
Greene, L. W., 461
Greene, N. M., 458
Greene, R., 177, 1109
Greenfeld, D., 201, 205, 215, 247, 293, 296
Greenfield, J. G., 489
Greenhill, L., 189, 1109
Greenough, W., 651, 657, 658, 660, 661, 670

Greenspan, S., 832, 889, 890, 957, 966, 967
Greenspan, S. I., 873, 929, 932, 936, 939, 940, 941, 1061, 1140, 1310
Greenspan, S. J., 1003
Greer, R., 253, 947, 948
Greig, T., 619
Greiner, N., 956
Grelotti, D., 520, 521, 522, 523, 524, 526, 670, 696
Grenot-Scheyer, M., 988
Gresham, F. M., 874, 1182
Grether, J., 44, 49, 59, 61, 63, 184, 291, 434, 462
Grezes, J., 693
Grice, P., 806
Grice, S. J., 370, 371, 549
Grier, R. E., 545
Griffin, C., 1058
Griffin, J. C., 1127
Griffin, R., 628, 629
Griffith, E., 102, 234, 372, 388, 612, 613, 614, 635, 663, 984
Griffiths, A. M., 547
Griffiths, M., 109
Griffiths, P. D., 430, 524
Grigorenko, E., 263, 354, 438, 691
Grigsby, J., 545
Grillon, C., 268, 477, 478, 479, 480, 482, 642
Grill-Spector, K., 523
Grimes, A. M., 476, 477
Grimme, A., 521, 522
Grinager, A. N., 733
Grinnell, E., 697
Griswold, D., 354, 375, 1018
Griswold, V. J., 499
Grizenko, N., 548
Groden, G., 553
Groden, J., 269, 869, 914, 984, 1016
Groen, A., 239, 949, 1048
Grøholt, B., 1243
Groom, J. M., 1034
Groothues, C., 180, 418, 436, 591
Gross, M. M., 315
Grossman, E., 693
Grossman, J., 106, 412, 800, 803
Grounds, A., 101, 299
Grover, W., 503
Grubber, J., 753
Gruber, B., 1010
Gruber, C., 83, 746, 753
Gruber, H. E., 464
Grufman, M., 177
Grynfeltt, S., 261
Gsodl, M., 549
Gualtieri, C. T., 501
Guela, C., 671
Guenin, K. D., 267, 1109
Guenther, S., 253
Gueorguieva, R., 1108
Guerin, P., 751
Guilloud-Bataille, M., 432, 462

Guisa Cruz, V. M., 1231
Gumley, D., 548
Gunter, H. L., 97, 375
Gupta, N., 74, 77, 78, 175
Guptill, J. T., 463, 490
Gur, R. C., 619
Gur, R. E., 619
Guralnick, M. J., 1034
Gurevich, N., 209
Gurling, H. M. D., 429
Gurney, J. G., 44, 57, 61
Gurrieri, F., 551
Gurunathan, N., 439, 631, 632, 634
Gusella, J. L., 690
Gustavson, K., 546
Gustein, S. E., 1020
Guthrie, D., 227, 316, 354, 478, 481, 489, 499, 553, 662, 745, 750, 832, 834, 837, 1305
Guthrie, R. D., 467
Gutierrez, E., 526
Gutierrez, G., 51, 545, 769
Gutknecht, L., 432
Gutstein, S., 929, 932, 936, 940, 941, 958, 967, 992
Guy, J., 431
Guze, B., 500, 536, 539
Gwirtsman, H., 460

Ha, Y., 668
Haas, R., 141, 144, 145, 147, 148, 154, 367, 499
Habers, H., 967
Hackney, D. B., 499
Hadano, K., 255
Haddad, C., 147
Hadden, L. L., 501, 536
Haddon, M., 1311
Hadjez, J., 459
Hadjikhani, N., 521
Hadwin, J., 259, 261, 682, 687, 872, 873
Haeggloef, B., 288
Hafeman, C., 1074
Hagberg, B., 48, 53, 54, 76, 126, 128, 129, 130, 131, 132, 136, 139, 142, 143, 144, 148, 154, 431, 535, 544, 594
Hagerman, R., 545, 546, 547, 844, 1110
Hagie, C., 1021
Hagiwara, R., 985, 996
Hagiwara, T., 354, 374, 375, 869, 1018
Häglöf, B., 204, 213
Hagopian, L. P., 907
Haier, R., 367, 617
Haigler, T., 539
Haines, J., 438, 543, 754
Hainline, L., 317
Hains, S. M. J., 317, 689
Haist, F., 522
Haith, M. M., 317, 684, 689
Hakeem, A., 670
Haley, S., 845

Halit, H., 549
Hall, D. A., 545, 546
Hall, G. B. C., 521
Hall, I., 299
Hall, L. J., 267
Hall, L. M., 459, 460, 461, 462, 1208
Hall, N., 369
Hall, R. V., 264, 1125, 1126
Hall, S. K., 255
Hall, T., 953, 1043, 1050
Hall, W., 546
Hallahan, D. P., 1073
Hallberg, L. R. M., 1057, 1074, 1076
Halle, J., 264, 819, 822, 883, 884, 900, 967, 1183
Hallett, M., 665, 839
Halliday, M. A. K., 337
Halligan, P. W., 646
Hallin, A., 212, 739
Hallmayer, J., 426, 428, 432, 433, 434, 437, 617, 754
Halloran, W., 1092
Hallum, E., 212
Halpern, C., 651, 655, 656, 657, 658, 661
Halsey, N. A., 1312
Halt, A. R., 463, 490
Haltiwanger, J., 845
Hamanaka, T., 255
Hamano, K., 661
Hamberger, A., 143, 462
Hamburger, J. D., 267
Hamburger, S. D., 27, 181, 263, 372, 388, 487, 606, 1016, 1106
Hamdan-Allen, G., 187, 251, 270
Hamel, B. C., 78
Hameury, L., 229, 232, 240, 366, 689, 708, 712, 751, 834
Hamill, D., 804
Hamilton, R., 901
Hamilton-Hellberg, C., 457
Hammeke,T. A., 844
Hammer, J., 618, 632, 634, 645, 1308
Hammer, M. S., 542
Hammer, S., 78, 435
Hammes, J. G. W., 384, 392
Hammill, D., 844
Hammond, J., 207
Hammond, M., 1034, 1060, 1062
Hamre-Nietupski, R., 1090
Hamre-Nietupski, S., 818, 1097
Hamstra, J., 526
Hanaoka, S., 135, 136
Hand, M., 291
Handen, B. L., 189, 906, 1110, 1111, 1112
Handleman, J. S., 239, 257, 708, 817, 819, 820, 870, 873, 949, 953, 1003, 1004, 1029, 1030, 1032, 1034,
1035, 1036, 1038, 1044, 1045, 1046, 1047, 1049, 1132, 1144
Hanefeld, F., 127, 129, 130, 131, 132, 138
Hanfeld, F., 464
Hanks, S. B., 150, 151, 152, 153, 154
Hanley, H. G., 454, 455, 456
Hanline, M., 1003
Hanna, G., 539
Hannah, G. T., 1128
Hannan, T., 319
Hannan, W. P., 544
Hannequinn, D., 258
Hannesdóttir, H., 1238
Hanrahan, J., 1034
Hans, S. L., 183
Hanselmann, H., 1239, 1240
Hansen, C., 130, 132, 137, 138
Hansen, N., 1238, 1239
Hansen, P. M., 905
Hansen, S., 462, 553
Hanson, D. R., 425
Hanson, E., 97, 104, 107, 375, 723
Hanson, R., 267
Hanson, S., 1074
Hanzerl, T. E., 823
Happé, E. F., 654, 655
Happé, F., 105, 106, 518, 524, 525, 526, 595, 615, 618, 630, 634, 635, 642, 643, 644, 645, 665, 666, 669
Happé, F. G., 253, 258, 326, 368, 640, 641, 642, 643, 644, 645, 682, 709, 730, 731, 832, 962
Hara, H., 325, 834
Harada, M., 172, 499
Harbauer, H., 1240, 1241
Harcherik, D., 456, 458, 460, 492, 539
Harchik, A. E., 916, 1098
Hardan, A., 297, 493, 494, 498, 499, 519, 660, 661, 667, 1305
Harden, A., 144
Harder, S. R., 823
Hardin, M. T., 838, 848
Harding, B., 139, 488, 489, 536, 546, 617, 618, 1305
Hardy, C., 551
Hardy, R. J., 554
Hare, D., 212
Harel, B., 251
Harenski, K., 660, 661
Hari, R., 389
Haring, N. G., 1010
Haring, T. G., 886, 904, 991, 1031, 1143
Hariri, A., 170, 173, 521, 526
Harlow, H. F., 1304
Harlow, M., 1304
Harmjanz, D., 548

Harms, L., 479, 480
Harnsberger, H. R., 548
Harper, J., 17, 214, 288, 289, 460, 741, 1076, 1077
Harper, L. V., 1061
Harper, V. N., 847, 848
Harrell, R., 912
Harrington, B., 1016
Harrington, H., 181
Harrington, R., 434, 438, 442, 710, 711
Harris, D. B., 795
Harris, F., 967, 1130
Harris, G. J., 355, 517
Harris, J. C., 142, 263
Harris, L. L., 1003
Harris, N., 368, 671
Harris, P., 383, 394, 395, 396, 399, 615, 630
Harris, R., 593
Harris, S. L., 239, 257, 290, 297, 708, 818, 820, 870, 872, 873, 890, 949, 953, 1004, 1029, 1030, 1032, 1033, 1034, 1035, 1036, 1038, 1044, 1045, 1046, 1047, 1049, 1055, 1060, 1061, 1071, 1074, 1077, 1132, 1144
Harris, S. W., 545
Harrison, D. J., 154
Harrison, J. E., 543, 545
Harrison, S., 526, 693
Harrower, J., 868, 929, 930, 932, 934, 937, 940, 941, 954, 1005, 1006, 1033, 1049
Harry, B., 988
Hart, B. M., 883, 950, 951, 967, 1130, 1144
Hart, C., 632
Hart, L. A., 438
Harter, M. R., 479
Harteveld, E., 183
Hartlep, P., 1125, 1126
Hartlep, S., 1125, 1126
Hartley, J., 353
Hartung, J., 800
Harvey, M. T., 542
Hasegawa, M., 140, 141
Hasegawa, T., 318
Hashimoto, O., 546
Hashimoto, T., 172, 461, 499, 539, 667
Hass, R., 140
Hassanein, K. M., 494
Hassold, T., 551
Hasstedt, S. J., 537
Hastings, R. P., 1055, 1070
Hatano, K., 662, 663
Hatfield, E., 383, 384, 836
Hattab, J., 463
Hattersley, J., 1244
Hatton, D., 546, 547, 833, 834, 849
Hattox, S. E., 458, 459
Hauck, J. A., 387, 388
Hauck, M., 323, 520
Hauser, E. R., 429, 754

Hauser, S. L., 553, 1305
Havercamp, S., 492, 499, 646, 660, 661
Haviland, J. M., 261, 690
Havlak, C., 151
Hawk, A. B., 550, 551
Hawkridge, S. M., 1103
Haxby, J., 520, 525, 696
Hay, D. F., 653
Hayashi, K. M., 494
Hayashi, T., 463, 1226
Hayden, D., 957
Hayden-Chumpelik, D., 951
Hayek, G., 143
Hayek, Y., 142
Hayes, C., 710, 712, 717, 718
Hayes, A., 547
Hays, S., 746, 753
Haywood, H. C., 872
Hazlett, E., 367, 496, 617
Haznedar, M., 496, 497, 525, 660, 667
He, X. S., 542
Head, D., 616
Heal, L., 207
Heap, I., 914
Heap, J., 1017
Hearsey, K., 302, 867, 932, 937, 940, 1043, 1049, 1050, 1067, 1177, 1178
Heaton, P., 642, 644
Heavey, L., 5, 8, 25, 61, 93, 316, 317, 419, 427, 442, 644
Heberlein, A. S., 526
Hebert, J. M., 433
Heckaman, K., 968, 1030
Hecox, K. E., 476
Hedrick, D., 83, 804
Hedrick, J., 551
Heemsbergen, J., 352, 426, 732, 733, 753, 756, 820
Heffelfinger, J., 551
Heflin, J., 929, 930
Heflin, L. J., 1032
Heiberg, A., 147, 149
Heider, F., 525, 697
Heimann, M., 384, 385, 386
Heimann, S. W., 1105
Hein, A., 691
Heinrichs, W., 545
Heinze, H. J., 646
Helayem, M., 553
Held, M., 131
Held, R., 691
Heller, A., 1092
Heller, T., 8, 70, 71, 72, 175, 1212, 1239
Hellgren, L., 28, 425
Hellings, J. A., 821, 1108
Hellreigel, C., 349
Helps, S., 1059
Helverschou, S. B., 542
Hemmeter, M. L., 889, 890
Hemphill, L., 353
Hemsley, R., 1244
Henderson, L., 588, 664, 665, 667, 670
Henderson, S., 588, 835

Hendrich, B., 431
Hendry, C. N., 23, 1312
Hendry, S. N., 80
Henggeler, S. W., 1063
Henighan, C., 147, 149
Heninger, G. R., 456, 1107
Hennessy, M. J., 154
Hennick, J. M., 1089
Henriksen, K. F., 130, 132, 137, 138
Henry, D., 842
Henry, L., 234, 370, 608, 611
Henry, R. R., 30
Hepburn, S., 31, 227, 232, 233, 235, 236, 237, 238, 251, 316, 321, 342, 366, 367, 384, 385, 386, 387, 388, 547, 707, 708, 721, 734, 753, 757, 799, 801, 833, 834, 835, 837, 843, 847, 947, 1007, 1011
Herault, J., 542, 1208
Herbert, D. A., 139
Herbert, J. T., 1004
Herbert, M., 355, 489, 493, 494, 496, 497, 498, 517, 519, 1061, 1305
Herbert-Jackson, E., 1143
Herbison, J., 953, 1043, 1050
Hering, E., 542
Herman, B., 459, 462, 1112
Herman, R., 553
Hermelin, B., 255, 263, 323, 388, 411, 596, 628, 640, 641, 642, 644
Heron, T. E., 1004, 1009
Herrington, J., 522, 523, 524, 526
Herrmann, D., 619
Hersen, M., 826
Hersh, J., 241, 544, 556
Hersov, L., 107, 124, 1244
Hertzig, M., 17, 184, 249, 261, 324, 409, 456, 458, 459, 460, 462, 520, 707, 749, 1208
Hervas, A., 48, 59, 62
Herzing, L. B. K., 429
Hess, C., 1092
Hess, L., 833, 834, 849
Hesselink, J. R., 367, 371, 499, 1282, 1305
Hetherington, H., 143
Hetzroni, O., 149
Heuschkel, R., 541
Heward, W. L., 1004, 1009
Hewett, F., 948
Heyes, C., 383, 389
Heyman, M. B., 541
Heyne, L. A., 870
Hicks, G., 476, 477, 479, 480
Higa, J., 481
Higgins, G., 143
Higgins, J. N., 430
Higgins, J. V., 551
Higgins, K., 322

Higley, J. D., 454
Higurashi, M., 141, 142
Hile, M. G., 915
Hilgenfeld, T., 354
Hill, A. E., 75
Hill, D., 318, 324, 387, 409, 520, 838, 946
Hill, E., 608, 611, 614, 837
Hill, J., 190, 628, 629, 631, 632, 1088
Hill, K., 259, 261, 682
Hill, S. D., 415, 467
Hill, W., 428
Hiller, S., 454
Hillman, R., 60, 435, 439, 501, 536
Hills, J., 545
Hillyard, S., 480, 482
Hinds, D., 426, 432, 433, 617
Hingtgen, J. N., 9, 384, 385, 387, 453, 836, 1011
Hington, J. N., 1198
Hinrichs, H., 646
Hippler, K., 24, 91, 96, 97
Hirasawa, K., 141
Hirata, J., 28
Hirsch, R. P., 710, 711
Hirsch, S. R., 1105
Hirschfield, L., 629
Hirstein, W., 459
Hitner, J. B., 900, 906
Hitzeman, R., 462
Hjelmquist, E., 234, 375, 1306
Ho, H., 29, 262, 288, 290, 291, 542, 595, 833, 1112
Hobbs, N., 12
Hobson, P., 324, 781
Hobson, R., 32, 227, 237, 253, 256, 260, 261, 344, 347, 353, 384, 386, 389, 390, 396, 407, 408, 411, 412, 413, 414, 415, 416, 417, 418, 436, 520, 554, 555, 643, 656, 672, 689, 731, 836
Hoch, H., 253, 868
Hock, M. L., 901
Hodapp, R., 1120
Hoder, E. L., 455
Hodgdon, L., 984
Hodge, S. E., 434
Hodge, S. M., 495
Hodges, J. R., 526
Hodgson, S., 1307
Hoehler, F. K., 462
Hoeksma, M., 480
Hoey, H., 544
Hof, P., 496, 497, 525, 667, 670
Hofacker, N., 143
Hoffbuhr, K., 130, 138, 139, 148, 151
Hoffman, E., 151, 696
Hoffman, E. A., 520, 525
Hoffman, E. L., 228, 231, 319, 409
Hoffman, E. P., 136

Hoffman, J. E., 693
Hoffman, T., 1023
Hoffman, W., 388, 492
Hoffmann, W., 64, 487, 606, 1016
Hofman, A., 556
Hofmeister, A. M., 916
Hogan, A., 315, 320, 651, 653, 654, 662, 663, 673, 800
Hogan, K., 233, 235, 236, 238, 251, 316, 708, 712, 734, 799, 801, 833, 834, 835, 947, 1007, 1011
Holden, J., 437
Holdgrafer, M., 45, 228, 323, 186, 664, 690, 740, 753, 832
Hole, K., 462
Hole, W. T., 461
Holguin, S., 544
Holland, J. G., 1125
Hollander, C. S., 460, 461
Hollander, E., 432, 433, 437, 439, 660, 754, 1111
Holliday-Willey, L., 201, 203
Hollis, C., 436
Holm, V. A., 127
Holmans, J., 431
Holmes, A. S., 1095
Holmes, D. L., 870, 899, 1089, 1093, 1095
Holmes, G., 489
Holmes, J. P., 267, 1105
Holmes, M., 431
Holmes, N., 214, 790, 1076, 1077
Holmgreen, P., 555
Holmgren, G., 546
Holroyd, S., 739
Holt, K. D., 1061, 1070
Holthausen, H., 143
Holttum, J. R., 499, 909
Holtzman, G., 49, 73, 80, 1312
Homatidis, S., 335, 550, 551, 749
Hommer, D., 454
Honda, H., 47, 435
Honeycutt, N., 371, 497, 660
Hong, D., 189, 839, 1310
Hong, J., 619
Honomichl, R. D., 503, 542
Hood, B., 234, 318, 616, 630, 663
Hoogstrate, J., 44, 49, 59, 184, 291
Hook, E., 547
Hooks, M., 345, 580, 595
Hooper, C., 263, 691
Hooper, J., 746
Hooper, K., 905
Hooper, S., 833, 834, 849
Hoover, J. A., 886
Hopkins, B., 1033
Hopkins, J. M., 1030, 1031
Hopkins, K. R., 1094

Horikawa, M., 540
Horne, W. C., 453, 454
Horner, R. D., 1126, 1130, 1143
Horner, R. H., 821, 822, 823, 824, 825, 897, 898, 899, 900, 903, 911, 934, 1010
Hornig, M., 542
Hornsey, H., 838
Hornykiewicz, O., 142
Horrigan, J. P., 1105
Horsley, J. A., 1126
Horvath, E., 549
Horvath, K., 541, 1112
Horwitz, B., 518
Hosack, K., 1092
Hoshika, A., 541
Hoshino, K., 17
Hoshino, Y., 46, 52, 71, 79, 227, 455, 456, 459, 460, 461, 463, 542, 707, 834, 1224, 1225, 1249
Hotopf, M., 551
Hou, J. W., 551
Hough, M. S., 258
Houghton, J., 1092, 1093
Houle, S., 665
Houlihan, D., 901
Houston, R., 583
Houwink-Manville, I., 138
Howard, M., 497, 499, 1088
Howard, R., 668
Howie, P. M., 106
Howlin, P., 24, 30, 33, 50, 100, 110, 113, 170, 174, 185, 202, 203, 204, 205, 206, 207, 208, 210, 211, 212, 213, 214, 215, 216, 255, 259, 261, 288, 290, 292, 293, 294, 295, 296, 297, 298, 299, 302, 304, 335, 342, 343, 345, 348, 349, 351, 373, 412, 436, 520, 535, 544, 547, 548, 587, 588, 652, 682, 687, 708, 724, 732, 760, 872, 873, 875, 961, 1055, 1056, 1057, 1064, 1078, 1088, 1244
Hoyson, M., 394, 708, 870, 953, 967, 968, 1030, 1046
Hoza, B., 177
Hresko, W., 804
Hsu, M., 499
Hsu, W. L., 342
Huang, C. T., 389
Huang, J., 539, 1307
Huang, Y. W., 458
Hubbard, C. R., 145
Huber, H., 1092
Huber, J., 588
Hubl, D., 521
Hudelot, C., 690
Hudson, A., 1200
Huffman, L. R., 261
Huggins, R. M., 545, 569

Hughes, A., 804
Hughes, C., 253, 267, 326, 368, 372, 373, 387, 609, 611, 612, 613, 614, 615, 616, 618, 642, 644, 836, 837, 868, 959, 1094
Hughes, D., 813
Hughes, J. R., 461, 462
Hughes, S. O., 255
Hulse, S. H., 644
Hulse, W. C., 583
Hulshoff Pol, H. E., 493, 499
Hultman, C. M., 539
Humbertclaude, V., 552
Humphrey, M., 585, 592
Humphrey, N., 660
Humphreys, L., 1060
Humphry, R., 849
Hundert, J., 1033
Hunnisett, E., 236
Hunt, A., 51, 545, 594
Hunt, C., 496
Hunt, F. M., 713
Hunt, J. M., 83, 148
Hunt, J. McV., 792
Hunt, P., 254, 883, 884
Hunter, K., 128, 146, 155
Huntley, M., 800
Hunyadi, E., 521, 523
Huotilainen, M., 481
Huppke, P., 131, 138
Hurkens, E., 171, 186, 187
Hurley, C., 886, 911, 1033
Hurst, J. A., 432, 1307
Hurtig, R., 257, 353, 598
Hurwic, M., 456, 457, 463
Huson, S. M., 553
Hutcheson, H., 438, 754
Hutcheson, J., 479
Hutchinson, J. M., 1128
Hutchinson, T., 319, 799, 942, 946, 947, 978, 1007
Hutt, C., 268
Hutt, S. J., 268
Huttenlocher, J., 337
Huttenlocher, P., 658, 660, 708
Hutton, D., 630
Hutton, J., 202, 205, 206, 210, 212, 213, 215, 216, 290, 292, 293, 295, 296, 297, 298, 299, 335, 342
Hutton, S., 1088
Huws, J. C., 261
Hviid, A., 44, 49, 52, 57, 435
Hwang, B., 253, 959
Hwang, C. P., 1055
Hyman, S., 134, 146, 152, 155, 436, 494, 1312
Hymas, N., 616

Iacoboni, M., 28, 389, 687, 691
Iacono, T., 884
Iancu, D. R., 542
Iannetti, P., 555
Iarocci, G., 1182

Idziaszczyk, S., 543, 545
Ierodiakonou, C., 1215
Iivanainen, M., 296, 297
Iliyasu, Z., 547
Ilmoniemi, R. J., 481
Imuta, F., 46, 540
Inaba, Y., 435
Inanuma, K., 542
Incorpora, G., 547
Inge, K. J., 1088
Ingenito, G. G., 1106
Ingenmey, R., 257
Ingersoll, B., 886, 887, 888, 889, 890
Inglis, A., 335
Ingram, D., 151
Ingram, J. L., 489, 553, 836
Ingram, R. E., 607
Innocent, A. J., 904
Inoue, M., 261
Insel, T., 266, 326, 327, 462, 1111, 1306
Iovannone, R., 1092
Ireland, M., 544
Ireton, H., 712
Ireys, H. T., 1062
Iriki, A., 691
Iro, M., 489
Irvin, L. K., 1092
Isaacs, C., 427
Isagai, T., 544
Isager, T., 50, 75, 76, 212, 296, 1238, 1239
Isarangkun, P. P., 462
Ishige, K., 46, 52
Ishii, T., 1224
Ishikawa, A., 127
Ishikawa, N., 135, 136
Ishikawa, T., 1094
Ishizaka, Y., 1225
Ismond, D. R., 476, 477
Isquith, P. K., 373, 794
Isserlin, M., 1239
Itard, J., 167
Itkonnen, T., 901
Ito, K., 389, 662, 663
Ittenbach, R. F., 1312
Ivancic, M. T., 908, 1126, 1143
Iversen, P., 459
Iverson, L. L., 453
Iverson, S. D., 453
Ivey, M., 75, 77
Iwamura, Y., 691
Iwasaki, N., 661
Iwata, B. A., 152, 155, 819, 822, 824, 825, 901, 907, 908, 910, 1126, 1127, 1128, 1143
Iyama, C. M., 129
Izaguirre, J., 838
Izard, C. E., 409, 411
Izeman, S. G., 1133

Jackendoff, R., 691
Jackowski, A., 523
Jackson, A., 186, 546
Jackson, C. T., 323
Jackson, D., 1125
Jackson, J., 849
Jackson, R. K., 9, 385, 387, 453, 1198

Jackson, S., 177, 268, 747, 748
Jacobi, D., 5, 107, 170, 173, 427
Jacobs, B., 140
Jacobs, H., 884, 899, 1004, 1129, 1140
Jacobs, J., 546
Jacobs, M. M., 429
Jacobsen, G., 1282
Jacobsen, K., 129, 147, 149
Jacobson, J., 252
Jacobson, L., 554, 901
Jacquemont, S., 545, 546
Jaedicke, S., 344, 520
Jaeken, J., 464
Jaenisch, R., 440
Jahr, E., 239, 254, 870, 874, 984
Jakobsson, G., 227, 232, 329, 425, 834
Jalal, S. M., 551
Jamain, S., 433
Jambaque, I., 545
James, A. L., 268
James, J. A., 544
James, J. E., 1060
James, M., 609
James, R., 433, 544
James, V., 60
James, W., 234
Jamieson, B., 394, 708, 967, 1030, 1046
Jamison, D. L., 79
Jan, M. M. S., 130
Janicki, M. P., 1089
Janisse, J., 752
Jankovic, J., 134, 150, 838, 839
Janner, J. P., 905
Janney, R., 868
Janols, L. O., 109
Janosky, J. E., 1112
Janota, I., 488, 489, 536, 617, 618
Jansen, D. H. J., 481
Jansen, L. M., 183
Janson, U., 554
Janssen, J., 493, 499
Janssen, P. A., 1103
Janusonis, S., 454
Janzen, J., 1004, 1016, 1017
Jarast, R., 1230
Jarman, P. H., 1128
Jaros, E., 463, 490
Jarrold, C., 234, 254, 344, 350, 370, 393, 394, 395, 396, 399, 608, 611, 616, 642, 643, 645, 1307
Jarvis, K., 342
Jaselskis, C., 27, 1107
Jasinowski, C., 902
Jasper, H., 663
Jasper, S., 253, 872, 1064, 1074
Jatlow, P., 1108
Jawad, A. F., 542
Jayakar, P., 503
Jayne, D., 911
Jeavons, P. M., 551

Jefferson, G., 912
Jelliffe, L. L., 462
Jellinger, K., 139, 140
Jellum, E., 535
Jenkins, E., 546
Jenkins, S., 542
Jenks, J., 542, 1112
Jennings, P., 960
Jennings, W. B., 414
Jensen, A. R., 434
Jensen, C. M., 1096
Jensen, J., 458, 459, 460, 608, 611
Jensen, V., 177, 949
Jensen, W. R., 47, 63
Jenson, W., 461, 534, 536, 539, 540, 543, 909, 916
Jepsen, R. H., 620
Jerdonek, M. A., 130
Jerger, J., 844
Jerger, S., 844
Jernigan, T., 367, 371, 499, 549, 1282, 1305
Jezzard, P., 521
Jick, H., 59, 61, 435, 541
Jimenez, F., 643
Jimerson, D. C., 458
Jiron, C. C., 616
Joanette, Y., 258
Jocelyn, L. J., 544
Jocic, Z., 616
Joe, C., 336
Johannesson, T. M., 109
Johansson, E., 476, 484
Johansson, G., 692
Johansson, M., 48, 62, 105, 109, 352, 525, 553, 615, 666
John, A., 734, 753, 757
Johnson, C., 655, 668, 669, 673, 1149
Johnson, C. N., 630
Johnson, C. R., 189, 267, 268, 367, 368, 369, 372, 373, 1110, 1111
Johnson, D., 97, 551
Johnson, E., 1055, 1070
Johnson, J., 875, 906, 912
Johnson, L., 253, 899
Johnson, M., 317, 318, 670, 671, 691, 695, 696
Johnson, R. J., 462, 553
Johnson, S., 630, 1004, 1005, 1006
Johnson, S. A., 646
Johnson, S. B., 863, 1181
Johnson, W. D., 539
Johnson, W. T., 456, 457, 537
Johnson-Frey, S. H., 524
Johnston, C., 153
Johnston, F., 548
Johrs, P., 1078
Jolliffe, T., 105, 201, 295, 628, 630, 631, 634, 635, 641, 642, 682, 1284
Jones, A. C., 543, 545
Jones, B. L., 486
Jones, G., 323
Jones, J. P. R., 212

Jones, M. B., 170, 173, 185, 187, 427, 437, 537, 754, 1058
Jones, P. B., 107
Jones, R., 261, 630, 831
Jones, T., 555, 657, 658, 660
Jones, V., 387
Jones, W., 13, 105, 106, 191, 234, 236, 248, 249, 250, 260, 275, 313, 325, 326, 368, 373, 375, 376, 412, 520, 526, 549, 595, 683, 684, 694, 696, 699
Jongvan, C., 200
Jonveaux, P., 130, 138
Jordan, H., 352, 426, 427, 428, 693, 732, 733, 753, 756, 820
Jordan, R., 256, 322, 371, 397, 399, 1011
Jorde, L., 47, 63, 537, 540
Jorgensen, E., 462
Joseph, A., 589, 838
Joseph, R., 234, 260, 291, 336, 368, 372, 373, 439, 520, 521, 609, 610, 615, 617
Joseph, S., 210, 265
Jou, R. J., 493
Jouve, J., 459
Joy, H., 991
Juhrs, P., 207, 298, 302, 1091, 1093
Jukes, E., 201, 204
Jundell, I., 1239
Jung, T., 483, 493
Juranek, J., 538, 550, 551
Jure, R., 555, 832
Jusczyk, P., 689
Just, M., 355, 487, 517, 518, 646
Juul-Dam, N., 539

Kaabachi, N., 553
Kaczmarek, L., 969, 990, 991, 1030
Kadesjö, B., 48, 53, 54, 184
Kadivar, K., 541
Kafantaris, V., 839, 840
Kagan, J., 983
Kahn, A. A., 460
Kahn, J. V., 149
Kahn, R. S., 183, 493, 499
Kain, W., 614
Kaiser, A., 883, 884, 889, 890, 950
Kaiser, M., 695
Kalachnik, J. E., 823, 848
Kaland, N., 105
Kalaria, R. N., 443
Kales, A., 458
Kalish, B. I., 744, 750
Kalmanson, B., 1310
Kalmijn, M., 460, 461
Kalsher, M. J., 819, 825
Kaminsky, L., 1057, 1074, 1077
Kamio, Y., 371, 1225
Kamoshita, S., 135, 136

Kamp, L. N. J., 1233
Kamps, D., 251, 264, 872, 886, 887, 913, 956, 991, 1030, 1031, 1032
Kanafani, N., 60, 435
Kanai, T., 458
Kancki, M., 46, 52
Kandt, R. S., 543, 545
Kane, J. M., 1106
Kaneko, M., 455, 456, 460, 461, 463, 542, 1224, 1225, 1249
Kaneko, S., 1225
Kaneko, W., 883, 884, 912, 937
Kanes, S. J., 1105
Kanner, L., xv, 6, 13, 17, 26, 32, 33, 74, 75, 79, 90, 91, 97, 167, 201, 204, 206, 210, 212, 214, 215, 224, 233, 249, 256, 288, 295, 296, 298, 299, 305, 312, 324, 327, 336, 344, 346, 347, 374, 406, 407, 419, 425, 111, 500, 584, 585, 596, 628, 641, 650, 652, 742, 744, 750, 831, 871, 925, 962, 1011, 1178, 1180, 1194, 1203, 1233, 1239, 1266, 1277, 1304
Kanodia, R., 463
Kanwisher, N., 520, 523, 696
Kao, B. T., 1064, 1065, 1074
Kaplan, A. R., 484
Kaplan, B., 320
Kaplan, D., 27, 839, 847, 1107
Kaplan, J. E., 1090
Kaplan, M., 832
Kappas, A., 690
Kapucu, O., 107
Kapur, S., 665, 1103
Karantanos, G., 1215
Karapurkar, T., 57, 63, 1070, 1123
Kardash, A., 17
Karlgren-Leitner, C., 544
Karmiloff-Smith, A., 236, 549, 656, 657
Karns, C., 489, 492, 493, 496, 499, 501, 519, 661
Karsh, K. G., 819, 916
Karumanchi, S., 459, 1111
Karumanchi, V., 459, 1111
Kasari, A., 946
Kasari, C., 233, 236, 239, 260, 261, 318, 319, 320, 323, 324, 325, 369, 409, 410, 411, 415, 416, 520, 630, 631, 652, 653, 655, 657, 659, 660, 662, 665, 671, 673, 707, 946, 1007, 1020, 1034
Kashanian, A., 499
Kashiwagi, H., 1223

Kashiwagi, Y., 541
Kassorla, I. C., 882
Kasteleijn-Nolst Trenite, D. G., 503
Kates, W. R., 269, 545, 547
Kato, T., 389, 662, 663
Katsovich, L., 1103, 1106
Katusic, S. K., 534
Katz, K., 964
Katz, M., 183
Katz, N., 834
Katz, R. C., 870
Katzung, V. M., 616
Kau, A. S., 547
Kauffman, J. M., 1073
Kauffmann, C., 267
Kaufman, A. S., 642, 788, 790
Kaufman, B., 958
Kaufman, N. L., 788, 789
Kaufman, S., 141
Kavanagh, M. E., 453, 455, 459
Kavanaugh, R. D., 394, 395
Kawano, Y., 540
Kawasaki, Y., 502, 503, 546, 1225
Kawashima, H., 541
Kawashima, K., 47, 661
Kawashima, R., 389, 662, 663
Kay, J. B., 697
Kaye, J., 59, 61, 435, 541
Kayihan, H., 153
Kaysen, D., 169, 181
Kazak, S., 5, 426, 427
Kazdin, A. E., 821, 822, 897, 915, 1062
Keane, J., 526, 663
Keaveney, L., 180
Keeble, S., 630
Keel, J. H., 207, 298, 302
Keeler, W. R., 417, 554
Keer, A. M., 127
Keetz, A., 884, 950
Kehres, J., 258
Keilitz, L., 1143
Keillor, J. M., 371
Keilp, J. G., 617
Keith, R. W., 844
Keliher, C., 905
Keller, K., 551
Keller, T., 355, 487, 517, 518, 646
Kellet, K., 885, 956
Kelley, L. A., 1108
Kelley, M., 251, 252, 257, 258, 259, 260, 316, 317, 352, 353
Kelley, R. I., 544
Kelly, K. M., 336
Kelly, L., 916
Kem, D. L., 189, 1106
Kema, I. P., 454
Kemmerer, K., 956, 991
Kemmotsu, N., 525
Kemner, C., 171, 183, 478, 480, 481, 482, 485, 493, 499, 684
Kemp, D., 821, 897, 911, 916, 926, 1088
Kemp, S., 793

Kempas, E., 432, 433
Kemper, T. L., 371, 372, 463, 488, 489, 490, 492, 493, 494, 496, 526, 536, 1014, 1305
Kempton, S., 617
Kendall, T., 1283
Kendler, K. S., 432, 438
Kenemans, J. K., 482
Kennedy, C. H., 267, 542, 886, 901, 904, 1143
Kennedy, D., 355, 494, 495, 517, 536, 538
Kenworthy, L., 373, 613
Keogh, M., 30, 335
Keogh, W., 149
Kerbeshian, J., 27, 28, 46, 52, 55, 71, 75, 77, 101, 135, 539, 588, 838, 1111
Kerdelhue, B., 459, 462
Kern, J. K., 542
Kern, L., 820, 823, 865, 866, 869
Kern, R. A., 1110
Kern, S. J., 436
Kern-Dunlap, L., 820, 1032
Kerns, K. A., 619
Kerr, A., 127, 136, 137, 139, 147, 148, 151, 153
Kerr, B., 556
Kerr, M. M., 1030
Kerwin, R. W., 107
Keshavan, M., 491, 493, 494, 498, 499, 500, 519, 660, 661, 667
Keskr, J., 909
Kestenbaum, C., 183
Ketelaars, C., 753
Ketelsen, D., 1031
Key, E., 1239
Keyes, J., 909
Keymeulen, H., 177
Khan, K., 542, 1112
Khoromi, S., 140
Kielinen, M., 48, 534, 544
Kientz, M., 366, 536, 832, 834, 843, 981, 983
Kienzl, E., 141, 142
Kiernan, W. E., 1088, 1093
Kiesewetter, K., 128
Kilgore, E., 1108
Kilifarski, M., 429, 432, 433, 439, 754
Killcross, A. S., 642
Killian, W., 139, 142, 145
Kilman, A., 103, 369, 374
Kilman, B. A., 24, 477, 479, 480, 482
Kiln, A., 73
Kilpatrick, M., 498, 551
Kilsby, M., 207
Kim, C. A., 553
Kim, J., 100, 101, 208, 269, 1014
Kim, K., 889
Kim, S.-J., 429, 439
Kimberg, D. Y., 388
Kimbrough-Oller, D., 800
Kimchi, R., 640, 643
Kimura, D., 633, 634

Kincaid, D., 1092
King, B. H., 1108, 1111
King, J., 183, 556
King, L., 1268
King, M., 460, 551
King, N., 1061, 1065
Kingstone, A., 663
Kinney, E. M., 871
Kinsbourne, M., 1067, 1177
Kirby, B. L., 113
Kirchner, D., 806
Kirk, K. S., 1111
Kirk, U., 793
Kirkham, N., 671
Kirkpatrick-Sanchez, S., 909, 910
Kirwin, P. D., 456
Kisacky, K. L., 886, 887
Kishino, T., 551
Kissel, R. C., 1128
Kita, M., 73, 74, 749, 1312
Kitahara, H., 127
Kitsukawa, K., 904
Kitt, C. A., 142
Kjelgaard, M., 342, 343, 344, 350
Kjellgren, G., 48, 62
Kjoerholt, K., 154
Klaiman, C., 523
Klare, G. R., 1143
Klauck, S. M., 130, 432, 433, 546
Kleczkowska, A., 546
Kleefstra, T., 78
Kleiman, K., 806
Kleiman, M. D., 499
Klein, D. F., 181, 182
Klein, K., 31, 105, 227, 232, 233, 234, 266, 707, 708, 733, 734, 741, 754, 755
Klein, L. S., 253, 392
Kleinhans, N., 525
Kleinman, J., 521, 522, 523, 524, 526, 716
Klevstrand, M., 155
Klicpera, C., 24, 91, 96, 97
Kliewer, C., 1031
Klima, E. S., 549
Klin, A., xix, 5, 7, 13, 14, 18, 19, 20, 24, 25, 28, 30, 31, 32, 33, 41, 45, 72, 74, 88, 91, 92, 93, 95, 96, 97, 99, 100, 102, 103, 104, 105, 106, 107, 108, 109, 110, 111, 113, 124, 170, 173, 174, 175, 179, 184, 186, 191, 213, 224, 225, 227, 232, 233, 234, 236, 238, 239, 248, 249, 250, 251, 256, 263, 268, 269, 275, 293, 294, 303, 313, 316, 317, 318, 319, 321, 323, 325, 326, 341, 343, 348, 350, 352, 353, 354, 365, 367, 368, 372, 373, 374, 375, 376, 412, 419, 498, 519, 520, 521,

522, 523, 524, 525, 526, 595, 609, 610, 615, 617, 628, 650, 651, 652, 657, 666, 671, 682, 683, 684, 686, 689, 691, 694, 696, 697, 698, 699, 730, 732, 734, 735, 736, 739, 740, 750, 772, 773, 777, 779, 782, 784, 789, 793, 800, 803, 809, 810, 813, 820, 832, 835, 889, 946, 960, 961, 962, 977, 979, 980, 982, 983, 984, 998, 1102, 1106, 1109, 1121, 1221
Klinger, L. G., 369, 371, 374, 642
Klinger, M. R., 369, 371
Klitz, W., 431
Kluckman, K., 454
Klug, M. G., 539
Klykylo, W. M., 457, 462
Knight, R. T., 524, 615, 1306
Knivsberg, A. M., 462
Knobler, H., 459
Knobloch, H., 50
Knoll, J. H., 551
Knott, F., 1057, 1077
Knouf, N., 523
Knowles, T., 267
Knox, S. H., 845
Kobagasi, S., 1281
Kobayashi, R., 73, 74, 80, 100, 202, 204, 206, 212, 213, 214, 288, 289, 291, 293, 296, 298, 1224, 1225, 1312
Kobayashi, S., 886
Koburn, A., 1108
Koch, D., 251, 416, 417
Kochanska, G., 386
Kocoglu, S. R., 130
Koczat, D., 485
Koechlin, E., 668, 669
Koegel, B. L., 1180
Koegel, L., 874, 875, 883, 886, 900, 911, 912, 913, 926, 929, 930, 932, 934, 937, 940, 941, 950, 951, 952, 953, 954, 961, 978, 1004, 1005, 1006, 1009, 1025, 1033, 1049, 1061, 1064, 1183
Koegel, R., 264, 268, 821, 823, 874, 875, 882, 883, 884, 886, 887, 888, 889, 890, 900, 906, 911, 912, 913, 926, 929, 930, 932, 934, 937, 940, 941, 950, 951, 952, 953, 954, 978, 1004, 1005, 1006, 1009, 1033, 1049, 1055, 1058, 1060, 1061, 1064, 1129, 1160, 1183

Koenig, K., 977, 1105, 1106, 1108
Koga, Y., 100
Kohen-Raz, R., 387, 388, 485, 486, 832, 839
Kohler, F., 886, 937, 938, 939, 940, 968, 990, 991, 1129, 1130
Kohler, R., 953
Kohn, A. E., 267, 1109
Kohn, Y., 299
Kokkinaki, T., 383
Kolachana, B. S., 526
Kolevzon, A., 753
Koller, R., 301
Kolmen, B. K., 1112
Kolodny, E., 77, 140
Kologinsky, E., 885, 1089
Koluchova, J., 591
Kolvin, I., 8, 9, 15, 17, 70, 79, 179, 180, 585, 592
Komatsu, F., 1225
Komori, H., 540
Komoto, J., 28
Kondo, I., 138
Koning, C., 323, 348
Konkol, O., 149
Konstantareas, M., 301, 335, 550, 551, 749, 1072
Koon, R., 607, 616
Koop, S., 461
Koos, O., 629
Kootz, J. P., 478
Kooy, R. F., 545
Kopin, I. J., 458
Kopp, J., 886
Koppenhaver, D., 154, 155, 802, 804
Korein, J., 460, 461
Korenberg, J. R., 548
Korf, J., 456
Korkman, M., 793
Korn, S., 7
Korvatska, E., 542, 1312
Korzilius, H., 898
Kosen, R. L., 1183
Koshes, R. J., 269
Koshimoto, T., 1225
Koslowski, L. T., 692
Kotsopoulos, S., 462, 544
Kozinetz, C. A., 136
Kozloff, M. A., 1055, 1060, 1065
Kozma, C., 552
Kraemer, G., 658
Kraemer, H., 21, 29, 314, 335, 437, 733, 754, 1307
Kraft, I. A., 462, 553
Krageloh-Mann, I., 140
Kraijer, D., 251, 753
Kramer, A., 668, 669
Kramer, J. H., 645
Kramer, M., 17
Kramer, N., 138
Krams, M., 371, 495, 497, 1305
Krantz, P., 261, 298, 299, 354, 867, 869, 871, 873, 875, 883, 884, 887, 913, 950, 953,

959, 968, 985, 995,
    1004, 1009, 1010,
    1029, 1030, 1035,
    1044, 1045, 1046,
    1047, 1061, 1127,
    1129, 1132, 1143
Krasny, L., 73, 77, 78
Kratochwill, T. R., 1059
Krause, I., 542
Krauss, M. W., 214, 288,
    289, 290, 293, 295,
    297, 323, 324, 1055,
    1059, 1075, 1077
Kravits, T., 251, 886, 887,
    913, 956, 991, 1030,
    1031
Krawczak, M., 543, 545
Krawiecki, N., 76
Kream, J., 456, 458
Kregel, J., 1089, 1091,
    1092, 1093, 1094
Kreitner, R., 1127
Kremer-Sadlik, T., 868
Kreppner, J. M., 180
Kreps-Falk, R., 552
Kresch, L. E., 27, 178
Kreutzer, J., 479, 482, 619
Kriehoff, I. I., 492
Kriegstein, K. V., 524
Kristiansson, M., 299
Kristoff, B., 708, 949,
    1004, 1032, 1034
Kroeker, R., 266
Kromberg, J. G., 555, 556
Krug, D. A., 476, 719, 731,
    733, 741, 747, 750,
    762, 1004, 1005, 1006,
    1007, 1008, 1009,
    1012, 1023, 1199
Kruger, A., 237, 318, 337,
    369, 383
Kubba, H., 555
Kuddo, T., 541
Kudo, S., 78
Kugiumutzakis, G., 383
Kuhaneck, H. M., 842
Kuhl, D. P., 545
Kuhl, P., 224, 225, 481,
    482, 833, 834, 837,
    846, 962
Kuhr, R., 1064, 1065, 1075
Kuipers, E., 619
Kulesz, A., 740
Kulldorff, M., 64
Kulomaki, T., 389
Kumar, A., 140
Kumari, V., 107, 493
Kumashiro, H., 227, 460,
    463, 542, 834, 1224,
    1225
Kumazawa, T., 1281
Kumra, S., 183
Kunce, L. J., 213
Kunihiro, T., 667
Kuoch, H., 869
Kuperman, S., 212, 494,
    499
Kupretz, S. S., 456
Kurita, H., 72, 73, 74, 76,
    79, 80, 167, 173, 224,
    270, 342, 749, 1224,
    1311, 1312

Kuriya, N., 540
Kurland, L. T., 51
Kuroda, Y., 461, 499, 539
Kurosawa, M., 435
Kurtz, M. M., 619
Kurtz, P. F., 903, 904, 908,
    909
Kurtzberg, A., 480, 482
Kurtzberg, D., 479, 480
Kurtzer, D., 479, 482
Kustan, E., 1106
Kustanovich, V., 1307
Kusunoki, T., 1225
Kutas, M., 482
Kutty, K. M., 462, 544
Kwiatkowski, D., 543
Kwiatkowski, J., 813
Kwon, H., 108, 170, 185,
    521, 526
Kwon, J., 325, 410, 652,
    671, 707
Kyllerman, M., 551
Kyrios, M., 617

Laan, L., 551
Laccone, F., 131, 138
Lachar, D., 1110, 1111
Lachman, S. R., 908
Lafargue, R. T., 27, 839,
    847, 1107
LaFluer, B., 130, 138, 139,
    148
La Franchi, S., 484
Lagercrantz, H., 139
Lagomarcino, T., 1089,
    1092, 1094
Lahey, M., 337, 813
Lahuis, B. E., 493, 499
Lai, C. S., 432, 1307
Lai, Z., 260, 549
Laing, E., 549
Lainhart, J., 28, 73, 77, 78,
    208, 210, 269, 270,
    427, 428, 439, 489,
    500, 501, 536, 539, 618
Laitenen, R., 823
Lake, R., 459
Lakesdown, R., 1284
Lakoff, G., 695
Lal, S., 456, 457
Lalande, M., 551
Lalli, J. S., 822, 901, 907
Lam, A. Y., 429
Lam, M. K., 758
Lamabrecht, L., 1124
Lamb, J., 432, 433, 438
Lamb, M. R., 645
Lambert, R., 107, 646
Lambrecht, L., 196, 228,
    233, 348, 541, 547,
    551, 655, 712, 731,
    739, 753, 756, 757,
    808
Lampe, M., 844
Landa, R., 170, 173, 195,
    197, 295, 352, 427,
    428, 439, 484, 485,
    489, 500, 501, 536,
    537, 538, 539, 808,
    809, 979, 1111
Landaburu, H. J., 908
Landau, B., 693

Landesman-Dwyer, S., 1245
Landgren, M., 544
Landis, B. H., 458
Landis, H. D., 459
Landon-Jimenez, D., 30,
    335
Landrus, R., 758, 1176,
    1216
Landry, R., 832
Landry, S., 236, 249, 251,
    254, 255, 256, 320,
    346, 351, 653, 947
Landsdown, R., 201
Lane, H., 583
Lane, J. B., 143
Lane, R., 668
Lane, S., 478
Lanfermann, H., 521
Lang, B., 613, 614, 615
Lang, C., 542, 1112
Lang, J., 20, 779
Langdell, T., 324, 384, 392,
    412, 413, 520, 652, 689
Lange, N., 355, 493, 494,
    496, 497, 498, 519,
    1305
Langer, S. N., 824, 899
Langstrom, D., 450
Langworthy-Lam, K., 838
Lanquetot, R., 899
Lansdown, R., 295
Lansing, M., 543, 757,
    1176
Lanuzza, B., 479, 481, 482
Lanzi, G., 539
LaPerchia, P., 539
Lappalainien, R., 143
Larcombe, M., 595, 745,
    755
Larmande, C., 240, 689,
    708, 751
Larnaout, A., 553
Laroche, C., 551
Laron, Z., 1220
Larrandaburu, M., 553
Larrieu, J. A., 177
Larsen, F. W., 203, 204,
    206, 212, 213
Larsen, J., 541
Larson, K., 539
Larsson, E. V., 886
Lasker, A., 484, 485
Laski, K. E., 950, 953,
    1004, 1009, 1061, 1129
Lassen, N. A., 140
Laszlo, A., 549
Latif, R., 137
Lattimore, J., 1128
Lauder, J. M., 454
Laulhere, T., 342, 542, 752,
    757, 762, 1112
Launay, J., 459, 462, 1112
Laurent, A., 367, 926, 927,
    928, 929, 932, 933,
    935, 936, 937, 938,
    939, 940, 941, 942,
    978, 979, 980, 981,
    982, 983, 986, 989,
    990, 995, 996, 997,
Lauritsen, M., 185, 188,
    430, 435, 453, 534,
    551

Laushey, K. M., 1032
Lavenex, P., 526, 1306
LaVigna, G. W., 902, 903,
    904, 905, 906, 907,
    966, 1076
Lavin, D. R., 795
Law, P. A., 1111
Lawlor, B. A., 437, 754
Lawrence, A., 609, 663
Lawrence, L. G., 208, 269
Lawry, J., 968
Laws, G., 549
Lawson, J., 628, 632, 634
Lawson, W., 201, 203
Layton, T., 948, 949, 955,
    957
Lazar, N. A., 373, 485, 496,
    525
Lazenby, A. L., 641
Le, L., 871, 885, 887
Lea, S. E., 692
Leach, D. J., 1070
Leaf, R., 864, 868, 870,
    874, 875, 891, 929,
    1004
League, R., 83, 800
Leary, M. R., 387, 838
Leaver, E., 483, 493, 663,
    671
Leavitt, B. R., 546
Lebel, L. A., 1106
Lebiedowska, M. K., 839
LeBlanc, L., 885, 906,
    956
Leboyer, M., 189, 326, 434,
    459, 462, 517, 618,
    1112
Leckman, J., 27, 456, 459,
    462, 546, 719, 720,
    750, 838, 848, 1103,
    1111, 1306
Le Couteur, A., 5, 8, 25,
    26, 28, 33, 45, 51, 65,
    76, 93, 95, 101, 107,
    108, 110, 167, 170,
    213, 214, 227, 228,
    232, 248, 265, 290,
    294, 315, 323, 341,
    342, 346, 347, 348,
    412, 419, 425, 426,
    427, 429, 434, 436,
    437, 438, 439, 442,
    462, 489, 500, 520,
    534, 536, 537, 538,
    539, 546, 547, 553,
    554, 594, 599, 617,
    632, 712, 722, 731,
    734, 740, 753, 754,
    775, 779, 832, 1124,
    1143, 1215, 1305
Lecuyer, C., 690
L'Ecuyer, S., 167, 169, 757
Ledda, M. G., 1103
Leddet, I., 751
LeDoux, J., 525, 526, 652,
    686
Lee, A., 237, 256, 260, 261,
    344, 347, 384, 389,
    390, 396, 411, 412,
    413, 414, 415, 416,
    418, 436, 520, 554,
    555, 689, 836

Lee, C., 154, 544
Lee, D., 268
Lee, E. B., 31, 227, 232, 233, 707, 708, 721, 734
Lee, E. W. H., 209
Lee, H. K., 515
Lee, J., 454
Lee, M., 463, 490, 549
Lee, S. S. J., 130
Lee, T., 643
Lee, Y. H., 484
Leehey, M., 545, 546
Leekam, S., 24, 93, 94, 167, 172, 236, 318, 348, 593, 594, 595, 615, 632, 641, 643, 650, 654, 655, 663, 735, 736, 745, 755, 756
Leenaars, A. A., 97
Leevers, H. J., 396, 399
Lefebre, D., 912
Legacy, S. M., 907
Le Grand, R., 696
Leibenluft, E., 181
Leiber, B., 127
Leigh, R. J., 484
Leiguarda, R., 107, 538
Leinikki, P., 541
Leininger, L., 101, 187
Leiter, R. G., 83, 790
Lekman, A., 139, 142
LeLaurin, K., 1130
Lelord, G., 459, 751, 1208
Lelwica, M., 690
Lemanek, K., 320, 321, 355, 408, 707, 732
Le Maréchal, K., 586, 588
Lembrecht, L., 45, 326
Lempert, H., 341
Lempp, R., 1240, 1241
Lenane, M., 169, 181, 183
Lennon, S., 27, 189, 1110
Lennox, C., 903
Lennox, D. B., 914
Lenoir, P., 229, 232, 240, 366, 689, 708, 712, 751, 834
Lensing, P., 1112
Leonard, B., 991, 1032
Leonard, H., 127, 143
Leonard, J., 645
Leonard, M. A., 253
Lepistö, T., 481, 482
Lerman-Sagie, T., 550
Lerner, M., 1109
Lerner, Y., 459
Lese, C. M., 551
Lesesne, C., 1062
Leshinsky-Silver, E., 550
Leslie, A., 186, 254, 259, 368, 393, 394, 615, 628, 629, 630, 631, 632, 652, 654, 655, 666, 669, 671, 690
Leslie, K. R., 524
Lettick, A. L., 301
Letts, C., 804
Lev, D., 550
LeVasseur, P., 869, 984
Leven, L. I., 453

Leventhal, B., 45, 348, 655
Leventhal, B. I., 474
Leventhal, B. L., 169, 170, 196, 228, 233, 326, 429, 439, 455, 456, 459, 539, 541, 547, 551, 712, 731, 732, 739, 753, 754, 756, 757, 761, 808, 1107, 1124
Levesque, S., 545
Levi, G., 1221, 1222, 1223
Levin, A. V., 696
Levin, C. G., 1003
Levin, J., 253
Levin, L., 821, 897, 916, 926, 1044, 1046, 1064, 1074
Levine, B., 619
Levine, D. N., 646
Levine, M., 1021
Levine, R. A., 545, 546
Levitas, A., 546
Levitt, J. G., 499, 549, 1305
Levy, D., 552
Levy, E. R., 1307
Levy, R., 1126, 1128
Levy, S., 539, 542
Levy, S. E., 1312
Levy, S. M., 1088, 1095
Lewin, S., 127
Lewine, J. D., 503
Lewis, C., 1057, 1077
Lewis, H., 394, 708, 1050, 1051
Lewis, J. C., 543, 545
Lewis, J. D., 542, 1112
Lewis, K. R., 134, 1088, 1093
Lewis, M., 149, 265, 267, 319, 838, 839, 847, 848
Lewis, S. E., 228, 231, 319, 409
Lewis, T. L., 696
Lewis, V., 237, 324, 370, 393, 394, 395, 412, 519, 689
Lewy, A., 235, 268, 320, 480, 656, 659, 959
Leysen, J. E., 1103
Lhermitte, F., 255
Li, J., 48, 54, 60, 435
Libby, S., 24, 93, 94, 322, 397, 399, 593, 594, 595, 735, 736, 745, 755, 756, 1011
Lichtenberger, L., 548, 549
Lickliter, R., 656, 657
Liddell, M. B., 443
Liddle, P. F., 518
Lieb-Lundell, C., 150, 151, 153
Liebowitz, M. R., 181, 182
Lieu, T. A., 436
Light, J., 956
Lightdale, J. R., 541, 542
Likins, M., 916
Lin, Q., 478
Linarello, C., 1029, 1030

Lincoln, A., 97, 100, 104, 107, 260, 375, 474, 549, 551, 642, 655, 656, 659, 660, 668, 835, 836
Lincoln, A. E., 24
Lincoln, A. J., 103, 183, 268, 367, 369, 374, 476, 477, 479, 480, 482, 494, 496, 499
Lindamood, T., 482
Lindauer, S. E., 821
Lindback, T., 462
Lindblom, R., 51, 227, 232, 329, 834
Lindem, K., 183
Lindenbaum, R. H., 51
Linder, T. W., 846
Lindgren, V., 474, 551
Lindhout, D., 556
Lindsay, R. L., 1102, 1109, 1111
Lindsay, W. R., 914
Lindstrom, E., 590
Lind-White, C., 542
Linetsky, E., 255
Ling, A. H., 318
Ling, D., 318
Lingam, R., 435, 541
Lingham, S., 464
Link, C. G., 1105
Links, P. S., 501
Linna, S. L., 48, 534, 544
Linnell, J., 435, 541
Linscheid, T., 460
Linschoten, L., 476
Lipkin, W. I., 542
Lisch, S., 27, 546
Lison, C. A., 886
Liss, M., 251, 616
Lissner, K., 1017
Lissner, L. S., 609
Lister Brook, S., 586, 598
Little, J., 794
Little, L., 250
Littleford, C., 321, 384, 385, 386, 708, 836, 837
Littlejohns, C. S., 101, 210, 265
Littlewood, R., 870
Litwiller, M., 1108
Liu, C., 541
Liu, D. H., 551
Liu, J., 432, 433, 438, 439, 754
Livesey, D., 619
Livingstone, S., 555
Livni, E., 1220
Lloyd, D. J., 555, 556
Lloyd, K. G., 142
Loban, W., 340
Lobato, D. J., 1064, 1065, 1074
Lobo, S., 48, 59, 62
Locascio, J. J., 462, 839, 840
Locke, P., 264, 803
Lockhart, L., 546
Lockshin, S. B., 1035, 1043, 1044, 1046, 1047, 1130, 1138

Lockyer, L., 8, 201, 204, 205, 206, 210, 213, 215, 247, 292, 293, 294, 296, 588, 641, 962
Loder, R. T., 154
Loening-Baucke, V., 541
Loesch, D. Z., 545, 569
Loew, L. H., 321
Lofgren, D. P., 183
Loftin, J., 1180
Logan, G. D., 608, 617
Lohr, J., 496
Loiselle, R. H., 553
Lombard, J., 549
Lombroso, P. J., 136, 138, 552
Long, E. S., 824
Long, F. L., 550
Long, J. S., 882, 887
Long, S., 966, 1180
Longaker, T., 1021
Longhi, E., 549
Longo, I., 78, 130, 551
Lonigan, C. J., 863, 1181
Lonnerholm, G., 462
Loomis, M. E., 1126
Loos, L., 888, 1004, 1005, 1006, 1007, 1008, 1009, 1012, 1058, 1129
Lopez, A. G., 991
Lopez, B., 236, 318, 641, 643
Lopez-Martin, V., 544
Lopreiato, J., 436
Lord, C., 5, 7, 13, 14, 18, 19, 29, 31, 32, 45, 72, 75, 92, 93, 96, 110, 169, 170, 174, 175, 179, 184, 186, 196, 202, 203, 204, 205, 206, 210, 214, 215, 216, 223, 224, 226, 227, 228, 229, 231, 232, 233, 234, 238, 239, 248, 251, 252, 265, 288, 289, 290, 291, 292, 293, 294, 295, 297, 298, 304, 312, 315, 316, 317, 322, 323, 324, 325, 326, 335, 336, 341, 342, 343, 344, 346, 348, 349, 350, 351, 352, 354, 365, 369, 375, 376, 385, 408, 409, 426, 429, 438, 439, 520, 537, 539, 541, 547, 551, 553, 554, 599, 650, 655, 660, 689, 691, 707, 708, 709, 712, 721, 722, 723, 730, 731, 732, 733, 734, 739, 740, 741, 749, 750, 753, 754, 755, 756, 757, 759, 761, 763, 775, 777, 778, 779, 780, 781, 784, 792, 793, 802, 808, 818, 820, 832, 834, 889, 926, 946, 947, 955,

960, 961, 962, 967, 969, 978, 980, 984, 988, 1004, 1005, 1030, 1031, 1033, 1036, 1071, 1076, 1077, 1124, 1132, 1143, 1177, 1215, 1216, 1221
Lord, J., 1096
Lorge, I., 348
Lorimer, P. A., 869, 913
Losche, G., 224, 237
Losh, M., 259, 260, 353
Lossie, A., 551
Loth, F. L., 171, 186, 187
Lotspeich, L., 108, 170, 185, 315, 426, 432, 433, 437, 440, 453, 521, 526, 617, 754
Lotter, V., 42, 44, 46, 52, 201, 204, 205, 206, 210, 212, 215, 288, 293, 296, 434, 545, 585, 594, 1076, 1243
Lou, H., 140, 144
Lovaas, N. W., 253
Lovaas, O., 926, 929, 932, 933, 937, 939, 940, 941
Lovaas, O. I., 155, 189, 253, 268, 288, 346, 708, 873, 874, 875, 876, 882, 883, 884, 887, 889, 891, 915, 948, 961, 966, 1003, 1004, 1005, 1006, 1008, 1012, 1029, 1035, 1038, 1043, 1047, 1048, 1049, 1051, 1055, 1060, 1061, 1089, 1132, 1141, 1142, 1180, 1181, 1284, 1310
Lovaas, O. L., 346
Love, S. R., 833, 914
Loveland, K., 236, 248, 249, 251, 252, 254, 255, 256, 257, 258, 259, 260, 261, 275, 316, 317, 320, 324, 346, 347, 350, 351, 352, 353, 354, 385, 399, 412, 478, 653, 670, 833, 947, 1110, 1111
Lovell, A., 632
Lovett, K., 1177
Lovett, P., 1177
Lowe, J. B., 548
Lowe, T. L., 50, 460, 463, 539, 553
Lubetsky, M., 189, 909, 1110, 1111
Lucarelli, S., 539
Lucci, D., 29, 30, 519, 520
Luce, S., 891, 906, 910, 936, 1003, 1008, 1030, 1128
Lucki, I., 453
Ludlow, L. H., 845
Ludowese, C. J., 551
Ludwig, R., 499
Lueger, R. J., 607, 616

Lugaresi, E., 152
Luiselli, J. K., 902
Luk, E., 617
Luk, F. L., 209
Luna, B., 185, 373, 484, 485, 496, 498, 525, 655, 668, 669, 673
Lund, C. E., 848
Lund, D., 1125
Lund, J., 548
Lundahl, A., 886
Lunetta, K. L., 431
Lung, F. W., 607
Lunsky, Y. J., 301
Luria, A. R., 608
Lurier, A., 1110, 1111
Lutchmaya, S., 634, 636
Luteijn, E., 177, 268, 747, 748
Luteijn, F., 747, 748
Luthert, P., 488, 489, 500, 536, 546, 617, 618, 1305
Lutz, J., 1239
Lutzker, J. R., 886, 911
Luu, C., 496
Luu, P., 668, 669, 670, 673
Luyster, R., 342
Lynch, N., 189, 462
Lyon, G. R., 981
Lyon, M. F., 138

Maag, J. W., 458, 459, 903
MacAndie, C., 555
Macdonald, H., 170, 171, 412, 426, 427, 434, 438, 442, 520, 534, 536, 537, 539, 586, 594, 617, 632
MacDonald, R. B., 900
MacDonald, R. F., 824, 899
MacDuff, G. S., 298, 299, 875, 913, 1127
MacDuff, M. T., 913, 1046, 1061
Mace, F. C., 822, 901
MacFarlane, M., 555
Machado, C. J., 526
Machado, N., 438, 541
Macintosh, K. E., 174, 213
Mack, K. K., 177
Mackay, M., 544
MacLean, C. J., 432
MacLean, J., 77, 78, 170, 173, 187, 1058
Maclean, J. E., 172, 173, 174, 427, 437, 731, 734, 753, 754
MacLean, W. E., Jr., 1183
Macleay, A., 460
Macleod, H. A., 127
MacMahon, B., 51, 76, 539, 1305
MacMillan, D. L., 874, 1182
MacNaughton, N., 136
MacPhie, I. L., 438
Maddalena, A., 545
Madsen, C. H., 1126, 1127
Madsen, K., 435
Madsen, K. M., 44, 49, 52, 57, 435

Maertens, P., 463
Maes, B., 546
Maestrini, E., 130, 430, 432, 438
Maestro, S., 225, 234, 236, 243
Magill-Evans, J., 232, 323, 348
Magito-McLaughlin, D., 897
Magliano, J. P., 354
Magnussen, P., 432, 433
Magnusson, K., 1243
Magnusson, P., 5, 49, 55, 59
Magnússon, P., 753
Magnusson, P. K. E., 432, 433
Maher, E., 550
Maher, J., 264
Maher, K. R., 460
Mahler, M., 9, 584, 587, 1243
Mahoney, W., 77, 78, 170, 172, 173, 174, 190, 437, 731, 734, 753, 754
Mailloux, Z., 835, 836, 846, 847
Main, B., 27, 588, 838
Maiti, A. K., 832
Majnemer, A., 535
Makeig, S., 483, 493, 663, 671
Makita, K., 71
Makris, N., 355, 489, 493, 494, 495, 517, 1305
Malecha, M., 267
Maley, A., 428
Maley, K., 1031
Malhotra, A. K., 431
Malhotra, S., 74, 76, 77, 78, 175
Malicki, D. M., 138, 432
Malik, M., 435, 541
Malin-Ingvar, M., 80, 82
Malkmus, D., 1092
Mallikarjuhn, M., 493, 498, 499, 661
Mallinger, A. G., 491, 500
Malone, R. P., 839, 840, 1102, 1105
Malott, R. W., 1125, 1126
Maltby, N., 520
Malvy, J., 751
Mamelle, N., 47, 52
Mamourian, A. C., 550
Mancina, C., 886, 887
Mancuso, V., 433, 474
Mandalawitz, M., 1004
Mandel, D., 849
Mandelbaum, D. E., 1307
Mandell, D. S., 1312
Mandlawitz, M. R., 1125, 1173
Manes, F., 494, 499, 519
Manfredi, M., 691
Mangelsdorf, M. E., 544
Mangiapanello, K., 871
Mangner, T., 490, 517
Mangun, G. R., 646
Manikam, R., 1029, 1030

Manjiviona, J., 33, 173, 174, 373, 387, 835
Mank, D., 1089, 1094, 1095
Mankoski, R., 32, 432, 439, 731, 733, 754, 755
Manly, J. T., 1062
Mann, J. J., 453
Mann, L. H., 1133
Mann, N. A., 321
Mann, S. M., 551
Mannheim, G. B., 27, 267, 367, 368, 610, 617, 1106
Manning, A., 964
Manning, J. T., 461
Manning-Courtney, P., 541, 542
Mannion, K., 1093
Mannuzza, S., 181, 182
Manolson, H., 958
Mansell, J., 1245
Manstead, A. S. R., 519
Mantel, N., 64
Mao, R., 551
Marans, S., 804
Marans, W. D., 74, 107, 100, 111, 721, 735, 772, 773, 782
Marchand-Martella, N., 1023
Marchant, R., 1244
Marchetti, B., 542
Marcin, C., 1231
Marcus, B. A., 906, 908
Marcus, J., 183
Marcus, L., 290, 351, 543, 721, 749, 757, 962, 1004, 1005, 1036, 1055, 1056, 1060, 1061, 1064, 1065, 1066, 1067, 1068, 1069, 1070, 1071, 1073, 1075, 1132, 1176, 1177, 1216
Marcy, S., 150, 153
Marendaz, C., 645
Marfo, K., 934
Margaretten, N. C., 542
Margarotte, G., 1177
Margerotte, G., 1177
Margolin, R. A., 1015
Mari, F., 78
Mari, M., 536
Marinelli, B., 478
Marin-Garcia, J., 550
Markham, C. H., 484
Markle, S. M., 1125
Markman, A. N., 690
Markowitz, J., 541, 1089, 1095
Markowitz, P., 1306
Marks, D., 536
Marks, R. E., 1110
Marks, S., 549, 1021
Markusic, D., 550
Marlow, A. J., 430, 438
Marois, R., 521, 522, 523, 524, 526
Marques-Dias, M. J., 553
Marquis, J., 347, 897
Marraffa, C., 536
Marriage, K., 101

Mars, A., 49, 52, 57, 60, 185
Marsden, D. D., 838
Marsh, J. T., 481
Marsh, R. D., 1105
Marshall, A. M., 883, 884
Marshall, J. C., 646
Martella, R. C., 1023
Martens, B. K., 915
Martin, A., 268, 269, 520, 524, 696, 762, 1102, 1105, 1106, 1108, 1109
Martin, G. L., 1125
Martin, J., 431, 663, 664, 669
Martin, N., 594, 819, 821, 823, 897, 1061, 1064
Martindale, B., 619
Martineau, J., 240, 459, 542, 689, 708, 751, 1208
Martinez, J., 544
Martinez, M., 432
Martinez-Bermejo, A., 544
Martin-Ruiz, C., 463, 490
Martinsson, T., 551
Martsolf, J. T., 539
Maruff, P., 617
Maruki, K., 141
Maruyama, G., 205
Masaaki, I., 140
Maslin-Cole, C., 238, 322, 416, 417, 1057
Mason, A., 484
Mason, D., 883, 950, 1046
Mason, S. S., 903
Mason, W. A., 526, 1306
Mason-Brothers, A., 47, 63, 299, 461, 500, 534, 536, 537, 539, 540, 545
Masser-Frye, D. S., 550
Masson, G., 486, 642
Masters, J. C., 744
Mateer, C. A., 619
Matese, M. J., 833
Matey, L., 1035, 1043, 1044, 1046, 1047, 1130, 1138
Matochik, J., 524, 525, 667
Matson, J., 251, 267, 719, 720, 721, 745, 749, 750, 751, 833, 909, 912, 914, 915, 951, 1029, 1030
Matsuba, C., 542, 1112
Matsuda, H., 667
Matsuishi, T., 46, 140, 540, 544
Matsuno, D., 455
Matsuoka, K., 886
Mattay, V. S., 526
Matthews, A. L., 819, 823
Matthews, N. J., 369, 371
Matthews, P. M., 521
Matthews, W. S., 251
Matthys, W., 177
Mattison, R. E., 335
Mattlinger, M. J., 260, 690
Maturana, H. R., 688
Maudsley, H., 583

Maughan, A., 1062
Mauldin-Jourdain, M. L., 526, 1306
Maurer, D., 696
Maurer, R., 367, 387, 488, 590, 674, 837, 838, 839, 840
Maurice, C., 891, 936, 1003, 1008
Mauthner, N., 613
Mavrolefteros, G., 181
Mavropoulou, S., 1217
Mawhood, L., 30, 33, 202, 203, 204, 206, 207, 210, 214, 216, 290, 292, 293, 294, 295, 298, 299, 302, 343, 348, 349, 351, 352, 426, 436, 588, 732, 733, 753, 756, 760, 820, 961
Mawson, D., 101, 299
Maxwell, A. P., 541
Maxwell, K., 539
Maybery, M., 428
Mayer, M., 812
Mayes, A., 497, 499
Mayes, L., 234, 236, 317, 318, 345, 518, 526, 739, 1014
Mayes, S. D., 93, 294, 374
Maynard, J., 543
Mays, L. Z., 542, 551, 752, 757, 762, 1112
Mazaleski, J. L., 901, 907
Maziade, M., 476, 477, 478
Mazure, C., 1103
Mazziotta, J. C., 140, 389
Mazzocco, M. M., 269, 545, 547
Mazzoncini, B., 1223
Mazzone, D., 539
McAfee, J., 872, 982, 992
McAleer, O., 616
McAlonan, G., 107, 493
McArthur, A. J., 144
McArthur, D., 235
McAtee, M. L., 897
McAuliffe, S., 1110
McBeath, M., 695
McBride, P. A., 453, 456, 458, 459, 460, 461, 462, 1208
McBurnett, K., 177
McCabe, A., 335
McCabe, E. R. B., 616
McCallon, D., 720, 721, 741, 748, 749
McCann, J., 1306
McCarthy, G., 483, 520, 525, 693
McCarthy, K. S., 542
McCarthy, P., 46
McCaughrin, W., 207, 1094
McCauley, J. L., 429
McCellan, J., 191
McClannahan, L., 261, 298, 299, 354, 867, 869, 871, 873, 875, 883, 884, 887, 913, 950, 959, 968, 985, 995,

1004, 1009, 1010, 1029, 1030, 1035, 1044, 1045, 1046, 1047, 1061, 1127, 1129, 1130, 1132, 1143
McClelland, R. J., 477
McComas, J. J., 253
McConachie, H., 554, 589
McConnachie, G., 821, 897, 916, 926
McConnell, S., 324, 967, 968, 991, 1031
McCormick, M. C., 435
McCormick, T. A., 344, 642
McCoy, J. F., 1125
McCracken, J., 182, 189, 208, 295, 428, 499, 549, 839, 1102, 1103, 1104, 1305, 1310
McCullough, K. M., 886
McCune-Nicholich, L., 391, 393
McDaniel, C., 692
McDermott, C., 544
McDermott, J., 520, 696
McDonald, J. A., 524
McDonald, M., 551
McDonald-McGinn, D., 552
McDonnell, J., 264, 1015
McDonough, L., 237, 253, 384, 393, 395
McDougle, C., 27, 178, 189, 211, 267, 454, 456, 526, 821, 1102, 1103, 1104, 1105, 1106, 1107, 1108, 1109, 1282
McDowell, L., 908
McDuff, M. T., 1004, 1009
McDuffie, A., 664, 665, 667, 670
McEachin, J., 708, 864, 868, 870, 874, 875, 891, 915, 926, 929, 1004, 1048
McEvoy, M. A., 968, 991, 1030, 1033
McEvoy, R., 234, 237, 255, 257, 258, 259, 260, 320, 346, 352, 353, 372, 384, 385, 387, 388, 536, 537, 607, 608, 612, 613, 616, 655, 663, 836, 837
McFadden, T., 813
McFarland, M., 1062
McGann, A., 145
McGarvey, L., 541
McGee, G., 324, 520, 799, 874, 875, 883, 884, 885, 887, 890, 899, 903, 929, 930, 932, 933, 934, 937, 938, 939, 940, 941, 950, 953, 1004, 1011, 1030, 1031, 1035, 1036, 1045, 1046, 1125, 1127, 1129, 1130, 1132, 1133, 1140, 1143

McGee, J., 946, 947, 955, 967, 969
McGhee, D. E., 1110
McGill, P., 1245
McGill-Evans, J., 845
McGillivary, L., 813
McGimsey, J., 819, 1183
McGinniss, M. J., 545
McGoldrick, M., 1068
McGonigle, J. J., 909, 1107
McGough, J., 189, 839, 1307, 1310
McGrath, A. M., 870, 876
McGrath, J., 844
McGrath, L., 32, 495, 521, 731, 733, 754, 755
McGrother, C., 548
McGuffin, P., 431
McGuire, L., 832, 833
McGuire, R. J., 210, 212, 587
McHale, S., 351, 820, 962, 1057, 1068, 1074
McInnes, L., 609
McIntosh, D. E., 1061
McIntosh, D. N., 844
McKay, B., 1103
McKean, T., 1089, 1281
McKeegan, G. F., 902
McKellop, J. M., 430
McKelvey, J. R., 107, 646
McKelvie, S. J., 643
McKenna, K., 169, 181
McKenna, M., 526
McKenna, P. J., 848
McKissick, F. C., 251, 415
McLaughlin-Cheng, E., 252
McLennan, J. D., 251
McMahon, R., 1060, 1062
McMahon, W., 368, 372, 433, 437, 461, 498, 534, 536, 539, 542, 545, 609, 610, 615, 616, 617, 618, 643, 722, 752, 754, 757, 762, 1111, 1112
McManus, E. J., 543
McMorrow, M. J., 910
McNally, R. J., 905
McNay, A., 585, 592
McNerney, E., 874, 875, 926, 941, 978, 1049
McNew, S., 653, 665, 667
McPartland, J., 5, 31, 113, 171, 233, 234, 235, 375, 388, 483, 612, 613, 656, 662, 663, 665, 668, 670, 690, 1078
McPhedran, P., 455
McQuade, R. D., 1106
McQuivey, C., 264
McSwain-Kamran, M., 1107
McSweeny, J., 256, 293, 343, 348, 352, 813, 962
McTarnaghan, J., 997, 998
McWhinney, B., 658
McWilliam, J., 617
Mead, G., 633, 686, 687, 695

Medeiros, J., 902
Meek, J. L., 456
Meek, M., 147, 149
Mees, H., 948, 1125
Meinberg, D. L., 871, 886
Meinhold, P. M., 903, 909
Meir, D., 459, 463
Meiselas, K. D., 838, 839, 847
Meisels, S. J., 709
Melbye, M., 435
Melero-Montes, M., 61, 435
Melhuish, E., 322, 689
Meli, C., 553
Melin, L., 719, 731, 750, 883, 884
Mellerup, T., 462
Melmer, G., 429
Melnick, M., 434
Melnyk, A. R., 145
Melone, M. B., 301
Meloni, I., 78, 130, 551
Meltzer, H., 49, 60, 1103
Meltzoff, A., 171, 224, 225, 233, 234, 235, 236, 237, 320, 326, 337, 383, 384, 385, 388, 390, 396, 397, 483, 526, 613, 651, 656, 657, 659, 670, 671, 672, 673, 689, 690, 692, 707, 799, 832, 833, 834, 836, 837, 846, 962
Menage, P., 542
Ménard, A., 642
Menard, E., 326, 642
Menchetti, B. M., 1094
Mendelson, L., 1310
Mendez, M. F., 255
Mendilaharsu, C., 1229
Mendoza, S. P., 526
Menolascino, F., 548
Menold, M. M., 429, 432, 433, 434, 439, 544, 551, 754
Menon, V., 170, 185, 521
Menscher, S., 911
Merckelbach, H., 758
Merette, C., 31, 170, 172, 477, 478, 731, 735, 754
Merewether, F. C., 348
Merhar, S., 1312
Merikangas, K., 431
Merjanian, P., 371
Merleau-Ponty, M., 687
Merlino, J., 907
Mermelstein, R., 351
Merrin, D. J., 336
Merrit, J., 463, 490
Merritt, A., 144, 145
Merry, S. N., 1110
Merson, R., 962
Mervis, C. B., 549
Meryash, D., 546, 594
Merzenich, M. M., 1308
Mesaros, R. A., 149
Mesibov, G., 113, 188, 189, 207, 213, 264, 266, 289, 290, 292, 298, 299, 301, 302, 324,

546, 547, 749, 758, 883, 915, 932, 937, 940, 1043, 1048, 1049, 1050, 1055, 1060, 1064, 1066, 1067, 1069, 1073, 1075, 1076, 1077, 1089, 1176, 1177, 1178, 1179, 1182, 1184, 1216
Messa, C., 662
Messenheimer, J. A., 1111
Messer, D., 322, 397, 399, 1011
Mestre, D., 486, 642, 839
Mesulam, M., 98, 613, 671
Metz, J. R., 883
Metzger, M., 660
Meundi, D. B., 457
Mewhorn, S. K., 551
Meyer, D. J., 1074
Meyer, E. C., 932, 980, 981, 982
Meyer, J., 372, 652, 654, 668, 669
Meyer, K. A., 267
Meyer, L., 988
Meyer, L. H., 870, 915, 916, 1031, 1034
Meyer, L. S., 1044, 1046
Meyer, M., 438, 810
Meyer, R. N., 1078
Meyerson, M. D., 553
Micali, N., 171
Michael, J., 819, 823, 963, 964, 1125
Michaelis, R., 140, 550, 551
Michal, N., 289, 749
Micheli, E., 1065, 1178
Micheli, R., 551
Michelman, J. D., 27, 209
Michelotti, J., 248
Michelson, A. M., 539
Michie, A., 914
Mick, E., 177
Miedaner, J., 152
Miladi, N., 553
Milberger, S., 183
Mildenberger, K., 177, 536
Milders, M., 236
Miles, J., 60, 435, 439, 501, 536
Miles, S., 107, 352, 353, 809, 810, 962
Miles, T., 101
Milham, M., 668, 669
Militerni, R., 80, 265, 266, 494
Miller, B., 267
Miller, D. E., 744
Miller, E., 48, 54, 60, 435, 541, 668
Miller, J., 24, 33, 93, 103, 104, 174, 186, 213, 258, 340, 373, 375, 544, 616, 682, 731, 735, 736, 805, 1056
Miller, L. J., 789, 844, 846
Miller, L. K., 640
Miller, M., 544, 553
Miller, M. L., 901
Miller, M. T., 553

Miller, N., 871, 1015, 1016
Miller, S. B., 539
Miller, S. L., 1308
Millichap, J. G., 75, 135
Millonig, J. H., 433, 474
Mills, D., 548, 1055
Mills, J., 821
Mills, J. B., 545
Mills, J. I., 1160
Mills, M., 322, 689
Mills Costa, N., 1228
Millstein, R., 208
Milner, B., 720
Milstein, J. P., 886, 995
Milstien, S., 141
Miltenberger, R. G., 820, 823, 907, 914
Milton, R., 1095
Minassian, O. L., 1307
Minchin, S., 494, 499
Minderaa, R., 171, 186, 187, 455, 456, 458, 459, 747, 748
Minow, F., 177, 536
Minshew, N., 97, 103, 181, 185, 257, 263, 264, 267, 268, 295, 344, 355, 367, 368, 369, 371, 372, 373, 387, 484, 485, 486, 487, 491, 493, 494, 496, 497, 498, 499, 501, 517, 518, 519, 525, 536, 546, 549, 646, 652, 655, 660, 661, 667, 668, 669, 673, 767, 832, 835, 1306
Minter, M., 418
Miotto, E. C., 373
Miozzo, M., 551
Miranda, M., 518
Miranda-Linne, F., 719, 731, 750, 883, 884
Mirenda, P., 149, 255, 256, 802, 803, 804, 866, 869, 884, 885, 934, 937, 941, 951
Mirsky, A. F., 367, 368, 476, 498, 614
Mises, R., 1207
Mishkin, M., 524
Missliwetz, J., 139, 145
Mistry, J., 383
Misumi, K., 47
Mitchell, C., 551
Mitchell, J., 151, 153, 461, 462
Mitchell, P., 642
Mitomo, M., 141
Mittenberger, R. G., 899
Mittler, P., 201, 204
Miyake, Y., 73, 74, 76, 80, 749, 1312
Miyazaki, M., 172, 461, 499, 539
Mizuguchi, M., 543
Mlele, T., 291
Mlika, A., 61
Mo, A., 476, 500, 536, 539
Moak, J. P., 129, 143
Mobbs, D., 170, 185, 521
Moberg, P. J., 619

Möbius, P. J., 552
Mock, M. A., 1021
Modahl, C., 342, 462, 544, 833
Moes, D., 262, 264, 897
Moeschler, J. B., 551
Moffett, M., 544
Moffitt, T. E., 181, 439, 443
Mohamed, S., 498
Mohandas, T. K., 550, 551
Mohkamsing, S., 545
Moilanen, I., 48, 534, 544
Molenaar, P. C. M., 434
Molina, B. S., 177
Molitoris, D., 541
Moller-Nielsen, A., 105
Molloy, C., 486, 541, 542
Molony, H., 546
Monaco, A. P., 430, 432
Monaghan, L., 520
Mondloch, C. J., 696
Monsch, A. U., 646
Monson, N., 616
Montagna, P., 152
Montague, J., 127, 147
Montan, N., 1031
Montgai, C. A., 1126, 1127
Monteiro, B., 555
Montero, G., 209
Monteverde, E., 1107
Montgomery, J., 321
Montgomery, M., 488, 489, 536, 617, 618
Montgomery, S. M., 438, 541
Montgomery, T., 555, 556
Monuteaux, M. C., 177
Moodley, M., 136
Moon, M. S., 1093
Moore, A., 1056, 1057, 1064
Moore, C., 236, 318, 650, 654, 655, 656, 663
Moore, D., 414
Moore, G. J., 549
Moore, J., 432
Moore, K. M., 463
Moore, M., 317
Moore, M. J., 684, 689
Moore, M. K., 383, 692
Moore, N. A., 1105
Moore, R. J., 1090
Moore, S. C., 1092, 1095
Moore, S. J., 555, 556
Moore, V., 31
Moore, W., 1076
Moraine, C., 78
Morales, M., 656, 1021
Mordzinski, C., 740
Morecraft, R., 671
Morel, M. L., 545
Moreno, H., 553
Morey, J., 44
Morford, M., 459
Morgan, C. N., 291
Morgan, D., 692
Morgan, D. B., 916
Morgan, D. E., 476
Morgan, K., 545, 652, 655, 657, 713, 714, 763

Morgan, R., 630
Morgan, S. B., 234, 251, 305, 316, 385, 392, 1069
Morgan, T., 31, 224, 232
Morgan, V., 693
Mori, T., 541
Morishita, R., 138
Moroz, T., 669, 671
Morrelli-Robbins, M., 1003
Morren, J., 898, 903
Morressy, P. A., 1183
Morrier, M., 799, 874, 875, 885, 929, 930, 932, 933, 934, 937, 939, 941, 950, 1035, 1036, 1045, 1046, 1132
Morris, J., 518
Morris, M., 462, 552, 1127
Morris, N., 1126, 1128
Morris, R., 30, 325, 369, 373, 410, 539, 616, 772, 773
Morrison, L., 251, 1031
Morrone, M. C., 692, 693
Mors, O., 185, 188, 534, 551
Mortensen, E. L., 105
Mortensen, P. B., 185, 188, 534, 551
Mortimer, A. M., 848
Mortimore, C., 628, 630, 631, 634, 682
Morton, J., 317
Morton, M., 619
Mortweet, S. L., 1059
Moscovich, M., 669, 671
Moser, H., 126, 127, 128, 132, 140, 142, 144, 147
Moser-Richters, M., 322
Moses, L. J., 614, 615
Moses, L. M., 130
Moses, P., 489, 524
Mosier, C., 383
Moss, E., 552
Moss, S. A., 610
Motil, K. J., 145
Motile, K. J., 139
Mottron, L., 107, 185, 234, 326, 368, 611, 642, 643, 644, 646, 656, 1182
Motulsky, A. G., 434
Mountain-Kimchi, K., 103, 374, 375
Mouren-Simeoni, M. C., 517
Mouridsen, S. E., 50, 75, 76, 203, 204, 206, 212, 213, 296
Moya, K. L., 646
Moyes, F. A., 835
Moyes, R. A., 872
Mozes, T., 171
Msall, M. E., 554
Mudford, O. C., 897, 1061, 1064
Muenz, L. R., 369, 487
Muglia, P., 1103
Müh, J. P., 432, 459, 542

Muhle, R., 1309
Muir, D. W., 317, 689, 690
Mukhlas, M., 47
Mulder, E., 454, 753
Mulick, J. A., 542, 752, 903, 909
Mullen, E. M., 791
Müller, R. A., 261, 497, 517, 521, 525, 526, 1306
Mullin, J. T., 689
Mullins, J. L., 914, 1016
Mulloy, C., 539
Mumme, D. L., 552
Mundy, P., 7, 185, 233, 235, 236, 237, 238, 239, 251, 253, 254, 260, 261, 315, 318, 319, 320, 321, 322, 324, 349, 369, 392, 394, 409, 411, 416, 520, 613, 630, 631, 650, 651, 652, 653, 654, 655, 656, 657, 658, 659, 660, 661, 662, 663, 664, 665, 667, 669, 670, 671, 672, 673, 684, 702, 707, 709, 721, 724, 738, 750, 800, 833, 915, 946, 947, 962, 1007, 1306
Munk, D. D., 540, 900
Munson, J., 5, 31, 171, 226, 233, 234, 236, 316, 319, 375, 387, 388, 429, 542, 612, 613, 656, 657, 662, 663, 665, 668, 670, 708, 757, 1112, 1311
Munson, R., 826
Munstermann, E., 546
Murakami, A., 367, 368
Murakami, J., 141, 367, 499, 610, 617, 655, 656, 659, 668, 832, 889
Murakami, Y., 540
Murakawa, K., 172, 499
Muraki, A. S., 499
Murata, S., 456, 459, 460, 461, 1225, 1249
Murata, T., 73, 74, 80, 100, 202, 204, 206, 212, 213, 214, 288, 289, 291, 293, 296, 298, 1312
Muratori, F., 225, 234, 236, 243
Murch, S., 435, 438, 541
Muris, P., 758
Murphy, C., 57, 63, 555, 883, 912, 1004, 1009, 1070, 1123
Murphy, D. G. M., 107, 493
Murphy, D. L., 459
Murphy, G., 214
Murphy, K. C., 543, 545
Murphy, L. B., 398
Murphy, M., 126, 127, 144, 147, 208, 269, 295, 428, 429, 434, 534,

536, 539, 546, 594, 1110
Murphy, W. D., 1143
Murray, A., 521, 523, 546
Murray, D. S., 542
Murray, P. J., 1110, 1111
Murray, R. M., 181
Murrie, D. C., 299
Murtaugh, M., 207
Musiek, F. E., 844
Musumeci, S., 479, 481, 482, 494, 499, 542, 1307
Mutirangura, A., 551
Muzik, O., 454, 490, 517, 752
Mycke, K., 1057, 1058, 1074
Myer, E., 142
Myers, B., 548
Myers, M., 542, 1112
Myers, R. M., 170, 315, 440, 754
Myklebust, H. R., 97
Myles, B., 113, 354, 366, 374, 375, 867, 868, 869, 872, 876, 913, 985, 986, 996, 1015, 1016, 1018, 1020, 1021, 1022
Myrianthopoulos, N. C., 434

Näätänen, R., 481, 482
Nabors, L., 541, 1112
Nacewicz, B. M., 521, 522
Nadasdy, Z., 630, 698
Nadel, J., 253, 260, 386, 690
Nader, R., 833, 834
Nagai, Y., 325, 834, 1225
Nagamitsu, S., 462
Naganuma, G., 152
Nagell, K., 336, 653
Nagy, E., 478
Nagy, J., 93, 97, 101, 586
Nahmani, A., 552
Nahmias, C., 521
Naidich, T. P., 543
Naidu, S., 126, 127, 128, 130, 132, 134, 136, 137, 140, 141, 142, 144, 146, 147, 151
Naik, B., 1108
Naitoh, H., 140
Nakahato, M., 455
Nakajima, E., 544
Nakamura, A., 389, 662, 663
Nakamura, H., 255
Nakamura, K., 389
Nakane, A., 463, 1226
Nakayasu, N., 270
Nakhoda-Sapuan, S., 871
Nalin, A., 142
Namerow, N. S., 619
Nanba, E., 543
Nanclares, V., 494, 499, 519, 740
Narasaki, M., 127
Narayan, M., 457
Naruse, H., 461, 463, 1226

Nash, C., 496
Nash, S., 227, 408
Nasr, A., 291
Nass, R., 503
Nation, K., 354
Nault, K., 540
Nave, G., 1023
Naviaux, R. K., 550
Navon, D., 640, 643
Naylor, S. T., 27, 178, 456, 1107, 1108
Nazzi, T., 337
Neal, A. R., 709
Neal, R., 651, 654, 658, 659, 660, 661, 662, 670, 671, 673, 684, 833
Neale, M. C., 432
Needleman, R., 344
Neef, N. A., 1030, 1126, 1138, 1143
Neff, N. H., 456
Neff, S., 499
Nehme, E., 107, 492, 499, 537, 538, 768
Neighbor, G., 693
Neill, W. T., 609
Neisser, U., 687
Neisworth, J. T., 713, 871
Nelson, C., 482, 657, 658, 660, 697
Nelson, D. S., 7, 51, 296, 1111
Nelson, E. C., 27
Nelson, J. E., 27, 1106
Nelson, K., 337, 977
Nelson, K. B., 436, 462, 539, 541
Nelson, K. E., 959
Nelson, L. G., 544
Nelson, M., 1034
Nelson, S., 489, 553, 836
Nemanov, L., 433
Nemeroff, C. B., 142
Neri, P., 692, 693
Ness, K. K., 44, 57, 61
Neuman, C. J., 415
Neuringer, A., 871
Neuschwander, J., 539
Neville, H., 549
Nevin, N. C., 551
New, E., 17, 184, 749
Newbury, D. F., 432, 438
Newcorn, J. H., 453
Newell, A., 690, 694
Newell, K. M., 847, 848
Newhart-Larson, S., 417, 554
Newhouse, L., 964
Newman, B., 871, 886
Newman, H. A., 462
Newman, S., 588
Newschaffer, C. J., 44, 57, 61
Newsom-Davis, I. C., 1059
Newson, E., 109, 201, 203, 204, 206, 586, 588
Newton, J. S., 822
Ney, J., 387
Nguyen, M. T., 538, 550
Nichols, K., 664
Nichols, S., 659, 673, 698

Nicholson, H., 520
Nicholson, J. C., 550
Nicholson, R., 183
Nicolao, P., 130, 138
Nicoletti, M. A., 491, 500
Nicoll, D., 434
Nicolson, K., 491
Nicolson, R., 544
Nie, J., 73, 77, 78
Niedermeyer, E., 144, 151
Niehaus, D., 266
Nielsen, J., 140, 144, 544, 1107
Nielson, J., 1282
Niemann, G., 140
Nientimp, E. G., 1030
Nietupski, J., 818, 1090, 1097
Nightingale, N., 105, 227, 229, 652, 655, 657, 713, 714, 763
Nigro, F., 547
Nigro, M. A., 144
Nihei, K., 140
Niimi, M., 47
Nijhof, G. J., 189
Niklasson, I., 552
Nimchinsky, E., 670
Ninomiya, H., 543
Nir, I., 459
Nishikawa, M., 667
Nissen, G., 1240, 1241
Niwa, S., 502, 503, 1225
Njardvik, U., 251
Njio, L., 30, 183
Nober, E., 657, 662
Noebels, J., 431, 432
Noemi, C., 1230
Nohria, C., 428
Noin, I., 345
Noirot, E., 689
Nolin, T., 257, 960
Noll, W. W., 551
Nomura, Y., 127, 140, 141, 142
Norbury, C., 33, 175, 176, 353, 641, 722, 740, 753, 810, 812, 813
Nordin, V., 205, 212, 288, 289, 290, 292, 293, 295, 297, 304, 478, 540, 544, 720, 748, 749, 750, 751, 753, 832
Nordquist, V., 968, 1030
Norlin, B., 544
Norman, D., 670
Norman, R. M., 489
Normandin, J. J., 489, 493, 494, 1305
Norris, C., 890
Norris, M., 554
Norris, R. G., 1089
North, W. G., 1111
Northup, J., 912, 916
Norton, J., 204, 206, 215, 288, 293, 320, 335, 835, 962, 1304
Noterdaeme, M., 177, 536
Nouri, N., 426, 432, 433, 617
Novick, B., 479, 480, 482
Novotny, S., 1111

Nowell, M. A., 499
Numato, Y., 463
Nunn, K., 80
Nurmi, E. L., 429
Nuzzolo-Gomez, R., 253
Nwokoro, N. A., 544
Nyberg, L., 372
Nydén, A., 103, 234, 299, 352, 375, 495, 748, 1306
Nye, J., 837
Nyhan, W. L., 464, 544
Nyholt, D. R., 432, 433
Nylander, L., 590
Nzeocha, A., 905

Oades, R., 479
Oakes, P., 261
O'Bara, M., 494
Oberfield, R., 838, 839, 847
Oberlander, T. F., 833, 834
O'Brien, D. J., 462, 1306
O'Brien, D. W., 1282
O'Brien, G., 189, 299, 300
O'Brien, L. M., 493, 494, 496, 497, 498, 519, 1305
O'Brien, M., 1143
O'Brien, R. A., 455, 458
O'Callaghan, E., 539
Ochocka, J., 1096
Ochs, E., 868
O'Connor, N., 255, 263, 388, 596, 628, 640, 641
O'Connor, T., 180, 430
Oda, H., 254
Oda, S., 47
Odell, J., 542
O'Dell, M., 883, 950, 952, 1004, 1009
Odom, S. L., 394, 967, 968, 991, 1011, 1029, 1030, 1031, 1033
O'Donovan, A., 539
Odor, S., 1021
O'Driscoll, G., 183, 189
Oduwaiye, K. A., 842
Oelsner, R. R., 1229
Oetting, J. B., 347
Offord, D. R., 733
Oftedal, G., 542
Oftelie, A., 267
Ogdie, M. N., 1307
Ogle, P. A., 1074
Ohashi, Y., 47
Ohnishi, T., 667
Ohno, K., 543
Ohno, Y., 455, 459, 460
Ohta, M., 325, 384, 834
Ohtaki, E., 540
Ohtani, Y., 540
Ohura, T., 461
Okada, F., 460
Oke, N. J., 912, 990, 991, 1032
Oksanen, H., 296, 297
Okuda, K., 261
Okun, M., 502
Oldendorf, W. H., 499
O'Leary, J. J., 438, 541

O'Leary, M., 142
Olivari, C., 1232
Oliver, J., 241
Ollendick, T., 30, 595, 1059
Oller, D., 235, 319
Oller, K., 349, 962
Olley, G., 953, 962
Olley, J. G., 351, 863, 866, 867, 868, 876, 1003, 1176, 1310
Olsen, C. L., 547
Olson, C., 317
Olson, L. M., 429
Olson, S. T., 476
Olsson, B., 132, 134, 135, 431
Olsson, I., 1303
Olsson, M. B., 1055
Olsson, V. A., 544
O'Malley Cannon, B., 938, 1036
O'Neill, D. K., 253
O'Neill, J., 201, 549
O'Neill, M., 831
O'Neill, R. E., 257, 822, 823, 824, 825, 887, 890, 900, 903, 906, 911, 912, 1061
Ong, B., 24, 167, 172
Onizawa, J., 455
Oosterlaan, J., 373
Oostra, B. A., 545
Opitz, J. M., 127, 128
Opitz, J. O., 544
Oram, M. W., 692
Oranje, B., 478
O'Reilly, B., 1093
O'Riordan, M., 630, 635, 642
Ornitz, E., 27, 209, 227, 316, 366, 367, 455, 476, 478, 484, 488, 540, 542, 553, 832, 834, 837, 981
Orr, S., 366
Orsini, D. L., 30
Orsmark, C., 109
Orsmond, G., 214, 288, 289, 290, 293, 295, 297, 323, 324, 1055, 1059, 1075, 1077
Ort, S., 492, 838, 848
Ortegon, J., 258, 261, 324, 412
Ortiz, E., 253
Osada, H., 76, 80
Osaki, D., 953, 1043, 1050
Osann, K., 342
Osborn, A. G., 548
Osborne, J. P., 543
Osborne, P., 1110
Oshima, M., 1225
Oshima, N., 463
Oskarsdottir, S., 552
Osnes, P. G., 827
Ostergaard, O., 544
Osterling, J., 5, 31, 171, 224, 225, 226, 233, 234, 235, 236, 237, 316, 319, 341, 366, 375, 384, 385, 387,

388, 396, 397, 398, 429, 526, 542, 595, 612, 613, 651, 654, 656, 657, 662, 663, 665, 668, 670, 671, 689, 707, 708, 799, 800, 832, 833, 834, 837, 846, 942, 946, 962, 987, 998, 1003, 1004, 1008, 1112, 1311
Östman, O., 212
Ostrosky, M., 884, 967, 968, 991, 1031
Ostry, D., 693
Oswald, D. P., 720, 870
Otsubo, H., 544
Otsuka, D. P., 304
Ounsted, C., 268, 585, 592
Ousley, O., 228, 229, 231, 233, 235, 236, 238, 251, 301, 316, 319, 321, 384, 385, 386, 409, 655, 708, 717, 718, 734, 799, 801, 835, 836, 837, 947, 1007, 1011
Ouston, J., 260, 261, 389, 412, 413, 520, 643, 689
Ouvrier, R., 80
Overall, J. E., 1102, 1112
Ovrutskaya, I., 542
Owely, T., 722
Owen, A., 609, 615, 663
Owen, L., 127
Owen, M. J., 443
Owen, V., 1004
Owley, T., 542, 752, 757, 762, 1112
Ownby, J. B., 1033
Ozanne, A. E., 148, 149
Ozbayrak, K. R., 107
Ozonoff, S., 13, 24, 33, 73, 77, 78, 93, 102, 103, 104, 105, 113, 115, 174, 186, 213, 234, 238, 251, 258, 261, 262, 264, 268, 322, 324, 326, 350, 368, 370, 372, 373, 375, 388, 391, 413, 416, 417, 487, 498, 539, 544, 607, 608, 609, 610, 611, 613, 614, 615, 616, 617, 618, 620, 631, 634, 635, 643, 653, 682, 731, 735, 736, 758, 786, 836, 837, 890, 984, 1050, 1056, 1057, 1061, 1064, 1078

Pabst, H. F., 499
Pace, G. M., 152, 155, 819, 825, 907
Pace, N. C., 542
Pacifico, L., 539
Padden, S., 481, 482
Padeliadou, S., 1217
Page, J., 385, 836, 847

Page, T., 464, 1126, 1128, 1143
Paine, C., 212
Painter, K. M., 151
Paisey, T. J., 905
Palermo, M. T., 265, 266
Palfai, T., 615
Palferman, S., 5, 8, 25, 93, 419, 427, 442
Palm, A., 143
Palmen, S. J. M. C., 491, 493, 499
Palmer, A., 301, 432, 433, 515, 1071, 1075
Palmer, D. S., 1034
Palmer, F., 800
Palmer, L. J., 431
Palmer, P., 5, 107, 170, 173, 182, 214, 269, 288, 289, 295, 427, 428, 492, 499, 617, 618, 646, 660, 661, 741, 1076, 1077
Palumbo, D., 1109
Palumbo, L. W., 902
Pan, J. W., 143
Panagiotaki, G., 549
Panagiotides, H., 171, 235, 483, 690
Panchalingam, K., 549
Pancsofar, E. L., 1091
Pandit, B. S., 48, 52, 54, 61, 63
Panerai, S., 494, 499, 758
Panksepp, J., 461, 656, 659, 662, 1112
Panman, L. E., 484
Pantelis, C., 617
Panyan, M., 1126, 1127, 1128
Panzer, S., 668, 669
Papademetris, X., 523
Papadimitriou, J. C., 541
Papageorgiou, M., 367, 368, 498, 614
Papageorgiou, V., 1216, 1217
Papanikolau, E., 427
Papanikolau, K., 5, 426, 427
Paradis, T., 899
Parano, E., 432, 433
Paravatou-Petsotas, M., 551
Paredes, S., 886, 887
Parente, R., 619
Parham, L. D., 835, 836, 843, 846, 847
Park, C., 632, 1076, 1185, 1311
Park, G. S., 594
Park, J., 550, 1129
Park, R. J., 430
Parker, D., 251, 265, 267, 839, 847, 1031
Parker, J., 1056, 1072
Parks, B. T., 903
Parks, D. R., 886, 913
Parks, S. L., 312, 730, 744
Parle, N., 619
Parmeggiani, A., 296, 502
Parmelee, T., 484
Parr, J. R., 432, 433, 438
Parrett, J., 886, 887, 913

Parrish, J. M., 1126, 1138
Parsons, M. B., 1033
Partington, J., 929, 932, 933, 937, 939, 941, 963, 964
Partington, M. W., 455
Parush, S., 834
Pascalis, O., 670
Pascotto, A., 552
Pascual-Castroviejo, I., 544
Pascualvaca, D., 367, 368, 498, 524, 525, 614, 667
Pasley, B. N., 518, 526
Passante, N., 746, 753
Passingham, R., 371, 495, 497, 1305
Passoni, D., 551
Pasto, L., 1182
Pastuszak, A. L., 553
Patel, M. R., 819, 821, 823
Patel, S. T., 462
Patil, A. A., 503
Patil, S., 188, 551
Patja, A., 541
Patja, K., 296, 297
Patta, P. C., 462
Pattavina, S., 1023
Patterson, B., 536
Patterson, E. T., 1127
Patterson, G., 1061
Patton, M. A., 544
Patzold, L. M., 542
Paul, G., 412, 483
Paul, M., 483
Paul, R., 17, 30, 31, 71, 79, 224, 232, 233, 234, 238, 251, 256, 293, 315, 316, 318, 319, 323, 335, 340, 341, 342, 343, 346, 348, 349, 350, 352, 353, 492, 561, 587, 691, 707, 783, 793, 801, 802, 804, 809, 810, 813, 832, 946, 960, 961, 962, 966
Pauli, R. M., 551
Paulk, M., 551
Pauls, D., 24, 27, 41, 91, 92, 95, 96, 102, 104, 109, 110, 124, 263, 691, 735, 736, 1111
Paulson, G. W., 555
Paulson, R. B., 555
Paunio, M., 541
Pavone, L., 539, 553
Pavone, P., 432, 433
Payton, J., 369, 484, 487, 546
Pearce, P., 958, 959
Pearl, G., 768
Pearlman-Avnion, S., 260
Pearlson, G., 107, 492, 499, 537, 538
Pearson, D., 258, 261, 324, 385, 412, 1110, 1111
Pearson, G. S., 169, 182
Pearson, J., 189
Peck, C., 934
Peck, S. M., 819, 823

Pedersent, C. B., 435
Peeters, T., 1177
Pefiesson, R. S., 1018
Pei, F., 225, 234, 236
Peirini, P., 668, 669
Pelham, W., 1109
Pelham, W., Jr., 177
Pelios, L., 898, 903
Pellicer, A. A., 541
Pelphrey, K., 412, 483, 491
Pelson, R. O., 476
Peltola, H., 541
Pelton, G. H., 267
Pencarinha, D., 208
Pence, A. R., 1034
Pencrinha, D., 269
Penge, R., 1223
Pennington, B., 324, 372, 373, 375, 485, 631, 634, 635, 663, 673
Pennington, B. E., 236
Pennington, B. F., 33, 104, 105, 185, 234, 237, 261, 262, 268, 320, 326, 350, 368, 369, 370, 371, 372, 375, 383, 384, 385, 386, 387, 388, 389, 391, 413, 487, 536, 537, 545, 606, 607, 611, 612, 613, 614, 615, 616, 618, 836, 837, 1050, 1306
Pennington, R., 655, 663, 1030
Pennisi, G., 479, 481, 482
Peppe, S., 1306
Peraino, J. M., 1088
Percy, A., 127, 128, 129, 130, 131, 132, 134, 135, 136, 138, 139, 140, 141, 142, 143, 144, 145, 150, 151, 152
Perdue, S., 183
Pereira, J., 136
Perel, J. M., 457, 463
Peretz, I., 326, 611, 642
Perez, E., 483, 552
Perez, J., 1305
Pergament, E., 544
Perkins, J., 1142
Perloff, B. F., 882, 883
Perman, J. A., 541
Perner, J., 105, 395, 613, 614, 615, 630, 632
Perot, A., 689
Perou, R., 1062
Perrett, D., 236, 266, 389, 521, 523, 526, 692
Perrine, K., 607
Perrot, A., 229, 232, 240, 366, 689, 708, 712, 751, 834, 1208
Perry, A., 147, 749, 762, 1076
Perry, B. D., 539
Perry, D., 27, 209, 295
Perry, E. K., 463, 490
Perry, R., 77, 177, 189, 463, 490, 492, 1102, 1104

Perry, T. L., 462, 553
Persson, B., 297, 758, 1177
Persson, E., 177, 546, 548
Perucchini, P., 536
Pescucci, C., 551
Peselow, E. D., 838, 839, 847
Pessoa, L., 526
Peters, A., 346
Peters, K. G., 617
Petersen, B. P., 909
Petersen, P. B., 433, 437, 536, 539
Petersen, S., 663
Peterson, B., 27, 754, 1103
Peterson, C., 660, 968, 991, 1089
Peterson, F. M., 915
Peterson, R. E., 455
Peterson, R. F., 883
Pethick, S., 337
Petit, E., 1208
Petkovic, Z. B., 459
Petrides, G., 589
Petrides, M., 693
Petropoulos, M. C., 48, 54, 60, 435
Petrucha, D., 503
Pettegrew, J. W., 549
Petterson, B., 434
Petti, T. A., 501
Petty, L. K., 27, 209
Peze, A., 386
Pezzullo, J., 548
Pfiffner, L. J., 177
Phelan, M. C., 550, 551
Phelps, D. L., 554
Phelps, L. A., 1091
Phelps, M. E., 140
Philbrick, L., 1003, 1004
Philippart, M., 129, 130, 135, 140, 144
Philippe, A., 432, 433, 462
Philips, W., 650, 661
Philipson, E., 544, 553
Phillips, M., 521, 526
Phillips, N. E., 499
Phillips, S., 480
Phillips, W., 318, 355, 537, 707, 834
Philofsky, A., 547
Piaget, J., 149, 224, 234, 236, 321, 382, 391, 392, 395, 656, 673, 695
Piazza, C. C., 128, 152, 908, 909, 912
Piazza, K., 134, 146
Picardi, N., 353
Piccinelli, P., 551
Piccolo, E., 873, 874
Pichal, B., 105
Pichichero, M. E., 436
Pickens, D., 693
Pickett, J., 212, 293, 295, 296, 297
Pickles, A., 5, 31, 32, 108, 170, 171, 180, 208, 228, 269, 295, 335, 341, 342, 343, 346,

385, 408, 426, 427,
428, 430, 434, 437,
534, 536, 537, 538,
539, 553, 586, 594,
617, 632, 655, 722,
730, 731, 732, 734,
740, 741, 753, 754,
763
Pickrel, S. G., 1063
Pickup, G. J., 171
Picton, T. W., 844
Pierce, C., 1148
Pierce, K., 250, 261, 266,
483, 493, 497, 521,
522, 525, 526, 654,
661, 663, 671, 837,
886, 887, 890, 913,
959, 990, 991, 1004,
1011, 1030, 1031, 1306
Pierce, S., 343, 345
Pierce, T., 322
Pieretti, M., 545
Pieropan, K., 886
Pietila, J., 1307
Piggot, J., 170, 185, 521
Piha, J., 1238
Pikus, A. M., 476, 477
Pilling, S., 619
Pillotto, R. F., 136
Pilowsky, T., 171, 433, 734,
748, 749, 753
Pincus, H. A., 11
Pine, D. S., 181
Pingree, C., 47, 63, 184,
299, 461, 534, 536,
537, 539, 540, 545
Pinker, S., 340
Pinter, E., 901
Pinter-Lalli, E., 822
Pinto, M. C. B., 1230
Pinto-Martin, J. A., 1312
Pisani, F., 479, 481
Pitcher, D. A., 494, 536,
538
Pitkanen, A., 525
Pitts-Conway, V., 886, 904,
1143
Piven, J., 5, 107, 123, 170,
173, 182, 188, 195,
197, 214, 250, 269,
288, 289, 295, 412,
427, 428, 439, 453,
483, 489, 491, 492,
493, 494, 496, 498,
499, 500, 501, 519,
536, 537, 538, 539,
551, 617, 618, 646,
660, 661, 741, 768,
808, 809, 1058, 1076,
1077, 1307
Pizzo, S., 550
Pizzuti, A., 545
Placidi, F., 542
Plaisted, K., 630, 635, 642,
643
Planer, D., 255
Plebst, C., 494, 499, 519,
740
Plesner, A.-M., 435
Pliner, C., 31, 73, 317, 708
Plioplys, A. V., 503
Plomin, R., 431

Ploof, D. L., 1110
Plotkin, S., 455
Plousia, M., 655
Plumb, I., 190, 631, 632
Plumet, M. H., 326, 521,
618
Pober, B. R., 548
Pocock, S. J., 429
Poe, M. D., 833, 843
Poirier, K., 78
Poland, J., 113
Polatkoff, S., 189
Poldrack, R. A., 1308
Polich, J., 479
Poline, J. B., 517
Polinsky, R. J., 458
Pollard, J., 234
Pomerleau, O., 1127,
1148
Pomeroy, J., 782, 1055,
1059, 1060, 1124,
1134, 1139
Pommer, D. A., 1127
Pomponi, M. G., 551
Pond, R., 800, 804
Ponnet, K., 105
Pons, R., 550
Pontius, W., 1304
Porat, S., 1218
Porges, S., 336, 832
Porparino, M., 1182
Porter, F. D., 544
Porterfield, P. J., 1143
Posar, A., 296
Posey, D. J., 189, 267, 454,
526, 1106, 1108, 1109
Posner, K., 1109
Posner, M., 610, 617, 663,
668, 669, 670, 671,
673
Potenza, M. N., 1105
Potkin, S. G., 617
Potter, C. A., 952
Potter, D., 653
Potter, M., 991
Potucek, J., 956, 991
Poulsen, C., 959
Poulson, C. L., 261, 871
Poustka, A., 130, 432
Poustka, F., 27, 294
Povinelli, D., 317
Powell, D. R., 264
Powell, J., 48, 52, 54, 61,
63, 666
Powell, S., 322, 371, 397,
399, 1011
Powell, T., 617, 1074
Power, R., 1064
Power, T., 264
Powers, J., 458
Powers, L., 1060, 1063,
1068, 1093
Powers, M., 113, 817, 818,
819, 820, 826, 1037
Powers, S., 1183
Pozdol, S. L., 712, 718
Pozner, A., 207
Prasad, A. N., 544
Prasad, C., 544
Prasher, V., 209, 295
Prassad, A., 553
Prather, E., 804

Prather, F., 83
Prather, M. D., 526
Pratt, C., 105, 352, 569,
630
Preece, D., 1177
Prego Silva, L. E., 1229
Premack, D., 629, 630
Presberg, J., 1108
Presburger, G., 552
Press, G. A., 141, 367, 371,
499, 610, 617, 832,
889, 1282, 1305
Prevor, M. B., 612
Pribor, E. F., 27
Price, B. H., 613
Price, D. L., 142
Price, J. L., 524, 525
Price, J. H., 27, 189, 267,
456, 821, 1107, 1108,
1111, 1282
Price, R., 693
Primavera, E., 934
Prince, S., 269, 914
Pring, L., 642, 644
Prior, J., 427, 428
Prior, M., 24, 27, 33, 93,
167, 172, 173, 174,
185, 261, 320, 348,
373, 387, 388, 459,
460, 487, 492, 536,
542, 593, 606, 744,
835, 1016, 1201
Pritchard, J. K., 426, 432
Prizant, B., 255, 257, 319,
346, 691, 713, 758,
759, 773, 777, 778,
799, 800, 890, 926,
927, 928, 929, 930,
932, 933, 935, 936,
937, 938, 939, 940,
941, 942, 946, 947,
961, 978, 979, 980,
981, 982, 983, 984,
985, 986, 987, 989,
990, 995, 996, 997,
1005, 1007, 1008,
1009, 1016
Proctor-Williams, K., 959,
966
Pronovost, W., 348, 813
Provence, S., 9, 29, 182,
183
Prutting, C., 351, 653, 806,
947
Przybeck, T., 746, 753
Puce, A., 483, 520, 525,
693
Puchalski, C., 396
Pueschel, S., 548, 553
Puleston, J. M., 438, 541
Pulsifer, M., 547
Pumariega, A. J., 267
Purcell, R., 617
Purdy, W. C., 456, 459
Purisch, A. D., 844
Purpura, D. P., 553, 1305
Putnam, L. E., 479
Putnam, N. H., 484
Putnam, S., 32, 731, 733,
754, 755
Pyck, K., 546
Pyles, D. A. M., 1128

Quach, H., 433
Quarrington, B., 539
Quemada, N., 1207
Quilitch, H. R., 1127, 1128
Quill, K., 259, 936, 966,
990, 1021
Quinn, A., 555, 556
Quinn, G. E., 554
Quinn, J., 936
Quintana, H., 27, 189, 1110
Quintana-Murci, L., 433
Quintieri, F., 539
Quisling, R., 502
Qumsiyeh, M. B., 551

Rabsztyn, A., 541
Racine, Y., 733
Raoux, C., 770, 772
Rademacher, J., 494, 536,
538
Rader, S., 608
Rafaelsen, O. J., 462
Raggett, P., 634
Ragland, E. U., 1030
Rahav, M., 1218
Rahbar, B., 251, 292, 294,
316
Ralford, K. L., 32, 429,
432, 433, 439, 754
Rainville, C., 185
Raivio, K. O., 464
Rakic, P., 454
Ramachandran, V. S., 459,
694
Ramberg, C., 352
Ramos, E. R., 551
Ramos, O., 126, 154, 431,
535, 594
Ramoz, N., 433, 474, 550
Ramsden, S., 130, 139
Ramstad, K., 548
Randall, P., 1056, 1072
Randolf, B., 368
Randolph, B., 234
Rank, B., 9, 16
Rankin, J., 547
Ranson, B. J., 494, 496,
498, 499
Rantala, H., 534, 544
Rao, J. M., 177
Rao, N., 758
Rapagna, S., 1034
Rapin, I., 30, 65, 76, 79,
80, 82, 97, 175, 202,
204, 205, 206, 212,
213, 214, 224, 288,
289, 290, 291, 292,
293, 295, 296, 298,
299, 385, 387, 388,
491, 502, 503, 534,
536, 537, 538, 539,
544, 555, 586, 832,
1305, 1307, 1309,
1311, 1312
Rapoport, J. L., 27, 169,
179, 181, 202, 203,
204, 206, 207, 208,
209, 210, 251, 266,
288, 290, 293, 294,
295, 297, 298, 299,
316, 492, 501, 1015,
1106

Rapoport, J. T., 267
Rapoport, M. D., 344, 352
Rapoport, S. I., 492, 518
Rapoport, S. L., 1015
Rapson, R. L., 383, 384, 836
Rashkis, S., 458
Rasing, E., 867, 899
Rasmussen, C., 813
Rasmussen, P., 548, 552, 588, 594
Rast, J., 901
Rastam, M., 101, 113, 432, 586, 590, 743, 760
Rastamm, M., 109
Raste, Y., 190, 631, 632
Ratering, E., 758
Ratey, J. J., 189
Ratliff-Schaub, K., 542, 1112
Ratner, H. H., 237, 318, 369, 383
Ratzoni, G., 299
Rauch, A. M., 544
Rausch, L. A., 551
Ravan, S. A., 32, 432, 433, 439, 551, 754
Ravitz, A., 459
Rawitt, R., 1111
Ray, B., 962
Rayfield, R., 1094
Raymond, G., 488
Raynes, H. R., 544
Realmuto, G., 782
Realmuto, G. M., 27, 458, 459, 460, 588, 589, 838, 1124, 1134, 1139
Realmuto, G. R., 463, 490
Reaney, S., 967, 968, 1031
Reaven, J., 953, 1043, 1050
Recasens, C., 462
Reddy, K. P., 541
Reddy, V., 253, 395, 833, 849
Redmond, D. E., Jr., 458
Redwood, L., 435
Reed, D., 635
Reed, H. K., 897, 898, 899
Reed, J., 1245
Rees, L., 462, 643
Reeser, R., 1010
Reeve, C. E., 863, 866, 867, 868, 876, 899
Reeve, E., 458
Reeve, S. A., 886
Reeves, D., 897, 1061, 1064
Regnier, M. C., 1129
Regolin, L., 692
Rehm, R., 268, 889
Reichelt, K. L., 462
Reichert, J., 429, 432, 433, 439, 474, 550, 754
Reichle, J., 149, 885, 910, 926, 939
Reichle, N. C., 297, 301, 302, 1075, 1076, 1256
Reichler, R., 289, 543, 546, 553, 554, 720, 721, 732, 734, 744, 748, 749, 757, 758, 818, 820, 1055, 1066, 1067,

1175, 1176, 1177, 1199, 1216
Reichlet, R., 667
Reid, D., 956, 1010, 1033, 1126, 1127, 1128, 1138
Reid, K., 804
Reid, M. J., 1060, 1062
Reif, W. E., 1127
Reik, W., 440
Reilly, J., 260, 549
Reilly, S., 145
Reimers, T., 912
Reinecke, D. R., 871, 886
Reinhartsen, D. B., 870
Reis, A. M., 553
Reis, K., 1051
Reiss, A. L., 141, 185, 269, 429, 524, 545, 547, 548
Reiss, J. E., 693
Reiss, M. L., 1128
Reite, M., 355, 493, 495
Reitzel, J.-A., 103
Remschmidt, H., 1241
Remy, P., 373
Renda, Y., 130
Rende, R., 17, 71, 79, 324, 707
Renner, B. R., 720, 734, 748, 749, 818, 820, 1176, 1199
Renner, H., 144
Renner, P., 369, 371
Repacholi, B., 150, 153
Repetto, G. M., 551
Repp, A. C., 540, 819, 900, 904, 915, 916, 934
Rescorla, L., 182, 183, 345, 748, 799, 800
Restall, G., 845
Rett, A., 8, 75, 126, 127, 129, 132, 134, 135, 139, 142, 144, 145, 147, 154, 431
Revecki, D., 45
Revell, W. G., 1094
Revicki, D., 75
Reynell, J., 83, 800
Reynolds, J., 551
Reynolds, N. J., 1130
Reznick, J., 337, 412, 483, 983
Reznick, S., 800
Rheinberger, A., 1032
Rheingold, H. L., 653
Rhodes, H., 550
Rhodes, L. E., 1095
Rhodes, P. H., 436
Riccardi, V. M., 127, 136, 141, 142, 152
Ricci, I., 551
Rice, C., 57, 63, 549, 1070, 1123
Rice, M., 149, 345
Rice, M. A., 144, 145
Rice, M. L., 345, 347
Rice, M. L. A., 145
Rich, B., 50, 75, 76, 212, 296
Rich, S., 169, 186, 187, 202, 203, 204, 206,

207, 210, 211, 288, 295, 297, 298, 299, 590
Richard, E., 868
Richards, B. S., 154
Richards, C. S., 545
Richards, H., 62
Richardson, A. J., 438
Richardson, E., 543
Richardson, J., 145
Richardson, M. P., 523, 525
Richdale, A., 459, 460, 542
Richelme, C., 494, 536, 538
Richler, J., 342, 439, 631, 632, 634
Richman, D. M., 819, 823
Richman, G. S., 825, 1128
Richters, M. M., 169, 180
Ricks, D. M., 324, 349, 392, 410, 595
Ricks, M., 415
Riddle, J. E., 545
Riddle, J. I., 1141, 1144, 1151
Riddle, M. A., 838, 848
Riederer, P., 139, 141, 142, 145
Riegelman, R. K., 710, 711
Riguet, C. B., 253, 392
Riikonen, R., 143, 545
Rimland, B., 268, 312, 455, 546, 596, 733, 744, 832, 1014, 1089, 1195
Rinaldi, J., 233, 234, 235, 236, 237, 384, 385, 388, 396, 397, 526, 613, 651, 656, 657, 670, 671, 689, 707, 799, 832
Rincover, A., 268, 1089, 1129
Rineer, S., 550, 551
Rinehart, N. J., 104, 610, 836
Ring, A., 1220
Ring, B., 326
Ring, H., 373, 419, 525, 526, 615, 652, 666
Ringdahl, J. E., 904
Ringman, J. M., 838, 839
Ringo, J. L., 519
Rinner, L., 1015, 1016
Riordan, M. R., 1128
Rios, P., 45, 170, 171, 228, 323, 412, 426, 427, 520, 536, 537, 554, 586, 594, 599, 632, 740, 753, 832, 1017
Risch, N., 170, 315, 426, 431, 432, 433, 440, 617, 754
Risi, S., 45, 110, 196, 214, 223, 224, 228, 233, 248, 326, 342, 343, 348, 541, 547, 551, 655, 709, 712, 731, 739, 753, 756, 757, 778, 779, 780, 781, 808, 1124, 1143
Risley, T. R., 883, 903, 948, 950, 951, 1006, 1125, 1126, 1130,

1133, 1141, 1143, 1144, 1148, 1151, 1154
Ritchie, K., 555
Ritvo, A., 741, 745, 762
Ritvo, E., 38, 47, 63, 184, 234, 251, 292, 294, 299, 316, 366, 367, 453, 455, 458, 461, 484, 488, 489, 499, 500, 534, 536, 537, 539, 540, 542, 545, 741, 745, 750, 762
Ritvo, R., 251, 292, 294, 299, 316
Rivera, C. M., 253
Rivier, F., 552
Rivinus, T. M., 79
Rizzolatti, G., 255, 389, 524, 673
Rizzolio, F., 78
Roache, J. D., 1110, 1111
Robaey, P., 643
Robb, S. A., 144
Robbins, F. R., 820, 899, 900, 916, 1003, 1058, 1129
Robbins, L. A., 1015, 1016
Robbins, T. W., 368, 372, 609, 615
Roberts, A. C., 609, 615
Roberts, B., 956
Roberts, J., 317, 345
Roberts, M., 1060
Roberts, R. J., 616
Roberts, S. B., 432
Roberts, S. E., 552
Roberts, W., 542
Robertson, D., 107, 419, 493, 521, 526, 652
Robertson, I. H., 619
Robertson, J., 32, 167, 169, 173, 754, 755, 757
Robertson, K. D., 440
Robertson, L. C., 645
Robertson, M., 628, 630, 631, 634, 682, 838
Robertson, S., 45, 108, 170, 228, 323, 426, 437, 554, 599, 632, 740, 753, 754, 832
Robins, D. L., 229, 521, 713, 716, 717
Robins, E., 15
Robinson, C., 1284
Robinson, H., 489
Robinson, J. F., 90
Robinson, M., 551
Robinson, R., 543
Robinson, S., 902, 1069
Robinson, T., 201, 295, 542
Rochat, P., 395, 398, 630
Roche, C., 544
Rochen-Renner, B., 543, 546, 553, 554
Rodger, R., 719, 720, 750
Rodgers, J. R., 552
Rodier, P., 385, 436, 489, 501, 553, 836
Rodrigue, J. R., 234, 251, 316, 385, 392
Rodrigues, L., 61, 316, 317

Rodriguez, A., 288, 298, 324
Roeder-Gordon, C., 1078, 1092, 1093
Roelofs, J. W., 482
Roeyers, H., 177, 236, 237, 373, 389, 390, 671, 1057, 1058, 1074
Rogan, P., 1088
Rogé, B., 439., 500, 501, 536
Roger, H., 435
Rogers, C., 548
Rogers, D., 589, 848
Rogers, M. F., 1021
Rogers, R. D., 615
Rogers, S., 13, 29, 32, 33, 73, 75, 104, 105, 185, 224, 225, 227, 229, 234, 236, 237, 238, 261, 316, 317, 320, 321, 322, 324, 336, 342, 350, 355, 366, 367, 368, 369, 370, 371, 372, 373, 375, 383, 384, 385, 386, 387, 388, 389, 394, 396, 397, 413, 416, 417, 419, 485, 487, 493, 495, 536, 537, 542, 547, 554, 607, 611, 612, 613, 614, 615, 618, 631, 634, 635, 655, 663, 673, 691, 692, 707, 708, 709, 716, 721, 723, 734, 753, 757, 833, 834, 836, 837, 843, 847, 863, 874, 939, 947, 950, 952, 953, 957, 959, 967, 987, 1003, 1004, 1008, 1043, 1050, 1051, 1057, 1112, 1181, 1182, 1193
Rogers-Warren, A., 826, 883, 884, 951
Rogoff, B., 383
Rogosch, F. A., 326
Roid, G. H., 844, 846
Roid, G. M., 789
Rojahn, J., 266, 909, 1110
Rojas, D., 355, 493, 495
Rojas, J., 656
Rolando, S., 147
Roley, S., 835, 836, 846, 847
Rolfe, U., 537
Rolider, A., 908, 909
Rolls, E., 518
Roman, J., 489
Romanczyk, R., 929, 936, 938
Romanczyk, R. G., 254, 874, 899, 901, 916, 949, 1035, 1043, 1044, 1046, 1047, 1130, 1138
Romanczyk, R. L., 819, 823
Romano, J., 553, 836
Romanski, L., 372, 520, 525, 665, 670
Romick, K. S., 908

Romine, L., 496
Romski, M., 956
Ronald, A., 1239
Rondan, C., 519, 520
Roosa, J., 996
Root, R., 206
Ropar, D., 642
Roper, L., 555
Rosch, E., 686, 687, 688, 690, 691
Rose, G. D., 900
Rose, K., 1183
Rosenbaum, J. L., 317
Rosenbaum, K., 185, 548
Rosenbaum, P., 535
Rosenberg, E., 1307
Rosenberg, L. E., 462
Rosenberger-Diesse, J., 464
Rosenblatt, B., 476
Rosenbloom, L., 73, 75
Rosenbloom, S., 492
Rosenblum, J. F., 1004, 1005, 1008
Rosenblum, S. M., 476
Rosenhall, U., 478, 484, 540, 832
Rosenkranz, J. A., 1306
Rosen-Sheidley, B., 429, 430, 432, 433, 436, 440, 453
Rosenthal, U., 476
Rosman, N. P., 499, 1305
Ross, A., 800
Ross, D., 457, 462, 948
Ross, G. S., 398
Ross, R., 485
Rossetti, L., 800
Rossi, F. G., 502
Rossi, P. G., 502
Rotatori, A. F., 261
Roth, D., 1096
Rothbart, M., 671
Rothermal, R., 454
Rothermel, R., 490, 517, 752
Rothman, S., 788
Rotholtz, D., 264
Rotholz, D. A., 906
Roubertie, A., 552
Roubertoux, P., 459, 461
Rouillard, P., 545
Rouleau, N., 611
Roulet, E., 80, 82
Rourke, B., 24, 33, 96, 97, 103, 104, 173, 234, 375, 498, 586, 628, 736, 985, 995
Rouse, B., 616
Rousseau, F., 545
Roussounis, T., 551
Routh, D. A., 645
Routsoni, C., 1215
Roux, S., 229, 232, 366, 394, 479, 712, 751, 834
Rovee-Collier, C., 640
Rovner, L., 909
Rowe, A., 373
Rowland, D., 526
Rowlett, R., 1107
Roy, E., 107, 474, 488, 1305

Roy, M., 31, 170, 172, 291, 477, 478, 731, 735, 754
Roy, P., 180
Royer, J., 251, 1030
Royers, H., 105
Rubia, K., 666, 667
Rubin, C., 149
Rubin, E., 31, 224, 232, 367, 375, 773, 926, 927, 928, 929, 932, 933, 935, 936, 937, 938, 939, 940, 941, 942, 977, 978, 979, 980, 981, 982, 983, 986, 987, 989, 990, 995, 996, 997, 998, 1005, 1008
Rubin, M., 1105
Ruble, L. A., 267, 301
Ruchelli, E. D., 541
Rucker, R. E., 1091
Rude, H. A., 1030, 1031
Ruhl, D., 546
Rumeau-Rouquette, C., 61
Rumsey, J., 27, 179, 181, 202, 203, 204, 206, 207, 208, 209, 210, 251, 263, 266, 268, 288, 290, 293, 294, 295, 297, 298, 299, 316, 344, 352, 367, 368, 372, 388, 476, 477, 487, 492, 518, 606, 610, 617, 839, 1015, 1016
Runco, M. A., 821
Ruoppila, I., 296, 297
Rusch, F., 207, 1089, 1091, 1092, 1094, 1095
Ruskin, E., 235, 236, 237, 253, 323, 342, 394, 397, 398, 655, 657, 662, 946, 1020, 1030
Russell, J., 234, 344, 350, 368, 370, 372, 373, 388, 608, 609, 611, 612, 613, 614, 615, 616, 635, 642, 836, 837
Russell, T., 666, 667
Russo, A., 1124
Russo, D. C., 1129
Russo, F., 552
Russo, L., 551
Russo, M., 77
Russon, A. E., 383
Rutgers, A. H., 322
Rutherford, J. B., Jr., 903
Rutherford, M., 88, 191, 321, 396, 397, 634
Ruttenberg, B. A., 744, 750
Rutter, M., 5, 6, 7, 8, 9, 10, 11, 12, 14, 15, 17, 18, 21, 23, 26, 28, 30, 31, 32, 33, 34, 45, 51, 65, 70, 72, 73, 76, 78, 79, 81, 91, 93, 95, 97, 107, 108, 110, 165, 167, 168, 169, 170, 175, 180, 201, 202, 203, 204, 205, 206, 207, 208, 209, 210, 212,

213, 214, 215, 216, 227, 228, 232, 237, 288, 290, 292, 293, 294, 295, 296, 297, 298, 299, 312, 313, 314, 315, 318, 322, 323, 324, 335, 336, 341, 342, 343, 344, 345, 346, 347, 348, 349, 351, 352, 355, 373, 408, 412, 418, 425, 426, 427, 428, 429, 430, 432, 434, 435, 436, 438, 439, 441, 442, 443, 453, 455, 462, 489, 500, 515, 520, 534, 536, 537, 538, 539, 546, 547, 553, 554, 584, 585, 588, 591, 592, 594, 599, 613, 628, 632, 650, 661, 731, 732, 740, 741, 753, 756, 760, 763, 775, 779, 780, 781, 783, 820, 832, 834, 1088, 1240, 1244
Rutter, M. J., 110
Rutter, M. L., 180, 189, 247, 248, 249, 255, 256, 265, 269, 707, 708, 712, 722, 731, 732, 733, 734, 740, 753, 756, 961, 962, 1124, 1143, 1201, 1215, 1216, 1244, 1305, 1306
Ryan, E., 496
Ryan, R., 102, 800
Rydelius, P.-A., 1238, 1241
Rydell, A.-M., 1243
Rydell, P., 255, 256, 777, 778, 890, 926, 927, 928, 929, 930, 932, 933, 934, 937, 938, 939, 940, 941, 961, 978, 979
Ryerse, C., 110, 317

Sabbagh, M., 258, 666
Saberski, L., 456
Sabo, H., 549
Sabry, M. A., 551
Sachdev, P., 839
Sacks, O., 590, 1283
Sadato, N., 665
Saeger, K., 455
Saelens, T., 539
Saelid, G., 462
Saemundsen, E., 5, 49, 55, 59, 753
Saez, L., 553
Safir, M. P., 73, 80, 1312
Safran, J. S., 1015
Saha, A. R., 1106
Sahakian, B. J., 609
Sahl, R., 297
Sai, F., 689
Sainato, D., 968, 1031
Saito, Y., 460
Saitoh, O., 367, 368, 494, 496, 499, 519, 1305

Sakaguchi, M., 1225
Sakuragawa, N., 140
Sale, P., 619
Saliba, E., 483
Saliba, J. R., 109
Saliba, K., 123, 519, 661
Salisbury, D. M., 16, 80, 82
Salthammer, E., 154
Saltmarsh, R., 608, 614
Salvia, J., 713
Salzberg, C. L., 912
Sam, I. L., 140
Samdperil, D. L., 1016
Sampen, S., 1125
Sampson, J., 543, 545
Samren, E. B., 556
Samson, Y., 373
Samuels, M., 151, 153
Sanchez, L., 739, 839, 1107
Sandberg, A., 234, 1306
Sanders, C., 253
Sanders, G., 461
Sanders, J. L., 305
Sanders, M. R., 1060, 1062
Sanders, R. S., 499
Sandler, A. D., 1112
Sandler, R. H., 541
Sandman, C. A., 189, 459,
    460, 461, 462
Sandow, D., 1094
Sandson, J., 608
Sandstrom, M., 540, 832
Sanford, M., 733
Sangiorgi, E., 551
Sankar, D. V. S., 464
Santangelo, S., 170, 173,
    489, 500, 501, 536
Santarcangelo, S., 910
Santogrossi, J., 885, 951
Santos, C. W., 1110, 1111
Santucci, M., 502
Sapuan, S., 956
Sarlo-McGarvey, N., 147
Sarne, Y., 459, 462, 1252
Sarokoff, R. A., 871
Sarria, E., 320
Sartorius, N., 17
Sasagawa, E., 254
Sasaki, M., 325, 834, 1176,
    1177
Sasaki, N., 141
Sassi, R. B., 491, 500
Sasso, G., 819, 823, 872,
    912, 916, 1030, 1031
Sasson, N., 412, 483
Sattler, J. M., 787, 792
Satz, P., 30
Saulnier, C., 777, 784, 793
Saunders, K., 64
Saunders, R. C., 526
Sauvage, D., 555, 751,
    1208
Savedra, J.,Perman, J., 134,
    146
Sayegh, L., 548
Sayi, A., 130
Scacheri, C., 130, 138, 139,
    148
Scafidi, F., 690
Scahill, L., 268, 269, 1102,
    1103, 1104, 1105,
    1106, 1108, 1109

Scahill, V., 634, 838
Scaife, M., 630, 653
Scalise, A., 542
Scambler, D., 229, 716,
    723
Scanlon, C., 1004
Scapagnini, U., 542
Scarborough, H. S., 345
Scariano, M. M., 1014,
    1077, 1277, 1280, 1281
Scarr, S., 656
Sceery, W. R., 27, 202,
    203, 204, 206, 207,
    208, 209, 210, 251,
    266, 288, 290, 293,
    294, 295, 297, 298,
    299, 316, 344, 352
Schaapveld, M., 903
Schachar, R., 183, 617
Schacter, D. L., 619
Schaefer, C. E., 1060, 1062,
    1065
Schaefer, G. B., 537
Schaeffer, B., 882, 883
Schaffer, B., 289, 749, 758,
    1176, 1216
Schaffer, R., 319, 323
Schain, R., 454, 455, 456,
    1195
Schall, J., 669, 670
Schanen, C., 78, 138
Scharre, J., 832
Schatz, A. M., 100, 367,
    835, 836
Schatz, J., 187, 251
Schaumann, H., 47, 49, 60,
    62, 227, 232, 329, 502,
    545, 834
Scheffer, I. E., 544
Scheibel, A., 140, 489
Scheier, C., 691
Schell, R., 819
Schellenberg, G. D., 165,
    171, 191, 651, 755
Schendel, D., 44, 49, 52,
    57, 435, 555
Schepis, M., 956, 1033
Scherer, N. J., 552
Schermer, A., 1031
Schery, T., 800
Scheuffgen, K., 641
Schicor, A., 458
Schiel, W., 143
Schiller, M., 322
Schindler, M. K., 315
Schlag, J., 668, 670
Schlag-Rey, M., 668, 670
Schlattmann, P., 64
Schleichkorn, J., 153
Schleien, S. J., 870
Schloss, P. J., 911
Schlosser, R., 802
Schmahmann, J. D., 1305
Schmall, B., 454
Schmeidler, J., 437, 753,
    754
Schmidek, M., 813
Schmidt, A. W., 1106
Schmidt, B., 142
Schmidt, D., 534
Schmidt, M., 1241
Schmidt, S., 800

Schmitz, N., 107, 493
Schmotzer, G., 546
Schnack, H. G., 493, 499
Schnecker, K., 141, 142
Schneider, H. C., 897
Schneiderman, G., 455
Schneier, F. R., 181, 182
Schoener, G., 691
Scholz, M., 646
Schopler, D., 354
Schopler, E., 10, 14, 17, 18,
    45, 64, 73, 75, 79, 169,
    186, 188, 202, 203,
    204, 206, 212, 213,
    215, 227, 238, 251,
    264, 289, 292, 293,
    294, 295, 297, 298,
    299, 302, 324, 336,
    369, 453, 539, 543,
    546, 553, 554, 667,
    707, 720, 721, 732,
    733, 734, 741, 744,
    748, 749, 757, 758,
    792, 818, 820, 889,
    926, 932, 937, 940,
    953, 978, 1004, 1005,
    1036, 1043, 1048,
    1049, 1050, 1055,
    1059, 1060, 1061,
    1064, 1065, 1066,
    1067, 1068, 1069,
    1070, 1071, 1074,
    1075, 1076, 1077,
    1089, 1132, 1175,
    1176, 1177, 1178,
    1179, 1180, 1182,
    1183, 1186, 1199,
    1216, 1310
Schouten, J., 520, 696
Schreck, K. A., 542, 752
Schreibman, L., 236, 237,
    250, 253, 261, 264,
    268, 346, 384, 393,
    394, 395, 494, 496,
    499, 821, 823, 867,
    882, 883, 884, 886,
    887, 888, 889, 890,
    912, 913, 916, 937,
    950, 953, 959, 961,
    966, 990, 991, 1004,
    1005, 1006, 1007,
    1009, 1011, 1030,
    1031, 1032, 1055,
    1058, 1060, 1061,
    1129, 1160, 1310
Schroeder, G. L., 883
Schroeder, M., 431
Schroer, R. J., 251, 501,
    550, 551
Schroth, G., 140
Schroth, P., 745, 750
Schuh-Wear, C. L., 1127,
    1128
Schuler, A., 254, 348, 691,
    773, 777, 926, 927,
    936, 938, 939, 941,
    961, 966, 967, 968,
    979, 980, 981, 983,
    984, 985, 988, 990,
    995, 997
Schuler, L., 553
Schulman, M., 30

Schultz, R., 13, 24, 91, 92,
    95, 96, 102, 104, 106,
    109, 110, 129, 138,
    143, 144, 145, 150,
    191, 234, 236, 248,
    249, 250, 275, 313,
    325, 326, 375, 412,
    419, 432, 526, 595,
    650, 651, 652, 665,
    670, 682, 683, 684,
    686, 689, 694, 696,
    699, 735, 736, 977,
    979, 982, 998
Schultz, R. A., 551
Schultz, R. B., 107, 108
Schultz, R. J., 136, 138,
    139, 145
Schultz, R. T., 5, 7, 14, 92,
    96, 105, 170, 191, 239,
    325, 365, 368, 372,
    373, 375, 376, 498,
    518, 519, 520, 521,
    522, 523, 524, 525,
    526, 696, 697, 777,
    889, 1103
Schultz, W., 670
Schulz, D. W., 1106
Schulz, S. C., 438, 463
Schumann, C. M., 108, 526
Schuntermann, P., 1056,
    1061, 1069
Schuster, J. W., 868
Schwab-Stone, M., 9, 10,
    17, 26
Schwafel, J., 476, 478, 481
Schwandt, W. L., 886
Schwartz, I., 969, 988,
    1030, 1031
Schwartz, L. S., 1128
Schwartz, M., 130, 132,
    137, 138, 492
Schwartz, S., 551
Schyns, P. G., 521, 522, 523
Scifo, R., 542
Sciscio, N., 552
Scotese-Wojtila, L., 539
Scott, F. J., 57, 254, 724
Scott, J. P., 1112
Scott, S., 429, 534, 536,
    546, 594, 663
Scotti, J. R., 915
Scourfield, J., 48, 59, 62
Scragg, P., 101, 299
Scriver, C. R., 462
Scuderi, C., 494, 499, 542,
    1307
Seal, B., 836, 955
Searle, J., 687
Sears, L., 241, 250, 267,
    498, 661
Sears, S. P., 467
Seashore, M. R., 50, 463,
    553
Secord, W., 807
Sedaghat, F., 522
Seeger, T. F., 1106
Seeman, P., 1103
Segawa, M., 127, 140, 141,
    142
Segebarth, C., 693
Seibert, J., 653, 654, 662
Seielstad, M., 431

Seifer, R., 322
Seiteberger, F., 139, 140
Sejnowski, T. J., 694
Sekhon, G. S., 551
Sekul, E. A., 127, 128, 129, 134, 135, 143, 144, 151
Selfe, L., 795
Seligman, M., 1060, 1064, 1068
Selman, R. L., 795
Seltzer, G. B., 906
Seltzer, M. M., 214, 288, 289, 290, 293, 295, 297, 323, 324, 1055, 1059, 1075, 1077
Selvin, S., 44, 49, 59, 61, 63, 184, 291
Semenuk, G., 458
Semprino, M., 552
Semrud-Clikeman, M., 619
Senft, R., 263, 691
Senju, A., 318
Sergeant, J. A., 373
Seri, S., 479, 481
Serra, M., 171, 177, 186, 187, 268
Sevcik, R., 956
Sevenich, R., 823
Sevin, B., 745, 749, 751, 951
Sevin, J., 719, 720, 721, 745, 749, 750, 751, 833, 951
Seymour, P. A., 1106
Seys, D. M., 1127
Sfaello, I., 517
Shabani, D. B., 267, 870
Shafer, K., 969, 990, 991, 1030
Shafer, M. S., 1030, 1088
Shaffer, D., 14, 15, 17, 200, 695, 762, 1240
Shah, A., 101, 209, 210, 214, 290, 299, 589, 597, 635, 642, 643, 790, 838, 839, 840
Shah, B., 189, 839, 1310
Shah, P., 1108
Shahbazian, M., 132, 137, 138, 431, 432
Shahmoon-Shanok, R., 1310
Shakal, J., 539
Shaked, M., 1058
Shallice, T., 670
Shalock, R. L., 1096
Shamow, N. A., 897
Shannak, K., 142
Shannon, M., 537
Shanske, A., 544
Shao, Y., 32, 429, 432, 433, 439, 753, 754
Shapiro, A. K., 588
Shapiro, B., 800
Shapiro, E. G., 44, 57, 61
Shapiro, E. S., 588
Shapiro, H., 712
Shapiro, T., 17, 184, 249, 251, 261, 321, 324, 346, 409, 416, 417, 453, 520, 707, 749
Sharbrough, F. W., 476, 479
Share, L. J., 645

Sharpe, P. A., 152
Sharpe, S., 613
Sharpley, C., 1058, 1064, 1065, 1069
Shattuck, P., 214, 288, 289, 290, 293, 324
Shavelle, R. M., 212, 293, 295, 296, 297
Shaw, D. W., 170, 172, 493, 496, 497, 498, 501
Shaw, S., 261
Shay, J., 839
Shaywitz, B. A., 453, 455, 456, 457, 459, 492, 744
Shea, E., 690
Shea, M. C., 822
Shea, V., 266, 292, 298, 299, 301, 302, 1050, 1061, 1069, 1073, 1184
Shearer, D. D., 886, 990
Shearer, T. R., 539
Shedlorski, J. G., 467
Sheehan, D. V., 1282
Sheely, R., 958, 967
Sheffield, V., 438, 754
Sheikh, R. M., 1105
Sheinkopf, S., 235, 319, 349, 800, 948, 962, 1008, 1064
Sheitman, B. B., 27, 839, 847, 1107
Shekhar, A., 526
Sheldon, J. B., 916, 1098
Sheldon, S., 544, 551
Shell, J., 1102, 1104
Shellenberger, S., 980
Shepard, B. A., 173
Shepherd, C., 51, 545, 594
Shepherd, M., 14, 15, 17, 1240
Sheppard, D. M., 1308
Sheppard, V., 1112
Sherer, M., 886, 887, 888, 908
Sheridan, S. M., 1063
Sherman, J. A., 883, 916, 1098
Sherman, M., 251, 321, 416, 417
Sherman, S. L., 546
Sherman, T., 7, 185, 233, 236, 237, 253, 254, 317, 318, 320, 321, 369, 392, 394, 653, 656, 665, 667, 669, 707, 738
Shernoff, E., 722, 752
Sherr, E. H., 544
Sherrard, E., 477
Sherwin, A. C., 167, 460
Sheslow, B. V., 373
Shestakova, A., 481, 482
Shevell, M. I., 107, 535, 646
Shewmon, D. A., 503
Shields, W. D., 354
Shields-Wolfe, J., 1088
Shigley, R. H., 1055, 1060, 1064, 1069, 1178
Shih, J. C., 539
Shimizu, Y., 47, 435, 546
Shinnar, S., 65, 76, 79, 80, 82, 202, 204, 205, 206,

212, 213, 214, 288, 289, 290, 291, 292, 293, 296, 298, 299, 502, 534, 538, 1305, 1307, 1311, 1312
Shinohara, M., 140
Shinomiya, M., 502, 503, 1225
Shiotsuki, M., 46
Shiotsuki, Y., 540
Shipley-Benamou, R., 886
Shirakawa, Y., 461, 539
Shirataki, S., 47, 1223
Shoaf, S. E., 454
Shoemaker, J., 1128
Shoenfeld, Y., 542
Shoji, H., 46, 540
Shook, J., 483
Shores, R., 968, 1030
Short, A., 17, 73, 79, 227, 707, 1048, 1050, 1182
Short, C. B., 336
Short, L., 633
Short, M., 543
Shoshan, Y., 926, 941, 1049
Showalter, D., 30
Shprintzen, R. J., 552
Shrader, C., 1021
Shriberg, L., 256, 293, 343, 348, 352, 813, 962
Shu, B. C., 607
Shubin, R. A., 543
Shukla, S., 267
Shulman, C., 224, 341, 342, 343, 474, 551, 730, 732, 734, 740, 748, 749, 753, 1176, 1178
Shulman, L., 76, 79, 80, 82, 1312
Shuster, A., 438
Shuster, L., 1281
Shyamsundar, M. M., 543
Shyi, G. C. W., 640
Shyu, V., 635, 844
Sicotte, N., 367, 617
Siebelink, B. M., 503
Siegal, B., 348, 592, 730, 732, 734, 739, 740, 750
Siegal, D. J., 263
Siegal, M., 660
Siegel, A., 1064
Siegel, B., xix, 13, 16, 17, 18, 19, 21, 29, 31, 45, 72, 73, 93, 174, 175, 179, 184, 232, 233, 234, 248, 294, 314, 317, 323, 335, 541, 542, 707, 708, 709, 713, 717, 718, 948, 984, 1008, 1056, 1069, 1221
Siegel, B. V., 496, 617
Siegel, B. V., Jr., 367
Siegel, D. J., 97, 103, 257, 263, 264, 295, 367, 387, 487, 835, 1306
Siegel, G., 293, 804, 883
Siegel, L., 1273
Sievers, P., 44, 57, 61
Sigafoos, J., 542, 870
Sigman, M., 7, 170, 173, 185, 233, 234, 235,

236, 237, 238, 251, 253, 254, 258, 260, 261, 318, 319, 320, 321, 322, 323, 324, 325, 335, 342, 350, 369, 382, 385, 386, 392, 394, 397, 398, 409, 410, 411, 415, 416, 520, 521, 526, 630, 631, 652, 653, 654, 655, 656, 657, 658, 659, 660, 662, 665, 667, 669, 670, 671, 673, 702, 707, 724, 738, 740, 741, 750, 751, 753, 755, 757, 833, 836, 946, 961, 962, 1007, 1011, 1020, 1030
Sigurdardóttir, S., 753
Sikich, L., 1111
Silahtaroglu, A., 130, 132, 137, 138
Silberg, J., 430
Siller, M., 254, 320, 335
Sillibourne, J., 550
Silva, A. E., 551
Silva, E., 551
Silveira, E. L., 553
Silver, E. J., 1062
Silver, M., 261
Silverman, J. M., 429, 432, 433, 437, 439, 474, 550, 753, 754
Silverstein, M. L., 181
Sim, C. H., 617
Sim, L., 426
Simell, O., 545
Simensen, R. J., 251, 501
Simeon, J., 501
Simeonsson, R. J., 351, 820, 962, 1057, 1068, 1074
Simion, F., 317, 318
Simizu, Y., 502, 503
Simmel, M., 525, 697
Simmonds, H. A., 464
Simmonoff, E., 632
Simmons, A., 373, 419, 435, 525, 526, 541, 615, 652, 666
Simmons, H., 49, 60
Simmons, J., 962
Simmons, J. Q., 256, 346, 882, 887, 1089, 1180, 1306
Simmons, J. Q., III., 393
Simon, E. W., 550, 551
Simon, J., 107, 492, 499, 539, 768
Simon, N., 6
Simonoff, E., 108, 170, 425, 426, 427, 430, 434, 438, 441, 442, 500, 536, 537, 538, 553
Simpson, G. M., 838, 848
Simpson, R., 113, 354, 374, 375, 867, 868, 869, 872, 907, 913, 929, 930, 985, 986, 996, 1018, 1021, 1022, 1123, 1129

Sims, A., 167, 169, 757
Simson, R., 479, 480
Sinclair, B. D., 499
Sinclair, J., 1022, 1284
Sinclair, L., 949
Singer, G. H. S., 1060, 1063, 1068, 1092
Singer, H. S., 137
Singer, J., 321, 323
Singer, W., 690, 695
Singh, N., 493, 501, 536, 646, 660, 762, 915
Singh, S., 74, 76
Singh, T., 536
Singh, V., 539, 542
Sinka, I., 804
Siperstein, R., 31, 73, 79
Siponmaa, L., 299
Siqueland, E., 689
Sirian, L., 613
Sirianni, N., 130, 136, 138, 139, 148
Sirota, K. G., 868
Sisson, L., 266, 967
Sitter, S., 177
Siu, V. M., 544
Sjogreen, L., 553
Sjöholm, E., 46
Sjöholm-Lif, E., 1243
Sjostedt, A., 551
Skender, M., 136, 144
Skinner, B. F., 1006, 1125, 1155
Skinner, C., 501
Skinner, M., 546, 547
Skinner, S. A., 550, 551
Skjeldal, O., 5, 48, 54, 55, 129, 130, 131, 132, 147, 149, 535
Skoff, B. F., 476
Skotko, B. G., 154, 155
Skudlarski, P., 522, 696
Skuse, D. H., 433, 434, 544
Slangen, J. L., 482
Slavik, B. A., 1014
Slifer, K. J., 825
Slifer, M., 753
Sloan, J., 1057, 1068, 1074, 1075, 1076
Sloan, M. E., 1126, 1138
Sloane, H. N., 1125
Sloman, L., 544
Slomka, G. T., 1107
Slonims, V., 127, 248
Small, A. M., 189, 460, 461, 462, 501, 739, 1102, 1104, 1107, 1112
Smalley, S., 51, 182, 185, 208, 295, 428, 430, 536, 537, 545, 549, 769, 1305, 1307
Smania, N., 691
Smári, J., 753
Smedegaard, N., 1238, 1239
Smeeth, L., 61, 316, 317
Smit, A. M., 503
Smith, A., 542, 633, 902
Smith, B., 266, 371, 408, 1056, 1057
Smith, C., 869, 926, 1062

Smith, C. E., 821, 897, 916
Smith, C. J., 429, 432, 433, 437, 439, 474, 550, 753, 754
Smith, E. O., 141
Smith, I. M., 44, 47, 100, 184, 237, 291, 294, 295, 320, 384, 387, 388, 389, 539, 835, 836, 837
Smith, K., 515, 874
Smith, L., 105, 147, 149, 369, 691, 695, 849
Smith, M., 51, 207, 503, 544, 545, 550, 551, 769, 1078
Smith, M. A., 46
Smith, M. D., 298, 302, 902, 904, 905, 916, 1091, 1093
Smith, N. J., 435
Smith, P., 61, 254, 393, 395, 396, 399, 1307
Smith, P. G., 316, 317
Smith, P. K., 394
Smith, R., 544, 1127, 1148
Smith, R. C., 848
Smith, R. G., 901, 907
Smith, S. M., 521
Smith, T., 155, 239, 253, 343, 708, 874, 915, 926, 929, 949, 951, 953, 987, 1004, 1007, 1009, 1012, 1044, 1048, 1058, 1132, 1141
Smits, A. P., 545
Smoker, W. R., 548
Snauwaert, D. T., 1092, 1093
Snead, R. W., 1108
Sneed, T. J., 1126
Snell, M., 821, 868
Snell, R. G., 543, 545
Snidman, N., 983
Snow, M. E., 17, 184, 261, 324, 409, 459, 460, 462, 520, 707, 749, 1208
Snowling, M., 255, 263, 641, 642
Snyder, D., 29, 30, 524
Snyder, J., 521
Snyderman, M., 788
Soares, D., 740
Soares, J. C., 1305
Sobel, N., 526
Sobesky, W. E., 545
Sobsey, D., 290, 1075, 1093
Sofic, E., 139, 141, 142, 145
Sofronoff, K., 1064, 1065
Sohlberg, M. M., 619
Sohmer, H., 476
Sokol, D. K., 463
Sokol, M. S., 1112
Sokolski, K. N., 541, 1112
Solimando, A., 660
Solnick, J. V., 1089
Solomon, O., 868
Somaia, M., 661

Sommerschild, H., 1243
Song, Y., 541
Soni, W., 666, 667
Sonksen, P., 554, 589
Soper, H. V., 30, 900
Soprano, A. M., 1228, 1230
Sörensen, S. A., 50
Sorgi, P., 189
Souders, M. C., 542
Sourkes, T. L., 456, 457
South, M., 213, 251, 375, 542, 616, 653, 722, 731, 736, 752, 757, 762, 1112
Southall, D., 151, 153
Sowers, J., 1093
Sowinski, J., 434
Spagnola, M., 1062
Sparen, P., 539
Sparks, B. F., 170, 172, 493, 496, 497, 498, 501, 536, 646, 660
Sparling, J. W., 224
Sparrevohn, R., 106
Sparrow, S., 24, 234, 315, 316, 367, 374, 595, 628, 682, 777, 793, 800, 804, 845
Sparrow, S. A., 315
Sparrow, S. S., 24, 25, 28, 33, 83, 91, 96, 97, 103, 104, 107, 108, 111, 170, 173, 177, 183, 186, 213, 225, 227, 238, 251, 252, 294, 316, 324, 325, 375, 412, 520, 689, 696, 719, 720, 735, 736, 738, 750, 754, 755, 772, 773, 777, 782, 783, 784, 789, 793, 835
Spaulding, P., 554
Spechler, L., 183
Speck-Martins, C. E., 553
Spector, S., 458
Speed, W. C., 438
Spellman, R. A., 550
Speltz, M. L., 1029
Spence, A., 946
Spence, M. A., 537, 550
Spence, S. J., 432, 433
Spencer, A., 318, 324, 409, 520, 740
Spencer, C., 431, 432
Spencer, E. K., 189, 838, 839, 840, 847
Spencer, E. S., 1112
Spencer, T., 1109
Spengler, P., 914
Spengler-Schelley, M., 964
Spiegle-Cohen, J., 660
Spielman, R. S., 431
Spiker, D., 170, 315, 415, 426, 432, 433, 437, 440, 617, 754
Spinner, N. B., 551
Spirtos, G., 553
Spitz, R., 317, 1304
Spitzer, R., 15, 16, 17, 45, 184, 592, 707, 708
Spong, A., 634

Sponheim, E., 5, 48, 54, 55, 432, 535, 542, 735, 736, 748
Sponseller, P. D., 150, 153, 154
Spradlin, J. E., 819, 822, 883, 884
Sprague, J. R., 822, 823, 824, 825, 903, 911, 1010
Sprague, R. L., 847, 848
Spratling, M. W., 549
Springer, J., 749, 1072
Spurkland, I., 1239
Square-Storer, P., 957
Squires, J., 710, 712
Squires, K., 479, 480
Squires, N., 480
Squires, T., 261
Srinath, S., 457
Srinivasan, M., 139
Sriram, N., 871, 956
St. George, M., 549
St. James, P. J., 258, 350
Stach, B. A., 147, 148
Stackhaus, J., 1032
Stackhouse, T., 237, 321, 342, 384, 385, 386, 387, 388, 837, 847
Stafford, N., 261
Staghezza, B., 732
Stahl, S. M., 454, 455, 456
Stahmer, A., 237, 253, 384, 393, 394, 395, 867, 884, 886, 888, 889, 890, 913, 1004, 1009, 1011
Staib, L., 523
Stanhope, S. J., 839
Stanley, J. A., 491, 500
Stansfield, B., 697
Stanton, A., 1074
Stapells, D. R., 844
Stark, J. A., 1088, 1093
Starkstein, S. E., 107, 494, 499, 519, 537, 538
Starr, A., 476, 479
Starr, E., 5, 426, 427
Stary, J. M., 463, 490
State, R. C., 27, 267, 1106
Stauder, J., 234, 368, 643
Stedge, D., 27, 189, 1110
Steege, M., 912, 916
Steel, R., 335
Steele, R., 204, 206, 215, 288, 293, 962, 1304
Steele, S., 521
Steenhuis, M. P., 177, 268
Steere, D. E., 1091
Steerneman, P., 758
Stefanatos, G., 541, 1112
Stefanos, G. A., 503
Steffenburg, S., 47, 49, 60, 62, 108, 186, 199, 202, 204, 213, 215, 291, 293, 296, 425, 534, 538, 545, 551, 553, 1305
Steffenburg, U., 129, 291, 551

Steffens, M., 235, 319, 349, 800, 962
Steg, J. P., 501
Stehli, A., 1281, 1284
Stein, D. J., 266
Stein, M. T., 81
Stein, R. E. K., 1062
Steinberg, M., 169
Steiner, V., 800, 804
Steingard, R., 28, 189, 1108, 1111
Steinhausen, H., 46, 184
Steinhoff, K., 1109
Steinschneider, M., 1306, 1307
Steir, D., 169, 175
Stella, J., 319, 657, 721, 724, 750, 800, 833, 947
Stellern, J., 794
Stellfeld, M., 435
Stenbom, Y., 132
Stephan, M., 556
Stephenson, J. B., 127, 136, 147, 148
Stergaard, O., 551
Stern, D., 225, 234, 236, 260, 319, 383, 673, 836, 980
Stern, L., 479
Sternbach, H., 460
Stevens, M., 1306, 1307
Stevenson, C. L., 871
Stevenson, C. S., 619
Stevenson, J., 418, 454, 554, 580, 595, 838, 848
Stevenson, R. E., 501, 538
Stevenson, R. J., 619
Stewart, K., 984
Stewart, M. A., 427
Stewart, M. P., 1032
Stewart, T. G., 489
Stich, S., 659, 673
Stiebel, D., 1064
Stier, D., 17, 72, 73, 79, 223, 593, 707
Stipek, D. J., 324, 415
Stirling, J., 520
Stockard, J. E., 476, 479
Stockard, J. J., 476, 479
Stoddart, K., 212
Stodgell, C. J., 494
Stoecker, J. J., 645
Stoel-Gammon, C., 960
Stoiber, K. C., 1059
Stokes, D., 101
Stokes, P. E., 460
Stokes, R., 950
Stokes, T. F., 826, 827
Stokwell, M., 501
Stone, D. H., 547
Stone, J. L., 1307
Stone, K. R., 384, 389
Stone, R. L., 464
Stone, V., 88, 524, 526, 615, 630, 634, 1306
Stone, W., 31, 225, 227, 228, 229, 231, 232, 233, 235, 236, 237, 238, 251, 316, 317, 319, 320, 321, 351, 355, 366, 384, 385,

386, 408, 409, 655, 707, 708, 712, 717, 718, 721, 732, 734, 799, 801, 833, 834, 835, 836, 837, 843, 947, 962, 1007, 1011, 1056, 1068
Stoof, J. C., 1103
Stores, G., 542
Storey, K., 822, 824, 825, 903, 968, 990, 991
Storm, K., 1095
Storoschuk, S., 31, 32, 335, 344, 408, 520, 731, 732, 740, 741, 753
Stott, C., 632, 645
Stott, D. H., 835
Stowe, J., 435, 541
Stowe, M. J., 1124
Stowe, R. M., 613
Stowitschek, J. J., 912, 1091
Strain, P., 708, 870, 897, 898, 899, 912, 937, 938, 939, 940, 953, 967, 968, 990, 991, 1004, 1011, 1030, 1031, 1035, 1045, 1046, 1047, 1057, 1061, 1064, 1074, 1129, 1130
Strandburg, R. J., 481
Stratton, J., 1017, 1018, 1019
Stratton, K., 435
Stratton, M., 847
Strauss, D. J., 212, 293, 295, 296, 297
Strayer, D. L., 368, 370, 372, 498, 608, 609, 611, 616, 617, 643, 836
Streedback, D., 1127
Streiner, D., 24, 93, 95, 100, 101, 110, 174, 213, 252, 269, 317, 343, 345, 719, 734, 735, 736, 743, 845, 1014
Stremel-Campbell, K., 1076
Striano, T., 395, 398
Strik, W., 521
Strogatz, M., 541
Stromer, R., 871
Stromland, K., 544, 553
Stromme, P., 544, 548
Strong, C., 813
Strouse, M. C., 916
Strunk, P., 1240, 1241
Strupp, K., 64
Stubbs, E. G., 476, 544
Student, M., 476
Stump, M. H., 547
Stuphorn, V., 669, 670
Sturmey, P., 60, 211, 719, 721, 745, 749, 750
Stuss, D., 371, 613, 669, 671
Subhani-Siddique, R., 542, 1112
Subramaniam, B., 141

Suckling, J., 107, 493, 666, 667
Suddendorf, T., 266, 389
Sudhalter, V., 30, 335, 345
Sue, C. M., 550
Sugayama, S. M., 553
Sugiura, M., 389, 662, 663
Sugiyama, T., 44, 47, 478, 1224
Sulkes, J., 1220
Sullivan, C. L., 870, 876
Sullivan, K., 259, 260, 344, 354, 549, 552, 698
Sullivan, M. W., 149
Sullivan, N., 723
Sullivan, R. C., 1089, 1257, 1263
Sulmont, V., 459, 461
Sulzer-Azaroff, B., 890, 953, 1011, 1030, 1031, 1130
Summers, C. G., 554
Summers, J. A., 1078
Summers, S. A., 1092, 1093
Sundberg, C., 963, 964
Sundberg, M., 929, 932, 933, 937, 939, 941, 963, 964
Sundram, B. S., 549
Sung, K., 486
Sungum-Paliwal, R., 266, 408
Sungum-Paliwal, S. R., 48, 52, 54, 61, 63
Suratt, A., 832, 833
Surian, L., 258, 352
Surratt, A., 912, 913, 951
Susnjara, I. M., 459
Sussman, F., 936, 958, 966
Susuki, I., 141
Sutcliffe, J. S., 545
Sutton, K., 956, 1112
Sutton, S., 669
Suwa, S., 461
Suzuki, H., 140
Svennerholm, B. A., 142
Svennerholm, L., 139, 457, 459
Svenson, B., 588
Sverd, J., 209, 456, 457, 463
Swaab-Barneveld, H., 169, 171, 412
Swanson, J., 617, 1109
Swartz, K. L., 838, 848
Swayne, S., 542
Swayze, S., 542
Swe, A., 214, 288, 289, 290, 293, 324
Swedo, S. E., 266
Sweeney, J., 185, 373, 456, 458, 484, 485, 496, 498, 832
Sweeney, M. H., 384, 389
Sweet, R. D., 588
Sweeten, T. L., 526
Sweetland-Baker, M., 257, 912
Sweetman, L., 544
Swettenham, J., 31, 48, 52, 54, 57, 60, 105, 227, 229, 231, 232, 233, 234, 235, 237, 266,

320, 342, 369, 384, 410, 434, 613, 634, 643, 652, 654, 655, 656, 657, 665, 707, 708, 709, 713, 714, 715, 716, 730, 732, 733, 734, 741, 754, 755, 763, 832, 837, 847, 947, 961, 1307
Swiderski, R. E., 1307
Swiezy, N., 267, 912, 1109
Swisher, C. N., 553
Swisher, C. W., 1305
Switala, A. E., 107, 474, 488, 1305
Sylvester, O., 462
Symons, F. J., 265, 267, 839, 847
Symons, L. A., 689
Syrota, A., 373
Sytema, S., 753
Szatmari, P., 8, 13, 17, 18, 19, 24, 31, 72, 77, 78, 88, 92, 93, 94, 95, 97, 100, 101, 103, 104, 109, 110, 118, 169, 170, 172, 173, 174, 175, 179, 183, 184, 185, 186, 187, 202, 203, 204, 206, 207, 210, 211, 213, 216, 232, 233, 234, 248, 252, 256, 257, 258, 269, 288, 295, 297, 298, 299, 317, 323, 348, 372, 373, 375, 427, 437, 477, 478, 491, 586, 590, 595, 606, 607, 628, 719, 730, 731, 732, 733, 734, 735, 736, 739, 740, 743, 750, 753, 754, 845, 984, 1014, 1058, 1066, 1074, 1221
Szatmark, I., 45
Szechter, L., 697
Szechtman, H., 521
Szekely, B., 459, 462
Szekely, G., 1220, 1252
Szentagothai, J., 489
Szivos, S. E., 207
Szurek, S., 209
Szymanski, E., 1091
Szymanski, L., 546, 594

Tableau, F., 459, 462
Tabuteau, F., 1112
Tachataki, M., 543, 545
Tachibana, R., 46, 52, 227, 455, 456, 459, 460, 461, 834, 1224
Tadevosyan, O., 439
Tadevosyan-Leyfer, O., 32, 731, 733, 754, 755
Taft, L. T., 594
Tager-Flusberg, H., 104, 106, 185, 234, 256, 257, 258, 259, 260, 291, 293, 336, 342, 343, 344, 345, 346, 347, 348, 350, 353, 354, 369, 373, 439,

Tager-Flusberg *(Continued)* 549, 630, 631, 641, 698, 960, 962, 1306
Taiminen, T., 102
Taira, R., 1223
Takagi, K., 1281
Takagi, N., 138
Takahashi, T., 60, 435, 501, 536
Takatsu, T., 455
Takekuma, K., 541
Takesada, M., 461, 463, 1226
Takeuchi, A. H., 644
Takeuchi, K., 262
Takita, H., 661
Talay-Ongan, A., 832, 833, 834, 843
Tallal, P., 1308
Tallis, J., 1228, 1230
Tamarit, J., 320
Tamis-LeMonda, C. S., 236
Tamminga, C. A., 1106
Tamulonis, D., 553
Tanaka, J. R., 520
Tanaka, J. W., 697
Tanaka, K., 50, 463, 553
Tanaka, M., 691
Tancredi, R., 551
Tanguay, P., 32, 51, 167, 169, 173, 181, 182, 183, 208, 295, 428, 476, 478, 481, 542, 545, 751, 754, 755, 757, 769, 782, 1124, 1134, 1139
Tani, Y., 458
Tankersley, M., 886, 887
Tanoue, Y., 47
Tantam, D., 92, 93, 94, 95, 97, 100, 101, 107, 109, 124, 179, 183, 184, 203, 204, 206, 208, 210, 212, 295, 297, 299, 519, 520, 586, 735, 979, 983
Tao, Kuo-Tai., 1203
Tao, L., 349
Tarabulsy, G. M., 690
Taras, M., 915, 938, 949
Tardieu, M., 77, 138
Tardif, C., 519, 520
Tarr, M., 696
Tassone, F., 545
Taubman, M., 886
Tayama, M., 172, 461, 499, 539
Taylor, A., 181, 342, 545, 569, 844
Taylor, B., 48, 54, 60, 253, 257, 435, 541, 868, 870, 871, 872, 1044, 1046, 1064, 1074
Taylor, C., 594, 755, 756, 870
Taylor, E., 79, 593, 615
Taylor, G., 263
Taylor, H. G., 295
Taylor, J., 901, 903
Taylor, M., 476, 483, 666
Taylor, N. D., 253, 392
Taylor, T., 669, 670

Teague, L. A., 1107
Teal, M. B., 730, 749
Teasdale, J., 668
Tebbenkamp, K., 872, 876, 1020
Teberg, A. J., 544
Teebi, A. S., 130
Teeter, P. A., 619
Teitelbaum, O., 387, 837
Teitelbaum, P., 387, 837
Temlett, J. A., 1103
Tempelaars, A., 543
Temple, E., 1308
Tendero, A., 544
ten Hove, F., 183
Tentler, D., 109
Terenius, L., 76, 142, 462
Terpstra, J. E., 322
Terro, F., 551
Terzic, I. M., 459
Terzic, J., 459
Tesch, D., 898, 903
Tessier, R., 690
Testa, M., 183
Teunisse, J. P., 324, 372, 610, 613, 644
Thaiss, L., 632, 666
Thal, D., 337, 800
Tharp, R. G., 1126
Thelen, E., 691, 695, 849
Themner, U., 177
Thibadeau, S., 1183
Thibault, G., 542
Thiemann, K. S., 887, 1033
Thirrupathy, K., 541
Thirumalai, S. S., 543
Thivierge, J., 31, 170, 172, 476, 477, 731, 735, 754
Thomas, G., 991
Thomas, H. V., 543, 545
Thomas, J., 1176
Thomas, M. A., 1092
Thomas, M. W., 543
Thomas, N. S., 551, 552
Thomas, S., 839, 1246
Thompsen, W., 44
Thompson, A., 170, 173, 190
Thompson, E., 686, 687, 688, 690, 691
Thompson, K. J., 551
Thompson, P. M., 1305
Thompson, R. A., 322
Thompson, R. J., 551, 552
Thompson, S. J., 237, 253, 384, 393, 395
Thompson, T., 461, 462
Thomsen, P., 101, 590
Thomson, J., 619
Thomson, M., 438, 541
Thorin, E., 1092
Thorndike, E. L., 1006
Thorne, G. L., 1126
Thorp, D. M., 394, 884, 1009, 1011
Thorpe, J., 548, 900
Thorsen, P., 44, 49, 52, 57, 435
Thorson, N., 264
Thulborn, K. R., 373, 485, 496, 525

Thurber, C., 259, 260, 348, 353
Thurm, A., 723
Thvedt, J., 907
Thyer, B. A., 905
Tidhar, S., 433
Tidmarsh, L., 53, 102
Tidswell, T., 613
Tiegerman, E., 934
Tien, A., 485, 607
Tierney, E., 544, 547, 762, 1102, 1103, 1104
Tigue, Z., 489, 492, 493, 499, 501, 519, 524, 661
Tildon, J. T., 541, 1112
Tilton, J. R., 321, 394
Timm, M., 968, 1030
Timonen, E., 534, 544
Tines, J., 1094
Tinline, C., 268, 588
Tint, G. S., 454
Tipper, S., 609
Tirosh, E., 49, 73, 80, 1 312
Tisdale, B., 489, 553, 836
Titus, E., 455
Titus, J. B., 539
Tobias, R., 431
Tobin, A., 83, 804
Tobing, L. E., 1055, 1057
Toci, L., 261
Todd, A. W., 897, 898, 899
Todd, R. D., 32, 95, 315, 440, 746, 754
Toga, A., 499
Toichi, M., 371
Tojo, Y., 318
Tolbert, L., 539
Tolkin-Eppel, P., 343
Tolosa, E. S., 108, 519
Tomasello, M., 236, 237, 318, 336, 337, 369, 383, 390, 395, 398, 630, 653, 654, 656, 657, 670, 978, 979
Tomblin, J. B., 257, 353, 598
Tomchek, S., 847
Tomkins, S., 543
Tomlins, M., 427
Tommasi, L., 692
Tommerup, N., 130, 132, 137, 138
Tompkins, L. M., 616
Tonge, B., 104, 265, 266, 542, 548, 610, 836, 1061, 1065, 1197, 1198, 1199, 1201
Toombs, K., 871, 876, 886
Toomey, K. E., 185
Topaloglu, H., 130
Topcu, M., 130, 153
Tordjman, S., 459, 460, 461, 462, 1208
Torrente, F., 438, 541
Torrisi, L., 551
Toruner, G. A., 130
Toth, K., 5, 31, 171, 233, 234, 375, 388, 612, 613, 656, 657, 662, 663, 665, 668, 670

Toth, S. L., 1062
Touchette, P. E., 824, 899
Tourrette, C., 394
Towbin, K. E., 28, 116, 169, 181, 182, 187, 189, 190
Townsend, J., 367, 368, 483, 493, 539, 610, 617, 655, 656, 659, 660, 663, 668, 671, 832, 889, 1305
Tpocu, M., 130
Trad, P. V., 249
Tramer, M., 1239
Tran, C. Q., 21, 77, 78, 130, 136, 138, 431, 432
Tranel, D., 497, 524, 526
Traphagen, J., 966
Trasowech, J., 257, 819, 823, 950, 953
Trauner, D. A., 100, 144, 145, 367, 835, 836
Traversay, J., 662
Travis, L., 961, 962, 1030
Treanor, J., 436
Trecker, A., 835, 849
Treffert, D., 46, 596
Tremblay, L., 670
Trentacoste, S. V., 1309
Trentalange, M. J., 538
Trescher, W. H., 547
Tress, B., 492
Trevarthen, C., 319, 325, 383, 673
Trevathan, E., 127, 128, 132, 134
Triggs, W., 502
Trillingsgaard, A., 105, 325, 551, 682
Trimble, M., 593
Tripathi, H. L., 142
Trivedi, M. H., 542
Trivedi, R., 140
Trivette, C., 932
Tronick, E. Z., 690
Tronick., 981
Troscianko, T., 692
Troutman, A. C., 903, 907, 908, 913
Truhan, A. P., 543
Trupin, E. W., 1110
Trygstad, O., 462, 539
Tryon, A. S., 886
Tsai, L., 18, 24, 27, 28, 30, 33, 50, 91, 93, 101, 102, 120, 187, 210, 248, 266, 299, 344, 373, 427, 434, 494, 499, 536, 539, 544, 547, 548, 593, 594, 734, 790
Tsai, M. C., 30
Tsatsanis, K., 367, 372, 374, 498, 520, 586, 665, 670, 789, 985, 995
Tsiouri, I., 947
Tsuang, M. T., 183
Tsuruhara, T., 461
Tu, J. B., 455
Tuchman, R., 65, 76, 79, 80, 82, 202, 204, 205,

206, 212, 213, 214,
224, 288, 289, 290,
291, 292, 293, 295,
296, 298, 299, 502,
503, 534, 538, 555,
657, 721, 724, 750,
832, 1305, 1307, 1311,
1312
Tucker, D., 247, 275, 651,
655, 669, 670
Tucker, R. M., 1308
Tudmay, A. J., 139
Tuff, L., 104, 174, 183,
372, 373, 375, 437,
606, 607, 628
Tulving, E., 370, 371, 669,
671
Tumuluru, R., 1110
Tunali, B., 257, 258, 259,
260, 264, 352, 353,
1064
Tunali-Kotoski, B., 258,
261, 324, 354, 385,
412
Turanli, G., 130
Turbott, S. H., 1110
Turic, D., 431
Turk, J., 544, 546
Turkeltaub, P. E., 518
Turnbull, A. P., 897, 1078,
1092, 1093, 1129
Turnbull, H. R., 1078,
1092, 1124
Turner, D., 476
Turner, L. M., 712, 718
Turner, M., 265, 608, 609,
616
Turnpenny, P., 555, 556
Turton, L., 1006
Tuten, H., 152
Twachtman-Cullen, D.,
293
Twardosz, S., 968, 1030
Tyano, S., 1220, 1252
Tye, N. C., 1105
Tyrano, S., 459, 462
Tzyy-Ping, J., 663, 671

Uchiyama, T., 435
Uddenfeldt, U., 109
Udenfriend, S., 455
Udwin, O., 549, 594
Uema, T., 667
Uhlmann, V., 541
Uller, C., 698
Ullstadius, E., 384, 385,
386
Ulvund, S., 369
Umansky, R., 150, 151, 153
Underwood, L. A., 905
Ungaro, P., 551
Unger, D. D., 1088
Unger, D. G., 264
Ungerer, J., 7, 185, 233,
234, 236, 237, 238,
251, 253, 254, 318,
320, 321, 322, 350,
369, 382, 385, 386,
392, 394, 397, 398,
416, 653, 656, 665,
667, 669, 707, 738,
740, 836

Ungerleider, L., 520, 526,
696
Unis, A., 542, 846, 1112
Urabe, F., 540
Usher, S., 908
Usui, S., 28
Uther, M., 481
Uyanik, M., 153
Uzgiris, I. C., 83, 148, 383,
386, 792

Vadasy, P. F., 1074
Vail, C., 1003
Vaisanen, M. L., 541
Valdez-Menchaca, M., 1049
Valdovinos, M. G., 821
Valle, M., 541
Vallortigara, G., 692
Van Acker, R., 134, 148,
149, 151, 152, 153
van Amelsvoort, T., 107,
419, 493, 521, 526,
652
van Bentem, P.-P. G., 455
van Berckelaer-Onnes, I.
A., 322
van Bokhoven, H., 78
Van Bourgondien, M., 124,
292, 297, 301, 302,
721, 749, 838, 1075,
1076, 1256
Vance, A., 617
Vance, H. B., 267
van Daalen, E., 723
van Daalen, H., 657, 662
Van den Ban, E., 30, 183
Van den Berghe, G., 464
Van den Berghe, H., 546
van den Bosch, R. J., 607
Van den Pol, R. A., 1143
Van den Veyver, I. B., 21,
77, 78, 130, 136, 137,
138, 431, 432
van der Does, A. W., 607
Van der Gaag, C., 521, 522,
523, 524, 526
Van der Gaag, J., 269
Van der Gaag, R., 5, 30,
166, 169, 171, 182,
183, 187, 190, 412,
482, 1111
Van der Geest, J. N., 171,
485, 684
Van der Heide, L., 519, 642
van der Hoeven, J., 269,
1111
Van der Lely, H., 258, 352
van der Linden, C., 1103
van der Linden, J. A., 183
Van der Wees, M., 169,
171, 412
Van de Water, J., 542, 1312
van Duijn, C. M., 556
Vandvik, I. H., 1239
van Engeland, H., 30, 171,
177, 183, 189, 249,
318, 319, 460, 478,
480, 481, 482, 485,
491, 493, 499, 657,
662, 684, 723
van Geert, P. L., 171, 186,
187

Vanhala, R., 432, 433, 481,
482
van Hooff, J., 249, 318, 319
Van Houten, R., 257, 821,
902, 907, 908, 909
van Ijzendoorn, M. H., 322
Van Kannen, D. P., 268
Van Krevelen, D., 90, 91,
93, 94, 105, 1233
Van Lancker, D., 344, 478,
481
van Lange, N. D. J., 454
Van Miller, S., 542
Van Oost, P., 236, 237,
389, 390
van Ree, J. M., 460
van Slegtenhorst, M., 543
van Spaendonck, K. P. M.,
372, 610, 613, 644
Van Walleghem, M., 546
Varela, F., 686, 687, 688,
690, 691
Varella-Garcia, M., 551
Vargas, F., 553
Vargha-Khadem, F., 432
Varilo, T., 432, 433
Varley, C. K., 1110
Varma, R., 493
Varma, R., 144
Vasa, S. F., 794
Vaughan, A., 663, 669, 671,
672
Vaughan, H., 479, 482
Vaughan, H., Jr., 479, 480,
482
Vayego-Lourenco, S. A.,
551
Vedora, J., 871
Veenstra-VanderWeele, J.,
429, 439, 515
Vega-Lahar, N., 690
Velting, O. N., 181, 182
Veltman, M. W., 551, 552
Venezia, M., 653, 654, 662
Venter, A., 186, 202, 203,
204, 206, 215, 216,
289, 292, 293, 294,
295, 297, 298, 335,
733, 741, 749, 978,
1076, 1077
Ventner, A., 354
Ventura, L. O., 553
Verbalis, A., 518
Verbaten, M., 171, 183,
478, 480, 481, 482,
485, 684
Verdecchia, M., 543
Verhoef, S., 543
Verkerk, A. J., 545
Verma, N. P., 144
Vernon, J., 1032
Verrier, A., 61
Verstraeten, T., 436
Verté, S., 373
Vesala, H., 296, 297
Vest, C., 498
Vest, L., 336
Vestal, C., 290, 295, 297,
1055, 1059, 1075, 1077
Vestergaard, M., 44, 49, 52,
57, 435
Vickers, S., 551
Vida, S., 548

Vidal, C. N., 494
Vieland, V. J., 1307
Vigorito, J., 689
Viken, A., 129
Vila, M. R., 550
Vilensky, J. A., 488, 839,
840
Villalobos, R., 503
Villareal, L., 1231, 1232
Vincent, J., 429
Vinet, M. C., 130, 138
Vinters, H. V., 140
Viozzi, L., 539
Visconti, P., 502
Visscher, P. M., 434
Vitale, L. J., 90
Vitiello, B., 762
Vogel, F., 434
Vogindroukas, I., 1216,
1217
Volden, J., 344, 354, 962
Volkmar, F. R., 5, 7, 8, 9,
10, 13, 14, 15, 16, 17,
18, 19, 20, 21, 23, 24,
25, 26, 27, 28, 30, 31,
32, 33, 41, 45, 50, 51,
53, 71, 72, 73, 74, 75,
76, 78, 79, 80, 81, 88,
91, 92, 93, 94, 95, 96,
97, 99, 100, 101, 102,
103, 104, 105, 106,
107, 108, 109, 110,
111, 113, 124, 169,
170, 173, 174, 175,
177, 178, 179, 180,
181, 182, 184, 186,
187, 189, 191, 200,
209, 210, 211, 213,
223, 224, 225, 227,
232, 233, 234, 236,
238, 239, 248, 249,
250, 251, 252, 263,
268, 269, 275, 293,
294, 296, 303, 312,
313, 314, 315, 316,
317, 318, 319, 322,
323, 324, 325, 326,
343, 345, 348, 350,
352, 353, 354, 365,
367, 368, 373, 374,
375, 376, 387, 388,
412, 419, 428, 429,
455, 456, 458, 459,
485, 486, 491, 492,
498, 519, 520, 521,
522, 523, 524, 525,
526, 534, 537, 538,
546, 547, 556, 561,
580, 587, 592, 593,
595, 628, 650, 651,
652, 683, 684, 689,
691, 694, 696, 697,
699, 707, 719, 720,
721, 730, 732, 734,
735, 736, 739, 740,
747, 748, 749, 750,
753, 754, 761, 772,
773, 777, 779, 782,
783, 784, 789, 793,
794, 800, 803, 809,
810, 813, 820, 821,
822, 832, 835, 839,

Volkmar, F. *(Continued)*
889, 906, 908, 912,
946, 960, 961, 962,
977, 979, 980, 982,
983, 984, 998, 1014,
1055, 1059, 1060,
1102, 1106, 1107,
1109, 1111, 1124,
1134, 1139, 1221,
1224, 1225, 1281,
1282, 1306
Volpe, A. G., 539
Volsen, S. G., 463, 490
Volterra, V., 149, 630
von Cramon, D. Y., 668,
669
von Knorring, A.-L., 204,
213, 288
von Tetzchner, S., 129,
147, 149, 155
von Thaden, K., 620
Vostanis, P., 266, 268, 408,
588, 1056, 1057, 1216,
1217
Vourc'h, P., 432
Vrancic, D., 494, 499, 519,
740
Vroomen, J., 519, 642
Vuilleumier, P., 523, 525
Vukicevic, J., 21, 314, 335,
708
Vygotsky, L., 982

Waage-Baudet, H., 454
Wacher, D. P., 904
Wachtel, R., 541, 800,
1112
Wacker, D., 819, 823, 912,
916, 926, 939
Wadden, N., 719, 720, 750
Wagner, A. E., 613
Wagner, E. A., 467
Wagner, H. N., 142
Wagner, S., 548, 867, 1130,
1149
Wagstaff, J., 551
Wahlberg, T., 261, 354
Wahlstrom, J., 429, 546,
548, 551
Wainwright, J., 832
Wainwright, L., 1307
Wainwright, M. S., 539
Wainwright-Sharp, J. A.,
268, 368, 610, 617,
1014
Waiter, G. D., 521, 523
Waits, M. M., 539
Wakabayashi, S., 251, 252,
289, 317, 547, 587
Wakefield, A., 435, 438,
541
Wakefield, J., 541
Wakstein, D., 348, 813
Wakstein, M., 348, 813
Waldenström, E., 588
Waldo, M. C., 744
Walker, A. S., 630, 689
Walker, D., 170, 173, 190,
264
Walker, H. A., 501
Walker, H. M., 1126
Walker, J., 236

Walker, K., 1006
Walker, M., 479
Walker, P., 454, 915
Walker, R. D., 484
Walker, V. G., 236
Walker-Andrews, A. S.,
261
Walker-Smith, J., 540, 541
Wall, S., 238, 322, 416,
1223
Wallace, B., 1093
Wallace, C., 651, 657, 658,
660, 661, 670
Waller, D., 459, 462, 1112
Walter, A., 269
Walter, D. O., 476
Walter, J., 440
Walter, R., 484
Walter, S., 8, 172, 173,
174, 731, 734, 753
Waltrip, C., 167, 169, 757
Wan, M., 21, 77, 78, 130,
136, 431
Wang, A. T., 170, 173
Wang, J. J., 252, 316
Wang, J.-J., 294, 793
Wang, L., 551
Wang, N. J., 551
Wang, P. P., 549, 552
Wang, Q., 543
Wang, T. A., 521, 526
Wang, T. R., 551
Wannamaker, S. W., 870
Wanska, S., 340
Want, S. C., 383
Wantanabe, M., 670
Ward, M., 1013, 1022,
1078, 1091
Ward-O'Brien, D., 1107,
1108
Ware, J., 723
Waring, R. H., 463
Waring, S. C., 144
Warren, J., 299, 651, 652
Warren, R., 539, 542
Warren, S., 883, 884, 888,
889, 930, 951
Warren, W., 542
Warreyn, P., 671
Warrington, E. K., 369,
371, 488
Wassink, T. H., 188, 1307
Watanabe, H., 542
Watanabe, M., 46, 52, 227,
455, 456, 460, 461,
834, 1224, 1249
Watanbe, Y., 458
Watemberg, N., 550
Waterhouse, L., 16, 29, 30,
169, 238, 323, 325,
344, 367, 410, 462,
519, 520, 592, 617,
833, 1306
Waters, E., 238, 322, 416,
1223
Watkins, J. M., 181, 183
Watkins, N., 1032
Watkiss, E., 551
Watling, R., 366, 536, 834,
843, 846
Watson, D., 477
Watson, J. B., 1006

Watson, J. S., 150, 153
Watson, L., 318, 324, 409,
520, 946
Watson, L. R., 833, 843
Watson, L. S., 1126
Watson, M., 546
Watson, P., 130, 139
Watson, R., 151
Watts, E., 1021, 1031
Waugh, M. C., 554
Weatherly, J. J., 1003
Weaver, A., 534
Weaver, B., 609
Weaver, L., 542
Webb, D. W., 543
Webb, E., 44, 48, 59, 62
Webb, P. J., 154
Webb, S., 165, 171, 191,
235, 483, 651, 690,
755
Webb, T., 137, 551
Weber, A. M., 430
Weber, D., 1212, 1213
Weber, R. C., 900
Webster, D. R., 464
Webster, J., 254
Webster-Stratton, C., 1060,
1061, 1062
Wechsler, D., 545, 731, 788
Wecker, L., 539
Weed, K. A., 1004
Weeks, D. E., 430, 431
Weeks, L., 127
Weeks, S., 261, 414, 520,
689
Wehby, J., 968, 1030
Wehman, P., 619, 1088,
1089, 1090, 1091,
1092, 1093, 1094
Wehmeyer, M., 151, 868
Wehner, B., 237
Wehner, E., 229, 234, 321,
342, 366, 367, 372,
384, 385, 386, 387,
388, 547, 612, 613,
614, 663, 716, 723,
833, 834, 837, 843,
847
Wei, T., 496, 497, 525, 667
Weidenbaum, M., 1093
Weider, S., 957, 966, 967,
1061
Weidmer-Mikhail, E., 100,
209, 295, 544, 551
Weimer, A. K., 100, 367,
835, 836
Weinberger, D. R., 526
Weiner, L. B., 544
Weinle, C., 542, 1112
Weintraub, A., 542, 1112
Weintraub, S., 98
Weir, F., 353
Weir, K., 16, 80, 82
Weir, R., 346
Weisberg, J., 524
Weisner, L. A., 556
Weiss, E., 1108
Weiss, M. J., 872, 873, 874,
1030
Weissbach, H., 455
Weissman, B. A., 459, 462,
1252

Weissman, D., 668, 669
Weisz, C. L., 149
Weitzman, E., 958, 959
Weizman, A., 459, 462,
1220, 1252
Weizman, R., 459, 462,
1220, 1252
Welch, J. P., 501
Welham, M., 93, 348, 593
Wellington, P., 833, 1011
Wellman, H., 630, 667
Wells, K. C., 1062
Welsh, M. C., 616
Wenar, C., 744, 750
Wendelboe, M., 539
Wenger, S., 546
Wenk, G., 134, 142, 146
Wentz, E., 113, 553, 586,
590, 743, 760
Wermuth, T. R., 1092
Werner, E., 225, 398, 689,
708
Werner, H., 320
Wernicke, C., 1232
Werry, J., 82, 180, 191, 915
Wert, B. Y., 871
Wertheimer, A., 1064,
1065, 1075
Wesecky, A., 150, 153
Wessels, M., 543
West, B. J., 901
West, D., 914
West, M., 619, 653, 1094
Westby, C., 813
Westerfield, M., 483, 493,
663, 671
Westlake, J. R., 484
Wetherby, A., 235, 236,
319, 351, 352, 653,
691, 707, 713, 758,
759, 773, 777, 778,
799, 800, 890, 926,
927, 928, 929, 930,
932, 933, 935, 936,
937, 938, 939, 940,
941, 942, 946, 947,
961, 978, 979, 980,
981, 982, 983, 985,
986, 989, 990, 995,
996, 997, 1007
Wetherley, A., 1007, 1008,
1009
Wetzel, R. J., 1126
Wexler, B. E., 619
Whalen, C., 236, 253, 867,
884, 886, 889
Wharton, P., 551
Wheeler, M. A., 371
Wheelwright, S., 48, 52,
54, 57, 60, 88, 105,
190, 191, 227, 229,
231, 373, 419, 434,
439, 461, 525, 526,
615, 628, 629, 631,
632, 633, 634, 645,
652, 666, 709, 713,
714, 715, 716, 847,
1307
Whisnant, J. P., 51
Whitaker, P., 991, 1061
Whitaker-Azmitia, P. M.,
454

White, G. B., 1281
White, L. M., 551
White, M. S., 1281
White, O., 366, 536, 826, 834, 843
White, R. L., 1032
Whitehouse, D., 263
Whitehouse, P. J., 142
Whitehouse, W., 48, 52, 54, 61, 63
Whiteley, P., 541
Whiten, A., 266, 389, 521, 523, 536, 630, 660
Whitley, F. P., 1143
Whitlock, B., 434, 534, 539
Whitman, B., 537
Whitman, T. L., 1126, 1128
Whitmont, S., 619
Whitney, R., 905
Whitney, Tu 1020
Whittaker, C. A., 952
Whittemore, V., 543
Whittington, C. J., 1283
Whittington, J., 552
Wichart, I., 142
Wickstrom, S., 394, 967, 969, 990
Widawski, M. H., 1108
Widiger, T. A., 11
Wiebe, M. J., 730, 749
Wieder, S., 832, 889, 890, 929, 932, 936, 939, 940, 941, 1003, 1140, 1310
Wiegers, A. M., 545
Wiersema, V., 462, 553
Wieser, M., 142
Wiesner, L., 31, 224, 232
Wigal, T., 1109
Wiggs, L., 542
Wignyosumarto, S., 47
Wigram, T., 127
Wiig, E., 807
Wijsenbeek, H., 1220
Wilcken, B., 143
Wilcox, B. L., 1124
Wilcoxen, A., 800
Wilder, D. A., 267, 870
Wilens, T., 1109
Wilgosh, L., 290, 1075, 1093
Wilkerson, D. S., 539
Wilkins, A. J., 503
Will, M., 1089
Willems, H., 758
Willemsen, R., 545
Willemsen-Swinkels, S. H. N., 189, 723
Willemsen-Swinkels, S. W., 183
Willen, J., 318, 630, 663
Willensen-Swinkel, S., 657, 662
Willey, L. H., 295
Williams, A. R., 1074
Williams, B. J., 544, 722, 752
Williams, C., 462, 551
Williams, D., 201, 832, 1014, 1017, 1022, 1284
Williams, D. E., 909, 910

Williams, D. F., 438
Williams, D. J., 619
Williams, E., 253, 395, 833, 849
Williams, G., 556
Williams, J., 227, 443
Williams, J. B. W., 17
Williams, J. C., 548
Williams, J. H., 266, 389, 521, 523, 536
Williams, J. M., 408
Williams, K., 80, 143, 540, 1014, 1015
Williams, M., 181, 800, 980
Williams, N., 431
Williams, P. D., 1074
Williams, P. G., 241, 267, 544, 556
Williams, R. E., 901
Williams, R. S., 553, 1305
Williams, S., 17, 419, 521, 526, 652, 668
Williams, S. C., 521, 526
Williams, S. C. R., 525
Williams, T., 1057, 1077
Williams, W. A., 454
Williamson, C. G., 939
Williamson, G., 367, 980, 981, 983
Williamson, P. C., 494
Willis, B. S., 1126, 1127, 1128
Willis, K. D., 152, 155
Willis, T. J., 903
Willoughby, J., 655, 673
Wilsher, C. P., 1110
Wilson, B., 619, 867
Wilson, F., 93, 95, 100, 101, 110, 213, 252, 269, 317, 734, 735, 736, 743, 845, 1014
Wilson, J., 79, 129, 139, 464
Wilson, R., 431, 545
Wilson, S., 82
Wimmer, H., 105, 630
Wimpory, D. C., 227, 408
Win, L., 523
Winborn, L. C., 904
Windsor, J., 293, 804
Wing, L., 7, 16, 24, 28, 30, 33, 43, 46, 49, 50, 52, 53, 62, 64, 88, 91, 92, 93, 94, 101, 102, 103, 106, 108, 109, 113, 166, 167, 172, 178, 184, 187, 208, 209, 210, 211, 214, 248, 249, 250, 265, 290, 295, 297, 312, 313, 317, 321, 323, 324, 344, 345, 348, 349, 392, 396, 408, 534, 535, 547, 548, 554, 580, 583, 584, 585, 586, 587, 588, 589, 592, 593, 594, 595, 596, 597, 598, 599, 600, 628, 629, 631, 653, 724, 734, 735, 736, 741, 743, 745,

749, 755, 756, 833, 838, 839, 840, 1014, 1056, 1066, 1069, 1175, 1182, 1189, 1197, 1216, 1243, 1244, 1245, 1246, 1305, 1306
Winking, D. L., 1093
Winklosky, B., 32, 731, 733, 754, 755
Winner, M., 992, 996
Winnergard, I., 552, 553
Winocur, G., 669, 671
Winograd, T., 687
Winsberg, B. G., 456, 457, 463
Winterling, V., 823, 865, 869, 900
Wisart, J., 548
Wise, S., 690
Wishart, J., 548
Wisniewski, L., 551
Wittchen, H. U., 181, 182
Wittenberger, M. D., 1110
Witt-Engerström, I., 76, 127, 128, 129, 132, 139, 142, 148, 431
Wiznitzer, M., 539, 1307
Wohlfahrt, J., 44, 49, 52, 57, 435
Wohlgemuth, D., 73
Wohlleben, B., 46, 184
Wojciulik, E., 520
Wolchik, S. A., 903
Wolery, M., 865, 868, 869
Wolf, C., 544
Wolf, E. G., 744, 750
Wolf, J., 323
Wolf, L., 296, 1068, 1074
Wolf, M., 821, 822, 825, 948, 967, 1006, 1125, 1126
Wolfberg, P., 967, 968, 980, 990, 991
Wolfe, B. E., 1181
Wolfensberger, W., 1246
Wolpert, C. M., 32, 429, 432, 433, 434, 439, 544, 551, 753, 754
Wolraich, M. L., 1109
Wong, C. Y., 455
Wong, D., 142, 428
Wong, S. E., 904
Wong, S. N., 476, 477
Wong, V., 476, 477
Wood, F. B., 438
Wood, K., 832, 833, 834, 843
Wood, R., 619, 1091
Woodcock, M., 137
Woodcock, T., 137
Woodhouse, J. M., 842
Woodhouse, W., 439, 536
Woodin, M., 552
Woodroffe, A., 544
Woods, A., 124, 207, 298, 302

Woods, C. G., 551
Woods, J., 759
Woods, R. P., 389
Woodyatt, G. C., 148, 149
Woolsey, J. E., 904
Worcester, J., 865, 866, 869
Wozniak, J., 208
Wray, J., 542
Wright, D. M., 1111
Wright, E. C., 589
Wright, H. H., 208, 269, 754
Wrozek, M., 427
Wszalek, T., 496
Wu, J. C., 367, 617
Wulf, G., 1014
Wynn, J., 239, 949, 1048
Wzorek, M., 170, 195, 197, 295, 427, 428, 439, 489, 500, 501, 536, 537, 538, 539, 808, 809

Xagoraris, A., 525
Xiang, F., 130, 138

Yachnis, A., 502
Yairi, E., 733
Yale, M., 664, 665, 667, 670
Yales, A., 459
Yamada, S., 140
Yamamoto, J., 261, 262
Yamamoto, T., 455, 459, 460, 543
Yamashita, F., 46, 540
Yamashita, I., 460
Yamashita, T., 539
Yamashita, Y., 140, 540, 544
Yamazaki, K., 460, 461, 463, 1223, 1226
Yan, S., 455
Yang, X.-L., 1203
Yankee, J., 833, 834, 849
Yano, S., 140
Yanossky, R., 499
Yardin, C., 551
Yashima, Y., 46, 52, 227, 456, 461, 463, 542, 834, 1224, 1225
Yashinaga, K., 202, 204, 206, 212, 213, 214
Yates, A., 1111
Yates, K., 371, 497, 660
Yaylali, I., 503
Yeargin-Allsopp, M., 49, 52, 57, 60, 63, 185, 555, 1070, 1123
Yeates, S., 46, 52, 321, 392, 396, 587, 598
Yeoh, H. C., 455
Yeung-Courchesne, G., 655, 656, 659, 668
Yeung-Courchesne, R., 141, 268, 367, 368, 371, 479, 480, 482, 499, 610, 617, 832, 889, 1282, 1305

Yilmaz, I., 153
Yin, X., 478
Yirmiya, N., 171, 260, 261,
    318, 320, 324, 325,
    409, 410, 411, 415,
    416, 433, 520, 630,
    631, 652, 653, 655,
    671, 707, 724, 734,
    741, 748, 749, 750,
    751, 753, 755, 946,
    1058, 1068
Ylisaukko-Oja, T., 432,
    433
Yntema, H. G., 78
Yoder, P., 235, 236, 386,
    664, 665, 667, 670,
    708, 734, 799, 801,
    884, 888, 889, 947,
    948, 949, 950, 955,
    957, 1007, 1011
Yokochi, K., 127
Yokota, A., 234, 251, 292,
    294, 316, 741, 745, 762
Yokota, K., 502, 503, 1225
Yokoyama, F., 456, 459,
    460, 1249
Yonan, A. L., 432, 433, 515
Yonan, J., 515
Yonclas, D. G., 235, 236,
    707
Yorbik, O., 667
Yoshen, Y., 978
Yoshikawa, H., 140
Yoshimoto, T., 172, 499
Yoshimura, I., 251, 252,
    289, 317
Yoshimura, K., 46, 540

Yoshinaga, K., 288, 289,
    291, 293, 296, 298
Young, A. H., 189
Young, A. W., 526
Young, D., 552, 1142
Young, G. C., 97
Young, H., 1004, 1005, 1006
Young, J. G., 50, 453, 455,
    458, 459, 460, 463,
    539, 553
Young, J. I., 431, 432
Young, N. B., 476
Young, S. N., 456, 457, 459
Youngman, P., 619
Youpa, D., 617
Yovel, G., 520
Yu, C.-E., 429
Yudovin, S., 354
Yule, E., 1244
Yule, W., 346, 549, 594,
    1244
Yusal, S., 739
Yuva-Paylor, L. A., 431,
    432
Yuwiler, A., 453, 455, 458,
    539
Yuzda, E., 108, 170, 500,
    534, 536, 632
Yuzda, F. Y., 425, 426, 434

Zaccagnini, J., 536
Zaccagnini, M., 539
Zackai, E., 551, 552
Zaeem, L., 432
Zager, D. B., 897
Zaharia, E. S., 1141
Zahl, A., 261

Zahn, T., 181, 266, 268
Zajdemann, H., 335
Zajonc, R., 695
Zaki, M., 130
Zakian, A., 751
Zalenski, S., 1029
Zalkin, H., 464
Zambito, J., 907
Zambrino, C. A., 539
Zametkin, A., 181, 524,
    525
Zametkin, J., 667
Zamichek, W., 538
Zanolli, K., 889
Zappella, M., 131, 142,
    143, 149, 150, 153,
    544
Zappert, J., 71
Zarcone, J. R., 821, 822,
    901, 907
Zarcone, T. J., 821
Zarifian, E., 459
Zee, D., 484, 485
Zeilberger, J., 1125
Zekan, L., 459
Zelazo, P., 325
Zelazo, P. D., 615
Zelazo, P. R., 1068
Zelnik, N., 542
Zemke, R., 849
Zercher, C., 254
Zetlin, A., 207
Zeuthen, E., 544
Zhang, H., 440, 543
Zhang, L., 545
Zhang, X., 130
Zhang, Z., 130, 138

Zhou, E. C., 454
Ziatas, K., 105, 352
Ziccardi, R., 489, 492, 493,
    499, 501, 519, 661
Zidel, S., 494, 536, 538
Ziegler, A., 80, 82
Ziegler, D. A., 489, 493,
    494, 496, 497, 498,
    517, 519, 1305
Ziegler, M. G., 459
Zigler, E., 206, 739, 1120
Zilber, N., 459
Zilbovicius, M., 373, 524
Zimbroff, D. L., 1106
Zimerman, B., 181
Zimmerman, A. W., 1111
Zimmerman, E. G., 27, 209
Zimmerman, I., 800, 804
Zimmerman, M. C., 476
Zimnitzky, B., 1108
Zingoni, A. M., 539
Zoghbi, H., 21, 77, 78, 127,
    130, 132, 134, 136,
    137, 138, 139, 141,
    142, 144, 145, 152,
    431, 432, 1312
Zohar, A. H., 552
Zollinger, B., 1221
Zoltak, B., 539
Zorn, S. H., 1106
Zubieta, J. K., 189
Zuddas, A., 1103
Al-Zuhair, A. G. H., 130
Zvi, J. C., 30
Zwaigenbaum, L., 77, 78,
    170, 173, 187, 190,
    427, 437

Subject Index

AAPEP. *See* Adolescent and Adult Psychoeducational
  Profile (AAPEP)
ABA. *See* Applied behavioral analysis (ABA)
ABC. *See* Autism Behavior Checklist (ABC)
Aberrant Behavior Checklist (ABC), 762
Abnormal Involuntary Movement Scale (AIMS), 848
Academic skills, functional (NRC instructional
  priorities), 928
Academic supports, 1018–1020. *See also* School(s)/
  school-based programs
Acculturation theory, 398
Achenbach System of Empirically Based Assessment,
  748
Achievement:
  academic, 294–295 (*see also* School(s)/school-based
    programs)
  clinical assessment, 786
Acting-Out scale, 747
Action level imitation, 383
Action on objects, 384
Active-but-odd group, 250, 586, 598–599
Adaptive Behavior Scale-School Version, American
  Association of Mental Deficiency (AAMD), 751
Adaptive functioning/behavior, 114, 238, 251, 294–295,
  792–793, 1178
Addison-Schilder disease, 76
ADHD. *See* Attention Deficit Hyperactivity Disorder
  (ADHD)
ADI-R. *See* Autism Diagnostic Interview-Revised (ADI-R)
Administrative organization (TEACCH), 1176
Adolescent and Adult Psychoeducational Profile
  (AAPEP), 743, 758
Adolescents with autism, 288–305
  and average intelligence, 303
  clinical issues, 300–304
  emotion, 411–414
  and mental retardation, 300–303
  outcome studies, 288–300
  peer relationships, 303
  school, 303, 1013–1023 (*see also* School(s)/school-based
    programs)
ADOS. *See* Autism Diagnostic Observation Schedule
  (ADOS)
Adulthood, transition to, 875–876, 1022–1023
Adults with autism, 288–305
  and average intelligence, 303–304
  college, 303–304
  consultants on care for, 1137
  deterioration in, 213–214, 289–290
  jobs/work (*see* Employment)
  and mental retardation, 300–303
  neuro-psychiatric conditions, 589–590

outcome studies, 288–300
sexuality, 304
work, 304
Advocacy, 1063, 1064, 1078, 1308–1309
Aerobic exercise, antecedent, 900
Affect, interpersonal coordination of, 409–410. *See also*
  Emotion(s)
Affective development, 324–325
Affective disorder, 428
Affective symptoms, 27–28
Ages and Stages Questionnaire, Second Edition (ASQ),
  712
Akathisia Ratings of Movement Scale (ARMS), 848
Allergies, 539
Aloof group, 249, 595–597
Alpine Learning Group, 1044–1045
Amalgamatic nucleus, 1229
Ambulation (Rett syndrome), 153
Americans with Disabilities Act (ADA), 1091
Aminoacidophathies, 76. *See also* Phenylketonuria (PKU)
Amino acids and acetylcholine, 462–463
Amygdala, 497, 525–526
Anatomic studies, 1305. *See also* Neuroimaging studies
Angelman/Prader-Willi syndromes, 76, 135, 551–552
Animal models and studies of portmortem brain tissues,
  440–441
Anorexia nervosa, 590
Antecedent interventions, 899–902
Antipsychotics, atypical, 1102–1106
Anxiety, 100–101, 178, 208, 269, 428, 1013–1015,
  1282–1283
Appearance, physical, 1057–1058
Applied behavioral analysis (ABA), 949, 959, 964, 1005,
  1006–1007, 1046, 1125–1126
Apprenticeships, 1147
Apraxia, 150–151, 387, 951
Argentina. *See* Latin America
Aripiprazole, 1106
Aristaless-related homeobox gene (ARX syndrome), 544
ASIEP. *See* Autism Screening Instrument for Educational
  Planning (ASIEP-2)
Asperger syndrome, 88–118
  alternative diagnostic concepts, 97–98
  autism versus, 92
  cachet of diagnosis, 1308
  classification/diagnosis, 89–90, 91–95, 165, 166, 167,
    169
    criteria, 735–736, 1306
    historical perspective, classification, 6, 8, 24–25,
      90–96, 169
  clinical assessment, 111–113
  clinical features, 94, 98–102

Asperger syndrome *(Continued)*
  differential diagnosis, 81, 173–174
  epidemiology, 53, 54, 102
  future research directions, 109–111
  genetics, 108–109
  ICD10 research diagnostic guidelines for, 93
  instruments, 760–762
  language, 335, 1306
  medical and neurobiological studies, 106–108
  natural history, 186–187
  neuropsychological studies, 102–104
  original clinical concept (Asperger's), 89–90, 96–97
  outcomes, 109–110, 213
  psychiatric disorders/conditions and, 28, 208, 209–210, 269
  social-cognitive studies, 104–106
  social skills interventions/curricula, 872
  terminology (versus "autistic psychopathy"), 584
  treatment and interventions, 113–116
  undiagnosed, 1245
  validity, 102–111, 872
  versus HFA (high-functioning autism), 91–92, 95–96, 103–104, 628–629
Asperger Syndrome Diagnostic Interview (ASDI), 113, 743, 760–761
Assessment, 705–706. *See also* Clinical evaluation in autism spectrum disorders
Assessment of Basic Language and Learning Skills (ABLLS), 929
Attachment, 238, 322–323
Attention, 28, 234–235, 367–369, 610, 1307. *See also* Joint attention
Attention Deficit Hyperactivity Disorder (ADHD), 265, 614, 616–617, 619, 629, 644, 1016
  differential diagnosis (PDD-NOS), 177
  executive function, 373
  stimulants, 1109–1111
  treatment studies, in developmentally disabled populations, 1110–1111
Attention Process Training (APT) program, 619
Attributions, first-order/second-order, 105
Atypical antipsychotics, 1102–1106
Atypical autism (PDD-NOS), 6, 25
Atypical PDD, 16
Auditory brainstem response (ABR), 844
Auditory potentials:
  brainstem evoked (exogenous), 476–478
  cognitive, 479–482
  long latency, 478–479
  middle latency, 478
Augmentative and alternative communication (AAC) strategies, 149, 801–803, 885, 941, 955–957
Australia, 1197–1201
Australian Scale for Asperger's Syndrome (ASAS), 743, 761
Austria and Germany, 1212–1215
Autism:
  classification/diagnosis (overview), 1–3
  diagnosis/classification, 1–3, 5–34
  differences in, 1283–1285
  differential diagnosis, 81, 94, 174–175
  epidemic, 1308
  essence of, 419
  history of concepts, 583–587
  versus mental retardation, 226
  past and future, 1304–1313
  primary/secondary, 7–8
  public policy perspectives, 1119–1121
  subtyping, 28–31
  theoretical perspectives, 579–581
Autism Behavior Checklist (ABC), 714–715, 719–720, 723, 740–741, 742, 747, 750–751, 754, 762, 1204

Autism Diagnostic Interview-Revised (ADI-R):
  defined/described, 753–755
  overview table, 743
  usage/comparison, 176, 214, 228, 232, 289, 293, 315, 326, 342, 712, 722, 734, 740, 743, 751, 760, 762, 780
Autism Diagnostic and Observation Scale, 820
Autism Diagnostic Observation Schedule (ADOS), 326, 739, 740–741, 743, 753, 756–757, 760, 762, 780
  ADOS-G (Generic), 176, 214, 228, 551, 712, 722
  PL-ADOS (Pre-Linguistic), 756
"Autism in schizophrenia" (1916 term), 89
Autism Screening Instrument for Educational Planning (ASIEP-2), 1006
Autism Screening Questionnaire/Social Communication Questionnaire (ASQ/SCQ), 714–715. *See also* Social Communication Questionnaire (SCQ)
Autism Services Center (ASC), Huntington, West Virginia, 1255–1264
Autism specialists, preparation of. *See* Training (preparation of autism specialists)
Autism spectrum disorders (ASDs), 88, 535, 586
Autistic continuum, 586, 1233
Autistic disorder, 25, 535
Autistic psychopathy, 584
Aversive/nonaversive interventions, 915–916
Avoidant personality disorder, 178, 179

Babbling, 91, 349
Backhanded bullying, 1022
BAEPs. *See* Brainstem auditory evoked potentials (BAEPs)
Barnes Akathisia Scale, 848
Baron-Cohen's "eyes task," 643
Basal ganglia, 497–498
Bayley Scales of Infants Development-II, 791
Beery Buktenica Developmental Test of Visual-Motor Integration (VMI), 794, 844
Behavior, development and, 221–222
Behavioral assessment (functional ecological approach), 817–827
  characteristics, 817–821
  domains, 821–825
  treatment plan development, 825–827
Behavioral Assessment Scale of Oral Functions in Feeding, 847
Behavioral competencies, and provider training, 1140, 1143–1146
  hands-on training, 1143–1146
  operational definitions, 1144
Behavioral curricula, 874–875
Behavioral Development Questionnaire, 820
Behavioral difficulties:
  adolescents/adults, 290
  Asperger syndrome, 89–90
  conduct disorder, 268
  deviance from normal, 14
  public (stressors confronting families), 1058
  violent/criminal behavior, 101
Behavioral interventions, 882–892, 897–917
  antecedent interventions, 899–902
  Asperger syndrome, 114–115
  augmentative and alternative communication strategies, 885
  aversive and nonaversive, 915–916
  in the community, 916
  computer applications, 916–917
  consequence-based interventions, 902–910
  differential efficacy of strategies, 914
  extinction procedures, 907
  functional communication training (FCT), 910–912
  future directions, 887–892
  interruption and redirection, 902–903

issues in (current and future), 914–917
language and communication skills, 910–912
maintenance and generalization, 887, 914–915
naturalistic, 883–885
versus nonbehavioral approaches, 890
noncontingent reinforcement, 907–908
parents/families, 1061, 1062
pivotal response training, 883–885, 888, 954 (see also Pivotal response training (PRT))
punishment procedures, 908–910
reinforcement-based interventions, 903–907
respondent conditioning procedures, 913–914
self-management, 885–886, 913
skill acquisition, 910–913
social skills, 912–913
social validity, 916
stimulus change procedures, 902
strategies, 882–887
structured, 883
teacher variables, 888
video instruction, 886–887
Behavioral momentum, 901
Behavioral studies, 1305–1307
Behavioral Summarized Evaluation-Revised (BSE-R) (overview table), 742, 751
Behavior Observation Scale (BOS), 745
Behavior Rating Instrument for Autistic and Atypical Children (BRIAAC), 742, 744
Behavior Rating Inventory of Executive Functions (BRIEF), 794
Behavior Rating Scale (BRS), 791
Behavior Summarized Evaluation-Revised (BSE-R), 751
Biological studies/findings. See Genetics; Neuroimaging studies
Biological vulnerabilities, anxiety and, 269
Blindness, congenital, 417–419, 553–555
Block Design test, 635, 642, 643
Blood 5-HT, 454–455
Blood oxygen level dependent (BOLD) signal, 517
Body mapping, 387, 389
Body movements, imitation of, 384–385
Brain. See also Central nervous system; Neuroimaging studies:
    animal models, portmortem studies, 440–441
    extreme male brain (EMB) theory, 634
    systems, and initiating social behavior, perception of social behavior, 645
    Type B (balanced), 633–634
    Type E (empathizing), 633–634
    Type S (systemizing), 633–634
    volume/weight, 488, 492–494
Brain behavior:
    correlates (play), 397
    joint attention and, 662–665
    theory of mind and, 665–668
Brainstem, 499
Brainstem auditory evoked potentials (BAEPs), 476–478
Brigance Screens, 712
Broad descriptive orientation (enhancing communication abilities), 930
Broader autism phenotype. See Phenotype, broader autism
Bruininks-Oseretsky Test of Motor Proficiency (BOTMP), 794, 846, 847
Bruxism, 902
Bullying, 1021–1022
Business community, developing active ties, 1097

Cambridge Neuropsychological Test Automated Battery (CANTAB), 609, 615, 618, 620
Canada, 1201–1203
Candidate genes (leads/strategies), 433–434, 440
"Can't" versus "won't" dilemma, 1057

Cardiff Acuity Test, 842
Cardiovascular, 459
CARS. See Childhood Autism Rating Scale (CARS)
Catatonia, 589–590
CATCH 22 (chromosome 22q11 deletion syndrome), 552
Categorical definitions:
    of autism, approaches to, 14–25
        DSM-III, 15
        DSM-III-R, 16–17
        DSM-IV and ICD-10, 17–18
        DSM-IV field trial, 18–21
        from ICD-9 to ICD-10, 17
    problems with, 583–600
Causality, models of, 655
CBCL, 748
Celiac antibodies, 539
Center-based programs, 1043–1047
    differences/similarities among programs, 1045–1047
    specific programs, 1044, 1047
    strengths/limitations, 1051–1052
    terminology (mainstreaming, inclusion, integration), 1047
Central coherence, 640–646
    cognitive style, normal variation, 644–645
    deficit accounts, 643–644
    evidence (at three levels of processing), 641–643
    extended phenotype of autism, 645
    savant skills, 644
    social development, 326
    theory, 635
    weak central coherence (WCC) hypothesis, 669
Central nervous system:
    function, 474–488
    structure, 488–500
Cerebellar hemispheres, 498–499
Cerebellar vermis, 499
Cerebellum, 498
Cerebral palsy, 50, 51
Cerebrospinal fluid, 459
CHARGE association, 544
Checklist for Autism in Toddlers (CHAT), 227, 229, 713–716, 723, 741
Checklist-based performance appraisals, 1152
Child-centered approaches, 959
Child Development Inventories (CDIs), 712
Childhood, disorders beginning in (conditions causing diagnostic problems), 587–589
Childhood Autism Rating Scale (CARS):
    defined/described, 720–721
    overview table, 714–715, 742
    use of/comparisons, 543, 546, 553, 657, 667, 723, 734, 744, 745, 748–750, 758, 820, 1176, 1204, 1227
    validity, 714, 740–741, 742
Childhood disintegrative disorder (CDD), 70–84
    associated medical conditions, 76
    autism and, 79–80
    behavioral and clinical features, 74–75
    case report, 83–84
    clinical features, 72–74
    course and prognosis, 75
    definition, 71–72
    development of diagnostic concept, 6, 17, 21–23, 25, 70–72
    differential diagnosis, 81–82, 175
    epidemiology, 53–56, 75, 185
    evaluation and management, 82–83
    genetics, 77–79
    neurobiological findings and etiology, 75–77
    onset (age/characteristics), 72–74
    Rett syndrome and, 78, 81
    validity as diagnostic category, 79–81

Childhood onset pervasive developmental disorder (COPDD), 15, 16, 71
Childhood psychosis, 1239–1240
Childhood schizophrenia. *See also* Schizophrenia:
  differential diagnosis, 81–82
  terminology/classification, 9, 584
Children of school age, with an autistic spectrum disorder, 247–276
  developmental issues, 245–265
  language and communication, 254–260
  psychiatric and behavioral problems, 265–270
Children's Global Assessment Scale, 762
Children's Psychiatric Rating Scale, 1107
Children's Social Behavior Questionnaire (CSBQ), 742, 747, 748
Children's Unit for Treatment and Evaluation (State University of New York at Binghamton), 1035, 1044, 1047, 1130, 1131
China, 1203–1206
Chromosomal abnormalities and genetically determined medical conditions, 429–430, 544. *See also* Genetics
Cingulate cortex, 496
Citalopram, 1109
Clancy Behavior Scale, 1204
Classification. *See* Diagnosis/classification
Classroom structure. *See* Curriculum and classroom structure
Clinical evaluation in autism spectrum disorders, 772–795
  comprehensive developmental approach, 773–776
  diagnostic formulation and differential diagnosis, 781–782
  diagnostic work-up, 778–781
  medical workups, 782–783
  psychological assessment, 777, 783–795
  speech, language, and communication, 777–778
Clinical Linguistic and Auditory Milestone Scale, 800
Clinical neurology, 500–503
Clinical web sites, 305
Clomipramine, 1106–1107
Clozapine, 1103
Cluster and factor analysis, 29–30
Cluster reports (epidemiological studies), 64–65
Coactive model of organism-environment interaction, 659
Cognition/cognitive:
  behavioral studies, 1306
  executive function, 619–620
  families, approach with, 1062, 1064
  outcomes (changes in ability), 205
  profiles (neuropsychological characterstics), 374–375
  remediation, 619–620
  Rett syndrome, 146–148
  skills, 872–873
  strengths/challenges (school-based programs), 1016–1017
  style, central coherence and normal variation in, 644–645
  theories (TEACCH philosophy/principles), 1178
  theory of mind and, 872–873
Cohen syndrome, 544
Collaborative Program of Excellence in Autism (CPEA), 1196
College:
  adolescents/adults with autism, 303–304
  student trainees/providers, 1137–1138
Colombia. *See* Latin America
Communication:
  language (*see* Language)
  nonverbal, 235–236
  preverbal, 235–236
  protoimperative/protodeclarative, 320
  requestive, 320
  vocalizations, 235

Communication abilities, enhancing, 925–942. *See also* Language interventions
  approaches, 928–931
  behavioral problems, relation to, 926–928
  challenges, 927
  dimensions, critical, 931–941
  NRC guidelines and other tenets of practice, 927–928
  priority of, in treatment, 925–926
Communication assessment, 799–814
  children with advanced language, 807–817
  early linguistic communication, 804–807
  prelinguistic, 799–804
Communication boards, 149
Communication Competence Checklist (CCC), 753
Communication Intention Inventory, 801
Communication and Symbolic Behavior Scale (CSBS), 743, 758–759, 800–801
Communicative Development Inventory, 800
Community:
  behavioral interventions, 916
  interpersonal supports for members of, 993–995
Community-integrated residential services for adults with autism (working model, mother's perspective), 1255–1264
  components of a successful residential program, 1257–1264
  historical perspective, 1256–1257
  introduction, 1255–1256
Comorbidity:
  Asperger syndrome, 100–102
  autism, 26
Competencies and coping (TEACCH principle), 1067–1068
Component process analyses, 607–611
Computational models, enactive mind (EM) framework versus, 686
Computer applications, behavioral interventions, 916–917. *See also* Technology/computers
Conduct problems. *See* Behavioral difficulties
Congenital rubella. *See* Rubella
Consequence-based interventions, 902–910
Contingencies or reinforcement, 827
Contingent electric shock as a punisher, 909
Continuum orientation, 930–931. *See also* Spectrum/continuum
Conversation. *See also* Communication; Language; Speech:
  manner assessing communication, 806–807
  skills (school-age children), 257–259, 873
Coordination disorder, developmental, 588
COPDD. *See* Childhood onset pervasive developmental disorder (COPDD)
Core characteristics, two triads, 629
Corpus callosum, 494–495
Cortical language areas, 495–496
Cortisol secretion, 460
Cost issues, 1143, 1169, 1170
Course of development, uneven/unusual (stressors confronting families), 1056
Coworker training/support, 1097
Criminal justice system, autism and, 299–300
Cronbach's alphas, 747
Cross-cultural issues. *See* Cultural issues
Cross-model matching and body mapping, 389
CSBQ. *See* Children's Social Behavior Questionnaire (CSBQ)
CSF 5-HIAA, 456–457
CSF HVA, 457
CTRF, 748
Cues, multiple, 954
Cultural issues:
  assessment/diagnosis, 32
  cross-cultural programs, 1174–1187

Curriculum and classroom structure, 863–877
  behavioral curricula, 874–875
  classroom structure, 866–867
  cognitive skills, 872–873
  comprehensive curricula, 873–875
  inclusion settings, 867–868
  outcomes, 865–867
  pivotal response training, 874 (see also Pivotal response training (PRT))
  play skills, 870, 1011, 1012 (see also Play)
  preschool curricula, 873–874
  publishers, 864
  settings, 867–868
  social skills, 868–872
  social validity, 876
  transition to adulthood, 875–876
Curriculum content (school-based programs), 1010–1012
  communication skills (expressive/receptive language and spontaneous language), 1010, 1012
  daily routines, 1010, 1012
  instructional strategies and curriculum areas (STAR program), 1012
  play skills, 1011, 1012
  preacademic skills, 1010–1011, 1012
  social interaction skills, 1011, 1012

Daily Living Skills, 793
Daily routines (school-based), 1010, 1012
DAMP (Disorders of Attention, Motor Control, and Perception) syndrome, 28, 182–184, 588
DAS. See Differential Abilities Scales (DAS)
DDDC. See Douglass Development Disabilities Center (DDDC)
Deafness, congenital, 553–555. See also Hearing
Declarative memory, 370
Deficit acceptance, 1178
DeGangi-Berk Test of Sensory Integration, 846
Deictic terms, use of, 347
Delaware Autistic Program, 1036
Delay, deviance versus, 227–229, 386–387, 397–398, 776
Delayed nonmatch to sample (DNMS), 663
Dementia infantilis, 8, 75
Dementia precoccissima catatonica, 584
Denmark. See Nordic nations
Denver Development Screening Test (DDST), 1204
Denver Model at University of Colorado, 712, 953, 1050–1051
Depression, 11, 100–101, 208
Detection of Autism by Infant Sociability Interview (DAISI), 227
Deterioration in adulthood, 213–214, 289–290
Development, behavior and, 221–222
Developmental, Individualized, Relationship-based (DIR) model, 873, 929, 932, 934, 939, 957, 959
Developmental approach, 14
Developmental change, 31
Developmental continuum (principles of TEACCH), 1068
Developmental delay, deviance versus, 227–229, 386–387, 397–398, 776
Developmental disorder(s):
  autism as (principles of TEACCH), 1066
  language disorders, 175, 587–588
  learning disability of the right hemisphere, 98
  "other" (problems of categorical classification systems), 587
  pervasive (see Pervasive developmental disorder (PDD))
Developmental-pragmatic approaches/strategies, 947, 953–955, 957–960, 966–967
Developmental psychosis, 1233–1234
Developmental regression, 30–31
Developmental sensitivity, 818
Diagnosis/classification, 1–3, 5–34

behavioral definition (versus biological), 1307
categorical definitions of autism:
  approaches to, 14–25
  problems with, 583–600
classification issues, 9–13
controversies, 25–33
development of autism as diagnostic concept, 6–9
diagnostic confusion, as stress to families, 1056
diagnostic process, 1, 9
dimensional versus categorical classification, 10–11
early diagnosis, 31–33, 232–233, 707–709, 1204
etiologies and causes, 12
general issues in diagnosis of autistic spectrum disorders, 730–741
history of concepts of autism, 583–587
labels, 2, 10
misconceptions about, 10–11
misuse of classification systems, 12
multidimensional diagnostic formulation, 594–599
  active-but-odd group, 250, 586, 598–599
  aloof group, 249, 595–597
  passive group, 249–250, 597–598
"official" status, diagnostic systems, 10
pervasive developmental disorder (PDD), term introduced (DSM-III, 1980), 2
research, role of, 13–14
spectrum with fuzzy borders and overlaps, autism as, 1307–1308
stigmatization, potential for, 12–13
theory, role of, 11
Diagnosis/classification systems, official, 2, 10, 591–594
Diagnostic instruments in autistic spectrum disorders, 730–763
  for Asperger syndrome, 760–762
  direct observation scales, 756–758
  first empirically developed rating scales and questionnaires, 744–745
  interviews, 753–756
  measuring change in core behaviors, 761–762
  overview tables, 742–743, 787
  psychometric issues, 735
  rating scales, currently used, 748–752
  recommended, 787
  related diagnostic and behavioral assessment instruments, 758–760
  reliability, 736–740
  scales measuring core deficits, 746–748
  validity, 740–741
Diagnostic interviews, 753–756
Diagnostic Interview for Social and Communication Disorders (DISCO), 594–595, 735–736, 743, 745, 755–756
Diagnostic problems, associated conditions causing, 587–591
  anorexia nervosa, 590
  attention deficit/hyperactivity disorder (ADHD), 588
  borderlines of normality, 591
  catatonia, 589–590
  deficits of attention, motor control, and perception (DAMP syndrome), 588
  developmental coordination disorder, 588
  developmental language disorders, 587–588
  disorders beginning in childhood, 587–589
  eccentric normality, 587
  generalized mental retardation, 587
  hearing impairments, 588–589
  neuro-psychiatric conditions in adults, 589–590
  obsessive-compulsive disorder (OCD), 590
  personality disorders (schizoid and schizotypal), 590
  psychosocial deprivation, 591
  schizophrenia, 590

Diagnostic problems, associated conditions causing
    (*Continued*)
    Tourette's syndrome, 588
    visual impairments, 589
Diagnostic and Statistical Manual of Mental Disorders
    (*DSM*) of the American Psychiatric Association, 2,
    71–72, 92, 184, 232, 592–594, 748
    DSM-IV/ICD-10 systems as epistemological backbone of
        this *Handbook*, 2
    problems of *DSM-IV/ICD-10* system of classification,
        592–594
    autism, 14–25
        definition of autism (in *DSM-IV* and *ICD-10*), 20–21
        definition of nonautistic PDDs, 21–25
        DSM-III, 15
        DSM-III-R, 16–17
        DSM-IV and *ICD-10*, 17–18
        DSM-IV field trial, 18–21
Didactic approaches, 947, 959, 963, 1141–1142, 1143
Differential Abilities Scales (DAS), 787, 789
Differential diagnosis, 25
    Asperger syndrome, 25
    autistic disorder, 25
    childhood disintegrative disorder, 25, 81–82
    involuntary movements, 847
    PDD-NOS, 25, 172–184
    Rett syndrome, 25, 132–135
Differential reinforcement procedures, 904–910
    of Alternative Behavior (DRA/DRAlt), 904, 905, 906,
        907
    of Incompatible Behavior (DRI), 904, 905, 906, 907,
        908, 909
    of Low Rates of Responding (DRL), 904, 906
    of Other Behavior (DRO), 904–905, 906, 907, 910
Difficult life events, 302–303
Dimensional versus categorical classification, 10–11
Direct observation scales, 756–758
DISCO. *See* Diagnostic Interview for Social and
    Communication Disorders (DISCO)
Discourse management, 806, 808
Discrete trial training (DTI), 883, 941, 948, 949, 959,
    1004, 1005, 1007–1009
Discriminant validity problem (EF hypothesis), 616–617
Disembodied cognition, 686, 690
Disintegrative PDDs, 33. *See also* Childhood disintegrative
    disorder (CDD); Rett syndrome
Disintegrative psychosis (Heller's syndrome), 8, 15, 71, 135
DMFC/AC (dorsal medial-frontal cortex), 645, 663–673
Dopamine, 457
Douglass Development Disabilities Center (DDDC), 1045,
    1046, 1047, 1131, 1132
Down syndrome, 50, 51, 235, 321, 345, 547–548
DRA/DRI/DRL/DRO. *See* Differential reinforcement
    procedures
Drawings, 794–795
DSM. *See Diagnostic and Statistical Manual of Mental
    Disorders* (*DSM*) of the American Psychiatric
    Association
Due process, 1167
Dyskinesia, 839, 848
Dyskinesia Identification System Condensed User Scale
    (DISCUS), 848
Dyslexia, 263, 618, 645
Dysmorphic features (minor physical anomalies; MPAs),
    501
Dyspraxia, 387

Early diagnosis, 31–33, 232–233, 707–709, 1204
Early inclusion, 1035–1038. *See also* Mainstream
Early infantile autism, 584
Early intervention, 238–239
Early Language Milestone Scale, 800

Early Social-Communication Scales (ESCS), 654, 662
Eating problems, 847
Eccentric normality (problems of categorical classification
    systems), 587
Echoes, 963, 965
Echolalia, 255–256, 346–347, 804, 805, 961, 964
Ecological approach, functional (behavioral assessment),
    817–827
Ecological model of autism, experiential effects on pretend
    play, 398–399
Ecological/setting event interventions (versus immediate
    antecedents), 899
Ecological validity, 826, 827
Ecuador. *See* Latin America
Education:
    Asperger syndrome, 986–998
    as intervention (overview), 1310
    legal issues (*see* Legal issues, educating children with
        autism)
    outcomes, 205–208
    personal perspective (Grandin), 1276–1277
    of public (press/TV/Internet), 1309
    Rett, 154–155
Educational interventions:
    with families, 1061, 1062
    models of, 1043–1053 (*see also* Center-based programs;
        Home-based programs; School(s)/school-based
        programs)
    social communication, 987–989
Education for All Handicapped Children Act of 1975, 867
Efficiency (behavioral assessment), 822
Effort (behavioral assessment), 822
Ego skin, 1230
Electroencephalograms (EEGs), 144–145, 503, 538, 663,
    665, 1204
Elizabeth Ives School for Special Children (New Haven,
    CT), 1287
Elementary and Secondary Education Act (No Child Left
    Behind), 863
Embarrassment, 415
Embedded Figures Task (EFT), 635, 642, 643, 645
Embodied cognition, 686, 690
Emergence of mind, 687
Emotion(s), 406–420
    abstract (sibling's perspective), 1271
    complex, 415–417
    conceptual issues, 406–408
    emotional expressiveness, 410–411
    Grandin (gradual change and my emotional life), 1283
    interpersonal coordination of affect, 409–410
    later childhood and adolescence, 411–414
    self-conscious, 414–417
    social impairment in congenitally blind children and
        Romanian orphans, 417–419
    stress/anxiety during adolescence, 1014–1015
    systematic studies, early years, 408–409
Emotional assessment, 794–795
Emotional regulation, 934, 939, 980–983
Emotional support (families), 1062, 1064
Emotional vulnerability, supports for, 1015
Empathizing:
    in autism spectrum conditions, 631
    mindblindness, 629–631
    normal development of, 630–631
    theory of mind and, 629–631
Empathizing-systemizing theory, 631–634
Empathy, defined, 629–630
Empirically supported treatments, 1038, 1059
Employment, 298–299, 304, 1087–1098
    average intelligence and, 304
    entrepreneurial supports, 1094–1095
    family, role of, 1092–1093

historical overview, 1089
legislation, 1089–1091
mental retardation and, 301–302
outcomes, 205–208
personal perspective (Grandin), 1277–1278
poll results, 1088
protected, 1313
recommendations toward greater employability,
    1096–1097
school-to-work transition process, 1091–1093
secure, 1095
service models, 1093–1096
sheltered workshops, 1095
supported, 207, 302, 1093–1094
Emulation, 383
Enactive mind (EM), 682–699
    computational models versus framework of, 686
    emergence of mental representations, 689–694
    explanation of term, 686
    social cognition as social action, 695–698
    social development, 326
    social world as open-domain task, 687–689
    temporal constraints on models of social adaptation,
        694–695
Entrepreneurial supports, 1094–1095
Environmental engineering/modifications, 899, 997
Epidemiology, 42–65, 434
    Asperger's syndrome, 53, 54
    autism and social class, 64
    autistic disorder, 46–49
    characteristics of autistic samples, 45–51
    childhood disintegrative disorder (CDD), 53–56, 75
    cluster reports, 64–65
    design/selection of studies, 42–45
    gender, 46–49
    immigrant status, ethnicity, social class, and other
        correlates, 62–65
    international (countries), 46–49
        Australia, 1197–1198
        China, 1203–1204
        Israel, 1219
    IQ, 46–49
    pervasive developmental disorders, 51–56, 184–185
    Rett syndrome, 135–136
    time trends, 56–62
Epigenetic mechanisms/models, 439–440, 655
Epilepsy, 50, 51, 82, 151, 295–296, 502–503, 544, 629
Episodic memory, 370
ERN (error-related negativity), 669
Erythrocyte glutathione peroxidase, 539
Escitalopram, 1109
ESCS. See Early Social-Communication Scales (ESCS)
Ethics (provider training), 1139
Ethnicity, 62–65
Etiology, 12, 75–77, 136–139, 185–186, 594, 1229–1231
Evaluation of Sensory Processing (ESP), 843
Evoked potentials, 475–483
Executive function (EF), 606–621
    coherence, 644
    component process analyses, 607–611
    deficits and broader autism phenotype, 617–618
    emerging issues, 612–617
    flexibility and inhibition, 608–611
    future directions, 617–620
    generativity hypothesis, 396
    imitation, 388
    language and intelligence, 616
    literature review, 606–611
    model of cognitive development in autism (theory of
        mind), 634–635
    neuropsychological characteristics, 372–374
    remediation, cognitive, 618–620

repetitive behavior, 616
skills, 234, 325–326
social processes and, 613–616
specificity to autism, 616–617
working memory, 611, 788
Exercise, physical, 900, 1015
Experience-expectant neural development, 657–658
Explicit memory, 370
Exploration and play, 236–237. See also Play
Extended school year, 1171
Extinction procedures, 901, 907, 910
Extreme emotional dysregulation, 940
Extreme male brain (EMB) theory, 634
Eye(s):
    "eyes task" (Baron-Cohen), 643
    gaze, 317–319, 962
    pointing (augmentative communication systems), 149
    tracking/movement studies, 318, 483–485, 683–684,
        688, 695

Faces, 149, 318, 385, 519–520, 696, 697
Facilitated Communication (FC), 1185. See also
    Augmentative and alternative communication (AAC)
    strategies
Fads/unproven therapies (stresses on families), 1059
False alarm errors, 610
False belief task, 615
Family(ies), 1055–1079. See also Parent(s)
    advocacy training/support, 1063, 1064
    behavioral approach, 1061, 1062
    cognitive approach, 1062, 1064
    education approach, 1061, 1062
    emotional support, 1062, 1064
    goals, 1060
    implications, 1065–1066
    instrumental support, 1063, 1064
    life cycle, autism and, 1068–1078
    modalities, 1064–1065
    parent(s) as cotherapist(s), 1061, 1062
    patterns/studies, 90, 137, 426–429, 437–438, 617–618,
        632–633
    principles, 1060–1061
    relationship enhancement methods, 1061–1063
    school-to-work transition process and, 1092–1093
    social classes, 7, 64
    stressors confronting, 1055–1059
    support, 989, 997–998, 1059–1066
    targeted outcomes, 1061–1064
    TEACCH approach (principles), 1066–1068
    techniques, 1065
FAPE standard (free appropriate public education),
    1163–1164
Feedback on provider work performance, 1127
Feeding problems, 146, 540–542
Fetal alcohol syndrome, 544
Fetal anticonvulsant syndrome, 555–556
Fetal valproate syndrome (FVS), 555–556
First words (normal language development), 337–340
Floor Time, 873, 889, 957
Fluoxetine (Prozac), 1107, 1282–1283
Fluvoxamine, 1107–1108
Foot deformities (Rett syndrome), 154
Fragile X syndrome (FXS), 26, 50, 51, 185, 429–430, 442,
    534, 537, 545–547
France, 1206–1212
Frontal lobe findings, 525
Functional adjustment, 775–776
Functional analysis, 949
Functional Analysis Screening Tool (FAST), 824
Functional Assessment and Curriculum for Teaching
    Everyday Routines (FACTER), 1023
Functional communication training (FCT), 910–912

Functional ecological approach, 817–827
Functional magnetic resonance imaging (fMRI), 355. *See also* Neuroimaging studies
Functional routines (FR), teaching, 1004, 1005
Functioning:
    levels (low, medium, high) autism spectrum conditions, and theory of mind, 628–629
    specific areas of (infancy and early childhood), 233–238
Fusiform face area (FFA), 520–523
Fusiform gyrus (FG), 695
Future research directions, 109–111, 440–441, 617–620, 887–892, 914–917, 1311–1313

Gait, 500
Gangliosidoses, 76
Gastrointestinal inflammation, 629
GAUTENA Autism Society, 1237
Gaze, 317–319, 962
Generalization and maintenance, treatment gains, 826, 887, 914–915, 928, 935–936
Generalized anxiety disorder, 178
Generativity hypothesis (play), 395–396
Genetic counseling, 441–443
Genetics, 425–444, 1309–1310
    animal models and studies of portmortem brain tissues, 440–441
    Asperger syndrome, 108–109
    biological findings, 439
    candidate gene strategies, 433–434
    childhood disintegrative disorder, 77–79
    chromosomal abnormalities and genetically determined medical conditions, 429–430
    clinical implications, 441–443
    epidemiological findings, 434
    epigenetic mechanisms, 439–440
    familial clustering, 437–438
    family studies, 426–429
    future directions, 440–441
    genetic partitioning of autism, 436–440
    genome-wide screens of sib pair samples, 432–433
    leads for candidate genes, 440
    linkage evidence, 438–439
    molecular genetics, 430–434
    multiplex-singleton comparisons: developmental regression, 438
    neurocognitive endophenotypes, 439
    nongenetic risk factors, 434–436
    quantitative genetics, 425–429
    quantitative trait loci (QTL) approaches, 440
    twin studies, 425–426
Germany and Austria, 1212–1215
Gesturing, protoimperative versus protodeclarative, 320
Gilliam Autism Rating Scale (GARS), 542, 714–715, 721–722, 723, 742, 751–752
Goldenhar syndrome, 544
Grading/tests, modifying, 1019
Grandin, Temple:
    contributions to public education on autism, 1184–1186, 1311
    personal perspective of autism, 1276–1285
Greece, 1215–1218
Group homes, 1312
Group work and class discussions, 1019
Guardianship (adolescents/adults), 301
Guilt, 415

Habilitation programs, 1183–1184
Hair analysis for trace elements, 538
Handedness, nonright-, 629
Handicaps, Behavior, and Skills schedule (HBS), 214, 745
Hand splinting, 152
Hanen approach, 958, 959

Head circumference, 500–501, 536
Headstart, 1037
Hearing:
    assessment, 537, 842
    impairment, 50, 540, 553–555, 588–589
    sound sensitivity, 1281–1282
Heller's syndrome (disintegrative psychosis), 8, 15, 71, 135
High probability (high *p*) requests, 901
Hippocampus, 496–497
Histidinemia, 544
HIV, 76
Holistic orientation, 1178–1179
Home-based programs, 1043, 1047–1049
    pivotal response training (PRT) at University of California at Santa Barbara), 1049
    strengths/limitations, 1051
    Young Autism Project at UCLA, 1047–1049
Home Life Checklist, 1023
Homework/assignments, modifying, 1019
Hydrotherapy (Rett syndrome), 153
Hyperlexia, 263, 354, 629, 691
Hypomelanosis of Ito, 544
Hypothalamic-pituitary adrenal axis, 459, 460–461
Hypothyroidism, 76
Hypotonia, 150

IBR skill. *See* Initiating behavior requests (IBR skill)
ICD-10. *See International Statistical Classification of Diseases and Related Health Problems* of the World Health Organization (*ICD/ICD-10*)
Iconic systems, 885
Id, 1229
IDEA (Individuals with Disabilities Education Act), 1090, 1091, 1124, 1161–1162, 1171
Identity development, 1022
If-then rules, embedded use of, 615
IJA/RJA (initiating/responding to joint attention) skills, 654, 655, 662, 663, 664, 667, 672
I LAUGH model, 992, 996
Imitation, 320–321, 382–391, 400–401, 889
    action level, 383
    action on objects, 384
    of body movements (intransitive acts), 384–385
    cross-model matching and body mapping, 389
    delay versus deviance, 386–387
    development and, 382–384
    developmental correlates, 385–386
    emulation, 383
    executive functions, 388
    kinesthesia, 388–389
    methodological issues, 390–391
    model of interpersonal development, 383
    motor problems in autism, 387–388
    neural mechanisms, 389–390
    oral-facial, 385
    possible mechanisms underlying imitation problem, 387–389
    praxis and body mapping, 387
    reciprocal, 889
    response facilitation, 383
    social development, 320–321
    stimulus enhancement, 383
    symbolic content, 388
Immigrant status (epidemiological studies), 62–65
Immune/immunological factors, 539, 542
Impairments in Communication and Social Interaction scale, 667
Incidental teaching, 951
Inclusion. *See* Mainstream
Index of Productive Syntax (IPSyn), 345
Individualization, 1035, 1066–1067, 1178

Individualized Education Program (IEP), 1073, 1164–1165, 1171
Individualized Family Service Plan (IFSP), 1164, 1168
Infant(s)/toddlers, autism in, 31–33, 223–240
    areas of functioning, 233–238
    autism versus mental retardation, 226
    autism versus typical and developmentally delayed peers, 225–226, 230
    communication, 230
    early diagnosis, 31–33, 232–233
    early intervention, 238–239
    methodological limitations, 231
    social interaction, 230
    stereotypical behaviors and repetitive patterns, 230
    symptoms in first year of life, 223–227
    symptoms in second and third years, 227–231
Infant(s)/toddlers with disabilities, services for:
    identification/assessment, 1168
    Individualized Family Service Plan (IFSP), 1164, 1168
    services for (legal issues), 1167–1169
    transition, 1168
Infant Behavioral Summarized Scale (IBSS), 229
Infant Behavior Summarized Evaluation (IBSE), 712
Infantile autism (terminology), 134, 314
Infantile spasms/West syndrome, 544
Infant/Toddler Checklist, 713
Infections, congenital/acquired, 76, 544. See also Rubella
Initial Communication Processes Scale, 800
Initiating behavior requests (IBR skill), 653, 662, 664, 665
Initiation of communication, 954
Instrument(s). See Diagnostic instruments
Instrumental support for families, 1063, 1064
Intellectual disability, 8
Intellectualization of affect, 89
Intelligence, autism and, 290–292, 628–629, 1313
    clinical assessment, 786, 787–792
    epidemiology, 46–49
    outcome and, 215–216
Intentional stance, 629
Interests, circumscribed/all absorbing, 94, 100
International perspectives, 1193–1247
    Australia, 1197–1201
    Canada, 1201–1203
    China, 1203–1206
    comparative analysis, 1193–1194, 1197
    France, 1206–1212
    Germany and Austria, 1212–1215
    Greece, 1215–1218
    Israel, 1218–1221
    Italy, 1221–1222
    Japan, 1223–1226
    Korea, 1226–1228
    Latin America, 1228–1233
    Netherlands, 1233–1235
    Spain, 1235–1238
    Sweden and other Nordic nations, 1238–1243
    United Kingdom, 1243–1247
    United States, 1194–1196
International Statistical Classification of Diseases and Related Health Problems of the World Health Organization (ICD/ICD-10), 2, 10, 591–594. See also Diagnosis/classification
    definition of autism (in DSM-IV and ICD-10), 20–21
    DSM-IV and ICD-10, 17–18
    DSM-IV/ICD-10 systems as epistemological backbone of this Handbook, 2
    from ICD-9 to ICD-10, 17
    ICD-10 PDD classification (overactive disorder with mental retardation), 6
    ICD10 research diagnostic guidelines, 93
    problems of DSM-IV/ICD-10 system of classification, 592–594

Interpersonal development, model of, 383
Interpersonal relationships versus relatedness, 417
Interpersonal supports (social communication), 989–995
    for members of the community, 993–995
    for peers, 990–992
    for teachers and professionals, 992–993
Interruption/redirection, 902–903
Interventions/treatment, 859–861, 1310–1311
    Asperger, 113–116
    behavioral approaches (see Behavioral interventions)
    education as, 1310 (see also Educational interventions)
    language/communication enhancement (see Communication abilities, enhancing; Language interventions)
    PDD-NOS, 187–190
    psychopharmacologic, 1310 (see also Psychopharmacology)
    treatment plan development, 825–827
Intestinal permeability studies, 539
Intradimensional-Extradimensional Shift Task (ID/ED), 609–610, 618, 620
Intraverbals, 964, 965
Intrinsic reinforcers, 947, 959
In vivo protocol, 810, 811
Involuntary movements, 838–840, 847–848
Isodicentric chromosome 15q syndrome, 550–551
Israel, 1218–1221
Italy, 1221–1222

Japan, 1223–1226
Job carving, 1097
Job duties, specification of (provider training), 1126
Joint attention, 650–674
    brain behavior research, 662–668
    brain volume in autism, 660–662
    deficits, 889, 1007
    defined, 650
    initiating/responding skills (IJA/RJA), 654, 655, 662, 663, 664, 667, 672
    neural plasticity and, 657–660
    neurodevelopmental models of autism, 650–674
    role of dorsal medial-frontal cortex in social and nonsocial behavior, 668–673
    skills, 946
    social communication, 979
    social development, 319–320
    social impairment and, 652–655
    social orienting model, 655–662
    theory of mind and, 665–668
Joubert syndrome, 544

Kanner's description, early controversies, 6–8
Karyotype and DNA analysis for Fragile X, 537
Kaufman-Assessment Battery for Children (K-ABC-II), 789, 794
Kinesthesia (imitation), 388–389
Kleinfelter's syndrome, 544
Knowledge:
    examples of "need to know" orientation competencies (provider training), 1139
    "knowing that" versus "knowing how," 687
    trainee skills and, 1138–1140
Korea, 1226–1228

Labels, 2, 10
Landau-Kleffner syndrome, 82, 135
Language. See also Communication:
    acquisition (sibling's perspective), 1266–1267
    behavioral interventions, 910–912
    deficits, 335, 427, 1306
    executive function, 616
    expressive versus receptive, 961

Language *(Continued)*
  neuroimaging studies of, 517–519
  supports for comprehension (school-based), 1018
Language/communication development, 335–356
  Asperger syndrome, 94, 99–100, 115
  in autism, 227, 292–294, 335–336, 341–356
    adolescents/adults, 292–294
    articulation, 343–344
    babbling, 349
    characteristics of speech, 256
    conversational skills, 257–259
    course and developmental change, 341–343
    deficits overlapping with other disorders, 335
    echolalia, 255–256, 346–347
    infancy and early childhood, 227
    intonational peculiarities, 348
    language comprehension in autism, 349–351
    language use, 351–354
    narrative storytelling, 259–260
    personal pronouns, 256–267, 347
    reading, 354–355
    school-age children, 254–260
    suprasegmental aspects of language, 347–349
    syntax and morphology, 345–346
    theories of origin, 355–356
    use of deictic terms, 347
    word use, 344–345
  deficits in relatives, 427
  in typical populations (non-autistic), 336–341
Language Development Survey, 800
Language disorder, autism versus (infancy and early
    childhood), 227
Language interventions, 946–970. *See also* Communication
    abilities, enhancing
  core communicative deficits:
  early language stage, 963–969
  methodological elements common to ABA approaches,
    949
  methods (three major approaches), 947, 959
  prelinguistic stage, 947–961
Latin America, 1228–1233
Law enforcement agencies, fostering awareness, 994–995
Lead level, 537
LEAP program (Learning Experiences, an Alternative
    Program for Preschoolers and Their Parents), 940,
    953, 1035–1036, 1045, 1046–1047
Learning characteristics/styles, 114, 983–986, 1007–1008
Learning/educational supports, 989, 995–997
Least restrictive environment (LRE), 1165–1166
Legal issues:
  classification, 9
  educating children with autism, 1161–1172
    FAPE standard (free appropriate public education),
      1163–1164
    IDEA (Individuals with Disabilities Education Act),
      1090, 1091, 1124, 1161–1162, 1171
    Individualized Education Program (IEP), 1164–1165,
      1171
    Individualized Family Service Plan (IFSP), 1164,
      1168
    least restrictive environment (LRE), 1165–1166
  employment for adolescents/adults with autism, 9,
    1089–1091
    Americans with Disabilities Act, 1091
    Vocational Rehabilitation Act of 1973 (employment),
      1090–1091
Leigh disease, 76
Leiter International Performance Scale Revised
    (Leiter-R), 374, 787, 789, 844
Lesch-Nyhan syndrome, 544
Levels of Narrative Development, 813
Life skills, 1023

Limbic system, 495–496, 497, 525–526
Lipofuscinosis, 76
Litigation, parent-initiated, 1124–1125
Living arrangements (adolescents/adults), 297–298
Loss/death of parent, 1273–1274
Luria-Nebraska Neurosopsychological battery, 844

Mainstream, 1029–1039
  definition, 1029
  early education and beyond, 1037–1038
  early inclusion, 1035–1036
  empirically supported interventions, 1038
  individualized, comprehensive programming, 1035
  laws/regulations, 1120
  models of inclusion, 1035
  outcomes of inclusion, 1034–1035
  peers, role of, 1037
  peers initiation, 1030
  planning inclusion activities, 1037
  settings, 867–868
  social skills, 1029–1033
  statewide services, 1036–1037
  teachers' and parents' perspectives, 1033–1034
  terminology (mainstream/inclusion/integration), 1029
  training inclusion providers, 1129–1130
Maintenance and generalization, 826, 887, 914–915, 928,
    935–936
Mands, 963, 965
Manual signs, 955
Mastery criterion (provider training), 1146–1147
Maternal drug/alcohol abuse, 436, 544
Maternal hypothyroidism, 436
May Center for Early Childhood Education, 1036
Mean Length of Utterance (MLU), 345, 805
Measles-mumps-rubella (MMR) vaccination, 435–436,
    541. *See also* Rubella
Measurement, qualitative/quantitative, 935–936
MECP2 gene, 130–132, 136, 148. *See also* Rett syndrome
Mediation, 1166
Medical conditions associated with autism, 7, 50, 543–556.
    See also specific conditions
  Angelman/Prader-Willi syndromes, 76, 135, 551–552
  CATCH 22, 552
  cerebral palsy, 50
  congenital blindness and deafness, 553–555
  congenital rubella, 50
  Down syndrome, 50, 547–548
  epidemiological studies, 50–51
  epilepsy, 50
  fetal anticonvulsant/valproate syndrome, 555–556
  fetal valproate syndrome (FVS), 555–556
  Fragile X, 50, 545–547
  hearing deficits, 50
  isodicentric chromosome 15q syndrome, 550–551
  mitochondrial disorders, 549–550
  Möbius syndrome, 552–553
  neurofibromatosis, 50
  phenylketonuria (PKU), 50, 553
  semantics (versus autism associated with medical
      conditions), 535
  syndromic associations, 544
  tuberous sclerosis, 50, 543–545
  velocardiofacial syndrome (VCFS), 552
  visual deficits, 50
  Williams-Beuren syndrome (WBS), 548–549
Medical conditions associated with CDD, 76
Medical evaluation in autism, 536–539, 782–783
  definitive hearing test, 537
  electroencephalography, 538
  karyotype and DNA analysis for Fragile X, 537
  lead level, 537
  metabolic testing, 538

neuroimaging studies, 538
physical and neurologic examination, 536–537
   head circumference, 536
   recurrence risk estimate for ideopathic autism, 537
   sensorimotor function, 536–537
tests of unproven value, 538–539
Medical signs/symptoms associated with autism, 539–543
Medications. *See* Psychopharmacology
Memory, 369–372, 388, 611, 788, 1279
Mental Development Index (MDI), 791
Mental representations (enactive mind), 689–694
Mental retardation:
   Asperger syndrome, 94
   autism and, 28, 51, 291, 300–303
   autism diagnosis more acceptable than, 1308
   autism versus (infancy and early childhood), 226
   categorical classification systems, problems of, 587
   differential diagnosis (PDD-NOS), 176–177
   difficult life event, 299–300
   guardianship, 301
   ICD-10 PDD classification (overactive disorder with
      mental retardation), 6
   lifestyle risk factors and, 297
   and mental retardation, 300–303
   self-help skills, 300–301
   sexuality, 301
   work, 301–302
Metabolic testing, 538
Metachromatic leukodystrophy, 76
Metaphoric language, 691
Methylphenidate, 1110
Mexico. *See* Latin America
Milieu teaching, 950–951, 959
Miller Assessment for Preschoolers (MAP), 844, 846, 847
Mindblindness/empathizing theory, 629–631
Mind-mind problem, 691
Mind reading, 629, 873
Minimal speech approach (MSA), 952, 959
Minor physical anomalies (MPAs), 501
Mirtazapine, 1109
Mismatch negativity (MMN), 481
Mitochondrial deficits/disorders, 76, 549–550
MMR vaccine. *See* Measles-mumps-rubella (MMR)
   vaccination
Möbius syndrome, 552–553
Modeling, 870
Modified Checklist for Autism in Toddlers (M-CHAT),
   229, 714–715, 716–717. *See also* Checklist for Autism
   in Toddlers (CHAT)
Modified Rogers Scale, 848
Molecular genetics, 430–434. *See also* Genetics
Monozygotic twinning as risk factor, 434
Montgomery County Public School System Preschool for
   Children with Autism, 1037
Mood stabilizers, 1111
More Than Words program, 958
Morphology, syntax and, 345–346
Mortality and causes of death, 212–213, 296–297
Motivation, 954, 1231
Motivation Assessment Scale (MAS), 824
Motor. *See also* Sensory and motor features in autism:
   apraxia, 500
   Asperger syndrome, 94, 100
   assessments, 845–848
   autism, 387–388
   clumsiness, 94
   features, 834–835
   imitation, 237–238
   skills and praxis, 845–847
Motor Free Visual Perception Test, 844
Mullen, 787, 791
Multiaxial diagnostic approaches, 14

Multidisciplinary training (TEACCH component), 1177
Multiple Complex (or Multiplex) Developmental Disorder
   (MCDD), 182–184, 186
Multiplex developmental disorder, 587
Multiplex-singleton comparisons, 438
Mutual regulation, 940

Naltrexone, 1111–1112
Narrative assessment, 810–813
Narrative Rubrics, 813
Narrative storytelling (school-age children), 259–260
National Research Council (NRC) guidelines, 927–928
Natural environments (staff performance), 1130
Naturalistic approaches, 883–885, 947, 950, 959, 964–966
Natural Language Paradigm (NLP), 929, 930, 937, 940,
   941, 952
Negative priming effect, 609
NEPSY, 787, 793–794
Netherlands, 1233–1235
Neural basis for autism (genetics), 443
Neural mechanisms (imitation), 389–390
Neurobiological factors, 75–77, 79, 140–141
Neurochemical abnormalities (tests of unproven value),
   539
Neurochemical alterations, Rett syndrome, 141–143
Neurochemical studies of autism, 453–465
   amino acids and acetylcholine, 462–463
   blood 5-HT, 454–455
   cardiovascular, 459
   cerebrospinal fluid, 459
   CSF 5-HIAA, 456–457
   CSF HVA, 457
   dopamine, 457, 458
   hypothalamic-pituitary adrenal axis, 459, 460–461
   neuroendocrine studies of serotonergic functioning, 456
   norepinephrine, 458–459
   peptide research, 461–462
   plasma, 457–458, 459
   purines and related compounds, 463–464
   serotonin, 453–456
   stress response systems in autism, 459
   thyroid hormone and TRH test, 460–461
   tryptophan metabolism, 455–456
   urine, 459
   urine 5-HIAA and 5-HT, 455
Neurocognitive endophenotypes, 439
Neurofibromatosis, 50, 51, 544
Neuroimaging studies, 515–527, 538
   blood oxygen level dependent (BOLD) signal, 517
   communication and language, 355, 517–519
   face perception deficits, 519–520
   fMRI, 516–517
   frontal lobe findings, 525
   fusiform face area (FFA), 520–523
   PDD-NOS, 171–172
   role of amygdala, 525–526
   social cognition, 524–525
   social perception, 520–524
Neurolipidosis, 76
Neurological/medical issues (overview), 423–424
Neurologic aspects of autism, 473–504
   central nervous system function, 474–488
   central nervous system structure, 488–500
   clinical neurology, 500–503
   dysmorphic features (minor physical anomalies; MPAs),
      501
   electroencephalograms (EEGs) in autism, 503
   epilepsy in autism, 502–503
   evoked potentials, 475–483
   head circumference, 500–501
   neurologic examination, 500
   neuropathology, 488–490

Neurologic aspects of autism (Continued)
  neuropsychologic profile, 486–488
  oculomotor physiology, 483–485
  pathogenesis, theories of, 490–491
  postural physiology, 485–486
  structural brain imaging, 491–500
Neuropathology, 139–140, 488–490
Neuropsychological assessment, 786, 793–794
Neuropsychological characteristics in autism and related
    conditions, 365–376
  attention, 367–369
  cognitive profiles, 374–375
  executive function, 372–374
  memory, 369–372
  sensory perception, 366–367
Neuropsychological studies, 102–104, 171, 486–488, 645
New situations (sibling's perspective), 1269
Nomothetic measures, 820
Noncontingent reinforcement, 907–908
Nonright-handedness, 629
Nonverbal communication, 89, 235–236
Nonverbal intelligence, 272
Nonverbal learning disabilities (NLD), 97
Nordic nations, 1238–1243
Norepinephrine, 458–459
Normality:
  borderlines of (problems of categorical classification
      systems), 591
  eccentric, 587
  physical appearance, 1057–1058
Nuclear autism, 184
Nutrition:
  feeding problems, 146, 540–542
  growth patterns and (Rett syndrome), 145–146

Observational assessments, 843–845
Observational studies (emotion), 409
Obsessive-compulsive disorder (OCD), 178, 265, 275, 590
Obsessive Desire for Sameness, 667
Obstetrical complications/risk factors, 434–435, 539–540
Oculomotor physiology, 483–485
"Official" status, diagnostic systems, 10
Olanzapine, 1105
Onset:
  age/type of, and problems of categorical classification
      systems, 593
  Asperger syndrome, 90, 94, 98–99
  childhood disintegrative disorder (CDD), 72–74
  criteria (autism versus Asperger syndrome), 92
Operant conditioning procedures, early educational
    applications of (provider training), 1125
Optimal arousal, 940
Oral-facial imitations, 385
Oral-motor apraxia or dyspraxia, 500
Organization(s):
  parent (international), 1206, 1211–1212, 1214–1215,
      1219, 1222–1223, 1228
  school-based, 1019–1020
Organizational behavior management (OBM), 1128
Organizational citizenship, 1139
Original narcissism, 1229
Orthogonal movement disorder exams, 847
Orthopedic aspects and intervention (Rett syndrome),
    150–154
Outcome(s), 201–217, 288–300
  adaptive behavior, 294–295
  adolescents/adults, 288–300
  Asperger syndrome, 109–110, 213
  changes in recent years, 203–205
  cognitive ability, changes in, 205
  criminal justice system, autism and, 299–300
  deterioration in adulthood, 213–214

  developmental course, 288–290
  education, 205–208, 294–295
  employment, 205–208, 298–299
  epilepsy, 295–296
  higher functioning individuals, and risk of psychiatric
      disturbance, 210–211
  of inclusion, 1034–1035
  intelligence, 290–292
  language, 292–294
  living arrangements, 297–298
  marriage, 299
  mortality/causes of death, 212–213, 296–297
  predictors of, 215–216
  psychiatric disorders, 208–212, 295
  social, 201–204
  suicide, 212
  victims of crime, 299

Parent(s). See also Family(ies):
  advocacy, 1308–1309
  associations (international), 1206, 1211–1212,
      1214–1215, 1219, 1222–1223, 1228
  collaboration with:
    provider training, 1129
    TEACCH component, 1067, 1176, 1178
  consent (education, legal issues), 1166
  as cotherapists, 1061, 1062
  death of, 1273–1274
  involvement, 775, 936
  litigation (impact on provider training), 1124–1125
  pathogenesis (history of autism), 7
  reports, 225, 227, 408–409, 712
  stressors confronting families, 1055–1059
  training, 1061
Paroxetine, 1108
Passive group, 249–250, 597–598
Pathogenesis, theories of, 490–491
Pathological demand avoidance syndrome (PDA), 586
Patty-cake, 320
Pay Attention! program, 619
Peabody Developmental Motor Scales (PDMS), 846
Peabody Picture Vocabulary Test (PPVT/PPVT-R/
    PPVT-III), 147, 293, 790, 804
Pediatric epilepsy syndromes, 544. See also Epilepsy
Pediatric Evaluation of Disability Inventory (PEDI), 845
Pediatric Speech Intelligibility Test, 844
Peekaboo, 320
Peers:
  interpersonal support for, 990–992
  relationships with, 303, 323–324, 1020
  role of, in interventions, 938–939, 968–969, 1037
Peptide research, 461–462
Perception-for-action systems, 691–693
Perceptual coherence, 642
Perceptual reasoning, 788
Performance appraisal (provider training), 1128, 1144
Perinatal factors, 539–540
Perseveration, 1231, 1307
Personality, clinical assessment, 786
Personality disorders:
  avoidant, 178, 179
  differential diagnosis (PDD-NOS), 178–180
  schizoid, 97, 178, 179, 586, 590
  schizotypal, 179, 590
Personal perspectives, 1253
  mother (working model, community-integrated
      residential services for adults with autism),
      1255–1264
  personal (Grandin), 1276–1285
  sibling, 1265–1275
  teacher, 1287–1303
Personal pronouns, 256–267

Pervasive developmental disorder (PDDs):
  conditions currently classified as (in *ICD-10* and *DSM-IV*), 6
  nonautistic, defined, 21–25
  term introduced (*DSM-III,* 1980), 2
Pervasive developmental disorder not otherwise specified (PDD-NOS), 165–191
  Asperger syndrome and, 173–174, 735
  Attention Deficit Hyperactivity Disorder (ADHD) versus, 177, 268
  biological studies of, 169–172
  case of James, 274–275
  classification issues, 2, 6, 16–17, 25, 233, 275
  conceptual background, 167–169
  differential diagnosis, 172–184
    Asperger syndrome, 173–174
    Attention Deficit Hyperactivity Disorder (ADHD), 177
    autistic disorder, 174–175
    childhood disintegrative disorder, 175
    childhood-onset conditions, 177–178
    developmental language disorders, 175
    generalized anxiety disorder, 178
    mental retardation, 176–177
    obsessive-compulsive disorder (OCD), 178
    other developmental disorders, 175–176
    other PDD entities, 172–175
    personality disorders, 178
    pragmatic language impairment (PLI), 175–176
    reactive attachment disorder, 180
    schizophrenia, 180–181
    semantic-pragmatic disorder, 175
    social phobias, 181–182
    table, conditions to be considered, 172
  epidemiology, 53, 184–185
  etiology, 185–186
  multiple meanings, 168–169
  natural history, 186–187
  nosology, 166
  self-injury, 189
  subgroups (two potential) within, 182–184
  treatment, 187–190
Pervasive Developmental Disorder Problems Scale, 748
Pervasive Developmental Disorders Rating Scale (PDDRS), 742, 746–747
Pervasive Developmental Disorders Screening Test (PDDST):
  Stage 1, 714–715, 717, 723
  Stage 2, 714–715, 717–718, 723
Pharmacotherapy. *See* Psychopharmacology
Phenocopies, 436
Phenomenological approach/systems, 12
Phenotype, broader autism, 32–33, 116, 427, 428, 617–618, 645, 1058, 1308
Phenotype versus genotype, 12
Phenylketonuria (PKU), 50, 51, 76, 136, 141, 553
Phonics, learning to read with, 1284
Phonology, 338
Physical and neurologic examination, 536–537
Piagetian stages, 148
Pica, 905–906
Picture Arrangement, 788
Picture Exchange Communication System (PECS), 155, 885, 891, 929, 955–957, 959, 964
Pivotal response training (PRT), 883–885, 888, 912, 929, 930, 941, 953
  behaviors, 954
  curriculum, 874
  defined, 1004
  school-based, 1004, 1005
  UCSB (UC at Santa Barbara), 1049
Plasma, 457–458, 459

Plasticity, neural, 657–660
Play, 236–237, 382, 391–400
  autism-specific findings in pretend play, 392
  brain behavior correlates, 397
  clinical evaluation, 795
  curricula/teaching skills, 870, 928, 1011, 1012
  deficient imaginative, 1307
  delay versus deficit, 397–398
  ecological model of autism, 398–399
  generativity hypothesis, 395–396
  impaired sensorimotor and functional play, 394–395
  intact symbolic abilities, 393–394
  methodological issues, 399–400
  normal development (language and communication), 339
  sibling's perspective, 1271
  social development, 321–322
  symbolic, 391–397
Positive Behavioral Support (PBS), 934–935
Postural physiology, 485–486
Prader-Willi. *See* Angelman/Prader-Willi syndromes
Pragmatic language impairment (PLI), 98, 175–176
Pragmatic Rating Scale (PRS), 808–810
Pragmatics, 339, 805–806, 962
Praise, behavior-specific (provider training), 1127
Praxis, 387, 845–847
Precedence rule, 92
Predictive value (negative/positive) of screening measures, 711–712
Pre-Linguistic Autism Observation Schedule, 740
Prelinguistic Communication Assessment, 801
Preschool curricula, 873–874
Preschool Language Scale, 800, 804
Pressure/squeeze machine, 1281, 1282
Preverbal communication, 235–236
Pride, asocial form of, 415
Princeton Child Developmental Institute (PCDI), 873, 875, 1035, 1045, 1047, 1131, 1132
Problem solving, 1016–1017, 1280
Procedural reliability, 826, 827
Process, diagnostic, 1, 9
Processing speed, 788
Professional relationships, family stress and, 1058–1059
Professional training. *See* Training (preparation of autism specialists)
Profile scatter (clinical assessment), 775
PROMPT system, 951–953, 957, 959
Pronoun use, 347, 804–805, 961
Prosody, 962
Prosody Voice Screening Protocol (PVSP), 813–814
Provider training. *See* Training (preparation of autism specialists)
Psychiatric conditions:
  adolescents/adults with autism, 295
  categorical classification systems, problems of, 587
  outcomes, 208–211
  personality disorders (*see* Personality disorders)
  psychopathology (Japan), 1224–1225
  psychosis/phychotic, 210, 1229
  risk of, and level of functioning, 210–211
  schizophrenia (*see* Schizophrenia)
Psychoanalytic conceptions, 1229
Psychodynamic treatment approaches, 1239, 1242–1243
Psychoeducational Profile-Revised (PEP-R), 543, 743, 757–758, 1227
Psychogenic theories/hypothesis, 7, 1304–1305
Psychological assessment. *See* Clinical evaluation in autism spectrum disorders
Psychomotor Development Index (PDI), 791
Psychopathy (terminology), 91
Psychopharmacology, 1102–1113
  aggression, 906
  anxiety, 269

Psychopharmacology *(Continued)*
  Asperger syndrome, 116
  atypical antipsychotics, 1102–1106
  Japan, 1226
  mood stabilizers, 1111
  naltrexone, 1111–1112
  secretin, 1112
  need for research, 1310
  PDD-NOS, 189
  personal perspective (Grandin), 1282–1283
  Rett syndrome, 143–145
  self-injury, 906
  serotonin reuptake inhibitors (SRIs), 1106–1109,
    1282–1283
  single-mechanism intervention research, 1183
  stimulants, 1109–1111
Psychosis, 210, 1229
Psychosocial deprivation (problems of categorical
    classification systems), 591
PTSD, 12
Public policy perspectives, 1119–1121
Publishers, curricula, 864
Punishment procedures, 908–910
Purines and related compounds, 463–464

Qualitative versus quantitative approaches, 935
Quality of care, defined, 1127
Quality of life improvements, 1134–1136
Quantitative genetics, 425–429, 440
Quantitative trait loci (QTL), 440
Quetiapine, 1105

Rainman, 1097, 1245, 1299, 1311
Rapid motor imitation (RMI) response approach, 948, 959
Reactive attachment disorder (differential diagnosis, PDD-
    NOS), 180
Reading, 354–355, 1284
Real-Life Rating Scale (RLRS), 742
Reception by feature, function, and class (RFFC), 964
Receptive (sequence of teaching verbal behavior), 965
Receptive-Expressive Emergent Language Scale (REEL),
    83, 800
Recreation:
  school-based, 1023
  sibling's perspective, 1270–1271
  sports, 994
Regional centers, 1176
Register variation, 806, 808
REHABIT program, 620
Reinforcement:
  assessment of natural communities of, 827
  behavioral interventions based on, 903–907
  differential, 904–910
    of Alternative Behavior (DRA/DRAlt), 904, 905, 906,
      907
    of Incompatible Behavior (DRI), 904, 905, 906, 907,
      908, 909
    of Low Rates of Responding (DRL), 904, 906
    of Other Behavior (DRO), 904–905, 906, 907, 910
Relationship development intervention (RDI) model, 929,
    940, 958–959
Relationship enhancement methods, 1061–1063
Relaxation techniques, 913, 1016
Reliability, 736–740
Repetitive behavior, 616, 635. *See also* Stereotypies
Research:
  future directions, 109–111, 440–441, 617–620,
    887–892, 914–917, 1311–1313
  gap between clinical application and, 1181–1182, 1186
  role of, 13–14
Residential services, 1076, 1077, 1205, 1255–1264
Residual autism, 15–16

Respondent conditioning procedures, 913–914
Response facilitation (imitation), 383
Responsibility/guilt (sibling's perspective), 1265–1266
Rett syndrome, 126–156, 500
  ambulation, 153
  apraxia-ataxia, 150–151
  clinical characteristics, 133
  clinical presentation and natural history, 126–129, 133
  cognitive and adaptive functioning, 146–148
  communication abilities, 148–150
  definition, 21
  diagnostic criteria, 129–130, 131, 132
  differential diagnosis features, 25, 81, 132–135
  drug therapy, 143–145
  educational implications, 154–155
  EEG characteristics, 145
  epidemiology, 135–136
  etiology, 136–139
  feeding problems, 146
  foot deformities, 154
  genetics (MECP2 mutation), 78–79, 130–132, 431–432
  growth patterns and nutrition, 145–146
  hydrotherapy, 153
  ICD-10 and *DSM-IV* inclusion, 6, 8, 11
  infantile autism compared to, 134
  neuroanatomy, 140–141
  neurochemical alterations, 141–143
  neurologic examination, 500
  neuropathology, 139–140
  orthopedic aspects and intervention, 150–154
  scoliosis, 154
  spasticity, 153
  stages, 128–129, 133
  stereotypic hand movements, 127, 150, 151–153
  variants, 130–132
Revised Knox Preschool Play Scale (PPS), 845
Reynell Developmental Language Scales, 83, 800, 804
Rigidity, 1307
Rimland Diagnostic Form for Behavior Disturbed Children,
    742–743, 744
Risk estimate, recurrence (for ideopathic autism), 537
Risk factors, nongenetic, 434–436
Risperidone, 1103–1105
Ritvo-Freeman Real Life Rating Scale (RLRS), 745
RJA/IJA (initiating/responding to joint attention) skills,
    654, 655, 662, 663, 664, 667, 672
Romanian children, 418–419
Rorschach Inkblot Test, 794
Rosetti Infant Toddler Language Scale, 800
Rubella:
  congenital, 7, 50, 51
  measles-mumps-rubella (MMR) vaccination, 435–436
Rumination, treatment of, 901–902

Safety (provider training), 1139
Safety net for student, 1015
Salaries, 1148
Salience, topology of, 688, 695
Sameness, insistence on, 667, 871
Savant skills, 354, 644
SCAN (Screening Test for Auditory Processing Disorders),
    844
Scanning patterns in response to social visual/verbal cues,
    685
SCERTS model. *See* Social Communication, Emotional
    Regulation, Transactional Support (SCERTS) model
Schizoid personality disorder, 97, 178, 179, 586, 590
Schizophrenia:
  Asperger syndrome, 101, 187
  classification:
    historical perspective, 8, 15, 27, 70, 89, 584
    problems of categorical systems, 590

differential diagnosis, PDD-NOS, 179, 180–181
echolalia, 255
outcomes, 209–210
retrospective studies, 428
Schizophrenic psychosis in childhood, 585
Schizophrenic syndrome of childhood, 585, 1243
Schizotypal personality disorder, 179, 590
School(s)/school-based programs, 303, 1003–1023, 1044,
    1049–1051, 1312
  academic supports, 1018–1020
  applied behavioral analysis (ABA), 1005–1007
  cognitive strengths and challenges, 1016–1017
  communication skills, 1010, 1012
  curriculum content, 1010–1011
  daily routines, 1010, 1012
  discrete trial training (DT), 1004, 1005, 1007–1009
  emotions, stress, anxiety during adolescence, 1014–1015
  functional routines (FR), 1004, 1005
  general skills and peer interactions, 1011
  instructional techniques, 1008–1010
  learning characteristics of children with autism related
      to curriculum needs, 1007–1008
  life skills and recreation, 1023
  models, 1044, 1049–1051
    Denver Model at University of Colorado, 1050–1051
    strengths/limitations, 1052
    TEACCH, 1049–1050
  organizations and time management, 1019–1020
  pivotal response training, 1004, 1005 (see also Pivotal
      response training (PRT))
  play skills, 1011, 1012
  preacademic skills, 1010–1011, 1012
  problem solving, 1016–1017
  progress in recent decades, 1312
  sensory differences, 1013–1014, 1015
  social interaction skills, 1011, 1012
  social supports, 1020–1022
  strategies, 1004–1008, 1011–1013
  teaching areas, 1011–1013
  transition to adulthood, 1022–1023
  visual thinking, 1017
School-age children. See Children of school age, with an
    autistic spectrum disorder
School Function Assessment (SFA), 845
School-to-work transition process, 1091–1093
Scoliosis, 154
Screeners versus instruments, diagnostic, 112–113
Screening measures (for autism in young children),
    707–724
  autism-specific, 713–717
  early identification of autism and, 707–709
  general characteristics, 709–712
  level 1, 712–717
  level 2, 717–723
  non-age-specific, 719–723
  nonspecific, 712–713
  overview table, 714–715 (see also specific measures)
  positive and negative predictive value, 711–712
  psychometric characteristics, 710–712
  retrospective analysis of home videotapes, 708
  sensitivity and specificity, 710–711
Screening Tool for Autism in Two-Year-Olds (STAT),
    714–715, 718–719, 723
Scripts, 871
Secretin, 1112, 1183
Seizures, 7, 76, 144. See also Epilepsy
Self-help skills, 300–301
Self-initiated actions, 673
Self-injurious behavior, 189, 901, 906, 909–910,
    1267–1268
Self-knowledge, identity development and, 1022
Self-management, 871–872, 885–886, 913

Self-monitoring (provider training), 1128
Self-organizing facility, 654
Self-regulation, 940, 954, 981
Self-support, 116
Semantic memory, 370
Semantic-pragmatic disorder, 97–98, 175
Semantics, 338
Sensitivity/specificity, 710–711
Sensory conditions, behavioral assessment and, 824
Sensory Experiences Questionnaire (SEQ), 843
Sensory Integration and Praxis Test (SIPT), 844, 846, 847
Sensory and motor features in autism, 536–537, 831–850
  clinical assessment, 840–848
  development, 831–840
  intervention considerations, 848–849
  motor assessments, 845–848
  play, and, 394–395
  questionnaires and structured interviews, 842, 843
  sensory assessment, 841–845
  sensory differences, and school-based interventions,
      1013–1014, 1015
  sensory features, 831–834
  sensory perception, 366–367
  sensory problems (Grandin), 1280–1282
Sensory Processing Assessment (SPA), 844
Sensory Profile, 843
Sensory Sensitivity Questionnaire-Revised, 843
Separation (sibling's perspective), 1271–1273
Sequenced Inventory of Communicative Development
    (SICD), 83, 804
Serotonin, 453–456
Serotonin reuptake inhibitors (SRIs), 1106–1109
Sertraline, 1108
Service-research interaction (TEACCH component),
    1175–1176
Setback phenomenon, 223
Severe developmental language disorder (SDLD), 588
Sex education, 1313
Sex hormones, 461
Sexual abuse allegations, 1185
Sexuality, 301, 304
Sheltered workshops, 1095
Shutdown, 940
Sibling's personal perspective, 1265–1275
Sib pair samples, genome-wide screens of, 432–433
Signing, manual, 885, 955
Simpson-Angus Scale for Extrapyramidal Symptoms, 848
Situations Options Choices Strategies and Stimulation
    (SOCCSS) program, 996
Skill acquisition/enhancement, 910–913, 1178
Skill-based learning opportunities, 937–938
Skinnerian categories of verbal behaviors, 963–964
Sleep disorders/disturbances, 503, 542–543
Small Wonders Preschool class, 1046
Smith-Lemli-Opitz syndrome, 544
Social anxiety, 428
Social Attribution Task (SAT), 666
Social class, 7, 62–65
Social cognition, 104–106, 519–525, 695–698
Social communication:
  atypical (stressors confronting families with autism),
      1057
  high-functioning autism and Asperger syndrome,
      917–999
    core challenges, 978–983
    educational programming, 986–998
    emotional regulation, 980–983
    environmental modifications, 997
    family support, 989
    family supports, 997–998
    interpersonal supports, 989–995
    joint attention, 979

Social communication *(Continued)*
    learning and educational supports, 989, 995–997
    learning style differences, impact on intervention
        planning, 983–986
    mutual regulation, 981
    self regulation, 981
    symbol use, 979
    transactional supports, 989
    visual and organizational supports, 995–997
Social Communication, Emotional Regulation,
    Transactional Support (SCERTS) model, 929,
    932–941, 959, 966, 988–989
Social Communication Questionnaire (SCQ), 714–715,
    722, 740, 753, 740
Social development in autism, 312–327
    social dysfunction as diagnostic feature, 313–316
    specific social processes, 317–325
    studying social behavior in autism, 316–317
    theoretical models of autistic social dysfunction,
        325–326
Social-emotional assessment, 794–795
Social-emotional maladjustment (SEM), and Asperger
    syndrome, 114
Social impairment/functioning, 89, 94, 99, 230, 652–655,
    1306
Social interventions, school-based, 1011, 1012, 1020–1021
Socialization (sibling's perspective), 1268–1269
Social orienting model, 655–657, 660–662
Social outcomes, 201–204
Social perception, 519–526
Social phobias (differential diagnosis, PDD-NOS),
    181–182
Social processes and executive function, 613–616
Social Responsiveness Scale (SRS), 742, 746
Social skills:
    behavioral interventions, 912–913
    curricula, 868–872
    mainstream, 1029–1033
    personal perspective (Grandin), 1279
Social stories, 869–870, 996
Social supports (school-based), 1020–1022
Social validity, 876, 916
Social world as an open-domain task (enactive mind),
    687–689
Son-Rise program, 958
Sound sensitivity, 1281–1282. *See also* Sensory and motor
    features in autism
Spain, 740, 1235–1238
Spasticity (Rett syndrome), 153
Special Olympics, 994
Spectrum/continuum:
    of autistic disorders, 88
    of interventions, 1183–1184
    orientation, 930–931
    of professionals, 1183
    of services, 1177
    of social roles, 1182–1183
Speech. *See also* Communication; Language:
    assessment, 777–778
    characteristics (school-age children), 256
    minimal speech approach (MSA), 952
    patterns of development, 335
    as predictor of outcome (age 5), 216
    responsiveness to, 805
    social (interest in), 319
Sports, 994
Squeeze machine (Grandin), 1281, 1282
Stanford-Binet, 374
STAR program, 1005–1006, 1008, 1012
State and local educational agencies (SEA, LEA), 1162
Statewide services, 1036–1037
Statistical approaches (subtyping), 29–30

Stay-put requirement (legal issues), 1167
Stereotyped movement disorder, 27
Stereotypies:
    autism, 27, 230, 500, 635, 847
    executive function and, 616, 635
    versus involuntary movements (tics/dyskinesias), 847
    research about, lack of, 1307
    Rett syndrome, 127, 150, 151–153
    treatment, noncontingent reinforcement, 908
Stigmatization, potential for, 12–13
Stimulants, 1109–1111
Stimulus/stimuli, 383, 902, 1231
Story Structure Decision Tree, 813
Strengths/needs, emphasis on, 820
Stress:
    exercise for, 1015
    response systems (sympathetic/adrenomedullary and
        hypothalamic-pituitary-adrenal axis function), 459
    sources of, for families, 1055–1059
Strong Narrative Assessment Procedure (SNAP), 813
Structural brain imaging (CNS function), 491–500
Structured behavioral interventions, 883
Structured classrooms/teaching, 937, 1067, 1177, 1178.
    See also Curriculum and classroom structure
Structured descriptive assessment (SDA), 824
Studies to Advance Autism Research and Treatment
    (STAART), 1196
Subacute sclerosing panencephalitis, 76
Subtyping autism, 28–31, 440
Suicide, 208, 212
Supervisory attention system (SAS), 670
Supported employment, 207, 302, 1093–1094. *See also*
    Employment
Symbiotic psychosis (Mahler), 8–9, 584
Symbolic behavior, 947
Symbolic content (imitation), 388
Symbolic play. *See* Play
Symbol use (social communication), 979
Syndromic associations, 544
Syntax, 338, 345–346, 963
System(s):
    abstract, 631
    aided/unaided (AAC), 801
    motoric, 631
    natural, 631
    organizable, 631
    social, 631
    technical, 631
Systemizing. *See* Empathizing-systemizing theory

Tact(s), 964, 965
Tactile Defensiveness and Discrimination Test-Revised
    (TDDT-R), 844
Task analysis, 949
TEACCH (Treatment and Education of Autistic and
    Related Communication Handicapped Children) at
    University of North Carolina, 1049–1050, 1174–1180
    components, 1175–1177
    educational interventions, 1049–1050
    philosophy and principles, 1177–1179
    principles (working with families), 1066–1068
    professional training, 1131, 1132
    related issues, 190, 207, 289, 302, 619–620, 867, 889,
        932–933, 953, 1036, 1037, 1043, 1055, 1061, 1064,
        1066–1068, 1070–1071, 1073, 1131, 1132, 1184,
        1237
    supported employment, 302
Teacher(s), 888, 948–950, 1033–1034
Teacher's personal perspective (adult outcomes),
    1287–1303
    data collection, 1287–1288, 1303
    implications, 1299–1302

students:
  Bill, 1288–1290
  David, 1290–1291
  Eric, 1297–1299
  Jimmy, 1292–1293
  John, 1293–1295
  Karen, 1291–1292
  Polly, 1295–1296
  Tom, 1296–1297
Teach Me Language, 959, 963–964
Team sports, 994
Teasing/bullying from peers, 1021–1022
Technology/computers, 115–116, 871, 916–917, 955, 1142
Temperament and Atypical Behavior Scale Screener (TABS Screener), 713
Temporal analysis (behavioral assessment), 824
Temporal constraints on models of social adaptation, 694–695
Test of Early Language Development, 804
Test of Playfulness (ToP), 845–846
Test of Visual Motor Skills-Revised (TVMS), 847
Test of Visual-Perceptual Skills (nonmotor) Revised, 844
Thalamus, 498
Thalidomide, 436, 544
Theoretical perspectives, 579–581
  categorical classification systems (problems), 583–600
  enactive mind, 682–699
  executive functions, 606–621
  joint attention and neurodevelopmental models of autism, 650–674
  language/communication, theories of origin, 355–356
  models of autistic social dysfunction (social development), 325–326
  role of theory in diagnosis/classification, 11
  weak central coherence account of autism, 640–646
Theory of mind, 628–636
  attributional component-629
  austism versus Asperger, 104–106
  autism spectrum conditions, 628–629
  central coherence theory, 635
  cognitive development, 634–635
  curricula, 872–873
  empathizing-systemizing theory, 631–634
  executive function and, 615
  executive function theory, 634–635
  extreme male brain (EMB) theory, 634
  impairment, 613
  joint attention, 660, 665–668
  mindblindness/empathizing theory, 629–631
  neuropsychological perspective, 519, 527
  social development, 325
  task, second-order, 698
  Williams-Beuren syndrome, 549
Thyroid hormone and TRH test, 460–461, 539
Time management, 1019–1020
Time trends (epidemiological studies), 56–62
  approaches, 58
  comparison of cross-sectional surveys, 59–60
  incidence studies, 61
  overview table, 57
  referral statistics, 58–59
  repeat surveys in defined geographic areas, 60–61
  successive birth cohorts, 61
Toddler Infant Motor Evaluation (TIME), 846
Toe walking, 500
Toilet training (sibling's perspective), 1267
Tooth grinding, 902
Topology of salience, 688, 695
Touch sensitivity (Grandin), 1280–1281
Tourette's syndrome/disorder, 27, 101, 255, 268, 354, 588, 838

Tower tasks, 373, 607, 615
Train-and-hope strategy, 826
Training (preparation of autism specialists), 1123–1155
  addressing current intervention trends, 1129–1130
  behavior analysis, 1125–1126
  behavior-specific praise, 1127
  best practices, 1130–1132
  big picture, 1139
  college student trainees/providers, 1137–1138
  comprehensive systems, 1130–1132
  consultants on adult care, 1137
  demand for qualified personnel, 1124–1125
  didactic training, 1141–1142, 1143
  dissemination, 1139, 1142–1143
  distinctive features, 1139
  empirical evolution of best practice provider preparation, 1125–1128
  ethics, 1139
  evaluating curriculum, 1153–1155
  feedback on work performances, 1127
  hands-on training, behavioral competencies, 1143–1146
  inclusion providers, 1129–1130
  job duties, specification of, 1126
  limitations of staff training research, 1132
  maintaining new skills, 1152–1153
  managing training system, 1153
  manuals, behavior modification, 1126
  mastery criterion, 1146–1147
  methods most effective, 1141–1147
  natural environments, 1130
  objectives, 1140, 1141
  operant conditioning procedures, 1125
  operational definitions of behavior competencies, 1144
  organizational behavior management (OBM), 1128
  organizational citizenship, 1139
  parent-professional relationships, 1129
  performance appraisals, 1128, 1144, 1152
  primary group factors, 1132–1134
  prioritizing according to immediate need, 1141
  privileges as positive reinforcement, 1127–1128
  professionalism, 1139
  quality of life, 1134–1136
  research/development, 1126–1128
  rewarding trainees/staff for exceptional performances, 1148–1150
  safety, 1139
  self-monitoring, 1128
  sequencing dilemmas, 1141
  supervision, ongoing, 1152–1153
  technological innovations, 1142
  trainee considerations, 1136–1140
  trainer selection/preparation, 1150–1152
  Walden Incidental Teaching Checklist, 1145
  Walden Special Art Activities (SA) Checklist, 1146
  workshops/lectures, 1126–1127
Transactional supports, 989
Triads, 586, 629
Tryptophan metabolism, 455–456
Tuberous sclerosis (TS), 26, 50, 51, 135, 185, 442, 543–545
Turner syndrome, 354, 544
Twin(s):
  monozygotic twinning as risk factor, 434
  studies (genetics), 425–426

UCLA Young Autism Project, 1131, 1132, 1141, 1142
United Kingdom, 1243–1247
United States, 1194–1196
Upright/inverted figures, 693–694
Urine, 455, 459, 539
Uzgiris-Hunt Ordinal Scale of Infant Development, 792

Vacations (sibling's perspective), 1270
Validity, 102–111, 740–741
Valproate syndrome, fetal (FVS), 555–556
Valproic acid, maternal use, 436
Velocardiofacial syndrome (VCFS), 552
Ventricles, 499–500
Verbal apraxia or apraxis of speech, 336
Verbal auditory agnosia, 502
Verbal behavior, 959, 963–964. *See also* Language
Verbal communication, idiosyncrasies in, 89
Verbal comprehension, 788
Verbal intelligence, 103
Verbal-semantic coherence (EF), 641
Victims of crime, 299
Video instruction, 886–887
Videotape analysis studies, 225–227, 708
Vineland Adaptive Behavior Scales (VABS), 83, 315, 316, 762, 787, 793, 800, 804, 845
Violent/criminal behavior, 101
Visual deficits, 50, 589
Visual-Motor Integration, Developmental (VMI) test, 847
Visual-Motor Skills-Revised-Upper Limits, 847
Visual/somatosensory cognitive potentials, 482–483
Visual supports (enhancing communication abilities), 936–937, 995–997
Visual thinking, 1017, 1278–1280
Visuo-spatial constructional coherence (EF), 642
Visuospatial orienting task, 610
Vocalizations (infancy and early childhood), 235
Vocational Rehabilitation Act of 1973, 1090–1091
Vocational training, 116. *See also* Employment

Voice output communication aids (VOCAs), 925, 937, 955
Voluntary movements/praxis (sensory/motor), 835–838

Walden model, 1045
    categorical orientation and, 929, 930
    communication enhancement, 929, 930, 940, 953
    inclusion, 1035–1036
    preschool curricula, 873–874
    professional training, 1131, 1132
        Incidental Teaching Checklist, 1145
        Special Art Activities (SA) Checklist, 1146
WCST. *See* Wisconsin Card Sorting Test (WCST)
Weak central coherence (WCC) hypothesis, 640–646, 669.
    See also Central coherence
Wechsler scales, 292, 374, 545, 643, 731, 787–789, 1204
Williams-Beuren syndrome (WBS), 548–549
Wisconsin Card Sorting Test (WCST), 606–609, 611, 614, 620
Word use, 344–345, 805
    slowed down version of normal, 961
    unusual and idiosyncratic, 962
Working memory, 611, 788
Workshops/lectures (provider training), 1126–1127

Yale Global Tic Severity Scale (YGTSS), 848
Yale In Vivo Pragmatic Protocol, 810, 811
Young Autism Project at UCLA, 1047–1049

Ziprasidone, 1105–1106
Zoloft, 1283